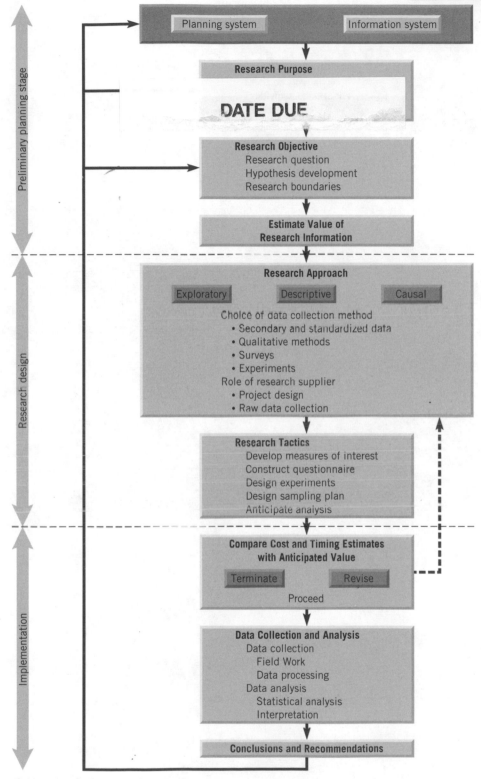

The research design process

MARKETING RESEARCH

FIFTH EDITION

DAVID A. AAKER
University of California, Berkeley

V. KUMAR
University of Houston

GEORGE S. DAY
University of Pennsylvania
Wharton School

John Wiley & Sons, Inc.

New York • Chichester • Brisbane • Toronto • Singapore

Dedicated with Love

To my wife, Kay

parents, Patta and Viswanathan

To my wife, Marilyn

ACQUISITIONS EDITOR   Timothy Kent
ASSISTANT EDITOR   Ellen Ford
MARKETING MANAGER   Debra Riegert
PRODUCTION EDITOR   Edward Winkleman
ART DIRECTION   Dawn L. Stanley
DESIGNER   Jenkins and Page
MANUFACTURING OPERATIONS MANAGER   Susan Stetzer
FREELANCE ILLUSTRATION COORDINATOR JR.   Gene Aiello

This book was set in 10/13 Palatino Light by TCSystems, Inc. and printed and bound by R. R. Donnelley (Crawfordsville). The cover was printed by Phoenix Color, Inc.

Recognizing the importance of preserving what has been written, it is a policy of John Wiley & Sons, Inc. to have books of enduring value published in the United States printed on acid-free paper, and we exert our best efforts to that end.

Library of Congress Cataloging-in-Publication Data
Aaker, David A.
    Marketing research / David A. Aaker, V. Kumar, George S. Day.—
5th ed.
        p.   cm.

    Includes index.

    ISBN 0-471-55254-2
    1. Marketing research.   I. Kumar, V.   II. Day, George S.
III. Title.
HF5415.2.A14   1995
658.8'3–dc20   94-40075
                                                                  CIP

Printed in the United States of America

10 9 8 7 6 5 4 3 2 1

PREFACE

etaphorically, if marketing can be looked on as a long train with multiple compartments, then marketing research would justly claim the dual roles of the engine that powers the train and the vestibule that links the individual compartments to form a cohesive functional unit. In other words, marketing research is pervasive—the *brain* and the *brawn* of any marketing organization.

Having said this, we realize that marketing research is a complex subject and therefore has to be introduced to the student one compartment at a time before the entire train can be visualized. We also realize the danger in this approach. The student can get overly excited or, even worse, overwhelmed by the individual units that he or she fails to see the proverbial "big picture"— the overarching framework, the subtle but essential interactions between units, and the ultimate purpose, namely, how marketing research can help organizations achieve their goals. Hence, this text takes a "macro-micro-macro" approach toward communicating the intricacies of marketing research and its usefulness to the marketing organization.

We begin with a macro-level treatment of what marketing research is, where it fits within an organization, and how it helps in managerial decision making. Here, we also discuss the marketing research industry, with a brief treatment of both suppliers and users. The body of the text takes a micro-level approach, detailing each and every step of the marketing research process. In describing the marketing research process, a decision-oriented perspective has been adopted to help students, who are future managers and researchers, make better decisions. Detailed discussions of the process with numerous examples from the industry characterize this micro phase. Finally, we wrap up with a macro-level treatment of the applications of marketing research. Here we address the traditional 4P research, as well as current issues such as brand equity and customer satisfaction research that fascinate marketers.

OBJECTIVES OF THIS TEXT

Our overall objectives in writing this text continue to be

1. To communicate in an interesting and informative manner the essence of marketing research to "future managers" and "future researchers." Both groups need to know when marketing research can and should be used,

what research alternatives exist, how to recognize effective and ineffective research, and how to interpret and apply the results.

2. To emphasize the current developments in marketing research, such as the distinction between domestic and international market research.

3. To use examples, applications, and illustrations throughout the book, in an effort to tie the material to the real world and thus provide interest and better understanding to the student.

4. To provide a clear and comprehensive treatment of modern data analysis topics. Each chapter includes simple numerical examples to help students get a hands-on feel for the material.

5. To provide thorough coverage of the most advanced and current marketing research methodologies, pointing out their limitations, as well as their potential for enhancing research results.

HIGHLIGHTS OF THIS EDITION

In line with these objectives, the Fifth Edition has undergone major changes. The more prominent of these changes are

▶ The text has been made current by the addition of discussions on new topics of interests and methods of practice in marketing research.

▶ Relevant and recent examples and citations that provide the state-of-the-art description of the marketing research process and the industry have been included.

▶ The international element of marketing research has been introduced to keep abreast with the emerging trends and changes in the marketplace. Particularly, an effort has been made to provide a clear distinction between domestic and international marketing research process and prepare the users of this text to face the challenges of multicountry research.

▶ The chapters on data analysis have been made more rigorous while retaining the clear exposition of the earlier editions. Essentially the data analysis sections have undergone major revisions. Individual topics in data analysis have been rearranged for sake of clarity, and a new chapter on discriminant and canonical analysis has been added.

▶ The section on applications of marketing research has been revamped. It now includes two chapters on the traditional 4P applications and a chapter on more recent developments such as competitive advantage, brand equity, total quality management, customer satisfaction, relationship marketing, and integrated marketing communications.

ORGANIZATION OF THE TEXT

The book is organized to reflect the "macro-micro-macro" approach toward imparting marketing research training to the student. The text consists of five parts. Parts I and V deal with the "macro" aspects of marketing research; Parts II, III, and IV deal with the micro aspects.

Part I, consisting of four chapters, deals with the nature and scope of marketing research. Here, the overall framework of marketing research is presented, and where and how marketing research fits in with the other aspects of marketing is explained. The nature of research industry and the suppliers is also discussed here.

Part II, consisting of Chapters 5 through 14, deals extensively with the various aspects of data collection. This part is further divided into four sections, one section devoted to each of the three fundamental types of marketing research: exploratory, descriptive, and causal. The final section addresses the issue of sampling.

Part III, consisting of three chapters, discusses the fundamental aspects and techniques in data analysis. These include preanalysis issues such as data editing, coding, and simple techniques such as hypothesis testing, chi-square analysis, and the analysis of variance.

Part IV is devoted exclusively to advanced and more sophisticated data analysis techniques such as correlation and regression analysis, discriminant analysis, factor analysis, cluster analysis, conjoint analysis, and multidimensional scaling. This part consists of four chapters, the last chapter dealing with the aspects of presenting the research results.

In Part V, the student is exposed to both the traditional and emerging applications of marketing research. This section has three chapters and provides the student with a comprehensive picture of marketing research, highlighting where and how the individual units of the research process fit in while solving marketing problems.

ACKNOWLEDGMENTS

Many debts have been accumulated during the years in which five editions of this book have taken shape. We are especially grateful to our students, who gave us feedback from the consumer's perspective and whose field research projects provided many of the illustrations and problems; to our colleagues, who stimulated us and brought new ideas and approaches to our attention; and to our clients, who gave us many opportunities to put ideas into practice and thus broaden our understanding of marketing research as it is currently practiced. It has been a continuing pleasure to associate with a class publisher, John Wiley & Sons, and to work with three Wiley editors—Rich Esposito, who nurtured the book through three editions, John Woods, who helped so much with the Fourth Edition, and Tim Kent, who worked hard to make the Fifth Edition a success in the market.

A host of other helpful and insightful reviews on the first four editions were received from Scott Armstrong, Ronald Beall, Andrew Brogowicz, Dave Bruzonne, Melvin Crask, William R. Dillon, Chris T. Ford, Gary T. Ford, Michael Hagerty, Chris Lovelock, Barry Mason, Douglas L. Maclachlan, Shelby McIntyre, Thomas Pilon, Peter Riesz, Gary Russell, Eli Seggev, Subrata Sen, Terence A. Shimp, Allan Shocker, Judy Wilkinson, Noel Zabriskie, Curt J. Donmeyer, A. Dwayne Ball, Jeffrey M. Ferguson, Zir Carmon, Anita Desembrana, John H. Summey, Alexandra Campbell, and Sanjit Sengupta.

The Fifth Edition was created with the help of

Frank Acito
Indiana University

Manoj Agarwal
SUNY-Binghamton

Greg Allenby
Ohio State

David Andrus
Kansas State University

Joseph Ballenger
Steven F. Austin State University

Kapil Bawa
McGill University

William Bearden
University of South Carolina

Liz Blair
Ohio University

Norman Bruvold
University of Cincinnati

Robert Dyer
George Washington University

Richard Easley
Baylor University

Andrew Forman
Hofstra University

Fran Franzak
Virginia Commonwealth University

Srinath Gopalakrishna
Pennsylvania State University

John Gwin
University of Virginia

Arun Jain
SUNY-Buffalo

Deborah Roedder John
University of Minnesota

Ram Kesavan
University of Detroit

Praveen Kopalle
University of Arizona

Jack Lesser
Miami University

Gary McCain
Boise State University

Janet Oglethorpe
University of Texas at San Antonio

Catherine Schaffer
University of Dayton

Bruce Seaton
Florida International University

Hirokazu Takada
University of California-Riverside

Jerry Thomas
San Jose State University

Gail Tom
California State University at Sacramento

We would like to express special thanks for the countless hours spent by Jaishankar Ganesh and Velavan Subramaniam through their assistance in the revision process. Considerable gratitude is expressed to the Marketing Department at the University of Houston, particularly to its Chairman, Dr. Keith Cox, for providing the necessary infrastructural support. A great appreciation is extended to Robert P. Leone for acting as a sounding board for all the ideas generated during the creation of this edition. We also thank Erich Joachimsthaler for facilitating the like minds to meet (in Spain) and conceive this Fifth Edition.

We also wish to thank the John Wiley group of Ellen Ford, Edward Winkleman, Andrea Bryant, and Debra Riegert for all the excellent service they provided during the creation of this edition.

Finally, we wish to express our sincere appreciation to our family for their constant support, encouragement, and sacrifices during the creation of this book.

David A. Aaker
V. Kumar
George S. Day

BRIEF CONTENTS

PART I
The Nature and Scope of Marketing Research, *1*

    Chapter 1 A Decision-Making Perspective On Marketing Research, *2*

    Chapter 2 Marketing Research in Practice, *22*

    Chapter 3 The Marketing Research Process, *42*

    Chapter 4 Research Design and Implementation, *71*

PART II
Data Collection, *113*

SECTION A
Secondary and Exploratory Research, *114*

    Chapter 5 Secondary Sources of Marketing Data, *114*

    Chapter 6 Standardized Sources of Marketing Data, *141*

    Chapter 7 Information Collection: Qualitative and Observational Methods, *173*

SECTION B
Descriptive Research, *199*

    Chapter 8 Information from Respondents: Issues in Date Collection, *199*

    Chapter 9 Information from Respondents: Survey Methods, *218*

    Chapter 10 Attitude Measurement, *253*

    Chapter 11 Designing the Questionnaire, *290*

SECTION C
Causal Research, *321*

    Chapter 12 Experimentation, *321*

SECTION D
Sampling, *358*

    Chapter 13 Sampling Fundamentals, *358*

    Chapter 14 Sample Size and Statistical Theory, *392*

PART III
Data Analysis, *441*

    Chapter 15 Fundamentals of Data Analysis, *442*

    Chapter 16 Hypothesis Testing: Basic Concepts and Tests of Associations, *467*

    Chapter 17 Hypothesis Testing: Means and Proportions, *491*

PART IV
Special Topics in Data Analysis, *535*

    Chapter 18 Correlation Analysis and Regression Analysis, *536*

    Chapter 19 Discriminant and Canonical Analysis, *573*

    Chapter 20 Factor and Cluster Analysis, *595*

    Chapter 21 Multidimensional Scaling and Conjoint Analysis, *629*

    Chapter 22 Presenting the Results, *660*

PART V
Applications, *679*

    Chapter 23 Traditional Applications of Marketing Research: Product and Price, *680*

    Chapter 24 Traditional Applications of Marketing Research: Distribution and Promotion, *706*

    Chapter 25 Applications of Marketing Research in the Nineties, *730*

Appendix: Tables
Standard Normal Probabilities, *761*
χ^2 Critical Points, *762*
F Critical Points, *764*
t Critical Points, *767*

Glossary, *769*

Index, *779*

CONTENTS

PART I   THE NATURE AND SCOPE OF MARKETING RESEARCH, *1*

CHAPTER 1 A Decision-Making Perspective On Marketing Research, 2

Learning Objectives, 2

Introduction, 2

General Motors, 2   American Express Focuses on Relationships—Not Products, 3   Store-Specific Marketing, 3

Role of Marketing Research in Managerial Decision Making, 4

Situation Analysis, 5   Strategy Development, 7 Marketing Program Development, 8 Implementation, 11

Factors That Influence Marketing Research Decisions, 11

Relevance, 12   Type and Nature of Information Sought, 12   Timing, 12   Availability of Resources, 12   Cost–Benefit Analysis, 13

Use of Marketing Research, 13

Does Marketing Research Guarantee Success?, 13

Ethics in Marketing Research, 14

The Sponsor's Ethics, 14   The Supplier's Ethics, 16 Abuse of Respondents, 16

The Respondent's Ethics and Rights, 16

International Marketing Research, 17

Summary, 18

Questions and Problems, 19

Case 1-1: Ethical Dilemmas in Marketing Research, 20

End Notes, 21

CHAPTER 2 Marketing Research in Practice, 22

Learning Objectives, 22

Information Systems, Decision Support Systems, and Marketing Research, 23

Databases, 23   Decision Support Systems, 24

Applying Information Systems to Marketing Research, 25

Marketing Decision Support Systems, 25

Characteristics of an MDSS, 27   Database, 27 Reports and Displays, 28   Analysis Capabilities, 28   Models, 28   Gaining Insights from an MDSS, 28

Suppliers of Information, 30

Corporate/In-house Marketing Research, 32 External Suppliers of the Research Industry, 33 Type and Nature of Services, 35

Criteria for Selecting External Suppliers, 36

The International Marketing Research Industry, 37

Career Opportunities in Marketing Research, 37

Summary, 38

Questions and Problems, 38

End Notes, 39

Appendix: Careers in Marketing Research, 40

CHAPTER 3 The Marketing Research Process, 42

Learning Objectives, 42

Overview of the Marketing Research Process, 42

The Preliminary Stages of the Marketing Research Process, 43

Step 1—Research Purpose, 43   Step 2—Research Objective, 49   Step 3—Estimating the Value of Information, 54

Planning a New HMO, 55

The International Marketing Research Process, 59

Framing Research Questions in an International Environment, 59

Summary, 60

Questions and Problems, 61

End Notes, 63

Appendix: The Value of Research Information Using Bayesian Decision Theory, *64*

Case 3-1: A VideOcart Test for Bestway Stores, *66*

Case 3-2: Sperry/MacLennan Architects and Planners, *67*

CHAPTER 4 Research Design and Implementation, *71*

Learning Objectives, *71*

Research Approach, *73*

Types of Research, 73   Detective Funnel, 76 Data Collection Methods, 77   Choosing a Research Approach for the HMO Study, 78

Research Tactics and Implementation, *79*

Measurement, 79   Sampling Plan, 80 Anticipating the Analysis, 80   Analysis of Value Versus Cost and Time Involved, 80

Errors in Research Design, *81*

Sampling Error, 81   Nonsampling Error, 81

Budgeting and Scheduling the Research Project, *83*

Research Proposal, *85*

Basic Contents of a Proposal, 86

Designing International Marketing Research, *86*

Issues in International Research Design, *88*

Determining Information Requirements, 88   Unit of Analysis, 90   Construct, Measurement, and Sample Equivalence, 90

Summary, *91*

Questions and Problems, *91*

End Notes, *92*

Case 4-1: Reynold's Tobacco's Slide-Box Cigarettes, *93*

Case 4-2: California Foods Corporation, *97*

Cases for Part I, *101*

Case I-1: Clover Valley Dairy Company, *101*

Case I-2: Southwestern Conquistador Beer, *103*

PART II DATA COLLECTION, *113*

SECTION A SECONDARY AND EXPLORATORY RESEARCH, *114*

CHAPTER 5 Secondary Sources of Marketing Data, *114*

Learning Objectives, *114*

Secondary Data, *115*

Uses of Secondary Data, *115*

Benefits of Secondary Data, *116*

Limitations of Secondary Data, *116*

Internal Sources of Secondary Data, *117*

Internal Records, 117

External Sources of Secondary Data, *119*

Published Data Sources, 119   Computer Retrievable Databases, 122   Accessing Computer Retrievable Databases, 124   Advantages of Computer Retrievable Methods, 125   Limitations of Computer Retrievable Methods, 125

Census Data, *126*

Understanding the Census, 127

Standard Industrial Classification System, *128*

Appraising Secondary Sources, *129*

Applications of Secondary Data, *131*

Demand Estimation, 131   Monitoring the Environment, 133   Segmentation and

Targeting, 133   Developing a Business Intelligence System, 134

Sources of Secondary Data for International Marketing Research, *134*

Problems Associated with Secondary Data in International Research, *135*

Data Accuracy, 135   Comparability of Data, 135

Applications of Secondary Data in International Research, *135*

Summary, *137*

Questions and Problems, *137*

End Notes, *138*

Case 5-1: Barkley Foods, *139*

CHAPTER 6 Standardized Sources of Marketing Data, *141*

Learning Objectives, *141*

Retail Store Audits, *142*

Nielsen Retail Index, 143   Audits and Surveys: National Total Market Audit, 144

Consumer Purchase Panels, *144*

Advantages of Panels, 145   Limitations of Consumer Panels, 147

Scanner Services and Single-Source
Systems, 148

*Scanner-Based Audit Services, 148   Single-
Source Systems, 151*

Media-Related Standardized Sources, 155

*Nielsen Television Index (NTI), 155   Arbitron
Diary Panel, 156   Starch Scores, 156
Multimedia Services, 156*

Applications of Standardized Sources of
Data, 157

*Measuring Produce Sales and Market
Share, 157   Measuring Advertisement Exposure
and Effectiveness, 157   Measuring Promotion
Effectiveness, 158   Estimation and Evaluation of
Models, 158*

Summary, 158

Questions and Problems, 159

End Notes, 160

Case 6-1: Promotion of Rocket Soups, 161

Case 6-2: Kerry Gold Products, Ltd., 163

Case 6-3: Paradise Foods, 163

**CHAPTER 7 Information Collection:
Qualitative and Observational Methods, 173**

Learning Objectives, 173

Need for Qualitative Research, 173

Qualitative Research Methods, 174

*Individual In-depth Interviews, 176   Focus-Group
Discussions, 177   Projective Techniques, 183
Limitations of Qualitative Methods, 189*

Observational Methods, 189

*Direct Observation, 190   Contrived
Observation, 190   Content Analysis, 190
Physical Trace Measures, 191   Humanistic
Inquiry, 191   Behavior Recording
Devices, 192   Limitations of Observational
Methods, 192*

Summary, 193

Questions and Problems, 193

End Notes, 195

Case 7-1: Mountain Bell Telephone Company, 196

Case 7-2: U.S. Department of Energy (A), 198

SECTION B   DESCRIPTIVE RESEARCH, *199*

**CHAPTER 8 Information from Respondents:
Issues in Data Collection, 199**

Learning Objectives, 199

Information from Surveys, 200

Sources of Survey Error, 200

*Nonresponse Errors Due to Refusals, 201
Inaccuracy in Response, 202   Interviewer
Error, 205*

Methods of Data Collection, 206

Factors Affecting the Choice of a Survey
Method, 207

*Sampling, 207   Type of Population, 208
Question Form, 209   Question Content, 209
Response Rates, 210   Costs, 210   Available
Facilities, 210   Duration of Data
Collection, 211*

Ethical Issues in Data Collection, 211

Summary, 213

Questions and Problems, 213

End Notes, 215

Case 8-1: Essex Markets (A), 216

Case 8-2: More Ethical Dilemmas in Marketing
Research, 216

**CHAPTER 9 Information from Respondents:
Survey Methods, 218**

Learning Objectives, 218

Collecting Data, 218

*Personal Interviewing, 218   Telephone Interviewing,
222   Mail Surveys, 227*

*Combinations of Survey Methods, 232   Trends
in Survey Research, 233   Choice of Survey Methods
for HMO Study, 238*

Surveys in the International Context, 238

*Personal Interviews, 238   Telephone
Interviews, 239   Mail Surveys, 240*

Summary, 241

Questions and Problems, 242

End Notes, 244

Case 9-1: Project DATA: An Urban Transportation
Study, 245

Case 9-2: Roland Development Corp., 246

CHAPTER 10 Attitude Measurement, 253

Learning Objectives, 253

What Are Attitudes?, 254

Cognitive or Knowledge Component, 254

Affective or Liking Component, 254   Intention or Action Component, 255

The Concept of Measurement and Scaling, 255

Properties of Measurement Scales, 255

Types of Attitude Rating Scales, 258

Single-Item Scales, 258   Multiple-Item Scales, 266   Stapel Scales, 270

General Guidelines for Developing a Multi-Item Scale, 272

Continuous-Rating Scales, 274

Interpreting Attitude Scales, 274

Choosing an Attitudinal Scale, 274

Accuracy of Attitude Measurements, 277

Validity, 277   Reliability, 278   Sensitivity, 279   Generalizability, 279   Relevancy, 280

Scales in Cross-National Research, 280

Summary, 281

Questions and Problems, 281

End Notes, 283

Case 10-1: Wine Horizons, 284

Case 10-2: National Kitchens, 285

CHAPTER 11 Designing the Questionnaire, 290

Learning Objectives, 290

Planning What to Measure, 291

Translating Research Objectives into Information Requirements, 292

Formatting the Question, 292

Open-Response Questions, 294   Closed-Response Questions, 295   Using Both Open-Response and Closed-Response Questions, 299

Question Wording: A Problem of Communication, 300

Asking Sensitive Questions, 302

Sequence and Layout Decisions, 305

Order Bias: Does the Question Create the Answer?, 306   Pretesting and Correcting Problems, 307   Pretest Design, 308   Role of the Pretest, 310

Questionnaire Design for International Research, 311

Choosing the Questions Format for Cross-National Research, 311   Problems Faced in Wording   Questions for International Research, 312

Summary, 314

Questions and Problems, 314

End Notes, 318

Case 11-1: Essex Markets (B), 319

Case 11-2: Smith's Clothing (A), 319

Case 11-3: Compact Lemon, 320

SECTION C   CAUSAL RESEARCH, *321*

CHAPTER 12 Experimentation, *321*

Learning Objectives, 321

Descriptive Versus Experimental Research, 322

What Are Causal Relationships?, 322   Limitations of Descriptive Designs, 323

What Constitutes Causality?, 324

Direction of Causation Issue, 324   Conditions for Valid Causal Inferences, 325

Issues in Experimental Research, 326

Basic Symbols and Notations, 326

Types of Experimental Designs, 328

Classical Designs, 328   Statistical Designs, 336

Laboratory and Field Experiments, 343

Threats to Experimental Validity, 345

Threats to Internal Validity, 345   Threats to External Validity, 346

Guidelines for Conducting Experimental Research, 347

Common Misuses of Experimental Research in Marketing, 349

Limitations of Experiments, 349

Cost, 350   Security, 350   Implementation Problems, 350   Uncertain Persistency of Results, 351

Summary, 352

Questions and Problems, 352

End Notes, 354

Case 12-1: Evaluating Experimental Designs, 355

Case 12-2: Barrie Food Corporation, 356

SECTION D   SAMPLING, *358*

CHAPTER 13 Sampling Fundamentals, *358*

Learning Objectives, 358

Sample or Census, 358

When Census Is Appropriate, 359   When a Sample Is Appropriate, 359   Error in Sampling, 359

Sampling Process, 360

Determining the Target Population, 361

Determining the Sampling Frame, 363   Selecting a Sampling Procedure, 366

Probability Sampling, 367

Selecting the Probability Sample, 367   Multistage Design, 373

Nonprobability Sampling, 375

Judgmental Sampling, 375   Snowball Sampling, 376
Convenience Sampling, 376   Quota Sampling, 377
Determining the Sample Size, 378   Nonresponse Problems, 378

Shopping Center Sampling, 380

Shopping Center Selection, 380   Sample Locations Within a Center, 380   Time Sampling, 381
Sampling People Versus Shopping Visits, 381

Sampling in the International Context, 382

Selecting the Sampling Frame, 382   Sampling Procedure, 383

Summary, 384

Questions and Problems, 385

End Notes, 388

Case 13-1: Exercises in Sample Design, 389

Case 13-2: Talbot Razor Products Company, 389

CHAPTER 14 Sample Size and Statistical Theory, 392

Learning Objectives, 392

Determining the Sample Size: Ad Hoc Methods, 392

Rules of Thumb, 393   Budget Constraints, 393
Comparable Studies, 394   Factors Determining Sample Size, 394

Population Characteristics/Parameters, 394

Sample Characteristics/Statistics, 395

Sample Reliability, 397

Interval Estimation, 399

Sample Size Question, 401

Determining the Population Standard Deviation, 402

Proportions, 402

Several Questions, 404

Stratified Sampling, 406

Multistage Design, 408

Sequential Sampling, 408

Summary, 408

Questions and Problems, 409

End Notes, 412

Cases for Part II, 414

Case II-1: Pacific Gas & Electric (A), 414
Case II-2: Bellboy, 422
Case II-3: Currency Concepts International, 435

PART III   DATA ANALYSIS, 441

CHAPTER 15 Fundamentals of Data Analysis, 442

Learning Objectives, 442

Preparing the Data for Analysis, 443

Data Editing, 443   Coding, 444   Statistically Adjusting the Data, 447

Strategy for Data Analysis, 448

Tabulation: Frequency Distribution, 449
Tabulation: Descriptive Statistics, 450   Difference Between Means or Percentages, 452

Cross-Tabulations, 453

Factors Influencing the Choice of a Statistical Technique, 454

Type of Data, 455   Research Design, 455
Assumptions Underlying Test Statistic, 457

An Overview of Statistical Techniques, 458

Presenting the Results, 462

Summary, 462

Questions and Problems, 463

End Notes, 464

Appendix, 465

CHAPTER 16 Hypothesis Testing: Basic Concepts and Tests of Associations, 467

Learning Objectives, 467

The Logic of Hypothesis Testing, 468

An Illustrative Example, 468

Steps in Hypothesis Testing, 469

Basic Concepts of Hypothesis Testing, 470

The Null and the Alternative Hypothesis, 470
Choosing the Relevant Statistical Test and the Appropriate Probability Distribution, 471
Choosing the Critical Value, 471

Cross-Tabulation and Chi-Square, 475

The Concept of Statistical Independence, 475
Chi-Square as a Test of Independence, 477
Measures of Associations for Nominal Variables, 481
The Chi-Square Goodness-of-Fit Test, 484

Summary, *486*

Questions and Problems, *486*

End Notes, *488*

Case 16-1: Medical Systems Associates: Measuring Patient Satisfaction, *488*

CHAPTER 17 Hypothesis Testing: Means and Proportions, 491

Learning Objectives, *491*

Commonly Used Hypothesis Tests in Marketing Research, *492*

Testing Hypotheses About a Single Mean, 492 Hypothesis Testing for Differences Between Means, 495 Hypothesis Testing of Proportions, 499 Hypothesis Testing of Difference Between Proportions, 500

The Probability Value (*p*-Values) Approach to Hypothesis Testing, *501*

Effect of Sample Size and Interpretation of Test Results, *502*

Relationship Between Confidence Interval and Hypothesis Testing, *503*

Analysis of Variance (ANOVA), *504*

One-Factor Analysis of Variance, 505 Expanding the ANOVA Table, 510

Summary, *513*

Questions and Problems, *514*

End Notes, *516*

Case 17-1: American Conservatory Theater, *517*

Case 17-2: Apple Appliance Stores, *519*

Cases for Part III, 521

Case III-1: The Vancouver Symphony Orchestra, *521*

Case III-2: Pacific Gas & Electric (B), *529*

Case III-3: Ralston Development Company, *530*

PART IV   SPECIAL TOPICS IN DATA ANALYSIS, *535*

CHAPTER 18 Correlation Analysis and Regression Analysis, 536

Learning Objectives, *536*

Correlation Analysis, *537*

Simple Correlation Coefficient, 537 Testing the Significance of the Correlation Coefficient, 541 Partial Correlation Coefficient, 542

Regression Analysis, *542*

Simple Linear Regression Model, 543 Multiple Regression, 552 Parameter Interpretation in Multiple Regression, 554 Tests of Significance and Their Interpretations, 555 Interactions, 562 Analyzing Residuals, 562 Predictive Validity, 563 Regression with Dummy Variables, 563

Summary, *564*

Questions and Problems, *565*

End Notes, *569*

Case 18-1: The Seafood Grotto, *570*

Case 18-2: Ajax Advertising Agency, *571*

Case 18-3: Election Research, Inc., *572*

CHAPTER 19 Discriminant and Canonical Analysis, 573

Learning Objectives, *573*

Discriminant Analysis, *573*

Determination of Significance, *579*

Interpretation, *579*

Multiple Discriminant Analysis, *583*

Discussion of Results, 583

Summary of Discriminant Analysis, *586*

Canonical Correlation Analysis, *587*

Summary of Canonical Correlation Analysis, *591*

Questions and Problems, *591*

End Notes, *593*

Case 19-1: Southwest Utility, *594*

CHAPTER 20 Factor and Cluster Analysis, 595

Learning Objectives, *595*

Factor Analysis, *596*

Purpose, 596 Methodology, 596 A Geometric Perspective, 597 Principal-Component Analysis, 598 Common-Factor Analysis, 607

Summary of Factor Analysis, *607*

Cluster Analysis, *610*

Problem Definition, 611 Measures of Similarity, 611 Clustering Approach, 612 Number of Clusters, 617 Evaluating and Profiling the Clusters, 620 Statistical Inference, 620

Summary of Cluster Analysis, *621*

Questions and Problems, *622*

End Notes, *623*

Case 20-1: Store Image Study, *624*

Case 20-2: Behavioral Research, *626*

Chapter 21 Multidimensional Scaling and Conjoint Analysis, *629*

Learning Objectives, *629*

Multidimensional Scaling, *629*

Attribute-Based Approaches, *630*

*Factor Analysis, 630   Discriminant Analysis, 631
Comparing Factor and Discriminant
Analysis, 632   Introducing Importance
Weights, 632   Correspondence Analysis, 632
Basic Concepts of MDS, 633   Evaluating the
MDS Solution, 633   Application of MDS with
Nonattribute Data, 636   Issues in MDS, 639*

Summary of MDS, *640*

Conjoint Analysis, *641*

*Overview of Conjoint Analysis, 642
Interpreting Attribute Importance, 644   Collecting
Trade-off Data, 645   Comparing Data Collection
Approaches, 646   Analyzing and Interpreting the
Data, 647   Validity Issues, 648   Application
Issues, 649*

Summary of Conjoint Analysis, *649*

Questions and Problems, *651*

End Notes, *652*

Case 21-1: Nester's Foods, *654*

Case 21-2: Pepsi-Cola, *655*

Case 21-3: The Electric Truck Case, *657*

Case 21-4: Fargo Instruments, *658*

Chapter 22 Presenting the Results, *660*

Learning Objectives, *660*

Guidelines for Successful Presentations, *661*

*Communicate to a Specific Audience, 661
Structure the Presentation, 661   Create Audience
Interest, 663   Be Specific and Visual, 664
Address Issues of Validity and Reliability, 665*

Written Presentation, *666*

The Organization of the Report, 667

Oral Presentation, *670*

*Don't Read, 671   Use Visual Aids, 671   Make
Sure the Start Is Positive, 672   Avoid Distracting
the Audience, 672   Involve the Audience, 673*

Summary, *673*

Questions and Problems, *674*

End Notes, *674*

Cases for Part IV, *675*

Case IV-1: Smith's Clothing (B), *675*

Case IV-2: Newfood, *675*

PART V   APPLICATIONS, *679*

Chapter 23 Traditional Applications of Marketing Research: Product and Price, *680*

Learning Objectives, *680*

New Product Research, *681*

*Concept Generation, 681   Product Evaluation and
Development, 684*

Forecasting, *692*

*Qualitative Methods, 693   Quantitative
Methods, 694   Causal Models, 695*

Pricing Research, *696*

*Research for Profit-Oriented Pricing, 697
Research for Share-Oriented Pricing, 697*

Summary, *698*

Questions and Problems, *701*

End Notes, *703*

Case 23-1: Brown Microwave, *704*

Case 23-2: National Chemical Corporation (B), *705*

Case 23-3: U.S. Department of Energy (B), *705*

Chapter 24 Traditional Applications of Marketing Research: Distribution and Promotion, *706*

Learning Objectives, *706*

Distribution Research, *706*

*Warehouse and Retail Location Research, 707
Number and Location of Sales Representatives, 711*

Promotional Research, *713*

*Advertising Research, 713   Purchase Behavior, 716
Tracking Studies, 717   Diagnostic Testing, 718
Copy Test Validity, 718   Budget Decision, 720
Media Research, 720   Sales Promotion Research, 721*

Summary, *723*

Questions and Problems, *724*

End Notes, *725*

Case 24-1: Levi Strauss & Co., *726*

CHAPTER 25 Applications of Marketing Research in the Nineties, *730*

Learning Objectives, *730*

Competitive Advantage, *731*

Assessing Competitive Advantage, 731

Brand Equity, *733*

Research Questions under Brand Equity, 734
Measuring Brand Equity, 735

Customer Satisfaction, *739*

Customer Satisfaction Measurement Process, 740

Total Quality Management, *744*

Information Requirements for Total Quality Management, 746   Marketing Research, 753

Relationship Marketing, *753*

Three Keys to Relationship Marketing, 753

Integrated Marketing Communications, *755*

Summary, *756*

Questions and Problems, *757*

End Notes, *758*

Appendix: Tables, *761*

Standard Normal Probabilities, *761*

χ^2 Critical Points, *762*
F Critical Points, *764*
t Critical Points, *767*

Glossary, *769*

Index, *779*

xvi

PART I

NATURE AND SCOPE OF MARKETING RESEARCH

1

A DECISION-MAKING PERSPECTIVE ON MARKETING RESEARCH

Learning Objectives

▶ Understand the need and use of marketing research in an organization.

▶ Comprehend how marketing research fits in the bigger schema of the marketing environment.

▶ Explain the role of marketing research in decision making.

▶ Discuss the factors that affect the marketing research decisions.

▶ Understand the implication of ethical issues in conducting research.

▶ Introduce international marketing research.

INTRODUCTION

Marketing is the process of planning and executing the conception, pricing, promotion, and distribution of ideas, goods, and services to create exchanges that satisfy individual and organizational objectives. The **marketing concept** requires that **customer satisfaction** rather than **profit maximization** be the goal of an organization.[1] In other words, the organization should be consumer oriented and should try to understand consumers' requirements and to satisfy them quickly and efficiently, in ways that are beneficial to both the consumer and the organization. This means that any research organization should try to obtain information on consumer needs and gather marketing intelligence to help satisfy these needs efficiently.

Marketing research is a critical part of such a marketing intelligence system; it helps to improve management decision making by providing relevant, accurate, and timely (RAT) information. Every decision poses unique needs for information, and relevant strategies can be developed based on the information gathered through marketing research. The following examples give the flavor of marketing research in action.

General Motors

In 1988 GM's share of the U.S. auto market dropped to 37 percent compared with 43 percent as recently as 1983. This decline was partly attributable to the sameness of the basic Buick, Pontiac, Oldsmobile, Chevrolet, and Cadillac models. In response, GM began to design and market cars for highly defined market niches rather than a mass market. To achieve this they needed to know the answers to such questions as: How is the market segmented? What features do these customer groups want? Are they willing to sacrifice one feature for another (say, acceleration versus fuel economy)? What are competitors doing that could be copied?

American Express Focuses on Relationships—Not Products[2]

American Express, the charge-card giant, is changing its focus from product marketing to relationship marketing; and that, in turn, will put more emphasis on the company's direct marketing. Recent customer research has revealed significant differences among cardholders, depending on the length of their tenure with American Express and the way they use their cards. The company plans to use these insights into the different consumer segments to increase loyalty and usage.

The direct marketing effort tries to take a more surgical approach. Instead of having different marketing groups that concern themselves with green, gold, or platinum charge cards, the company has set up "relationship management" to get to know the different cardholder niches. For example, AmEx now plans to focus on seniors, a group that hasn't received a great deal of individual attention. The company realizes that because of the group's affluence and its tendency toward leisure travel, it warrants a different message than, for instance, the frequent business traveler segment. "It is the way the customer battle will be won in the 1990s," says the executive vice president and general manager of advertising for AmEx's charge-card division.

Store-Specific Marketing[3]

Welcome to the latest in "**micromarketing.**" These days, consumer-product companies are concluding that it isn't enough to focus on a region or a state or even a city. Increasingly, the target is narrowing to a bull's-eye no bigger than an individual neighborhood or a single store. "Store-specific marketing is going to be the future of successful retailers," says a packaged goods specialist for Andersen Consulting in Chicago. The trend is possible thanks to new insights provided by the spread of checkout scanners, which are generating more sophisticated data on consumers buying habits. Also, a few big food companies and research firms have begun collecting data on individual stores and shoppers in ways that marketers could only dream of a few years ago.

For example, using a network of food brokers and store surveyors, **Market Metrics** of Lancaster, Pennsylvania, collects statistics on 30,000 supermarkets around the country. In addition to compiling economic, social, and ethnic shopper profiles for each store, Market Metrics tracks traffic patterns, per-capita food expenditures and neighborhood population density, as well as store size, sales volume, and even the exact measurement of space devoted to health and beauty products and dairy, meat, and other departments. Combining those statistics with consumption pattern studies—the demographic profiles of people who buy any of 1,300 packaged goods—Market Metrics can rank specific stores on how well they should sell everything from strained baby food to upscale pasta sauce. That helped **Borden, Inc.,** which makes Classico pasta sauce, to increase sales. The company had Market Metrics generate a list of the best stores for Classico consumers. It showed, among other things, that in West Coast markets, Classico would sell strongly in about 75 to 80 percent of the stores, while in more rural areas, the number was 50 percent or less. "We can now spend our money more efficiently," says the product manager for Borden.

There are thousands of such examples, because virtually every private and public-sector organization encounters the same pressures for more and better information about its markets. Whether the organization serves customers in competitive market environments or clients in a public sector enterprise, it is necessary to understand and satisfy the changing needs of diverse groups of people.

> *Marketing research is the function that links an organization to its market through information. This information is used to identify and define marketing opportunities and problems; generate, refine, and evaluate marketing actions; monitor marketing performance; and improve the understanding of marketing as a process. Marketing research specifies the information required to address these issues; designs the method for collecting information; manages and implements the data-collection process; interprets the results; and communicates the findings and their implications.*
>
> American Marketing Association
> Official Definition of *Marketing Research*

This definition highlights the role of marketing research as an aid to decision making. An important feature is the inclusion of the specification and interpretation of needed information. Too often, marketing research is considered narrowly as the gathering and analyzing of data for someone else to use. Firms can achieve and sustain a competitive advantage through the creative use of market information. Hence, marketing research is defined as an information input to decisions, not simply the evaluation of decisions that have been made. But, market research alone does not guarantee success; the intelligent use of market research is the key to business achievement. A competitive edge is more the result of how information is used than of who does or doesn't have the information.[4]

ROLE OF MARKETING RESEARCH IN MANAGERIAL DECISION MAKING

Marketing decisions involve issues that range from fundamental shifts in the positioning of a business or the decision to enter a new market, to narrow tactical questions of how best to stock a grocery shelf. The context for these decisions is the market planning process that proceeds sequentially through four stages: situation analysis, strategy development, marketing program development, and implementation. This is a never-ending process, so the evaluation of past strategic decisions serves as an input to the situation assessment. Figure

FIGURE 1-1
Marketing planning process

1-1 suggests some elements of each stage. During each stage, marketing research makes a major contribution to clarifying and resolving issues, and then choosing among decision alternatives. The following sections describe these steps in more detail and describe the information needs that marketing research satisfies.

Situation Analysis

Effective marketing strategies are built on an in-depth understanding of the market environment of the business, and the specific characteristics of the market. The depth of these information needs can be seen from the list in Table 1-1 showing the requirements of a major consumer packaged goods manufacturer.

The macroenvironment includes political and regulatory trends, economic and social trends, and technological trends. Marketing researchers tend to focus on those trends that impact on the demand for products and services. For example, the most important influences on the demand for consumer packaged food products during the 1980s and early 1990s were

▶ Demographic shifts, including a record number of aging adults who were increasingly affluent and active.

▶ Rapid changes in family structure as a result of delayed marriages, working wives, and a high divorce rate.

▶ Shifts in values as consumers became preoccupied with their own economic and emotional well-being.

These trends resulted in increased concerns about the quality of food, nutritional value, personal fitness, and "naturalness." Equally influential were shifts in food, consumption patterns toward "grazing," or snacking, and more away-from-home eating.

TABLE 1-1

Scope of Situation Assessment for a Consumer Goods Manufacturer

1. Market Environment
   a. Technologies? How else will customers satisfy their needs?
   b. Economic trends? Disposable income?
   c. Social trends? What are the trends in age, marital status, working women, occupations, location, and shifts away from the center city? What values are becoming fashionable?
   d. Political and regulatory? New labeling and safety requirements.

2. Market Characteristics
   a. Market size, potential, and growth rate?
   b. Geographic dispersion of customers?
   c. Segmentation: How many distinct groups are there? Which are growing?
   d. Competition? Who are the direct rivals? How big are they? What is their performance? What is their strategy, intentions, and likely behavior with respect to product launches, promotions, and the like?
   e. Competitive products? Their nature and number?
   f. Channel members? What is the distribution of sales through supermarkets and other outlets? What are the trends? What are they doing to support their own brands?

3. Consumer Behavior
   a. What do they buy? A product or service? A convenience, shopping, or specialty good? A satisfaction . . . ?
   b. Who buys? Everybody? Women only? Teenagers (i.e., demographic, geographic, psychographic classification)?
   c. Where do they buy? Will they shop around or not? Outlet types?
   d. Why do they buy? Motivations, perceptions of product and needs, influences of peers, prestige, influence of advertising, media?
   e. How do they buy? On impulse, by shopping (i.e., the process they go through in purchasing)?
   f. When do they buy? Once a week? Everyday? Seasonal changes?
   g. Anticipated change? Incidence of new products, shifts in consumers' preferences, needs?

Understanding the customers—who they are, how they behave, why they behave as they do, and how they are likely to respond in the future—is at the heart of marketing research. Increasingly, marketing researchers are being asked to turn their talents to understanding the behavior and intentions of competitors. Since much data is available from public sources, marketing researchers are well positioned to work with other functions as part of competitor analysis teams.

A major responsibility of the marketing research function is providing information that will help detect problems and opportunities, and then, if necessary, to learn enough to make decisions as to what marketing program would result in the greatest response. An opportunity might be presented by the sense that customers are increasingly dissatisfied with existing products. Marketing research could be asked to detect the dissatisfaction, perhaps determine how many people are dissatisfied, and learn the level and nature of that dissatisfaction.

Various research approaches are used to analyze the market. Perhaps the simplest is to organize information already obtained from prior studies, from magazine articles that have been filed, and from customers' comments to a firm's sales representatives. Another approach is to have small groups of customers, called **focus groups,** discuss their use of a product. Such discussion groups can provide many ideas for new marketing programs.

When a problem or opportunity has been identified and it is necessary to understand it in greater depth, a survey is often employed. For example, to understand the competitive position of Quebec in the tourism market, a survey was conducted to determine the benefits sought by visitors and nonvisitors, as well as the risks they perceived. The results identified a large group who felt highly insecure in new and/or foreign environments and were not attracted by the appeals of uniqueness in culture, traditions, and architecture that Quebec used to differentiate its product. Exhibit 1-1 is a classic example of a company finding a niche based on the customer's current concerns.

Strategy Development

During this stage the management team of the business decides on answers to three critical questions. Marketing research provides significant help in finding the answers to these questions:

1. What business should we be in? Specifically, what products or services should we offer? What technologies will we utilize? Which market segments should we emphasize? What channels should we use to reach the market? These are far-reaching choices that set the context for all subsequent decisions.

    These questions have become especially compelling in markets that are mature and saturated, including not only most packaged goods but also household appliances, automobiles, and services such as banking and air travel. One sure route to growth in this competitive environment is to create highly targeted products that appeal to the tastes of small market segments. Research supports this search for niches with large-scale quanti-

EXHIBIT 1-1

EcoSport Finds Opportunities ''Going Green''

NPD Group research on environment showed that more than 55 percent of people care a great deal about recycling. Businesses, ranging from disposable diaper makers such as P&G and Kimberly Clarke to McDonald's, have realized the advantages of **green** marketing. The latest entrant to realize that going green pays off is EcoSport, a New York–based clothing manufacturer and distributor. The difference between EcoSport and other clothing manufacturers is that the firm uses certifiably organically grown cotton in all of its products. It has a catalog and a growing following. The owners, David and Marylou Marsh Sanders, have always been environmentally concerned parents, and combining that concern with Marylou's clothing company yielded EcoSport. ''When you support our clothing, you're supporting a whole new change in agriculture,'' is how Marylou described going green in clothing. Initially, the Sanderses turned to the environmentally correct Greenpeace group and offered it a T-shirt for its catalog. Since then, it's been nothing short of an explosion for the firm in terms of more and more distribution avenues opening up, more products being developed, and mainstream status getting nearer. EcoSport started as a T-shirt manufacturer in 1990. Then came sweatshirts, long-sleeve T-shirts, polo shirts, football jerseys, pocket T-shirts, baby blankets, skullcaps, and one-piece jumpsuits with more than $3 million in annual sales.

Source: ''Makers of Organic Clothes Find Mainstream Outlets,'' *Marketing News,* March 1, 1993, pp. 1 and 2.

tative market studies that describe buying behavior, consumer beliefs and attitudes, and exposure to communications media. Large samples are needed to delineate the segments, indicate their size, and determine what the people in each segment are seeking in a product.

2. How will we compete? Next the management team has to decide why the business is better than the competition in serving the needs of the target segment, and what has to be done to keep it in front. Competitive superiority is revealed in the market as either differentiation along attributes that are important to target customers, or the lowest delivered cost position. Otis Elevator is able to dominate the elevator business by using information technologies to provide superior service response and preventive maintenance programs that reduce elevator breakdowns—attributes that customers appreciate.

    Marketing research is essential for getting answers to three key questions about differentiation: What are the attributes of the product or service that create value for the customer? Which attributes are most important? How do we compare to the competition?

    The attributes of value go well beyond physical characteristics, to encompass the support activities and systems for delivery and service that make up the augmented product. In the lodging market, the key attributes are honoring reservations on time, good value for the money, and the quality and amenities of the guest rooms. Each market has unique attributes that customers employ to judge the competitive offerings, which can be understood only through careful analysis of usage patterns, and decision processes within that market. This knowledge comes from informed sources and in-depth customer surveys.

    An understanding of competitive advantage also requires detailed knowledge of the capabilities, strategies, and intentions of present and prospective competitors. Marketing research contributes here in two ways: identifying the competitive set, and collecting detailed information about each competitor. Some ways of undertaking competitive intelligence work are discussed later in the book. Exhibit 1-2 talks about how marketing research helped a chemical manufacturer to find out about customer preferences and the positioning of a product.

3. What are the objectives for the business? An objective is a desired performance result for a business that can be quantified and monitored. There are usually objectives for revenue growth, market share, and profitability. Increasingly, firms are adopting objectives for service levels (e.g., speed of response to quotations) and customer satisfaction. Marketing research is needed to establish both the market share and the level of customer satisfaction. Sometimes share information—we have x percent of the y market— is readily available from secondary sources. This is not always possible if the served market is different from the standard definition, or if share is defined in dollar sales terms rather than unit volume.

Marketing Program Development

Programs embrace specific tasks, such as developing a new product or launching a new advertising campaign. An action program usually focuses on a single objective in support of one element of the overall business strategy. This is

EXHIBIT 1-2

> # Understanding a Specialized
> # Industrial Market
>
> A chemical manufacturer in southern Europe began integrating forward into specialty chemicals in 1981. Its first move was almost abortive, for it entered the complex market for **factifiers,** a key component of adhesives, with little idea of customer requirements and no clear positioning. Belatedly, they undertook a major study of about 120 European adhesives manufacturers. Exploratory interviews with the buyer and major specifier in some of these prospects identified six product specific attributes affecting choice: softening paint, viscosity, color stability, starting color, tack, and price. Beyond these quantifiable variables, they found that the supplier's product range, service support, geographical coverage, and overall reputation for reliability determined which supplier to choose. The research also found that adhesive makers had to buy from several sources of factifiers because none could meet the requirements of the diversity of applications from packaging and woodworking to nonwoven goods. Eventually they found nine different profiles of values (attributes) being sought. Then the size, growth, strength of the competition and the manufacturer's relative ability to compete was judged for each segment, as a prelude to choosing a target market.

Source: Drawn from Peter Doyle and John Sauders, "Market Segmentation and Positioning in Specialized Industrial Markets," *Journal of Marketing,* 49, Spring 1985, pp. 24–32.

where the bulk of ongoing marketing research is directed. An idea of the possibilities of and needs for research can be gathered from Table 1-2, which describes some of the representative program decisions that utilize information about market characteristics and customer behavior.

To illustrate some of the possible research approaches that are employed, we will focus on the series of market research studies that were conducted to help Johnson Wax Company successfully introduce Agree Cream Rinse in 1977 and Agree Shampoo in 1978. The story begins with a major market analysis survey of hair-care practices conducted in the early seventies. The study showed that there was a trend away from hair sprays, but a trend toward shampooing hair more frequently and a growing concern about oily hair. This led to a strategic decision to enter the shampoo and creme rinse market with products targeted toward the oiliness problem. This decision was supported by other studies on competitive activities in the market and on the willingness of the retailers to stock new shampoos.[5]

A total of 50 marketing research studies conducted between 1975 and 1979 supported the development of these two products. A series of focus group discussions was held to understand the oiliness problem and people's perceptions of existing shampoo products. The firm was particularly interested in learning about teenagers, since most of its products were sold to homemakers. One goal of these focus groups was to get ideas for a copy theme. Subsequently, more focus groups were held to get reactions to the selected advertising theme, "Helps Stop the Greasies." Several tests of advertising were employed in which customers were exposed to advertisements, and their reactions were obtained. In fact, over 17 television commercials were created and tested.

More than 20 of the studies helped to test and refine the product. Several blind comparison tests were conducted, in which 400 women were asked to use the new product for two weeks and compare it to an existing product. (In

TABLE 1-2
Developing the Marketing Program—Representative Decisions That Draw on Marketing Research

1. Segmentation decisions
   Which segment should be the target?
   What benefits are most important for each segment?
   Which geographic area should be entered?

2. Product decisions
   What product features should be included?
   How should the product be positioned?
   What type of package is preferred by the customers?

3. Distribution decisions
   Which type of retailer should be used?
   What should be the markup policy?
   Should a few outlets be employed or many?

4. Advertising and promotion decisions
   What appeals should be used in the advertising?
   In which vehicles should the advertising be placed?
   What should the budget be?
   What sales promotions should be used, and when should they be scheduled?

5. Personal selling decisions
   What customer types have the most potential?
   How many salespeople are needed?

6. Price decisions
   What price level should be charged?
   What sales should be offered during the year?
   What response should be made to a competitor's price change?

a **blind test** the products are packaged in unlabeled containers and the customers do not know which contains the new product.)

Several tests of the final marketing program were conducted. One was in a simulated supermarket where customers were asked to shop after they had been exposed to the advertising. The new product, of course, was on the shelf. Another test involved placing the product in an actual supermarket and exposing customers to the advertising. Finally, the product was introduced using the complete marketing plan in a limited test area involving a few selected communities including Fresno, California, and South Bend, Indiana. During the process, the product, the advertising, and the rest of the marketing program were being revised continually. The effort paid handsome dividends: The Agree Creme Rinse took a 20 percent share of the market for its category and was number one in unit volume, and the Agree Shampoo also was introduced successfully. In the 1980s Gillette introduced the Mink Difference Shampoo, containing mink oil, for the older market, and for the younger segment, Silkience, a self-adjusting shampoo that provided differential conditioning, depending on the user's hair type.

Implementation

The beginning of the phase is signaled by a decision to proceed with a new program or strategy and by the related commitments to objectives, budgets, and timetables. At this point the focus of marketing research shifts to such questions as

> *Did the elements of the marketing program achieve their objectives?*
> How did sales compare with objectives?
> In what areas were sales disappointing? Why?
> Were the advertising objectives met?
> Did the product achieve its distribution objectives?
> Are any supermarkets discontinuing the product?
> *Should the marketing program be continued, revised, or expanded?*
> Are customers satisfied with the product?
> Should the product be changed? More features added?
> Should the advertising budget be changed?
> Is the price appropriate?

For research to be effective at this stage, it is important that specific measurable objectives be set for all elements of the marketing program. Thus, there should be sales goals by geographic area; distribution goals, perhaps in terms of the number of stores carrying the product; and advertising goals, such as achieving certain levels of awareness. The role of marketing research is to provide measures against these objectives and to provide more focused studies to determine why results are below or above expectations.

Often underlying this phase of marketing management is uncertainty about the critical judgments and assumptions that preceded the decision. For example, in 1982 Xerox, Canon, and IBM all launched new products into the office copier market. Prior to this, some companies had emphasized very large copiers, while others had ignored this end of the market. One reason for these differences in strategic emphasis was a fundamental assumption as to whether customers tended to centralize or decentralize their processing of copies. In response to this uncertainty, the companies undertook research studies with the dual purpose of measuring the acceptability of the new product entries and of monitoring the copy processing policies of the target customers.

There is overlap among the phases of the marketing process. In particular, the last phase, by identifying problems with the marketing program, and perhaps opportunities as well, eventually blends into the situation analysis phase of some other follow-up marketing program.

FACTORS THAT INFLUENCE MARKETING RESEARCH DECISIONS

Marketing research is not an immediate or an obvious path to finding solutions to all managerial problems. A manager who is faced with a particular problem should not instinctively resort to conducting marketing research to find a solution to the problem. There are several factors that a manager should consider before ordering that a marketing research be done. In several situations, it is best not to conduct a marketing research. Hence, the primary decision to be made is whether or not market research is called for in a particular situation. The factors that influence this initial decision include the following.

Relevance

Research should not be conducted to satisfy curiosity or confirm the wisdom of previous decisions. **Relevance** comes through support of strategic and tactical planning activities; that is, by anticipating the kinds of information that will be required. This information is the backbone of the ongoing information system. As new circumstances arise and decision alternatives become more specific, research projects may be undertaken. Throughout the planning of these projects, the focus must be constantly toward decisions.

Type and Nature of Information Sought

The decision whether to conduct marketing research depends on the type and nature of the information sought. If the information required for decision making already exists within the organization, in the form of results of a study conducted for a different problem or in the form of managerial experience and talents, marketing research is not called for. Under these circumstances, further research would be redundant and a waste of money. For example, Procter & Gamble, using its prior knowledge of the U.S. coffee market, launched Folger's Instant Coffee nationally, after some preliminary research. The same is true for many organizations that have accumulated rich experience in a particular market and already possess the information required to solve a certain problem.

Timing

Research decisions are constrained by the march of events. Often these decisions are fixed in time and must be taken according to a specified schedule, using whatever information is available. If a new product is to be launched in the spring, all the research-based decisions on price, product formulation, name, copy appeals, and other components must be conducted far in advance. One role of the planning system is to schedule needed market research so that it can be conducted in time to influence decisions. The formulation of responses to competitive actions puts the greatest time pressure on researchers, for the results are always wanted "yesterday." There are, of course, many situations where the timing of decisions is contingent upon the research results. Even so, there is still time pressure stemming from the recognition that failure to take corrective action or pursue an opportunity as quickly as possible will result in opportunity costs.

Availability of Resources

Though this factor appears to be obvious, in several instances managers have called for marketing research without properly understanding the amount of resources available—including both financial and human resources. Lack of funds can result in an improper and inefficient execution of a marketing research project. The results of such research often are inaccurate. Again, if funds are available to conduct proper research but are insufficient to implement the results of the research, the marketing research is made useless. Also, the availability of a talent pool is a critical issue in deciding whether or not to conduct extensive marketing research. This is particularly so when the research is being conducted by an external source. When poorly qualified researchers are hired, the weaknesses in their training and lack of insight produces unimpressive and often inapplicable results.

Cost–Benefit Analysis

Before conducting marketing research, a prudent manager would perform a cost–benefit analysis to determine the value of the information sought through the research. Willingness to acquire additional decision-making information by conducting marketing research depends upon a manager's perception of the incremental quality and value of the information vis-a-vis its cost and the time it would take to conduct the research. Hence, before conducting marketing research, it is necessary to have some estimate of the value of the information sought through research. Such an estimate will help determine how much, if anything, should be spent on the research.

USE OF MARKETING RESEARCH

Although research is conducted to generate information, managers do not readily use the information to solve their problems. The factors that influence a manager's decision to use research information are (1) research quality, (2) conformity to prior expectations, (3) clarity of presentation, (4) political acceptability within the firm, and (5) challenge to the status quo.[6] Researchers and managers agree that the technical quality of research is the primary determinant of research use. Also, managers are less inclined to utilize research that does not conform to prior notions or is not politically acceptable.[7] However, a researcher should not alter the findings to match a manager's prior notions. Further, managers in consumer organizations are less likely to use research findings than their counterparts in industrial firms.[8] This is due to a greater exploratory objective in information collection, a greater degree of formalization of organizational structure, and a lesser degree of surprise in the information collection.

Does Marketing Research Guarantee Success?

It is easier to conduct research and generate information than to understand the consequences of the information. Many companies with excellent marketing research experience have failed in their efforts to capture the actual needs of the consumers. For example, Coca-Cola conducted numerous studies before introducing the New Coke. The study results revealed that New Coke tasted better than the original Coke. Yet, the product failed in the marketplace because of the strong emotional/loyalty attachment to the original Coke.[9] Realizing that the market needs a low-calorie beer, Gablinger introduced the first low-calorie beers. However, the poor taste of the beer led to its downfall. Later, Anheuser-Busch and Miller Brewing achieved great success by emphasizing the benefits of good taste and a less-filling product (rather than fewer calories, although what the market wanted was a low-calorie beer).[10] RCA used price as the major incentive to attract customers to buy their videodiscs. However, what RCA failed to realize through its research was that although consumers were price conscious, ultimately the benefit of reusing the video cassettes outweighed the benefit of the marginal price difference. Therefore, RCA was forced to withdraw the product from the market. Sony thought that its Betamax video format was of better quality and charged a higher price for the product. Unfortunately, consumers were attracted to VHS-format VCRs because of price and multiple brand choices. As a result, Sony lost its dominant position in the market. Consumers may state that quality is important; however, if they cannot perceive the difference in quality between two technologies (such as Betamax and VHS), then price becomes a key factor, and the rest is history.

ETHICS IN MARKETING RESEARCH

Ethics refers to moral principles or values generally governing the conduct of an individual or group. Researchers have responsibilities to their profession, clients, and respondents, and must adhere to high ethical standards to ensure that both the function and the information are not brought into disrepute. The Marketing Research Association, Inc., Chicago, Illinois, has instituted a code of ethics that serves as a guideline for marketing ethical decisions (Exhibit 1-3 provides the Code of Professional Ethics and Practices instituted by the Marketing Research Association).[11] The Council of American Survey Research Organization (CASRO) has also established a detailed code of marketing research ethics to which its members adhere.[12] Normally, in a marketing research project, three parties are involved: (1) the client who sponsors the project, (2) the supplier who designs and executes the research, and (3) the respondent who provides the information. The issue of ethics in marketing research involves all three players in a research project.

The Sponsor's Ethics

The sponsor, or the research client, has to abide by a number of ethical or moral rules and regulations when conducting a research study. The more common sources of ethical problems in the client establishment stem from the following sources:

Overt and Covert Purposes. Most researchers have encountered situations where the main purpose of their efforts was to serve someone's organizational goals. Thus, research can be used to postpone an awkward decision or to lend respectability to a decision that has been made already. A related purpose is to avoid responsibility. When there are competing factions, the manager who

EXHIBIT 1-3

Code of Ethics of Marketing Research Association

The Code of Professional Ethics and Practices

1. To maintain high standards of competence and integrity in marketing and survey research.
2. To maintain the highest level of business and professional conduct and to comply with Federal, State and local laws, regulations and ordinances applicable to my business practice and those of my company.
3. To exercise all reasonable care and to observe the best standards of objectivity and accuracy in the development, collection, processing and reporting of marketing and survey research information.
4. To protect the anonymity of respondents and hold all information concerning an individual respondent privileged, such that this information is used only within the context of the particular study.
5. To thoroughly instruct and supervise all persons for whose work I am responsible in accordance with study specifications and general research techniques.
6. To observe the rights of ownership of all materials received from and/or developed for clients, and to keep in confidence all research techniques, data and other information considered confidential by their owners.
7. To make available to clients such details on the research methods and techniques of an assignment as may be reasonably required for proper interpretation of the data, providing this reporting does not violate the confidence of respondents or clients.
8. To promote the trust of the public for marketing and survey research activities and to avoid any procedure which misrepresents the activities of a respondent, the rewards of cooperation or the uses of data.
9. To refrain from referring to membership in this organization as proof of competence, since the organization does not so certify any person or organization.
10. To encourage the observance of principles of this code among all people engaged in marketing and survey research.

Source: Reprinted by permission of the Marketing Research Association, Inc., Chicago, IL.

---

must make a difficult choice looks to research to guide the decision. This has the further advantage that if the decision is later proven wrong, the manager can find someone else to blame.

Sometimes a covert purpose will open the way to ethical abuses that present hard dilemmas to researchers. The most serious abuses are created when there is subtle (or not so subtle) pressure to design research to support a particular decision or enhance a legal position.

Dishonesty in Dealing with Suppliers. A few client companies have been known to indulge in "picking the brains" of research suppliers by asking them to submit elaborate bids that detail the research design and methodology the supplier would adopt in conducting the research. Later, the client firms use these ideas and conduct the research on their own. Another technique that client firms sometimes use against suppliers is to make a false promise of future contracts in an effort to obtain a low price for the current project.

Misuse of Research Information. The client firm should not misuse information gathered through marketing research projects. The common form of misuse comes from comparative advertisements or product performance claims that stem from data that are statistically not significant. Though puffery in advertisements is a normal practice, gross misuse of research data is ethically unacceptable.

Too often researchers find themselves dealing with demands by sales or other personnel for access to results and the names and telephone numbers of respondents. The intention, of course, is to use the research study for the entirely different—and usually unethical—purpose of generating sales leads. The only time this is acceptable is when the interviewer specifically asks whether the respondent will accept a follow-up sales call, or would like more information, and acts precisely on the respondent's answer.

Sadly, there are a number of situations where the research study is simply a disguise for a selling pitch. Many people have received phone calls, ostensibly to ask some research questions, but that lead only to a canned sales message for life insurance, encyclopedias, or mutual funds. This is not only unethical behavior because it has no merits on its own, but it is also a serious abuse of respondent rights. Not surprisingly, respondents are more suspicious after a few of these encounters and may refuse to participate in any research study.

The Supplier's Ethics

The more common ethical issues from the research supplier are

▶ *Violating client confidentiality.* Disclosing any information about the client that the supplier has gathered from the research project amounts to a violation of client confidentiality.

▶ *Improper execution of research.* Suppliers are required to conduct marketing research projects in an objective manner, free from personal biases and motives. Improper execution also includes biased sampling, ignoring relevant data, or misusing statistics, all of which lead to erroneous and misleading results. Exhibit 1-4 talks about a lawsuit that has raised many ethical issues in marketing research.

Abuse of Respondents

This perhaps is the most controversial and frequent problem that crops up regarding ethics in conducting research. Any form of violation of a respondent's rights amounts to unethical treatment or abuse of the respondent.

THE RESPONDENT'S ETHICS AND RIGHTS

A respondent who of his or her own free will agrees to participate in a marketing research project has the ethical obligation to provide the supplier, and hence the client, with honest and truthful answers. The respondent can abstain from answering a sensitive question, but falsifying the answer is ethically improper.

Any respondent who participates in a research project, has the following rights:

▶ The right to privacy.

▶ The right to safety.

▶ The right to know the true purpose of the research.

▶ The right to the research results.

▶ The right to decide on which questions to answer.

EXHIBIT 1-4

Beecham Products vs Yankelovich, Clancy Shulman

Beecham Products used the marketing research firm Yankelovich, Clancy Shulman (YCS) to test Delicare, its new cold-water detergent, in a simulated laboratory test market. A laboratory test market involves people being exposed to the advertising of a new product and then shopping in a room that is set up to resemble an area of a supermarket. The percentage of people who buy the brand in this simulated environment and the percentage who say they will repurchase it after using it are among the inputs used to predict sales of the new brand.

The Delicare test resulted in a prediction by YCS that Delicare would gain a dominant 45 to 52 percent share of the market from Woolite, the brand leader with 90 percent of the $103 million market. The only condition was that Beecham would have to spend $18 million in advertising to launch the brand.

Beecham relied on these results for Delicare's national launch. Despite heavy introductory and spending, the performance was far below the projection, and market share hovered around 20 percent. Beecham management was furious and sued YCS for $24 million in damages, accusing the firm of negligence and professional malpractice. A key contention in the suit was that incorrect data were used in the YCS computer model used to predict market performance. The correct percentage of homes that use fine-fabric detergents is 30 percent, but the suit claimed the researcher used an inaccurate figure of 75 percent.

The researchers rebutted with a lengthy catalog of shortcomings by Beecham, including premature termination of ad support; using different ads than were tested; and failing to get adequate distribution of trial sizes. They argued that it is no wonder that the forecast was faulty. The suit, which was settled out of court, sent shockwaves through the research industry and raised several serious issues. Exactly what is the responsibility of a marketing research firm? If it makes a mistake in designing a study, does it accept responsibility for all decisions that were influenced by the study? Does the client, in this case Beecham, have the responsibility to understand every assumption that underlies a recommendation so that they can detect errors?

Source: "A Case of Malpractice in Marketing Research," *Business Week*, October 19, 1987; and "YXS Strikes Back," *Adweek's Marketing Week*, December 7, 1987.

INTERNATIONAL MARKETING RESEARCH

The increase in international trade and the emergence of global corporations resulting from increased globalization of business have had a major impact on all facets of business, including marketing research. The increase in global competition, coupled with the formation of regional trading blocs such as the European Community (EC) and the North American Free Trade Agreement (NAFTA), have spurred the growth of global corporations and the need for international marketing research. The need to collect information relating to international markets, and to monitor trends in these markets, as well as to

EXHIBIT 1-5

Brewing Euro-Style Beer

Miller Brewing Co. is developing a top-secret product believed to be a European-style beer that may eventually be marketed in the United States. Miller, the second largest brewer in the United States behind Anheuser-Busch, already markets a darker version of Lowenbrau, a super-premium brand. Also, the brewer markets some core bands outside North America. Miller Genuine Draft is sold in Ireland and the United Kingdom, while Miller Lite is also sold in the United Kingdom.

But industry observers and consultants believe that a European-style beer would clearly fare better with European palates. "Most U.S. companies have tried to sell American-style beer in Europe, and that's gone over like a lead balloon," says the president of Bevmark, a beverage consultancy. European consumers prefer darker, richer beer with fuller, richer flavors. The Philip Morris company plans to attract European consumers with its launch of a dark premium beer in Europe.

Source: "Miller's Dark Secret," *Adweek's Marketing Week*, June 29, 1992, pp 1, 7.

conduct research to determine the appropriate strategies that will be most effective in international markets, are expanding rapidly. The marketing research industry in the United States is increasingly growing into an international industry, with more than one-third of its revenues coming from foreign operations.

The increase in the importance of global business has caused an increase in awareness of the problems related to international research. *International marketing research can be defined as marketing research conducted to aid in making decisions in more than one country.*[13] As such, the basic functions of marketing research and the research process do not differ from domestic and multicountry research; but the international marketing research process is much more complicated and the international marketing researcher faces problems that are unique, in that normally a domestic researcher does not face such problems. Exhibit 1–5 talks briefly about the problems beer manufacturers face in marketing to different countries.

Throughout this book, we will be discussing the international aspect of the marketing research process, and, when applicable, we will be highlighting the differences between domestic and international research.

Summary

Marketing research links the organization with its market environment. It involves the specification, gathering, analysis, and interpretation of information to help management understand that particular market environment, identify its problems and opportunities, and develop and evaluate courses of marketing action. The marketing management process involves situation analysis, strategy development, and marketing program development and implementation. Each of these areas includes a host of decisions that need to be supported by marketing research information. Marketing research, to be effective, should be relevant, timely, efficient, accurate, and ethical.

Questions and Problems

1. How might the following use marketing research? Be specific.
   a. A small sporting goods store
   b. Continental Airlines
   c. Ohio State University
   d. Houston Astros baseball team
   e. Sears Roebuck
   f. A major television network (CBS, NBC, or ABC)
   g. Compaq Computers
2. How might marketing research be used to support each of the steps in Figure 1-1 that describes the marketing planning process? For example, how could it help select the served market segment?
3. What are some ethical problems that marketing researchers face in designing and conducting field studies?
4. In some companies strategic planning and marketing research functions both report to the same executive and may be more or less integrated. What are the advantages to locating the research function in this part of the organization? What arguments could be made in opposition to this arrangement?
5. Most companies have entire marketing research studies, or portions of entire studies, such as interviewing, done by outside suppliers. What factors will determine whether a firm decides to "make versus buy"; that is, to contract out most or all of a study or conduct it themselves?
6. How does marketing research directed toward strategy development differ from that directed toward marketing program development?
7. Fred Burton, the owner of a small tennis club in Wichita, Kansas, feels that a demand exists for indoor courts that presently is not being served. He is considering employing a marketing research company to conduct a study to ascertain whether a market exists for the indoor facilities.
   a. What factors should Mr. Burton consider before ordering market research to be conducted?
   b. What are the possible pitfalls that the marketing research company must avoid while conducting the study?
   c. After obtaining the market research recommendations, Mr. Burton decided not to use the information generated by the market research study. Which factors could have influenced his decision not to use the research information?
8. Linda Phillips, an engineering student, has designed an innovative piece of equipment to help the physically disabled to communicate. The equipment incorporates a system of electronic signals emitted with a slight turn of the head. She feels that this product could have commercial success if marketed to health care organizations, but she has had no past experience in marketing management and does not know how to undertake the market planning and evaluation process. Acting as Ms. Phillips's marketing consultant, suggest a course of action to help her bring this innovative product to its market.

CASE 1–1
Ethical Dilemmas in Marketing Research[1]

The following scenarios present a set of ethical dilemmas that might arise in marketing research. Your assignment is to decide what action to take in each instance. You should be prepared to justify your decision. Bear in mind that there are no uniquely right answers: Reasonable people may choose different courses of action.

1. You are the market research director of a pharmaceutical company, and the executive director suggests to you that company interviewers telephone physicians under the name of a fictitious market research agency. The purpose of the survey is to help assess the perceived quality of the company's products, and it is felt that the suggested procedure will result in more objective responses.

What action would you take?

2. You are employed by a marketing research firm and have conducted an attitude study for a client. Your data indicates that the product is not being marketed properly. This finding is badly received by the client's product management team. They request that you omit that data from your formal report, which you know will be widely distributed, on the grounds that the verbal presentation was adequate for their needs.

What do you do?

3. You are a study director for a research company undertaking a project for a regular client of your company. A study you are working on is about to go into the field when the questionnaire you sent to the client for final approval comes back drastically modified. The client has rewritten it, introducing leading questions and biased scales. An accompanying letter indicates that the questionnaire must be sent out as revised. You do not believe that valid information can be gathered using the revised instrument.

What action would you take?

4. A well-respected public figure is going to face trial on a charge of failing to report his part ownership of certain regulated companies while serving as a provincial minister. The defense lawyers have asked you, as a market research specialist, to do a research study to determine the characteristics of people most likely to sympathize with the defendant and hence to vote for acquittal. The defense lawyers have read newspaper accounts of how this approach has been used in a number of instances.

What action would you take?

5. You are the market research director for a large chemical company. Recent research indicates that many of your company's customers are misusing one of its principal products. There is no danger resulting from this misuse, though the customers are wasting money by using too much of the product at one time. You are shown the new advertising campaign by the advertising agency. The ads not only ignore this problem of misuse, but actually seem to encourage it.

What action would you take?

6. You are a student in a marketing research course. The professor assigns a project where each student is required to conduct personal interviews with executives of high technology companies concerning their future plans. The professor has stated that all the information is confidential and will only be used in the research course. However, two days after you are assigned the project, you overhear your professor mentioning to a colleague that this research project will be sold to a major technology firm in the industry.

What action would you take?

---

[1] These vignettes were provided through the courtesy of Professor Charles Weinberg, University of British Columbia, and are reproduced with his permission.

End Notes

1. A. K. Kohli and B. J. Jaworski, "Market Orientation: The Construct, Research Propositions, and Managerial Implications," *Journal of Marketing*, 54, April 1990, pp. 1–18.
2. "AmEx Builds Its Relationships," *Adweek's Marketing Week*, June 8, 1992, p. 10.
3. "Marketers Zero In On Their Customers," *The Wall Street Journal*, 1991.
4. Adapted from P. Vincent Barabba and Gerald Zaltman, *Hearing the Voice of the Market*, Massachusetts: Harvard Business School Press, 1991.
5. "Key Role of Research in Agree's Success is Told," *Marketing News*, January 12, 1979, p. 14.
6. Rohit Deshpande and Scott Jeffries, "Attitude Affecting the Use of Marketing Research in Decision Making: An Empirical Investigation," in *Educator's Conference Proceedings*, series 47, ed. Kenneth L. Bernhardt et al. Chicago: American Marketing Association, 1981, pp. 1–4.
7. Rohit Deshpande and Gerald Zaltman, "Factors Affecting the Use of Market Research Information: A Path Analysis," *Journal of Marketing Research*, 19, February 1982, pp. 14–31; Rohit Deshpande and Gerald Zaltman, "A Comparison of Factors Affecting Researcher and Manager Perceptions of Market Research Use," *Journal of Marketing Research*, 21, February 1984, pp. 32–38; Michael Hu, "An Experimental Study of Managers' and Researchers' Use of Consumer Research," *Journal of Academy of Marketing Science*, Fall 1986, pp. 44–51; and Hanjoon Lee, Frank Acito, and Ralph Day, "Evaluation and Use of Marketing Research by Decision Makers: A Behavioral Simulation," *Journal of Marketing Research*, 24, May 1987, pp. 187–196.
8. Rohit Deshpande and Gerald Zaltman, "A Comparison of Factors Affecting Use of Marketing Information in Consumer and Industrial Firms," *Journal of Marketing Research*, 24, February 1987, pp. 114–118.
9. Betsy D. Gelb and Gabriel M. Gelb, "Coke's Lesson to the Rest of Us," *Sloan Management Review*, Fall 1986.
10. Robert D. Hisrich and Michael P. Peters, *Marketing Decisions for New and Mature Products*, New York: MacMillan Publishing Co. 1991, p. 427.
11. "Code of Ethics of Marketing Research Association," *Marketing Research Association Inc.*, Chicago, Il.
12. "CASRO Code of Standards for Survey Research," *The Council of American Survey Research Organizations*, Annual Journal 1992, pp. 19–22.
13. Douglas P. Susan and Samuel C. Craig, *International Marketing Research*, Prentice Hall Series in Marketing, 1983, p. 24.

2 MARKETING RESEARCH IN PRACTICE

Learning Objectives

▶ Discuss briefly the practice of marketing research.

▶ Expose the students to the concept of *information systems and decision support systems.*

▶ Explain *marketing decision support systems.*

▶ Introduce the various suppliers of marketing research information and the types of services offered by them.

▶ Briefly talk about the criteria to be used for selecting among suppliers.

▶ Introduce the career options available in the marketing research industry.

In practice, a marketing research department's goal can be grouped into three major categories:[1] programmatic, selective, or evaluative. Programmatic research is performed to develop marketing options through market segmentation, market opportunity analysis, or consumer attitude and product usage studies. Selective research is done to test different decision alternatives such as new product concept testing, advertising copy testing, pre-test marketing, and test marketing. Evaluative research is carried out to evaluate performance of programs, including tracking advertising recall, corporate and brand image studies, and measuring customer satisfaction with the quality of the product and service. As the number of products and types of services introduced into the market increase, the need for marketing research explodes and the future of marketing research appears to be both promising and challenging.[2]

Unquestionably, marketing research is a growth industry. In the last decade, real expenditures on marketing research (that is, after adjusting for inflation) more than doubled! This is largely a consequence of economic and social changes that have made better marketing an imperative.

> *With marketing the new priority, marketing research is the rallying cry. Companies are trying frantically to get their hands on information that identifies and explains the needs of powerful new consumer segments now being formed. Kroger Co., for example, holds more than 250,000 consumer interviews a year to define consumer wants more precisely. Some companies are pinning their futures to product innovations, others are rejuvenating timeworn but proven brands, and still others are doing both.[3]*

Not only are the companies that always did marketing research doing a great deal more, but the breadth of research activities also continues to expand:

▶ Senior management is looking for more support for its strategic decisions; therefore, researchers are doing more acquisition and competitor studies, segmentation and market structure analyses, and basic strategic position assessments.

▶ Other functions, such as the legal department, now routinely use marketing research evidence. Corporate Affairs wants to know shareholders', bankers', analysts', and employees' attitudes toward the company. The service department continuously audits service delivery capability and customer satisfaction.

▶ Entire industries that used to be protected from the vagaries of competition and changing customer needs by regulatory statutes are learning to cope with a deregulated environment. Airlines, banks, and financial services groups are looking for ways to overcome product proliferation, advertising clutter, and high marketing costs brought on by more sophisticated customers and aggressive competitors.

In this chapter we will look at how companies use the information gathered by marketing research, at the various ways they obtain this marketing research information, and at the career opportunities available in the marketing research industry.

INFORMATION SYSTEMS, DECISION SUPPORT SYSTEMS, AND MARKETING RESEARCH

An **information system (IS)** is a continuing and interacting structure of people, equipment, and procedures designed to gather, sort, analyze, evaluate, and distribute pertinent, timely, and accurate information to decision makers.

While marketing research is mainly concerned with the actual content of the information and how it is to be generated, the information system is concerned with managing the flow of data from many different projects and secondary sources to the managers who will use it. This requires databases to organize and store the information and a decision support system (DSS) to retrieve data, transform it into usable information, and disseminate it to the users.

Databases

Information systems contain three types of information. The first is the recurring day to day information; for example, the market and accounting data that flow into the organization as a result of market analysis research and accounting activities. Automobile firms use government sources for monthly data on new-car sales by brand and geographic area. In addition, surveys are conducted yearly to determine the age and types of automobiles currently driven, the lifestyles of the drivers (their activity and interest patterns), their media habits, and their intentions to replace their cars. The accounting department will submit sales and inventory data for each of its dealers on a continuing basis, to update and supplement the information system.

A second type of information is intelligence relevant to the future strategy of the business. Automobile firms, for example, will collect reports about new sources of fuel to power automobiles. This information could come from scientific meetings, trade organizations, or perhaps from government reports. It also might include information from salespersons or dealers about new-product tests being conducted by competitive firms. Intelligence is difficult to develop, because it usually involves diverse and changing sets of topic and information sources and is rarely collected systematically.

A third input to the information system is the research studies that are not of a recurring nature. The potential usefulness of a marketing research study can be multiplied manyfold if the information is accessible instead of filed and forgotten. However, the potential exists that others may use the study, although perhaps not in the way it was originally intended.

Decision Support Systems

Databases have no value if the insights they contain can't be retrieved. A decision support system (DSS) not only allows the manager to interact directly with the database to retrieve what is wanted, it also provides a modeling function to help make sense of what has been retrieved.

A common example of a DSS in action is that used by many industrial salespeople—especially those selling products that require significant customization. The salesperson frequently will be asked whether or not the price and delivery time of a unique product configuration will meet or exceed a competitor's promises. Without leaving the customer's office, the salesperson can plug a lap-top computer into a phonejack and begin communicating with a database stored in the main computer memory. The salesperson types in the product configuration and desired delivery data, and these requirements are compared to the costs, inventory, and assembly time contained in the data bank. In a matter of minutes, the salesperson can propose a price and delivery date—and perhaps close the sale.

Each firm has to develop or adapt models to support its own decision problems. For example, Avon Products, Inc., the door-to-door cosmetics firm, has unique problems as the result of a part-time sales force of almost 400,000 representatives theoretically covering half of the 80 million households in North America. This sales force carried a large product line that each year had 1600 new or reformulated products added. The following computer models were added to their DSS to help cope with these problems:[4]

▶ A sales force turnover model, which revealed that the most significant variable influencing the rate was the level of appointment fee that the representatives pay for the initial material.

▶ An order model that explains the components of the average order and isolates the actionable variables such as the size and timing of the catalog and the gift incentives.

▶ A procurement model that helps determine how much of a new product to buy, when to purchase it, and the risks that are involved.

Applying Information Systems to Marketing Research

Often the process of developing and using models and information systems reveals gaps in the data bank that have to be closed. These emergent needs for information become a marketing research problem; for example,

▶ Performance (sales, market share, contributions, patronage) may be unsatisfactory relative to objectives. Perhaps the condition can be traced to a specific geographic area, but the underlying reasons still must be sought before action can be taken.

▶ A competitor may launch a new product or employ a new advertising appeal, with unknown consequences for the firm's competitive position.

▶ An unavoidable increase in costs puts pressures on profitability (or, in the case of a transit system, increases the subsidy requirements to an unacceptable level). Various possible increases in fares or prices must be evaluated.

▶ An upsurge in interest in health and nutrition may suggest to a snack company a new product line directed toward responding to this interest. Concept testing might be a first step in exploring this opportunity.

Given the sometimes chaotic and usually uncertain nature of most market environments, a large number of problems and some opportunities can emerge. Few will ever be given formal consideration: There may be no further need for clarification, the implications may not appear serious, or the response may appear evident in the judgment of the decision maker. Our interest is in those problems or opportunities that need to be clarified, whose consequences are uncertain, or that involve the development of new programs, products, or services.

The information system serves to emphasize that marketing research should not exist in isolation as a single effort to obtain information. Rather, it should be part of a more systematic and continuous effort by the organization to improve the decision-making process. Exhibit 2–1 describes the "third wave" in marketing research, telling us how marketing research has progressed from the rudimentary to the sophisticated.

MARKETING DECISION SUPPORT SYSTEMS

A typical marketing manager regularly receives some or all of the following data: factory shipments or orders; syndicated aggregate (industry) data services; sales reports from the field sales force; consumer panel data; scanner data;

EXHIBIT 2-1

The Third Wave in Marketing Research

The term **Third Wave,** coined from Alvin Toffler's book of the same name, has come to symbolize the contemporary transition from current ways of viewing and doing things to a new age. The coming changes will shape not only the way information is used, but also our fundamental conception of the role of marketing research in assisting management decisions.

In the **First Wave,** seat-of-the-pants decision making progressed to data-based decisions. Much of the initial interest in marketing research came about during the transition from a sales-oriented to a marketing-oriented business environment. The need to support marketing decisions with data drove much of the initial interest in research. Although a data-based approach makes logical sense, the seeds of dissatisfaction were buried deep within the philosophy. As more data became available, a large problem arose: A handful of data was helpful; a truckload was not necessarily better.

In the **Second Wave,** the progression was from data-based decisions to information-based decision making. Rather than review a multitude of individual facts, the role of marketing research evolved to manipulate data to summarize the underlying patterns. If we could understand the relationships and patterns in the data, so the logic went, this would lead to the insights necessary to drive marketing decisions. Unfortunately, much of the criticism of marketing research today is a result of this excessive focus on methodology and statistics. The problem now with marketing research was not centered on incompetent analysis, but the lack of a decision maker's perspective and the inability to provide actionable insights consistently once the data were analyzed correctly.

Now with the **Third Wave,** we progress from information-based decision making to system-based decisions. The Third Wave involves a number of developments centered on automated decision systems (ADS) that put the power of marketing information directly into the hands of nontechnical decision makers. It is a three-way marriage between marketing analysis, computer and information technologies, and the formal marketing planning process. The team approach, including marketing researchers, systems engineers, and marketing management, provides the synergy needed to build useful computer-based systems that help managers through the marketing planning and evaluation process. Through pooling expertise and applying information technologies, the full potential of marketing information can be realized in the Third Wave.

Source: "Third Wave of Marketing Research on the Horizon," *Marketing News,* March 1, 1993, p. 6.

---

demographic data and internal cost and budget data. These data may also come in various levels of detail and aggregation. Often they use different reporting periods and incompatible computer languages. Add to this sales estimates about competing brands and advertising, promotion, and pricing activity, and there is a data explosion.

But managers don't want data. They need decision-relevant information in accessible and preferably graphical form for (1) routine comparisons of current performance against past trends on each of the key measures of effectiveness, (2) periodic exception reports to assess which sales territories or accounts have not matched their previous years' purchases, and (3) special analyses to evaluate the sales impact of particular marketing programs, and to predict what would happen if changes were made. In addition, different divisions would like to be linked to enable product managers, sales planners, market researchers, financial analysts, and production schedulers to share information.

The purpose of a **marketing decision support system (MDSS)** is to combine marketing data from diverse sources into a single database which line managers can enter interactively to quickly identify problems and obtain standard, periodic reports, as well as answers to analytical questions.

Characteristics of an MDSS

A good MDSS should have the following characteristics:

1. *Interactive:* The process of interaction with the MDSS should be simple and direct. With just a few commands the user should be able to obtain the results immediately. There should be no need for a programmer in between.
2. *Flexible:* A good MDSS should be flexible. It should be able to present the available data in either discrete or aggregate form. It should satisfy the information needs of the managers in different hierarchical levels and functions.
3. *Discovery Oriented:* The Marketing Decision Support System should not only assist the managers in solving the existing problems but should also help them to probe for trends and ask new questions. The managers should be able to discover new patterns and be able to act on them using the MDSS.
4. *User Friendly:* The MDSS should be user friendly. It should be easy for the managers to learn and use the system. It should not take hours just to figure out what is going on. Most MDSS packages are menu driven and are easy to operate.

A typical MDSS is assembled from four components (see Figure 2-1).

Database

This contains data from all sources, and it is stored in a sufficiently disaggregated way so that it can be analyzed by product item, sales district, trade account, and time period. The best systems have databases that can be easily updated with new information and have sufficient flexibility that data can be readily analyzed in new ways. Since most analyses deal with a subset of a larger database, the supporting software should permit random access to any and all data to create appropriate subsets.

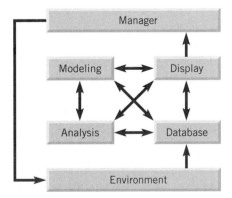

FIGURE 2-1
The four components of an MDSS

Reports and Displays

The capabilities of an MDSS range from simple ad hoc tables and reports to complex plots, charts, and other graphic displays. Any report or display can include calculations such as variances and running totals, or the results of statistical procedures found in the system. Typical reports produced with an MDSS include status reports that track current trends, exception reports on troubled brands and markets, and variance reports showing budget and actuals for sales and profits. The report in Figure 2-2 answers the question: In which regions is the Mama Mia brand not keeping up with the industry trend? Figure 2-2 shows that the product category sales were up 5.8 percent, whereas Mama Mia sales were up only 2.0 percent. On a more detailed level, product category sales were up 13.1 percent in Cleveland and 1.7 percent in Miami, while Mama Mia sales rose 6.5 percent in Cleveland and fell 0.3 percent in Miami.

Analysis Capabilities

These are used to relate the data to the models, as well as clarify relationships, identify exceptions, and suggest courses of action. These capabilities should include the ability to make calculations such as averages, lags, and percentage changes versus a previous period, and to conduct seasonal analyses and standard statistical procedures such as regression, correlation, and factor analysis. These procedures will be covered in subsequent chapters of this book.

Models

These represent assumptions about how the world works, and specifically how brand sales, shares, and profits respond to changes in elements of the marketing mix. Models are used to test alternative marketing programs, answer "what if" questions, and assist in setting more realistic objectives. For example, managers want help with such questions as: What is the impact on profitability of achieving wider distribution? What is the optimal call level for each sales representative for each account and prospect? What objectives should be set for coupon redemption and the profitability of promotion programs? The models used to address these questions can range from forecasts to complex simulations of relationships among marketing, economic, and other factors.

Using an MDSS offers the organization a number of advantages. It results in substantial cost savings, because it helps in making better and quicker decisions. The presence of an MDSS forces the decision maker to view the decision and information environment within which he or she operates; hence, it leads to a better understanding of the decision environment. Since the managers can now retrieve and utilize information that was never accessible before, it results in the enhancement of decision-making effectiveness. Using a MDSS results in better quality and quantity of data being collected and hence increases the value of information to the managers.

Gaining Insights from an MDSS

When an OTC (over-the-counter) drug manufacturer suffered a decline in national unit market share for its drug "Alpha," management turned to an MDSS for insights. They suspected the losses would be traced to actions of the

MARKETING DECISION
SUPPORT SYSTEMS

two main competitors. "Beta" was a private label competitor that was sold at half the price of Alpha. The other competing brand, "Delta," was produced and marketed by another division of the same company, following a rather similar strategy. Initial data from the decision support system seemed to confirm management's initial suspicions. Alpha's share had dropped from 5.0 percent to 2.5 percent, and Delta's share had more than doubled from 2.0 percent to

Comparison Matrix
Issue 203 Ending 04.02.88

% Change in Category Sales vs Year Ago			% Change in Mama Mia Sales vs Year Ago	
28.7			Memphis	9.8
20.3			San Antonio	14.0
13.3			Oklahoma City	10.5
13.1			Cleveland	6.5
12.8			Kansas City	9.3
12.8			Detroit	4.1
11.6			Cincinnati/Dayton	4.1
10.9	Indianapolis	0.0		
10.1			Houston	6.3
9.6	Milwaukee	−0.4		
9.3	Norfolk/Richmond	0.9		
9.3			Phoenix/Tucson	6.4
Above 9.3			Minneapolis/St. Paul	8.4
8.5			Omaha/Des Moines	6.3
8.5			St. Louis	12.1
8.4				
7.9	Pittsburg	−1.5	Buffalo	7.1
7.8			New Orleans	7.7
7.8				
7.8	Albany/Schnectedy	−4.5	New York	3.1
7.1			Salt Lake City	11.1
7.1			Boston/Providence	7.7
7.0			Dallas/Ft. Worth	6.7
6.6			Jacksonville/	7.8
6.0	Syracuse	1.3		
5.9			Charlotte	4.0
U.S. Average 5.8				
5.3			Portland	3.6
4.8			Nashville/Knoxville	3.2
4.6	Birmingham/Mobile	−0.9		
4.4			Denver	2.6
3.9	Baltimore/Washington	−3.1		
2.9			Seattle/Tacoma	7.1
Below 2.7			Atlanta	10.1
1.7	Miami	−0.3		
1.2	Chicago	1.3		
0.3	Los Angeles/San Diego	−0.2		
−0.6	Philadelphia	−4.7		
−2.3	Raleigh/Greensboro	−0.2		
−5.2	San Francisco	−9.6		
	Below	2.0 U.S. Average	Above	

FIGURE 2-2
Comparison of brand performance with industry trend

4.5 percent. However, subsequent analysis of the database showed that this information was misleading and shouldn't be followed.

The premise of the further analysis was that any competitive effects should be evident at the regional as well as the national level. To test this possibility, the market share changes of Alpha were related to share changes of Beta and Delta, by region, for a six-month period.

The results in Figure 2-3 certainly confirmed the adverse effects of Beta on Alpha. In almost every region, a share decrease for Alpha was associated with a share increase for Beta. A different picture emerged when a similar analysis (in Figure 2-4) was done with Delta. In the regions where Alpha's share had decreased the least, Delta's share had increased the most. Conversely, Alpha's share had decreased the most in those regions where Delta had gained the least share. Clearly, Delta was not the source of Alpha's problems; more likely, Delta was helping Alpha by combining the two brands' sales force efforts. This analysis prevented a potentially damaging interdivisional dispute and helped focus management's attention on the proper target competitor.

SUPPLIERS OF INFORMATION

In general, there are two basic types of sources through which managers can acquire the necessary information for decision making:

1. The corporate or in-house marketing research department.
2. External suppliers.

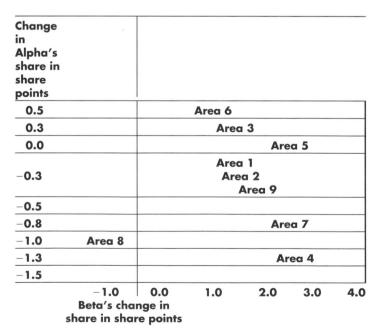

FIGURE 2-3
Regional market share changes—Alpha and Beta

Change in Alpha's share in share points								
0.50								
0.25						Area 2	Area 7	
0.00		Area 5						
		Area 6						
−0.25			Area 9					
		Area 1		Area 3				
−0.50	Area 8							
−0.75								
−1.00			Area 4					
−1.25								
	0.0	0.5	1.0	1.5	2.0	2.5	3.0	3.5

Change in Delta's
share in share
points

FIGURE 2-4

Regional market share changes—Alpha and Delta

Usually, managers use a mix of in-house and external approaches to solve a certain problem. Both can feed information directly to their clients who are users with decision-making needs. More often, the outside suppliers will get their direction and provide information to an inside research group. These inside suppliers translate the problems of their clients into specific information requirements, decide how the information will be collected and by whom, and then interpret the findings. Figure 2-5 shows the interaction between the participants in a marketing research activity.

The purpose of this section is to briefly discuss the nature and attributes of the providers of marketing research services, the types of services they

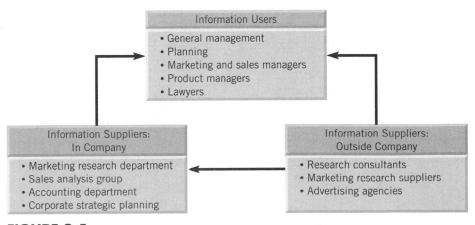

FIGURE 2-5

Participants in marketing research activities

provide, and the factors that influence the choice of a suitable supplier for a given situation. Figure 2-6 gives a concise summary of the different types of information suppliers within the marketing research industry.

Corporate/In-house Marketing Research

The location of the marketing research department within an organization and the strength of the department vary from firm to firm and to a very great extent depend on the requirements for information and the organizational structure of the firm. Some firms have a single centralized research department, housed in the corporate headquarters, which provides the information required to the various business units scattered geographically and/or functionally. The other extreme is the completely decentralized operation, wherein each business unit or geographic unit has its own research department. The type of structure adopted depends on the amount of information required, the frequency with which it is required, the uniqueness of the information, and the time available to collect it. In most major organizations, especially in multinational corporations, a mix of both these structures can be found.

Not all organizations (regardless of size) have an in-house research establishment. Even among those that have an in-house research department, it is not unusual for them to seek the assistance of external suppliers. Virtually all

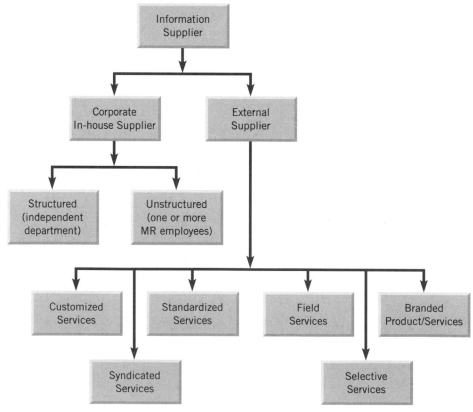

FIGURE 2-6
Information, suppliers, and services

research users will at some time use the services of outside research specialists. Their role may be limited to raw-data collection, depending on the research approach, questionnaire, and sampling method provided by the client. At the other extreme, the client may assign the entire problem to an outside consultant who is responsible for every step to the completed report and action recommendations. Other possibilities are to bring in outside specialists for special problems (such as a sampling expert to draw a complex sample), or to employ services that have special facilities or data.

Many related considerations will influence the decision to go outside:

1. Internal personnel may not have the skills or experience. Few but the largest companies have specialists in all areas, from psychologists able to conduct focus-group interviewing, to electronics engineers with MBAs who have studied the telecommunications equipment market.

2. Outside help may be called in to boost internal capacity in response to an urgent deadline.

3. It may be cheaper to go outside. Specialists who have encountered similar problems with other clients probably are more efficient in dealing with the problem, and because they are not on the staff there is no risk of under-utilization of their time.

4. Shared cost and multiclient studies coordinated by an outside supplier offer considerable savings possibilities. Multiclient studies are feasible when several organizations have related needs for information about a major topic, such as the future of electronic funds transfer systems. Each client will pay an agreed share of the total cost. The ultimate in shared cost studies are the large standardized data collection services, such as store audits of product sales activity or omnibus surveys, which combine questions from several clients.

5. Often, outside suppliers have special facilities or competencies (an established national interviewing field force, conference rooms with one-way mirrors, banks of telephone lines, or test kitchens) that would be costly to duplicate for a single study.

6. Political considerations may dictate the use of an outside research specialist whose credentials are acceptable to all parties in an internal policy dispute. Research people within the organization may be well advised to avoid being on one side or the other of a sensitive issue.

7. Marketing research is used increasingly in litigation or in proceedings before regulatory or legislative bodies. The credibility of the findings generally will be enhanced if the study is conducted by a respected outsider. Also, this kind of research often is subjected to critical questioning or cross-examination and is likely to stand up only if designed to high standards, which may exceed those used within the organization for routine decision-making purposes.

External Suppliers of the Research Industry

The marketing research industry in the United States consists of several hundreds of research firms ranging from small, one-person operations to large corporations having operations in multiple countries. Table 2-1 provides a list

TABLE 2-1
Top 25 U.S. Research Organizations

Rank 1993	1992	Organization	Headquarters	Phone	Total research revenues (millions)	Percent change from 1992	Percent and revenues from outside U.S. ($ in millions)	
1	1/2	D&B Marketing Information Services	Cham, Switzerland	(41 42) 362 244	$1,868.3	−1.2%	61.0%	$1,139.7
2	3	Information Resources Inc.	Chicago, IL	(312) 726-1221	334.5	21.1	15.0	50.2
3	4	The Arbitron Co.	New York, NY	(212) 887-1300	172.0	−3.4		
4	6	Walsh International/PMSI	Phoenix, AZ	(602) 381-9500	115.4	32.1	34.4	39.7
5	5	Westat Inc.	Rockville, MD	(301) 251-1500	113.1	−0.5		
6	7	Maritz Marketing Research Inc.	St. Louis, MO	(314) 827-1610	74.4	6.7		
7	8	The NPD Group	Port Washington, NY	(516) 625-0700	66.0	15.6	23.8	15.7
8	10	NFO Research Inc.	Greenwich, CT	(203) 629-8888	51.9	10.2		
9	11	Elrick & Lavidge Inc.	Atlanta, GA	(404) 885-8657	47.1	0.6		
10	12	Market Facts Inc.	Arlington Heights, IL	(708) 590-7000	45.6	12.0		
11	9	The M/A/R/C Group	Las Colinas, TX	(214) 506-3400	44.7	−17.1		
12	13	Walker Group	Indianapolis, IN	(317) 843-3939	38.1	−3.0	1.9	.7
13	19	Abt Associates Inc.	Cambridge, MA	(617) 492-7100	36.4	33.8		
14	14	MRB Group	London, England	(44-81) 579-5500	35.0	2.8		
15	18	The National Research Group Inc.	Los Angeles, CA	(213) 549-5000	34.5	25.5	15.0	5.2
16	15	NOP Information Group	Livingston, NJ	(201) 717-0500	33.0	3.4		
17	16	Intersearch Corp.	Horsham, PA	(215) 657-6400	32.2	7.0		
18	17	The BASES Group	Covington, KY	(606) 655-6000	31.0	10.7	5.0	1.6
19	20	Millward Brown Inc.	Naperville, IL	(708) 505-0066	29.0	15.1		
20	—	Opinion Research Corp.	Princeton, NJ	(908) 281-5100	26.6	−8.6	27.9	7.4
21	21	Burke Marketing Research	Cincinnati, OH	(513) 241-5663	26.1	7.0	2.9	.8
22	25	Roper Starch Worldwide Inc.	Mamaroneck, NY	(914) 698-0800	24.9	9.2	4.0	.9
23	26	J.D. Power & Associates	Agoura Hills, CA	(818) 889-6330	24.5	17.1		
24	28	Creative & Response Research Svcs.	Chicago, IL	(312) 828-9200	23.8	28.1		
25	24	Research International USA	New York, NY	(212) 679-2500	22.7	−.1	30.4	6.9

Source: "The 1994 Honomichl Business Report On The Marketing Research Industry," Marketing News, June 6, 1994.

of the top 25 marketing research firms, their annual revenues for the year 1993, and the percent change from the previous year.[6] The table also gives an estimate of the total revenue from foreign operations. As can be seen from the table, the total revenue of the top 25 firms exceeds $3 billion, and more than one-third of this revenue is estimated to come from foreign operations.

The marketing research industry in the United States is not only huge and profitable, but is also a growing industry with research spendings within the United States, showing a 7.6 percent real growth (after adjusting for inflation) for the year 1992 and a 6.3 percent real growth for 1993. Figure 2-7 gives a comparison of the growth in research spending within the United States for the years 1987 to 1993.[7] According to Jack Honomichl, the president of Marketing Aid Center Inc., Barrington, Illinois, and the author of the *Annual Industry Review,* much of this growth can be traced to three factors: **pharmaceutical/health care, customer satisfaction measurement,** and **revenues from foreign operations.**

Type and Nature of Services

External suppliers that collectively comprise the marketing research industry can be further classified into six different groups, depending on the type and nature of the services they provide. Based on Figure 2-6, the major types of services provided by external suppliers of information are discussed in the paragraphs that follow.

Customized Services. Firms that specialize in customized services work with individual clients to help them develop and implement a marketing research project from top to bottom. They work with the management on any given problem and go through the entire research process, including analyzing and presenting the final results.

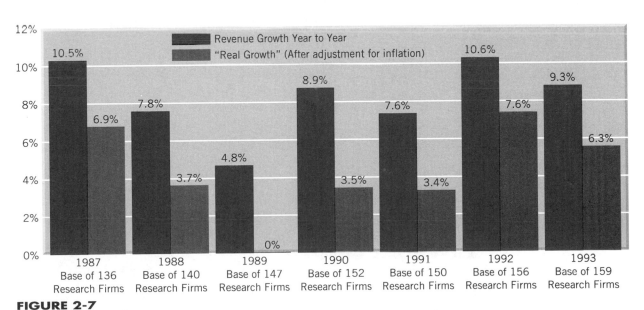

FIGURE 2-7
Growth in research spending within the U.S.
Source: "Combined Revenues for '93 Hit $3.7 Billion," *Marketing News,* June 6, 1994

Syndicated Services. These are companies that routinely collect information on several different issues and provide it to firms that subscribe to their services. The Nielsen Television Index, which provides information on audiences viewing different TV programs, is an example of such services. These suppliers also provide information on retail sales, household purchasing patterns, and so on, which they collect through scanner data.

Standardized Services. These are market research projects conducted in a standard, pre-specified manner and supplied to several different clients. The Starch Readership Survey is a typical example of such a service; it provides clients information regarding the effectiveness of print advertisements, in the form of Starch scores.

Field Services. These suppliers concentrate only on collecting data for research projects. They specialize in various survey techniques such as mail surveys, telephone surveys, or personal surveys. These organizations range from small one-person establishments to large multinational **wide area telephone service (WATS)**-line interviewing services, and have extensive facilities for personal interviews in homes and shopping malls. Some of these firms specialize in qualitative data collection methods such as **focus** group interviews, and **projection** techniques.

Selective Services. Some companies specialize in just one or two aspects of marketing research, mainly concerned with data coding, data editing, or data analysis. These generally are small firms, sometimes referred to as lab houses, with expertise in sophisticated data analysis techniques. The proliferation of software for marketing research projects has led to an increase in such types of lab houses. Any enterprising individual with expertise in computer and sophisticated multivariate analysis techniques can acquire the required software packages and establish a firm specializing in data analysis.

Branded Products Services. Some firms have developed specialized data collection and analysis procedures to address specific types of research problems, which they market as branded products. *PRIZM,* a Claritas Corporation product that forms clusters of the population on the basis of life-style and zip code classifications, is an example of one such branded product. Based on this technique, the entire U.S. population has been divided into forty clusters. Author Michael J. Weiss, in his popular book *Clustering of America,* provides a vivid portrait of the nation's forty neighborhood types—their values, life-styles, and eccentricities.

CRITERIA FOR SELECTING EXTERNAL SUPPLIERS

Once the decision has been made to go outside, there still remains the question of which consultant or supplier to retain. What criteria should a firm adopt in selecting an external research supplier? Several academic scholars have conducted research studies to identify the factors that are important in the selection of external suppliers. A crucial factor in the choice is the judgment as to whether the supplier or consultant actually can deliver the promised data, advice, or conclusions. This judgment should be made only after the following steps have been followed:

1. A thorough search for names of people and companies who have acknowledged expertise in the area of the study.[8]
2. The selection of a small number of bidders on the basis of recommendations of colleagues or others who have had similar needs.
3. Personal interviews with the person who would be responsible for the project, asking for examples of work on similar problems, their procedures for working with clients, and the names of previous clients who could provide references.
4. A check of the references of each potential supplier, with special attention to comments on their depth of competence and expertise, their creativity in dealing with problems, and the quality and adequacy of resources available.
5. Selection on the basis of how well the problem and objectives have been understood,[9] the comments by the references, and whether the quoted price or fee is a good value in light of the research approach that is proposed. Seldom is the lowest quotation going to be the best value. To minimize the problem of comparability, have all bidders respond to the same study specifications.[10]

THE INTERNATIONAL MARKETING RESEARCH INDUSTRY

The growing importance of the international components of the marketing research industry revenue reflects the fact that the United States accounts for only 39 percent of the marketing research expenditures worldwide. Western Europe accounts for 40 percent of the research expenditures, Japan accounts for nearly 10 percent, and the remainder is accounted for by the rest of the world. Almost all major countries in the world, including the newly industrialized and developing countries, have major marketing research organizations. The leading market research companies in the United States such as A.C. Nielsen Co. have subsidiaries in several countries. The top ten marketing research firms in the world are given in Table 2-2.

CAREER OPPORTUNITIES IN MARKETING RESEARCH

Marketing research offers several promising career opportunities, depending upon one's level of education, experience, interests, and personality. Interesting and exciting careers are available both within research supplier organizations— typically, the external supplier of marketing research services such as A.C.

TABLE 2-2
Top Ten Marketing Research Companies of the World

Research company	Turnover (mill.ECU)[1]	Countries with office[2]	Head office	Ownership
1. A.C. Nielsen	868	32	USA	Dun & Bradstreet, USA
2. IMS International	454	62[3]	USA/UK	Dun & Bradstreet, USA
3. IRI	214	4[3]	USA	Public Company, USA
4. GfK	178	26	D	Public Company, D
5. Arbitron	138[4]	1	USA	Ceridian Corp., USA
6. Sofrès/Cecodis	131	8	F	Fimalac-led Group, F
7. Research International	113	40	UK	WPP, UK
8. Westat	88	1	USA	Private Company, USA
9. Infratest/Burke	87[5]	13	D	Private Company, D
10. Video Research	82	1	J	Dentsu et al., J

Sources: ESOMAR Annual Market Study, major research companies, J. Honomichl/Marketing News.

1) Excluding associates.
2) Including associates.
3) No 1992 information available; these data refer to the 1991 market situation.
4) Estimate (J. Honomichl).
5) Turnover relates to the year ending 9/92.

Nielsen, Information Resources Inc. (IRI), J. D. Power and Associates, and so on—and within companies that have their own research department. A brief description of marketing research jobs, the required level of education, the real level of experience, and the average annual compensation are provided in the Appendix.[11]

Summary

The focus of marketing research has shifted from adhoc methods to collecting data and helping managers make informed, knowledgeable decisions. The MDSS is the latest in the series of developments that help marketing managers use the information they obtain in a more meaningful manner. Marketing research is a key component of the MDSS as it provides one of the inputs into the system. Marketing research can be done either in-house or can be bought from outside suppliers. There are a number of market research companies that provide many services—both syndicated and customized.

Questions and Problems

1. a. How do marketing information systems aid marketers in their decision making?
    b. What are the types of information that can be obtained from marketing information systems?

2. What are the inherent characteristics of an effective marketing-decision support system?

3. A marketing manager needs to find the causes for the decline in market share of his/her company's product. The manager decides to conduct marketing research.
   a. How should he/she go about finding a supplier of research services?
   b. Suppose the manager decides to introduce the product in Europe. A study needs to be conducted to assess the acceptance of the product in various markets. What criteria should the manager use in selecting a research supplier?

End Notes

1. Sil Seggev, "Listening Is Key to Providing Useful Marketing Research," *Marketing News,* January 22, 1982, p. 6.

2. Kenneth R. Wade, "The When/What Research Decision Guide," *Marketing Research: A Magazine of Management & Applications,* 5, Summer 1993, pp 24–27.

3. "Marketing: The New Priority," *Business Week,* November 21, 1983, p. 96.

4. Cyndee Miller, "Computer Modelling Rings the Right Bell for Avon," *Marketing News,* May 9, 1988, p. 14.

5. Paul Boughton, "Marketing Research Partnerships: A Strategy for the '90s," *Marketing Research: A Magazine of Management and Applications,* 4, December 1992, pp 8–13.

6. "The 1994 Honomichl Business Report on the Marketing Research Industry," *Marketing News,* June 6, 1994, p. H4.

7. "Combined Revenues for '93 Hit $3-7 billion," *Marketing News,* June 6, 1994.

8. Useful Sources are *Greenbook: International Directory of Marketing Research Houses and Services,* New York: American Marketing Association, Annual; *Consultants and Consulting Organizations Directory,* Detroit: Gale Research Co., Triennial with Annual Supplements; and *Bradfords Directory of Marketing Research Agencies in the U.S. and Around the World,* Fairfax, Virginia: Bradford Publishing Co., 1984. A list of the top 300 companies that specialize in focus group interviewing techniques can be obtained from the January issues of *Marketing News.*

9. *Marketing News* provides a directory of software for marketing research application.

10. Raymond D. Speer, "Follow These Six Steps to Get Most Benefits from Marketing Research Consultant Project," *Marketing News,* September 18, 1981, pp. 12, 13. *The Marketing News* on a regular basis gives a directory of international marketing research firms.

11. Sources: Thomas C. Kinnear and Ann R. Root, *1988 Survey of Marketing Research,* Chicago: American Marketing Association; and Carl McDaniel and Roger Gates, *Contemporary Marketing Research,* Minneapolis: West Publishing Co., p. 26. *Marketing News* on a regular basis publishes a directory of marketing research firms, within research users such as Coca-Cola, AT&T, etc., in their in-house research department.

Careers in Marketing Research

Description of Marketing Research Jobs	Level of Education	Level of Experience	Range of Compensation
Research Director/Vice President of Marketing Research: This is the senior position in research. The director is responsible for the entire research program of his or her company. Accepts assignments from superiors or from clients, or may on own initiative develop and propose research undertakings to company executives. Employs personnel and executes general supervision of research department. Presents research findings to clients or to company executives.	Graduate degree	10+ years	$60,000–$80,000
Assistant Director of Research: This position usually represents a defined "second in command," a senior staff member having responsibilities above those of other staff members.	Graduate degree	5+ years	$55,000–$70,000
Statistician/Data Processing Specialist: Duties are usually those of an expert consultant on theory and application of statistical techniques to specific research problems. Usually responsible for experimental design and data processing.	Graduate degree	2+ years	$40,000–$60,000
Senior Analyst: Usually found in larger research departments. Participates with superior in initial planning of research projects, and directs execution of projects assigned. Operates with minimal supervision. Prepares, or works with analysts in preparing questionnaires. Selects research techniques, makes analyses, and writes final report. Budgetary control over projects and primary responsibility for meeting time schedules rests with the senior analyst.	Graduate degree	3+ years	$40,000–$50,000

Description of Marketing Research Jobs	Level of Education	Level of Experience	Range of Compensation
Analyst: The analyst usually handles the bulk of the work required for executing research projects. Often works under senior analyst's supervision. The analyst assists in preparing questionnaires, pretests them, and makes preliminary analyses of results. The analyst handles most of the library research or work with company data.	College degree	2+ years	$30,000–$40,000
Junior Analyst: Working under rather close supervision, junior analysts handle routine assignments. Editing and coding of questionnaires, statistical calculations above the clerical level, and simpler forms of library research are among their duties. A large portion of the junior analyst's time is spent on tasks assigned by superiors.	College degree	0–1 years	$25,000–$30,000
Librarian: The librarian builds and maintains a library of reference sources adequate to the needs of the research department.	College degree	0–1 years	$30,000–$35,000
Clerical Supervisor: In larger departments, the central handling and processing of statistical data are the responsibilities of one or more clerical supervisors. Duties include work scheduling, and responsibility for accuracy.	Vocational degree	2–4 years	$20,000–$25,000
Field Work Director: Usually only larger departments have a field work director, who hires, trains, and supervises field interviewers.	High school	3–5 years	$30,000–$40,000
Full-time Interviewer: The interviewer conducts personal interviews and works under direct supervision of the field work director. Few companies employ full-time interviewers.	Some high school	0–1 years	$18,000–$22,000
Tabulating and Clerical Help: These people perform the routine, day-to-day work of the department.	Some high school	0–1 years	$18,000–$22,000

3 THE MARKETING RESEARCH PROCESS

Learning Objectives

▶ Be familiar with the various stages of the marketing research process.

▶ Highlight the importance of the problem/opportunity identification stage of the research process.

▶ Understand the issues related to hypotheses development.

▶ Explain the concept of **value of information,** and its role in deciding when marketing research is beneficial.

▶ Introduce the international marketing research process.

How is the market research project conceived, planned, and executed? The answer, in part, is through a research process, consisting of stages or steps that guide the project from its conception through the final analysis, recommendation, and ultimate action. The **research process** provides a systematic, planned approach to the research project and ensures that all aspects of the research project are consistent with each other. It is especially important that the research design and implementation be consistent with the research purpose and objectives. Otherwise, the results won't help the client.

In this chapter and Chapter 4, the research process is described. This chapter provides an overview of the research process, a discussion of the research purpose and research objectives, and a consideration of the value of research information. Chapter 4 gives an overview of the research design and its implementation. Together, these two chapters are the foundation for the rest of the book.

OVERVIEW OF THE MARKETING RESEARCH PROCESS

Research studies evolve through a series of steps, each representing the answer to a key question:

1. *Why* should we do research? This establishes the research purpose as seen by the management team that will be using the results. This step requires

understanding the decisions to be made and the problems or opportunities to be diagnosed.

2. *What* research should be done? Here the management purpose is translated into objectives that tell the researchers exactly what questions need to be answered by the research study or project.

3. *Is it worth* doing the research? The decision has to be made here on whether the value of the information that will likely be obtained is going to be greater than the cost of collecting it.

4. *How* should the research be designed to achieve the research objectives? Design issues include the choice of research approach—reliance on secondary data versus conducting a survey or experiment—and the specifics of how to collect the data. Chapter 4 deals with how to approach these issues.

5. *What* will we do with the research? Once the data have been collected, how will it be analyzed, interpreted, and used to make recommendations for action?

The necessary steps are linked in a sequential process (see Figure 3-1). Although the steps usually occur in this general order, we must emphasize that "early" decisions are always made by looking ahead to "later" decisions. The early decisions are constantly being modified to account for new insights and possibilities presented by later decisions. Also, the steps don't function in isolation. Rather, they are embedded in the ongoing planning process of the business, which culminates in the development of strategies, programs, and action. This planning process provides the purposes of the research. In turn, planning is supported by the information system, which (1) anticipates the type of information required by decision makers, and (2) organizes data that have been collected to ensure their availability when needed.

The development of a research purpose that links the research to decision making, and the formulation of research objectives that serve to guide the research, are unquestionably the most important steps in the research process. If they are correct, the research stands a good chance of being both useful and appropriate. If they are bypassed or wrong, the research almost surely will be wasteful and irrelevant. These aspects of research, too often neglected by researchers, will be discussed in detail in this chapter. The next chapter deals with research design; the chapters in Part II discuss the various methods to collect data; and the chapters in Part III of the book deal with analysis and interpretation of the data.

THE PRELIMINARY STAGES OF THE MARKETING RESEARCH PROCESS

Step 1—Research Purpose

Seldom will research problems come neatly packaged—with obvious information requirements, clear-cut boundaries, and pure motives on the part of the decision makers. They are more likely to be poorly defined, only partially understood, and missing possible decision alternatives that should be analyzed.

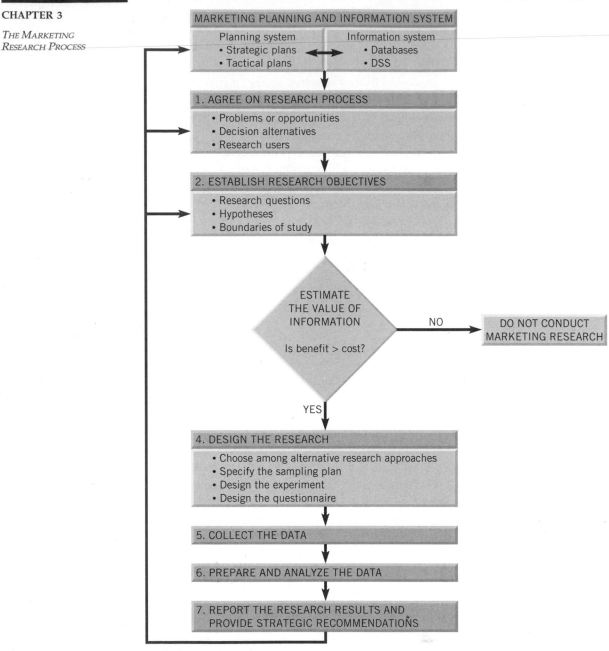

FIGURE 3-1
The marketing research process

Launching a research study with such shaky inputs is a recipe for unusable findings and unhappy clients. It is in the best interest of both the researcher and the managers paying for the research to be sure that the research purpose is fully understood. One of the hallmarks of a competent researcher is the ability to get to the heart of the management problem.

Consider the seemingly straightforward request by the chairperson of an association of community merchants for a research project. The objective of this project was to help reduce the propensity of residents in the community to do their shopping in two nearby communities. Clearly, the purpose of the research was to identify and evaluate various ways to increase the local merchants' share of shopping by residents. Further probing, however, revealed that the statement of the problem was at least partially inaccurate.

Only late in the research process was it learned by the researcher that the chairperson was having real difficulty convincing the other local merchants there was a serious enough outflow of local trade to warrant joint action to reverse the flow. This certainly changed the purpose of the research. Now the researcher would have to measure the level of retail trade outflow, in addition to finding the reasons for the outflow. This required a major change in the research design, but had the change not been made the results would have been of little value to the client.

The **research purpose** comprises a shared understanding between the manager and the researcher of the following:

1. Problems or opportunities to be studied.
   ▶ Which problems or opportunities are anticipated?
   ▶ What is the scope of the problems and the possible reasons?

2. Decision alternatives to be evaluated.
   ▶ What are the alternatives being studied?
   ▶ What are the criteria for choosing among the alternatives?
   ▶ What is the timing or importance of the decision?

3. Users of the research results.
   ▶ Who are the decision makers?
   ▶ Are there any covert purposes?

Problem or Opportunity Analysis. Research often is motivated by a problem or opportunity. The fact that sales are below expectations in the East might be a problem requiring research. The fact that people are consuming fewer sweets might be a problem or a potential opportunity for a candy company. Increased leisure time might be viewed as an opportunity by a recreation-oriented organization. In such cases the research purpose should specify the problem or opportunity to be explored. Identifying and defining the problem/opportunity is a crucial first step in the marketing research process. Especially in situation analysis contexts, exploratory research is needed to identify problems and opportunities. What sales areas are showing weak performance? What segments represent opportunities because they are dissatisfied with current products or because they are underusing the product? Even in exploratory research, however, it will be helpful to identify the nature of the problem or opportunity that is motivating the research. Further, the goal should be to move from exploratory research to research more focused on a decision. Exhibit 3-1 describes how Seagram capitalized on an opportunity.

The manager needs to make certain that the real problem is being addressed. Sometimes the recognized problem is only a symptom, or perhaps merely a part of a larger problem. A sobering illustration of this is the plight of Compton

EXHIBIT 3-1

Tropicana Identifies Opportunity and Gains a Headstart

It isn't often that the No. 3 brand in a $3 billion category simply drops out and leaves $210 million in annual sales up for grabs. So when Procter & Gamble Co. scuttled its money-losing Citrus Hill orange juice last September, the two top competitors—Seagram Co.'s Tropicana and Coca-Cola Co.'s Minute Maid—seized a rare opportunity and launched a juicy fight. Early results show Tropicana is winning handily in the biggest and fastest growing part of the orange-juice market—ready-to-drink juice in cartons and other containers. Supermarket sales data from Information Resources Inc.'s InfoScan service show that in the $2 billion ready-to-drink market, Tropicana's Pure Premium's share increased by 3.7 percentage points for a 12-week period ended December 27, 1992. Minute Maid's Premium Choice, by contrast, has gained only three-tenths of a share point in the same category.

Marketing consultants attribute Tropicana's lead in the battle of Citrus Hill to sheer aggressiveness. Tropicana began its battle planning immediately after rumors swept through the grocery trade that Citrus Hill's withdrawal was imminent. Tropicana hired a research firm to create a list, by zip code, of some 11 million middle-class households that were likely Citrus Hill buyers. When the withdrawal became official, Tropicana moved quickly: Within weeks, 11 million homes received coupons for 40 cents off a typical $2.79 carton of Tropicana, promising, "If you liked Citrus Hill orange juice, you'll love the great taste of Tropicana." From the first mailing of 11 million homes, Tropicana got back roughly 15 percent of its coupons, about double its typical response. Industry analysts attribute Minute Maid's loss to its inability to identify and capitalize on the opportunity quickly.

Source: Adapted from "Tropicana Squeezes Out Minute Maid To Get Bigger Slice of Citrus Hill Fans," *The Wall Street Journal*, February 4, 1993, pp. B1, B5.

Corp.,[1] a manufacturer of capital equipment costing between $10,000 and $25,000. The company was dominant in its market, with a share as large as the next two biggest competitors. All the companies sold their equipment through a network of independent distributors, each of which sold the products of at least two competitors. For several years this market leader had been losing share. In an attempt to reverse the trend, they changed advertising agencies. When the new agency funded a study of end users, they found to their surprise that the previous agency had done a superb job in creating awareness and favorable attitudes. However, many of the equipment purchasers who favored Compton were actually buying the competing brands. This problem had little to do with the performance of the advertising agency. A new study, oriented toward the distributors, found that Compton's distributor-relations program was very weak relative to competitors. One competitor emphasized sales contests, another offered cash bonuses to salespeople, and a third was particularly effective with technical sales assistance directed to difficult accounts. Not surprisingly, these factors influenced the distributors when they were asked for advice, or when the prospective purchaser didn't have a firm commitment to Compton equipment.

In this case, the real problem ultimately was isolated, but only after much time and energy had been directed toward the wrong problem. It is important, when defining the problem, to think broadly about the possible causes—or influential variables. This may justify a separate exploratory research study. Further, what appears to be a genuine problem/opportunity may not be researchable. For example, if a company that manufactures washing machines is interested in determining the replacement rates for all the machines sold within the last three years, it may not be worthwhile to pursue the issue. Since most household washing machines have a lifetime ranging from five to ten years, the problem of identifying the replacement rate for working machines sold within the last three years may be a nonresearchable problem.

Decision Alternatives. For research to be effective, it must be associated with a decision. Marketing research is committed to the principle of utility. In general, if research is not going to have an effect on decisions, it is an exercise in futility. The researcher should always be sensitive to the possibility that either there are no decision alternatives—and therefore no decision—or that the research findings will not affect the decision, usually because of resource or organizational constraints. In such circumstances, the research will have no practical value and probably should not be conducted.

When a decision potential does exist, it is important to identify it explicitly, because the research then can be designed for maximum effectiveness. For example, researchers frequently are asked to assess the potential of a market that is unfamiliar to the company. But what are the decisions the manager faces? Is the manager thinking of acquiring a company serving that market? Has the lab produced a new product that might be sold as a component to the industry serving that market? The answers will have a significant influence on the design of the research.

A most useful way to clarify the decision motivating the research is to ask: (1) What alternative actions are being considered? (2) What actions would be taken, given the various feasible outcomes of the research? This line of questioning can be very enlightening for the decision maker, as well as for the researcher, in terms of clarifying exactly what the research can accomplish. The story in Exhibit 3-2 illustrates how both can learn from a focus on decisions.

EXHIBIT 3-2

Political Campaign Research

The meeting between Hugh Godfrey and two project directors from Pollsters Anonymous, a well-known survey research company, had taken a surprising turn. Here were two researchers suggesting that no research be undertaken.

Godfrey was campaign manager for John Crombie, a university professor and erstwhile Democratic challenger of the Republican incumbent for the local House of Representatives seat. He and his candidate were anxious to undertake a program of research. They thought it would be a good idea to have surveys in May and September (five months and six weeks prior to the election) of voter awareness of the candidate, attitudes toward him, issue salience, and intentions to vote. The results would be helpful in clarifying the candidate's position and deciding on media expenditures. Positive results would be useful in soliciting campaign contributions, which loomed as a big problem.

During the meeting the researchers had asked what Godfrey expected to find. He was sure that the initial survey would reveal low awareness, and would confirm other information he had that there was a low level of voter registration among Democrats in the area. The next question was whether any foreseeable results would persuade him not to spend all his available resources on a voter registration drive. He had to admit also that the preliminary estimate of $6000 for a May survey was a large chunk of his available funds. In fact, he was thinking, "With the money I would spend on the survey, I could hire enough canvassers to get at least 1500 to 2000 registrations."

Sometimes the decision involved is highly specific. A copy test is used to select a copy alternative. A concept test is employed to determine if a concept should be developed further. Sometimes the decision can be very general. What markets should be the primary targets of our organization? Should our marketing program be changed? It is desirable to be as specific as possible because the research purpose then will be more effective in guiding the development of the research design. However, even if the decision is necessarily general, it needs to be clearly stated.

Criteria for Choosing Among Alternatives. It is essential for the researcher to know how the decision maker will choose among the available alternatives. Suppose a product manager is considering three possible package redesigns for a health-care product with declining sales. This would seem to be a straightforward research undertaking, as the decision alternatives are completely specified. Yet, the product manager could use some or all of the following criteria to choose the best of the three alternative packages:

1. Long-run sales.
2. Trial purchases by users of competing brands.
3. Amount of shelf space assigned to the brand.
4. Differentiation from competitive packages.
5. Brand-name recognition.

The researcher and decision maker need to discuss all possible criteria in advance, and choose those that are appropriate. If the criterion for comparison is long-run sales results, the research approach will be much more elaborate than if the choice were based simply on brand-name recognition.

Timing and Importance. These are always pivotal questions in the research process. How crucial is the decision? If the wrong decision is made, what will the consequences be? Obviously, the decision to go national with a new government program represents a much larger commitment than the decision to pursue a new program idea a bit further. Other questions are concerned with the timing of the decision. What is the time pressure on the decision? Is information needed quickly or is there time to develop an optimal research design?

Research Users

Decision Makers. When the research results will be used to guide internal problem solving, the researcher must know the objectives and expectations of the actual decision makers. The bigger the problem, the more difficult this becomes, for not only are a large number of people likely to be involved, but the contact person may simply be acting as a liaison whose interpretation of the problem and the need for research may be secondhand. The major benefit from making an effort to reach all the decision makers is that the research purpose is likely to be specified more adequately. These contacts also will tell the researcher (especially an outside supplier who is called in to undertake the work) a good deal about the resources that are available to deal with the problem. This is very helpful in developing a realistic proposal.

Increasingly, marketing research is entering the public domain, which introduces a new set of users who frequently have very different criteria for evaluating research results; for example,

▶ A public utility presents a research study to a regulatory body in support of a request for a rate change or the introduction of a change in service level.

▶ An industry trade association conducts research designed to influence proposed legislation or trade regulations. The Direct Mail Marketing Association has sponsored a study of mail-order buyers in response to a proposed Federal Trade Commission order that would require sellers to offer a refund if they could not ship the ordered goods within a month.

▶ A regional transit agency wants to build public support for the continuation of an experimental program involving "dedicated" bus lanes (part of a road or highway on which no automobile traffic is permitted). The research demonstrating the effectiveness of the program is to be presented to various public bodies and citizen groups.

In most cases, the research in the above examples is used to support a decision alternative. However, the examination of the results often is conducted in an adversarial setting, which means more criticism of shortcomings and necessitates a higher quality of research.

Overt and Covert Purposes. It would be naive to presume that research is always conducted to facilitate rational problem-solving activity or that the decision maker always will be willing or able to share reasons for initiating the research. As discussed in Chapter 1, there are times when the main purpose of marketing research was to serve someone's organizational goals or for other unethical purposes. None of these abuses can be condoned. Often they are specifically prohibited by industry codes of ethics. When they are not, one's moral standards become the compass for deciding what is right.

Step 2—Research Objective

The **research objective** is a statement, in as precise terminology as possible, of what information is needed. The research objective should be framed so that obtaining the information will ensure that the research purpose is satisfied.

Research objectives have three components. The first is the **research question.** It specifies the information the decision maker needs. The second and third elements help the researcher make the research question as specific and precise as possible. The second element is the **development of hypotheses** that are basically alternative answers to the research question. The research determines which of these alternative answers is correct. It is not always possible to develop hypotheses, but the effort should be made. The third is the **scope**

or boundaries of the research. For example, is the interest in only current customers or in all potential customers?

Research Question. The **research question** asks what specific information is required to achieve the research purpose. If the research question is answered by the research, then the information should aid the decision maker.

An illustration comes from a company in the toiletries and cosmetics business, which was interested in acquiring a smaller firm with an apparently complementary product line. One anticipated benefit of the acquisition was the opportunity to eliminate one of the sales forces. The *purpose* of the research was to assess whether the company could use its existing sales force to distribute the products of the acquired company. The corresponding research *objective* was to determine how much the retail distribution patterns of the two companies overlapped. There was some preliminary evidence that suggested (that is, hypothesized) that distribution coverages would differ by geographic area and store type. The resulting study found that there was very little overlap, for the acquiring company emphasized major metropolitan areas, whereas the other company was largely represented in smaller cities and suburbs.

It is possible to have several research questions for a given research purpose. Thus, if the purpose is to determine if a specific advertisement should be run, the following research questions could be posted:

▶ Will the advertisement be noticed?

▶ Will it be interpreted accurately?

▶ Will it influence attitudes?

These questions correspond to the criteria used to evaluate the advertising alternatives. Similarly, if the purpose is to determine how to improve the services of a bank, possible research questions might be

▶ What aspects of the current service are customers most pleased with and with which are they most dissatisfied?

▶ What types of customers use the various services?

▶ What benefits do people seek from banks?

Each of these questions should pass the test of being relevant to the purpose. For example, if customer types are identified that use a service like traveler's checks, it may be possible to modify that service to make it more convenient or attractive to them.

Sometimes the researcher can select a major objective and some supporting objectives. An example is a study conducted for the Department of Defense to address the problem of declining strength of the National Guard and the reserve components such as the Army Reserve.[2] The research purpose was to determine what job characteristics (product dimensions) would increase the enlistment levels and the reenlistment levels of various demographic types. Job characteristics such as salary, fringe benefits, educational opportunity, travel, job image, and hair regulations were among the possible policy variables that could be adjusted. The overall objective of the study, to examine motivation factors in enlistment and reenlistment, led to several supporting objectives. The first of these was to measure young people's propensity to serve (or reenlist). The second was to determine current perceptions of the reserve in terms of 12 key attributes. The third was to determine the relative importance of the 12 key job attributes that could provide the basis for influencing young men and women to join and remain in the service.

The researcher will always try to make the research question as specific as possible. Suppose the research question as to which customer types use the various bank services could be replaced by the research question: What are the lifestyle and attitude profiles of the users of credit cards, automatic overdraft protection, and travelers' checks? This increase in specificity will aid the researcher in developing the research design by suggesting whom to survey and what questions to include. The role of the research objective is to provide guidance to the research design. The more specific the research question is, the more practical guidance will be provided.

When a research question is set forth, it is sometimes difficult to realize that the question can and should be made more specific. The remaining two elements of the research objective—hypothesis development and the research boundaries—provide exercises to help the researcher make the research question more specific.

Hypothesis Development. A **hypothesis** is a possible answer to the research question. The researcher should always take the time and effort to speculate as to possible research question answers that will emerge from the research. In doing so, the fact that everyone already knows the answer sometimes becomes apparent. More often, the effort will add a considerable degree of specificity to the research question.

A hypothesis could speculate that sales are down in the Northeast because the level of competition has been abnormally high there during the past two months. Such a hypothesis provides considerable detail to a research question that asks what the problem is in the Northeast. It guides the research by ensuring that competitive promotions are included in the research design. One important role of a hypothesis is to suggest variables to be included in the research design—in this case, competitive promotion.

A research problem might be to estimate the demand for a new product. The hypothesis that the product will do well in the North but not in the South adds the concept of geographic location to the problem. It suggests that the sampling plan should include people from both regions. If the hypothesis suggests that the product will not do well in the South because it is not compatible with the southern lifestyle, it becomes evident that the research should measure not only purchase intentions, but also how the product would be used.

Normally, there will be several competing hypotheses, either specified or implied. If all the hypotheses were known in advance to be true, there would be little reason to conduct the research. Thus, one objective of research is to choose among the possible hypotheses. A good illustration of the role of competing hypotheses is the problem recently faced by a cable television company. A cable TV company picks up TV and radio signals with a large, sophisticated antenna and "pipes" the high-quality signals through cable into subscribers' homes. This company provided service to 75 percent of the households within the total service area. The problem facing the company was that there were several areas where the penetration rate was far below average. The population in these areas represented about 15 percent of the total service area. Bringing these areas closer to the average would significantly improve profitability. Before remedial action could be taken it was necessary to establish the reasons for the low penetration. Various reasons were suggested by management, including

1. Good television reception is available without cable.
2. Residents are illegally connecting their sets to the cable network.
3. There is a very transient population.
4. Residents have had poor previous experience with cable service.
5. The price is too high, given the incomes in the area.
6. The sales force coverage has been inadequate.
7. A large percentage of the residents of the area are in age or social class groups that watch little television.

The challenge for the researcher is to devise a research approach that will gather information that can test each of these hypotheses. Hypotheses are not appropriate for all situations. As the upcoming discussions on exploratory research in Chapter 4 will make it clear, there may be insufficient information for developing hypothesis. There are also times when the most reasonable hypothesis statement is simply a trivial restatement of the research question. For example:

Research

Question: Will the advertisement attract attention?

Hypothesis: It will attract attention.

In such cases the hypothesis will not add anything to the research and should simply be omitted. Hypothesis development should not be viewed as an item on a checklist to be quickly satisfied but rather as an opportunity to communicate information and to make the research question more specific.

How does the researcher generate hypotheses? The answer is that whatever information is available is used to speculate on which answers to the research questions are possible and which are likely. There are three main sources of information the researcher can use to develop hypotheses, as Figure 3-2 illustrates. First, the researcher can draw on previous research efforts; in fact, it is not uncommon to conduct exploratory research to generate hypotheses for

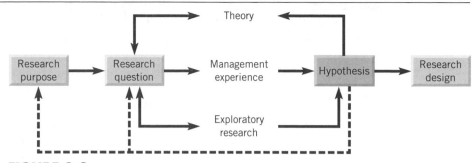

FIGURE 3-2
Hypothesis development

future large-scale research efforts. The research purpose might be deciding whether to conduct the large-scale studies.

A second source of hypotheses is theory from such disciplines as psychology, sociology, marketing, or economics. Thus, economic theory might suggest the importance of price in explaining the loss of retail sales. Marketing theory could indicate that distribution was important in predicting new-product acceptance. The use of attitude as a measure of advertising impact might be suggested by psychological theory.

A third and perhaps the most important source of hypotheses is the manager's experience with related problems, coupled with a knowledge of the problem situation and the use of judgment. This source is illustrated by the manufacturer who has discovered an unusual increase in selling costs. Past experience with similar problems, plus a preliminary investigation into the reasons for the problem, point to an increase in the proportion and number of small orders received. The tentative hypothesis is: Small orders (suitably defined) have increased in both number and proportion, and this increase, coupled with a higher cost of processing these orders, has raised selling costs. The research would then be directed at the questions of (1) the extent of increase in small orders (and the reasons for the increase) and (2) the additional unit costs involved in processing orders of different sizes.

Research Boundaries. Hypothesis development helps make the research question more precise. Another approach is to indicate the scope of the research or the **research boundaries.** Is the interest in the total population restricted to men or to those on the West Coast? Is the research question concerned with the overall attitude toward the proposed new automobile, or is it necessary to learn customer attitudes about trunk space, handling, gas economy, styling, and interior appearance?

Much of the dialogue between the researcher and the decision maker will be about clarifying the boundaries of the study. For example, a manager may wish to study the effects of the 1992 European trade agreement on industry conditions. During the process of hypothesis development, the possible effects may be isolated. This still leaves a number of areas of ambiguity. What is meant by "condition"—profitability, competitive position in world markets, labor relations, or what? How is the "industry" to be defined? What geographic areas are to be considered? What time period is to be appraised?

A final question of research scope regards the desired precision or accuracy of the results. This will, of course, depend on the research purpose. If a multimillion-dollar plant is to constructed on the basis of the research results, a high degree of accuracy will be required. If, however, the decision involves the investment of a small sum in research and development on a new product idea, then a crude judgment as to the potential of the product would be acceptable.

Step 3—Estimating the Value of Information

Before the research approach can be selected, it is necessary to have an estimate of the value of the information; that is, the value of obtaining answers to the research questions. Such an estimate will help determine how much, if anything, should be spent on the research.

The value will depend on the importance of the decision as noted in the research purpose, the uncertainty that surrounds it, and the influence of the research information on the decision. If the decision is highly significant in terms of the investment required or in terms of its impact upon the long-run success of the organization, then information may have a high value. However, uncertainty that is meaningful to the decision also must exist if the information is to have value. If the outcomes are already known with certainty, or if the decision will not be affected by the research information, the information will have no value.

To illustrate and expand on these concepts, consider the simplified examples in Figure 3-3. In Case A, the decision to introduce a new product is shown as a decision tree. The first two branches represent the decision alternatives— to introduce the product or to decide not to introduce it. The second branch represents the uncertainty. Our descriptive model indicates that if the product is successful, a profit of $4 million will result. The indication is that there is a probability of 0.6 (obtained from prior experience) that the product will be

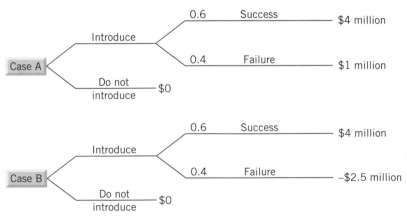

FIGURE 3-3
Illustrative decision models

successful. However, if the product is not successful, the profit would be only $1 million, an event that will occur with probability 0.4. These subjective probabilities have been calculated based on prior knowledge of the situation. How much should we be willing to pay for perfect information in this case? If someone could tell us, in advance, and with certainty, whether the product would be successful or not, how much would we pay for that information? The correct answer is nothing! The fact is that regardless of the information our decision would be the same. We would introduce the product, for even if the product were not well accepted, we would still make $1 million. In this case, not only is the decision insignificant to the organization, it is nonexistent. There is only one viable alternative. Without alternatives there is no decision contest, even if uncertainty exists; therefore, there is no need for additional information.

In Case B, the estimate is that, if the product is not successful, a loss of $2.5 million will occur. Since the expectation of the new product's eventual performance is still, on balance, positive, the product would be introduced.* However, in this case, perfect information now would have value. If we knew in advance that the product definitely would not be accepted, we would decide against introducing it and save $2.5 million. Since our best estimate of the probability of the product not being accepted is 0.4, the value of the information would be 0.4 times $2.5 million, or $1 million. Thus, if this decision contest could be repeated many times, perfect information would save us $2.5 million about 40 percent of the time and would save us nothing (since it would not alter our decision) about 60 percent of the time. On average, it would save us $1 million. By spending money on research, we might improve the knowledge of how the product will be accepted. But market research is unlikely to be as good as perfect information, and therefore its value will be less than $1 million. Obviously, if the cost associated with an unsuccessful product were lower, or if the probability of an unsuccessful product were smaller, the value of information would be less. (The appendix to this chapter extends this example to include the possibility of using a concept test to predict whether or not the product will succeed. A method is developed to determine the value of the concept test to the decision maker.)

PLANNING A NEW HMO

To see how a research purpose and a set of research objectives are developed, we join a meeting that took place at the Fraser General Hospital in September 1988.

The five doctors had a dilemma. They had spent a useful morning confirming that their hospital had the resources to operate a Health Maintenance Organization. These resources were substantial, as would be expected in a big teaching and research hospital with a strong regional reputation. The concept of an HMO is briefly explained in Exhibit 3-3.

* The expected value of introducing the product would be 0.6(4M) + 0.4(−2.5M) = 1.4M.

EXHIBIT 3-3

What is an HMO?

There are two basic kinds of health coverage. The Health Maintenance Organization (HMO) is the best example of the *prepaid group practice* type. This involves fixed monthly payments directly to a group of doctors or clinic who is then responsible for all the health needs covered by the plan. The other is the *insurance* type that involves a company that collects premiums from subscribers who can go to any clinic or doctor they choose. The insurance company pays for the services covered by the policy. In both cases there may be limits to the coverage os such items as hospitalization, drugs, and office visits. The big drawback of the HMO is restriction of the choice of physicians and hospitals to those affiliated with the HMO. Generally, the total annual cost of an HMO to the consumer is lower than for group insurance plans. One reason is that the flat-fee formula discourages doctors from hospitalizing patients longer than necessary. Also the emphasis on preventative care produces fewer seriously ill patients.

The September 10, 1988 meeting was one in a long series of informal talks, investigations, and efforts to build support for the idea within the hospital. These efforts had brought them to a critical point: Their problem was how to determine whether there was enough market demand in the region to support another HMO. Although each member of the planning group was convinced of the prospective benefits to the community, the hospital teaching program, and the bed utilization rate, they knew they needed persuasive evidence before the hospital trustees would provide start-up funds. After all, the trustees were even reluctant to approve funds for initial planning. What would it take before they would approve an initial investment in excess of $400,000?

The trustees weren't the only hurdle. Each of the doctors in the HMO planning group knew at least one colleague who was openly skeptical because of the presence of competitive health care programs. There was a well-established HMO about eight miles away, plus several clinics operating on a fee-for-service basis. Many of the clinic doctors had privileges at the Fraser General Hospital.

At lunch, the planning group was joined by Herb Ellis, a partner in a local research and consulting firm. He had been invited by one of the doctors who knew him socially. During lunch, the doctors enthusiastically described the HMO concept, what it meant to subscribers—especially those on low incomes, and some of the innovations, such as consumer inputs to operations and procedures.

After lunch, John Akitt, a surgeon and the originator of the HMO proposal, reviewed some of the tentative decisions that would influence the market analysis. First, they intended to offer fairly comprehensive services from the beginning, including internal medicine, pediatrics, surgery, orthopedics, obstetrics, and gynecology. However, they weren't sure whether they should also offer dentistry and optometry at an additional fee. Such an array of services was felt to be competitively necessary, but when combined with a high doctor-enrolled-ratio to ensure a high service level, the result was very high fixed costs.

All the doctors agreed that one way to keep initial costs down was to concentrate on larger employer groups. This meant that a two-stage marketing effort would be required—first to get the employer to agree to offer the HMO plan as a subsidized benefit and then to persuade the employees to switch from their present health care plan. The largest employer in the vicinity was the state university, two miles away, with over 13,000 faculty, staff, and married students who could join a health plan. The university's vice president of finance appeared committed to offering the HMO plan. There were three other large employers nearby, representing an additional 20,000 possible enrollees. However, they had been much less enthusiastic about offering the Fraser Hospital HMO as a benefit, and implied that they wouldn't consider it until it had been successfully operating for a few months. This was upsetting to the doctors, for a sizable enrollment base had to be generated quickly if the HMO was to achieve its objectives. Still, if there was a significant adoption of the HMO within the university, they felt they could get close to the break-even target in the short run.

As the discussion progressed, Ellis realized that the extent and rate of acceptance of the HMO would depend on the marketing effort and the fee level. Marketing was a real problem since solicitation of patients was, strictly speaking, unethical. This probably did not prevent personal selling and other communications efforts to explain the differences between fee-for-service and HMO plans. Pricing seemed to be a big factor; the prepaid feature of the HMO meant the prospective enrolled would see a bigger monthly salary bite, although over the long run total health costs would be lower. Since a large proportion of costs were fixed, a high enrollment target could help to lower fees. Otherwise, to lower fees it would be necessary to reduce services, which would make the HMO less attractive. Without knowledge of the price sensitivity of the market, it would be hard to establish a fee structure. But who was the target market? Here the doctors had many conflicting opinions and the meeting became quite heated. Was the HMO concept most attractive to young families, older families with or without children, or enrollees in the competitive HMO? No one was sure just how big an area an HMO could serve. Although some existing HMOs attracted only people within a 10-mile radius of the hospital, there was a feeling that convenience and driving time were more important than distance.

At this point Herb Ellis felt he had some understanding of the doctors' marketing problems. Rather than discuss research approaches, he asked for another meeting at which specific research purposes and objectives could be discussed. These would be the basis for a research proposal. He already knew that a big constraint on his planning would be the available budget. There was no way that more than $10,000 could be found to finance marketing research, no matter what the economic value of the research information to the hospital.

Prior to a second meeting with the planning committee, Herb Ellis had done some background reading on the HMO concept, talked to several doctors in private practice, and informally interviewed four members of the competitive HMO. With this background he was ready to discuss preliminary research purposes and objectives, which could be used to guide the design of the study.

During the second meeting with the hospital planning committee, quick agreement was reached that the primary purpose of the study was to address the decision as to whether the proposal for an HMO should be pursued to the point of making major investments in its implementation. The following research objective consists of the research question and a statement of the study scope.

Research

Question: What is the demand for the new HMO?

Scope: Limited to students, staff, and faculty of the University.

The study was limited to University students, staff, and faculty, for several reasons. First, the University administration was favorably disposed toward the plan, giving it the best chance of success in that environment. If support from that group was not in evidence, then the prospects would be dim in other organizations. Second, the budget limitation made it unlikely that any worthwhile research could be conducted with more than one organization. No geographical limits were placed on the study, as it was thought that distance from the home to the HMO would have only a weak influence on individual interest in the proposed HMO.

Much more time was spent on developing the supporting purposes and objectives, with Ellis constantly challenging the usefulness of each proposed purpose and objective. Because of the tight budget constraint, he was fearful that overly ambitious objectives would be difficult to achieve with the alternative research designs he had in mind. Finally, the following set of supporting purposes and objectives was developed:

Purpose: What target market segments should the HMO emphasize?

Objective: Identify the market segments most interested in the proposed HMO. Estimate their probable rate of utilization of medical services from their past medical experience.

Purpose: What services should be provided at what price level?

Objective: Identify the attributes or characteristics of health plans that would have the greatest influence on an individual's choice among alternatives.

During the meeting a number of hypotheses were advanced as to who was the most likely to be interested in the plan. Of course, they would have to express strong interest in the plan as described to them. In addition, good prospects would be those who were dissatisfied with the coverage or quality of their present plan, didn't have a long-standing relationship with a family doctor, had favorable attitudes toward the Fraser General Hospital, and weren't enrolled in other plans through their spouses. At the end of the meeting, the chairperson indicated a need for a proposal in time for the trustees' meeting on October 3. If the proposal were approved, they would need the results of the study no later than the first week in February.

THE INTERNATIONAL MARKETING RESEARCH PROCESS

As we mentioned earlier in Chapter 1, the basic functions of marketing research and the various stages in the research process do not differ between domestic and international research. But, the international marketing research process is much more complicated than the domestic research process. This complication stems from operating in different and diverse environmental contexts—ranging from the technologically advanced and stable United States, to more mature Western European markets, to the fast-changing environments in the newly industrialized countries such as Hong Kong and South Korea, to the developing economies such as India and Brazil, to transforming economies such as the former U.S.S.R. and Eastern Europe, and to less-developed countries on the African continent. Exhibit 3-4 clearly illustrates the differences between the United States of America and Canada.

Framing Research Questions in an International Environment

Problems may not always be couched in the same terms in different countries or cultural contexts. This may be due to differences in socioeconomic conditions, levels of economic development, or differences in any of the macroenvironmental factors.

EXHIBIT 3-4

Are Canadians Our Cousins up North?

The United States and Canada are not only geographical neighbors, but with nearly $200 billion in trade flowing between the U.S. and Canada, the two countries are each others' largest trading partners. Also, nearly 90 percent of the total Canadian population lives within 100 miles of the U.S. border. So, can a U.S. based manufacturer treat the Canadian market as a mere extension of the domestic market? Absolutely not!! Despite their proximity and close trade ties, important differences exist between the two countries. These include demographic, economic, and cultural differences. For a start, the Canadian population is about 27 million people, or roughly 10 percent of the U.S. population and, interestingly, over 60 percent of population is accounted for by two major provinces—Ontario and Quebec. Ontario has a socialist government which is pro-labor and imposes more restrictions on business than other provincial governments or the United States. The costs of doing business are, in general, higher in Canada. It has a 7 percent federal goods and service tax, and provincial taxes ranging around 8–10 percent. First-class mail costs $0.42 per letter. Bilingual labeling is required. Personal and corporate income taxes are higher, as are transportation and distribution costs and interest rates. Apart from these macro level differences, there are differences in the way business is done. For example, offering a sales promotion like a contest entails special legal requirements. Also, these legal requirements might vary from province to province.

The cultural differences are as important as the demographic, economic, political, and legal differences. More than 80 percent of the Quebec population uses French as its first language, and Quebec nationals are committed to sovereignty status. Canadians are extremely sensitive to environmental issues, and even municipal governments have strict local environmental ordinances. To make matters worse, Canada uses the metric system!!

Source: "Do Your Homework Before You Start Marketing in Canada," *Marketing News*, September 14, 1992, pp. 22, 23; and "Promotions in Canada Have Special Legal Requirements," *Marketing News*, December 7, 1992, p. 14.

Several academic scholars have identified and have pointed out the major reason for the failure of businesses and marketing research projects in a foreign environment. The result has been the **Self-Reference Criterion (SRC)** adopted by researchers in defining the problem in a foreign country. SRC assumes that the environmental variables (cultural and others) that are prevalent in the researcher's domestic market are also applicable to the foreign country. This is a major cause for the failure of research projects, since defining the problem is the most crucial step in the marketing research process.

One of the most frequent objectives of international marketing research is **foreign market opportunity analysis.**[3] When a firm launches its international activities, information can be accumulated to provide basic guidelines. The aim is not to conduct a painstaking and detailed analysis of the world, but to gather information on questions that would help management narrow down the possibilities for international marketing activities. Possible questions an international marketing researcher might ask to achieve the above-mentioned objective include:

▶ Do opportunities exist in foreign markets for the firm's products and services?

▶ Which foreign markets warrant detailed investigation?

▶ What are the major economic, political, legal, and other environmental facts and trends in each of the potential countries?

▶ What mode of entry does the company plan to adopt to enter the foreign market?

▶ What is the market potential in these countries?

▶ Who are the firm's present and potential customers abroad?

▶ What is the nature of competition in the foreign markets?

▶ What kind of marketing strategy should the firm adopt?

Summary

The research process consists of a series of stages or steps that guide the research project from its conception through to the final recommendations. An overview of the domestic marketing research and the International marketing research processes was presented. This chapter discussed the research purpose and the research objective in detail. Chapter 4 will provide a discussion of the research design and implementation stages. Together, the two chapters will provide a structure for the rest of the book.

The specification of the research purpose involves first the identification of the decision involved, its alternatives, and the importance of its timing. Sometimes the decision is as general as "Should our marketing program be changed?" In such cases it is also useful to specify the problem or opportunity that is motivating the research, or the environmental surveillance objective. The purpose statement also should consider who the research users are. There are times when identifying the research users and understanding their decisions and motives can significantly improve the effectiveness of the research.

The research objective involves the identification of the research questions. The answer to an appropriate research question should be relevant to the research purpose, and the question should be as specific as possible. In particular, hypotheses should be developed whenever possible. The research boundaries specification is also part of the research objective statement.

Even at the early stages of research conceptualization, it is useful to consider what value the resulting information is likely to have. This exercise can lead to a decision to forego the research, or at least make a judgment about the appropriate scale of the research project.

Questions and Problems

1. Jim Mitchell, a high-profile business person, is considering running for State Governor against a two-term incumbent. Mitchell and his backers do not want to enter the race unless there is a reasonable chance of winning. What are some research questions and hypotheses that, if answered, could help him make the decision?

2. At the beginning of Chapter 1, there are three examples of management information needs: General Motors, Borden Inc., American Express, and Market Metrics. Review each of these situations and develop an appropriate set of research purposes and objectives.

3. In the United Kingdom, cars are polished more frequently when the owners do not have garages. Is the lack of a garage a good variable for predicting sales of car polish? Are there other hypotheses that might explain this finding?

4. Can you think of additional research objectives for the HMO study?

5. You have been retained by a manufacturer of major appliances to investigate the probable color preferences for stoves and refrigerators in the coming year. What is the purpose of the research? Are there different purposes that might require different research approaches?

6. The president of a small chain of women's clothing stores was concerned about a four-year trend of decreasing profits. The stores have been characterized as being rather conservative over the years in respect to their product line, store decor, and advertising. They have consistently avoided trendy clothes, for example. Their market is now becoming extremely competitive because several aggressive fashion stores are expanding and are aiming at the young fashion-conscious buyer. As a result of this competition and the disappointing profit trend, the president is considering making the product line appear less conservative and more oriented to the young buyer. Before making such a risky change, the president felt it prudent to conduct some marketing research to learn the exact status of his chain. What should be the research purpose? Compose a set of research questions what would be helpful.

7. Explain the role of an information system. How would the possible role differ for Avon Products and Johnson Wax Company? (Refer to the Agree Shampoo example in Chapter 1 for background.)

8. Consider the example in Figure 3-4 in the Appendix. What would be the expected value of perfect information if the loss would be $1 million instead

of $2.5 million? How about if the loss would be $10 million instead of $2.5 million? What would it be if the probability of failure would be .2 instead of .4? Explain in words what is meant by the expected value of perfect information and what its implication is.

9. Consider the example explained in Figure 3-4 in the Appendix. Determine the value of research information under the following situations:
   a. Pr(Neg|F) = .9 and Pr(Pos|F) = .1 and all else remains the same
   b. Pr(Pos|S) = .7 and Pr(Neg|S) = .3 and all else remains the same
   c. Pr(Pos|S) = .9, Pr(Neg|S) = .1, Pr(Neg|F) = .9, Pr(Pos|F) = .1

10. ExoArt inc., a small U.S.-based manufacturer of exotic jewelry, feels that a market exists for its product in foreign markets. However, the company's managers have no experience in the international environment, and do not know how to proceed in forming a marketing strategy for international markets. They have decided to contact a marketing research firm to help with the process. The researchers recommend a "foreign market opportunity analysis" as a starting point for the company's internationalization.
    a. What is the aim of a foreign market opportunity analysis?
    b. Which questions might a researcher ask to gather information for the analysis?
    c. What is the most probable cause of failure for a business or marketing research project in a foreign enviroment?

11. a. Are there any differences between the basic functions of marketing research in a domestic environment and those in an international environment?
    b. Why is the international research process considered more complicated than the domestic research process?

12. Crystal-Clear Lens, Inc., a newly formed mail-order contact lens company, has struggled to obtain break-even sales after five years in the eyewear market. The company's founders felt that a high demand would exist for mail order supply as a low cost alternative to purchasing the lens at optical outlets. These retail outlets usually are within a close geographical proximity to an affiliated optician. This allows customers to have their eyesight examined by the optician and then take the prescription to the optical outlet to purchase their eyeglasses or contact lens. Many retail outlets offer coupons that refund the cost of the eye examination upon the purchase of the contact lens, and offer several free follow-up visits after the sale to check that the correct prescription has been made. The mail-order process requires customers to send in their prescription after the eye examination, whereupon the contact lens will be supplied within two weeks of receipt of the order. The managers at Crystal-Clear Lens, Inc. have employed you as their marketing research consultant, to determine the reasons for the low sales.
    a. What would be the research purpose of this study?
    b. How does the **research purpose** differ from the **research objective?** Illustrate this difference in terms of the Crystal-Clear Lens example.
    c. What specific information would be required to achieve the research purpose? (i.e., State the **research question**).
    d. State some preliminary hypotheses to answer the research question.

End Notes

1. Adapted from Irving D. Canton, "Do You Know Who Your Customer Is?" *Journal of Marketing,* April 1976, p. 83.

2. "Conjoint Analysis of Values of Reserve Component Attitudes," *a report prepared for the Department of Defense by Market Facts,* Chicago: November 1977.

3. Adapted from R. Michael Czinkota and Ilkka A. Ronkainen, *International Marketing,* 3rd edition, Dryden Press, 1993.

The Value of Research Information Using Bayesian Decision Theory

In the discussion surrounding Figure 3-3, the value of perfect research information for Case B was determined to be $1 million. Perfect research information would indicate with certainty that the product would be a success or a failure. In this appendix, the more realistic question as to the value of imperfect research information will be addressed.

The Case B example of Figure 3-3 is shown at the top of Figure 3-4. A decision to introduce a new product has two possible outcomes. A "success" is given a prior probability of 0.6 and will result in a profit of $4 million. A "failure" is given a prior probability of 0.4 and will result in a profit of −$2.5 million. Symbolically,

$$\text{Product Success} = S = \$4 \text{ million}$$
$$\text{Product Failure} = F = -\$2.5 \text{ million}$$
$$\text{Probability of Success} = Pr(S) = 0.6$$
$$\text{Probability of Failure} = Pr(F) = 0.4$$

The expected value of introducing the product is then the sum of the two possible payoffs, each weighted by its probability of occurring:[1]

$$EV = \text{Expected Value} = S \times Pr(S) + F \times Pr(F)$$
$$= (\$4 \text{ million}) \times 0.6 + (-\$2.5 \text{ million}) \times 0.4$$
$$= \$1.4 \text{ million}$$

This expected value is shown in Figure 3-3 between the two outcomes: success and failure. The alternative of not introducing will result in a profit of zero. Thus, the product will be introduced. If it were possible to obtain perfect information about the outcome of the product introduction then the potential would be created to avoid the result of losing $2.5 million. The maximum amount that would be paid for perfect information would be $2.5 million times .4, the probability that a failure will result, which amounts to $1 million. Only when a failure results will the decision be affected; therefore, the firm will save some money.

Figure 3-4 has added the alternative of evaluating the new product with a concept test, such as a focus-group interview in which a group of eight to ten people are asked to discuss the concept. Let us assume that the concept test will either be positive (Pos) or negative (Neg). Now assume that the concept test is not a perfect indicator of the ultimate result. In particular, those who have worked with this concept test several times before believe that for successful products the concept test is positive 80 percent of the time (and thus negative 20 percent of the time). For the failed products, the concept test is believed to be negative 60 percent of the time (and thus positive 40 percent of the time). In terms of conditional probabilities,

$$\text{Probability of a Pos concept test}$$
$$\text{given a successful product}$$
$$= Pr(Pos \mid S) = .8$$

$$\text{Probability of a Neg concept test}$$
$$\text{given a successful product}$$
$$= Pr(Neg \mid S) = .2$$

$$\text{Probability of a Neg concept test given a failed product}$$
$$= Pr(Neg \mid F) = .6$$

$$\text{Probability of a Pos concept test given a failed product}$$
$$= Pr(Pos \mid F) = .4$$

The expected value of the "introduce the product immediately" option is $1.4 million. We need to determine the expected value of the concept text alternative in order to determine how much value, if any, there will be in conducting the test. To proceed we first need to determine

$Pr(Pos)$ = Probability of a positive concept test

$Pr(Neg)$ = Probability of a negative concept test

$Pr(S \mid Pos)$ = Probability that the product will be successful given a positive concept test

$Pr(F \mid Pos)$ = Probability that the product will be a failure given a positive concept test

$Pr(S \mid Neg)$ = Probability that the product will be successful given a negative concept test

$Pr(F \mid Neg)$ = Probability that the product will be a failure given a negative concept test

The first two terms are obtained from the following formula.[2]

$$Pr(Pos) = Pr(Pos \mid S)Pr(S) + Pr(Pos \mid F)Pr(F)$$
$$= .8 \times .6 + .4 \times .4 = .64$$

---

[1] To understand expected value consider the following game. Ten balls numbered from one to 10 are placed in a bowl. One ball is selected at random. If the number is 1, 2, 3, 4, 5, or 6, you receive $4 million. If it is 7, 8, 9, or 10, you must pay $2.5 million. If you played this game thousands of times you would earn $1.4 million, on the average, each time the game was played.

[2] The formulas are easily expanded if there are more than two outcomes to the decision. For example, suppose that there were three outcomes. Success (S), Failure (F), and Indeterminant (I). The formula would then be

$$Pr(Pos) = Pr(Pos \mid S) \times Pr(S) + Pr(Pos \mid I) \times Pr(I) + Pr(Pos \mid F) \times Pr(F)$$

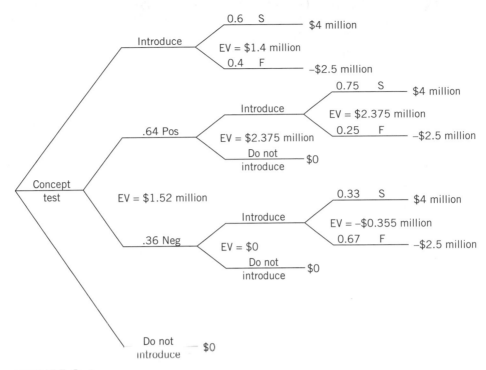

FIGURE 3-4
The concept test option

$$Pr(Neg) = Pr(Neg \mid S)Pr(S) + Pr(Neg \mid F)Pr(F)$$
$$= .2 \times .6 + .6 \times .4 = .36$$

To obtain the balance of the expressions we apply a formula known as Bayes theorem, which is the basis of Bayesian Decision Theory:

$$Pr(S \mid Pos) = \frac{Pr(Pos \mid S) \times Pr(S)}{Pr(Pos)} = \frac{.8 \times .6}{.64} = .75$$

$$Pr(F \mid Pos) = \frac{Pr(Pos \mid F) \times Pr(F)}{Pr(Pos)} = \frac{.4 \times .4}{.64} = .25$$

$$ePr(S \mid Neg) = \frac{Pr(Neg \mid S) \times Pr(S)}{Pr(Neg)} = \frac{.2 \times .6}{.36} = .33$$

$$Pr(F \mid Neg) = \frac{Pr(Neg \mid F) \times Pr(F)}{Pr(Neg)} = \frac{.6 \times .4}{.36} = .67$$

The information is now at hand to evaluate the concept test alternative. We first consider what happens if there is a positive concept test and the product is introduced. The probability of obtaining a successful product, which would earn $4 million, is $Pr(S \mid Pos)$ or .75. The failure probability is of course $Pr(F \mid Pos)$ or .25. The expected value, the sum of the two outcomes each weighted by its probability, is then

$$S \times Pr(S \mid Pos) + F \times Pr(F \mid Pos) = (\$4 \text{ million})$$
$$\times .75 + (-\$2.5 \text{ million}) \times .25 = \$2.375 \text{ million}$$

Since $2.375 million is more than the value of the "do not introduce" alternative, the product would be introduced after a positive concept test, and an expected value of $2.375 million would result, as shown in Figure 2-4.

A similar analysis reveals that the expected value of introducing the product after a negative concept test would be

$$(\$4 \text{ million}) \times .33 + (-\$2.5 \text{ million}) \times .67$$
$$= -\$.355 \text{ million}$$

Thus, given a negative concept test, the preferred alternative would be "do not introduce," which would yield zero.

Therefore an expected value of $2.375 million (associated with a positive concept test) will occur with a probability of .64 [recall that $Pr(Pos) = .6$]. Further, an expected value of zero (associated with a negative concept test) will occur with probability .36. The expected value of a concept test alternative is thus

$$(\$2.375 \text{ million}) \times .64 + (\$0) \times .36 = \$1.52 \text{ million}$$

Note that

$$\text{Expected Value of ''Concept Test'' Alternative} = \$1,520,000$$

$$\text{Expected Value of ''Introduce'' Alternative} = \$1,400,000$$

$$\text{Difference} = \$120,000$$

Thus the value of a concept test is $120,000, considerably less than value of perfect information ($1 million), but still substantial. A researcher should be willing to pay up to $120,000 for a concept test. Of course, if another concept test could be found that would predict success or failure more accurately, then its value would be higher, as the reader could demonstrate.

CASE 3-1
A VideOcart Test for Bestway Stores

The executives of Bestway Stores were intrigued with a proposal they had received from Information Resources Inc., the developer of the VideOcart, to participate in a market test of the new point-of-sale technology. They were debating whether to agree to let IRI conduct a test in 3 of their 300 stores. Their reasons for doing it were not because they especially wanted to help IRI, but rather to learn about the benefits and shortcomings of this approach to in-store displays as a possible competitive weapon. As an input to the decision, the marketing research department was asked to design a study that would assess the desirability of deploying the new display technology in all their stores once the test was finished. The test was to last about 12 months.

How Does a VideOcart Work?
Here is what a consumer would find:

After a long day at work, you rush to the supermarket to pick up dinner. As you wheel a grocery cart down the aisle, an ad for Brand X coffee flashes on a liquid-crystal screen perched on your cart's handlebar. The ad reminds you that you need coffee, so you drop a can of Brand X into your cart and push on to the next aisle.

Much of what the Bestway Stores' management knew about the VideOcart came from a press conference. They learned that IRI would beam a commercial via satellite to a pick-up dish at each store. The signal would be sent out by a low-power FM transmitter to each cart, and stored in the memory of a computer located in the handlebar of the cart.

According to an IRI spokesperson,

The ads will be shown at breaks in an information and entertainment program for consumers and won't interrupt the program. The sequence of the ads shown will be determined by the route of the cart through the store.

As a shopper pushes a VideOcart down the aisles, the manufacturer's ads for brands on the shelves being passed at that moment will be "triggered" at a rate of about two per aisle (about 32 per store) and appear on the flat, 6-by-8 in. liquid crystal display mounted on the handles of the cart. Tie-in promotion ads also will be able to be used—for instance, a hotdog bun ad when the cart is near the hot dogs.

But only about 15 percent of VideOcart's display time will be devoted to ads. The rest will be a friendly medium in which to display ads including a continually changing video newsmagazine, news to create a new shopping experience, store specials and maps, trivia questions, and videogames to play while waiting to check out.

The video seen on the screen isn't television but will use attention-getting graphics created on a personal computer.

The Test of the VideOcart
Besides gathering sales data, the test markets will be used to perfect consumer programming and fine tune the technology. IRI also will be checking on factors such as the ideal length of ads, shopper interest in games and information, how the shopper interacts with the unit, and opportunities for the grocers to contribute programming. VideOcart's computer capabilities also will offer supermarkets some advantages, including sounding an alarm if a cart is taken too far from the store, as in an attempt to steal it. The stores also could use VideOcart to transmit information such as the shortest checkout line, the next number up at the deli counter, or that a red Ford in the parking lot has its light on.

We will put the needed equipment into the supermarkets—including a satellite dish on the roof—at no cost to the retailers and eventually will pay the supermarkets a royalty four to six times greater than they're now receiving from other shopping cart ads. We're not asking for an exclusive in the supermarkets, but we're out to make that other type of shopping cart ad irrelevant.

The VideOcarts will be designed to be weatherproof and childproof. The retailers will have to recharge the batteries on the carts each night.

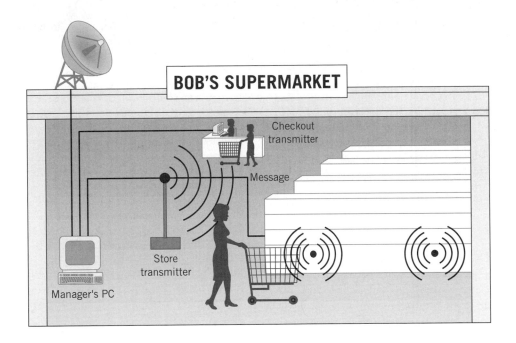

BOB'S SUPERMARKET

Checkout transmitter

Message

Store transmitter

Manager's PC

The carts should be equipped for under $500 per cart. The average supermarket has about 100 carts and IRI would turn about 75 of them into VideOcarts, which we expect shoppers will seek out because they'll make shopping efficient and fun.

VideOcart will offer excellent media efficiency compared to other alternatives. Once national, the medium will reach 60 percent of all shoppers in a week at the cost per thousand of a free-standing newspaper insert— $4–$5 per thousand households.

VideOcart ads will be able to be created in a few hours and somewhat inexpensively using microcomputer graphics software. The learning curve to master the tech-nology should be short and IRI will provide technical support and counsel.

The Assignment

The marketing research manager pondered about this project and wondered what really had to be learned to draw up a statement of purpose. With this in hand the design of the research would be a lot easier. Time was short, for management needed to know how the research manager was going to get usable information. If it looked too difficult or expensive they might not agree to a test in their stores.

CASE 3-2
Sperry/MacLennan Architects and Planners

In August 1988 Mitch Brooks, a junior partner and director of Sperry/MacLennan (S/M), a Dartmouth, Nova Scotia, architectural practice specializing in recreational facilities, is in the process of developing a plan to export his company's services. He intends to present the plan to the other directors at their meeting the first week of October. The regional market for architectural services is showing some signs of slowing, and S/M realizes that it must seek new markets. As Sheila

Sperry, the office manager and one of the directors, said at their last meeting, "You have to go wider than your own backyard. After all, you can only build so many pools in your own backyard."

About the Company

Drew Sperry, one of the two senior partners in Sperry/MacLennan, founded the company in 1972 as a one-man architectural practice. At the end of its first year, the company was incorporated as H. Drew Sperry and Associates; by then Sperry had added three junior architects, a draftsman, and a secretary. One of those architects was John MacLennan, who would later become a senior partner in Sperry/MacLennan.

Throughout the 1970s, the practice grew rapidly as the local economy expanded, even though the market for architectural services was competitive. With the baby boom generation entering the housing market, more than enough business came its way to enable Sperry to develop a thriving architectural practice, and by 1979 the company had grown to 15 employees and had established branch offices in Charlottetown and Fredericton. These branch offices had been established to provide a local market presence and meet licensing requirements during this aggressive growth period.

But the growth could not last. The early 1980s was not an easy time for the industry, and many architectural firms found themselves unable to stay in business through a very slow period in 1981–82. The company laid off all but the three remaining partners: Drew, Sheila Sperry, and John MacLennan. However, one draftsman and the secretary refused to leave, working without pay for several months in the belief that the company would win a design competition for an aquatics center in Saint John; their faith in the firm is still appreciated today.

Their presistence and faith was rewarded in 1983. Sperry won the competition for the aquatics facility for the Canada Games to be held in Saint John. Sperry had gained national recognition for its sports facility expertise, and its reputation as a good design firm specializing in sports facilities was secured.

From the beginning, the company found recreational facilities work to be fun and exciting. To quote Sheila Sperry, this type of client "wants you to be innovative and new. It's a dream for an architect because it gives him an opportunity to use all the shapes and colors and natural light. It's a very exciting medium to work in." So they decided to focus their promotional efforts to get more of this type of work and consolidate their "pool designer" image by associating with Creative Aquatics on an exclusive basis in 1984. Creative Aquatics provided aquatics programming and technical operations expertise (materials, systems, water treatment, safety, and so on) to complement the design and planning skills at Sperry.

The construction industry rebounded in 1984; declining interest rates ushered in a mini building boom, which kept everyone busy for the 1984–87 period. Mitch Brooks joined the practice in 1987. The decision to add Brooks as a partner, albeit a junior one, stemmed from their compatibility. Brooks was a good production architect, and work under his supervision came in on budget and on time, a factor compatible with the Sperry/MacLennan emphasis on customer service. The company's fee revenue amounted to approximately $1.2 million in the 1987 fiscal year; however, salaries are a major business expense, and profits after taxes (but before employee bonuses) accounted for only 4.5 percent of revenue.

Now it is late August, and with the weather cooling, Mitch Brooks reflects on his newest task, planning for the coming winter's activities. The company's reputation in the Canadian sports facility market is secure. The company has completed or has in construction five sports complexes in the Maritimes and five in Ontario, and three more facilities are in design. The awards have followed, and just this morning, Drew was notified of their latest achievement—the company has won the $10,000 Canadian Architect Grand Award for the Grand River Aquatics and Community Center near Kitchener, Ontario. This award is a particularly prestigious one because it is given by fellow architects in recognition of design excellence. Last week Sheila Sperry received word that the Amherst, N.S., YM-YWCA won the American National Swimming Pool and Spa Gold Medal for pool design against French and Mexican finalists, giving them international recognition. Mitch Brooks is looking forward to his task. The partners anticipate a slight slowdown in late 1988, and economists are predicting a recession for 1989. With 19 employees to keep busy and a competitor on the West Coast, they decided this morning that it is time to consider exporting their hard-won expertise.

The Architecture Industry

Architects are licensed provincially, and these licenses are not readily transferable from province to province. Various levels of reciprocity are in existence. For this reason, joint ventures are not that uncommon in the business. In order to cross provincial boundaries, architecture firms in one province often enter into a joint venture arrangement with a local company.

It is imperative that the architect convince the client that he or she has the necessary experience and capability to undertake the project and to complete it satisfactorily. S/M has found with its large projects that the amount of time spent meeting with the client requires some local presence, although the design need not be done locally.

Architects get business in a number of ways. "Walk-in" business is negligible, and most of S/M's contracts are the result of one of the following five processes:

1. A satisfied client gives a referral.
2. A juried design competition is announced. (S/M has found that these prestigious jobs, even though they offer "runners-up" partial compensation, are not worth entering except to win, since costs are too high and the compensation offered other entrants too low. Second place is the same as last place. The Dartmouth Sportsplex and the Saint John Aquatic Center were both design competition wins.)
3. A client publishes a "Call for Proposals" or a "Call for Expressions of Interest" as the start of a formal selection process. (S/M rates these opportunities;

unless it has a 75 percent chance of winning the contract, it views the effort as not worth the risk.)

4. A potential client invites a limited number of architectural firms to submit their qualifications as the start of a formal selection process. (S/M has a prepared qualification package that it can customize for a particular client.)

5. S/M hears of a potential building and contacts the client, presenting its qualifications.

The fourth and fifth processes are the most common in buildings done for institutions and large corporations. Since the primary buyers of sports facilities tend to be municipalities or educational institutions, these are the ways S/M acquires a substantial share of its work. Although juried competitions are not that common, the publicity possible from success in landing this work is important to S/M. The company has found that its success in securing a contract is often dependent on the client's criteria and the current state of the local market, with no particular pattern evident for a specific building type.

After the architect signs the contract, there will be a number of meetings with the client as the concept evolves and the drawings and specifications develop. Therefore, continuing client contact is as much a part of the service sold as the drawings, specifications, and site supervision and, in fact, may be the key factor in repeat business.

Developers in Nova Scotia often are not loyal buyers, changing architects with every major project or two. Despite this, architects are inclined to think the buyer's loyalty is greater than it really is. Therefore, S/M scrutinizes buyers carefully, interested in those that can pay for a premium product. S/M's philosophy is to provide "quality products with quality service for quality clients," and thus produce facilities that will reflect well on the company.

The Opportunity

In 1987, a report entitled "Precision, Planning, and Perseverance: Exporting Architectural Services to the United States," identified eight market niches for Canadian architects in the United States, one of which was educational facilities, in particular post-secondary institutions. This niche, identified by Brooks as most likely to match S/M's capabilities, is controlled by state governments and private organizations. Universities are known not to be particularly loyal to local firms and so present a potential market to be developed. The study reported that "post-secondary institutions require design and management competence, whatever the source" (p. 39). Athletic facilities were identified as a possible niche for architects with mixed-use-facility experience. Finally, the study concluded that "there is an enormous backlog of capital maintenance

and new building requirements facing most higher education institutions" (p. 38).

In addition to the above factors, the study indicated others that Brooks felt were important:

1. The United States has 30 percent fewer architectural firms per capita than Canada.

2. The market shares many Canadian values and work practices.

3. The population shift away from the Northeast to the sunbelt is beginning to reverse.

4. Americans are demanding better buildings.

Although Brooks knows that Canadian firms have always had a good reputation internationally for the quality of their buildings, he is concerned that American firms are well ahead of Canadian ones in their use of CADD (computer-assisted design and drafting) for everything from conceptual design to facility management. S/M, in spite of best intentions, has been unable to get CADD off the ground, but is in the process of applying to the Atlantic Canada Opportunities Agency for financial assistance in switching over to CADD.

Under free trade, architects will be able to freely engage in trade in services. Architects will be able to travel to the United States and set up an architectural practice without having to become qualified under the American Institute of Architects; as long as they are members of their respective provincial associations and have passed provincial licensing exams and apprenticeship requirements, they will be able to travel and work in the United States and import staff as required.

Where to Start?

At a meeting in Halifax in January 1988, the Department of External Affairs had indicated that trade to the United States in architectural services was going to be one positive benefit of the Free Trade Agreement to come into force in January 1989. As a response, S/M has targeted New England for its expansion, because of its geographical proximity to S/M's home base in the Halifax/Darmouth area and also because of its population density and similar climatic conditions. However, with all the hype about free trade and the current focus on the United States, Brooks is quite concerned that the company might be overlooking some other very lucrative markets for his company's expertise. As part of his October presentation to the board, he wants to identify and evaluate other possible markets for S/M's services. Other parts of the United States, or the affluent countries of Europe where recreational facilities are regularly patronized and design is taken seriously, might provide a better export market, given S/M's string of design successes at home and the international recognition afforded by the Amherst facility design award. Brooks feels that designing two sports facilities a year in a new market would be an acceptable goal.

In his search for leads, Brooks notes that the APPA (Association of Physical Plant Administrators of Universities and Colleges) charges $575 for a membership, which provides access to its membership list once a year. But this is only one source of leads. And of course there is the U.S. Department of Commerce, Bureau of the Census, as another source of information for him to tap. He wonders what other sources are possible.

S/M appears to have a very good opportunity in the New England market because of all of its small universities and colleges. After a decade of cutbacks on spending, corporate donations and alumni support for U.S. universities has never been so strong, and many campuses have sports facilities that are outdated and have been poorly maintained. But Mitch Brooks is not sure that the New England market is the best. After all, a seminar on exporting that he attended last week indicated that the most geographically close market, or even the most psychically close one, may not be the best choice for long-run profit maximization and/or market share.

Questions for Discussion

1. What types of information will Brooks need to collect before he can even begin to assess the New England market? Develop a series of questions you feel are critical to this assessment.
2. What selection criteria do you believe will be relevant to the assessment of any alternative markets? What preliminary market parameters are relevant to the evaluation of S/M's global options?
3. Assuming that S/M decides on the New England market, what information will be needed to implement an entry strategy?

Source: This case was adapted with permission from the case prepared by Dr. Mary R. Brooks, of Dalhousie University.

4 RESEARCH DESIGN AND IMPLEMENTATION

Learning Objectives

▶ Understand the definition and purpose of research design.

▶ Be familiar with the different types of research designs.

▶ Identify the appropriate data collection method for a given research design.

▶ Describe and briefly discuss the various sources of errors in a design.

▶ Get introduced to the concepts of budgeting and scheduling a project.

▶ Describe the elements of a research proposal.

▶ Get introduced to the issues in international marketing research design.

A **research design** is the detailed blueprint used to guide a research study toward its objectives.

The process of designing a research study involves many interrelated decisions. The most significant decision is the choice of **research approach,** because it determines how the information will be obtained. Typical questions at this stage are: Should we rely on secondary sources such as the census? What is more appropriate, an exploratory approach with group discussions or a survey? Is a mail, telephone, or personal interview survey better for this problem?

Tactical research decisions are made once the research approach has been chosen. Here the focus is on the specific measurements to be made or questions to be asked, the structure and length of the questionnaire, and the procedure for choosing a sample to be interviewed. These tactical decisions also are constrained by time and budget availability. So before a study can be implemented, the estimated costs must be compared to the anticipated value.

To design something also means to ensure that the pieces fit together. The achievement of this fit among objectives, research approach, and research tactics is inherently an iterative process in which earlier decisions are constantly reconsidered in light of subsequent decisions. This may mean a revision of the research objectives as new insights are gained into the complexities of the population to be sampled, or a reassessment of the research approach in light of realistic cost estimates. Consequently, few researchers find they have designed their research studies in the neat and linear fashion that is implied by Figure 4-1; however, this figure is a useful overview of major research design topics to be introduced in this chapter. Also in this chapter we will discuss the

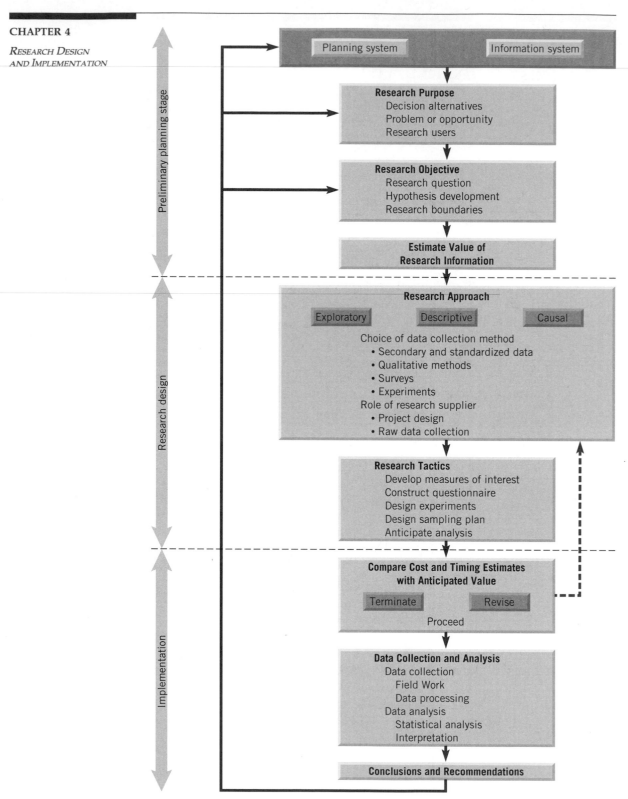

FIGURE 4-1
The research design process

research proposal as a vehicle for summarizing significant decisions made during the research design process.

RESEARCH APPROACH

The choice of a research approach depends on the nature of the research that one wants to do. In this section the various types of research approaches, data collection methods, and the factors affecting their choice are discussed.

Types of Research

All research approaches can be classified into one of three general categories of research: exploratory, descriptive, and causal. These categories differ significantly in terms of research purpose, research questions, the precision of the hypotheses that are formed, and the data collection methods that are used.

Exploratory Research. Exploratory research is used when one is seeking insights into the general nature of a problem, the possible decision alternatives, and relevant variables that need to be considered. Typically, there is little prior knowledge on which to build. The research methods are highly flexible, unstructured, and qualitative, for the researcher begins without firm preconceptions as to what will be found. The absence of structure permits a thorough pursuit of interesting ideas and clues about the problem situation.

Exploratory research hypotheses are either vague and ill defined, or do not exist at all. Table 4-1 illustrates this point with three examples. In the first example, the research question asks what alternative ways there are to provide lunches for school children. It was precipitated by information suggesting problems with existing school lunch programs. In this case, there simply is no information that would suggest the most tentative of hypotheses. In the second, the research question is to determine what benefits people seek from the product. Since no previous research considered consumer benefits, it is difficult to even provide a list of them. In the third, the hypothesis is advanced that a root cause of customer dissatisfaction is an image of impersonalization. However, this hypothesis is extremely tentative and provides at best only a partial answer to the research question.

Exploratory research is also useful for establishing priorities among research questions and for learning about the practical problems of carrying out the research. What kinds of questions will respondents be able to answer? What are the barriers to contacting the appropriate respondents? When should the study be conducted? An example of exploratory research is given in Exhibit 4-1.

A variety of productive exploratory approaches will be discussed in Chapters 5, 6, and 7, including literature reviews, individual and group unstructured interviews, and case studies.

Descriptive Research. Descriptive research embraces a large proportion of marketing research. The purpose is to provide an accurate snapshot of some aspect of the market environment, such as

TABLE 4-1
Three Research Approaches

Research Purpose	Research Question	Hypothesis
Exploratory research 1. What new product should be developed? 2. What product appeal will be effective in advertising? 3. How can our service be improved?	What alternative ways are there to provide lunches for school children? What benefits do people seek from the product? What is the nature of any customer dissatisfaction?	Boxed lunches are better than other forms. Constructs unknown. Suspect that an image of impersonalization is a problem.
Descriptive research 4. How should a new product be distributed? 5. What should be the target segment? 6. How should our product be changed?	Where do people now buy similar products? What kinds of people now buy the product, and who buys our brand? What is our current image?	Upper-class buyers use specialty stores, and middle-class buyers use department stores. Older people buy our brand, whereas the young married are heavy users of competitors'. We are regarded as being conservatives and behind the times.
Causal research 7. Will an increase in the service staff be profitable? 8. Which advertising program for public transit should be run? 9. Should a new budget or "no frills" class of airfare be introduced?	What is the relationship between size of service staff and revenue? What would get people out of cars and into public transit? Will the "no frills" airfare generate sufficient new passengers to offset the loss of revenue from existing passengers who switch from economy class?	For small organizations, an increase of 50% or less will generate marginal revenue in excess of marginal costs. Advertising program A generates more new riders than program B. The new airfare will attract sufficient revenue from new passengers.

EXHIBIT 4-1

Marketing Research Goes Undercover

More Americans are eschewing material wealth for the simpler life, and Foote Cone & Belding (FCB), a leading marketing research agency, figures the best way to research this "downshifting" trend is to examine back-to-basics consumers in their natural habitat: the small town. In 1989, the company targeted a small Illinois town code-named "Laskerville" (named for FCB founder Albert Lasker), where the research unit could go undercover to observe and interact with everyday citizens. At Laskerville, researchers conduct sophisticated marketing research that includes eavesdropping, reading local newspapers, and even attending funerals. The birth of Laskerville was motivated by the need for better ways to research trends and values among consumers. There are no notes, tape recorders, or surveys allowed. The basic gist of the research is to simply chat with the locals and be on the lookout for clues as to what they are thinking and feeling. Popular hangouts for folks in Laskerville include town meetings, church meetings, barber shops, funerals, and car dealerships. Though the methodology was "messy," FCB apparently has gotten valuable results from the research.

Source: "Researchers Go Undercover To Learn About 'Laskerville'," *Marketing News*, May 11, 1992, p. 11.

► The proportion of the adult population that supports the United Fund.

► Consumer evaluation of the attributes of our product versus competing products.

► The socioeconomic and demographic characteristics of the readership of a magazine.

► The proportion of all possible outlets that are carrying, displaying, or merchandising our products.

In descriptive research, hypotheses often will exist, but they may be tentative and speculative. In general, the relationships studied will not be causal in nature. However, they may still have utility in prediction.

In the fourth example in Table 4-1, the research question is concerned with where people buy a particular type of product. One hypothesis is that upper-class families buy this type of product in specialty stores and middle-class families use department stores. There is no explicit cause–effect relationship. The question is simply to describe where people buy. With this hypothesis it is clear that if data are gathered, it will be important to include indicators of social class and to be prepared to analyze the data with respect to stores classified as specialty and department stores. Thus, the development of the hypothesis provides guidance to the researcher by introducing more detail to the research question. Similarly, in the sixth example, the hypothesis suggests that when image is being measured, it is necessary to include measures of innovativeness.

Causal Research. When it is necessary to show that one variable causes or determines the values of other variables, a causal research approach must be used. Descriptive research is not sufficient, for all it can show is that two variables are related or associated. Of course, evidence of a relationship or an association is useful; otherwise, we would have no basis for even inferring that causality might be present. To go beyond this inference we must have reasonable proof that one variable preceded the other and that there were no other causal factors that could have accounted for the relationship.

Suppose we had evidence that territories with extensive sales coverage, as measured by the number of accounts per salesperson, had higher per capita sales. Are there sufficient grounds for a decision to increase the sales coverage in areas where sales currently are weak? The answer would depend first on whether past increases in sales coverage had led to increases in sales. Perhaps the allocation of the sales force annual budget was based on the previous year's sales. Then we might conclude that past sales increases led to an increase in sales coverage—a conclusion with dramatically different implications. Secondly, we would have to be sure that there were not other reasons for differences in sales between territories. Perhaps the weak sales territories had special requirements because of climate differences, and our product was at a disadvantage; or perhaps the weak territories were served by competitors with local advantages. In either case, adding more salespeople to weak sales territories would not improve sales, for the basic problems still would be present.

Because the requirements for proof of causality are so demanding, the research questions and relevant hypotheses are very specific. The examples in Table 4-1 show the level of detail that is desirable. Exhibit 4-2 describes an application of causal research.

Detective Funnel

Each of the three types of research—exploratory, descriptive, and causal—has a distinct and complementary role to play in many research studies. This is most evident in studies that are initiated with this question: Why are our sales (share, patronage, contributions) below our objectives or below last year's performance? The first step is to use exploratory techniques to generate all possible reasons for the problem (as shown in the drawing on page 77). Thereafter, a combination of descriptive and causal approaches is used to narrow the possible causes. Hence, the research is used in exactly the same way that a detective proceeds to eliminate unlikely suspects. Descriptive research evidence is often sufficient to filter out many of the possible causes.

For example, a municipal transit company, seeking to understand why ridership has declined suddenly, can quickly dispose of weather-related factors by examining weather records to see whether the recent weather pattern has been unusual. Similarly, evidence from customer records can be used to determine whether or not telephone complaints about the quality of service have increased. Also, their surveys of customers will reveal that service frequency and fares are the two most important factors in evaluating transit service, whereas

EXHIBIT 4-2

Is Everyday Low Pricing Leading to Everyday Low Profits?

Over the past six months, Procter & Gamble has announced that 50 percent of its volume was on "value pricing"—its name for everyday low prices—and that it expects to save $175 million from the shift. But a new report from Salomon Brothers offers a more sobering picture of P&G's trendline at the checkout stand. In 10 of 11 household product categories it tracked, P&G's dollar market share in supermarkets fell in 1992. The million dollar question now facing the retail industry is, "Should supermarkets adopt the everyday low prices (EDLP) strategy? Does the EDLP strategy provide greater profits over traditional pricing strategies?"

A group of researchers from the University of Chicago conducted an experiment to find answers to these questions. The researchers manipulated prices in 19 product categories in 88 stores of Dominick's Finer Foods, Inc., based in Chicago, and patronized by an estimated one million people each week. Some stores used the standard pricing approach, called "high–low" in the industry. Others were converted to everyday low pricing, in which prices were reduced and kept low. In their analysis of everyday low pricing, the researchers moved prices up and down 10 percent in the key categories—which included beer, cereals, cigarettes, detergents, frozen entrees, juices, and soft drinks—and accounted for 30 percent of an average store's sales. In stores with everyday low pricing in those categories, prices were dropped an additional 10 percent. In stores with a high-low strategy, prices were raised 10 percent to test consumer response.

The result: Stores featuring everyday low pricing rang up slightly more sales but much less profit than the high–low stores. Overall, profits in the categories that used everyday low pricing were about 17 percent below what grocers would have made with the traditional high–low approach, the researchers calculate. They attribute the difference to the higher profit margins on items that aren't on sale.

Source: Adapted from Jon Berry, "So How is P&G's Share? Lagging, New Study Says," *Brandweek*, April 19, 1993, p. 16, and Richard Gibson, "Broad Grocery Price Cuts May Not Pay," *The Wall Street Journal*, Friday, May 7, 1993, pp. B1, B8.

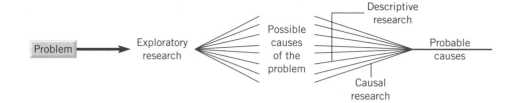

riders are indifferent to the amount and type of advertising inside buses. If fares haven't risen or the costs of competitive transportation modes such as car parking or operating costs haven't declined, then attention can be focused on service frequency. Whether this is the causal factor depends on whether there was a reduction in frequency that preceded the decline in ridership.

Data Collection Methods

The research designer has a wide variety of methods to consider, either singly or in combination. They can be grouped first according to whether they use secondary or primary sources of data. Secondary data are already available, because they were collected for some purpose other than solving the present problem. Included here are (1) the existing company information system; (2) databanks of other organizations, including government sources such as the Census Bureau or trade association studies and reports; and (3) syndicated data sources, such as consumer purchase panels, where one organization collects reasonably standardized data for use by client companies. These secondary sources are discussed in Chapters 5 and 6. **Primary data** are collected especially to address a specific research objective. A variety of methods—ranging from qualitative research to surveys to experiments—may be employed. These methods are described in more detail in Table 4-2. Some methods are better suited to one category of research than another.

TABLE 4-2

Relationship Between Data Collection Method and Category of Research

	Category of Research		
Data Collection Method	**Exploratory**	**Descriptive**	**Causal**
Secondary sources			
information system	a	b	
databanks of other organizations	a	b	
syndicated services	a	b	b
Primary sources			
qualitative research	a	b	
surveys	b	a	b
experiments		b	a

a = Very appropriate method.   b = Somewhat appropriate method.

Because different methods serve different purposes, a researcher often will use several in sequence, so the results from one method can be used by another. For example, in investigating the potential for a new frozen dessert product, a researcher may begin by consulting secondary sources, such as census statistics or industry trade association statistics, or by studying the performance of similar products that have been launched into the same market. Then qualitative research would be used to gain insights into the benefits sought by customers and into sources of dissatisfaction with the existing products. These tentative insights could be confirmed with telephone survey interviews of a representative sample of potential buyers. Finally, a controlled store experiment might be used to test the appeal of different packages. Data collection methods also vary depending on the managerial style and the culture of the organization. Exhibit 4-3 describes the method the Japanese use to collect data.

Choosing a Research Approach for the HMO Study

Seldom is a data-collection method perfectly suited to a research objective. A successful choice is one that has the greatest number of strengths and the fewest weaknesses, relative to the alternatives. Often this is achieved by combining several methods to take advantage of their best features and minimize their limitations. This was what Herb Ellis had to do to get the amount of information required by the research objectives and still remain within the budget limit.

From the beginning it was clear that the overall research approach would involve preliminary qualitative research followed by a survey, to expose the concept of a health maintenance organization to a large representative sample and test the specific hypotheses. Ellis proposed to conduct two focus groups to establish the vocabulary used by the target respondents and the attributes they used to evaluate a health plan, as well as explore their knowledge and

EXHIBIT 4-3

Data Collection—The Japanese Way

Cultural and individual preferences play a major role in determining the research technique and the method of data collection adopted for a given research project. U.S. managers, in general, prefer gathering large quantities of data through surveys, which provides numbers that can be manipulated statistically. In contrast, managers in Japan prefer the "soft" approach. For example, when Sony conducted a market survey to determine consumers' preference for a lighweight portable cassette player, results showed that consumers wouldn't buy a tape player that didn't have the recording function. Regardless of these results, Sony's chairman Akio Morita went ahead with his plans for introducing the Walkman, and the rest is history.

Sony's disdain for surveys and other scientific research tools that U.S. managers believe in is shared by other large Japanese consumer goods manufacturers such as Matsushita and Toyota. Of course, Japanese corporations do want accurate and useful information about their markets; they just go about it differently. Japanese-style market research relies heavily on two kinds of information: soft data obtained from visits to dealers and other channel members and hard data about shipments, inventory levels, and retail sales. Japanese managers believe that these data better reflect the behavior and intentions of flesh-and-blood consumers.

Source: Adapted from Johansson, K. Johnny, and Ikujiro Nonaka, "Market Research the Japanese Way," *Harvard Business Review*, May–June 1987, p. 16.

expectations of health plans and their reasons for past or prospective changes. The problem was deciding the kind of survey to conduct.

The principal survey options were mail questionnaires and personal or telephone interviews. Each, however, had a serious drawback. Personal interviews using trained interviewers were simply too costly and would have been feasible only with a sample that was too small to identify adequately the differences among the three segments. Telephone interviews would have been difficult to conduct, both because of the length of the questionnaire and the evident need for multiple-category questions, which are awkward to communicate verbally. The questionnaire could have been administered by mail, but experience suggested that the response rates would be low unless substantial incentives and follow-ups were used.

The solution was a self-administered questionnaire, with door-to-door delivery and pick-up by untrained survey assistants. The advantage of the telephone in reaching large samples economically was utilized both to establish contact and then get agreement to participate. During the initial phone call, arrangements were made to deliver and pick up the questionnaire. Before the pick-up, a reminder phone call was made to ensure that the questionnaire had been completed. In some instances the respondent was given a stamped, addressed envelope so the questionnaire could be returned by mail.

The research approach was successful in achieving a high response rate at a low cost per completed interview. The key to success was in matching the approach to the objectives of the study and the characteristics of the population, notably, the presence of an up-to-date listing, the limited geographic area to be covered, and the participants' inherent interest in the subject of the survey.

RESEARCH TACTICS AND IMPLEMENTATION

Once the research approach has been chosen, **research tactics** and **implementation** follow: the specifics of the measurements, the plan for choosing the sample, and the methods of analyses must be developed.

Measurement

The first step is to translate the research objective into information requirements and then into questions that can be answered by anticipated respondents.

For example, one of the objectives in the HMO study is to estimate probable demand for the proposed HMO. This means that information will be needed on (1) the respondents' overall evaluation of the proposed HMO, (2) their preference for the proposed HMO relative to their present health plan, and (3) their likelihood of adopting the new plan if it becomes available. As we will see in Chapters 9, 10 and 11, there are many ways to ask questions to obtain this kind of attitudinal information.

Once the individual questions have been decided, the measuring instrument has to be developed. Usually this instrument is a questionnaire, but it also may be a plan for observing behavior or recording data. The researcher designing an effective questionnaire must be concerned with how sensitive questions on topics such as income can be asked, what the order of the questions should be, and how misinterpretations can be avoided.

Sampling Plan

Most marketing research studies will be limited to a sample or subgroup of the total population relevant to the research question, rather than a census of the entire group. The sampling plan describes how the subgroup is to be selected. One approach is to use probability sampling, in which all population members have a known probability of being in the sample. This choice is indicated whenever it is important to be able to show how representative the sample is of the population. Other critical decisions at this stage are the size of the sample, as this has direct implications for the project budget, and the means of minimizing the effect on the results of sample members who cannot be reached or refuse to cooperate.

Anticipating the Analysis

When one is bogged down in the details of tactical research problems, it is easy to lose sight of the research objectives. Before actual data collection begins, the researcher must be alert to the possibility that the data will be inadequate for testing the hypotheses, or will be interesting but incapable of supporting action recommendations. Once the data have been collected, it is too late to lament, "Why didn't we collect data on that variable?" or "Why didn't we foresee there wouldn't be enough respondents to test that hypothesis?"

With these concerns in mind, the researcher should plan how each of the data items is to be analyzed. One useful device is to generate fictional (dummy) data from the questions in the measurement instrument. These dummy data can be analyzed for the study, to ensure that the results of the analysis address the objectives. For example, a great deal of preliminary data analysis consists of cross-tabulating one question by a second question. Each of the anticipated tables should be reviewed in terms of its relevance to the research question. Any shortcomings identified here will help guide the changes to the questionnaire before it is sent into the field.

Analysis of Value Versus Cost and Time Involved

At this stage of the design, most of the cost has yet to be expended. Yet the research is now completely specified and a reliable cost estimate should be available. Thus, a more detailed cost–benefit analysis should be possible to determine if the research should be conducted as designed or if it should be conducted at all.

One component of cost to be considered is the time involved. A research study can take six months or more. It may be that such a time period will delay a decision, thus creating the risk that a set of attractive conditions will be missed. For example, if the research designed to test a new product takes too long, a competitor may preempt the market with its own version of the product.

The analysis can conclude that either the research design is cost effective and should proceed or that it is not and should be terminated. Usually, instead of termination, consideration will be given to a revised research design that will be less costly. Perhaps a smaller sample could be used or a laboratory experiment substituted for a field experiment. Throughout the whole research process, new information is uncovered that makes it useful to alter the purpose, the research question, the research approach, or some aspect of tactics. Indeed, it is much more accurate to think of the research process as a series of iterations and reconsideration, rather than an ordered sequence of well-defined steps.

ERRORS IN RESEARCH DESIGN

The usefulness of a research project depends on the overall quality of the research design and the data collected and analyzed based on the design. Several potential sources of error can affect the quality of a research process. The errors can influence the various stages of the research process and can result in inaccurate or useless research findings. Errors specific to each stage of the research process are mentioned in subsequent chapters. In this section, we present a broad overview of the various types of errors that can affect a research design, with a brief description of each type.

The total error in a research study is the difference between the true mean value (within the population) of the variable being studied and the observed mean value obtained through the research study. This error has two main components:

Sampling Error

Sampling error is the difference between a measure obtained from a sample representing the population and the true measure that can be obtained only from the entire population. This error occurs because no sample is a perfect representation of a given population, unless the sample size equals the population. This issue will be dealt with in greater detail in Chapters 13 and 14.

Nonsampling Error

Nonsampling error includes all other errors associated with a research project. There may be several different reasons for these errors; they can be broadly classified into four groups: (1) design errors, (2) administering errors, (3) response errors, and (4) nonresponse errors.

Design Errors. These errors, also called researcher-induced errors, are mainly due to flaws in the research design. There are several different types of design errors:

Selection Error. Selection error occurs when a sample obtained through a nonprobability sampling method is not representative of the population. For example, if a mall interviewer interested in shopping habits of the visitors to the mall avoids interviewing people with children, he or she is then inducing a selection error into the research study.

Population Specification Error. Population specification error occurs when an inappropriate population is chosen from which to obtain data for the research study. For example, if the objective of a research study is to determine what brand of dog food people buy for their pets, and the research draws a sample from a population that consists predominantly of cat owners, a population specification error is induced into the study.

Sampling Frame Error. A sampling frame is a directory of population members from which a sample is selected. A sampling frame error occurs when the sample is drawn from an inaccurate sampling frame. For example, if a researcher interested in finding the reasons why some people have personal computers in their homes selects the sample from a list of subscribers to *PC World*, he or she is inducing a sample frame error into the study.

Surrogate Information Error. Surrogate information error is the difference or variation between the information required for a marketing research study and the information being sought by the researcher. The famous (or rather infamous) New Coke taste tests are a classic example of surrogate information error. The researchers in that case were seeking information regarding the taste of the New Coke versus the Old Coke, but the study should have determined consumers' attitudes toward a change in the product and not just their taste preferences.

Measurement Error. Measurement error is the difference or the variation between the information sought by a researcher for a study and the information generated by a particular measurement procedure employed by the researcher. Measurement error can occur at any stage of the measurement process, from the development of an instrument to the data analysis and interpretation stage. For example, if a researcher interested in the individual income of the respondent words the question as annual household income, a measurement error is being induced into the research study.

Experimental Error. An experiment is designed to determine the existence of any causal relationship between two variables. Any error caused by the improper design of the experiment induces an experimental error into the study.

Data Analysis Error. Data analysis error can occur when the data from the questionnaires are coded, edited, analyzed, or interpreted. For example, a wrong coding of data or a wrong usage of a statistical analysis procedure can induce a data analysis error into the study.

Administering Errors. All errors that occur during the administration of a survey instrument to the respondents are classified as **administering errors.**

They are caused by mistakes committed by the person administering the questionnaire. They may be caused by three major factors:

Questioning Error. This error arises while addressing questions to the respondents. If the interviewer does not word the question exactly as designed by the researcher, a questioning error is induced.

Recording Error. This error arises from improperly recording the respondent's answers. If the interviewer misinterprets the response or hears it inaccurately, this induces a recording error into the study.

Interference Error. This error occurs when an interviewer interferes with or fails to follow the exact procedure while collecting data. For example, if the interviewer fabricates the responses to a survey, it induces an interference error.

Response Errors. Response errors, also called data errors, occur when the respondent—intentionally or unintentionally—provides inaccurate answers to the survey questions. This might be due to the respondent's inability to fully comprehend the question or it may be due to fatigue, boredom, or misinterpretation of the question. Response errors can also occur when a respondent who is unwilling or embarrassed to answer a sensitive question provides an inaccurate or false response.

Nonresponse Errors. Nonresponse errors occur if (1) some members of a sample were not contacted, and hence their responses were not included in the study or (2) some of the members contacted provide an incomplete or no response to the survey instrument. The primary reasons for this error occurring include the unwillingness of respondents to participate in the study and the inability of the interviewer to contact the respondents.

Figure 4-2 provides a schematic diagram of the various types of errors possible in a research study.

BUDGETING AND SCHEDULING THE RESEARCH PROJECT

Decisions regarding the allocation of resources—time, money, and human resources—form an equally important part of the planning for a research project. In any organization there are constraints and limitations on the availability and use of these resources. Given these constraints, the budgeting and scheduling activities ensure that the resources are used effectively and efficiently. The cost–benefit analysis that precedes the research design phase gives management a preliminary idea of the worth of a marketing research project. By comparing the expected research information with its anticipated costs—both time and money—management can decide whether or not a particular

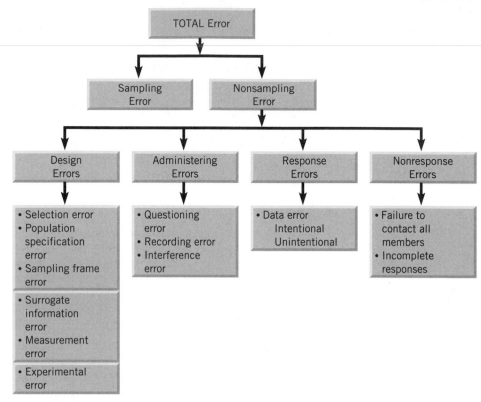

FIGURE 4-2
Errors in research design

project is worth conducting. After deciding that the benefits exceed the costs, we enter into the blueprint stage, or the research design stage.

Two common approaches of budgeting for a marketing research project are estimating the dollar costs associated with each research activity, and determining the activities to be performed, in hours, and then applying standard cost estimates to these hours. The former approach typically is used when a marketing research project is relatively unusual or expensive. The latter approach is used for routine marketing research projects or when the researcher has considerable knowledge of research activity costs.

The analysis can conclude that either the research design is cost effective and should proceed, or that it is not and should be terminated. Usually, instead of termination, consideration will be given to a revised, less costly research design. Perhaps a smaller sample could be used, or a laboratory experiment substituted for a field experiment.

Since certain research activities (most notably data analysis) cannot be initiated before other activities (data collection) are completed, research activities must be closely coordinated for a research project to be completed on time and within the budget. Scheduling makes certain that appropriate personnel and resources are available to carry out the necessary research activities, so that the entire research process is completed as economically and efficiently as possible. One approach to scheduling is an activity flowchart, a schematic representation or diagram that sequences the required research activities.

Scheduling helps marketing researchers answer one vital question: Who is responsible for accomplishing what research activity within what time period? This is a critical question for any marketing research project, for it not only allocates a person to a task but also provides a time frame within which the task is to be accomplished. Essentially it identifies the personnel accountable for a particular task.

There are several creative managerial techniques that can be used for scheduling a research project. The most often used of these techniques are (1) **critical path method (CPM),** (2) the **program evaluation and review technique (PERT),** (3) **GANTT charts,** and (4) **graphical evaluation and review techniques (GERT).**

CPM is a network approach that involves dividing the marketing research project into multiple components and estimating the time required to complete each component/activity. **PERT** is a probability based scheduling approach that recognizes and measures the uncertainty of the project completion times. **GANTT charts** are a form of activity flow chart that provide a schematic representation incorporating the activity, time, and personnel requirements for a given research project. An illustration of the use of a GANTT chart for a marketing research project is given in Figure 4-3. **GERT** is essentially a second generation PERT approach to scheduling, in which both the completion probabilities and activity costs to be built into a network representation.

RESEARCH PROPOSAL

A **research proposal** described a plan for conducting and controlling a research project. While it has an important function as a summary of the major decisions in the research process, it is useful for a number of other reasons as well. Adminis-

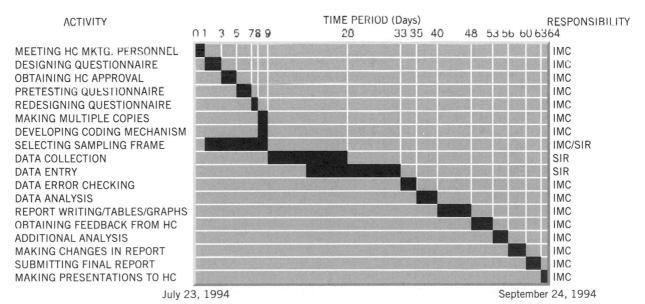

FIGURE 4-3
GANTT chart for the 1994 Houston Cellular Study

tratively, it is the basis for a written agreement or contract between the manager and researcher, as well as a record of what was agreed upon. As such it provides a vehicle for reviewing important decisions. This helps ensure that all parties are still in agreement on the scope and purpose of the research, and it reduces later misunderstandings. Frequently, proposals are used to make a choice among competing suppliers and to influence positively the decision to fund the proposed study. For these latter purposes, a proposal should be viewed as a persuasive device that demonstrates the researcher's grasp of the problem and ability to conduct the research, and also highlights the benefits of the study.

Like other communications, the structure and coverage of a proposal must be tailored to the situation. However, the following content outline has been used widely, as it ensures that likely questions will be anticipated.

Basic Contents of a Proposal

Executive Summary. A brief overview of the contents of the proposal. It may be the only part some people read, so it should be sufficient to give them a basic understanding of the proposal.

Purpose and Scope. A description of the management problem, the possible reasons for the problem, and the decision alternatives being studied.

Objectives. Defines the information to be obtained in terms of research questions to be answered. This information must be related explicitly to the management problem.

Research Approach. Presents the important features of the research methods to be used, with justification of the strengths and limitations of the chosen method relative to the alternatives. All aspects of the research that might be elements of a contract should be discussed, such as sample size, quality-control procedure, and data-collection method. Details of questionnaire format, sample selection procedures, and so forth, should be confined to an appendix.

Time and Cost Estimates. This encompasses all negotiated aspects, including total fees, payments, provisions, treatment of contingencies such as the clients' decision to expand or cancel the study, and the schedule for submission of interim, draft, and final reports.

Appendixes. Any technical matters of interest to a small minority of readers should be put at the back end of the proposal.

An example of a research proposal is given in Exhibit 4-4.

DESIGNING INTERNATIONAL MARKETING RESEARCH

As we explained earlier in Chapters 1, 2, and 3, international marketing research is conducted to aid in marketing decisions in more than one country. As such, designing a research process for international marketing decision making is

EXHIBIT 4-4

A Research Proposal to the IRS

Purpose of the Research

The general purpose of the study is to determine the taxpaying public's perceptions of the IRS role in administering the tax laws. In defining the limits of this study, the IRS identified the study areas to be addressed. A careful review of those areas led to the identification of the following specific research objectives: (1) To identify the extent to which taxpayers cheat on their returns, their reasons for doing so, and approaches that can be taken to deter this kind of behavior; (2) To determine taxpayers' experience and level of satisfaction with various IRS services; (3) To determine what services taxpayers need; (4) To develop an accurate profile of taxpayers' behavior relative to the preparation of their income tax returns; (5) To assess taxpayers' knowledge and opinions about various tax laws and procedures.

Research Design

The survey research method will be the basic research design. Each respondent will be interviewed in his or her home. The personal interviews are generally expected to last between 35 and 45 minutes, although the length will vary depending on the respondent's previous tax-related experiences. For example, if a respondent has never been audited, questions on audit experience will not be addressed; or, if a respondent has never contacted the IRS for assistance, certain questions concerning reactions to IRS services will be skipped.

Some sample questions that will be asked are

Did you (or your spouse) prepare your federal tax return for (year)?

_____ Self

_____ Spouse

_____ Someone else

Did the federal income tax package you received in the mail contain all the forms necessary for you to fill out your return?

_____ Yes

_____ No

_____ Didn't receive one in the mail

_____ Don't know

If you were calling the IRS for assistance and no one was able to help you immediately, would you rather get a busy signal or be asked to wait on hold?

_____ Busy signal

_____ Wait on hold

_____ Neither

_____ Don't know

During the interview a self-administered questionnaire will be given to the taxpayer to ask certain sensitive questions such as: Have you ever claimed a dependent on your tax return that you weren't really entitled to?

_____ Yes

_____ No

Sample Design

A survey of approximately 5,000 individuals located in 50 counties throughout the country will provide the database for this study. The sample will be selected on a probability basis from all households in the continental United States.

Eligible respondents will be adults, over the age of 18. Within each household an effort will be made to interview the individual who was most familiar with completing the federal tax forms. When there is more than one taxpayer in the household, a random process will be used to select the taxpayer to be interviewed.

Data Gathering

The field workers of a consulting research organization will conduct the interview.

Data Analysis

Standard editing and coding procedures will be utilized. Simple tabulations and cross-tabulations will be utilized to analyze the data.

Report Preparation

A written report will be prepared, and an oral presentation of the findings will be made by the research analyst, at IRS convenience.

Budget and Time Schedule

Any complete research proposal should include a schedule of how long it will take to conduct each stage of the research and prepare a statement of itemized costs.

Source: Based on A General Taxpayer Opinion Survey, Office of Planning and Research, Internal Revenue Service, March 1980.

considerably more complex than designing it for a single country. Conducting research in different countries implies much greater attention to issues such as

1. Understanding the nature and type of information sought.
2. Defining the relevant unit of analysis.
3. Formulating problems, variable specifications, and categories.
4. Identifying and selecting sources of information.
5. Availability and comparability of data.
6. Achieving equivalence of samples and measures across countries and cultures.
7. Identifying the degree of centralization of the research.
8. Coordinating research across countries.
9. Finding errors in the research design.
10. Learning the cost of conducting research in multiple countries.

Exhibit 4-5 gives a brief synopsis of the pitfalls a researcher can encounter while conducting international marketing research.

ISSUES IN INTERNATIONAL RESEARCH DESIGN

Regardless of the basic research design selected (exploratory, descriptive, or causal), researchers need to be familiar with and experienced in handling several issues or problems somewhat unique to the conduct of marketing research within and across countries and cultural groups. Three issues critical to international research design are (1) determining information requirements, (2) determining the unit of analysis, and (3) achieving equivalence of construct, measurement, and sample.[3]

Determining Information Requirements

In determining the information required for international marketing research, a primary consideration is the specific level and type of decision for which the research is being conducted. In general, the types of decisions fall into two broad categories—**strategic decisions** and **tactical decisions.** These two types differ significantly in their information requirements and the level in the organization structure where the decision making is done.

Global strategic decisions are mostly made at corporate headquarters, and they normally concern issues pertaining to foreign market selection, market entry, mode of entry, market expansion strategies, and decisions related to global standardization versus local adaptation of marketing mix strategies. Such decisions involve the entire organization and determine the overall allocation of company resources across country markets. If a firm is involved in more than one product category, the decisions involve not only country markets but also product markets within countries. The information required for global strategic

EXHIBIT 4-5

A Practitioner's View of the Key Pitfalls in Conducting International Research

The key pitfalls to avoid when conducting an international marketing research project are

1. **Selecting a domestic research company to do your international research:** There are just a handful of domestic research companies that are both dedicated to and expert in international research. It is important that international projects be coordinated by a team whose sensitivity and knowledge of foreign markets will ensure a well-executed study. Emphasis should be placed on selecting a research company with a solid reputation and extensive experience in the design, coordination, and analysis of global research.

2. **Rigidly standardizing methodologies across countries:** Attempting to be consistent with a methodological approach across countries is desirable, but among other things two key questions need to be asked in order to determine whether a particular methodology will yield the best results: (a) Does the culture lend itself to that methodology? For example, relationships in Latin America are based on personal contact. Hence, when conducting business-to-business surveys, personal interviews, though expensive, are more efficient than telephone interviews; (b) Does the local infrastructure hinder the use of that methodology? For example, telephone surveys are very common in the United States. But in Russia the telephone system is notoriously inefficient. The Moscow office for the *Economist* conducted an informal study to determine how ineffective the phone system is. The Moscow office kept a log of international calls made in a 30-day period. A total of 786 calls were attempted, of which 754 resulted in no connection, 6 calls were cut off halfway through, and 2 were wrong numbers. Also, the cost of using this inefficient system is exorbitant. To install the phone it costs $2,865; one year's service costs $485, and a one-minute call from Moscow to London costs $3.30.[1]

3. **Interviewing in English around the world:** When conducting business-to-business research, even if the executives in the foreign country speak English, interviewing in English might result in inaccurate responses. Are the subjects accurately and fully comprehending the questions, or are there nuances to the question that are not being understood? Are their answers to open-ended questions without detail and richness due to their apprehension about responding in a non-native language? Moreover, has their attention been diverted to a consideration of accents (theirs and/or the interviewer's) rather than the research questions at hand? Hence, even though translating the questionnaire may be costly and time-consuming, it results in more accurate responses.

4. **Setting inappropriate sampling requirements:** Several country-specific variables influence the selection of appropriate sampling procedures in a multi-country marketing research. For example, although random sampling is statistically the most reliable technique to use, it may be impractical in a given foreign market. Reasons may include the face that in many of the less developed countries the literacy rate is very low. Hence, while sampling for surveys that require the respondent to be literate, random sampling might not work.

5. **Lack of consideration given to language:** Translations into the appropriate local languages need to be carefully checked. When possible, a quality-control procedure of "back translation" should be followed. The prime issue is to ensure translation of the questionnaire so that there is equivalent meaning and relevance in all the countries where the project is being conducted.

6. **Lack of systematic international communication procedures:** One of the biggest problems of international research is communicating clearly with the local research companies. Do they understand the objectives of the study? Do they understand the sampling criteria? And do they understand what is expected from them? All too often, assumptions are made concerning the above issues that lead to major problems in the study's execution.

7. **Misinterpreting multi-country data across countries:** Analysis of the study's data must focus on the international market from which the data were gathered. Survey comparisons across countries should be made with the understanding of how the particular countries may differ on many key factors, including local market conditions, the maturity of the market, and the local competitive framework for the study category.

8. **Not understanding international differences in conducting qualitative research:** When conducting qualitative research such as focus groups, group discussions, and in-depth interviews, the researcher must be aware of the importance of culture in the discussion process. Not all societies encourage frank and open exchange and disagreement among individuals. Status consciousness may result in situations in which the opinion of one is reflected by all other participants. Disagreement may be seen as impolite, or certain topics may be taboo.[2] Also, in some countries like parts of Asia, mixed sex and age groups do not yield good information in a consumer group discussion. Younger people, for example, often defer to the opinions of older people. If groups cannot be separated by age and sex, one-to-one interviews should be done.

Source: Adapted from Daphne Chandler, "8 Common Pitfalls of International Research," *The Council of American Survey Research Organizations Journal*, 1992, p. 81.

decisions is governed by the company's overall objectives and has implications pertaining to the company's long-term survival.

On the other hand, tactical decisions are concerned with microlevel implementation issues, and the information required for tactical decision making is obtained mostly from primary data. These decisions are primarily concerned with marketing mix strategies with country/product markets. For example, what type of advertising copy would be effective in a given culture, and so on. The decisions are made at the functional or subsidiary level rather than at the corporate level.

Unit of Analysis

In conducting marketing research in more than one country, another major issue to be sorted out is at what level the analysis is to be done. Should it be done at (1) the global level, taking all countries simultaneously (a very complicated and seldom undertaken unit of analysis); (2) the regional level, considering groups of countries as being relatively homogeneous in terms of macroenvironmental factors (for example, the European Union and the North American Free Trade Agreement can be considered regional trading blocs); (3) the country level, where each country is taken as a separate unit; or (4) similar segments across countries (a recent trend that is gaining popularity). In this last type of analysis, the researcher targets homogeneous segments having similar tastes and preferences, across countries.

Construct, Measurement, and Sample Equivalence

Construct equivalence deals with how both the researcher and the subjects of the research see, understand, and code a particular phenomenon. The problem confronting the international researcher is that, because of sociocultural, economic, and political differences, perspectives may be neither identical nor equivalent. The international researcher constantly is faced with the self-reference criterion problem and its implications in formulating a research design. Construct equivalence is concerned with the question, "Are we studying the same phenomenon in countries X and Y?" For example, in the United States, bicycles are predominantly used for recreation; in the Netherlands and various developing countries, they provide a basic mode of transportation. This implies that the relevant competing product set must be defined differently. In the United States it will include other recreational products, whereas in the Netherlands it will include alternative modes of transportation.

Measurement equivalence deals with the methods and procedures the researcher uses to collect and categorize essential data and information. Construct and measurement equivalence are highly interrelated. Measurement is the operationalization of the constructs to be used. Measurement equivalence is concerned with the question, "Are the phenomena in countries X and Y measured the same way?" For example, while Americans measure distance in miles, in most of the other countries of the world it is measured in kilometers.

Because of sociocultural, economic, and political differences among or between countries, the international researcher faces two problems not encountered by the domestic researcher: (1) identifying and operationalizing comparable populations, and (2) selecting samples that are simultaneously representative of other populations and comparable across countries. **Sampling equivalence** is concerned with the question, "Are the samples used in countries

X and Y equivalent?" For example, children in the United States are legitimate respondents, because they exercise substantial influence in the purchase of cereals, toys, desserts, and other items, whereas in the Oriental cultures it is the parent who decides on most of these issues.

Apart from these issues, other aspects of the research process such as identifying sources of data, availability, and comparability of data from different countries, problems associated with primary data collection across countries, and so forth, add to the complexity of the international research process. Also, these issues add to the non-random error component of the research process. These issues will be dealt with in greater detail in the subsequent chapters.

Summary

In this chapter the focus has shifted from the manager's problems and information needs—as expressed in the research purpose and objectives—to the strategic and tactical decisions that will achieve the objectives of the research approach. The various research approaches include qualitative research, surveys, observation, and experimentation. Tactical research design decisions include the choice of a research supplier, the questionnaire development, the design of the experiment, the sampling plan, and the anticipation of data analysis. Implementation involves a final cost–benefit check, plus data collection, data analysis, and the development of conclusions and recommendations. Also, issues relevant to the design of international marketing research projects are discussed in this chapter.

An important distinction can be made between exploratory, descriptive, and causal research. Exploratory research, which tends to involve qualitative approaches such as group interviews, is usually characterized by ill-defined or nonexistent hypotheses. Descriptive research, which tends to use survey data, is characterized by tentative hypotheses that fall short of specifying causal relationships. Causal research, which tends to rely upon experimentation, involves more specific hypotheses involving causal relationships. Possible sources of errors in research designs are presented, and the concepts of budgeting and scheduling a research projected are discussed in great detail.

The major decisions during the research process are summarized in the research proposal. This step is essential to ensuring that the manager's problems have been translated into a research study that will help obtain relevant, timely, and accurate information—and not cost more than the information is worth.

Questions and Problems

1. Is a research design always necessary before a research study can be conducted?
2. In what ways do exploratory, descriptive, and causal research designs differ? How will these differences influence the relative importance of each research approach at each phase of the marketing program development process described in Chapter 1?

3. What alternative research approaches should Herb Ellis consider for the HMO study? What are the strengths and weaknesses of the possible approaches?

4. A manufacturer of hand tools uses industrial supply houses to reach its major markets. The company is considering a new automatic inventory-control procedure. How would you proceed with an exploratory study in advance of a larger study of the dealers' reactions to this new procedure?

5. What problems can you foresee in a test of the hypothesis that federal food stamps issued to low-income individuals are being used to supplement food budgets rather than replace former spending on food?

6. The problem of a large Canadian cable TV company was described in Chapter 3. A number of hypotheses were offered by management to account for the poor penetration in several areas comprising 15 percent of the population of the total service area. If you were the researchers assigned to study this problem, how would you proceed? Specifically, is the statement of purpose of the research adequate? What alternative research designs should be considered? Will one design be adequate to test all the hypotheses?

7. Smith Computers, Inc., a U.S.-based manufacturer of personal computers has developed a microcomputer, using the new pentium microchip technology, but at a fraction of the cost of its competitors. The company has an in-house marketing research department and a study has been ordered to assist in developing the marketing program for this product.
   a. Which type of research would be most appropriate for this study?
   b. What are the possible errors that could be made in designing the research project?
   c. Scott Peters, the head of the marketing research department, must prepare a research proposal. Suggest a content outline that will ensure that all likely questions will be addressed?
   d. Peters has also been given the task of identifying foreign market opportunities for this product. What critical issues must be considered in formulating the research design?

8. What possible problems might be encountered by a domestic research company in conducting an international research study?

9. a. How is a cost–benefit analysis useful to the management in deciding whether or not to conduct a marketing research study?
   b. What are the two approaches to budgeting for a market research project?
   c. For what situation is each approach most suitable?

End Notes

1. "Hung Up," *Economist*, July 20, 1991, p. 50.
2. R. Michael Czinkota, and A. Ronkainen Ilkka, *International Marketing*, 3rd edition, Florida: The Dryden Press, 1993, pp. 550, 551.
3. Adapted from Toyne Brian and Peter G. P. Wal-

ters, *Global Marketing Management: A Strategic Perspective*, 2nd edition, Massachusetts: Allyn and Bacon, 1993; and Douglas P. Susan and Samuel C. Craig, *International Marketing Research*, New Jersey: Prentice-Hall, Inc., 1983.

CASE 4-1
Reynold's Tobacco's
Slide-Box Cigarettes[1]

There is a tendency for management to think of marketing research as an expense, perhaps a necessary expense, but an expense nevertheless. With corporate attention being focused more and more on the bottom line, one question is often asked, "What is the impact of current or potential new activities on profit?" This case will focus on how marketing research can aid in decision making and enhance the bottom line.

To give you some basic understanding of the business situation, the cigarette industry is very mature. Many big opportunity areas for product differentiation have already been thoroughly explored and mined by the major manufacturers. There are different product attributes, ranging from different flavors (menthol and non-menthol), to different "tar" levels (full flavor, light/low "tar," ultra-low "tar"), to different lengths (king size to 120mm), and even different circumferences (superslims to wide circumference). Imagery is another means of differentiating products, so there are upscale cigarettes, masculine cigarettes, feminine cigarettes, etc. Finally, price is another important dimension differentiating brands. Combining all these methods of differentiating products results in literally hundreds of unique types of cigarettes available to smokers, ranging from superslim ultra low tar 120s in a box to a traditional nonfilter 70-mm cigarette.

With this in mind, you would think that there are few new ideas under the sun for tobacco manufacturers. That may be, but ideas that have the potential to draw business from competition and increase our company's share of the market are constantly being examined.

One such new idea was a brand that Reynold's had in test market. This new brand was developed to capture Marlboro smokers with imagery that was more sociable and had more appeal to both male and female adult smokers than the solitary cowboy image. From a product standpoint, the new brand's smoothness was emphasized in contrast to the rich flavor emphasized in Marlboro advertising. Marlboro's conventional crush-proof box has always been a key feature of the brand. Rather than offering the new brand in an identical packaging configuration, Reynold's Tobacco's R&D department developed a slide-box, a unique configuration that operated something like a matchbox. This feature was intended as yet another point of difference to attract Marlboro smokers to the the new brand.

Concept product test results of the new brand (Table 1) in a conventional crush-proof box, versus the slide-box, indicated that the slide-box would enhance the new brand's appeal among prospect smokers.

When Reynolds management saw these results, they said, "If this slide-box is better than the conventional crush-proof box, we shouldn't just limit it to a new brand that may or may not make it out of the test market. To really capitalize on the apparent appeal of the slide-box, we should put it on our established products." The direction to put it on our established brands is not as clear as it may sound at first blush. There were several questions to be resolved: Which brands? Which styles of which brands? Should the slide-box replace any current conventional crush-proof box or should it be an additional offering? How would a slide-box launch fit in with other planned programs? How big an announcement should this be? (All media forms? Point-of-sale advertising only?) Should pack graphics be redesigned to emphasize the change or should they just be translated from existing graphics? How much volume will the slide-box generate and, therefore, how much new equipment needs to be purchased?

Given the excitement over this proposition, tentative plans were made regarding which brands would use the slide-box, volume projections were calculated, and equipment was ordered. The long equipment-lead-time provided us with time to resolve some of the key questions surrounding the slide-box. The most critical question was which brand or brands should use the slide-box. The issue here was one of image compatibility; that is, whether the inherent image of the slide-box is compatible with the current or desired image of the brand. Another critical question was what was its source of appeal. If it was indeed a better package, what were specific benefits that we could advertise to prospect smokers?

A good deal of what we do in the marketing research department is implement standardized methodologies to answer recurring marketing questions: How does a product compare to competition? How effective is this new ad campaign? How appealing is this premium? The issues and questions surrounding the slide-box were new to them. So they developed a custom research design that they felt would generate required consumer input on the slide-box.

The research was designed with two objectives. The first objective was to determine which of RJR's major established brands has an image consistent with the image projected by the slide-box; and the second objective was to determine the degree of interest in this new slide-box packaging among each of these brands' prospect smoker groups. In designing the study, they knew that they needed to analyze the data by each brand's prospect group. So they designed the sample

[1] Adapted with permission from a case originally written by H. Daniel Murphy and Mary E. Brownell, "*How Research Can Save Your Company Time and Money!: A Case Study*," The Council of American Survey Research Organizations Annual Journal, 1992, pp. 107–112.

TABLE 1
Concept Product Test Results

	Conventional Crush-Proof Box	Slide-Box
Positive Purchase Interest	56→	64
Intended Frequent Use	59→	68
As usual brand	20	24
Occasionally	39	44
Package Increased		
Purchase Interest	51→	73
Increased a lot	27	53
Increased a little	24	20
Overall Positive Taste Rating	72→	80

→ = Significant at 80% confidence level or greater.

in two phases. First, a large random sample of adult smokers was drawn. Then additional augment interviews were conducted to give them large enough bases of specific types of smokers. As a result, the sample for the study consisted of 767 adult smokers, 600 of whom were selected randomly, and an additional 167 interviews to fill out specific prospect group quotas.

Given the sample size and the fact that Reynolds wanted representation across the country, they conducted personal interviews in twenty geographically dispersed markets during June 1991. The biggest challenge in designing this research was to evaluate the image of the packaging itself without allowing any influence of the image of any brand. Hence, they showed smokers a sample of the packaging without any graphics. Further, since they wouldn't be able to evaluate people's responses to the slide-box packaging in a vacuum, they also showed them prototypes of current packaging, i.e., conventional crush-proof box and soft pack, also without any graphics. This provided benchmarks to help them interpret the results.

They agreed that there are two aspects of packaging on which the packs should be evaluated: benefits of the packaging itself (such as protecting the contents, being easy to open or close, etc.), and the image of the types of smokers who would use such packaging (such as white-collar versus blue-collar). They showed respondents prototypes of each of the three types of packaging attributes and user imagery. Importantly, each smoker interviewed was given a fresh prototype and allowed to open it. After they had obtained this information, they then had each of the brands in their study rated on these same user characteristics.

Finally, they directly asked the smokers in their study how appropriate the three types of packages were for the brands of cigarettes included in their study. The order in which all packs and brands were presented was rotated to avoid any order bias. The results of the overall evaluation of packs are given in Table 2.

The outcomes of the perception studies are illustrated in Figures 1, 2, and 3.

They found that the slide-box had functionality

TABLE 2
Overall Evaluation of Packs

	Slide-Box Pack	Conventional Crush-Proof Box	Soft Pack
	%	%	%
Favorable	60	70	42
Unfavorable	26	8	26

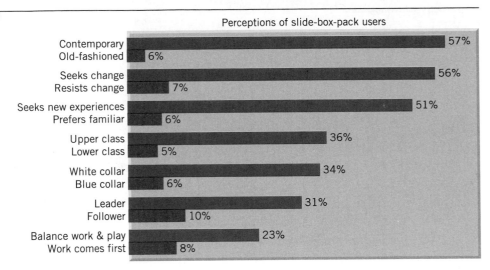

FIGURE 1
Perceptions of slide-box-pack users

problems as compared to the conventional crush-proof box. It was seen as having cosmetic advantages, such as being attractive, modern, being its own case and having an edge over the conventional crush-proof box. And, once opened, hard to keep closed. Thus, the cigarettes are more apt to fall out. The slide-box was also seen as less convenient to use. And importantly, the slide-box was perceived to be more gimmicky than the conventional crush-proof box. It is important to note that although these problems were pervasive, in that all target groups felt this way, it was conceivable that these pack problems might go away as smokers become more experienced with using this configuration.

It was also important that the user image of the slide-box was, with one exception, not felt by respondents to be compatible with the user imagery of the brands for which the pack was being considered. The analysis found that only one of the established brand's prospect group was most likely to find the slide-box

as appropriate for the brand as the conventional crush-proof box and to believe that brand's smokers and slide-box users share many similar characteristics. Both groups were pictured as white-collar, upper-class women seeking changes and new experiences. The only inconsistency was that respondents perceived the slide-box user as European. Their image of the slide-box user was more consistent with their image of their current brand than their image of the conventional crush-proof-box user.

The results of the appropriateness of packs of cigarette brands are presented in Table 3.

The new brand was not included in this national study as it was only in test market at this time. However, the new brand's prospect group did not rate the slide-box as highly overall as they rated the conventional crush-proof box. Figure 4 provides the differences in perception of slide-box-pack users among the new brand smokers.

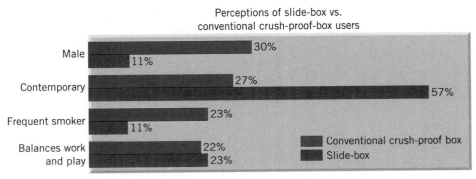

FIGURE 2
Perceptions of slide-box vs. conventional crush-proof-box users

Perceptions of slide-box vs. soft-pack users

Frequent smoker	36%
	11%
Old fashioned	34%
	8%
Prefers familiar	29%
	6%
Resists change	28%
	7%
Older	34%
	12%
Blue collar	22%
	6%

■ Soft pack
■ Slide-box

FIGURE 3
Perceptions of slide-box vs. soft-pack users

TABLE 3
Appropriateness of Packs of Cigarette Brands

% Saying Extremely/Very Appropriate

	Established Brand A	Established Brand B	Established Brand C	Established Brand D	Most Often Brand
Slide-Box	32	47	49	39	48
Conventional Crush-Proof Box	55	64	51	62	73
Soft Pack	61	44	39	55	44

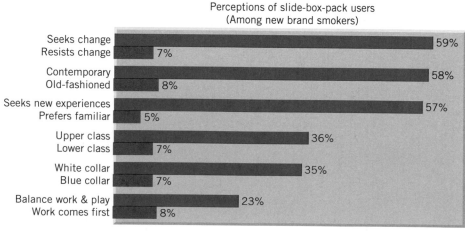

Perceptions of slide-box-pack users
(Among new brand smokers)

Seeks change	59%
Resists change	7%
Contemporary	58%
Old-fashioned	8%
Seeks new experiences	57%
Prefers familiar	5%
Upper class	36%
Lower class	7%
White collar	35%
Blue collar	7%
Balance work & play	23%
Work comes first	8%

FIGURE 4
Perceptions of slide-box-pack users (among new brand smokers)

Questions for Discussion

1. Why are the results of the second study different from the first?

2. Based upon these findings, What is your recommendation to the company?

CASE 4-2
California Foods Corporation

In early 1990, the international marketing manager at California Foods Corporation (CFC), Lois Verbrugge, was considering how to react to the continuing decline of CFC grape juice sales in the Puerto Rican market. In 1989, the marketing staff in the international division estimated that sales of CFC grape juice had fallen off by approximately 30 percent from the previous year. To determine why this loss of volume had taken place, extensive consumer research was utilized. But, as of February, Ms. Verbrugge and her staff had not come up with any clear-cut remedies for CFC's problems in the Puerto Rican market.

Company Background

CFC was a wholly owned subsidiary of the Federation of Grape Growers' Associations. The federation purchased the California Foods Corporation in 1956 as part of a strategy to integrate its business forward into the processing and distribution of grape products. CFC continued in 1990 to operate as a agribusiness largely as it had in 1956. The federation supplied the grapes, and CFC handled all processing and marketing of the products. CFC's sales had increased every year since the takeover by the federation. CFC was generally considered the foremost leader in the juice industry. It set the standards for progressive marketing techniques and new product development for the industry. With sales reaching a quarter billion dollars in 1989, the growers and CFC were the largest grape growing, processing, and marketing enterprise in the world.

Originally, CFC had produced only grape-related products: grape jams, grape jelly, frozen grape concentrate, grape drink, and grape preserves. In recent years, however, CFC had expanded to include nongrape products, too. Between 1970 and 1982, CFC introduced thirty-six new products. In 1990, CFC incorporated a complete line of fruit juices with a selection of fruit drinks and a line of fruit-flavored preserves.

CFC's International Division

CFC distributed an assortment of products to foreign markets with the majority of sales derived from juices and fruit drinks. It marketed its products to over forty countries. Major markets included Puerto Rico, Mexico, and Japan. CFC products were distributed by food brokers and distributors to retail stores and food service institutions. In 1988, the International Division experienced record sales and greater than expected profitability. Sales slipped slightly during 1989, largely the result of sales erosion in the Puerto Rican market.

The Juice and Drinks Market in Puerto Rico

Most of the juice consumption in Puerto Rico was composed of imported products. Some of the more popular brands competing for market share were CFC, Seneca, Pueblo, and Grand Union. There was only one domestic grape juice producer, selling under the name Richy. Richy had been in business for a few years, but its impact on the market had been minimal. Table 4 outlines the imported volumes of juices and drinks into Puerto Rico over the last three years.

As the table reveals, grape juice imports (California Foods' and others) were declining rather sharply. Still, the grape juice market was by far the largest juice market in Puerto Rico.

The "fruit drink" category was quite large too and was growing, especially the miscellaneous/all-others subgroup, which included Tang's imported powdered grape and orange drinks. Because many Puerto Ricans equated powdered grape with grape juice, it was possible that at least some of CFC grape juice's volume loss could be traceable to these imports, although no hard evidence existed.

Frozen concentrates represented another competing group that was large and had shown strong growth in the preceding three years. Again, the miscellaneous/all-others subgroup had shown steady growth. Perhaps some of CFC grape juice's loss could be attributable to a shift of sales across generic categories.

CFC's Entry into Puerto Rico

CFC's first experience in Puerto Rico came in the 1950s when it introduced CFC grape juice. At that point, grape juice was practically unheard of by the majority of Puerto Ricans. Despite this, the introduction was a resounding success and CFC grape juice became the best-selling juice in Puerto Rico.

Rumor had it that CFC grape juice's success was traceable to the Puerto Rican beliefs that grape juice

TABLE 4
Juices and Drinks Imported into Puerto Rico

	Thousands of Cases (Not Equivalents)			Percent of Change
	1987	1988	1989	1988–1989
Fruit juices				
Vegetable juice	20.6	23.4	23.9	+2.1
Tomato juice	45.5	21.2	26.3	+24.6
Apple juice	84.5	109.0	105.6	−3.1
Citrus juice	203.5	198.7	183.4	−7.7
Nectars	—	5.0	1.8	−64.0
Pineapple juice	22.5	22.9	29.1	+27.1
Prune juice	25.8	23.3	29.5	+26.6
Grape juice CFC	569.1	586.5	412.1	−29.7
Other	40.6	37.1	26.6	−28.3
Fruit drinks				
RJR	114.1	161.0	116.3	−27.8
Borden*	92.9	124.4	132.6	+6.6
Miscellaneous/all others†	260.5	296.4	356.0	+20.4
Fruit juice—frozen and concentrated				
Citrus Central	184.8	236.6	219.5	−7.2
CFC	34.4	24.4	32.5	+33.2
Miscellaneous/all others	378.1	431.5	499.8	+15.8

* Includes Orange Burst instant breakfast drink, Wyler's ades.
† Includes Tang powdered grape and orange drinks.
Source: Maritime Reports (Washington, D.C.: U.S. Government Printing Office, 1990).

was good for men's virility and for women's hemoglobin during their menstrual cycles. Pseudomedicinal drinks were concocted by mixing eggs with grape juice. The resulting mixture was referred to as an "egg punch." To take advantage of this seemingly unique consumer behavior, CFC launched an "egg punch" campaign in 1985. One television spot showed a young Puerto Rican man at a disco drinking an egg punch and subsequently departing with an attractive young woman. Print advertising featured a mother nursing her newborn and copy expounding the nutritional value of grape juice.

Grape juice was indeed CFC's biggest seller in Puerto Rico. Sales for 1989 were 412,000 cases. Frozen concentrated grape juice accounted for sales of 32,000 cases during 1989. Other CFC products were Calfood fruit drink, California instant powdered grape drink, CFC grape soda, and CFC strawberry soda.

Consumer Research

In order to ascertain the causes of CFC's rapid decline in grape juice sales, an "Awareness, Usage, and Attitude Study" was compiled in February 1990 to update the marketing department's understanding of Puerto Rican grape juice consumers. Two hundred personal interviews were done with people who had used grape juice during the previous two years. The study was ministered by a Puerto Rican consulting group. Results are listed in Table 5.

The results of the study showed that the demand for orange juice had increased tremendously since 1988. Both current and previous study users of CFC grape juice were drinking much more orange juice by 1990. In addition, the percentage of respondents who did not use orange juice was practically nil.

Current users of CFC juice continued to drink large quantities of grape juice, as the figures reveal. In fact, 86 percent of all CFC users said that they drank as much, or more, grape juice in 1989 as they had previously. However, among the previous CFC users, there were many more who had decreased their consumption of grape juice than had increased it. Therefore, it was implied that they were not switching from one grape juice brand to another, but drinking more orange juice instead. Over 57 percent of previous CFC users drank more orange juice by 1990 than they had in early 1988.

TABLE 5

Consumption Results of Sample of Puerto Rican Grape Juice Users During 1988 and 1989

Juices	Previous Users (n = 45)				Current CFC Users (n = 155)			
	More	**Same**	**Less**	**Don't Use**	**More**	**Same**	**Less**	**Don't Use**
Orange	57.7%	28.9%	11.1%	2.3%	43.5%	42.2%	11.7%	2.6%
Grape	13.3	37.8	24.5	24.4	38.9	47.4	13.0	0.7
Pineapple	22.2	26.7	33.3	17.8	23.3	29.9	31.1	15.7
Grapefruit	15.6	11.1	51.2	22.1	5.2	16.9	45.4	32.5
Fruit drinks	17.7	20.0	35.5	26.8	13.6	29.2	23.3	33.9
Fruit nectar	20.0	35.6	26.7	17.7	13.6	30.5	30.5	25.4
Powdered drinks	31.1	17.8	24.4	26.7	9.1	32.5	34.4	24.0

The main motive for the purchase of grape juice by mothers in the sample was because their children had asked for and/or liked it. The study also revealed that Puerto Ricans perceived grape juice to be both tasty and nutritious. On the negative side, respondents who were buying less grape juice had a variety of reasons for not buying it; most notably, very high price and preference for other juices were mentioned.

It was discovered that previous CFC users replaced grape juice with three other types of beverages: other canned juices (pineapple, orange, grapefruit), natural juices (orange, grapefruit, tamarind, lemon), and carbonated drinks (Pepsi, Coca-Cola, and the like).

Researchers had asked the question "Why aren't you using more CFC grape juice?" The most frequent response indicated that CFC's price was too high and that the respondents tried to buy products that were more economical. Secondary reasons suggested that they did not like the taste and preferred other flavors to grape. Table 6 summarizes consumers' reasons for buying either less or no grape juice in general and of CFC's in particular.

CFC had performed a similar consumer study in 1985 to determine grape juice drinkers' attitudes toward CFC grape juice. One section of the 1985 questionnaire involved consumers' opinions of the characteristics of CFC grape juice. Likewise, part of the 1990 survey was devoted to similar questioning. In both studies, respondents rated CFC grape juice on the basis of eight criteria, on a scale from 1 to 6. The figures in Table 7 represent average ratings for each of the product characteristics.

Both studies seemed to suggest that CFC grape juice had been, and still was, well regarded in the Puerto Rican market. There had not been too much change in the general opinion that CFC grape juice was a good-tasting, nutritious, high-quality product. In consumers' minds even the price had become more reasonable in relation to the generally stormy economic conditions. So what seems to be the problem with CFC grape juice in the Puerto Rican market?

The study data appear to support the notion that CFC grape juice is held in high esteem in Puerto Rico, yet a solution to CFC's sales problem is needed. With this in mind, Ms. Verbrugge arranged a meeting with Jeff Hartman, Market Research Manager, to discuss and review the situation. Ms. Verbrugge wanted to examine the problem in more detail and was prepared to commit additional funds for marketing research. Before making any decision, however, she wanted Mr. Hartman's assessment of the situation.

Source: Reprinted with permission from Subash C. Jain, International Marketing Management, California: Southwestern Publishing Co., 1993.

TABLE 6
Respondents' Reasons for Not Buying Grape Juice

	Reasons for No Longer Serving Grape Juice	Reasons for No Longer Serving CPC Grape Juice
High price	22.6%	23.2%
Only use it occasionally	9.7	4.4
Prefer other flavors	29.0	22.2
Harmful to stomach/diet	12.9	10.3
Prefer natural juices	16.1	6.7
Not accustomed to using it	n.a.	8.9
Prefer powdered drinks	n.a.	8.7
Other	9.7	15.6
Total	100.0%	100.0%

TABLE 7
Averaged Ratings of CFC Grape Juice (Scale of 1 to 6)

	1990 Study (*n* = 200)	1985 Study (*n* = 200)
Sweetness	4.95	3.96
Taste	4.96	4.73
Economy	3.86	3.47
Nutrition	5.06	5.24
Naturalness	4.91	5.05
Best for children	4.97	4.92
Best for adults	4.88	4.74
Quality	5.13	5.17

CASE I-1
Clover Valley Dairy Company

In the fall of 1978, Vince Roth, General Manager of the Clover Valley Dairy Company, was considering whether a newly developed multipack carrier for yogurt was ready for market testing and, if so, how it should be tested.

Since 1930, the Clover Valley Dairy Company had sold, under the trade name Valleyview, milk, ice cream, and other milk byproducts—such as yogurt, cottage cheese, butter, skim milk, buttermilk, and cream—in Camden, New Jersey. The raw milk was obtained from independent farmers in the vicinity of Camden and was processed and packaged at the Clover Valley Dairy.

Clover Valley's sales had grown steadily from 1930 until 1973 to an annual level of $3.75 million. However, between 1973 and 1977, a series of milk price wars cut the company's sales to $3.6 million by 1977. During this time, a number of other independent dairies were forced to close. At the height of the price wars, milk prices fell to 75 cents per half gallon. In the spring of 1977, an investigation of the milk market in Camden was conducted by the Federal Trade Commission and by Congress. Since then, prices had risen so that Clover Valley had a profit for the year to date.

Clover Valley served approximately 130 grocery store accounts, which were primarily members of a cooperative buying group or belonged to a 10-store chain that operated in the immediate area. Clover Valley no longer had any major chain accounts, although in the past they had sold to several. Because all three of the major chains operating in the area had developed exclusive supply arrangements with national or regional dairies, Clover Valley was limited to a 30 percent share of the Camden area dairy product market.

Although Clover Valley had a permit to sell its products in Philadelphia, a market six times the size of Camden, management decided not to enter that market and instead concentrated on strengthening their dealer relationships. In addition, it was felt that, if a price war were to ensue, it might extend from Philadelphia into the Camden area.

With the healthier market and profit situation in early 1978, Clover Valley began to look for ways to increase sales volume. One area that was attractive because of apparent rapid growth was yogurt. During the previous three years, management had felt that this product could help to reverse Clover Valley's downward sales trend, if given the correct marketing effort. However, the financial problems caused by the loss of the national grocery chains and the price war limited the firm's efforts. As a result, Mr. Roth felt that Clover Valley had suffered a loss of share of yogurt sales in the stores they served.

Since 1975, Mr. Roth had been experimenting with Clover Valley's yogurt packaging with the hope that a new package would boost sales quickly. All dairies in Clover Valley's area packaged yogurt in either 8-oz or 1-lb tubs made of waxed heavy paper. Clover's 8-oz tub was about 5 in. high and $2\frac{1}{2}$ in. in top diameter, tapering to $1\frac{3}{4}$ in. at base.

The first design change to be considered was the use of either aluminum or plastic lids on the traditional yogurt tubs. However, these were rejected because the increased costs did not seem to be justified by such a modest change. Changing just the lid would not make their tubs appear different from their competitor's tubs, it was felt.

By 1976, Mr. Roth had introduced a completely different package for Clover Valley's yogurt. The 8-oz tubs were replaced by 6-oz cups, designed for individual servings. In addition, the new cups were made of plastic and had aluminum foil lids. The 1-lb tubs were unchanged. No special promotional effort was undertaken by Clover Valley, but unit sales of the new 6-oz cups were more than triple the unit sales of the old 8-oz tubs (see Exhibit I-1). While the increased sales volume was welcomed, the new plastic cups increased unit packaging costs from 7.2 cents to 12.0 cents. This more than offset the saving of 4 cents because of the reduction in the amount of yogurt per container. Retail prices were reduced from 41 cents to 34 cents for the new 6-oz cup, while the price for the 1-lb tub remained at 75 cents. The increased sales then increased the total dollar contribution to fixed costs from yogurt by only 5 percent. (All dairies priced their yogurt to give retailers a 10 percent margin on the retail selling price. Competitor's retail prices for their 8-oz tubs remained at 41 cents.)

Mr. Roth felt that both the change to plastic and the convenience of the smaller size were responsible for the increased sales. However, he was disappointed with the high packaging costs and began to look at ways of reducing them, without changing the package much further. He felt another package change would be too confusing to consumers. Because of the economies of scale needed to produce plastic containers, costs could be reduced if more units were produced and sold. Mr. Roth felt that packaging a number of

EXHIBIT I-1

Clover Valley Dairy Company: Sales Results

	1974	1975	1976	1977	1978
Unit Sales of Yogurt—8-oz Tubs (6-oz After June 1977)					
January		1,203	3,531	7,899	18,594
February		996	3,651	7,629	20,187
March		960	3,258	6,677	20,676
April		853	3,888	6,081	20,199
May		861	4,425	5,814	18,420
June		915	4,044	12,726[a]	14,424
July		978	3,546	13,422	16,716
August		1,254	3,696	15,105	16,716
September		1,212	3,561	23,601	18,657
October	1,740	1,485	4,731	23,214	
November	1,437	2,928	4,499	22,146	
December	1,347	3,528	6,177	17,916	
Unit Sales of Yogurt—1-lb Tubs					
January	3,882	3,715	3,937	3,725	2,971
February	4,015	3,596	3,833	3,510	3,232
March	4,061	3,670	3,285	3,344	2,866
April	3,573	3,405	3,333	3,503	3,392
May	3,310	3,482	3,609	3,101	2,390
June	3,252	3,376	3,366	3,537	2,094
July	3,383	3,366	2,837	2,827	2,589
August	3,721	3,307	2,616	3,103	2,384
September	3,415	3,275	2,729	2,871	2,895
October	3,276	3,450	2,816	3,028	
November	3,865	4,650	3,375	2,796	
December	4,110	3,908	3,386	3,086	

[a] 6-oz tubs.

cups together would make the 6-oz cups easier to carry home, which might increase sales, and would certainly reduce packaging costs.

By 1978, work had begun on developing a multi-pack holder to hold six cups together. A single strip of aluminized plastic would serve both as holder and as the top for two rows of three yogurt cups. A single cup could be readily separated from the others in the pack. Dairy personnel constructed wooden models of several different cups for use with the holder and with plastic-molding experts, choosing one that would mold easily and cheaply. Eventually, some of these carriers were made to order for testing in the plant and among Clover Valley employee families.

Several problems soon became apparent. The holder did not always fasten securely to all six cups in the multipack. While the holder strip was being put on, the side walls of the cups were slightly compressed, causing some cups to crack at the edges. When consumers tried to remove one of the cups, they sometimes pulled the top from an adjacent cup. The problem was the strength of the aluminized plastic, which made it difficult to tear even when perforated.

The multipack was redesigned and again tested in the plant and by employee families. It appeared that the new package was performing satisfactorily. Negotiations with Cover Valley's carton supplier resulted in an estimated price of 8.5 cents for the first

100,000 units. Thereafter unit costs would drop to 7.5 cents per 6-oz cup.

Mr. Roth decided that the best multipack carrier presently possible had been designed. His attention then turned to methods of testing the new packs for consumer acceptance. Mr. Krieger, his father-in-law and president of Clover Valley, sent him the following letter concerning market testing:

Dear Vince,

Concerning the market test of the new cups and carriers, I have a few suggestions that may be helpful, although the final decision is yours. I think we should look for a few outlets where we are not competing with the other dairies, perhaps the Naval Base of Bill's Market. Actually, if we use Bill's, then the test could be conducted as follows:

1. *Give Bill a special deal on the multipacks for this weekend.*
2. *In the next two weeks, we'll only deliver the multipacks and no single cups at all.*
3. *In the third week we'll deliver both the packs and the single cups.*
4. *During the third weekend we'll have someone make a survey at the store to determine its acceptance.*
5. *Here is how it could be conducted:*
   a. *Station someone at the dairy case.*
   b. *After the shoppers have chosen either single cups or the multipacks, question them.*
   c. *If they chose the multipacks, ask them why.*
   d. *If they chose the single cups ask them why they didn't buy the packs.*
   e. *Thank them for their help and time.*

Yours,

CHARLES KRIEGER
   (signed)

Questions for Discussion

1. Should the new multipack carrier be tested?
2. If a test is judged necessary, what should be the criteria for success or failure?
3. How useful is the proposed test in addressing the management problem? What changes, if any, would you recommend?

CASE 1-2
Southwestern Conquistador Beer[1]

Introduction

Larry Gomez was just beginning to realize the problem was more complex than he thought. The problem, of course, was giving direction to Lawson and Associates regarding which research projects should be completed by February 20, 1989, to determine the market potential of a Conquistador beer distributorship for Southwestern Oregon. With data from this research, Larry would be able to estimate the feasibility of such an operation before the March 5 application deadline. Larry knew his decision of whether or not to apply for the distributorship was the most important career choice he had ever faced.

Larry Gomez

Larry was just completing his M.B.A. From his standpoint, the Conquistador announcement of expansion into Oregon could hardly have been better timed. He had long ago decided the best opportunities and rewards were in smaller, self-owned businesses.

Because of a family tragedy some three years ago, Larry found himself in a position to consider small business opportunities such as the Conquistador distributorship. Approximately $300,000 was held in trust for Larry, to be disbursed when he reached age 30. Until then, Larry and his young family lived on an annual trust income of about $22,000. It was because of this income that Larry decided to leave his sales engineering job and return to graduate school for his M.B.A.

The decision to complete a graduate program and operate his own business had been easy to make. While he could have retired and lived off investment income, Larry knew such a life would not be to his liking. Working with people and the challenge of making it on his own, Larry thought, were preferable to enduring an early retirement.

Larry would be 30 in July, about the time money would actually be needed to start the business. In the meantime, he had access to about $7500 for feasibility research. While there certainly were other ways to spend the money, Larry and his wife agreed the opportunity to acquire the distributorship could not be overlooked.

[1] Adapted with permission from a case originally written by Professor James E. Nelson of Montana State University.

Conquistador, Inc.

Conquistador had entered the U.S. beer market with distribution originally limited to New Mexico, Texas, California, and Arizona. The beer was still produced in Mexico, and retained its original and distinctive taste and packaging. These features plus an appealing image had generated a wide and enthusiastic following among some Hispanic market segments and college students. This success had prompted the company to expand their distribution as rapidly as possible into the states adjoining the original markets.

Larry was aware of Conquistador's popularity with consumers. From both personal experience and published articles, Conquistador's consumers were characterized as almost fanatically brand loyal despite the beer's premium price. As an example, ticket counter employees at the Los Angeles airport regularly reported seeing out-of-state passengers carrying one or more cases of Conquistador on board for home consumption in non-Conquistador states. Local acceptance, Larry thought, would be no less enthusiastic.

Because of this high consumer acceptance, the Conquistador company spent less on advertising than did competitors. Consumer demand seemed to pull the product through the distribution channel.

Lawson Research Proposal

Because of the press of studies, Larry contacted Lawson and Associates in January for assistance. The firm, a Portland based general research supplier, had conducted other feasibility studies in the Pacific Northwest.

In January Larry met John Rome, Senior Researcher, and extensively discussed the Conquistador opportunity and appropriate research. Rome promised a formal research proposal (Exhibit I-2) for the project that Larry now held in his hand. It certainly was extensive, Larry thought, and reflected the professionalism he expected. Now came the hard part, choosing the more relevant research from the proposal, because he certainly couldn't afford to pay for it all. Rome had suggested a meeting for Friday which gave Larry only three more days to decide.

Larry was at first overwhelmed. All of the research would certainly be useful. He was sure he needed estimates of sales and costs in a form allowing managerial analysis, but what data and in what form? Knowledge of competing operations' experience, retailer support, and consumer acceptance also seemed crucial for feasibility analysis. For example, what if consumers were excited about Conquistador but retailers were indifferent, or the other way around? Finally, several of the studies would provide information also useful in later months of operation in the areas of promotion and pricing, for example. The problem now appeared more difficult than before.

It would have been nice, Larry thought, if he only had some time to perform part of the suggested research himself. There was just too much in the way of class assignments and other matters to allow him that luxury. Besides, using Lawson and Associates would give him research results from an unbiased source. Anyway, there would be enough for him to do once he received the results.

Investment and Operating Data

Larry was not completely in the dark regarding investment and operating data for the distributorship. In the previous two weeks he had visited two beer wholesalers in his hometown, who handled Olympia and Hamms beer, to get a feel for their operation and market experience. It would have been nice to interview a Conquistador wholesaler, but Conquistador management had strictly informed all of their distributors to provide no information to prospective applicants.

While no specific financial data were discussed, general information had been provided in a near cordial fashion because of the noncompetitive nature of Larry's plans. Based on his conversations, Larry had made the following estimates:

Inventory		$240,000
Equipment		
Delivery trucks	$152,000	
Forklifts	20,000	
Recycling and	20,000	
miscellaneous		
equipment		
Office equipment	8,000	
Total equipment		200,000
Warehouse		320,000
Land		40,000
Total investment		$800,000

A local banker had reviewed Larry's financial capabilities and had seen no problem in extending a line of credit on the order of $350,000. Other family sources also might loan as much as $200,000 to the business.

As a rough estimate of fixed expenses, Larry planned to have four route salespersons, a secretary, and a general warehouseperson. Salaries for these people and himself would be about $225,000 annually plus some form of incentive compensation he had yet to determine. Other fixed or semifixed expenses were estimated at

Equipment depreciation	$ 40,000
Warehouse depreciation	16,000
Utilities and telephone	16,000
Insurance	12,000
Personal property taxes	10,000

EXHIBIT I-2

Lawson and Associates Research Proposal

January 15, 1989

Mr. Larry Gomez
1198 West Lamar
Portland, Oregon

Dear Larry,

It was a pleasure meeting you last week and discussing your business and research interests in Conquistador wholesaling. From further thought and discussion with my colleagues, the Conquistador opportunity appears even more attractive than when we met.

Appearances can be deceiving, as you know, and I fully agree that some formal research is needed before you make an application. Research that we recommend would proceed in two distinct stages and is described below:

Stage One: Research Based on Secondary Data

Study A: National and Oregon per capita Beer Consumption for 1986, 1987, and 1988

> Description: Per capita annual consumption (in gallons) of beer for the total population and population age 21 and over is provided.
>
> Source: Various publications
>
> Cost: $300

Study B: Population Estimates for 1988 to 1993 for Five Oregon Counties in Market Area

> Description: Annual estimates of total population and population age 21 and over is provided for the period 1988 to 1993.
>
> Source: U.S. Bureau of Census and Sales Management Annual Survey of Buying Power
>
> Cost: $450

Study C: Conquistador Market Share Estimates for 1990–1993

> Conquistador market share based on total gallons consumed in the five-county market area is estimated for each year in the period 1990 to 1993. These data will be projected from Conquistador's experience in California, Texas, New Mexico, and Arizona.
>
> Source: Various publications
>
> Cost: $600

Study D: Estimated Liquor and Beer Licenses for the Market Area 1989–1993

> Description: Projection of the number of on-premise sale operations and off-premise sale operations is provided.
>
> Source: Oregon Department of Revenue, Liquor Division
>
> Costs: $300

Study E: Beer Taxes Paid by Oregon Wholesalers for 1987 and 1988 in the Market Area

> Description: Beer taxes paid by each of the five currently operating competing beer wholesalers is provided. This can be converted to gallons sold by applying the state gallonage tax rate.

(continued)

(continued)

Source: Oregon Department of Revenue, Liquor Division

Cost: $1200

Study F: Financial Statement Summary of Wine, Liquor, and Beer Wholesalers for 1988

Description: Composite balance sheets, income statements, and relevant measures of performance provided for 152 similar wholesaling operations are provided.

Source: Robert Morris Associates annual statement studies

Cost: $50.00

Stage Two: Research Based on Primary Data

Study G: Consumer Study

Description: Study G involves focus-group interviews and a questionnaire to determine consumer past experience, acceptance, and intention to buy Conquistador beer. Three interviews would be conducted in three counties in the market area. From these data, a mail questionnaire would be developed and sent to 1000 adult residents in the market area utilizing direct questions and a semantic differential scale to measure attitudes towards Conquistador beer, competing beers, and an ideal beer.

Source: Lawson and Associates

Cost: $3300

Study H: Retailer Study

Description: Focus-group interviews would be conducted with six potential retailers of Conquistador in one county in the market area to determine their past beer sales and experience and their intention to stock and sell Conquistador. From these data, a mail questionnaire would be developed and sent to all appropriate retailers in the market area to determine similar data.

Source: Lawson and Associates

Cost: $1800

Study I: Survey or Retail and Wholesale Beer Prices

Description: Study I involves in-store interviews with a sample of fifteen retailers in the market area to determine retail and wholesale prices for Budweiser, Hamms, Michelob, Olympia, and a low-price beer.

Source: Lawson and Associates

Cost: $1500

Examples of the form of final report tables are shown in Exhibit I-3. This should give you a better idea of the data you will receive.

As you can see, the research is extensive and, I might add, not cheap. However, the research as outlined will supply you with sufficient information to make an estimate of the feasibility of a Conquistador distributorship, the investment in which is substantial.

I have scheduled 9:00 A.M. next Friday as a time to meet with you to discuss the proposal in more detail. Time is short, but we firmly feel the study can be completed by February 20, 1989. If you need more information in the meantime, please feel free to call.

Sincerely,

John Rome
Senior Research Analyst

Maintenance and janitorial		5,600
Miscellaneous		2,400
Total		$102,000

According to the two wholesalers, beer in bottles and cans outsold keg beer by a three-to-one margin. Keg beer prices at the wholesale level were about 45 percent of prices for beer in bottles and cans.

Meeting

The entire matter deserved much thought. Maybe it was a golden opportunity, maybe not. The only thing certain was that research was needed. Lawson and Associates was ready, and Larry needed time to think. Today is Tuesday, Larry thought, only three days until he and John Rome get together for direction.

Exhibit I-3
Examples of Final Research Report Tables

TABLE A
National and Oregon Resident Annual Beer Consumption 1986–1988 (gallons)

	U.S. Consumption		Oregon Consumption	
Year	Based on Entire Population	Based on Population over Age 21	Based on Entire Population	Based on Population over Age 21
1986				
1987				
1989				

Source: Study A.

TABLE B
Population Estimates for 1988–1993 for Five Oregon Counties in Market Area

	Projected Entire Population					
County	1988	1989	1990	1991	1992	1993
A						
B						
C						
D						
E						

Projected Population Age 21 and Over

County	1988	1989	1990	1991	1992	1993
A						
B						
C						
D						
E						

Source: Study B.

TABLE C
Conquistador Market Share Estimates for 1990–1993[a]

Year	Market Share (%)
1990	
1991	
1992	
1993	

Source: Study C.
[a] Conquistador 1988 market shares for Arizona, California, New Mexico, and Texas are _____&, _____%, _____%, _____%, and _____%, respectively.

TABLE D
Liquor and Beer License Estimates for Market Area for 1989–1993

Type of License	1989	1990	1991	1992	1993
All beverages					
Retail beer and wine					
Off-premise beer only					

Type of License	1989	1990	1991	1992	1993
Veterans beer and liquor					
Fraternal					
Resort beer and liquor					

Source: Study D.

TABLE E
Beer Taxes Paid by Beer Wholesalers in the Market Area for 1987 and 1988

Wholesaler	1987 Tax Paid ($)	1988 Tax Paid ($)
A		
B		
C		
D		
E		

Source: Study E.

TABLE F
Financial Statement Summary for 152 Wholesalers of Wine, Liquor, and Beer in 1988

Assets	Percentage
Cash	
Marketable securities	
Receivables net	
Inventory net	
All other current	
Total current	
Fixed assets net	
All other noncurrent	*Ratios*
Total 100.0	Quick
	Current

Liabilities	Debts/Worth
Due to banks—short-term	Sales/Receivables
Due to trade	Cost sales/Inventory
Income taxes	Profit before taxes (%) based on total assets
Current maturities, long-term debt	
All other current	
Total current debt	
Noncurrent debt unsubordinated	
Total unsubordinated debt	
Subordinated subtotal	
Tangible net worth	
Total 100.0	

Income Data

Net sales

Cost of sales

   Gross profit

All other expenses net

              Profit before taxes _____

Source: Study F (Robert Morris Associates, Copyright © 1989).

Note: Robert Morris Associates cannot emphasize too strongly that its figures may not be representative of the entire industry for the following reasons:

1. The only companies with a chance of being included in Table F are those for whom their submitting banks have recent figures.
2. Even from this restricted group of potentially includable companies, those which are chosen, and the total number chosen, are not determined in any random or otherwise statistically reliable manner.
3. Many companies in Table F have varied product lines. Bankers have categorized them by their primary product line, and some "impurity" in the data will be introduced. Thus, the figures should not automatically be considered as representative of norms.

TABLE G
Consumer Questionnaire Results

Consumed Conquistador in the Past (%)	Yes (%)	No (%)	Usually Buy Beer at (%)

Attitudes toward Conquistador	Usually Buy Beer at
Strongly like	Liquor stores
Like	Taverns and bars
Indifferent/No opinion	Supermarkets
Dislike	Corner grocery
Strongly dislike	
Total ‾100.0‾	Total ‾100.0‾

Weekly Beer Consumption (%)   **Features Considered Important When Buying Beer**

Weekly Beer Consumption	Features Considered Important
Less than 1 can	Taste
1–2 cans	Brand name
3–4 cans	Price
5–6 cans	Store location
7–8 cans	Advertising
9 cans or more	Carbonation
	Other
Total ‾100.0‾	Total ‾100.0‾

Intention to Buy Conquistador (%)

Intention to Buy Conquistador
Certainly will
Maybe will
Not sure
Maybe will not
Certainly will not
Total ‾100.0‾

Semantic Differential Scale[a]

	Extremely	Very	Somewhat	Somewhat	Very	Extremely	
Masculine	____	____	____	____	____	____	Feminine
Healthful	____	____	____	____	____	____	Unhealthful
Cheap	____	____	____	____	____	____	Expensive
Strong	____	____	____	____	____	____	Weak
Old-fashioned	____	____	____	____	____	____	New
Upper-class	____	____	____	____	____	____	Lower-class
Good taste	____	____	____	____	____	____	Bad taste

Source: Study G.

[a] Profiles would be provided for Conquistador, three competing beers, and an ideal beer.

TABLE H
Retailer Questionnaire Results

Brands of Beer Carried (in percent)	1988 Beer Sales (in percent)
Olympia	Olympia
Budweiser	Budweiser
Rainier	Rainier
Hamms	Hamms
Brand E	Brand E
Brand F	Brand F
Brand G	Brand G
Total 100.0	Total 100.0

Semantic Differential Scale[a]

	Extremely	Very	Somewhat	Somewhat	Very	Extremely	
Masculine	____	____	____	____	____	____	Feminine
Healthful	____	____	____	____	____	____	Unhealthful
Cheap	____	____	____	____	____	____	Expensive
Strong	____	____	____	____	____	____	Weak
Old-fashioned	____	____	____	____	____	____	New
Upper-class	____	____	____	____	____	____	Lower-class
Good taste	____	____	____	____	____	____	Bad taste

Source: Study H.

[a] Profiles would be provided for Conquistador, three competing beers, and an ideal beer.

Intention to sell Conquistador: Certainly will

Maybe will

Not sure

Maybe will not

Certainly will not

Total 100.0

TABLE I
Retail and Wholesale Prices for Selected Beers in the Market Area

Beer	Wholesale[a] Six Pack Price ($)	Retail[b] Six Pack Price ($)
Budweiser		
Hamms		
Michelob		
Olympia		
Low-price special		

Source: Study I.
[a] Price that the wholesaler sold to retailers.
[b] Price that the retailer sold to consumers.

PART II

DATA COLLECTION

5

SECONDARY SOURCES OF MARKETING DATA

Learning Objectives

▶ Define and introduce the various secondary data sources.

▶ Discuss the uses, benefits, and limitations of secondary data.

▶ Describe the various sources and forms of secondary data.

▶ Provide a brief overview of the sources of secondary data used in international marketing research.

▶ Help the student get a feel for the applications of secondary data in domestic and international marketing research.

The previous chapters identified many data sources. These only suggest the vast array of possibilities that can literally submerge the manager and researcher in numbers. The real problem with this data explosion is not the quantity but the variability of the sources with respect to quality, availability, cost, timeliness, and relevance to the needs of the decision maker. In this chapter, we begin the task of identifying and assessing the data which answer the decision maker's specific questions.

One of the hallmarks of a competent marketing researcher is familiarity with the basic sources pertaining to the market being studied, coupled with sensitivity to their respective strengths and weaknesses. This means that time will not be lost in an aimless search for nonexistent data, and neither time nor money will be wasted on a premature decision to go into the field to obtain the data.

Figure 5-1 shows the principal sources available to a researcher who is responding to a research question or considering what data to collect in order to anticipate future information needs. This chapter is concerned primarily with externally available **secondary sources,** where the specification, collection, and recording of the data are done by someone other than the user. We will take a particularly close look at census data, because it is so fundamental to understanding all aspects of a market economy. This becomes evident when census data are used to analyze market demand. We will also look at **standardized data** (Chapter 6) which are collected especially for a set of information users with a common need. Standardized data are both purpose-specific and expensive, but still much cheaper than having each user do it singly. Often, the immediate and unique needs of a decision maker require collecting original, or **primary data,** which is the topic of the rest of the book.

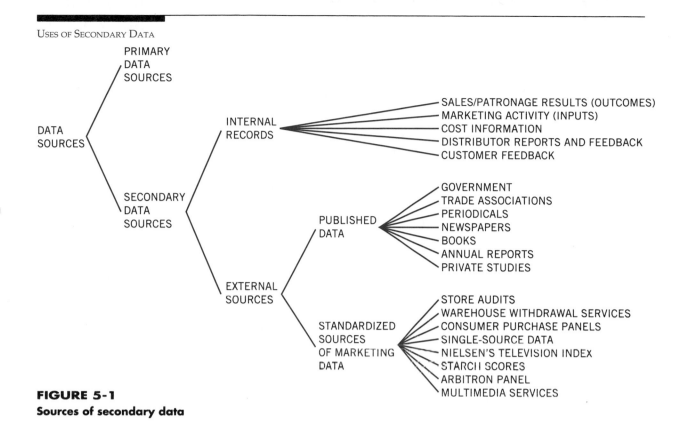

FIGURE 5-1
Sources of secondary data

SECONDARY DATA

Secondary data are data that were collected by persons or agencies for purposes other than solving the problem at hand. They are one of the cheapest and easiest means of access to information. Hence, the first thing a researcher should to is search for the secondary data available on the topic. The amount of secondary data available is overwhelming, and researchers have to locate and utilize the data that are relevant to their research. Most search procedures follow a distinctive pattern, which begins with the most available and least costly sources. Figure 5-1 shows the various sources of secondary data. The order from top to bottom roughly corresponds to the order in which the alternative sources should be considered, or to the likelihood of that type of data being incorporated into the marketing information system. That is, almost all information systems initially are based on routinely collected internal data, and expand through the inclusion of data from published and standardized sources.

USES OF SECONDARY DATA

Secondary data can be used by researchers in many ways. In this section we look at the various ways in which it can be used:

1. Secondary data may provide enough information to actually resolve the problem being investigated. Suppose a marketing researcher needs to know

the income of households in a particular market area; all he or she has to do is to look into the appropriate Census Bureau report.

2. Secondary data can be a valuable source of new ideas that can be explored later through primary research.

3. Examining available secondary data is a prerequisite to collecting primary data. It helps to define the problem and formulate hypotheses about its solution. It will almost always provide a better understanding of the problem, and its context frequently will suggest solutions not considered previously.

4. It will be of use in the collection of primary data. Examining the methodology and techniques employed by other investigators in similar studies may be useful in planning the present one. It will help to suggest improved methods.

5. Secondary data also helps to define the population, select the sample in primary information collection, and define the parameters of primary research.

6. Secondary data can also serve as a reference base against which to compare the validity or accuracy of primary data. It may also be of value in establishing classifications that are compatible with past studies so that trends may be more readily analyzed.

BENEFITS OF SECONDARY DATA

The most significant benefits secondary data offer a researcher are savings in cost and time. Secondary data research involves just spending a few days in the library extracting the data and reporting them. This should involve very little time, effort, and money compared to primary research. Even if the data were to be bought from another source, it will turn out to be cheaper than collecting primary data, because the cost of data collection would be shared by all those using the data.

Certain research projects may not be feasible for the firm; in such cases, recourse to secondary data will be the only solution. For example, if a firm needs some information on the entire population of the United States, it will be neither physically nor financially possible for the company to obtain it. Historical data is always secondary data. If a firm wants to obtain information on something that happened in the past, it cannot conduct primary research to obtain it.

In some cases secondary data can be more accurate than primary data. For example, if a company wants information on the sales, profits, and so forth, of other companies, it can get more reliable and accurate information from government-released sources than from the companies themselves.

LIMITATIONS OF SECONDARY DATA

Despite the many potential benefits of secondary data, they also have a number of limitations. By its very definition, secondary data is data that were collected in the past for purposes other than the current research. Hence, problems of fit are likely to occur between the data required for current research and the available data. The available data can have a different unit of measurement from what is required. For example, consumer income can be measured and reported at the individual, family, or household level. Even assuming that the data use the same unit of measurement, there still may be differences in the class definitions. For example, if the problem demands classification of income of individuals in increments of $10,000 ($0–$10,000, $10,001–$20,000, and so on), it does not help the researcher if he or she gets data where it is classified in increments of $7,500 ($0–$7,500, $7,501–$15,000, and so on).

The researchers have no knowledge of how the data were collected nor do they have any control over it. Therefore, they do not know anything about its accuracy or its bounds of error. They must make a number of assumptions before they can use it for actual analysis. It is also very difficult to evaluate the accuracy of the data already collected, because one can gauge its accuracy only by assessing such research characteristics as the methodology used or evidence of conscientious work. In many cases the secondary data may not be sufficient to meet the data requirement for the research at hand. In these cases, researchers may have to use primary research.

Finally, secondary data may be outdated, and hence cannot be used in current research. Data about attendance at theaters five years ago will probably be irrelevant to determine the type of motion pictures to be produced next spring, because motion picture preferences continually change. Another problem frequently faced by researchers using secondary data is one of publication currency. The time from data collection to data publication is often long; hence, the data are outdated even when they are first available. An example is the government census, which takes three years to get published. The benefits and limitations of secondary data are summarized in Table 5-1.

INTERNAL SOURCES OF SECONDARY DATA

Internal Records

A company's **internal records** accounting and control systems provide the most basic data on marketing *inputs* and the resulting *outcomes*. The principal virtues of these data are ready availability, reasonable accessibility on a continuing basis, and relevance to the organization's situation.

TABLE 5-1
Benefits and Limitations of Secondary Data

Benefits	Limitations
1. Low cost.	1. Collected for some other purpose.
2. Less effort expended process.	2. No control over the data collection.
3. Less time taken.	3. May not be very accurate.
4. Sometimes more accurate than primary data.	4. May not be reported in the required form.
5. Some information can be obtained only from secondary data.	5. May be outdated.
	6. May not meet data requirements.
	7. A number of assumptions have to be made.

Data on *inputs*—marketing effort expended—can range from budgets and schedules of expenditures to salespeople's call reports that describe the number of calls per day, who was visited, problems and applications discussed, and the results of the visit.

Extensive data on *outcomes* can be obtained from the billing records on shipments maintained in the accounting system. In many industries the resulting sales reports are the single most important piece of data used by marketing managers, because they can be related (via exception reporting methods) to plans and budgets to determine whether performance is meeting expectations. Also, they may be compared with costs in order to assess profitability.

New developments in information technology that tie customers more tightly to suppliers are improving the timeliness and depth of the sales information available to managers. For example, American Hospital Supply has supplied hospitals with computers so that hospital order entries go directly to the sales department, where they are stored in a computer and can be immediately accessed and analyzed for trends and transaction details. Salespeople at Wrangler Womenswear can connect their portable computers to the corporate computer, to send and retrieve messages, enter orders, and receive up-to-date sales information.

Using Internal Data Effectively. Many diagnostic studies potentially can be undertaken with various combinations of internal and external data, to address such questions as

► What is the effect of marketing inputs (number of sales calls or types of distribution channels) on outcomes such as profitability and unit sales within regions or sales territories?

► Is our sales performance within key market segments or types of retailers improving or deteriorating?

► Are current sales and marketing expenditures above or below the levels set in the annual budget and sales plan?

Such insightful analyses, however, often are thwarted because of limitations in the accounting system and distortions in the data.

The first problem is that accounting systems are designed to satisfy many different information needs. As a result, the reporting formats frequently are rigid and inappropriate for marketing decisions. Often the accounting data are too highly aggregated into summary results and are not available for key managerial units, such as geographic areas, customer types, or product types. Efforts to break down sales and profitability data by different units may involve special, time-consuming studies. It is also possible that production, sales, and profit figures are each measured in slightly different time frames, which are all at variance with external data such as bimonthly store-audit data.

A second problem is the quality of the data found in the internal records. On the input side, the reports of salespeople's call activity may be exaggerated if they are being evaluated on this basis. Indeed the well-known optimism of salespeople may unconsciously pervade all the data from this source. Accounting data are not exempt from such problems. The usual interpretation of a sales invoice is compromised if liberal return privileges are permitted or if the product is purchased at one location but delivered to or used in another. In general, whenever there is a long distribution channel, with several places where inventories can be accumulated, the data on orders received or invoices billed may not correspond to actual sales activity.

Customer Feedback. Increasingly, companies are augmenting their internal records with systematic compilations of product returns, service records, and customer correspondence, in a manner that permits easy retrieval. Responding to the voice of the customer has become critical in order to maintain or increase market share in today's competitive environment.[1] Complaint letters are being used as sources of data on product-quality and service problems. One reason is the insight they can provide into the problems of small groups with unusual requirements, reactions, or problems. For example, a premarket skin abrasion test of a new talc-base bath powder uncovered no problems, but the complaint letters that poured in shortly after the reformulated product was introduced revealed serious problems among a small group with sensitive skin.

Yet, complaint letters present an incomplete and distorted picture. People who write such letters are not typical clients or customers. They are most likely to be highly educated, articulate, and fussy, with more than average amounts of free time. A letter of complaint is actually a rather infrequently used method of resolving a dissatisfaction; instead, people are more likely to switch brands, shop in a different store, or complain to their friends. Manufacturers are almost completely cut off from knowledge of customer unhappiness, because most complaints are voiced to retailers and there is little systematic feedback from retailers to manufacturers.

Customer Database. Many companies have started to build **customer databases** on their own. A customer database is raw information on the customer that can be sorted and enhanced to produce useful information. Records of frequent customers and their transactions are maintained and the companies use this data to find out what is common among its customers. This data can also be used to find out about the customers product preferences, form of payment, and so on. Holiday Inn has created a customer database for its Priority Club members in order to track their activities and transactions with regard to the company.[2] These customer databases are now being used extensively by marketing managers for formulating **relationship marketing** strategies. This is discussed in greater detail in the final chapter of the book.

EXTERNAL SOURCES OF SECONDARY DATA

Published Data Sources

Published data are by far the most popular source of marketing information. Not only are the data readily available, but often they are sufficient to answer the research question; for example,

▶ A marketing manager studying developments in the wine industry will use trade association data to learn how the total consumption of wine is broken down, by type of customers, geographic area, type of wine, brand name, and distribution client. These data are available annually and sometimes quarterly, so significant trends can be isolated readily.

▶ A person starting a new specialty shop will use census data on family characteristics and income to support a likely location for the shop.

▶ Local housing planners rely on census data dealing with the characteristics of housing and households in their locality to judge the need for new housing construction or housing rehabilitation.

The prospective user of published data also is confronted with the problem of matching a specific need for information with a bewildering array of secondary data sources of variable and often indeterminate quality. What is needed first is a flexible search procedure that will ensure that no pertinent source is overlooked and, second, some general criteria for evaluating quality. These issues will be dealt with in the next two sections.

Finding Published Sources. The major published sources are the various government publications (federal, state, provincial, and local), periodicals and journals, and publicly available reports from such private groups as foundations, publishers, trade associations, unions, and companies. Of all these sources, the most valuable data for the marketing researcher come from the government census and various registration requirements. The latter encompass births, deaths, marriages, income tax returns, unemployment records, export declarations, automobile registrations, and so on.

How should someone who is unfamiliar with a market or research topic proceed? In general, two basic rules are suggested to guide the search effort: (1) start with the general and go to the specific and (2) make use of all available expertise.[3] The four main categories are authorities, general guides and indices, compilations, and directories.

Authorities. Knowledge of pertinent sources—and of their limitations—comes from continued experience. Thus, the best starting point is someone else who has been doing research on the same subject. Trade associations and specialized trade publications are particularly useful, for they often compile government data and collect additional information from their subscribers or members.[4] If information about a specific geographic area is sought, the local chamber of commerce is a good place to begin. When the problem or topic is too large or ill defined, there is no substitute for a well-informed reference librarian.

General Guides and Indices. Within this category there is a hierarchy of generality. At the top are the *"guides to the guides,"* such as Constance Winchell, *Guide to Reference Books*, the *Bibliographic Index: A Cumulative Bibliography of Bibliographies*, the *Cumulative Book Index*, and *Guide to Special Issues and Indices of Periodicals*, by Doris B. Katz et al., editors.

At the next level of reference materials are the guides to general business information sources. Several important bibliographies are the *Encyclopedia of Business Information Sources, Encyclopedia of Geographic Information Sources,* and the *Statistical Reference Index.* At a third level of generality, business periodical indices (e.g., *Psychological Abstracts, Wall Street Journal*) contain references to a large number of journals, periodicals, and newspapers.

For studies of international markets there is the *International Bibliography of Marketing and Distribution.* Each country has its own reference guides to domestic periodicals. For example, in Canada there is the (*Annual*) *Statistics Canada Catalogue,* the *Canadian Business Index,* and in the United Kingdom there is the *Annual Abstract of Statistics.* Most countries have reference guides to state and provincial jurisdictions. For example, *Canadiana* includes a regular listing of provincial and municipal government publications.

Marketing researchers often overlook valuable information on trends and conditions in specific markets, which is produced by firms such as Frost and Sullivan, Predicasts, Euromonitor, Economist Intelligence Unit, Stanford Research Institute, and A. D. Little. Although these reports may be expensive, they usually are much cheaper than primary research. These reports are indexed and described in

▶ Findex (Find / SVP), with over 13,500 reports on file from over 500 publishers.

▶ Off-the-Shelf-Publications (Commack, NY), which provides a monthly catalog of market reports.

▶ *Research Alert,* a biweekly publication that reports on 550 studies each year dealing with trends in consumer markets, attitudes, and life-styles.

Compilations. These are intermediate sources, in that they facilitate access to the original sources. This is particularly desirable with statistical information. The standard work in this area is the *Statistical Abstract of the United States,* which contains selections from the various censuses as well as data collected by other agencies. For example, data on the number of industrial robots installed worldwide, by country, are compiled by the U.S. International Trade Commission. General-purpose marketing statistics are published in volumes such as *Market Guide, Marketing Economics Guide,* and the *Rand McNally Commercial Atlas and Marketing Guide.* Other valuable compilations are the *Sales and Marketing Management* annual statistical issues detailing the "Survey of Buying Power," which includes industrial incomes, sales of six types of retail stores, market potential indices for states, countries, and metropolitan areas, and similar statistics for Canada.

Directories. These are useful for locating people or companies that could provide information. Trade directories supply a wealth of information on individual companies, including addresses, names of executives, product range, and brand names. Information on parent companies and / or subsidiaries often is provided. The *Thomas Register of American Manufacturers* lists such data on more than 150,000 manufacturing firms. *Who Owns Whom,* (North American Edition) lists 6,500 parent companies and 100,000 domestic and foreign subsidiaries and associated companies. Some *directories* are narrowly focused, such as *McKitrick's Directory of Advertisers,* or the *Pulp and Paper Directory of Canada.* There are a number of directories such as the *World Who's Who in Finance and Industry,* and *Standard and Poor's Register of Corporations, Directors and Executives* (covering the United States and Canada), which provide general biographical information on individuals.

It is important to realize that only a few of the better-known sources have been described or mentioned here. The researcher is always best advised to seek the assistance of a qualified reference librarian whenever a new area or topic is being studied.

Computer Retrievable Databases

Even with the array of printed bibliographies, directories, and indices, a search can be very time consuming. Recent advances in computer technology have resulted in more efficient methods of cataloging, storing, and retrieving published data. The growth in the number of databases available electronically through computers has been dramatic. It is estimated that over 4750 on-line databases are available to researchers and analysts working in almost every area of business, science, law, education, and the social sciences. Many of these databases are now accessible from personal computers, as well as terminals equipped with an appropriate telephone linkage. Increasingly, the software developed for the user's communication with the database system is designed to be user-friendly. As a result, use of these electronic information sources has expanded rapidly to facilitate almost any search for information and is no longer limited to computer specialists.

The large number of databases can be overwhelming. Databases can be classified by type of information contained or by the method of storage and retrieval. The Figure 5-2 gives a comprehensive view of the classification.

Classification of Databases Based on Content of Information

Reference Databases. Reference databases refer users to articles and news contained in other sources. They provide on-line indices and abstracts and are therefore referred to as bibliographic databases. This is a quick and efficient method for researching a subject before obtaining a large amount of detailed information. Reference databases provide three distinct search features:

1. They are up-to-date summaries or references to a wide assortment of articles appearing in thousands of business magazines, trade journals, government reports, and newspapers throughout the world.
2. The information is accessed by using natural language key words, rather than author or title. For example, the word "steel" will cause the computer to retrieve all abstracts that contain that word.
3. Key words can be combined in a search for articles that cover a number of related topics.

Source Databases. Source databases provide numerical data, a complete text, or a combination of both. These include the many economic and financial

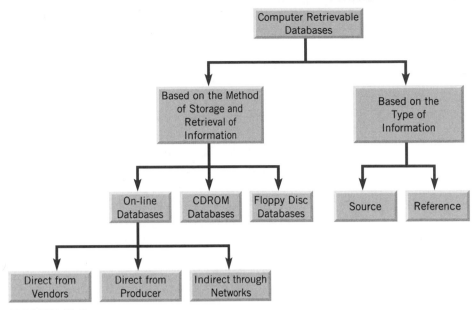

FIGURE 5-2
Classifying computer retrievable databases

databases and the textual source databases that contain the complete texts of newspaper or journal articles.

As opposed to the indices and summaries contained in the reference database, source databases provide complete textual or numerical information. They can be classified into (1) full-text information sources, (2) economic and financial statistical databases, and (3) on-line data and descriptive information on companies.

Nexis is a full-text database that includes the text of stories and articles in the major wire services, 10 newspapers including the *New York Times* and the *Washington Post,* 48 magazines and journals, and the *Encyclopedia Britannica.*

The economic and financial statistical databases were among the first databases to be offered on-line. Several of the more widely known statistics vendors (e.g., Chase Econometrics/Interactive Data Corp, Predicasts Forecasts, and Predicasts Worldcasts) provide general economic information as well as specific industry analyses and forecasts.

1. *BI/DATA TIME SERIES:* A computerized database containing 300 economic, demographic, trade, and other time series for 131 countries.
2. *DONNELLY DEMOGRAPHICS:* U.S. demographic information including the latest census, current year estimates, and five-year projections from zip-code level to the U.S. summary.

In addition to the various major databases providing financial information about companies and stocks, such as *Standard and Poor's Compustat* services and the *Value Line Database,* there are a number of on-line sources of nonfinancial information about companies. Examples are

1. Economic Information Systems—*EIS Industrial Plants* and *EIS Nonmanu-facturing Establishments:* These provide the following information for 150,000 industrial plants with over 20 employees, and for 350,000 nonmanufacturing establishments: address, SIC industry code, value of shipments, employment-size class, share of market estimates, and headquarters address.

2. Dun and Bradstreet's—*Dun's Market Identifiers:* Directory of over 1 million public and private companies with 10 or more employees, listing address, products, sales executives, corporate organization, subsidiaries, industry information, and sales prospects.

Another useful way of classifying databases might be based on their method of storage and retrieval. They can be classified as **on-line databases, CDROM databases,** and **floppy disk databases.**

Classification of Databases Based on Storage and Retrieval Methods

On-Line Databases. On-line databases are those that can be accessed in real time directly from the producers of the database or through a vendor. In order to access on-line databases, all one needs is a personal computer, a modem, and a telephone line. On-line data bases drastically reduce the time required for a search and bring data right to the desk.

CDROM Databases.[5] **Compact disc read only memory (CDROM)** technology has revolutionized the technology of storing and retrieving of information. Storing and retrieving is no longer restricted to large mainframe machines accessed by modems. Now, large amounts of information can be stored on compact discs and can be read by personal computers. A single CDROM can hold approximately 600 megabytes of information (as much as the contents of 1800 floppy disks) or 250,000-plus pages of text. The main advantage of CDROM over on-line is that there are no on-line connect time charges or long-distance telephone charges. The most powerful CDROM applications usually are sold by annual subscription or one-time fee for unlimited data access. Typically, the user receives a disc with updated information each week, month, or quarter. Almost all the reference and source databases that are available on-line are also available on CDROM.

Floppy Disk Databases. As the name suggests, floppy disk databases store information on floppy disks. These are the least popular of the databases, and with the prices of CDROM technology coming down at a rapid rate these types of databases may be totally replaced by the CDROM databases. The *Current Contents* on-diskette series is an example of a floppy disk database.

Accessing Computer Retrievable Databases

On-line databases are accessible both from their producers and increasingly from on-line information services. Most on-line services have a fee for access to each database, a charge for the amount of information retrieved, and possibly supplemental charges, depending on the nature of the information or the contract arrangements. A one-hour search for on-line information costs an average of $150, whereas a five-minute search of a familiar database source costs approximately $8 to $10.[6] The four leading vendors of on-line databases are BRS (Bibliographic Retrieval Service), DIALOG, NEWS, and SDC/ORBIT. In order to access the information on a CDROM disc, it is necessary to have a CDROM drive connected to a personal computer (or access to one available in a public library).

Advantages of Computer Retrieval Methods

The main advantage of these methods is the scope of the information available on databases. They now cover several thousand U.S. and worldwide information sources. A second advantage is the speed of information access and retrieval. Often, much of the information is available from a computer before it is available in published form, because of the time required for printing and mailing printed material. Third, commercially available search procedures provide considerable flexibility and efficiency in cross-referenced searching. For example, by using the *EIS Industrial Plants* database, it is possible to locate plants that simultaneously meet several criteria, such as geographic location, industry code, and market share. The future of computer retrievable databases is exciting. Exhibit 5-1 gives us an idea about the computer retrieval databases of the future.[7]

Limitations of Computer Retrievable Methods

The main limitations of the reference databases are their reliance on the accuracy of the abstract author, the dependence on the journal and article selection policy of the database producer, and the idiosyncracies of the search procedures of the different databases as well as the different database network vendors.[8]

Because the computer search is based on finding certain key words within the abstract, there is the possibility that some important information is missed if an abstract is missing a key word. On the other hand, a lot of irrelevant data may be generated if certain key words used to limit a search are not cited in an abstract. For example, a manufacturer of minicomputers who is interested only in developments pertaining to minicomputers may not want to retrieve the entire database on computers. However, the abstract may contain the word "computer" regardless of size, and accessing information on minicomputers would also yield general computer information.

Another limitation arises from the enormous amount of information now available on-line. It is often quite difficult to know which of the myriad sources has the correct information most readily accessible. Finally, the researcher using on-line database retrieval services must weigh the benefits of the research procedure, including timeliness, speed, and scope of information retrieval, against the costs of searching and accessing computer retrievable databases.

EXHIBIT 5-1

Three Dimensional Databases?

Lately, *virtual reality* (VR) has become a buzzword in the media. For those who may not have heard about it, VR involves technologies that promise to revolutionize the human–computer interface, as well as the way we search, display, and assimilate the information we have stored in databases. By donning VR's "goggles-and-glove" hardware, you enter a three-dimensional world generated from real-time computer graphics. Although VR is still in its infancy, it is likely to become the ultimate multimedia computing experience.

The Origins of Virtual Reality
The premise of virtual interface technology at its most basic level seems obvious. We live in a three-dimensional word. However, in order to convey information about this world, we translate it into two-dimensions such as words and symbols. Then we have to translate this 2-D information back into 3-D, at least in our own minds, in order to use it in the real world. Why not speed up the learning process by eliminating the intermediate 2-D translation wherever possible? This is a radical idea, particularly for folks in the information industry who tend to be verbally-oriented. The presentation of the data could do with some sprucing up.

However, there is a far more important and pressing issue here than a convenient interface for accessing information or displaying it in a pretty package. Who among us can deny that we have reached the point of information overload? Granted, with all of this information literally at our fingertips, participants in the on-line information industry might be the worst of the information junkies. Just reading e-mail can become a full-time job if you-re not careful. The point is, we have just about reached the limit of the amount of information we can assimilate unless we change the way we think.

Virtual Reality and On-Line
So what does virtual reality have to do with the on-line industry? Virtual interface technology may well be the means by which we interact with databases in the future. Instead of being limited to a keyboard that we use to "dialog" with the computer (i.e., type in commands, keywords, numbers, or menu options, our body and all or most of its senses may be the central component of the interface. Virtual world technology may provide a key to assimilating complex information stored in databases. Instead of displaying the results of a database search on a screen, we may be able to step "through the looking glass" and immerse ourselves in the data. This presentation of data could take advantage of all of our senses.

Virtual reality is well-suited to representing complex numeric data. For example, you could protray the stock market as a wheat field, with each stalk of wheat representing a different stock. Price fluctuations or other factors could be portrayed by the stalks growing and shrinking. You could literally walk through this virtual field of real-time stock data. This 360-degree view of data represented pictorially and in three dimensions is simpler to follow and remember. Obviously, this type of representation would also make it much easier to identify patterns and trends. While some would argue that you can do almost the same thing on a computer screen, I take exception to that. I think that the 360-degree field of vision and being able to interact with the data in a three-dimensional virtual world will make all the difference.

Source: Carmen Miller, "Virtual Reality and Online Databases: Will 'Look' and 'Feel' Literally Mean 'Look' and 'Feel'?" *Online*, 1992.

CENSUS DATA

The demographic, economic, and social statistics contained in great detail in the census are key aspects of many marketing studies; for example,

> Company Y must decide where to locate a new shopping mall and which kinds of stores to install. These decisions will require (1) **census of population** information about the populations with access to the proposed locations, (2) **census of retail trade** information about likely competitors and local wage levels, and (3) **census of construction industries**

information about land development, contractors, and construction costs, available by state and metropolitan area.

Understanding the Census

All countries conduct a mandatory enumeration of important facts about their population and the economic and social environment. The major national and international census data collection agencies and some of their major publications are the U.S. Bureau of the Census, Statistics Canada, Statistical Office of the European Communities (Social Statistics, Industrial Statistics), Great Britain Central Statistical Office (*Annual Abstract of Statistics*), Japan Bureau of Statistics (*Japan Statistical Yearbook*), and the United Nations (*Statistical Yearbook*).

The U.S. Bureau of the Census is illustrative of the scope of these undertakings. There are actually eight regular **economic censuses,** taken in the years ending with the numbers 2 and 7, and **censuses of population** and **housing** that are taken every 10 years in the year ending with 0. The eight economic censuses compile detailed statistics on the structure and functioning of the major economic sectors: agriculture, construction industries, manufacturers, mineral industries, retail trade, service industries, transportation, and wholesale trade.

Two major innovations were introduced in the 1990 census. One is the availability of census data on CDROM. For a fee, the census bureau provides detailed summaries of the information it obtains on CDROM. The bureau also sells computer software that may be used for accessing and tabulating data on the CDROM. The second major innovation in the 1990 census is the introduction of the Topologically Integrated Geographic Coding and Referencing (TIGER) system. The TIGER system gives the user the ability to generate a digitized street map of the entire 3.6-million-square-mile map of the United States. Specifically, with use of the TIGER system, one can literally chart every block in every county in the United States, both topographically and demographically. Five versions of the TIGER maps are available from the government. These include the prototype and precensus versions, both issued in 1989; the Initial Voting Codes version released in October 1990, which blankets the United States by election districts; and the initial and final post-census versions, the latter released in the early part of 1991. TIGER covers 3,286 counties in the United States, including addresses from the most populated urban areas to the most rural areas. One of TIGER's most popular uses is to plot store locations.

To use census data effectively one must be able to locate quickly the specific information relevant to the research topic. The *Index to Selected 1990 Census Reports* and the *Index to 1990 Census Summary Tapes* list all the titles of tables available from the 1990 census in either printed or tape form. Each table is described in terms of the variable and the level of aggregation used. For example, one table may be described as "education by sex" with an indication of the level of aggregation available.

Census data can be obtained at many levels of aggregation (see Figure 5-3). The smallest identifiable unit is the **city block** bounded by four streets and some other physical boundaries. City blocks then are combined arbitrarily to form block groups. The block groups then are collected together to make up

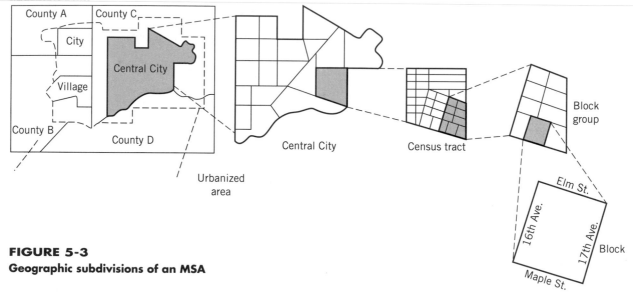

FIGURE 5-3
Geographic subdivisions of an MSA

census tracts, which are generally used to approximate neighborhoods. *Census tracts* have populations of above 4000 and are defined by local communities. In urban areas, census tracts are combined to form metropolitan statistical areas (MSAs), which are counties containing a central city with populations of at least 50,000.

The general concept of a metropolitan area is one of a large population nucleus, together with adjacent communities that are determined to have a high degree of economic and social integration with that central nucleus. In June 1983 the federal government replaced the old **standard metropolitan statistical area (SMSA)** designation with new definitions. To maintain comparability, data for an earlier period are revised where possible to reflect the MSA boundaries of the more-recent period. In addition to the new standard MSAs, the largest defined areas are **consolidated metropolitan statistical areas (CMSA),** which are metropolitan complexes containing separate component areas. (There are 335 MSAs and 68,000 census tracts and 254,000 block groups in the United States [including Puerto Rico].)

Finally, the whole country is divided into four large regions (Northeast, Midwest, South, and West). In addition, census data are available by civil divisions, such as states, counties, cities, and wards.

STANDARD INDUSTRIAL CLASSIFICATION SYSTEM

The key to obtaining census data in the industrial and services market is the **Standard Industrial Classification System (SIC).** This is a uniform numbering system for classifying establishments according to their economic activities.

The total economy is first divided into 11 divisions, such as mining, manufacturing, retail trade, and public administration. Within each of these divisions, the major industry groups are classified by two-digit numbers. Thus, **SIC 22** includes all manufacturers of textile mill products within division D, which contains all manufacturing industries. Industry subgroups are defined by a third digit, and detailed industries are defined by a fourth digit. Table 5-2 illustrates the different levels. Each plant or establishment is given the SIC number that comes closest to describing the principal activity at the location.[9]

There are many sources of SIC-related data. The most detailed source is the *U.S. Census of Manufacturers*, which provides data shown to the five- and seven-digit level. Because it is published at four- and five-year intervals, it is frequently out-of-date. Other Census Bureau sources are *U.S. Industrial Outlook and County Business Patterns*, as well as many directories that publish information on individual companies within SIC categories. Other sources are

▶ *Predicasts Quarterly* reports on past industry trends and summaries of long-term growth forecasts, by a seven-digit SIC number.

▶ *Dun's Market Identifiers* service is a continuous file on approximately 3,250,000 U.S. and Canadian establishments. For each establishment, such information as the name, address, telephone number, number of employees at the location, credit rating, and so forth is provided.

▶ Mailing-list companies such as Polk and National Business Lists Co. provide mailing lists and labels on SIC-classified establishments.

APPRAISING SECONDARY SOURCES

Users of secondary sources rapidly develop a healthy skepticism. Unfortunately, there are many reasons why a forecast, historical statistic, or estimate may be found to be irrelevant or too inaccurate to be useful. Before such a judgment can be made, the researcher should have answers to the following questions:

1. *Who?* This question applies especially to the reputation of the collecting agency for honest and thorough work and the character of the sponsoring

TABLE 5-2
Standard Industrial Classification System

Classification	SIC Number	Description
Major group	57	Home furniture, furnishings, and equipment stores
Industry subgroup	571	Home furniture and furnishing stores
Detailed industry	5712	Furniture stores
	5713	Floor covering stores

Source: Standard Industrial Classification Manual (1987), Published by the Executive Office of the President, Office of Management and Budget, U.S.

organization, which may influence the interpretation and reporting of the data. A related question is whether either organization has adequate resources to do a proper job. The problems do not end here, for the original data source (that provided the count, estimate, or other basis for the reported result) may have its own motives for biasing what it reports. A company that is pressed by a trade association, chamber of commerce, or government agency may be unwilling to report the true state of affairs or to take the time to collect the data, which may result in a biased guess.

2. *Why?* Data that are collected to further the interests of a particular group are especially suspect. Media buyers, for example, soon learn to be wary of studies of media. It is easy to choose unconsciously those methods, questions, analysis procedures, and so forth that favor the interests of the study sponsor, and it is unlikely that unfavorable results will be exposed to the public.

3. *How?* It is impossible to appraise the quality of secondary data without knowledge of the methodology used to collect them. Therefore, one should immediately be suspicious of any source that does not describe the procedures used—including a copy of the questionnaire (if any), the nature and size of the sample, the response rate, the results of field validation efforts, and any other procedural decisions that could influence the results. The crucial question is whether any of these decisions could bias the results systematically.

   The need for caution is illustrated by a study to determine the best locations for new bank branches. The researchers initially used the projections of population in different parts of the city, which were provided by the city planning commission. These ostensibly valuable data had to be discarded when it was found that the commission had arrived at their projections by subdividing on maps the areas to be developed and multiplying each area by the density of families in the already-established areas of the city. When this methodology was discovered, a proper projection was made by canvassing every real estate developer in the area regarding his future plans. The difference between the two projections was great, both in extent and timing of population increases.

4. *What?* Even if the available data are of acceptable quality, they may prove difficult to use or inadequate to the need. One irritating and prevalent problem is the classifications that are used. Wide variations in geographic, age, and income groupings across studies are common; there is no accepted definition for the minimum number of stores in a supermarket chain, for example.

5. *When?* There is nothing less interesting than last week's newspaper. Sooner or later, the pace of change in the world in general, and in markets in particular, renders all secondary data equally obsolete and uninteresting except to the historian. The rate of obsolescence varies with the types of data, but in all cases the researcher should know when the data were collected. There may be a substantial lag between the time of collection and the publication of the results.

6. *Consistency?* With all the possible pitfalls in secondary data, and the difficulty in fully identifying them, the best defense is to find another source

that can be used as a basis for comparison. Ideally, the two sources should use different methodologies to arrive at the same kind of data. In the likely event that there is some disagreement between the two sets of data, the process of reconciliation should first identify the respective biases in order to narrow the differences and determine which set is the most credible.

APPLICATIONS OF SECONDARY DATA

Secondary data are widely used for a number of marketing research problems. We have already discussed the various sources of secondary data and how to appraise them. In this section we will look at the various applications of secondary data. Table 5-3 gives a comprehensive framework of the types of sources to be used for different applications.

Demand Estimation

Most marketing resources, especially sales effort, service coverage, and communication activity, are allocated by region, segment, or territory. The key to efficient allocation is knowledge of the potential of each segment relative to other segments. Hence, demand estimation is a key determinant of the allocation of resources. Demand can be estimated from secondary data by the methods described in the paragraphs that follow.

Direct Data Methods. These are based on a disaggregation of total industry data. The sales information may come from government sources, industry surveys, or trade associations. For example, the National Electrical Manufactur-

TABLE 5-3
Applications of Secondary Data

Demand Estimation	Monitoring the Environment
1. Census data 2. Standard industrial classification (SIC) 3. Trade associations data 4. Experts and authorities	1. Press releases 2. Legislation and laws 3. Industry news 4. Business and practitioner literature, such as magazines

Segmentation and Targeting	Developing a Business Intelligence System
1. PRIZM 2. CLUSTER PLUS 3. ACORN 4. DMI 5. SIC 6. TIGER	1. Competitor's Annual Reports 2. Press releases

ers Association reports shipments of refrigerators to retailers. Now, such data are useful for establishing relative market potentials only if the sales can be broken down by the organization's sales or operating territories. Fortunately, industry refrigerator-shipment data are available by trading area. This permits a direct comparison of the share of company sales and industry sales in each territory.

Corollary Data Methods. One solution to the absence of industry sales data for each territory is to use another variable that is (1) available for each sales territory or region and (2) is correlated highly with the sales of the product. For example, the territory demand for child care services or baby food is correlated highly with the number of births in the area during the previous three years. Thus, the share of births in all geographic areas within the territory of interest would be a good proxy for the relative market potential within that territory.

Companies use other methods that are peculiar to their product and sales environment to forecast sales. An example of such a method is given in the Exhibit 5-2. In the example, Hansen Company, a manufacturer of quick connective couplings for air and fluid power transmission systems use what they call "sales-per-employee ratio" to forecast sales.

EXHIBIT 5-2

Relative Sales Potentials

What can be done if a reliable estimate of total industry sales is unavailable, the customers cannot provide a good estimate of their purchases of the product, and the product is used in many industries, so there are no obvious corollary variables? This was the situation confronting the Hansen Company, a manufacturer of quick connective couplings for air and fluid power transmission systems, who distributed these products through a national network of 31 industrial distributors. To be able to evaluate and control their activity, the company badly needed data on the relative performance of their distributors. Its approach was based on the only reliable data that were available to it—sales of company products, by distributor. To utilize these data, it made the assumption that it should be possible for Hansen distributors to attain the same *sales-per-employee ratio* in noncustomer establishments as in customer establishments. To establish the sales-per-employee ratio that would serve as a performance standard, the following steps were taken:

1. A random sample of 178 accounts was drawn from a census of all customer accounts buying $2000 or more from the seven best distributors (where "best" was defined in terms of perceived effectiveness of management and utilization of an up-to-date data processing system).
2. Each account was assigned to a two-digit SIC group on the basis of its principal output or activity.
3. Data on the number of employees in each account were obtained primarily from industrial directories.
4. Sales-per-employee ratios were computed for each SIC group within the set of seven distributors.
5. Sales-per-employee ratios for each SIC group were multiplied by the total employment in all establishments in each of the 31 distributor territories. The employment data came from the current edution of the *County Business Patterns* publication of the U.S. Census.

The output of these five steps was a table for each distributor, patterned after the following table, which gives the results for distributor A.

The resulting sales potential was compared with actual sales, which for distributor A amounted to $86,218 in 1988. That is, actual sales performance was 52.6 percent of sales potential. The sales performance for all distributors ranged from 125.0 percent to 15.4 percent, with an average of 50.3 percent. It is not surprising that the distributor with sales of only 15.4 percent of potential was subjected to a very careful review, which revealed that the salespeople did not really know how to sell the product to major accounts in the area.

Monitoring the Environment

One of the most important uses of secondary data is to monitor the environment in which the company is functioning. Monitoring the environment is very crucial these days, because it is highly volatile and because attitudes, fashions, and fads keep changing so often. To keep itself abreast of all the latest developments, a company has to be in constant touch with newspapers, general magazines, and periodicals. It has to know all the latest legislation and laws that may affect it. To know about the most recent trends in the industry, a firm has to look in the latest journals in the field. Thus, constant monitoring of the environment through a surveillance of all the relevant indicators is very important to compete effectively in this dynamic environment.

Segmentation and Targeting

Market segmentation is common among businesses seeking to improve their marketing efforts. Effective segmentation demands that firms group their customers into relatively homogeneous groups. The *Standard Industrial Classification* (SIC) and *Dun's Market Identifiers* (DMI) are used by companies selling industrial goods to segment their markets.

One of the latest developments with regard to segmentation for consumer products is geocoding, or a cluster demographic system, which identifies groups of consumers who share demographic and life-style characteristics. Several services now can link U.S. census data on a zip-code basis to life-styles, to help marketing researchers identify the best areas in which to concentrate their efforts. Among the services are PRIZM (by Claritas), CLUSTER PLUS (by Donnelly Marketing Information Services), and ACORN (CACI, Inc.).

About 1000 consumer characteristics can be used to build clusters of homogeneous groups. Demographic variables include age, marital status, size of household, and income. Behavioral characteristics include amount of TV watched, amount of white bread consumed, types of magazines read, and so on. Geographic areas range from cities and countries to zip codes, census tracts, and block groups.

The **Potential Rating Index Zip Markets (PRIZM)** system is based on evidence that people with similar cultural backgrounds and circumstances will gravitate naturally toward one another. Each of the 35,600 zip markets was first described according to 34 key demographic factors. These zip markets then were clustered into 40 distinct groups, which were each very homogeneous within themselves and very different from other groups.

Since every market is composed of zip-code areas, it is possible to estimate the sales potential of a market by zip market clusters. As an example, a power tool manufacturer was able to create a PRIZM profile of product warranty cards mailed by recent buyers. This told the manufacturer which zip code areas should be chosen as target markets and helped to allocate media spending and sales-force effort.

The **ACORN** system (an acronym for "A Classification of Residential Neighborhoods") assigns 256,000 block groups or neighborhoods to 44 clusters with less colorful descriptions. Within the larger group of "Wealthy Areas" there are three clusters: "Established Suburbs," "Newer Suburbs," and "Mixed-

Housing Inner Suburbs.'' Both ACORN and Donnelly rejected colorful descriptions, because they tend to focus on a single tendency that is not shared by all residents in the cluster. They also contend that zip codes are too heterogeneous to classify properly. On average, 68 percent are apparently misclassified using zip codes rather than block groups. They further argue that block groups are better because they do not shift from year to year, unlike zip-code boundaries.

Developing a Business Intelligence System

A **business intelligence system** is basically a system that contains data on the environment and the competitors. It forms an integral part of the marketing decision support system. Both primary and secondary data form a part of the business intelligence system. As has already been said, data on the environment can be obtained from a variety of sources. Data on competitors can be obtained from their annual reports, press releases, patents, and so on.

SOURCES OF SECONDARY DATA FOR INTERNATIONAL MARKETING RESEARCH[10]

Secondary data are a key source of information for conducting international marketing research. This is in part due to their ready availability, the high cost of collecting primary data versus the relatively low cost of secondary data, and the usefulness of secondary data in assessing whether specific problems need to be investigated, and if so, how. Further, secondary data sources are particularly valuable in assessing opportunities in countries with which management has little familiarity, and in product markets at an early stage of market development.

A wide variety of secondary data sources are available for international marketing research. These range from sources that provide general economic, social, and demographic data for almost all countries in the world, to sources that focus on specific industries worldwide.

A host of sources of macroeconomic data are to be found, ranging widely in the number of countries or regions covered. Many of these are based on or derived from United Nations and World Bank data. *Business International, Euromonitor,* and *Worldcasts* divisions of Predicasts also publish annual information on the macroeconomic variables.

The preceding macroeconomic data sources, with the exception of *Euromonitor,* relate to the general business environment. They therefore do not provide much indication as to market potential for specific industries. A number of sources of industry-specific data are available. They are United Nations Yearbooks, publications of the U.S. Department of Commerce, the *Economist,* and the *Worldcasts.*

Numerous other sources specific to individual countries or product markets are also to be found. The U.S. Department of Commerce, for example, publishes *International Marketing Handbook,* which provides profiles and special information about doing business in various countries. Information regarding regulations, customs, distribution channels, transportation, advertising and marketing research, credit, taxation, guidance for business travelers abroad, and so forth, are compiled in their "Overseas Business Reports." Governments or other bodies frequently publish national yearbooks or statistical data books. Various private sources also publish regional and country handbooks. The World of Information, for example, publishes the *African Guide*, the *Middle East Review*, and so on.

PROBLEMS ASSOCIATED WITH SECONDARY DATA IN INTERNATIONAL RESEARCH

There are two major problems associated with secondary data in international marketing research. They are the accuracy of data and the comparability of data obtained from different countries.

Data Accuracy

Different sources often report different values for the same macroeconomic factor like the GNP, per capita income, or the number of television sets in use. This casts some doubt on the accuracy of the data. This may be due to different definitions followed for each of those statistics in different countries. The accuracy of data also varies from one country to another. Data from the highly industrialized nations are likely to have a higher level of accuracy than that from developing countries, because of the difference in the sophistication of the procedures adopted. The level of literacy in a country also plays a role in the accuracy of the macroeconomic data collected in that country.

Comparability of Data

Business statistics and income data will vary from country to country because the countries have different tax structures and different levels of taxation. Hence, it may not be right to compare these statistics across countries. Population censuses may not only be inaccurate, but also may vary in frequency and the year in which they are collected. Although in United States they are collected once every 10 years, in Bolivia there was a 25-year gap between two censuses. So most population figures are based on estimates of growth that may not be accurate and comparable. Measurement units are not necessarily equivalent from country to country. For example, in Germany the expense incurred on buying a television would be classified as entertainment expense whereas in the United States it would be classified as furniture.

APPLICATIONS OF SECONDARY DATA IN INTERNATIONAL RESEARCH

Secondary data are particularly useful in evaluating country or market environments, whether in making initial market-entry decisions or in attempting to assess future trends and developments. They thus form an integral form of the international marketing research process. More specifically, three major uses of secondary data are in

1. Selecting countries or markets that merit in-depth investigation.
2. Making an initial estimate of demand potential in a given country or a set of countries.
3. Monitoring environmental changes.

Secondary data can be used to systematically screen market potential, the risks, and the likely costs of operating in different countries throughout the world. Two types of generalized procedures are used. The first procedure classifies countries on two dimensions—the degree of demographic and economic mobility, and the country's domestic stability and cohesion. The second procedure calculates multiple factor indices for different countries. For example, *Business International* publishes information each year, on three indices showing (1) **market growth,** (2) **market intensity,** and (3) **market size,** for countries in Western and Eastern Europe, the Middle East, Latin America, Asia, Africa, and Australia. Customized models, which are geared to specific company objectives and industry characteristics, can also be developed using secondary data.

Once the appropriate countries and markets to be investigated in depth have been determined, the next step is to make an explicit evaluation of demand in those countries or markets.[11] This is important when considering initial market entry, because of the high costs and uncertainty associated with entering new markets. Here the management has to make an initial estimate of demand potential, and also to project future market trends.

There are four types of data analyses that are unique to demand estimation in an international context. The first and the most simplistic is the lead-lag analysis. It uses time series (yearly) data from a country to project sales in other countries. A second procedure is the use of surrogate indicators. This is similar to the use of general macroindicators, but develops the macroindicators relative to a specific industry or product market. An example of a surrogate indicator would be the number of child births in the country as an indicator of the demand potential for diapers. A third technique, which relies on the use of cross-sectional data (data from different countries), is analogous to the use of barometric procedures in domestic sales forecasting. This assumes that if there is a direct relationship between the consumption of a product, service, or commodity and an indicator in one country, the same relationship will hold in other countries to estimate the demand. The fourth and the most complex forecasting model is the econometric forecasting model. These models use cross-sectional and time-series data on factors underlying sales for a given product market for a number of countries to estimate the certain parameters. Later, these models can be used to project the market demand.

A third use of secondary data in an International context is for monitoring environmental changes. Monitoring environmental changes requires surveillance of a number of key indicators. These should be carefully selected and tailored to the specific product or range of products with which management is concerned. Two types of indicators are required. The first monitors the general health and growth of a country and its economy and society; the second, those of a specific industry or product market. A variety of procedures can be used to analyze the impact of environmental factors on world trends or industrial countries, and on product markets, as well as the implications for market growth and appropriate marketing strategies. These range from simple trend projections or tracking studies and the use of leading indicators, to the more complex scenario evaluation studies.

Summary

The theme of this chapter is the wealth of data available to marketing researchers. Many management problems can be resolved by recourse to the firm's internal records or to secondary sources such as government statistics, trade association reports, periodicals, books, and private studies. With the growing power of computers, these data are increasingly easy to access in databases. The low cost and convenience of these database sources leave no excuse for not starting a marketing research study with a thorough scan of what is already available. Invariably, the researcher will be surprised at the extent of what is already available without any effort. Even if it is not entirely suitable, the secondary data sources can provide useful pointers on how to design a better research study.

Questions and Problems

1. You are opening a new retail store that will sell personal computers and software. What secondary data are available in your area to help you decide where to locate the store? Would the same data be relevant to someone opening a convenience copying center?

2. A large chain of building supply yards was aiming to grow at a rate of three new yards per year. From past experience, this meant carefully reviewing as many as 20 or 30 possible locations. You have been assigned the task of making this process more systematic. The first step is to specify the types of secondary information that should be available for the market area of each location. The second step is to identify the possible sources of this information and appraise their usefulness. From studies of the patrons of the present yards, you know that 60 percent of the dollar volume is accounted for by building contractors and tradesmen. The rest of the volume is sold to farmers, householders, and hobbyists. However, the sales to do-it-yourselfers have been noticeably increasing. About 75 percent of the sales were lumber and building materials, although appliances, garden supplies, and home entertainment systems are expected to grow in importance.

3. For each of these products, which industry associations would you contact for secondary data? (a) Foreign convenience dinners, (b) numerically controlled machine tools, (c) irrigation pipe, (d) imported wine, (e) compact disc players, and (f) children's shoes.

4. Obtain data on beer consumption in your state or province for the latest available year. Calculate the per-capita consumption for this area and compare it to that for the country as a whole. What accounts for the difference?

5. Educational Edge, a small company with limited resources, is interested in segmenting potential markets for its erasable transparencies.

    a. Which type of data would be best suited to obtain the required information?

    b. What are the possible sources of information to aid in the segmentation decision?

    c. What are the benefits and limitations of using secondary data for this purpose?

6. Howard Enterprises, a small family-owned manufacturer of unique lamps has begun to receive unsolicited inquiries about its product from foreign countries. The company has been operating exclusively in the domestic environment, but these inquiries have become numerous enough to suggest that a market for these specialty lamps may exist abroad. J. P. Howard, the company head, decided to contact Peter Franks, an old college friend of his, who is now the head of marketing research for a multinational company, to ask for his advice on how to proceed in evaluating foreign country markets. Mr. Howard recommends that Howard Enterprises should select countries that merit in-depth investigation and proceed to make an initial estimate of the demand potential in these countries.

    a. Considering the limited resources that are available to Mr. Howard's company, explain how secondary data can be used to help Mr. Howard follow his friend's recommendation.

    b. What are the possible limitations of secondary data of which Mr. Howard (in the above question) must be aware when conducting the marketing research?

End Notes

1. Ellen R. Kidd, "Establishing Quality Focus in a Multi-Cultural Organization," presented at the Third Congress on Competitive Strategies.

2. Paula A. Francese and Leo M. Renaghan, "Finding the Customer," *American Demographics,* January 1991, 48–51.

3. More extensive discussion of data sources and how to locate them can be found in Lorna Daniels, *Business Information Sources* (Berkeley, California: University of California Press), 1985; Lorna Daniels, Notes on Sources of External Marketing Data in B. Shapiro, R. Dolan and J. Quelch; Marketing Management Vol. ii, Appendix, Homewood, IL: Richard D. Irwin, Inc., 1985; Barbara E. Brown, *Canadian Business and Economics: A Guide to Sources of Information,* Ottawa: Canadian Library Assn., 1984; and Leonard M. Fuld, *Competitor Intelligence,* New York: Wiley, 1985.

4. A comprehensive listing of these associations can be found in the *Encyclopedia of Associations,* National Gale Research Co., 1984: and in Leonard M. Fuld, *Competitor Intelligence* (New York: Wiley), 1985.

5. For more information see, Jennifer. Langlois, *CD-ROM 1992: An Annotated Bibliography of Resources* (Westport, Connecticut: Meckler), 1992.

6. For information on how to use online databases in an effective manner see Barbara Quint, "Inside a Searcher's Mind: The Seven Stages of an Online Search," Parts 1 and 2, *Online,* May and July 1991.

7. Carmen Miller, "Virtual Reality and Online Databases: Will 'Look' and 'Feel' Literally Mean 'Look' and 'Feel'?" *Online,* 12, November 1992.

8. An interesting compilation of reasons why a database search might not meet with success is provided in Jeff Pemberton, "Faults and Failures—25 Ways That Online Searching Can Let You Down," *Online,* September, 1983.

9. These numbers are obtained from the Office of Management and Budget, 1987 Standard Industrial Classification Manual, Washington, D.C.: U.S. Government Printing Office, 1987.

10. For a more detailed discussion see Susan P. Douglas and C. Samuel Craig, *International Marketing Research*, (Englewood Cliffs, New Jersey: Prentice Hall), 1983.

11. V. Kumar, A. Stam, and E. A. Joachimsthaler, "An Interactive Multicriteria Approach to Identifying Potential Foreign Markets," *Journal of International Marketing*, Vol 2, No. 1, pp. 29–52, 1994.

CASE 5-1
Barkley Foods

Joyce Stevenson, the manager of marketing research for Barkley Foods, had just left an emergency meeting with the firm's president. An opportunity to buy an established line of gourmet (high quality/high priced) frozen dinners had arisen. Because there were other interested buyers, a decision had to be made within three or four weeks. This decision depended on judgments about the future prospects of the gourmet frozen dinner market and whether Barkley could achieve a competitive advantage. The marketing research group was asked to provide as much useful information as possible within a 10-day period. Although uncomfortable with the time pressure involved, Joyce was pleased that marketing had finally been asked to participate in the analysis of acquisition prospects. She had pressed for such participation and now she had to deliver.

Because of prior work on frozen fruit juices, Joyce had some knowledge of the gourmet frozen market. It was pioneered by Stouffer who introduced the "Lean Cuisine" line of entrees in 1981. Since then, other firms have entered the industry with complete gourmet dinners (including Swanson's Le Menu and Armour's Dinner Classics). The distinction between entrees, dinners, and the three main types of food offered—conventional, ethnic (i.e., Benihana Restaurant Classics), or low-calorie (i.e., Weight Watchers or Light & Elegant)—define relevant submarkets. Joyce hypothesized that the gourmet frozen food buyer differs from the buyer of conventional "TV dinners" in several respects. The gourmet frozen food buyers are generally young, upper socioeconomic group people who probably have microwaves, are more health conscious, and are likely to be working women and others who want the sophisticated cuisine but lack the time to prepare it.

Barkley Foods was a diversified food company with sales of 2.3 billion dollars. Over 80 percent of its sales came from branded packaged food products sold nationally through grocery stores. Its largest product areas were canned tomato products, frozen orange juice, cake mixes, and yogurt. Barkley was known to have strengths in operations (product preparation), distribution (obtaining distribution and managing the shelves), and advertising. Their brands typically held a solid second place position in the supermarket. There was no effort at umbrella brand identification, so each product area was carried by its own brand.

Joyce Stevenson had previously been in strategic planning, and reviewed the type of information and analysis that would be required to support a strategic decision like this one. She wrote down the following four sets of questions to guide the thinking of the research group:

1. Market Analysis
▶ What is the size, current growth rate, and projected growth rate, of the industry and its relevant subsets (such as ethnic dinners) for the next five and ten years?
▶ What are the important industry trends?
▶ What are the emerging production technologies?
▶ What are the distribution trends?
▶ What are current and future success factors (a competitive skill or asset needed to compete successfully)?

2. Environmental Analysis
▶ What demographic, cultural, economic, or governmental trends or events could create strategic threats or opportunities?
▶ What major environmental scenarios (plausible stories about the future) can be conceived?

3. Customer Analysis
▶ What are the major segments?
▶ What are their motivations and unmet needs?

4. Competitor Analysis
- ▶ Who are the existing and potential competitors?
- ▶ What are their current or forecasted levels of sales, market shares, and profits?
- ▶ What are their strengths and weaknesses?
- ▶ What strategies are they following, and how are they differentiating themselves in the market?

Questions for Discussion

1. What secondary data sources would be useful? What types of questions might be answered by each?

2. Identify one piece of information from the library that would be helpful and relevant. How did you locate it?

3. What other mechanisms would you use to gather information?

6

STANDARDIZED SOURCES OF MARKETING DATA

Learning Objectives

▶ Introduce the various sources of standardized sources of marketing data available.

▶ Provide a description of each of the well-known sources of standardized marketing data.

▶ Discuss the sources and applications of scanner data.

▶ Develop a framework for the various applications of standardized data sources.

The more specific and topical the need for information, the smaller the likelihood that relevant secondary data will be found. The researcher then has the choice of designing a special study or taking advantage of standardized data collection and analysis procedures. The latter alternative generally exists whenever several information users have common information needs and when the cost of satisfying an individual user's need is prohibitive. These conditions are most often encountered with consumer goods sold to large, diffuse markets and repurchased at frequent intervals. A further condition—especially important for data sources such as store audits and continuous consumer panels—is that the information needs are recurrent and can be anticipated. Thus, the data supplier can enter into long-term relationships with clients and be sure of covering the heavy fixed costs. The clients get continuity of data series, which is essential for monitoring and evaluation purposes.

This chapter describes and evaluates the major syndicated sources of marketing data, including store audits, warehouse withdrawal services, consumer purchase panels, and scanner-based systems. Each source has a distinctive profile of strengths and weaknesses that reflects differences in orientation, types of measures, and their location in the distribution channel. To get a full picture of the market situation of a product category or brand, it is usually necessary to use several sources in combination. Unfortunately, when this is done the result is more often confusion rather than clarity of insight, because of information overload. This is such a prevalent problem that the last section of this chapter will be devoted to recently developed decision support systems that help reduce the confusion.

The usage of standardized data sources has been revolutionized by so-called **single-source data** from scanner systems. This means that all data on product purchases and causal factors, such as media exposure, promotion influence, and consumer characteristics, come from the same households. These data are being made possible through advances in information technology whose full impact is only slowly being understood. At the moment it does not appear that single-source data will fully displace other standardized sources, but it will be used in conjunction with them to generate important new insights.

To understand the basic motivation for using standardized sources, consider the problems of a manufacturer of cold remedies who has to rely on factory shipment data for sales information. Management is especially interested in the reaction to a new convenience package that was introduced at the beginning of the cold season in December. By the end of January, the following information had been received from the accounting department:

Week Ending	Factory Shipments
December 28	12,700 Cases
January 4	19,800 Cases
January 11	18,200 Cases
January 18	14,100 Cases
January 25	11,050 Cases

All the usual problems of interpreting time series data are compounded in this example by the ambiguities in the data. The peak in factory shipments during the week ending January 4 represents a substantial amount of "pipeline filling," and an unknown amount of product sold for pipeline filling still remains on the shelves. Also unknown is competitive performance during this period: Did the new package gain sales at the expense of competition, or was there a loss of market share? Shipment data provide no diagnostic information, so these questions remain: How many retail stores used the special displays of the new product? Were competitors making similar or more effective offers? Was there a carry-over of last year's stock in the old package? Without answers to these questions, the manager is in no position to either correct problems or continue the strong points of the campaign.

RETAIL STORE AUDITS

Every two months a team of auditors from a research firm visits a sample of stores to count the inventory on hand and record deliveries to the store since the last visit. Sales during the two-month period, for any desired classification of the product category (including brands, sizes, package types, flavors, etc.), are arrived at by computing

Beginning Inventory + Deliveries Ending Inventory = Sales for the Period

These **retail store audit** results then are projected—to arrive at nationwide and regional estimates of total sales, inventories, and so forth—and reported to the client between six and eight weeks after the end of the period. During each store visit, the auditor also may collect such observable information as shelf prices, display space, the presence of special displays, and in-store promotion activities.

Nielsen Retail Index

The A. C. Nielsen Co. is the biggest research company in the world, primarily because of its auditing services. There are four major reporting groups: (1) grocery products, (2) drugs, (3) mass merchandisers, and (4) alcoholic beverages. Within the grocery products group, the auditors cover a 1300-store sample, which is weighted toward high-volume stores. One of every 39 of the large chain stores is taken in the sample, while only one of every 360 small independent stores is taken. These stores are paid for their cooperation.

The data provided by Nielsen, or other auditing companies such as Audits and Surveys, are incredibly rich. Table 6-1 summarizes the information that is provided routinely in the bimonthly report. For most companies this becomes the basis of their marketing information system. Beyond basic analyses of market position and competitive activity, the data can be used to analyze the impact of marketing activities. Since products purchased regularly are reported

TABLE 6-1
Contents of a Nielsen Store Audit Report

Each of the following variables can be subdivided as follows:
   a. Sales districts.
   b. Size of county (A, B, C, or D).
   c. Type of store (e.g., chain versus large-medium-small independents).
   d. Thirty-two largest metropolitan markets.

1. **Sales** (volume, trend, and share) on the basis of retail dollars and units, pounds or equivalent cases for total market, and major brands by sizes, flavors, types, etc., as appropriate to the category.

2. **Distribution**
   a. Percentage of all stores, and all commodity sales, carrying each brand, and size.
   b. Out-of-stock conditions.
   c. Retail inventories.
   d. Stock cover (the length of time the stocks will last, assuming current rates of sales).
   e. Source of delivery (wholesaler, rack jobbers, manufacturer, chain warehouse, or inter-store transfers).

3. **Selling prices** and volume sold at each price or deal.

4. **Retailer support** in terms of shelf facings, special displays, in-store advertising, and newspaper advertising.

5. **Media advertising** for total market and major brands.

6. **Special analyses** (illustrative).
   a. Analyses of combinations of brands stocked to determine the extent to which individual brands compete together.
   b. Cumulative distribution of new products.

separately from those items sold with a promotional offer, it is possible to judge the effect of a promotion by comparing several periods of data.

Audits and Surveys: National Total Market Audit

This is a bimonthly audit that focuses on products, regardless of the type of retail outlet carrying the product. This is especially useful for categories such as personal-care products, batteries, and candy and confectionery, which are sold through many types of outlets other than grocery stores or drugstores. The audit samples 4000 outlets to obtain brand-by-brand retail (consumer) sales, dealer purchases, retail inventory, distribution, and out-of-stocks. Clients purchase only the outlet types and sample size to suit a particular need. Because this audit is conducted regularly, it provides continuous measures of how well a brand is doing in terms of share, distribution coverage, inventory in stock, and so forth.

For infrequently purchased products, such as housewares, writing instruments, and sunglasses, where bimonthly audit data are less important than a very large sample of outlets, Audits and Surveys conducts an annual "Retail Census of Product Distribution." This census entails personal store visits to 40,000 retail outlets of all types from catalog showrooms to variety stores. The detail collected from each type of store on a product, such as bakeware and cookware, permits manufacturers to analyze the strengths and weaknesses of their distribution. With the census results, for example, a manufacturer of hair sprays can ask, "Is the wholesaler getting my brand into the smaller stores in more remote areas, or merely skimming the cream off the market?"

CONSUMER PURCHASE PANELS

From store audits and warehouse withdrawal services, we can learn how much product is moving through the distribution channel. As this information is one step removed from the actual purchase transaction, we still don't know who bought, how frequently they bought, or whether the seeming stability of market shares reflects stable purchasing patterns or a great deal of switching back and forth between brands and stores in response to short-term promotional efforts. To answer these questions, we need detailed records of purchasing activity by the same people over an extended period of time. Here are two methods for collecting this data:

1. The **home audit** approach in which the panel member agrees to permit an auditor to check the household stocks of certain product categories at regular intervals. A secondary condition is that the panel member save all used cartons, wrappers, and so on, so that the auditor can record it.
2. In the **mail diary** method the panel member records the details of each purchase in certain categories and returns the completed diary by mail at regular intervals (biweekly or monthly). The detail that can be collected is

illustrated for two of the 88 clothing, food, and personal care products recorded by members of the American Shoppers Panel (see Figure 6-1).

Both types of panels are used extensively in Europe, whereas in the United States and Canada the mail diary method is dominant. When comparisons have been possible, the two methods have produced equally accurate market share and trend data.[1]

MRCA (Market Research Corporation of America) has operated a mail diary panel since 1941. The MRCA data on consumer purchases of items sold in food and drugstores are obtained from a panel of approximately 7500 families throughout the United States. For each purchase, the following information is recorded by the participating families:

Date and day of week
Brand name
Number of items purchased
Type of container (glass, tin, and so on)
Exact weight or quantity
Where purchased (including store name)
Normal transaction or deal
Price paid

The 7500 families used in the sample are selected on a probability basis to be representative of the total population on major characteristics such as geographic region, city size, income, presence of children, education, size of family, and age of homemaker. When a family is selected for the panel, a personal call is used to enlist its cooperation and train it in the reporting procedures. Each family receives compensation in the form of points, which are exchangeable for merchandise.

Each month MRCA delivers a report for the preceding month, showing total consumer purchases of each brand in the category, plus sales overall, which can be converted into volume and dollar market shares. Each quarter, an analysis of purchases by regions and by type of retail outlet is provided.

Other organizations like the NPD, Inc., and the National Family Opinion (NFO) also maintain diary panels. In fact, the National Purchase Diary Panel maintains the largest diary panel in the United States. More than 14,500 households record their monthly purchases in about 50 product categories. The National Family Opinion also maintains special-purpose diary panels. For example, NFO has a beverages panel consisting of 12,000 households, which provide quarterly information on beverage consumption.

Advantages of Panels

The data from a panel can be analyzed as a series of snapshots—providing information on *aggregate* sales activity, brand shares, and shifts in buyer characteristics and types of retail outlets from one month to the next. But, just as a motion picture is more revealing than a snapshot, it is the ability to measure

NOTE: Extra space page 1. Free Gifts and Samples, inside front cover.

Form 1: RAZOR BLADES

Write in BRAND NAME as shown on label

RAZOR BLADES

Including free blades with purchase of razor or travel and shaving kits.

Write in all of the words which together describe the complete brand name.

Columns:
- Date of month purchase was made
- HOW MANY of each kind did you buy? — Write in number of packages or other containers
- HOW MUCH DID YOU PAY? — TOTAL CASH PAID, Don't include taxes ($ / ¢)
- Was this a special price or merchandise offer? — IF NO, Check here ✓
- If YES, describe kind, such as: Price-Off marked on package • Store Coupon from newspaper • Other Coupon from newspaper • Coupon from magazine or received in mail • Gift on or in package • Special refund offer such as cash refund or merchandise offer • Store sales • Other deals — Total ¢ off if any
- WHERE DID YOU PURCHASE? — NAME OF STORE (or company if purchased from door-to-door or home delivery salesperson)
- KIND OF STORE, Check (✓) one or write in: GROCERY OR FOOD, DRUGS, DISCOUNT, Other—Describe
- CHECK (✓) ONE: BLADES ONLY, RAZOR INCLUDING BLADES, KIT INCLUDING BLADES
- CHECK (✓) ONE Type of Blade: SINGLE EDGE, DOUBLE EDGE, INJECTOR, CONTINUOUS EDGE (BRAND), BONDED, TWIN (2) BLADED CARTRIDGE, OTHER
- Write in: Number of blades or cartridges per package or number of shaving edges per continuous band
- CHECK (✓) ONE Kind of Blade: BLUE, SUPER BLUE, STAINLESS STEEL, CHROMIUM, PLATINUM, TUNGSTEN, THINS, OTHER
- WRITE IN AGE, SEX OF PURCHASER: Age, Sex
- WRITE IN AS MANY AS APPLY TO THE ITEM, AGE AND SEX OF USERS: User No. 1 (Age, Sex), User No. 2 (Age, Sex), User No. 3 (Age, Sex), User No. 4 (Age, Sex), User No. 5 (Age, Sex), User No. 6 (Age, Sex)

NOTE: Extra space page 1. Free Gifts and Samples, inside front cover.

Form 2: CARBONATED SOFT DRINKS

Write in BRAND NAME as shown on label

CARBONATED SOFT DRINKS

Write in all of the words which together describe the complete brand name.

CARBONATED SOFT DRINKS DIARY TIPS: First of all, enter in the diary only those purchases which are brought home from the store. This includes items which may later be taken on a picnic or to the beach as well as items which are consumed at home. • Do not enter items which are consumed at the place of purchase. Usually, these include vending machine purchases, restaurants, refreshment stands, ball games, etc. • When you make a purchase entry, fill in the answers under every column all the way across the page. • Be sure to enter purchases brought home by all family members.

Columns:
- Date of month purchase was made
- HOW MANY of each kind did you buy? — Write in number of packages or other containers
- HOW MUCH DID YOU PAY? — TOTAL CASH PAID, Don't include taxes ($ / ¢)
- Was this a special price or offer? — IF NO, Check here ✓
- If YES, describe kind, such as: store sale, cents off coupon, gift on or in package, etc. How much savings in total? — DESCRIBE SPECIAL PRICE OR OFFER, Total ¢ off
- WHERE DID YOU PURCHASE? — NAME OF STORE (or company if purchased from door-to-door or home delivery salesperson)
- KIND OF STORE Check (✓) or write in: GROCERY OR FOOD, Other—Describe
- WEIGHT (SIZE) SHOWN ON LABEL: Write in the amount of weight per item of container and tell us the kind of weight, such as pounds, and or ounces, pints, quarts, etc.
- Check (✓) one TYPE OF PACK: SINGLES, 2 PACK, 4 PACK, 6 PACK, 8 PACK, CASE, OTHER
- Check (✓) one TYPE OF CONTAINER: Glass bottle (RETURN, THROW AWAY), PLASTIC BOTTLE, CAN
- WRITE IN FLAVOR: Such as: Orange, Chocolate, Cola, Lemon, Cherry, etc. COPY FROM LABEL
- Check (✓) one: REGULAR, LOW CALORIE

FIGURE 6-1

Illustrations of recording forms used in mail diary panels

changes in the behavior of *individuals* that is the real advantage of a panel. Knowledge of the sequence of purchases makes it possible to analyze

▶ Heavy buyers and their associated characteristics.

▶ Brand switching rates and the extent of loyal buying. (Evidence of stable purchase activity in the aggregate usually masks a great deal of individual movement.)

▶ Cumulative market penetration and repeat purchase rates for new products. (The success of new products depends jointly on the proportion who have tried them once and then purchased them a second, third, or fourth time.)

A **continuous purchase panel** is an excellent vehicle for conducting quasi-experiments. A change in price, advertising copy, or package can be implemented in one region, and the results compared with that of other regions where no change was made. Also, because of the lengthy relationship with members of continuous panels, there is much more opportunity to collect classification and attitudinal information to help understand the observed changes in behavior.

In comparison with interview methods, although not with audits, the continuous purchase panel has the advantage of accuracy. Several studies have found that interview respondents will exaggerate their rate of purchasing (an effect that is most pronounced for infrequently purchased products) and dramatically oversimplify brand-switching behavior. Apparently, survey respondents tend to equate their most recent brand buying behavior with their "normal" behavior—whether or not this is accurate.

Limitations of Consumer Panels

The limitations all relate to the vulnerability of panels to various biases. The first encountered is **selection bias,** because of the high rates of refusal and the resulting lack of representativeness. It is estimated that panel recruitment rates may vary from as low as 10 to 15 percent when the initial contact is made by mail in the United States, to 50 percent or more for personal contacts made on behalf of panels in Great Britain.

A related problem is **mortality effect,** which may mean a dropout rate in excess of 20 percent a year. Some of this is unavoidable, because it is attributable to moves and illness. To reduce both the refusal and mortality rates, all panels offer some incentive for continuing participation; these include direct money payments and stamp schemes in exchange for gifts.

There is little doubt that those who refuse or drop out differ from those who participate and remain. In particular, those not interested in the topic are the most likely to drop out. These losses are replaced by new members with similar characteristics. This amounts to a matching procedure, and of course it is not possible to match on all important characteristics. In a subsequent chapter we will examine the problem of refusals, which afflicts all forms of survey work. As a consequence, however, all panels underrepresent the very rich, the very poor, and the transitory.

Panels also are subject to a variety of **testing effects.** There is a definite tendency for new panel members to report unusual levels of purchasing because of the novelty of the reporting responsibility. This effect is so pronounced that the first month's results usually are discarded. Surprisingly, there is little evidence to suggest that there is any long-run conditioning behavior that would lead to great brand loyalty or price consciousness that would produce systematically biased data.

Finally, it should be kept in mind that usually one person does the recording of purchases. Whenever a product, such as cigarettes or toothpaste, is purchased by several members of the household, there is a good chance that some purchases will be missed. These products are also troublesome to analyze, for what appears to be brand switching simply may be the purchasing of different brands for (or by) different members of the household.

SCANNER SERVICES AND SINGLE-SOURCE SYSTEMS

It is no understatement to say that standardized sources of marketing data for consumer goods are being revolutionized by the **universal product code (UPC)** scanner. By the end of 1992, 80 percent of the commodity value of groceries, 85 percent of the commodity value of mass merchandises, and 40 percent of the commodity value for drugs came through scanner-equipped retail stores.[2]

Within markets equipped with scanner checkouts, purchases are recorded by passing them over a laser scanner, which automatically reads the bar-coded description (the universal product code) printed on each package. This in turn activates the cash register, which relates the product code to its current price—held in computer memory—and calculates the amount due. All the pertinent data on the purchase then are stored in the computer and can be accessed instantly for analysis. In addition to price, the memory stores information on coupon use, so marketers can quickly measure consumer response to using coupons across product categories. Information about shelf space, end-of-aisle displays, use of cooperative advertising, and the like can be retained on these scanners and then measured with respect to impact on sales, item movement, and net contribution.

As mentioned earlier, the impact of scanners is being felt in the conduct of retail audits, where in-person audits will soon be obsolete, and in the growth of single-source services that track the behavior of individual households, from the TV set to the checkout counter. In 1986, manufacturers spent about $10 million for these services; by 1987, it had grown to $50 million; and in 1991 they spent over $200 million. By the end of 1992, this figure had grown to $300 million.

Scanner-Based Audit Services

The most immediate benefits of **scanner data** are a high degree of accuracy, time savings, and the ability to study very short time periods of sales activity. To appreciate these benefits, consider the introduction of a new food product into a test market monitored by a scanner-based audit service.

According to the standard bimonthly reports from the store audit service, there was steady progress in building the market share. During the second bimonthly period (see graph below), share more than doubled, as retailer advertising and coupon promotions were stepped up.

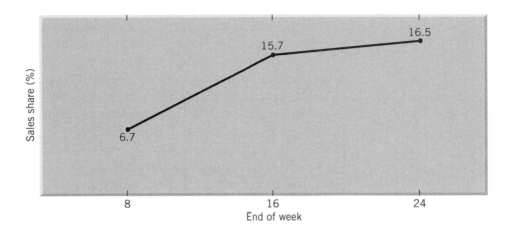

The results from the third period normally would not be available for six to eight weeks. With scanning data, however, weekly reports on this product were available within two to three weeks of the period's end. These weekly reports were also far more revealing, as we see from the data shown in Figure 6-2 for the same time period following the launch. The first 11 weeks followed a fairly typical new-brand cycle, with share by week 10 only half of the initial peak. Back-to-back price and coupon promotion in weeks 12 and 13 boosted shares to twice the introductory level. Shares then declined, until a further promotion in week 18. Fortunately, postpromotion shares were always higher than prepromotion shares through week 22. The sharp decline in week 23 was traced to a shortage of the most popular size of package, which was rectified during the next week.

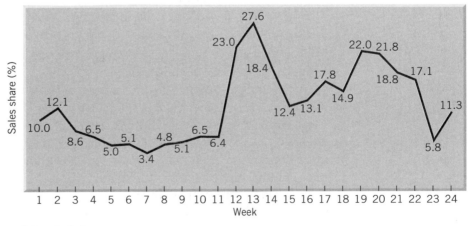

FIGURE 6-2
Weekly results from scanner service

There are three scanner-based audit services providing nationally, or locally, representative results within two weeks of the end of the reporting period. Each service provides full detail on each universal product code in a product category: product description, size, price, unit movement and unit share, and dollar sales and share as well as availability in stores, shelf-space allocation, and usage of coupons. This data can be made available in virtually any combination of stores, to look at sales by chain, geographic area, or even individual store.

Nielsen's SCANTRACK now appears to be the largest service, with access to 3000 scanner-equipped stores. Both SCANTRACK and NFI (Nielsen Food Index) reports can be accessed directly by a manager with a personal computer and a modem, who will be able to tap directly into the Nielsen on-line system. For categories such as candy, snacks, and tobacco, where a large proportion of sales are made in stores without scanners, the supermarket scanner data can be combined with in-person audit data. However, by the end of early 1990s, it is expected that there will be enough drugstores, convenience stores, and mass merchandisers who will install scanners to generate and use scanner data for various business applications. Then the revolution in standardized data sources will truly be in place.

Applying Scanner Data. Scanner data are used mainly to study the behavior of the consumer when different elements of the marketing mix are varied. They are also used to study and forecast the sales of a new product. For example, in 1991 Frito Lay, Pepsico's $4.2-billion-a-year snack-food division, tested its new multigrain snack called *Sun Chips* for 10 months in the Minneapolis area. The company experimented with 50 ridges and a salty, nutty flavor, and introduced the product on supermarket shelves. Using scanner data, the company discovered how many shoppers actually took home their first bag of Sun Chips in a given week and who went back a second and third time. This "depth of repeat" gives the company a much clearer sense of the product's potential.[3]

Even retailers are using scanner data. They not only purchase scanner data but also conduct their own tests.[4] They conduct a number of experiments to analyze historical demand at various pricing levels and determine the prices at which they can maximize their total contribution. One retail grocer offered Minute Rice at five different prices over a period of 16 weeks, and the sales results are shown in the next page[5]:

With costs of $.69 per box, the store could see that profit was maximized at a price of $1.19. Lower prices did not generate sufficient incremental volume to overcome the drop in per-unit profit. This kind of analysis can now be done routinely for thousands of retail store items. This helps retailers control their operations more closely, and some feel it will significantly enhance their power over manufacturers.

Safeway is an example of a retailer who does a lot of scanner-based research. Safeway used scanner data to test alternative placement of products within a store. Results showed, for example, that foil-packaged sauce mixes should not be displayed together, but should be spread around the store according to their

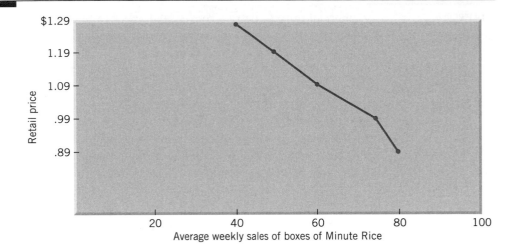

contents (spaghetti sauce mix near bottled spaghetti sauce, gravy mix near canned gravy, etc.). In 1990, Safeway created Safeway Scanner Marketing Research Services (SSMRS). Its first product was StoreLab. Clients can test the effectiveness of off-shelf displays, shelf extenders, in-store signs, new package designs or sizes, and consumer bonus packages.[6]

Single-Source Systems

These systems are basically straightforward. They usually are set up in reasonably self-contained communities, with their own newspaper and cable TV, and are roughly representative of the country's demographics.[7]

After recruiting a test panel of community households, with small payments or coupons as inducements, the researcher monitors each home's TV sets and quizzes household members periodically on what newspapers and magazines they have read. This provides detailed records of exposure to programming and specific commercials.

Each panel member presents an identification card at a scanner-equipped grocery store each time a purchase is made. This card alerts the checkout terminal to send an item-by-item record of those purchases to a computer file. Then researchers can relate the details of a household's purchase of each product to previously collected classification information about the household and any promotional stimuli to which they were exposed.

These panel households can also be individually targeted for newspaper advertising, so a marketer could experiment with different combinations of advertising copy and/or exposure, discount coupons, and in-store price discounts and promotions. The effects of these different programs can be unobtrusively monitored in the supermarket, and each panel member's purchase is compared with what they had purchased before the test. To control for competitive activity, the service also tracks the amount of feature, display, and couponing activity in each supermarket.

Television advertising exposure also can be controlled through the cable system. For example, it is possible to transmit a Duncan Hines cake mix commercial only to Betty Crocker customers to find out if they can be induced to switch. The process of collecting data and providing it to the manufacturers and retailers is shown in Figure 6-3.

A typical application of single-source systems is an experiment by the Campbell Soup Company. Using an index of 100 for the average household's V-8 consumption, Campbell found that demographically similar TV audiences were consuming vastly different quantities of V-8. In early 1987, for example, "General Hospital" audiences had a below-average 80 index, while "Guiding Light" audiences had an above-average 120 index. The results were surprising, because "General Hospital" had a slightly higher representation of 25- to 54-year-old women, who were known from other research to be heavier buyers of V-8. With this sort of information at hand, it will become possible to rearrange media schedules to raise the average index.[8]

The possibilities for research are limited only by the ingenuity of the researchers.[9] Suppose the research purpose is to decide whether a product sample should be an alternative or an accompaniment to TV commercials for

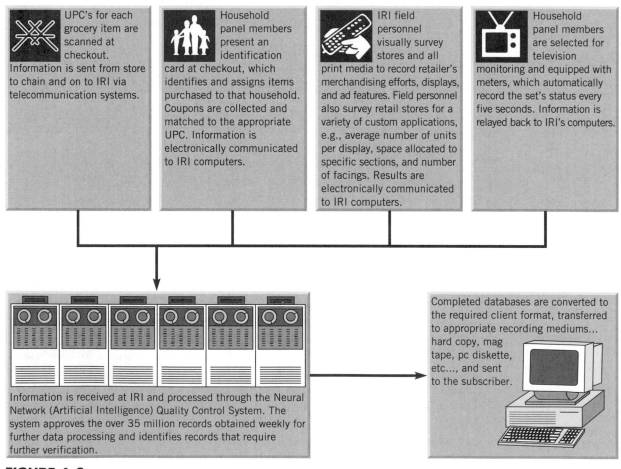

FIGURE 6-3

The process of scanner data collection by IRI
Source: Information Resources, Inc.

a child-oriented cereal. The household test panel could be divided into four matched groups and given different combinations of samples and advertising. Sales results could then be monitored, but it would also be possible to determine whether the group that was also exposed to advertising would be more brand loyal in subsequent weeks.

The advantages of single-source data for this kind of market response study—compared with conventional market tests—are (1) availability of extensive pretest records, (2) immediate availability of test results, and (3) ability to compare the purchases of households receiving a specific ad during the test with their own purchases prior to the test as well as with purchases of those who had not been exposed to the new product ad.

The disadvantage is that single-source systems can track purchases only at grocery stores and drugstores that are equipped with scanners. Furthermore, the test services don't know whether viewers actually are watching a television set when it is on, or whether they leave the room during the commercial break. Test participants who are paid volunteers might also unconsciously bias the results, because they know they are sending a message to advertisers. An unresolved question is whether the tests conducted in small, self-contained markets can predict nationwide results. Finally, there are significant differences in results among competing single-source services that raise questions about the quality of the findings.

Comparing Single-Source Services. One of the most advanced services is BehaviorScan, by Information Resources, Inc., (IRI).[10] It has 3000 households wired in each of the different minimarkets across the United States, from Pittsfield, Massachusetts, to Visalia, California. It pioneered the service and has had the most experience in conducting tests. IRI's system used the identification card described earlier, so that details of their transactions can be recorded, by household, on presentation of the card to cashiers at participating stores. IRI also has another product known as InfoScan. InfoScan is a scanner-based, national and local market tracking service for the consumer packaged goods industry. BehaviorScan provides data about different markets, whereas InfoScan provides data on different products. Retail sales, detailed consumer purchasing information, and promotional activity are monitored and evaluated for all UPC products. InfoScan collects weekly purchase data from 2700 supermarkets, 500 drugstores such as Walgreens and Eckerd, and also 250 mass merchandisers like Wal-Mart, Kmart, and Target.

For several years A. C. Nielsen had been testing a single-source service, and had 15,000 homes by 1989. In 1992, Nielsen had increased its panel size to 40,000 households. Nielsen, along with another new entrant, Scan America (a joint venture of Control Data and Selling Areas Marketing, Inc., a subsidiary of Time Inc.) offered a very different technology. Unlike BehaviorScan participants, Nielsen families recorded their purchases at home by passing a penlike wand over goods bearing bar codes, keying in other information about coupons at the same time. The information was transmitted daily through a device attached to participants' television sets. Because Nielsen's system is not dependent on retailers who cooperate, it allows tracking of purchases from a wider range of stores, but it has been criticized for requiring that participants be actively involved in entering the data. Another important difference in the service is that Nielsen can send test commercials over the air so that members of the sample don't have to be cable subscribers.[11]

Expert Systems Based on Single-Source Services. The rapid increase in the use of scanner technology has brought forth a peculiar problem to the marketing analyst. Although about a decade ago researchers were struggling to obtain data to conduct research, they now are faced with exactly the opposite problem. Users of scanner data have been overwhelmed with massive amounts of data. Therefore, suppliers of scanner data have created expert systems to give the data more utility for the managers. These expert systems are designed to cut the mass of scanner data down into actionable pieces of information. There are many expert systems that give solutions to specific problems. Both IRI and A.C. Nielsen have developed a number of these expert systems to make the decision process easier. A partial list is provided below.

Information Resources, Inc.[12]

▶ **Apollo Space Management Software** provides suggestions for optimizing shelf allocations for each item in the section of a retail store. It analyzes scanner data from the InfoScan database to review the amount of shelf space, price, and profit components of product category shelf sets, such as dishwashing soaps or cereals. Apollo also can produce photo-quality schematics using its library of 120,000 product images and dimensions. Thus, the retailer gets a visual picture of what the shelf reallocation will look like.

▶ **CoverStory** provides a cover memo, like the one a marketing researcher would write, to describe the key events reflected in a database. The system locates the important "news" and writes a memo for managers, complete with charts, tables, and graphs.

▶ **Sales Partner** is designed to help manufacturers sell to retailers, by using the retailers' own scanner data. It sorts through the data to provide the most convincing arguments a sales representative can direct to the retailer.

A. C. Nielsen[13]

▶ **Promotion Simulator** is an easy-to-use software application that automatically simulates future promotion strategies. It uses historical Nielsen data to calculate the effect of the promotional plans on manufacturer and retailer profitability, given the price points and retail conditions in the plan.

▶ **Spotlight** is an expert system that runs through the database, calculating volume and share changes, and searching for the key merchandising and competitive factors that influence those factors. Then it summarizes the findings in a presentation-quality report.

▶ **Sales Advisor** automatically highlights the need-to-know information and enables the sales force to add their own personal insights to presentation-quality output. Sales Advisor produces finished summaries and presentations of sales and marketing data.

MEDIA-RELATED STANDARDIZED SOURCES

Another area in which there is a great deal of commerical information available for marketers relates to advertising and media. A number of services have evolved to measure consumer exposure to the various media and advertisements. A few of them are described below.

Nielsen Television Index (NTI)

The NTI is probably the best known of all the commercial services available in this category. As a system for estimating national television audiences, NTI produces a "rating" and corresponding share estimate. A **rating** is the percent of all households that have at least one television set tuned to a program for at least six out of every 15 minutes that the program is telecast. **Share** is the percent of households that have a television set that is tuned to a specific program at a specific time.

From 1987 onward, Nielsen has been using "people meters" instead of the traditional diary to obtain this information. The **people meter,** which is attached to the television set, continuously monitors and records television viewing in terms of when the set was turned on, what channels were viewed, how long the channels were tuned in, and who in the household was watching that channel.[14] The data are stored in the people meter and later are transmitted via telephone lines to a central processing facility.

The NTI panel consists of approximately 2,000 households, matched according to United States' national statistics. The viewing- and audience-characteristics data from these households are combined to produce a report entitled the NTI-NAD (Nielsen Television Index—National Audience Demographics). The NTI-NAD report gives ratings broken down by the following demographics:

Households
Women employed outside the house
Women 18+, 12–24, 18–34, 18–69, 25–54, 35–64, and 55+ age groups
Men 18+, 18–34, 18–69, 25–54, 35–65, and 55+ age groups
Teenagers
Children ages 2 and older, and ages 6 to 11

The Nielsen NTI-NAD data are used by media planners to analyze alternative network programs. Next, the cost efficiency of each program is calculated. Cost efficiency represents a television program's ability to deliver the largest target audience at the smallest cost. A cost per thousand (CPM) calculation is computed by taking

$$\frac{\text{Cost of a commercial}}{\text{Number of target audience delivered}} = \text{CPM}$$

Arbitron Diary Panel

A subsidiary of Control Data, Arbitron maintains both national and regional radio and TV panels. The panel members are chosen by randomly generated telephone numbers, to ensure that households with unlisted numbers are reached. Those household members who agree to participate when called are sent diaries in which they are asked to record their radio listeing behavior over a short duration. Most radio markets are rated only once or twice a year; however, some larger ones are rated four times a year. The TV diary panel is supplemented with a sample of households that have agreed to attach an electronic meter to their television sets. Arbitron produces custom reports for clients. Typically, these are based on an interactive computer-based system called Arbitron Information on Demand (AID).

Starch Scores

The previous two sources of marketing data dealt with radio and television ratings, whereas Starch scores deal with the print media. The Starch Readership Service measures the readership of advertisements in magazines and newspapers.[15] Some 75,000 advertisements in 1000 issues of consumer and farm magazines, business publications, and newspapers are assessed each year, using 100,000 personal interviews.

The Starch surveys employ the **recognition method** to assess a particular ad's effectiveness. Four degrees of reading are recorded:

1. *Nonreader:* A person who does not remember having previously seen the advertisement in the issue.
2. *Noted:* A person who remembered seeing the advertisement in the issue.
3. *Associated:* A person who not only "noted" the advertisement, but also saw or read some part of it that clearly indicated the brand or advertiser.
4. *Read Most:* A person who read 50 percent or more of the written material in the ad.

Because newspaper and magazine space cost data are also available, a "readers per dollar" variable can be calculated. The final summary report from Starch shows each ad's (one-half page or larger) overall readership percentages, readers per dollar, and rank when grouped by product category.

Multimedia Services

The Simmons Media/Marketing Services uses a national probability sample of some 19,000 respondents and serves as a comprehensive data source, allowing the cross-referencing of product usage and media exposure. Four different interviews are conducted with each respondent, so that magazine, television, newspaper, and radio can all be covered by the Simmons Service. Information is reported for total adults and also for males and females separately.

Media-mark Research also makes available information on exposure to various media and on household consumption of various products and services. Its annual survey of 20,000 adult respondents covers more than 250 magazines, newspapers, radio stations and television channels, and over 450 products and services.

APPLICATIONS OF STANDARDIZED SOURCES OF DATA

Standardized data sources are used widely in a number of marketing research problems. We have already discussed the various sources of standardized data. In this section we will look at the some of the applications of standardized data. Table 6-2 gives a comprehensive framework of the types of sources to be used for different applications.

Measuring Product Sales and Market Share

A critical need in today's increasingly competitive environment is for firms to have an accurate assessment of their performance. Marketing performance typically is measured by the company's sales and market share. Firms can track their own sales through analyses of their sales invoices. An alternative source that can be used is the on-line bibliographic data sources. The measurement of sales to the final customers historically has been done by the use of diary panels and retail store audits. Scanner data is now being widely used for this purpose.[16]

Measuring Advertisement Exposure and Effectiveness

With media costs rising exponentially, and the options for advertising increasing dramatically with the advent of cable television, measurement of advertising exposure and effectiveness and program ratings has become critical.

TABLE 6-2
Applications of Standardized Data Sources

Measuring Promotion Effectiveness	Measuring Ad Exposure and Effectiveness
1. Scanner Data 2. Diary Panels	1. Starch Scores 2. NTI 3. Arbitron 4. Multimedia Services

Measuring Product Sales and Market Share	Estimation and Evaluation of Models
1. Diary Panels 2. Retail Audits 3. Scanner Data 4. Internal Records 5. SIC	1. Scanner Data 2. Starch Scores 3. Diary Panels 4. Internal Records

Advertising exposure and effectiveness in the print media are tested by Starch scores[17] and in the audio-visual media by Nielsen Television Services and Arbitron. Ratings of the various network and cable programs can be found in the Nielsen Television Index, and those of the radio programs in the Arbitron panels. Multimedia services like the Simmons Media/Marketing Services and Media-mark Research conduct research on overall media exposure and effectiveness. Scanner data also have been used extensively for modeling ad exposure and measuring ad effectiveness.[18]

Measuring Promotion Effectiveness

Only after the advent of scanner data have marketers begun to fathom the power of promotion in increasing product sales and market share. This is evident from the fact that the number of coupons, samples, displays, and features at the retail outlets have increased tremendously over the past four years. Before scanner data was introduced in a big way, promotion effectiveness was measured by diary panels of the NPD group. Since store-level scanner data and scanner panels were introduced by IRI and Nielsen, measurement of promotion effectiveness has been revolutionized. The effect of promotions now can be directly observed through scanner data.[19]

Estimation and Evaluation of Models

Models are essentially explanations of complex phenomena, expressed by symbols. They can be mathematical, verbal, graphical, or a figure. Marketing researchers build models to explain the various marketing phenomena and to draw managerial implications from them. The models can either be at the aggregate level or at the individual level. Scanner data are used to evaluate the efficacy of the model and estimate the response of the market to changes in the marketing-mix elements.[20] Standard industrial classifications (SICs) and diary panels are used for this purpose.

Summary

Between the generally available secondary sources (which are economical and quickly found but perhaps not relevant), and primary data (which are designed to be directly relevant but consume considerable time and money), there are various standardized information services. These exist whenever there are economies of scale in collecting data for a number of users with similar information needs. The most widely used services are still retail store audits and consumer panels. With recent developments in information technology, and especially the widespread adoption of store checkout scanners, the usage of these services is quickly shifting to scanner audits. New capabilities for understanding consumer response by integrating measures of purchase behavior and communications exposure in single-source data are also changing the conduct of research very rapidly.

The remainder of this book will emphasize the collection and analysis of primary data, for it is here that the greatest problems and opportunities are found. Knowledge of the methods of primary data collection is also essential to informed usage of secondary sources.

Questions and Problems

1. Which of these two, a product audit (such as the Audits and Surveys National Market Audit) or a store audit (such as the Nielsen Retail index), would be more suitable for the following products: (1) peanut butter, (2) cameras, (3) engine oil additives, and (4) chewing gum? Why?

2. The manager of a supermarket in Hoboken, New Jersey, has two local newspapers competing for weekly ads. The salesperson for newpaper A claims that, although A's rates are significantly higher than Paper B's, Paper A has the best circulation in the market. Also, readership studies show that area residents really scrutinize the paper's pages. The salesperson for Newspaper B concedes that the publication doesn't have the widest circulation, but points to readership studies showing the ads are equally effective. "Why pay twice as much for an ad, when my paper can do as strong a job for less money?" This problem has been unresolved for some time. Recently, the store had nine scanner checkouts installed. The manager would like your advice on how to use the store's scanner sales data to compare the effectiveness of the two newspapers.

3. What combination of standardized services would you use to monitor the effects of your existing cereal brands when a new cereal brand is being introduced? Why? Would you use the different services to monitor trial and repeat purchases of the new cereal product in a test market?

4. The sales and market shares for the same brand in the same period are often different when they are measured by a scanner audit rather than a consumer panel. How would you account for the differences? What would you do about them?

5. Campbell Soup used BehaviorScan data to discover that viewers of two daytime serials had very good appetites. "Search for Tomorrow" viewers bought 27 percent more spaghetti sauce than average, but 22 percent less V8 vegetable juice. Viewers of "All My Children" bought 10 percent less spaghetti sauce than average, but purchased 46 percent more V8 than the norm for all viewers. How would you go about explaining the differences between these two programs that led to the comsumption differences? What action would you recommend to Campbell Soup management?

6. Wash O'Well, a leading detergent company in Canada is unable to explain the reason why its new zeolite-based detergent has not captured the anticipated market share since its launch in Minneapolis, Minnesota in 1992. The company has decided to focus on point-of-sale activities; for example, which brands have distribution in which stores, what shelf location each brand occupies, the kinds of displays in effect, and so forth. The marketing manager has been instructed to recommend a suitable source of standardized data.
   a. What are the various data source alternatives available to Wash O'Well?
   b. Discuss the advantages and limitations of each of them and recommend the data source most suitable for Wash O'Well's needs.

7. a. What are the two types of consumer panels used for gathering marketing research data?
    b. Which type of panel is most frequently used in the United States.
    c. What are the advantages and disadvantages of using a consumer panel?

End Notes

1. Seymour Sudman and Robert Ferber, *Consumer Panels* (Chicago: American Marketing Association), 1979.
2. Source: A. C. Nielsen.
3. Susan Caminiti, "What the Scanner Knows About You," *Fortune*, December, 3, 1990.
4. James Sinkula, "Status of Company Usage of Scanner Based Research," *Journal of the Academy of Marketing Science*, Spring 1986, 17.
5. This example was adapted from Leonard M. Lodish and David J. Reibstein, "New Gold Mines and Mine Fields in Marketing Research," *Harvard Business Review*, January–February 1986, 168–182.
6. "Safeway Launches New StoreLab Testing Service," *Marketing News*, January 8, 1990, 45.
7. The following articles give a good overview of the single-source systems: David Curry "Single Source Systems: Retail Management Present and Future," *Journal of Retailing*, Spring 1989, 1–20; Melvin Prince, "Some Uses and Abuses of Single Source Data for Promotional Decision Making," *Marketing Research*, December, 1989, 18–22; "Futuristic Weaponary," *Advertising Age*, June 11, 1990, 5–12.
8. Joanne Lipman, "Single Source Ad Research Heralds Detailed Look at Household Habits," *Wall Street Journal*, February 16, 1988, 35.
9. Examples of recent applications of scanner data include Peter S. Fader and Leigh McAllister, "An Elimination by Aspects Model of Consumer Response to Promotion Calibrated on UPC Scanner Data," *Journal of Marketing Research*, 27, August 1990, 322–332; Eric Waarts, Martin Carree, and Beren Wierenga, "Full Information Maximum Likelihood Estimation of Brand Positioning Maps Using Supermarket Scanning Data," *Journal of Marketing Research*, 28, November, 1991, 483–490.
10. The information on BehaviorScan is drawn from a pamphlet from Information Resources Incorporated.
11. A good article that compares the two single-source suppliers is Leon Winters, "Home Scan vs. Store Scan Panels: Single Source Options for the 1990s," *Marketing Research*, December 1989, 61–65. Also see, "Now Its Down to Two Equal Competitors,"
    Superbrands 1991: A Supplement to Adweeks's Marketing Week, 28 and "IRI, Nielsen Slug It Out in Scanning Wars," *Marketing News*, September 2, 1991, 1.
12. Source: Information Resources Incorporated.
13. Source: A.C. Nielsen.
14. Soong Roland, "The Statistical Reliability of People Meter Readings," *Journal of Advertising Research*, February–March 1988, 50–56.
15. *Starch Readership Report: Scope, Method and Use* (Mamaroneck, New York: Starch INRA Hooper), undated.
16. V. Kumar, and T. Heath, "A Comparative Study of Market Share Models Using Disaggregate Data," *International Journal of Forecasting*, July, 1990, 163–174.
    Francis J. Mulhern and Robert P. Leone, "Implicit Price Bundling of Retail Products: A Multiproduct Approach to Maximizing Store Profitability," *Journal of Marketing*, October, 1991, 63–76.
17. George M. Zinkhan and Betsy D. Gelb, "What Starch Scores Predict," *Journal of Advertising Research*, August—September, 1986, 45–50.
18. Gerald J. Tellis, "Advertising Exposure, Loyalty, and Brand Purchase: A Two-State Model of Choice," *Journal of Marketing Research*, May, 1988, 134–144.
19. Sunil Gupta, "Impact of Sales Promotions on When, What, and How Much to Buy," *Journal of Marketing Research*, November, 1988, 342–355.
    V. Kumar and R. Leone, "Measuring the Effect of Retail Store Promotions on Brand and Store Substitution," *Journal of Marketing Research*, May, 1988, 178–185.
    Robert C. Blattberg and Scott A. Neslin, *Sales Promotion: Concepts, Methods, and Strategies* (Englewood Cliffs, N.J.: Prentice Hall), 1990.
20. V. Kumar, A. Ghosh, and G. Tellis, "A Decomposition of Repeat Buying," *Marketing Letters*, 1992, 407–417.
    Peters S. Fader, James M. Lattin, and John D. C. Little, "Estimating Nonlinear Parameters in the Multinomial Logit Model," *Marketing Science*, Fall, 1992, 372–385.

CASE 6-1
Promotion of Rocket Soups[1]

Soups provide an interesting case history through which to examine the impact of sales promotion. Soups are sold primarily through food stores and frequently are promoted by both the manufacturer and the retailer. This case is based on 40 weeks of scanner sales history in one city. Please answer all of the questions at the end of the case.

Background

Soups are purchased by over 75 percent of all households. On the average the time between purchases is around 40 days. Sales promotion, including features, displays, and price reductions, is extremely important in this category, with around 55 percent of annual category sales moving with some sort of sales promotion. Shelf-price reductions, when they are used, average about 30 percent.

The major competitors in this category are

Brands	Share
Rocket	19.7
Stellar	40.3
Tasty	13.4
Lovely	3.5
Happy	18.1
Smile	5.0

The data for this case were collected from grocery store scanner installations in one market area, and consist of

1. Weekly store sales by brand.
2. Predominant price charged by brand by store.
3. Occurrence of promotional activity by brand by store.

The data have been summarized across all stores in the market on a weekly basis, for a total of 60 weeks. Table 1 is the week-by-week summary.

At the weekly level, Table 2 shows the data on the amount of volume moved by various promotions at various prices. However, since the stores in the market are of varying sizes, direct evaluation of promotional effects is difficult. Therefore, the sales effects are normalized (adjusting for store sizes statistically). Table 3 shows the normalized sales volume by promotional type. The commonly used methods for store-level scanner data are (1) brand volume per $1,000.000 total all commodity volume spending, and (2) brand volume per 1,000 register checkouts.

During the time of data collection, some extremely "hot" promotional activity occurred as the result of a Rocket promotional program. Some retailers decided to use Rocket soup as a loss-leader in addition to the manufacturer promotions, and combined both. These activities resulted in substantial variations in price, volume, and share of Rocket.

Case Questions

Question 1
According to Table 1, Weeks 5, 12, 22, 23, 36, and 37 are highly important sales weeks for Rocket. Weeks 2, 8, and 31 are important sales weeks for the competition. If data on promotional activity are not known, its presence is usually inferred by abnormally high sales of the brand or category, a cut in price, or both. Reviewing these weeks, and nearby weeks, discuss the impacts on Rocket and its competitors on

1. Total category volume.
2. Total category dollar spending.
3. Each other's volume (Rocket's and competitors').
4. Sales in the weeks following high volume movement.

Question 2
Table 2 shows overall promotional activity. Sales during Week 12 are at an average price near zero. This typically arises out of a retail promotion of the type: "Free box of Rocket given with total purchases of $10.00 or more." Table 3 shows sales levels adjusted for the percentage of stores in each class, and for their relative sizes. Discuss any difficulties you see in assessing the impact of the Week 12 promotion on

1. Incremental volume to Rocket.
2. Promotional volume borrowed from future sales.

Question 3
Using Table 3, plot only the non-promoted sales versus the non-promoted price. Discuss the probable percent impact on Rocket sales from a 10 percent increase or decrease in price.

---

[1] This case was prepared by V. Kumar for the purpose of classroom discussion. For similar cases, please refer to *Analyzing Sales Promotion*, by Totten and Block (1994), Dartnell Corp.: Chicago.

TABLE 1
City Sales of Soup by Week (Price Is Volume Weighted Average)

Week	Rocket Volume	Rocket Dollars	Category Volume	Category Dollars	Rocket Price	Rocket Share	Competitive Volume
1	306	250	5,984	4,356	0.82	5.1	5,678
2	345	384	14,288	9,780	1.11	2.4	13,943
3	873	694	6,201	4,893	0.79	14.1	5,328
4	900	715	5,657	4,447	0.79	15.9	4,757
5	4,404	2,772	7,673	5,453	0.63	57.4	3,269
6	456	388	5,027	4,196	0.85	9.1	4,571
7	444	395	5,570	4,687	0.89	8.0	5,126
8	513	507	11,519	8,305	0.98	4.5	11,006
9	483	441	4,661	3,917	0.91	10.4	4,178
10	615	548	4,803	4,381	0.89	12.8	4,188
11	624	571	5,038	4,632	0.91	12.4	4,414
12	16,113	705	19,633	3,982	0.04	82.1	3,520
13	1,056	811	4,476	3,967	0.76	23.6	3,420
14	381	375	3,863	3,599	0.98	9.9	3,482
15	534	526	5,014	4,677	0.98	10.6	4,480
16	1,821	870	6,487	5,257	0.47	28.1	4,666
17	390	384	3,642	3,350	0.98	10.7	3,252
18	405	398	3,743	3,441	0.98	10.8	3,338
19	1,152	1,012	5,042	4,865	0.87	22.8	3.890
20	348	342	4,733	4,248	0.98	7.4	4,385
21	378	372	3,862	3,448	0.98	9.8	3,484
22	5,319	5,129	8,352	7,839	0.96	63.7	3,033
23	2,280	1,691	7,086	5,311	0.74	32.2	4.806
24	1,194	962	5,931	4,878	0.80	20.1	4,737
25	1,020	837	5,708	4,666	0.82	17.9	4,688
26	342	336	7,780	5,849	0.98	4.4	7,438
27	1,509	1,378	5,385	5,191	0.91	28.0	3,876
28	420	413	7,352	5,533	0.98	5.7	6,932
29	528	520	7,516	5,661	0.98	7.0	6,988
30	942	676	6,416	5,461	0.71	14.7	5,474
31	957	711	15,599	7,578	0.74	6.1	14,642
32	1,014	738	4,937	4,294	0.72	20.5	3,923
33	1,059	990	5,664	5,213	0.93	18.7	4,605
34	351	385	9,045	7,302	1.09	3.9	8,694
35	384	418	5,435	4,932	1.09	7.1	5.051
36	4,122	3,084	8,672	7,699	0.74	47.5	4,550
37	9,108	4,466	13,165	8,694	0.49	69.2	4,057
38	498	542	5,643	5,103	1.09	8.8	5,145
39	459	500	5,555	5,150	1.09	8.3	5,096
40	486	529	4,485	4,285	1.09	10.8	3,999

Using Table 3, plot the relationship between sales on display-only, and display-only price. What similarities and differences in sales levels and response to price do you see in comparing the display-only response to the nonpromotional response?

CASE 6-2
Kerry Gold Products, Ltd.

In late May of 1986 the research manager for Kerry Gold Products met with the product manager for margarine to review the company's first experience with Nielsen scanner data. A year-long test in a single chain organization, which began in April of 1985 had been completed recently.

The first purpose of their review was to interpret the findings. They decided to concentrate on the results of the first 18 weeks of the tests, which are summarized in Figure 1. The size of the bars represents the weekly unit sales for Kerry Gold brand and the three competing brands also sold by the chain organization. In addition to the weekly data there were summary data on share of total sales for the first and second halves of the year. This distinction was important because Kerry Gold had spent relatively little on promotion in the second half of the year. Since Nielsen had full records of all sales on deal, they were also able to examine their share of sales during weeks when no brands offered price-reduction promotions. These data are shown in the two righthand columns in the preceding table.

While reviewing these results the research manager also was wondering whether scanner data would be useful for other grocery products sold by Kerry Gold. Many of them were as heavily promoted as margarine. Judgments on the desirability of consumer promotions for these products usually were based on a combination of store audit data plus periodic controlled experiments.

CASE 6-3
Paradise Foods[1]

by Steven H. Star
and Glen L. Urban

Introduction

Bill Horton sat alone in his office late Friday afternoon anxiously leafing through computer printouts, even though he could recite their contents from memory. Horton was waiting for his boss, Bob Murphy, to report back the decision on a subject the marketing committee had been debating for more than four hours. The issue—whether Paradise Foods should authorize national rollout of a new product, Sweet Dream, to complement its established frozen specialty dessert, LaTreat. Horton was product manager for Sweet Dream, and Murphy was the group manager responsible for all new products in Paradise's dessert line.

"I'm glad you're sitting," Bob quipped uncomfortably as he entered Bill's office. "The news isn't good. The committee decided not to go ahead."

"I don't believe it," Bill protested, "I started to worry when the meeting dragged on, but I never thought they'd say no. Damn. Eighteen months down the drain."

"I know how you feel, but you have to understand where the committee was coming from. It was a real close call—as close as I can remember since I've had this job. But the more carefully they considered your tests results, the more it looked like the returns just weren't there."

---

[1] Steven H. Star is director of the marketing center at MIT's Sloan School of Management. Glen L. Urban is Dai-Ichi Kangyo Bank Professor of Management and deputy dean of the Sloan School. This case is reprinted with permission from *Harvard Business Review*, September–October, 1988.

TABLE 2

City Sales of Soup by Week (Price Is Volume Weighted Average Sales by Promotional Type)

Week	Volume with no Promotion	Price with no Promotion	Volume with Display Only	Price with Display Only	Volume with Feature Only	Price with Feature Only	Volume with Feature and Display	Price with Feature and Display
1	306	0.82	0	.	0	.	0	.
2	345	1.11	0	.	0	.	0	.
3	477	0.75	396	0.85	0	.	0	.
4	420	0.75	480	0.84	0	.	0	.
5	222	0.69	0	.	0	.	4,182	0.63
6	399	0.83	57	0.99	0	.	0	.
7	375	0.87	69	0.99	0	.	0	.
8	471	0.98	42	1.07	0	.	0	.
9	405	0.90	78	0.99	0	.	0	.
10	486	0.87	129	0.99	0	.	0	.
11	537	0.90	87	0.99	0	.	0	.
12	486	0.79	102	0.85	0	.	15,525	0.02
13	384	0.75	0	.	0	.	672	0.78
14	381	0.99	0	.	0	.	0	.
15	534	0.99	0	.	0	.	0	.
16	267	0.87	153	0.98	0	.	1,401	0.35
17	390	0.99	0	.	0	.	0	.
18	405	0.98	0	.	0	.	0	.
19	315	0.81	672	0.89	60	0.98	105	0.98
20	348	0.99	0	.	0	.	0	.

TABLE 2 (continued)

Week	Volume with no Promotion	Price with no Promotion	Volume with Display Only	Price with Display Only	Volume with Feature Only	Price with Feature Only	Volume with Feature and Display	Price with Feature and Display
21	378	0.98	0	.	0	.	0	.
22	201	0.69	0	.	0	.	5,118	0.98
23	0	.	702	0.86	1,578	0.69	0	.
24	819	0.86	375	0.69	0	.	0	.
25	366	0.74	654	0.86	0	.	0	.
26	252	0.98	90	0.99	0	.	0	.
27	117	0.99	288	0.99	585	0.89	519	0.88
28	327	0.98	93	0.99	0	.	0	.
29	309	0.98	219	0.99	0	.	0	.
30	588	0.74	354	0.69	0	.	0	.
31	450	0.73	507	0.75	0	.	0	.
32	333	0.69	283	0.69	195	0.79	198	0.79
33	555	0.87	504	1.01	0	.	0	.
34	303	1.10	43	1.12	0	.	0	.
35	384	1.09	0	.	0	.	0	.
36	132	0.89	0	.	0	.	3,990	0.74
37	0	.	2,409	0.74	0	.	6,699	0.40
38	498	1.09	0	.	0	.	0	.
39	459	1.09	0	.	0	.	0	.
40	486	1.09	0	.	0	.	0	.

TABLE 3

City Sales of Soup by Week (Price Is Volume Weighted Average Normalized Volume Sales by Promotional Type)

Week	Normalized Volume no Promotion	Price with no Promotion	Normal Volume Display Only	Price with Display Only	Normal Volume Feature Only	Price with Feature Only	Normal Volume Feature and Display	Price with Feature and Display
1	0.21	0.82	0.00	.	0.00	.	0.00	.
2	0.20	1.11	0.00	.	0.00	.	0.00	.
3	0.45	0.75	0.66	0.85	0.00	.	0.00	.
4	0.50	0.75	0.63	0.84	0.00	.	0.00	.
5	0.60	0.69	0.00	.	0.00	.	3.94	0.63
6	0.33	0.83	0.32	0.99	0.00	.	0.00	.
7	0.24	0.87	0.36	0.99	0.00	.	0.00	.
8	0.31	0.98	0.27	1.07	0.00	.	0.00	.
9	0.30	0.90	0.34	0.99	0.00	.	0.00	.
10	0.36	0.87	0.50	0.99	0.00	.	0.00	.
11	0.41	0.90	0.41	0.99	0.00	.	0.00	.
12	0.50	0.79	0.45	0.85	0.00	.	3.95	0.02
13	0.38	0.75	0.00	.	0.00	.	1.14	0.78
14	0.25	0.99	0.00	.	0.00	.	0.00	.
15	0.26	0.99	0.00	.	0.00	.	0.00	.
16	0.34	0.87	0.65	0.98	0.00	.	2.05	0.35
17	0.25	0.99	0.00	.	0.00	.	0.00	.
18	0.27	0.98	0.00	.	0.00	.	0.00	.
19	0.70	0.81	1.85	0.89	0.15	0.98	0.48	0.98
20	0.21	0.99	0.00	.	0.00	.	0.00	.

TABLE 3 (continued)

Week	Normalized Volume no Promotion	Price with no Promotion	Normal Volume Display Only	Price with Display Only	Normal Volume Feature Only	Price with Feature Only	Normal Volume Feature and Display	Price with Feature and Display
21	0.27	0.98	0.00	.	0.00	.	0.00	.
22	0.57	0.69	0.00	.	0.00	.	4.79	0.98
23	0.00	.	0.64	0.86	3.77	0.69	0.00	.
24	0.65	0.86	0.98	0.69	0.00	.	0.00	.
25	0.55	0.74	0.80	0.86	0.00	.	0.00	.
26	0.21	0.98	0.28	0.99	0.00	.	0.00	.
27	0.43	0.99	0.82	0.99	1.55	0.89	0.79	0.88
28	0.26	0.93	0.29	0.99	0.00	.	0.00	.
29	0.24	0.93	0.67	0.99	0.00	.	0.00	.
30	0.48	0.74	1.15	0.69	0.00	.	0.00	.
31	0.45	0.73	0.95	0.75	0.00	.	0.00	.
32	0.55	0.69	0.93	0.69	0.96	0.79	0.55	0.79
33	0.52	0.87	0.88	1.01	0.00	.	0.00	.
34	0.22	1.10	0.35	1.12	0.00	.	0.00	.
35	0.25	1.09	0.00	.	0.00	.	0.00	.
36	0.37	0.89	0.00	.	0.00	.	2.98	0.74
37	0.00	.	1.92	0.74	0.00	.	18.61	0.40
38	0.29	1.09	0.00	.	0.00	.	0.00	.
39	0.26	1.09	0.00	.	0.00	.	0.00	.
40	0.29	1.09	0.00	.	0.00	.	0.00	.

TABLE 4

Brand	Share of Total Sales (%)				Share of Sales in Nonpromotional Weeks (%)	
	1st $\frac{1}{2}$ yr		2nd $\frac{1}{2}$ yr		1st $\frac{1}{2}$ yr	2nd $\frac{1}{2}$ yr
Kerry Gold	39	(34)	13	(7)	18.9	19.3
B	17	(8)	42	(35)	30.4	30.3
C	29	(13)	28	(18)	33.1	33.9
D	15	(11)	17	(12)	17.6	16.5
	100	(66)	100	(72)	100	100

* Figures in parentheses are deal merchandise shares of market. In the first half of the year, 66 percent of total unit sales in the category were on deal.

"Not there? All they had to look at was Appendix B in my report—the data from Midland and Pittsfield. Sweet Dream got a 3% share after 26 weeks. A trial rate of 15%. A repurchase rate of 45%. If national performance were anywhere close to that, we'd have our launch costs back in 14 months. Who can argue with that?"

"I'm on your side here, but I only had one vote," Bob said defensively. "We both knew what Barbara's position was going to be—and you know how much weight she carries around here these days." Barbara Mayer was the Paradise group manager responsible for established dessert products. She became a "grouper" in 1985, after two enormously successful years as LaTreat's first product manager.

"And to be honest, it was tough to take issue with her," Bob continued. "What's the point of introducing Sweet Dream if you end up stealing share from LaTreat? In fact, Barbara used some of your data against us. She kept waving around Appendix C, griping that 75% of the people who tried Sweet Dream had bought LaTreat in the previous four weeks. And repurchase rates were highest among LaTreat heavy users. You know how the fourteenth floor feels about LaTreat. Barbara claims that adjusting for lost LaTreat sales means Sweet Dream doesn't recover its up-front costs for three years."

LaTreat

Launched in 1983, LaTreat was the first "super premium" frozen dessert to enter national distribution. It consisted of 3.5 ounces of vanilla ice cream dipped in penuche fudge and covered with almonds. An individual bar sold for just under $2 and a package of four was $7. Unlike LaTreat, which came on a stick, Sweet Dream resembled an ice cream sandwich.

It consisted of sweet-cream ice cream between two oversized chocolate chip cookies and coated with dark Belgian chocolate. Its price was comparable to LaTreat's.

Under Barbara Mayer, annual sales of LaTreat soon reached $40 million, and it began making a significant contribution to dessert groups profits. It accounted for almost 5% of the market despite a price about 50% higher than standard frozen specialties. Lately, however, competition had stiffened. LaTreat faced tough challenges from three direct competitors as well as several parallel concepts (like Sweet Dream) at various stages of test marketing. The total frozen specialties market had grown fast enough to absorb these new entrants without reducing LaTreat sales, but revenues had been essentially flat through 1986 and 1987.

Bill understood the importance of LaTreat, but he was not the type to mince words. "You and I both know things are more complicated than Barbara would have people believe," he told Bob. "There wasn't the same cannibalization effect in Marion and Corvallis. And we never did a test in Midland and Pittsfield where Barbara's people were free to defend LaTreat. We might be able to have it both ways . . ."

Bob interrupted. "Bill, we could stay here all night on this. But what's the point? The committee's made its decision. You don't like it, I don't like it. But these aren't stupid people. It's hard to argue with the dessert group's batting average over the last five years. This may ring hollow right now, but you can't take this personally."

"That's easy for you to say," Bill sighed.

"You know how this company works," Bob reminded him. "We don't hold withdrawal of a new product against the manager if withdrawal is the

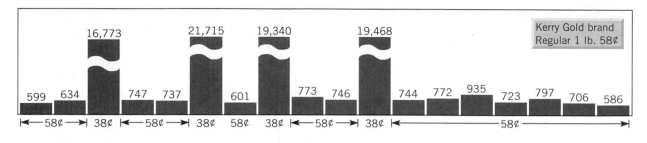

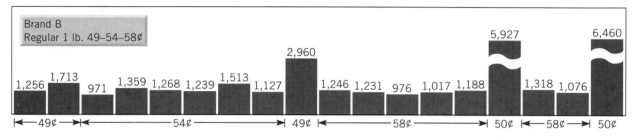

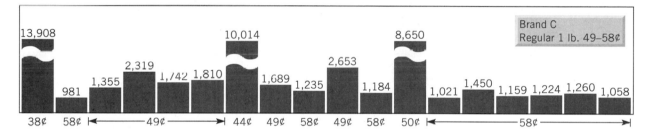

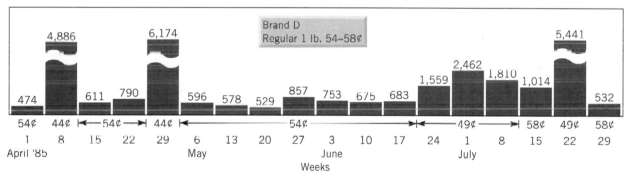

FIGURE 1
Unit sales per week (and prevailing price for the brand during the week)

right decision. Hell, it happened to me ten years ago with that dumb strawberry topping. It made sense to kill that product. And I was better off at the company for it. The fact is, the committee was impressed as hell with the research you did—although to be honest, you may have overwhelmed them. A 40-page report with 30 pages of appendixes. I had trouble wading through it all. But that doesn't matter. You did a good job, and the people who count know that.''

"I appreciate the sentiment, but that's not why I think this is the wrong decision. Sweet Dream is a go on the merits."

"Go home, play some golf this weekend," Bob counseled. "Things won't seem so bleak on Monday."

Bill never made it to the country club. Instead, he spent the weekend worrying about his future at Paradise and puzzling over how the marketing committee could have reached its no-launch decision.

Sweet Dream Proposal

Paradise Foods was a large, successful manufacturer of packaged foods and household products whose markets were becoming increasingly competitive. Bill believed that Paradise was vulnerable in this treacherous environment because of its failure to keep pace with technological change—in particular, the increasing sophistication of marketing research based on computer modeling, supermarket scanner data, and targetable cable television. Paradise certainly used these tools, but to Bill's way of thinking, top management didn't embrace them with the same enthusiasm as other companies.

When Bill became produce manager for Sweet Dream, he promised himself he would do a state-of-the-art research job. The plan was to compare the performance of Sweet Dream in two test markets exposed to different advertising and promotion strategies. The campaign in Midland, Texas, and Pittsfield, Massachusetts struck an overtly self-indulgent tone—"Go Ahead, You Deserve It"—and used limited price promotion to induce trial. The campaign in Marion, Indiana, and Corvallis, Oregon, emphasized superior quality—"Taste the Goodness"—and used promotion aggressively. Sunday newspapers in the two cities frequently carried 50-cents-off coupons, and Sweet Dream boxes included a 75-cent rebate voucher.

Bill used two computer-based research services—InfoScan and BehaviorScan—to evaluate Sweet Dream's performance and long-term potential.[2] InfoScan tracks product purchases on a national and local basis for the packaged-goods industry. It collects point-of-sale information on all bar-coded products sold in a representative sample of supermarkets and drugstores. It generates weekly data on volume, price, market share, the relationship between sales and promotional offers, and merchandising conditions. Bill subscribed to InfoScan to monitor competitive trends in the frozen specialties segment.

BehaviorScan is used in marketing tests to measure the effect of marketing strategies on product purchases. In a typical BehaviorScan test, one group of consumer panelists is exposed to certain variables (i.e., print or television advertisements, coupons, free samples, instore displays), while other participating consumers serve as a control group. Company analysts use supermarket scanner data on both groups of consumers (who present identification cards to store checkout clerks) to evaluate purchasing responses to marketing campaigns. A typical BehaviorScan test lasts about one year.

Bill Horton's research program had generated a stack of computer printouts several feet high. He had spent much of the spring trying to unravel the complex interactions between different advertising and promotion strategies for Sweet Dream, the various promotion deals Paradise was running on LaTreat, and the proliferation of other frozen specialties. Despite Bob's advice to relax, Bill spent Sunday afternoon in front of his home computer, massaging the data one last time.

Competitive Analysis

On Monday, Bill arrived at his office a few minutes late. He was surprised to find Barbara Mayer waiting on him.

"Sorry to drop in on you first thing," she said, "but I wanted to let you know what a fantastic job you did on the Sweet Dream test. I'm sure you were disappointed with the committee's decision, and in a way I was too. It would have been great to work together on the rollout. But the data were pretty clear. We didn't have a choice."

"Well, I thought the data were clear too—but in the opposite direction."

"Come on, Bill, you can understand the logic of the decision. The Midland and Pittsfield numbers were fine, but they were coming at the expense of LaTreat. There wasn't so much cannibalization in Marion and Corvallis, but the Sweet Dream numbers weren't as good either. Trial was acceptable, but repurchase was low. We might make money, but we'd never meet the hurdle rate. Every so often a product just falls between two stools."

"So we'll do more tests," Bill countered. "We can play with the positioning in Marion and Corvallis. Or we can start from scratch somewhere else. I can have us wired to go in three weeks."

"We've already taken 18 months on Sweet Dream," Barbara said. "The committee felt it was time to try new concepts. I don't think that's so unreasonable."

"You're forgetting two things," Bill replied. "First, with freezer space as tight as it is, the longer it takes to come up with another product, the harder the stores are going to squeeze us. Second, other people are going to find out how well Sweet Dream did in Midland and Pittsfield. We're the only ones who get the BehaviorScan numbers, but you know the competition is monitoring our tests. What do you think Weston & Williams is going to do when it sees the results? It'll have a Sweet Dream clone out in a few months if we don't launch."

Weston & Williams (W & W) was a leading supplier of household products that was diversifying into foods, including desserts. It had a reputation as a conservative company that insisted on exhaustive prelaunch research. But the trade press recently had reported on W & W's decision to rush Pounce—a combination detergent, colorfast bleach, and fabric soft-

---

[2] InfoScan and BehaviorScan are actual services offered by Information Resources, Inc.

ener—to the market on the basis of very preliminary tests and data from a competitior's test markets. W & W had thus become the first national entrant in the "maxiwash" category.

"Bob made that argument Friday," Barbara said. "But you can guess how far he got. The guys upstairs have a tough enough time taking our own computer data seriously. They don't buy the idea that someone else is going to jump into the market based on our tests. Plus, that would be a huge risk. Pounce may have given Weston & Williams all the gray hair they can stand for a few years."

"From what I can tell, Barbara, the only issue that counted was cannibalization." Bill's voice betrayed a rekindled sense of frustration. "I understand you want to protect LaTreat. I understand the company wants to protect LaTreat. But it seems to me we're protecting a product that is getting tired."

"What are you talking about?" Barbara objected. "Profits aren't growing as fast as they used to, but they're not dropping either. LaTreat is solid."

Sales Analysis

"Come on, Barbara. Your people have really been promoting it in the last two quarters—shifting money out of print and TV and into coupons and rebates. Total spending hasn't changed, so profits are OK. But LaTreat has gotten hooked on promotion. And all the wrong kinds of promotion. You've got people accelerating future purchases and price-sensitive types jumping in whenever LaTreat goes on sale. Who needs that?"

"Where are you getting this stuff?" Barbara demanded, "I didn't see it in your report."

"I spent the weekend running some more numbers," Bill replied. "Take a look at this."

Bill punched a few buttons on his computer keyboard and called up a series of graphs. The first docu-

mented the growing percentage of LaTreat sales connected with promotional offers. A second graph disaggregated LaTreat's promotion-related sales by four buyer categories Bill had created from Behavior-Scan data. "Loyalists" were longtime customers who increased their purchases in response to a deal. "Trial users" bought LaTreat for the first time because of the promotion and who seemed to be turning into loyal customers. "Accelerators" were longtime customers who used coupons or rebates to stock up on product they would have bought anyway. "Switch-on-deal" customers were nonusers who bought LaTreat when there were promotions but demonstrated little long-term loyalty. Bill's graph documented that a majority of LaTreat's coupon redeemers fell into the last two categories, with "loyalists" accounting for a shrinking percentage of sales.

Finally, Bill called up his ultimate evidence—a graph that adjusted LaTreat sales to eliminate the effect of promotions. (See Figure 2).

"I'm amazed you spent your weekend doing this," Barbara said, "but I'm glad you did. It'll help us think through future marketing strategies for LaTreat. But it doesn't change what the committee decided. It's time to move on."

"I'm not so sure," Bill replied. "I hope you don't mind, but I think I should show these data to Bob. Maybe he can convince the committee to reconsider. After all, if LaTreat is weakening, its going to show up in your profit figures sooner or later."

"Data don't make decisions, Bill, people do. And the people on the marketing committee have been in the industry a lot longer than you. Their gut tells them things your computer can't. Besides, you and I both know that when you collect this much data, you can make it show just about anything. Go ahead and talk to Bob, but I'm sure he'll see things the same way I do."

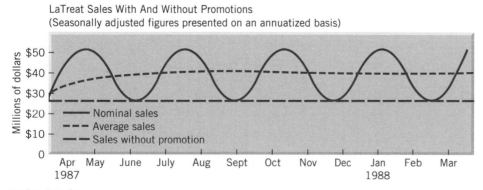

FIGURE 2

LaTreat sales with and without promotions (seasonally adjusted figures presented on an annualized basis)

171

Assignment

1. What (if any) issues did Bill Hutton overlook in evaluating Sweet Dream?

2. Do you think Sweet Dream should be launched? Give the rationale for your answer. Is there any additional research you feel should be conducted before a final decision in the Sweet Dream launch is made?

7

INFORMATION COLLECTION: QUALITATIVE AND OBSERVATIONAL METHODS

Learning Objectives

▶ Explain the need for qualitative research.

▶ Introduce the different types of qualitative research methods.

▶ Discuss in-depth interviews, focus group, and projective techniques in detail.

▶ Be familiar with the various observational methods.

This chapter shifts the focus from the utilization of already-available secondary data to the collection of primary data for a specific purpose. Seldom is enough known about a marketing problem or situation for the researcher to be able to proceed directly to the design of a structured study that would yield representative and quantifiable results. Hence, qualitative data collection is done to obtain a basic feel for the problem before proceeding to the more analytical portion of the study.

A variety of qualitative methods can be used for such exploratory purposes. Specifically, we will discuss individual and group interviews and case studies. The category of qualitative methods includes projective techniques that are used when self-reports are likely to be misleading. Although projective techniques are utilized during exploratory research, they are also used as a primary data-collection method.

Observational methods are also discussed in this chapter. The observation of ongoing behavior is a widely used exploratory method, as well as an effective way to collect quantitative information when direct questioning is not possible.

NEED FOR QUALITATIVE RESEARCH

The purpose of qualitative research is to find out what is in a consumer's mind. It is done in order to access and also get a rough idea about the person's perspective. It helps the researcher to become oriented to the range and complexity of consumer activity and concerns. Qualitative data are collected to know more about things that cannot be directly observed and measured. Feelings, thoughts, intentions, and behavior that took place in the past are a few examples of those things that can be obtained only through qualitative data-collection methods. It is also used to identify likely methodological problems in the study, and to clarify certain issues that were not clear in the problem. Sometimes it may not be possible or desirable to obtain information from respondents by using fully structured or formal methods. Qualitative data collection methods are used in such situations. People may be unwilling to answer some questions when directly confronted with them. Questions that they perceive as an invasion of privacy, that they think will embarrass them, or that may have a negative impact on their ego or status will not be answered. Examples of such sensitive questions could be: "Are you a compulsive drinker of alcohol? Do you use drugs to relieve stress or anxiety?" Sometimes, accurate answers will not be forthcoming because they are a part of the subconscious mind and cannot be directly tapped into. They are disguised from the outer world through the mechanism of ego defenses, like rationalization. For example, a person may have purchased an expensive sports car to overcome a feeling of inferiority. However, if asked, "Why did you purchase this sports car?" he or she may say, "I got a great deal," or "My old car was falling apart." It has been shown that information of this sort can be better obtained from qualitative methods, such as focus-group discussion or projective techniques, than through a formal, structured-survey method of data collection.

The basic assumption behind qualitative methods is that an individual's organization of a relatively unstructured stimulus indicates the person's basic perceptions of the phenomenon and his or her reaction to it.[1] The more unstructured and ambiguous a stimulus is, the more subjects can and will project their emotions, needs, motives, attitudes, and values. The structure of a stimulus is the degree of choice available to the subject. A highly structured stimulus leaves very little choice: the subject has unambiguous choice among clear alternatives. A stimulus of low structure has a wide range of alternative choices. If it is ambiguous, the subjects can "choose" their own interpretations.

QUALITATIVE RESEARCH METHODS

Collectively, these methods are less structured and more intensive than standardized questionnaire-based interviews. There is a longer, more flexible relationship with the respondent, so the resulting data have more depth and greater richness of context—which also means a greater potential for new insights and perspectives. The numbers of respondents are small and only partially representative of any target population, making them preludes to, but not substitutes for carefully structured, large-scale field studies. There are three major categories of acceptable uses of qualitative research methods:

Exploratory
▶ Defining problems in more detail.

▶ Suggesting hypotheses to be tested in subsequent research.

▶ Generating new product or service concepts, problem solutions, lists of product features, and so forth.

▶ Getting preliminary reactions to new product concepts.

▶ Pretesting structured questionnaires.

Orientation

▶ Learning the consumer's vantage point and vocabulary.

▶ Educating the researcher to an unfamiliar environment: needs, satisfactions, usage situations, and problems.

Clinical

▶ Gaining insights into topics that otherwise might be impossible to pursue with structured research methods.

The range of possible applications of these methods can be seen from the following examples:

1. A telephone equipment supplier wanted to know what features to incorporate in an answering device located in a telephone substation (rather than in the home or office). From several group discussions came ideas for many features such as variable-length messages and accessibility from any telephone. Specific features and price expectations were tested in a subsequent survey.

2. Before Beckman Instruments entered the process-control-equipment market, it conducted four separate group interviews with instrumentation engineers. Participants came to the three-hour sessions in part because of the opportunity to talk with others in the field. Their complaints and comments about lack of readability of scales and unreliability of recording equipment were very influential in subsequent design decisions.[2]

3. General Motors uses consumer and dealer focus groups,[3] as well as extensive questionnaires, to identify the best features of their own and of competitors' automobiles. These give insight on "world class" elements they want to meet or exceed. For example, the design of air filter covers for the GM10 line of cars was inspired by Mazda; the seat adjustment was made by a long bar under each front seat; and electrical fuses were put in the glove box—an idea used by Saab.

Among the heaviest users of qualitative data are Japanese firms. They prefer "soft data" collected by managers during visits to dealers and customers, because it gives them a much better feel for a market's nuances. Talks with dealers who know their customers result in realistic, context-specific information. These talks directly relate to consumer attitudes, or the way the product has been or will be used, rather than being remote from actual behavior.[4] If Japanese firms do conduct surveys, they will interview only people who have actually experienced the product or service, rather than asking a random sample about general attitudes. When Toyota wanted to learn what Americans preferred in small, imported cars, they asked groups of Volkswagen Beetle owners what they liked and disliked about that particular car.

Individual In-Depth Interviews

Individual in-depth interviews are interviews that are conducted face to face with the respondent, in which the subject matter of the interview is explored in detail. There are two basic types of in-depth interviews. They are **nondirective** and **semistructured,** and their differences lie in the amount of guidance the interviewer provides.

Nondirective Interviews. Here the respondent is given maximum freedom to respond, within the bounds of topics of interest to the interviewer. Success depends on (1) establishing a relaxed and sympathetic relationship; (2) the ability to probe in order to clarify and elaborate on interesting responses, without biasing the content of the responses; and (3) the skill of guiding the discussion back to the topic outline when digressions are unfruitful, always pursuing reasons behind the comments and answers. Such sessions normally are one to two hours long and may be tape recorded (always with the permission of the respondent) for later interpretation.

Semistructured or Focused Individual Interviews. Here the interviewer attempts to cover a specific list of topics or subareas. The timing, exact wording, and time allocated to each question area are left to the interviewer's discretion.

This mode of interviewing is especially effective with busy executives, technical experts, and thought leaders. Basic market intelligence, such as trends in technology, market demand, legislation, competitive activity, and similar information are amenable to such interviews. The open structure ensures that unexpected facts or attitudes can be pursued easily.

This type of interview is extremely demanding, and much depends on the interviewer's skill. First, the interviewer must be sufficiently persuasive to get through the shield of secretaries and receptionists around many executives, in order to get an appointment. The major challenge is to establish rapport and credibility in the early moments of the interview, and then maintain that atmosphere. For this, there is no substitute for an informed, authoritative person who can relate to respondents on their own terms. This can be achieved by asking the respondent to react to specific information provided by the interviewer. Care should be taken to avoid threatening questions. A good opener might be, "If you had to pick one critical problem affecting your industry, what would it be?" Cooperation sometimes can be improved by offering a quid pro quo, such as a summary of some of the study findings.

A difficult problem with these interviews is the matter of record keeping. Some executives dislike tape recorders, so it may be necessary to use a team of interviewers who alternate between asking questions and recording responses. To keep the interview as short as possible, it is usually best to leave behind a structured questionnaire for any specific data that are wanted, because this can be assigned to staff for answering. Finally, since the appropriate respondents for these studies are often difficult to identify, and may encompass many parts of an organization, it is always advisable to ask for recommendations about which other people it might be useful to interview.

Individual in-depth interviews are also used in consumer markets to identify key product benefits and trigger creative insights. There are three techniques that are being widely used now. The first technique, **laddering,**[5] is well suited here. In this technique, questioning progresses from product characteristics to user characteristics. A good starting point is with a repertory (sometimes called Kelly's Triad). If the topic were airlines, respondents might be asked to compare one airline, in a set of three, to the other two: How do airlines A and B differ from C? How do A and C differ from B? And so on. Each attribute, such as a "softer seat," is then probed to see why it is important to the respondent; then that reason is probed, and so on. The result might be the following kind of dialogue:

Interviewer: "Why do you like wide bodies?"
Respondent: "They're more comfortable."
Interviewer: "Why is that important?"
Respondent: "I can accomplish more."
Interviewer: "Why is that important?"
Respondent: "I will feel good about myself."

Notice that the dialogue has moved from a very tangible aspect of an airline to its contribution to self-esteem.

The second technique is called **hidden-issue** questioning. In hidden issue questioning, the focus is not on socially shared values but rather on personal "sore spots"; not on general life styles but on deeply felt personal concerns. The third technique, **symbolic analysis,** attempts to analyze the symbolic meaning of objects by comparing them with their opposites. For example, the following question could be asked, "What would it be like if you could no longer use airlines?" Responses like "Without planes, I would have to rely on long distance calls and letters." may be received. This would suggest that one of the attributes that can be highlighted in an ad campaign for airline could be face-to-face communication. Sometimes an interviewer may have to go outside his country to interview people or have to design questionnaires that are to be administered in other parts of the world. Issues that an interviewer commonly faces when interviewing in another culture are described in Exhibit 7-1.[6]

Focus-Group Discussions

A focus group discussion is the process of obtaining possible ideas or solutions to a marketing problem from a group of respondents by discussing it. The emphasis in this method is on the results of group interaction when focused on a series of topics a discussion leader introduces. Each participant in a group of five to nine or more persons is encouraged to express views on each topic, and to elaborate or react to the views of the other participants. The objectives are similar to unstructured in-depth interviews, but the moderator plays a more passive role than an interviewer does.

The **focus-group discussion** certainly offers the participants more stimulation than an interview; presumably this makes new ideas and meaningful comments more likely.[7] Among other advantages, it is claimed that discussions

EXHIBIT 7-1

> ## Qualitative Interviewing in the International Context
>
> Evaluation has become an international activity. International and cross-cultural short-term evaluation site visits are much more subject to misinterpretations and miscommunications than traditional, long-term anthropological fieldwork. The data from interviews are words. It is tricky enough to be sure what a person means when using a common language, but words can take on a very different meaning in other cultures. In Sweden, I participated in an international conference discussing policy evaluations. The conference was conducted in English, but I was there for two days, much of the time confused, before I came to understand that their use of the term *policy* corresponded to my American use of the term *program*. I interpreted policies, from an American context, to be fairly general directives, often very difficult to evaluate because of their vagueness. In Sweden, however, policies are very specific programs.
>
> The situation becomes more precarious when a translator or interpreter must be used because of language differences. Using an interpreter for conducting interviews is fraught with difficulty. Special and very precise training of translators is critical. It is important that questions be asked precisely as you want them asked, and that full and complete answers be translated. Interpreters often want to be helpful by summarizing and explaining responses. This contaminates the interviewee's actual response with the interpreter's explanation to such an extent that you can no longer be sure whose perceptions you have—the interpreter's or the interviewee's.
>
> There are also words and ideas that simply can't be translated. People who regularly use the language come to know the unique cultural meaning of special terms, but they don't translate well. One of my favorites from the Caribbean is "liming." It means something like hanging out, just being, doing nothing—guilt free. In conducting interviews for a program evaluation, a number of participants said they were just "liming" in the program. But that was not meant as a criticism. Liming is a highly desirable state of being, at least to participants. Funders might view the situation differently.
>
> The high esteem in which science is held has made it culturally acceptable in Western countries to conduct interviews on virtually any subject in the name of science. Such is not the case worldwide. Evaluation researchers cannot simply presume that they have the right to ask intrusive questions. Many topics may be taboo. I have experienced cultures where it is simply inappropriate to ask questions to a subordinate about a superordinate. Any number of topics may be taboo, or at least indelicate, for strangers—family matters, political views, who owns what, how people came to be in certain positions, and sources of income.
>
> There are also different norms governing interactions. I remember with great embarrassment going to an African village to interview the chief. The whole village was assembled. Following a brief welcoming ceremony, I asked if we could begin the interview. I expected a private, one-on-one interview. He expected to perform in front of and involve the whole village. It took me a while to understand this, during which I kept asking to go somewhere else so we could begin the interview. He did not share my concern about preference for privacy. What I expected to be an individual interview soon turned out to be a whole village focus group interview! In many cultures it is a breach of etiquette for an unknown man to ask to meet alone with a woman. Even a female interviewer may need the permission of a husband, brother, or a parent to interview a village woman.

Source: Michael Quinn Patton, *Qualitative Evaluation and Research Methods.* Second Edition. Thousand Oaks, CA (Sage Publications, 1990).

often provoke more spontaneity and candor than can be expected in an interview. Some proponents feel that the security of being in a crowd encourages some participants to speak out.

Types of Focus Groups. Focus groups can be classified into three types. **Exploratory focus groups** are commonly used at the exploratory phase of the market research process to aid in precisely defining the problem. They can also be viewed as pilot testing. Exploratory groups can also be used to generate hypotheses for testing or concepts for future research.

Clinical focus groups involve qualitative research in its most scientific form. The research is conducted as a scientific endeavor, based on the premise that a person's true motivations and feelings are subconscious in nature. The moderator probes under the level of the consumer's consciousness. Obviously, clinical groups require a moderator with expertise in psychology and sociology. But their popularity is diminished because of the difficulty of validating findings from clinical groups and because unskilled operators attempt to conduct clinical groups.

The reality in the kitchen or supermarket differs drastically from that in most corporate offices. **Experiencing focus groups** allows the researcher to experience the emotional framework in which the product is being used. Thus an experiencing approach represents an opportunity to "experience" a "flesh and blood" consumer.

There are no hard-and-fast rules for choosing focus groups rather than individual in-depth interviews for qualitative studies. The comparison that follows in Table 7-1, may help you to make the choice.[8]

Key Factors for Focus-Group Success. As a rule, three or four group sessions usually are sufficient. The analyst invariably learns a great deal from the first discussion. The second interview produces much more, but less is new. Usually, by the third or fourth session much of what is said has been heard before, and there is little to be gained from additional focus groups. Exceptions to this rule occur if there are distinct segments to cover, such as regional differences in tastes, the differences between women working in the home and outside the home, or the differences between married or unmarried women.

A focus group is not an easy technique to employ. Further, a poorly conducted or analyzed focus group can yield very misleading results and waste a good deal of money.[9] In 1993 the recruitment costs, payments to participants, space rental, moderation, and analyst fees easily could be in the range of $3000 per focus group for consumer studies.[10] The typical cost for an industrial focus group is approximately $4000. The key success factors are (1) planning the agenda, (2) recruiting participants, (3) effective moderation, and (4) analysis and interpretation of the results.

Planning the Agenda. This starts by translating the research purpose into a set of managerially relevant questions, which ensures that client and moderator agree on specific objectives before the study begins. From these questions, the group moderator can prepare a discussion guide that serves as a checklist of the specific issues and topics to be covered. However, this list is strictly for general guidance, it is not desirable to have formal questions that are read to the group.

An important issue is the order in which the moderator introduces topics. Usually, it is best to proceed from a general discussion to increasingly specific questions, for if the specific issue is addressed first it will influence the general discussion. It is also easier for respondents to relate to a specific issue when it has been preceded by a general discussion. For example, Mother's Cookies was interested in concept-testing a new fruit-filled cookie, and a proposed

TABLE 7-1
Comparison of Focus Groups and Individual In-Depth Interviews

	Focus Groups	**Individual In-Depth Interviews**
Group interactions	Group interaction is present. This may stimulate new thoughts from respondents.	There is no group interaction. Therefore, stimulation for new ideas from respondents comes from the interviewer.
Group/peer pressure	Group pressure and stimulation may clarify and challenge thinking.	In the absence of group pressure, the thinking of respondents is not challenged.
	Peer pressure and role playing may occur and may be confusing to interpret.	With one respondent, role playing is minimized and there is no peer pressure.
Respondent competition	Respondents compete with one another for time to talk. There is less time to obtain indepth details from each participant.	The individual is alone with the interviewer and can express thoughts in a noncompetitive environment. There is more time to obtain detailed information.
Influence	Responses in a group may be "contaminated" by opinions of other group members.	With one respondent, there is no potential for influence from other respondents.
Subject sensitivity	If the subject is sensitive, respondents may be hesitant to talk freely in the presence of several other people.	If the subject is sensitive, respondents may be more likely to talk.
Interviewer fatigue	One interviewer can easily conduct several group sessions on one topic without becoming fatigued or bored.	Interviewer fatigue and boredom are problems when many individual interviews are needed.
Amount of information	A relatively large amount of information can be obtained in a short period of time with relatively small cost.	A large amount of information can be obtained, but it takes time to obtain it and to analyze the results. Thus, costs are relatively high.
Stimuli	The volume of stimulus materials that can be used is somewhat limited.	A fairly large amount of stimulus material can be used.
Interviewer schedule	It may be difficult to assemble eight or ten respondents if they are a difficult type to recruit (such as very busy executives).	Individual interviews are easier to schedule.

Source: Adapted from *Focus Groups: Issues and Approaches.* (New York: Advertising Research Foundation, 1985).

introductory promotion involved tickets to a circus. The moderator started with a general discussion about snacks and then moved to the use of cookies as snacks and the question of buying versus making cookies. Only after this general discussion was the more specific topic addressed.

The set of topics covered may change after each focus-group experience. The moderator and client may decide that a question is not generating useful, nonrepetitive information, and drop it in the remaining focus group. Or a new, interesting idea may emerge, and reactions may be sought from subsequent groups.[11]

Recruitment. When recruiting participants, it is necessary to provide for both similarity and contrast within a group. As a rule, it is undesirable to combine participants from different social classes or stages in the life cycle, because of differences in their perceptions, experiences, and verbal skills.[12]

Within an otherwise homogeneous group, it may be helpful to provide for a spark to be occasionally struck by introducing contrasting opinions. One way to do this is to include both users and nonusers of the product or service or brand. But if the product carries social connotations, this mixing up may suppress divergent opinions; for example, buyers of large life insurance policies may believe that nonbuyers are irresponsible. Some moderators believe that having conflicting opinions within a group may invite either a "rational" defense or a "withdrawal" of those who think their opinions are in a minority.

One controversial source of participants is the "experienced" panel, whose members have been trained in ways that contribute to the dialogue in the group. Those who oppose this practice feel that "professional" respondents who show up repeatedly are so sensitized by the interview experience that they are no longer representative of the population.[13]

Although groups of 8 to 12 have become customary, smaller groups may be more productive.[14] With 12 panelists for example, after subtracting the time it takes to warm up (usually about 3 min) and the time for the moderator's questions and probes, the average panelist in a 90-min focus group has 3 min of actual talking time. The experience becomes more like a group survey than an exploration of experiences, feelings, and beliefs. It is also a very expensive form of survey, so cutting group size makes sound economic sense.

The Moderator. Effective *moderating* encourages all participants to discuss their feelings, anxieties, and frustrations as well as the depth of their convictions on issues relevant to the topic, without being biased or pressured by the situation.[15] The following are critical moderating skills:

▶ Ability to establish rapport quickly by listening carefully, demonstrating a genuine interest in each participant's views, dressing like the participants, and avoiding the use of jargon or sophisticated terminology that may turn off the group.

▶ Flexibility, observed by implementing the interview agenda in a way the group finds comfortable. Slavish adherence to an agenda means the discussion loses spontaneity and degenerates into a question-and-answer session.

▶ Ability to sense when a topic has been exhausted or is becoming threatening, and to know which new topic to introduce to maintain a smooth flow in the discussion.

▶ Ability to control group influences to avoid having a dominant individual or subgroup that might suppress the total contribution.

Common techniques for conducting successful focus group interviews include the **chain reaction, devil's advocate,** and **false termination.** In the **chain reaction** technique, the moderator builds a cumulative effect by encouraging each member of the focus group to comment on a prior idea suggested by someone else in the group by adding to or expanding on it. When playing **devil's advocate,** the moderator expresses extreme viewpoints; this usually provokes reactions from focus group members and keeps the discussion moving forward in a lively manner. In **false termination,** the moderator falsely concludes a focus group interview, thanks group members for participating, and inquires whether there are any final comments. These "final comments" frequently lead to new discussion avenues and often result in the most useful data obtained. Exhibit 7-2 gives an idea of what could go wrong in a focus group interview.

Analysis and Interpretation of the Results. This is complicated by the wealth of disparate comments usually obtained, which means that any analyst can find something that agrees with his or her view of the problem. A useful report of a group session is one that captures the range of impressions and observations on each topic and interprets them in the light of possible hypotheses for further testing. When reporting comments, it is not sufficient merely to repeat what was said without putting it into a context, so that the implications are more evident.

Several features of group interactions must be kept in mind during the analysis. An evaluation of a new concept by a group tends to be conservative;

EXHIBIT 7-2

Fear and Loathing in a Chrysler Focus Group

A reporter, Nancy Nichols, participated in a ride-and-drive test of a Plymouth Acclaim LX. Her account is as follows:

We were asked to sit in the front and rear seats and rate a gaggle of the cars' features on a scale of 1 to 10. Rating the cars' appearance, headroom and legroom made sense to me. But I was dumbfounded when they asked me to rate the rear-door panels. After all those years spent in the back seat of my two-tone Chrysler Newport, I can't even remember what the rear-door panel looked like, and I was similarly unimpressed with the ones I saw at the clinic.

By mid-morning I was beginning to feel a nagging pressure, as if this was some kind of quiz I must pass. Gripped by fear and ambivalence, I gave all the rear-door panels a neutral rating and went on to the next part of our clinic.

I test drove each of the cars with an interviewer from an independent company who knew little about how the cars operated. We fumbled around finding our seat belts as she told me the route we would follow. Her questions sometimes seemed inappropriate. For example, she asked me about the car's ability to corner when the two sharp corners in our route hadn't come up yet. Later, as we entered the highway, she told me to take the car up to 55 miles an hour and evaluate the road and engine noise. If I had followed her orders we would have rear-ended a semi-truck.

It wasn't until we left the cars and began our one-on-one interview that she angered me. She looked at me—a high-income career woman, exactly the type who makes more than half the car-purchase decisions in America—and said, "I am really glad I got a nice little girl like you."

My rage blurred the rest of my answers to her questions. The focus group that followed was a cross between group therapy and late-night television. A Geraldo Rivera look-alike rolled up his sleeves and said, "I want you to talk about the driving experience."

He called us all by our first names to build intimacy. As if it might unravel some ancient mystery, he turned to me and asked, "Nancy, what does it mean to you when the wheels squeak?"

As I would imagine happens in many focus groups, the discussion was dominated by two knowledgeable and opinionated automotive buffs. They didn't like the plastic around the key or the feel of the steering wheel and they were vehement—almost passionate—about these things. Their comments made sense and Chrysler was listening.

Source: *Ad Week's Marketing Week,* May 15, 1989, p. 61.

that is, it favors ideas that are easy to explain and not necessarily very new. There are further problems with the order of presentation when several concepts, products, or advertisements are being evaluated. If group participants have been highly critical of one thing, they may compensate by being uncritical of the next.

Trends in Focus Groups. The number of focus groups being conducted is growing at a rapid pace. There may be over 50,000 focus groups conducted annually. The quality of focus groups' facilities have also become better. Instead of tiny viewing rooms with small one-way mirrors, plush two-tiered observation areas that wrap around the conference room to provide an unobstructed view of all the respondents are being used. Telephone focus groups have emerged recently. This technique has been developed for respondents who are difficult to recruit, like doctors. These focus groups use the conference calling facility to conduct the discussion.

Another emerging trend is in **two-way focus groups.**[16] This allows one target group to listen to and learn from a related group. In one application, physicians viewed a focus group of arthritis patients discussing the treatment they desired. A focus group of these physicians was then held to determine their reactions. A new focus-group television network entitled the Focus Vision Network may represent a third trend. Instead of flying from city to city, clients can view the focus groups in their offices. Live focus groups are broadcast by video transmission from a nationwide network of independently owned focus facilities. But the cost of this option is quite high.[17] Focus Vision also plans to unveil an international network of focus facilities. Thus, global focus groups will be possible in the near future.[18]

Projective Techniques

The central feature of all projective techniques is the presentation of an ambiguous, unstructured object, activity, or person that a respondent is asked to interpret and explain.[19] The more ambiguous the stimulus, the more respondents have to project themselves into the task, thereby revealing hidden feelings and opinions. These techniques often are used in conjunction with individual nondirective interviews.

Projective techniques are used when it is believed that respondents will not or cannot respond meaningfully to direct questions about (1) the reasons for certain behaviors or attitudes, or (2) what the act of buying, owning, or using a product or service means to them. People may be unaware of their own feelings and opinions, unwilling to make admissions that reflect badly on their self-image (in which case they will offer rationalizations or socially acceptable responses), or are too polite to be critical to an interviewer.

Originally, projective techniques were used in conjunction with clinical "motivation research" studies. One such study was done on Saran Wrap, a plastic food wrap, when it was first introduced. Because it was very clingy, it was effective in sealing food, but also quite difficult to handle. As a result, strong negative attitudes toward the product became evident. To clarify the reasons for this dislike, a series of in-depth, nondirective clinical interviews was conducted. During the fifties, there were many homemakers who disliked and even hated their role of keeping house and cooking. At that time, prior to the resurgence of the women's movement, there was no acceptable outlet among women for this dislike. It could not be verbalized openly, and women were too inhibited to admit it to themselves. The study concluded that many homemakers found an outlet for this dislike by transferring it to Saran Wrap. The frustrations they had with the use of the product came to symbolize their frustrations with their role and life-style. As a result of the study, the product was made less clingy, and nonkitchen uses were stressed.

The underlying assumption of the clinical approach is that people often cannot or will not verbalize their true motivations and attitudes. They may be embarrassed to reveal that they dislike cooking. Alternatively, they may have suppressed this dislike and not even be conscious of it.[20] They simply may believe that their dislike is caused by the plausible judgment that Saran Wrap is awkward to use. The difficulty with clinical research is that the true motivations are seldom clear. Indeed, two different clinical analysts working from different theoretical backgrounds may arrive at totally different interpretations. These problems have brought considerable disrepute to motivation research. At present, this type of research is relegated to a distinctly secondary role; however, projective techniques for asking indirect questions, when direct questions may not provide valid answers, are used more extensively. The following categories of projective techniques will be discussed: (1) word association, (2) completion tests, (3) picture interpretation, (4) third-person techniques, and (5) role playing.

Word Association. Here the respondent is asked to give the first word or phrase that comes to mind after the researcher presents a word or phrase. The list of items used as stimuli should include a random mix of such neutral items as "chair," "sky," and "water," interspersed with the items of interest, such as "shopping downtown," "vacationing in Greece," or "Hamburger Helper." An interviewer reads the word to the respondents and asks them to mention the first thing that comes to mind. The list is read in quick succession to avoid time for defense mechanisms to come into play. Responses are analyzed by calculating (1) the frequency with which any word is given as a response, (2) the amount of time that elapses before a response is given (3) the number of respondents who do not respond at all to a test word within a reasonable period of time.

The result of a word-association task often is hundreds of words and ideas. To evaluate quantitatively the relative importance of each, a representative set of the target segment can be asked to rate, on a five-point scale, how well the word fits the brand, from "fits extremely well" to "fits not well at all." It is also useful to conduct the same associative research on competitive brands. When such a scaling task was performed for McDonald's on words generated from a word-association task, the strongest associations were with the words Big Macs, Golden Arches, Ronald, Chicken McNugget, Egg McMuffin, everywhere, familiar, greasy, clean, food, cheap, kids, well-known, French fries, fast, hamburgers, and fat. In the same study, Jack-in-the-Box had much lower associations with the words everywhere, familiar, greasy, and clean, and much higher associations with tacos, variety, fun, and nutritious.[21]

The **word association** technique has also been particularly useful for obtaining reactions to potential brand names. Consumers associate a brand with (1) product attributes, (2) intangibles, (3) customer benefits, (4) relative price, (5) use/application, (6) user/customer, (7) celebrity/person, (8) life-style personality, (9) product class, (10) competitors, and (11) country/geographic area.[22] This technique is being used extensively to explore these associations. Word association has also been used for obtaining reactions to and opinions about advertising slogans. For example, Bell Telephone found that one theme for advertising, "The System is the Solution," triggered negative, big-brother-is-watching-you reactions among some people.

Completion Tests. The simplest test involves giving a respondent an incomplete and ambiguous sentence, which is to be completed with a phrase. Again, the respondent is encouraged to respond with the first thought that comes to mind. Sentences are usually in the third person ("The average person considers television ———————." "People drawing unemployment compensation are ———————."), but may refer directly to the object or activity ("Insurance of all kinds is ———————.") The **completion test** can be expanded readily to involve the completion of a story presented as an incomplete narrative or simply as a cartoon. In one such study, people were shown a crude picture of two women shopping in a supermarket, each pushing a shopping cart (Figure 7-1). Told that one woman is purchasing dry soup mix, they were asked to tell a story about her and to describe what she is saying to the second woman.

FIGURE 7-1
Two women shopping
Source: From "Dreams, Fairy Tales, Animals, and Cars," by Sidney J. Levy, in *Psychology and Marketing* 2, Summer 1985, pp. 67–81, copyright © 1985 by John Wiley & Sons, Inc.

They were also asked to tell what the second woman is like. Based on this, user profiles for the soup mix were developed.[23]

Picture Interpretation. The **picture interpretation** technique is based on the Thematic Apperception Test (TAT). The respondent is shown an ambiguous picture in the form of a line drawing, illustration, or photograph, and asked to describe it. This is a very flexible technique, for the pictures can be adapted readily to many kinds of marketing problems. An example of picture interpretation was a study that gave the respondents two scenes.[24] One involved a break after a daytime hike on a mountain, while the other was during a small evening barbecue with close friends. During the scene the beer served was either Coors or Lowenbrau. Respondents were asked to project themselves into the scene and indicate, on a five-point scale, the extent to which they would feel "warm," "friendly," "healthy," and "wholesome." The study was designed to test whether the advertising of Coors and Lowenbrau had established associations with their use-contexts—Coors with hiking, wholesomeness, and health, and Lowenbrau with a barbecue-type setting, friends, and warmth. The results showed that Coors was evaluated higher in the mountain setting and Lowenbrau in the barbecue setting, as expected, but that the other (word) associations were not sensitive (related) to the setting. For example, in the hiking context, Coors was higher on the "warm" and "friendly" dimensions, as well as on "healthy" and "wholesome."

Third-Person Techniques. By asking how friends, neighbors, or the average person would think or react in the situation, the researcher can observe, to some extent, the respondents projecting their own attitudes onto this **third person,** thus revealing more of their own true feelings. Magazines successfully use this technique to identify which articles to feature on the cover, to stimulate newsstand sales. Direct questioning as to the articles of greatest interest to the respondent tends to be confounded by socially desirable responses. For example, articles on complex issues of foreign affairs are rated highly interesting to the respondent during direct questioning, but are not thought to be of interest to the neighbors.

Another variant of this technique provides a shopping list or a description of a person's activities, and asks respondents to describe the person. The respondents' attitudes toward the activities or items on the list will be reflected in their descriptions of the person. Usually, two lists are prepared and presented to matched sets of respondents; these could be grocery shopping lists, in which all items are identical except that Nescafe instant coffee on the first list is replaced by Maxwell House (drip grind) coffee on the second list;[25] or the contents of a billfold, which differ only in the inclusion of a Bank Americard on one list. Differences in the descriptions attributed to the two lists can reveal the respondents' underlying attitudes toward the product or activity that is being studied.

Role Playing. Here a respondent assumes the role or behavior of another person, such as a salesperson in a store. This person then can be asked to try to sell a product to consumers, who raise objections. The method of coping with objections may reveal the respondents' attitudes, if they project themselves fully into the **role playing** without feeling uncomfortable or embarrassed.

Another technique with similar expressive objectives is the **role rehearsal** procedure used as part of a focus-group discussion. The participants in a focus group are encouraged, by offering them an incentive, to alter their behavior pattern in some extreme way. Abelson describes a study in which homemakers were asked to serve chicken to their families three times a week for a year, in return for $15.00 a week and an agreement to not tell the family about the arrangement.[26] The reaction of the participants to this offer, as they "rehearsed" the problems and objections they would likely encounter, gave useful insights into their own attitudes toward chicken. This technique is used toward the end of the focus-group session, and when the exercise is finished, respondents must be told that the offer was fictional.

Case Studies. A case study, in the research sense, is a comprehensive description and analysis of a single situation. The data for a case study usually are obtained from a series of lengthy, unstructured interviews with a number of people involved in the situation, perhaps combined with available secondary and internal data sources.

Case studies are very productive sources of research hypotheses. This approach was used by a food company to suggest the attributes that might characterize successful district sales managers. A successful and an unsuccessful manager from otherwise similar territories (that is, the territories had similar market structure, potential, and competitive situations) were studied closely for two weeks. They were interviewed, observed during sales calls and trips with their salespeople, and given a series of personality tests. The differences were used to develop a series of surveys that were administered to all the managers.

There are circumstances where a case study may be the only way to understand a complex situation. For example, the decision-making processes in large organizations may be imperfectly understood by a single participant. This problem makes it difficult to understand the sequence of decisions leading to, for example, the choice of a telephone service that customers use to call for reservations or information, or to place purchase orders. A telecommunications manager may be simply a technical consultant on the telephone system for the using company and not know how the system is used in the business. The functional managers in marketing or operations actually may make the decision to offer the service to customers but not know the intricacies of the switching network. To get a picture of the company's use of the service, all parties must be interviewed. Exhibit 7-3 makes a case for case studies.

Other Projective Techniques. Many other projective techniques have been developed and used in recent years. BBDO Worldwide has developed a trademarked technique called Photo Sort. Consumers express their feelings about brands through a specially developed photo deck showing pictures of different

EXHIBIT 7-3

A Case for Case Studies

Which would you rather bet your company's strategy on: what consumers say or what they do? Surveys, focus groups, and mall intercepts attempt to develop an understanding of customers' motivations by collecting reactions to researchers' questions. The major criticism of these methods is that what they gather are mere opinion statements that don't reveal actual behavior. Instead of gathering poorly considered opinion statements, the case-study approach builds insight into marketing behavior by pursuing—and verifying—the stories behind specific recent purchases in a given product category. It builds the full stories of how 50 supermarket shoppers selected their peanut butter last Tuesday, or how 25 companies replaced their PBX systems last month.

Key arguments for the case-study approach are

▶ Case studies uncover motivations through demonstrated actions, not through statements of opinions.
▶ They're conducted in the surroundings where a product is bought or used to achieve greater immediacy (and accuracy) of response.
▶ They use observation and documentation to stimulate questions and corroborate responses.
▶ They access multiple decision makers.
▶ They require the talents of "marketing detectives" rather than "census takers."

Source: "Study What People Do, Not What They Say," *Marketing News*, January 6, 1992, pp. 15, 32.

---

types of people, from business executives to college students. Respondents connect the people with the brands they think they use. Another photo-sort technique entitled the Pictured Aspirations Technique (PAT) has been created by Grey Advertising. This device attempts to uncover how a product fits into consumers' aspirations. Consumer drawings are used to unlock motivations or express perceptions. Researchers ask consumers to draw what they are feeling or how they perceive an object. An example of how consumer drawing was used to elicit the inner feelings of the consumer is given in Exhibit 7-4.

EXHIBIT 7-4

Consumer Drawings Reveal Frustration of Women

McCann-Erickson advertising agency wanted to find out why Raid roach spray outsold Combat insecticide disks in certain markets. In interviews, most users agreed that Combat is a better product, because it kills roaches without any effort on the user's part. So the agency asked the heaviest users of roach spray—low-income southern women—to draw pictures of their prey. The goal was to get at their underlying feelings about this dirty job.

All of the 100 women who participated in the agency's interviews portrayed roaches as men. "A lot of their feelings about the roach were very similar to the feelings that they had about the men in their lives," said Paula Drillman, executive vice-president at McCann-Erickson. Many of the women were in common-law relationships. They said that the roach, like the man in their life, "only comes around when he wants food." The act of spraying roaches and seeing them die was satisfying to this frustrated, powerless group. Setting out Combat disks may have been less trouble, but it just didn't give them the same feeling. "These women wanted control," Drillman said. "They used the spray because it allowed them to participate in the kill."

Source: Rebecca Piirto, *Beyond Mind Games*, Ithaca, New York: American Demographic Books, 1991, p. 52.

Limitations of Qualitative Methods

Most of the limitations of these methods stem from the susceptibility of the results to misuse, rather than their inherent shortcomings. There is a great temptation among many managers to accept small-sample exploratory results as sufficient for their purposes, because they are so compelling in their reality. The dangers in accepting the unstructured output of a focus group or from brief series of informal interviews are twofold. First, the results are not necessarily representative of what would be found in the population, and hence cannot be projected. Second, there is typically a great deal of ambiguity in the results. The flexibility that is the hallmark of these methods gives the moderator or interviewer great latitude in directing the questions; similarly, an analyst with a particular point of view may interpret the thoughts and comments selectively to support that view. In view of these pitfalls, these methods should be used strictly for insights into the reality of the consumer perspective and to suggest hypotheses for further research.

OBSERVATIONAL METHODS[27]

Observational methods are limited to providing information on current behavior. Too often, this limitation becomes an excuse for not considering observational methods; because many researchers don't get to use these methods, they may not appreciate their considerable benefits. Nevertheless, there are strong arguments for considering the observation of ongoing behavior as an integral part of the research design. Some of these are

▶ **Casual observation** is an important exploratory method. Managers continually monitor such variables as competitive prices and advertising activity, the length of lines of customers waiting for service, and the trade journals on executives' desks, to help to identify problems and opportunities.

▶ **Systematic observation** can be a useful supplement to other methods. During a personal interview, the interviewer has the opportunity to note the type, condition, and size of the residence, the respondent's race, and the type of neighborhood with regard to mixed types and qualities of homes and apartments. Seldom is this data source adequately exploited in surveys.

▶ Observation may be the least expensive and most accurate method of collecting purely behavioral data such as in-store traffic patterns or traffic passing a certain point on a highway system. Thus, people's adherence to pedestrian safety rules before and after a safety campaign can be measured most easily by counting the number of people who cross against the light or outside the sidewalks.

▶ Sometimes observation is the only research alternative. This is the case with physiological phenomena or with young children who cannot articulate their preferences or motives. Thus, the Fisher Price Company operates a nursery school in a residential area as a means of field testing potential new toys.

Direct Observation

This method is frequently used to obtain insights into research behavior and related issues, such as packaging effectiveness. One firm uses an observer, disguised as a shopper, to watch grocery store shoppers approach a product category; to measure how long they spend in the display area, and to see whether they have difficulty finding the product; and whether the package is read, and if so, whether the information seemed hard to find. This kind of **direct observation** can be highly structured, with a detailed recording form prepared in advance, or very unstructured. When making an unstructured observation, the observer may be sent to mingle with customers in the store and look for activities that suggest service problems. This is a highly subjective task, because the observer must select a few things to note and record in varying amounts of detail. This inevitably will draw subjective inferences from the observed behavior. For example, just what was meant by the frown on the face of the shopper waiting at a cash register?

Regardless of how the observation is structured, it is desirable that the respondents not be aware of the observer.[28] Once conscious of being observed, people may alter their behavior, but in very unpredictable ways. One-way mirrors, disguises, and cameras are some of the common solutions. Care should be taken, however, that there is not an invasion of privacy.

Contrived Observation

These methods can be thought of as behavioral projective tests; that is, the response of people placed in a **contrived observation** situation will reveal some aspects of their underlying beliefs, attitudes, and motives. Many direct-mail offers of new products or different kinds of books fall into this category, as do tests of variations in shelf space, product flavors, and display locations. The ethics of such offers can be very dubious, as in the example where a manufacturer decides to produce a product only after receiving an acceptable number of orders from a direct-mail advertisement.

A variant of this method uses buying teams, disguised as customers, to find out what happens during the normal interaction between the customer and the retailer, bank, service department, or complaint department. This method has provided useful insights into the discriminatory treatment of minorities by retailers, and the quality of public performance by employees of government agencies, banks, and airlines. One is hard pressed to think of other ways of finding out about the knowledgeability, helpfulness in meeting customers' needs, and efficiency of the staff. Clouding this picture are some serious, unresolved questions of ethics.

Content Analysis

Content analysis is an observation technique used to analyze written material into meaningful units, using carefully applied rules.[29] It is defined as the objective, systematic, and quantitative description of the manifest content of communication. It includes observation as well as analysis. The unit of analysis may be words, characters, themes, space and time measures, or topics. Analytical categories for classifying the units are developed, and the communication is broken down according to prescribed rules. Marketing research applications involves observing and analyzing the content or message of advertisements, newspaper articles, television and radio programs, and the like. For example, a study hypothesized that because of the growing number of elderly Americans, advertisers would use more elderly models in their promotions. After a content analysis of all the advertisements, the researchers found that the use of elderly people in advertisements has indeed increased.

Physical Trace Measures

This approach involves recording the natural "residue" of behavior. These **physical trace measures** are rarely used, because they require a good deal of ingenuity and usually yield a very gross measure. When they work, however, they can be very useful.[30] For instance, (1) the consumption of alcohol in a town without liquor stores has been estimated from the number of empty bottles in the garbage;[31] (2) an automobile dealer selected radio stations to carry his advertising by observing the most popular dial settings on the radios of cars brought in for servicing; (3) one magazine readership research method employs small glue spots in the gutter of each page spread of a magazine, so broken glue spots are used as evidence of exposure; and (4) a museum gauges the popularity of individual exhibits by measuring the rate of wear on the floor tiles in front of the exhibit and by the number of nose smudges on the glass of the case around the exhibit.

The **home-audit** approach to purchase panels (described in Chapter 6) is yet another type of physical trace measure. The auditor describes the inventory in several prespecified categories. This method is not very useful if used on a one-shot basis, for it then requires a very tenuous assumption that possession indicates purchase and usage. However, if the inventory is made over an extended period and supplemented with a record of cartons and wrappers, an indication of the rate of purchase is possible.

Humanistic Inquiry

Humanistic inquiry is a controversial research method that relies heavily on observation, and is now being used in marketing with increasing frequency.[32] The humanistic approach advocates immersing the researcher in the system under study rather than as in the traditional scientific method, in which the researcher is a dispassionate observer. Throughout the immersion process, the humanistic researcher maintains two diaries, or logs. One is a theory-construction diary that records in detail the thoughts, premises, hypotheses, and revisions in the researcher's thinking. The second set of notes the researcher maintains is the methodological log. Detailed and time-sequenced notes are kept on the investigative techniques used during the inquiry, with special attention to biases and distortions a given technique may have introduced. To access whether the interpretation is drawn in a logical and unprejudiced manner from the data gathered and the rationale employed, humanistic inquiry relies on the judgment of an outside auditor or auditors.

Behavior Recording Devices

Various **behavior recording devices** have been developed to overcome particular deficiencies in human observers. The most obvious example is the traffic counter, which operates continuously without getting tired, and consequently is cheaper and probably more accurate than humans. For the same reasons, as well as for unobtrusiveness, cameras may be used in place of human observers. Someone still has to interpret what is recorded on the film, but the options exist of sampling segments of the film, slowing the speed, or having another observer view it for an independent judgment.

Of the mechanical devices which do not require respondents' direct participation, the A.C. Nielsen "people meter" is best known. The **people meter** is attached to a television set to continually record to which channel the set is tuned. It also records who is watching. Arbitron recently developed a pocket people meter that is no larger than an electronic pager and can recognize the unique code that broadcasters embed in the soundtrack of radio or television programs.[33] Technological advances such as the Universal Product Code (UPC) have made a major impact on mechanical observation. The UPC system, together with optical scanners, allow for mechanical information collection regarding consumer purchases, by product category, brand, store type, price, and quantity.

Some types of observation are beyond human capabilities. All physiological reactions fall into this category. Therefore, devices are available to measure changes in the rate of perspiration as a guide to emotional response to stimuli (the psychogalvanometer), and changes in the size of the pupils of subjects' eyes, which are presumed to indicate the degree of interest in the stimulus being viewed (the pupilometer). These devices can be used only in laboratory environments, and often yield ambiguous results.

Experience with **eye movement recorders** has been more successful. This device records the experience of viewing pictures of advertisements, packages, signs, or shelf displays, at a rate of 30 readings per second. The recorded eye movements show when the subjects starts to view a picture, the order in which the elements of the image were examined and reexamined, and the amount of viewing time given each element. One application is for testing the visual impact of alternative package designs.

Voice pitch analysis examines changes in the relative vibration frequency of the human voice to measure emotion.[34] In voice analysis, the normal or baseline pitch of an individual's speaking voice is charted by engaging the subject in an unemotional conversation. The greater the deviation from the baseline, the greater is said to be the emotional intensity of the person's reaction to a stimulus. For example, voice pitch analysis has been used in package research, to predict consumer brand preference for dog food.[35]

Limitations of Observational Methods

The vast majority of research studies use some form of questionnaire. Observation methods, despite their many advantages, have one crucial limitation: they cannot observe motives, attitudes, or intentions, which sharply reduces their diagnostic usefulness. To be sure, these cognitive factors are manifested in the observed behavior, but so are many other confounding factors. For example, the Zippo Lighter Company seemingly has a valuable measure of advertising effectiveness in the volume of its lighters sent in for repair. Despite the mention of the free repair privilege in the advertising, it is questionable whether such a measure can unambiguously test for impact.

Observational methods suffer other limitations as well. They are often more costly and time consuming, and may yield biased results if there are sampling problems or if significant observer subjectivity is involved. However, these biases usually are very different in character from those that affect obtrusive, questionnaire methods. This is one of the underexploited strengths of observation methods: They help to increase our confidence in questionnaire measures if they yield similar results when used as a supplement.

Summary

Exploratory research is an essential step in the development of a successful research study. In essence, this kind of research is insurance that major elements of the problem or important competing hypotheses will not be overlooked. It further ensures that both the manager and the researcher will see the market through the consumer's eyes. Fortunately, research design is an iterative and not a sequential process, so major initial oversights are not necessarily irreversible. In particular, the exploratory technique of semistructured interviews should be reemployed later when the structured study is pretested. Properly handled, a pretest should provide opportunities for respondents to express their frustrations with the specific questions, as well as identify deficiencies in the scope of the questions.

In this chapter we also discussed observational methods. These are useful during the exploratory stage of the research design but are even more valuable as a data collection method. The advantages of observational methods will become even more apparent in Chapter 8 as we examine the errors that are inherent when an interviewer starts to interact with a respondent.

Questions and Problems

1. What are the significant differences between nondirective and semistructured individual interviews? In what circumstances would a nondirective interview be more useful than a semistructured interview?

2. You have conducted two group meetings on the subject of telephone answering devices. In each group there were seven prospective users of such devices, and in the two groups there were four users of telephone answering services. (These services use an operator to intercept calls and record messages.) When the client's new product development manager heard the tapes and read the transcripts of the two meetings, the first reaction was, "I knew all along that the features I wanted to add to our existing model would be winners, and these people are just as enthusiastic.

Let's not waste any more research effort on the question of which features are wanted.'' What do you say?

3. There have been a number of complaints in your city that minorities are discriminated against by local major appliance retailers (with respect to prices, trade-ins, sales assistance, and credit). How would you use the techniques described in this chapter to study this question?

4. A local consumer organization is interested in the differences in food prices among major stores in the area. How should it proceed in order to obtain meaningful comparisons?

5. Toothpaste manufacturers have found consistently that if they ask for detailed information on the frequency that people brush their teeth, and then make minimal assumptions as to the quantity of toothpaste used on each occasion, as well as spillage and failure to squeeze the tube empty, the result is a serious overstatement of toothpaste consumption. How would you explain this phenomenon? Would it be possible to design a study to overcome these problems and obtain more accurate estimates of consumption? Describe how such a study would be conducted.

6. The school board of St. Patrick's High School is concerned about the rise of student violence involving guns during the past two months. During an emergency meeting, Father Hennessy, the school's principal, insisted that steps be taken to return student behavior to its traditionally exemplary level. He suggested that this rise in the level of violence was for reasons beyond the experience of most of the school board members, and recommended that they needed to gather some background information on the situation in order to address the problem knowledgeably. The school board agreed with his proposal and decided to commission a market research study to question students on whether they carried guns and their underlying motivation for doing so. The research firm, Church and Associates, has decided to use focus groups or individual in-depth interviews to obtain the required information.

   a. Which of the above-mentioned techniques is suitable for this purpose? Give reasons.

   b. Church and Associates has recommended separate focus-group discussions involving the faculty. How can the moderator effectively encourage all the participants to discuss their feelings on the topic?

   c. What possible questions could be asked in an in-depth interview?

7. What difficulties might be encountered when conducting a qualitative interview in an international context?

8. When would you recommend observational methods? Why?

9. How can a pretest add to the quality of a marketing research study?

End Notes

1. Fred N. Kerlinger, *Foundations of Behavioral Research,* 3rd ed. (New York: Holt, Rinehart and Winston), 1986.

2. "Beckman Gets Customers to Design its Products," *Business Week,* August 17, 1974, 52.

3. David Kiley, "At long Last, Detroit Gives Consumers the Right of Way," *Adweek,* June 6, 1988, 26–27.

4. Johny K. Johansson and Ikujiro Nonaka, "Market Research the Japanese Way," *Harvard Business Review,* May–June 1987, 16–22.

5. Jeffrey F. Durgee, "Depth-Interview Techniques for Creative Advertising," *Journal of Advertising Research,* January 1986, 29–37.

6. Michael Quinn Patton, *Qualitative Evaluation and Research Methods,* (Newbury Park: Sage), 1990. For additional discussion of cross-cultural research and evaluation, see Patton, Michael Quinn, *Culture and Evaluation: New Directions for Program Evaluation,* (San Francisco: Jossey-Bass), 1985; Lonner, Walter J. and John W. Berry, *Field Methods in Cross Cultural Research* (Newbury Park, California. Sage Publications), 1986.

7. Martin Lautman, "Focus Groups: Theory and Method," *Advances in Consumer Research 9, October 1981,* 54.

8. See, Thomas Greenbaum, "Focus Groups vs. One-on-Ones. The Controversy Continues, *Marketing News,* September 2, 1991, 16.

9. Peter Tuckel, Elaine Leppo, and Barbara Kaplan, "Focus Groups Under Scrutiny: Why People Go and How it Affects Their Attitudes Towards Participation," *Marketing Research,* 12 June 1992.

10. For a comprehensive listing of the providers of focus group facilities, see, "1992 Marketing News Directory of Focus Group Facilities and Moderators," *Marketing News,* January 6, 1992.

11. David W. Stewart and Prem N. Shamdasani, *Focus Groups: Theory and Practice* (Newbury Park, California: Sage Publications), 1990.

12. Nelson E. James and Nancy Frontczak, "How Acquaintanceship and Analyst Can Influence Focus Group Results," *Journal of Advertising, 17* (1988):41–48.

13. Wendy Hayward and John Rose, "We'll Meet Again . . . Repeat Attendance at Group Discussions—Does it Matter?" *Journal of Advertising Research Society,* July 1990, 377–407.

14. For more discussion, see Edward F. Fern, "The Use of Focus Groups for Idea Generation: The Effects of Group Size, Acquaintanceship, and Moderator on Response Quantity and Quality," *Journal of Marketing Research,* 19 February 1982, 1–13.

15. Naomi R. Henderson, "Trained Moderators Boost the Value of Qualitative Research," *Marketing Research,* 20, June 1992.

16. Michael Silverstein, "Two Way Focus Groups Can Provide Startling Information," *Marketing News, January 4, 1988, 31.*

17. "Network to Broadcast Live Focus Groups," *Marketing News,* September 3, 1990, 10, 47.

18. Cindy Miller, "Anybody Ever Hear of Global Focus Groups?" *Marketing News,* May 27, 1991, 14.

19. Harold H. Kassarjian, "Projective Methods," in Robert Ferber, ed., *Handbook of Marketing Research* (New York: McGraw-Hill), 1974, 3–87; Sidney J. Levy, "Dreams, Fairy Tales, Animals, and Cars," *Psychology and Marketing,* 2, Summer 1985, 67–82.

20. Robert K. Schnee, "Quality Research: Going Beyond The Obvious," *Journal of Advertising Research,* 28, February–March 1988.

21. David A. Aaker, *Managing Brand Equity: Capitalizing on the Value of a Brand Name* (New York: Macmillan), 1991.

22. Ibid.

23. Sidney J. Levy, "Dreams, Fairy Tales, Animals, and Cars," *Psychology and Marketing,* 2, Summer 1985, 67–81.

24. David A. Aaker and Douglas M. Stayman, "Implementing the Concept of Transformational Advertising," *Psychology and Marketing,* May–June 1992, 237–253.

25. This was the design of the classic study by Mason Haire, "Projective Techniques in Marketing Research" *Journal of Marketing,* 14, 1950, 649–656. However, recent validation studies have found that differences in the two descriptions also are influenced by the relationship of the two test products to the items in the shopping list, so the interpretation is anything but straightforward. See also James C. Andersen, "The Validity of Haire's Shopping List Projective Technique," *Journal of Marketing,* 15, November 1978, 644–649.

26. Herbert Abelson, "A Role Rehearsal Technique for Exploratory Research," *Public Opinion Quarterly,* 30, 1966, 302–305.

27. The analysis of secondary records, as discussed in the previous chapter, is an observational method. In this chapter, however we are restricting ourselves to the observation of ongoing behavior.

28. Cliff Scott, David M. Klien, and Jennings Bryant, "Consumer Response to Humor in Advertising: A Series of Field Studies Using Behavioral Observation," *Journal of Consumer Research,* 16, March 1990, 498–501.

29. An excellent summary article of content analysis is Richard Kolbe and Melissa Burnett, "Content

Analysis Research: An Examination of Applications with Directives for Improving Research Reliability and Objectivity," *Journal of Consumer Research*, September 1991, 243–250. Other examples of content analysis are Mary Zimmer and Linda Golden, "Impressions of Retail Stores: A Content Analysis of Consumer Images," *Journal of Retailing*, Fall 1988, 265–293; and Terence Shimp, Joel Urbany, and Sakeh Camlin, "The Use of Framing and Characterization for Magazine Advertising of Mass Marketed Products," *Journal of Advertising*, January 1988, 23–30.

30. For a fuller discussion see, Sechrest Lee, *New Directions for Methodology of Behavior Science: Unobtrusive Measurement Today* (San Francisco: Jossey Bass), 1979.

31. Joseph A. Cote, James McCullough, and Michael Reilly, "Effects of Unexpected Situations on Behavior-Intention Differences: A Garbology Analysis," *Journal of Consumer Research*, 12, September 1985, 188–194.

32. Elizabeth Hirschman, "Humanistic Inquiry in Marketing Research: Philosophy, Method and Criteria," *Journal of Marketing Research*, August 1986, 237–249. For more detailed information, see Yvonna Lincoln and Edward Guba, *Naturalistic Inquiry* (Beverly Hills, California: Sage Publications), 1985.

33. "Arbitron to Develop 'pocket people meter'," *Marketing News*, January 4, 1993.

34. Nancy Nighswonger and Claude Martin, Jr., "On Voice Analysis in Marketing Research," *Journal of Marketing Research*, August 1981, 350–355.

35. Glen Brickman, "Uses of Voice Pitch Analysis," *Journal of Advertising Research*, April 1980, 69–73.

CASE 7-1
Mountain Bell
Telephone Company[1]

Jim Martin, marketing research manager for Mountain Bell, studied the final research design for the hospital administrator study that had been prepared by Industrial Surveys, a marketing research firm in Denver. He realized that he needed to formulate some recommendations with respect to some very specific questions. Should individual personal interviewers be used as suggested by Industrial Surveys, or should a series of one to six focus-group interviews be used instead? Was the questionnaire satisfactory? Should individual questions be added, deleted, or modified? Should the flow be changed? Exactly who should be sampled, and what should the sample size be?

Research Setting

About 20 field salespeople at Mountain Bell Telephone Company were involved in sales of communication equipment and services to the health-care industry. Because of job rotations and reorganizations, few salespeople had been in their present positions for more than three years. They were expected to determine customer needs and problems and to design responsive communication systems. In addition, there was a health care industry manager, Andy Smyth, who had overall responsibility for the health care industry mar-

keting effort at Mountain Bell, although none of the sales personnel reported directly to him. He prepared a marketing action plan and worked to see that it was implemented. The marketing action plan covered

Sales objective by product and by segment
Sales training programs
Development of sales support materials and information

Andy Smyth was appointed only recently to his current position, although he had worked in the health care market for several years while with the Eastern Bell Telephone Company. Thus, he did have some firsthand knowledge of customer concerns. Further, there was an AT&T marketing plan for the health care industry which included an industry profile; however, it lacked the detailed information needed, especially at the local level. It also lacked current information as to competitive products and strategies.

Mountain Bell had long been a quasimonopoly, but during the past decade had seen vigorous aggressive competitors appear. Andy Smyth thought it imperative to learn exactly what competitive products were making inroads, in what applications, and the basis of their competitive appeal. He also felt the need for some objective in-depth information as to how major Mountain Bell customers in the health care industry perceived the company's product line and its salesforce. He hypothesized that the salesforce was generally weak in terms of understanding customers'

[1] This case was prepared by D. Aaker and J. Seydel as a basis for class discussion.

communication needs and problems. He felt that such information would be particularly helpful in understanding customers concerns and in developing an effective sales training program. He hoped that the end result would be to make the salesforce more customer oriented and to increase revenues from the health care market.

While at Eastern Bell, Andy Smyth had initiated a mail survey of hospital administrators that had been of some value. Several months before, he had approached Jim Martin with the idea of doing something similar at Mountain. Jim's reaction was that the questionnaire previously used was too general (i.e., one question was: What basic issues confront the health care area?) or too difficult to answer (How much do you budget monthly for telecommunications equipment or service? 0–$1000; $1000—$2000; etc.) Further, he felt that indepth individual interviews would be more fruitful. Thus, he contacted Industrial Surveys, which, after considerable discussion with both Jim and Andy, created the research design. They were guided by the following research objectives:

1. What are the awareness and usage levels of competitive telecommunications products by the hospital?
2. What is the perception of Mountain Bell's salesforce capabilities as compared to other telecommunications vendors?
3. What is the decision-making process as it pertains to the identification, selection, and purchase of telecommunications equipment?
4. What concerns/problems impact most directly upon the hospital's (department's) daily operations?
5. What are the perceived deficiencies and suggestions for improvement of work/information flow?

Research Design

Research interviews will be conducted in seven Denver area hospitals with the hospital administrator and, where possible, with the financial officer and the telecommunications manager. A total of 14 interviews are planned. Interviews will be held by appointment, and each respondent will be probed relative to those questins that are most appropriate for his/her position and relevant to the study's overall objectives. The cost will be from $6500 to $8500, depending on the time involved to complete the interviews. The questionnaire to be used follows:

A. Awareness and Usage of Competitive Telecommunications Equipment
   1. What departments presently use non-Bell voice communications equipment (paging, intercom, message recording, etc.)? What were the main considerations in selecting this equipment?
   2. What departments use non-Bell data terminals (CRTS)? What are the major functions/activities that this equipment is used for? What were the main considerations in selecting this equipment?
   3. How do you view the capabilities of Bell System voice-communications equipment to meet your operations needs?
   4. How do you view the capabilities of Bell System data terminals to meet your records- and information-retrieval needs?
   5. What do you feel are Mountain Bell's main strengths and/or weaknesses in meeting your hospital's overall telecommunications needs?

B. Perceptions of the Mountain Bell Salesforce
   1. What should a telecommunications specialist know about the hospital industry in order to adequately address your voice-communications and data-processing needs?
   2. Have you ever worked with any Mountain Bell marketing people in terms of your communications needs? If so, how knowledgeable do you perceive the Mountain Bell salesforce to be with respect to both the health care industry and their telecommunications equipment? How do they compare to non-Bell vendors of such products?

C. Purchasing Decision
   1. What is the standard procedure for selecting and authorizing a telecommunications purchase? Is this based primarily on the dollar amount involved or type of technology?
   2. Who has the greatest input on the telecommunications decision (department manager, administrator, physicians, and so on)?
   3. What are the most important considerations in evaluating a potential telecommunications purchase (equipment price, cost-savings potential, available budget, and so on)?
   4. What supplier information is most important in facilitating the purchasing decision? How effective has the Mountain Bell salesforce been in providing such information?

D. Specification of the most important problems or concerns relating to effective hospital management.
   1. What are the most important problems or concerns confronting you in managing the hospital?
   2. What type of management data are required in order to deal effectively with these problems or concerns?
   3. How are these data presently recorded, updated, and transmitted? How effective would you say your current Information Retrieval System is?
   4. Do you have any dollar amount specifically budgeted for data or telecommunications improvements in 1979–1980? What specific information

or communication functions are you most interested in upgrading?

E. Achieving maximum utilization of hospital facilities.

1. Do you experience any problems in obtaining accurate, up-to-date information on the availability of bed space, operating rooms, or lab services?

2. Do you see _____ hospital as competing with other area hospitals or HMOs in the provision of health care services? If so, with which hospitals? Do you have a marketing plan to deal with this situation?

F. Efficient Use of Labor Resources

1. How variable is the typical daily departmental workload, and what factors most influence this variance?

2. How do you document and forecast workload fluctuations? Is this done for each hospital department?

3. To what extent (if any) do you use outside consulting firms to work with you in improving the delivery of hospital services?

G. Reimbursement and Cash Flow

1. Which insurer is the primary provider of funds? How is reimbursement made by the major insurers?

2. What information do you need to verify the existence and type of insurance coverage when an individual is being processed for admission or outpatient hospital services? What, if any, problems are experienced in the verification and communication of insurance information?

CASE 7-2
U.S. Department of Energy (A)

Judy Ryerson, the head of the windmill power section of the U.S. Department of Energy, was considering what types of qualitative marketing research would be useful to address a host of research questions.

The U.S. Department of Energy was formed to deal with the national energy problem. One of its goals was to encourage the development of a variety of energy sources, including the use of windmill power. One difficulty was that almost nothing was known about the current use of windmill power and the public reaction to it as a power source. Before developing windmill power programs, it seemed prudent to address several research questions to obtain background information and to formulate testable hypotheses.

Current Use of Windmills in the United States

How many power generating windmills are there? Who owns them? What power generating performance is being achieved? What designs are being used? What applications are involved?

Public Reaction

What are the public attitudes to various power sources? How much premium would the public be willing to pay for windmill power sources, both in terms of money and in terms of "visual pollution?" What is the relative acceptance of six different windmill designs ranging from the "old Dutch windmill" design to an eggbeater design?

Assignment

Design one or more qualitative research designs to address the search questions and to develop hypotheses for future testing. If focus-group interviews are considered, provide a set of questions to guide the moderator.

8

INFORMATION FROM RESPONDENTS: ISSUES IN DATA COLLECTION

Learning Objectives

▶ Briefly mention the different kinds of information that are collected through surveys.

▶ Introduce the various errors that occur while conducting a survey.

▶ Briefly mention the various factors that influence the selection of the various survey methods.

▶ Discuss the ethical issues involved in collecting data from respondents.

The survey is the overwhelming choice of researchers for collecting primary data. The methods already discussed—qualitative and observational research and secondary data analysis—are more likely to be used to improve or supplement the survey method than to take its place.

The principal advantage of a survey is that it can collect a great deal of data about an individual respondent at one time. It is perhaps only stating the obvious to say that for most kinds of data the respondent is the only, or the best, source. The second advantage of this method is versatility; surveys can be employed in virtually any setting—whether among teenagers, old-age pensioners, or sailboat owners—and are adaptable to research objectives that necessitate either a descriptive or causal design.

These advantages are not easy to achieve. Effective implementation requires considerable judgment in the choice of a survey method, whether a personal or telephone interview or a mail questionnaire. There also are some distinct disadvantages to surveys that stem from the social interaction of interviewer and respondent. Indeed, a survey cannot be developed or properly interpreted without a knowledge of the errors that may intrude into the data during this interaction. These and other related issues are discussed in this chapter as a prelude to the analysis of the methods of collecting survey data, the principal focus of the next chapter.

INFORMATION FROM SURVEYS

Surveys can be designed to capture a wide variety of information on many diverse topics and subjects. Attitudes are very often the subject of surveys. Information on attitudes frequently is obtained in the form of consumers' awareness, knowledge, or perceptions about the product, its features, availability, and pricing, and various aspects of the marketing effort. Surveys can also capture the respondent's overall assessment and the extent to which the object is rated as favorable or unfavorable. Information can be obtained about a person's image of something. Each person tends to see things a little differently from others, so no two images are apt to be exactly alike. Decisions are also the topic of research but the focus is not so much on the results of decisions in the past but more on the *process* by which respondents evaluate things. Those seeking survey information are often keenly interested in those aspects of the decision process that people use to choose actions. Marketers are often concerned with *why* people behave as they do. Most behavior is directed toward satisfying one or more human needs. Thus, the answer to the question of "why" is often obtained by measuring the relationship between actions and needs, desires, preferences, motives, and goals.

Measuring behavior usually involves four related concepts: what the respondents did or did not do; where the action takes place; the timing, including past, present, and future; and the frequency or persistence of behavior. In other words, it often means assessing *what, where, when,* and *how often.* Surveys can also be conducted to determine respondents' life-styles. Groupings of the population by life-style can be used to identify an audience, constituency, target market, or other collections of interest to the sponsor. Social contact and interaction are often the focus of survey research or bear heavily on other issues relevant to the survey. So the family setting, memberships, social contacts, reference groups, and communications of respondents frequently are measured or assessed within the survey research process. Demographic factors often obtained through surveys include such variables as age, sex, marital status, education, employment, and income, among others. Personality reflects consistent, enduring patterns of behavior and it is more deeply rooted than life-style. Personality can be measured using rating methods, situational tests, projective techniques, and inventory schemes. Motivation and knowledge are also frequently measured using surveys.

SOURCES OF SURVEY ERROR

The process by which respondents are questioned appears deceptively simple. The reality, however, is closer to Oppenheim's opinion that ". . . questioning people is more like trying to catch a particularly elusive fish, by hopefully casting different kinds of bait at different depths, without knowing what is going on beneath the surface."[1]

The problem of getting meaningful results from the interview process stems from the need to satisfy reasonably the following conditions:

▶ Population has been defined correctly.

▶ Sample is representative of the population.

▶ Respondents selected to be interviewed are available and willing to cooperate.

▶ Respondents understand the questions.

▶ Respondents have the knowledge, opinions, attitudes, or facts required.

▶ Respondents are willing and able to respond.

▶ Interviewer correctly understands and records the responses.

These conditions often are not satisfied because of interviewer error, ambiguous interpretation of both questions and answers, and errors in formulating responses. These types of errors are shown in Figure 8-1 as filters or screens that distort both the question and response. Ambiguity, usually a consequence of poor question wording, is covered in Chapter 11. In this section, we will deal with the factors that influence prospective respondents' willingness to cooperate and provide accurate answers to whatever questions are asked.

Nonresponse Errors Due to Refusals

Refusal rates are highly variable. They can be as low as three to five percent of those contacted for a short interview on a street corner or at a bus stop, to 30 or 35 percent and higher for lengthy personal and telephone interviews or mail questionnaires, which are of little interest to most subjects. High refusal rates are a major source of error, for those who refuse to be interviewed are likely to be very different from those who cooperate. People cooperate for a number of reasons, such as trying to be friendly and helpful, to interact socially when they are lonely or bored, to know more about the subject, or to experience something novel. Many people also cooperate when they expect a reward or a direct benefit.

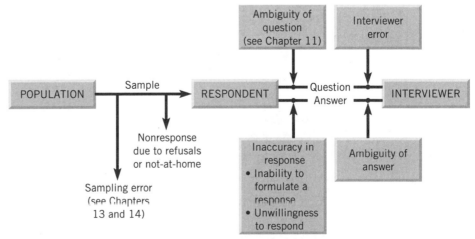

FIGURE 8-1
Sources of error in information from respondents

People refuse to answer survey questions for a number of reasons. Fear is the main reason for refusal.[2] Other reasons might be that some may think of surveys as an invasion of privacy; the subject matter may be sensitive (such as death, sexual habits, etc.); or there may be hostility toward the sponsor.[3] Refusal rates can be reduced if the reason for refusals is related to a phenotypic source. A **phenotypic source** of refusals refers to characteristics of the data collection procedure (which questions are asked, how they are asked, the length of the interview, and so on). These elements vary from study to study and can be controlled to a certain extent. But if the source of refusals is genotypic, then it is difficult to control for them. A **genotypic source** refers to the indigenous characteristics of respondents (such as age, sex, and occupation). One avenue to reducing this type of refusal is to try to interview respondents in ways that are less intrusive in their lives.[4] Other methods, like multiple callbacks (mailings), guaranty of anonymity, increasing surveyor credibility, incentives for completed responses, randomized responses, and shortening the survey through matrix designs, can increase response rates.[5] An example of the effect of nonresponse errors is given in Exhibit 8-1.

Inaccuracy in Response

Respondents may be unable to give any response, or *unwilling* to give a complete and accurate response.

Inability to Respond. Respondents may not know the answer to a question because of ignorance or forgetting, or may be unable to articulate it. All three problems create further errors when respondents contrive an answer because they don't want to admit they don't know the answer or because they want to please the interviewer. Respondents are likely to be ignorant when asked some questions. Some homemakers, for example, may not be aware of the financial status of the family (such as insurance, investments, and benefits).

EXHIBIT 8-1

Nonresponse Bias Leads to Wrong Prediction in Presidential Opinion Poll

An example of significant bias as a result of low response to mail questionnaires is the often-cited *Literary Digest* presidential poll in 1936. The two candidates were Alfred E. Landon of the Republican Party and Franklin D. Roosevelt of the Democratic Party. The *Literary Digest* conducted a mail survey and predicted a victory for Landon in the election. But Roosevelt won by a big margin in a landslide victory for the Democrats. The story is told that the sample was drawn from telephone books, and the Republicans (Landon's party) were more likely to have telephones in 1936. Hence, this biased the sample toward Republicans. In addition, the failure of the poll to predict correctly was attributed to nonresponse; only a minority of those asked to return questionnaires did so. As is typical of mail surveys, those who returned the questionnaire wanted the underdog Landon to win. The Landon supporters were particularly likely to want to express their views, whereas the Roosevelt supporters, since they were the majority, did not bother to respond to the survey.

Source: Bryson M., "The Literary Digest Poll: Making of a Statistical Myth," *American Statistician*, November 1976, 184–185.

The likelihood of forgetting an episode such as a visit to a doctor, a purchase, and so forth, depends on both the recency of the occurrence and the importance of the event, as well as on what else was happening at the same time.[6] Ideally, questions should be asked only about recent behavior. If retrospective questions are required, the accuracy of recall can be improved by questioning the respondent about the context in which an event occurred. Memories may be sharpened by aided-recall techniques. These attempt to stimulate recall with specific cues, such as copies of magazines, pictures, or lists. It is always preferable to ask about specific occasions of an activity.

It is essential to keep in mind that most respondents want to be cooperative; when in doubt they prefer to give too much rather than too little information. Memory distortions compound this source of error by **telescoping** time, so that an event is remembered as occurring more recently than it actually did.[7] Another common memory error is **averaging,** whereby something is reported as more like the usual, the expected, or the norm. This is a particular problem for researchers trying to study the exceptions to the ordinary. General Foods' researchers interested in the homemaker's variations in evening meals found it very difficult to overcome the respondent's tendency to say "It was Sunday, so it must have been roast beef." In studies of evening meals at General Foods, researchers reduced the averaging problem by asking respondents a series of questions that helped them to reconstruct the event. A third memory pitfall is called **omission,** where a respondent leaves out an event or some aspect of an experience. Respondent fatigue and poor interviewer rapport are demotivating, and result in increased omitting. The use of graphic aids to recall or recognition measures will help to reduce omission.

Finally, respondents may be unable to respond because they cannot formulate an adequate answer. This is especially true of direct questions about motivations. Many choice decisions are made without conscious consideration of the reasons. So when people are asked why they responded to a charitable appeal, bought a particular brand of analgesics, or watched a certain television program, the reasons they give are likely to be incomplete and superficial. An alternative is to use indirect methods such as the projective techniques described in Chapter 7.

One technique that is being used to judge the probability of response inaccuracies is to measure the time lag between the time a question is asked and when it is answered. Studies show that a too-slow response may mean the question is too difficult to understand, whereas an immediate response probably means that it was either misunderstood or hurriedly answered.

Unwillingness to Respond Accurately. During the interview a number of **response bias** factors may come into play to subvert the positive motivations that were present when the respondent agreed to participate. Questionnaires that are lengthy and boring are especially vulnerable to these biases.

1. *Concern About Invasion of Privacy.* Although most respondents don't regard a survey, per se, as an invasion of privacy, their tolerance may not extend to detailed personal questions. As many as 20 percent of the respondents

in a telephone or personal interview survey may refuse to answer an income question, and others may distort their answer. To some extent, assurances of confidentiality and full explanations of the need for the data will reduce this problem.

2. *Time Pressure and Fatigue.* As a lengthy interview proceeds, the accuracy of responses is bound to decline. Those respondents who initially were reluctant to participate because they were busy become anxious about the time that seems to be required. Not surprisingly, they may decide that giving abrupt answers and avoiding requests for clarification are the best ways to terminate the interview quickly. Even those who willingly and fully respond to all questions will become fatigued eventually if the interview is too long. The resulting bias is most likely random, but is sometimes in a consistent direction if the respondent decides to retaliate by grouping all answers about some point on a scale.[8]

3. *Prestige Seeking and Social Desirability Response Bias.* There is mounting evidence that respondents will distort their answers in ways that (they believe) will enhance their prestige in the eyes of the interviewer and will not put them at variance with their perception of the prevailing norms of society. Consequently, questions that have implications for prestige—such as income, education, time spent reading newspapers, tastes in food, or even place of residence—may be biased subtly in ways that reflect well on the respondent.

4. *Courtesy Bias.* There is a general tendency to limit answers to pleasantries that will cause little discomfort or embarrassment to the interviewer, or to avoid appearing uncooperative. We have seen already how this bias can inflate responses to aided-recall questions. It also is encountered in concept-testing situations when a respondent gives a "courtesy endorsement" to the description of a new idea, even though he or she may have little interest in the idea.[9]

5. *Uninformed Response Error.* Simply asking someone a question implies that the interviewer expects the respondent to have an answer. This expectation, plus a desire to appear cooperative, may induce respondents to answer a question despite a complete lack of knowledge about the topic. When a sample of the general public was asked a question about a fictitious organization, the National Bureau of Consumer Complaints, an astonishing 75 percent of those who returned the questionnaire expressed an opinion about the effectiveness of the organization in obtaining relief for consumers.[10]

6. *Response Style.* Evaluative questions requiring a good–bad, positive–negative judgment are afflicted by systematic tendencies of certain respondents to select particular **styles** or **categories of response** regardless of the content of the question. For example, there is an acquiescence response set, which is the tendency to favor affirmative over negative responses. This is different from "yea-saying," which is a tendency to give exaggerated responses; that is, good becomes very good and bad becomes very bad. For example, Wells found that yea-sayers consistently gave higher ratings to favorably evaluated advertisements and were more likely to exaggerate self-reports of product purchases.[11]

Interviewer Error

Interviewers vary enormously in personal characteristics, amount of previous experience, style of interviewing, and motivation to do a thorough job. The differences among interviewers also mean a great deal of variability in the way interviews are conducted.

Respondent's Impression of the Interviewer. For most respondents a personal interview is a sufficiently novel experience that the interviewer becomes a major source of clues to appropriate behavior. The interviewer must be seen as a person who is capable of understanding the respondent's point of view, and of doing so without rejecting his or her opinion. This kind of rapport is most likely to be established quickly when respondent and interviewer share basic characteristics such as sex, age, race, and social class.

The attitudes the interviewer reveals to the respondent during the interview can greatly affect their level of interest and willingness to answer openly. Especially important is a sense of assurance and ease with the task. Communication will be inhibited further if the interviewer appears flippant or bored, constantly interrupts the person when speaking, or is too immersed in note-taking to look up.[12] Obviously, proper selection of interviewers, coupled with good training, can reduce many of these problems.

Questioning, Probing, and Recording. The way an interviewer asks a question and follows up by probing for further details and clarification will be colored by (1) the interviewer's own feelings about the "appropriate" answer to the questions and (2) expectations about the kind of answers that "fit" the respondent. For example, when interviewing a person with limited education, the interviewer might shift unconsciously from a question worded, "Have any of your children attended college?" to "I don't imagine any of your children have gone to college. Have they?" In one study it was found that one interviewer obtained 8 percent while another interviewer obtained 92 percent choosing the same option.[13]

Perhaps the most common interviewer error is insufficient probing. The respondents may not be expected to have much to say about the subject or may have given an answer that the interviewer thinks is "right."

Fraud and Deceit. Modest interviewer compensation and the problem of monitoring the activities of personal interviewers out in the field, or telephone interviewers calling from their home, provide ample incentive for cheating. This may be as serious as outright fabrication of an entire interview or judicious filling in of certain information that was not obtained during the interview. Because it is such a serious potential source of error, most commercial research firms validate 10 to 15 percent of the completed interviews. This entails interviewing a sample of those who were reported to have been interviewed, to verify that an interview actually took place and that the questions were asked.

Improving Interviewer Quality. New approaches to improving data collection quality are being constantly tried in order to overcome some of the interview problems that have been mentioned. Field briefings can be improved by prepar-

"That's the worst set of opinions I've heard in my entire life."

Drawing by Weber, © 1973, The New Yorker Magazine, Inc.

ing videotaped briefings to show to interviewers, to ensure a consistent message to all interviewers prior to data collection. Actual interviews can be recorded by camera at a particular site, and all interviewers can be rotated through that site to check on the quality of interviewing. Finally, if electronic quality checks are too expensive, research firms can hire independent field personnel to check quality.

The array of problems and sources of error, summarized in Table 8-1, have the greatest effect on the personal interview method. The best solution by far is to minimize the problems by proper recruiting, selecting, training, motivation, and control of interviewers. Yet the potential for poor-quality interviews is enormous.[14]

While other methods of data collection are less prone to interview error, they have offsetting problems, as we will see in Chapter 9.

METHODS OF DATA COLLECTION

The choice of a data collection method is a critical point in the research process. The decision is seldom easy, for there are many factors to be considered and many variations of the three basic **survey methods**: (1) personal interview, (2) telephone interview, and (3) mail survey. In this section, we will look briefly

TABLE 8-1
Sources of Error in Interview Surveys

1. *Nonresponse errors due to refusals.*
   a. Fear of the consequences of participation.
   b. Resentment of an invasion of privacy.
   c. Anxiety about the subject.

2. *Inaccuracy in responses.*
   a. Inability to give a response.
      i. Ignorance of the answer.
      ii. Memory problems.
      iii. Problems in formulating an answer.
   b. Unwillingness to respond accurately.
      i. Concern about invasion of privacy.
      ii. Time pressure and fatigue.
      iii. Desire to enhance prestige.
      iv. Desire to appear cooperative.
      v. Biased response style.

3. *Errors caused by interviewers.*
   a. Provision of clues to "appropriate" responses.
   b. Inadequate questioning and probing.
   c. Fraud and deceit.

at the different methods of data collection and the factors affecting the choice of method.

Because each research problem will have a different ranking of importance, and no data collection method is consistently superior, few generalizations can be made. Much depends on the researcher's skill in adapting the method to the circumstances. Overall, however, the telephone and the mail survey methods are the dominant methods for conducting surveys. In the 1990 Walker Industry Image Study, it was found that 69 percent of the respondents had participated in mail surveys, 68 percent had participated in telephone surveys, 32 percent in mall intercept surveys, and 15 percent in door-to-door interviews. The characteristics of each survey method are explained briefly in Table 8-2.

FACTORS AFFECTING THE CHOICE OF A SURVEY METHOD

One of the most important decisions a researcher must make is the way in which the data will be collected. The decision to choose among the various survey methods already discussed is affected by a number of factors.[15] Some of them are described in the paragraphs that follow.

Sampling

The way a researcher plans to draw a sample is related to the best way to collect the data. Certain kinds of sampling approaches make it easier or more difficult to use one or another data collection strategy. If one is sampling from

TABLE 8-2
Basic Survey Methods and Their Characteristics

Survey Method	Characteristics
Personal Interviews	The interviewer interviews the respondent in person. There is direct contact between the interviewer and the respondent. The environment (mood of the respondent and the interviewer, the time and place of the interview, etc.) affects the data collection process to a large extent. Costliest, and the most time-consuming form of data collection.
Telephone Interviews	The interviewer interviews the respondent over the telephone. The interviewer has only verbal contact with the respondent. The environment plays a relatively minor role in the data-collection process. Data-collection cost is in between that of a personal interview and a mail survey.
Mail Surveys	The questionnaire is administered through the mail. The interviewer has no contact with the respondent. The environment plays no role in the data-collection process. The least expensive form of data collection.

a list, the information on the list matters. Obviously, if a list lacks either good mailing addresses or good telephone numbers, trying to collect data either by mail or phone is complicated. Random-digit dialing has improved the potential of telephone data collection strategies by giving every household with a telephone a chance to be selected.

Of course, it is possible to use random-digit dialing strategies, which are explained in Chapter 9, merely to sample and make initial contact with households, followed by collecting data using some other mode. Once a household has been reached, one can ask for an address, to permit either a mail questionnaire to be sent or an interviewer to visit. Such designs are particularly useful when one is looking for a rare population, because both the sampling and the screening via telephone are relatively less expensive than doing the same task with a personal interviewer.

Another sampling issue to consider is designating a respondent. If the sample frame is a list of individuals, any procedure, including mail, is feasible. Many surveys, however, entail designating a specific respondent at the time of data collection. If a questionnaire is mailed to a household or organization, the researcher has little control over who actually completes it. Therefore, the involvement of an interviewer is a critical aid if respondent designation is an issue.

Type of Population

The reading and writing skills of the population and its motivation to cooperate are two salient considerations in choosing a mode of data collection. Self-administered approaches to data collection place more of a burden on the respondent's reading and writing skills than do interviewer procedures.

Respondents who are not very well educated, whose reading and writing skills in English are less than facile (but who can speak English), people who do not see well, and people who are somewhat ill or tire easily will find an interviewer-administered survey easier than filling out a self-administered form. Another problem for mail surveys is getting people to return a completed questionnaire. People who are particularly interested in the research problem tend to be most likely to return questionnaires.[16]

Question Form

Generally speaking, if one is going to have a self-administered questionnaire, one must reconcile oneself to close-end questions; that is, questions that can be answered by simply checking a box or circling the proper response from a set provided by the reseacher. Second, and more important, self-administered open answers often do not produce useful data. With no interviewer present to probe incomplete answers for clarity and for meeting consistent question objectives, the answers will not be comparable across respondents, and they will be difficult to code.

There are question forms (including those with complex descriptions of situations or events and those requiring pictures or other visual cues) that cannot be adapted to the telephone. If such measurement is a critical part of a survey, some form other than the telephone probably is needed.

Question Content

Researchers have argued persuasively that one or another of the strategies should have an advantage when dealing with sensitive topics. Self-administered procedures are thought to be best, because the respondent does not have to admit directly to an interviewer a socially undesirable or negatively valued characteristic or behavior. Others have argued that telephone procedures lend an air of impersonality to the interview process that should help people report negative events or behaviors. Moreover, random-digit dialing at least provides the option of having a virtually anonymous survey procedure, because the interviewer need not know the name or location of the respondent. Still others argue that personal interviews are the best way to ask sensitive questions, because interviewers have an opportunity to build rapport and establish the kind of trust that is needed for respondents to report potentially sensitive information.

An entirely different aspect of question content that may affect the mode of data collection is the difficulty of the reporting task. In some surveys, researchers want to ask about events or behaviors that are difficult to report with accuracy, because they extend over a period of time or are quite detailed. In such cases, reporting accuracy may benefit from a chance to consult records or to discuss the questions with other family members. The standard interview is a quick question-and-answer process that provides little such opportunity; this is especially true for telephone interviews. Self-administered procedures provide more time for thought, for checking records, and for consulting with other family members.

Response Rates

The rate of response is likely to be much more salient than other considerations in the selection of a data collection procedure. Obviously, one of the strengths of group-administered surveys, when they are feasible, is the high rate of response. Generally speaking, when students in classrooms or workers in job settings are asked to complete questionnaires, the rate of response is nearly 100 percent.

There is no doubt that the problem of nonresponse is central to the use of mail surveys. If one simply mails questionnaires to a general population sample without an appropriate follow-up procedure, the rate of return is likely to be less than 20 percent.

The effectiveness of telephone strategies in producing high response rates depends in part on the sampling scheme. Response rates in some urban areas benefit from using the telephone, whereas suburban and rural rates are usually lower for telephone surveys than when a personal interviewer is used. Using the telephone permits better coverage of units in buildings with security systems and neighborhoods where interviewers are reluctant to go in the evening.

Costs

The great appeal of mail and telephone survey procedures is that in most cases they cost less than personal interviews. Survey costs depend on the multitude of factors. Some of the more salient factors are the amount of professional time required to design the questionnaire, the questionnaire length, the geographic dispersion of the sample, the availability and interest of the sample, the callback procedures, respondent selection rules, and the availability of trained staff. Although on the surface mail survey costs might appear to be lowest, the cost of postage, of clerical time for mailing, and of printing questionnaires turns out not to be trivial. Moreover, if there are telephone follow-ups, the expense gets higher.

Available Facilities

The facilities and staff availability should be considered in choosing a data-collection mode. Developing an interviewing staff is costly and difficult. Attrition rates are generally high for newly trained interviewers. Many new interviewers are not very good at enlisting the cooperation of respondents, producing high refusal rates at the start. In addition, people who are good at training and supervising interviewers are not easy to find. Thus, one very practical consideration for anyone thinking about doing an interviewer-conducted survey is the ability to execute a professional data-collection effort.

The available facilities are a crucial factor in the choice of a survey method in the international context. The question that has to be evaluated is whether local researchers must be used in conducting the survey or whether to use foreign researchers. In considering whether to use local researchers or import foreign researchers with specific skills, a number of factors need to be evaluated. This question arises particularly in the context of developing countries where research staff with specific skills, such as the ability to conduct in-depth interviews or focus groups, or skills in research design and analysis, may not be readily available.

The major advantage of using local researchers for qualitative research or in research design is that they will know the local culture and people, as well as the language, and hence be best able to understand local cultural differences.

On the other hand, the local researchers may have more limited research experience than foreign staff and may not have the same specialist skills. In interviewing, they may have difficulties in adopting a neutral or objective stance relative to respondents, or may lack familiarity with the design of a sophisticated research instrument. In some cases, there may be a scarcity of local researchers with even the minimum required skills, thus necessitating consideration of importing foreign researchers.

A second issue is that of training field interviewers. This is particularly critical in cases where a pool of experienced interviewers is not readily available. In political and social surveys conducted in developing countries, extensive training programs have been developed for interviewing. Upscale individuals in leadership positions, such as village headmen, teachers, and country prefects, have been found to be good interviewers in these situations.

Duration of Data Collection

The time involved in data collection varies by mode. Mail surveys usually take two months to complete. A normal sequence involves mailing the questionnaires and waiting for the responses. If the response rate is poor, then some more questionnaires are mailed and, finally, some telephone or in-person follow-up is done if the second wave of mailing also does not produce a good response rate. At the other extreme, it is quite feasible to do telephone surveys in a few days. Surveys done in a very short period of time pay a cost in nonresponse, because some people cannot be reached during any short period. However, telephone surveys routinely can be done more quickly than mail or personal interview surveys of comparable size.

ETHICAL ISSUES IN DATA COLLECTION

Survey research is an objective process and therefore has explicit guidelines and principles. However, it takes place in a subjective context, and thus is vulnerable to distortion by its producers and perceivers. Misrepresentation of the research itself through the use of inadequate sampling procedures or volunteers to obtain so-called "survey" information will be discussed in Chapter 13.

Misrepresentation of the data-collection process stems from two principal sources. The first is the representation of a marketing activity other than research, as research. The second is the abuse of respondents' rights during the data-collection process under the rationale of providing better quality research.

Consumers expect to be sold and to be surveyed, and they expect to be able to tell the difference without great difficulty. When a selling or marketing activity uses the forms and language of survey research in order to mask the real nature of the activity being performed, it violates the public trust. Classic examples of this type of practice are

1. *The use of survey techniques for selling purposes.* In this case, a person answers a few questions only to find him/herself suddenly eligible to buy a specific product or service. The misuse of the survey approach as a disguise for sales canvassing is a widespread practice that shows no signs of abating.

2. *The use of survey techniques to obtain names and addresses of prospects for direct marketing.* These efforts are usually conducted by mail. Questionnaires about products or brands are sent to households, and response is encouraged by the offer of free product samples to respondents. The listing firms compile the information by implying to the prospective customer that he or she has been interviewed in a market study.[17]

In both of these cases, the consumer is not told that the company conducting the survey is in a business other than research. The harm caused by this practice is that legitimate research is given a bad name in the eyes of consumers. Both response rates and response quality are jeopardized.

Even companies practicing legitimate research can violate the rights of respondents by deliberately engaging in a number of practices such as

▶ Disguising the purpose of a particular measurement, such as a free draw or free product choice question.

▶ Deceiving the prospective respondent as to the true duration of the interview.

▶ Misrepresenting the compensation in order to gain cooperation.

▶ Not mentioning to the respondent that a follow-up interview will be made.

▶ Using projective tests and unobtrusive measures to circumvent the need for a respondent's consent.

▶ Using hidden tape recorders to record personal interviews (or recording phone conversations without the respondent's permission).

▶ Conducting simulated product tests in which the identical product is tried by the respondent except for variations in characteristics, such as color, that have no influence in the quality of a product.

▶ Not debriefing the respondent.[18]

Many of these practices cannot be condoned under any circumstances, and others present the conscientious researcher with a serious dilemma. Under certain circumstances, disguising the nature of the research hypotheses may be the only feasible method to collect the necessary data. Yet these practices have the potential to create biased data and suspicion or resentment that later may be manifested in a refusal to participate in subsequent studies.

Both the misrepresentation of research and the abuse of respondents' rights during the legitimate research interviewing process involve consumer deception. This has two implications. From a business perspective, if public willingness to cooperate with the research process is adversely affected, the long-term statistical reliability of marketing research is jeopardized. From a social perspective, consumer deception violates basic business ethics. The responsibility of business to society rests on a fundamental concern for the advancement of professional business practices. Marketing research depends on mutual trust and honesty between the business community and society. Deception undermines the trust by using people as mere instruments to accomplish unstated purposes.

Other ethical issues in data collection arise even when the respondent is not being deceived. One of the most important is invasion of privacy. A basic criterion of good research is respect for the privacy of the individual. Yet, legitimate research is always to some extent intrusive in nature. Excessive interviewing in certain metropolitan areas, especially in those popular for test markets, can be perceived by consumers as violating their basic right to privacy. A recent telephone survey with 300 respondents found that 57 percent had been interviewed at some time in the past and 50 percent had been interviewed during the past year. This type of overinterviewing may result in consumers feeling resentful and less willing to fully cooperate. If they suspect that participation in one interview leads to further requests for interviews, they will be more likely to refuse.

Summary

There is bound to be a number of errors when surveys are conducted, some of which can be controlled and others that cannot be controlled. A researcher should know all the potential sources of errors and should try to reduce their impact on the survey findings. This is a good research practice and will lead to more robust results.

The choice of a survey method, that is, whether to use mail, or telephone or personal interviews, is determined by a number of factors. A knowledge of these factors will make it easier for the researcher to decide among the various methods. The most important factors are the sampling plan to be employed, the type of population to be surveyed, the response rates required, the budget for the survey, and the available resources. There may be a number of factors that may be important for the choice of survey method other than those discussed here. It depends on the particular study, but the factors listed in the text are the most common ones.

All data-collection methods are susceptible to misrepresentation by the researchers. Two principle sources of this misrepresentation are disguising the true purpose of a marketing activity, such as selling, by calling it marketing research, or abusing respondents' rights during a legitimate data-collection process. Both of these practices involve a disregard of professional business ethics. Maintaining high standards of business ethics while collecting data is the obligation of all responsible researchers.

Questions and Problems

1. How would you overcome some of the problems you might anticipate in designing a survey to establish the kind of paint used by the "do-it-yourself" market when the members of this sample last redecorated a room?

2. How would you balance the requirements of improving the quality of interviews against any ethical considerations that may arise?

3. Is the biasing effect of an interviewer more serious in a personal or telephone interview? What steps can be taken to minimize this biasing effect in these two types of interviews?

4. People tend to respond to surveys dealing with topics that interest them. How would you exploit this fact to increase the response rate in a survey of attitudes toward the local urban transit system, in a city where the vast majority of people drive to work or to shop?

5. If you were a marketing research manager, would you permit the following if they were important to the usefulness of a study?
   a. Telling the respondent the interview would take only two or three minutes when it usually took four minutes and a follow-up ten-minute interview was employed.
   b. Telling the respondent the questionnaire would be anonymous but coding it so that the respondent could be identified (so that additional available information about the respondent's neighborhood could be used).
   c. Secretly recording (or videotaping) a focus-group interview.
   d. Saying the research was being conducted by a research firm instead of your own company.

6. You are product manager for brand M butter, a nationally known brand. Brand M has been declining in absolute level of sales for the last four consecutive months. What information, if any, that could be obtained from respondents would be useful for determining the cause or causes of this decline?

7. What are the general advantages and disadvantages associated with obtaining information by questioning and by observation? Which method provides more control over the sample?

8. Houston Resources Consultancy has been contracted to conduct a job-satisfaction survey among the 2470 employees of United Machine Tools, Inc., Dayton, Ohio. The management insists that the questionnaire be comprehensive and incorporate all the views of the respondent in order to improve the work environment.
   a. What factors should Houston Resources Consultancy consider in choosing the survey method to be used?
   b. Which question form would be most likely to supply management with the information it has requested?
   c. Design a sample questionnaire that Houston Resources Consultancy will use in conducting the job-satisfaction survey.
   d. What possible sources of survey error might be encountered?
   e. United Machine Tools, Inc., has a wholly owned subsidiary at Madras, India. What additional factors must Houston Resources Consultancy consider in choosing the survey method to assess the job-satisfaction levels of the employees at the Madras plant?

9. Mark Hirst, a high school student in Sydney, Australia, developed an innovatively shaped surfboard that radically increased the number of

maneuvers a surfer could perform in low surf. In his enthusiasm to research the market, he developed a comprehensive seven-page questionnaire to be completed by customers and distributed it among surf supply stores.

a. How will the length of the questionnaire affect the response rate?

b. What possible biases could arise from Mark's sampling method?

10. Families for the Future, a nonprofit organization formed to promote a return to the family values of the 1950s in the United States, is conducting a mail survey to determine the level of domestic violence and its causes. The organization plans to survey families in urban areas in four cities across the United States.

a. What are the possible sources of survey error in this study?

b. How might the study be redesigned to eliminate these errors?

End Notes

1. A. N. Oppenheim, *Questionnarie Design and Attitude Measurement* (New York: Basic Books), 1966.

2. George S. Day, "The Threats to Marketing Research," *Journal of Marketing Research*, 12, November 1975, 462–467.

3. Frederick Wiseman and Mariane Schafer, "If Respondents Won't Respond, Ask Nonrespondents Why," *Marketing News*, September 9 1977, 8–9; Susan Kraft, "Who Slams the Door on Research," *American Demographics*, September 1991, 14.

4. A. Ossip, "Likely Improvements in Data Collection Methods—What Do They Mean for Day-to-Day Research Management?" *Journal of Advertising Research*, Research Currents, October/November 1986, RC9–RC12.

5. Arthur Saltzman, "Improving Response Rates in Disk-By-Mail Surveys," *Marketing Research: A Magazine of Management & Applications*, 5, Summer 1993, 32–39.

6. Charles F. Cannel, Lois Oksenberg, and Jean M. Converse, "Striving for Response Accuracy: Experiments in New Interviewing Techniques," *Journal of Marketing Research*, 14, August 1977, 306–315.

7. W. Cook, "Telescoping and Memory's Other Tricks," *Journal of Advertising Research*, 87, February–March 1987, 5–8.

8. James Julbert and Donald R. Lehmann, "Reducing Error in Question and Scale Design: A Conceptual Framework," *Decision Sciences*, 6, January 1975, 166–173.

9. Bill Iuso, "Concept Testing: An Appropriate Approach." *Journal of Marketing Research*, 12, May 1975, 228–231.

10. Del I. Hawkins and Kenneth A. Coney, "Uninformed Response Error in Survey Research," *Journal of Marketing Research*, 13, August 1981, 370–374.

11. William D. Wells, "The Influence of Yeasaying Response Style," *Journal of Advertising Research*, 1, June 1963, 8–18.

12. Donald P. Warwick and Charles A. Lininger, *The Sample Survey: Theory and Practice* (New York: McGraw-Hill, 1975) pp. 198, 203.

13. J. Freeman and E. W. Butler, "Some Sources of Interviewer Variance in Surveys," *Public Opinion Quarterly*, Spring 1976, 84–85.

14. Good discussions of what can be found in Warwick and Lininger are in Robert Ferber, ed., *Handbook of Marketing Research* (New York: McGraw-Hill), 1974, pp. 2.124–2.132, 2.147–2.159.

15. This section is adapted from Floyd J. Fowler, Jr., *Survey Research Methods* Newbury Park, (California: Sage Publications), 1993.

16. T. Heberlein and R. Baumgartner, "Factors Affecting Response Rates to Mailed Questionnaires: A Quantitative Analysis of the Published Literature," *American Sociological Review*, 1978, 447–462.

17. ARF Position Paper, "Phony or Misleading Polls," *Journal of Advertising Research*, Special Issue, 26, January 1987, pp. RC3–RC8.

18. George S. Day, op. cit.

CASE 8-1
Essex Markets (A)[1]

Essex Markets was a chain of supermarkets in a medium-sized California city. For six years it had provided its customers with unit pricing of grocery products. The unit prices were provided in the form of shelf tags that showed the price of the item and the unit price (the price per ounce, for example). The program was costly. The tags had to be prepared and updated. Further, because they tended to become dislodged or moved, considerable effort was required to make sure that they were current and in place.

A study was proposed to evaluate unit pricing. Among the research questions in the study were the following:

▶ What percentage of shoppers was aware of unit pricing?

▶ What percentage of shoppers used unit pricing?

▶ With what frequency was unit pricing in use?

▶ What types of shoppers used unit pricing?

▶ For what product classes was it used most frequently?

▶ Was it used to compare package sizes and brands or to evaluate store-controlled labels?

It was determined that a five-page questionnaire completed by around 1000 shoppers would be needed. The questionnaire could be completed in the store in about 15 minutes, or the respondent could be asked to complete it at home and mail it in.

Questions for Discussion

Specify how the respondents should be approached in the store. Write out the exact introductory remarks that you would use. Should the interview be in the store, or should the questionnaire be self-administered at home and mailed in, or should some other strategy be employed? If a self-administered questionnaire is used, write an introduction to it. What could be done to encourage a high response rate.

CASE 8-2
More Ethical Dilemmas in Marketing Research[2]

The following scenarios are similar to those you saw in Chapter 1, but bear directly on the rights of respondents in a research study. As before, your assignment is to decide what action to take in each instance. Be prepared to justify your decision.

1. Your company is supervising a study of restaurants conducted for the Department of Corporate and Consumer Affairs. The data, which have already been collected, include specific buying information and prices paid. Respondent organizations have been promised confidentiality. The ministry demands that all responses be identified by business name. Their rationale is that they plan to repeat the study and wish to limit sampling error by returning to the same respondents. Open bidding requires that the government maintain control of the sample.

   What action would you take?

2. You are a project director on a study funded by a somewhat unpopular federal policing agency. The study is on marijuana use among young people in a community and its relationship, if any, to crime. You will be using a structured questionnaire to gather data for the agency on marijuana use and criminal activities. You believe that if you reveal the name of the funding agency and/or the actual purposes of the study to respondents, you will seriously depress response rates and thereby increase nonresponse bias.

   What information would you disclose to respondents?

3. You are employed by a market research company. A manufacturer of female clothing has retained

---

[1] Prepared by Bruce McElroy and David A. Aaker as a basis for class discussion.

[2] Provided with the premission of Professor Charles Weinberg, University of British Columbia.

your firm to conduct a study for them. The manufacturer wants you to know something about how women choose clothing, such as blouses and sweaters. The manufacturer wants to conduct group interviews, supplemented by a session which would be devoted to observing the women trying on clothing, in order to discover which types of garments are chosen first, how thoroughly they touch and examine the clothing, and whether they look for and read a label or price tag. The client suggests that the observations be performed unobtrusively by female observers at a local department store, via a one-way mirror. One of your associates argues that this would constitute an invasion of privacy.

What action would you take?

4. You are the market reasearch director in a manufacturing company. The project director requests permission to use ultraviolet ink in precoding questionnaires on a mail survey. Although the accompanying letter refers to a confidential survey, the project director needs to be able to identify respondents to permit adequate cross-tabulation of the data and to save on postage costs if a second mailing is required.

What action would you take?

9 INFORMATION FROM RESPONDENTS: SURVEY METHODS

Learning Objectives

▶ Introduce the different kinds of survey methods.

▶ Discuss the survey methods and describe the process involved in each method.

▶ Enumerate the advantages and disadvantages of the survey method.

▶ Discuss the future trends in survey methods.

▶ Elucidate the problems that the researcher faces in conducting international surveys.

There as many survey methods as there are different forms of communication technology. As the technology for communication progresses, the number of survey methods also proliferates. Recent advances in fax technology and in electronic mail have introduced many new possibilities for conducting error-free surveys. Hence, a researcher has to know the mechanics of each method clearly, and also how it performs compared to the other methods. The choice between different survey methods is never an easy one. The factors affecting the choice of a survey method were discussed in Chapter 8, but without a thorough knowledge of the various methods, it will always be difficult to choose among them. In this chapter, the three most prevalent methods of conducting surveys—personal interviews, telephone interviews, and mail surveys—are discussed in detail. The latest trends in survey methods are also discussed. Conducting international surveys leads to a number of new problems that are not encountered in domestic research. These problems and possible solutions are also discussed briefly.

COLLECTING DATA

Personal Interviewing

The different methods of conducting personal interviews can be classified based on the respondents to be contacted and on the means of contacting them. In this section the different types of personal interview methods are discussed, as well as their advantages and limitations.

Process. The personal interviewing process is characterized by the interaction of four entities: the researcher, the interviewer, the interviewee, and the interview environment. Each of the three has certain basic characteristics, both inherent and acquired. Each also has general research knowledge and experience, which vary a great deal among them. Collectively, these characteristics influence the interviewing process and, ultimately, the interview itself. During a personal interview, the interviewer and the interviewee interact and simultaneously influence one another in an interview environment. The choice of an interview environment is made by the researcher, depending on the type of data to be collected. A brief discussion of the various personal interview methods, classified according to interview environment, follows.

Door-to-Door Interviewing. This method, where consumers are interviewed in person in their homes, has traditionally been considered the best survey method. This conclusion was based on a number of factors. First, the **door-to-door interview** is a personal, face-to-face interview with all the attendant advantages—feedback from the respondent, the ability to explain complicated tasks, the ability to use special questionnaire techniques that require visual contact to speed up the interview or improve data quality, the ability to show the respondent product concepts and other stimuli for evaluation, and so on. Second, the consumer is seen as being at ease in a familiar, comfortable, secure environment.

The door-to-door interview remains the only viable way to do long, in-depth, or detailed interviews and certain in-home product tests. In addition, the door-to-door survey is the only way currently available to obtain anything approaching a probability sample in a study that involves showing concepts or other stimuli to consumers.

Executive Interviewing. The term **executive interviewing** is used by marketing researchers to refer to the industrial equivalent of door-to-door interviewing. This type of survey involves interviewing business people at their offices, concerning industrial products or services.

This type of interviewing is very expensive. First, individuals involved in the purchase decision for the product in question must be identified and located. Once a qualified person is located, the next step is to get that person to agree to be interviewed and to set a time for the interview.

Finally, an interviewer must go to the particular place at the appointed time. Long waits are frequently encountered; cancellations are not uncommon. This type of survey requires the very best interviewers, because frequently they must conduct interviews on topics about which they know very little.

Mall Intercept Surveys. Shopping-center interviews are a popular solution when funds are limited, and the respondent must see, feel, or taste something. Often, they are called **shopping mall intercept surveys,** in recognition of the interviewing procedures. Interviewers, stationed at entrances or selected locations in a mall, randomly approach respondents and either question them at that location or invite them to be interviewed at a special facility in the mall.

These facilities have equipment that is adaptable to virtually any demonstration requirement, including interview rooms and booths, kitchens with food preparation areas, conference rooms for focus groups, closed-circuit television and sound systems, monitoring systems with one-way mirrors, and on-line video-screen interviewing terminals.

Since interviewers don't travel and respondents are plentiful, survey costs are low. However, shopping center users, not representative of the general population, visit the center with different frequencies, and shop at different stores within the center.[1] These problems can be minimized with the special sampling procedures described in Chapter 13. The number of people who agree to be interviewed in the mall will increase with incentives.[2]

Self-Administered Questionnaires. In the **self-administered interview** method, no interviewer is involved. Even though this reduces the cost of the interview process, this technique has one major disadvantage: There is no one present to explain things to the respondent and clarify responses to open-ended questions. This results in the answers to most of the open-ended questions being totally useless. But some have argued that the absence of an interviewer results in the elimination of interviewer bias.

Self-administered interviews are often used in the malls or other central locations where the researcher has access to a captive audience. Airlines frequently use this technique to get information about their services; the questionnaires are administered in flight. Many hotels, restaurants, and other service businesses provide brief questionnaires to patrons, to find out how they feel about the quality of service provided.

Purchase Intercept Technique (PIT).[3] This technique is different from but related to the mall intercept approach. The **purchase intercept technique** combines both in-store observation and in-store interviewing to assess shopping behavior and the reasons behind that behavior. Like a mall intercept, PIT involves intercepting consumers while they are in a shopping environment; however, PIT is administered at the time of an observable, specific product selection, as compared to consumers in a mall location. The researcher unobtrusively observes the customer make a purchase in a particular product category; then the researcher intercepts the customer for an interview as soon as the purchase has been made.

The major advantage of PIT is that it aids buyer recall. Interviewing at the point of purchase minimizes the time lapse between the purchase and data collection, and can provide a neutral set of memory cues for the respondent while the purchase is still salient. Apart from difficulties in gaining access to stores, the principal disadvantage of PIT is that it samples only purchasers and not anyone else who might be influencing the decision on what to buy or where to shop.

Omnibus Surveys. Omnibus surveys are regularly scheduled (weekly, monthly, or quarterly) personal interview surveys with questions provided by a number of separate clients. The questionnaires, based on which the interviews are conducted, will contain sequences of questions on different topics. Each sequence of questions is provided by one client, and the whole questionnaire is made up of such sequences of questions, on diverse topics, from different clients.

There are impressive advantages to the omnibus approach whenever only a limited number of personal interview questions are needed. The total costs are minimized, since the rates are based on the number of questions to be asked and tabulated, and the cost of the survey is shared by the clients. The results are available quickly, because all the steps are standardized and scheduled in advance. The regularity of the interview schedule and the assurance that the independent samples are matched make this a suitable base for continuous "tracking" studies and before–after studies. Some omnibus operators offer split-run facilities, so that half of the sample receives one stimulus (one version of a question or concept) and the other matched half gets another version. Also, by accumulating over several waves of interviews, it is possible to conduct studies of low-incidence activities, such as the extent of salt-free diets, and shortwave transmitter ownership.

Advantages. An interviewer, face to face with a respondent, can do a great deal to arouse initial interest and thereby increase the rate of participation and continuing rapport. To reduce the likelihood of a respondent refusing to finish the interview with an interviewer, it is also feasible to ask complex questions and enhance their meaning with pictorial and mechanical aids, clarify misunderstandings, and probe for more complete answers. For these reasons, the **personal interview** usually is preferred when a large amount of information is required and the questions are complex or involve tasks such as sorting cards into ordered piles or evaluating visual cues such as pictures of product concepts or mock-ups of advertisements.

The personal interview questionnaire has a high degree of flexibility. For example, if the answer to "Have you ever heard of (a community agency)?" is "yes," the interviewer asks questions A and B, but if the answer is "no," the interviewer asks about the next agency.

Generalizations about the **accuracy** of personal interview responses are hazardous. On one hand, interviewer probes and clarifications maximize respondent understanding and yield complete answers, especially to open-ended questions. Possibly offsetting these advantages are the problems of prestige seeking, social desirability, and courtesy biases discussed earlier. In relative terms, it seems that for questions about neutral topics, all three methods are equally satisfactory, whereas for embarrassing topics the personal interview is at a disadvantage.

Finally, there is an advantage to having a personal interview when an explicit or current list of households or individuals is not available. The interviewer can be assigned to specific census tracts, blocks, or residences as defined by census data. Once a residence is chosen, the researcher can control who is interviewed and how much assistance is obtained from others in the household.

Limitations. Personal interview studies are time consuming, administratively difficult, and costly. The time requirements are understandable in light of the need to travel between interviews, set up appointments, and perhaps schedule return visits to complete interrupted interviews. Only 30 to 40 percent of an interviewer's time on the job is devoted to interviewing itself. One can use more interviewers to reduce the elapsed time, but then problems of quality control increase. Because of the time and administrative problems, the cost per completed personal interview tends to be higher than it is for mail or telephone surveys. Direct comparisons of the costs of different methods are difficult, in part because of the wide variability in the implementation of each method.

Table 9-1 provides some approximate indices of the direct cost of a completed interview, to help compare data collection methods. In 1994, an index value of 1.0 corresponded to a cost of $20.00. Thus, in 1994, one could expect a 40- to 60-minute personal interview on a national basis, with one call-back and 10 percent validation, to cost between $50 (2.5 × $20.00) and $70.00 (3.5 × $20.00). This cost assumes that the study was conducted by a commercial research supplier and a general population was interviewed. But if the sample to be interviewed consists of a particular segment, like physicians, then a 40- to 60-minute interview would cost close to $200 per interview.

Until recently, it was thought that the personal interview method was always the best way to reduce nonresponse bias. Interviewers can track down hard-to-find respondents and minimize refusals by being physically present at the door. Unfortunately, the costs of the call-backs needed to achieve high response rates are becoming excessive. This is especially a problem in the inner-city areas, which interviewers are reluctant to visit and may refuse to enter at night even when they work in teams.

Telephone Interviewing

The telephone interview gradually has become the dominant method for obtaining information from large samples, as the cost and nonresponse problems of personal interviews have become more acute. At the same time, many of the

TABLE 9-1

Comparative Indices of Direct Costs per Completed Interview (including travel and telephone charges, interviewer compensation, training, and direct supervision expenses)

Data Collection Method	Index of Cost[a]
1. **Mail survey** (costs depend on return rate, incentives, and follow-up procedure).	0.3–0.8
2. **Telephone interviews.**	
a. 7-minute interview with head of household in metropolitan area.	0.5–0.8
b. 15-minute interview with small segment of national population from a central station.	1.3–1.7
3. **Personal interviews.**	
a. 10-minute personal interview in middle-class suburban area (1 call-back and 10 percent validation).	1.5–1.8
b. 40- to 60-minute interview of national probability sample (1 call-back and 10 percent validation).	2.5–3.5
c. Executive (VIP) interviews.	4.0–15.0+

[a] In 1994, an index value of 1.0 corresponded to a cost of $20.00.

accepted limitations of telephone interviewing have been shown to be of little significance for a large class of marketing problems.

Process. The telephone interviewing process generally is very similar to personal interviewing. Only certain unique aspects of telephone interviewing such as selecting the telephone numbers, the call outcomes, the introduction, when to call, and call reports are described below.

Selecting Telephone Numbers. There are three basic approaches to obtaining telephone numbers when selecting study participants for telephone interviews. A researcher can use a prespecified list, a directory, or a random dialing procedure. Prespecified lists—membership rosters, customer lists, or lists purchased from commercial suppliers of telephone numbers—are sometimes used for selected groups of people. This use, however, is not widespread in marketing research.

The traditional approach to obtaining numbers has been to use a directory, one provided by either a telephone company or a commercial firm (for instance, the Polk crisscross directory). However, a directory may be inadequate for obtaining a representative sample of consumers or households. On the average, 15 to 20 percent of the U.S. households that have telephones are not included in telephone directories.[4] People voluntarily not listed in a telephone directory tend to have characteristics somewhat different from those listed.

To overcome telephone directory nonrepresentativeness, many researchers now use **random-digit dialing** when they interview consumers by telephone. In its most general form, complete random-digit dialing is a nondirectory procedure for selecting all 10 (area code, prefix or exchange, suffix) telephone number digits at random. Although this approach gives all households with telephones an approximately equal chance of being called, it has severe limitations. It is costly to implement, both in dollars and time, since not all possible telephone numbers are in service, and therefore many telephoning attempts are to nonexistent numbers. Additionally, complete random-digit dialing does not discriminate between telephone numbers in which a researcher is interested and those of no interest (numbers out of the geographical study area and those of business or government).

A variation of the random-digit dialing procedure is **systematic random-digit dialing** (SRDD). In SRDD, a researcher specifies those telephone area codes and exchanges, or prefixes, from which numbers are to be selected. Thus, government, university, business, or exchanges not of interest (out of the geographical study area) are avoided. The researcher determines a starting number (seed point) plus a sampling interval—a constant number systematically added to the starting number and subsequent numbers generated, to obtain the list of telephone numbers to be called. For metropolitan areas, it is necessary to generate approximately four times as many telephone numbers as completed interviews desired because of not-in-service numbers and the like. An illustration of the SRDD process is described in Exhibit 9-1.

SRDD has several advantages. Because there is a random starting point, each telephone number has an equal chance of being called. Second, since

EXHIBIT 9-1

An Illustration of the SRDD Process

Suppose an interviewer wants to poll a thousand (n = 1000) respondents on the eve of the presidential election in a particular area (with the area code prefix as 743). There are a total of ten thousand (k = 10,000) numbers with the prefix 743; i.e., 743-0000 to 743-9999. The first step in the SRDD process is to compute the sampling interval (I) given by k/n, which in this case is equal to ten. The interviewer then randomly chooses a telephone number in the interval 743-0000 to 743-0010. Once a number is chosen (say 743-0005), then to generate additional numbers, the value of 'I' is added to each of the previously selected number. In other words, the telephone numbers to call would be 743-0005, 743-(0005 + I), 743-(0005 + 2I). . . . 743-(0005 + (n − 1)I).

telephone exchanges tend to cover specific geographic areas, a spatial focus is possible. Third, if the same number of telephone calls is attempted from each exchange studied, the resulting sample tends to have the same geographical dispersion as the original population. Finally, SRDD can be incorporated into a standard computer program.

Another version of random-digit is **plus-one dialing,** a directory-assisted, random-digit-dialing telephone number selection procedure. Plus-one dialing consists of selecting a random sample of telephone numbers from one or more telephone directories, then adding the constant "1" to the last four digits of each number selected. This procedure increases the chances of an existing telephone number being obtained and also allows unlisted numbers to be included in the sample.

Call Outcomes. Once the telephone numbers have been selected, a call is made. Once a call has been attempted, eight possible outcomes can occur. The possible outcomes of a call attempt are as follows: the telephone being not in service, the number dialed is busy, no one answers the phone, the number called may be a fax number, an answering machine could come on, the call may be answered by someone other than the person to be contacted, the call may result in contacting a person outside the sampling frame (telephone line has been given to someone else when the respondent relocated), and, finally, the call may be answered by the actual respondent. Table 9-2 discusses the various call outcomes and the method to handle each outcome.

The Introduction. One of the most important aspects of telephone interviewing, and the key to a successfully completed interview, is the introduction. For the interview to be successfully completed, the interviewer must gain immediate rapport with potential study participants. Gaining rapport requires a pleasant telephone voice (being male or female does not seem to matter) and a good introduction. It is important that the introduction introduce the topic of study and be brief. An overly long introduction tends to decrease cooperation and elicit refusals to participate.

When to Call. To efficiently obtain a representative sample of study participants, telephone interviews should be attempted at times when prospective

TABLE 9-2
Call Outcomes and Recommendations to Deal with Them

Call Outcome	Recommendation
The telephone is not in service.	Eliminate the number from further consideration.
The number dialed is busy.	Call the number again later, because the characteristics of the people whose lines are busy will be different from those whose lines are not.
No one answers the call.	Call the number back later, because the characteristics of the people who are not at home will be different from those who are at home.
The number called is a fax number.	Send a fax to the respondent requesting for his time to conduct the interview, and get his or her telephone number.
An answering machine comes on.	Leave a message in the answering machine saying who you are and the purpose of your call. Call the number again after some time.
The call is answered by someone other than the respondent.	Find out when the respondent will be available and call back at that time.
The person contacted is not in the sampling frame.	Eliminate the number from further consideration.
The call is answered by the person to be contacted.	Conduct the interview.

interviewees will most likely be available. For consumer interviews, telephone interviews should probably be attempted between 6 P.M. and 9 P.M. on weekdays, and 10 A.M. to 8 P.M. on weekends. Calling before 6 P.M. on weekdays decreases the chances of reaching working individuals, and calling after 9 P.M. incurs the wrath of those who are early to bed. On the other hand, the best time to reach homemakers or contact individuals at work is between 9 A.M. and 4:30 P.M.

Call Reports. A **call report** is a form that has telephone numbers to be called and columns for interviewers to document their telephoning attempts—what day and time the call was made, the outcome, the length of the call, and so forth. Call reports provide records of calling experiences and are useful for managing data collection.

Advantages. Telephone interviews may be conducted either from a central location, at prescribed hours under close supervision, or from the interviewer's home, unsupervised and at their own hours. The former is preferred because problems can be isolated quickly and greater uniformity is possible. Supervisors can double-record interviews by listening on an extension and can gradually weed out incompetent interviewers.

Regardless of how the telephone interviews are conducted, the obvious advantages are the same: (1) more interviews can be conducted in a given time period, because no time is lost in traveling and locating respondents; (2) more hours of the day are productive, especially the evening hours when working women and singles are likely to be at home and apartment doors are locked; and (3) repeated call-backs at different times of the day can be made at very low cost. The key to the low costs for the latter surveys is the **wide area telephone service (WATS),** which provides unlimited calls to a given zone in Canada or the United States for a fixed monthly charge.

Overall, the telephone method dominates the personal interview with respect to speed, absence of administrative problems, and cost per completed interview. As we saw in Table 9-1, the costs of a telephone survey seldom will exceed two-thirds of the comparable costs of a personal interview.[5] Costs can be reduced further with omnibus surveys.

For better or worse the telephone is an "irresistible intruder." A ringing telephone literally compels us to answer. Long-distance calling brings a further dimension of urgency and importance to reaching the desired respondent. (This tends to counteract the fact that it is easier for a person to terminate midway through a telephone interview.) The telephone is a particularly effective method for gaining access to hard-to-reach people such as busy executives. The receptionist who thwarts the personal interviewer will readily connect a telephone interview request. Thus, Payne found that 94 percent of the interviews attempted with responsible persons in the 600 largest companies were successfully completed.[6] The intrusiveness of the telephone, plus the ease of making call-backs, means there should be less sample bias due to nonresponse.

For most topics there is likely to be little difference in the accuracy of responses between telephone and personal interviews. The Survey Research Center (University of Michigan) found that similar aggregate results were obtained by the two methods in their quarterly interview of consumer intentions. However, less differentiated responses were obtained over the telephone.[7]

During the telephone interview, the respondent's only impression of the interviewer is that conveyed by the voice. The lack of rapport is offset to a

Reprinted courtesy of Beta Research. Copyright ©1987, 88 Robert Leighton.

degree by lessened interviewer bias and greater anonymity of the situation. However, the research on whether the respondent will reply with greater candor to personal questions (such as alcohol consumption) is mixed.

Limitations. Relatively few of the problems with the telephone method are completely insurmountable. The most obvious problem is the inability to employ visual aids or complex tasks. For example, it does not appear feasible to ask respondents to retain in their minds the names of nine department stores and then ask them to choose one store. There have been solutions to this problem, including separate mention of individual stores and asking the respondent to treat the telephone push-button as a 10-point rating scale (from "1" for *like it very much* to the "0" for *don't like it at all*). A related problem with the telephone is that the interviewer must rely solely on verbal cues to judge the reaction and understanding of respondents.

There is some controversy about the amount of information that can be collected in a telephone interview. Most telephone interviews are kept as short as five to ten minutes, because of the belief that a bored or hurried respondent would be likely to hang up the phone. However, there is a tendency for the respondents to underestimate the length of time spent on a telephone call. Therefore, 20- to 30-minute interviews are increasingly frequent and successful, but only with interesting topics and capable interviewers.

A further limitation of telephone interviewing is the potential for sample bias, which is a consequence of some people being without phones, having unlisted phones, and telephone directories being unable to keep up with a mobile population. A subsequent chapter on sampling will discuss some of the solutions to these sampling problems, as well as the use of callbacks to reduce the frequency of not-at-homes.

Mail Surveys

The third major survey method is the **mail survey.** In this survey mode, questionnaires traditionally are mailed to potential study participants, who complete and return them by mail.

The Process. Superficially, interviewing by mail consists of identifying and locating potential study participants, mailing them questionnaires, and waiting for completed questionnaires to be returned. Substantively, the process is a series of distinct and often difficult decisions regarding the identification of study participants and the mail interview package—outgoing envelope, cover letter, questionnaire, return envelope, and the incentives, if any, to be used.

Unlike personal and telephone interviews, mail interviews require at least broad identification of the individuals to be sampled before data collection begins. Without such an identification, and an associated mailing address, mail interviews are not feasible. Therefore, an initial task is to obtain a valid mailing list of potential study participants. Mailing lists can be obtained from customer lists, association or organization membership rosters, telephone directories, publication subscription lists, or commercial "list houses." Regardless of its source, the mailing list must be current and relate closely to the group being studied. As might be expected, obtaining a useful mailing list is especially difficult when a list representative of the general population is desired.

Decisions must also be made about the various elements to be contained in a mail survey. Although many of these decisions involve relatively mechanical elements, each decision influences both the response rate and the response quality. Some decisions that are to be considered are as follows:

Type of return envelope.
Postage.
Method of addressing.
Cover letter.
Questionnaire length, content, layout, color, and format.
Method of notification; should there be a follow-up?
Incentive to be given.

One decision area is method of notification. In both preliminary and follow-up notification, a researcher communicates with potential mail interview respondents more than once. Preliminary notification may also be used to screen, or qualify, individuals for study inclusion. This communication may be by postcard, letter, or telephone. Follow-up communication methods include sending potential study participants postcards or letters, or telephoning them a few days after they receive the questionnaire to remind them to complete and return it as soon as possible.

Advantages. The most likely reason for choosing a **mail survey** is cost, but there are other reasons also, as illustrated by the decision of the Census Bureau to switch from a personal interview to a census by mail to gain "better results, including a shortening of the period for collecting the data and more reliable answers supplied directly by respondents instead of through a more-or-less inhibiting intermediary, the enumerator."[8] This approach worked well for the 1970 census, when forms were mailed to 60 percent of American households, of which 87 percent were completed voluntarily. More recent tests, to larger segments of the population, have not been so encouraging.

There is consistent evidence that mail surveys yield more accurate results—among those completing the survey. Because the mail questionnaire is answered at the respondent's discretion, the replies are likely to be more thoughtful and others can be consulted for necessary information. Mail surveys generally are superior when sensitive or potentially embarrassing topics, such as sexual behavior and finances, are covered (so long as the respondent is convinced that the answers will be taken in confidence). For example, a study of Boston residents, which compared the three basic methods of data collection, found that each of them gave equivalent results for neutral topics. But on sensitive topics where socially undesirable responses were possible, there were large differences. On the question of legalizing abortion, 89 percent of mail survey respondents were in favor, compared to 62 and 70 percent of telephone and personal interview respondents, respectively.[9]

Limitations. The absence of an interviewer means that a large number of variables are controlled inadequately, including

▶ The identity of the respondent. (Was it the addressee who answered, or an assistant or a spouse?)

▶ Whom the respondent consults for help in answering question.

▶ The speed of the response. (The usual time lag before receipt of a questionnaire delays the study and makes the responses vulnerable to external events taking place during the study.)[10]

▶ The order in which the questions are exposed and answered. (The respondent can look ahead to see where the questions are leading, so it is not possible to funnel questions from the general to the specific, for example.)

▶ Respondent understanding of the questions. (There is no opportunity to seek clarification of confusing questions or terms, so many respondents return their questionnaire partially completed.)

One consequence of these problems is that long questionnaires with complicated questions cannot be used without diminishing the response rate. As a rule of thumb, six to eight pages is the upper limit on topics of average interest to respondents.[11]

Mail surveys are limited to situations where a mailing list is available and the cost of the list is not prohibitive. Unfortunately, there are a number of possible flaws in all such lists: obsolescence, omissions, duplications, and so forth. This makes it difficult to find the ideal list, which consists entirely of the type of person to be contacted, and also represents all of those who exist. Great care must be taken at this stage to ensure that the study objectives can be achieved without excessive compromise.

If the boon of mail surveys is cost, then the bane is *response rates*. The response rate gives an indication of the number of questionnaires that have been returned. The Council of American Survey Research Organizations defines response rates as the ratio of the number of completed interviews with responding units to number of eligible responding units in the sample.[12] But implementing the definition may be simple or complex, depending on the methods used to select the sample.[13] The problem is not that acceptable response rates cannot be achieved, but rather that the rate is hard to forecast and there is substantial risk that an acceptable rate may not be achieved.

Many factors combine to influence the response rate, including (1) the perceived amount of work required, which in turn depends on the length of the questionnaire and the apparent ease with which it can be completed; (2) the intrinsic interest of the topic; (3) the characteristics of the sample; (4) the credibility of the sponsoring organization; and (5) the level of induced motivation. A poorly planned mail survey on a low-interest topic may achieve only a 10 to 15 percent response rate. Under the right circumstances, 90 percent response rates are also possible.

Coping with Nonresponse to Mail Surveys. Nonresponse is a problem, because those who respond are likely to differ substantially from those who do not respond. The best way to protect against this bias is to improve the response rate. The most consistently effective methods for achieving high response rates involve some combination of monetary incentives and follow-ups or reminders.[14] The inclusion of a 25-cent coin in the mailing, which is the usual reward, has been found to improve response rates by increments of 18 to 27 percent when compared to returns when no incentive is used. Comparable improvements have been obtained from the single or multiple follow-up letter. Although each follow-up brings additional responses, the optimum number seems to be two. It is a moot point whether it is worthwhile to include another questionnaire in the follow-up letter. Other techniques for improving response rates, such as providing a stamped, return envelope and a persuasive cover letter, appear to have a lesser but still worthwhile effect. Surprisingly, there is no clear evidence that personalization of the mailing, promises of anonymity, color, and methods of reproduction make much difference.

Another approach to the nonresponse problem is to determine the extent and direction of bias by studying the differences between those who respond and those who do not. This sometimes can be done by taking a subsample of the nonrespondents and using a variety of methods to get a high response rate from this group. Of course, when the questionnaire is anonymous or time is short, this cannot be done. In this situation it may be possible to compare the results of the survey with "known" values for the population, using such variables as age and income. Alternatively, one can use extrapolation methods, which assume that those who respond less readily are more like nonrespondents.[15] "Less readily" can be defined as either being slower-than-average in answering a simple mailing, or responding to the extra prodding of a follow-up mailing. With data from two waves of mailings, a trend can be established in the pattern of answers; nonrespondents can be assumed to be like either the last respondent to the second wave or like a projected respondent at the midpoint of the nonresponse group. This is represented graphically in the response rate chart.

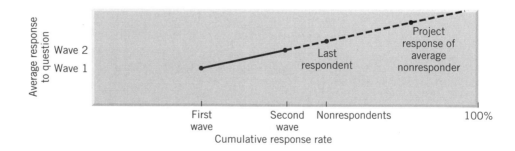

Mail Panels. A **mail panel** means a representative national sample of people who have agreed to participate in a limited number of mail surveys each year. A number of these panels are operated by firms such as Market Facts, Home Testing Institute, and National Family Opinion, Inc. The latter firm, for example, offers a number of panels that contain 130,000 people. The major advantage is the high response rate, which averages 75 to 85 percent.

A typical mail panel is the Conference Board Survey of Consumer Confidence. Each quarter, a large sample, drawn from the National Family Opinion Panel, is sent a questionnaire in the card format shown in Figure 9-1. This card is sent with cards from as many as 10 other studies, which spreads the costs of the survey. Since the questions and the sampling procedures are the same every quarter, the Conference Board has a standard measuring stick for tracking fluctuations in consumer attitudes and buying intentions.

Panels are recruited to match the general population with respect to geographic location, city size, age of homemaker, family income, and so on. Hence, it is possible to draw special samples of particular occupation groups (such as lawyers), age categories (such as teenagers), and geographic areas. Large samples can be obtained quickly in test-market areas, for example. Inevitably, those people who agree to serve on such panels will be different from the rest of the population—perhaps because they are more interested in such research, have

Answer This Side First

1. How would you rate the present general business conditions in your area?
   - ☐ GOOD   ☐ NORMAL   ☐ BAD
   a. SIX MONTHS from now do you think they will be:
   - ☐ BETTER?   ☐ SAME?   ☐ WORSE?

2. What would you say about available jobs in your area right now?
   - ☐ PLENTY ☐ NOT SO MANY ☐ HARD TO GET
   a. SIX MONTHS from now do you think there will be:
   - ☐ MORE?   ☐ SAME?   ☐ FEWER?

3. How would you guess your total family income to be SIX MONTHS from now?
   - ☐ HIGHER   ☐ SAME   ☐ LOWER

4. Does anyone in your household plan to buy a house in the next SIX MONTHS?
   - ☐ YES   ☐ NO   ☐ MAYBE
   a. If YES: ☐ NEW? ☐ LIVED IN? ☐ DON'T KNOW?

5. Does anyone in your household plan to buy a car in the next SIX MONTHS.?
   - ☐ YES   ☐ NO   ☐ MAYBE
   a. If YES: ☐ NEW? ☐ USED? ☐ DON'T KNOW?
   MAKE? _____   ☐ DON'T KNOW?
   CONTINUE →

ANSWER OTHER SIDE FIRST

6. Please check which, if any, of the items you plan to buy in the next SIX MONTHS, and which *brand* you are most likely to choose:

   BRAND PREFERENCE

   Refrigerator ....01☐ _____
   Washing Machine ....02☐ _____
   Black/White TV...........03☐ _____
   Color TV ....04☐ _____
   Vacuum Cleaner ....05☐ _____
   Ranges........................06☐ _____
   Clothes Dryer ....07☐ _____
   Air Conditioner ....08☐ _____
   Dishwasher ....09☐ _____
   Microwave Oven ....10☐ _____
   Sewing Machine..........11☐ _____
   Carpet (over 4' × 6')...12☐ _____
   - ☐ NONE OF THESE

7. Do you plan to take a vacation *away from home* between NOW and the next SIX MONTHS?
   - ☐ YES   ☐ NO   ☐ UNDECIDED
   a. Where will you spend *most* of your time while on vacation?
   - ☐ HOME STATE ☐ OTHER STATE(S) ☐ FOREIGN COUNTRY
   b. How will you mainly travel?

AIRPLANE	CAR	TRAIN	BOAT	BUS
☐	☐	☐	☐	☐

   Name of airline: _____

FIGURE 9-1
Conference Board Mail Panel Survey of Consumer Confidence

more time available, and so forth. Little is known about the impact of such differences on questionnaire responses.

Combinations of Survey Methods

Since each of the basic methods of data collection has different strengths and weaknesses, it is sometimes desirable to combine them and retain the best features of each while minimizing the limitations. Some of the feasible combinations (or sequences) are illustrated below:

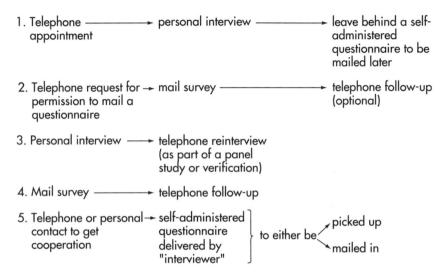

1. Telephone ⟶ personal interview ⟶ leave behind a self-
   appointment   administered
                                                     questionnaire to be
                                                     mailed later

2. Telephone request for ⟶ mail survey ⟶ telephone follow-up
   permission to mail a   (optional)
   questionnaire

3. Personal interview ⟶ telephone reinterview
                         (as part of a panel
                         study or verification)

4. Mail survey ⟶ telephone follow-up

5. Telephone or personal ⟶ self-administered ⎤
   contact to get   questionnaire   ⎬ to either be ⟶ picked up
   cooperation   delivered by   ⎭   ⟶ mailed in
                             "interviewer"

With the exception of the reinterview panel design of sequence 3, each of the above combinations has proven very effective in increasing the response rate. Indeed, sequence 1 is virtually mandatory for personal interviews with executives, as we noted in the previous chapter. The virtues of the other sequences are not quite so obvious.

The **telephone prenotification approach** is essentially a phone call to ask permission to mail a questionnaire. The key is the telephone presentation, which must not only gain an agreement to participate but make sure the prospective respondent is serious about cooperating. In one study in which 300 households were phoned, 264 households (88 percent) agreed to the mailing and 180 (60 percent) returned usable questionnaires.[16] If the return rate is not acceptable, a follow-up phone call can be made.

The **lockbox approach** is designed to circumvent the screens that receptionists and secretaries set around busy executives. The mail is used to deliver a small locked metal box containing a questionnaire and other interviewing materials such as flashcards, exhibits, and pictures. A covering letter, attached to the box, explains the purpose of the survey and tells the prospective respondent that an interviewer will conduct a telephone interview in a few days. The letter also tells the respondent that the box is a gift but that the combination to the lock will not be provided until the time of the interview. Ostensibly, this is so that the respondent will not be biased by seeing the interview materials in advance. However, it is clear that the value of the gift depends on participation in the survey. Also, the locked box stimulates respondent curiosity. As a result, the originator of this technique has been able to obtain response rates of 50 to 70 percent, even with notoriously difficult respondents such as attorneys in private practice who sell time for a living and are loath to participate in "free interviews."[17]

The **drop-off approach** is an illustration of sequence 5, which is particularly well suited to studies within compact geographic areas. For public transit studies, the questionnaire can be hand-delivered to sampling points, such as every 25th house within areas that have access to a transit line. It also can be used for subjects living in designated political precincts or within a given radius of a specific retail outlet or other service. The major advantages are (1) only lightly trained interviewers are required to gain the cooperation of the respondents, deliver the questionnaires, and arrange a return visit; (2) response rates are high, generally between 70 and 80 percent, in part because of the initial commitment to cooperate, coupled with the realization that the person who dropped the survey will be returning to pick up the completed questionnaire; (3) several questionnaires can be left in each household, if all adults are part of the sample; (4) lengthy questionnaires can be used without affecting the response rate; and (5) it is a very cost-effective method.[18]

Table 9-3 presents a comprehensive set of advantages and disadvantages of the various methods discussed above.

Trends in Survey Research

Surveys will continue to dominate as a method of data collection for marketing research, at least for the next few decades. But rapid advancement in technology is changing the very nature of data collection and survey methods. Computers and interactive technology are revolutionizing the way surveys are conducted. This section will look into some survey methods that have become popular in the last few years, and also the future of survey research.

Computer-Assisted Telephone Interviewing (CATI). Computers are being used increasingly to control the administration and sequence of questions asked by an interviewer seated at a terminal. This use of computers provides researchers with a way to prevent many interviewer errors, such as choosing the wrong respondent in a household, failing to ask a question that should be asked, or asking a series of questions that isn't appropriate for a particular respondent. If the respondent selection procedure or the skip patterns in a questionnaire are complicated, these interviewer errors are more likely to happen. When control of the question sequence is turned over to the computer, the interviewer theoretically is free to concentrate fully on reading the questions, recording the answers, and establishing rapport with the respondent.

There are some limitations to computer-controlled telephone interviewing. It is generally more expensive to use the computer than to administer the traditional paper-and-pencil questionnaire. For that reason, use of a computer-controlled system is recommended when a large number of surveys must be done or when the questionnaire will be used many times in a tracking study.

A second limitation relates to the problems involved in using a mechanical system and to human error in its programming and operation. A program must be written and carefully debugged for each questionnaire. The computer

TABLE 9-3
Advantages and Disadvantages of Survey Methods

Type of Survey Method	Advantages	Disadvantages
Personal Interviewing	• There are some sample designs that can be implemented best by personal interview (e.g., area probability samples). • Personal interview procedures are probably the most effective way of enlisting cooperation for most populations. • Advantages of interviewer administration—answering respondent questions, probing for adequate answers, accurately following complex instructions or sequences—are realized. • Multimethod data collection—including observations, visual cues, and self-administered sections—are feasible. • Rapport and confidence building are possible (including any written reassurances that may be needed for reporting very sensitive material). • Probably longer interviews can be done in person.	• It is likely to be more costly than the alternatives. • A trained staff of interviewers that is geographically near the sample is needed. • The total data collection period is likely to be longer than telephone procedures. • Some samples (those in high-rise buildings or high-crime areas, elites, employees, students) may be more accessible by some other mode.
Telephone Interviewing	• Lower costs than personal interviews. • Random-digit-dialing (RDD) sampling of general populations. • Better access to certain populations, especially as compared to personal interviews. • Shorter data collection periods. • The advantages of interviewer administration (in contrast with mail surveys). • Interviewer staffing and management easier than personal interviews—smaller staff needed, not necessary to be near sample, supervision and quality control potentially better. • Likely better response rate from a list sample than from mail.	• Sampling limitations, especially as a result of omitting those without telephones. • Nonresponse associated with RDD sampling is higher than with personal interviews. • Questionnaire or measurement constraints, including limits on response alternatives, use of visual aids, and interviewer observations. • Possibly less appropriate for personal or sensitive questions if no prior contact.

system must be able to handle the demands of a large number of interviewers. At the worst, several days of interviewing may pass before someone notices that a mistake has been made and the questionnaire program is incorrectly skipping over a crucial series of questions. Valuable interviewing time and money may be lost if the computer system becomes overloaded and "crashes." At its best, computer-controlled telephone interviewing can produce faster, more complete, data to the researcher.

Computer Interactive Interviewing. In this type of interview method the respondent directly interacts with the computer. The respondent is asked to sit before the computer and to answer the questions as they appear on the screen. This type of interview is being widely used in malls. Customers are intercepted and qualified in the mall and then brought to a test facility in the

TABLE 9-3 (*Continued*)

Type of Survey Method	Advantages	Disadvantages
Self-Administration	• Ease of presenting questions requiring visual aids (in contrast to telephone interviews). • Asking questions with long or complex response categories. • Asking batteries of similar questions. • The fact that the respondent does not have to share answers with an interviewer.	• Especially careful questionnaire design is needed. • Open questions usually are not useful. • Good reading and writing skills by respondents are needed. • The interviewer is not present to exercise quality control with respect to answering all questions, meeting question objectives, or the quality of answers provided.
Mail Procedures	• Relatively low cost. • Can be accomplished with minimal staff and facilities. • Provides access to widely dispersed samples and samples that for other reasons are difficult to reach by telephone or in person. • Respondents have time to give thoughtful answers, to look up records, or to consult with others.	• Ineffectiveness of mail as a way of enlisting cooperation (depending on group to be studied). • Various disadvantages of not having interviewer involved in data collections. • Need for good mailing addresses for sample.
Dropping Off Questionnaires	• The interviewer can explain the study, answer questions, and designate a household respondent, in contrast to mail. • Response rates tend to be like those of personal interview studies. • There is more opportunity to give thoughtful answers and consult records or other family members than in personal or telephone interview surveys.	• This procedure costs about as much as personal interviews. • A field staff is required (albeit perhaps a less thoroughly trained one than would be needed for personal interviews).

Source: Adapted from Floyd J. Fowler, Jr., Survey Research Methods, Newbury Park: Sage, 1993.

mall. They are seated at a computer terminal, given some instruction on what to do, and the administrator enters the sequence to start the interview. The interview then proceeds in the same manner as the CATI described before, the only difference being that the information is being directly input into the computer by the respondent. Computer interactive interviewing has resulted in better responses from respondents and, in some instances, 30 to 40 percent cost savings.[19] Exhibit 9-2 gives an example of how and why Hallmark converted its survey process from a paper and pencil one to a computer-interactive one. Many hardware and software developments continue to make this form of interviewing more feasible.

Recent Developments in Software and Hardware[20]

There have been many recent developments in this area which have helped researchers to use the computer more effectively. A few of them are discussed here:

▶ **GRiDPAD** is a pen computer that has an 8-by-10-inch screen with a wand attached. Respondents use the wand to touch answer categories that appear

EXHIBIT 9-2

Hallmark Switches to Computers

Managers at Hallmark Cards need a lot of survey data to make sure their sentiments are up-to-date. For years, the company armed its interviewers only with a pencil and paper. Conducting and processing a 200-interview study in this way took up to 35 days. When Hallmark executives asked the research department to complete over 23,000 interviews in 1988, almost five times more than it had done in 1985, Hallmark switched to computer interviewing.

Hallmark launched a new line of cards called Shoebox Greetings in 1985 with old-fashioned paper-and-pencil interviews. To select 400 to 500 cards for this launch, Hallmark needed to have consumers evaluate 1500 different designs. Researchers asked respondents to rate cards on a six-point scale that ran from excellent to poor, and to indicate which cards they were most likely to buy. Respondents also gave demographic information about themselves and the people for whom they might buy cards.

This kind of study requires a room big enough to hold four or five six-foot tables. The tables are divided into ten sections, each of which contains five cards. Respondents walk past the tables and evaluate each card by writing the number of the card and its score on a form. Then they choose up to eight cards they would be most likely to buy. They record the number of the card, and their relationship to and the age of the person who would receive the card. When 100 interviews have been turned in, Hallmark employees check to see that card numbers have been entered correctly, that all cards have been evaluated, and that no card has been evaluated more than once. Editing alone takes about 8 hours. Coding, keypunching, and verification takes another day and a half. Then the reports are run and given to the analyst.

By 1988, the volume of testing had become extremely demanding. At least one test was required each week, and some weeks required three or four. Hallmark faced a choice: either hire more employees or find a faster alternative. In the computer method, interviewers place their greeting cards next to the computer in ten stacks of five, and each card remains in its respective group throughout the study. Respondents read the card numbers and their scores to the interviewer; during the evaluation phase, respondents hold up the eight cards they would be most likely to buy and the age and relationship of the person for whom they would buy the card. The session ends with a few questions about the respondent's attitudes and demographics. The programmed questionnaire automatically alerts interviewers if an invalid number is entered. An internal counter warns the interviewer not to move on until all 50 cards are evaluated.

Interviewing customers by computer is both faster and more accurate than using paper and pencil. The pencil-and-paper interview method has several disadvantages. First, respondents can see all of their previous scores. This can bias their responses because they may not want to rate everything too high or too low. Second, laying all of the cards on a table at one time can cause some respondents to compare one card with another. This is why the highest-scoring cards scored lower in the computer evaluation than they did in the pencil-and-paper test.

The computer method encourages respondents to evaluate cards individually, because they see only one card at a time. Comparing the computer test with the pencil-and-paper test reveals that the average scores are relatively close. But the range of scores varies less with computers. And because respondents hold out their favorite cards as they go through the stack, computer interviewing is more like the shopping experience.

Source: Diane L. Pyle, "How to Interview Your Customers." *American Demographics*, December 1990, 44–45.

on the screen (no more keyboards, no more mice). Advanced Data Research (ADR) produces software that can be used with GRiDPAD. Auto manufacturers were among the first to take advantage of the new system.

▶ **FormPro** enables the researcher to create a custom-made, scannable questionnaire using standard paint and drawing tools. The finished questionnaire is then printed on a laser printer using special scanning paper.

▶ **ScanPro** reads forms from FormPro as well as those not made with FormPro. ScanPro, together with an optical mark reader, enables the researcher to scan a questionnaire and produce a standard ASCII file for later use with statistical software packages, spreadsheets, databases, and so on.

▶ **ScanPhone** is a high-tech telephone that enables consumers to scan and transmit bar codes. This may offer new opportunities to researchers, because in the future even questionnaires may be scanned.

Fax Surveys.[21] As a consequence of their deep penetration of some markets, fax machines have become feasible tools for use by marketing researchers in addressing certain research questions. Although it is probably premature to consider fax as a practical means of collecting data from consumer households, it can be used now for research with industrial, commercial, or institutional respondents. Under certain conditions, marketing researchers may prefer faxes over mail surveys.

Although many surveys do not have urgent deadlines, if fax provides quicker responses than mail, then faxes should be considered in place of mail in situations where rapid response is desirable. For instance, a firm needing immediate feedback on a product recall, a proposed price change, or a last-minute ad campaign decision would be pleased to save three to five days of survey time. Fax correspondence appears to have a greater urgency by its nature, and people may actually take the time to respond sooner to fax correspondence than to mail correspondence after receiving it.

Unless each questionnaire is unique, only one cover letter and questionnaire need be printed for fax transmittal. This results in savings in paper and printing costs. In some cases a hard copy of the questionnaire material need not be printed, because a computer can transfer the document to the fax machine. This capability eliminates the need to print labels or type addresses, purchase envelopes, and so on, all of which can add considerable cost in terms of time, labor, and materials. If surveys are to be done within an area having the same telephonic area code, then fax surveys will be much cheaper than mail surveys. Another potential cost advantage of fax surveys is that data can be returned by fax directly by computer, which in turn affords on-line access to and analysis of that portion of the data, thus skipping data-entry costs.

Fax surveys have some limitations. Unlike telephone interview costs, fax costs are affected by the quality of both the sending and receiving equipment. Additionally, transmission time will increase proportionately with the number of pages sent. Using monetary incentives to encourage response is not as easy with fax as it is with mail surveys, and it is not possible to provide self-addressed, postage-paid return envelopes with fax questionnaires.

Electronic Mail (E-Mail) Surveys. In March 1993, Telecommunications Incorporated, a leading cable company announced that its goal was to connect all of America with fiber optic cable within the next few years. Moreover the technological goal of the Clinton administration is to create the "data super-highway." This will revolutionize the methods by which researchers collect data. With the arrival of fiber optics technology and interactive multimedia computing, the paper-and-pencil methods of data collection may well become obsolete in the near future. Researchers will be able to e-mail the questionnaires into the respondents' computers and get their responses directly back into their own computers without any human interference at all. This will drastically reduce the errors committed in the surveys. E-mail surveys can become one of the most effective and popular survey methods of the future. With the use of Internet becoming more prevalent globally, e-mail surveys can be used for international surveys. The use of fax and e-mail surveys increases as other countries become more industrialized. They are bound to become important data-collection methods in the future.

Choice of Survey Methods for HMO Study

The HMO study described in earlier chapters successfully used a modification of the drop-off method. The changes were made so that advantage could be taken of the availability of a complete address list of all faculty, staff, and married students. This population was scattered over an area with a 20-mile radius, so it was not practical for the survey assistant to make unannounced personal visits. The specific procedure was as follows:

1. A telephone contact was made with each household named in the sample, to determine the head of the household and obtain that person's agreement to participate. To minimize nonresponse bias, at least five telephone call-backs were made.
2. During the telephone call, arrangements were made to deliver the questionnaire and a pick-up time was set.
3. Before the pick-up, a reminder phone call was made to see if the questionnaire had been completed.
4. If the questionnaire was not ready at the promised time, arrangements were made for a second pick-up time.

Only three percent of the sample of 1500 persons refused to participate on the first contact. Fourteen percent were ineligible, not at home after calls, or had disconnected phones. Another 9 percent refused to complete the questionnaire they had received, usually citing lack of time (this is not surprising, as the questionnaire had 14 pages and more than 200 variables). The overall response rate of 74 percent reflected the interest of most respondents in the subject and the subtle pressure to respond from the knowledge that someone was calling to pick up the questionnaire.

SURVEYS IN THE INTERNATIONAL CONTEXT

While conducting surveys for international research, a number of differences between the domestic and the international environment have to be taken into account. In this section the differences between domestic and international research and the problems faced by the researcher in conducting international research are discussed briefly for the three major survey methods.

Personal Interviews

Personal interviewing tends to be the dominant mode of data collection outside the United States.[22] Lower wage costs imply that personal procedures are cheaper than in the United States. On the other hand, use of personal interviewing requires the availability of field staff fluent in the relevant language.

Often, however, given the lack of a pool of trained interviewers in other countries, companies with local research units or international research organizations may train and develop their own field staffs. This provides greater control over the quality of the interviewing conducted in different countries. This is in marked contrast to the practice of "buying field and tab services" from an outside organization that is common in the United States. These interviewers are not necessarily required to work exclusively for a given research supplier, though often they may do so of their own choice.

The ease with which the cooperation of respondents can be obtained may, however, vary from one country or culture to another. In Latin countries, and particularly in the Middle East, interviewers are regarded with considerable suspicion. In Latin countries, where tax evasion is more prevalent, interviewers are often suspected of being tax inspectors. In the Middle East, where interviewers are invariably male, interviews with housewives often have to be conducted in the evenings when husbands are at home.

Telephone Interviews

In international marketing research, the advantages of this survey method are not always as evident. Low levels of telephone ownership and poor communications in many countries limit the coverage provided by telephone surveys. In addition, telephone costs are often high, and volume rates may not be available. Again, this depends on the specific country and the target population. Consequently, the desirability of conducting a telephone survey will depend to a large extent on the nature and purpose of the survey.

In industrial international marketing research, the use of telephone surveys may be quite effective. Most businesses, other than some small or itinerant retailers or craftspersons, are likely to have telephones.

With the decline of international telephone costs, multicountry studies can also be conducted from a single location. This significantly reduces the time and costs associated with negotiating and organizing a research project in each country, establishing quality controls, and so on. Although the additional costs of making international telephone calls are incurred, these may not be highly significant when a centralized location is used.[23]

International calls also obtain a higher response rate. Results obtained by using this technique have been found to be highly stable. Interviewer and client control is considerably greater. The questionnaire can be changed and modified in the course of the survey, and interviewing can be extended or stopped to meet the client's requirements. It is necessary to find interviewers fluent in the relevant languages, but in most European countries, this is rarely a problem.

In consumer research, the feasibility of using telephone surveys depends on the level of private telephone ownership in a country, and the specific target population. In countries such as India, which is predominantly rural, the telephone penetration is only 1 percent, and hence telephone surveys may not be the ideal method to adopt.[24] Even in relatively affluent societies such as Great Britain, where the telephone penetration is only 80 percent, telephone interviewing is not widely used because many practitioners are still skeptical about it.[25] The Eastern European countries and countries in the newly formed

Commonwealth of Independent States have a poor telecommunication system. In such countries, conducting telephone surveys may not be a good idea.

Mail Surveys

As in the case of telephone interviews, in international marketing research, the advantages and limitations of mail surveys are not always clear, because of the absence of mailing lists, poor mail services, and high levels of illiteracy. In many markets the efficacy of mail surveys, however, depends on the specific product market being investigated (that is, industrial versus consumer), and also the nature of the survey. Response rates are a problem in international mail surveys, too. When international mail surveys are conducted, the response rates vary depending on the country to which the questionnaires are mailed. The response rate for a mail survey conducted by ESOMAR in 1992 is given in Table 9-4, and these rates should not be viewed as representative of the country's response rates.

Mail surveys typically can be used effectively in industrial international marketing research. Mailing lists such as those from Bottin International, or directories for specific industries, are generally available.

In consumer research, and particularly in developing countries, the use of mail surveys may give rise to some problems. Mailing lists comparable to those in the domestic market may not be available, or not sold, and public sources such as telephone directories may not provide adequate coverage. Lists that are available, that is, magazine subscription lists or membership association lists, may be skewed to better-educated segments of the population. In addition, in some countries, the effectiveness of mail surveys is limited not only by low

TABLE 9-4
Response Rates in the ESOMAR 1992 Price Study

	Sample Selected	Effective Returns	% of Response
North America	22	11	50.00
Latin America	17	16	94.12
Eastern Europe	17	10	58.82
Turkey	11	10	90.91
North Africa	6	4	66.67
Middle East	9	6	66.67
Australasia	9	6	66.67
India	5	4	80.00
Pacific Rim	12	11	91.67
Japan	12	5	41.67
South Africa	3	3	100.00
Total	123	86	Overall = 69.92

Source: European Society for Opinion and Marketing Research Prices Study, 1992.

literacy levels, but also by the reluctance of respondents to respond to them.[26] As noted previously, levels of literacy are often less than 40 or 50 percent in some Asian and African markets, thus limiting the population that can be reached by mail. Mail surveys are also hazardous in countries such as Brazil, where it has been reckoned that 30 percent of the domestic mail is never delivered; or Nicaragua, where all the mail has to be delivered to the post office. Even in countries where literacy levels and mail services make the use of mail surveys feasible, a tendency to regard surveys as an invasion of privacy may limit their effectiveness.

Thus, while mail surveys may be used effectively in industrial marketing research, in consumer research they may be appropriate only in industrialized countries where levels of literacy are high, and mailing lists are more available.

Summary

The choice of a data-collection method involves a series of compromises in matching the often conflicting requirements of the situation with the strengths and limitations of the available methods.

While each situation is unique to some degree, the following represent the major constraints to be satisfied:

Available budget.
Nature of the problem and the complexity of the required information.
Need for accuracy.
Time constraints.

Part of the skill of research design is adapting a basic data collection method, whether personal or telephone interview or mail survey, to those constraints. This process of adaptation means exploiting the advantages as well as blunting the limitations, which to some extent makes generalizations suspect. Nonetheless, it is useful to summarize the relative merits of the basic survey methods, as in Table 9-3, to put the methods into perspective. Of course, these summary judgments do not reflect the myriad of special factors that may be influential in specific cases, such as the availability of a sampling frame, the need to ask sensitive questions, and the rarity of the population to be sampled.

The greatest potential for effective adaptation of method to situation lies with combinations of methods, or specialized variants of basic methods. The latter include omnibus surveys and mail panels, which are particularly good for tracking studies, or where limited responses from specific populations are required and budget constraints are severe. Some combinations of methods, such as the drop-off method, similarly confer impressive advantages by combining some of the advantages of personal interviews and mail surveys. As with specialized variants, however, their usefulness often is restricted to certain settings.

Survey research is bound to be the most dominant data-collection method in the future. The future of survey research is exciting. With technology growing at such a tremendous pace, newer and better methods to conduct surveys, such as computer interactive surveying, are becoming more common. With the dawn of the age of multimedia computing, e-mail surveys are also likely to become more prevalent. Another trend in the survey research area is internationalization. This introduces a number of new challenges to the marketing researcher, who has to contend with language, cultural, and a host of other problems.

Questions and Problems

1. What kind of data collection procedure would you recommend to research the question of why female shoppers choose a particular retail store at which to buy clothing?

2. Even with the use of expensive gifts and call-backs, all three interview methods produce low response rates, usually under 30 percent. What are some ways to increase these response rates?

3. What biases, if any, might be introduced by offering to give respondents $5.00 when they return a mail questionnaire? Would these biases be different if a gift with retail value of $5.00 were included with the questionnaire?

4. What can an interviewer do during the first 30 seconds of an interview to maximize the cooperation rate of (a) a personal interview and (b) a telephone interview? Assume the appropriate respondent is the head of the household.

5. What are the advantages of the telephone prenotification approach over a conventional mail survey?

6. Write a cover letter to a mail survey of householders that contains a number of questions regarding the utilization of various kinds of burglary protection devices.

7. You are a senior analyst in the marketing research department of a major chemical company. Your company has accidentally stumbled upon a chemical that, when combined with plastic, gives it near metallic properties. You have been asked to find out various uses for this chemical and also forecast its total market potential.
   a. What information if any, that could be obtained from respondents, would be useful for this research?
   b. What techniques are applicable for obtaining each item of information?
   c. Design a survey to obtain the information desired. Prepare all instructions, collection forms, and other materials required to obtain such information.
   d. Estimate the cost of conducting the survey you have designed.

8. You are a publisher of national repute and you would like to find the potential for an academic book. You have decided to conduct a survey among college professors for this purpose. What form of survey method would you use? What trend do you see in the future for this survey method?

9. What are the advantages and disadvantages of computer interactive interviewing compared to the traditional methods of surveying?

10. What are the problems faced by researchers when they are conducting research in developing countries?

11. You are the manufacturer of a major consumer product in the United States. You plan to enter the following countries with your products within the next two years:

Russia, France, South Africa, Brazil, China, Japan, Mexico, Canada, India, and Germany.

Based on the demographic data and the infrastructural data about these countries, determine the best survey method to be adopted in each of these countries.

12. Idaho Ideal Potatoes, Ltd., developed a new guacamole-flavored potato chip and wanted to ascertain the national sales potential for this unique product offering. However, he found the response rate to be extremely low (10 percent) and found that many of the returned surveys had been incorrectly completed.

   a. How might the company have more effectively collected the relevant data?

   b. What are the advantages and disadvantages of using telephone surveys and focus groups for this kind of study?

   Due to stringent budget constraints, the marketing research director decides to limit the survey to residents of San Antonio, Texas.

   c. What possible biases could be reflected in the survey results?

   Idaho Ideal Potatoes, Ltd., has decided to simultaneously offer their new potato chip in foreign markets and wishes to survey potential sales demand for the product in the United Kingdom.

   d. How is the choice of survey method altered to suit the company's research of foreign markets?

13. Wildlife Treasures, Inc.'s head of marketing, Judy Gomez, has been informed by the board of directors that they would like a marketing research study conducted to determine the cause of the plateau in sales performance over the past two years. The company is a producer of art and ornaments depicting African wildlife, and currently supplies specialty stores throughout the United States. A considerably restricted budget has been allocated to the project. Ms. Gomez is expected to survey all of these stores in order to determine how sales in the domestic market can be increased. The board of directors has been generous in its time allowance for the study, preferring a thorough marketing research effort to a hasty one.

   a. Suggest a suitable survey method for the study and justify your answer.
      Ms. Gomez believes that a possible remedy to Wildlife Treasures, Inc.'s stagnant sales performance may be an entry into foreign markets. Because the company has received some unsolicited inquiries from European tourists, she feels that a market may exist in Europe for its specialty good.

   b. Given the restraints of the study, how can Ms. Gomez conduct a survey to determine potential markets across Europe?

14. In the above example, Ms. Gomez would like to utilize the company's recently updated computer system for the marketing research study. What features would need to be available in order to use the computer system for this purpose?

End Notes

1. Seymour Sudman. "Improving the Quality of Shopping Center Sampling," *Journal of Marketing Research*, 17, November 1980, 423–431.

2. Frederick Wiseman, Marianne Schafer, and Richard Schafer. "An Experimental Test of the Effects of a Monetary Incentive on Cooperation Rates and Data Collection Costs in Central-Location Interviewing," *Journal of Marketing Research*, November 1983, 439–442.

3. S. M. McIntyre and S. D. F. G. Bender. "The Purchase Intercept Technique in Comparison to Telephone and Mail Surveys," *Journal of Retailing*, 62, Winter 1986, 364–383.

4. Tyzoon T. Tyebjee. "Telephone Survey Methods: The State of the Art," *Journal of Marketing*, Summer 1979, 68–78; Patricia E. Moberg, "Biases in Unlisted Phone Numbers," *Journal of Advertising Research*, August–September 1982, 51–55.

5. Stanley L. Payne. "Data Collection Methods: Telephone Surveys," in Robert Ferber, ed., op. cit., pp. 2.105–2.123.

6. Payne, op. cit., 2.116.

7. J. B. Lansing and J. N. Morgan. *Economic Survey Methods*, (Ann Arbor, Michigan: University of Michigan, Institute of Social Research), 1971, 203–243.

8. Quoted from Census Bureau sources by Paul L. Erdos. "Data Collection Methods: Mail Surveys," in Robert Ferber, ed., *Handbook of Marketing Research*, op, cit., pp. 2–91.

9. Results from other comparative studies have not been so clear-cut. See, for example, W. Locander, S. Sudman, and N. Bradburn. "An Investigation of Interviewer Method, Threat and Response Distortion," *Journal of the American Statistical Association*, June 1976, 262–275.

10. Michael J. Houston and Neil M. Ford. "Broadening the Scope of Methodological Research on Mail Surveys," *Journal of Marketing Research*, 13, November 1976, 397–403.

11. Paul L. Erdos, op cit.

12. Council of American Survey Research Organizations, *On the Definition of Response Rates*, Special Report (Port Jefferson, New York: CASRO), 1982.

13. Frederick Wiseman and Maryann Billington. "Comment on a Standard Definition of Response Rates," *Journal of Marketing Research*, August 1984, 336–338.

14. Leslie Kanuk and Conrad Berenson. "Mail Surveys and Response Rates: A Literature Review," *Journal of Marketing Research*, 12, November 1975, 440–453. Jeanine M. James and Richard Bolstein, "The Effect of Monetary Incentives and Follow-up Mailings on the Response Rate and Response Quality in Mail Surveys," *Public Opinion Quarterly*, 54, Fall 1990, 346–361.

15. J. Scott Armstrong and Terry S. Overton. "Estimating Nonresponse Bias in Mail Surveys," *Journal of Marketing Research*, 14, August 1977, 396–402.

16. Marvin A. Jolson. "How to Double or Triple Mail-Survey Response Rates," *Journal of Marketing*, 41, October 1977, 78–81.

17. David Schwartz. "Locked Box Contains Survey Methods, Helps End Some Woes of Probing Industrial Field," *Marketing News*, January 27, 1978, 18.

18. Christopher H. Lovelock, Ronald Stiff, David Cullwick, and Ira M. Kaufman. "An Evaluation of the Effectiveness of Drop-Off Questionnaire Delivery," *Journal of Marketing Research*, 13, November 1976, 358–364.

19. For more details on cost savings refer to, John P. Liefeld. "Response Effects in Computer-Administered Questioning," *Journal of Marketing Research*, 25, November 1988, 405–409.

20. Lewis C. Winters. "Questionnaires in the 1900s: Wands and Scannable Forms are 'In'," *Marketing Research*, June, 1992. 46.

21. John P. Dickson and Douglas L. MacLachlan. "Fax Surveys?" *Marketing Research*, September 1992, 26–30.

22. D. Monk. "Marketing Research in Canada," *European Research*, November 1987, 274, and J. J. Honomichl, "Survey Results Positive," *Advertising age*, November 1984, 23.

23. M. De Houd. "International Computerized Telephone Research: Is It Fiction?" *Marketing Research Society Newsletter*, January 1982, 14–15.

24. D. Sopariwala. "India: Election Polling in the World's Largest Democracy," *European Research*, August 1987, 174–177.

25. R. M. Worcester. "Political Opinion Polling in Great Britain: Past, Present and Future," *European Research*, May 1987, 143–151.

26. Erdener Kayanak. "The Use of Marketing Research to Facilitate Marketing within Developing Countries," *International Marketing Management* (New York: Praeger Publishers), 1984, 155–171.

CASE 9-1
Project DATA: An Urban Transportation Study

The Downtown Agency for Transportation Action project (Project DATA) was a collaborative approach to the problem of improving the high-density movement of people and goods within downtown Cleveland.[1] In August 1968, the survey researcher employed by Project DATA was wondering how to collect downtown origin and destination (DOD) data for input to a comprehensive model of traveler behavior in downtown Cleveland. Problems had been compounded by a poor response rate to a recent test of the preferred method of data collection, a mail-back questionnaire distributed to rapid-transit users, bus patrons, and automobile travelers. Consequently, the researcher had to decide in a short time whether to stay with the mail-back questionnaire method or try some other, more costly, procedure. To not change would involve persuading the other members of the research team that the problems encountered in the pretest could be overcome and that the mail-back method would yield sufficiently accurate results.

Background

Downtown Cleveland represented one of the most important concentrations of people in the Midwest. It generally was defined as an area encircled by the Cuyahoga River Valley, the Innerbelt Freeway, and Lake Erie. For the purposes of Project DATA, this definition was modified slightly to include the downtown-oriented activity centers adjacent to the southeast corner of the area outside the Innerbelt Freeway. These centers include the future location of Cuyahoga Community College and the St. Vincent Hospital and its parking area.

There had been considerable progress in making downtown Cleveland more accessible through rail rapid transit and freeways; however, facilities to expedite the movement of people and goods within the downtown area were being installed at a much slower rate. Transportation planners had tended to treat downtown Cleveland as a terminus point for regional line-haul transportation. Yet, the downtown covered a broad land area with several separate activity centers and a solid network of business, commercial, and entertainment facilities. Except for a downtown loop bus system, there was little transportation among these centers.

The lack of transportation was regarded as a contributing factor in the deterioration of downtown Cleveland and many other urban areas. After the Hough riots, Cleveland was chosen by the U. S. Department of Transportation as the site of the first large-scale effort to design a comprehensive central urban transportation network. A number of systems were under consideration, including: (1) train-type systems, (2) small automatic taxis, and (3) continuous systems. Each was to be evaluated by a model that would simulate the decision processes of different user segments. The model would consider where and how users move from one place to another for various trip purposes within the downtown area. The DOD data being collected by Project DATA were to be the base for the calibration of the simulation model. In addition, the data would be used in the development of interim projects to improve the existing downtown transportation system. Thus, there was considerable urgency behind the request for the data.

Designing the DOD Study

The first step was to establish the purpose of the study. After extensive discussions, it was agreed that the following types of information were needed:

1. The numbers and socioeconomic characteristics of people who move to, from and within downtown Cleveland
2. The locations of the activity centers within downtown Cleveland to which these people are moving
3. The methods of travel used to move these people to, from, and within downtown
4. The trip purposes of the people movements
5. The time distribution of the people-movement patterns throughout a 24-hour period

A number of alternative methods for collecting the DOD information were considered. These included mail-back questionnaires distributed to people at key locations within the downtown area, personal interviews conducted at these same key locations, telephone surveys, trip diaries distributed to people to complete over extended periods of time, mailback questionnaires sent to houses, personal home interviews, newspaper coupons to be completed and returned by mail, and a system of distributing and collecting precoded computer cards to reflect origins and destinations of trips within the downtown area.

An evaluation of the various survey designs was made by the Project DATA staff. It decided that a mail-

[1] Funds and assistance for the project were provided by Case Western Reserve University, Battelle Memorial Institute, City of Cleveland, Cleveland-Seven County Transportation-Land Use Study, Cleveland Transit System, Cuyahoga County, and U.S. Department of Housing and Urban Development.

back questionnaire distributed at key locations within the downtown area was the most realistic approach to collecting the needed information, taking into account the time and financial constraints of the project. To test this decision, a pilot survey was conducted. The objectives were:

1. To evaluate the ability of the survey forms and questions to obtain the required data
2. To determine the approximate survey-response rates that could be expected from the various categories of people so that a proper data-sampling frame could be formulated
3. To ascertain where in the downtown area the survey questionnaires should be distributed
4. To determine the best procedures for distributing the questionnaires to the users of various modes of transportation

The pilot survey utilized the questionnaire shown in Figure 1. Four hundred were distributed to rapid-transit users as they went through the turnstiles in Terminal Tower. Another 600 were given to bus riders as they passed an imaginary downtown cordon line. Those questionnaires were distributed only during the A.M. and P.M. peak traffic periods. A final 400 questionnaires were distributed within two major parking lots by placing them under windshield wipers after the automobiles had been parked. The results of the pilot survey are summarized in Figures 2, 3, and 4.

Questions for Discussion

1. Critique the questionnaire. Does it provide the required data?
2. Evaluate the overall research design with respect to possible sources of bias in the results and the reasons for the poor response rate.
3. Specify how you would improve this mailback survey.
4. Suggest an alternative design and cite its advantages and shortcomings.

CASE 9-2
Roland Development Corp.

Roland Development was a leading builder of homes in the Western United States. Its emphasis was on condominiums and townhouses, which were forecast to have an attractive future in these markets. These housing types lent themselves to standardization and cost reduction possibilities. Further, rising land costs were causing the share of single-family detached houses to decline significantly. Meanwhile the share of market for single-family attached houses (houses with common walls, floors or roofs) was expected to double in the next five years. Roland was well positioned to exploit these trends by following a strategy that differed from competition in three areas:

▶ Market segmentation. Roland typically segmented the market more finely than other home builders, and then designed homes to meet the specific needs of these groups.
▶ Direct selling. Shoppers in some department stores could find full-scale, fully furnished Roland homes on display.
▶ Low prices for a complete housing package (including all the furnishings and necessary financing).

The company had begun to expand its limited line of condominiums and townhouses to provide design and square footage combinations that would appeal to higher-income households. The management was especially pleased with the elegance, convenience, and durability of the four new models they were planning to launch. Several problems remained to be solved. The first was the identification of a creative strategy that would position the new models and attract the largest number of purchases. That is, the company wanted to know what main ideas and themes should be used in the advertising of the new models. Another problem was to identify those segments of the market with the highest probability of purchasing the new models. The company asked the YKG Group, a large national research firm, to submit a written proposal for research which would provide Roland's management with information useful in solving these two problems. Their proposal is summarized below.

Research Proposal
The recommended research design would use a consumer panel and employ both telephone interviews and mail questionnaires. The research firm felt that the needed information could be obtained only from that very small proportion of the population who might buy such a home. Each of several different market segments would be studied to determine how they positioned the new models in relation to competing homes already on the market. The likelihood of pur-

Downtown Agency for Transportation Action

Project Data
University Circle Research Center
1000 Cedar Avenue
Cleveland Ohio 44106

Project DATA needs to know how people travel to, from, and, especially, *within* downtown Cleveland. "Downtown" is the open area in this map

Our goal is a better transportation system—including improved pedestrian facilities—for the downtown. We would appreciate your assistance in completing the questions on the other side of this form according to the instructions below. THANK YOU.

xxxxxxxxxxxxxxxxxxxxxxxxxxxxxxxxxxxxxxxxxxxxxxxxxxxxxxxxxxxxxxxxxxxxxxxxxxxxxxxxxxxxxxxxxxxxxxxxxxxxxxxxxxxxxx
xxxxxxxxxxxxxxxxxxxxxxxxxxxxxxxxxxxxxxxxxxxxxxxxxxxxxxxxxxxxxxxxxxxxxxxxxxxxxxxxxxxxxxxxxxxxxxxxxxxxxxxxxxxxxx

First Class
Permit No. 2086
Cleveland, Ohio

BUSINESS REPLY MAIL
No Postage Stamp Necessary if Mailed in the United States

Postage Will Be Paid By

Case Western Reserve University
Cleveland, Ohio 44106
University Circle

Attention: Dr. James B. Reswick, Project DATA

INSTRUCTIONS:

1. Please complete the questions on the other side of this form. Only a small number of these forms are being distributed at this time. We need this information in order to design a large-scale survey that will be conducted this summer and fall. Your cooperation will make a significant difference to the project.

2. After completing the questionnaire, please fold it lightly along the dotted lines so that the address in the center of the page above is showing.

3. Please drop it into any mailbox—no postage is required.

THANK YOU FOR PARTICIPATING IN PROJECT DATA

FIGURE 1
Project DATA transportation questionnaire

chasing a Roland model would also be determined during the study for each of the three-market segments and also for each of several different advertising themes. This information would help Roland identify the most promising market segments for the new models, as well as the creative advertising strategy that would most appeal to them.

The proposed research design consisted of three phases: (1) the members of a large consumer mail panel would be screened to locate qualified prospects for the new models; (2) a relatively small sample of qualified prospects would be interviewd "in-depth"

to identify possible advertising themes; and (3) a large sample of qualified respondents would be surveyed by mail to test their response to alternative creative strategies.

Phase 1. The YKG Group maintained a bank of over 200,000 families who agreed to cooperate in research projects undertaken by this firm. Considerable information existed about each family, including geographical location, occupation and age of male and female heads of family, total family income, presence and age of children, and so on. Roland managers felt that the four new models would most likely appeal to middle

1. Please list ALL trips you made downtown TODAY. We are especially interested in short walking trips such as: going to lunch, coming from lunch, a walk from the parking lot to the office, etc.

	Name of Place Where Trip Starts and Address if Possible	Time Trip Starts	Name of Place Where Trip Ends and Address if Possible	Time Trip Ends	Purpose of Trip (Please use codes below)	Method of Travel
Trip TO the downtown area					☐	☐
First Trip IN downtown area					☐	☐
Second Trip in downtown area					☐	☐
Third Trip					☐	☐
Fourth Trip					☐	☐
Fifth Trip					☐	☐
Sixth Trip					☐	☐
Trip FROM the downtown area					☐	☐

2. How many persons accompanied you downtown today? ☐

   How many of these persons were children under 12? ☐

   ↓ "Purpose of Trip"   ↓ "Method of Travel"

   1. work   1. auto driver
   2. personal business   2. auto passenger
   3. shopping   3. bus
   4. social-recreation   4. rapid transit
   5. school   5. taxi
   6. eat   6. walk
   7. medical or dental   7. other
   8. serve passenger
   9. to home
   10. other

3. How often do you usually come downtown? (Please Check One)
   1. Every Weekday (Mon-Fri) ☐
   2. Several Times a Week ☐
   3. Once a Week ☐
   4. Once a Month ☐
   5. Other (Please Specify) ☐ _____

4. Name Address _____
   (Number)   (Street)   (City)   (Zip)

5. Male ☐ Female ☐ : Number of Persons in Your Household? ☐ Your Age? ☐ No. of Autos in Household? ☐

6. Approximate Family Yearly Income: (Please Check One)
   Under $3500 ☐; $3500–6500 ☐; $6500–9500 ☐; $9500–12500 ☐; $12500–15500 ☐;   Over $15,500 ☐

7. What could be done to make your trips within downtown Cleveland easier, faster, or more pleasant?
   _____
   _____

8. We would appreciate any suggestions you may have for making this questionaire clearer or easier to answer. For instance, were any of the questions confusing? Why?
   _____
   _____

FIGURE 1 (continued)

248

Mode	Number of Questionnaires Returned	Number of Questionnaires Handed Out	Percentage Return
CTS Rapid Transit	20 (A.M.)	100	20
	19 (P.M.)	100	19
Shaker Rapid Transit	23 (A.M.)	100	23
	16 (P.M.)	100	16
CTS Bus Route 32 (suburban express)	23 (A.M.)	100	23
	15 (P.M.)	100	15
CTS Bus Route 9 (suburban local)	22 (A.M.)	100	22
	16 (P.M.)	100	16
CTS Bus Route 14 (low-income inner-city area local)	5 (A.M.)	100	5
	1 (P.M.)	100	1
Department Store Parking Lot (relatively high parking turnover rate)	10	200	5
Muny Parking Lot (caters primarily to all-day parkers)	16	200	8
Totals	186	1,400	

FIGURE 2
Distribution and response of pilot survey

and upper-income families of size two, three, or four, with a household head 30 years of age or over. For this reason, the first phase of the proposed research involved mailing a short questionnaire to all panel members with those characteristics. The questionnaire asked panel members to indicate the likelihood of their purchasing a home in the next two to three years and also to report their attitude toward buying a townhouse or condominium.

It was expected that this screening process would locate some 3000 to 5000 families who would be prospects to buy the new models over the next few years. To be considered a prospect, a family had to report being likely to purchase a home in the next two to three years, as well as having a favorable attitude toward a condominium or townhouse. Among these prospects three market segments would be identified. A high-income family would be a "very good" prospect if it was "very likely" to buy a home; a medium-income family would be a "good" prospect if it was "very likely" to buy a new home; and a high-income family would be a "fair" prospect if it was "somewhat" likely to buy a new home. All other responses were considered to indicate nonprospects.

Phase 2. In this phase about 200 qualified prospects would be interviewed using a combination of telephone and mail. These families would be mailed pictures, specifications, and line drawings of the

company's new models of condos and townhouses, although they would not be identified by the Roland name. The line drawings would include front and rear views of each unit's exterior as well as sketches of each room. The specifications would include the number of square feet, wall thickness, heating and cooling equipment capacities, appliance brands and models, slab thickness, type of roof covering, and other features.

After reviewing these materials, respondents' reactions and impressions would be obtained through telephone interviews using open-ended questions. Interviewers would be told that the objective was to obtain qualitative data useful for ascertaining how potential buyers perceived the new models with respect to appearance, comfort, elegance, convenience, durability, ease and economy of maintenance, and other criteria. Interviewers would be instructed to record verbatim responses and were told that it was very important to do so because none of the responses would be tabulated or analyzed statistically. Responses to the open questions would then be studied to identify four or five ideas of themes that might be considered for use as creative strategies in advertising the new models.

Phase 3. This phase would be undertaken after four of the best advertising themes had been identified. Some 2400 families would be selected from the list of

1. A common error for rapid transit respondents was that they failed to record Terminal Tower as their first destination in the central business district (CBD).

2. A common error for all respondents was that they often failed to record return trips, especially the return lunch trip.

3. It appears that a relatively large number of people (especially bus riders) do not leave the building they work in during the day. Or, these people did not understand how to fill out the form.

4. The people that returned the questionnaire can be generally categorized into two major groups: (a) those that completely understood how to fill out question 1, and (b) those that completely misunderstood how to fill out question 1.

5. A few people recorded "work," "restaurant," and so on as their origin and destination points, rather than an address or the specific name or the place or location.

6. Several people did not record the number of the home address; only street, city and zip code.

7. A relatively large number of respondents failed to answer question 2.

8. For the majority of the respondents, filling the trip purpose and method of travel codes presented no problems. In fact, many people improvised on the quesionnaire to provide additional data.

9. In a few instances people did not record trip times. Again, it appears that these cases were oversights. Generally, people recorded this information quite accurately. For example, walking trips lasting two or three minutes were being recorded. The longer the trip—usually the trips to and from the CBD—the more tendency there was to round off the trip time to 15- or 30-minute intervals.

10. The majority of respondents filled out the income question with no comments. However, several people residing in higher income areas questioned the necessity of the information in relation to transportation. Eleven of the 180 respondents failed to answer this question.

11. There is some confusion on the income question. For example, there were many 20- and 21-year-olds making over $15,000 annually, based on the result of the survey.

12. A few respondents (seven) did not record their age.

13. Public transportation respondents receiving the questionnaire on the outbound trip (P.M.) had a tendency to record only that trip. In addition, the (P.M.) return rate of the questionnaire was considerably less than the (A.M.) (inbound) trip.

14. Several bus-rider respondents obviously failed to record their first trip in the CBD between the bus stop and their first CBD destination. In other cases, this error was difficult to identify, since it is unknown to us how far it is from the bus stops to their first CBD destinations on Euclid Avenue. (Bus routes surveyed were Euclid Avenue routes.)

15. Many bus respondents misunderstood question 2 and recorded the total number of people on the bus.

16. A surprisingly large number of people enter the CBD via one mode and exit using another mode.

17. Bus riders are very concerned about trips to and from the CBD and wonder why we are concerned with only downtown transportation needs.

FIGURE 3
Analysis of problems by Project DATA staff

prospects obtained from Phase 1—approximately 800 "very good" prospects, 800 "good" prospects, and 800 "fair" prospects.

All of the families in each of the three market segments would be sent pictures, line drawings, and specifications (including prices) of the new Roland models as well as those of major competing models, all identified by brand name. Each of these three groups of prospects would then be randomly divided into four subsamples of 200, each of which would receive one, and only one, of the four advertising themes identified for the new models. Thus, the study design would consist of three samples of 800 families each. In turn, each sample would be broken into four subsamples, each of which would receive a different advertising theme.

Analysis. The effect of each advertising theme on each prospect segment would be evaluated on three measures—the degree to which it (1) resulted in the new line being rated as "most appealing," (2) led respondents to request further information about the company's products, and (3) led respondents to indicate that they would be most likely to select one of the company's homes if they were to make such a purchase in the near future. For each advertising theme-prospect segment combination the research would yield three percentages. For example, for theme #1 and the "very good" prospects, the research might show that 38 percent of the respondents found a model in the new line "most appealing" among all the models reviewed: that 26 percent requested further information about the Roland models; and

1. Question #1 refers to "today," while #3 refers to "usual" habits. I go downtown every day, but I do not always drive. Also, times of leaving and arriving vary.

2. I think this questionnaire is easily followed.

3. Good questionnaire—easy to answer.

4. The first group of questions could be made more explicit.

5. They were confusing on many trips because I don't do the same thing every day at lunch time.

6. Question #2.

7. Everything is clear.

8. Very good—not confusing.

9. If answers must be confined to the blocks, it might be well to point this out.

10. Questionnaire seems clear enough.

11. Not confusing.

12. Add a few more lines for #7 and place a line for the date.

13. Could not be made any clearer.

14. No provision of alternates—sometimes walk/bus; no space allowed for total trip home as buses connecting with rapid for suburbs cannot be included in "downtown area" trips. I need two bus trips plus rapid to get home.

15. Understand as is.

16. Question #4 is revelatory; you should ask for nearest intersection.

17. Question #2a could be reworded—glad you're interested!

18. Question #2 doesn't make it possible to answer if a bus trip and one is unaware of survey. Question #7—why discuss only downtown? The trip to town is depressing.

19. All questions clear enough.

20. No clearcut place for occasional trips.

21. It was difficult for me to answer Question #1.

22. It is fine.

23. Clarify Question #1 and #2—add extra part to "from downtown area" for intermediate trip, e.g., Terminal–Windemere–home (one trip or two?)

24. Home address—why necessary?

25. Use of "grid" and block number instead of address would make the form easier and more meaningful.

26. The questionnaire was very simple to fill out. I hope you get as many back as you gave out.

27. My family does not reside in Cleveland, therefore, perhaps question #6 is irrelevant.

28. You didn't provide for combined bus and rapid or car and rapid use.

29. No confusion.

30. Questionnaire was clear.

31. Upper right-hand corner should have more blocks for more than one method of travel or purpose of trip.

32. Method of travel does not indicate if more than one method is used; i.e., bus, transfer to rapid, transfer to bus again, or walk.

33. Provide a way of indicating more than one method of travel for the same trip, such as transfers to and from a bus or rapid transit.

34. Why worry about short walking trips? Alleviate the problems of getting into and out of the downtown area from the suburban residential sections.

35. I should like to know the purpose of this questionnaire and whether something constructive will come of it. I think the questionnaire is clear—I hope useful.

36. Believe inquiry as to whether or not service from home to downtown was frequent enough at hour necessary to leave would be pertinent.

FIGURE 4
Survey criticisms by respondents (unedited responses to question 8)

37. Referring back to Question #1—List trips within downtown area for a 30-day period giving people more of an opportunity to use "Purpose of Trip" and "Method of Travel."

38. Much more time could be spent in the organization of this questionnaire.

39. What does the yearly family income have to do with the transportation problem?

40. Very specific and clear.

41. Why income of family?

42. Not confusing, but embarrassing and totally unnecessary, i.e., why the question of sex (male and female) necessary? Also, why the interest about incomes? Or if a person is alone or how many in the household? These, to me, seem totally irrelevant questions.

43. I found the questionnaire clear enough.

44. It seems a much better questionnaire than the usual.

45. Perfectly clear.

46. No distinction between going to work and business calls during day.

47. Method of travel and purpose should indicate that more than one answer is okay. Also more space for multiple answers.

48. Complication where two travel modes are used—see Question #1 "Trip"—definition not immediately clear.

49. Design a way to emphasize that you are only interested in a certain part of downtown.

50. Question #7 might be worded as below to eliminate unwanted responses. This may, however, confuse your strictly ambulatory respondents. (Question #7 reworded: What could be done to our transportation system to make your trips within downtown Cleveland easier, faster, and more pleasant)?

51. Extremely amateurish from a professional standpoint—too detailed, too time-consuming, too personal (address, identify with income).

52. Question #4 is not necessary.

53. Question #1 doesn't indicate whether you mean total trip or first or second leg—to my office is two steps.

54. It would seem easier to ask approximately how long a trip took than the times. I never pay much attention to timing my trips by the clock—especially shopping.

55. Questions were all clear.

56. Good questionnaire—okay.

FIGURE 4 (continued)

that 17 percent indicated that they "most likely would purchase" one of the new Roland models. By comparing these three percentages for each advertising theme-prospect segment combination, it would be possible to identify the most promising combinations. These results could be weighed by the relative size of each prospect segment to decide which creative strategy would be most effective in generating sales interest in the new models.

Questions for Discussion

1. Would you recommend that Roland accept the YKG Group proposal?
2. If yes, what conclusions can be drawn from the data in Phase 3 of the research?
3. If the proposal is not accepted, what alternative designs should be considered?

10 ATTITUDE MEASUREMENT

Learning Objectives

▶ Introduce the concept of measurement and scaling in marketing research.

▶ Briefly discuss the different scales in measurement.

▶ Introduce the different types of scales used for measuring attitudes.

▶ Give a description of each of the well-known scales that are used to measure attitudes.

▶ Provide an approximate heuristic for choosing an attitude scale.

▶ Discuss the concept of reliability, validity, and generalizability.

Most questions in marketing research surveys are designed to measure attitudes. For example, each of the following situations involves the measurement of some aspect of a respondent's attitude:

1. An appliance manufacturer wants to know how many potential buyers are aware of a brand name. (What brand names do they think of in connection with dishwashers?)
2. Administrators concerned with formulating an energy policy want to know what proportion of the voters agree that car buyers should pay an extra tax of several hundred dollars on cars that get poor gasoline mileage.
3. A food manufacturer is interested in the intentions of a sample of consumers to buy a possible new product after the concept has been described to them.

Common to each of these examples is a need to learn something about the basic orientation or attitude of present or prospective customers. Their attitudes are based on the information they have, their feelings (liking and disliking), and their intended behavior.

What management really wants to understand—and ultimately influence—is behavior. For many reasons, however, they are likely to use attitude measures instead of behavior. First, there is a widely held belief that attitudes are precursors of behavior. If consumers like a brand, they are more likely to choose that brand over one they like less. Second, it is generally more feasible to ask attitude questions than to observe and interpret actual behavior. Attitude measures offer the greatest advantage over behavior measures in their capacity for diagnosis or explanation. Attitude measures can be used to help learn which features of a new product concept are acceptable or unacceptable, as well as the perceived strengths and weaknesses of competitive alternatives. Insights can be gained into the process by which choice decisions are made: What alternatives are known and considered? Why are some rejected? What problems are encountered with the products or services that are used?

This chapter is concerned primarily with the measurement of attitudes. Some measurement approaches were encountered in earlier chapters. Projective techniques and physiological methods, discussed in Chapter 7, are indirect methods for inferring a person's attitude. By far the most popular approach is the direct self-report, in which the respondent is asked a series of questions. The two previous chapters describe the survey methods appropriate for such self-reports. This chapter and the next are devoted specifically to attitude measurements, in recognition of their importance to marketing and of the special problems of specifying and identifying attitudes.

WHAT ARE ATTITUDES?

Attitudes are mental states used by individuals to structure the way they perceive their environment and guide the way they respond to it. There is general acceptance that there are three related components that form an attitude: a cognitive or knowledge component, a liking or affective component, and an intentions or actions component. Each component provides a different insight into a person's attitude.

Cognitive or Knowledge Component

The **cognitive/knowledge component** represents a person's information about an object. This information includes awareness of the existence of the object, beliefs about the characteristics or attributes of the object, and judgments about the relative importance of each of the attributes.

Consider the knowledge people might bring to planning a ski vacation in the Rockies. They might remember the names of several ski areas without prompting: Aspen, Snowmass, Alta, and Park City, for example. This is unaided recall awareness. The names of additional ski areas are likely to be remembered when the travel agent mentions them. This is **aided recall awareness.**

Knowledge of ski areas is not limited to awareness, however. From the experience of friends, brochures, magazine articles, and other sources, a person would have formed beliefs or judgments about the characteristics or attributes of each of these ski areas. These attributes might range from the difficulty of the slopes to the type of social life and the cost of accommodations. Often, these beliefs incorporate explicit comparative judgments, such as which ski area is the most difficult or the cheapest, within a set. Another kind of belief is an overall similarity judgment: Are Aspen and Snowmass more similar to each other than Aspen and Alta, for example?

Affective or Liking Component

The affective/liking component summarizes a person's overall feelings toward an object, situation, or person, on a scale of *like–dislike,* or *favorable–unfavorable.* When there are several alternatives to choose among, then liking is expressed in terms of preference for one alternative over another. Preferences can be measured by asking which is "most preferred" or the "first choice," which is the "second choice," and so forth. Affective judgments also can be made about the attributes of an object, such as a ski area. Someone may like all other aspects of an area but dislike the location because it requires too much traveling.

Intention or Action Component

The **intention/action component** refers to a person's expectations of future behavior toward an object. Is he or she "very," "somewhat," or "not at all" likely to go to Aspen for a ski week next winter? Intentions usually are limited to a distinct time period that depends on buying habits and planning horizons. The great advantage of an intentions question is that it incorporates information about a respondent's ability or willingness to pay for the object, or otherwise take action. One may prefer Aspen over all other ski areas in the Rockies but have no intention of going next year because of the cost.

THE CONCEPT OF MEASUREMENT AND SCALING

Measurement can be defined as a standardized process of assigning numbers or other symbols to certain characteristics of the objects of interest, according to some prespecified rules. Measurement often deals with numbers, because mathematical and statistical analyses can be performed only on numbers, and they can be communicated throughout the world in the same form without any translation problems. There are two characteristics of the measurement process that make it a standardized process of assignment. First, there should be one-to-one correspondence between the symbol and the characteristic in the object that is being measured. Second, the rules for assignment should be invariant over time and the objects being measured.

Scaling is the process of creating a continuum on which objects are located according to the amount of the measured characteristic they possess. An illustration of a scale that is often used in research is the dichotomous scale for sex. The object with male/female characteristics is assigned a number 1 and the object with the opposite characteristics is assigned the number 0. This scale meets the requirements of the measurement process in that the assignment is one-to-one and it is invariate with respect to time and object. Measurement and scaling are basic tools used in the scientific method and are used in almost every marketing research situation.

Properties of Measurement Scales

The assignment of numbers is made according to rules that should correspond to the properties of whatever is being measured. The rule may be very simple, as when a bus route is given a number to distinguish it from other routes. Here, the only property is identity, and any comparisons of numbers are meaningless. This is a **nominal scale.** At the other extreme is the **ratio scale** which has very rigorous properties. In between the extremes are **ordinal** and **interval scales,** as shown in Table 10-1.

Attitude variables, such as beliefs, preferences, and intentions, are also measured with rating scales. These scales provide respondents with a set of numbered categories that represent the range of possible judgments or positions. An attitude scale involves measurement in the same sense that a thermometer measures temperature or a ruler measure distance. In each of these cases, measurement means the assignment of numbers to objects or persons to represent quantities of their attributes. For example, the attributes of a person include his income, social class, attitude, and so forth. Therefore, it is very important to understand the differences among the types of scales and to be able to identify them in practice, for their properties put significant restrictions on the interpretation and use of the resulting measurements.

Nominal Scale. Objects are assigned to mutually exclusive, labeled categories, but there are no necessary relationships among the categories; that is, no ordering or spacing is implied. If one entity is assigned the same number as another, they are identical with respect to a nominal variable. Otherwise, they are just different. Sex, geographic location, and marital status are nominally scaled variables. The only arithmetic operation that can be performed on such a scale is a count of each category. Thus, we can count the number of automobile dealers in the state of California or the number of buses seen on a given route in the past hour.

TABLE 10-1
Types of Scales and Their Properties

Type of Measurement Scale	Types of Attitude Scale	Rules for Assigning Number	Typical Application	Statistics/ Statistical Tests
Nominal	Dichotomous "yes" or "no" scales	Objects are either identical or different	Classification (by sex, geographic area, social class)	Percentages, mode/ chi-square
Ordinal or Rank Order	Comparative, Rank order, Itemized Category, Paired Comparison	Objects are greater or smaller	Rankings (preference, class standing)	Percentile, median, Rank-order correlation/ Friedman ANOVA
Interval	Likert, Thurstone, Stapel, Associative, Semantic-Differential	Intervals between adjacent ranks are equal	Index numbers, temperature scales, attitude measures	Mean, standard deviation, product moment correlations/ t-tests, ANOVA, regression, factor analysis
Ratio	Certain scales with special instructions	There is a meaningful zero, so comparison of absolute magnitudes is possible	Sales, incomes, units produced, costs, age	Geometric and harmonic mean, coefficient of variation

Ordinal Scale. This scale is obtained by ranking objects or by arranging them in order with regard to some common variable. The question is simply whether each object has more or less of this variable than some other object. The scale provides information as to how much difference there is between the objects.

Because we don't know the amount of difference between objects, the permissible arithmetic operations are limited to statistics such as the median or mode (but not the mean). For example, suppose a sample of 1000 consumers ranked five brands of frozen mixed vegetables according to quality. The results for Birds-Eye brand were as follows:

Quality Rank	Number of Respondents Giving Ranking to Birds-Eye
Highest	150
Second	300
Third	250
Fourth	200
Lowest	100
Total	1000

The "second" quality category is the mode; the "third" category is the median; however, it is not possible to compute a mean ranking, because the differences between ordinal scaled values are not necessarily the same. The finishing order in a horse race or class standing illustrates this type of scale. Similarly, brands of frozen vegetables can be ranked according to quality, from highest to lowest.

Interval Scale. Here, the numbers used to rank the objects also represent equal increments of the attribute being measured. This means that differences can be compared. The difference between 1 and 2 is the same as between 2 and 3, but is only half the difference between 2 and 4. The location of the zero point is not fixed, since zero does not denote the absence of the attribute. Fahrenheit and Celsius temperatures are measured with different interval scales and have different zero points. Interval scales have very desirable properties, because virtually the entire range of statistical operations can be employed to analyze the resulting number, including addition and subtraction. Consequently, it is possible to compute an arithmetic mean from interval-scale measures.

A recurring question regarding most attitude measures is whether or not they are interval scales. Usually it is doubtful that the intervals between categories are exactly equal, but they may not be so unequal as to preclude treating the whole as an interval scale. A good example is a "willingness to buy" scale with 10 categories labeled from 1 to 10. If this were an interval scale, we could say that two people with scores of 2 and 4, respectively, differed by the same degree of "willingness" as two other people with scores of 8 and 10. Further, only ratios of the differences in scale values can be meaningfully interpreted but not ratios of the absolute scale values. For example, the difference between 8 and 10 is twice the difference between 2 and 3 but 6 on the "willingness" scale does not represent three times the value of 2 in terms of the degree of willingness.

Ratio Scale. This is a special kind of interval scale that has a meaningful zero point. With such a scale—of weight, market share, or dollars in savings accounts, for example—it is possible to say how many times greater or smaller one object is than another. This is the only type of scale that permits us to make comparisons of absolute magnitude. For example, we can say that an annual income of $15,000 is two times as large as an income of $7500.

There have been some contemporary efforts to adapt ratio scales to the measurement of social opinion. Some researchers have attempted to use magnitude estimation scales to overcome the loss of information that results when categories arbitrarily constrain the range of opinion. Magnitude scaling of attitudes has been calibrated through numeric estimation. The following is an example of numeric estimation of social opinion:[1]

> *I would like to ask your opinion about how serious you think certain crimes are. The first situation is, "A person steals a bicycle parked on the street." This has been given a score of 10 to show its seriousness. Use this situation to judge all others. For example, if you think a situation is 20 times more serious than the bicycle theft, the number you tell me should be around 200, or if you think it is half as serious the number you tell me should be around 5, and so on.*
>
> *COMPARED TO THE BICYCLE THEFT AT SCORE 10, how serious is:*
>
> A parent beats his young child with his fists. The child requires hospitalization. A person plants a bomb in a public building. The bomb explodes and 20 people are killed. . . .

Magnitude scaling of this type has shown some interesting results, but there are problems with the technique. The researcher must be sure that the respondents have the competence to make these proportional judgments, which means that respondents must be allowed to practice before attempting the actual research questions.

TYPES OF ATTITUDE RATING SCALES

There are many ways to present a respondent with a continuum of numbered categories that represent the range of possible attitude judgments. Figure 10-1 shows one of the ways the various attitudinal scales used in marketing research can be classified. They can be generally classified as single-item scales and multiple-item scales.

Single-Item Scales

As the name itself suggests, single-item scales are those that have only one item to measure a construct. Under the single-item scales, the itemized-category scale is the most widely used by marketing researchers. In some situations, comparative scales, rank-order scales, or constant-sum scales have advantages. Each of these major types of rating scales will be discussed in turn.

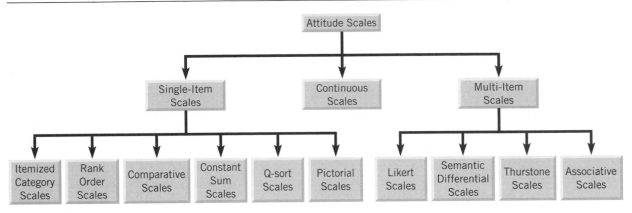

FIGURE 10-1
Classification of attitude scales

Itemized-Category Scales. The following scale from the HMO study is an **itemized-category scale.** There are four categories from which respondents can choose to indicate their overall level of satisfaction with their present health insurance plan:

_____ Very Satisfied _____ Quite Satisfied _____ Somewhat Satisfied _____ Not at all Satisfied

This satisfaction scale has the following characteristics:

1. All categories are labeled.
2. The respondent is forced to make a choice; there is no provision for neutral opinion or "don't know" responses.
3. There are more favorable than unfavorable categories, so the scale is unbalanced.
4. There is no explicit comparison of the respondents' present plan with other health insurance plans.

The design of the satisfaction scale requires decisions along several dimensions, as shown in Figure 10-2. Another feature of this scale is that there is no attempt to make the intervals between categories even approximately the same. A quite different scale would have resulted had the decision been to label only the polar or end categories, balance the favorable and unfavorable categories, and provide an obvious neutral category.

A numerical scaling of the response categories from +2 to −2, as presented in the following chart, could help to achieve a quasi-interval scale. While evidence is mixed, it appears that an adequate approximation of an interval scale can be achieved with this procedure.[2]

Very Satisfied   **Very Dissatisfied**

+2	+1	0	−1	−2

1)	Extent of category description	All categories labeled Polar categories labeled
2)	Treatment of respondent uncertainty or ignorance	Forced choice (no neutral point) Neutral point Provision of "don't know" category
3)	Balance of favorable and unfavorable categories	Equal Unbalanced
4)	Comparison judgment required	Yes No

FIGURE 10-2
Types of itemized-category scales

Yet another set of choices is illustrated by the following scale, which was used to ask respondents in the HMO study about the various medical services (including private clinics, private doctors, and an existing HMO), on a number of attributes, one of which was quality of care provided:

Q28 " . . . we are interested in your opinions about the medical services offered in this area . . .

(a) Quality of medical care provided: (check one for each provider)"

	Excellent	Very good	Average	Below average	Don't know
Private doctors in area	☐	☐	☐	☐	☐
Private clinics	☐	☐	☐	☐	☐
Health organizations in the area	☐	☐	☐	☐	☐

The scale used for this question is unbalanced, with all categories labeled and a "don't know" category provided, and implies a comparison with other health care providers. The decision to use an unbalanced scale was based on an assumption of positively skewed attitudes toward all health care providers. This assumption was borne out by the results, which showed that only 15 percent rated private doctors as average or below average. However, 31 percent replied "don't know" to this question, indicating they did not have sufficient experience to form a judgment. This could be thought of as a form of awareness question. In general, a "don't know" category should be provided whenever respondents have insufficient experience to make a meaningful attitude judgment.

Comparative Scale. Another version of the preceding scale would label the categories "excellent," "very good," "good," "fair," and "poor," thereby eliminating the implicit comparison. The problem with a comparative scale is that the reference point is unclear and different respondents may use different reference points or standards. Are private doctors rated "excellent" or "very good" because they are superior to the existing alternatives, or because they measure up to an ideal form of medical care provider? In marketing studies where competitive alternatives are being evaluated, some form of explicit or implicit comparison should be built into the scale; for example:

Compared to private clinics in the area the doctors in private practice provide a quality of medical care which is

Very Superior		Neither Superior nor Inferior		Very Inferior
_____	_____	_____	_____	_____

A recent review of research on the question of the appropriate number of response categories concluded[3]

▶ "Scales with two or three response alternatives generally are inadequate in that they are incapable of transmitting very much information and they tend to frustrate and stifle respondents."

▶ There is little to be gained from using more than nine categories.

▶ An odd rather than an even number of categories is preferable when the respondent legitimately can adopt a neutral position.

Rank-Order Scale. These scales require the respondent to arrange a set of objects with regard to a common criterion: advertisements in terms of interest, product features in terms of importance, or new-product concepts with regard to willingness to buy in the future. The result is an ordinal scale with the inherent limitations of weak scale properties. Ranking is widely used in surveys, however, because it corresponds to the choice process occurring in a shopping environment where a buyer makes direct comparisons among competing alternatives (brands, flavors, product variations, and so on).

Rank-order scales are not without problems. Ranking scales are more difficult than rating scales because they involve comparisons, and hence require more attention and mental effort. The ranking technique may force respondents to make choices they might not otherwise make, which raises the issue of whether the researcher is measuring a real relationship or one that is artificially contrived.

Due to the difficulties of rating, respondents usually cannot meaningfully rank more than five or six objects. The problem is not with the rankings of the first and last objects but with those in the undifferentiated middle. One solution, when there are several objects, is to break the ranking task into two stages. With nine objects, for example, the first stage would be to rank the objects into classes: top three, middle three, and bottom three. The next stage would be to rank the three objects within each class.

When using paired comparisons, the objects to be ranked are presented two at a time, and the respondent has to choose between them according to some criterion such as overall preference or willingness to buy. Before a ranking of all objects can be obtained, all possible combinations of pairs have to be presented. This means that for n objects there are $\{n(n-1)/2\}$ comparisons. This is very manageable for five objects (10 comparisons), but with more objects, the task can get out of hand. When 10 brands, for example, there are 45 paired comparisons. Paired-comparisons data have some potential analytical advantages, which will become apparent in Chapter 21 when we discuss multi-dimensional scaling. A serious problem, however, is that the comparison of two objects at a time is seldom the way choices are made in the marketplace; thus, an item may do well in a paired-comparison situation, but perform poorly in an actual market situation.[4] Despite these limitations, however, rankings still have much to recommend them if a researcher is interested in how consumers rank alternatives.

Q-Sort Scaling. When the number of objects or characteristics that are to be rated or ranked is very large, it becomes rather tedious for the respondent to rank order or do a pairwise comparison. If the respondent is forced to do a rank ordering or a pairwise comparison, a number of problems and biases creep into the study. To deal with such a situation, the **Q-sort scaling process** is used. In Q-sort scaling the respondents are asked to sort the various characteristics or objects that are being compared into various groups, such that the distribution of the number of objects or characteristics in each group follows a normal distribution. For example, let us take the case of a toy manufacturing company such as Toys 'R Us developing a new product. After a marathon brain-storming session, the new-product team has come up with a hundred different products, each with minor variations in their features, and wants to test and find out from consumers which feature combination is the most preferred and will generate the maximum sales. The best scaling procedure that can be used in this context is Q-sort scaling. The procedure to be adopted is as follows:

> *Each respondent is handed one hundred cards, each containing a product with various features. The respondent is then asked to sort the cards into twelve different piles in such a way that one pile contains what they feel is the most preferred among the products that have been developed, and another pile contains the least preferred of the products that have been developed. The other ten piles will contain cards with products that vary gradually from those with higher preference to those with lower preference. The number of cards in each pile is normally distributed as shown in Figure 10-3. In this particular case, only five cards can be placed in the most and the least preferred product piles. After placing all the cards in the piles, the respondent is asked to rank-order only those products in the most-preferred pile or in the top few sets of piles.*

In Q-sort scaling, a relatively large number of groups or piles should be used (10 or more). This increases the reliability or precision of the results.

Constant-Sum Scale. The constant-sum scale requires respondents to allocate a fixed number of rating points (usually 100) among several objects, to reflect

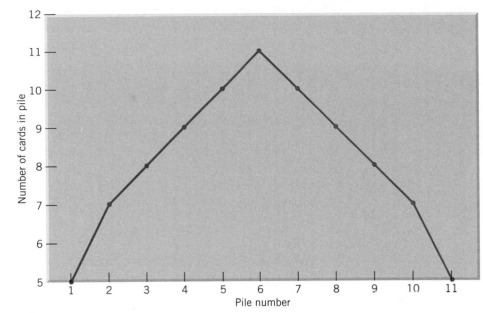

FIGURE 10-3
Plot of number of cards in each pile

the relative preference for each object.[5] It is widely used to measure the relative importance of attributes, as in the following example:

Please divide 100 points among the following characteristics so the division reflects the relative importance of each characteristic to you in the selection of a health care plan.

Ability to choose a doctor	_____
Extent of coverage provided	_____
Quality of medical care	_____
Monthly cost of the plan	_____
Distance to clinic or doctor from your home	_____

The most attractive feature of this scale is the quasi-interval nature of the resulting scale. However, just how close it comes to a true interval scale has not been fully established. The scale is limited in the number of objects or attributes it can address at one time. Respondents sometimes have difficulty allocating points accurately among more than a few categories.

Pictorial Scales. Pictorial scales are those in which the various categories of the scale are depicted pictorially. The respondents are shown a concept, or read an attitudinal statement and asked to indicate their degree of agreement or interest by indicating the corresponding position on the pictorial scale. Therefore, in designing a format, it is of prime importance to design one that the respondent will comprehend and will enable him to respond accurately. Commonly used pictorial scales are the **thermometer scale** and the **funny faces scale.** Pictorial scales are used mainly when the respondents are young children or people who are illiterate.

Issues in Designing Single-Item Scales. Attitude rating scales are widely used to test the effectiveness of advertising copy or compare the performance of new product concepts and segment markets. Despite years of experience with these applications, the design of the rating scale is usually an ad hoc judgment based on the researcher's preferences and past experiences in similar situations. The various decisions that a researcher has to make regarding the form and structure of the scale while designing a scale are described briefly below:

1. *Number of scale categories.* Theoretically, the number of rating-scale categories can vary from two to infinity. A continuous rating scale has infinite categories, whereas the number of categories in a discontinuous scale depends on several factors, like the capabilities of the scalers, the format of the interview, and the nature of the object.[6] For example, if the survey is done by telephone, then the number of categories that a scale can have is very limited, because the memory of the respondent is limited.

2. *Types of poles used in the scale.* All rating scales have verbal descriptors or adjectives that serve as end points or anchors. The scale can have a single pole or two poles. An example of a two-pole scale is "sweet . . . not sweet," and an example of a scale with a single pole is the Stapel scale, which is discussed later. The advantage of the single-pole scale over the scale with the double pole is ease of construction, as one need not look for adjectives to achieve bipolarity. But the disadvantage is that we do not know what each category represents in a single-pole scale.

3. *Strength of the anchors.* By strength of the anchor, we refer to the intensity of the adjective that is used to anchor the scale. A rating-scale anchor could vary from "extremely colorful" to "very colorful" to "colorful." Anchor strength has been found to shape scale-response distributions; the stronger the anchors, the less likely scalers are to use the extreme scale categories, so the resulting scale response distribution will be more peaked.

4. *Labeling of the categories.* Another decision that has to be made while developing scales is whether to label every category of the scale or to label only the extreme categories. Labeling all categories reduces the scale's ambiguity.[7] Evidence also shows that using such terms as "very" or "somewhat" markedly influences responses to scales.[8]

5. *Balance of the scale.* A related decision is whether category labels should be balanced or unbalanced. A balanced four-category scale to measure the smell of a perfume could be

The smell of Morning Dew is . . .

____ Very Good ____ Good ____ Bad ____ Very Bad while a corresponding unbalanced scale might be expressed as

_____ Superb   _____ Very Good   _____ Good   _____ Average

Generally, a balanced scale is preferred to an unbalanced scale in order to obtain meaningful results.

There is little argument on the criteria a rating scale ideally should satisfy. The results should be reliable and valid, and there should be a sharp discrimination among the objects being rated and a sensitivity to advertising or product stimuli. These criteria are seldom employed in practice. Part of the reason is the sheer variety of rating scales. The real problem is the absence of empirical evidence on the performance of the various rating scales on these criteria. However, one study of different scales did shed some useful light on the subject, and can help us narrow down the set of acceptable scales.[9]

Respondents in the study were given various subsets of the scales, and asked to rate six brands in each of six package goods categories such as coffee, analgesics, detergents, and toothpaste. Three criteria were used to compare the performance of the scales: (1) response distribution, which is the ability to avoid having responses pile up in the end categories; (2) discrimination among brands in the category; and (3) concurrent validity—how well the ratings related to current brand usage.

Three scales were found to be particularly attractive:

Brand Awareness Scale. This question asked: "When I mention detergents, what brand do you think of? Any others? Have you heard of (interviewer mentions other brands of interest that were not reported)?

_____   First unaided mention
_____   Second unaided mention
_____   Other unaided mention
_____   Aided recall
_____   Never heard of

This scale was consistently the best discriminator among brands and had high concurrent validity. By design, it yielded uniform distributions of responses.

Verbal Purchase Intent Scale. The question asked: "What is the chance of your buying (brand) the next time you purchase this product?

Definitely buy	Probably buy	Might buy	Probably not buy	Definitely not buy
_____	_____	_____	_____	_____

This balanced scale made efficient use of the five categories, distributing the responses quite uniformly. The labels were easy for the respondents to handle. On average it discriminated well.

Paired Comparison Scale. The brands to be rated were presented two at a time, so each brand in the category was compared once to every other brand. In each pair the respondents were asked to divide 10 points among the brands, on the basis of how much they liked one compared to the other. A score was then totaled for each brand. Although this scale performed well on the criteria, it is cumbersome to administer. Another possible limitation is that the frame of reference is always the other brands in the set being tested. These brands may change over time.

There are several features shared by all three of the most effective scales:

▶ They restrict the numbers of highly positive ratings that could be given, either by forcing a choice or directly comparing brands.

▶ They provide a limited number of categories that have verbal anchors. Respondents prefer words to numbers, and especially avoid negative numbers. Also, including more than seven categories may actually reduce the scale's power to discriminate.

▶ The stimulus to the respondent is simple and unambiguous. One of the worst performing scales presented a picture of a thermometer with 10 categories of liking; each was labeled by a number from zero to 100, as well as an assortment of verbal anchors. For example, 80 was labeled "like very much" while 50 was "indifferent" and 30 was "not so good."

Although these issues are useful, and should be carefully considered, the best guidance still comes from carefully tailoring the scale to the research objectives, followed by thorough pretesting for comprehension and discrimination.

Multiple-Item Scales

Attitudes toward complex objects such as health plans, automobiles, credit instruments, or transportation modes have many facets. Thus, it is often unrealistic to attempt to capture the full picture with one overall attitude scale question. For example, the public appears to support the general idea of income tax reform but opposes the elimination of the most popular tax loopholes. While beliefs in any specific issue, aspect, or characteristic are useful indicators of the overall attitude, there may be unusual reasons that make the single belief unrepresentative of the general position.[10] To cope with this problem, a variety of methods have been developed to measure a sample of beliefs toward the attitude objects (such as agreement or disagreement with a number of statements about the attitude object) and combine the set of answers into some form of average score. The most frequently employed of these methods are **Likert, Thurstone,** and **semantic-differential** scales. An adaptation of these methods, with particular relevance to marketing problems, is **associative scaling.**

Likert Scale. A **Likert** scale requires a respondent to indicate a degree of agreement or disagreement with a variety of statements related to the attitude or object. It is also called a **summated** scale, for the scores on the individual items are summed to produce a total score for the respondent. The Likert scale usually consists of two parts, the item part and the evaluative part. The item part is essentially a statement about a certain product, event, or attitude. The evaluative part is a list of response categories ranging from "strongly agree" to "strongly disagree." An important assumption of this scaling method is that each of the items (statements) measures some aspect of a single common factor; otherwise, the items cannot legitimately be summed. In other words, the resulting scale is unidimensional. The Likert scaling method, then, refers to the several steps in the procedure for culling out the items that don't belong. The result is a series of 5 to 20 or more statements and questions, of which those given below are illustrative.

	Agree Strongly	Agree Somewhat	Neither Agree nor Disagree	Disagree Somewhat	Disagree Strongly
1. There needs to be much improvement in the health insurance available for people like me.	☐	☐	☐	☐	☐
2. I have a variety of very good health plans from which to choose.	☐	☐	☐	☐	☐
3. I haven't heard of a health insurance plan that will protect me against a disastrous illness.	☐	☐	☐	☐	☐

Thurstone Scale. This procedure also is known as the method of **equal-appearing intervals,** since the objective is to obtain a unidimensional scale with interval properties.

The first step is to generate a large number of statements or adjectives reflecting all degrees of favorableness toward the attitude objects. Then, a group of judges is given this set of items (as many as 75 to 100 in all) and asked to classify them according to their degree of favorableness or unfavorableness. Usually, this is done with an 11-category bipolar scale, with "very favorable" at one end and "very unfavorable" at the other, and a neutral position in the middle. The judges are instructed to treat the intervals between categories as equal and to make evaluations of each item without expressing their own attitudes. The scale value of each item is the median position to which it is assigned by the judges. Items that have been placed in many different categories are discarded as ambiguous because there was no consensus among the judges. The resulting scale consists of 10 to 20 items that are distributed uniformly along the scale of favorability. The scale then is administered as part of a survey by asking each respondent to select those statements which best reflect his or her feelings toward the attitude object. The respondent's attitude score is the average of the scale scores of the chosen statements.

Because of the two-stage procedure, a **Thurstone scale** is both time-consuming and expensive to construct; however, the scale itself is easy to administer and requires a minimum of instructions. But because there is not an explicit response to each item in the scale, it does not have as much diagnostic value as a Likert scale. Thurstone scales also have been criticized because the scale values themselves may depend on the attitudes of the original judges. This seems to be a problem only with topics that elicit strong feelings, such as abortion or school integration.

Semantic-Differential Scale. This scaling procedure is used widely to describe the set of beliefs that comprise a person's image of an organization or brand. It is also an insightful procedure for comparing the images of competing brands, stores, or services.[11] Respondents are asked to rate each attitude object in turn on a number of five- or seven-point rating scales, bounded at each end by polar adjectives or phrases. Some researchers prefer unipolar scales while others use bipolar scales. In either case, the respondent chooses the end point only if that adjective is closely descriptive of that object. However, the midpoint of the scale has two different meanings, depending on the type of scale. With unipolar scales, the midpoint is simply a step on the scale from "sweet" to "not sweet," whereas on a bipolar scale, it is a neutral point.

Low price	____	____	____	____	____	High price
Consistent quality	____	____	____	____	____	Spotty quality
Tangy	____	____	____	____	____	Smooth
Bitter	____	____	____	____	____	Not bitter

There may be as many as 15 to 25 **semantic-differential scales** for each attitude object. The scales in the following chart were used in a beer brand image study in a U.S. regional market. (Only four of a total of 10 scales are shown.) Each of 10 brands was evaluated separately on the same set of 10 scales, for comparison.

This set of scales is characteristic of most marketing applications of the semantic differential.

1. The pairs of objects or phrases are selected carefully to be meaningful in the market being studied and often correspond to product/service attributes.[12] Exploratory research generally is required to ensure that important attributes are represented and described in words that are familiar to respondents.[13]

2. The negative or unfavorable pole is sometimes on the right side and sometimes on the left. This rotation is necessary to avoid the halo effect in which the location of previous judgments on the scale affects subsequent judgments made because of respondent carelessness.

3. The category increments are treated as interval scales, so group mean values can be computed for each object on each scale. As with Likert scaling, this assumption is controversial, but is adopted because it permits more powerful methods of analysis to be used.

The semantic differential also may be analyzed as a summated rating scale. Each of the seven scale categories is assigned a value from −3 to +3 or 1 to 7, and the scores across all adjective pairs are summed for each respondent. Individuals then can be compared on the basis of their total scores. Summation is not usually advisable, however, for a good deal of specific information is lost in the aggregate score, which may be distorted if there are several scales that measure roughly the same thing.

Profile Analysis. Profile Analysis is an application of the **semantic differential** scale. Visual comparisons of the images of different objects can be aided by plotting the mean ratings for each object on each scale. To show what can be done, Figure 10-4 compares the ratings for two well-known national brands of beer and a regional brand, on six of the ten scales. Even with three brands and only six of ten attributes, the interpretation of the profiles is not easy. With more brands and attributes, the overall comparisons of brands are even harder to grasp. A second difficulty is that not all attributes are independent, that is, several of the attributes may be measuring approximately the same dimension. For example, to most beer drinkers there is not likely to be much difference in the meaning of the "tangy–smooth" and "bitter–not bitter" scales. This is borne out by the similarity of the scores of the three brands on these two scales in Figure 10-4. Fortunately, there are several procedures using multidimensional

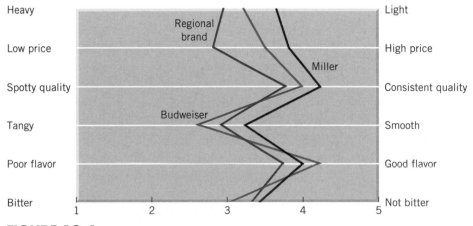

FIGURE 10-4
Profile analysis of three beer brands

scaling techniques that can deal effectively with these problems and yield easily interpreted spatial maps that describe the overall image of a brand. These are discussed in detail in Chapters 20 and 21, which deal with methods for analyzing interdependencies among variables.

Stapel Scales

This is a simplified version of the semantic-differential scale, which uses only one pole rather than two opposite poles. Respondents are asked to indicate the object by selecting a numerical response category. The higher the positive score, the better the adjective describes the object. A typical format for this scale is shown for Coors beer as it would be adapted to the measurement of beer brand attitudes.

The main virtue of this scale is that it is easy to administer and construct. Also, this scale is easier to construct, for there is no need to provide adjectives or phrases to assure bipolarity.[14]

Coors Beer

Heavy	+3 +2 +1 −1 −2 −3	Consistent quality	+3 +2 +1 −1 −2 −3	Tangy	+3 +2 +1 −1 −2 −3

Associative Scaling. Although the semantic-differential and Stapel scales are used widely for image studies, they have substantial limitations in markets where the average respondent is likely to be knowledgeable only about a small subset among a large number of choice alternatives. They also can be cumbersome and time-consuming to administer when there are a number of attributes and alternatives to consider. An alternative approach, **associative scaling,** designed to overcome these limitations, asks the respondent simply to associate one alternative with each question. The questions in Figure 10-5 illustrate how this approach is employed in a telephone survey of retail-store images.

The technique is argued to be particularly appropriate to choice situations that involve a sequential decision process. For example, supermarkets have to be within a reasonable distance to be considered, and within that set the choice is made on the basis of which chain is best in satisfying their needs. Of course, the technique does not answer the questions of how consumers make trade-offs when there are several important dimensions and no alternative is superior across the board. Thus the benefits of low cost and ease of telephone administration are purchased at a possible cost of reduced validity in representing the market structure. For this reason the associative technique is best suited to market tracking, where the emphasis is on understanding shifts in relative competitive positions.

Which store

	Eaton's Store or Catalog	The Bay	Simpsons	Sears Store or Catalog	Horizon	Sayvette	Towers	Woolco	Zellers	Any Other	None DK	More Than One Answer
1. Has the lowest overall prices?	1	2	3	4	5	6	7	8	9	0	B	X
2. Has the highest overall prices?	1	2	3	4	5	6	7	8	9	0	B	X
3. Is the easiest one to get to from your home?	1	2	3	4	5	6	7	8	9	0	B	X
4. Has the most knowledgeable, helpful sales clerks?	1	2	3	4	5	6	7	8	9	0	B	X
5. Has the highest-quality products?	1	2	3	4	5	6	7	8	9	0	B	X
6. Has the lowest-quality products?	1	2	3	4	5	6	7	8	9	0	B	X
7. Gives you the best overall value for the money?	1	2	3	4	5	6	7	8	9	0	B	X
8. Gives you the worst overall value for the money?	1	2	3	4	5	6	7	8	9	0	B	X
9. Has the best advertising?	1	2	3	4	5	6	7	8	9	0	B	X
10. Is the best for the latest, most fashionable merchandise?	1	2	3	4	5	6	7	8	9	0	B	X
11. Has the largest overall merchandise selection or assortment?	1	2	3	4	5	6	7	8	9	0	B	X
12. Do you shop at most often?	1	2	3	4	5	6	7	8	9	0	B	X

FIGURE 10-5
Retail store image questions (Telephone Questionnaire)

GENERAL GUIDELINES FOR DEVELOPING A MULTI-ITEM SCALE

Multi-item scales very often are used in social sciences research to measure abstract constructs. The characteristic that is to be measured is generally referred to as the construct. Most of the well-known scales that measure constructs such as IQ, consumer confidence, and so on, are multi-item scales. Developing a multi-item scale is a complex procedure and requires quite a lot of technical expertise. Figure 10-6 presents the various steps in the development of a multi-item scale. The stages of development are discussed below.

1. *Determine clearly what it is that you want to measure.* The scale should be well grounded in theory. Relevant social science theories should always be considered before developing the scale. The construct to be measured

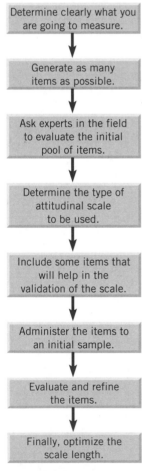

FIGURE 10-6
Steps in multi-item scale development

and the scale itself should be specific. The meaning and the definition of the construct should be clearly distinguishable from other constructs.

2. *Generate as many items as possible.* Items essentially are statements that are relevant to the construct. The content of each item should reflect primarily the construct of interest. If items are being written anew, they should be written with as much creativity as possible. The greater the number of initial items generated, the better the final scale will be. The items that are developed should not be too long, nor should they pose any reading difficulty to the respondent.

3. *Ask experts to evaluate the initial pool of items.* Experts are people who have worked or are currently working on the phenomenon that is being studied. They can be either business managers or academics who are doing research on that particular phenomenon. Having experts review the item pool can confirm or invalidate the definition of the construct. Experts can also give inputs on the relevancy, clarity, and conciseness of the items. Based on the experts' evaluation, the initial pool of items is modified. Some items are dropped while others are added, and a few of the existing ones are changed.

4. *Determine the type of attitudinal scale to be used.* The next step in the multi-item scaling process is to decide on the type of scale to be employed. The various scales such as the Likert scale, semantic differential scale, Thurstone, and associative scales have already been discussed. In fact, the type of attitudinal scale to be used has to be decided quite early on, because the wording of the items varies with each scale format.

5. *Include validation items in the scale.* Certain items are added to the scale in order to improve the scale's validity and also to detect certain flaws in it. An example of items that can be included in the scale to increase the validity of the results are those that are socially desirable. Some respondents answer in a certain fashion because they want to be perceived as socially desirable. In order to weed out such answers, the items of social desirability are added to the scale. Those responses that correlate highly with social desirability are then dropped.

6. *Administer the items to an initial sample.* Once it has been determined which construct-related items are to be included in the scale, the next step is to administer the scale to an initial sample. This is done to check the validity of the items. This will yield the best results if the sample size is large and the sample is representative of the population.

7. *Evaluate and refine the items of the scale.* The ultimate quality that is sought in an item is high correlation with the true score of the latent variable that is being measured. The properties that the items of a scale should possess are high intercorrelation, high-item scale correlation, high-item variances, a mean close to the center of the range of possible scores, and a high coefficient alpha. The items in the scale are then evaluated on the basis of these criteria.

8. *Optimize scale length.* The larger the scale the greater the reliability, but shorter scales are easier for the respondent to answer. Hence, a balance has to be struck between brevity and reliability, and the optimal scale

length has to be determined. Certain items in the scale are dropped or modified, then the final scale is ready to be administered to the respondent.

Continuous-Rating Scales

In **continuous-rating scales,** the respondents rate the objects by placing a mark at the appropriate position on a line that runs from one extreme of the criterion variable to the other.[15] They are also referred to as graphical rating scales. The main advantage of the continuous-rating scale is that it is easy to construct. However, scoring is cumbersome and unreliable and these scales do not provide much new information. Hence, continuous-rating scales are not widely used in marketing research.

INTERPRETING ATTITUDE SCALES

Conclusions obtained from attitude-scale measurements are strictly limited by the properties of the scale that is used. Failure to recognize these limits can lead to serious misinterpretation, as we see from the example in the boxed insert. The problem was created by assuming a ratio scale, where there was really only an interval scale. In Exhibit 10-1, an example is given of how attitudinal scales can be misinterpreted.

CHOOSING AN ATTITUDINAL SCALE

The choice of an appropriate scale is complicated by two problems:

1. There are many different techniques, each with its own strengths and weaknesses.
2. Virtually any technique can be adapted to the measurement of any one of the attitude components.

While these problems are significant impediments to broad generalizations, it is also true that all techniques are not equally suitable for all purposes. Table 10-2 summarizes some useful rules of thumb as to which scale types are likely to be best suited to the various components of attitudes. What is most evident from this table is the versatility of the itemized-category scale, which itself has many variations. Ultimately, the researcher's choice will be shaped by (1) the specific information that is required to satisfy the research objectives, (2) the adaptability of the scale to the data-collection method and budget constraints, and (3) the compatibility of the scale with the structure of the respondent's attitude.

The value of careful selection and adaptation of scales will be demonstrated here by a study of attitudes toward automobile dealers. The data came from a mail survey of people who had purchased a new car from an automobile dealer between one and two years earlier.[16] Each respondent rates 14 attributes

EXHIBIT 10-1

Interpreting Attitude Scales: A Problem for the Advertising Review Board

The Phoenix Drug Co. currently sells the leading brand of tranquilizers, known as Restease. A competitor, Montfort Drug Co., recently announced a tranquilizer brand called Calm, which they claim to be 50 percent more effective in reducing tensions than the leading brand.

As product manager for Restease you are concerned and also angry, because you don't believe there is a significant difference in effectiveness. Your first action is to complain to the National Advertising Review Board, an advertising industry sponsored body that investigates advertising claims and can put considerable pressure on advertisers to change their claims.

As part of the investigation of your complaint, the research director from Montfort Drug is asked by the NARB to present the research findings that support the claim. Among the findings are the results of an apparently well-designed comparison test with large sample sizes. In the test, one group of product users was given Restease capsules. After a month, each user was asked to rate the effectiveness of the brand as follows:

For easing tension I found Restease to be:

Very effective	Effective	Neither effective nor ineffective	Ineffective	Very ineffective
☐	☐	☐	☐	☐

Another group of product users, identical in all respects to the first group, was given Calm capsules and asked to rate the effectiveness of this brand on the same scale.

The research director for Montfort Drug coded the scale with a +2 for "very effective," +1 for "effective," 0 for "neither effective nor ineffective," −1 for "ineffective," and −2 for "very ineffective." The director correctly points out that this is a well-accepted coding convention. When the data for the two groups are summarized, the average response for the Calm user groups is calculated to be +1.2, while the average for Restease is +0.8. Because the 0.4 difference is 50 percent more than the +0.8 level achieved by Restease, the director concludes that the claims of superior effectiveness are valid.

While you are listening to this argument, the research director from your company has taken the same data and calculated that Calm is only 10.5 percent more effective, rather than 50 percent as claimed. Immediately you examine the figures. The only difference is that the "very effective" category has been coded +1, and "very ineffective" assigned +5, with the middle category assigned +3. It is argued that this is an equally acceptable coding procedure. The two different coding schemes are as follows:

Very effective	Effective	Neither effective nor ineffective	Ineffective	Very ineffective
☐	☐	☐	☐	☐
+2	+1	0	−1	−2
+1	+2	+3	+4	+5

Soon you will be asked to present the basis of your complaint to the Review Board. What do you say about the capacity of the data presented by your competitor to support its claim of superiority?

Source: Adapted from, B. Venkatesh, "Unthinking Data Interpretation Can Destroy Value of Research," *Marketing News* (January 27, 1978), 6.9.

TABLE 10-2
Comparison of Two Rating Techniques

Attribute	Median Importance Rating	Illustrative Constant-Sum Scale	
		Customer A	Customer B
1. Job done right the first time	3.8	35	25
2. Fast action on complaints	3.6	15	20
3. Prompt warranty work	3.6	10	15
4. Able to do any job needed	3.6	10	10
5. Service available when needed	3.4	15	20
6. Courteous and friendly service	3.4	15	10
		100	100

of the dealer's service department, on two separate scales. The first scale asked how *important* the attribute was (on a four-point scale ranging from "extremely important" to "not important"). The second scale asked how well the service department *performed* (on a four-point scale from "excellent" to "poor"). Each attribute was located in the grid shown in Figure 10-7, according to its median score on the two scales.

To illustrate how the grid can be used, quadrant A includes those attributes, such as "low prices on service" (attribute 10), which are very important, and

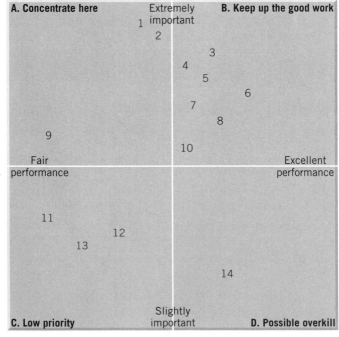

FIGURE 10-7
Importance–performance grid

where performance is rated only fair. By contrast, in quadrant B, customers place a high value on "courteous and friendly service" (attribute 6) and "prompt warranty work" (attribute 3), and are pleased with the dealer's performance. In quadrant C, the dealer's performance is rated low in terms of providing courtesy buses and rental cars, but fortunately these are not perceived as important services.

While the importance–performance grid yields useful insights, this application suffered from the inability of the four-point rating scale to discriminate. Ten of the 14 attributes had median ratings between 3.3 and 3.8 on this scale, where 4 means "extremely important" and 3 is "important." A constant-sum scale, on the other hand, might have resulted in sharper distinctions among attributes, as shown in Table 10-2 giving two possible patterns of responses of service customers thinking hard about which of six attributes were really important.

ACCURACY OF ATTITUDE MEASUREMENTS

Attitude measures, in common with all measures used in marketing, must be both accurate and useful. In this section, the focus is on those aspects of attitude measures that contribute to accuracy: validity, reliability, and sensitivity.

Validity

An attitude measure has validity if it measures what it is supposed to measure. If this is the case, then differences in attitude scores will reflect differences among the objects or individuals on the characteristic being measured. This is a very troublesome question; for example, how is a researcher to know whether measured differences in the attitudes of managers, consumer activists, and consumers toward marketing practices, regulation, and the contribution of the consumer movement are true differences? There have been three basic approaches to this question of validity assessment.

Face, or consensus, validity is invoked when the argument is made that the measurement so self-evidently reflects or represents the various aspects of the phenomenon that there can be little quarrel with it. For instance, buyers' recognition of advertisements is usually accepted at face value as an indication of past ad exposure. This faith typically is supported by little more than common sense, despite evidence that recognition scores are influenced by reader interest.

Criterion validity is more defensible, for it is based on empirical evidence that the attitude measure correlates with other "criterion" variables. If the two variables are measured at the same time, **concurrent validity** is established. Better yet, if the attitude measure can predict some future event, then **predictive validity** has been established. A measure of brand preference or buying intentions is valid if it can be shown through sales records to predict future sales. This is the most important type of validity for decision-making purposes, for the very nature of decisions requires predictions of uncertain future events.

While face, concurrent, and predictive validity provide necessary evidence of overall validity, often they are not sufficient. The characteristic of these three approaches is that they provide evidence on **convergent validity.** That is, an attitude measure can adequately represent a characteristic or variable if it correlates or "converges" with other supposed measures of that variable. Unfortunately, an attitude measure may converge with measures of other variables in addition to the one of interest. Thus, it is also necessary to establish **discriminant validity** through "low correlations between the measure of interest and other measures that are supposedly not measuring the same variable or concept." Advertising recognition measures often fail this second test. While they correlate or converge with past ad exposure, which is what we want, they also are correlated with number of magazines read and product interest.

Construct validity can be considered only after discriminant and convergent validity have been established.[17] It is achieved when a logical argument can be advanced to defend a particular measure. The argument aims first to define the concept or construct explicitly and then to show that the measurement, or operational definition, logically connects the empirical phenomenon to the concept. The extreme difficulty of this kind of validation lies in the unobservable nature of many of the constructs (such as social class, personality, or attitudes) used to explain marketing behavior. For example, is occupation a good operational definition of social class, or does it measure some other characteristic? One way to assess construct validity is to test whether or not the measure confirms hypotheses generated from the theory based on the concepts. Since theory development is at a youthful stage in marketing, the theory itself may be incorrect, making this approach hazardous. This is one reason why little construct validation is attempted in marketing. A more significant reason is the lack of well-established measures that can be used in a variety of circumstances. Instead, marketing researchers tend to develop measures for each specific problem or survey and rely on face validity.

Reliability

So far we have been talking about systematic errors between an observed score (X_o) and a true score (X_t), which will determine whether a measure is valid. However, the total error of a measurement consists of this systematic error component (X_s) and a random error component (X_r). Random error is manifested by lack of consistency (unreliability) in repeated or equivalent measures of the same object or person. As a result, any measurement can be expressed as a function of several components:

$$X_o = X_t + X_s + X_r$$
Observed score = true score + systematic error + random error

To interpret this equation, remember that a valid measure is one that reflects the true score. In this situation, $X_o = X_t$ and both X_s and X_r are zero. Thus, if we know the measure is valid, it has to be reliable. The converse is not necessarily true. A measure may be highly reliable, $X_r = 0$, and still have a substantial systematic error that distorts the validity. But, if the measure is not reliable, it cannot be valid since at a minimum we are left with $X_o = X_t + X_r$. In brief, reliability is a necessary but not a sufficient condition for validity.

Although **reliability** is less important, it is easier to measure, and so receives relatively more emphasis. The basic methods for establishing reliability can be classified according to whether they measure stability of results over time or internal consistency of items in an attitude scale.[18]

Stability over time is assessed by repeating the measurement with the same instrument and the same respondents at two points in time and correlating the results. To the extent that random fluctuations result in different scores for the two administrations, this correlation and hence the reliability will be lowered. The problems of this test–retest method are similar to those encountered during any pretest–post-test measurement of attitudes. The first administration may sensitize the respondent to the subject and lead to attitude change. The likelihood of a true change in attitude (versus a random fluctuation) is increased further if the interval between the test and the retest is too long. For most topics, this would be more than two weeks. If the interval is too short, however, there may be a carryover from the test to the retest: attempts to remember the responses in the first test, boredom or annoyance at the imposition, and so forth. Because of these problems, a very short interval will bias the reliability estimate upward, whereas longer periods have the opposite effect.

The equivalence approach to assessing reliability is appropriate for attitude scales composed of multiple items that presumably measure the same underlying unidimensional attitude. The split-half method assumes that these items can be divided into two equivalent subsets that then can be compared. A number of methods have been devised to divide the items randomly into two halves and compute a measure of similarity of the total scores of the two halves across the sample. An average split-half measure of similarity—coefficient alpha—can be obtained from a procedure that has the effect of comparing every item to every other item.

Sensitivity

The third characteristic of a good attitude measure is **sensitivity,** or the ability to discriminate among meaningful differences in attitudes. Such sensitivity is achieved by increasing the number of scale categories; however, the more categories there are, the lower the reliability. This is because very coarse response categories, such as "yes" or "no," in response to an attitude question can absorb a great deal of response variability before a change would be noted using the test–retest method. Conversely, the use of a large number of response categories when there are only a few distinct attitude positions would be subject to a considerable, but unwarranted, amount of random fluctuation.

Generalizability

Generalizability refers to the ease of scale administration and interpretation in different research settings and situations.[19] Thus, the generalizability of a multi-item scale is determined by whether it can be applied in a wide variety of data collection modes, whether it can be used to obtain data from a wide variety of individuals, and under what conditions it can be interpreted. As in the case of reliability and validity, generalizability is not an absolute but rather is a matter of degree.

Relevancy

Relevancy of a scale refers to how meaningful it is to apply the scale to measure a construct. Mathematically, it is represented as the product of reliability and validity.

$$\text{Relevance} = \text{Reliability} \times \text{Validity}$$

If reliability and validity are evaluated by means of correlation coefficients, the implications are

▶ The relevance of a scale can vary from 0 (no relevance) to 1 (complete relevance).

▶ If either reliability or validity is low, the scale will possess little relevance.

▶ Both reliability and validity are necessary for scale relevance.

SCALES IN CROSS-NATIONAL RESEARCH

The previous sections of this chapter discussed the various types of scales that are typically used in domestic marketing research. The question remains whether the same scales can be administered to respondents all over the world.[20] Low educational or literacy levels in some countries will have to be taken into account when the decision is taken to administer the same scale. Literacy and educational levels have a certain impact on the response formats of the scales employed. Moreover, culture in a country can also affect the responses and may induce some cultural biases.

Research has been conducted to find out whether there is a pan-cultural scale. The semantic differential scale seems to come closest to being a truly pan-cultural scale. It consistently gives similar results in terms of concepts or dimensions that are used to evaluate stimuli, and also accounts for a major portion of the variation in response when it is administered in different countries. An alternative approach that has been attempted is to apply techniques that use a base referent, a self-defined cultural norm. This type of approach is likely to be particularly useful in evaluating attitudinal positions where evidence exists to suggest that these are defined relative to the dominant cultural norm.

Another issue that is important in international research is whether response formats, particularly their calibration, need to be adapted for specific countries and cultures. For example, in France a 20-point scale is commonly used to rate performance in primary and secondary schools. Consequently, it has been suggested that 20-point scales should also be used in marketing research. In general, verbal scales are more effective among less-educated respondents, but a more appropriate procedure for illiterate respondents would be scales with pictorial stimuli. For example, in the case of life-style, pictures of different life-style segments may be shown to the respondents, and they may be asked to indicate how similar they perceive themselves to be to the one in the picture. Some other devices such as the **funny faces** and the **thermometer** scale are also used among the less-educated respondents.

Summary

This chapter has dealt with attitudes, defined as the mental orientation of individuals that structures the way they respond to their environment. This concept is useful to marketers only to the extent that the various components of attitudes can be measured "accurately."

Measurement was defined here as the assignment of numbers to objects or persons to represent quantities of their attributes. The problem is to establish how to assign numbers. This leads to an examination of the properties of different scales of measurement—nominal, ordinal, interval, ratio—and establishes a useful basis for evaluating various attitude scales, including itemized-category, rank-order, semantic-differential, Thurstone, and Likert scales. Each of these methods involves a direct self-report, which means that they should be supplemented with the behavioral and indirect measures discussed in Chapter 7.

To this point we have not been explicit as to what is meant by an "accurate" measurement of any kind. Intuitively it means freedom from error. More formally, an accurate measure is both valid and reliable. The nature of these concepts and the special issues involved in their application are discussed in the appendix to this chapter.

Questions and Problems

1. Advertising is an expenditure that ultimately must be justified in terms of its effect on sales and profits; yet most evaluations of advertising are in terms of the effects on attitudes. How do you account for this apparent mismatch?
2. What is measurement? What are the scales of measurement and what information is provided by each?
3. Identify the type of scale and justify your answer.
   a. During which season of the year were you born?
      _____ Winter _____ Spring _____ Summer _____ Fall
   b. How satisfied are you with the Ford Taurus that you have bought?
      _____ Very satisfied _____ Satisfied _____ Neither satisfied nor dissatisfied _____ Dissatisfied _____ Very dissatisfied
   c. On an average, how many cigarettes do you smoke in a day?
      _____ Over 1 pack _____ 1/2 pack to 1 pack _____ Less than 1/2 pack
   d. Rank the following according to your preference
      _____ Tide _____ Surf _____ Cheer _____ Wisk _____ Bold
4. One trend expected to have a large impact on marketing in the 1990s is the aging of the baby boomer population. This aging will likely result in changing consumer attitudes in a variety of areas. What types of attitude changes would be of most interest or concern to a product manager for a branded food product?

5. How would you select a set of phrases or adjectives for use in a semantic-differential scale to evaluate the image of banks and other consumer financial institutions? Would the procedure differ if you were going to use a Likert scale?

6. Develop a battery of attitude scales to predict whether or not people who currently smoke will try to quit smoking within the next year.

7. Suppose paired-comparison choices of most-preferred brand were made among three brands (A, B, and C), by a sample of 100 respondents. The results of 25 choosing A and 75 choosing B would be represented as $A_{25}B_{75}$. One possible set of results from the three paired comparisons might be $A_{50}B_{50}$, $B_{50}C_{50}$, and $A_{50}C_{50}$. Is this set of results consistent with any one of the following results of the choice of most-preferred brand from an array of the three brands? Why?

   $A_{25}B_{25}C_{50}$
   $A_{33}B_{33}C_{33}$
   $A_{50}B_0C_{50}$

8. Under what circumstances can attitude measures be expected to be good predictors of subsequent behavior? Is there any value to measuring attitudes in situations where attitudes are likely to be poor predictors?

9. Explain the concepts of reliability and validity in your own words. What is the relationship between them?

10. Develop a multi-item scale to measure student's attitudes toward the present system of grading. How would you assess the reliability and validity of this scale?

11. In March of 1977 the U.S. Federal Energy Administration (FEA) conducted a personal interview survey of a sample of homes where there was a heating load (that is, the outside temperature was below 65°F). The average indoor temperature of these homes, as measured by a calibrated thermometer was 70° + or −2°F during the day and 69° + or −2°F at night. This represented little or no change from the previous two years; yet, during an independent telephone survey, the FEA found that people said they were keeping their homes at 66°F during the day and 64°F at night.

    a. What are some of the possible hypotheses for this difference between stated and actual temperatures?

    b. What questions would you ask during a telephone survey to clarify the stated house temperature and learn about people's attitudes toward reducing the house temperature?

12. In February 1975, the Gallup poll asked, "Do you approve or disapprove of the way Ford is handling his job as president?" and found 55 percent approved and 28 percent disapproved. A poll by Harris at the same time asked, "How do you rate the job President Ford is doing as president—excellent, pretty good, only fair, or poor?" Forty-six percent gave "positive" responses (excellent or pretty good), and 52 percent were negative (only fair or poor). How do you explain the differences? What are the implications of your explanation for public opinion polls as guides to political leaders?

13. It has been said that for decisional research purposes the investigator is interested in predictive validity, to the exclusion of reliability or any other kind of validity. Do you agree? Explain.

14. Carter Toys, the U.S.-based manufacturer of the popular PollyDolly, feels that a strong sales potential exists for the doll in foreign markets. The management has identified the selection of suitable foreign country markets as being its first priority. Worldwide Research Corp. has been employed to conduct a survey of the three countries that are currently under consideration: The United Kingdom, Japan, and Kenya.
    a. Can the same questionnaire be used to survey all three countries? Give reasons for your answer.
    b. What factors must be considered in selecting a suitable scale to be used in each country?
    c. Recommend the most suitable scale for use in each country?

15. Ben Gatsby is a jewelry craftsman who specializes in high-quality religious artifacts. Recently, he has received a growing number of requests from customers for nonreligious artifacts and is considering an expansion of his product line to meet this new demand. Mr. Gatsby has decided to contact a local marketing research company to solicit its help in formulating a marketing strategy for the new product development. They inform him that the first task is to establish whether an unmet demand exists for the nonreligious items. They suggest that in order to evaluate consumer's jewelry purchase behavior, an attitudinal study should be undertaken. Mr. Gatsby does not understand why attitudes have to be measured when he is interested only in the consumers' behavior. Imagine you are the marketing research consultant and explain to Mr. Gatsby the rationale behind this research method.

16. a. How are attitude rating scales most commonly applied in marketing research?
    b. What decisions must a researcher make in designing a single-item scale for these purposes?

End Notes

1. M. Lodge. "Magnitude Scaling: Quantitative Measurement of Opinions" (Beverly Hills, CA: Sage), 1981.

2. C. E. Osgood, G. Suci, and P. Tannenbaum. *The Measurement of Meaning* (Urbana, IL: University of Illinois Press), 1957.

3. Eli P. Cox, "The Optimal Number of Response Alternatives for a Scale: A Review," *Journal of Marketing Research,* 17, November 1980, 407–422.

4. A. B. Blankership. "Let's Bury Paired Comparisons," *Journal of Advertising Research,* 6, March 1966, 13–17.

5. J. P. Guilford. *Psychometric Methods* (New York: McGraw-Hill), 1954.

6. M. M. Givon and Z. Shapira. "Response to Rating Scales: A Theoretical Model and Its Application to the Number of Categories Problem," *Journal of Marketing Research,* November 1984, 410–419. Eli P. Cox, III, "The Optimal Number of Response Alternatives for a Scale: A Review," *Journal of Marketing Research,* 17, November 1980, 407–422.

7. H. H. Friedman and J. R. Leefer. "Label Versus Position in Rating Scales," *Journal of the Academy of Marketing Science,* Spring 1981, 88–92. R. I. Haley and P. B. Case. "Testing Thirteen Attitude Scales for Agreement and Brand Discrimination," *Journal of Marketing,* Fall 1979, 20–32.

8. See, for instance, Norman Bradburn and Carrie Miles. "Vague Quantifiers," *Public Opinion Quarterly,* Spring 1979, 92–101.

9. Russell I. Haley and Peter B. Case. "Testing Thirteen Attitude Scales for Agreement and Brand Discrimination," *Journal of Marketing,* 43, Fall 1979, 20–32.

10. C. A. Moser and G. Kalton. *Survey Method in Social Investigation,* 2nd ed. (London: Heinemann), 1971.

11. Naresh K. Malhotra. "A Scale to Measure Self-Concepts, Person Concepts and Product Con-

cepts," *Journal of Marketing Research,* 18, November 1981, 456–464.

12. The scale was developed originally by Osgood, et al. op cit., as a method for measuring the meaning of an object to an individual. They explored a wide variety of adjective pairs that were sufficiently general to be applicable to diverse concepts and objects. From their results they identified three dominant dimensions along which judgments are made, and labeled them the evaluative, potency, and activity dimensions.

13. Several methods for eliciting attribute descriptors are described in John Dickson and Gerald Albaum. "A Method For Developing Tailor-Made Semantic Differentials for Specific Marketing Content Areas," *Journal of Marketing Research,* 14, February 1977, 87–91.

14. Dennis Menezes and Nobert F. Elbert. "Alternative Semantic Scaling Formats for Measuring Store Image: An Evaluation," *Journal of Marketing Research,* 16, February 1979, 80–87.

15. C. L. Narayana. "Graphic Positioning Scale: An Economical Instrument for Surveys," *Journal of Marketing Research,* 14, February 1977, 118–122. S. I. Lampert. "The Attitude Pollimeter: A New Attitude Scaling Device," *Journal of Marketing Research,* November 1979, 578–582.

16. John A. Martilla and John C. James. "Importance—Performance Analysis," *Journal of Marketing,* January 1977, 77–79.

17. F. M. Andrews. "Construct Validity and Error Components of Survey Measures," *Public Opinion Quarterly,* Summer 1984, 432.

18. J. Paul Peter. "Reliability: A Review of Psychometric Basis and Recent Marketing Practices," *Journal of Marketing Research,* 16, February 1979, 6–17.

19. For a discussion of *generalizability* theory and its applications in marketing research, see Joseph O. Rentz. "Generalizability Theory: A Comprehensive Method for Assessing and Improving the Dependability of Marketing Measures," *Journal of Marketing Research,* 24, February 1987, 19–28.

20. Most international research studies conducted use different kinds of scales in their research. A few recent examples are Daniel C. Fieldman and David C. Thomas. "Career Management Issues Facing Expatriates," *Journal of Business Studies,* Second Quarter 1992; Earl Naumann, "Organizational Predictors of Expatriate Job Satisfaction," *Journal of Business Studies,* First Quarter 1993, 61–81.

CASE 10-1
Wine Horizons

Wine Horizons was a medium-sized New York State winery that emphasized sparkling wines. The company was not known to the public as a producer of good-quality domestic champagne because all of their output was sold to well-known hotels and restaurants that put their own labels on the bottles. However, their still (nonsparkling) wines were sold under the Wine Horizons label and were moderately well known.

The management of the company had been planning for some time to launch a line of champagnes under their own brand name. They were seriously considering whether the launch should be based on a packaging innovation. The specific proposal was to package their champagne in six-packs of seven-ounce bottles in an easy-to-carry container, at a retail price of approximately $9.00. The seven-ounce quantity was chosen as it was the equivalent of two average-sized champagne glasses, thus making one bottle a convenient serving for one or two people. This size and price were expected to make the champagne an attractive alternative to imported beers in a variety of social situations.

Before a decision could be made, the management team had to be satisfied that there was an adequate market for the new packaging. They also wanted to know the occasions during which the target market would be likely to use the product, and whether these people would expect to find it in the imported beer or wine section of their retail outlet. To answer these questions the firm Ritchey and Associates was retained to conduct a market study. A meeting to review their attitude questionnaire was just beginning.

Developments in the Wine Industry

The wine industry had enjoyed significant growth in recent years. The growth of white wines had been especially strong, but sparkling wines had also experienced an upward trend. Champagne sales had grown, but less than sparkling wines in general. The reason for the increased popularity of white wines was not known, but many in the industry believed it was due to a general trend toward "lightness" on the part of consumers, as reflected in their increased use of light beers, light wine, bottled mineral water, health foods, and low-tar cigarettes. Whatever the reason, wine was being chosen more frequently as a beverage alternative to beer and liquor in various formal and informal social situations. It was also believed that champagne was not sharing in wine's growth because of the difficulty in keeping champagne fresh after the bottle was opened—a large, opened bottle of champagne would lose all its carbonation in a few hours and "go flat."

Two wineries had recently begun test-marketing wine in small packages. One winery was offering chablis, rosé, and burgundy in six-packs of cans, with each can containing six ounces of wine. Another winery was test-marketing chablis in six-packs of 6.5-ounce bottles. The new packaging seemed to be selling reasonably well in test areas, and retailers reportedly had a favorable attitude toward the new packaging. Compared with "single" small bottles or cans of wine—which were considered a nuisance—retailers felt that the six-packs were more profitable and more convenient to stack and display.

The Research Study
The objectives of the study were to (1) measure consumers' acceptance of wine in six-packs, (2) identify the type of person who was a potential purchaser and user of champagne in six-packs, (3) determine where in the store they would expect to find such champagne, and (4) determine the size of the potential market. The sample would be champagne drinkers who were 21 years of age or older. Also, the research would be limited to markets where the six-packs of wine were already being tested. It was further decided that the data would be collected with personal interviews using a shopping mall intercept method. This would permit the interviewer to show a picture of the proposed six-pack and to use cards to list answer categories in complex questions. Only malls that contained liquor stores would be selected. The interviewers would be located in the vicinity of the liquor store and would attempt to interview adults leaving the stores.

A six-part questionnaire (see Exhibit 1) was designed to obtain the desired information. The major issues to be resolved were whether this questionnaire and the mall intercept design would identify potential users and yield a valid estimate of the potential market for the six-packs.

Questions for Discussion

1. Will the proposed questionnaire and research design achieve the research objectives?
2. What alternative questions could be used to assess attitudes and intentions-to-buy? Which approach would yield the most valid responses?

CASE 10-2
National Kitchens

For several years the management of National Kitchens, a diversified packaged foods manufacturer, had been watching the rapid growth in sales of microwave ovens. They were particularly interested in the prospects for ready-to-eat soup in glass jars. The attraction of glass packaging was that the soup could be heated in a microwave oven in its original container. However, a single-serving ready-to-eat soup in a glass jar was expected to cost $1.10 as compared to $.90 for a comparable canned soup. While the price premium for glass was thought to be excessive, there were some new data on the acceptability of this price premium that had just been provided by a glass manufacturer.

The Research Study
The glass manufacturer had designed a brief questionnaire to evaluate consumer attitudes to glass packaging for a variety of microwave oven cooking jobs. This questionnaire was mailed to 600 names obtained from the warranty cards returned to one microwave oven manufacturer. The results had just been tabulated and were being shown to National Kitchens.

The questionnaire obtained information on microwave usage. Two key questions directly addressed the issue of ready-to-eat soup in glass:

15. Would you purchase ready-to-eat soup in a single-serving container (approximately 10 ounces) that could be put directly into your microwave oven and poured into a bowl after heating? Assume the same price per serving as canned soup.
    ☐ Yes About how many individual servings per month. _____
    ☐ No Why not? _____
16. Please review question 15 and indicate below whether or not you would be willing to pay 20 cents more per individual serving for the product.
    ☐ Yes
    ☐ No

Of the 600 questionnaires, 312 were returned. The responses to questions 15 and 16 that related to soup in glass are summarized in Table 1.

EXHIBIT 1

Hello! My name is _____ . I'm an interviewer with the marketing research firm of Ritchey and Associates, and we are conducting a study concerned with certain alcoholic beverages. Would you please take a few minutes to answer some questions? I assure you that your answers will be kept *completely confidential*.

1. Are you 21 years of age or older? (ASK ONLY IF NECESSARY)

   _____ Yes   _____ No (TERMINATE)

2. Do you drink any alcoholic beverages?

   _____ Yes   _____ No (TERMINATE)

3. What different kinds of alcoholic beverages do you drink?

   _____ Beer   _____ Liquor (any kind)

   _____ Wine   _____ Other

   _____ Champagne (to Q5)

4. Do you drink champagne?

   _____ Yes   _____ No (TERMINATE)

5. About how often do you drink champagne? (CLARIFY RESPONSE IF NECESSARY)

   _____ Once a week or more often   _____ About once in 2–3 months

   _____ About twice a month   _____ About twice a year

   _____ About once a month   _____ About once a year

                                                     _____ DK

6. On what types of occasions do you drink champagne?

   _____ Dinner for two   _____ Picnics

   _____ Small dinner party   _____ After athletic activities

   _____ Parties   _____ Just relaxing

   _____ Special holidays   _____ Other (specify) _____

   _____ Dinner

7. Do you consider champagne to be an appropriate beverage to serve at informal occasions, or is it only for formal occasions?

   _____ Appropriate for informal occasions

   _____ Only for formal occasions   _____ For both occasions

EXPLAIN: I'm now going to ask you some questions about wine, not champagne. These are questions about some new packaging that has recently been used by some brands of wine.

EXHIBIT 1 (continued)

8. Are you aware that some wine is now being sold in packages consisting of six small cans and bottles, each containing about 6 ounces?

_____ Yes   _____ No (to Q10)   _____ DK (to Q10)

9. Have you ever purchased wine sold in such packaging or drank wine from one of these small containers?

_____ Purchased   _____ Both

_____ Drank   _____ Neither

10. Do you think it's a good idea to sell wine in packages consisting of six small cans or bottles—that is, are you in favor of it?

_____ A good idea, in favor of   _____ Indifferent (to Q12)

_____ Not a good idea   _____ Undecided (to Q12)

11. Why?

EXPLAIN: Wine Horizons is one of the largest private label bottlers of champagnes in the United States. For example, it supplies well-known hotel chains and restaurants with their own brand of champagne. Wine Horizons is planning to market this package (SHOW PICTURE) of six small bottles of champagne.

12. Do you think it's a good idea to sell champagne in packages consisting of six small bottles—that is, are you in favor of it?

_____ A good idea, in favor of (to Q14)   _____ Indifferent (to Q14)

_____ Not a good idea   _____ Undecided (to Q14)

13. Why not?
14. Would you consider purchasing such a package of champagne at the retail price of $9.00?

_____ Yes (to Q16)   _____ No

_____ Maybe, possibly (to Q16)   _____ DK

15. Why not?
16. For what kinds of occasions would you use these small bottles of champagne?

_____ Dinner for two   _____ Picnics

_____ Small dinner party   _____ After athletic activities

_____ Parties   _____ Just relaxing

_____ Special holidays   _____ Other (specify) _____

_____ Dinner

EXHIBIT 1 (continued)

17. Would you use them for any of the occasions shown on this list? (SHOW CARD)

_____ Dinner for two   _____ Picnics

_____ Small dinner party   _____ After athletic activities

_____ Parties   _____ Just relaxing

_____ Special holidays

_____ Dinner

18. In what types of retail stores would you expect to find this product being sold?

_____ Liquor stores   _____ Other (specify) _____

_____ Supermarkets

19. In what section of the store would you expect to find this package of champagne, that is, what other products would you expect to find alongside it?

_____ Other champagnes   _____ Beer

_____ Wine   _____ Other (specify) _____

TABLE 1
Summary of Question Responses

Number of Servings per Month	Q. 15: No. of Responses	Q. 16: No. Responding that They Would Pay 20 Cents More per Serving
0 ("No")	103	185 = would not pay 20 cents more
1	8	3
2	12	7
3	5	3
4	26	19
5	9	6
6–10	31	14
11–15	19	9
16–20	56	38
21–30	11	9
31–40	17	8
41–50	14	10
50+	1	1

Questions for Discussion

1. What have you learned about the potential market for soup in glass jars?

2. What else would you like to know?

3. How else would you assess people's attitudes toward this concept?

289

11 DESIGNING THE QUESTIONNAIRE

Learning Objectives

▶ Introduce the concept of questionnaire design.

▶ Be familiar with the process of questionnaire design.

▶ Help recognize the characteristics of a good questionnaire.

▶ Learn how to deal with sensitive questions.

▶ Discuss the issues of questionnaire design in the international context.

Questionnaire construction is properly regarded as a very imperfect art. There are no established procedures that will lead consistently to a "good" questionnaire. One consequence is that the range of potential error contributed by ambiguous questions may be as much as 20 or 30 percentage points.[1] Fortunately, such extreme errors can be reduced sharply by common sense and insights from the experience of other researchers. A major objective of this chapter is to present systematically the "rules of thumb" that have been acquired with experience.

A good questionnaire accomplishes the research's objectives. Surveys must be custom-built to the specification of given research purposes, and they are much more than a collection of unambiguous questions. There are a number of constraints imposed on the development of an appropriate questionnaire. For example, depending on the data collection method the number, form, and ordering of the specific questions are determined. The respondent's willingness and ability to answer, discussed in Chapter 8, also exerts an influence in the final questionnaire format. The wording and sequence of questions can facilitate recall and motivate more accurate responses.

Although each questionnaire must be designed with the specific research objectives in mind, there is a sequence of logical steps that every researcher must follow to develop a good questionnaire:

1. Plan what to measure.
2. Formulate questions to obtain the needed information.
3. Decide on the order and wording of questions and on the layout of the questionnaire.
4. Using a small sample, test the questionnaire for omissions and ambiguity.
5. Correct the problems (and pretest again, if necessary).

We will use this sequence to organize the remainder of this chapter. Figure 11-1 gives the flow chart of this process.

PLANNING WHAT TO MEASURE

The most difficult step is specifying exactly what information is to be collected from each respondent. Poor judgment and lack of thought at this stage may mean that the results are not relevant to the research purpose or that they are incomplete. Both problems are expensive, and may seriously diminish the value of the study.

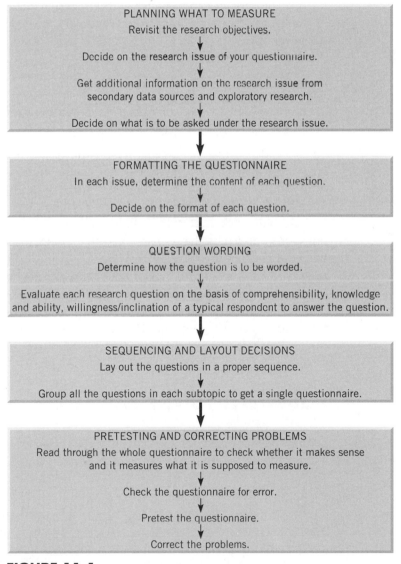

PLANNING WHAT TO MEASURE
Revisit the research objectives.

Decide on the research issue of your questionnaire.

Get additional information on the research issue from secondary data sources and exploratory research.

Decide on what is to be asked under the research issue.

FORMATTING THE QUESTIONNAIRE
In each issue, determine the content of each question.

Decide on the format of each question.

QUESTION WORDING
Determine how the question is to be worded.

Evaluate each research question on the basis of comprehensibility, knowledge and ability, willingness/inclination of a typical respondent to answer the question.

SEQUENCING AND LAYOUT DECISIONS
Lay out the questions in a proper sequence.

Group all the questions in each subtopic to get a single questionnaire.

PRETESTING AND CORRECTING PROBLEMS
Read through the whole questionnaire to check whether it makes sense and it measures what it is supposed to measure.

Check the questionnaire for error.

Pretest the questionnaire.

Correct the problems.

FIGURE 11-1
The process of questionnaire design

To combat the lack of relevance problem, it is necessary to ask constantly, "How will this information be used?" and ultimately to anticipate the specific analyses that will be made. It is also important to have a clear idea of the target population. Questions that are appropriate for college students may not be appropriate for homemakers. Understanding is related to respondent socioeconomic characteristics.[2]

When a questionnaire is incomplete in important aspects and is sent into the field, the error is irreversible. To avoid this awful situation, careful thought is required; this is facilitated by

1. Clear research objectives, which describe as fully as possible the kind of information the decision maker needs, the hypotheses, and the scope of the research.
2. Exploratory research, which will suggest further relevant variables and help the researcher absorb the vocabulary and point of view of the typical respondent.
3. Experience with similar studies.
4. Pretesting of preliminary versions of the questionnaire.

Translating Research Objectives into Information Requirements

At the end of Chapter 4 we saw how the research objectives for the HMO study were established. These objectives are summarized in Table 11-1. Before individual questionnaire items can be written, these objectives have to be translated into specific information requirements. Here is where the hypotheses play an especially important role. Since hypotheses suggest possible answers to the questions implied by the research objectives, there must be questionnaire items that could elicit those possible answers. For example, the HMO study included specific hypotheses as to which characteristics or features of a health plan would influence the choice of plan. Each of these characteristics needed to be represented by a question, so that the hypotheses could be tested. From the information requirements specified on the right-hand side of Table 11-1, one can see how the process advanced.

FORMATTING THE QUESTION

Before specific questions can be phrased, a decision has to be made as to the degree of freedom to be given respondents in answering the question. The alternatives are: (1) open-ended with no classification, where the interviewer tries to record the response verbatim; (2) open-ended, where the interviewer uses precoded classifications to record the response; or (3) the closed, or structured, format in which a question or supplementary card presents the responses the respondent may consider.[3] These options can be illustrated with the following brief sequence of questions from a personal interview survey:

TABLE 11-1
Research Objectives for HMO Study

Research Objectives	Information Requirements
1. What is the probable demand for the proposed HMO?	1. General attitudes and awareness with respect to health care and the concept of prepaid plans; and specific attitudes and knowledge regarding existing health plans.
2. Which market segments will be most interested in the proposed HMO?	2. Process by which the present plan was selected; sources of information and influences.
3. What will be the probable rate of utilization of medical services by the most interested segment?	3. Satisfaction with present plan (a) overall (b) with respect to specific characteristics of the plan, and (c) intentions to change.
4. Which aspects of health plans have the greatest influence on the choice process?	4. Reaction to proposed HMO design (a) overall evaluation (b) evaluation of specific characteristics (c) preference, compared to present plan (d) likelihood of adoption (e) influence of changes in price and benefits
	5. Classification variables including demographics; distance from HMO; time in area; expected stay in area; and utilization of medical services by individual family members.

Q10 Is there any particular type of information about life insurance that you would like to have, that you do not now have, or don't know enough about?

Q11 What kind of information?

PROBE: What else?

The first question uses a precoded classification, since a "yes" or "no" answer is strongly implied. The second question is completely open-ended, and the goal is to achieve an exact transcription. Only 20 percent of a national sample said "Yes" to question 10, and 44 percent of these responded only in very general terms to the follow-up question. This meant that only 11 percent of the total sample said they had a need for specific information, such as rate, or family benefits in case of disability or accident. It is likely that different results would have been obtained if either Q10 or Q11 had been converted to a closed-ended response, such that respondents were handed a card describing many different kinds of information and asked to indicate which they would like to have or didn't know enough about.

Open-Response Questions

There are advantages and disadvantages to open-response (or unstructured) questions. The advantages stem from the wide range of responses that can be obtained and the lack of influence in the responses from prespecified categories. Respondents often appreciate this freedom, as illustrated by the surprising frequency with which people write marginal comments in mail surveys when they don't feel the response categories adequately capture their feelings. Because of these advantages, open-ended questions are useful in the following circumstances:

▶ As an introduction to a survey or to a topic. A question such as, "In general, how do you feel about [color TV, this neighborhood, the bus service in this area]," will acquaint the respondent with the subject of the survey, open the way for more specific questions, and make the respondent more comfortable with the questioning process.

▶ When it is important to measure the salience of an issue to a respondent. (Asking "What do you think is the most important problem facing this country today?" will give some insight into what currently is bothering the respondent.)

▶ When there are too many possible responses to be listed, or they cannot be foreseen; for example, "What were some of the reasons why you decided to pay cash (for a major appliance purchase?)" or "What do you especially like about living in this neighborhood?"

▶ When verbatim responses are desired to give the flavor of people's answers or to cite as examples in a report.

▶ When the behavior to be measured is sensitive or disapproved (such as estimates of drinking or sexual activities). Reported frequencies are higher on an open format where there are no prespecified response categories. When respondents are given a choice of a low-frequency category on a closed format, they are less willing to admit to higher frequencies.[4]

The disadvantages of open-response or open-ended questions are numerous. The major problem is that variability in the clarity and depth of responses depends to a great extent on (1) the articulateness of the respondent in an interview situation, or the willingness to compose a written answer to a mail survey, and (2) the personal or telephone interviewer's ability to record the verbatim answers quickly—or to accurately summarize—and to probe effectively. A third area arose in Chapter 8 where we saw that the interviewer's expectations will influence what is selected for recording or when to stop probing. Open-ended questions are also time-consuming, both during the interview and during tabulation. Classifications must be established to summarize the responses, and each answer must be assigned to one or more categories. This involves subjective judgments that are prone to error. To minimize this source of error, it may be desirable to have two editors independently categorize the responses and compare their results. This adds further to the cost.

Another problem that occurs frequently in an open-ended question is that the answer given to it expands or contracts, depending on the space or time available for it. When the students are given a full page for a question, they have a tendency to fill up the whole page. But if there is only half a page left, they will write the answer in the space available. Open-ended questions must be designed so that the available answer space and time coincides with question importance.

In addition, respondents may not always use the same frame of reference when answering an open-ended question, and these different frames of reference may not be readily discernable by the researcher. This problem is illustrated in the results of an experiment on work values that compared the following two questions[5]:

Q1 People look for different things in a job. What would you most prefer in a job?

Q2 People look for different things in a job. Which one of the following five things would you most prefer in a job?

1. Work that pays well.
2. Work that gives a sense of accomplishment.
3. Work where there is not too much supervision and you make most decisions by yourself.
4. Work that is pleasant and where the other people are nice to work with.
5. Work that is steady with little chance of being laid off.

In the open-response format, many respondents said that pay was the most important aspect of a job. There was evidence that some of them meant "high pay," whereas others meant "steady pay." Since both answers were expressed in the same words, it was impossible to separate the two different frames of reference. Answers to the closed-response format did not have this problem, since "work that pays well" and "work that is steady" were two distinct options. Open-response questions run the risk that the researcher may not always be able to accurately tap differences among respondents.

In view of the disadvantages and the lack of convincing evidence that open-ended questions provide more meaningful, relevant, and nonrepetitive responses, it is advisable to close up as many questions as possible in large-scale surveys.

Closed-Response Questions

There are two basic formats for **closed-ended** (or **structured**) **questions.** The first asks respondents to make one or more choices from a list of possible responses. The second is a rating scale where the respondent is given a continuum of labeled categories that represents the range of responses. Research organizations, such as McCollum/Spielman, use both formats to ask diagnostic questions about commercials—both the message (theme, basic idea, unique selling point) and the presentation (setting, demonstration devices, music, and so forth). The following sample of ad testing questions illustrates what can be done:

Choice from a List of Responses
Which one of the following words or phrases best describes the kind of person you feel would be most likely to use this product—based on what you saw and heard in this commercial?

_____ Young   _____ Single

_____ Old   _____ Married

_____ Modern   _____ Homemaker

_____ Old-fashioned   _____ Career woman

Appropriate Single-Choice Rating on a Scale
Please tell us your overall reaction to this commercial.

_____ A great commercial, would like to see it again   _____ A pretty good commercial

_____ Just so-so, like a million others   _____ Another bad commercial

Based on what you saw and heard in this commercial, how interested do you feel you would be in buying the product?

_____ Definitely would buy   _____ Probably would buy   _____ May or may not buy

_____ Probably would not buy   _____ Definitely would not buy

Here is a statement about world peace. "World leaders are basically working to establish peace between countries." Do you agree, disagree, or do you not have an opinion about that?

_____ Definitely Agree   _____ Moderately Agree   _____ Neither agree nor disagree

_____ Moderately Disagree   _____ Definitely Disagree   _____ No opinion

Regardless of the type of closed-response format, the advantages are the same. Such questions are easier to answer, in both an interview and a mail survey; require less effort by the interviewer; and make tabulation and analysis easier. There is less potential error due to differences in the way questions are asked and responses recorded. Normally, a closed-response question takes less time than an equivalent open-ended question. Perhaps the most significant advantage of these questions in large-scale surveys is that the answers are directly comparable from respondent to respondent (assuming each interprets the words the same way). Comparability of respondents is an essential prelude to the use of any analytical methods.

There are significant limitations to closed-response questions. There is considerable disagreement among researchers on the type of response categories that should be listed. One area of controversy is whether or not middle alternatives should be included in the questions. It is not unusual for 20 percent of respondents to choose a middle alternative when it is offered, although they would not have volunteered this answer had it not been mentioned. Hence, if one wants to design questions that will help make a clear, actionable decision, then it is best not to include the neutral category in the question.

One way of handling this problem is to include the 'don't know' alternative, so that respondents are not forced to choose one opinion. Another way of handling this distortion of responses is by providing a scale that captures intensity of a respondent's feeling about a particular question.[6] The measurement of intensity is useful not only as a follow-up for items with logical middle positions but for attitude questions generally. Strength of feeling has been shown to predict both attitude stability and attitude consistency. Two of the most commonly used intensity indicators are the Likert and semantic differential scales.

Another potential limitation of the closed-response question arises from the fact that an answer will be received for a question, no matter how irrelevant the question is in that context.[7] Hence, if a large number of categories are included in the closed-response question, all the categories will receive a certain percentage of responses. This may not produce meaningful results. Therefore, care should be taken to include only the relevant categories.

An extreme form of the closed-ended question is the dichotomous question. A dichotomous question has only two response categories. For example,

SEX:
_____ Male   _____ Female

Dichotomous questions are mainly used to collect demographic and behavioral data when only two answers logically exist. They are not used to collect psychological data because they tend to provide oversimplified, often forced, answers. Dichotomous questions are also prone to a large amount of measurement errors; because alternatives are polarized, the wide range of possible choices between the poles is omitted.

A researcher must constantly strive to overcome the many limitations of closed-response questions. First, good questions are hard to develop and exploratory work is necessary to ensure that all potentially important response alternatives are included. In one experiment, respondents were first asked who should manage company benefit funds, the company, the union, or government? When these three alternatives were given, only 15 percent of the respondents suggested combinations. However, when the combinations were mentioned explicitly, the number choosing these alternatives jumped to 52 percent.[8] Second, the very nature of rigid closed responses provides fewer opportunities for self-expression or subtle qualifications, and they are not nearly so involving for the respondent.

Finally, the list of alternative response categories provides answers that respondents might not have considered. In this situation, the respondent might choose a "responsible" alternative. The respondent may also try to avoid a difficult choice or judgment by selecting the easiest alternative, such as "don't know." Where there is a distinct possibility of such biasing occurring in a personal or telephone interview survey, it may be desirable to precede the closed-response question with an open-response question. This is done often in brand-name awareness studies. The respondent is asked first what brands are associated with the product (unaided recall), and then is given a list of brands and asked to choose those that are known (aided recall).

Number of Response Categories. The number of categories can range from a two-point scale all the way to a 100-point scale. Some questions—especially those dealing with points of fact—admit only two possible answers: Did you purchase a new car in the past year? Did you vote in the last election? However, in most situations a dichotomous question will yield misleading results. Sometimes an either/or choice is not possible, and the correct answer may be both. In a survey of shaving habits, the question was asked, "Do you shave with an electric razor or a safety razor?" Some people apparently use both, the specific choice depending on the situation.[9] Attitudinal questions invariably have intermediate positions. A simple question such as "Are you considering changing your present health insurance plan?" revealed that 70 percent were not, 8 percent definitely were, and the remaining 22 percent were uncertain or might consider a change in the future. These subtleties are very important in interpreting such a question.

As a general rule, the range of opinion on most issues can be captured best with five or seven categories. Five categories are probably the minimum needed to discriminate effectively among individuals. One popular five-point scale is the Likert scale. This number of categories can be read by the interviewer and understood by the respondent. A seven- or nine-category scale is more precise but cannot be read to respondents with the assurance that they won't get confused.

Multiple-choice questions present special problems. Ideally, the response categories provided for such questions should be mutually exclusive and should exhaust the possibilities. Sometimes it is neither possible nor desirable to include all the possible alternatives. A listing of all the brands in a housewares product category, such as hand mixers, might include 50 or more names if all distributor-controlled and import brands were included. Since this is impractical, only the top five or six are listed, and the rest are consigned to an "other" category, which is accompanied by a "please specify" request and a space to enter the brand name.

A common type of question requires numerical data in response: What is your annual income? How far is it to your work? How many stores did you visit? Usually, it is preferable to group the possible answers into categories; for example, under $4000, $4000 to $7000 . . . $20,000 and over. This is a somewhat less sensitive way of asking an income question and facilitates coding. If the numbers falling in the response categories are not known or it is important to know the exact number (of children, pets, and so forth) for later analysis, this does not apply.

Order of Response Categories. The order of presentation of categories to respondents in personal or telephone interview situations sometimes can have a big influence on results. A classic study in 1974 provided clear evidence for this. One way of asking a person's income over the telephone is to start by asking "Is your income more than $2000?" and increasing the figure in increments of $2000 until the first "no" response. Alternatively, one can start with the highest income category and drop the figure until the first "yes" response. The study found that the median income when the first category was $2000 was $12,711; however, when the income question started with the high category, $17,184 was the median income.[10] One explanation for this remarkable difference is that respondents find the question threatening and try to get it out of the way by making a premature terminal response. A much better approach is to begin with the median income figure and use a series of branching questions, such as, "Is it over (the median income)?" and if the answer is "No," then asking, "Is it under (half the median income)?" and so forth. This gives a relatively unbiased measure of income and the lowest proportion of refusals.

Another ordering problem is encountered with mail survey questions, in which respondents tend to select categories that are in the middle position of a range of values. This is especially prevalent with questions of fact, such as the number of checkouts at a local store. Respondents who do not know the answer will choose the center position as a safe guess. This also can happen with questions about information that is unique to the respondent, such as the distance to the nearest department store. When the question is constructed with multiple categories, with the middle category representing an estimate of the average distance, the natural tendency to choose the middle position may lead to inaccurate responses. One solution is to place the average or expected distance at various positions in the sequence of categories.[11]

Handling Uncertainty and Ignorance. One awkward question concerns the handling of "don't know" and neutral responses. There are many reasons why respondents do not know the answer to a question, such as not knowing, forgetting, or an inability to articulate. If an explicit "don't know" response category is provided, it is an easy option for those in the latter group. But often "don't know" is a legitimate response and may yield very important insights. Thus, the option always should be provided as a response to questions about knowledge or opinions when there is some likelihood of ignorance or forgetting. Sometimes this response category is used by those who are unwilling to answer a question. In personal and telephone interviews, it may be advisable to provide the interviewer with an additional "no answer" category to correctly identify these people. A neutral response category such as "not sure" or "neither like nor dislike" also may be desirable for those people who genuinely can't make a choice among specific opinion statements.

If there is likelihood of both ambivalence and ignorance, then both a neutral category and a "don't know" category are appropriate.

Using Both Open-Response and Closed-Response Questions

The choice between open-and closed-response questions is not necessarily an either/or distinction. Open-response questions can be used in conjunction with closed-response questions to provide additional information. Using an open-response question to follow up a closed-response question is called a *probe*. Probes can efficiently combine some advantages of both open and closed questions. They can be used for specific prechosen questions or to obtain additional information from only a subset of people who respond to previous questions in a certain way. A common example of the latter is to ask respondents who choose "none of the above" a follow-up question to expand on their answer.

There are two general purposes for the use of probes in a questionnaire. The first is to pinpoint questions that were particularly difficult for respondents. Adequate pretesting of questions reduces this need to use probes. The second purpose is to aid researcher interpretation of respondent answers. Answers to open-response follow-ups can provide valuable guidance in the analysis of closed-response questions.

QUESTION WORDING: A PROBLEM OF COMMUNICATION

The wording of particular questions can have a large impact on how a respondent interprets them. Even small changes in wording can shift respondent answers, but it is difficult to know in advance whether or not a wording change will have such an effect. Our knowledge of how to phrase questions that are free from ambiguity and bias is such that it is easier to discuss what not to do rather than give prescriptions. Hence, the following guidelines are of greatest value in critically evaluating and improving an existing question:

1. *Is the vocabulary simple, direct, and familiar to all respondents?* The challenge is to choose words that can be understood by all respondents, regardless of education level, but do not sound patronizing. The most

"I'm undecided, but that doesn't mean I'm apathetic or uniformed."

Drawing by Barsotti; © 1980. The New Yorker Magazine, Inc.

common pitfall is to use technical jargon or specialized terms. Many respondents will not be able to identify their "marital status," but can say whether they are married, single, divorced, and so forth. Special care must be taken to avoid words that have different meanings for different groups. This can be readily appreciated in cross-cultural studies, where translation problems are profound, but it also is applicable within a country. One socioeconomic group may refer to the evening meal as dinner, while others call this meal supper and have their dinner at noon.

2. *Do any words have vague or ambiguous meanings?* A common error is not giving the respondent an adequate frame of reference, in time and space, for interpreting the question. Words such as "often," "occasionally," and "usually" lack an appropriate time referent, so respondents choose their own, with the result that answers are not comparable. Similarly, the appropriate space or locale often is not specified. Does the question, "How long have you lived here?" refer to this state, county, city, neighborhood, or particular house or apartment? Some words have many interpretations; thus, a respondent might interpret income to mean hourly pay rate, weekly salary, or monthly income, either before or after taxes and deductions, and could include or exclude sources of income other than wages and the incomes of other family members.

3. *Are any questions "double-barreled"?* There are questions in which a respondent can agree with one part of the question but not the other, or cannot answer at all without accepting a particular assumption. In either case, the answers cannot be interpreted. For example, what can be learned from such questions as, "Do you plan to leave your job and look for another one during the coming year?" or, "Are you satisfied with the cost and convenience of this (service)?" The second type of error is a bit more elusive to find, as the following example from a Harris poll demonstrates. The question was, "Have you often, sometimes, hardly ever, or never felt bad because you were unfaithful to your wife?" One percent said often, 14 percent said sometimes or hardly ever, and 85 percent said they never felt bad because of this.

4. *Are any questions leading or loaded?* A leading question is one that clearly suggests the answer or reveals the researcher's (or interviewer's) opinion. This can be done easily by adding "don't you agree?" or "wouldn't you say?" to a desired statement. A loaded question introduces a more subtle bias. A common type of loading of possible responses is through failure to provide a full range of alternatives; for example by asking, "How do you generally spend your free time—watching television, or what?" Another way to load a question is to provide the respondent with a reason for one of the alternatives: "Should we increase taxes in order to get more housing and better schools, or should we keep them about the same?" A second form of loading results from the use of emotionally charged words. These are words or phrases such as "fair profits," "radical," or "luxury items," which have such strong positive or negative overtones that they overshadow the specific content of the question. Organizations and groups also have emotional associations, and using them to endorse a proposition

will certainly bias the response: "A committee of experts has suggested . . . ; Do you approve of this, or do you disagree?" For this reason it is also risky to reveal the sponsor of the study. If one brand or company is identified as the sponsor, the respondents will tend to exaggerate their positive feelings toward the brand.

Questions that involve appeals or threats to the respondent's self-esteem may also be loaded.[12] A question on occupations usually will produce more "executives," if the respondent chooses from one of a small number of occupational categories rather than being asked for a specific job title.

5. *Are the instructions potentially confusing?* Sheatsley counsels against lengthy questions that explain a complicated situation to a respondent and then ask for an opinion. In his experience, "If the respondent is not aware of these facts, you have probably confused or biased him more than you have enlightened him, and his opinion won't mean much in either case." The question should be directed more toward measuring the respondent's knowledge or interest in the subject.

6. *Is the question applicable to all respondents?* Respondents may try to answer a question even though they don't qualify to do so or may lack an opinion. Examples of such questions are, "What is your present occupation?" (assumes respondent is working), "Where did you live before you moved here?" (assumes a prior move), or, "For whom did you vote in the last election?" (assumes that respondent voted). The solution to this is to ask a qualifying or filter question and limit further questioning to those who qualify.

7. *Split-ballot technique.* Whenever there is doubt as to the appropriate wording, it is desirable to test several alternatives. For instance, the responses to a question may vary with the degree of personalization. The question, "Do you think there should be government-run off-track betting in this state?" is different from, "Is it desirable to have government-run off-track betting in this state?" Sometimes the choice can be resolved by the purpose of the study; the impersonal form being preferred if the study aims at measuring the general tenor of public sentiment. Where the choice is not obvious, the best solution is to use one version in half of the questionnaire and the second version in the remaining half. Any significant differences in the results can be helpful in interpreting the meaning of the question.

8. *Are the questions of an appropriate length?* It is not always the case that shorter questions are better, although one common rule of thumb is to keep the number of words in any question under twenty. Under certain circumstances, a question may have to be long in order to avoid ambiguity, but these should be the exception rather than the rule. A questionnaire filled with only long questions is more fatiguing to answer and more difficult to understand.

Asking Sensitive Questions

One virtually can guarantee meaningless responses by directly asking such questions as, "Have you ever defaulted on a credit account?" "Do you smoke pot at least once a week?" or, "Have you ever been involved in an unreported automobile accident?" However, sometimes a research question will involve sensitive areas. Exhibit 11-1 gives an example of what happened when Mastercard sought confidential information from its clients. There are a variety of approaches that can be used to attempt to get honest answers. For example, long, open-ended questions with familiar wording have been found effective when asking threatening questions that require quantified responses. The only limit is the creativity of the researcher. Alan Barton made this point best when in 1958 he composed the following parody on ways to ask the question, "Did you kill your wife?"[13] His approach is adapted to a different situation. Here the respondent is a responsible adult who is being questioned about his or her consumption of Kellogg's Frosted Flakes (a potentially embarrassing situation).

1. *The Casual Approach:* "Have you eaten 'Frosted Flakes' within the last week?"
2. *The Numbered Card:* "Would you please read off the number on this card that corresponds to what you had eaten for breakfast in the last week?" (Hand card to respondent.)
   1. Pancakes
   2. Frosted Flakes
   3. Other (what)?
   (GET CARD BACK FROM RESPONDENT BEFORE PROCEEDING!)
3. *The Everybody Approach:* "As you know, many people have been eating Frosted Flakes for breakfast. Do you eat Frosted Flakes?"
4. *The "Other People" Approach:*
   a. "Do you know of any adult who eats Frosted Flakes?"
   b. "How about yourself?"
5. *The Sealed Ballot Technique:* In this version you explain that the survey respects people's right to anonymity in respect to their eating habits, and that they themselves are to fill out the answer to the question, seal it in an envelope, and drop it in a box conspicuously labeled "Sealed Ballot Box" carried by the interviewer.

EXHIBIT 11-1

MasterCard Asks Sensitive Questions

The $60-million MasterCard International review took a controversial turn when the agencies and buying services in the review received a questionnaire that requested what some considered to be highly confidential client information about past media buys. "It's very specific," said one agency media head involved in the review. "Imagine as specific as you can imagine. They want affidavits, invoices. Everything." The questionnaire designed by New York consulting firm Morgan, Anderson & Company, went out to Fallon McElligot, Lintas and Ammirati & Puris—all in MasterCard's creative review—and an undisclosed number of other media shops.

Sources who have seen the document say it requests specifics such as costs per rating point, post-buy analyses, and cost projections. "We're going to answer every question," said the media executive. "Whether it's the answer they want is another story. They have the right to know what our performance is. But I would tell them I didn't want the business before I gave them confidential client information."

Source: Richard Brunelli, "MasterCard Questionnaire Seeks Confidential Client Information," *Media Week*, July 13, 1992.

6. *The Kinsey Technique:* Stare firmly into respondent's eyes and ask in simple, clear-cut language such as that to which the respondent is accustomed, and with an air of assuming that everyone has done everything, "Do you eat Frosted Flakes for breakfast?"

Randomized Response Technique. There is good evidence that accurate answers to sensitive questions sometimes can be obtained with the randomized response technique. The respondent is asked to answer one or two randomly selected questions without revealing which question has been answered. One of the questions is sensitive, the other is innocuous, such as, "Does your birthday occur during the month of October?" The respondent selects which of the two questions to answer by flipping a coin or looking at the last number of his or her driver's license or Social Security card to see if it is odd or even. Since the interviewer records a "yes" or "no" answer without knowing which question has been answered, the respondent feels free to answer honestly.[14]

Suppose a sample of 1000 respondents has been given a card with two possible questions:

A. Have you smoked marijuana during the past year?
B. Is the last digit of your driver's license equal to seven?

After flipping a coin to choose which question to answer, 30 percent, or 300, respond "yes." How can the proportion who responded "yes" to question *A* be determined from this information? First, we know that each question has an equal probability of being chosen, because a coin flip was used. Therefore p(question *A* is chosen) = p(question *B* is chosen) = 0.5. In other words 0.5 times (total sample of 1000) = 500 respondents answered question *A*, and 500 answered question *B*. We also can estimate that 10 percent of those answering question *B* would have said "yes," because they would have had a seven as the last digit of their license. This also means that only 50 of those choosing question *B* would have answered yes, since 0.10 times 500 = 50. This formula is presented in the following table:

Question	Estimated Sample Size	×	Estimated Percentage "Yes"	=	Estimated Response "Yes"
A. Have you smoked marijuana during the past year?	500	×	?	=	?
B. Is the last digit of your driver's license equal to seven?	500	×	10	=	50
The total population	1000	×	30	=	300

We also know, however, that 300 respondents actually answered "yes." In order for this to have happened, there must have been 250 respondents who answered "yes" to the sensitive question. Thus we can estimate that 250/

500 = 50 percent of the sample had smoked marijuana in the past year. To summarize, the unknown proportion, x, answering "yes" to a sensitive question, can be determined from the following formula.

$$p(\text{yes}) = p(\text{question } A \text{ is chosen}) * p(\text{yes answer to question } A)$$
$$+ p(\text{question } B \text{ is chosen}) * p(\text{yes answer to question } B)$$

therefore,

$$0.30 = (0.50)(x) + (0.50)(0.10)$$
$$0.50x = 0.30 - 0.05 = 0.25$$
$$x = 0.25/0.50 = 0.50$$

SEQUENCE AND LAYOUT DECISIONS

The order, or sequence, of questions will be determined initially by the need to gain and maintain the respondent's cooperation and make the questionnaire as easy as possible for the interviewer to administer. Once these considerations are satisfied, attention must be given to the problem of **order bias**—the possibility that prior questions will influence answers to subsequent questions.

The basic guidelines for sequencing a questionnaire to make it interesting and logical to both interviewer and respondent are straightforward:

1. Open the interview with an easy and nonthreatening question. This helps to establish rapport and build the confidence of the respondent in his or her ability to answer.[15] For most routine interviewing it is better to start this way than offer a lengthy explanation of the survey. It may even be desirable to design a throwaway question for this purpose: "We're doing a survey on medical care. The first question is, what do you usually do when you have a cold?"

2. The questionnaire should flow smoothly and logically from one topic to the next. Sudden shifts in topic are to be avoided, as they tend to confuse respondents and cause indecision. When a new topic is introduced, a transition statement or question should be used, explaining how the new topic relates to what has been discussed previously or the purpose of the study.

3. For most topics it is better to proceed from broad, general questions to the more specific. Thus, one might ask. "What are some of the things you like about this community? What things don't you like?" and proceed to, "How about the transportation facilities generally?" and finally, "Should they add another bus or widen the highway?" This funnel approach helps the respondent put the specific question in a broader context and give a more thoughtful answer.

4. Sensitive or difficult questions dealing with income status, ability, and so forth, should not be placed at the beginning of the questionnaire. Rather, they should be introduced at a point where the respondent has developed

some trust and confidence in the interviewer and the study. In short interviews they can be postponed until the end of the questionnaire.

The physical layout of the questionnaire also will influence whether the questionnaire is interesting and easy to administer. For self-administered questionnaires, the quality of the paper, the clarity of reproduction, and the appearance of crowding are important variables. Similarly, the job of the interviewer is considerably eased if the questionnaire is not crowded, if precise instructions are provided, and if flow diagrams with arrows and boxes are used to guide the interviewer through filter questions. The manner in which a typical questionnaire is organized is given in Table 11-2.

Order Bias: Does the Question Create the Answer?

We have indicated already that it is usually preferable to ease a respondent into a subject by beginning with some general, orienting questions. However, when the topic is unfamiliar to the respondents—or their involvement with the subject is low or little—the nature of the early questions will impact significantly on subsequent answers.

A new-product concept test is the most prevalent example of research on an unfamiliar subject. Respondents typically are given a description of the new

TABLE 11-2
Organization of a Typical Questionnaire

Location	Type	Function	Example
Starting questions	Broad, general questions	To break the ice and establish a rapport with the respondent	Do you own a VCR?
Next few questions	Simple and direct questions	To reassure the respondent that the survey is simple and easy to answer	What brands of VCR did you consider when you bought it?
Questions up to a third of the questionnaire	Focused questions	Relate more to the research objectives and convey to the respondent the area of research	What attributes did you consider when you purchased your VCR?
Major portion of the questionnaire	Focused questions; some may be difficult and complicated	To obtain most of the information required for the research	Rank the following attributes of a VCR based on their importance to you.
Last few questions	Personal questions that may be perceived by the respondent as sensitive	To get classification and demographic information about the respondent	What is the highest level of education you have attained?

product and asked to express their degree of buying interest. As one study showed, however, this interest will depend on the sequence of the preceding questions.[16] The new product was described as a combination pen-and-pencil selling for 29 cents. Four different types of questions were asked of four matched sets of respondents before the buying-interest question was asked:

Questions Preceding Buying Interest Question	Percentage of Respondents "Very Much Interested" in Buying New Product
1. No question asked	2.8
2. Asked only about advantages	16.7
3. Asked only about disadvantages	0.0
4. Asked about both advantages and disadvantages	5.7

The nature of the preceding questions definitely establishes the frame of reference to be used by the respondent. The issue for the questionnaire designer is to decide which is the most valid frame of reference; that is, which corresponds most closely to the type of thinking that would precede an actual purchase decision in this product category. The same problem confronts survey researchers dealing with social issues that are not of immediate relevance to the respondent. The "cautionary tale" by Charles Raymond in the accompanying Exhibit 11-2 shows how questions create answers in these settings.[17]

Order bias is also a concern when the answer to one question has an obvious implication for the answer to another. Thus, fewer people say their taxes are too high after being asked a series of items about whether government spending should be increased in various areas.[18] This may be explained in a number of different ways. Respondents may attempt to maintain consistency in their answers. Another explanation is that earlier questions may make some experiences or judgments more salient to the respondent than they would otherwise be.

The difficulty with this type of order bias is that even where context is shown to have an effect, it is frequently unclear that one order is better than another. Instead, each order may reveal a different facet of the issue being studied.

Pretesting and Correcting Problems

The purpose of a **pretest** is to ensure that it meets the researcher's expectations in terms of the information that will be obtained from the questionnaire. First drafts of questionnaires tend to be too long, often lacking important variables, and subject to all the hazards of ambiguous, ill-defined, loaded, or double-barreled questions. The objective of the questionnaire pretest is to identify and correct these deficiencies.

Effective pretesting demands that the researcher be open to criticism and be willing to pursue the deficiencies. Thus, a good starting point is for the

EXHIBIT 11-2

When Questions Create Answers

Suppose I were to call you on the telephone as follows: "Hello, this is Charles Ramond of the XYZ Poll. We are trying to find out what people think about certain issues. Do you watch television?"

Whatever your answer, the next question is, "Some people say that oil tankers are spilling oil and killing the fish and want to pass a law against this, do you agree or disagree?" Your answer is duly recorded and the next question is, "Have you ever read or heard anything about this?"

Again, your answer is recorded and finally I ask "Do you think anyone should do anything about this? Who? What?"

And now the main question, "I'd like you to rate some companies on a scale from minus five to plus five, minus five if you totally dislike the company, plus five if you totally like it and zero if you are in between or indifferent. First, U.S. Steel." You give a number and I say, "The gas company." You give another number and I say, "Exxon."

You see what is happening. Or do you. Suppose I now tell you that this form of questioning is given only to a random half of a large sample called the experimental group. To the control group, the interview is as follows: "Hello, this is Charles Ramond from XYZ Poll. We are trying to find out what people think about certain things. Do you ever watch TV?" You answer and then I ask, "Now I'd like you to rate some companies on a scale from minus five to plus five. . . ." And the difference in the average rating between the experimental and control group can be attributed to them having thought about tankers spilling oil and killing the fish, for that is the only difference in the way the two groups were treated.

Questions Shape the Attitudes

I think you can see for yourselves, merely by following this interview pattern, how you might very well rate companies differently after having rehearsed your "attitude" toward oil pollution than without having done so. In case it is difficult for you to imagine how you would respond under these two conditions, I can assure you that random halves of well-drawn samples of certain elite publics rated large companies very differently, depending on whether they were in the experimental or control group. They did so in survey after survey, consistently over time, thereby showing the reliability of the phenomenon.

researcher to take the respondent's point of view and try to answer the questions.

Pretest Design

Because a pretest is a pilot run, the respondents should be reasonably representative of the sample population. However, they should not all be "typical," for much can be learned from those at the extremes of the sample. Will the questions work with those with a limited education, strong negative opinions, or little understanding of the subject? Only small samples are necessary—15 is sufficient for a short and straightforward questionnaire, whereas 25 may be needed if the questionnaire is long and complex with many branches and multiple options. Even when the field survey will be done by mail, the pretest should be done with a personal or telephone interview to get direct feedback on problems. Only the best, most insightful, and experienced interviewers should be used for this work.

A personal interview pretest can use either a debriefing or protocol approach. In the debriefing approach, the questionnaire is administered first, just as it would be in the full-scale study. For example, a mail survey would be filled out without assistance from the interviewer; however, the interviewer should be instructed to observe and note reactions of confusion, resistance, or uneasiness. When the interview is completed, the interviewer should debrief the respondent by asking what he or she was thinking about when forming each answer, whether there were any problems of understanding, and whether any aspects of the subject were not covered by the questions.

In the protocol method, the subject is asked to "think aloud" as he or she is filling out the questionnaire. The interviewer records these thoughts, and at the end of the pretest asks for further clarification of problems where necessary. The latter approach seems to work better when the pretest is being done by telephone rather than face-to-face. Respondents offer more frequent and extensive comments over the telephone because they lack nonverbal means of communication.

Pretesting Specific Questions. There are some very specific reasons for pretest questions. Four common tests for specific questions are as follows:[19]

1. *Variation.* Testing items for an acceptable level of variation in the target population is one of the most common goals of pretesting. The researcher is on the lookout for items showing greater variability than will be useful in detecting subgroups of people. Very skewed distributions from a pretest can serve as a warning signal that the question is not tapping the intended construct.

2. *Meaning.* This is probably the most important pretesting purpose. The intended meaning of the questions for the investigators may not be the meaning the respondents interpret it to be, for two important reasons. The first is that respondents may not necessarily hear or even see every word in a question. This can result in a distortion of the meaning of the question, as when, for example, the "im" is missed from the word "impossible." The second reason for problems with meaning is that a respondent is likely to modify a difficult question in a way that makes it easier for him or her to respond. This can happen in several ways: people may pay more attention to the part of the question they think is more sensible and answer only that part; or they may take the parts of the question that are meaningful to them and reassemble a different question and answer that. Studies have shown that respondents often transform obscure questions into ones that seem sensible to them in order to minimize the amount of effort required.

3. *Task Difficulty.* A meaningful and clear question can still be difficult to answer if the question requires that a respondent make connections or put together information in unfamiliar ways. A question such as "How many pounds of laundry detergent have you consumed this past year?" is likely to be too difficult for most respondents to answer, since they probably do not total up their consumption of laundry detergent by the pound or even by the year.

4. *Respondent Interest and Attention.* This is an area of pretesting that is often overlooked by researchers. Excessive repetition within a question or use of the same format within a question can reduce the amount of attention paid to questions by respondents. Researchers should at least make note

of questions that respondents found especially interesting and especially dull.

Pretesting the Questionnaire. Some research concerns about the questionnaire as a whole, such as the order of questions, have already been mentioned. Other concerns that should be pretested are as follows:

1. *Flow of The Questionnaire.* Testing the "flow" of the questionnaire is often a matter of intuitive judgment. Since respondents do not know what the next question will be, questions must appear in a logical sequence and be part of a coherent flow. Transitions from one topic to another must also be pretested to ensure that they are clear and logical.

2. *Skip Patterns.* Many questionnaires have instructions on what questions to skip, depending on the answer to a previous question. Whether the skip patterns are to be followed by the respondent (as in a mail survey) or by the interviewer (as in a personal interview), they must be clear and well laid out. In this context, a questionnaire is a little like a road map with signs. Researchers who have been involved with the questionnaire design may not spot any inconsistencies or ambiguities in the skip patterns simply because they already know the "road map."

3. *Length.* Each section of the questionnaire should be timed to ensure that none of them is too long. While respondents are willing to spend more time on questionnaires when they have a personal interest in the topic, there is an upper limit to the duration that is considered reasonable. Unless the length is pretested, the research may experience problems with respondent fatigue, interview break-off, and initial refusal if respondents know in advance the expected length.

4. *Respondent Interest and Attention.* Capturing and maintaining the interest of a respondent throughout the entire questionnaire is a major design challenge. Often the answering task is varied throughout the questionnaire, to engage a respondent's active attention. The extent to which this is successful can and should be pretested.

Role of the Pretest

There are limits to how well a pretest can detect errors. One study found that pretest respondents were virtually unable to detect loaded questions, and most did not recognize when response alternatives were missing or questions were ambiguous.[20] For example, less than 10 percent of a pretest sample pointed out the ambiguity of the following question: "Do you think things will be better or worse next summer than they are now?" Five response options were provided ranging from much better to much worse.

Although it requires only one perceptive or confused respondent to identify problems or improvements, respondents are not the only source of insights. Interviewers are equally important to the pretesting process. Once the interviewers have reported their experiences, they also should be asked for their suggestions. There is a danger that some interviewers will make changes in the field on their own initiative if they believe it will make their job easier.

This can create serious problems if some interviewers make the change and others do not.

Finally, the pretest analysis should return full-circle to the first step in the design process. Each question should be reviewed once again and asked to justify its place in the questionnaire. How will the answer be used in the analysis? Is the pattern of answers from the pretest sensible, or difficult to interpret? Does the question add substantial new information or unnecessarily duplicate the results from another question? Of course, the last step in the process may be another pretest, if far-reaching changes have been necessary.

QUESTIONNAIRE DESIGN FOR INTERNATIONAL RESEARCH

Choosing the Question Format for Cross-National Research

The issue of question format is an important one when constructing a questionnaire for cross-cultural or cross-national research.[21] The researcher lacks experience with purchasing behavior or relevant determinants of response in another country or cultural context. Use of open-ended questions may thus be desirable in a number of situations. Since they do not impose any structure or response categories, open-ended questions avoid the imposition of cultural bias by the researcher. Furthermore, they do not require familiarity with all the respondents' possible responses.

In addition, differences in levels of literacy may affect the appropriateness of using open-ended questions as opposed to closed questions. Since open-ended questions require the respondent to respond on his or her own terms, they also require a moderate level of sophistication and comprehension of the topic on the part of the respondent; otherwise, responses will not be meaningful. Open-ended questions will, therefore, have to be used with care in cross-cultural and cross-national research, in order to ensure that bias does not occur as a result of differences in levels of education.

Another consideration is whether direct or indirect questions should be utilized. Direct questions avoid any ambiguity concerning question content and meaning. On the other hand, respondents may be reluctant to answer certain types of questions. Similarly, they may tend to provide responses perceived as socially desirable or those they feel are desired by the interviewer. Use of indirect questions may aid in bypassing such biases. In this case, rather than being directly stated, the question is posed in an indirect form.

For example, respondents might be asked to indicate, rather than their own preferences, those they would anticipate from the majority of respondents, neighbors, or other relevant reference groups. Thus the decision to use a direct or an indirect format for a particular question depends on the respondent's perception of the topic. If the topic is perceived as sensitive by the respondent, then it is better to use an indirect format rather than a direct one. The sensitivity of a topic may vary from culture to culture. Hence a direct question in one country may have to be asked as an indirect one in a different country.

Another important consideration in instrument design is the extent to which nonverbal, as opposed to verbal, stimuli are utilized in order to facilitate respondent comprehension. Particularly where research is conducted in countries or cultures with high levels of illiteracy, as for example, Africa and the Far East, it is often desirable to use nonverbal stimuli such as show cards. Questionnaires can be administered orally by an interviewer, but respondent comprehension will be facilitated if pictures of products, concepts, or test packs are provided.

Various types of nonverbal stimuli may be used in conjunction with questionnaires, including show cards, product samples, or pictures. It should be noted that nonverbal stimuli are often used in other data collection techniques. The main focus here, however, is on their use in surveys in order to ensure that respondents understand verbal questions, relevant products, and product concepts.

Problems Faced in Wording Questions for International Research

When conducting cross-national research, the wording of questions has to be changed according to the country in which the questionnaire is being administered. Certain categories, such as sex and age, are the same in all countries or cultures, and hence, equivalent questions can be posed. Somewhat greater difficulties may be encountered with regard to other categories such as income, education, occupation, or the dwelling unit, since these are not always exactly comparable from one culture or country to another. In addition to the fact that in some countries men may have several wives, marital status can present problems, depending on how the question is put. The growing number of cohabiting couples, especially those who are divorced, creates a particular problem in this regard. What is included in the category of income may vary from country to country, and incomes vary considerably within countries.

Similarly—with regard to education—types of schools, colleges, or universities are not always comparable from one country to another. Also, certain occupational categories may not be comparable from one country to another. In general, however, the major distinctions or broad categories tend to be the same; that is, farm workers, industrial workers, blue-collar workers, office or white-collar workers, self-employed persons, lower and upper management, and the professionals. Alternatively, comparable social hierarchies can be identified. Another category where differences may occur is in the dwelling unit. In the major Western societies, dwelling units are primarily apartments or multistory houses. In African countries, however, dwelling units may be huts, whereas in Far Eastern countries many homes are one-story units.

In developing questions related to purchase behavior and consumption or usage behavior, and to specific product markets, two important issues need to be considered. The first concerns the extent to which such behavior is conditioned by a specific sociocultural or economic environment and hence is likely to vary from one country or cultural context to another. Each culture, society, or social group has its own particular conventions, rituals, and practices relating to behavior in social situations, such as entertaining family or friends on festive occasions—for example, graduation or Christmas. Rules relating to the exchange of gifts and products are, for example, governed by local cultural conventions. Thus, while in some cultures wine may be an appropriate gift for a dinner host or hostess, in others, flowers are preferred. Consequently, questions relating to the gift market, and products positioned as gifts, will need to be tailored to these specific behavior patterns. Significant differences also occur in the retail distribution network. In many developing countries, for example, there are few self-service outlets or supermarkets, except in major cities, and most purchases are made in small Mom-and-Pop-type stores. Such shopping patterns affect the formulation of questions relating to the location and timing of purchasing, as well as the importance of investigating salesperson influence on purchase decisions.

In addition to such differences in usage and purchase behavior, relevant product class boundaries or competing and substitute products vary from one country to another. For example, washing machines and other household appliances may be competing with domestic help and professional washer-women, as well as with other brands of washing machines.

The most significant problems in drawing up questions in multicountry research are likely to occur in relation to attitudinal, psychographic, and life-style data. Here, as has already been pointed out, it is not always clear that comparable or equivalent attitudinal or personality constructs—such as aggressiveness, respect for authority, and honor—are relevant in all countries and cultures. Even where similar constructs exist, it is far from clear whether they are most effectively tapped by the same question or attitude statement. Problems that were encountered in conducting an actual cross-cultural research project are described in Exhibit 11-3.

EXHIBIT 11-3

An Example of Questionnaire Construction
in International Research

A study was conducted to find out the influence of the role of stress on industrial salespeople's work outcomes in the United States, Japan, and Korea. The brief discussion that follows tells us how the questionnaire was constructed and the difficulties faced in constructing the questionnaire.

When conducting comparative studies, each version of the questionnaire should be equivalent across countries: that is, the terms in each version of the survey instrument should be relevant to the specific country surveyed. To maintain equivalence, a questionnaire that is translated from one language to another needs to be back-translated into the original language. Those doing the back-translation should be familiar with the different languages, the different cultures, and the usage of the concepts and their meanings in the different countries. Following the above guidelines, in this study the English version of the questionnaire was translated into Japanese and Korean and back translated into English by Japanese and Korean nationals, respectively. Despite the care that was taken to preserve the meaning and intent of the scale items across three questionnaires, there is a chance that questionnaire equivalence was not achieved, and even if this had occurred its degree cannot not be assessed. The questionnaire items used to assess the key constructs have been employed in previous research. These scales originally were developed using U.S.-based samples: admittedly, then, their substantive meaning derived from work in the United States may not be portable to samples in other countries.

Source: Dubinsky, Alan J., Michaels, Ronald E., Kotabe, Masaaki, Chae Un Lim, Hee Cheol Moon, "Influence of the Role of Stress on Industrial Sales People's Work Outcomes in the U.S., Japan and Korea," *Journal of International Business Studies*, 23, First Quarter, 1992.

Summary

As with most steps in the research process, the design of the questionnaire is highly iterative. Because it is an integral part of the research design, the objective is to seek consistency with the other elements of the design, notably the research purpose, the budget, and the methods of analysis. Additional constraints are imposed by the data-collection method and the respondent's ability and willingness to answer questions about the subject.

Within these constraints the questionnaire writer practices this art through the adroit choice of wording, response format, sequencing of questions, and layout of the questionnaire. Success in this activity comes from experience, an ability to look at the subject and the wording of the questions from the respondent's perspective, and a good understanding of the objectives of the research.

The difficulties in designing a good questionnaire have encouraged researchers to use previously published survey questions wherever possible. There are many published compilations of survey questions that can be consulted to save time and effort. This does not mean, however, that only previously published questions can or should be used, since it is the specific research purpose that ultimately determines the questionnaire design.

Guidelines for writing and organizing questionnaires have been presented here. Since they are a distillation of the experience of many researchers, adherence to these principles will narrow the range of problems. Ultimately, a good questionnaire is one that has been thoroughly pretested. There can be no substitute for this step in the process.

Even though the process of designing questionnaires for international research is essentially the same, there are certain key differences that have been discussed earlier. A classic trade-off situation exists with respect to the use of closed- versus open-response format in international research. While closed-response will lead to an imposition of the researcher's cultural biases on the respondent, open-response questions require a certain level of education and familiarity with the subject, which may not be present among respondents in many countries. Another area where a researcher is likely to encounter problems in cross-cultural research is in question wording. Words that represent a construct in one culture may turn out to be totally different in another culture when they are translated or, worse, a particular construct may not have a word at all in the language of that culture. A researcher conducting cross-cultural research has to overcome many such problems in questionnaire design.

Questions and Problems

1. A researcher investigating the general happiness of respondents in a particular age and socioeconomic group is considering using the following two questions in a questionnaire:
   a. All things considered, how happy would you say you were these days? Would you say that you were very happy, pretty happy, or not too happy?
   b. All things considered, how would you describe your marriage? Would you say your marriage is very happy, pretty happy, or not too happy?

What are some concerns you might have about the order in which these questions might be asked? Which order would you suggest?

2. "Questionnaire design for descriptive research is more difficult than for an exploratory research." Discuss this statement.

3. "As long as a question pertains to at least one of the research objectives, it must be included in the questionnaire." Do you agree or disagree with this statement? Explain your answer.

4. Open-response questions sometimes are used to establish the salience or importance of issues such as irritation from clutter due to excessive advertisements and station announcements during TV programs. Why would you want to use this type of response format rather than a closed-response question?

5. How do the responses from an unaided-recall question on brand awareness compare to those from an aided-recall question?

6. Use the formula for the randomized response model to estimate the percentage of respondents who indicated they did not report all of their income to the federal tax authorities in a survey in which a total of 16 percent answered "yes." Also, 10 percent of the sample were estimated to have their birthdays in June (and so would have answered "yes" to the innocuous question) and a coin toss was used to choose which of the two questions to answer.

7. What can a researcher do to make the request for information seem legitimate?

8. Evaluate the following questions and suggest improvements:

   a. Please check the following activities in which you participate as a private citizen interested in politics.

      Read books and articles on the subject _____

      Belong to political party _____

      Attend political rallies _____

      Write letters to legislators, newspapers, or government officials _____

      Other (please specify) _____

   b. When you eat dinner out, do you sometimes eat at the same place?

      _____ Yes   _____ No

   c. Is the current level of government regulation on environmental protection adequate or inadequate?

      _____ Adequate   _____ Inadequate

d. Where do you buy most of your clothes? _____

e. Do you think that Con Edison is doing everyting possible to reduce air pollution from their electricity-generating stations?

_____ Yes   _____ No

f. Please indicate how much of an average issue of *Sunset* magazine you usually read:

1. Less than 1/3 _____   3. Over 1/2   _____

2. 1/3 to 1/2   _____

g. List the magazines you read regularly ("read" means reads or looks at; "regularly" means almost as often as the magazine is published).

h. What kind of hobbies do you have?

i. Everybody knows that teenagers and their parents have lots of arguments. What are some of the things you and your parents have argued about lately?

9. A large automobile manufacturer has asked you to develop a questionnaire to measure owners' satisfaction with the servicing of their vehicles. One sequence of questions will deal with satisfaction with the design, construction, operating costs, performance, and amount of service required. In order to interpret these results, it has been decided to ask further questions to isolate the responsibility for car problems. That is, do car owners tend to blame the manufacturers, the service work by the dealer, or poor upkeep and driving habits of car owners? What kind of questions would you ask to determine this information?

10. Based on the following list of research questions, determine the research objective(s) of this questionnaire: Are any of the questions unnecessary and if so, why?

a. How many hours per week do you work, on average?

b. What type of magazines do you read?

c. Do you feel you have enough "free time" away from work?

d. What kind of hobbies do you have?

e. Would you describe yourself as a well-rounded person?

11. Develop three double-barreled questions related to eating habits and restaurant preferences. Also develop correct versions of each question.

12. What are some recommended ways by which one can ask sensitive information? Where in the questionnaire should one ask for sensitive information?

13. A research company has decided to pretest a personal interview questionnaire prior to collecting the actual data. Interviewers will conduct the pretest interviews. Design a separate questionnaire containing from five to ten questions that you feel the interviewer should fill out after each pretest interview. The objective of this separate questionnaire is to provide the research company with sufficient information to evaluate any problems with the personal interview questionnaire.

14. The Student Disciplinary Committee of Clint State University are extremely concerned about the increasing incidence of cheating in both in-class and out-of-class student assignments. They have approached a marketing research class to conduct a survey of Clint State students. They wish to know
    i) How predominant this behavior is campuswide.
    ii) Whether it occurs most frequently among freshman, sophomores, juniors, or seniors.
    iii) Some of the reasons for this behavior.
    iv) Possible solutions to the problem.
    a. What are the information requirements for the study?
    b. How should the questions be formatted? (Hint: consider the topic of the study.) Give reasons for your answer.
    c. How could order bias affect the results of this survey?
    d. It has been decided that the questionnaire should be pretested.
        i) What are the reasons for pretesting a questionnaire?
        ii) Suggest a suitable group of respondents for the pretest.
    As part of its assimilation in the present global environment, the marketing research class is paying close attention to research techniques for international markets. To meet this objective, the professor has instructed the students to undertake a similar study amongst students of a university in France.
    e. What is the most appropriate question format for this research?
    f. What are the possible problems that may be encountered by the class in the international research project?

15. The finance committee of St. Dunstan's Church has reported a fall in the level of donations to the church at Sunday services, despite the fact that attendance has not declined. In an effort to boost donations, the committee has decided to conduct personal interviews of all church members in their homes to determine each member's habits regarding donations to the church.
    a. How might this survey method bias the results of the study? Each member of the committee has been given a questionnaire from which to conduct the personal interviews. The first four questions were as follows:
        i) How often do you attend Sunday services per year?
        ii) Do you realize that the church's only form of income is the donations from its members?
        iii) Do you donate to the church every Sunday?
        iv) How much, on average, do you donate?
    b. How would the following factors affect the results of this study?
        i) Question order.
        ii) Question wording.
        iii) Subject matter.
        iv) Interviewer's affiliation to the church.

End Notes

1. Stanley L. Payne. *The Art of Asking Questions* (Princeton, New Jersey: Princeton University Press), 1951.

2. Jagdip Singh, Roy D, Howell, and Gary K. Rhoads. "Adaptive Designs for Likert-Type Data: An Approach for Implementing Market Surveys," *Journal of Marketing Research,* 27, August 1990, 304–321.

3. Gregory J. Spagna. "Questionnaires: Which Approach Do You Use?" *Journal of Advertising Research,* 24, February–March 1984, 67–70.

4. J. M. Converse and Stanley Presser, *Survey Questions, Handcrafting the Standardized Questionnaire,* Sage University Paper, Series on Quantitative Applications in the Social Sciences, 07–063, (Beverly Hills; Sage Publications) 1986.

5. H. Schuman and S. Presser. *Questions and Answers in Attitude Surveys: Experiments in Question Form, Wording and Context,* (New York: Academic Free Press), 1981.

6. George F. Bishop. "Experiments with the Middle Response Alternatives in Survey Questions," *Public Opinion Quarterly,* Summer 1987, 220–232.

7. George F. Bishop, Alfred J. Tuchfarber, and Robert W. Oldendick. "Opinions on Fictitious Issues: The Pressure to Answer Survey Questions," *Public Opinion Quarterly,* Summer 1986, 240–250.

8. Stanley L. Payne. *The Art of Asking Questions,* op. cit., p. 87.

9. Boyd, Westfall, and Stasch. *Marketing Research,* 4th ed., (Homewood, IL: Irwin), 1980.

10. W. B. Locander and J. P. Burton. "The Effect of Question Form on Gathering Income Data by Telephone," *Journal of Marketing Research,* 13, May 1976, 189–192.

11. Niels J. Blunch. "Position Bias in Multiple-Choice Questions," *Journal of Marketing Research,* 21, May 1984, 216–220, has argued that position bias in multiple-choice questions cannot be eliminated by rotating the order of the categories.

12. Such questions are vulnerable to the prestige seeking and social-desirability-response bias discussed in Chapter 7.

13. A. J. Barton. "Asking the Embarrassing Question," *Public Opinion Quarterly,* Spring 1958, 67–68.

14. Cathy Campbell and Brian L. Joiner. "How to Get the Answer Without Being Sure You've Asked the Question," *The American Statistician,* 27, December 1973, 119–231; and James E. Reinmuth and Michael D. Guerts, "The Collection of Sensitive Information Using a Two-Stage Randomized Response Model," *Journal of Marketing Research,* 12, November 1975, 402–407.

15. R. L. Kahn and C. F. Cannell. *The Dynamics of Interviewing,* New York: Wiley, 1957.

16. Edwin J. Gross. "The Effect of Question Sequence on Measures of Buying Interest," *Journal of Advertising Research,* 4, September 1964, 41.

17. Charles Raymond. "When Questions Create Answers," Speech to the Annual Meeting, *Advertising Research Foundation,* New York, May 1977.

18. C. F. Turner and K. Krauss. "Fallible Indicators of the Subjective State of the Nation," *American Psychologist,* 33, September 1978, 456–470.

19. J. M. Converse and Stanely Presser. *Survey Questions, Handcrafting the Standardized Questionnaire,* op. cit.

20. Shelby Hunt, Richard D. Sparkman, and James B. Wilcox. "The Pretest in Survey Research: Issues and Preliminary Findings," *Journal of Marketing Research,* May 1982, 269–273.

21. E. D. Jaffe and I. D. Nebenzahl, "Alternative Questionnaire Formats for Country Image Studies," *Journal of Marketing Research,* November 1984, 463–471.

CASE 11-1
Essex Markets (B)[1]

Essex Markets, a small chain of supermarkets, was planning a study to evaluate their program of supplying unit price information on shelf tags. Among the research questions were:

What percentage of the shoppers were aware that unit pricing was being supplied?

What percentage of the shoppers used unit pricing and with what frequency?

Assume that shoppers will be intercepted in checkout lines. Write a series of questions that will allow you to answer the research questions.

[1] Prepared by Bruce McElroy and David A. Aaker as a basis for class discussion.

CASE 11-2
Smith's Clothing (A)

John Simpson, the head of Simpson Research, was attempting to design a marketing research study that would address the research questions posed by Jim Andrews, the president of Smith's Clothing, during their morning meeting. The research questions seemed rather well defined:

1. Which women's clothing stores compete with Smith's?
2. What is the image of Smith's, and how does this image compare with that of its competitors? In other words, how is Smith's positioned with respect to its competitors?
3. Who is the Smith customer and how does she differ from that of Smith's competitors?

Although no final judgment had been made, Andrews was leaning toward an in-home, self-administered questionnaire. He was not certain, however, whether a questionnaire could be developed that would be responsive to the research questions. The population of interest was operationally defined to be those women whose family income exceeded the median income. Simpson's immediate task was to draft a questionnaire and to develop a tentative sampling plan.

Smith's was a six-store chain of women's clothing stores located in Bayview, a large, growing city in the Southwestern United States. The chain had provided fine clothing for the upper class of Bayview for over 40 years. Twenty years previously, Smith's had opened its first suburban store. Having closed its downtown store ten years ago, it now had five suburban stores and one in a nearby community of 60,000 people. Smith's had avoided trendy fashions over the years, in favor of classic, lasting designs. During the last ten years a set of five or six aggressive, high-fashion retail-

ers had expanded into or within Bayview. Thus, despite the fact that the market for fine women's clothes had expanded enormously during the past decade, the competition had grown much more intense.

Andrews was justifiably concerned about the performance of his stores. Profits at five of the six stores had fallen during each of the past four years. The sixth store had been opened only 18 months before and had not achieved its target growth rate. Although the chain was still profitable, if the existing trend continued it would soon be losing money.

This performance had stimulated Andrews to engage in serious reappraisal of the whole operation. In particular, he was reviewing the chain's rather conservative policy toward the product line, advertising, store decor, and store personnel. He felt that it might be time to consider stocking some trendy fashions and attempting to increase the store's appeal to women in their teens and twenties. A working hypothesis was that Smith's had a higher appeal relative to other stores to women over 40 and was less attractive to younger women. He realized that any such move was risky in that it would jeopardize the existing customer franchise without any guarantee that new customers would compensate. Before making any such move he felt that it was critical to learn exactly how Smith's was now positioned. He also felt that he needed a much more reliable fix on the current Smith customers in terms of their age, the stores in which they shop, their preferences, and their purchase profile. With such information he would be in a much better position to identify alternatives and evaluate them.

Assignment

Develop a research design including:
1. The type of survey to be employed
2. A questionnaire

CASE 11-3
Compact Lemon

Ben Johnson, a marketing research staff member, has been asked to provide a quantitative estimate of the demand for a new product concept, tentatively called *Compact Lemon*. The concept involves a powerful spray cleaner with a lemon scent to be used to clean trash compactors. The product will involve a heavy duty cleaner that will clean easier than current competitors which are not in a spray form and will provide the added benefit of a deodorizer.

Johnson has a research proposal for a telephone survey—a national random sample of 600 homeowners screened to be owners of compactors would be phoned via a WATS line. Johnson wonders (1) whether the proposed questionnaire will deliver the necessary information and (2) what improvements could be made.

Proposed Questionnaire for Telephone Survey

1. Do you own a compactor?
2. How often do you use your compactor?
3. Is it satisfactory?
4. Any problems?
5. Have you noticed any odor problems? (Skip if covered in question 4.)

Our client is considering a new product. The concept involves a powerful lemon scented cleaner in a convenient spray container to be used to clean trash compactors. This heavy duty cleaner will clean easier because it is in spray form and will provide the added benefit of a deodorizer.

6. Which of the following would describe your likelihood to buy the product?
   Would buy it
   Would very likely buy it
   Would not very likely buy it
   Would not buy it
7. What is your reaction to this idea? (Probe—any other reactions?)
8. How often do you use deodorizers in the home?
9. How many people are living in your home?
10. What is your age?
11. Do you have children under eight years old?
12. Which are you?
    a. Home owner?
    b. Home renter?
    c. Apartment renter?

12 EXPERIMENTATION

Learning Objectives

▶ Define experimentation and discuss the distinction between experiments and other types of research approaches.

▶ Understand the concept of causality and the conditions required to infer causality.

▶ Discuss the basic issues and terminologies involved in experimental research.

▶ Distinguish between classical designs and statistical designs.

▶ Understand the differences between preexperimental, true experimental and quasi-experimental designs.

▶ Identify and comprehend the advantages and limitations of the different types of experimental designs.

▶ Distinguish between laboratory and field experiments.

▶ Comprehend the concept of validity as applied to experimental research, and distinguish between internal and external validity.

▶ Provide guidelines for conducting experimental research and understanding the limitations of experimental research.

▶ Recognize the different threats to validity that are controlled by each type of design.

▶ Become familiar with common marketing applications of experimental research.

A utility company wants to encourage people to insulate their homes. It is recognized that insulation will conserve energy, reduce utility bills, improve living comfort, and retard fires. A decision is needed as to which of these appeals should be used in the campaign. More particularly, an advertisement using both the utility bill and comfort appeals has been developed, and a decision is needed as to whether the advertisement should be the basis of a statewide promotion.

In previous chapters several research approaches have been discussed, such as the use of secondary data, small-sample interviewing, observation, and surveys. All these can provide helpful insights in answering these questions and others. However, they are useful primarily as elements of exploratory or descriptive research efforts. They are not well suited to making definitive judgments about which appeal, if any, will work or about how much impact an advertisement will have. To determine the answer to these more demanding causal questions, experimentation, the subject of this chapter, is employed.

Experiments are defined as studies in which conditions are controlled so that one or more independent variable(s) can be manipulated to test a hypothesis about a dependent variable. In other words, in experimental research, the researcher manipulates the independent/experimental variable(s) and then measures the effect of this manipulation on the dependent variable(s). Thus, experiments are research investigations in which implementation involves an active intervention by the observer beyond that required for measurement. In the case of the utility company, the simplest experiment would be to run the advertisement and then measure its impact. The act of running the advertisement would be the experimental intervention or treatment. Ultimately, there is no substitute for actually trying the advertisement to see how it works. As we shall see, such a simple experiment has limitations, and it usually would be useful and worthwhile to consider other research designs.

This chapter provides an overview of the basic concepts and issues relating to experimentation. We will discuss a few of the most often used experimental designs and some marketing applications that use experiments to obtain causal inferences.

DESCRIPTIVE VERSUS EXPERIMENTAL RESEARCH

The key principle of experimental work is **manipulation** of a treatment variable (say X), followed by observation of response variable (say Y). If a change in X, causes Y to change in the hypothesized way, then we are tempted to say X causes Y. However, this causal inference rests on soft ground, unless the experiment has been properly designed to **control** for other variables.[1] As discussed in chapter 4, though descriptive research can show that two variables are related or associated, it is not sufficient to establish a causal inference. Of course, evidence of a relationship or an association is useful; otherwise, we would have no basis for even inferring that causality might be present. But to go beyond this inference, we must have reasonable proof that one variable precedes the other and that there were no other causal factors that could have accounted for the relationship.

What Are Causal Relationships?

A concern with causality appears throughout marketing decision making. For example,

▶ What effect have recent price increases had on product class sales?

▶ Does the number of sales calls per month affect the size of the order placed?

Underlying the research questions just given is the need to understand a **causal relationship** between an action and a probable outcome. These could be actions taken in the past (if we are in an evaluative or problem-solving mode) or predictions about future actions. If the focus is on the future, then the primary interest is in comparing the outcomes of decision alternatives.

Limitations of Descriptive Designs

Why can't a descriptive research design answer these needs for causal insights? In the first place, most descriptive research does exactly as it says—it provides a snapshot picture of some aspect of the market environment at a specific point in time. Thus, we use surveys, store audits, observation studies, analyses of financial records, and so on, to give us information about such variables as brand shares, distribution coverage, and the demographic characteristics of heavy buyers. There is no hint of a causal insight to be obtained from such data. Yet, under some circumstances descriptive information can be used to infer—but rarely to establish—the presence of causal relationships.

The first step toward establishing causality usually is a calculation of the strength of association of two or more variables measured during the descriptive study. If a causal link exists between two variables, they would be expected to be associated. Thus, we might find that a high quality of service is associated with health maintenance organizations that have small staffs.

Another way is to measure association with data over time. For example, historical data may show an association between advertising expenditures and sales. Does this finding mean that advertising causes sales? Unfortunately, this question is not easily answered. There is still the possibility of a third causal variable, like distribution, being involved. Increased distribution might require more advertising support and may generate sales. There is also a direction of a causation issue. It could be that the advertising expenditures are budgeted as a fixed percent of sales. Thus, a forecast of sales increases may lead to increases in advertising expenditures, so the more correct model could be

Sales change *causes* advertising expenditure change

instead of

Advertising expenditure change *causes* sales change

Clearly, what is needed is some idea of the time sequence of events; that is, did the change in advertising activity actually precede the observed change in sales? With a positive answer to this question we get closer to the characteristics of a proper causal design.

The following quotation provides a clear distinction between experimental research and other research approaches:

Experimentation differs from alternative methods of marketing research in that in experimentation the researcher manipulates the independent variable or variables before measuring the effect upon the dependent variable. For example, the effect of price changes on sales volume of a particular product can be examined by actually varying the price of the product. A nonexperimental approach would be to ask consumers whether they would buy more of the product if its price were lowered. The manipulation of independent variables, together with procedures of controlling extraneous variation . . . forms the basis of the power of experimental research relative to other research techniques. The better the researcher's control over the experimental variables and extraneous variations, the more confident the researcher can be that he [or she] is in fact determining cause and effect relationships.[2]

Hence, of all the various types of research approaches that may suggest causality between two variables, the greatest assurance that a causal inference is sound stems only from experimental research.[3] Specifically, experimentation consists of manipulating levels or amounts of selected independent variables (causes) to examine their influence on dependent variables (effects).

Although, theoretically a completely controlled experiment can indicate 100 percent causality, in practice seldom can causal inference be conclusively established. Because experimental designs is concerned with detecting and quantifying causal relationships, it is appropriate and rather necessary to have a discussion on what constitutes causality and what the conditions are for valid causal inferences.

WHAT CONSTITUTES CAUSALITY?

Causation, strictly speaking, means that a change in one variable will produce a change in another. In this context, the definition will be broadened somewhat to include the concept of a precondition influencing a variable of interest. For example, we could conceive that credit-card usage is determined partly by a person's sex. In this case, sex could be conceptualized as causal in nature, despite the fact that it would be impossible to take a group of people and change their sex to observe if a change in credit-card usage was "produced." The weaker term "influence" often will be used when it is more appropriate than the term "cause," but the logic of the analysis normally will remain the same.

Given the causation concept, that a change in one variable will produce a change in another, it is reasonable to conclude that, if two variables are causally linked, they should be associated. If association provides evidence of causation, then, conversely, the lack of association suggests the absence of cessation. Thus, an association between attitude (A) and behavior (B) is evidence of a **causal relationship**:

$$\text{Attitude} \rightarrow \text{Behavior}$$

Direction of Causation Issue

If a causal link between two variables is thought to exist, a reasonable question is: Which variable is the causal (or independent) variable and which is the "caused" (or dependent) variable?

One approach to determining the direction of causation is to draw on logic and previous theory. In this context it is useful to observe whether one of the variables is relatively fixed and unalterable. Variables like sex, age, and income are relatively permanent. If, for example, an association is found between age and attendance at rock concerts, it would be unrealistic to claim that attendance at rock concerts causes people to be young. In this case age could not be a "caused" variable because it is fixed in this context. However, it could be that age is an important determinant of who attends rock concerts.

A second approach is to consider the fact that there is usually a time lag between cause and effect. If such a time lag can be postulated, the causal variable should have a positive association with the effect variable lagged in time.

Conditions for Valid Causal Inferences

As the preceding discussion on competing explanations indicate, the concept of causality is complex. The scientific notion of causality is very different from the common-sense, everyday notion.[4] The following table summarizes the difference between the common-sense and the scientific notion of causality.

Common Sense Notion	Scientific Notion
• There is a single cause of an event, i.e., X is the only cause of Y.	• There can be more than one cause, i.e., X would only be one of the multiple causes of Y.
• There is a deterministic relationship between X and Y.	• There is only a probabilistic relationship between X and Y.
• The causal relationship between X and Y can be proved.	• The causal relationship can never be proved; we can only infer that X is a cause of Y.

Thus, the scientific notion holds that causality is inferred; it is never demonstrated conclusively.[5] Then what kind of evidence can be used to support causal inferences?

The following types of evidence are relevant to evaluating causal relationships:

▶ **Condition of concomitant variation**
  –Evidence that a strong association exists between an action and an observed outcome.

▶ **Condition of time order of occurrence**
  –Evidence that the action preceded the outcome.

▶ **Absence of competing causal explanations**
  –Evidence that there is no strong competing explanation for the relationship—that a high level of internal validity exists.

In addition, if the resulting causal inference is to be useful to management, it should be

▶ Generalizable beyond the particular setting in which it was found; that is, it should have a high level of external validity.

▶ Persistent in that it will hold long enough to make management action worthwhile.

As discussed earlier, even if the above-mentioned conditions are fulfilled—that is, there is evidence of concomitant variation, time order of occurrence, and absence of competing explanations—scientifically, the presence of a causal relationship can never be proved. The presence of strong evidence only increases our confidence in inferring the presence of a causal relationship. The results from controlled experimental research studies, conducted in different environmental settings, increases the reliability of our inference.

ISSUES IN EXPERIMENTAL RESEARCH

Experimental research involves decision making on three major issues:

1. What type of experimental design should be used?
2. Should the experiment be performed in a "laboratory" setting or in the "field"?
3. What are the internal and external threats to the validity of the experiment and how can we control for the various threats to the experiment's internal and external validity.

We will discuss the various types of experimental designs and how these designs take care of the threats to experimental validity. In the subsequent section, we will discuss the difference between laboratory and field experiments and the conditions that dictate the choice of one over the other. We will also discuss the threats to the internal and external validity of the experiment. Table 12-1 introduces the basics terminologies that one often used in experimental design.

Basic Symbols and Notations[6]

We introduce six notations that are commonly used while conducting experiments. They are observation (O) and exposure (X).

> O denotes a formal **observation** or measurement of the dependent variable that is made as part of the experimental study. Symbols O_1, O_2, and so on, will be used when two or more measurements of the dependent variable are involved during the experiment.
>
> X denotes **exposure** of test units participating in the study to the experimental manipulation or treatment. Symbols X_1, X_2, and so forth, will be used when the test units are exposed to two or more experimental treatments.

Note: The ordering of O's and X's from left to right will represent the time sequence in which they occur.

> EG denotes an **experimental group** of test units that get exposed to the experimental treatment. Symbols EG_1, EG_2, etc., will be used when the experiment has more than one experimental group.

CG denotes a **control group** of test units participating in the experiment but not exposed to the experimental treatment. Symbols CG_1, CG_2, etc., will be used when the experiment involves more than one control group.

R denotes **random** assignment of test units and experimental treatments to groups. Randomization ensures control over extraneous variables and increases the reliability of the experiment.

TABLE 12-1

Basic Concepts and the Language of Experimental Design

Independent Variable: The variable that can be manipulated, changed or altered by the experimenter, independently of any other variable. The independent variable is hypothesized to be the causal influence.

Dependent Variable: The variable whose value is dependent on the experimenter's manipulations. It is the criterion or the standard by which the results of the experiment are judged. Changes in the dependent variable are presumed to be the effect of changes in the independent variable.

Test Unit: A subject or entity whose responses to experimental treatments are being observed and measured.

Manipulation: Creating different levels of the independent variable is known as manipulating the variable. In the experiment, the independent variable is manipulated, and the effect of each level of manipulation on the dependent variable is observed.

Experimental Treatments: Experimental treatments are the alternative manipulations of the independent variable being investigated. For example, low exposure level, medium exposure level, and high exposure level might be experimental treatments in an advertising experiment.

Experiment: Studies in which conditions are controlled so that one or more independent variables can be manipulated to test a hypothesis about a dependent variable. In other words, in experimental research, the researcher manipulates the independent/experimental variable(s) and then measures the effect of this manipulation on the dependent variable(s).

Experimental Group: The group of subjects exposed to the experimental treatment is termed the experimental group.

Control Group: The group of subjects not exposed to the experimental treatment are termed the control group.

Extraneous Variable: Variables other than the manipulated variable that affect the response of the test units and hence the results of the experimental research. These variables interfere with the changes in the dependent variable and thus confound the results of the experiment. Hence they are also known as **confounding** variables.

Selection Bias: If an experimental group is systematically different in some relevant way from the population being studied, it invalidates the results of the experiment. This is known as selection bias. Also, if the subjects assigned to the experimental group differ systematically from the subjects assigned to the control group, then the result of the experiment could be attributed to the differences between the groups rather than to the experimental manipulations.

Randomization: A procedure in which the assignment of subjects and treatments to groups is based on chance. Randomization ensures control over extraneous variables and increases the experiment's reliability.

Blocking: Even after adopting random assignments of subjects and treatments to groups, it is possible at times for the experimental groups to differ in a systematic manner on some relevant variable. Blocking is a procedure by which a nonmanipulated variable is introduced into the experiment to ensure that the groups are equalized on that variable.

Matching: Matching is a procedure for the assignment of subjects to groups that ensures each group of respondents is matched on the basis of pertinent characteristics. Matching helps reduce the experimental error that arises out of selection bias.

Treatment Effect: Conducting the experiment by itself can alter the effects of the manipulations and thus affect the results of the experiment. This is known as treatment effect.

Hawthorne Effect: A form of treatment effect wherein the results of the experimental research are altered unintentionally by the subjects being aware that they are participating in an experiment.

Demand Characteristics: Another type of treatment effect, which refers to design procedures that unintentionally alert the subject about the experimenter's hypothesis. If participants recognize the experimenter's expectation or demand, they are likely to act in a manner consistent with the experimental treatment, and this introduces error in the experiment's results.

Experimental Design: A set of procedures that guide an experimental study by specifying
(a) what independent variables are to be manipulated, (b) what dependent variables are to be measured, (c) what levels of the experimental treatment are to be used, (d) how to select test units and assign them to different groups, (e) how to control for selection bias, and (f) how to minimize the influence of extraneous variables on the results of the experiment.

M denotes that both the experimental group and the control group are **matched** on the basis of some relevant characteristics. Matching helps reduce the experimental error that arises out of selection bias.

TYPES OF EXPERIMENTAL DESIGNS

Experimental designs can be broadly categorized into two groups—classical designs and statistical designs. The basic difference between these two types of experimental designs is that classical designs consider the impact of only one treatment level of an independent variable at a time, whereas statistical designs allow for examining the impact of different treatment levels of an independent variable and also the impact of two or more independent variables.[7] Figure 12-1 provides a detailed classification of the more commonly used experimental designs.

Classical Designs

Classical designs can be further categorized into three groups: pre-experimental, true experimental and quasi-experimental designs.

Pre-Experimental Designs. Pre-experimental designs, as the name suggests, are somewhat exploratory types of studies that have almost no control over the influence of extraneous factors on the results of the experiment. In the strict sense of the term, pre-experimental studies cannot be classified under

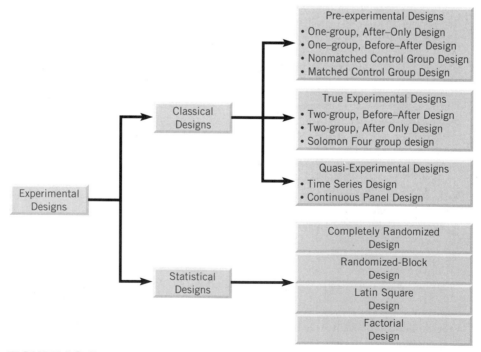

FIGURE 12-1
A classification of experimental designs

experimental research as they have little or no value in establishing causal inferences. But pre-experimental studies can lead to hypotheses about causal relationships, and this is precisely the reason we discuss these designs. Once the basic hypotheses about causal relationships between variables are developed, additional research can be performed to establish causality with greater confidence.

The most commonly used pre-experimental designs are (a) one-group, after-only design; (b) nonmatched control-group design; (c) matched control-group design; and (d) one-group, before–after design.

One-Group, After-Only Design. The simplest experiment is simply to apply the experimental treatment to a subject or group and measure the results. The utility company might run a two-week advertising campaign in Modesto, California, during January, advocating insulation. They then might measure the number of requests for price quotations insulation firms received. A high number of requests would serve to justify the advertising expenditure and support a decision to expand it to other cities. This experimental design can be described with the following notation:

$$EG \quad X \quad O$$

That is, an observation is made after an experimental group has been exposed to an experimental treatment.

One problem with this design is that it leaves open the possibility that the results could be explained by events external to the design. For example, insulation requests might arise from the fact that California was unseasonably cold during the test period, that utility bills are always high during January and high bills prompt interest in insulation, or that *Time* magazine had a cover story on energy during the period. Such a possibility of confounding effects that are external to the design are termed **history effects**.[8] In marketing studies, a prime source of history effects are the actions of competitors, retaliatory or otherwise. In some situations competitors deliberately run special promotions in markets in which others are experimenting, to foul them up. The longer the time period involved, the greater the likelihood that history will account for the observed results. A one-year trial run of a marketing program in a single city probably would generate many history effects.

Another problem analogous to history is **maturation**,[9] which refers to changes within respondents that are a consequence of time, including aging, growing tired, or becoming hungrier. For example, suppose the experimental treatment is a one-year delinquency prevention program. At the year's end the program is evaluated by measuring the number of subjects who have jobs and the incidence of crime. If 18-year-olds are more likely than 17-year-olds to hold jobs and avoid crime, then the findings may be the result of the young people maturing during the year, and not because of the delinquency program.

Nonmatched Control Group Design. One approach to control for history and maturation effects is to introduce a control group. Data on insulation requests might be readily available for Reading, California. Thus, the number of requests obtained in Reading could be compared with that of Modesto. This design would be:

$$EG \qquad X \qquad O_1$$
$$\text{...........................}$$
$$CG \qquad\qquad O_2$$

The top line refers to the Modesto group and the bottom line to the Reading group, which, of course, receives no experimental treatment. The results of interest would then be $O_1 - O_2$. A dotted horizontal line means that the groups are separate, and that the experimental treatment does not reach the control group. If people in Modesto read the Reading newspaper, such would not be the case.

Another major problem that existed in the first design and is not solved by the second is termed **selection bias.**[10] It may be that the response to the experiment is strictly a function of the city selected, Modesto. Modesto has many characteristics that could influence the experiment, including its location, its income, its quality of insulation firms, and its climate. If two, three, or more test cities and a like number of control cities were used, the selection bias very likely would be reduced, but it still would be there. Perhaps all of the test cities would be in the northern part of the state and the control cities in the southern part.

Selection bias is particularly severe when self-selection occurs, as when the test group consists of those who volunteered to participate in a program or research study. For example, suppose a group of students agreed to participate in a physical fitness program. To evaluate the program, the number of push-ups that the group can do is compared to the number possible by those who did not volunteer to be part of the experimental group. Those who did volunteer are likely to be in better condition before the program, and the results simply might reflect this selection bias.

Matched Control Group Design. One approach to reducing selection bias is to match the experimental and control groups. Thus, if average temperature is expected to affect a community's reaction to insulation advertising, cities are matched as to their average temperature. A control city is picked that would be similar to Modesto in terms of temperature. Of course, another city may be found that would match Modesto in other dimensions besides temperature, like the percentage of homes not insulated, or demographic variables. The design can be denoted as

$$EG \qquad M \qquad X \qquad O_1$$
$$\text{...}$$
$$CG \qquad M \qquad\qquad O_2$$

where M indicates that the two groups are matched with respect to some variable of interest.

The use of matched control groups is very beneficial when the sample design and cost considerations limit the size of the sample. It is very costly to run a test marketing program with subsequent measurement in a city or a small group of cities, and the researchers are often constrained to a single test city or at most two or three. In such cases, attempting to match the control city or cities with the test city or cities might be appropriate.

One-Group, Before–After Design. The designs considered thus far have been "after-only" designs, because they had no "before measures." Another approach to improving the control is to add a *before measure*:

$$EG \quad O_1 \quad X \quad O_2$$

The *before measure* acts as a control, because if the city was large the O_1 measure also would be large. The interest is then in the change from O_1 to O_2, correcting for seasonal patterns.

The *before measure* can be added to any design already presented. It will enhance sensitivity by adding another method to control for confounding variables. When the observation is obtrusive, several potential threats to internal validity emerge. Consider, for example, a laboratory experiment to test an advertisement aimed at reducing the incidence of smoking among teenage women. Attitudes and perceptions toward smoking are measured, the group is exposed to the advertisement, and the attitudes are measured again, immediately or perhaps after several days. The *before measure* in such an experiment may produce the following validity threats:[11]

1. *Before Measure Effect.* The *before measure* effect may alert the respondents to the fact that they are being studied. The result can be a tendency to give more socially desirable responses and behavior, such as reducing the claimed and actual smoking frequency. Further, the before measure can stimulate or enhance an interest in the subject of the study. It can, therefore, generate heightened curiosity and attention and even lead to discussing the topic with friends and changing the behavior. Thus, the mere fact that a prior measurement was taken can have an effect on any measurement taken after the treatment.
2. *Mortality Effect.* This is due to the possibility that some subjects may stop participating in the experiment, or may not respond when sought out for a follow-up interview. This dropout, or mortality, effect usually is not uniform across the sample being studied. Busy people, high-income households, and urban area residents are always more difficult to reach.
3. *Instrumentation Effect.* This is the result of a change in the measuring instrument. An instrumentation effect may be as simple as a change in question wording between interviews or the use of a different interviewer for the follow-up interview. A more subtle problem is a consequence of interviewers changing as they gain experience and virtually becoming different instruments.

True Experimental Designs. Most of the problems mentioned above (and in the earlier chapter that pertains to the internal validity of the experiment) to a large extent can be controlled by adopting a *random assignment* procedure. Randomization is assigning members of a universe to experimental treatments in such a way that, for any given assignment to a treatment, every member has an equal probability of being chosen for that assignment.[12] The basic purpose of random assignment is to assign subjects to treatments so that individuals with varying characteristics are spread about equally among the treatments, in an effort to neutralize the effect of extraneous variables. Experimental designs that adopt the random assignment procedure are called **true experimental designs,** and those designs are generally far superior to pre-experimental designs in making causal inferences with confidence. Thus, the defining feature of the true experimental design is the random assignment procedure.[13]

True experimental designs have two key features that enable researchers to exercise tight control over extraneous influences: the presence of one or more control groups and, more importantly, the random assignment of test units to various experimental and control groups. But random assignment is not a panacea; it is merely a procedure for minimizing the odds of systematic differences between groups at the start of an experiment. However, the ability of random assignment to lower those odds depends on the number of units available for assignment. The larger the initial sample size, the more successful random assignment will be in achieving equivalence across groups. But, for most marketing applications, complete random assignment may not always be practical, even if a sufficiently large sample of units is available. Studies conducted under these circumstances cannot employ experimental designs that are strictly true, and hence their findings must be interpreted with caution.[14]

The more commonly used true experimental designs are (a) two-group, before–after design, (b) two-group, after-only design, and (c) the Solomon four-group design.

Two-Group, After-Only Design. In the matched control group design (a pre-experimental design) we saw that matching helps in reducing selection bias, and thus provides relatively more control in the experiment. But the problem with matching is that test units cannot be matched on all relevant dimensions. They can be matched on one, two, and sometimes several dimensions, but in most contexts there are many dimensions that potentially could influence the results. Further, some or even most of these might be unknown or ones for which information is not available. For example, response to insulation might be due to people's attitude toward home improvement. If no information existed on people's attitudes, it would not be possible to develop sets of matched cities on this dimension.

Randomly assigning test units or subjects to test and control groups provides a mechanism that, when the sample size is sufficient, serves to match test and control groups on all dimensions simultaneously. Suppose we had 50 cities to use in our test, we randomly assign 25 to the test condition, and use the remaining 25 as a control. Because of the randomization, it would be unlikely that the test cities were larger, colder, or of higher income than the control cities. All of these factors should tend to average out. Of course, as the sample size increases, the degree of matching achieved by randomization also will increase.

A randomized two-group after-only design can be denoted as

$$
\begin{array}{cccc}
EG & R & X & O_1 \\
\hdashline
CG & R & & O_2
\end{array}
$$

where R indicates that the test units are randomly assigned to the test and control groups. Randomization is particularly appropriate whenever the sample size is large enough so that the randomization will result in the test and control groups being similar.

An advantage of this design over the two-group, before–after design is that the interaction effect of testing that is present in the earlier design is absent in this design, because there are no pretest measurements.

Two-Group, Before–After Design. The addition of a control group in the randomized case of the one-group, before–after design (a pre-experimental design) generates the following true experimental design:

$$
\begin{array}{ccccc}
EG & R & O_1 & X & O_2 \\
\hdashline
CG & R & O_3 & & O_4
\end{array}
$$

This design provides a control group that helps control for history and maturation effects and, in addition, controls for the reactive effect of O_1 on O_2 (part of the *before measure* effect). The output of interest would be the difference obtained by subtracting O_2 from O_1 and O_4 from O_3. However, the design fails to control for the effect of the *before measure* upon X, the experiment treatment (the other part of the *before measure* effect). It may be that the *before measure* will sensitize the respondents so that their reaction to the experimental treatment will be distorted. After giving their attitudes about smoking, the teenage women subjects might react quite differently to an anti-smoking advertisement than if they had not given their attitudes. Exhibit 12-1 describes how Campbell Soup used these types of design for its experiment.

Solomon Four-Group Design.[15] A possible solution to the problem present in the two-group, before-after design is to augment the design with an after-only design as follows:

$$
\begin{array}{ccccc}
EG & R & O_1 & X & O_2 \\
\hdashline
CG & R & O_3 & & O_4 \\
\hdashline
EG & R & & X & O_5 \\
\hdashline
CG & R & & & O_6
\end{array}
$$

EXHIBIT 12-1

The Campbell Soup Experiments

The Campbell Soup Company conducted a series of 19 before–after, randomized control-group experiments in the 1970s to evaluate alternative advertising strategies for many of their products, including Campbell's Condensed Soups, Soup for One Soups, Chunky Soups, Franco American Pasta, Swanson Frozen Dinners and "V-8" Cocktail Vegetable Juice. The studies tested increased advertising, shifts to different media, shifts to different markets, and new creative approaches.

One year-long experiment for Campbell's Chunky Soups evaluated the shift of 25 percent of the spot TV budget to outdoor in two test markets—Indianapolis and Houston. Sales were measured for each four-week period using warehouse withdrawals as reported by the SAMI system, during the experiment and for the prior three years. Prior sales were used to adjust sales for seasonal variations (caused in part by regular seasonal promotions) and for any trend over time. An increase in sales of 8 percent was found after eight months, an increase that was attributed to outdoor-reached people not exposed to TV advertising.

Several conclusions emerged from the experiments. First, in five tests of increased advertising expenditures, consumers did not respond to being told the same thing more often. Second, three of five experiments, including the Chunky Soup experiment, in which the test advertising reached more people, did result in increased sales. Third, improved creative efforts did result in increased sales in three of five experiments that tested new advertising. Fourth, in the experiments where significant sales increases occurred, they usually occurred within a relatively short time period, three or four periods.

Source: J. O. Eastlack, Jr. and Ambar G. Rao, "Conducting Advertising Experiments in the Real World: The Campbell Soup Company Experience," *Marketing Science*, Winter 1989, Vol. 5, No. 3, 245–259.

This design is usually prohibitively expensive, but it does provide the power to control for the *before measure* effect of O_1, on both X and O_2. This design provides several measures of the experimental effect {i.e., $(O_2 - O_4)$, $(O_2 - O_1) - (O_4 - O_3)$, $(O_6 - O_5)$}. If there is agreement among these measures, the inferences about X can be much stronger. If there is no agreement, it is still possible to measure directly the interaction of the treatment and *before measures* effects {$(O_2 - O_4) - (O_5 - O_6)$}.

Quasi-Experimental Designs. Quasi-experimental designs offer the researcher some degree of control (greater than pre-experimental designs) but there is no random assignment of subjects as there is for true experimental designs. Nevertheless quasi-experimental designs usually provide more measurements and more information than a typical pre-experimental design. The most popular and most frequently used quasi-experimental designs are the **time-series designs.**

Time-Series Designs. *Time-series designs* are similar to the one-group, before–after design except that a series of measurements are employed during which an experimental treatment occurs. Symbolically, time-series designs can be shown as

$$EG \ O_1 \ O_2 \ O_3 \ O_4 \ X \ O_5 \ O_6 \ O_7 \ O_8$$

There are two variants of this design, depending on whether the measurements are all from the same sample or from separate samples.

Trend Studies are measures over time that come from a succession of *separate* random samples from the same population and yield much of the basic information on which marketing decisions are made.

The data from trend studies can be analyzed only in the aggregate form in which they are collected. The question is whether the measures following the experimental treatment are a continuation of earlier patterns or whether they mark a decisive change. In Figure 12-2, a decisive change is apparent only in Case C.

The insights from trend studies can be expanded considerably if several trends can be analyzed simultaneously. For example, an estimate of the price elasticity of demand for a product can be obtained if parallel trends of prices and market shares or sales are available.

The availability of data spanning a number of time periods means that *maturation* is unlikely to be a possible cause of the observed effect. *History* and *instrument* changes remain as possible threats to validity. Of the two threats, the possibility that a simultaneous event produced the change is clearly the most difficult to rule out. If one is to use this design, there must be continuing sensitivity to plausible competing explanations.[16] Ideally, this should be done prior to the experimental treatment, so that the data needed to confirm or disconfirm the competing hypotheses are available. This may entail recording the weather, prices of related products, and so forth.

Continuous Panel Studies.[17] These collect a series of measurements on the same sample of test units, over an extended period of time. They offer insights into choice behavior that cannot be obtained from any other source. Each person whose behavior or attitude changed can be identified, instead of the information being buried in the aggregation of a time series. This is especially important in product categories where stable sales often obscure large, but compensating, gains and losses of individual buyers.

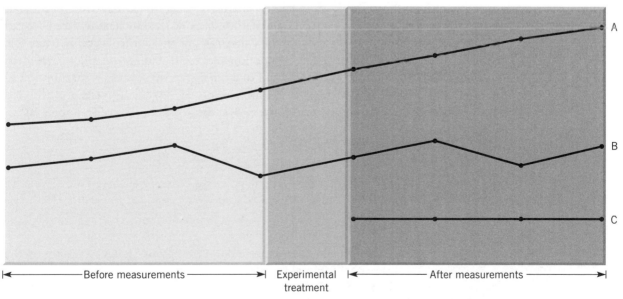

Before measurements | Experimental treatment | After measurements

FIGURE 12-2
A time-series design

Since panel data normally are collected directly from an individual, there is a significant threat to internal validity from the before-measure effect. When a person is asked about a subject and knows that further interviews will be made, the result is an unusual degree of awareness and sensitivity. Fortunately, this seems to decay over time, and within three to five months the preceding interview actually is forgotten. Also, these threats are not present while using scanner panel data. Other threats to validity include history, changes in instrumentation, and nonrandom selection.

Statistical Designs

As mentioned earlier, statistical designs differ from classical designs in that they allow for examining the impact of different treatment levels of an experimental variable, and also the impact of two or more independent variables. In general, statistical designs are "after-only" designs, and they require relatively complex data analysis procedures for sorting out the separate effects of multiple independent variables and/or treatment levels. Two principal aspects of statistical designs are (a) the experimental layouts by which treatment levels are assigned to test objects, and (b) the techniques that are used to analyze the results of the experiment. We briefly discuss now the major types of layouts used to obtain data. The analysis techniques, known generically as *analysis of variance* (ANOVA) and *analysis of covariance* (ANCOVA), will be discussed later in the data analysis chapters. The most often used statistical designs are: (a) completely randomized design, (b) randomized block design, (c) Latin square design, and (d) factorial design.

Completely Randomized Design. The completely randomized design is the simplest type of statistical design. In this design the experimental treatments are assigned to test units on a random basis. Any number of treatments can be assigned by a random process to any number of test units. Direct-mail tests of advertising appeals are an ideal setting for this design. The mailing list can be sampled randomly to obtain the experimental and control groups. Suppose, for example, three different promotion pieces to a series of plays are to be tested. The question is, which will deliver the most orders. A mailing list of 20,000 people is available. A random sample of 1200 is selected and divided randomly into three groups of 400 each. The experiment would appear as

$$EG_1 \quad R \quad X_1 \quad O_1$$
$$\dots\dots\dots\dots\dots\dots\dots\dots$$
$$EG_2 \quad R \quad X_2 \quad O_2$$
$$\dots\dots\dots\dots\dots\dots\dots\dots$$
$$EG_3 \quad R \quad X_3 \quad O_3$$

where the X_1 refers to the first experimental treatment "level," namely on the first of the three promotional pieces; X_2 refers to the second level; and so on. Here there is no separate control group. Each of the three treatments acts as a control for the others. The point of the experiment is to compare the three experimental treatments.

A variant of this design combines the treatment and the observation in the same questionnaire. In fact, this is the preferred method of obtaining reactions to different marketing options using surveys. For example, a study was conducted to determine the demand for a bus service at various price levels. One approach would have been to ask prospective patrons if they would ride the bus if the fare was 25 cents, 50 cents, or $1. However, it might have been unrealistic to ask a respondent to make a judgment on a 50-cent fare after he or she has just considered a 25-cent fare. To avoid this problem, each respondent was given only one price. Each pricing alternative was presented to a randomly chosen third of a representative sample from the service area of the new bus route. The modified design then was

$$
\begin{array}{ccc}
EG_1 & R & (X_1, O_1) \\
\cdots\cdots\cdots\cdots\cdots \\
EG_2 & R & (X_2, O_2) \\
\cdots\cdots\cdots\cdots\cdots \\
EG_3 & R & (X_3, O_3)
\end{array}
$$

Once the nature of the service and the fare level were described to each respondent, a measure of intentions or preferences relative to existing modes of transportation was obtained.

Randomized Block Design. A randomized-control-group design employs the randomization process for all variables, since there should be no tendency for an experimental group to differ systematically from the others on any dimension. However, there will be differences as long as the sample size is not extremely large. For example, even with 1200 in the sample, the group that received the first promotion piece might happen to be wealthier, more interested in the plays selected, or more urban than suburban. Thus, it could be argued that a superior performance by the first promotional piece actually could have been caused by those characteristics of the sample. Matching ensures that on the matched variable or variables there is/are no difference(s) between test samples. Randomization controls for all variables, not just the matched ones, but ensures only that the groups will tend to be similar.

Randomization and matching are combined in the **randomized block design.** The research identifies which one of the variables is the most important and controls for it by adding a block effect. This means that the control variable is used to define groups and the randomized experiment is conducted within each group. Symbolically, the randomized block design might be

$$
\begin{array}{cccc}
EG_1 & R & X & O_1 \\
\cdots\cdots\cdots\cdots\cdots \\
CG_1 & R & & O_2 \\
\hline
EG_2 & R & X & O_3 \\
\cdots\cdots\cdots\cdots\cdots \\
CG_2 & R & & O_4
\end{array}
$$

The solid line separates the two experiments.

For example, suppose that the urban respondents were expected to react more favorably than suburban respondents to a promotion for subscriptions to a series of plays. It is important to ensure that the experimental groups do not differ on this dimension. When a **block effect** is added, the experiment simply is repeated for both urban respondents and suburban respondents. Thus, 600 randomly selected urban respondents would be divided randomly into three test groups who are shown three different types of promotions. The subscripts refer to the three different test groups. Similarly, 600 randomly selected suburban subjects would be divided randomly into three groups. This experiment could be represented as follows:

$$
\begin{array}{lccccc}
& EG_1 & R & X_1 & O_1 & n = 200 \\
& & \cdots\cdots\cdots\cdots\cdots\cdots & & \\
\text{Urban} & EG_2 & R & X_2 & O_2 & n = 200 \\
& & \cdots\cdots\cdots\cdots\cdots\cdots & & \\
& EG_3 & R & X_3 & O_3 & n = 200 \\
\\
\hline
\\
& EG_1 & R & X_1 & O_1 & n = 200 \\
& & \cdots\cdots\cdots\cdots\cdots\cdots & & \\
\text{Suburban} & EG_2 & R & X_2 & O_2 & n = 200 \\
& & \cdots\cdots\cdots\cdots\cdots\cdots & & \\
& EG_3 & R & X_3 & O_3 & n = 200 \\
\end{array}
$$

The results might be presented in the form of a table as shown below.

Percentage Who Ordered Tickets

Treatment	Urban	Suburban	Means
A	11	4	7.5
B	24	11	17.5
C	24.5	15.5	20
Means	20	10	15

If in the original experiment, which did not block the urban-suburban factor, the group that received promotion B happened to have a higher percentage of urban respondents than the other group, it could have appeared superior to treatment C. However, when the blocked design is used, treatment C is superior.

The results provide evidence that treatment C is the best; however, it is not much better than treatment B. The difference is close enough that it might be due to chance. The treatment C respondents might just happen to be better prospects, and if the sample size was increased tenfold, promotions B and C actually might be the same. Hypothesis testing provides precise answers to such considerations and will be discussed later.

Another separate motivation for matching on the urban-suburban dimension might be to see if there were differences in reaction to the three promotions.

Perhaps a segmentation strategy might emerge that would indicate that one promotion was best for urban dwellers and another for suburban. The analysis of such **interactive effects** will be presented in a later section when factorial designs are discussed. It should be emphasized that this motivation is completely distinct and different from the experimental design motivation, to ensure that the respondents' location does not confound the results.

There is no reason why several control variables cannot be used. To the urban-suburban control variable, a prior-attendance control variable (attended frequently, attended, did not attend) and an age-control variable (older, middle-aged, and younger) could be added. The experiment then simply is repeated for each cell. For example, a group of respondents who are urban, have attended frequently in the past, and are middle-aged, will be divided into three groups, and the three experimental treatments will be applied to each group. The problem is, of course, that as the number of control variables increases so do the number of cells and the required sample size. In our example there are $2 \times 3 \times 3$, or 18 cells. The usual solution to this problem is the Latin square design.

Latin Square Design. The **Latin square design** is a method to reduce the number of groups involved when interactions between the treatment levels and the control variables can be considered unimportant. We will use a laboratory nutritional labeling experiment to describe and illustrate the Latin square design.[18]

The goal of the experiment was to contribute to the judgment of those proposing and evaluating several public policy nutritional labeling alternatives. In particular, the research goal was to determine the impact of variations in nutritional information on canned pea labels on shopper perceptions and preferences. Four levels of information were tested. The first provided only a simple quality statement. The second listed some major nutrient components and indicated whether the product was high or low on them. The third provided the amounts of each nutrient. The fourth listed all nutritional components, and was the most complete.

There were two control or block variables, the store and the brand. Four brands of canned peas, each with associated prices, were used. Four locations, each adjacent to a supermarket, were used, and 50 shoppers were interviewed in each. It was felt that interactions among the nutritional information treatments and the brands or stores would be insignificant, so the Latin square could be used. The design is shown in Figure 12-3. Note that treatment level I appears with each store once and only once, and with each brand once and only once. Thus, the results for treatment level I should not benefit from the fact that one of the brands is rated higher than the others or that shoppers from one of the stores are more sensitive to nutrition.

Each respondent was exposed to four cans of peas. For example, at store 1, respondents were exposed to Private Brand A at 21 cents with the treatment III label information, to Private Brand B at 22 cents with treatment II, and so on. After being exposed to the four cans, the respondents were asked to evaluate each on six different nine-point scales. Thus, this experiment illustrates the use

	Stores 1	2	3	4
Private Brand A 21 cents	III	IV	I	II
Private Brand B 22 cents	II	III	IV	I
Major Brand A 25 cents	I	II	III	IV
Major Brand B 26 cents	IV	I	II	III

FIGURE 12-3

A Latin square design: the treatment levels I, II, III, and IV

Source: Adapted from Edward H. Asam and Louis P. Bucklin, "Nutritional Labeling for Canned Goods: A Study of Consumer Response." *Journal of Marketing, 37* (April 1973), 36.

of multiple measures of the results. The mean score for each treatment level is shown below in a table. Again, the issue as to whether the results are "statistically significant" will be deferred until later chapters.

Mean Scores for Attitudes and Preference Scales for Four Different Levels of Nutritional Information on Can Labels

Nutritional Treatment	Scale: Like	Good Buy	Tasty	Tender	Wholesome	Preference
Level I	4.73	4.88	5.05	5.78	4.86	2.47
Level II	4.49	4.38	4.87	5.39	4.90	2.28
Level III	4.63	4.71	4.87	5.65	5.13	2.55
Level IV	4.86	4.91	5.07	5.99	5.32	2.69

In a randomized block design, each cell would require four experimental groups, one for each treatment level. In the Latin square design, each cell requires only one treatment level so that a minimum of 16 groups is required instead of 64. The Latin square normally would have a separate sample for each cell. In this study, the same 50 respondents from store 1 were used for all the cells in the first column. Each respondent reacted to four brands. Thus, the store block served effectively to control for not only the store but for many other characteristics of the sample. As a result the experiment was more sensitive. However, the experience of rating one brand may have had a carry-over effect on the task of rating another, which could generate some bias.

The Latin square design allows one to control two variables without requiring an expanded sample. It does require the same number of rows, columns, and treatment levels, so it does impose constraints in that respect. Also, it cannot be used to determine interaction effects. Thus, if nutritional information should have a different effect on private label brands than major brands, this design would not discern such differences.

Factorial Designs. In the statistical designs discussed so far, only one experimental variable was involved. In the factorial design, two or more experimental variables are considered simultaneously. Each combination of the experimental treatment levels applies to randomly selected groups.

Suppose that a consumer product was to be tested in 36 cities. Three levels of advertising were to be tested: a high level, a low level, and no advertising. In addition, two price levels are to be considered, a high price and a low price. The resulting factorial experiment could be denoted as

EG_1	R	X_1 (Hi Adv - Hi Price)	O_1	$n = 6$
EG_2	R	X_2 (Hi Adv - Low Price)	O_2	$n = 6$
EG_3	R	X_3 (Low Adv - Hi Price)	O_3	$n = 6$
EG_4	R	X_4 (Low Adv - Low Price)	O_4	$n = 6$
EG_5	R	X_5 (No Adv - Hi Price)	O_5	$n = 6$
EG_6	R	X_6 (No Adv - Low Price)	O_3	$n = 6$

The output of the experiment will provide not only the effects of advertising but also the effects of the price variable. Suppose the findings were as shown in the table below.

Sales in an Experiment Involving Advertising and Price

	High Price	Low Price	Average Sales
High advertising	105	133	119
Low advertising	103	124	113.5
No advertising	101	112	106.5
Average sales	103	123	113

Thus, in one experiment the effects of two variables are determined. The real power of a factorial design, however, is that it provides the ability to determine interactive effects.

Interactive Effects. Figure 12-4*a* shows the results in graphical form. The judgment about advertising can be refined now. When the product is priced high, the advertising effect almost disappears, whereas when the product is priced low the advertising effect is much larger. This illustrates an interaction effect between two experimental variables. The effect of the advertising level is termed a **main effect,** the main effect due to advertising. Similarly, the effect of price is termed the **main effect of price.** The **main effect** is distinguished from the **interactive effect** of pairs of experimental variables.

In Figure 12-4*a* there is a price effect, because the low-price results are higher on the average than the high-price results. There is also an **advertising effect,** as the average results for the various advertising levels differ. As has been noted already, there is also an **interaction effect.** Figure 12-4*b* is an example of the case where there is both an advertising and price effect but no interaction.

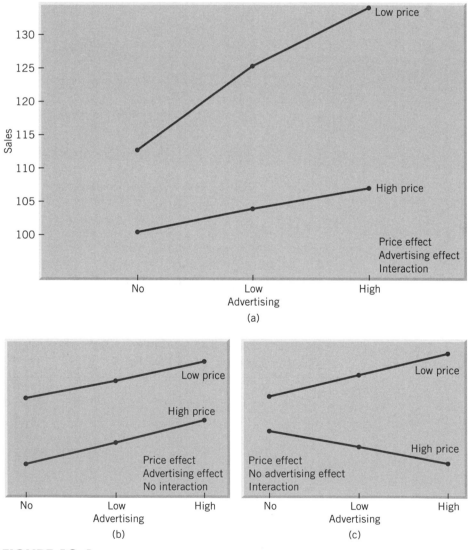

FIGURE 12-4
Interactive effects

The two main effects are additive here. Figure 12-4c shows a case where there is a price main effect but no advertising main effect. The average sales for each level of advertising are the same. There is, however, an interactive effect between advertising and price, an even more pronounced effect than the one observed in Figure 12-4a.

The factorial design could be expanded to include three or more variables. Each then would generate a main effect and each pair would generate a possible interactive effect. Of course, there needs to be an experimental group for each combination of experimental treatment levels. Thus, if three levels of advertising, two levels of price, and two promotion alternatives were involved, a total of 12 possible conditions would have to be tested. That would require a sample size of at least 12, which might be expensive if test cities were involved. Further, if each cell is to provide a reliable estimate of that treatment combination, several test cities might be desired. If the respondents were people instead of cities, several hundred might be required in each experimental group. Thus, one of the problems of factorial designs is that the number of experimental groups can get large rather quickly. Of course, the Latin square concept can be employed to reduce the number somewhat, if interactions can be neglected.

Factorial designs also could be expanded to include block effects. Thus, either the advertising and price experiment or the Budweiser experiment could have been duplicated, once for large cities and once for small ones, for example. Furthermore, factorial designs could be created using matching instead of randomization to develop the experimental groups. An example of a factorial experiment is given in Exhibit 12-2.

LABORATORY AND FIELD EXPERIMENTS

Experimental research can also be broadly divided into two main categories: laboratory experiments and field experiments. The first, laboratory experiments, as the name suggests, are experiments in which the experimental treatment is introduced in an artificial or laboratory setting. In this type of research study, the variance of all or nearly all of the possible influential independent variables not pertinent to the immediate problem of the investigation is kept to a minimum. This is done by isolating the research in a physical situation apart from the routine of ordinary living and by manipulating one or more independent variables under rigorously specified, operationalized, and controlled conditions. For example, a shopper might be exposed to a new product in a simulated supermarket, or two groups of hospital users might be asked to react to two different pricing plans for the delivery of medical services.

The second, field experiments, are conducted in the "field." A field experiment is a research study in a realistic situation in which one or more independent variables are manipulated by the experimenter under carefully controlled conditions as the situation will permit.[19] For example, one television advertisement is run in Omaha and another in Dayton. The next day viewers in the two cities are called to determine their response. A **field experiment** is the experimental treatment or intervention introduced in a completely natural

EXHIBIT 12-2

The Battle for Shelf Space

It has been a general belief among retailers and manufacturers that shelf space in retail outlets shares a positive relationship with product sales, and that product displays attract the attention of potential buyers and thus stimulate their demand for goods. Based on this notion, manufacturers yearn for more shelf space for their products in the hope that it will help maximize their brands' revenue and profit. On the other hand, the retailer is interested in maximizing the store profits and not necessarily the profits of any particular brand. With the growing power of the retailer, this conflict in interests has led to what is known in the industry as the "battle for shelf space." Manufacturers are forced to pay "slotting allowances" to retailers for them to carry their brands.

Recently, we conducted a field experiment to determine whether there is really a positive correlation between shelf space and product sales. The objective of the study was to determine whether there exists a relationship between shelf space, location of store (located either in a low-, middle-, or high-income area), and product sales; and if so, whether the location of the store (located either in a low-, middle-, or high-income area) moderates the relationship between shelf space and product sales. Because this was a field experiment, controlling for other factors or variables was a must to ensure the validity and reliability of the research results.

The cooperation of the store managers of a major retail chain was sought. Any variations from differences in retail chains were eliminated by conducting the experiment in outlets controlled by the same retail chain. Seasonality was controlled for by carrying out the experiment within a 2-month time period when no major holidays occurred. Also, the experiment was repeated in another time period and the data resulting from replication was also analyzed. This was done to see whether the observed effect was consistent over different time periods. During this time period, we ensured that there were no promotions for the brand under study. Promotional activities of competing brands were also monitored, and no major competing brands were fixed at their normal levels. To account for factors such as differences in size of the stores, the data analysis involved not only analyzing the actual sales data but the data were also adjusted by the product category sales and the all commodity volume (ACV) sales of each store. Also, to account for any change in sales of this product category for reasons other than change in shelf space, the product category sales in six other stores (control group) was monitored during the period of the experiment.

The cooperation of the store manager and the dairy manager of each of the six stores was personally solicited in executing the prescribed shelf treatments to the brand under study. The shelf facings for the chilled orange juice brand were varied each week. Since the normal number of shelf facings in this market for orange juice was three facings (as confirmed by the manufacturers and the store managers), we decided to study the effect of two, three, and four shelf facings (one below the normal and one above the normal); there seemed to be a realistic assumption that they would perform, given the constraints. The stores were closely monitored every day of the week to ensure proper execution of the shelf treatments. Any irregularity in the shelf treatments was brought to the notice of the dairy managers and was immediately rectified.

A 3×3 factorial design was used, with shelf facings and store location (neighborhood type) being the major factors. The experiment was carried out over a three-week period and was replicated over another three-week period. The shelf facings in each store were randomly assigned so that no two stores in the same income level had the same number of shelf facings in any given time period. The research results revealed that there is a distinct positive relationship between shelf space and product sales, and that this effect is independent of location. This study provides more evidence for the belief that shelf space is positively related to product sales. Although the research findings were conclusive in that they were consistent over time and place, these results cannot be generalized to encompass all the product categories in the supermarket. Also, because the shelf treatments for the orange juice brand under study were altered only between 2, 3, and 4 facings it is not possible to predict the relationship for greater than 4 facings or for less than 2 facings.

Source: Excerpts of an experimental study conducted by V. Kumar and Keith K. Cox, University of Houston, Houston, Texas, 1992–93.

setting. The respondents usually are not aware that an experiment is being conducted; thus, the response tends to be *natural.*

The **laboratory experiment** tends to be *artificial.* Furthermore, there is a **testing effect,** in that respondents are usually aware of being in a test and therefore are sensitized and tend not to respond naturally. Thus, the question always arises: What will happen outside the laboratory? Are the results projectable to the real world? Does the result have **external validity?** External validity refers to the applicability of the experimental results to situations external to the actual experimental context. Field experiments tend to have much greater external validity than laboratory experiments. Laboratory experiments, however, tend to be much less costly and allow the experimenter greater control over the experiment, thus reducing alternative explanations of the results and increasing internal validity. **Internal validity** refers to the ability of the experiment to unambiguously show relationships. For example, a large response to the Omaha advertisement might be caused by the number of people in Omaha, the weather when the advertisement was run, or the scheduling of civic activities. Although, by improving the experimental design, it is possible to reduce the number of competing explanations of the results of field experiments, they still tend to have less internal validity than laboratory experiments.

The purpose of an experiment usually is to detect or confirm causal relationships and to quantify them. The validity issue is, thus, extremely important. Of course, enhanced validity has associated costs and, as with other research approaches, the goal is not to maximize validity, regardless of cost. The goal, rather, is to make the appropriate trade-off between validity and cost. The design of an experiment allows considerable room for making such trade-offs.

THREATS TO EXPERIMENTAL VALIDITY[20]

An experiment is intended to provide information regarding the causal influence of an experimental treatment on the measure of interest. The **internal validity** of the experiment depends upon the extent to which competing explanations for the results are avoided. The **external validity** of the experiment refers to the extent that the causal inferences can be generalized from the experimental environment to the environment of the decision maker.

Threats to Internal Validity[21]

The major source of threat to internal validity comes from eight different classes of extraneous variables, which if not controlled might produce effects confounded with the effects of the experimental stimulus:

1. *History:* Events external to the experiment that affect the responses of the people involved in the experiment.
2. *Maturation:* Changes in the respondents that are a consequence of time, such as aging, getting hungry, or getting tired.
3. *Testing:* The effects of taking a test upon the results of a subsequent test.

4. *Instrumentation:* The measuring instrument may change, as when different interviewers are used.
5. *Statistical Regression:* Operates where groups have been selected on the basis of their extreme scores.
6. *Selection Bias:* An experimental group is systematically different in some relevant way from the population being studied.
7. *Mortality:* Respondents dropping out of the experiment, while the experimental research is in progress.
8. *Selection-Maturation Interaction:* In certain experimental designs, the selection-maturation interaction effect might be mistaken for the effect of the experimental variable.

Threats to External Validity[22]

Laboratory experiments have the greatest external validity problem because of the *artificiality* of the setting and arrangements. The exposure to an experimental treatment, such as a mock-up of a new product in a laboratory, can be so different from conditions in the real world that projections become very difficult and risky. Consider the plight of a researcher seeking to design a laboratory experiment to yield quick feedback on the effect of a company rebuttal to adverse publicity. An example is a government report on Alka-Seltzer, which contended that because it contained aspirin it was damaging to some of the stomach conditions it was designed to treat. Since "bad news" is thought to have superior attention-getting ability, a valid laboratory experiment would provide for selective exposure, attention, or perception of the attack and the rebuttal. This problem has defeated several ingenious researchers.

In addition to the problem of artificiality in laboratory experiments, most of the previous list of eight internal validity threats also apply to external validity. In particular, selectivity bias can be very serious. In field experiments the test market site, the stores chosen to test, and the people interviewed as part of the experiment are sometimes not representative of the entire market or population. In a laboratory experiment, the respondents are often not a good representation of the population, especially if the experiment requires considerable effort and if self-selection is involved. As Banks notes, "The greater the demand upon respondents in terms of either the effort expended or the period of time covered by the experiment, the greater the likelihood that the subject who cooperates throughout the study is atypical."[23]

Also, a significant **before measure** effect may diminish external validity. If the **before measure** increases respondent sensitivity to the treatment, then the results will not be typical of the "real world." This problem can be severe in experiments that ask respondents to record purchases in a diary. These consumer panel members invariably pay closer attention to the choices in the categories being recorded, and they may buy greater-than-usual quantities in order to have something to record. The novelty does wear off, and purchase behavior is thought to return to normal, but that can occur after the experiment is over.

In general, the major factors that jeopardize external validity of the experiment are

1. *The reactive or interaction effect of testing,* in which a pretest might increase or decrease the respondent's sensitivity or responsiveness to the experimental variable, and thus make the results obtained for a pretested population unrepresentative of the effects of the experimental variable for the unpretested universe from which the experimental respondents were selected.

2. *The interaction effect of selection biases and the experimental variable.*

3. *Reactive effects of experimental arrangements,* which would preclude generalization about the effect of the experimental variable on persons being exposed to it in nonexperimental settings.

4. *Multiple treatment interference,* likely to occur whenever multiple treatments are applied to the same respondents, because the effects of prior treatments usually are not erasable.

This enumeration of sources of invalidity is bound to be incomplete. Some threats are too specific to a given setting to be generalized easily. The sources of invalidity (internal and external) that are still a potential threat for classical experimental designs are provided in Table 12-2. For example, the likelihood that competitors will distort the results of market tests (by aggressive promotional activity, additional sales force effort, or even doing nothing when they certainly would take action if the new product were launched into a regional or national market) is an ever-present "history" problem in this particular setting.

What is important is not the completeness of the checklist of threats but a heightened sensitivity to the possibility of threats so that

1. The extent and the direction of the bias in results can be considered when it becomes time to use the relationship obtained from the experiment to make a decision.

2. The possibility of design improvements can be anticipated.

3. Other methods of measurement with different restraints on validity can be employed. The virtue of multiple measures or approaches to the same phenomena is that the biases of each may cancel each other.

GUIDELINES FOR CONDUCTING EXPERIMENTAL RESEARCH[24]

To design and analyze an experiment, it is necessary that everyone involved in it have a clear idea in advance of exactly what is to be studied, how the data are to be collected, and at least a qualitative understanding of how these data are to be analyzed. An outline of the recommended procedure is as follows:

1. *Recognition of and statement of the problem.* This may seem to be a rather obvious point, but in practice it is often not simple to realize that a problem requiring experimentation exists, nor is it simple to develop a clear and generally accepted statement of this problem. A clear statement of the

TABLE 12-2
Sources of Invalidity

	A	B	C	D	E	F	G	H	I	J	K	L
				Internal						**External**		
Pre-Experimental Designs:												
1. One-group, After-Only Design	−	−				−	−				−	
2. One-group, Before-After Design	−	−	−	−	?	+	+	−	−	−		?
3. Nonmatched Control Group Design	+	?	+	+	+	−	−	−	−			
4. Matched Control Group Design	+	?	+	+	+	+	−	−				
True Experimental Designs:												
4. Two-group, Before-After Design	+	+	+	+	+	+	+	+	−	?	?	
5. Solomon Four Group Design	+	+	+	+	+	+	+	+	?	?	?	
6. Two-group, After-Only Design	+	+	+	+	+	+	+	+	?	?	?	
Quasi-Experimental Designs:												
7. Time Series Design	−	+	+	?	+	+	+	+	−	?	?	

Adapted from Donald T. Campbell and Julian C. Stanley, *Experimental and Quasi-Experimental Designs for Research,* Chicago: Rand McNally and Company, 1963.

A = History **B** = Maturation **C** = Testing **D** = Instrumentation
E = Statistical Regression **F** = Selection **G** = Mortality
H = Interaction Of Selection And Maturation, etc.
I = Reactive Or Interaction Effect Of Testing
J = Interaction Of Selection Biases And The Experimental Variable
K = Reactive Effect Of Experimental Arrangements
L = Multiple Treatment Interference

(−) Indicates A Definite Weakness **(+)** Indicates That The Factor Is Controlled
(?) Indicates A Possible Source of Concern **( )** Indicates That The Factor Is Not Relevant

problem often contributes substantially to a better understanding of the phenomena and the final solution of the problem.

2. *Choice of factors and levels.* The experimenter must choose the factors to be varied in the experiment, the ranges over which these factors will be varied, and the specific levels at which runs will be made. Thought must be given to how these factors are to be controlled at the desired levels and how they are to be measured.

3. *Selection of the response variable.* In selecting the response variable, the experimenter should be certain that this variable really provides useful information about the process under study.

4. *Choice of experimental design.* If the first three steps are done correctly, this step is relatively easy. Choice of design involves the consideration of sample size (number of replicates), the selection of a suitable run order for the experimental trials, and the determination of whether or not blocking or other randomization restrictions are involved.

5. *Performing the experiment.* When running the experiment, it is vital to monitor the process carefully to ensure that everything is being done according to plan. Errors in experimental procedure at this stage will usually destroy experimental validity.

6. *Data analysis.* Statistical methods should be used to analyze the data so that results and conclusions are objective rather than judgmental in nature. If the experiment has been designed correctly and if it has been performed according to the design, then the statistical methods required are not elaborate. (Data analysis is covered in great detail in Part III of the text).

7. *Conclusion and recommendations.* Once the data have been analyzed, the experimenter must draw practical conclusions about the results and recommend a course of action. Graphical methods are often useful in this stage, particularly in presenting the results to others. Follow-up runs and confirmation testing should also be performed to validate the conclusions from the experiment.

Common Misuses of Experimental Research in Marketing[25]

Experimental and quasi-experimental design approaches have their own uses, methodological sets, benefits, and pitfalls. Each family of techniques is highly appropriate for specific uses, but neither is amenable to slavish application for all marketing purposes. Some examples of the most common misuses include

▶ Concluding from a test of two media-spending levels that sales are inelastic with regard to media and that advertising can be turned off entirely.

▶ Observing that a 10 percent price increase has no impact, so sales are not responding to price, and the price can be increased 25 percent.

▶ Deciding that an umbrella display for a number of brands won't work because a similar display that was tested for a single brand didn't pay off.

LIMITATIONS OF EXPERIMENTS

Experimentation is a powerful tool in the search for unambiguous relationships that we hope may be used to make valid predictions about the effects of marketing decisions, and to develop basic theories. The laboratory experiment is the preferred method because of its internal validity; however, because of acute external validity problems in the laboratory setting, managers are reluctant to rely upon it. Unfortunately, the field experiment is beset by a number of problems whose net effect has been to limit the vast majority of marketing experiments to short-run comparisons across stores, home placements of product variations, and so forth. Relatively few large-scale experiments with social programs, marketing programs, or advertising campaigns are conducted in any given year. What are the reasons?

Cost

Cost and time pressures are the first hurdle. Even "simple" in-store tests require additional efforts to gain cooperation; to properly place the display, price, or promotion; to measure the uncontrolled variables; and then to audit the resulting sales differences. The measurement costs alone are often substantial. When larger interventions, such as comparing alternative advertising themes in multiple geographic areas are contemplated, management may be very wary that the benefits will exceed the costs. These costs are likely to be considerable if any amount of reinterviewing or special manipulation of advertising, product, or other controllable variables is required.

Another cost is the fact that the research delays management decisions. For some experiments the impact of the experimental treatment can extend over a long time period, as much as a year or even longer. Consider the Budweiser advertising experiments, which were run for a full year. The researcher is often placed in a difficult position. If the experiment, especially the *after observation*, is not allowed sufficient time, the validity of the results might suffer. On the other hand, if the experiment is too lengthy, the resulting delays in making and implementing policy might be unacceptably long. One way to avoid the constraint of time pressure is to conduct an ongoing program of experimentation in anticipation of recurring decisions. Thus, some companies are building up data files of responses to marketing programs in a variety of contexts.

Security

Still another cost is that of security. A field experiment naturally involves exposing a marketing program in the marketplace, so it is difficult to hide from competitors who are in contact with their own field sales force, store personnel, research suppliers, and trade sources. For example, one consumer products company constructed product displays in several stores in one city for one eight-hour period on one Friday. At the end of the day, all traces of the test had been removed. However, by Monday the major trade magazine and most competitors knew of the test and the details of the test product.

Implementation Problems

Implementation problems abound in the conduct of experiments. First, it may not be easy to gain cooperation within the organization. Regional managers resist proposals to experiment with varying the size and call frequency of a sales force. They do not want to subject their market area to a reduced sales effort. Administrators of social programs may resist efforts to assign people randomly to treatments. They want to decide the assignments according to who can benefit most from the service and which service is most suitable. A second problem to which experiments involving market areas are especially susceptible is *contamination*, because of an inability to confine the treatment to the designated experimental area. Buyers from one geographic area may visit an adjacent area or receive media messages that overflow from that area. It is seldom possible to partition geographic market areas so that the sales measurements and treatments exactly coincide.

Experiments involving people as test units may become contaminated because people in the control group associate with people assigned to the program and learn what they have been doing. A third problem is that the variability in behavior across test units can be so large that it is difficult to detect the effects of the experiment. Of course, some of the variability can be removed by *blocking* or by *matching*, but it will not be eliminated. The question is: Can it be reduced enough so that the experimental effects can be discerned?

The ultimate problem, however, is that there may be no person or geographic area available to serve as a control. This is the case with industrial markets composed of a few large buyers who communicate among each other or are geographically dispersed. Any effort to limit a new-product introduction to a subset of such a market would be unsuccessful. The same problem occurs in attempting to assess the effects of federal legislation, which goes into effect in all parts of the country at the same time. Also, practitioners may be unwilling to deny access to a social program because they believe that it is counter to their professional obligation.

Uncertain Persistency of Results

This is the final category of the problems that limit the acceptance and usage of field experiments. For an experimental result to be useful, it must hold long enough to be acted on to advantage. The two factors most damaging to an assumption of persistency are high rates of technological, economic, or social change in the market environment, and aggressive competitive behavior. During the experiment the competition may elect to monitor the test independently and learn as much as possible—or take unusual action, such as a special consumer promotion, to confound the results. Similarly, when the test is expanded to a regional or national market, the competitors may either do nothing or retaliate. This means that there are at least four combinations of circumstances, each with different implications for the nature of the causal relationship being studied:

	Possible Competitive Responses After Experiment	
	No Response	Retaliation
No response	1	3
Retaliation	4	2

The persistency, and hence the value of the experimental results, will be uncertain to the degree that the decision maker cannot assess (1) the probability of each of the four possible events; (2) the magnitude of the retaliatory action, if any; or (3) the number of direct competitors taking action.

Summary

Experiments are defined as studies in which conditions are controlled so that one or more independent variables can be manipulated to test a hypothesis about a dependent variable. The key principle of experimental work is *manipulation* of a treatment variable (say X), followed by observation of response variable (say Y). If a change in X causes Y to change in the hypothesized way, then we are tempted to say X causes Y. However, this causal inference rests on soft ground, unless the experiment has been properly designed to *control* for other extraneous or spurious variables. (The term **spurious association** involves the possibility that two variables—such as advertising and intention— are both caused by a third variable, usage. Spurious association can be detected by developing association measures for subgroups defined by the spurious variable (i.e., users and nonusers)). The problem is to identify the spurious variable and establish controls for the effect of these variables on the dependent variable. Hence to establish causality between two variables, the following types of evidence are required: (a) **Condition of Concomitant Variation,** (b) **Condition of Time Order of Occurrence,** and (c) **Absence of Competing Causal Explanations.**

Experimental research can be broadly divided into two main categories: laboratory experiments and field experiments. Laboratory experiments are often relatively inexpensive and provide the opportunity to exercise tight control. In a laboratory, for example, an exposure to a concept can be controlled, whereas in the more realistic field context there are many factors that can distort an exposure, such as weather, competitive reactions, and family activities. However, the laboratory experiment suffers from the testing effect and from the artificiality of the situation. Thus, the external validity (the ability to generalize from the experiment) is limited. Field experiments have greater external validity but are more costly to run (in expense, time, and security), are difficult to implement, and lack the tight control possible in the laboratory. As a result their internal validity is often a problem.

Questions and Problems

1. How is experimental research different from descriptive research?
2. What is a spurious association? How do you distinguish between spurious association and the existence of an intervening variable?
3. When does association imply causation? Under what conditions? Could there ever be a causal relationship without association present?
4. Explain the following terms:
   a. Experimental treatments
   b. Manipulation

c. Extraneous variable
d. Selection bias
e. Randomization
f. Blocking
g. Matching

5. In a laboratory experiment (designed to test a new brand), people are exposed to advertisements for a new brand and then are asked to buy a brand from that product class from a supermarket aisle that has been set up as realistically as possible. After they use the brand, they are asked if they would like to repurchase it. When would such an experiment be preferred over a field experiment?

6. Distinguish between the internal and external validity of an experiment. List the various threats to internal validity and briefly describe each of these threats.

7. A blind taste test was responsible in part for the decision by Coca-Cola to introduce the "new Coke," a product that ran into resistance by those loyal to "old Coke" (now Coke Classic). On a blind taste test, unlabeled colas would be tasted and the respondent would report taste preferences. Evaluate the validity of this experiment.

8. Contrast the following pairs of concepts by defining and illustrating each:
   a. History versus instrumentation effects
   b. Maturation versus mortality effects
   c. Testing versus before measure effects
   d. Selection bias versus self-selection

9. NuSystems, Inc., a computer software distributing company, has recently completed an innovative sales training program in order to boost recently lagging sales. The head of the marketing department is interested in discovering how effective this new training has been in improving the performance of sales personnel and increasing sales.
   a. Would experimental or descriptive research methods be most suitable for this purpose? Give reasons for your answer.
   b. What kind of association exists between the variables?

10. In an effort to identify the reasons for the rise in teenage violence in the United States, Concerned Citizens of America (CCA) has decided to examine the relationship between exposure to rap music and incidents of teen violence. They have decided to utilize an experimental technique to establish whether a relationship exists.
    a. Suggest how such an experiment could be undertaken. Include a description of how the experiment would be conducted, from the problem statement to the conclusion.
    b. What are the possible limitations of this type of research?

11. a. In the preceding question, suggest ways in which this experiment could be conducted as:
      i) a field experiment
      ii) a laboratory experiment
    b. Which type of experiment would best serve the purpose of the study? Give reasons for your answer.

12. Which type of experimental design offers the most effective control of internal sources of validity?

13. A group of known smokers are sent literature on the harmful effects of smoking on weekly basis for one year. At the end of the year, a poll is taken to see how many of the smokers stopped smoking during the year. The results are used to establish the effectiveness of this literature campaign in encouraging smokers to stop smoking.
    a. This is an example of what kind of experiment design?
    b. What are the potential hazards in drawing the above conclusion from this type of experiment?

14. A leading manufacturer of ladies' lingerie has maintained its high share in the panty hose market over the past five years but has experienced a dramatic decrease in sales. This has led Cheryl Martin, the VP of Marketing to conclude that the market for panty hose as a whole must be shrinking. In an effort to determine whether a shift in women's attitudes or life-styles is responsible for the shrinkage of the market for pantyhose, she has decided to conduct a nationwide telephone survey of women across the country.
    a. How can the adoption of a random assignment procedure help maintain the internal validity of the experiment?
    b. Suggest a randomization technique that would be appropriate for this study.

15. a. What are the possible threats to the validity of a trend analysis?
    b. How can these threats be eliminated by the experimental design process?

End Notes

1. Steven R. Brown and Lawrence E. Melamed. *Experimental Design and Analysis* (Newbury Park, California: Sage Publications), 1990.

2. Keith K. Cox and Ben M. Enis. *Experimentation for Marketing Decisions* (Scranton, Pennsylvania: International Textbook), 1969, p. 5.

3. A. Parasuraman, *Marketing Research* (Reading, Massachusetts: Addison-Wesley Publishing Company), 1986, p. 267.

4. David A. Kenny, *Correlation and Causality* (New York: John Wiley & Sons), 1979.

5. Gilbert A. Churchill, Jr. *Marketing Research: Methodological Foundations,* 5th edition (New York: Dryden Press), 1991, 167–168.

6. This system of notation was introduced by Donald T. Campbell and Julian C. Stanley. *Experimental and Quasi Experimental Designs for Research* (Chicago: Rand McNally), 1963.

7. E. Paul Green, S. Donald Tull, and Gerald Albaum. *Research for Marketing Decisions*, 5th edition (New Jersey: Prentice–Hall, Inc.), 1988.

8. Refer to our discussion on the threats to experimental validity in this chapter.

9. ibid.

10. ibid.

11. ibid.

12. Fred N. Kerlinger. *Foundations of Behavioral Research* (New York: Holt, Rinehart and Winston), 1973, p. 114.

13. Louise H. Kidder and Sellitz Wrightsman. *Cook's Research Methods in Social Relations* (New York: Holt, Rinehart and Winston), 1981, p. 18.

14. Adapted from A. Parasuraman. *Marketing Research* (Massachusetts: Addison Wesley), 1991.

15. This design is named after R. L. Solomon who first proposed it in his article "An Extension of Control Group Design," *Psychological Bulletin*, 46 (1949), 137–150.

16. For a stimulating discussion of this method of strength in causal inferences, see Eugene J. Webb, Donald T. Campbell, Richard D. Schwarz, and Lee Lechrest. *Unobtrusive Measures: Nonreactive Research in the Social Sciences* (Chicago: Rand McNally), 1966.

17. The term "panel" sometimes refers to a consumer jury, whose members provide a reaction to some proposed product on a one-shot basis.

18. Adapted from Edward H. Asam and Louis P. Bucklin. "Nutritional Labeling for Canned Goods: A Study of Consumer Response," *Journal of Marketing*, 37 (April 1973), 36.

19. Ibid. p. 369.
20. Adapted from Donald T. Campbell and Julian C. Stanley. *Experimental and Quasi-Experimental Designs for Research* (Chicago, Illinois: Rand McNally), 1963.
21. Source: Donald T. Campbell and Julian C. Stanley. *Experimental and Quasi-Experimental Designs for Research*, (Chicago, Illinois: Rand McNally), 1963, and Thomas D. Cook and Donald T. Campbell. *Quasi-Experimentation: Design and Analysis Issues for Field Settings*, (Boston, Massachusetts: Houghton Mifflin), 1979.

22. Ibid.
23. Seymour Banks. *Experimentation in Marketing,* (New York: McGraw-Hill), 1965, p. 33.
24. Adapted from Douglas C. Montgomery. *Design and Analysis of Experiments,* (New York: John Wiley & Sons), 1991, 9–11.
25. John L. Carefoot. "Modeling and Experimental Designs in Marketing Research: Uses and Misuses," *Marketing News*, June 7, 1993, H19.

CASE 12-1
Evaluating Experimental Designs

A description of a variety of experimental designs follows. For each design: (1) indicate the type of experiment that is being used, (2) briefly discuss the threats to **internal** and **external validity** and identify those you regard as the most serious, and (3) describe how you would improve the design to overcome the problems you have identified.

1. In the Bayer deceptive advertising case an issue was whether people were influenced by some Bayer advertisements to believe that Bayer was more effective than other aspirins in relieving pain. In an experiment designed to address that issue, a Bayer print advertisement was shown to 428 people projectable to the U.S. adult population, and two television advertisements were shown to 240 people recruited from local organizations (which received $1.00 for each participant) in nine communities in Massachusetts, Missouri, and Georgia. After being exposed to the advertisements, respondents were asked to identify the main points of the advertisement, what the advertisement meant by its major claim, and whether the advertisement suggested that Bayer is more effective at relieving pain than any other brand of aspirin. The percentage of respondents were tabulated who, in response to the open-ended questions, said (1) that Bayer is best and (2) that Bayer is better than other aspirins. Whether the respondents made explicit reference to effectiveness also was noted. These percentages were used to address the issue. For example, across all surveys it was found that 10 percent felt that a main point of the advertisement was that Bayer is best or better than other aspirins *in effectiveness*. Also across all surveys, 71 percent felt that the advertisement suggested that Bayer works better than any other aspirin.

2. In 1982, the instrument group of National Chemical decided to change from a modest advertising effort aimed at generating leads for its sales force to a more substantial program aimed at increased awareness and preference. A major vehicle for this campaign was *Chemical Process Instrumentation,* a leading trade magazine. To evaluate the advertising, a survey was made of the readers of that magazine before and after the one-year campaign. In each case a systematic sample of 2500 readers was sent questionnaires. Responses were obtained from 572 for the before sample and 513 for the after sample. Among the questions were:
   ▶ List the companies you consider to be the leading manufacturers of the following products.
   ▶ Check the one manufacturer (for each product) that you would first consider when purchasing the item.

The results showed

	Before	After
Percentage aware of National Chemical	23	46
Percentage prefer National Chemical	8	11

The results were averaged across the major products carried by National Chemical.

3. An account executive notices that a client is sponsoring a program that will be shown on about three-fourths of the network's station lineup. This provides a possibility for testing the effectiveness of the new commercials being used. The executive's letter

to the research supervisor reads, in part: "What if we picked several markets that will receive the program and several that won't? Then within each of these we can measure attitudes and purchasing among a randomly selected group of consumers. After the broadcast we can interview other randomly selected groups on the same questions."

4. A manufacturer of products sold in food stores wished to find out whether a coupon good for 10 cents off the purchase price of its product could win new users. Coupons were mailed to half the households in the city's upper-80-percent income groups. Ten days before mailing, phone interviews were conducted with 200 randomly selected households scheduled to receive the coupon and 200 randomly selected who would not receive it. Whoever answered the phone was questioned about brand awareness and past purchasing within the product category. One month later callbacks were made to 400 households. Of the original group, 165 coupon receivers and 160 nonreceivers were asked the awareness and purchase questions again. In addition, 100 coupon recipients and 100 nonrecipients who were not previously questioned were interviewed on this occasion. The latter also were picked randomly from the receiver and nonreceiver populations.

5. Evaluate the McCollum/Spielman procedure described in Chapter 24.

6. Evaluate the Market Ware Corp'n Visionary shopper described in Chapter 23, Exhibit 23-1.

CASE 12-2
Barrie Food Corporation

Al Blankenship (of Carter-Wallace) has just given an enthusiastic account of a new technique for evaluating television commercials. Your boss—the marketing research manager for a large food manufacturer—who is in the audience with you, wants you to analyze the technique carefully and make a recommendation on the use of the technique. The transcript of Blankenship's remarks follows:

Jim stopped in my office one day early this year, bursting with an idea he had to test the effectiveness of television commercials. He told me that in fall, 1976, WCAU-TV had telecast a program which discussed the pros and cons of the proposed roofed-over sports stadium for the city. Viewers were asked to telephone their reactions to a special number to indicate whether they were in favor of or opposed to the sports palace. Jim and his group had been assigned the job of keeping a running total of the vote.

He had become intrigued, he said, that this sort of approach might be used to measure the effectiveness of television commercials. In a balanced experiment, you could have an announcer, immediately following the test commercial, ask people to telephone in to request a sample of the product. Differences in rate of response between different commercials would measure their effectiveness.

My reaction was immediate and positive. This was really getting close to a behavioral measurement of response to advertising. But it lacked a crucial control. How could you be sure that the same number of people had been exposed to each commercial? The technique required a measurement of the size of audience exposed to each test commercial.

In this situation, I thought of C. E. Hooper, since one of Hooper's specialties is measurement of audience size. If audience size could be built in as a control, it seemed to me that the technique was solid. I got Jim together with Bruce McEwen, Executive Vice President of Hooper. Bruce was just as excited as I had been.

However, following our discussion, I began to cool off. I was afraid that the audience size measurement made the whole thing too cumbersome, and that the cumbersomeness might somehow introduce error. There was something a bit sloppy about the methodology. I did not warm up to the idea, the more I thought about it, that the viewer was going to get a free sample merely by a telephone call. This was not real life. I was afraid that the free offer bit would result in such a high level of response that it would be impossible to differentiate between commercials.

Several weeks later it hit me. What we needed was an easy method of controlling audience size and who received the special offer, and a way to make the viewer pay at least something for his [or her] product. Couponing, properly designed, could provide the solution.

A simple method was devised, and pretesting was conducted on the couponing aspects to make sure that the price level was right. The entire test procedure required four steps: a screening telephone call, a coupon mailout, a telephone postcall, and measurement of coupon redemption.

The precall is made within a stated time period in advance of the television show that is to carry the test advertising. The respondent is asked about his or her viewing plans for the forthcoming period. The last brand purchased of each of several product groups is asked about. The product group for the brand of the test commercial is included.

Immediately following screening, each person stating that he or she intended to watch the test vehicle is sent a special coupon, good for the product advertised at a special, low price. This coupon is sent in the manufacturer's envelope, and so far as the recipient knows, has no connection with the survey. This is not a store coupon. To be redeemed, it must be sent to the manufacturer. However, it is made as easy as possible to redeem. A postage-paid return envelope is included, and all the recipient must do is insert the proper coins in a card prepared for this purpose, which includes his name and address. The coupon has an expiration date of one week from date of mailing, to prevent responses that are meaningless trickling in over a long time period. The procedure makes it possible to consider coupon responses only from those who viewed the program, which is crucial.

The day following the telecast, a call is made to each person who has said that he or she expected to view the particular program. The only purpose of the call is to determine whether the person has actually viewed the particular show. No question about advertising or about brands is asked.

13 SAMPLING FUNDAMENTALS

Learning Objectives

▶ Distinguish between census and sample.

▶ Know the differences between sampling and nonsampling errors.

▶ Learn the concepts of the sampling process.

▶ Describe probability and nonprobability sampling procedures.

▶ Determine sample size with ad hoc methods.

▶ Learn to deal with nonresponse problems.

▶ Understand sampling in the international context.

Marketing research often involves the estimation of a characteristic of some population of interest. For instance, the average level of usage of a park by community residents might be of interest; or information might be needed on the attitudes of a student body toward a proposed intramural facility. In either case, it would be unlikely that all members of the population would be surveyed. Contacting the entire population—that is, the entire census list—simply would not be worthwhile from a cost–benefit viewpoint. It would be both costly and, in nearly all cases, unnecessary, since a sample usually is adequately reliable. Further, it often would be less accurate, since nonsampling errors, like nonresponse, cheating, and data-coding errors, are more difficult to control. A **population** can be defined as the set of all objects that possess some common set of characteristics with respect to a marketing research problem.

SAMPLE OR CENSUS

A researcher typically is interested in the characteristics of a population. For example, if the proportion of people in a city watching a television show has to be determined, then the information can be obtained by asking every household in that city. If all the respondents in a population are asked to provide information, such a survey is called a **census.** The proportion of television viewers generate from a census is known as the **parameter.** On the other hand, a subset of all the households may be chosen and the relevant information could be obtained from that. Information obtained from a subset of the households is known as the **statistic** (from sample). Researchers then attempt to make an inference about the population parameter with the knowledge of the relevant sample statistic. A critical assumption in the process of inference is that the sample chosen is representative of the population. Estimation procedures and hypotheses tests are the types of inferences that link sample statistics and the corresponding population parameters.

When a Census Is Appropriate

A census would be appropriate if the population size itself is quite small. For example, a researcher may be interested in contacting all the firms in the petroleum industry to obtain information on the use of a particular software. A census also is conducted if information is needed from every individual/object in the population. For example, if the researcher is interested in determining the number of foreign students enrolled in a university, it is necessary to get information from all the departments in the university because of possible variations within each department. Further, if the cost of making an incorrect decision is high or if sampling errors are high, then a census may be more appropriate than a sample.

When a Sample Is Appropriate

Sampling may be useful if the population size is large and if both the cost and time associated with obtaining information from the population is high. Further, the opportunity to make a quick decision may be lost if a large population must be surveyed. Also, with sampling, in a given time period, more time can be spent on each interview (personal), thereby increasing the response quality. Additionally, it is easy to manage surveys of smaller samples and still exercise quality control in the interview process.

Sampling may be sufficient in many instances. For example, if a company is interested in obtaining reactions to installing a check-cashing operation within the premises, a sample of employees may be adequate. If the population being dealt with is homogeneous, then sampling is fine. Finally, if taking a census is not possible, then sampling is the only alternative. For example, if a researcher is interested in obtaining consumer response from all over the world to a new advertising theme for Coca-Cola, a census is not possible.

Error in Sampling

Execution of a research project always introduces some error in the study. As stated in Chapter 4, the total error in a research study is the difference between the true value (in the population) of the variable of interest and the observed value (in the sample). The total error in the study has two major components: sampling and nonsampling errors. If the difference in value (error) between the population parameter and the sample statistic is only because of sampling, then the error is known as **sampling error.** If a population is surveyed and error is observed, this error is known as a **nonsampling error.** Nonsampling errors can be observed in both a census and a sample.[1] Some of the common sources of nonsampling errors include measurement error, data-recording error, data analysis error, and nonresponse error. The sources of nonsampling errors are discussed in greater detail in Chapter 4.

Because of their nature, sampling errors can be minimized by increasing the sample size. However, as sample size is increased, the quality control of the research study may become more difficult. Consequently, nonsampling errors can increase (for example, the number of nonresponses can go up), thereby setting up a classic trade-off between sampling and nonsampling errors. Since nonsampling errors can occur from various sources, it is difficult to identify and control them. Therefore, more attention should be given to reducing them.

SAMPLING PROCESS

When a decision is made to use a sample, a number of factors must be taken into consideration. The various steps involved in the sampling process are given in Figure 13-1. The major activities associated with the sampling process are: (1) identifying the target population, (2) determining the sampling frame, (3) resolving the differences, (4) selecting a sampling procedure, (5) determining the relevant sample size, (6) obtaining information from respondents, (7) dealing with the nonresponse public, and (8) generating the information for decision-making purposes.

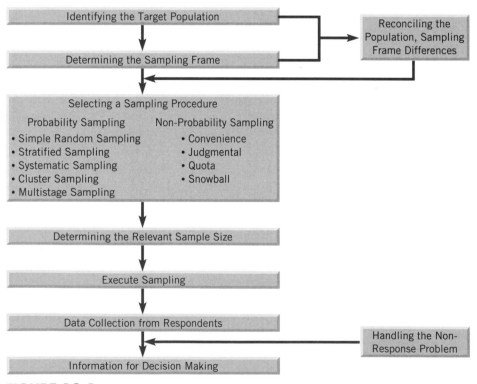

FIGURE 13-1
The sampling process

Determining the Target Population

Sampling is intended to gain information about a population. Thus, it is critical at the outset to identify the population properly and accurately. If the population is fuzzily defined, the results will be fuzzy also. If the population is defined improperly, the research probably will answer the wrong question as a result. For example, if some research questions involve prospective car buyers and the population contains all adults with driver's licenses, the research output will be unlikely to provide the relevant information.

A target population for a toy store can be defined as "all households with children living in Houston." The ambiguities with this definition are many:

▶ How do you define children? Are they below 10 years, 13 years, or 16 years?

▶ How do you define Houston? Does it include only the metropolitan area, or suburbs are also included?

▶ Who in the household is going to provide the information?

Therefore, the definition of a target population should contain information on sampling elements (children or parent), sampling units (households with children), and area of coverage (Standard Metropolitan Statistical Area [SMSA] or greater Houston).

Although the definition of the **target population** is important, it often is neglected because it seems obvious and noncontroversial. But considerable effort in identifying the target population usually will pay off. The following guidelines should be considered

Look to the Research Objectives. If the research objectives are well thought out, the target population definition will be clear as well. Recall from Chapter 3 that the research objectives include the research question, the research hypothesis, and a statement of the research boundaries. Each of these elements contributes to refining the definition of the target population. For example, the research question might involve how business firms in Chicago would react to a particular pricing method for advertising in the Yellow Pages of the telephone directory. The hypothesis might indicate that retailers of different types needed to be sampled. The consideration of the research boundary could restrict the population to metropolitan Chicago. Thus, the target population would be retail business firms in metropolitan Chicago.

Consider Alternatives. It is rare to find a study for which there are no alternative, reasonable, target population definitions. The task really is to identify and evaluate several of the alternatives instead of simply assuming that the first one mentioned is appropriate. For example, suppose the task is to determine the relative importance of such features as compactors, saunas, and patios, in medium-priced homes. The target population could be present owners of medium-priced homes, shoppers in middle-income shopping centers, those who might upgrade their homes, or clients of real estate firms. The choice will depend on the research objectives. The key point is to recognize that alternative definitions exist.

Know Your Market. If the research objective is to learn about the market response to some element of the marketing program, it is necessary to know something about the market. One may hope that some previous research will provide this type of information. Without it, the population definition will have to be unnecessarily broad and, therefore, will lead to an unnecessary increase in research expenses. For example, if a shopping center management were considering whether restaurants should be added to the center, the opinions of customers and potential customers would be desired. A key question for the population definition, especially if potential customers were to be reached, would be how large an area the shopping center draws. If previous studies show, for instance, that the center draws from a three-mile radius, that information will help in defining the target population.

Consider the Appropriate Sampling Unit. The target population consists of sampling units. A **sampling unit** may contain people, stores, households, organization transactions, products, or whatever. One task is to specify which sampling unit is appropriate. Is the interest in museums or in museum directors? Sometimes the choice is not clear. Should a study of banking activity or of leisure time activities use individuals or households? The choice will depend on the purpose of the study and perhaps on some judgments about consumer behavior. For example, if decisions about banking or leisure activities are thought to be family decisions, then the household might be the appropriate sampling unit. A respondent would report for the family. The assumption would be that family members are enough alike that responses within a family would tend to be similar. If, however, the decisions are assumed to be relatively independent among household members, then the sampling unit would be individuals instead of households.

Specify Clearly What Is Excluded. The specification of the target population should make clear what is excluded. A study of voting intentions on certain candidates and issues might restrict the sampling population to those of voting age and even to those who intend to vote or those who voted in the last election. If the election were in Cook County, for instance, it would be reasonable to restrict the population to those eligible to vote in Cook County.

Don't Overdefine. The population, of course, should be compatible with the study purpose and the research questions; however, the researcher should not arbitrarily overdefine the population. For example, a population of working wives between the ages of 25 and 30, earning more than $15,000 may be artificially restrictive. Such a restrictive population can generate a very costly design, because so many people need to be screened out to obtain the desired sample.

Should Be Reproducible. The population definition should be not so restrictive that it may not be reproducible at a later point in time. For example, if a researcher defines population as "all households living in the Kleine school district as of June 4, 1994," it would be hard to reproduce at a later date because of the time factor in the population definition. However, in certain studies, the time period may be a critical factor in the population definition.

Consider Convenience. When there is a choice, preference should be given to populations that are convenient to sample. Suppose that the population was to include those who are bothered by airplane noise. One population compatible with the research purpose might be those who live within one mile of an airport. This population would be easy and convenient to sample. Of course, the population should not be distorted for the sake of creating a convenient sample. A population of subscribers to *Sports Illustrated* may be convenient to sample, but may not be appropriate for the research purpose.

Determining the Sampling Frame

It is important to distinguish between the population and the sampling frame. The **sampling frame** usually is a list of population members used to obtain a sample. There might be a list of magazine subscribers, retail hardware stores, or college students; even a map can serve as a list.[2] Actually, the description of a sampling frame does not have to enumerate all population members. It may be sufficient to specify the procedure by which each sampling unit can be located. For instance, a member of a probability sample of school children could be obtained by randomly selecting a school district, a school, a classroom, and, finally, a pupil. The probability of picking any given pupil could be determined, even if a physical list were not created that included all students in the population.

Creating Lists. The biggest problem in simple random sampling is obtaining appropriate lists. The Donnelley Company maintains a list drawn from telephone directories and automobile registrations, which contains around 88 percent of U.S. households. Such a list can be used to get a national sample for a mail survey. Within a community, the local utility company will have a fairly complete list of the households.

The problem, of course, is that lists do not exist for specialized populations. For example, there is no list of high-income people, mothers, tennis players, or cyclists. A solution for this problem that is usually unsatisfactory is just to use a convenient list. For example, for tennis players, a list of subscribers to *Tennis World* or membership lists in tennis clubs might be available. Obviously, neither would be representative of the entire tennis-playing population, but still might be useful for some purposes. When lists that do not match the population are used, biases are introduced that should be considered. For instance, readers of *Tennis World* will be much more involved and knowledgeable than the average tennis player. A list of residents of a given community will not include new arrivals nor people living in dwellings built since the list was created. Thus, whole new subdivisions can be omitted. If such omissions are important, it can be worthwhile to identify new construction areas and design a separate sampling plan for them.

Sometimes several lists are combined in the hope of obtaining a more complete representation of the population. For example, subscribers to *Tennis World* and *Tennis Today* might be combined with a list of those who had purchased tennis equipment through a mail-order catalog. This approach, however, introduces the problem of duplication. Those appearing on several lists will have an increased chance of being selected. Removing duplication can be expensive and must be balanced against the bias that is introduced.

Another problem with lists is simply that of keeping them current. Many industrial firms maintain lists of those who have expressed interest in their products, and these are used in part for the mailing of promotional material. Similarly, many organizations, such as charities, symphony groups, and art galleries, have lists of various types; but these lists can become outdated quickly as people move and change jobs within an organization.

Creating Lists for Telephone Interviewing. As might be expected, there is extensive use of telephone directories as a basis for generating a sample. The concern with the use of directories is that population members may be omitted because they have changed residences, requested an unlisted number, or simply do not have a telephone.[3]

The incidence of unlisted numbers is extensive and varies dramatically from area to area. The percentage of unlisted phones in the major metropolitan areas ranges from 12.4 percent in West Palm Beach, Florida, to 64.6 percent in Las Vegas, Nevada, according to a study done by Survey Sampling, a firm that provides telephone samples for the market research industry.[4] Table 13-1 lists the top twenty metropolitan areas with the highest levels of unlisted numbers. Nationally, 30.4 percent of the phones were unlisted in 1993, up from 21.8 percent in 1984 and 10 percent in 1965.

About 20 percent of the unlisted numbers comprise people who have moved and have not had a chance to get a number listed. The other 80 percent (unlisted by choice) are people motivated to avoid crank or prank callers, telemarketers, bill collectors, or other unwanted callers. Those with unlisted numbers differ from other telephone subscribers. Demographically, these households tend to be younger, more urban, and less likely to own single-family dwelling units. Households that are unlisted by choice tend to have a higher-than-average income. Households that are unlisted by circumstance tend to be lower income. Lower-income households own fewer automobiles, are less educated, and tend to be non-white. One study showed that of those requesting unlisted telephones, 42 percent were female, whereas 32 percent of the other subscribers were female.

One way to reach unlisted numbers, dialing numbers randomly, can be very costly, because many of the numbers will be unassigned or will be business numbers.[5] A variant starts from a sample of listed telephone numbers. The number called is then the number drawn from the directory, plus some fixed number like 10. Of course, this method still will result in reaching some non-working numbers. A study using this approach, conducted in two Colorado communities (Sterling and Boulder), resulted in 10 percent nonworking numbers in Sterling and 29 percent in Boulder.[6]

TABLE 13-1
Top 20 Unlisted Markets (Of the Top 100 Metropolitan Areas)

Sacramento, CA PMSA	64.7
Los Angeles-Long Beach, CA PMSA	64.6
Oakland, CA PMSA	64.4
Fresno, CA	64.0
San Jose, CA PMSA	63.2
San Diego, CA	61.1
Riverside-San Bernardino, CA PMSA	60.3
Orange County, CA PMSA	60.1
Ventura, CA PMSA	58.7
Bakersfield, CA	58.0
Las Vegas, NV-AZ	57.7
San Francisco, CA PMSA	57.1
Jersey City, NJ PMSA	47.9
Tacoma, WA PMSA	42.5
Portland-Vancouver, OR-WA PMSA	40.7
Detroit, MI PMSA	40.3
Tucson, AZ	39.9
Miami, FL PMSA	38.2
Phoenix-Mesa, AZ	38.2
Honolulu, HI	37.9

Source: "Sacramento Most Unlisted Market For 1993," Survey Sampling, Inc: March 1994.

The method of adding a fixed number to a listed telephone number will not include those who are in a new series of numbers being activated by the telephone company. Seymour Sudman of The Survey Research Laboratory of the University of Illinois, a researcher long interested in sampling issues, therefore suggests that the last three digits in a listed telephone number be replaced by a three-digit random number. He indicates that the coverage will then increase and that half of the resulting numbers generally will be nonworking numbers.[7]

Another approach is to buy lists from magazines, credit card firms, mail-order firms or other such sources. One problem is that each such list has its own type of biases.

Sometimes it is possible to define the population to match the sampling frame exactly. Usually, however, an exact match is not possible and the task is to consider what portions of the population are excluded by the sampling frame and what biases are therefore created. For example, a list of a city's residents will exclude those in new housing developments. The question is, how many are in this category, and will their responses to the survey be different than the others? The existence of such biases usually will not affect the study's usefulness, as long as the biases are identified and the interpretation of the results takes them into consideration.

Dealing with Population-Sampling-Frame Differences. When a sampling frame does not coincide with a population definition, three types of problems arise: the subset problem, the superset problem, and the intersection problem. A **subset** problem occurs when the sampling frame is smaller than the population. In other words, some of the elements in the population will not be present in the sampling frame. For example, if a researcher is using the Dun & Bradstreet small business list for contacting all firms with less than a thousand employees, then a subset problem occurs. The D & B small business list contains names of firms with less than 500 employees. To deal with the subset problem, a researcher may have to redefine the population in terms of sampling frame or get information from other sources to match up with population.

A **superset** problem occurs when the sampling frame is larger than the population but contains all the elements of the population. For example, a researcher may be interested in contacting the buyers of Revlon lipstick. However, if the sampling frame contains a list of buyers of all of Revlon cosmetics, then a superset problem occurs. To deal with a superset problem, a researcher may pose a filter question such as "Do you buy Revlon lipsticks"; if "yes," that person will be included in the sample.

Finally, the most serious of these types of problems, an **intersection problem,** occurs when some elements of the population are omitted from the sampling frame, and when the sampling frame contains more elements than the population. Assume a researcher is interested in contacting small business owners with at least $4 million in sales. If the researcher uses the American Business list which contains all businesses (not strictly small businesses) with over $5 million in sales, an intersection problem results. To deal with such problems, a researcher may not only have to redefine the population but also may have to pose a better question.

Selecting a Sampling Procedure

There are many ways of obtaining a sample and many decisions associated with generating a sample. A researcher should first choose between using a Bayesian procedure and a traditional sampling procedure. Next, a decision is made to sample with or without replacement. Most of the marketing research projects employ a traditional sampling method without replacement, because a respondent is not contacted twice to obtain the same information. Among traditional sampling procedures, some are informal or even casual. Passers-by may be queried as to their opinions of a new product. If the response of everyone in the population is uniform—they all either love it or hate it—such an approach may be satisfactory. If you want to determine whether the water in a swimming pool is too cold, it isn't necessary to take a random sample; you just have to test the water at any one place, because the temperature will be constant throughout.

In most cases, however, the situation is more complex. There are several questions to be answered and a wide variability in responses. It is then necessary to obtain a representative sample of the population consisting of more than a handful of units. It is possible, even necessary in some cases, to obtain a sample representative of the population just by using judgment and common sense.

The preferred approach, however, is to use probability sampling (where some randomization process is used) to obtain a representative sample. In **probability sampling,** all population members have a known probability of being in the sample. In most probability sampling procedures, a sampling frame is needed and information on objects/sampling units is necessary prior to employing the sampling process.

Probability sampling has several advantages over nonprobability sampling. First, it permits the researcher to demonstrate the sample's representativeness. Second, it allows an explicit statement as to how much variation is introduced, because a sample is used instead of a census of the population. Finally, it makes possible the more explicit identification of possible biases.

In the next two sections, probability sampling will be described first, followed by a description and comparison of nonprobability sampling methods.

PROBABILITY SAMPLING

Probability sampling involves four considerations. First, the target population—the group about which information is being sought—must be specified. Second, the method for selecting the sample needs to be developed. Third, the sample size must be determined. The sample size will depend upon the accuracy needs, the variation within the population, and the cost. Finally, the nonresponse problem must be addressed.

Selecting the Probability Sample

Various methods can be used to select a probability sample. The simplest, conceptually, is termed **simple random sampling.** It not only has practical value, but it is a good vehicle for gaining intuitive understanding of the logic and power of random sampling.

Simple Random Sampling. Simple random sampling is an approach in which each population member, and thus each possible sample, has an equal probability of being selected. The implementation is straightforward. Put the name of each person in the population on a tag and place the tags in a large bowl. Mix the contents of the bowl thoroughly and then draw out the desired number for the sample. Such a method, using birth dates, was, in fact, used to select the order in which men would be drafted for military service during the Vietnam War. Despite the fact that the bowl was well mixed, the early drawing revealed a much higher number of December dates than January dates, indicating that the randomizing process can be more involved than it seems. The apparent reason was that the December tags were put in last, and the mixing was not sufficient to create a random draw. The solution was to randomize the order in which the dates were placed in the bowl.[8]

The use of a table of random numbers usually is much more practical than the use of a large bowl. A random-number table is a long list of numbers, each of which is computer generated by randomly selecting a number from 0 to 9. It has the property that knowledge of a string of 10 numbers gives no information about what the eleventh number is. Suppose a sample is desired from a list of 5000 opera-season-ticket holders. A random-number table such as that shown in Table 13-2 might provide the following set of numbers:

$$7569/0783/4710/3749/7741/2960/0016/9347$$

Using these numbers, a sample of five would be created that would include these ticket holders:

$$0783/4710/3749/2960/0016$$

The numbers above 5000 are disregarded, because there are no season-ticket holders associated with them.

The researcher can start anywhere in the random-number table, as long as the choice is made before looking at the numbers. It isn't fair to discard some numbers from the table because "they don't look random" or because they are not "convenient" for some reason or other.

If the original list of season-ticket holders were randomly arranged, a result equivalent to the computer-generated list could be obtained by taking the first ticket holders in the list. However, there is always the danger that the list may have some subtle deviations from a random order. Perhaps it was prepared according to the order in which the tickets were purchased; thus, the more interested and organized patrons would be early on the list. The use of random numbers eliminates such concerns.

Accuracy–Cost Trade-off. The trade-off between the cost of employing a probability sampling procedure and the resulting accuracy can best be described by the term **sampling efficiency,** or **efficiency of sampling,** which is defined as the ratio of accuracy over cost. In general, the higher the cost, the higher the

TABLE 13-2
A Set of Random Numbers

55	38	32	99	55	62	70	92	44	32
87	63	93	95	17	81	83	83	04	49
11	59	44	39	58	81	09	62	08	66
82	93	67	50	45	60	33	01	07	98
31	40	45	33	12	36	23	47	11	85
24	38	77	63	99	89	85	29	53	93
57	68	48	78	37	87	06	43	97	48
44	84	11	59	73	56	45	65	99	24
65	60	59	52	06	03	04	79	88	44
98	24	05	10	07	88	81	76	22	71
59	67	80	91	41	63	18	63	13	34
76	59	07	83	47	10	37	49	54	91
77	41	29	60	00	16	93	47	54	91
28	04	61	59	37	31	66	59	97	38

Reprinted courtesy of Beta Research. Copyright © 1987, 88
Robert Leighton.

accuracy. The simple random sampling process has some sampling efficiency associated with it. Researchers are always interested in increasing the sampling efficiency, and the various attempts to increase it have resulted in different probability sampling techniques. The feasible ways to increase the sampling efficiency include: (1) holding the accuracy constant and decreasing the cost, (2) holding the cost constant and increasing the accuracy, (3) increasing the accuracy at a faster rate than the rate of cost increase, and (4) decreasing the accuracy at a slower rate than the rate of cost decrease. The subsequent probability sampling procedures are the result of the attempts to increase the sampling efficiency in the above-described ways.

Stratified Sampling. In simple random sampling, a random sample is taken from a list (or sampling frame) representing the population. Often, some information about subgroups within the sample frame can be used to improve the efficiency of sampling. **Stratified sampling** improves the sampling efficiency by increasing the accuracy at a faster rate than the cost increase. The rate of increases of both accuracy and cost depends on the variable(s) used to form the groups and the strength of association between the measure of interest (e.g., attitudes) and the variable(s) used to form the groups.

Suppose information is needed on the attitudes of students toward a proposed new intramural athletic facility. Let us assume that there are three groups of students in the school: off-campus students, dormitory dwellers, and those living in fraternity and sorority houses. Assume, further, that those living in fraternities and sororities have very homogeneous attitudes toward the proposed facility; that is, the variation, or variance, in their attitudes is very low. Suppose also, that the dormitory dwellers are less homogeneous and that the off-campus students vary widely in their opinions. In such a situation, instead of allowing the sample to come from all three groups randomly, it will be more sensible to take fewer members from the fraternity/sorority group and draw more from the off-campus group. We would separate the student body list into the three groups and draw a simple random sample from each of the three groups, resulting in stratified sampling.

The sample size of the three groups will depend on two factors. First, it will depend on the amount of attitude variation in each group. The larger the variation, the larger the sample. Second, the sample size will tend to be inversely proportional to the cost of sampling. The smaller the cost, the larger the sample size that can be justified. (Sample-size formulas for stratified sampling are introduced in Chapter 14.)

In developing a sample plan, it is wise to look for natural subgroups that will be more homogeneous than the total population. Such subgroups are called "strata." Thus, there will be more homogeneity within the "strata" compared to between the "strata." In fact, the accuracy of stratified sampling is increased if there are dissimilarities between the groups, and similarities within the groups, with respect to the measure of interest.

The major difference among the different types of stratified sampling processes is in the selection of sample sizes within each group. The different types of stratified sampling are described below.

Proportional Stratified Sampling. In this type of sampling procedure the number of objects/sampling units chosen from each group is proportional to the number in the population. **Proportional stratified sampling** can further be classified as **directly proportional** and **inversely proportional stratified sampling.** Examples of both types of proportional stratified sampling are provided here.

Directly Proportional Stratified Sampling. Assume that a researcher is evaluating customer satisfaction for a beverage that is consumed by a total of 600 people. Among the 600 people, 400 are brand loyal and 200 are variety-seekers. Past research indicates that the level of customer satisfaction is related to consumer characteristics, such as being either brand-loyal or variety-seeking. Therefore, it should be beneficial to divide the total population of 600 consumers into two groups of 400 and 200 each, and randomly sample from within each of the two groups. If a sample size of 60 is desired, then a 10 percent directly proportional stratified sampling is employed.

Consumer Type	Group Size	10 Percent Directly Proportional Stratified Sample Size
Brand Loyal	400	40
Variety Seeker	200	20
Total	600	60

Inversely Proportional Stratified Sampling. Assume, now, that among the 600 consumers in the population, say 200 are heavy drinkers and 400 are light drinkers. If a researcher values the opinion of the heavy drinkers more than that of the light drinkers, more people will have to be sampled from the heavy drinkers group. In such instances, one can use an inversely proportional stratified sampling. If a sample size of 60 is desired, a 10 percent inversely proportional stratified sampling is employed.

Consumer Type	Group Size	10 Percent Inversely Proportional Stratified Sample Size
Heavy drinker	200	40
Light drinker	400	20
Total	600	60

In the inversely proportional stratified sampling, the selection probabilities are computed as follows:

Denominator $= > \dfrac{600}{200} + \dfrac{600}{400} = 3 + 1.5 = 4.5$

Heavy Drinkers proportion and sample size $= > \dfrac{3}{4.5} = 0.667; 0.667 \times 60 = 40$

Light Drinkers proportion and sample size $= > \dfrac{1.5}{4.5} = .333; 0.333 \times 60 = 20$

Disproportional Stratified Sampling. In stratified sampling, when the sample size in each group is not proportional to the respective group sizes, it is known as **disproportional stratified sampling.** When multiple groups are compared and their respective group sizes are small, a proportional stratified sampling would not yield a sample size large enough for meaningful comparisons, and a disproportional stratified sampling is used. One way of selecting sample sizes within each group would be to have equal group sizes in the sample. In the example of heavy and light drinkers, a researcher could have selected 30 people from each of the two groups.

In general, stratified sampling is employed in many research projects, because it is easy to understand and execute.

Cluster Sampling. In **cluster sampling,** the sampling efficiency is improved by decreasing cost at a faster rate than accuracy. Like stratified sampling, cluster sampling is a two-step process. Unlike stratified sampling, the process of cluster sampling involves dividing the population into subgroups, here termed as clusters instead of strata. This time, however, a random sample of subgroups/clusters is selected and all members of the subgroups are interviewed. Even though cluster sampling is very cost effective, it has its limitations. Cluster sampling results in relatively imprecise samples, and it is difficult to form heterogenous clusters because, for example, households in a block tend to be similar rather than dissimilar.[9]

Cluster sampling is useful when subgroups that are representative of the whole population can be identified.

Suppose a sample of high school sophomores who took an English class was needed in a Midwestern city. There were 200 English classes, each of which contained a fairly representative sample with respect to student opinions on rock groups, the subject of the study. A cluster sample would randomly select a number of classrooms, say 15, and include all members of those classrooms in the sample. The big advantage of cluster sampling is lower cost. The subgroups or clusters are selected so that the cost of obtaining the desired information within the cluster is much smaller than if a simple random sample were obtained. If the average English class had 30 students, a sample of 450 could be obtained by contacting only 15 classes. If a simple random sample of 450 students across all English classes were obtained, the cost probably would be significantly greater. The big question, of course, is whether the classes are representative of the population. If the classes from the upper-income areas have different opinions about rock groups than classes with more lower-income students, then the assumption underlying the approach would not hold. The differences between stratified sampling and cluster sampling are striking. A comparison between the stratified sampling process and the cluster sampling process is given in Table 13-3.

Systematic Sampling. Another approach, termed **systematic sampling,** involves systematically spreading the sample through the list of population members. Thus, if the population contained 10,000 ($=N$) people and a sample size of 1000 ($=n$) were desired, every tenth ($=I$, sampling interval) person would be selected for the sample. A starting point could be randomly chosen between the first name and the Ith name initially, and then every I^{th} name would be chosen. Although in nearly all practical examples such a procedure would generate a sample equivalent to a simple random sample, the researcher should be aware of regularities in the list. Suppose, for example, that a list of couples in a dance club routinely placed the female's name first. Then selecting every tenth name would result in a sample of all males.

In general, the sampling efficiency of systematic sampling is improved by lowering costs while maintaining accuracy relative to simple random sampling.

TABLE 13-3
A Comparison of Stratified and Cluster Sampling Processes

Stratified sampling	Cluster sampling
Homogeneity within group	Homogeneity between groups
Heterogeneity between groups	Heterogeneity within groups
All groups are included	Random selection of groups
Random selection of group members	All group members included
Sampling efficiency improved by increasing accuracy at a faster rate than cost	Sampling efficiency improved by decreasing cost at a faster rate than accuracy

However, the sampling efficiency of systematic sampling depends on the ordering of the list.

If the list of elements in the sampling frame is arranged in a random order (alphabetical), then the accuracy of systematic sampling may be equal to that of simple random sampling. If the elements (firms) are arranged in a monotonic order (increasing sales revenues), then the accuracy of systematic sampling would exceed that of a simple random sampling, because the sample would be representative (include firms from low to high sales revenues) of the population. Finally, if the elements are arranged in a cyclical order (days of the week) and a sampling interval of seven is selected, then a researcher studying the consumer visits to a theater would be collecting data from the same day of the week, resulting in a lower accuracy than simple random sampling.

One situation in which systematic sampling is risky is the sampling of time periods. Suppose the task was to estimate the weekly traffic flow on a certain street. If every twelfth 10-minute period were selected, then the sampling point would be the same each day, and periods of peak travel or low usage easily could be missed.

A common use of systematic sampling is in telephone surveys. A number like seventeen could be obtained from a random-number table. Then the seventeenth name on each page of a telephone directory would be a sample member. (Actually, a random number of inches from the top of the page would be used, so that names would not have to be counted.) Of course, more than one name could be selected from each page if a larger sample were needed, or every other (or every third or fourth) page could be used if a smaller sample were desired.

Multistage Design

It is often appropriate to use a **multistage design** in developing a sample. Perhaps the most common example is in the case of area samples, in which a sample of some area such as the United States or the state of California is desired.

Suppose the need was to sample the state of California. The first step would be to develop a cluster sample of counties in the state. Each country would have a probability of being in the cluster sample proportionate to its population. Thus, the largest county—Los Angeles County—would be much more likely to be in the sample than a rural county. The second step would be to obtain a cluster sample of cities from each county selected. Again, each city is selected with a probability proportionate to its size. The third step is to select a cluster sample of blocks from each city, again weighing each block by the number of dwellings in it. Finally, a systematic sample of dwellings from each block is selected, and a random sample of members of each dwelling is obtained. The result is a random sample of the area, in which each dwelling has an equal chance of being in the sample. Note that individuals living alone will have a greater chance of being in the sample than individuals living in dwellings with other people.

To see how a cluster sample of cities is drawn so that the probability of each being selected is proportionate to its population, consider the following

"And don't waste your time canvassing the whole building, young man. We all think alike."

Drawing by Stevenson; Copyright © 1980. The New Yorker Magazine, Inc.

example. Suppose there are six cities in Ajax County. In Table 13-4, the cities, plus the rural area, are listed together with their population sizes and the "cumulative population." The cumulative population serves to associate each city with a block of numbers equal in size to its population. The total population of Ajax County is 100,000. The task is to select one city from the county, with

TABLE 13-4
Cities in Ajax County

City	Population	Cumulative Population
Concord	15,000	1–15,000
Mountain View	10,000	15,001–25,000
Filmore	60,000	25,001–85,000
Austin	5,000	85,001–90,000
Cooper	2,000	90,001–92,000
Douglas	5,000	92,001–97,000
Rural area	3,000	97,001–100,000

the selection probability proportionate to the city population. The approach is simply to obtain a random number between 1 and 100,000. Taking the fourth row of Table 13-2 and starting from the right we get the number 89,701. The selected city would be the only with a cumulative population corresponding to 89,701: Austin. Clearly, the largest city, Filmore, would have the best chance of being drawn (in fact, a 60 percent chance), and Cooper the smallest chance (only 2 percent).

Large marketing research firms develop a set of clusters of dwellings after each U.S. census. The clusters may be counties or some other convenient grouping of dwellings. Perhaps 100 to 300 such areas are selected randomly. Each area will have a probability of being selected proportional to the population within its boundaries. This set of clusters then would be used by the marketing research firm for up to 10 years for their national surveys. For each area, data are compiled, on blocks and on living units within blocks. For rural areas, these firms hire and train interviewers to be available for subsequent surveys. Respondents from each area are selected on the basis of a sampling scheme such as stratified sampling or on the basis of a multistage scheme.

NONPROBABILITY SAMPLING

In probability sampling, the theory of probability allows the researcher to calculate the nature and extent of any biases in the estimate and to determine what variation in the estimate is due to the sampling procedure. It requires a sampling frame—a list of sampling units or a procedure to reach respondents with a known probability. In **nonprobability sampling,** the costs and trouble of developing a sampling frame are eliminated, but so is the precision with which the resulting information can be presented. In fact, the results can contain hidden biases and uncertainties that make them worse than no information at all. These problems, it should be noted, are not alleviated by increasing the sample size. For this reason, statisticians prefer to avoid nonprobability sampling designs; however, they often are used legitimately and effectively.

Nonprobability sampling typically is used in situations such as (1) the exploratory stages of a research project, (2) pretesting a questionnaire, (3) dealing with a homogeneous population, (4) when a researcher lacks statistical knowledge, and (5) when operational ease is required. It is worthwhile to distinguish among four types of nonprobability sampling procedures: judgmental, snowball, convenience, and quota sampling.

Judgmental Sampling

In **judgmental sampling** an "expert" uses judgment to identify representative samples. For example, patrons of a shopping center might serve to represent the residents of a city, or several cities might be selected to represent a country.

Judgmental sampling usually is associated with a variety of obvious and not-so-obvious biases. For example, shopping center intercept interviewing can oversample those who shop frequently, who appear friendly, and who have extra time. Worse, there is no way of really quantifying the resulting bias and uncertainty, because the sampling frame is unknown and the sampling procedure is not well specified.

There are situations where judgmental sampling is useful and even advisable. First, there are times when probability sampling is either not feasible or prohibitively expensive. For example, a list of sidewalk vendors might be impossible to obtain, and a judgmental sample might be appropriate in that case.

Second, if the sample size is to be very small—say, under 10—a judgmental sample usually will be more reliable and representative than a probability sample. Suppose one or two cities of medium size were to be used to represent 200 such cities. Then it would be appropriate to pick judgmentally two cities that appeared to be the most representative with respect to such external criteria as demographics, media habits, and shopping characteristics. The process of randomly selecting two cities could very well generate a highly nonrepresentative set. If a focus-group interview of eight or nine people were needed, again, a judgmental sample might be a highly appropriate way to proceed.

Third, sometimes it is useful to obtain a deliberately biased sample. If, for example, a product or service modification were to be evaluated, it might be possible to identify a group that, by its very nature, should be disposed toward the modification. If it were found that they did not like it, then it could be assumed that the rest of the population would be at least as negative. If they liked it, of course, more research probably would be required.

Snowball Sampling

A snowball sampling is a form of judgmental sampling that is very appropriate when it is necessary to reach small, specialized populations. Suppose a long-range planning group wanted to sample people who were very knowledgeable about a new specialized technology, such as the use of lasers in construction. Even specialized magazines would have a small percentage of readers in this category. Further, the target group may be employed by diverse organizations, like the government, universities, research organizations, and industrial firms. Under a snowball design, each respondent, after being interviewed, is asked to identify one or more others in the field. The result can be a very useful sample. This design can be used to reach any small population, such as deep-sea divers, people confined to wheelchairs, owners of dunebuggies, families with triplets, and so on. One problem is that those who are socially visible are more likely to be selected.

Convenience Sampling

To obtain information quickly and inexpensively, a convenience sample may be employed. The procedure is simply to contact sampling units that are convenient—a church activity group, a classroom of students, women at a shopping center on a particular day, the first 50 recipients of mail questionnaires, or a few friends and neighbors. Such procedures seem indefensible, and, in an absolute sense, they are. The reader should recall, however, that information must be evaluated not "absolutely," but in the context of a decision. If a quick reaction to a preliminary service concept is desired to determine if it is worthwhile to develop it further, a convenience sample may be appropriate. It obviously would be foolish to rely on it in any context where a biased result could have serious economic consequences, unless the biases could be identified. A convenience sample often is used to pretest a questionnaire.

Quota Sampling

Quota sampling is judgmental sampling with the constraint that the sample include a minimum number from each specified subgroup in the population. Suppose a 1000-person sample of a city is desired and it is known how the population of the city is distributed geographically. The interviewers might be asked to obtain 100 interviews on the east side, 300 on the north side, and so on.

Quota sampling often is based on such demographic data as geographic location, age, sex, education, and income. As a result, the researcher knows that the sample "matches" the population with respect to these demographic characteristics. This fact is reassuring and does eliminate some gross biases that could be part of a judgmental sample; however, there are often serious biases that are not controlled by the quota sampling approach. The interviewers will contact those most accessible, at home, with time, with acceptable appearance, and so forth. Biases will result. Of course, a random sample with a 15 to 25 percent or more nonresponse rate will have many of the same biases. Thus, quota sampling and other judgmental approaches, which are faster and cheaper, should not always be discarded as inferior.

Researchers using quota sampling in order to meet the quotas sometimes overlook the problems associated with adhering to the quotas. For example, the researcher may match the marginal frequencies but not the joint frequencies. Assume that an oil company is interested in finding out if women assume responsibility for vehicle maintenance. The company is interested in interviewing women aged below 35 and with age equal to and above 35, as well as working women and nonworking women. Suppose the distribution of the population of women in a city ($N = 1000$) is as follows:

Population Characteristics

	<35 Years	35 Years and Above	Total	Percentage
Working Women	300	200	500	50
Nonworking Women	200	300	500	50
Total	500	500	1000	100
Percentage	50	50	100	

Assume that the researcher is interested in interviewing 100 women from this city and develops a quota system such that 50 percent of the sample should be working women and 50 percent of the sample should also be under 35 years old. A quota matrix can be developed for a sample size of 100.

	<35 Years	35 Years and Above	Total	Percentage
Working Women	50	0	50	50
Nonworking Women	0	50	50	50
Total	50	50	100	100
Percentage	50	50		

Sample Characteristics

In the above illustration, although the marginal frequencies (50% and 50%) in the sample match with those of the population, the joint frequencies (in each cell—30%, 20%, 20%, 30%) do not match. Researchers should take precautions to avoid making such errors when using quota sampling.

Determining the Sample Size

How large should the sample be? This question is simple and straightforward, but to answer it with precision is not so easy. Statistical theory does provide some tools and a structure with which to address the question, which will be described in more detail in Chapter 14.

Nonresponse Problems

The object of sampling is to obtain a body of data that are representative of the population. Unfortunately, some sample members become nonrespondents because they (1) refuse to respond, (2) lack the ability to respond, (3) are not at home, or (4) are inaccessible.

Nonresponse can be a serious problem. It means, of course, that the sample size has to be large enough to allow for nonresponse. If a sample size of 1000 is needed and only a 50 percent response rate is expected, then 2000 people will need to be identified as possible sample members. Second, and more serious, is the possibility that those who respond differ from nonrespondents in a meaningful way, thereby creating biases.

The seriousness of **nonresponse bias** depends on the extent of the nonresponse. If the percentage involved is small, the bias is small. Unfortunately, however, as the discussion in Chapter 9 made clear, the percentage can be significant. For example, a review of 182 telephone studies found a refusal rate of 28 percent.[10] Further, this level is likely to increase with the increase in the use of telemarketing, and the problem is generally more severe in home personal interviews and worse in mail surveys, where nonresponse of 90 percent is not uncommon.

The nonresponse problem depends on how the nonrespondents differ from the respondents particularly upon the key questions of interest. The problem is that the very act of being a nonrespondent often implies a meaningful difference. Nonrespondents to in-home interviews tend to be urban dwellers, single or divorced, employed, and from the higher social classes. A comparison of 100 nonrespondents to a telephone interview with 100 respondents revealed that responses were associated with older age, lower income, nonparticipation in the work force, interest in the question, and concern with invasion of privacy.[11] Clearly, the nonresponse problem can be substantial and significant in many studies, although its impact will depend on the context.

What can be done about the nonresponse problem? A natural tendency is to replace each nonrespondent with a "matched" member of the sample. For example, if a home is included in the sample but the resident is not at home, a neighbor may be substituted. The difficulty is that the replacement cannot be matched easily on the characteristic that prompted the nonresponse, such as being employed or being a frequent traveler. Three more defensible approaches are (1) to improve the research design to reduce the number of nonresponses, (2) to repeat the contact one or more times (callbacks) to try to reduce nonresponses, and (3) to attempt to estimate the nonresponse bias.

Improving the Research Design. In Chapter 9, the problem of refusals was discussed in some detail, along with suggestions on how to improve the research design to reduce the incidence of refusals. The challenge in personal and telephone interviewing is to gain initial interest and to generate rapport through interviewer skill and the design and placement of questions. In mail surveys, the task is to motivate the respondent to respond, through incentives and other devices. The number of not-at-homes can be reduced by scheduling calls with some knowledge of the respondents' likely activity patterns. For example, midday is obviously a bad time to reach employed homemakers. Sometimes it is useful to make a telephone appointment for an in-home interview, although this tactic may tend to increase the refusal rate.

Callbacks. Callbacks refer to overt new attempts to obtain responses. The use of callbacks is predicated on the assumption that they will generate a useful number of additional responses and that the additional responses will reduce meaningfully a nonresponse bias. If the nonresponse is due to refusals or the inability to respond, callbacks may not reduce significantly the number of nonrespondents. They are most effective for the not-at-home nonrespondent. For some surveys, it may be worthwhile to use as many as six callbacks to reduce the number of nonrespondents to acceptable levels, although the first and second callbacks are usually the most productive.[12] The efficiency of the callbacks will be improved by scheduling them at different times of the day and week.

In a mail survey, the callback is particularly important, because the nonresponse level can be high. As was noted in Chapter 9, it is common practice to remind nonrespondents at regular intervals.

Estimating the Effects of Nonresponse. One approach is to make an extra effort to interview a subsample of the nonrespondents. In the case of a mail survey, the subsample might be interviewed by telephone. In a telephone or personal survey, an attractive incentive, such as a worthwhile gift, might be employed to entice a sample of the nonrespondents to cooperate. Often, only some of the critical questions thought to be sensitive to a nonresponse bias are employed in this stage.

The Politz approach is based on the fact that not-at-homes can be predicted from a knowledge of respondents' frequency of being away from home.[13] The respondents are asked how many evenings they are usually at home (if the interviewing is to be done in the evening). This information serves to categorize them into groups that can serve to represent the not-at-home respondents. For instance, if a respondent usually is at home only one night a week, it might be assumed that there are six more similar ones among the nonrespondents. On any given night, there would be only one chance in seven of finding one home. Thus, on the average, six homes with people with this tendency to be away would have to be contacted to find one person at home. This respondent is therefore assumed to represent six of the nonrespondents. There are uncertainties introduced by this approach, but it does provide a way to proceed, especially when callbacks are costly.

SHOPPING CENTER SAMPLING

Shopping center studies in which shoppers are intercepted present some difficult sampling problems. As noted in Chapter 9, well over 20 percent of all questionnaires completed or interviews granted were store-intercept interviews.[14] One limitation with shopping center surveys is the bias introduced by the methods used to select the sample. In particular, biases that are potentially damaging to a study can be caused by the selection of the shopping center, the part of the shopping center from which the respondents are drawn, the time of day, and the fact that more frequent shoppers will be more likely to be selected. Sudman suggests approaches to minimize these problems and, in doing so, clarifies the nature of these biases.[15]

Shopping Center Selection

A shopping center sample usually will reflect primarily those families who live in the area. Obviously, there can be great differences between people living in a low-income neighborhood and those in a high-income, professional neighborhood. It is usually good policy to use several shopping centers in different neighborhoods, so that differences between them can be observed. Another concern is how representative the cities used are. When possible, several diverse cities should be used.

Sample Locations Within a Center

The goal usually is to obtain a random sample of shopping center visits. Because of traffic routes and parking, one entrance may draw from very different neighborhoods than another. A solution is to stratify by entrance location and to take a separate sample from each entrance. To obtain an overall average, the resulting strata averages need to be combined by weighing them to reflect the relative traffic that is associated with each entrance.

Suppose that a survey is employed to determine the average purchase during a shopping trip. Assume that there were two shopping mall entrances. Entrance A, which drew from a working-class neighborhood, averaged 200 shoppers per hour; while Entrance B, which drew from a professional suburb, averaged 100 shoppers per hour. Thus, 67 percent of shoppers used Entrance A and 33 percent of shoppers used Entrance B. Assume further that the Entrance A shoppers spent $60 on the average, while the Entrance B shoppers averaged $36. These statistics are tabulated as follows:

The estimate of the average dollar amount of the purchase made by a shopping center visitor would be the Entrance A average purchase plus the Entrance B average purchase, weighted by the proportion of shoppers represented, or

$$(0.67 * 60) + (0.33 * 36) = \$52$$

Sometimes it is necessary to sample within a shopping center, because the entrances are inappropriate places to intercept respondents. The location used to intercept shoppers can affect the sample. A cluster of exclusive women's stores will attract a very different shopper than the Sears store at the other end of the mall. A solution is to select several "respresentative" locations, determine from traffic counts about how many shoppers pass by each location, and then weigh the results accordingly.

A major problem is that refusals can increase if respondents are asked to walk a specific distance to an interviewing facility. The cost of increasing nonresponse may outweigh any increase in the sample's representativeness.

Time Sampling

Another issue is the time period. For example, people who work usually shop during the evening, on weekends, or during lunch hours. Thus, it is reasonable to stratify by time segments—such as weekdays, weekday evenings, and weekends— and interview during each segment. Again, traffic counts can provide estimates of the proportion of shoppers that would be in each stratum, so the final results can be weighted appropriately.

Sampling People Versus Shopping Visits

Obviously, some people shop more frequently than others and will be more likely to be selected in a shopping center sample. If the interest is in sampling shopping center visits, then it is appropriate to oversample those who shop more. If the goal is to develop a sample that represents the total population, however, it becomes important to adjust the sample so that it reflects the infrequent as well as the frequent shoppers.

One approach is to ask respondents how many times they visited the shopping center during a specified time period, such as the last four weeks. Those whose current visit was the only one during the time period would receive a weight of one. Those who visited two times would have a weight of one-half; those who visited three times would have a weight of one-third; and so on.

One industry researcher measured the impact of weighting results by the frequency of visiting a shopping center on the analysis of its four commercial studies.[16] He found that the weighing procedure did not affect either the demographic profiles or the values of the key questions in each study. He concluded that a frequent shopper bias should be a problem warranting the use of a weighing procedure only where there is some reason to suspect that the bias will affect a key question. For example, if a test of a Sears commercial was conducted in a mall with a Sears store, there could be a problem.

Another approach is to use quotas, which serve to reduce the biases to levels that may be acceptable. One obvious factor to control is respondents' sex, since women shop more than men. The interviewers can be instructed simply to sample an equal proportion of men and women. Another factor to control would be age, as those aged 25 to 45 tend to make more visits to shopping centers than do either younger or older shoppers.[17] Still another would be employment status, as unemployed people spend more time shopping than those employed.[18] The quotas would be set up so that the number sampled would be proportional to the number of the population. If 55 percent of the people were employed, then the quota should ensure that 55 percent of the sample was employed.

SAMPLING IN THE INTERNATIONAL CONTEXT

Sampling in the international context requires certain special care and is seldom an easy task. The major problems here are the absence of information on sampling frames in other countries, and one of sampling equivalence. The procedure to be followed when sampling for an international research is described briefly below.

Selecting the Sampling Frame

In domestic research, in order to determine the sampling frame, one has to first decide on the target population. Once the target population has been determined, the availability of a list of population elements from which the sample may be drawn should be assessed. In the international context, this frequently presents difficulties because of the paucity of information available in other countries. Even when sampling frames such as municipal lists, directories, and telephone books are available, they do not provide adequate coverage, particularly in less-developed countries, and hence give rise to frame error.

Another point of difference between sampling in the domestic and international context is that in the international context sampling may take place at a number of geographical levels. The most aggregate level is the world, the next being regions such as the Pacific Rim or Europe, following which are the country level units and then the subunits within each country. The level at which the sample is drawn will depend to a large extent on the specific product market, the research objectives, and the availability of lists at each level. Table 13-5 gives a few examples of lists for different levels of the sampling frame.

TABLE 13-5
The Different Levels of Sampling Frames

Levels	Examples of Sampling Lists
World	Bottin International Kelly's Manufacturers and Merchants Directory Financial Times, International Business and Company Yearbook
Regions	Directory of European Associations Europa Yearbook Regional Associations
Countries	National Associations Banking Associations Population Lists Telephone Listings
Cities	Municipal Lists Church Organizations List of Government Organizations Public Administration

Source: Susan P. Douglas and Samuel C. Craig, "International Marketing Research," Prentice Hall: Englewood Cliffs, New Jersey, 1983.

Once the sampling frame has been determined, the next step is to determine the specific respondent to be interviewed. The specific respondent in each country has to be identified as they may vary from country to country. For example, in some cultures (such as the oriental cultures) the parents buy toys without even consulting the children, whereas in some other cultures (Western cultures) the child is the decider. Hence, while conducting research about toys in some countries, the respondent will be adults, whereas in some it will be children.

Sampling Procedure

The next step in the sampling process is to determine the appropriate sampling procedure. In international research, the first decision that has to be taken in this context is whether research has to be conducted in all countries or whether results and findings are generalizable from one country to another. Ideally, it would be best if research is conducted in all the countries where marketing operations are planned. But given the high costs of multicountry research there is a trade-off between the number of countries in which the research can be conducted and the cost of the research project. In many cases, findings in one country can be used as a proxy for another. For example, the market response pattern in Denmark will be similar to those in the other Scandinavian countries.

Once the number of countries, or other sample units and the sequence in which they are to be investigated have been determined, the next step is selecting the appropriate **sampling technique.** The most appropriate sampling technique for domestic research is that of **random** or **probabilistic sampling,** but this may not always be true in the international context. Random sampling is a good technique only if there are comprehensive lists available of the target population. If such information does not exist, then conducting random sampling will lead to errors in sampling. Hence, probabilistic sampling techniques may not be the best for international research.

Researchers facing a paucity of information have two options open to them. Either they can obtain the required information themselves and construct a sampling list from which they can randomly sample, or they can adopt a **nonprobability sampling technique.** In the international context nonprobability sampling techniques are used more frequently than probability sampling techniques because of lack of information. Techniques such as convenience sampling, judgmental sampling, and quota sampling are used. One technique that is very popular in international research is the **snowball sampling technique.** In this technique, the initial respondents are selected at random and additional respondents are selected based on information given by the initial respondents. Two-phase sampling procedures also are frequently employed in order to reduce costs. In two-phase sampling, the data collection process is done in two stages. In the first phase, data is collected from the customers on certain characteristics such as purchase behavior, demographic variables, and so forth. Based on this information, a sampling frame is developed, and then a second sample is drawn from this frame.

A related issue that a researcher in the international context faces is whether to use the same sampling procedure across countries. Sampling procedures vary in reliability across countries. Therefore, instead of using one single sampling procedure in all the countries, it may be preferable to use different methods or procedures that have equivalent levels of accuracy or reliability. Further, costs of different sampling procedures may also differ from country to country. Hence, cost savings can be achieved by choosing the cheapest method in that country. Cost savings also can be achieved by using the same method in many countries, so that the cost of analysis, coding, and so on may be reduced because of economies of scale. Hence, the researcher has to weigh all these issues and make a decision.

Another important decision facing an international researcher concerns sample size. Given a fixed budget, the researcher has to decide on the number of countries he or she has to sample, and also on the number of respondents in each country. To statistically estimate sample sizes, some measure of population variance is required. Since this may not be available, in many instances the researcher determines the sample size on an ad hoc basis.

Summary

There are two methods by which one can obtain information on the population of interest. Census is the process of obtaining information about the population by contacting every member in the population. Sampling is the process of estimating a population parameter by contacting only a subset of the population. Sampling is adopted because of the limitations of time and money. In some cases a census may not be possible and sampling may be the only alternative.

The first step in the sampling process is to define the target population. The target population has to be defined in such a manner that it contains information on sampling elements, sampling units, and the area of coverage. In order to define the target population, certain simple rules of thumb should be adopted, such as looking to the research objectives, reproducibility, and convenience.

The next step is to determine the sampling frame. The sampling frame is usually a convenient list of population members that is used to obtain a sample. A number of biases will result if the sampling frame is not representative of the population. Hence, care should be taken to choose an appropriate list. There is extensive use of telephone directories as a basis for generating lists, but problems such as changed residences, unlisted numbers, and so forth, introduce biases in the sample.

Next, the mechanism for selecting the sample needs to be determined. There are essentially two different methodologies for sample selection. One is known as **probability sampling** where the probability theory is used to determine the appropriate sample. The **simple random sampling, cluster sampling, stratified sampling, systematic sampling,** and **multistage designs** are among the various available choices in probability sampling.

Nonprobability sampling methods, such as **judgmental sampling, snowball sampling,** and **quota sampling,** are appropriate in the right context, even though they can be biased and lack precise estimates of sampling variation. **Shopping-center sampling** is used widely, in part because it is relatively inexpensive. Biases in shopping-center samples can be reduced by adjusting the samples to reflect shopping-center characteristics, the location of the shoppers within the shopping center, the time period of the interviewing, and the frequency of shopping.

The fourth consideration in the process is determining the **sample size.** In Chapter 14 we will examine the various approaches to determining sample size.

The final consideration is **nonresponse bias.** Nonresponse bias can be reduced by improving the research design to reduce refusals and by using callbacks. Sometimes the best approach is to estimate the amount of bias and adjust the interpretation accordingly.

Sampling in international research poses some special problems. The absence of reliable sampling lists brings in a number of biases into the study. Moreover adopting the same sampling method in different countries may not yield the best results. Even if one adopts the same sampling procedure across all countries, sampling equivalence will not necessarily be achieved.

Questions and Problems

1. Develop a population list or sampling frame for an attitude study when the target population is
   a. All those who rode on a public transit system during the last month.
   b. Retail sporting good stores.
   c. Stores that sell tennis rackets.
   d. Watchers of evening television.
   e. High-income families.

    f. Adults over 18 years of age in California.

    g. Dwelling units with compactors.

    h. Users of unit pricing during the past week.

2. In Question 1, consider how the various populations might be stratified.

3. A manufacturer wanted to get opinions from 4000 hardware store managers on a new type of lawn mower. An associate provided a list of such stores, divided into 400 large and 3600 small stores. He drew a random sample of 200 stores and was disappointed to find only 19 large stores in the sample, since they represented more than 30 percent of the potential volume. A friend suggested that he draw a second sample. What do you recommend? What other pieces of information would you like to have?

4. A telephone survey is planned to determine the day-after recall of several test commercials to be run in Fargo, North Dakota. Design a telephone sampling plan.

5. The owners of a seven-store drugstore chain want to sample shoppers of their chain and shoppers of a competing chain, so that they can administer a 10-minute questionnaire. Develop alternative sampling plans. Recommend one and defend your recommendation.

6. A town planning group was concerned about the low usage of a library by its citizens. To determine how the library could increase its patronage, they planned to sample all library-card holders. Comment.

7. Assume that you have a list of 80 managers of research and development departments, who are numbered from 1 to 80. Further, you want to talk to a random sample of seven of them. Use the following random numbers to draw a sample of seven. Draw four additional samples. Calculate the average number in each case.

60311428243730443968059455937559 4967

76391450608085041765794444744 1288200

8. A concept for a new microcomputer designed for use in the home is to be tested. Because a demonstration is required, a personal interview is necessary. Thus, it has been decided to bring a product demonstrator into the home. The city of Sacramento has been selected for the test. The metropolitan-area map has been divided into a grid of 22,500 squares, 100 of which have been selected randomly. Interviewers have been sent out to call on homes within the selected square until five interviews are completed. Comment on the design. Would you make any changes?

9. The U.S. Department of Energy would like a census of power-generating windmills. How could such a census be obtained?

10. Use the random numbers in Table 13-2 to select a city from the set in Table 13-4.

11. A shopping center sample was used to evaluate a new product. Given the following data, what is your estimate of the proportion of people that say they will buy the product?

Time Period	Location of Shopping Center	Normal Store Traffic	Sample Size	Proportion of Sample Saying They Will Buy It
Weekdays	A	500	100	50
Evenings	A	200	100	25
Weekends	A	400	100	20
Weekdays	B	600	100	60
Evenings	B	250	100	30
Weekends	B	550	100	35

12. Discuss the differences between stratified sampling and cluster sampling.
13. Briefly describe the concept of sampling efficiency and discuss the ways in which it could be improved.
14. The sampling efficiency of systematic sampling can be greater than, less than, or equal to single random sampling. Discuss.
15. Identify a situation where you would be in favor of using a nonprobability method over a probability sampling method.
16. Discuss the differences between proportionate and disproportionate stratified sampling.
17. Pete Thames, the general manager of the Winona Wildcats, a minor league baseball team, is concerned about the declining level of attendance to the team's games in the past two seasons. He is unsure whether the decline is due to a national decrease in the popularity of baseball or factors that are specific to the Wildcats. Having worked in the marketing research department of the team's major league affiliate, the New Jersey Lights, Thames is prepared to conduct a study on the subject. However, because it is a small organization, there are limited financial resources available for the project. Fortunately, the Wildcats have a large group of volunteers who can be used to implement the survey. The study's primary objective is to discover the reasons why Winona residents are not attending games. A list of 1200 names, which includes all attenders for the past two seasons, is available as a mailing list.
    a. What is the target population for this study?
    b. What is the appropriate sampling frame for this study of the attitudes of both attenders and nonattenders?
    c. Which kind of sample would provide the most efficient sampling?
    d. Why would this method of sampling be the most efficient in this situation?
18. a. How does the sampling procedure employed in an international environment differ from that used domestically?
    b. What issues are relevant to a researcher's decision to use the same sampling procedure across countries?
19. Jane Walker is the founder and CEO of Sport Style, a sporting goods manufacturing company based in Louisville, Kentucky, that specializes in leather goods. The company currently is under contract to exclusively supply one of the leading sporting goods companies with Sport Style

accessories. That large multinational company markets the products under its own major company label as part of its "Made in the USA" promotional campaign. Sport Style has expanded its product line to include golf gloves; premium quality leather grips for tennis, squash, racquetball, and badminton rackets; and sports bags. The contract for exclusive supply will expire within the next year.

Ms. Walker has recently felt that Sport Style specialized products may not be best served by this method of distribution, and she believes that her company's sales revenue could drastically increase if Sport Style were to market its goods under its own label as a specialty good. This would allow the company to eliminate the intermediaries and their portion of the selling price. The specialty goods could be offered at the same price as is currently being asked, but without the intermediary Sport Style would get a larger proportion of the final retail sales price. Ms. Walker has decided to undertake a marketing research study to determine whether a market exists among retail outlets and sporting goods distributors for these specialty items, under the Sport Style brand name.

a. Define the target population for this study.
b. Suggest a suitable sampling frame.
c. Recommend a sampling procedure for this study and support your answer.

End Notes

1. H. Assael and J. Keon. "Non sampling Vs. Sampling Errors in Sampling Research," *Journal of Marketing,* Spring 1982, 114–123.
2. Edward Blair. "Sampling Issues in Trade Area Maps Drawn from Shopper Surveys," *Journal of Marketing,* 47, Winter 1983, 98–106.
3. For a comparison of directory-based sampling with other methods of sampling, see R. Czaja, J. Blair, and J. P. Sebestik. "Respondent Selection in a Telephone Survey: A Comparison of Three Techniques," *Journal of Marketing Research,* August 1982.
4. *Sacramento Most Unlisted Market for 1993,* Survey Sampling Inc., March 1994.
5. Clyde L. Rich. "Is Random Digit Dialing Really Necessary?" *Journal of Marketing Research,* 14, August 1977, 301–304.
6. E. Laird Landon, Jr. and Sharon K. Banks, "Relative Efficiency and Bias of Plus-One Telephone Sampling," *Journal of Marketing Research,* 14, August 1977, 294–299.
7. Seymour Sudman, *Applied Sampling* (New York: Academic Press), 1976, 0. 65.
8. Sudman, op. cit., p. 50.
9. Geographic clustering of rare populations, however can be an advantage. See Sudman, "Efficient Screening Methods for the Sampling of Geographically Clustered Special Populations," *Journal of Marketing Research,* 22, February 1985, 20–29.
10. Frederick Wiseman and Philip McDonald. "The Nonresponse Problem in Consumer Telephone Surveys" (Cambridge, Massachusetts: Marketing Science Institute), 1978.
11. Jolene M. Struebbe, Jerome B. Kernan, and Thomas J. Grogan. "The Refusal Problem in Telephone Surveys," *Journal of Advertising Research,* June/July 1986, 29–37.
12. In the late sixties the Survey Research Center, University of Michigan, found that when they made six or more calls, they reached 25 percent of the final sample on the first call, 33 percent on the first callback, and 17 percent on the second callback. The remaining 25 percent were reached on subsequent callbacks. William C. Dunkelberg and George S. Day. "Nonresponse Bias and Call-backs in Sample Surveys," *Journal of Marketing Research,* 10, May 1973, 160–168.
13. Alfred N. Politz and Willard R. Simmons. "An Attempt to Get 'Not-At-Homes' into the Sample Without Callbacks," *Journal of the American Statistical Association,* 44, March 1949, 9–31, and 45, March 1950, 136–137.
14. "Shoppers Grant 91 Million Interviews Yearly," *Survey Sampling Frame,* published by Survey Sampling, Inc., Spring 1978, p. 1.
15. Seymour Sudman. "Improving the Quality of Shopping Center Sampling," *Journal of Marketing Research,* 17, November 1980, 423–431.

16. Thomas D. DuPont, "Do Frequent Shoppers Distort Mall-Intercept Results?," *Journal of Advertising Research*, August/September 1987, 45–51.

17. Sudman, op. cit., 430.
18. Ibid., 430.

CASE 13-1
Exercises in Sample Design

In each of the following situations you are asked to make recommendations as to the type of sample to be used, the method of selecting the sample, and the sample size:

1. The manager of the appliance department of a local full-line department store chain is planning a major one-day nonprice promotion of food processors, supported by heavy advertising in the two local newspapers. The manager asks you to recommend a method of sampling customers coming into the department. The purpose is to assess the extent to which customers were drawn by the special advertisement, and the extent to which the advertisement influenced their intentions to buy. A pretest of the questionnaire indicates that it will take about three minutes to administer. The manager is especially interested in learning whether there are significant differences in the response to the questionnaire among (a) males versus females, (b) gift buyers versus other buyers, and (c) age groups.

2. A major airline wants to run a preliminary study on the attitudes of university students toward air travel. The company's research director already has submitted an interview plan and has estimated that, on average, each interview will require between an hour and an hour-and-a-half to administer. It is esti-

mated that the cost of interviewing and interpretating the interview will be roughly $75.00 per respondent.

3. A small Caribbean island relied heavily on tourist income. There was a need to develop a study so that an estimate could be provided each month as to
   a. The number of tourists
   b. The length of stay
   c. Their activities
   d. Their attitudes toward some programs and activities

The plan was to conduct a short interview with each respondent and to leave with them a short questionnaire to be completed and mailed after returning home.

Several sampling plans were considered. One would be to generate a random sample of hotel rooms and to interview each occupant. Another involved sampling every nth person that passed a predetermined point in the city. Still another was to sample departing planes and ships. There were about six plane departures and three ship departures per day. Design a sampling plan so that each month 500 tourists are obtained in the sample.

4. A sample of homeowners in the state of Illinois is desired for a major segmentation study conducted by a large financial institution. A lengthy personal interview lasting over one hour will be conducted with each respondent. A sample size of 3000 is targeted.

CASE 13-2
Talbot Razor Products Company

One of the products marketed by Talbot was an after-shave lotion called Enhance. This brand was sold through drugstores, supermarkets, and department stores. Sales exceeded $30 million per year but were barely profitable because of advertising expenses that exceeded $9 million. For some time the company and its advertising agency had felt the need to undertake a study to obtain more data on the characteristics of

their users as contrasted to those of other leading brands. Both the company and the agency believed that such information would help them find better ways to promote the Enhance brand.

Preliminary discussions between the advertising department and the research department of the advertising agency resulted in the following study objectives:

1. To determine the characteristics of Enhance users versus competitors' by such factors as age, income, occupation, marital status, family size, education, social class, and leisure time activities.

2. To determine the image of the Enhance brand versus competitors on such attributes as masculinity, expensiveness, and user stereotypes (such as young men, factory workers, young executives, and men living in small towns).
3. To discover the meaning to consumers of certain words that were used to describe after-shave lotions.
4. To examine the media habits of users by television programs, magazines, and newspapers.

In discussing the sampling universe, the advertising manager thought the study results should be broken down by heavy versus light users of Enhance. In the manager's opinion, as few as 15 to 20 percent of the users might account for 60 percent of the total purchases. It was not clear how many containers a user would have to buy during a specified time period to qualify as a heavy or a light user. The research director and the advertising manager disagreed on a definition of user: the research director thought that anyone who had used the Enhance product within the past year should qualify as a user and, therefore be included in the study, while the advertising manager thought that a user should be defined as one who had purchased the product within the past three months. In fact, the advertising manager went on to say, "I am really interested only in those people who say that the Enhance brand is their favorite brand or the brand that they purchase more than any other."

After much discussion about what constituted or should constitute a user, the research director pointed out that the advertising manager was being unrealistic about the whole sampling problem. A pilot study was conducted to determine how many qualified users could be obtained out of every 100 persons interviewed in Sacramento, California. While the findings were not completely representative, they did provide a crude estimate of the sampling problem and the costs that would result from using any kind of a probability sample. The research director said,

In the Sacramento study we were interested only in finding out how many males 18 years of age or older used after-shave, what brands they had purchased during the past year and the past three months, and what brand they bought most frequently. All interviewing took place during the evening hours and the weekend. The findings revealed that only about 70 percent of the male respondents were at home when the interviewer made the call. Of those who were home and who agreed to cooperate, only 65 percent were users of after-shave: that is, affirmatively answered the question: "Do you ever use after-shave?" Of those who used after-shave, only 7 percent had purchased the Enhance brand within the past three months, while 15 percent reported having purchased it within the past year. The costs of the Sacramento job figured out to about $6.00 per contact including the

not-at-homes, refusals, and completed interviews, all as contacts. The sample size for the Sacramento pilot study was 212 male respondents, and the field costs were $1272. These costs will be increased substantially if the sample includes smaller towns and farm interviews.

The research director believed that the best sample size they could hope for would be one that provided about 100 interviews with Enhance users plus 100 interviews with users of other brands in each of 10 to 15 metropolitan areas. This would provide a total sample size of 2000 to 3000 and would require contacts with between 40,000 and 50,000 respondents. The research director indicated that this size sample would permit breakdown of the results for the United States by heavy versus light users.

The advertising manager, who did not think this would be an adequate national sample, said,

I can't present these results to my management and tell them that they are representative of the whole country, and I doubt if the sample in each of the 10 to 15 metropolitan areas is big enough to enable us to draw reliable conclusions about our customers and noncustomers in that particular area. I don't see how you can sample each metropolitan area on an equal basis. I would think that the bigger areas such as New York and Chicago should have bigger samples than some of the smaller metropolitan areas.

The research director explained that this way of allocating the sample between areas was not correct since the size of the universe had no effect on the size of the sample. According to the director,

If we do it the way you are suggesting, it will mean that in some of the big metropolitan areas we'll end up with 150 to 200 interviews, while in some of the smaller ones, we'll have only 50 or 75 interviews. Under such conditions it would be impossible to break out the findings of each metropolitan area separately. If we sample each area equally, we can weigh the results obtained from the different metropolitan areas so as to get accurate U. S. totals.

When the discussion turned to costs, the advertising manager complained,

I can't possibly tell my management that we have to make 40,000 to 50,000 calls in order to get 2000 to 3000 interviews. They're going to tell me that we're wasting an awful lot of money just to find users. Why can't we find Enhance users by selecting a sample of drugstores and offering druggists some money for getting names and addresses of those men who buy after-shave. We could probably locate Enhance users for maybe 35 to 50 cents each.

The research director admitted that this would be a much cheaper way, but pointed out that it is not known what kind of sample would result, and therefore it would be impossible to tell anything at all about the reliability of the survey. The advertising manager thought management would provide no more than $30,000 for the study. The research director estimated that the results could be tabulated, analyzed, a report written, and the results presented to management for about $7000, thus leaving around $23,000 for fieldwork.

Questions for Discussion

1. How should the sampling universe be defined?
2. How large a sample should be collected?
3. How should the sample be distributed geographically?

14 SAMPLE SIZE AND STATISTICAL THEORY

Learning Objectives

▶ Discuss some ad hoc methods of determining sample size.

▶ Introduce the concepts of population characteristics and sample statistics.

▶ Discuss confidence intervals and interval estimation.

▶ Show how to calculate sample size for a simple random sample.

▶ Calculate sample sizes for stratified sample and also for multistage designs.

A practical question in marketing research often involves determining sample size. A survey cannot be planned or implemented without knowing the sample size. Further, the sample-size decision is related directly to research cost, and therefore must be justified.

This chapter presents several practical approaches to obtaining sample size. These approaches are extremely sensible, will lead to reasonable sample-size decisions, and, in fact, often are used in marketing research. There is, however, a formal approach to determining sample size using statistical theory. It is useful to understand this formal approach for several reasons. First, in some contexts it can be applied directly to make more precise sample-size decisions. Second, it can provide worthwhile guidance even when it may not be easy to apply the statistical theory. Finally, the discussion serves to introduce some important concepts and terms of sampling that, together, will generate a deeper understanding of the process. Among these terms and concepts are **population characteristics, sample characteristics, sample reliability,** and **interval estimation.** Each of them will be introduced, and then the question of **sample size** will be considered.

DETERMINING THE SAMPLE SIZE: AD HOC METHODS

The size of a sample can be determined either by using statistical techniques or through some ad hoc methods. Ad hoc methods are used when a person knows from experience what sample size to adopt or when there are some constraints, like budgetary constraint, which dictate the sample size. This section discusses a few common ad hoc methods for determining sample size.

Rules of Thumb

One approach is to use some rules of thumb. Sudman suggests that the sample should be large enough so that when it is divided into groups, each group will have a minimum sample size of 100 or more.[1]

Suppose the opinions of citizens regarding municipal parks were desired. In particular, an estimation is to be made of the percentage who felt that tennis courts were needed. Suppose, further, that a comparison was desired among those who (1) used parks frequently, (2) used parks occasionally, and (3) never used parks. Thus, the sample size should be such that each of these groups had at least 100 people. If the frequent park users, the smallest group, were thought to be about 10 percent of the population, then under simple random sampling a sample size of 1000 would be needed to generate a group of 100 subjects.

In almost every study, a comparison between groups provides useful information and is often the motivating reason for the study. It is therefore necessary to consider the smallest group and to make sure that it is of sufficient size to provide the needed reliability.

In addition to considering comparisons between major groups, the analysis might consider subgroups. For example, there might be an interest in breaking down the group of frequent park users by age, and comparing the usage by teenagers, young adults, middle-aged persons, and senior citizens. Sudman suggests that for such minor breakdowns the minimum sample size in each subgroup should be 20 to 50.[2] The assumption is that less accuracy is needed for the subgroups. Suppose that the smallest subgroup of frequent park users, the senior citizens, is about 1 percent of the population and it is desired to have 20 in each subgroup. Under simple random sampling, a sample size of about 2000 might be recommended in this case.

If one of the groups or subgroups of the population is a relatively small percentage of the population, then it is sensible to use **disproportionate sampling.** Suppose only 10 percent of the population watches educational television, and the opinions of this group are to be compared with those of others in the population. If telephone interviewing were involved, people might be contacted randomly until 100 people who do not watch educational television were identified. The interviewing then would continue, but all respondents would be screened, and only those who watch educational television would be interviewed. The result would be a sample of 200, half of which watch educational television.

Budget Constraints

Often there is a strict **budget constraint.** A museum director might be able to spare only $500 for a study, and no more. If data analysis will require $100 and a respondent interview is $5, then the maximum affordable sample size is 80. The question then becomes whether a sample size of 80 is worthwhile, or if the study should be changed or simply not conducted.

393

Comparable Studies

Another approach is to find similar studies and use their sample sizes as a guide. The studies should be **comparable** in terms of the number of groups into which the sample is divided for comparison purposes. They also should have achieved a satisfactory level of reliability.

Table 14-1, which is based on a summary of several hundred studies, provides a very rough idea of typical sample size. Note that the typical sample size tends to be larger for national studies than for regional studies. A possible reason is that the national studies generally address issues with more financial impact, and therefore require a bit more accuracy. Note, also, that samples involving institutions tend to be smaller than those involving people or households. The reason is probably that institutions are more costly to sample than people.

Factors Determining Sample Size

Sample size really depends on four factors. The first is the number of groups and subgroups within the sample that will be analyzed. The second is the value of the information in the study in general, and the accuracy required of the results in particular. At one extreme, the research need not be conducted if the study is of little importance. The third factor is the cost of the sample. A cost–benefit analysis must be considered. A larger sample size can be justified if sampling costs are low than if sampling costs are high. The final factor is the variability of the population. If all members of the population have identical opinions on an issue, a sample of one is satisfactory. As the variability within the population increases, the sample size also will need to be larger.

POPULATION CHARACTERISTICS/ PARAMETERS

Let us assume that we are interested in the attitudes of symphony season-ticket holders toward changing the starting time of weekday performances from 8:00 P.M. to 7:30 P.M. The population comprises the 10,000 symphony

TABLE 14-1
Typical Sample Sizes for Studies of Human and Institutional Populations

Number of Subgroup Analyses	People or Households		Institutions	
	National	**Regional or Special**	**National**	**Regional or Special**
None or few	1000–1500	200–500	200–500	50–200
Average	1500–2500	500–1000	500–1000	200–500
Many	2500+	1000+	1000+	500+

Source: Seymour Sudman. *Applied Sampling* (New York: Academic Press), 1976, p. 87.

season ticket holders. Their response to the proposal is shown in Figure 14-1. Of these ticket holders, 3000 responded "definitely yes" (which is coded as +2). Another 2000 would "prefer yes" (coded as +1), and so on. The needed information is the average, or **mean,** response of the population (the 10,000 season-ticket holders), which is termed

$$\mu = \text{the population mean} = 0.3$$

This population mean is one population characteristic of interest. Normally, it is unknown, and our goal is to determine its value as closely as possible, by taking a sample from the population.

Another population characteristic of interest is the population **variance,** σ^2, and its square root, the population **standard deviation, σ.** The population variance is a measure of the population dispersion, the degree to which the different season ticket holders differ from one another in terms of their attitude. It is based on the degree to which a response differs from the population average response, μ. This difference is squared (making all values positive) and averaged across all responses.[3] In our example, the population variance is

$$\sigma^2 = \text{the population variance} = 2.22$$

and

$$\sigma = \text{the population standard deviation} = 1.49$$

SAMPLE CHARACTERISTICS/STATISTICS

The problem is that the population mean is not known but must be estimated from a sample. Assume that a simple random sample of size 10 is taken from the population. The 10 people selected and their respective attitudes are shown in Figure 14-2.

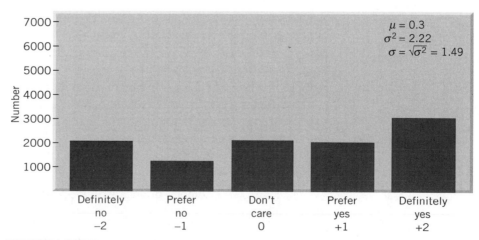

FIGURE 14-1
The population opinion on symphony starting time (7:30 P.M. on weekdays)

Attitude

1.	John T.	$X_1 = +1$
2.	Lois M.	$X_2 = +2$
3.	Steve K.	$X_3 = +2$
4.	Paul A.	$X_4 = 0$
5.	Carol Z.	$X_5 = +1$
6.	Judy D.	$X_6 = +1$
7.	Tom E.	$X_7 = -1$
8.	Sharon P.	$X_8 = +1$
9.	Jan K.	$X_9 = -2$
10.	Ed J.	$X_{10} = 0$

FIGURE 14-2
A sample of symphony season-ticket holders

$$\overline{X} = \frac{1}{10}\sum_{i=1}^{10} X_i = 0.5$$

$$s^2 = \frac{1}{n-1}\sum_i (X_i - \overline{X})^2 = \frac{14.50}{9} = 1.61$$

$$s = \sqrt{s^2} = 1.27$$

Just as the population has a set of characteristics, each sample also has a set of characteristics. One sample characteristic is the sample average, or mean:

$$\overline{X} = \frac{1}{n}\sum_{i=1}^{n} X_i = 0.5$$

Two means now have been introduced, and it is important to keep them separate. One is the population mean (μ), a population characteristic. The second is the sample mean ($\overline{X}$), a sample characteristic. Because the $\overline{X}$ is a sample characteristic, it would change if a new sample were obtained. The sample mean ($\overline{X}$) is used to estimate the unknown population mean (μ).

Another sample characteristic or statistic is the sample variance (s^2), which can be used to estimate the population variance (σ^2). Under simple random sampling, the sample variance is

$$s^2 = \text{sample variance} = \frac{1}{n-1}\sum_{i=1}^{n} (X_i - \overline{X})^2 = 1.61$$

Note that s^2 will be small if the sample responses are similar, and large if they are spread out. The corresponding sample standard deviation is simply[4]

$$s = \text{sample standard deviation} = \sqrt{s^2} = 1.27$$

Again, it is important to make a distinction between the population variance (σ^2) and the sample variance (s^2).

SAMPLE RELIABILITY

Of course, all samples will not generate the same value of $\overline{X}$ (or s). If another simple random sample of size 10 were taken from the population, $\overline{X}$ might be 0.3 or 1.2 or 0.4, or whatever. The point is that $\overline{X}$ will vary from sample to sample.

Intuitively, it is reasonable to believe that the variation in $\overline{X}$ will be larger as the variance in the population σ^2 is larger. At one extreme, if there is no variation in the population, there will be no variation in $\overline{X}$. It also is reasonable to believe that as the size of the sample increases, the variation in $\overline{X}$ will decrease. When the sample is small, it takes only one or two extreme scores to substantially affect the sample mean, thus generating a relatively large or small $\overline{X}$. As the sample size increases, these extreme values will have less impact when they do appear, because they will be averaged with more values. The variation in $\overline{X}$ is measured by its **standard error,**[5] which is

$$\sigma_{\overline{x}} = \text{standard error of } \overline{X} = \sigma_x/\sqrt{n} = 1.49/\sqrt{10} = 0.47$$

(σ_x can be written simply as σ). Note that the standard error of $\overline{X}$ depends on n the sample size. If n is altered, the standard error will change accordingly, as Table 14-2 shows.

The variable X has a probability distribution, as reflected in Figure 14-1. The sample mean, $\overline{X}$, also has a probability distribution. It is customary to assume that the variation of $\overline{X}$ from sample to sample will follow the normal distribution.[6] Figure 14-3 shows the familiar bell-shaped normal probability distribution. In other words, it indicates that $\overline{X}$ usually will be close to the population mean (μ) and that it is just as likely to be larger than μ as smaller. The top drawing in Figure 14-3 shows how the area under the normal curve is divided. The area corresponds to probability; that is, the area under the

TABLE 14-2
Increasing Sample Size

Sample Size	σ_x	$\sigma_{\overline{x}} = \sigma_x/\sqrt{n}$
10	1.49	0.470
40	1.49	0.235
100	1.49	0.149
500	1.49	0.067

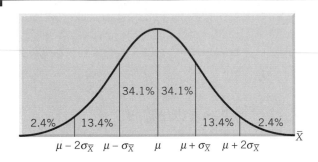

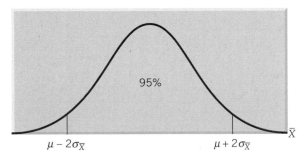

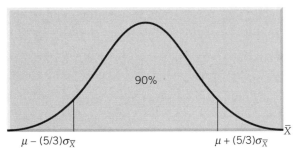

FIGURE 14-3
The normal distribution of $\overline{X}$

curve between two points is the probability that $\overline{X}$ will be between those two points. For example, in the middle figure, 95 percent of the area is shown. Thus, the probability that $\overline{X}$ lies within $2\sigma_{\overline{x}}$ of the population mean (μ) is 0.95. Similarly, the bottom figure shows 90 percent of the area under the normal curve. Its interpretation is that the probability is 0.90 that $\overline{X}$ is within $5/3\ \sigma_{\overline{x}}$ of the population mean (μ).[7]

Thus, the concept of a standard error now can be illustrated in the context of Figure 14-3. There is a 0.95 probability that $\overline{X}$ will fall within ±2 standard errors of the population mean. In our symphony example from Figure 14-1, suppose we drew 100 different samples of 10 people. About 95 percent of the resulting sample means ($\overline{X}$) would be within ±2 standard errors ($\sigma_{\overline{x}} = 0.47$) of the population mean ($\mu = 0.3$). Figure 14-3 is sometimes called a sampling distribution, since it indicates the probability of getting a particular sample mean.

Table 14-2 illustrates how the standard error of $\overline{X}$, ($\sigma_{\overline{x}}$), decreases as the sample size gets larger. Thus, with a large sample, $\overline{X}$ will tend to be close to μ, and the distribution of $\overline{X}$ will change accordingly. Figure 14-4 shows the

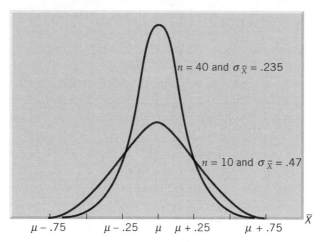

FIGURE 14-4
The effect of increasing sample size on the normal distribution of $\overline{X}$

effect of sample size change from 10 to 40 on the distribution of $\overline{X}$. If the sample size were increased further, the $\overline{X}$ probability distribution would get taller and narrower.

A source of confusion is the fact that two probability distributions are being discussed. It is very important to keep them separate. The first is the distribution of response over the population, as illustrated by Figure 14-1. The population standard deviation, σ, reflects the dispersion of this distribution. The second is the distribution of $\overline{X}$, illustrated by Figures 14-3 and 14-4 (the dispersion of which is reflected by σ_X). To conceptualize the X distribution (distribution of the sample), it is necessary to conceive of many replications of the sample.

INTERVAL ESTIMATION

The sample mean, $\overline{X}$ is used to estimate the unknown population mean (μ). Because $\overline{X}$ varies from sample to sample, it is not, of course, equal to the population (μ). There is a sampling error. It is useful to provide an interval estimate around $\overline{X}$ that reflects our judgment of the extent of this sampling error:

$$\overline{X} \pm \text{sampling error} = \text{the interval estimate of } \mu$$

The size of the interval will depend on the confidence level. If it were necessary to have a 95 percent confidence level, the interval estimate containing the true population mean would be

$$\overline{X} \pm 2\sigma_{\overline{x}} = \overline{X} \pm 2\sigma_x/\sqrt{n} = 95\% \text{ interval estimate of } \mu$$

(recall that $\sigma_{\overline{x}} = \sigma_x/\sqrt{n}$). The interval size is based on $2\sigma_{\overline{x}}$ because, as Figure 14-3 shows, the probability that X will be within $2\sigma_{\overline{x}}$ of the population mean is 0.95. In our example, the interval would be

$$\overline{X} \pm 2\sigma_{\overline{X}} = 0.5 \pm 2 \times 0.47 = 0.5 \pm 0.94$$

since $\sigma_{\overline{X}} = \sigma_X / \sqrt{n} = 0.47$. Note that this interval includes the true population mean (recall from Figure 14-1 that $\mu = 0.3$). About 95 percent of samples will generate an interval estimate that will include the true population mean.

If the desire were to have a 90 percent confidence level, then the interval estimate containing the true population mean would be

$$\overline{X} \pm 5/3 \, (\sigma_{\overline{X}}) = \overline{X} \pm (5/3) \, \sigma_x / \sqrt{n} = 90 \, \% \text{ interval estimate of } \mu$$

Again, the interval is based on $5/3$ $(\sigma_{\overline{x}})$ because, as shown in Figure 14-3, there is a 0.90 probability that $\overline{X}$ is within $5/3$ $(\sigma_{\overline{x}})$ of the true population mean, μ. In our example, the 90 percent interval estimate is

$$\overline{X} \pm 5/3(\sigma_{\overline{x}}) = 0.5 \pm 5/3(0.47) = 0.5 \pm 0.78$$

Note that the interval is smaller, but that we are less confident that it would include the true population mean.

If the population standard deviation ($\sigma_x = \sigma$) is not known, it is necessary to estimate it with the sample standard deviation, s.[8] Thus, the 95 percent interval estimate would be

$$\overline{X} \pm 2s / \sqrt{n} = 95 \, \% \text{ interval estimate with } \sigma \text{ unknown}$$

In our example, it would be

$$0.5 \pm 2(1.27 / \sqrt{10}) = 0.5 \pm 0.80$$

since from Figure 14-2, s was determined to be 1.27.

To summarize, the interval estimate of the population mean, μ, can be written as

$$\overline{X} \pm \text{sampling error, or } \overline{X} \pm z\sigma_x / \sqrt{n}$$

where

$z = 2$ for a 95 percent confidence level
$z = 5/3$ for a 90 percent confidence level
$\sigma_x =$ population standard deviation (s is used if σ_x is unknown)
$n =$ the sample size

Thus, the size of the interval estimate will depend on three factors. The first is the confidence level. If we are willing to have a lower confidence level for the interval estimate to include the true unknown population mean, then the interval will be smaller. The second factor is the population standard deviation. If there is little variation in the population, then the interval estimate of the population mean will be smaller. The third is the sample size. As the sample size gets larger, the sampling error is reduced and the interval will get smaller.

SAMPLE SIZE QUESTION

Now we are finally ready to use these concepts to help determine sample size. To proceed, the analyst must specify

1. Size of the sampling error that is desired.
2. Confidence level; for example, the 95 percent confidence level.

This specification will depend on a trade-off between the value of more accurate information and the cost of an increased sample size. For a given confidence level, a smaller sampling error will "cost" in terms of a larger sample size. Similarly, for a given sampling error, a higher confidence level will "cost" in terms of a larger sample size. These statements will become more tangible in the context of some examples.

Using the general formula for the interval estimate (recall that σ and σ_x are the same)

$$\overline{X} \pm \text{sampling error, or } \overline{X} \pm z\sigma/\sqrt{n}$$

We know that

$$\text{Sampling error} = z\sigma/\sqrt{n}$$

Dividing through by the sampling error and multiplying by $\sqrt{n}$

$$\sqrt{n} = z\sigma/(\text{sampling error})$$

and squaring both sides, we get an expression for sample size:

$$n = z^2\sigma^2/(\text{sampling error})^2$$

Thus, if we know the required confidence level, and therefore z, and also know the allowed sampling error, then the needed sample size is specified by the formula.

Let us assume that we need to have a 95 percent confidence level that our sampling error in estimating the population mean does not exceed 0.3. In this case, sampling error = 0.3, and, since the confidence level is 95 percent, $z = 2$. In our example from Figure 14-1, the population standard deviation is 1.49, so the sample size should be

$$n = 2^2(1.49)^2/(0.3)^2 = 98.7 \approx 99$$

Changing the Confidence Level. If the confidence level were changed from 95 percent to 90 percent, the sample size could be reduced, because we do not have to be as certain of the resulting estimate. The z term would then be 5/3 and the sample size would be

$$n = (z\sigma)^2/(\text{sampling error})^2 = (5/3)^2(1.49)^2/(0.3)^2 = 68.5 \approx 69$$

Changing the Allowed Error. If the allowed error were increased, the sample size also would decrease, even if a 95 percent confidence level was retained. In our example, if the allowed error were increased to 0.5, then the sample size would be

$$n = (z\sigma)^2/(\text{sampling error})^2 = 4(1.49)^2/(0.5)^2 = 35.5 \approx 36$$

Population Size. It should be noted that the sample-size calculation is independent of the size of the population. A common misconception is that a "good" sample should have a relatively high percentage of the sampling frame included. Actually, the size of the sample will be determined in the same manner whether the population is 1000 or 1,000,000. There should be no concern that the sample contain a reasonable percentage of the population. Of course, if the population is small, the sample size could be reduced.[9] Obviously, the sample size should not exceed the population.

Determining the Population Standard Deviation

The procedure just displayed assumes that the population standard deviation is known. In most practical situations it is not known, and it must be estimated by using one of several available approaches.

One method is to use a sample standard deviation obtained from a previous comparable survey or from a pilot survey. Another approach is to estimate σ subjectively. Suppose the task is to estimate the income of a community. It might be possible to say that 95 percent of the people will have an income of between $4,000 and $20,000. Assuming a normal distribution, there will be four population standard deviations between the two figures, so that one population standard deviation will be equal to $4,000.

Another approach is to take a "worst-case" situation. In our example, the largest population variance would occur if half the population would respond with a +2 and the other half with a -2.[10] The population variance would then be 4, and the recommended sample size, at a 95 percent confidence level and a 0.3 allowable error, would be 178. Note that the sample size would be larger than desired, and thus the desired accuracy would be exceeded. The logic is that it is alright to err on the side of being too accurate.

PROPORTIONS

When proportions are to be estimated (the proportion of people with negative feelings about a change in the symphony's starting time, for example), the procedure is to use the sample proportion to estimate the unknown population proportion, π. Because this estimate is based on a sample, it has a population variance, namely,

$$\sigma_p^2 = \pi(1 - \pi)/n$$

where

π = population proportion

p = sample proportion (corresponding to $\overline{X}$), used to estimate the unknown

σ^2_p = population variance of p

The formula for sample size is then

$$n = z^2\pi(1 - \pi)/(\text{sampling error})^2$$

As Figure 14-5 shows, the worst case (where the population variance is at its maximum) occurs when the population proportion is equal to 0.50:

$$\pi(1 - \pi) = 0.25$$
$$\pi = 0.50$$

Because the population proportion is unknown, a common procedure is to assume the worst case. The formula for sample size then simplifies to

$$n = z^2(0.25)/(\text{sampling error})^2$$

Thus, if the population proportion is to be estimated within an error of 0.05 (or 5 percentage points) at a 95 percent confidence level, the needed sample size is

$$n = 2^2(0.25)/(0.05)^2 = 400$$

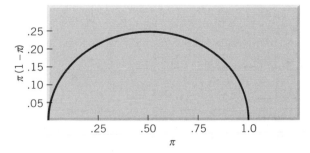

FIGURE 14-5
A graph of π $(1 - \pi)$

since z equals 2, corresponding to a 95 percent confidence level, and the allowed sampling error equals 0.05. Figure 14-6 summarizes the two sample size formulas.

Sampling error (also known as *accuracy* or *precision* error) can be defined in relative rather than absolute terms. In other words, a researcher might require that the sample estimate be within plus or minus G percentage points of the population value. Therefore,

$$D = G\mu$$

The sample size formula may be written as

$$n = \sigma^2 z^2 / (\text{Sampling error})^2$$
$$n = \sigma^2 z^2 / D^2$$
$$= c^2 z^2 / G^2$$

where

$$c = (\sigma / \mu)$$

known as the coefficient of variation.

If a researcher has information on the coefficient of variation, required confidence level, the desired precision accuracy level, then the estimation of sample size can be readily obtained from the chart in Exhibit 14-1. One has to place a number corresponding to the desired information level and read of the sample size. For example, if $c = 0.30$, confidence level = 95% and the desired precision = 0.034, then the required sample size, n, is equal to 300.

Several Questions

A survey instrument or an experiment usually will not be based on just one question. Sometimes hundreds can be involved. It usually will not be worthwhile to go through such a process for all questions. A reasonable approach

---

In general,

    Sample size = $n = z^2 \sigma^2 \div (\text{sampling error})^2$

where

    $z = 2$ for a 95 percent confidence level
    $z = \frac{5}{3}$ for a 90 percent confidence level
    $\sigma = $ population standard deviation

and

    sampling error = allowed sampling error

For proportions,

    Sample size = $n = z^2(.25) \div (\text{sampling error})^2$

FIGURE 14-6
Some useful sample-size formulas

EXHIBIT 14-1

Calculation of Sample Size

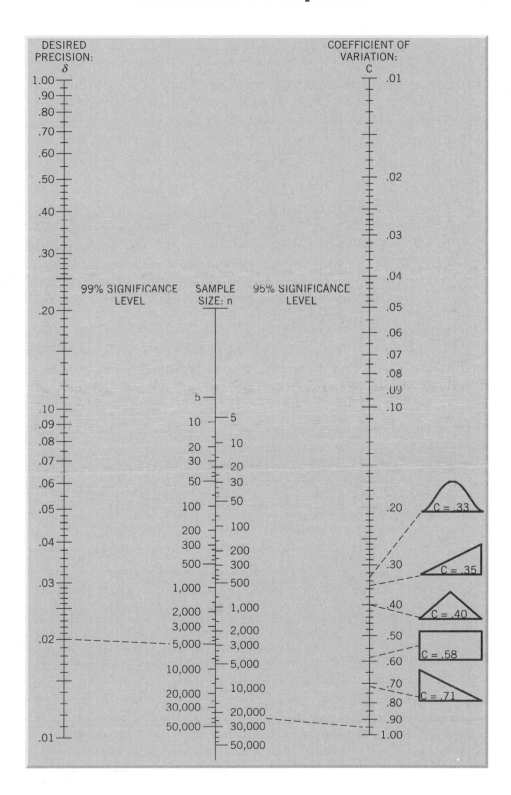

would be to pick a few representative questions and determine the sample size from them. The most crucial ones with the highest expected variance should be included.

STRATIFIED SAMPLING

In **stratified sampling** the population is divided into subgroups or strata and a sample is taken from each. Stratified sampling is worthwhile when one or both of the following are true:

1. The population standard deviation differs by strata.
2. The interview cost differs by strata.

Suppose we wanted to estimate the usage of electricity to heat swimming pools. The population of swimming pools might be stratified into commercial pools at hotels and clubs and individual home swimming pools. The latter might have a small variation, and thus would require a smaller sample. If, however, the home-pool owners were less costly to interview, that would allow more of them to be interviewed than if the two groups involved the same interview cost.

How does one determine the best allocation of the sampling budget to the various strata? This classic problem of sampling was solved in 1935 by Jerzy Neyman.[11] His solution is represented by the following formula:

$$n_i = \frac{\pi_i \sigma_i / \sqrt{c_i}}{\Sigma(\pi_i \sigma_i / \sqrt{c_i})} n$$

where

$n = $ the total sample size

$\pi_i = $ the proportion of population in stratum i

$\sigma_i = $ the population standard deviation in stratum i

$c_i = $ the cost of one interview in stratum i

$\Sigma_i = $ the sum over all strata

$n_i = $ the sample size for stratum i

Figure 14-7 presents information on a survey of the monthly usage of bank teller machines. The population is stratified by income. The high-income segment has both the highest variation and the highest interview cost. The low- and medium-income strata have the same interview cost but differ with respect to the standard deviation of bank-teller usage. The column at the right shows the breakdown of the 1000-person sample into the three strata. Note that the high-income stratum is allocated 235 people. If a simple random sample of size 1000 had been taken from the population, about 200 would have been

Income Stratum (i)	Proportion (π_i)	Standard Deviation (σ_i)	Interview Cost (c_i)	$\pi_i\sigma_i/\sqrt{c_i}$	n_i
Low	.3	1	25	.06	177
Medium	.5	2	25	.20	588
High	.2	4	100	.08	235
				$.34 = \sum_i \pi_i\sigma_i \div \sqrt{c_i}$	1000 = n

FIGURE 14-7
Allocating sample size to strata

taken from the high-income group, since 20 percent of the population is from that stratum.

The formula shows how to allocate the sample size to the various strata; however, how does one determine the sample size in the first place? One approach is to assume that there is a budget limit. The sample size is simply adjusted upward until it hits the budget limit. The budget should be figured as follows:

$$\text{Budget} = \sum_i c_i n_i$$

The second approach is to determine the sampling error and decide whether it is excessive. If so, the sample size would be increased. The sampling error formula is:

$$\text{Sampling error} = z\sigma_{\bar{x}}$$

and is based on the standard error of $\overline{X}$, which is found as follows:

$$\text{Standard error of } \overline{X} \text{ or } \sigma_{\bar{x}} = \sqrt{(\sum_i \pi_i\sigma_i/n_i)}$$

It is based on the variances of the individual strata. In the example given in Figure 14-7,

$$\sigma_{\bar{x}} = 0.7$$

As was illustrated in the last chapter, the estimate of the population mean under stratified sampling is a weighted average of the sample means found in each stratum sample:

$$\text{Estimate of the population mean} = \sum_i \pi_i \overline{X}_i$$

where

$$\overline{X}_i = \text{the sample mean for stratum } i$$

MULTISTAGE DESIGN

If other sampling designs are employed, the logic used to generate the optimal sample size will still hold; however, the formula can get complicated. For example, in an area design, the first step might be to select communities at random. Then the procedure could be to select census tracts, then blocks, and finally households. In such a design the expression for determining the standard error of X becomes hopelessly complex. The solution is to replicate the entire sampling plan and obtain two, three, or four independent estimates of $\overline{X}$. These different estimates can be used to estimate the standard error of $\overline{X}$.

SEQUENTIAL SAMPLING

Sometimes a researcher may want to take a modest sample, look at the results, and then decide if more information, in the form of a larger sample, is needed. Such a procedure is termed **sequential sampling.** For example, if a new industrial product were being evaluated, a small probability sample of potential users might be contacted. Suppose it were found that their average annual usage level at a 95 percent confidence level was between 10 and 30 units, and it was known that for the product to be economically viable the average would have to be 50 units. This is sufficient information for a decision to drop the product. If, however, the interval estimate from the original sample were from 45 to 65, the information would be inadequate for making that decision, and an additional sample might be obtained. The combined samples then would provide a smaller interval estimate. If the resulting interval were still inadequate, the sample size could be increased a third time. Of course, although sequential sampling does provide the potential of sharply reducing costs, it can result in increased costs and a delayed decision.

The concept of sequential sampling is useful because it reminds the researcher that the goal of marketing research is providing information to help in decision making. The quality of the information must be evaluated in the decision-making context. Too often, information tends to be evaluated absolutely (it is intellectually comfortable to be "certain"). Instead, it should be judged with respect to its use.

Summary

This chapter started off by discussing some ad hoc methods of determining sample size, and then introduced some useful concepts and applied them to the problem of determining sample size. A population characteristic, such as the attitude of symphony season-ticket holders, is to be estimated by the sample. A sample statistic, such as the average attitude of a sample of season-ticket holders, is used to estimate the population characteristic. The sample statistic will have a variance (it will not be the same each time a sample is drawn), and this will be a measure of its reliability. The estimate, based on the sample statistic, has an interval associated with it that reflects its variance and the confidence level of the researcher. The sample size then is determined by the confidence level desired, the allowed estimate error, and the variance of the population as per the following formula:

$$n > (z\sigma)^2/(\text{sampling error})^2$$

In stratified sampling, the sample size of each stratum will depend on the variance and the interviewing cost within each stratum.

Questions and Problems

1. A group of 25,000 design engineers was asked a series of questions concerning the importance of various attributes of a milling machine. The group had the following response to the question, "How important is it that the machine be capable of working with both hard and soft metals?"

Scale	Description	Frequency	Percentage
5	Extremely important	5000	20
4	Important	8000	32
3	Desirable	6000	24
2	Only a small plus	2000	8
1	Of no consequence	4000	16
		25,000	100

a. What is the average response of this population?
b. What is the variance and standard deviation? (See end note 1.)
c. A sample of size 25 yielded the following numbers: 4, 4, 1, 2, 3, 5, 4, 2, 3, 3, 3, 4, 4, 4, 1, 1, 5, 5, 4, 1, 3, 4, 4, 5, 2. Determine the sample mean, the sample variance, and the sample standard deviation.
d. Calculate the standard error of the sample mean, $\sigma_{\bar{X}}$. How would your calculation change if the sample size were 100 instead of 25? Why? Estimate the $\sigma_{\bar{X}}$ using s instead of σ.
e. Repeat parts (a) and (b) assuming that half the population of 25,000 engineers had responded "extremely important" and half had responded "of no consequence."

2. A sample of size 100 was taken from the population represented in Figure 14-1. The results showed that

$$\bar{X} = 0.52$$
$$s^2 = 2.62$$

a. Determine a 90 percent interval estimate for μ. (Recall from Figure 14-1 that [$\sigma = 1.49$].)
b. Determine a 95 percent interval estimate for μ.
c. Repeat (a) and (b) using s^2 instead of σ^2.

d. What sample size would be needed to reduce the sampling error to 0.10 if a confidence level of 95 percent were desired? Use the fact that $\sigma = 1.49$.

3. If the proportion of people who intend to vote Democratic were to be estimated at a 95 percent confidence level, what sample size should be taken
   a. If the accuracy is to be ± 0.01 (or one percentage point)?
   b. If the accuracy is to be ± 0.03?
   c. If the accuracy is to be ± 0.06?
   d. Repeat the above for a 90 percent confidence level.

4. A promotion campaign is being planned to encourage people to reduce heat in their houses at night. In order to measure the campaign's impact, we want to determine the proportion of people who reduce their heat at night, π. A telephone sample will be taken before and after the campaign.
   a. What sample size is required if an accuracy of ± 0.03 is desired at a 90 percent confidence level?
   b. At a 95 percent confidence level?
   c. How would your answer to part (b) change if you knew that the proportion would not exceed 0.3? What if it would not exceed 0.1?
   d. Assume that a "before" measure was taken with a sample size of 400 and the sample proportion was 0.3. Generate a 90 percent confidence-level estimate for the population proportion. (Hint: Recall that $\sigma_p^2 = [\pi(1 - \pi)/n]$.)

5. A new consumer product is proposed. It is thought that 25 percent of the population will buy it. A critical question is how frequently buyers will use it. A judgment has been made that 95 percent of them will use it between one and 17 times per month. On that basis, the population standard deviation is estimated to be 4.
   a. Explain how the standard deviation estimate was obtained.
   b. What sample size is required if an accuracy of ± 1 is needed at the 90 percent level? At the 95 percent level? (The sampling error should not exceed 1.)
   c. Repeat (b) for an accuracy of ± 0.4.
   d. What considerations should be introduced in selecting the confidence level and desired accuracy?

6. The problem is to estimate the sales for the coming year for a maker of industrial equipment. The forecast is based on asking customers how much they are planning to order next year. To use the research budget efficiently, the customers are stratified by the size of their orders during the past year. The following is some relevant information based on the past year:

Strata Customer Size	Proportion (π_i)	Standard Deviation (σ_i)	Interview Cost (c_i)
Large	.1	40	64
Medium	.2	3	64
Small	.7	2	64
Number of customers: 5000			

a. Assume that a total of 300 interviews are to be conducted. How would you allocate those interviews among the three strata?

b. If a simple random sample of size 300 were obtained from the population, about 10 percent, or 30 interviews, would be from the large-customer stratum. Why did you recommend in part (a) that more than 30 interviews be conducted from this stratum?

c. The survey was conducted, and the average values (in thousands) for each stratum were as follows:

$$\overline{X}_1 = 100$$
$$\overline{X}_2 = 8$$
$$\overline{X}_3 = 5$$

What would your estimate be of the population mean, the average sales that will be received from all customers next year?

d. Given the context of part (c), what would be the variance of your estimate of the population mean? Do you think that this variance would be larger or smaller than the variance of your estimate of the population mean if you had taken a simple random sample of size 300 from the total population? Why?

e. What is the total interviewing cost, given a cost per interview of $64, and 300 interviews?

f. Assume now that it has been decided that the small customers can be contacted by telephone, making their cost per interview only $9 each. Repeat the analysis that you did for part (a). How would you allocate 300 interviews now?

g. Now, under part (f), what is the total interviewing cost?

h. How many interviews could you conduct, assuming that you had the same amount of money determined under part (e), that you allocated the interviews according to your answer in part (f), and that the costs were as in part (f)?

7. In the Winona Wildcats study presented in Chapter 13 (Question 17), Pete Thames, the team's general manager has decided to use a stratified sample. One sample group includes only those who attended Wildcats games during the past two years. The other sample group represents nonattenders. The Wildcats hope to draw fans from Winona and surrounding areas, which have a combined population of 144,000.

a. What proportion of those included in the sample should be in the stratum of nonattenders, assuming that a directly proportional method of stratification will be used?

b. What is the actual number of people in the nonattender sample?

c. What will be the size of the entire sample used in the study?

8. The owner of Galaxy Pizza, a pizza delivery business in Mercury, South Dakota, (population 100,000) believes that there may be a demand for a service that provides customers with their choice of movie videos along with the pizza delivery. Galaxy Pizza currently delivers only to customers within a ten-mile radius of the store, but guarantees delivery within thirty minutes.

a. What sampling frame would the owner use to establish how many households lie within this delivery area?

It was found that 1000 households are within the current delivery area, which is 5 percent of the total number of households in Mercury. The owner wants to conduct this study throughout the city, and has decided to collect a random sample of 2000 households.

b. What percentage of the total population will be represented in the sample?

c. Recommend a sampling method that is most suitable for this study, and support your answer.

End Notes

1. Seymour Sudman. *Applied Sampling*, New York: Academic Press, 1976, 50.
2. Ibid., 30.
3. Here follows one method for calculating the population mean and variance. Note the responses (R) are weighted by the response frequency (f). Thus, the response +1 is weighted by 0.20, because it occurs 0.20 of the time in the population. For a further discussion, see any introductory statistics book.

6. Such an assumption is not as extreme as it may seem. The $\bar{x}$ distribution will be normal if the distribution of the underlying population is normal, or if the sample size gets large. The last condition is due to the central-limit theorem. In practice, if the population distribution is fairly symmetrical in appearance, a "large" n can be 30, 20, or even smaller, depending on the accuracy required by the situation. Even with an n of 10, the error introduced by assuming that $\bar{x}$ is distributed normally is often not of practical importance, and the reality is that there is often no practical alternative.

Response (R)	Response Frequency (f)	Weighted Average (Rf)	Population Mean (μ)	(R − μ)	(R − μ)²	(R − μ)²f
+2	0.3	0.6	0.3	1.7	2.89	0.87
+1	0.2	0.2	0.3	0.7	0.49	0.10
0	0.2	0	0.3	0.3	0.09	0.02
−1	0.1	−0.1	0.3	1.3	1.69	0.17
−2	0.2	−0.4	0.3	2.3	5.29	1.06
Total		0.3 = μ				2.22 = σ²

4. The term $n - 1$ appears in the expression for the sample variance so that s^2 will be an unbiased estimate of the population variance. The reader need not be concerned about this fact; it has little practical significance. If the population size, termed N, is small relative to the sample size, n, a "finite population correction factor" of N − n/ N − 1 should be added. Thus, if N is 1000 and n is 100, the correction factor would be 0.9. If N is more than 10 times the sample size, the correction factor is rarely significant.

5. We also could use the term population standard error of $\bar{x}$. The word "population" is omitted in this context to make the discussion less cumbersome.

7. Actually, the numbers 2 and 5/3 are approximations. The correct numbers from a normal distribution table are as follows:

Number of σ_x	Probability
2.575	0.99
1.96	0.95
1.64	0.90
1.282	0.80

8. Actually, the use of s adds a bit more uncertainty to the interval estimate. If the sample size is small, and if it is important to be extremely precise in

the confidence interval estimate, this uncertainty can be accounted for explicitly by replacing the normal distribution with the t-distribution, which makes the interval larger. For example, using the t-distribution, the 95 percent interval estimate would involve a factor of 2.23 for a sample size of 10, a factor of 2.06 for a sample size of 20, and a factor of 2.00 for a sample size of 60. As n gets larger, the t-distribution approaches the normal distribution.

9. When sampling with relatively small populations, the standard error of $\bar{x}$ is

$$(\sigma/\sqrt{n})\sqrt{\frac{N-n}{N-1}}$$

where N is the size of the population. If the sample size is a meaningful percentage of N (such as 30 to 50 percent) then it might be worthwhile to reduce the sample size.

10. The population variance would be $0.5\,(2-0)^2 + 0.5(-2-0)^2 = 0.5 \times 4 + 0.5 \times 4 = 4$, since 0.5 of the population responded with a +2, and the population mean, or average, would be zero. See end note 1 for a calculation formula.

11. Jerry Neyman, "On the two different aspects of the representative method: The method of stratified sampling and the method of purposive selection," *Journal of the Royal Statistical Society*, 1934, 97, 558–606.

CASES FOR PART II
Data Collection

CASE II-1
Pacific Gas & Electric (A)[1]

Pacific Gas & Electric (PG&E) was interested in determining what could be done to encourage the installation of solar water heaters. As a first step it was decided that some exploratory marketing research should be conducted. As a result, a research proposal for a telephone survey to determine homeowners' knowledge, attitudes, and intentions toward solar water heaters was on the desk of John Glenning, a marketing research analyst of PG&E. John needed to decide whether the methodology, including the sampling plan and the questionnaire, was sound. He further needed to decide whether a telephone interview was the appropriate research approach. Focus-group interviews had been very helpful in developing a home insulation program several years earlier, and he felt that a real alternative was to commission several focus groups.

Solar Water Heaters

Solar water heaters have been in use for a long time. In fact, they were very popular in Florida during the early thirties. They are extremely simple, as Exhibit II-1 illustrates. Cold water is pumped onto the roof of a house, where it circulates through "collector panels" that are heated by the sun. Hot water then returns to a storage tank. A conventional gas or electric water heater will raise the water temperature, if necessary, on cloudy days. The water heater application of solar energy is attractive because solar water heaters are much more economical than solar space (house) heaters and because the market potential for solar swimming pool heaters is limited.

The expected rate of return that a homeowner can expect from the installation of a solar water heater will depend on a set of assumptions about how the unit is financed and what energy source it will replace. Generally, the investment is unattractive if gas currently is used, but it can be attractive if water is now heated with electricity. If a utility were to install and lease units to homeowners, the investment's attractiveness might improve since the payments could be stretched out and since the utility probably would have lower installment costs than a conventional dealer. One

possibility to be explored is whether PG&E should be involved in leasing and installing solar water heaters.

PG&E's Solar Program

PG&E's solar program, budgeted at over half a million dollars, had two primary objectives. The first was to gather and analyze information on available solar energy systems' cost-effectiveness, dependability, and acceptability to PG&E customers. The second was to inform customers of the information obtained.

Projects undertaken toward these objectives included solar demonstration homes, monitoring of other solar installations, product testing, and customer information programs. Three demonstration solar houses were built, and five more were planned. A part of PG&E advertising had been devoted to solar applications. An energy conservation trailer was displayed at fairs and shopping centers. Over 90,000 copies of a booklet entitled *Sun Energy* were distributed.

Two approaches toward encouraging homeowner installation of solar water heaters had been proposed. The first, now under active consideration by PG&E, was the use of advertising and other customer information programs to communicate information regarding solar water heaters and to get homeowners to consider installing them. One purpose of the proposed research was thus to determine who should be the target audience, what their characteristics and their information needs were, and what appeals would be most effective. The second approach was to involve PG&E in the solar heating business. This involvement could take a variety of forms. One possibility was to develop a pilot program in which PG&E would install and lease solar water heaters to homeowners. Another purpose of the research was to evaluate the practicality of such a pilot program. At the time, the only known solar leasing program was operated by the Municipal Utility of Santa Clara, which installed plastic solar swimming-pool heaters for a $200 installation fee and a monthly fee payable during the six-month swimming season.

Research Objectives

Several specific types of research information were desired. First, a knowledge of homeowners' awareness, knowledge, attitudes, and intentions concerning resi-

[1] Written by Darrell R. Clarke and David A. Aaker as a basis for class discussion.

EXHIBIT II-1

Solar Hot-Water Heating System

Cool water is drawn from supply line (1), and pump (2) circulates water through collector panels (3). Hot water leaving panels (4) is transferred to storage tank (5). Preheated water circulates to backup heater (6) for additional heating, if necessary, before distribution through hot-water outlets.

dential applications of solar energy, particularly water heaters was needed to determine appropriate objectives of customer information programs. Second, knowing what information was desired by consumers and from what sources would guide customer information programs. Third, an estimate of the effect on intentions of alternative financing methods in general and a PG&E leasing program in particular had to be developed. Fourth, descriptions of the different customer groups on the basis of awareness, knowledge, attitudes, and intentions were required.

Several specific hypotheses were developed, based in part on some marketing research conducted by the San Diego Gas and Electric Company. The hypotheses were intended to make the issues represented by the research questions more specific and to summarize current thinking about customers' positions toward solar energy.

1. Interest in and general awareness of solar energy is high, but knowledge of specific applications, including solar water heaters, is rather low.

2. Solar energy is regarded as expensive and not yet fully perfected.

3. Attractions of solar energy include saving money, conserving energy, helping the environment, and being innovative. Cost payback is a very important consideration in any solar energy decision.

4. Utilities are generally perceived as reliable sources of information and equipment.

5. Solar leasing by utilities will be attractive to one segment because less investment is required and because a utility company would be trusted to assure performance. Another segment will be opposed to utility involvement with solar programs.

6. There should be a positive association between knowledge and intention, because information should influence intentions and because interested people seek out information.

7. People interested in installing solar water heaters tend to be young, affluent, well-educated, con-

EXHIBIT II-2

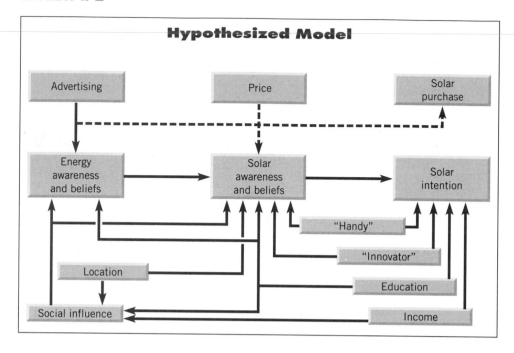

Hypothesized Model

cerned about energy, "handy" people who enjoy trying new things, and owners or friends of owners of swimming pools.

These hypotheses, together with other opinions, served as the basis for a tentative model of the decision process associated with solar water heaters. This model is shown in Exhibit II-2.

Methodology

The research approach was a telephone interview of a sample of 200 homeowners in the San Francisco Bay Area. The questionnaire is shown in the next section. A telephone survey was selected because it is relatively free of bias and is economical and fast.

The target population for the survey was all PG& E customers in the San Francisco Bay Area who own their own detached homes. The sample was obtained from the telephone directories of the six Bay Area counties. Thus, there were to be 70 respondents in the largest county and 14 in the smallest. Within each county a sample was drawn by systematically sampling from the telephone directory. If a telephone interviewer needed 25 respondents and the directory allocated to her or him contained 250 pages, then one respondent would be obtained from every tenth page. On each selected page the interviewer would measure a fixed amount, such as three inches from the top of the first column. The interviewer would then begin calling people starting at that point and continue until a completed interview was obtained.

Telephone Interview Format

Respondent No. __ ___ (1–3)

City _____ _____ (4)

SOLAR ENERGY SURVEY

Hello, I'm _____ from Drexel Research Corporation, a national consumer research firm. We're taking a survey in your area about home energy use and would like to ask you a few questions. May I please speak to the head of the household? (*IF THE HEAD OF THE HOUSEHOLD IS NOT AVAILABLE, THANK THE PERSON ON THE PHONE AND TERMINATE THE INTERVIEW. IF THE HEAD OF THE HOUSEHOLD IS REACHED, REINTRODUCE YOURSELF AND PROCEED.*)

1. Do you own or rent the home in which you live?

    Own _____ (CONTINUE) _____ ☐
    Rent _____ (TERMINATE)

1a. Is that home a single family dwelling?

    Yes _____ (CONTINUE) _____ ☐
    No _____ (TERMINATE)

2. I'm going to read you a few statements about energy conservation and for each one I'd like you to tell me whether you agree or disagree with it. (READ STATEMENTS BELOW)

    (FOR EACH STATEMENT "AGREE" WITH, ASK:) Do you agree completely or somewhat?
    (FOR EACH STATEMENT "DISAGREE" WITH, ASK:) Do you disagree somewhat or completely?

		AGREE		DISAGREE		
		Completely	Somewhat	Completely	Somewhat	
a.	It is important for the United States to have an energy conservation program.	___ 1	___ 2	3	___ 4	(6)
b.	What an individual consumer does or does *not* do to save energy has a meaningful effect on the energy shortage.	___ 1	___ 2	___ 3	___ 4	(7)
c.	New supplies of natural gas will be discovered before any serious shortages develop.	___ 1	___ 2	___ 3	___ 4	(8)

3. I'd like to know how well the following statements describe you. Please tell me whether you agree completely, agree somewhat, disagree somewhat, or disagree completely with . . . (READ LIST)

	Agree Completely	Agree Somewhat	Disagree Somewhat	Disagree Completely	
I generally like to try new ideas at work and in my life.	___ 1	___ 2	___ 3	___ 4	(9)
I like to experiment with new ways of doing things.	___ 1	___ 2	___ 3	___ 4	(10)
I like to build things for my house.	___ 1	___ 2	___ 3	___ 4	(11)

I like to fix things around the house.	____ 1	____ 2	____ 3	____ 4	(12)
I wait for new things to be proven before trying them.	____ 1	____ 2	____ 3	____ 4	(13)

4. Now I'd like to talk about solar energy. Please tell me all the ways that you can think of that solar energy can be used in the home. (PROBE AND CLARIFY)

_____ (14)

_____ (15)

_____ (16)

_____ (17)

5a. Have you seen any advertisements or brochures about solar energy devices recently?

Yes ____ (CONTINUE) ____ 1 (18)

No ____ (SKIP TO Q. 5c) ____ 2

5b. Whom was the advertisement or brochure from?

_____ (19)

_____

5c. Have you read any articles about solar energy recently in magazines or newspapers?

Yes ____ 1 (20)

No ____ 2

6a. Have you seen any displays of solar equipment?

Yes ____ (CONTINUE) ____ 1 (21)

No ____ (SKIP TO Q. 7a) ____ 2

6b. Where did you see this display?

_____ (22)

7a. Have you ever seen a solar heating unit on a house or building?

Yes ____ (CONTINUE) ____ 1 (23)

No ____ (SKIP TO Q. 8) ____ 2

7b. Where was that?

_____ (24)

_____

8. Have you ever discussed solar energy with your friends?

Yes ____ 1 (25)

No ____ 2

9a. Have you ever considered buying a solar water heater for your home?

Yes ____ (CONTINUE) ____ 1 (26)

No ____ (SKIP TO Q. 10) ____ 2

9b. What kind was that? (PROBE AND CLARIFY)

_____ (27)

_____

_____ (28)

10a. What would be the main *advantage* of having a solar water heater in your home? (PROBE) What other advantages?

_____ (29)

_____

_____ (30)

10b. And what would be the main *disadvantage* of having a solar water heater? (PROBE)
What other disadvantages?

_____ (31)
_____
_____ (32)

11a. About how much would you estimate your average monthly utility bill
is for gas and electricity? $ _____ (33)

11b. About how much per month do you think you might save on your gas
and electricity bill if you had a solar water heater? $ _____ (34)

12a. As you may know, water in a solar water heater is pumped through solar collector panels and the roof
and stored in a tank. This water is then heated additionally by the existing water heater if it isn't hot
enough—say on a cloudy day. A solar water heater costs about $1500 installed, and can save $4 to $5 per
month on your gas bill. How interested do you think you might be in buying and installing a solar water
heater in your home? Would you say you would be . . . (READ LIST)

Definitely interested in buying one _____	(CONTINUE) _____	1	(35)
Somewhat interested in buying one _____	(SKIP TO Q. 13a) _____	2	
Not at all interested in buying one _____	(SKIP TO Q. 13a) _____	3	

12b. If you did purchase a solar water heater, would you pay cash for it or finance it?

Pay cash _____   1   (36)
Finance _____   2

13a. Have you heard that you can deduct 10 percent of the cost of any solar equipment you buy from your
state income tax?

Yes _____   1   (37)
No _____   2

13b. Would this tax deduction make you more likely to buy a solar water heater, less likely to buy one, or
wouldn't make any difference one way or the other?

More likely _____   1   (38)
Less likely _____   2
No difference _____   3

14a. If you could lease a water heater for a lower monthly charge than a loan payment, would you rather lease
one than buy one?

Yes _____ (CONTINUE) _____   1   (39)

No _____ | SKIP TO | _____   2
No difference _____ | Q. 15a | _____   3

14b. Who would you prefer to *lease* a solar water heater from . . . (READ LIST)

Utility company _____ (ASK Q. 14c, THEN SKIP TO Q. 15a)   1   (40)

Government _____ | SKIP TO | _____   2
Some other company _____ | Q. 14d | _____   3

14c. Why would you prefer to lease from a utility company? (PROBE AND CLARIFY)

_____ (41)
_____
_____ (42)

14d. Why wouldn't you want to lease it from a utility company? (PROBE AND CLARIFY)

_____ (43)
_____
_____ (44)

15a. What information would you need to have before deciding on buying a solar water heater? (PROBE AND CLARIFY)

_____ (45)
_____
_____ (46)

15b. Which of the following would you consider to be the most reliable source of information on solar water heaters . . . (READ LIST)

Solar heater company _____	1	(47)
Government _____	2	
Utility company _____	3	

16a. Do you have a swimming pool?

Yes _____ (CONTINUE) _____	1	(48)
No _____ (SKIP TO Q. 17) _____	2	

16b. Is your pool heated?

Yes _____ (CONTINUE) _____	1	(49)
No _____ (SKIP TO Q. 16d) _____	2	

16c. How is your pool heated?

Gas heater _____	1	(50)
Solar heater _____	2	
Other (specify) _____	x	

16d. Do you have a pool cover?

Yes _____	1	(51)
No _____	2	

Now I need to ask some questions about you and your home so we can classify your answers with those of the others on this survey.

17. What is the total number of rooms in your home, excluding bathrooms? # _____ (52)

18. Approximately how old is your home? (DO NOT READ LIST)

Years		(53)
1 or less _____	1	
2 _____	2	
3 _____	3	
4–7 _____	4	
8–10 _____	5	
11–15 _____	6	
16–20 _____	7	
Over 25 _____	8	
Don't know _____	9	

19. How many people are living in your home, including yourself? # _____ (54)

20. Are you—(READ LIST)

Married _____	1	(55)
Single, widowed, or divorced _____	2	

21. Are there any children under the age of 18 living at home with you?

Yes _____ 1 (56)

No _____ 2

22. Into which of the following groups does your age fall? (READ LIST)

Under 25 _____ 1 (57)

25–35 _____ 2

36–49 _____ 3

50–64 _____ 4

65 and over _____ 5

(DO NOT READ) Refused _____ 0

23. Which of the following best describes the amount of formal education you had the opportunity to complete? (READ LIST)

Grade school _____ 1 (58)

Some high school _____ 2

Graduated high school _____ 3

Some college _____ 4

Graduated college _____ 5

24. Which of the following categories best describes the approximate market value of your home? (READ LIST)

Under $25,000 _____ 1 (59)

$25,000–$34,999 _____ 2

$35,000–$49,999 _____ 3

$50,000–$59,999 _____ 4

$60,000–$75,000 _____ 5

Over $75,000 _____ 6

(DO NOT READ) ← [Don't know _____ 0

Refused _____ 0

25. Which of the following groups best represents your total annual family income before taxes? (READ LIST)

Under $10,000 _____ 1 (60)

$10,000–$14,999 _____ 2

$15,000–$19,999 _____ 3

$20,000–$24,999 _____ 4

$25,000–$35,000 _____ 5

Over $35,000 _____ 6

(DO NOT READ) Refused _____ 0

26. (RECORD ONLY:) Sex

Male _____ 1 (61)

Female _____ 2

CASE II-2

BELLBOY [1]

The Southwestern Bell Telephone Company (SWB) has applied to the FCC for permission to initiate a new service known as BELLBOY in the Dallas/Fort Worth area. As a regulated monopoly, SWB is under the control of the FCC with respect to new services. (See Exhibit II-4 for a recent ruling). The proposed BELLBOY system is a compact, lightweight, one-way signaling device about the size of a candy bar. It is carried when the user is away from the office telephone. Someone can contact the user by simply dialing a special number which gives a "beep" signal from the BELLBOY. The user then would call the office from any nearby phone.

In order to be granted a permit to operate the service in the new area, SWB must submit to the FCC evidence of a "substantial unmet demand" for the service in the relevant market. If the evidence submitted is not contested and seems reasonable to the FCC, then the permit will be granted. Exact procedures have not been established yet as to what constitutes acceptable demonstration of "unmet demand," except for the fact that in one similar case New York Telephone used a survey technique to secure a license.

Accordingly, SWB has hired a consultant who has conducted the following survey (Exhibit II-5).

Two companies that already provide a similar one-way signaling service in the Dallas/Fort Worth area are very disturbed by the impending competition from the telephone monopoly; these companies view the market as small but well served at present. Therefore, lawyers have been hired to contest the SWB application before the FCC. These lawyers, in turn, have called upon you, as an expert in survey techniques, to criticize the SWB survey. The following information is provided:

▶ Exhibit II-3 Internal memorandum from the lawyers

▶ Exhibit II-4 Quote from a recent and relevant FCC ruling

▶ Exhibit II-5 The survey report done for SWB by Peters Marketing Research

▶ Exhibit II-6 BELLBOY Telephone Interview

EXHIBIT II-3

Memorandum

October 7, 1976

To: PBP File No. 1498
2230

From: AB

Re: Southwestern Bell's amendment dated September 29,
1976, to the Dallas-Forth Worth guardband application
which has been protested by Page A Fone and FWS

On October 4 we transmitted to you a copy of the referenced amendment which includes what in effect amounts to a further survey of need. I believe that this survey should be critically evaluated or refuted or at least weakened to the full extent possible so that we will establish a complete record for a possible court appeal. It seems to me that the survey is a sort of a theoretical exercise which does not demonstrate in any practical sense that there is a need for Bell's paging service. Nevertheless, the Commission may be inclined to accept it uncritically unless we attack it successfully; and *in view of the New York Telephone Company holding that a survey of need will be accepted unless the existing carriers raise substantial and material questions regarding it*, we have no choice but to contest it if at all possible.

One thought that has occurred to me with respect to the three price levels used in the survey is that *there has been no showing that any one of these prices is just and reasonable as it must be under the accepted common carrier pricing standards.* Thus, a response by any member of the public

[1] This case is used with the permission of Professor A. Bruno and Professor S. G. McIntyre, Santa Clara University.

EXHIBIT II-3 (continued)

to any one of the three prices does not establish a valid basis for determining the need because any one of the three prices might be unrealistic, meaning that the proposed service could not actually be offered at those prices. Also, as you pointed out in one of the recent pleadings, *this type of a survey merely establishes the existence of a continuing market, not the existence of a need or demand for additional services.*

Finally, perhaps we should ascertain from Page A Fone and FWS what efforts they have been making recently to aggressively promote their paging services. If such promotion has not resulted in an upsurge of orders, this would suggest that there is no *unsatisfied* demand, regardless of what the survey shows. This would also constitute a "substantial and material question" about the validity of the survey.

AB: In

EXHIBIT II-4

Quote from FCC Ruling

Statement by the Federal Communications Commission in the matter of Application of New York Telephone Co. for Permit for a new one-way signaling Base Station on 152.84 MH in Buffalo, N.Y. (June 19, 1974)

"We shall apply the following policy in consideration of applications by common carriers in this service: if the applicant for a new frequency can *demonstrate substantial unsatisfied need* for service by one or more of the alternative methods set forth in Long Island Paging and existing carriers fail to raise *substantial and material questions* regarding that need showing, then no hearing will be required on this issue. Where a prospective carrier surveys a particular market and demonstrates that substantial unsatisfied demand exists despite the presence of other carriers offering the same or similar services, his application will be granted."

EXHIBIT II-5

BELLBOY Attitudinal Evaluation Survey (Dallas/Fort Worth)

1. Test Summary

A. Objectives

The objectives of this study were to determine:

The interest in BELLBOY service among businesses in the Dallas/Fort Worth metropolitan area.

Among those interested it was further desired to determine:

▶ The types of companies and types of jobs in those companies that could benefit most from BELLBOY service;

▶ Reaction to three possible monthly charges

EXHIBIT II-5 (continued)

B. Method and Sample Selection

Three hundred and eighty-two telephone interviews were conducted with the *individual in charge of communication needs* at businesses throughout the Dallas/Fort Worth metropolitan area.

The telephone numbers of the businesses were supplied by Southwestern Bell Telephone Company and sample selection was implemented by Southwestern Bell Telephone Company on a systematic random basis selecting every *Nth* number.

Each business contacted was selected from the lists provided on a systematic random basis to comprise the primary sample. In addition, total remaining listings were randomly selected to form the sub-sample to be used as necessary for substitution to the primary sample.

A primary listing was replaced with a subsample listing only after one of the following circumstances was encountered which would have precluded a 'completed' interview:

▶ Three unsuccessful attempts had been made to contact the 'key' individual on three different days, or three times a day

▶ A refusal on the part of the respondent

▶ Unavailability of the 'key' person throughout the alloted calling time

▶ Disconnected/not in service telephone numbers and

▶ A Southwestern Bell Telephone number selected as part of the sample

All telephoning was conducted by Peters Marketing Research personnel during late July and early August 1975.

C. Interview Procedure

Upon reaching the randomly preselected company, an attempt was made to speak with the person at that company who handled communications. If that person were not available a callback was made at a later time.

On reaching the desired individual, it was explained that we were conducting a survey for the telephone company about a new service called BELLBOY, and wanted to obtain their opinions concerning this new service.

Next, BELLBOY service was briefly explained and the respondent indicated their general interest in the service, assuming it would be reasonably priced.

Those not interested were questioned concerning their reasons for lack of interest. The interview was then concluded.

Those interested in BELLBOY service were asked to briefly describe their company's business and to indicate anticipated benefits from the BELLBOY service.

Reaction to the number of potential users at three price levels was then determined.

2. Management Summary

A. In total, approximately one-fourth of all companies contacted indicated an interest in using the BELLBOY service, assuming the price was reasonable.

Projecting this response pattern to the entire Dallas/Fort Worth Metropolitan area which consists of 74,789 (approximate) business customers/potential customers can be derived as follows:

Low Estimate
11,218—composed of those indicating a "yes" response.

High Estimate:
14,210—composed of those indicating a "yes" response and one-half of those indicating a "maybe" response.

EXHIBIT II-5 (continued)

Respondents Interested or Not Interested in Using This Service

	Percentage of Sample[a]	Projected Number of Customer Companies
Yes	15	11,218.35
Maybe	8	5,983.12
No	77	57,587.53
Total	100	74,789
Base	(382)	(74,789)

[a] See Table 1.

B. Those companies that indicated yes or maybe were asked to indicate the number of employees who could be possible users of BELLBOY at specified prices.

As seen from the following table, potential usage of BELLBOY service by more employees increases as the alternative prices decrease at all but one level.

Potential Usage by Price[a]

Number of Employees	At $24 (%) Total (%)	Yes (%)	Maybe (%)	At $20 (%) Total (%)	Yes (%)	Maybe (%)	At $16 (%) Total (%)	Yes (%)	Maybe (%)
1–3	36	36	35	47	50	42	54	64	35
4–5	5	4	7	7	5	11	9	7	14
6–10	5	3	4	6	7	3	11	8	14
11–25	2	2	3	2	2	3	1		3
26–75	—	—	—	—	—	—	1	2	—
Over 75	1	—	3	1	—	3	1	—	3
Don't know	1	—	3	1	—	3	1	—	3
None	50	53	45	36	36	35	22	19	28
Total	100	100	100	100	100	100	100	100	100

[a] See Tables 6, 7, 8.

C. In an effort to evaluate the effect of the monthly charge on company usage and subsequent revenues, the following two projected monthly revenue tables have been developed. Figures shown are percentages developed in the previous table and applied to the 74,789 Dallas/Fort Worth metropolitan business customers.

It is apparent from the tables regarding the high (yes + 1/2 maybe) estimate that, with increased market penetration brought about by price reduction, total revenues at first decrease (at the $20.00 per unit level) and then increase (at the $16.00 per unit level). Total revenues increase for each lower price schedule when considering the low (yes only) estimate.

Also apparent, in terms of our customer mix at the prices evaluated, is the relatively small size of the average customer, and the importance in terms of revenue of the very large customer.

D. As indicated by Table 9, those companies by type of business most interested in BELLBOY were service, retailing, construction, and professional organizations.

425

EXHIBIT II-5 (continued)

E. As might be expected, the jobs in which companies indicated the primary needs were those where employees were consistently away from the office or where a key employee would need to be contacted. See Table 4.

F. Those companies not interested in the BELLBOY service often indicated that they were "always in the office" and did not need to contact anyone outside. Other companies indicated that there was "just no need" for the service. Some companies also stated their business was 'too small' and did not have enough employees to warrant the service. See Table 3.

It should be remembered that no sales effort was employed as part of this project. Obviously, it could be anticipated that many companies expressing a lack of interest might alter their opinion if the advantages of BELLBOY were made more apparent through personal sales contact.

Projected Monthly Revenues High Estimate
of Potential Market (14,210 companies)

Number of Companies	At $24.00 per Month, per Unit Average Number of Employees	Number of BELLBOY Units	Monthly Revenue
5086	2	10,172	$244,128
658	4.5	2,961	71,064
681	8	5,448	130,752
314	18	5,652	135,648
90	100	9,000	216,000
Total 6829	—	33,233	$797,592
Average number of BELLBOY units per customer—4.87			

Projected Monthly Revenues High Estimate
of Potential Market (14,210 companies)

Number of Companies	At $20.00 per Month, per Unit Average Number of Employees	Number of BELLBOY Units	Monthly Revenue
6866	2	13,732	$274,640
890	4.5	4,005	80,100
875	8	7,000	140,000
314	18	5,652	113,040
90	100	9,000	180,000
Total 9035	—	39,389	$787,780
Average number of BELLBOY units per customer—4.36			

EXHIBIT II-5 (continued)

**Projected Monthly Revenues High Estimate
of Potential Market (14,210 companies)**

| | At $16.00 per Month, per Unit | | |
| | Average | | |
Number of Companies	Number of Employees	Number of BELLBOY Units	Monthly Revenue
8227	2	16,454	$263,264
1204	4.5	5,418	86,688
1316	8	10,528	168,448
90	18	1,620	25,920
224	50.5	11,312	180,992
90	100	9,000	144,000
Total 11,151	—	54,332	$869,312

Average number of BELLBOY units per customer—4.87

**Projected Monthly Revenues Low Estimate
of Potential Market (11,218 companies)**

| | At $24.00 per Month, per Unit | | |
| | Average | | |
Number of Companies	Number of Employees	Number of BELLBOY Units	Monthly Revenue
4039	2	8,078	$193,872
449	4.5	2,020.5	48,492
561	8	4,488	107,712
224	18	4,032	96,768
Total 5273	—	18,618.5	$446,844

Average number of BELLBOY units per customer—3.53

**Projected Monthly Revenues Low Estimate
of Potential Market (11,218 companies)**

| | At $20.00 per Month, per Unit | | |
| | Average | | |
Number of Companies	Number of Employees	Number of BELLBOY Units	Monthly Revenue
5609	2	11,218	$244,360
561	4.5	2,524.5	50,490
785	8	6,280	125,600
224	18	4,032	80,640
Total 7179	—	24,054.5	$481,090

Average number of BELLBOY units per customer—3.35

EXHIBIT II-5 (continued)

**Projected Monthly Revenues Low Estimate
of Potential Market (11,218 companies)**

	Number of Companies	At $16.00 per Month, per Unit Average Number of Employees	Number of BELLBOY Units	Monthly Revenue
	7180	2	14,360	$229,760
	785	4.5	3,532.5	56,520
	897	8	7,176	114,816
	224	50.5	11,312	180,992
Total	9086	—	36,380.5	$582,088

Average number of BELLBOY units per customer—4.00

TABLE 1
Respondents Interested or Not Interested in Using This Service (Base: 382)

Base: 382	(%)
Yes	15
Maybe	8
No	77
Total	100

Based on answers to the question: (Q.3) "If the monthly rate for this service was reasonable from your standpoint, would you be interested in using this service in the operation of your business?"

TABLE 2
Respondents Who Are or Are Not Familiar with a One-Way Pocket Signaling Unit

	Companies Interested (%) (Base: 87)	Companies Not Interested (%) (Base: 295)
Yes	62	50
No	38	50
Total	100	100

Based on answers to the question: (Q.2) "Are you familiar with a one-way pocket signaling unit?"

TABLE 3
Reasons Respondents Are Not Interested in BELLBOY Service (Base: 295)

Reason	Number Giving This Reason (%)
Always in office/no need to contact anyone outside	29
Just don't need/not interested	24
Business too small/not that many employees	11
Always able to reach/keep close contact	10
Have own communications system	6
Have two-way radios/mobile phones/car radios	5
System has too short a range/doesn't cover enough territory	5
Have system like this	4
Don't want interruptions when away from office	3
Salespeople call in/employees call us	3
Other	4
Total	104

Based on answers to the question: (Q.4) "You probably have a good reason why you feel BELLBOY service would not interest you. Would you mind telling me what it is?"

TABLE 4
Types of Jobs That Might Benefit from the BELLBOY Service

	Total (%)	Yes (%)	Maybe (%)
Base:	(87)	(58)	(29)
Employees in the field/salespeople/people on the road	51	52	48
Supervisor/manager/owner/president	40	45	31
Service people	15	16	14
Professional	9	9	10
Administrative/office personnel	5	7	—
Total	120	129	103

Based on answers to the question: (Q.5) "What types of jobs do the people have that might benefit from BELLBOY service?"

TABLE 5

Number of Employees Who Work at Jobs That Might Benefit from BELLBOY Service

	Base:	Total (%) (87)	Yes (%) (58)	Maybe (%) (29)
One		20	21	21
Two		14	16	10
Three		20	24	14
Four		10	12	7
Five		12	12	10
Six		5	3	7
Seven–nine		5	7	—
Ten to twenty		6	3	10
Twenty-one and over		7	2	17
Refused		1	—	4
Total		100	100	100

Based on answers to the question: (Q.6) "About how many employees do you have in these types of jobs?"

TABLE 6

Number of Employees Who Could Be Possible Users of the Service for $24.00 per Month

	Base:	Total (%) (87)	Yes (%) (58)	Maybe (%) (29)
One to three		36	36	35
Four to five		5	4	7
Six to ten		5	5	4
Eleven to twenty-five		2	2	3
Twenty-six to seventy-five		—	—	—
Over seventy-five		1	—	3
Don't know		1	—	3
None		50	53	45
Total		100	100	100

Based on answers to the question: (Q.7) "If the price for each BELLBOY unit was about $1.15 per business day or about $24.00 per month, how many employees could be possible users of this service?"

TABLE 7

Number of Employees Who Could Be Possible Users of the Service for $20.00 per Month

Base:	Total (%) (87)	Yes (%) (58)	Maybe (%) (29)
One to three	47	50	42
Four to five	7	5	11
Six to ten	6	7	3
Eleven to twenty-five	2	2	3
Twenty-six to seventy-five	—	—	—
Over seventy-five	1	—	3
Don't know	1	—	3
None	36	36	35
Total	100	100	100

Based on answers to the question: (Q.8) "If the price were lowered to $.95 per business day, or about $20.00 per month per unit, how many employees would be possible users of this service?"

TABLE 8

Number of Employees Who Could Be Possible Users of the Service for $16.00 per Month

Base:	Total (%) (87)	Yes (%) (58)	Maybe (%) (29)
One to three	54	64	35
Four to five	9	7	14
Six to ten	11	8	14
Eleven to twenty-five	1	—	3
Twenty-six to seventy-five	1	2	—
Over 75	1	—	3
Don't know	1	—	3
None	22	19	28
Total	100	100	100

Based on answers to the question: (Q.9) "If the price were lowered to $.75 per business day, or about $16.00 per month per unit, how many employees would be possible BELLBOY users?"

TABLE 9
Type of Company Business

Base:	Total (%) (87)	Yes (%) (58)	Maybe (%) (29)
Service	34	34	35
Retailing	30	31	28
Construction	10	9	14
Professional	9	10	17
Real Estate	6	5	7
Manufacturing	3	5	—
Other	14	12	17
Total	106	106	118

Based on answers to the question: (Q.10) "It would be helpful if you could briefly describe your company's business."

TABLE 10
Number of Employees in Company

Base:	Total (%) (87)	Yes (%) (58)	Maybe (%) (29)
One	2	3	—
Two	2	2	3
Three	7	10	—
Four	11	15	3
Five	10	9	14
Six	6	7	4
Seven	5	5	4
Eight	5	5	4
Nine to Twenty	25	26	24
Twenty-one to thirty	6	9	—
Thirty-one to forty	2	2	3
Forty-one to fifty	1	—	3
Fifty-one to ninety-nine	4	—	10
One hundred and over	13	5	28
Don't know	1	2	—
Total	100	100	100

Based on answers to the question: (Q.11) "About how many employees does your company have in (CITY NAME _____)?"

EXHIBIT II-6

BELLBOY Telephone Interview

RESPONDENT NAME _____

TELEPHONE
COMPANY _____ AREA CODE _____ PHONE _____
CALLS: DATE/TIME   1st _____ 2nd _____ 3rd _____

INTRODUCTION
Hello, I'm _____ of Peters Marketing Research. We are conducting a study for the TELEPHONE COMPANY and I would like to talk with the person that handles _____ (CO. NAME) communications needs. Have I reached that person?

Yes (_____)
No (_____)

[a] IF YES, GET NAME AND GO TO "*AGREEMENT*"
[b] IF NO, GET NAME, ASK TO BE CONNECTED, AND GO BACK TO "*INTRODUCTION*"
[c] IF NO, AND THE PERSON CANNOT BE CONTACTED, GET NAME AND *CALL BACK*

AGREEMENT
Mr./Ms. _____, as I mentioned, the TELEPHONE COMPANY has asked us to conduct a study and gather information about a new service that might be offered. This new service is entitled BELLBOY.

1.   Would you mind if I asked a few questions to get your opinion concerning this service?

Okay   (_____) GO TO Q.2
Not okay   (_____) TERMINATE INTERVIEW

2.   Are you familiar with a one-way pocket signaling unit?

Yes   (_____)
No   (_____) GO TO EXPLANATION

EXPLANATION OF BELLBOY SERVICE
Well, briefly, Southwestern Bell's BELLBOY is a compact, lightweight, one-way signaling device about the size of a candy bar. There are others that are similar but the BELLBOY unit fits easily into your pocket. BELLBOY is carried whenever you are away from your office. Your people can contact you simply by dialing a number which gives you a "beep" signal from your BELLBOY. The "beep" tells you someone wants to reach you. You then would call your office from any nearby telephone.

3.   If the monthly rate for this service was reasonable from your standpoint, would you be interested in using this service in the operation of your business?

Yes   (_____) GO TO Q.5
No   (_____) GO TO Q.4, THEN TERMINATE

4.   You probably have a good reason why you feel BELLBOY service would not interest you; would you mind telling me what it is?

_____
_____
_____
_____
_____
_____

5.   What types of jobs do the people have that might benefit from the BELLBOY service?
6.   About how many employees do you have in these types of jobs? _____
7.   If the price for each BELLBOY unit was about $1.15 per business day or about $24.00 per month, how many employees could be possible users of this service?

EXHIBIT II-6 (continued)

ENTER ACTUAL ANSWER

0	(_____)	11–25	(_____)
1–3	(_____)	26–75	(_____)
4–5	(_____)	Over 75	(_____)
6–10	(_____)	Don't know	(_____)

8. If the price were lowered to $.95 per business day, or about $20.00 per month per unit, how many employees would be possible users of this service?

ENTER ACTUAL ANSWER

0	(_____)	11–25	(_____)
1–3	(_____)	26–75	(_____)
4–5	(_____)	Over 75	(_____)
6–10	(_____)	Don't know	(_____)

9. If the price were lowered to $.75 per business day, or about $16.00 per month per unit, how many employees would be possible BELLBOY users?

ENTER ACTUAL ANSWER

0	(_____)	11–25	(_____)
1–3	(_____)	26–75	(_____)
4–5	(_____)	Over 75	(_____)
6–10	(_____)	Don't know	(_____)

10. It would be helpful if you could briefly describe your company's business.
_____
_____
_____

11. About how many employees does your company have in (CITY NAME)
_____ ?

CASE II-3
Currency Concepts International[1]

Dr. Karen Anderson, Manager of Planning for Century Bank of Los Angeles, settled down for an unexpected evening of work in her small beach apartment. It seemed that every research project Century had commissioned in the last year had been completed during her ten-day trip to Taiwan. She had brought three research reports home that evening to try to catch up before meeting with the bank's Executive Planning Committee the next day.

Possibly because the currency-exchange facilities had been closed at the Taiwan Airport when she first arrived, Dr. Anderson's attention turned first to a report on a project currently under consideration by one of Century Bank's wholly owned subsidiaries, Currency Concepts International (CCI). The project concerned the manufacture and installation of currency-exchange automatic teller machines (ATMs) in major foreign airports.

CCI had been responsible for the development of Century Bank's very popular ATM ("money machine"), now installed in numerous branches of the bank, as well as in its main location in downtown Los Angeles. The current project was a small part of CCI and Century Bank's plan to expand electronic banking services worldwide.

As she started to review the marketing research effort of Information Resources, Inc., she wondered what she would be able to recommend to the Executive Planning Committee the next day regarding the currency-exchange project. She liked her recommendations to be backed by solid evidence, and she looked forward to reviewing results of the research performed to date.

Activities of Information Resources, Inc.

Personnel of Information Resources, Inc., had decided to follow three different approaches in investigating the problem presented to them: (1) review secondary statistical data; (2) interview companies that currently engage in currency exchange; and (3) conduct an exploratory consumer survey of a convenience sample. **Secondary Data.** The review of secondary data had three objectives:

1. To determine whether the number of persons flying abroad constitutes a market potentially large enough to merit automated currency exchange

2. To isolate any trends in the numbers of people flying abroad

3. To determine whether the amount of money that these travelers spend abroad is sizeable enough to provide a potential market for automated currency exchange

The United States Department of Transportation monitors the number of people traveling from United States airports to foreign airports. These statistics are maintained and categorized as follows: citizen and noncitizen passengers, and civilian and military passengers. Since this study was concerned only with Americans who travel abroad, only citizen categories were considered. Furthermore, since American military flights do not utilize the same foreign airport facilities as civilian passenger flights, the military category was also excluded. The prospect that non-Americans might also use these facilities causes the statistics to be somewhat conservative. The figures, for 1978, were summed for each foreign airport, the results by geographical area are shown in Exhibit II-7. The top ten gateway cities from all American ports are shown in Exhibit II-8.

The second objective, to determine any growth trends in air travel, was addressed by studying the number of Americans flying abroad in the last five years. Exhibit II-9 shows the number of American travelers flying to various geographic areas and the associated growth rates in each of those areas. Europe, clearly has the greatest number of travelers; and, although it

EXHIBIT II-7
American Citizens Flying Abroad in 1978 to Foreign Ports of Entry with Over 25,000 Arrivals

Europe	3,725,952
Caribbean	1,930,756
Central America	1,356,496
South America	301,347
Far East	516,861
Oceania	133,584

Note: Included in these area totals are all ports of entry that receive more than 25,000 passengers annually (68 per day). Ports of entry with a lower through-put rate were excluded.
Source: United States Department of Transportation. *United States International Air Travel Statistics,* 1978, Washington, D.C.

---

[1] This case is printed with permission of the author, Grady D. Bruce of the California State University, Fullerton.

EXHIBIT II-8
Most Frequented Foreign Ports of Entry from All American Ports

Port	Passengers
1. London, England	1,420,285
2. Mexico City, Mexico	641,054
3. Frankfurt, Germany	446,166
4. Hamilton, Bermuda	378,897
5. Nassau, Bahamas	361,791
6. Tokyo, Japan	320,827
7. Freeport, Bahamas	309,288
8. Paris, France	295,823
9. Rome, Italy	272,186
10. Acapulco, Mexico	226,120

Source: Based on data provided in United States Department of Transportation, *United States International Air Travel Statistics,* 1978, Washington, D.C.

did not show the greatest percentage growth in 1978, it does have the largest growth in absolute numbers. Generally, growth rates in overseas air travel have been good for the last four years; at this time, these trends appear to be positive from the standpoint of a potential market. However, there are also some potential problems on the horizon. As the world's energy situation increasingly worsens, there is the possibility of significant decreases in international travel.

In order to address the third objective, whether the amount of money spent by American travelers abroad constitutes a potential market, per capita spending was examined. Exhibit II-10 shows per capita spending, by geographic area, for the last five years as well as yearly percentages of growth. The category that includes the Far East, "other areas," shows the highest per capita spending. This may be the result of the relatively low prices found in the Far East.

Europe shows the second-highest figures for per capita spending; this area also exhibited strong growth in the last year. These figures indicate that Americans are spending increasing amounts of money aboard; even when inflation is taken into consideration, these figures are positive.

Information Resources, Inc., concluded, therefore, that Europe holds the greatest market potential for the new system. As Dick Knowlton, coordinator of the research team, said, "Not only are all of the statistics for Europe high, but the short geographic distances between countries can be expected to provide a good deal of intra-area travel."

Company Interviews. In an attempt to better understand the current operations of currency exchange in airports, four major firms engaged in these activities were contacted. While some firms were naturally reluctant to provide information on some areas of their operations, several were quite cooperative. These firms, and a number of knowledgeable individuals whose names surfaced in initial interviews, provided the information that follows.

In both New York and Los Angeles, there is only one bank engaged in airport currency exchange: Deak-Perera. American Express, Bank of America, and Citibank, as well as Deak-Perera, are engaged in airport currency exchange in a variety of foreign locations. Approval of permits to engage in airport currency

EXHIBIT II-9
Growth in Number of Americans Flying Abroad 1974–1978 (Thousands)

	1974	% Change	1975	% Change	1976	% Change	1977	% Change	1978
European and Mediterranean	3,325	(4.2)	3,185	10.6	3,523	11.3	3,920	5.2	4,105
Western Europe	3,118	(4.1)	2,990	10.0	3,245	11.2	3,663	6.9	3,914
Caribbean and Central America	2,147	(3.8)	2,065	6.6	2,201	—	2,203	7.4	2,365
South America	423	5.7	447	(2.5)	436	10.8	483	6.6	515
Other Areas	572	14.9	657	12.2	737	6.4	784	2.7	805
Total	9,585	8.5	9,344	36.9	10,142	39.7	11,053	28.8	11,704

Source: United States Department of Commerce, Survey of Current Business, June 1979, Washington, D.C.

EXHIBIT II-10
Per Capita Spending by Americans Traveling Abroad 1974–1978

	1974	% Change	1975	% Change	1976	% Change	1977	% Change	1978
Europe	542	11.1	602	1.3	610	—	612	17.2	717
Caribbean and Central America	319	19.4	381	(6.6)	356	—	359	4.5	375
South America	494	9.5	541	(1.7)	532	(1.1)	526	12.9	594
Other Areas	786	1.9	802	0.9	809	3.7	839	20.0	1,007
All Areas	486	12.6	547	—	545	1.8	555	14.6	635

Source: United States Department of Commerce, Survey of Current Business, June 1979, Washington, D.C.

exchange activity rests with the municipal body that governs the airport, and is highly controlled. It appears that foreign currency exchange is a highly profitable venture. Banks make most of their profits on the spread in exchange rates, which are posted daily.

Both Citibank and Bank of America indicated that they attempt to ensure their facilities availability to all flights. The more profitable flights were found to be those that were regularly scheduled, rather than chartered. The person more likely to use the facilities was the vacationer rather than the businessperson. Neither bank could give an exact figure for the average transaction size; estimates ranged from $85 to $100.

It was the opinion of bank/Deak employees, who dealt with travelers on a daily basis, that the average traveler was somewhat uncomfortable changing money in a foreign country. They also believed it to be particularly helpful if clerks at the exchange counter converse with travelers in their own language. A number of years ago Deak attempted to use a type of vending machine to dispense money at Kennedy Airport. This venture failed; industry observers felt that the absence of human conversation and assurance contributed to its lack of success.

Most of the exchanges performed the same types of services, including the sale of foreign currency and the sale of travelers checks. The actual brand of travelers checks sold varies with the vendors.

American Express has recently placed automated unmanned travelers check dispensers in various American airports. This service is available to American Express card holders and the only charge is 1 percent of the face value of the purchased checks; the purchase is charged directly to the customer's checking account. As yet, the machines have not enjoyed a great deal of use, although American Express has been successful in enrolling its customers as potential users.

Methods of payment for currency purchases are similar at all exchanges. Accepted forms of payment include: actual cash, travelers checks, cashier checks drawn on local banks, and Master Charge or Visa cards. When using a credit card to pay for currency purchases, there is a service charge added to the customer's bill, as with any cash advance.

Traveler Interviews. To supplement and complement the statistical foundation gained by reviewing secondary data sources, the consumer interview portion of the study was purposefully designed to elicit qualitative information about travelers' feelings toward current and future forms of exchanging currency. Approximately sixty American travelers were interviewed at both the San Francisco and Los Angeles International Airports, due to the accessibility of these locations to Information Resources' sole location. An unstructured, undisguised questionnaire was developed to assist in channeling the interview toward specific topics (see Appendix A). Questions were not fixed and the question order was dependent on the respondent's answers. Basically, the guide served to force the interview conversation around the central foreign currency exchange theme. The interviews were conducted primarily in the arrival/departure lobbies of international carriers and spanned over four weeks, beginning in mid-December 1979. A deliberate attempt was made to include as many arriving as departing passengers to neutralize the effect of increasing holiday traffic. Additionally, to reduce interviewer bias, three different interviewers were used. Interviews were intentionally kept informal. And Dick Knowlton cautioned the interviewers to remain objective and "not let your excitement over the product concept spill over into the interview and bias the responses."

The interviews were divided almost evenly between those who favored the concept and those who did not. Those who did perceive value in the concept tended also to support other innovations such as the automated teller machine and charging foreign currency on credit cards. Those who would not use the currency exchange terminals wanted more human interaction and generally did not favor automation in any form; a fair proportion also had had previous problems exchanging foreign currency. However, even those who did not favor the currency exchange idea did seem to prefer the system of having twenty-four-hour availability of the machines, and of using credit cards to get cash under emergency situations.

The respondents represent a diverse group of individuals ranging in age from eighteen to eighty years, holding such different positions as oil executive, photographer, housewife, and customs officer. Primarily bound for Europe, Canada, and Mexico, the interviewees were mainly split between pleasure-seekers and those on business. Only three individuals interviewed were part of tour groups, and of these three, only one had previously traveled abroad. The majority of the others had been out of the United States before and had exchanged currency in at least one other country. Many had exchanged currency in remote parts of the world, including Morocco, Brazil, Australia, Japan, Tanzania, and Russia. Only five individuals had not exchanged money in airports at one time or another. The majority had obtained foreign currency in airports and exchanged money in airports primarily in small denominations for use in taxi cab fares, bus fares, phones, and airport gift shops, as well as for food, tips, and drinks. Most respondents agreed a prime motive for exchanging money in airports was the security of having local currency.

Exchanging currency can become a trying ordeal for some individuals. They fear being cheated on the exchange rate; they cannot convert the foreign currency into tangible concepts (for example, "how many yen should a loaf of bread cost?"); they dislike lines and associated red tape; and many cannot understand the rates as posted in percentages. Most individuals exchange money in airports, hotels, or banks, but sometimes there are no convenient facilities at all for exchanging currency.

People like to deal with well-known bank branches, especially in airports, because they feel more confident about the rate they are receiving. However, major fears of individuals are that money exchange personnel will not understand English and that they will be cheated in the transaction. Furthermore, a few people mentioned poor documentation when they exchange currency in foreign airports.

The travelers were divided as to whether they exchange currency before or after they arrive in the foreign country, but a few said that the decision depended on what country they were entering. If a currency, such as English pounds, could easily be obtained form a local bank before leaving the United States, they were more likely to exchange before leaving. However, in no case would the traveler arrange for currency beyond a week in advance. Most prefered

to obtain the foreign currency on relatively short notice—less than three days before the trip. Of the individuals on tours, none planned to obtain currency in the foreign airport. Apparently, the tour guide had previously arranged for the necessary transportation from the airport to the hotels, and there would be only enough time to gather one's luggage and find the bus before it would depart, leaving no time to enjoy the facilities of the airport which required foreign currency. All three tour individuals did mention that they planned to obtain foreign currency once they arrived at the hotel. All individuals mentioned that they had secured their own foreign currency, but a few of the wives who were traveling with their husbands conceded that their spouses usually converted the currency in the foreign airport.

Very few of the interviewees had actually used an automated teller machine, but the majority had heard of or seen the teller machines on television. Those who had used the automated machines preferred their convenience and were generally satisfied with the terminal's performance. Many of those who had not used the automated teller machines mistrusted the machine and possible loss of control over their finances. Concerns about security and problems with the machines breaking down were also expressed. One woman described the teller machines as being "convenient, but cold." Apparently, many people prefer having human interaction when their money is concerned.

As noted earlier, approximately thirty of the respondents would favor the exchange terminals over their normal airport currency exchange routine, while the same number would have nothing to do with the machines. However, the majority of potential users qualified their use by such features as competitive rates, knowing the precise charges, or knowing they could get help if something went wrong. Individuals who indicated no preference were included in the favorable category, simply because they would not refuse to try the machine. Most of the indifferent people seemed to indicate they would try such a machine if some type of introductory promotional offer was included, such as travel information, currency tips, or a better rate.

With virtually unanimity, the respondents felt that twenty-four-hour availability made the currency exchange machines more attractive, yet that alone would not persuade the dissenters to use the terminals. Some individuals felt that a machine simply could not give the travel advice that could be obtained at the currency exchange booths.

The opportunity to charge foreign currency against a major credit card, such as Master Charge or Visa, was a definite plus in the minds of most respondents. One individual clearly resented the idea, however, feeling that he would "overspend" if given such a convenient way to obtain cash. Respondents offered a number of suggestions concerning implementations of the product concept and a number of specific product features:

1. Add information about the country.
2. Provide small denominations, and include coins.
3. Have it communicate in English.
4. Put in travelers checks to get cash.
5. Put in cash to get foreign currency.
6. Post rates daily.
7. Keep rates competitive and post charges.
8. Have television screen with person to describe procedure.
9. Place the machines in hotels and banks.
10. Have a change machine nearby that can convert paper money.
11. Place machine near existing currency exchange facilities for convenience when normal lines become long.
12. Demonstrate how to use the machine.
13. Use all bank credit cards.

Appendix A

Interview Guide for International Travelers (U.S. Citizens)

These interviews should remain as informal as possible. The object is not to obtain statistically reliable results, but to get ideas that will help to stimulate research. These questions are not fixed; the order, however, is sometimes dependent on answers the respondents give.

Introduce yourself

1. Are you going to be traveling to a foreign country? Arriving from a foreign country? A United States resident?
2. Where is / was your final destination?
3. Why are you traveling (business, pleasure, a tour)?
4. How often do you travel outside of the United States?
5. Have you ever exchanged currency in a foreign country. (If no, go to #6.) Where? Does anything in particular stand out in your mind when you exchanged currency?
6. Have you ever changed money in an airport? (If no, go to #7.)
7. Where do you plan to exchange currency on this trip?
8. Where do you change money normally?
9. Have you ever had any problems changing currencies? Explain circumstances.
10. Normally, would you change money before entering a country or after you arrive? If before, how long in advance? Where? (Probe.)
11. Are you familiar with automated teller machines that banks are using? (If not, explain.) Have you used one of these machines?
12. What are your feelings toward these machines?
13. If a currency exchange terminal, similar to an automated teller machine, was placed in your destination airport, would you use the machine or follow your normal routine?
14. Would 24-hour availability make the currency exchange machines more attractive? Woud you use the terminals at night?
15. None of the currency exchange machines currently exists. What features or services could be provided so that you might choose to use a terminal rather than other currency exchange facilities?
16. If you could charge the foreign currency received to a major credit card, such as Master Charge or Visa, would you be more likely to use the machine?
17. Demographics—Age range (visual)
    Occupation?
    Sex?
    Traveling alone?

PART III

DATA ANALYSIS

15

FUNDAMENTALS OF
DATA ANALYSIS

Learning Objectives

▶ Familiarize with the fundamental concepts of data analysis.

▶ Understand the need for preliminary data preparation techniques such as data editing, coding, and statistically adjusting the data where required.

▶ Describe the various statistical techniques for adjusting the data.

▶ Discuss the significance of data tabulation.

▶ Identify the factors that influence the selection of an appropriate data analysis strategy.

▶ Familiarize with the various statistical techniques available for data analysis.

▶ Explain the need for a brief explanation of the various multivariate techniques.

The HMO study introduced in Chapter 4 resulted in a survey from which 1145 usable questionnaires were obtained. This represents a stack of paper literally over 10 feet high. Data analysis plays an important role in turning this quantity of paper into defensible, actionable sets of conclusions and reports. It is actually a set of methods and techniques that can be used to obtain information and insights from the data.

An understanding of the principles of data analysis is useful for several reasons. First, it can lead the researcher to information and insights that otherwise would not be available. Second, it can help avoid erroneous judgments and conclusions. Third, it can provide a background to help interpret and understand analysis conducted by others. Finally, a knowledge of the power of data analysis techniques can constructively influence research objectives and research design.

Although data analysis can be a powerful aid to gaining useful knowledge, it cannot rescue a badly conceived marketing research study. If the research purpose is not well conceived, if the research questions are irrelevant, or if the hypothesis is nonviable or uninteresting, the research will require an abundance of good fortune to be useful. Further, data analysis rarely can compensate for a bad question, an inadequate sampling procedure, or sloppy fieldwork.

Data analysis has the potential to ruin a well-designed study. Inappropriate or misused data analysis can suggest judgments and conclusions that are at best unclear and incomplete, and at worst erroneous. Thus, it can lead to decisions inferior to those that would have been made without the benefit of the research. One important reason for studying data analysis, therefore, is to avoid the pitfalls associated with it.

The purpose of Parts III and IV of this book is to describe data analysis techniques, so that when the appropriate situation arises the researcher can draw on them. Another goal is to provide an understanding of the limitations of the various techniques, to minimize the likelihood that they will be misused or misinterpreted. The techniques and approaches revealed in this chapter are used routinely in nearly all descriptive and causal research. It is, therefore, important for the reader to understand them.

The type of data analysis required will be unique to each study; however, nearly all studies involving data analysis will require the editing and coding of data, will use one or more data analysis techniques, and will have to be concerned with presenting the results effectively.

In this chapter some preliminary data preparation techniques such as data editing, coding, and statistically adjusting the data for further analysis, will be discussed first. Basic ways to tabulate individual questions from a questionnaire (one-way tabulation) then will be developed. The discussion on tabulation will also include graphical representation of tabulated data. Next, the focus will turn to the question of tabulation among sample subgroups (cross-tabulation). Further, we will provide a discussion of the various factors that influence the selection of an appropriate data analysis strategy. This chapter will also present an overview of the various statistical techniques that a researcher can use in analyzing data.

PREPARING THE DATA FOR ANALYSIS

The raw data obtained from the questionnaires must undergo preliminary preparation before they can be analyzed using statistical techniques. The quality of the results obtained from the statistical techniques and their subsequent interpretation depend to a great degree on how well the data were prepared and converted into a form suitable for analysis. The major data preparation techniques include (a) data editing, (b) coding, and (c) statistically adjusting the data (if required).

Data Editing

The role of the editing process is to identify omissions, ambiguities, and errors in the responses. It should be conducted in the field by the interviewer and field supervisor, as well as by the analyst, just prior to data analysis. Among the problems to be identified are the following:

Interviewer error	Interviewers may not be giving the respondent the correct instructions.
Omissions	Respondents often fail to answer a single question or a section of the questionnaire, either deliberately or inadvertently.

Ambiguity	A response might not be legible or it might be unclear (which of two boxes is checked in a multiple-response system).
Inconsistencies	Sometimes two responses can be logically inconsistent. For example, a respondent who is a lawyer may have checked a box indicating that he or she did not complete high school.
Lack of cooperation	In a long questionnaire with hundreds of attitude or image questions, a respondent might rebel and check the same response (in an agree–disagree scale, for example) in a long list of questions.
Ineligible respondent	An inappropriate respondent may be included in the sample. For example, if a sample is supposed to include only women over 18, others should be excluded.

When such problems are identified, there are several alternatives available.[1] The preferred alternative, where practical, is to contact the respondent again. This is often quite feasible and should be done by the interviewer if the questions involved are important enough to warrant the effort. Another alternative, to throw out the whole questionnaire as not usable, might be appropriate if it were clear that the respondent either did not understand the survey or was not cooperating. A less extreme alternative is to throw out only the problem questions and retain the balance of the questions. Some respondents will bypass questions like income or age, for example, and cooperate fully with the other questions. In the parts of the analysis involving income or age, only those respondents who answered those questions will be included, but in the rest of the analysis all respondents could be included. Still another alternative is to code illegible or missing answers into a category such as "don't know" or "no opinion." Such an approach may simplify the data analysis without materially distorting the interpretation. Alternatively, for any respondent one can input missing values for certain variables through the use of mean profile values, or infer the values by matching the respondent's profile to that of another similar respondent.

A by-product of the editing process is that it helps in evaluating and guiding the interviewers; an interviewer's tendency to allow a certain type of error to occur should be detected by the editing process.

Coding

Coding the closed-ended questions is fairly straightforward. In this process, we specify exactly how the responses are to be entered. Figure 15-1 is an example of an auto maintenance questionnaire, and Figure 15-2 illustrates the corresponding coding mechanism. The survey was mailed to 500 participants, and 150 responded.

As shown in Figure 15-2, the first three columns are used for identifying the respondents. The column reference is synonymous with variable identification; the questionnaire number is also indicated to provide a direct link between the question number, the variable identification, and the column numbers. Each question is described briefly in a separate column, and the range of permissible values provides the key information of the value to be entered for the particular type of response.

Directions: Please answer the questions below by placing a check mark (√) in the appropriate boxes or, where applicable, by writing your response in the space provided.

1. Are you solely responsible for taking care of your automotive maintenance needs?
    ☐ Yes   ☐ No
    If you answered "no" to question No. 1, who is and what is that person's relation to you?
    _____

2. Do you perform simple auto maintenance yourself? (*e.g., tire pressure, change wiper blades, change air filter, etc.*)
    ☐ Yes   ☐ No

3. If you answered "no" to question No. 2, where do you take your car for servicing?
    _____

4. How often do you either perform maintenance on your automobile or have it serviced?
    ☐   Once per month
    ☐   Once every three months
    ☐   Once every six months
    ☐   Once per year
    ☐   Once (*please specify*) _____

5. When do you handle maintenance related automobile problems?
    ☐   Through scheduled maintenance
    ☐   As problems arise
    ☐   Postpone as long as possible
    ☐   Other (*please specify*) _____
    ☐   I do not keep track of it

6. If scheduled maintenance is done on your automobile, how do you keep track of what has been done?
    ☐   Auto dealer or mechanic's records
    ☐   Personal records
    ☐   Mental recollection
    ☐   Other (*please specify*) _____
    ☐   I do not keep track of it

7. Please rank the following list of car maintenance activities in order of importance. (*1 = most important; 2 = second most important; 3 = third most important; etc.*)

    _____ Tire maintenance

    _____ Oil change

    _____ Brake maintenance

    _____ Check belts and hoses

    _____ Check spark plugs

8. Are there any other maintenance activities that should be included in the above list?
    _____
    _____

AUTO MAINTENANCE QUESTIONNAIRE

FIGURE 15-1
Auto Maintenance Questionnaire

Once the response values are entered into a computer file, a statistical software program can be employed to generate diagnostic information. However, before any data analysis is performed, the data have to be checked for any error that might have come from the process of data entry. Once the data are error free, statistical adjustments to the data can be made.

Column No.	Column Ref.	Question No.	Question Description	Range of Permissible Values
1–3	A		ID No. of Questionnaire	001–150
4	B	1	Responsible for maintenance	0 = no, 1 = yes, 9 = blank
5	C	1	Who is responsible	0 = husband, 1 = boyfriend, 2 = father, 3 = mother, 4 = relative, 5 = friend, 6 = other, 9 = blank
6	D	2	Perform simple maintenance	0 = no, 1 = yes, 9 = blank
7	E	3	Where for service	
8	F	4	How often is maintenance performed	Once per: 0 = month, 1 = three months, 2 = six months, 3 = year, 4 = other, 9 = blank
9	G	4	Other for "how often"	
10	H	5	When are problems handled	0 = scheduled maintenance, 1 = as problems arise, 2 = postpone as long as possible, 3 = other, 9 = blank
11	I	5	Other for "when problems handled"	
12	J	6	How maintenance is tracked	0 = not tracked, 1 = auto dealer/mechanics' records, 2 = personal records, 3 = mental recollection, 4 = other, 5 = doesn't keep track, 9 = blank
13	K	6	Other for "how maintenance is tracked"	
14	L	7	Rank in order of importance: tire	0 = blank, 1 = most important, 2 = second most important, 3 = third, 4 = fourth, 5 = fifth
15	M	7	Rank in order of importance: oil	0 = blank, 1 = most important, 2 = second most important, 3 = third, 4 = fourth, 5 = fifth
16	N	7	Rank in order of importance: brake	0 = blank, 1 = most important, 2 = second most important, 3 = third, 4 = fourth, 5 = fifth
17	O	7	Rank in order of importance: belts	0 = blank, 1 = most important, 2 = second most important, 3 = third, 4 = fourth, 5 = fifth
18	P	7	Rank in order of importance: plugs	0 = blank, 1 = most important, 2 = second most important, 3 = third, 4 = fourth, 5 = fifth
19	Q	8	Any that should be included in No. 7	

FIGURE 15-2
Coding instructions for the Auto Maintenance Questionnaire

Coding for open-ended questions is much more difficult. Usually a lengthy list of possible responses is generated and then each response is placed into one of the list items. Often the assignment of a response involves a judgment decision if the response does not exactly match a list item. For example, a question such as "Why did you select your instrument from Ajax Electronics?" might elicit literally hundreds of different responses, such as *price, delivery, accuracy, reliability, familiarity, doesn't break down, can get it repaired, features, includes spare parts, a good manual, appearance, size,* and *shape.* Decisions must be made about the response categories. Should "reliability" and "doesn't break down" be in the same category, or do they represent two different responses? The difficulty of coding and analyzing open-ended responses provides a reason to avoid them in the questionnaire whenever possible.[2]

Statistically Adjusting the Data

There are many adjustments that can be made to the data in order to enhance its quality for data analysis. The most common procedures for statistically adjusting data are as follows:

Weighting. **Weighting** is a procedure by which each response in the database is assigned a number according to some prespecified rule. Most often, weighting is done to make the sample data more representative of a target population on specific characteristics. Categories underrepresented in the sample are given higher weights, while overrepresented categories are given lower weights. Weighting also is done to increase or decrease the number of cases in the sample that possess certain characteristics.

Weighting may also be used for adjusting the sample so that greater importance is attached to respondents with certain characteristics. For example, if a study is conducted to determine the market potential of a new sports drink, the researcher might want to attach greater weight to the opinions of the younger people in the market, who will be the heavy users of the product. This could be accomplished by assigning weights of 2.0 to persons in the sample who are under age 30 and 1.0 to respondents over 30. Weighting should be applied with caution, and the weighting procedure should be documented and made a part of the project report.[3]

Variable Respecification. **Variable respecification** is a procedure in which the existing data are modified to create new variables, or in which a large number of variables are collapsed into fewer variables. The purpose of this procedure is to create variables that are consistent with the study's objectives. For example, suppose the original variable represented the reasons for purchasing a car, with ten response categories. These might be collapsed into four categories: performance, price, appearance, and service. Respecification also includes taking the ratio of two variables to create a new variable, taking square root and log transformations, and using dummy variables.

Dummy variables are extensively used for respecifying categorical variables. They are also called **binary, dichotomous, instrumental,** or **qualitative** variables. The general rule is that if there are "*m*" levels of the qualitative variable, we use "*m-1*" dummy variables to specify them. The reason for using only *m-1* dummy variables is that only *m-1* levels (or categories) are independent, and the information pertaining to the *m*th level can be obtained from the existing *m-1* dummy variables. A product could have been purchased in either the first half or the second half of the year (a qualitative variable with two levels). The purchase time could be represented by a single dummy variable.[4]

It will take a value of 1 if it was bought in the first half of the year, and 0 in the second half.

Scale Transformation. Yet another common procedure for statistically adjusting data is scale transformation. **Scale transformation** involves the manipulation of scale values to ensure comparability with other scales. In the same study, different scales may be employed for measuring different variables. Therefore, it would not be meaningful to make comparisons across the measurement scales for any respondent. Even if the same scale is employed for all the variables, different respondents may use the scale differently. Some respondents may consistently use the lower end of a rating scale, whereas others may consistently use the upper end. These differences can be corrected by appropriately transforming the data.[5]

One of the most common scale transformation procedures is **standardization.** Standardization allows the researcher to compare variables that have been measured using different types of scales. For example, if sales are measured in actual dollars, and price in cents, then the actual value of the variance for the sales variable will be higher compared to price, because of the units of measurement. To compare the variances, both variables can be brought down to a common unit of measurement. This can be achieved by forcing the variables, by standardization, to have a mean zero and a standard deviation of one. Mathematically, this is done by first subtracting the mean, X, from each score and then dividing by the standard deviation, s_x. Standardization can be done only on interval or ratio-scaled data. The formula for standardized score, z_i, is

$$z_i = (X_i - \overline{X})/s_x$$

STRATEGY FOR DATA ANALYSIS

Usually the first step in data analysis, after data preparation, is to analyze each question or measure by itself. This is done by tabulating the data. Tabulation consists simply of counting the number of cases that fall into the various categories. Other than aiding in "data cleaning" aspects, such as identifying the degree of omissions, ambiguities, and errors in the responses, the primary use of tabulation is in (a) determining the empirical distribution (frequency distribution) of the variable in question and (b) calculating the descriptive (summary) statistics, particularly the mean or percentages.

Next, the data are subjected to cross-tabulations to assess if any association is present between two (typically) nominal variables. If the variables are measured as interval or ratio, they are transformed to nominally scaled variables for the purpose of cross-tabulation. For example, the income of a household can be rescaled to <\$30,000 and >\$30,000 to cross-tab with another nominally scaled variable. For analyzing relationships between two or more variables, **multivariate analysis** (discussed later) can be performed.

Tabulation: Frequency Distribution

A **frequency distribution** simply reports the number of responses that each question received, and is the simplest way of determining the empirical distribution of the variable. A frequency distribution organizes data into **classes,** or groups of values, and shows the number of observations from the data set that falls into each of the classes. Figure 15-3 provides a frequency distribution for two of the questions from the HMO study. A key question is the enrollment plan question in which the respondents are asked if they would enroll in the described plan. The number of people in each response category is shown. Thus, 124 responded "Yes, I would enroll." The figure shows two other methods of presenting the frequency distribution. One is the percentage breakdown of the various categories; the percentage often is easier to interpret than the actual numbers (rounding errors cause the percentage total to differ from 100 percent). The other is a visual bar-graph presentation known as a **histogram.**

A **histogram** is a series of rectangles, each proportional in width to the range of values within a class and proportional in height to the number of items falling in the class. If the classes we use in the frequency distribution are of equal width, the vertical bars in the histograms are also of equal width. The height of the bar for each class corresponds to the number of items in the class. The actual distribution of the variable can be visualized easily through the histogram. The actual distribution can then be compared to some theoretical

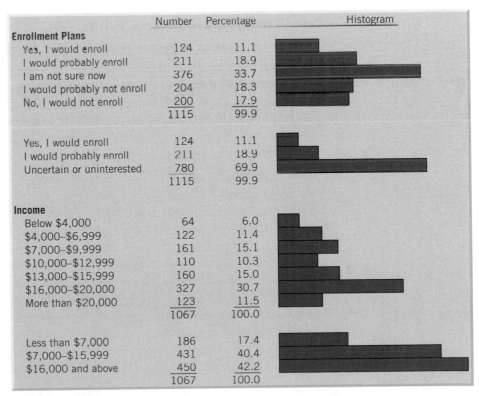

FIGURE 15-3
Frequency distribution

distribution to determine whether the data are consistent with some a priori model.

For many questions it is useful to combine some of the question categories. For example, in Figure 15-3 the enrollment question is shown with three of the responses combined into an "uncertain or uninterested" category. The logic is that a response of "I am not sure now" probably means that the respondent will not enroll. Responses to a new concept usually need to be discounted somewhat to correct for initial curiosity and a desire to please the survey sponsor. Decisions to combine categories should be supported by some kind of logic or theory. The resulting combinations also should result in categories that contain a worthwhile number of respondents. Usually, it is not useful to work with categories with only a few respondents. In fact, one purpose of combining categories is to develop larger respondent groups. Note that the two lowest income categories had relatively small respondent groups before they were combined.

Why not start with only three categories in each case? The questionnaire then would be shorter and easier to complete. One reason for not doing so is that before the study is conducted there may be no knowledge as to how the respondents are distributed. If too few categories are planned, all the respondents may end up in one of them and none in the others. Furthermore, extra categories might make responses more realistic. In the enrollment plan question in Figure 15-3, if there were not five responses available, people might have a greater tendency to check the "I would probably enroll" category.

Tabulation: Descriptive Statistics

Descriptive statistics are statistics normally associated with a frequency distribution that helps summarize the information presented in the frequency table. These include (a) measures of central tendency (mean, median, and model), (b) measures of dispersion (range, standard deviation, and coefficient of variation), and (c) measures of shape (skewness and kurtosis).[6] Here we restrict our discussion to the more commonly used statistics—the mean and the percentage.

Means and Percentages. In some situations it is desirable to use a single number to describe the responses to a question. In such circumstances, the sample mean or percentage is used. The sample **mean** is simply the average number, obtained by dividing the sum of the responses to a question by the sample size (the number of respondents to that question). The **percentage** is the proportion who answered a question a certain way, multiplied by 100.

Table 15-1 illustrates a study of the reaction of members of a community to a transit system. As part of the study, four life-style and attitude questions were asked, using a seven-point, agree–disagree scale. The first column of Table 15-1 gives the mean or average score among the 62 respondents. They indicate that the sample in general is concerned with gasoline costs and is not excited about jogging. When the response is based on two alternatives, or when a single alternative is the focus of the analysis, the percentage is used. For example, Question 5 in Table 15-1 reports that 36 percent of the shoppers live close to a transit station. The balance of Table 15-1 will be discussed shortly.

TABLE 15-1
Rapid Transit User

	Mean Score	Transit System User[a] $\bar{X}_U$	Nonuser[b] $\bar{X}_H$	Difference Between Sample Means $\bar{X}_U - \bar{X}_H$
Agreement on a 7-point scale (7 is strongly agree; 1 is strongly disagree) to the statements:				
1. I dislike driving.	3.7	4.3	2.9	1.4
2. I like to jog.	3.9	3.8	4.0	−0.2
3. I am concerned about gasoline costs.	5.3	6.1	4.4	1.7[c]
4. I am concerned about air pollution.	4.6	4.6	3.9	0.7
Percentage who answer affirmatively to the question:				
5. Do you live within three miles from a transit station?	36%	50%	25%	25%[d]
Sample size	62	28	34	

[a] Average score over the 28 respondents using the transit system.
[b] Average score over the 34 respondents not using the transit system.
[c] Significant at the 0.01 level.
[d] Significant at the 0.10 level.

When to Use What. Descriptive statistics can provide accurate, simple, and meaningful figures by summarizing information in a large set of data. The summary measures can sometimes communicate the information in an entire distribution. There is an obvious trade-off between the use of the frequency distribution and the use of a single number. The frequency distribution can be unwieldy but does provide more information. For example, Table 15-2 shows the response to an attitude question. The average response indicates that the sample is fairly neutral about abstract art. Underlying that mean response, however, is the frequency distribution that indicates that a substantial group

TABLE 15-2
A Question Response[a]

		Response	Frequency	Percentage
	Disagree	−3	300	30
		−2	120	12
I prefer abstract art exhibitions to nonabstract art exhibitions.		−1	50	5
		0	50	5
		+1	100	10
		+2	300	30
	Agree	+3	80	8

[a] Mean response = −0.3.

likes abstract art, a larger group dislikes it, and, in fact, very few people actually are neutral. In situations where the population is not likely to be clustered around the mean, the frequency distribution can be useful.

When nominal scales are involved, frequency distributions must be employed. Recall that a **nominal scale** is one in which numbers merely label or identify categories of objects. For example, suppose respondents were asked if they lived in an urban area, a suburban area, or a rural area. There would be no way to determine an average number to represent that sample (although the percentage who live in rural areas could be used).

Difference Between Means or Percentages

The second step in most data analysis procedures is to repeat the analysis of a single question for various subgroups of the population. Thus, the interest might be in the heavy user, and the analysis would be done for this group. More likely, it would be done for the heavy user, the light user, and the nonuser; then the results would be compared. Responses often are more meaningful and useful when a comparison is involved. For instance, in this case it might be of interest to determine how those who use the transit system differ from those who do not use it.

Table 15-1 presents the sample means of the five questions for the users and the nonusers. The sample percentages answering positively to the location question also are presented for each group. The differences between the responses for the two groups provide some interesting insights. The difference between the sample means for Question 1, for example, indicates that the transit user tends to dislike driving more than the transit nonuser. The Question 2 difference indicates that the user shows only a small tendency to enjoy jogging more than the nonusers. The other comparisons suggest that the user is more concerned about gasoline costs and air pollution and lives closer to a transit station.

The difference between means is concerned with the association between two questions, the question defining the groups (transit usage in this case) and another question (question 1 on disliking driving, for example). In terms of the scale definitions, the question defining the groups would be considered a **nominally scaled** question and the question upon which the means are based would be considered an **intervally scaled question.** Of course, the analysis could use three, four, or more groups instead of just two. For example, comparisons could be made among nonusers of the traffic system, light users, medium users, and heavy users.

A variety of variables besides usage can be used to identify subgroups of interest. For example, in a segmentation study we might focus on

▶ Loyal buyers versus nonloyal buyers.

▶ Those interested in abstract art versus those not interested.

▶ Customers of a competing store versus others.

▶ Those aware of our art gallery versus others.

▶ High-income versus moderate-income versus low-income groups.

If our initial analysis involved means (or percentages), the focus would turn to the difference between means (or percentages). If the initial analysis involved frequency distributions, then cross-tabulation, the subject of the next section would be the focus.

CROSS-TABULATIONS

The appropriate statistical analysis technique for studying the relationships among and between nominal variables is termed **cross-tabulation.** It also is called cross-tabs, cross-classification, and **contingency table analysis.** In cross-tabulation, the sample is divided into subgroups in order to learn how the dependent variable varies from subgroup to subgroup. Cross-tabulation tables require fewer assumptions to construct, and they serve as the basis of several statistical techniques such as chi-square and log-linear analysis. Percentages are computed on each cell basis or by rows or columns. When the computations are by rows or columns, cross-tabulation tables usually are referred to as contingency tables, because the percentages are basically contingent on the row or column totals.

Figure 15-4 illustrates cross-tabulation with two examples from the HMO study. The focus here is on the question of enrollment intentions. Often, a usage or intentions question is the key question in a study.

To illustrate cross-tabulations in a probability framework, if the above data (intentions to enroll, by income) were representative of U.S. households (they are not), the probability of a household most interested in enrolling is 0.11 (121/1067). However, the probability of a household most interested in enrolling, given that the household's income is less than $7000, is 0.20 (38/186).

INTENTIONS TO ENROLL—BY INCOME	Less than $7,000		$7,000–$15,999		$16,000 and above			
Most interested	20.4%	(38)	11.6%	(46)	7.6%	(37)	11.3%	(121)
Moderately interested	19.4%	(36)	11.9%	(47)	17.9%	(87)	16.0%	(170)
Uncertain or uninterested	60.2%	(112)	76.5%	(302)	74.5%	(362)	72.7%	(776)
	100%	(186)	100%	(395)	100%	(486)	100%	(1067)

(The differences between income groups are significant at .01 level.)

INTENTIONS TO ENROLL—BY AGE	Under 30 Years		30–40 Years		Over 40 Years			
Most interested	14.0%	(60)	12.5%	(40)	6.6%	(24)	11.1%	(124)
Moderately interested	21.9%	(94)	20.0%	(64)	14.5%	(53)	18.9%	(211)
Uncertain or uninterested	64.1%	(276)	67.5%	(216)	78.9%	(288)	70.0%	(780)
	100%	(430)	100%	(320)	100%	(365)	100%	(1115)

(The differences between age groups are significant at .01 level.)

FIGURE 15-4
Cross-tabulations—the HMO study

We wish to determine if various income groups differ in their intentions. One way to define groups is by using the income question, or variable. The top of Figure 15-4 shows an intentions-by-income cross-tabulation. It presents the frequency distribution breakdown for the degree of intentions within each of the three income groups. If the three groups were similar, each of their frequency distributions should be expected to be similar to that of the total sample (marginal frequencies shown at the right). The results do not support this view. In fact, the higher-income people are less likely to be interested than the middle-income groups, and the low-income group is the most interested. More than 20 percent of the low-income group was classified as "most interested," as contrasted with only 7.6 percent of the high-income group. When the intentions by income cross-tabulated data are subjected to statistical analysis to evaluate the association between income groups and degree of intentions, the results indicate that there are differences among the three income groups in the degree of intentions to enroll.

The bottom of Figure 15-4 shows the intentions, by age cross-tabulation. Again, the frequency distribution within each of the subgroups must be compared to the frequency distribution for the total sample, shown at the right. The youngest group has somewhat more interest than the middle group, and both have considerably more interest than the older group.

Cross-tabulation is the analysis of association between two variables that are nominally scaled. Of course, any interval-scaled variable can be used to define groups and therefore form a nominally scaled variable. For example, income and age are intervally scaled (actually, ratio scaled), but in the context of Figure 15-4, they are used to define categories and thus are nominally scaled. Most marketing research studies go no further than cross-tabulation, and even those studies that do use more sophisticated analytical methods still use cross-tabulation as an important component. Hence, along with the data-preparation techniques, understanding, developing, and interpreting cross-tabulation are the fundamental needs of data analysis.[7]

Chapters 16 through 21 will discuss in detail the various statistical tests and techniques that can be used to analyze the data obtained from questionnaires. Before we launch a formal discussion of these sophisticated statistical techniques, it will be beneficial to discuss the various factors that influence the choice of an analysis technique. This will help us to identify the appropriate technique(s), based on our needs. Finally, we will end this chapter with an overview of the various statistical techniques that are available to the researcher and a brief discussion on how these techniques are classified.

FACTORS INFLUENCING THE CHOICE OF STATISTICAL TECHNIQUE

Data analysis is not an end in itself. Its purpose is to produce information that will help to address the problem at hand. Several factors influence the selection of the appropriate technique for data analysis. These include: (*a*) type of data, (*b*) research design, and (*c*) assumptions underlying the test statistic and related considerations.[8]

Type of Data

The type of data plays a central role in the choice of a statistical technique to be employed in data analysis. As pointed out already, a useful classification of data involves nominal, ordinal, interval, and ratio scales of measurement. The **nominally** scaled type of data are the most primitive form of data from the perspective of data analysis. They are just numbers assigned to objects, based only on the fact that the objects belong to particular categories. Very few formal statistical analyses can be done on nominal data, and the only meaningful measure of central tendency is the mode.

The **ordinal scale** represents a higher level of measurement than the **nominal,** because the numerals assigned to reflect order also serve to identify the objects. The **median** and **mode** are now both legitimate measures of central tendency. Most nonparametric tests can be performed on ordinal data. Even though parametric tests cannot be used on ordinal data, in many research studies one sees them being used erroneously.

Interval and **ratio-scaled** data (also called **metric** data) are the best from the perspective of data analysis. A wide range of both parametric and nonparametric tests can be performed on these types of data. The mean, the median, and the mode are now legitimate measures of central tendency. Measures of dispersion and measures of shape are meaningful only on these types of data. Hence, researchers should always try to collect interval or ratio-scaled data.

Research Design

A second consideration that affects the choice of analysis technique is the research design used to generate the data. Some of the decisions the analyst has to face involve the dependency of observations, the number of observations per object, the number of groups being analyzed, and the control exercised over the variables of interest.

Sample Independence. The type of statistical test that can be done depends on whether the research design uses dependent or independent samples. Let us clarify this statement with the following example. Suppose that you were interested in determining the effectiveness of an advertisement. Also, assume that the measure of effectiveness was attitudes toward the product advertised, and that the interval scale was used to measure attitude, and, in particular, that the research design was

$$X \quad O_1$$
$$O_2$$

where O_1 represents the attitudes of those who saw the advertisement, and O_2 the attitudes of those who did not see the advertisement. In this case, the samples are independent. The O_2 measures do not depend on the O_1 measures. An appropriate test of significance would allow for the independence of the samples. In this case, the t test for the difference in two means would be appropriate.

Consider another research design that is represented by

$$O_1 \quad X \quad O_2$$

Again, there are two sets of observations, O_1 and O_2. However, now they are obtained from the same individuals, before and after seeing the advertisement. The measurements are not independent, and the observations must be analyzed in pairs. The focus is on differences in attitudes per individual before and after exposure to the advertisement. A paired difference t test should be used in this case.

Number of Groups. The choice of a statistical method for data analysis also depends on the number of groups that are in the experimental design. Suppose that you were interested in the relative effectiveness of two different advertisements, and you decided to explore the question through a controlled experiment. In the experiment, some respondents receive X_1, others get X_2, and a third group receives neither. The design can be represented as

$$
\begin{aligned}
X_1 & \quad O_1 \\
X_2 & \quad O_2 \\
& \quad O_3
\end{aligned}
$$

This design parallels that for the single advertisement, except for the addition of the alternative advertisement X_2. Now, however, there are three groups or three means to be compared (two experimental and one control), whereas previously there were two (one experimental and one control). The t test for the difference in two means is no longer applicable; the problem is best handled through analysis-of-variance procedures.

Number of Variables. The number of variables in the study (measurements per object) also affects the analysis procedure. Let us consider the single advertisement example again. Previously, we used attitudes toward the advertised product as the measure of the advertisement's effectiveness. In order to check on the validity of this measure, we now wish to contrast the "exposed" and "unexposed" groups, not only in terms of their differences in attitude, but also in terms of the sales of the product to each group. The design has not changed. It is still represented as

$$
\begin{aligned}
X & \quad O_1 \\
& \quad O_2
\end{aligned}
$$

only now O_1 and O_2 represent measures of both sales and attitudes.

A univariate technique cannot be applied in this case, because it will lead to erroneous conclusions. We need to have some means of looking at the differences among groups when several characteristics are considered simultaneously. This type of problem is handled using multivariate statistical procedures.

Variable Control. Another important factor that affects the choice of technique for analysis involves the control of variables in the design, which can affect the result. Let us consider the one-advertisement design again.

$$X \quad O_1$$
$$O_2$$

in which the emphasis is on the differences in attitudes between the two groups. This attitudinal difference between the two groups can be the result of some variable other than exposure to the advertisement. One variable that would certainly seem to determine attitudes is previous usage of the product. If so, in the experimental design, the analyst would like to control for prior usage, to minimize its effect. A good way of doing this would be to make the experimental and control groups equal with respect to prior usage, by matching, by randomization, or by some combination of these approaches. If this control procedure is followed, the t test for analyzing the difference in two means can legitimately be employed. If the control is not affected but if attitudes do depend on prior use of the product, the conclusions produced using the t test will be in error, to the extent that the two groups differ in their previous use of the product.[9]

Assumptions Underlying Test Statistic

The assumptions underlying the test statistic also affect the choice of a statistical method of analysis. For example, the assumptions of a two-sample t-test are as follows:

1. The samples are independent.
2. The characteristic of interest in each population have normal distribution.
3. The two populations have equal variances.

The t test is more sensitive to certain violations of these assumptions than others. For example, it still works well with respect to violations of the normality assumption, but is quite sensitive to violations of the equal-variance assumption. When the violation is too severe, the conclusions drawn are inappropriate. Hence, if the assumptions on which a statistical test is based are violated or are not met, those tests should not be performed, because they will give meaningless results. If the samples are not independent or have unequal variances, a modified t test can still be employed. Ultimately, the researcher's knowledge about statistical techniques does matter in the selection of the technique for data analysis.

AN OVERVIEW OF STATISTICAL TECHNIQUES

The entire gamut of statistical techniques can be broadly classified as univariate and multivariate techniques, based on the nature of the problem. **Univariate techniques** are appropriate when there is a single measurement of each of the n sample objects, or when there are several measurements of each of the n observations but each variable is analyzed in isolation. On the other hand, **multivariate techniques** are appropriate for analyzing data when there are two or more measurements of each observation and the variables are to be analyzed simultaneously.

Univariate techniques can be further classified based on the type of data—whether they are **nonmetric** or **metric.** As mentioned earlier, nonmetric data are measured on a nominal or ordinal scale, whereas metric data are measured on an interval or ratio scale. Nonparametric statistical tests can be used to analyze nonmetric data. Nonparametric tests do not require any assumptions regarding the distribution of data.

For both nonmetric and metric data, the next level of classification involves determining whether a single sample or multiple samples are involved. Further, in the case of multiple samples, the appropriate statistical test depends on whether the samples are independent or dependent. Figure 15-5 provided an overview of the univariate analysis techniques.

For metric data, t tests and z tests can be used for one or two samples. For more than two samples, the analysis of variance (ANOVA) is used. For nonmetric data, with a single sample, chi-square, Kolmogorov-Smirnov (K-S), and RUNS tests can be used. For two or more independent samples, chi-square, rank sum tests, K-S, and ANOVA (Kruskal-Wallis ANOVA) should be used.

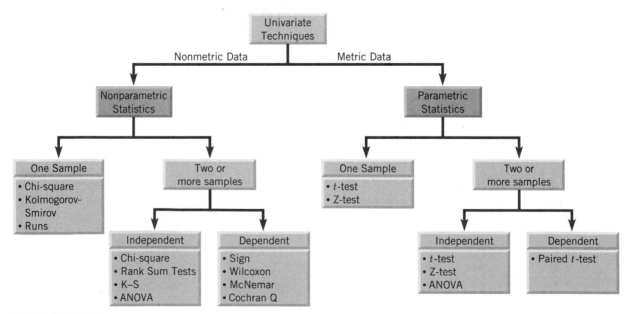

FIGURE 15-5
Classification of univariate statistical techniques

For two or more dependent samples, sign test, Wilcoxon test, McNemar, and Cochran Q tests can be used. A detailed discussion of nonparametric statistics is beyond the scope of this book.[10]

Multivariate statistical techniques can be broadly defined as "a collection of procedures for analyzing the association between two or more sets of measurements that were made on each object in one or more samples of objects." If only two sets of measurements are involved, the data typically are referred to as **bivariate**.[11] The multivariate techniques can be classified based on the following logic:

▶ Can the data be partitioned into dependent and independent variable sets? If so, classify according to the number of variables in each set. If not, classify the technique as an interdependence technique.

▶ In the case of interdependence techniques, classification is done based on the principal focus of the analysis. Is the focus on the object (person / thing / event) or is it on the variable?

Based on the first factor, the **multivariate** techniques can be broadly classified as **dependence** techniques or **interdependence** techniques. Dependence techniques are appropriate when one or more variables can be identified as dependent variables and the remaining as independent variables. The appropriate choice of dependence techniques further depends on whether there are one or more dependent variables involved in the analysis.

In interdependence techniques, the variables are not classified as dependent or independent; rather, the whole set of interdependent relationships is examined. The interdependence techniques can be further classified as focusing on variables or objects; that is, as variable interdependence or interobject similarity techniques. Figure 15-6 provides an overview of the various multivariate analysis techniques.

Subsequent chapters will discuss in detail most of the techniques represented in Figures 15-5 and 15-6. The chi-square tests for independence and

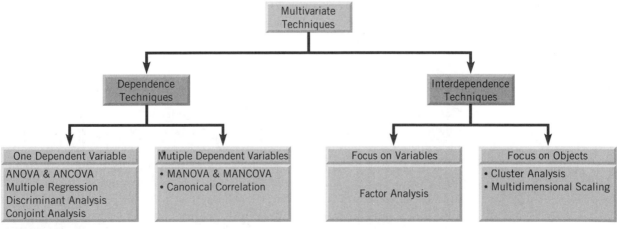

FIGURE 15-6
Classification of multivariate satistical techniques

goodness-of-fit and the analysis of variance (ANOVA) will be discussed in Chapter 16, and the hypothesis testing (t test and z test) will be discussed in Chapter 17. Chapter 18 will focus on correlation and regression analysis. Chapters 19 through 21 will very briefly describe the various multivariate techniques that are available to the marketing researcher.

Why use multivariate analysis, anyway? Clearly, substantial information can be obtained without using such complex techniques; however, there are several reasons why multivariate analysis is useful.

Multiple Linear Regression. A manager is interested in determining which factors predict the dollar value of the firm's personal computer sales. Aggregate data on population size, income, educational level, proportion of population living in metropolitan areas, and so on, have been collected for 30 areas. As a first step, a multiple linear regression equation is computed, where dollar sales is the outcome factor and the other factors are considered as candidates for predictor factors. A linear combination of the predictor factors is used to predict the outcome or response factor.

ANOVA. Suppose that a retail chain is interested in determining whether it should run a quarter-page, half-page or a full-page advertisement for a product. In order to choose the size of the ad that will bring in the most store traffic, the chain decides to conduct an experiment to determine the ad's effect on store traffic. The number of customers visiting the store on three different occasions (when each of the different sized ads is used) can be collected for all the stores belonging to the chain, and ANOVA can be performed to see if there are any differences in the store traffic across ad length.

Discriminant Analysis. A large sample of consumers over 50 years of age from a small city has been contacted to see if they had a proper retirement savings plan. A survey was conducted to obtain information on the respondents' savings behavior, and psychographic and demographic variables. The investigator would like to determine a linear function of these and possibly other measurements that would be useful in predicting who would and who would not have a proper (adequate) retirement savings plan. That is, the investigator wishes to derive a classification (discriminant) function that would help determine whether or not a middle-aged consumer is likely to have a proper retirement savings plan.

Canonical Correlation. A psychiatrist wishes to correlate measures of market orientation with marketing performance, from data obtained from a number of firms. This problem is different from a multiple linear regression example, because more than one outcome factor is being predicted. The investigator wishes to determine the linear function of the market orientation variables such as interdepartmental conflict, interdepartmental connectedness, concern for the ideas of other departments, and so forth, which is most highly correlated with a linear function of marketing performance variables: profit, sales, sales growth, market share, and so on. After these two linear functions, called **canonical**

variables, are determined, the investigator will test to see whether there is a statistically significant (canonical) correlation between scores from the two linear functions, and whether a reasonable interpretation can be made of the two sets of coefficients from the functions.

Factor Analysis. An investigator has asked each respondent in a survey whether he or she strongly agrees, agrees, is undecided, disagrees, or strongly disagrees with 15 statements concerning attitudes toward inflation. As a first step, the investigator will do a factor analysis on the resulting data, to determine which statements belong together, in sets that are uncorrelated with other sets. The particular statements that form a single set will be examined to obtain a better understanding of attitudes toward inflation. The scores derived from each set or factor will be used in subsequent analysis to predict consumer spending.

Cluster Analysis. Investigators have made numerous measurements on a sample of consumers who have been classified as being brand loyal. They wish to determine, on the basis of their measurements, whether these consumers can be classified by type of brand loyalty. That is, is it possible to determine distinct types of brand-loyal consumers by performing a cluster analysis on measures of purchase behavior on various purchase occasions?

Unlike the investigator of consumers who do or do not have a proper retirement savings plan, these investigators do not have a set of individuals whose type of brand loyalty can be known before the analysis is performed. Nevertheless, they want to separate the consumers into separate groups and to examine the resulting groups to see whether distinct types do exist and, if so, what their characteristics are.

Multidimensional Scaling (MDS). It might be useful to determine how schools are perceived—which ones are perceived as similar and which ones are considered different. Is Stanford more like the University of California at Berkeley because of location and educational quality, or is Stanford perceived as being more like Harvard or MIT, two private schools? The general problem of positioning objects such as universities in an interpretable, multidimensional space is termed **multidimensional scaling (MDS).** The resulting locations or positions on the relevant perceptual dimensions serve to define new dimensions.

Conjoint Analysis. **Conjoint analysis** is an analysis-of-dependence technique. The dependent variable is the preference judgment a respondent makes about a new concept. The independent variables are the attribute levels that were specified. Thus, one motivation is prediction: What sales or usage level will a new concept achieve? A second motivation is understanding relationships: What is the effect on preference of changing one of the attribute levels?

Simultaneous Equation Regression Analysis. Consider a regression model with price, advertising, and perceived product quality (the three independent variables) influencing sales (the dependent variable). Suppose that sales also influenced advertising, because the advertising budget was in part set as a percentage of sales, and that advertising (which emphasized quality) and price also affected perceived product quality. Instead of a single regression equation, it would then be more appropriate to work simultaneously with three regression equations and three associated dependent variables (sales, advertising, and product quality). A single regression equation, for example, would not reflect the indirect impact of advertising through its impact on product quality, and would confuse the sales-to-advertising influence with the advertising-to-sales influence.

Unobservable Variables in Regression Analysis. In single or simultaneous regression analysis, there could be several indicators of one of the key variables; for example, the performance of salespeople, the dependent variable, could be based on supervisor ratings, customer ratings, sales gain over the last year, and sales gain over plan. The question is, how to combine the four indicators (the observables) to provide a measure of salesperson performance (the unobservable). The answer, provided by the model, is to weight each indicator according to its relationship to the independent variables.

If there is only one regression equation involved, and the unobservable variable is the dependent variable, the approach is termed **canonical correlation** (defined earlier). In the more usual case, in which multiple dependent variables and thus multiple equations are involved, the approach often is termed **causal modeling,** since the interest is in causal relationships, or LISREL analysis. LISREL is the name of the computer program that is used to estimate the parameters of such models.

Information on the choice of a statistical package to perform the statistical analysis is given in the appendix of this chapter.

Presenting the Results

Eventually, the researcher must develop some conclusions from the data analysis and present the results. The presentation, whether oral, written, or both, can be critical to the ultimate ability of the research to influence decisions. We will address this in Chapter 22, where we provide several guidelines that will lead to effective presentations and where we also offer some special tips for making written and oral presentations.

Summary

The first phase in data analysis involves editing, coding, and statistically preparing the data for analysis. Editing involves identifying omissions, ambiguities, inconsistencies, lack of cooperation, and ineligible respondents. Coding involves deciding how the responses are going to be entered. There are several techniques that can be used to statistically adjust the data. These include (*a*) **weighting,** (*b*) **variable respecification,** and (*c*) **scale transformation.**

There are a variety of data analysis techniques available. The most basic is to analyze each question by itself. A **frequency distribution** provides the most complete information and often leads to decisions to combine response categories. Several descriptive statistics such as the **mean, median, mode, standard deviation,** and **variance** can be obtained from these distributions. In most marketing research applications, only the sample means and/or percentages are reported.

Responses at times are much more meaningful and useful when a comparison is made. The usual step is to tabulate questions among subgroups, and this involves two of the questions from the questionnaire. Thus, the sample mean or the frequency distribution is obtained for subgroups such as transit users and transit nonusers, and they are compared to identify the differences. Guidelines are developed for selecting the appropriate statistical techniques. A discussion on the overview of statistical analysis is provided.

Questions and Problems

1. A poll of just over 1000 Californians selected by an area sampling plan were asked early in Governor Brown's tenure whether they felt that Governor Brown was doing a good, fair, or poor job as governor. They were then asked why they held those opinions. The results were coded into 35 response categories. Each respondent's answer was coded in from one to six of the categories. A total of 1351 responses were coded. The most frequently used categories (besides "No Answer," given by 135 of the respondents) were the following:
    i. Not bad or good; OK so far; Too soon to tell (253).
    ii. Doing his best (123).
    iii. Trying to help people; cares about people (105).
    iv. Cutting down government expenses (88).
    v. Like or agree with his ideas (69).
    vi. Not afraid to take a stand (61).
    Do you think the responses are being analyzed properly? A respondent who gives a lengthy reply that includes as many as six coded responses will have more weight than a respondent who gives a short direct response that is coded into only one category. Is that appropriate? Are there any alternatives? Code the following responses categories listed above, and into others you feel are appropriate.
    a. I like his position on welfare. It's probably the most critical problem facing the state. On the other hand he is not helping the business climate. All the regulations are making it impossible to bring in industry. It's really too soon to make a judgment, however.
    b. He's reducing unemployment, improving the economy. I like his ideas about welfare and cutting down government expense. However, I don't like his position on the smog device bill. On balance, he's doing OK.
    c. He's too much of a politician. He will swing with the political currents. He has started some needed government reorganization, however.
    d. I dislike his stand on education. He is really not interested in education, perhaps because he has no children. He's young and immature. He takes strong stands without getting his facts straight.

e. He's concerned about the farm workers. He's doing a good job. I like him.

2. Analyze Figure 15-4. What conclusions can you draw? What are the implications? What additional data analysis would you recommend, given your conclusions?

3. In the HMO study the "Intentions to enroll" by "Intentions to have more children" cross-tabulation is shown in the following table. Interpret it in the context of Figure 15-4.

Intentions to Enroll By Intentions to Have More Children

	Yes, Intend to Have Children		Not Sure		Do Not Intend to Have Children		Total	
Most interested	14.1%	(39)	14.9%	(97)	9.1%	(13)	11.1%	(121)
Moderately interested	25.6%	(71)	17.6%	(114)	16.8%	(25)	18.9%	(170)
Uncertain or uninterested	60.3%	(167)	67.5%	(438)	74.1%	(110)	70.0%	(776)
	100%	(277)	100%	(649)	100%	(148)	100%	(1,067)

4. Consider the PG&E (A) case. Plan an analysis strategy. What cross-tabulations would you run? What difference-between-means calculations? What correlations would be useful? Identify some questions for which you would use means (or percentages) and others for which you might consider the entire frequency distribution in your analysis. Using the case data, identify two key questions and determine the frequency distribution.

End Notes

1. See Naresh K. Malhotra. "Analyzing Marketing Research Data with Incomplete Information on the Dependent Variable," *Journal of Marketing Research*, 24 (February 1987), 74–84.

2. For a more detailed discussion on coding, see Philip S. Sidel. "Coding," in Robert Ferber (Ed.), *Handbook of Marketing Research* (New York: McGraw-Hill), 1974; Pamela L. Alreck and Robert B. Settle. *The Survey Research Handbook* (Homewood, Illinois: Irwin), 1985, 254–286; and J. Pope. *Practical Marketing Research* (New York: AMACOM), 1981, 89–90.

3. For more information on weighting, see Trevor Sharot. "Weighting Survey Results," *Journal of Marketing Research Society*, 28, July 1986, 269–284.

4. See L. Bruce Bowerman and Richard T. O'Connell. *Linear Statistical Models: An Applied Approach* (Boston: PWS-KENT Publishing Company), 1990.

5. See Ronald E. Frank. "Use of Transformations," *Journal of Marketing Research*, August 1966, 247–253.

6. The biggest advantage of the standard deviation is that it enables us to determine, with a great deal of accuracy, where the values of a frequency distribution are located in relation to the mean. This can be done using **Chebyshev's theorem,** which states that irrespective of the shape of the distribution, at least 75 percent of the values will fall within plus and minus two standard deviations from the mean of the distribution, and at least 89 percent of the values will lie within plus

and minus three standard deviations from the mean. If the distribution is a symmetrical, bell-shaped curve, then using Chebyshev's theorem we can say that:

▶ About 68 percent of the values in the population will fall within plus and minus one standard deviation from the mean.

▶ About 95 percent of the values will fall within plus and minus two standard deviations from the mean.

▶ About 99 percent of the values will fall within plus and minus three standard deviations from the mean.

For a detailed discussion on fundamental statistics see Richard I. Levin. *Statistics for Management*, (Englewood Cliffs, New Jersey: Prentice-Hall), 1987, or any business statistics textbook.

7. See O. Hellevik. *Introduction to Causal Analysis: Exploring Survey Data by Crosstabulation* (Beverly Hills, California: Sage Publications), 1984.

8. Adapted from Gilbert A. Churchill, Jr. *Marketing Research: Methodological Foundations* (Orlando, Florida: Dryden Press) 1991.

9. See Paul E. Green and Donald S. Tull. "Covariance Analysis in Marketing Experimentation," *Journal of Advertising Research*. 6, June 1966, 45–53.

10. For a detailed discussion of nonparametric tests, refer to Wayne W. Daniel. *Applied Nonparametric Statistics*, PWS-KENT Publishing Company, 1990.

11. Paul E. Green. *Analyzing Multivariate Data* (Hinsdale, Illinois: The Dryden Press), 1978.

Appendix

Choice of a Statistical Package

Whether the investigator decides to use a PC or a mainframe, there is a wide choice of statistical packages available. Unlike the situation for word processing where a handful of packages have captured a large share of the market, there are numerous statistical packages available, some written for a particular area of application (such as survey analysis) and others quite general. One feature that distinguishes among the statistical packages is whether they were originally written for mainframe computers or for the PC. Packages written for mainframe computers tend to be more general and comprehensive. They also take more computer memory to store and are often more expensive. Originally, the programs written for the mainframe computers were just adapted for the PC, but recent versions include more interactive features and menu-driven options. The cost of a PC package is less of a factor if a site license is purchased by the school, business, or governmental unit where one works, in which case the cost can be shared by a number of users.

User's Manual

Each of the three computer packages has multiple manuals. In the following we list the manuals used in this book. (The editions listed also refer to the versions of the programs used.)

BMDP

BMDP PC Supplement: Installation and Special Features, 1988 (installing BMDP programs and running them on a PC).
BMDP Data Entry, 1990, (data entry procedures).
BMDP Data Management Manual, 1988 (data management procedures).
BMDP Statistical Software Manual, Volumes 1 and 2, 1988 (general statistical programs).

SAS

SAS/FSP Guide Version 6, 1987 (data entry).
SAS Introductory Guide for Personal Computers Release 6.03, 1988 (useful for new users).
SAS Procedures Guide Release 6.03, 1988 (provides descriptions of elementary statistics, reporting, scoring, and utility procedures).
SAS Language Guide for Personal Computers Release 6.03, 1988 (describes DATA and PROC steps, syntax and use of SAS statements, and other options).
SAS/STAT Guide for Personal Computers Version 6, 1987 (describes multivariate statistical procedures).
SUGI Supplemental Library User's Guide Version 5, 1986 (describes additional SAS statistical procedures mostly available on mainframe computers).

SPSS

SPSS Data Entry II, 1988 (data entry).
SPSS-X User's Guide, 3rd edition, 1988 (complete guide, from syntax to statistical procedures, for the mainframe version),
SPSS/PC + V2.0, Base Manual, 1988 (for the PC descriptions of multivariate statistical procedures).
SPSS/PC + V3.0 Update Manual, 1988 (for the PC-describes changes and new features added in Version 3, compared to Version 2 of SPSS/CE +).

Further information and manuals can be obtained by writing to one of the following sources:

BMDP Statisical Software, Inc.
1440 Sepulveda Blvd.
Los Angeles, CA 90025

SPSS, Inc.
Suite 3000
444 North Michigan Ave.
Chicago, IL 60611

SAS Institute, Inc.
SAS Circle Box 8000
Cary, NC 27512-8000

16

HYPOTHESIS TESTING: BASIC CONCEPTS AND TESTS OF ASSOCIATIONS

Learning Objectives

▶ Understand the logic behind hypothesis testing.

▶ Familiarize with the concepts basic to the hypothesis-testing procedure.

▶ Describe the steps involved in testing a hypothesis.

▶ Interpret the significance level of a test.

▶ Understand the difference between Type I and Type II errors.

▶ Describe the chi-square test of independence and the chi-square goodness-of-fit test.

▶ Discuss the purpose of measuring the strength of association.

When an interesting, relevant, empirical finding emerges from data analysis based on a sample, a simple, yet penetrating, hypothesis test question should occur to every manager and researcher as a matter of course: Does the empirical finding represent only a sampling accident? For example, suppose a study was made of wine consumption. Data analysis revealed that a random sample of 100 California residents consumes more wine per family than a random sample of 100 New York residents. It could be that the observed difference was caused only by a sampling error; in actuality, there may be no difference between the two populations. If the difference found in the two samples could be caused by sampling fluctuations, it makes little sense to spend additional time on the results or to base decisions on it. If, on the other hand, the results are not simply caused by sampling variations, there is a reason to consider the results further.

Hypothesis testing begins with an assumption, called a hypothesis, that is made about a population parameter. Then, data from an appropriate sample are collected and the information obtained from the sample (sample statistics) is used to decide how likely it is that the hypothesized population parameter is correct. The hypothesis test question is thus a screening question. Empirical results should pass that test before the researcher spends much effort considering them further.

The purpose of hypothesis testing is not to question the computed value of the sample statistic but to make a judgment about the *difference* between two sample statistics or the sample statistic and a hypothesized population parameter. For example, in many marketing research situations the need arises to test an assumption regarding a certain value for the population mean. To test the assumption's validity, data from a sample are gathered and the sample mean is calculated. Then the difference between the sample mean and the hypothesized value of the population mean is calculated. The smaller the difference, the greater the likelihood that the hypothesized value for the population mean is correct. The larger the difference, the smaller the likelihood.

Unfortunately, the difference between the hypothesized population parameter and the actual sample statistic is more often neither so large that the hypothesis automatically is rejected nor so small that it is not rejected just as quickly. So in hypothesis testing, as in most significant real-life decisions, clear-cut solutions are the exception, not the rule. The mechanism that is adopted to make an objective decision regarding the hypothesized parameter forms the core of hypothesis testing.

A primary objective of this chapter will be to provide a real understanding of the logic of hypothesis testing. The hope is that the reader will become conditioned to asking whether the result was an accident. Just thinking of the question at the appropriate time is winning half the battle. Further, an effort will be made to help the reader think in terms of a model or set of assumptions (such as, there is no difference between California and New York in per capita wine consumption) in very specific terms. Hypothesis testing provides an excellent opportunity to be rigorous and precise in thinking and in presenting results.

In the first section, the logic of hypothesis testing is developed in the context of an example. This is followed by sections describing the steps in the hypothesis-testing process and the concepts basic to the hypothesis-testing procedure. The final section presents the hypothesis tests used in cross-tabulations. Here the chi-square statistic, which is useful in interpreting a cross-tabulation table, is developed. Also, the two major applications of the chi-square test—as a goodness-of-fit measure, and as a test of independence—will be discussed.

THE LOGIC OF HYPOTHESIS TESTING

An Illustrative Example

To guide the development and control of wilderness areas and national parks, a large-scale survey was conducted. A total of nearly 10,000 people participated and answered a series of questions about their usage of wilderness areas and their opinions on public-policy alternatives regarding them. One key question was how to control the number of people asking to use some of the popular rafting rivers. At one extreme, a very restrictive policy was proposed using a permit system that would preserve the wilderness character of the parks but would deprive many people of the opportunity to use them as a national resource. At the other extreme, there would be unrestricted access. One question asked for opinions about this policy spectrum as it applied to several wilderness areas.

The scale was as follows:

Highly Restrictive									No Restrictions
0	1	2	3	4	5	6	7	8	9

The average response of the 10,000 respondents was 5.6.

The researcher who conducted this survey wanted to test the theory that those who did white-water rafting would favor fewer restrictions. To test this hypothesis, 35 such people were identified in the study, which had an average response rate of 6.1. Thus, the evidence supports the contention that those engaging in white-water rafting did tend to support a no-restrictions policy more than did the rest of the population.

But how convincing is the evidence? After all, the opinions of a sample of only 35 rafters is known. The difference between 5.6 (the 10,000 respondent average) and 6.1 (the white-water rafters' average) might be more a case of luck than proof that the white-water rafters had different opinions. The extent to which the statement about the population is believable depends on whether the sample from which the information was generated is large or small (other things being equal). If the average response rate of the 35 white-water rafters was, say, 8.6, then the hypothesis that those who did white-water rafting favor fewer restrictions cannot be rejected. On the other hand if the average response of rafters was 2.7, then without any hesitation, the hypothesis can be rejected. But with an average response rate of 6.1, we can neither accept nor reject the hypothesis with absolute certainty; a decision about the hypothesis has to be taken based not on intuition, but on some objective measure. To what extent the statement about the population parameter is believable depends on whether the information generated from the sample is a result of few or many observations. In other words, evidence has to be evaluated statistically before arriving at a conclusion regarding the hypothesis. *This is the logic behind hypothesis testing.*

STEPS IN HYPOTHESIS TESTING

The steps involved in the process of hypothesis testing are illustrated in Figure 16-1. As shown in the figure, problem definition leads to the generation of hypotheses. The relevant probability distribution is then chosen. The corresponding critical value is determined from the information on the significance level, degrees of freedom, and one- or two-tailed test. The appropriate test statistic (calculated from the sample data) is then compared with the relevant critical value, and if the test statistic falls in the critical region (i.e., in general, when the test statistic equals or exceeds the critical value), the null hypothesis is rejected.

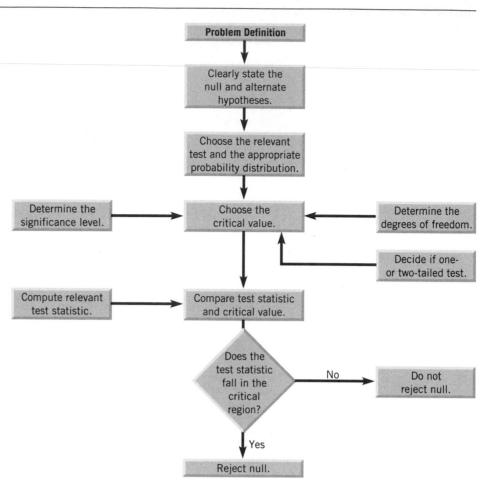

FIGURE 16-1
Hypothesis testing process

BASIC CONCEPTS OF HYPOTHESIS TESTING

The Null and the Alternate Hypothesis

Let us continue with the wilderness survey example. To test the theory that people who did white-water rafting would be in favor of fewer restrictions, the researcher has to formulate—just for argument—the **null hypothesis**[1] that the opinions of white-water rafters do not differ from those of the general population (the 10,000 respondents); and that if all the white-water rafters were contacted their average response would be 5.6 instead of 6.1. This null hypothesis (mathematically represented as H_o) will be tested against the **alternate hypothesis** (mathematically represented as H_a); that is, the contention that people who did white-water rafting would favor fewer restrictions.

As mentioned earlier, the purpose of hypothesis testing is not to question the computed value of the sample statistic but (for example) to make a judgment about the difference between that sample statistic and the hypothesized population parameter.

Choosing the Relevant Statistical Test and the Appropriate Probability Distribution

The next step in hypothesis testing is selecting the appropriate probability distribution. The choice of the appropriate probability distribution depends on the purpose of the hypothesis test. The purpose could vary, from comparing sample and population to comparing two sample characteristics such as means, proportions, variances, and so on. Table 16-1 provides the conditions under which various statistical tests can be used for different purposes. For a given purpose, a particular form of a statistical test may or may not be appropriate, depending on the sample size and whether or not the population standard deviation is known. In marketing research applications, typically, we deal with large samples ($n \geq 30$), which allows us to draw valid conclusions.

Hence, the next logical step, after stating the null and alternative hypotheses, is to decide upon the criteria (for choosing the critical or the table values for a statistical test) to use for making the decision whether to accept or reject the null hypothesis. (Strictly speaking, one should use the terminology "not reject" instead of "accept"; however, for simplicity's sake, we use the term "accept.") The three criteria referred to are the (1) **significance level,** (2) **degrees of freedom,** and (3) **one- or two-tail test.**

Choosing the Critical Value

Significance Level. Say that the hypothesis is to be tested at the 10 percent level of significance. This means that the null hypothesis will be rejected if the difference between the sample statistic and the hypothesized population parameter is so large that this or a larger difference would occur, on the average, only ten or fewer times in every 100 samples (assuming the hypothesized population parameter is correct). In other words, assuming the hypothesis to be true, *the significance level indicates the percentage of sample means that is outside the cut-off limits, also called the critical value.*[2]

There is no single rule for selecting a significance level (α). The most commonly chosen levels in academic research are the 1-percent level, the 5-percent level, and the 10-percent level. Although, it is possible to test a hypothesis at any level of significance, bear in mind that the significance level selected is also the risk assumed of rejecting a null hypothesis when it is true. *The higher the significance level used for testing a hypothesis, the higher the probability of rejecting a null hypothesis when it is true.* This is called the **Type I error.**

Alternately, accepting a null hypothesis when it is false is called a **Type II error** and its probability is represented as β (beta). Whenever a choice of the significance level for a test of hypothesis is made, there is an inherent trade-off involved between these two types of errors. The probability of making one type of error can be reduced only if the manager/researcher is willing to increase the probability of making the other type of error.

Figure 16-2 provides a graphical illustration of this concept.[3] From this figure it can be seen that as the significance level increases the acceptance region becomes quite small (.50 of the area under the curve in Figure 16-2c). With an acceptance region this small, rarely will a null hypothesis be accepted when it is not true; but at a cost of being this sure, the probability that a null

TABLE 16-1
Hypothesis Testing and Associated Statistical Tests

Hypothesis Testing	No. of Groups/ Samples	Purpose	Statistical Test	Assumptions/Comments
Frequency distributions	one	Goodness of fit	χ^2	
	two	Tests of independence	χ^2	
Proportions	one	Comparing sample and populations proportions	Z	If σ is known, and for large samples
		Comparing sample and populations proportions	t	If σ is unknown, and for small samples
	two	Comparing two sample proportions	Z	If σ is known
		Comparing two sample proportions	t	If σ is unknown
Means	one	Comparing sample and population mean	Z	If σ is known
		Comparing sample and population mean	t	If σ is unknown
	two	Comparing two sample means	Z	If σ is known
		Comparing two sample means (from independent samples)	t	If σ is unknown
		Comparing two sample means (from related samples)	t	If σ is unknown
	two or more	Comparing multiple sample means	F	Using analysis of variance framework (discussed in next chapter)
Variance	one	Comparing sample and population variances	χ^2	
	two	Comparing sample variances	F	

Legend: σ = population standard deviation.

472

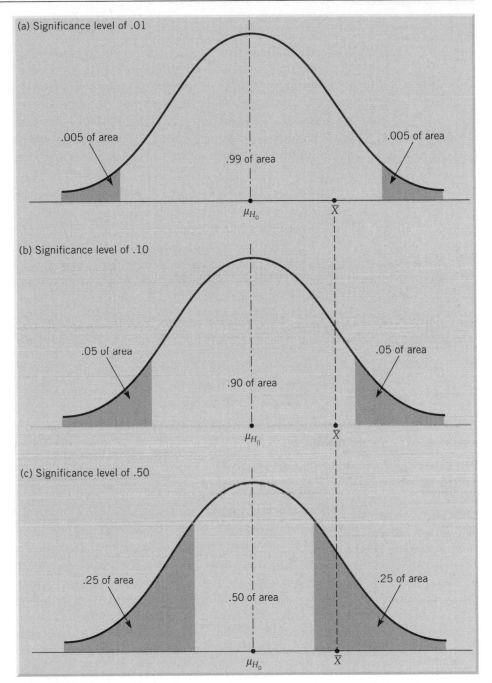

FIGURE 16-2
Relationship between Type I and Type II errors

hypothesis will be rejected when it is true will increase. In other words, in order to lessen the probability of committing a Type II error, the probability of committing a Type I error necessarily has to be increased.

To deal with this trade-off, researchers decide the appropriate level of significance by examining the costs or penalties attached to both types of errors.

For example, if making a Type I error (rejecting a null hypothesis when it is true) involves taking the time and trouble to reexamine the batch of packaged food products that should have been accepted, but making a Type II error (accepting a null hypothesis when it is false) means taking a chance that the consumers purchasing the product may suffer from food poisoning, obviously the company management will prefer a Type I error to a Type II error. As a result, it will set high levels of significance in its testing. Likewise, if the cost of committing a Type I error is overwhelming when compared to the cost of committing a Type II error, the researcher will go for low values of α.

The Power of a Hypothesis Test. Ideally, a good test of a hypothesis ought to reject a null hypothesis when it is false. In other words, β (the probability of accepting a null hypothesis when it is false) should be as low as possible, or $1-\beta$ should be as high a value as possible (preferably close to 1.0). A high value of $1-\beta$ indicates that the hypothesis test is working very well. Since the value of $1-\beta$ provides a measure of how well the test works, it is also known as the **power of the hypothesis test.**

Thus, the power of a statistical test of a null hypothesis is the probability that it will lead to the rejection of the null hypothesis; that is, the probability that it will result in the conclusion that the phenomenon exists. The power of a statistical test depends on three parameters: the significance level of the test, the reliability of the sample results, and the "effect size" (that is, the degree to which the phenomenon exists).[4]

Degrees of Freedom. Degrees of freedom (df) refers to the number or bits of "free" or unconstrained data used in calculating a sample statistic or test statistic.

Degrees of freedom is traditionally represented as $n - k$, where n is the total number of information bits available and k is the number of linear constraints or restrictions required when calculating a sample statistic or test statistic. In a simple random sample of n observations, there are n degrees of freedom if no restrictions are placed upon the sample. A sample mean $\overline{X}$ has n degrees of freedom, since there are no constraints or restrictions applied to the sample when calculating its value. However, there are $(n - 1)$ degrees of freedom associated with a sample variance because 1 degree of freedom is "lost" due to the restriction that it is necessary to calculate a mean before calculating the variance. Stated somewhat differently, the first $n - 1$ observations in a sample can be selected freely, but the nth value must be chosen so that the constraint of an identical mean value is satisfied. In general, the larger the degrees of freedom, the greater the likelihood of observing differences or relationships among variables.

One- or Two-Tail Test. When conducting a one-sided hypothesis test, the researcher determines whether a particular population parameter is larger or smaller than some predefined value. In this case, only one critical value (and region) of a test statistic is used. In a two-sided hypothesis test, the researcher determines the likelihood that a population parameter is within certain upper and lower bounds. Depending on the statistical technique applied, one or two critical values may be used.

The next section discusses the statistical test used to measure associations.

CROSS-TABULATION AND CHI-SQUARE

Chapter 15 presented the data analysis technique of cross-tabulating two questions. Recollect that the Figure 15-4 illustrated cross-tabulation with the focus on the enrollment intention question. In this case, the appropriate null hypothesis would be that there was no relationship between the respondents' enrollment intention and the income group to which they belong. Such a hypothesis can be tested based on a measure of the relationship between the questions of the cross-tabulation table, termed the chi-square statistic. In this section the chi-square and its associated test will be introduced formally. Typically, in marketing research applications, the chi-square statistic is employed either as a **test of independence** or as a **test of goodness of fit.**

A **test of statistical independence** is employed when the manager or the researcher wants to know whether there are associations between two or more variables in a given study. On the other hand, in situations where the manager needs to know whether there is a significant difference between an observed frequency distribution and a theoretical frequency distribution, the goodness-of-fit test is employed. In this section, we will discuss each of these applications of the chi-square statistic in detail. Before introducing the chi-square statistic as a test of independence, it is useful to develop and illustrate the notion of **statistical independence.** The concept of independence is really central not only to the chi-square statistic but to all association measures.

The Concept of Statistical Independence

Two variables are statistically independent if a knowledge of one would offer no information as to the identity of the other. Consider the following experiment, illustrated in Table 16-2. Suppose that in a repeated choice task conducted in New York City, a product was preferred in such a manner that it would yield a choice share of 0.40 (4 out of 10 individuals would choose the product). Suppose, further, that we have a group of consumers in Los Angeles that has 20 percent loyals, 30 percent variety seekers, and the rest deal-prone consumers. The experiment consists of executing the choice task and drawing a consumer from the group. The outcome of the choice task is independent of the draw from the group of consumers. Before the experiment begins, the chance of getting a loyal consumer is 0.20. After the choice task, the probability of getting a loyal is still 0.20. The knowledge of the outcome of the choice task does not affect our information as to the outcome of the consumer draw; therefore, the choice task is statistically independent of the consumer draw.

What Is Expected Value. If the previous experiment were repeated many times, we would expect 20 percent of the outcomes to include a loyal consumer. The number of "loyal" outcomes that we would expect would be $0.20n$, where

TABLE 16-2
An Experiment and Its Expected Outcome

		Choice Task in New York			
		Choose	Not Choose	Outcomes Expected	Probability
Drawing a customer in Los Angeles	Loyal	$E_1 = 16$[a]	$E_2 = 24$	40	0.20
	Deal prone	$E_3 = 40$	$E_4 = 60$	100	0.50
	Variety seekers	$E_5 = 24$	$E_6 = 36$	60	0.30
				200	
	Outcome expected	80	120		
	Probability	0.40	0.60		

[a] E_i = expected cell size under independence.

n is the number of experiments conducted. In each experiment we would expect 40 percent of consumers to choose the product, and 60 percent not to choose the product. Then the number of experiments resulting in drawing a loyal consumer and choosing the product would be "expected" to be $\{(0.40) * (0.20n)\}$.

If n is equal to 200 and E_i is the number of outcomes expected in cell i, then for cells 1, 2, and 3 we have

$$E_1 = (0.40) * (0.20n) = 16$$
$$E_2 = (0.60) * (0.20n) = 24$$
$$E_3 = (0.40) * (0.50n) = 40$$

The reader should determine E_4, E_5, and E_6. The expected number of outcomes in cell i, E_i, is the number that would be expected, on average, if the experiments involving independent variables were repeated many times. Of course, cell 1 will not have 16 entries; sometimes it will have more and sometimes fewer. However, on average, it will have 16.

Chi-Square as a Test of Independence

Consider Table 16-3, which shows the results of a survey of 200 opera patrons who were asked how frequently they attended the symphony in a neighboring city. The frequency of attendence was partitioned into the categories of never, occasionally, and often; thus it became a nominally scaled variable. The respondents also were asked whether they regarded the location of the symphony as convenient or inconvenient. The resulting cross-tabulation shows the percentage breakdown of attendance in each location category. The observed number of respondents in cell i, termed O_i, also is shown. Thus, 22 people in cell 1 attended the symphony often and felt that the location was convenient ($O_1 = 22$).

The row totals and column totals and the proportions (p_A and p_L) are tabulated in the margin. Note that they are the frequency distribution for the respective variables. For example, the column total indicates that 80 respondents (0.40 of all the respondents) felt the location was convenient and 120 (0.60 of all the respondents) felt it was inconvenient.

The null hypothesis associated with this test is that the two (nominally scaled) variables are statistically independent. The alternate hypothesis is that the two variables are not independent. Formally,

Null hypothesis H_o: attendance at symphony is independent of the location
Alternative hypothesis H_a: attendance at symphony is dependent on the location

The Chi-Square Distribution. If the variables are statistically independent—that is, if the null hypothesis is true—then the sampling distribution of the chi-square statistic can be closely approximated by a continuous curve known as a **chi-square distribution**. The chi-square distribution is a probability distribution and, therefore, the total area under the curve in each chi-square distribution is 1.0. As in the case of the t distribution, there are different chi-square distributions associated with different degrees of freedom. The chi-square dis-

TABLE 16-3

A Cross-Tabulation of Opera Patrons

		Location (L)			
		Convenient	**Not Convenient**	**Row Total**	P_A
Attendance at symphony (A)	Often (more than 6 times a season)	1 27.5% $\overline{O_1 = 22}$	2 15% $\overline{O_2 = 18}$	20% (40)	.20
	Occasionally	3 60% $\overline{O_3 = 48}$	4 43.3% $\overline{O_4 = 52}$	50% (100)	.50
	Never	5 12.5% $\overline{O_5 = 10}$	6 41.7% $\overline{O_6 = 50}$	30% (60)	.30
	Column total P_L	100% (80) .40	100% (120) .60	100% (200) 1.00	1.00

$$x^2 = \sum \frac{(O_i - E_i)^2}{E_i} = 20$$

Note: E_i equals the expected cell values and O_i equals the observed cell values.

478

tribution is one of the statistical distributions that is completely determined by its degree of freedom. The mean of the distribution is equal to v, the degrees of freedom and the variance of the chi-square distribution is equal to $2v$. The chi-square values based on the distribution is provided in Appendix Table A-2.

The degrees of freedom, v, for the chi-square test of independence is obtained using the formula $v = (r - 1) * (c - 1)$, where r is the number of rows in the contingency table and c is the number of columns. For large values of v, the distribution is approximately normal.

The Chi-Square Statistic. The *chi-square statistic* (χ^2) is a measure of the difference between the actual numbers observed in cell i, termed O_i, and the number expected if the null hypothesis were true; that is, under the assumption of statistical independence, E_i. The chi-square statistic is defined as

$$\chi^2 = \sum_{i=1}^{k} \frac{(O_i - E_i)^2}{E_i}$$

with $(r - 1)(c - 1)$ degrees of freedom
where

$\quad\quad O_i$ = observed number in cell i
$\quad\quad E_i$ = number in cell i expected under independence
$\quad\quad r\;$ = number of rows
$\quad\quad c\;$ = number of columns

If the two variables (location and attendance) were independent, then the expected frequencies in each cell would be

$$E_i = p_L * p_A * n$$

where p_L and p_A are proportions defined in the Table 16-3. Thus, for the data in Table 16-2,

$$E_i = .40 * .20 * 200 = 16$$

The appropriate χ^2 statistic is computed as

$$\chi^2 = \frac{(22 - 16)^2}{16}$$
$$+ \frac{(18 - 24)^2}{24} + \frac{(48 - 40)^2}{40} + \frac{(52 - 60)^2}{60} + \frac{(10 - 24)^2}{24} + \frac{(50 - 36)^2}{36} = 20.03$$

The degrees of freedom in this case is given by (rows $- 1$) $*$ (columns $- 1$), which is $(3 - 1) * (2 - 1) = 2$, and if the test is done at a significance level $\alpha = 0.05$, the table value of χ^2 can be found to be 5.99. Since the calculated value of χ^2 (20.03) is greater than the table value (5.99), the *null hypothesis* is rejected. The researcher can thus conclude that the attendance at the symphony is dependent on the location of the symphony. Figure 16-3 shows a graphical description of the chi-square test.

Interpreting the Chi-Square Test of Independence. The chi-square test of independence is valid only if the sample size is large enough to guarantee the similarity between the theoretically correct distribution and the χ^2 sampling distribution. If the expected frequencies are too small, the value of χ^2 will be overestimated and will result in too many rejections of the null hypothesis. *As a general rule, the results of the chi-square test are valid only if the value of expected frequency in each cell of the contingency table is at least 5.* If the table contains more than one cell with an expected frequency of less than 5, the chi-square test can still be used by combining these in order to get an expected frequency of 5 or more. But in doing this, the degrees of freedom is reduced and thus will gain less information from the contingency table.

Although the rejection rule in a chi-square hypothesis test is to reject the null hypothesis if the computed chi-square value is greater than the table value and vice-versa, if the computed chi-square value is zero, we should be careful to question whether *absolutely no difference* exists between observed and expected frequencies. If the manager / researcher has reasons to believe that some difference *ought* to exist, he or she should examine either the way the data were collected or the manner in which measurements were taken, or both, to be certain that existing differences had not been obscured or missed in collecting sample data.

Strength of Association. The strength of the association can be measured by the contingency coefficient (C). This index is also related to chi-square, as follows:

$$C = \sqrt{\frac{\chi^2}{\chi^2 + n}}$$

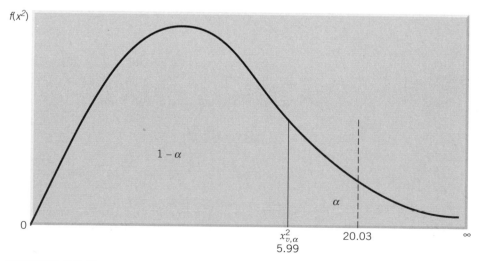

FIGURE 16-3
Cutoff points of the chi-square distribution function

The contingency coefficient varies between 0 and 1. The 0 value occurs in the case of no association (that is, the variables are statistically independent) but the maximum value of 1 is never achieved. Rather, the maximum value of the contingency coefficient depends on the size of the table (number of rows and number of columns). For this reason it should be used only to compare tables of the same size. The value of the contingency coefficient for our example is

$$C = \sqrt{\frac{20.03}{20.03 + 200}}$$
$$= 0.30$$

Limitations as an Association Measure. The chi-square statistic provides a measure of association between two variables, but it has several limitations. First, it is basically proportional to the sample size, which makes it difficult to interpret in an absolute sense (free from the effect of sample size) and to compare cross-tabulations with different sample sizes. However, in a given analysis it is often necessary to compare different cross-tabulations with the same sample size. Second, it has no upper bound; thus, it is difficult to obtain a feel for its value. Furthermore, the chi-square value does not indicate how the two variables are related. A further discussion of the use of chi-square as an association measure and some alternatives are presented in the appendix to this chapter. Chapter 18 presents a detailed discussion of the more commonly used measures of association, such as the correlation and regression analysis.

Measures of Association for Nominal Variables

We saw earlier in this chapter that the chi-square statistic is seriously flawed as a measure of the association of two variables. The essence of the problem is that the computed value of chi-square can tell us whether there is an association or a relationship, but gives us only a weak indication of the strength of the association. The principal purpose of this section is to describe a measure, Goodman and Kruskal's tau, which overcomes many of the problems of chi-square. First we look at some efforts to correct the problems of the chi-square measure. To illustrate these measures we return to Table 16-3. According to the chi-square test ($\chi^2 = 20$), the relationship between location and attendance in Table 16-3 is highly significant. That is, there is a probability of less than .001 that the observed relationship could have happened by chance. Now we wish to know whether there is a sufficiently strong relationship to justify taking action.

| | | Location | | |
		Convenient	Not Convenient	Row Total
	Often	22	18	40
Attendance at	Occasionally	48	52	100
symphony (Y)	Never	10	50	60
	Column total	80	120	200

Measures Based on Chi-Square. The most obvious flaw of chi-square is that the value is directly proportional to the sample size. If the sample in the previous table were 2000, rather than 200, and if the distribution of responses were the same (that is, all cells were 10 times as large), the chi-square would be 200 rather than 20. Two measures have been proposed to overcome this problem; they are the contingency coefficient (C), which was discussed earlier, and the phi-squared (ϕ^2).

$$\text{Phi-squared: } \phi^2 = \chi^2/n = \frac{20.03}{200} = 0.10$$

Other measures include Cramer's V which is a modified version of the phi-squared coefficient and is used for larger tables (greater than 2×2).

$$V = \sqrt{\frac{\phi^2}{\min{(r-1)(c-1)}}}$$

$$= \sqrt{\frac{\chi^2/n}{\min{(r-1)(c-1)}}}$$

$$= \sqrt{\frac{0.10}{2}}$$

$$= 0.223$$

While the phi-squared correlation has no upper limit for larger tables, Cramer's V adjusts the ϕ^2 by the minimum of the number of columns or rows in the table. This adjustment results in V ranging from 0 to 1, and a higher value indicates a stronger association. For a 2×2 table, Cramer's V is identical to the coefficient, phi (ϕ).

Both measures are easy to calculate but, unfortunately, are hard to interpret. On the one hand, when there is no association they are both zero. But when there is an association between the two variables, there is no upper limit against which to compare the calculated value. In a special case, when the cross-tabulation has the same number of rows r and columns c, an upper limit of the contingency efficient can be computed for two perfectly correlated variables as $(r-1)/r$.

Goodman and Kruskal's Tau. The **Goodman and Kruskal's tau** is one of a class of measures that permits a **proportional reduction in error** interpretation. That is, a value of tau between zero and one has a meaning in terms of the contribution of an independent variable, such as location, to explaining variation in a dependent variable such as attendance at the symphony.

The starting point for the calculation is the distribution of the dependent variable. Suppose we were given a sample of 200 people and, without knowing anything more about the people, were given the task of assigning them to one of the three categories, as follows:

**Number in
Category**

Attendance at	1. Often	40	(20%)
symphony (Y)	2. Occasionally	100	(50%)
	3. Never	60	(30%)
Total		200	

The only way to complete the task is to randomly draw 40 from the 200 for the first category, and then 100 for the second category, and so forth. The question is, how many of the 40 people who actually belong in the first category would wind up in that category if this procedure were followed? The answer is 40 times (40/200), or eight people. This is because a random draw of any size from the 200 will on average contain 20 percent who attend the symphony often.

For the purpose of computing tau, our interest is in the number of errors we would make by randomly assigning the known distribution of responses. For the first category this is $40 - 8 = 32$ errors; similarly, for the second ("occasionally") category we would make 100 (100/200) = 50 errors; and for the third category there would be 60 (140/200) = 42 errors. Therefore, we would expect to make $32 + 50 + 42 = 124$ errors in placing the 200 individuals. Of course, we do not expect to make exactly 124 errors, but this would be the best estimate if the process were repeated a number of times.

The next question is whether knowledge of the independent variable will significantly reduce the number of errors. If the two variables are independent, we would expect no reduction in the number of errors. To find out, we simply repeat the same process we went through for the total sample *within each category of the independent variable* (that is, within each column). Let us start with the 80 people who said the location of the symphony was convenient. Again we would expect an average, when randomly assigning 22 people from the "convenient location" group to the "often attend" category, to have 22 (58/80) = 16 errors. In total, for the "convenient location" group we would expect 16 + 48 (32/80) + 10 (70/80) = 44 errors. We next take the 120 in the "not convenient" group and randomly assign 18 to the first category, 52 to the second category, and 50 to the third category of the dependent variable. The number of errors that would result would be

$$18 (102/120) + 52 (68/120) + 50 (70/120) = 74 \text{ errors}$$

With knowledge of the category of the independent variable X to which each person belonged, the number of errors is $44 + 78 = 118$. This is six errors fewer than when we didn't have that knowledge. The tau measure will confirm that we haven't improved our situation materially by adding an independent variable, X:

$$\text{tau} = \frac{\text{(number of errors not knowing } X) - \text{(number of errors when } X \text{ is known)}}{\text{number of errors not knowing } X}$$

$$= \frac{124 - 118}{124} = 0.05$$

We now have a measure that is theoretically more meaningful, since a value of 0 means no reduction in error and a value of 1.0 indicates prediction with no error. However, a value of 1.0 can be achieved only when all cells but one in a column are empty, and such a condition is often impossible, given the marginal distributions. Thus, most tables have a ceiling on tau that is less than 1.0. For example, for the tables on symphony attendance, the best relationship we would expect to get—given the table's marginal distributions— is as follows:

		Location (X) Convenient	Not Convenient	Total
	Often	40	0	40
Y	Occasionally	40	60	100
	Never	0	60	60
	Total	80	120	200

The tau for this table is 0.19. The ceiling value of 0.19 for tau, in a table that satisfies the known marginals, indicates that there is little basis for expecting a strong relationship in this table. This value helps to put our calculated value in perspective.

The Chi-Square Goodness-of-Fit Test

In marketing, there are situations when the manager/researcher is interested in determining whether a population distribution corresponds to a particular form such as a normal or a Poisson distribution. Also, there are situations where the manager wants to know whether some observed pattern of frequencies corresponds to an "expected" pattern. In such situations, the chi-square test can be used as a goodness-of-fit test to investigate how well the observed pattern fits the expected pattern.

For example, an automobile manufacturer, planning the production schedule for the next model year, is interested in knowing in how many different colors of the car should be produced, and how many in each of the various shades. Past data indicate that red, green, black, and white are the fast-moving shades and that for every 100 cars, 30 red, 25 each of green and black, and 20 white cars were sold. Also, of the 2500 current-year model cars sold to date, 680 were red, 520 were green, 675 were black, and the remaining 625 were white. Based on this sample of 2500 cars, the production manager feels there has been a substantial shift in consumer preference for color and that the next model year production should not follow the 30:25:25:20 ratio of the previous years. The manager wants to test his hypothesis at an α level of 0.05. The purchases are independent and fall into 4 (=k) mutually exclusive categories, and, as such, the chi-square goodness-of-fit test can be employed to test this hypothesis. Formally,

H_O: The observed color preference coincides with the expected pattern.
H_a: The observed color preference does not coincide with the expected pattern.
$\alpha = 0.05$.

The chi-square statistic is calculated using the formula

$$\chi^2 = \Sigma_{i=1}^{k} \frac{(O_i - E_i)^2}{E_i}$$

where

O_i = observed number in cell i
E_i = number in cell i expected under independence
k = number of mutually exclusive categories

The degrees of freedom for this test is determined to be $v = (k - 1) = 3$. The expected value for each category is calculated using $E_i = p_i * n$. For the case of the red cars this will be 0.3*2500 = 750. Hence, the chi-square statistic can be calculated to be

$$\chi^2 = \frac{(680 - 750)^2}{750} + \frac{(520 - 625)^2}{625} + \frac{(675 - 625)^2}{625} + \frac{(625 - 500)^2}{500} = 59.42$$

The chi-square at $\alpha = 0.05$ for 3 degrees of freedom is obtained from the tables as 7.81. Since the calculated value of χ^2 (59.42) is greater than the table value (7.81), the *null hypothesis* is rejected. The production manager can thus conclude that consumer preference for colors has definitely changed.

As mentioned earlier, the results of the chi-square goodness-of-fit test are valid only if the expected number of cases in each category is five or more, although this value can be less for some cells. Also, in the case of problems where the researcher is interested in determining whether the population distribution corresponds to either a normal or Poisson or binomial distribution, certain additional restrictions might be imposed on the calculations of the degrees of freedom. For example, if we have 6 categories, v is calculated to be $6 - 1 = 5$. If, however, the sample mean is to be used as an estimate for the population mean, an additional degree of freedom has to be sacrificed. Also, if the sample standard deviation is to be used as an estimate for the population standard deviation, another degree of freedom has to be sacrificed. In this case v will be equal to 3. The rule of thumb to determine the degrees of freedom for the goodness of fit test is to *first employ the (k − 1) rule* and then subtract an additional degree of freedom for each population parameter that has to be estimated from the sample data.

Summary

Hypothesis testing begins with an assumption, called a *hypothesis*, that is made about a population parameter. Then data from an appropriate sample are collected, and the information obtained from the sample (sample statistics) is used to decide how likely it is that the hypothesized population parameter is correct. The purpose of hypothesis testing is not to question the computed value of the sample statistic but to make a judgment about the *difference* between (a) the sample statistics, and (b) the sample statistic and a hypothesized population parameter. There are several points worth remembering about hypothesis testing:

1. Hypothesis testing is a screening test. If the evidence does not pass this test, it may not be worth much attention. If it does pass this test, then it might at least be worth further analysis.
2. Hypothesis testing really measures the effect of sample size. A large sample has a tendency to always yield "statistically significant" results, whereas a small sample will not. Thus, the test really does no more than provide a measure of sample size.
3. Hypothesis testing does not establish whether the null hypothesis is true or false; it only quantifies how persuasive the evidence is against it. A low *p*-value indicates impressive evidence, and a high *p*-value indicates that the evidence is not impressive.

It is common to test an hypothesis concerning a single mean or proportion and the difference between means (or proportions) in data analysis, particularly when experimentation is involved. The hypothesis-testing procedure for differences in means differs, depending on the following criteria:

a. Whether the samples are obtained from different or related samples.
b. Whether the population standard deviation is known or not known.
c. If the population standard deviation is not known, whether or not they can be assumed to be equal.
d. Whether it is a large sample ($n \geq 30$) or not.

A cross-tabulation has associated with it a chi-square test of the relationship between the two variables. A goodness of fit test can also be performed with the chi-square analysis.

Questions and Problems

1. A study was conducted to determine the relationship between usage of a library and age of users. A sample of 400 was polled and the following cross-tabulation was generated. The numbers in parentheses are the observed cell sizes (O_i).

Age of Library Users

		Under 25	25 to 45	Over 45	Row Total	Prop.
Library usage	Heavy	26.2% (21) $E_1 = 17.8$	19.5% (41) $E_4 =$	24.5% (27) $E_7 =$	22.3% (89)	.223
	Medium	32.5% (26) $E_2 =$	18.1% (38) $E_5 =$	31.8% (35) $E_8 =$		
	Light	41.3% (33) $E_3 =$	62.4% (131) $E_6 =$	43.6% (48) $E_9 =$		
	Column total	100% (80)			100% (400)	1.00
	Proportion	.20		1.00		

a. Complete the table.

b. Interpret the term $E_1 = 17.8$.

c. Calculate the χ^2 value.

d. Is the χ^2 value significant? At what level? What exactly is the null hypothesis?

e. This data set proves that the usage of the library differs by age. True or false? Why?

2. P&G sampled 400 people to determine their cereal purchase behavior on a particular trip to the store. The results of the study are as follows:

Purchaser	Brand A	B	C	D
Buys the brand	45	50	45	60
Doesn't buy the brand	55	50	55	40

Are preferences and brands related?

3. It is known that on a particular high school campus, 62 percent of all students are juniors, 23 percent are seniors, and 15 percent are freshmen and sophomores. A sample of 80 students attending a concert was taken. Of these sample members, 74 were juniors, 17 were seniors, and 9 were freshmen and sophomores. Test the null hypothesis that the distribution of students attending the concert was the same as the distribution of students on campus.

4. An admissions dean has noted that, historically, 70 percent of all applications for a college program are from in-state, 20 percent are from neighboring states, and 10 percent are from other states. For a random sample of 100 applicants for the current year, 75 were from in-state, 15 were from neighboring states, and 9 were from other states. Test the null hypothesis that applications in the current year follow the usual pattern.

5. The accompanying table shows, for independent, random samples of boys and girls, the numbers who play for more or less than 2.5 hours per day.

Test at the 10 percent level the null hypothesis of no relationship between a child's sex and the hours of play.

Number of Hours of Play per Day

	Less Than 2.5	2.5 or More
Boys	18	10
Girls	17	13

End Notes

1. The term *null hypothesis* arises from earlier agricultural and medical applications of statistics. In order to test the effectiveness of a new fertilizer or drug, the tested hypothesis (the null hypothesis) was that it had *no effect*; that is, there was no difference between treated and untreated samples.

2. For a more detailed description of significance tests, see Alan G. Sawyer and Paul J. Peter. "The Significance of Statistical Significance Tests in Marketing Research," *Journal of Marketing Research*, May 1982, 122–131.

3. See Richard I. Levin. *Statistics for Management*, (Englewood Cliffs, New Jersey: Prentice-Hall, Inc.), 1987.

4. For a more detailed discussion on the power of a test, see *The Concept of Power Analysis*, Chapter 1, pp. 1–16, of J. Cohen. *Statistical Power for the Behavioral Sciences*, Academic Press: New York, 1969.

CASE 16-1
Medical Systems Associates: Measuring Patient Satisfaction[1]

Between 1950 and 1969, per capita consumer expenditures for nursing home services grew at a faster rate than any other health service category. During this period serious doubts were raised as to the quality of nursing home care and service. These concerns were confirmed by an HEW investigation in 1971 that led to substantial adverse publicity. Ray Baxter of Medical Systems Associates (MSA) felt that most of the problems stemmed from the "product-orientation" of the nursing homes; that is, they were "more concerned with selling the services and facilities they had than with providing a service mix designed to satisfy the needs and wants of the patients." A study grant was received from HEW to test this broad proposition, and in particular (1) to study the process by which patients chose nursing homes and (2) to identify the determinants of patient satisfaction. In early 1972 Baxter had completed the fieldwork and was wondering what he could conclude about the latter objective from the relationships he had observed in the data.

Study Design

The primary vehicle for data collection was a 12-page personal interview questionnaire containing more than 200 variables. The questionnaire was generally divided into six major conceptual areas as follows:

1. Socioeconomics.
2. Life-style measures (past and present).
3. Attitudes, interests, and opinions.
4. Nursing home selection process.
5. Evaluation of nursing home environment.
6. Perceived health.

Questionnaire development required considerable trial and revision. Questions had to be worded to be compatible with low educational levels because the median school grade attained by patients was under eight years. Five-point rating scales did not work, because the respondents rejected the supplied category descriptions and substituted broader descriptions of favorable, neutral, and negative. Standard projective techniques did not work well, apparently because many of the respondents were highly introspective.

The final questionnaire was administered in late 1971 to a stratified random sample of 122 patients in

TABLE 1
Cross-Classification Results: Environmental Rating Index Versus Selected Variables[a]

	Environmental Rating Index		
Variable	Low	Medium	High
NURSING HOME RELIGIOUS AFFILIATION			
Church-supported	15.8%	34.1%	45.9%
Nonsectarian	84.2	65.9	54.1
	100.0	100.0	100.0
Sample Size	(19)	(41)	(61)
"HAVE YOU MADE ANY NEW FRIENDS HERE?"			
Yes	84.2	71.8	96.7
No	15.8	28.2	3.3
	100.0	100.0	100.0
Sample Size	(18)	(39)	(60)
NUMBER OF FRIENDS			
"Just a couple"	31.2	21.4	5.1
"Just a few"	31.2	14.3	20.3
"Quite a few"	37.6	64.3	74.6
	100.0	100.0	100.0
Sample Size	(16)	(28)	(59)

[a] All variables are associated with the ERI at a level of .05 or greater using the χ^2 test of significance.

16 nursing homes in Wisconsin. These homes were selected from a universe of 93 homes. The sampling plan was designed to insure representativeness along the following dimensions:

1. Type of ownership (individual, partnership, corporate, nonprofit)
2. Level of care (skilled, limited, personal)
3. Type of assistance approval (Medicare and Medical Assistance, Medical Assistance only, and no assistance)
4. Size (small—less than 100 patients; medium—100 to 200 patients; and large—more than 200 patients)

In order to maintain approximate proportionate representativeness of the sample with the universe, the number of patients randomly selected from each sample-member nursing home was based on the size of the home.

Prior to the contact of respondents by the field interviewers, telephone calls or visits were made to the administrators of each nursing home in the sample, eliciting their cooperation. In general, administrators proved to be highly cooperative.

In contacting respondents, the interviewer was provided with a prearranged random sampling proce-

dure, which he or she was instructed to follow. Upon completion of the basic interview, the interviewer requested that the respondent sign two "release forms" permitting the researchers subsequently to obtain financial data and to discuss medical details with the respondent's doctor.

Analysis
The issue of the measurement of patient satisfaction and identification of determining variables was complicated by the special nature of the respondents. As Baxter noted, "Very few persons not in nursing homes want to be in a nursing home. And how satisfied are people with nursing homes when they have given up an established lifestyle because they now need services they would prefer to not need? Most persons, in and out of nursing homes, would opt for good health and independence. Because a nursing home represents an undesired portion of a life cycle, the problem, then, is to measure the satisfaction level of people who are, in an important sense, dissatisfied."

Three approaches were used to measure "conditional satisfaction," as it was termed. One was the *acceptance* of the necessity of entering a nursing home. The second was their *adjustment* to the disruption of established routines. The third was the patients' direct *evaluation* of their physical (medical), attitudinal, and environmental satisfaction. Each of the elements in the evaluation measure was represented by a separate index, based upon combinations of responses to various questions, as follows:

1. An Environmental Rating Index (ERI) was based upon answers to 14 questions involving satisfaction with such aspects of the nursing home as room size, physical layout, staff courtesy, medical care, cleanliness of facilities, food preparation, and so forth.
2. A Psychological Adjustment Index was based upon a series of attitudinal questions involving such issues as perceived self-usefulness, self-perceived level of activity, perceived life-style change, self-perceived reaction of others to nursing home patients, perceived difficulty in adjusting to nursing home life (upon arrival), desire to relocate, and so on.

3. A Physical Well-Being Validity Index was based upon a comparison of patients' self-perceived level of health with that indicated by medical records.

The focus of the initial analysis was on the determinants of the Environmental Rating Index (ERI). Cross-classification analyses with chi-square tests of significance were run for combinations of many variables with the ERI. Only three of the variables showed any statistical significance. (These variables, and the strength of the relationships, are summarized in the table on page 489.)

None of the other variables, such as the modernity of the home, size of the home, reasons for being in the nursing home, selection process, or patient mobility, were found to be significantly associated with the ERI. As Ray Baxter reviewed these results he was wondering what conclusions he could draw, and whether other analyses would be required to examine the basic "product orientation" hypothesis with the ERI.

17

HYPOTHESIS TESTING:
MEANS AND PROPORTIONS

Learning Objectives

▶ Get exposed to the more commonly used hypothesis tests in marketing research—tests of means and proportions.

▶ Understand the probability-values (*p*-values) approach to hypothesis testing.

▶ Understand the relationship between confidence interval and hypothesis testing.

▶ Describe the effect of sample size on hypothesis testing.

▶ Discuss the use of the analysis of variance technique.

▶ Describe one-way and *n*-way analysis of variance.

Suppose a brand manager is interested in determining if the company's brand is preferred over a competing brand. The manager chooses two cities, Houston and Philadelphia, to obtain preference ratings from a sample of 100 consumers of that product category in each city. The mean preferred ratings for that brand and the competing brand were computed as 4.2 and 4.4, respectively. The question is whether 4.4 is better than 4.2; in statistical terms, whether 4.4 is significantly different from 4.2, given the information on respective sample sizes, standard deviations, and the significance level.

In another scenario, 77 percent of the 280 consumers surveyed in Los Angeles favored Lay's potato chips, and 84 percent of the 260 consumers surveyed in New York favored Lay's. An import question facing the brand manager is whether these two proportions are different from one another; in statistical terms, are these two proportions significantly different from each other, given the sample information and significance level.

These examples are just a two illustrations of the many questions that face all businesses. Managers resort to using hypothesis testing of means and proportions, described next. The first section discusses the commonly used hypothesis tests in marketing research. The next section describes the **probability-value** (*p*-value) approach to hypothesis testing. The section that follows discusses the relationship between **confidence interval** and **hypothesis testing.** Also, in this chapter we will discuss another important statistical technique that is commonly used in experimental studies—the *analysis of variance,* or *ANOVA.* The analysis of variance is a statistical technique that allows the researcher to test for statistically significant differences between treatment means, and to estimate the differences between the means. Here, we will discuss in detail both one-factor and the *n*-factor analysis of variance.

COMMONLY USED HYPOTHESIS TESTS IN MARKETING RESEARCH

Testing Hypothesis About a Single Mean

One of the most commonly occurring problems in marketing research is the need to make some judgment about the population mean. This can be done by testing the hypothesized value of the population mean. A discussion on the hypothesis test of the mean will not be complete until we clarify a few issues pertaining to the test. Table 16-1 described the factors that influence the choice of the appropriate probability distribution. Broadly speaking, the choice of the distribution depends on (a) the purpose of hypothesis testing, (b) the size of the sample, and (c) whether or not the population standard deviation is known. When the population standard deviation (σ) is known, the sample size doesn't really matter, because the normal distribution and the associated z tables can be used for either of the cases. But when the population standard deviation is not known, the size of the sample dictates the choice of the probability standard distribution. Hence, this section will discuss applications pertaining to both the z and the t distributions. Also, it was mentioned earlier that the test could be either a two-tailed test or an one-tailed test, depending on the nature of the hypothesis. Examples of both tests will be presented in this section.

Samples with Known σ

Two-Tailed Test. Superior Shields, a manufacturer of automobile windshields, is faced with a problem. The company has to manufacture windshields that can obtain a quality rating of 5000 points (the average of the competition). But any further increase in the ratings raises production costs significantly and will result in a competitive disadvantage. Based on past experience, the manufacturer knows that the standard deviation of the quality rating is 250. To check whether this company's windshields meet the competitive standards for quality, the management picks a random sample of 100 industrial customers and finds that the mean quality rating from the sample is 4960. Based on this sample, the management of Superior Shields wants to know whether its product meets the competitive standards and is neither higher nor lower. Management wants to test its hypothesis at a 0.05 level of significance.

Statistically, the data in this case can be presented as follows:

Null hypothesis	$H_o: \mu = 5000$	hypothesized value of the population mean (competitive standards)
Alternative hypothesis	$H_a: \mu \neq 5000$	the true mean value is not 5000
Sample size	$n = 100$	
Sample mean	$\bar{x} = 4960$	
Population standard deviation	$\sigma = 250$	
Significance level	$\alpha = 0.05$	

Since the population standard deviation is known, and the size of the sample is large enough to be treated as infinite, the normal distribution can be used. The first step, then, is to calculate the standard error of the mean. This is done using the formula:

$$\text{Standard Error of Mean } \sigma_{\bar{x}} = \sigma/\sqrt{n}$$
$$= 250/10 = 25$$

Because this is a two-tailed test with a significance level α of 0.05, using the normal distribution table, the z value for a .975 $\{1 - (0.05/2)\}$ of the area under the curve is found to be 1.96. The calculated z score is

$$z = \frac{\bar{x} - \mu}{\sigma_{\bar{x}}} = \frac{(4960 - 5000)}{25} = -1.6$$

Figure 17-1 provides a graphical description of the hypothesis test. The rejection rule is to reject the null hypothesis in favor of the alternative hypothesis if $|z_{calc}| > z_{\alpha/2}$. Because 1.6 < 1.96, the management of Superior Shields is convinced that its windshields meet the competitive standards of a quality rating of 5000 points.

One-Tailed Test. Mr. James Ginter, the purchase manager of a big automobile manufacturer, wants to buy windshields that have quality ratings of *at least* 5000 points, and he doesn't mind paying the price for a good quality windshield. But Mr. Ginter is skeptical about the claims of Superior Shields that its windshields meet the competitive level. To convince Mr. Ginter, Superior Shields offers to pay for the survey of a sample of 50 consumers. The quality ratings from the sample reveal a mean of 4970 points. The problem facing Mr. Ginter now is whether or not to accept the claims of Superior Shields based on the sample mean. Also, Mr. Ginter wants the probability of a Type II error occurring

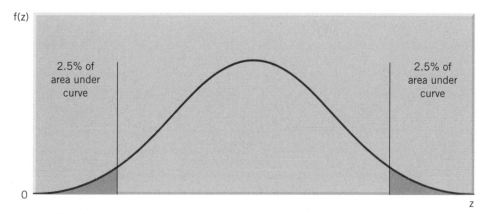

FIGURE 17-1
The normal distribution

(accepting the null hypothesis when it is false) to be as low as possible; hence, he wants the test to be done at a 0.01 level of significance.

Statistically, the new data can be presented as follows:

Null hypothesis	$H_o: \mu \geq 5000$	hypothesized value of the population mean
Alternative hypothesis	$H_a: \mu < 5000$	the true mean value is less than 5000
Sample size	$n = 50$	
Sample mean	$\bar{x} = 4970$	
Population standard deviation	$\sigma = 250$	
Significance level	$\alpha = 0.01$	
Standard error of mean	$\sigma_{\bar{x}} = \sigma/\sqrt{n}$	
	$= 250/7.07 = 35.36$	

Since this is now a one-tailed test (left-tailed test) with a significance level α of 0.01, using the normal distribution table, the z value for .990 $(1 - 0.01)$ of the area under the left or right tail of the curve can be found to be 3.08. The calculated z score is

$$z = \frac{\bar{x} - \mu}{\sigma_{\bar{x}}} = \frac{(4970 - 5000)}{35.36} = -0.85$$

Figure 17-2 provides an illustration of this test. The rejection rule for a left-tailed test is to reject the null hypothesis in favor of the alternative hypothesis if $z_{calc} < -z_\alpha$. Since $-0.85 > -3.08$, we fail to reject the null hypothesis.

Samples with σ Not Known. Now assume that Superior Shields provided Mr. Ginter with a sample of only 25 consumers for the previous example, and that the mean quality ratings from the sample were 4962 points. Also, assume that Superior Shields did not have prior knowledge of the population standard deviation, and the sample standard deviation was found to be 245.

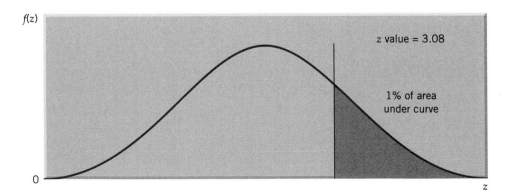

FIGURE 17-2
The normal distribution

Statistically, the data can now be presented as follows:

Null hypothesis	$H_o: \mu \geq 5000$	hypothesized value of the population mean
Alternative hypothesis	$H_a: \mu < 5000$	the true mean value is less than 5000
Sample size	$n = 25$	
Sample mean	$\bar{x} = 4962$	
Sample standard deviation	$s = 245$	
Significance level	$\alpha = 0.01$	

Because the population standard deviation is not known, the sample standard deviation can be used as an estimate of the population standard deviation. Also, since an estimate for the population standard deviation is being used, the standard error of the mean will also be an estimate, given by

$$S_{\bar{x}} = \frac{s}{\sqrt{n}} = \frac{245}{\sqrt{25}} = 49$$

As discussed earlier, if σ is not known, the appropriate probability distribution will be the t distribution. The appropriate t distribution will have n-1 (in our case 24) degrees of freedom. The table value can be obtained by looking at the t table under the 0.01 column for the 24 degrees of freedom row. The t value thus obtained is 2.492.

The calculate t value is given by

$$t_{calc} = \frac{\bar{x} - \mu}{s_{\bar{x}}} = \frac{(4962 - 5000)}{49} = -0.78$$

The rejection rule for a left-tailed t test is to reject the null hypothesis in favor of the alternative hypothesis if $t_{calc} < -t_{\alpha}^{n-1}$. Here, $-0.78 > -2.492$; hence, Mr. Ginter again will fail to reject the null hypothesis that the mean quality rating of Superior Shields' windshields is greater than or equal to 5000 points.

Hypothesis Testing for Differences Between Means

As discussed in Chapter 16, often in business research the manager or the researcher is more interested in making a statement regarding the difference between two population means or proportions. Testing differences in two or more means is commonly used in experimental research. The statistical technique used when testing more than two means is called the **analysis of variance** or more commonly, as **ANOVA** (discussed later in this chapter). This section will explore the hypothesis tests pertaining to differences in two means and proportions.

For example, the mayor of a city wanted to test whether the daily wages received by the male and female employees of large organizations in that city are the same for the same job description. To test this hypothesis, a random sample of 400 male and 576 female employees were selected, and the average wages recorded. The mean and standard deviation of the wages for the males are $105.70 and $5.00, respectively, whereas for the females the corresponding

HYPOTHESIS TESTING:
MEANS AND PROPORTIONS

numbers are \$112.80 and \$4.80. A significance level of 0.01 is desired. As was the case in the hypothesis testing of a single mean, the hypothesis testing procedure for differences in means differs depending on the following criteria:

a. Whether the samples are obtained from unrelated or related samples.
b. Whether the population standard deviation is known or not known.
c. If the population standard deviation is not known, whether they can be assumed to be equal or not.

The logic behind the hypothesis tests and the basic concepts of the tests remain the same for all the above-mentioned conditions. What varies is the statistical formula used to compute the standard error of the difference between the means. Also, for small sample sizes in the testing of means and proportions, the t distribution is used.

Case 1: Unrelated (independent) samples with known σ. In the "salary comparison" example, the null hypothesis will be that the mean salary of male employees is equal to the mean salary of the female employees of the same job description. Hence, in this case $\mu_1 - \mu_2 = 0$. Thus, the null hypothesis will be

$$H_o: \mu_1 - \mu_2 = c(=0)$$

For a two-tailed test, the alternative hypothesis will be

$$H_a: \mu_1 - \mu_2 \neq c \text{ and the rejection rule is}$$
$$\text{Reject } H_o \text{ if } |Z_{calc}| > Z_{\alpha/2}.$$

Since we use large sample sizes, we can adopt the approximation of using the sample standard deviation instead of the population standard deviation. The standard error of difference in means

$$s_{\bar{x}_1-\bar{x}_2} = \sqrt{\frac{S_1^2}{n_1} + \frac{S_2^2}{n_2}} = \sqrt{\frac{(5.00)^2}{400} + \frac{(4.80)^2}{576}} = \$0.32$$

where
s_1 = std. deviation of sample 1
s_2 = std. deviation of sample 2
n_1 = size of sample 1
n_2 = size of sample 2

and the calculated value of Z is

$$Z_{calc} = \frac{(\bar{x}_1 - \bar{x}_2) - (\mu_1 - \mu_2)}{s_{\bar{x}_1-\bar{x}_2}} = \frac{(105.70 - 112.80) - 0}{0.32} = -22.19$$

where

$$(\bar{x}_1 - \bar{x}_2) \quad = \quad \text{difference between sample means}$$
$$(\mu_1 - \mu_2) \quad = \quad \text{difference between the population means}$$

For $\alpha = .01$ and a two-tailed test, the Z table value is 2.58. Since the $|Z_{calc}|$ is greater than $Z_{\alpha/2}$, the null hypothesis is rejected. This means that the mean daily wages of males and females are not equal.

If the null hypothesis is $H_o : \mu_1 \leq \mu_2$, the alternative hypothesis will be

$$H_a : \mu_1 - \mu_2 > c \text{ and the rejection rule is}$$
$$\text{Reject } H_o \text{ if } Z_{calc} > Z_a$$

If the null hypothesis is $H_0 : \mu_1 \geq \mu_2$, the alternative hypothesis will be

$$H_a : \mu_1 - \mu_2 < c \text{ and the rejection rule is}$$
$$\text{Reject } H_o \text{ if } Z_{calc} < -Z_\alpha$$

For unknown σ, whether or not it is assumed to be equal across the two samples, t distribution is used. Table 17-1 gives information on the computation of test statistic, degrees of freedom (df), and standard error.

Case 2: Related (dependent) samples test. Instant Fit, a health club, advertises that on average its clientele lose at least 20 pounds within the first 30 days of joining the club. A health-conscious chief executive of an organization wants

TABLE 17-1
Procedure for Testing of Two Means

Unknown σ Assumed To Be Equal	Unknown σ Not Assumed To Be Equal
Compute	Compute
$$t = \dfrac{(\bar{x}_1 - \bar{x}_2) - (\mu_1 - \mu_2)}{s_{\bar{x}_1 - \bar{x}_2}}$$	$$t = \dfrac{(\bar{x}_1 - \bar{x}_2) - (\mu_1) - (\mu_2)}{s_{\bar{x}_1 \ \bar{x}_2}}$$
Where	Where
$$s_{\bar{x}_1 - \bar{x}_2} = s_p \sqrt{\dfrac{1}{n_1} + \dfrac{1}{n_2}}$$	$$s_{\bar{x}_1 - \bar{x}_2} = \sqrt{\dfrac{s_1^2}{n_1} + \dfrac{s_2^2}{n_2}}$$
Where	Where
$$s_p^2 = \dfrac{(n_1 - 1)s_1^2 + (n_2 - 1)s_2^2}{n_1 + n_2 - 2}$$	$$g = \dfrac{\dfrac{s_1^2}{n_1}}{\dfrac{s_1^2}{n_1} + \dfrac{s_2^2}{n_2}}$$
and	and
$\text{df} = n_1 + n_2 - 2$ (degrees of freedom)	$$\text{df} = \dfrac{(n_2 - 1)(n_2 - 1)}{(n_2 - 1)g^2 + (1 - g)^2(n_1 - 1)}$$

The rejection rule is same as before.

to provide his employees with free memberships to Instant Fit as part of the organization's employee benefit program, but the chief finance officer is rather skeptical about Instant Fit's advertising claims. In an effort to satisfy the finance officer, Instant Fit provides him with the "before and after" weight data of 10 of its clients. The finance officer wants to test the claim at a significance level of 0.05. Formally, the data can be presented as

Null hypothesis $\quad\quad\quad\quad H_o: \mu_1 - \mu_2 \geq 20$
Alternative hypothesis $\quad\;\; H_a: \mu_1 - \mu_2 < 20$
Significance level $\quad\quad\;\; \alpha = 0.05$

In this case, the t test for differences between means is not appropriate because the test assumes that the samples are independent. Conceptually, Instant Fit has not provided two independent samples of before and after weights, inasmuch as the weights of the same 10 persons were recorded twice. The appropriate procedure for this case is to obtain the mean and standard deviation of the "difference"; that is, the data have to be viewed as *one sample of weight losses.*

This can be done by defining a variable D, which is the difference between the before and after weights of each individual in the sample. Assume that the data provided by Instant Fit are as follows:

Before:	237	135	183	225	147	146	214	157	157	144
After:	153	114	181	186	134	166	189	113	188	111
Then D:	84	21	2	39	13	−20	25	44	−31	33

Let $\overline{D}$ be the mean of the difference variable D and let $s_{\overline{D}}$ be the standard deviation of the difference. Now, the

Null hypothesis $\quad\quad\quad\quad H_o: \overline{D} \geq 20$
Alternative hypothesis $\quad\;\; H_a: \overline{D} < 20$

The appropriate test statistic would be

$$t = \frac{\overline{D} - d}{s_{\overline{D}}/\sqrt{n}}$$

where
$\quad\quad d$ = hypothesized valued difference, in our case $d = 20$
$\quad\quad n$ = sample size (10)

$$\overline{D} = \frac{1}{n}\sum_{i=1}^{n} D_i = \frac{210}{10} = 21$$

$$s_D^2 = \frac{1}{n-1}(\sum_{i=1}^{n} D_i^2 - n\overline{D}^2) = \frac{1}{9}(14202 - 10(21)^2) = 1088$$

$$s_{\overline{D}} = 32.98$$

Thus,

$$t = \frac{21 - 20}{32.98/\sqrt{20}} = 0.096$$

The rejection rule is the same as before.

If $\alpha = .05$, for 9 (i.e., $n - 1$) degrees of freedom and one-tail test, the t critical value is -1.833. Because the t calculated value of $0.096 \geq -1.833$, the null hypothesis is not rejected. Therefore, Instant Fit's claim is valid.

Hypothesis Testing of Proportions

There are instances in marketing research where the management is concerned not with the mean but with proportions. Consider, for example, the quality assurance department of a light bulb manufacturing company. The manager of the department, based on his experience, claims that 95 percent of the bulbs manufactured by the company are defect free. The CEO of the company, a quality-conscious person, checks a random sample of 225 bulbs and finds only 87 percent of the bulbs to be defect free. The CEO now wants to test the hypothesis (at the 0.05 level of significance) that 95 percent of the bulbs manufactured by the company are defect free.[1]

The data for this test can be statistically described as

$p_o = 0.95$: hypothesized value of the proportion of defect free bulbs
$q_o = 0.05$: hypothesized value of the proportion of defective bulbs
$p - 0.87$: sample proportion of defect free bulbs
$q - 0.13$: sample proportion of defective bulbs

Null hypothesis	$H_o : p = 0.95$
Alternative hypothesis	$H_a : p \neq 0.95$
Sample size	$n = 225$
Significance level	$\alpha = 0.05$

The first step in the hypothesis test of proportions is to calculate the standard error of the proportion using the hypothesized value of defect-free and defective bulbs; that is,

$$\sigma_{\bar{p}} = \sqrt{\frac{p_o q_o}{n}} = \sqrt{\frac{0.95 * 0.05}{225}} = 0.0145$$

The two-tailed test of proportions is graphically illustrated in Figure 17-3. Since np and nq are each larger than 5, the normal approximation of the binomial distribution can be used. Hence, the appropriate z value for 0.975 of the area under the curve can be obtained from the z tables as 1.96. Thus, the limits of the acceptance region are

$$p_0 \pm 1.96\sigma_{\bar{p}} = 0.95 \pm (1.96 * 0.0145) = (0.922, 0.978)$$

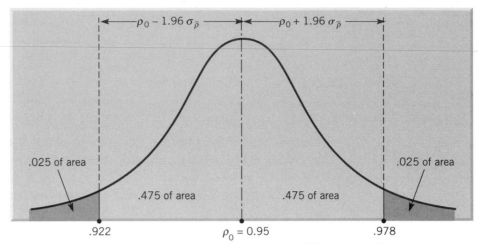

Two-tailed hypothesis test of a proportion at the .05 level of significance

FIGURE 17-3
The normal distribution

Inasmuch as the sample proportion of defect-free bulbs, 0.87, does not fall within the acceptance region, the CEO should reject the quality assurance manager's claims (the null hypothesis). A one-tailed test of hypothesis of proportions can be performed similarly.

Hypothesis Testing of Difference Between Proportions

John and Linda, sales executives for a big computer company, have been short-listed as the finalists in their company's annual sales competition. John and Linda have identical track records, and the winner of the competition will be selected based on his or her "conversion ratio" (i.e., the number of prospects converted into sales). The sales manager randomly picks 100 of John's prospects and finds that 84 of them have been converted to customers. In Linda's case, 82 of her sample of 100 prospects have been converted. The sales manager needs to know (at $\alpha = 0.05$) whether there is a difference in the conversion ratio, based on the sample proportions. Statistically, the data in this case can be represented as

$p_J = 0.84 = $ John's conversion ratio based on this sample of prospects
$q_J = 0.16 = $ Proportion that John failed to convert
$n_1 = 100 = $ John's prospect sample size
$p_L = 0.82 = $ Linda's conversion ratio based on her sample of prospects
$q_L = 0.18 = $ Proportion that Linda failed to convert
$n_2 = 100 = $ Linda's prospect sample size

Null hypothesis $H_0: p_J = p_L$
Alternative hypothesis $H_a: p_J \neq p_L$
Significance level $\alpha = 0.05$

As in the case of the pooled variance estimate of difference in means, the best estimate of p (the proportion of success) if the two proportions are hypothesized to be equal, is

$$\hat{p} = \frac{\text{Total number of successes in the two samples weighted by the respective sample sizes}}{\text{Total number of observations in the two samples}}$$

$$\hat{q} = 1 - \hat{p}$$

In this example,

$$\hat{p} = \frac{(n_1 p_J) + (n_2 p_L)}{n_1 + n_2} = \frac{(100 * 0.84) + (100 * 0.82)}{200} = 0.83$$

$$\hat{q} = 0.17$$

Now an estimate of $\sigma_{p_J - p_L}$ can be obtained using

$$\hat{\sigma}_{p_J - p_L} = \sqrt{\frac{\hat{p}\hat{q}}{n_1} + \frac{\hat{p}\hat{q}}{n_2}}$$

$$= \sqrt{\frac{(.83)(.17)}{100} +_k \frac{(.83)(.17)}{100}}$$

$$= 0.053$$

The Z value can be calculated using

$$Z_{calc} = \frac{(p_J - p_L) - (0)}{\hat{\sigma}_{p_J - p_L}} = \frac{.02}{.053} = 0.38$$

The Z value obtained from the table is 1.96 (for $\alpha = .05$). Hence, we fail to reject the null hypothesis.

THE PROBABILITY VALUES (*p*-VALUES) APPROACH TO HYPOTHESIS TESTING

In the hypothesis tests discussed so far, the manager or researcher tested the null hypothesis at a prespecified level of significance α. While discussing the Type I and Type II errors, it became clear that the choice of α will depend on the manager's concern for reducing either of these errors. In other words, there is a trade-off involved between the cost of each of these two kinds of errors, and the managers' choice of the significance level α will be guided by this cost–benefit analysis. However, knowledge of the nature of this trade-off still does not provide the manager with a foolproof method of selecting the appropriate α. The p value, or the probability-value approach provides the manager/ researcher with an alternative method of testing a hypothesis without having to prespecify α. The p-value can be defined as the largest significance level at which we would accept H_o.

Difference Between Using α and p Value. In hypothesis testing where α is prespecified, the researcher is trying to answer the question, "Is the probability of what has been observed less than α?" and reject or fail to reject accordingly. Alternatively, by using the p values, the researcher can answer the question, "How unlikely is the result that has been observed?" Once the probability value for the test is reported, the decision maker can weigh all the relevant factors and decide whether to accept or reject H_o, *without being bound by a prespecified significance level.*

For example, in a hypothesis test of a population mean, let the data be as follows:

Null hypothesis	$H_o: \mu = 25$
Alternative hypothesis	$H_a: \mu \neq 25$
Sample size	$n = 50$
Sample mean	$\bar{x} = 25.2$
Standard deviation	$\sigma = 0.7$

The standard error of mean can be calculated using

$$\sigma_{\bar{x}} = \frac{\sigma}{\sqrt{n}} = \frac{.7}{\sqrt{50}} = 0.1$$

The z statistic can be calculated using

$$Z = \frac{\bar{x} - \mu}{\sigma_{\bar{x}}} = \frac{(25.2 - 25)}{0.1} = 2.0$$

From the z table, the probability that z is greater than 2.0 can be found to be .0228 (value corresponding to z = 2.0).

Since this is a two-tailed test the p value = 2 × 0.0228 = 0.0456. *In other words, the p-value of 0.0456, is precisely the largest significance level at which we fail to reject the null hypothesis. For any other value of $\alpha > 0.0456$, we will reject* H_o.

If, instead, the hypothesis testing as done using a prespecified value of α, then

at $\alpha = .05$ the researcher will reject the null hypothesis, and
at $\alpha = .01$ the researcher will fail to reject

In general, the smaller the p-value, the greater is the researcher's confidence in the sample findings.

EFFECT OF SAMPLE SIZE AND INTERPRETATION OF TEST RESULTS

Considering sample size is important to the interpretation of hypothesis tests. The p-value generally is sensitive to sample size, in that if the sample size increases, the p-value usually will become smaller. In the example discussed in Chapter 16, suppose that the white-water-rafter sample size was 900 instead of 25 and that the average response was 5.8. The p-value then would be less than 0.01.[2] Thus, it could be concluded that the white-water rafters' response was indeed significantly higher (at the 0.01 level) than 5.6.

However, it may well be of no interest if the response of white-water rafters differs only slightly from the response of others. The hypothesis test does not provide information as to whether the evidence put forth is meaningful—only whether it is likely to have been a statistical accident. If the sample size becomes large, the probability of getting "lucky" or "unluckly" with the sample becomes small. Conversely, if the sample size is small, the probability of a statistical accident will be higher. The p-value can be conceived as a mechanism to report the impact of the sample size on the reliability of the results. If the sample size is large, a low p-value should be expected; if the sample size is small, a high p-value is more likely.

If there are more than two groups involved, differences in means across multiple groups can be analyzed through a procedure called the **analysis of variance.**

RELATIONSHIP BETWEEN CONFIDENCE INTERVAL AND HYPOTHESIS TESTING

In the white-water rafter example, can one determine whether the white-water rafters' average response of 6.1, which will be termed $\overline{X}$ (the sample mean), is the same as the population mean response of 5.6?

$$H_o: \mu = 5.6$$
$$H_a: \mu \neq 5.6$$

To answer this question, an estimate of the sample standard error of $\overline{X}$ has to be obtained using the formula

$$s_{\overline{x}} = \frac{s}{\sqrt{n}} = \frac{2.5}{\sqrt{35}} = 0.42$$

where s, the standard deviation of the sample was determined to be 2.5 in this example. Although, the population standard deviation is not known, the normal distribution can be used, because we have an estimate based on the sample standard deviation. The appropriate z value for $\alpha = 0.05$ can be obtained from the z table (Appendix A-1 Table), and is found to be 1.96. Now the critical values or the cut-off limits can be calculated using the formula

$$\mu_0 \pm 1.96 s_{\overline{x}} = 5.6 \pm (1.96*0.42) = (4.78, 6.42)$$

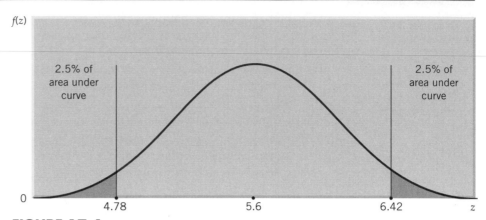

FIGURE 17-4
The normal distribution

Because 6.1 falls within the limits, *we fail to reject* the null hypothesis. Figure 17-4 provides a graphical illustration of the hypothesis test. From the *z* table, it can be determined that 95 percent of all the area under the curve is included in the interval extending 1.96 $\sigma_{\bar{x}}$ on either side of the hypothesized mean. In 95 percent of the area, then, there is no significant difference between the sample statistic and the hypothesized population parameter. If the sample statistic falls into the shaded area under the curve, representing 5 percent of the total area (2.5 percent in each tail), then we would reject the null hypothesis.

The term "fail to reject" is used instead of "accept" because, even though the sample statistic falls within the critical values, this does not prove that the null hypothesis is true; *it simply does not provide statistical evidence to reject it.*

Alternatively, acceptance or rejection of the hypothesis can be done without the need for calculating the critical values. This is done by calculating the *z* statistic. The *z* statistic is obtained using the formula

$$z = \frac{\overline{X} - \mu}{s_{\bar{x}}} = \frac{6.1 - 5.6}{0.42} = 1.19$$

Then one should apply the rejection rule, which states: *For a two-tailed test (for which the alternate hypothesis would be* H_a: $\mu \neq$ *c, the hypothesized value), the rejection rule is to reject the null hypothesis if* $|z_{calc}| > z_{\alpha/2}$; *for a right-tailed test of hypothesis, reject the null hypothesis if* $z_{calc} > z_\alpha$ *(where* z_α *is obtained from the z tables).* There are similar rules for a left-tailed test: *For a left-tailed test (for which the alternate hypothesis would be* H_a: $\mu <$ *c, the hypothesized value), the rejection rule is to reject the null hypothesis if* $z_{calc} < -z_\alpha$.

ANALYSIS OF VARIANCE (ANOVA)

Consider the following pricing experiment. Three prices are under consideration for a new product: 39 cents, 44 cents, and 49 cents. To determine the influence the various price levels will have on sales, three samples of five supermarkets are randomly selected from the geographic area of interest. Each sample is assigned one of the three price levels. Figure 17-5 shows the resulting sales levels in both graphic and tabular form. The 39-cent stores, the first row, had sales of 8, 12, 10, 9, and 11, and averaging 10 units. The 44-cent stores, the second row, averaged 8 units; and the 49-cent stores, the third row, averaged 7 units. Obviously, determining the optimal price will require an extensive analysis involving a host of considerations. However, before the analysis begins, it is appropriate to consider the basic concepts of experiment analysis.

In experimental design, the dependent variable is called the **response variable** and the independent variables are called **factors.** The different levels of a factor are called **treatments.** The purpose of most statistical experiments is to (a) determine whether the effects of the various treatments on the response variable are different, and (b) if so, to estimate how different they are. In our pricing experiment, the response variable is sales, the factor being the price, and the treatment being the three levels of the price—39 cents, 44 cents, and 49 cents.

One-Factor Analysis of Variance

Suppose that we wish to study one qualitative factor with levels 1, 2, . . . r. (In the case of the pricing experiment, the number of levels is 3.) That is, we wish to study the effects of these r treatments on a response variable (in this

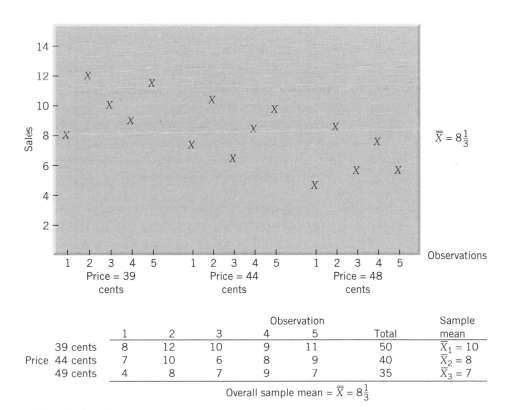

	Observation						Sample
	1	2	3	4	5	Total	mean
39 cents	8	12	10	9	11	50	$\bar{X}_1 = 10$
Price 44 cents	7	10	6	8	9	40	$\bar{X}_2 = 8$
49 cents	4	8	7	9	7	35	$\bar{X}_3 = 7$

Overall sample mean = $\bar{\bar{X}} = 8\frac{1}{3}$

FIGURE 17-5

A pricing experiment

case sales). The ANOVA of a one-factor model is sometimes called a **one-way analysis of variance.** As a preliminary step in one-way ANOVA, we wish to determine whether or not there are any statistically significant differences between the treatment means $\mu_1, \mu_2, \mu, \ldots \mu_r$ (μ_r being the mean value of the population of all possible values of the response variable that could potentially be observed using treatment "r"). To do this we test the null hypothesis

$$H_o: \mu_1 = \mu_2 = \mu_3 = \ldots = \mu_r$$

(This hypothesis says that all treatments have the same effect on the mean response.)

against the alternative hypothesis,

$$H_1: \text{at least 2 of } \mu_1, \mu_2, \ldots \mu_r \text{ are different}$$

(This hypothesis says that at least two treatments have different effects on the mean response.)

Essentially, in the case of the pricing experiment, the null hypothesis would be that the price levels have no effect on sales. The differences between sample means could be caused by the fact that a sample of only five was employed for each price level. The alternate hypothesis is that there is a price effect—that sales would not be the same for each of the price levels if they were applied to all stores.

To test these hypotheses, we need to compute the ratio between the "between-treatment" variance and "within-treatment" variance. Here, we define **between-treatment variance** as the variance in the response variable for different treatments. On the other hand, **within-treatment variance** is defined as the variance in the response variable for a given treatment. If we can show that "between" variance is significantly larger than the "within" variance, then we can reject the null hypothesis.

Variation Between Price Levels. Consider the pricing experiment illustrated in Figure 17-5. To test the null hypothesis, first focus on the variation among price levels ($\overline{X}_1 = 10$, $\overline{X}_2 = 8$, and $\overline{X}_3 = 7$). Then consider the variation within price levels (for example, the stores with the 39-cent price level had sales of 8, 12, 10, 9, and 11). Under the null hypothesis that price levels have no effect on sales, each of these estimates should be similar. If the estimate based on variation among stores of different price levels is inflated, doubt will be cast on the null hypothesis.

The "between" variance estimate is based on the variation between the sample mean values of each row (price level), which is calculated using the formula

$$SS_r = \sum_{p=1}^{n} n_p (\overline{X}_p - \overline{\overline{X}})^2$$

where

SS_r = sum of squares between price levels (rows), also called the treatment sum of squares or the variation explained by the price level.

$\overline{X}_p$ = mean sales at price level p (e.g., $\overline{X}_1 = 10$)

$\overline{\overline{X}}$ = overall mean (in this case = $8^1/_3$)

n = number of observations at each price level ($n = 5$)

p = treatment or price level ($p = 1, 2, 3$)

r = number of treatments or price levels ($r = 3$)

Hence, in this example, the treatment sum of squares can be calculated to be

$$SS_r = 5[(10 - 25\ 3)^2 + (8 - 25\ 3)^2 + (7 - 25\ 3)^2] = 23.3$$

Clearly, as the difference between means gets larger, so will the treatment sum of squares. The "between" variance estimate is termed MSS_r (the mean sum of squares between price levels and is an estimate of the variance among stores), and is obtained by dividing the SS_r by its associated degree of freedom (df), which here is the number of treatments (rows) less one. Thus,

$$MSS_r = SS_r/(r - 1)$$
$$= 23.3/2 = 11.65$$

Variation Within Price Levels. The "within" variance estimate is based on the variation within each price level (row), which is calculated using the formula

$$SS_u = \sum_{i=1}^{n_p} \sum_{p=1}^{r} (X_{ip} - \overline{X}_p)^2$$

where

SS_u = sum of squares unexplained by the price level (row), also called the error sum of squares or the variation within the price levels.

X_{ip} = sales of observations (stores) i at price level p

n_p = number of observations at each price level ($n_p = 5$ for all p's)

p = treatment or price level ($p = 1, 2, 3$)

r = number of treatments or price levels ($r = 3$)

Hence, in this example, the error sum of squares (or unexplained variations) can be calculated to be

$$SS_u = (8 - 10)^2 + (12 - 10)^2 + \cdots + (7 - 7)^2$$
$$= 34$$

The "within" variance estimate is termed MSS_u (the mean sum of squares unexplained by the price level and is an estimate of the variance within stores) and is generated by dividing SS_u by its associated degrees of freedom,[3] which is here equal to $r(n-1)$ or 12 (also equal to total sample size [N] minus the total number of treatment levels [p]). Thus,

$$MSS_u = SS_u/r(n-1)$$
$$= 34/12 = 2.8$$

Having calculated the variation explained by the treatment (price level) and the variation unexplained by it, an addition of these two factors would give the total variation or the sum of squares total (SS_t). Thus,

$$SS_t = SS_r + SS_u$$
$$= 23.3 + 34 = 57.3$$

ANOVA Table. The expressions derived above are summarized in Table 17-2, which presents an *analysis of variance* and is termed an *ANOVA* table. The ANOVA table is a conventional way to present a hypothesis test regarding the difference between several means. The table indicates, at the left, the source of the variation. The first row summarizes the determination of MSS_r, which is based on the variation between rows (the explained variation, or the variation explained by the price level). The second row summarizes the determination of MSS_u, which is based on the within-row variation (variation unexplained by the price levels). The third row represents the total variation based on the deviations of the individual sales results from the overall mean. All the variation is thus accounted for.[4]

TABLE 17-2
Price Experiment ANOVA Table

Source of Variation	Variation (Sum of Squares) (SS)	Degrees of Freedom (df)	Variance Estimate Mean Sum of Squares (MSS)	F-ratio
Between price levels explained variation	$SS_r = \sum_{p=1}^{n} n_p (\bar{X} - \bar{X})^2$ $= 23.3$	$r - 1 = 2$	$MSS_r = \dfrac{SS_r}{2} = 11.65$	$\dfrac{MSS_r}{MSS_u} = 4.16$
Within price levels unexplained variation	$SS_u = \sum_{i=1}^{5} \sum_{p=1}^{3} (X_{ip} - \bar{X}_p)^2$	$r(n_p - 1) = 12$	$MSS_u = \dfrac{SS_u}{12} = 2.8$	
Total	$SS_t = \sum_{i=1}^{5} \sum_{p=1}^{3} (X_{ip} - \bar{X})^2$ $= 57.3$	$n - 1 = 14$		

F-Statistic and p-Value. We now consider the ratio of the two estimates of the variance (the "between" and "within") of the store sales. This ratio is termed an *F-ratio* or *F-statistic*:

$$F = MSS_r / MSS_u$$
$$= 11.65 / 2.8 = 4.16$$

If the null hypothesis that price levels have no effect on sales is true, then our variance estimates using the difference between the sample means, MSS_r, should be the same as those based on the within-row (price-level) variations. The F-ratio should then be close to one. If, however, the hypothesis is not true and the different price levels generate different sales levels, the MSS_r term will have two components. One component will reflect the variance among stores; the other will reflect the different price effects. As a result, the F-ratio will tend to become large.

The p-value is the probability that the F-ratio would be larger than 4.16, given the null hypothesis. To generate the p-value, the F-probability distribution is used. Associated with each F-ratio are the numerator (MSS_r) degrees of freedom (2), and the denominator (MSS_u) degrees of freedom (12). Knowing this pair of degrees of freedom, a table of the F-distribution (Table A-3 at the back of the book) can be used to determine, at least approximately, the p-value. The F-distribution table provides the following p-values for our case, in which the degrees of freedom are 2 and 12.

F-Statistic	p-Value
1.46	0.25
2.81	0.10
3.89	0.05
6.93	0.01

Thus, the p-value associated with 4.16 is not in the table, but would be about 0.04. If the null hypothesis were true, there would be a 0.04 probability of getting an F-statistic of 4.16 or larger. Therefore, the evidence that the null hypothesis is not true is fairly substantial. The observed difference between sample means could have occurred by accident even if the null hypothesis were true, but the probability is low (1 chance in 25). Since the p-value is less than 0.05, we can say that the F-statistic is significant at the .05 level. *Note: The ANOVA approach and the regression approach to one-factor analysis of variance give the same value for the "F-statistic."*

Strength of Association. A good descriptive statistics for measuring the strength of association is to compute ρ (*Rho*), the ratio of the sums of squares for the treatment (SS_r) to the total sums of squares (SS_t). *Rho* is a measure of the proportion of variance accounted for in the sample data. In our example, $\rho = 23.3 / 57.3 = 0.407$. In other words, 40.7 percent of the total variation in the data is explained by the treatment (price levels). However, since the sample value (ρ) tends to be upward biased, it is useful to have an estimate of the population strength of association (ω^2, omega squared) between the treatment and the dependent variable. A sample estimate of this population value can be computed as:

$$\hat{\omega} = \frac{(SS_r - (r-1)MS_u)}{(SS_t + MS_u)} = \frac{(23.3 - 2(2.8))}{(57.3 + 2.8)} = 0.295$$

In other words, 29.5 percent of the total variation in the data is accounted for by the treatment.

Expanding the ANOVA Table

In Chapter 12 we saw how an experiment involving a treatment variable such as price could be expanded. It is possible to control experimentally for one or more variables, such as store size or city, by adding one or more *block effects*. In essence, the experiment is repeated for each block (that is, large stores and small stores). It also is possible to add more treatment variables. In either case, more than one nominally scaled variable is introduced, and there are several *difference between sample means* relationships. To handle such experiments, the ANOVA table is expanded.

To illustrate, consider the experiment Keith Hunt conducted on corrective advertising, which is advertising required by the FTC to "correct" a previous advertisement deemed deceptive.[5] The advertisement in question introduced F-310, a gasoline additive. The FTC claimed, in part, that the product did not significantly reduce pollution as claimed and that the demonstration involving a balloon attached to the exhaust emissions of two cars was rigged, in that one car had a dirty engine and the other emitted invisible pollutants. The effect of various "corrective advertisements" had policy implications for the FTC, which wanted a fair and effective remedy for deceptive advertising but did not want to be harsh and punitive.

Three types of corrective advertisements were tested:

1. *Explicit.* A specific statement explicitly pointing out the deceptive characteristics of the advertisement in question.
2. *General.* A general statement about the deception of the advertisement.
3. *No corrective advertisement.* A bland statement by the FTC on gasoline additives with no mention of the company.

Prior to being exposed to one of the corrective advertisements, the respondents were exposed to one of three "inoculation" advertisements. An inoculation advertisement is hypothesized to mitigate the effect of the corrective advertising, either by giving high levels of support (**supportive inoculation**) or by giving weak doses of the corrective advertisement, which are refuted (**refutational inoculation**). Three inoculation treatments were used:

1. *Refutation.* This advertisement warned of the upcoming corrective ad and refuted it. "If every motorist used F-310 for 2000 miles, air pollutants would

be reduced by thousands of tons per day. The FTC doesn't seem to think that is significant. We think it is."

2. *Supportive.* This contains no mention of the FTC or the upcoming corrective advertisement but does restate the positive arguments.
3. *No inoculation.* This advertisement makes no mention of the positive arguments.

A 3×3 factorial design was used, as outlined in Figure 17-6. Each of the nine cells had 22 respondents, each of which was exposed to the "deceptive" advertisement, the inoculation treatment, and the corrective advertisement. The criterion measure was the degree of agreement or disagreement, on a 28-point scale (where larger numbers indicate greater agreement), with the statement, "I like Chevron with F310." Figure 17-6 shows the sample mean for each of the nine cells. The hypothesis test involves determining the probability of obtaining the observed differences between the sample means, under the hypothesis that the population means were the same.

The expanded ANOVA table is shown in Table 17-3. Notice that each of the two treatments, inoculation and corrective advertising, now has an associated variation (sum of squares) and variance estimate (mean sum of squares). Consider first the inoculation treatment. The F-ratio for inoculation is

$$F\text{-ratio} = MSS_{inoculation} / MSS_{unexplained}$$
$$= 35.2/34.4 = 1.02$$

The associated p-value would be approximately 0.36. Thus, the evidence against the null hypothesis of no inoculation effect is not impressive. The evidence is the fact that the three sample means found in Figure 17-6 (16.7, 16.9, and 15.4) are not equal. However, although they are not equal, they are close enough so that we cannot reject the null hypothesis that the population means are equal.

Type of Inoculation	Type of Corrective Advertising			Sample Means
	Explicit	General	No Corrective Advertising	
Refutational inoculation	(1)	(2)	(3)	16.7
Supportive inoculation	(4)	(5)	(6)	16.9
No inoculation	(7)	(8)	(9)	15.4
Sample means	10.1	18.2	20.4	
Cell size = 22				

FIGURE 17-6
A factorial design

TABLE 17-3
Expanded ANOVA Table

Source of Variation	Variation (SS)	Degrees of Freedom (df)	Mean Sum of Squares (MSS)	F-Ratio	p-Value Less Than
Inoculation	70.5	2	35.2	1.02	.36
Corrective advertising	3,882.4	2	1,941.2	56.43	.001
Interaction between treatments	503.7	4	125.9	3.66	.007
Unexplained variation	6,496.6	189	34.4		
Total	10,953.2	197			

Consider next the corrective advertising. The *F*-ratio is calculated for the corrective advertising treatment in the same manner:

$$F\text{-ratio} = MSS_{Corrective\ Advertising} / MSS_{unexplained}$$
$$= 1941.2/34.4 = 56.43$$

The associated *p*-value is less than 0.001. Thus, the evidence is extremely impressive against the null hypothesis that there is no corrective advertising effect. The evidence is the fact that the three sample means found in Figure 17-6 (10.1, 18.2, and 20.4) are not equal. Thus, the null hypothesis that there is no corrective advertising effect can be rejected at the 0.001 level. A closer look at the three sample means in Figure 17-6 reveals that it is the explicit corrective advertising that is effective at changing attitudes. This finding is potentially important in designing remedies for deceptive advertising.

There is an advantage to analyzing the two treatments in the same analysis of variance table. By including both, the unexplained variation is reduced, as is the associated mean sum of squares (MSS_u). As a result, there will be less "noise" in the data, the results will be more sensitive, and the *F*-ratios will be larger.

Interaction. There is a third term in Table 17-3, the interaction between the two treatments. An **interaction effect** means that the impact of one treatment, such as inoculation, will not be the same for each condition of the other treatment. Figure 17-7 shows the results graphically. Note that inoculation affects the attitude created by explicit corrective advertising, but it really has little effect under the "no corrective advertising" and the "general corrective advertising" conditions. There is thus an **interaction effect** present. If there was no interaction, the shape of the three lines shown in Figure 17-7 would be the same. Their levels would differ, but their shapes would be the same.

The hypothesis of no interaction can be tested in the ANOVA table given in Table 17-3 by determining the appropriate *F*-ratio for interaction.

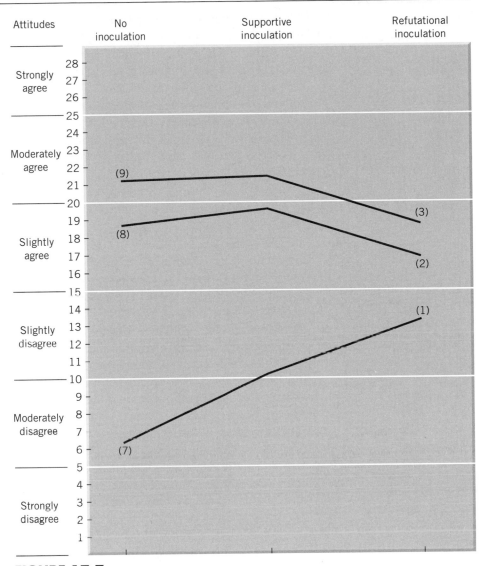

FIGURE 17-7
Attitude toward Chevron with F-310
Source: Adapted from H. Keith Hunt, "Effects of Corrective Advertising," *Journal of Advertising Research,* 13 (October 1973), 15–22.

$$F\text{-ratio} = MSS_{\text{interaction}} / MSS_{\text{unexplained}}$$
$$= 125.9/34.4 = 3.66$$

The associated *p*-value is approximately .007. Thus, the evidence against the null hypothesis of no interaction is very impressive.[6]

Summary

The chapter discussed the more commonly used hypothesis testing of means and proportions. It proposed the use of various statistical tests, depending on factors such as whether one or two groups are involved and whether the population or sample standard deviation is used. It also discussed the probability value approach to hypothesis testing and the relationship between confidence interval and hypothesis testing. Finally, for comparison of multiple group means, it proposed an analysis of variance framework.

The goal of one-factor ANOVA is to estimate and compare the effects of the different treatments on the response variable. The purpose of most statistical experiments is to (a) determine whether the effects of the various treatments on the response variable are different, and (b) if so, to estimate how different they are. The ANOVA table can be expanded to accommodate n-factor or n-way analysis of variance.

Questions and Problems

1. In Table 15-1, the statement concerning gasoline costs generated a larger difference (1.7) than the other three statements. Could you therefore conclude that it was the statement that best distinguished the unit-price user from the unit-price nonuser? What assumptions are involved in that conclusion?

2. The Consumer Fraud Council claims that Skippy Foods does not put the required weight of peanut butter in its 10-ounce jar. For evidence, a sample of 400 jars are selected randomly, weighed, and found to average 9.9 ounces. The p-value, 0.07, is associated with the hypothesis that the population mean (μ) is usually 10 ounces and the production process is not generating "light" bottles. Has the council proved the point? Evaluate the evidence. Is the evidence statistically significant at the 0.10 level? At the 0.05 level? Should the Consumer Fraud Council recommend a boycott?

3. A new product was tested in Fresno with a 25-cent coupon and in Tulsa with a 50-cent coupon. A sample of 100 people was contacted in each test city. A total of 40 percent of those contacted in Tulsa had tried the new product, whereas only 30 percent of those contacted in Fresno had tried it, a 10 percent difference. Prior to making the decision as to which coupon to use in the marketing program, a hypothesis was suggested.
   a. What should the null hypothesis be?
   b. What should the alternate hypothesis be?
   c. The probability of obtaining this result under the null hypothesis, namely, that the trial level in Tulsa was 10 percent higher than that in Fresno, was determined to be 0.06. What is the p-value?
   d. Is the result significant at the 0.10 level? At the 0.05 level? Would you reject the null hypothesis at the 0.10 level? At the 0.05 level?
   e. Does the hypothesis show that there will be more trials with a 50-cent coupon? Do you feel that a 50-cent coupon should be used?

4. A manufacturer claims that through the use of a fuel additive, automobiles should achieve, on average, an additional 5 miles per gallon of gas. A random sample of 100 automobiles was used to evaluate this claim. The sample mean increase in miles per gallon achieved was 4.4, and the sample standard deviation was 1.8 miles per gallon. Test the null hypothesis that the population mean is at least 5 miles per gallon. Find the p-value of this test, and interpret your findings.

5. A beer distributer claims that a new display, featuring a life-size picture of a well-known athlete, will increase product sales in supermarkets by an average of 40 cases a week. For a random sample of 25 supermarkets, the average sales increase was 31.3 cases and the sample standard deviation was 12.2 cases. Test, at the 5 percent level, the null hypothesis that the population mean sales increase is at least 40 cases, stating any assumption you make.

6. Of a sample of 361 owners of retail service and business firms which had gone into bankruptcy, 105 reported having no business experience prior to opening the business. Test the null hypothesis that at most 25 percent of all members of this population had no business experience before opening the business.

7. In a random sample of 400 people purchasing state lottery tickets, 172 sample members were women. Test the null hypothesis that half of all purchasers are women.

8. A random sample of 200 members of the American Marketing Association was asked which continuing professional education course had most appeal. Of these sample members, 70 opted for international marketing research-related courses. Test the null hypothesis that 45 percent of all members of the association hold this view against the alternative that the true percentage is lower.

9. A questionnaire was designed to compare the level of students' familiarity with two types of product. For a random sample of 120 students, the mean familiarity level with burglar alarms was found to be 3.355, and the sample standard deviation was 2.03. In an independent random sample of 100 students, the mean familiarity level for television was 9.5, and the sample standard deviation was 2.1. Assuming that the two population distributions are normal and have the same variance, test the null hypothesis that the population means are equal.

10. A random sample of consumers is taken, and their mean preference for visiting a sports event is found to be 5.1 (on a 1 to 7 scale, where 7 denotes most preferred). In the previous surveys, the mean preference has always been 5.0. Has the mean preference changed now? (Use $\alpha = .10$ and $\sigma = 0.1$)

11. In a test-marketing study, the average sales for a new brand of shampoo in 9 stores is 1.95 units (each unit is 100 bottles). The retail management was expecting to sell on the average 2.0 units. Was the management's expectation realized? (Use $\alpha = .05$ and $\sigma = .06$)

12. An experiment was conducted to determine which of three advertisements to use in introducing a new personal computer. A total of 120 people who were thinking of buying a personal computer was split randomly into three groups of 40 each. Each group was shown a different advertisement and each person was asked his or her likelihood of buying the advertised brand. A scale of 1 (very unlikely) to 7 (very likely) was used. The results showed that the average likelihood of purchase was

Advertisement A. 5.5
Advertisement B. 5.8
Advertisement C. 5.2

The ANOVA table was as follows:

Source of Variation	SS	df	MSS	F-Ratio	p-Value
Due to advertisements	12	2	6.0		
Unexplained	234	117	2.0		
Total	246	119			

  a. What is the appropriate null hypothesis? The alternate hypothesis?
  b. What is the F-ratio? The p-value?
  c. Is the result significant at the 0.10 level? The 0.05 level? The 0.01 level?
  d. Are there any differences among the impacts of the three advertisements?

13. Using Problem 12, assume that each of the three groups of respondents had been divided into two groups: younger (under 30) and older (over 30). The revised ANOVA table was as follows:

Source of Variation	SS	df	MSS	F-Ratio	p-Value
Due to advertisements	12	2	6.0		
Due to age	24	1	24.0		
Unexplained	210	116	1.81		
Total	246	119			

  a. What are the F-ratio and p-value associated with the hypothesis test that there is no advertisement effect? Why is it different than that in Problem 6? Notice that the total SS and the advertisement SS have not changed.
  b. Test the hypothesis that there is no age effect.

End Notes

1. Companies practicing total quality management (discussed in Chapter 25) usually go for zero defects, or six sigma quality, rather than 5 percent defects used in this example.
2. If the sample standard error again was found to be 2.5, then

$$t = \frac{(\bar{x} - u)}{\frac{s_{\bar{x}}}{\sqrt{n}}} = \frac{(5.8 - 5.6)}{\frac{2.5}{\sqrt{900}}} = 2.4$$

A t-value of 2.4 would have associated with it a p-value less than 0.01.

3. For a more detailed description of the analysis technique, see Geoffrey Kepel. *Design and Analysis:*

A Researcher's Handbook (Englewood Cliffs, New Jersey: Prentice Hall), 1973.

4. The reader also might note that the total degrees of freedom, which is the total sample size of 15 less one, or 14, is equal to the sum of the degrees of freedom associated with the first two rows of the ANOVA table.

5. H. Keith Hunt. "Effects of Corrective Advertising," *Journal of Advertising Research*, 13 October 1973, 15–22.

6. For a more detailed discussion on the analysis of experimental designs, see Douglas C. Montgomery. *Design and Analysis of Experiments* (New York: John Wiley & Sons, Inc.), 1991.

CASE 17-1
American Conservatory Theater[1]

The American Conservatory Theater (ACT), a major repertory theater located in San Francisco, was completing its tenth season. The management team at ACT decided to conduct a major research study, intended to help their planning effort. A questionnaire was developed and mailed to their approximately 9000 season subscribers. A return rate of 40 percent was obtained. A sample of 982 of these returned questionnaires was selected for analysis.

One of the major interests of ACT management was in developing an understanding of the dynamics of the process whereby individuals became ACT subscribers. To assist in this process the sample was divided into four groups according to their behavior pattern over the past five seasons:

1. Continual subscribers (32 percent)—subscribed all five seasons
2. Gradual subscribers (31 percent)—one or more seasons of attendance followed by becoming a subscriber
3. Sudden subscribers (21 percent)—became a subscriber without attending prior performances
4. Miscellaneous patterns (16 percent)

The existence of a substantial "sudden subscriber" group was surprising and ran counter to conventional belief among theater managers that people were first enticed to attend a few performances at a particular theater and only after they had had some positive experiences with this theater would they become subscribers.

The next step in the research study was to attempt to identify characteristics of the continual, gradual, and sudden subscriber groups that might be of use in understanding the segment differences and as inputs in the development of audience building and retention programs. Five variables appeared to be useful in this regard:

1. Years resident in the San Francisco Bay Area, measured on a scale ranging from 1 = two years or less, to 5 = more than 20 years.
2. Age of subscriber, measured on a scale ranging from 1 = 25 years or less, to 5 = more than 65 years old.
3. Household income, measured on a scale ranging from 1 = $15,000 per year or less, to 4 = more than $50,000 per year.
4. Whether the subscriber spent more than 20 hours a week watching TV, measured as a dummy variable: 1 if yes, 0 if no.
5. Attendance at six other cultural institutions (i.e., ballet, Civic Light Opera, DeYoung Museum, Museum of Modern Art, opera, and symphony) in San Francisco. The attendance score is the number of the six different activities that the respondent attended at least once in the previous year.

Table 1 shows the differences between the mean scores for the three groups for these five variables.

Each respondent was asked which two benefits from a list of eight were the best reasons for purchasing

TABLE 1
Subscriber Groups

	Mean Scores		
	Continual	**Gradual**	**Sudden**
Years resident (1 to 5 scale)[a]	4.32	3.68	3.53
Age (1 to 5 scale)[a]	3.34	2.74	2.86
Income (1 to 4 scale)	2.54	2.39	2.38
Cultural activities (0 to 6 scale)[a]	2.84	2.95	2.08
Twenty hours of TV (0 to 1 dummy variable)	0.31	0.26	0.38
Sample size	314	304	206

[a] Indicates that the differences between means are significant at the .01 level.

[1] Prepared by Adrian B. Ryans, Charles B. Weinberg, and David A. Aaker as a basis for class discussion.

517

TABLE 2
Benefits Obtained by Subscribing to ACT

Subscriber Group	Ease of Ordering (%)	Guaranteed Ticket (%)	Price Discount (%)	Priority Seating (%)	Discount on Special Plays (%)	More Certain to Attend (%)	New Play Series (%)	Support for Art (%)	Total Mentions
Continual subscriber	7.5	16.4	12.4	22.0	1.1	25.9	2.9	11.8	549
Gradual subscriber	8.2	16.5	12.5	22.2	1.1	28.5	3.0	7.9	558
Sudden subscriber	11.0	13.9	10.4	25.7	1.6	30.7	1.6	5.1	374
Total Sample	8.6	15.8	12.0	23.0	1.2	28.1	2.6	8.6	1481

Benefit[a]

[a] Each respondent could check a maximum of two benefits. Percentages are based on total number of benefits checked.

a subscription. One of the benefits listed was the subscription price discount (ACT offered subscribers seven plays for the price of six). The percentage of each subscriber group that mentioned each benefit is shown in Table 2.

Questions for Discussion

1. Does it surprise you that there are so many "sudden subscribers"? Why would a person subscribe (at a cost that could be as high as $50 per person) instead of first trying it out? After reviewing Table 1 in what aspects would you say that such a person differed from other subscribers? Interpret the footnote in Table 1.

2. What does Table 2 say about the difference between the three groups? What are the other implications of Table 2 for ACT?

CASE 17-2
Apple Appliance Stores

An experiment using a randomized design was conducted by the Apple Appliance chain of 300 retail stores. Four levels of advertising provided the experimental treatment: none, low, medium, and high. In addition, the stores were divided by store size into small, intermediate, and large. A random sample of eight stores was taken from each of the three store-size groups. Each set of eight stores was divided randomly into four groups of two stores for the experimental treatment, as summarized by the following:

Stores sales were measured during the six-month period after the experiment started. Sales also were determined during the same period in the previous year. The differences between the sales during the two periods was the variable of interest. A plot of the sales change is shown in Figure 1.

In Table 3, an analysis of variance is shown. Exactly what statistical questions are answered by the table? What additional, unanswered questions may be of interest?

		Store size			
		Small	**Medium**	**Large**	**Total**
	None	2	2	2	6
	Low	2	2	2	6
Advertising level	Medium	2	2	2	6
	High	2	2	2	6
	Total	8	8	8	

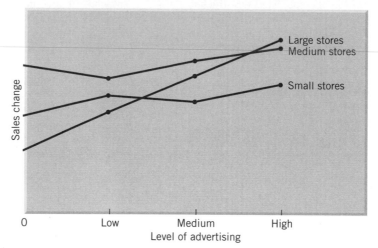

FIGURE 1
Effect of advertising on sales

TABLE 3
Analysis of Variance of Sales Changes

Source of Variation	Sum of Squares	Degrees of Freedom (df)	Mean Sum of Squares	*F*-ratio
Advertising	360	3	120	3.0[a]
Store size	88	2	44	1.1
Interaction	984	6	164	4.1[b]
Unexplained variation	480	12	40	
Total	1912	23		

[a] Significant at the 0.10 level.
[b] Significant at the 0.05 level.

CASES FOR PART III
Data Analysis

CASE III-I
The Vancouver Symphony Orchestra[1]

Daniel Gardiner and Charles Weinberg

At an afternoon meeting at the Vancouver Symphony Orchestra (VSO) offices, three executives, concerned with the marketing of the VSO, were discussing some of the challenges they currently faced.[2]

Ed Oscapella: We've got to do something and do it fast to get out of this difficult situation. Time is running out of the 1987/88 season.

Jane Corbett: From my point of view, I've got to find out who wants what: Do subscribers want something different from nonsubscribers? If so, what? We've got all this information that needs analyzing and I'm hoping it will be useful in marketing the 1987/88 season.

E. Douglas Hughes: I've got to decide on an appropriate theme or themes to communicate to the segment(s) we go after. We've got to give the printers sufficient lead time to get our brochures out so I need to know what to focus on in the promotion.

Armed with the computer data from a recent audience survey completed January 6, 1987 (four weeks earlier), the three knew that they had to sift through all the information very carefully. Within two weeks, they had to come up with a set of specific and actionable recommendations. The VSO's Board had already voted to cancel many concerts in June so as to lower its deficit.

All three agreed that perhaps their immediate task was to build ticket sales for the remaining four months of the 1986/87 season. The guest artist and concert schedule from February through June is shown in Exhibit III-2. During this time period, two subscription series were offered. The first was a six-concert "Seagram Pops" series. The second was a five-concert celebration series. In the prior year, a "Musically Speaking" series and "Jubilee" series were both offered.

Background

Situated midway between Asia Pacific countries and the United Kingdom and approximately 40 miles north of the United States, Vancouver is Canada's third largest city. Home to more than 1.3 million people, Vancouver is the largest metropolitan area in Western Canada and is an emerging center of international trade and investment.

Vancouver is rated one of the five most beautiful cities in the world and in addition to varied recreational and sports attractions, Vancouver has many cultural and theatrical attractions as well. These include the Vancouver Museum, the Queen Elizabeth Playhouse, the Arts Club, the Vancouver Art Gallery, the Vancouver Opera Society, and the Vancouver Symphony Orchestra.

The VSO is one of the oldest cultural institutions in Vancouver, with its inaugural concert held in 1897. Regular seasons were offered in the 1930s when the orchestra came under the patronage of Mrs. B. T. Rogers. The orchestra's original repertoire included mostly big band music. Over the years, the repertoire expanded to reflect more classical and romantic symphonic works, changing in response to the tastes of the various musical directors. As well, the regular season was lengthened and the number of scheduled programs and series increased.

The orchestra, among the 10 largest in North America, has been plagued with financial, managerial, and artistic problems over the past two years. Subscription revenue has steadily declined in the last five years, putting pressure on the symphony to emphasize sales of single tickets and to heavily promote each event. With 122 scheduled performances in the 1986/87 season, a 15 percent decrease in regular subscribers (to the "Jubilee" and "Musically Speaking" series), the sluggish economic climate in Vancouver post-Expo '86 and a deficit of $811,000, the Vancouver Symphony Orchestra faced an enormous challenge just to maintain the status quo, let alone reduce its deficit.

---

[1] Ed Oscapella, Executive Director; Jane Corbett, Director of Marketing; and E. Douglas Hughes, Director of Communications for the Vancouver Symphony Orchestra. See Exhibit III-1 for a brief biographical background of each of these staff members.

[2] The data for this case are available. See your professor.

EXHIBIT III-1

Background of Selected VSO Staff Members

Edward P. Oscapella, Executive Director, came to the VSO in March 1986, bringing with him a wealth of experience to various positions with arts organizations across Canada. A University of Toronto graduate in Music (Performance), Oscapella served as general manager of the Grand Theater in London, Ontario, and before that, the Toronto Dance Theater. He also was vice-president and general manager of Haber Artist Management, at the time the largest artist booking agency in Canada. Oscapella also served as grants coordinator for the Touring Office for the Canada Council, and for a short period of time was under contract as executive assistant to the Director of Marketing for CBC Radio and Television.

Jane Corbett, Director of Marketing, arrived at the VSO after several years of marketing experience with the Canadian Opera company in Toronto and at Vancouver Opera. Born in London, Ontario, Corbett took an M.B.A. at York University, and then began her professional career in musicology, working for the Guelph Civic Museum and for El Museo Archeologico de Cuenca in Spain. In 1985, Corbett made the move to Vancouver where she is now well-known in the arts community.

E. Douglas Hughes, Director of Communications, has assumed many guises in the arts, working as a CBC radio producer, an arts liaison officer for the Art Gallery of Ontario, a speechwriter for officials at B.C Hydro, a music journalist for the *Toronto Star,* the *Toronto Telegram,* the *Province* (Vancouver), and various magazines, a script writer for the CBC and private radio stations, a public relations director for the Toronto Symphony, the Winnipeg Art Gallery, Alberta Culture, the Banff Centre, Vancouver Opera, and the Vancouver Playhouse, and as a writer and host for many concert hall and theater presentations. Born in Saint John, New Brunswick, Hughes originally set out to become a concert pianist, studying at the Royal Conservatory of Music in Toronto, and the Royal Academy in London, England. He first joined the VSO in 1983, returning in 1986 after a year as Media Liaison Officer for the Royal Bank/EXPO 86 World Festival.

While small consolation, symphony orchestras throughout North America were going through difficult times (*Newsweek,* January 5, 1987, pp. 54–56). In September 1986, the Oakland Symphony declared bankruptcy and closed its doors; others, such as the San Diego Symphony and the one in Halifax, Nova Scotia, had suspended operations for a season or more. The Chicago Symphony, despite playing to a 98 percent capacity, was able to pay back only 62 percent of its $20 million operating budget. On the other hand, the symphonies in Montreal and Hamilton were enjoying record attendance levels and renewed financial support.

Decline in Attendance

At one point in the 1970s, the VSO enjoyed the largest subscription base of any orchestra in North America. However, the number of subscribers has been steadily declining. In 1985/86, subscriptions dropped by 18 percent. In 1986/87, the decrease in subscriptions could approach 20 percent, for an overall decline since 1984/85 of over 30 percent. Plans were being made to revise the subscription packages for the 1987/88 season in order to reverse this trend. However, the program for the current season was set.

Single-ticket sales had also been decreasing, but at a slower rate than subscriptions and were becoming relatively more important in terms of total attendance. They accounted for 36,701 tickets sold in the 1985/86 season. In 1984/85, regular subscribers accounted for 79 percent of the total attendance. However, the proportion of subscribers for 1986/87 was projected at only 70 percent of total attendance.

The Free Concert

One of the ways to offset declining revenues may be to focus on nonsubscribers. After a date to make a recording of the VSO was postponed, it was decided in early December that a "free concert" be given in order to obtain "trial" by the nonsubscriber group. This concert was held in the evening on Tuesday, January 6, 1987. People had to go to the VSO's administrative office located three miles away from the Orpheum Theater (where the VSO performed) to pick up tickets. After being heavily promoted on a local FM radio station, the concert was an immediate "sellout" with all 2761 tickets distributed. So as to obtain information about the concert-goers in a cost-effective manner, a questionnaire was developed and given to audience members. Because of time constraints, an initial draft of the questionnaire was pretested only on VSO office employees. A photo-reduced copy of the survey is shown in Exhibit III-3 along with relevant response

EXHIBIT III-2

VSO Guest Artist and Concert Schedule
February–June 1987

Date	Series	Conductor[a]	Soloist
Feb. 7, 9	CS#1	R. Barshai	I. Kipnis, harpsichord
Feb. 13	Recital		V. Ashkenazy, piano
Feb. 15, 16, 17	J#8	R. Barshai	C-L Lin, violin
Feb. 19, 20, 21 (2)	Bal #2		P. N. Balet Vanc-Canata Singers
Feb. 24(2)	School	P. McCoppin	K. Rudolph, pic., E. Volpe, hp.
Feb. 27, 28, Mar. 2, 3	POP#2	S. Dankworth	No soloists
Mar. 8, 9, 10	J#9	H. Holliger	Cond & ob solist
Mar. 12	Recital		M. Perahia, piano
Mar. 14, 16	CS#2	G. Sebastion	B. Tuckwell, hn
Mar. 18	Benefit Concert		M. J. Fox, T. Banks, B. Zarankin, piano/E. Northcott
Mar. 19, 20, 21(2)	Bal #3	E. Stafford	Royal Winnipeg Ballet
Mar. 24	SP Bal	P. McCoppin	R. Nureyev and Friends
Mar. 29, 30, 31	J#10	Y. P. Tortelier	W. Klien, piano
April 3, 4, 6, 7	POP#3	R. Hayman	The Cambridge Buskers
April 6	Tea & Trumpets	P. McCoppin	E. Northcott, sop, O. Lowry, host
April 12, 13, 14	J#11	K. Akiyama	L. Lortie, piano
April 18, 20	CS#3	T. Otaka	A. de Larrocha, piano
April 21	SP	P. McCoppin B. Buckley	Visions: Mission Andromeda
Apr. 24, 25, 27, 28	POP#4	M. Miller	No soloists
May 3, 4, 5	J#12	R. Barshai	Bach Choir: J. Coop, piano: M. Collins, sop; S. Graham, mezzo; G. Evans, tnr; D. Garrard, bass
May 9, 11	CS#4	R. Barshai	E. Mathis, sop
May 22, 23, 25, 26	POP#5	J. Everly and Bach Choir	S. Woods, spo/M. Paris, mezzo D. Eisler, trn/B Hubbard, bari
May 30, June 1	CS#5	K. Akiyama	C. Parkening, guitar-May 30 Norbert Kraaft, guitar-June 2
May 31	F. Pops#3	P. McCoppin	Jarvis Benoit Quartet
June 5, 6, 8, 9	POP#6	K. Akiyama	M. Martin, soprano; B. Zarankin, piano Y. Guilbert, piano

[a] Rudolf Barshai is Music Director and Principal Conductor and Kazuyoshi Akiyama is Conductor Laureate of the VSO.
Source: VSO files.

EXHIBIT III-3

Audience Questionnaire

VANCOUVER SYMPHONY

Audience Questionnaire

Dear Patron,

We at the Vancouver Symphony Orchestra want very much to provide the best possible musical experience for our audiences and the Vancouver community as a whole. In our continuing efforts to improve our performances and make your concert-going as satisfying and enjoyable as possible, we ask that you take a little time to answer the following questions. Your opinions and suggestions are extremely important and will be most useful in helping us to evaluate our programs, as well as our manner of presentation.

When you leave tonight's concert, please be so kind as to place the completed questionnaire in one of the special boxes located near the exits and the VSO Gift Shop. If you do not have time to complete it this evening, we would request that you mail it to us at your convenience. On behalf of the members of the orchestra and the staff, thank you very much for your assistance.

Edward Philip Oscapella
Executive Director
Vancouver Symphony Orchestra

400 East Broadway, Vancouver, B. C., V5T 1X2—875-1661

1.[a] Are you a subscriber (i.e., purchase series tickets) to the VSO.

19%	1-1	___ Yes, currently
29	1-2	___ No, but formerly
51	1-3	___ Never subscribed

2. Have you ever purchased tickets to an individual VSO event?

22%	2-1	___ Yes, since September 1986
51	2-2	___ Yes, but only before September 1986
26	2-3	___ No

3. Since September 1986, how many times have you attended a VSO performance?

56%	3-1	___ I haven't attended a VSO performance since September 1986
18	3-2	___ Attended once
12	3-3	___ Attended 2–3 times
7	3-4	___ Attended 4–5 times
5	3-5	___ Attended more than 5 times

4. If you have ever attended previous VSO performances, we would like to know why. Please indicate the THREE most important reasons from the list below. (1 = Most Important, 2 = Second-Most Important, 3 = Third-Most Important). Write 1, 2, or 3 on the appropriate lines.

i.[b]	ii.	iii.	
42%[a]	19%	39%	(4-) ___ I wanted to see and hear classical music preformed live
2	16	81	(5-) ___ The VSO under Maestro Rudolf Barshai is an excellent orchestra
7	44	49	(6-) ___ I think the Orpheum is an excellent setting for great music
13	31	54	(7-) ___ The choice of music appealed to me
13	37	50	(8-) ___ I wanted to see famous guest artists and conductors

EXHIBIT III-3 (continued)

Please list any additional reasons below:

(9-) ___ _____
(10-) ___ _____
(11-) ___ _____

5. Overall, what is your rating of the VSO on the following characteristics? Put a checkmark on the appropriate lines.

	EXCELLENT (4)	GOOD (3)	FAIR (2)	POOR (1)	
___ Performance of Orchestra	65%[a]	33%	1%	0%	(12-)
___ Guest Artists	43	53	2	2	(13-)
___ Music Selection	22	59	10	8	(14-)
___ Acoustics in Orpheum	56	39	3	1	(15-)
___ Prices of Tickets	13	46	35	6	(16-)
___ Convenience of Parking	12	41	33	13	(17-)
___ General Atmosphere of Orpheum	63	34	2	1	(18-)
___ Service from VTC-CBO	26	57	13	4	(19-)

6. Please give us your opinion about the amount of each type of music played by the VSO.

	TOO MUCH (3)	ABOUT RIGHT (2)	TOO LITTLE (1)	
___ Classical (e.g., Bach, Mozart)	6%[a]	72%	22%	(20-)
___ 20th century century music (e.g., Debussy, Stravinsky)	14	71	14	(21-)
___ Pops (e.g., Mantovani, Williams)	20	62	18	(22-)
___ Canadian (e.g., Schaeffer)	24	60	16	(23-)

7. Below are presented eight pairs of events characterized by reputation of performer, seating arrangements and single ticket prices. Assuming everything else about each pair is identical, please check your preference in each case.

International Performers & $20 price	$\frac{44\%^a}{24\text{-}1}$ vs. $\frac{56\%}{24\text{-}2}$	New, Promising Performers & $8 price	Orchestra & $20 price	$\frac{26\%}{28\text{-}1}$ vs. $\frac{74\%}{28\text{-}2}$	Balcony & $8 price
Orchestra & $20 price	$\frac{30}{25\text{-}1}$ vs. $\frac{70}{25\text{-}2}$	Balcony & $14 price	International Performers & $20 price	$\frac{63}{29\text{-}1}$ vs. $\frac{37}{29\text{-}2}$	New, Promising Perfomers & $14 price
International Performers & $14 price	$\frac{77}{26\text{-}1}$ vs. $\frac{23}{26\text{-}2}$	New, Promising Performers & $8 price	Orchestra & $14 price	$\frac{46}{30\text{-}1}$ vs. $\frac{54}{30\text{-}2}$	Balcony & $8 price
International Performers & Balcony	$\frac{67}{27\text{-}1}$ vs. $\frac{33}{27\text{-}2}$	New, Promising Performers & Orchestra	International Performers & Orchestra	$\frac{59}{31\text{-}1}$ vs. $\frac{41}{31\text{-}2}$	International Performers & Balcony

EXHIBIT III-3 (continued)

8. What concert times do you prefer?

12%ª	32-1	___ Matinees (2:30 P.M.)
34	32-2	___ 7:30 P.M.
55	32-3	___ 8:00 P.M.
7	32-4	___ 8:30 P.M.

9. What day of the week do you prefer to attend concerts?

18%ª	33-1	___ Sunday
21	33-2	___ Monday
27	33-3	___ Tuesday
17	33-4	___ Wednesday
17	33-5	___ Thursday
25	33-6	___ Friday
32	33-7	___ Saturday

10. From where do you get most of your information about VSO events?

47%ª	34-1	___ From VSO mailings
46	34-2	___ From ads in daily newspapers (e.g., *Sun, Province*)
3	34-3	___ From ads in community newspapers
32	34-4	___ From radio ads
3	34-5	___ From television ads
10	34-6	___ From reviews and feature stories
	34-7	___ Other-please specify $\frac{\text{word-of-mouth 9\%}}{\text{nonword-of-mouth 3}}$

11. Which daily newspaper do you read most often?

71%ª	35-1	___ *Vancouver Sun*
24	35-2	___ *Province*
7	35-3	___ *Globe and Mail*
6	35-4	___ Other—*please specify* _____

12. Are you

39%ª	36-1	___ Male
61	36-2	___ Female

13. To which age group do you belong?

2%ª	37-1	___ Under 18
6	37-2	___ 18–24
16	37-3	___ 25–34
17	37-4	___ 35–44
21	37-5	___ 45–54
22	37-5	___ 55–64
19	37-7	___ 65 and over

14. Please specify your postal code V ___ ___ ___ ___ ___ See EXHIBIT
    38 39 40 41 42

15. If you prefer to purchase tickets to individual events (as opposed to subscription tickets) why is this so? Please indicate below.

    _____
    _____
    _____
    _____
    _____

EXHIBIT III-3 (continued)

16. All things considered, what would it take to get you to attend VSO performances on a regular basis?

_____

_____

_____

_____

_____

THANK YOU FOR YOUR COOPERATION IN COMPLETING THIS QUESTIONNAIRE, AND THANK YOU FOR YOUR PATRONAGE OF THE VANCOUVER SYMPHONY.

When you leave tonight's concert, please place the completed questionnaire in one of the special boxes located near the exits and the VSO Gift Shop. If you do not have time to complete it this evening, we would request that you mail it to us at your convenience.

Audience Survey
c/o Vancouver Symphony Society
400 East Broadway
Vancouver, B.C.
VST 1X2

[a] Percentages given in questionnaire are for all respondents.
[b] i = most important; ii = 2nd or 3rd most important; iii = not ranked in top 3.

frequencies for each question for the entire sample. Respondents had the choice of dropping off the instrument at various places in the Orpheum or mailing it in later. A total of 614 completed questionnaires from the 2400 people actually in attendance were returned. Since almost everyone attended in groups of two or more, this was considered a good response rate by management.

The data from the survey is in a file called VSO. Exhibit III-4 provides a sequential listing of the variables in the file and each variable corresponds to a specific question in the survey. For example, SUBSCRBR is the first variable and corresponds to Question 1 on the questionnaire. POSTCOD5 is the last variable and refers to the sixth digit of the respondent's postal code as asked by Question 14. RESPID refers to respondent identification and was inserted after receiv-

ing the research instruments. It is to be noted that no quantitative analysis can readily be performed on Questions 15 and 16.

Given all this information, Ed, Jane, and Doug sat down to analyze it and work on a report for the Board of Directors. They knew that any recommendation(s) they make must be supported by the data.

Questions for Discussions

1. What are the strengths and weaknesses of this market research project?
2. What information can you derive from the data? State _specifically_ the managerial questions you are hoping to resolve and how the data would help you. Make at least one specific recommendation based on the results of this research.

EXHIBIT III-4

Variable Listing

VARIABLE	REC	START	END	VARIABLE	REC	START	END
SUBSCRBR	1	1	1	MATINEE	1	32	32
INDPURCH	1	2	2	SVNTHRTY	1	33	33
ATTEND	1	3	3	EIGHT	1	34	34
LIVEMUS	1	4	4	EGHTHRTY	1	35	35
VSOGOOD	1	5	5	SUNDAY	1	36	36
ORPGOOD	1	6	6	MONDAY	1	37	37
CHOICE	1	7	7	TUESDAY	1	38	38
FAMOUS	1	8	8	WEDNESDAY	1	39	39
OTHER1	1	9	9	THURSDAY	1	40	40
OTHER2	1	10	10	FRIDAY	1	41	41
OTHER3	1	11	11	SATURDAY	1	42	42
ORCHSTRA	1	12	12	VSOMAIL	1	43	43
GUESTS	1	13	13	PAPERADS	1	44	44
SELETION	1	14	14	COMMPAPR	1	45	45
ACOUSTIC	1	15	15	RADIOADS	1	46	46
PRICES	1	16	16	TVADS	1	47	47
PARKING	1	17	17	STORIES	1	48	48
ATMSPERE	1	18	18	OTHRSRCE	1	49	49
SERVICE	1	19	19	VANCSUN	1	50	50
CLASICAL	1	20	20	PROVINCE	1	51	51
TWENTITH	1	21	21	GLBEMAIL	1	52	52
POPS	1	22	22	OTHRPAPR	1	53	53
CANADIAN	1	23	23	GENDER	1	54	54
PAIR1	1	24	24	AGEGROUP	1	55	55
PAIR2	1	25	25	POSTCOD1	1	56	56
PAIR3	1	26	26	POSTCOD2	1	57	57
PAIR4	1	27	27	POSTCOD3	1	58	58
PAIR5	1	28	28	POSTCOD4	1	59	59
PAIR6	1	29	29	POSTCOD5	1	60	60
PAIR7	1	30	30	RESPID	1	61	61
PAIR8	1	31	31				

CASE III-2
Pacific Gas & Electric (B)[3]

The research proposal described in the Pacific Gas & Electric (A) case (Case II-1) was implemented. The resulting data are available on floppy disk.[4] The coding information for the open-ended questions follows. First, develop a data analysis strategy. Second, conduct the analysis. Third, present your conclusions and insights. Fourth, what additional research, if any, would you conduct? It can be useful to combine responses. For example, "solar awareness" could be defined as "high" if at least one application was named and $1–$10 was given as the range of expected monthly savings, "low" if no applications were named and a different savings rate was specified, and "medium" otherwise.

City		Q4 Solar Uses		Q5b AD. Source	
Category	**Code**	**Category**	**Code**	**Category**	**Code**
Walnut Creek	0	Water	1	PG&E	1
Novato	1	Pool	2	Home or news magazine	2
Martin	2	House	3	TV	3
San Francisco	3	Cooling	4	Environmental magazine	4
San Mateo	4	Electric	5	Newspaper	5
Palo Alto	5	Plants	6	Display	6
San Jose	6	Windows	7	Company	7
Fremont	7	Not proven	8	Popular science magazine	8
Oakland	8	Everything	9	Several	9
Richmond	9	No response	0	No response	0

Q6b Displays		Q7b Solar Heating Unit		Q9b	
Category	**Code**	**Category**	**Code**	**Category**	**Code**
PG&E	1	Media	1	Unnamed company	1
Show	2	Local house	2	Undecided	2
Display house	3	Display house	3	Looked at cost	4
Store	4	Relative-friend	4	Water	5
Media	5	Out of area	5	Build himself	7
School	6			Pool	7
Friend	7			No response	0
Company	8				
No response	0				

---

[3] Written by Darrell R. Clarke and David A. Aaker as a basis for class discussion.

[4] The floppy disk is available from your professor.

Q10a Advantages		Q10b Disadvantages		Q11 Cost/Savings	
Category	**Code**	**Category**	**Code**	**Category**	**Code**
Cheaper	1	Weather	1	1–10	1
Conserve energy	2	Cost	2	11–20	2
Safer	4	Performance	3	21–30	3
Uses	5	Needs back-up	4	31–40	4
Utility independent	6	Unproved	5	41–50	5
Performance	7	Ugly or bulky	6	51–60	6
Wrong	8	Unneeded	7	61–70	7
Are none	9	Future uncertain	8	71–80	8
No responses	0	No response	0	81+	9
				No response	0

Q14c Why Utility		Q14d Why Not Utility		Q15a Desired Information[a]	
Category	**Code**	**Category**	**Code**	**Category**	**Code**
In the business	1	Charge too much	1	Cost	1
Reliable	2	Too big	2	Performance	2
Less bureaucracy	3	Dislike private	3	Appearance-size	3
Dislikes government	4	Shouldn't	4	Durability	4
Pay with bill	5	Keep utility out	5	Technical	5
Husband works for	6	Private better	6	Installation	6
No response	0	No response	0	General	7
				Authority	8
				Why need	9
				No response	0

[a] Note: Column 62, the last column in the data presentation, is the last response to Q15a.

CASE III-3
Ralston Development Company

As the researchers from Acton Associates left his office, Joe Ralston felt he had been given the means to win a battle but he still wasn't sure he could win the war. While a survey of Beaverdale residents, conducted by Acton, had clearly supported his concept of a regional shopping center over a competitive proposal, the results were less convincing as a demonstration of citizen support for a major shopping center development. He had to decide quickly whether to introduce the results into the planning commission hearing scheduled the following week. While the main item on the agenda was whether to provide for a regional shopping center in the Beaverdale general plan, a choice of location also would be made. For five months he had been working full time to influence these decisions in favor of his company.

Joe Ralston had an enviable record as a developer of large regional shopping centers across Canada. His record had never been quite so threatened as by the situation he now faced. The basic problem was the absence of opportunities for new centers, as a result of weak economic conditions, oversaturation of retail

EXHIBIT III-5

Description of Proposal R (Given Verbally to Respondents)

Questions 1 and 3. "Which newspapers were read regularly and at which shopping center was most of the shopping done?"

Question 4. "Have you heard of any plans to build a large shopping center with four or five large department stores, in the nearby area?"

	n	%
Yes	215	52.8
No	182	44.7
Don't know	10	2.5
Total	407	11%

Question 5. "How do you think most people in Beaverdale feel about the need for a shopping center, with four or five large department stores, in the nearby area?" (PROBE)

	n	%
Haven't discussed it/never came up	92	22.0%
Others favor it/welcome it	54	12.9
Want nice-looking buildings/quality	5	1.2
Want all in one area	2	0.5
Want for convenience/less driving/save gas	51	12.2
Like idea of more centers	26	6.2
Not needed/over-run with shopping centers	131	31.3
Mixed feelings	9	2.1
Traffic is problem/congestion	15	3.6
Oversaturation of stores	8	2.0
Want to save trees/green area	10	2.4
Nothing/just moved to area	10	2.4
No answer	6	1.4

Question 6. "Which of these best describes your opinion of the need for such a shopping center?" (*Hand Card to Respondent*) Answer to Q4:

	Have heard	Have not heard	Total
Very much needed	28 (13.0%)	15 (8.2%)	43
Somewhat needed	72 (33.5)	50 (27.5)	122
Not much needed	42 (19.5)	39 (21.4)	81
Not at all needed	72 (33.5)	69 (37.9)	141
No answer	1 (0.5)	9 (4.9)	10
	215 (100%)	182 (100%)	397

Question 7. HAND RESPONDENT DIAGRAM ☐ R OR ☐ S: *Read Carefully and Consistently the Matching Statement to Respondent. Ask Questions, Then Show Other.*
(The same questions were asked for both R and S. For example: for R only the respondent was asked: "What do you like about the one marked R?" and "What do you dislike about the one marked R?" Then the same questions were asked about S. The open-ended responses are not tabulated here.)

EXHIBIT III-5 (continued)

Question 8. Leave Both Diagrams in Front of Respondent. Hand Correct Preference Scale.

    8a. In choosing between ☐ R and S or ☐ S and R (order was random) which box says how you feel?

Question 6

	Shopping center needed	Center not needed	Total
Strongly prefer R	44 (26.3 %)	45 (19.7 %)	89 (22.5%)
Somewhat prefer R	36 (21.6)	74 (32.4)	110 (27.8)
No preference	22 (13.2)	66 (28.9)	88 (22.3)
Strongly prefer S	32 (19.2)	30 (13.2)	62 (15.7)
Somewhat prefer S	33 (19.8)	13 (5.7)	46 (11.6)
Total	167 (100%)	228 (100%)	395 (100%)
(Note R = Ralston Development Company proposal and S = Santini proposal)			

    8b. There are three alternatives. One of the two proposed shopping centers or no shopping center in either location: Which do you most prefer? Which do you least prefer?

		Q8b: Most prefer			
		R (Ralston)	S (Santini)	**Neither**	**Total**
Q8b: Least Prefer	R	—	88 (88.9%)	39 (30.0%)	127 (32.3%)
	S	145 (87.9%)	—	72 (55.4%)	217 (55.1%)
	Neither	20 (12.1%)	11 (11.1%)	19 (14.6%)	50 (12.7%)
	Total	165 (100%)	99 (100%)	130 (100%)	394 (100%)

		Q8b: Most prefer			
		R (Ralston)	S (Santini)	**Neither**	**Total**
Q6: Need for Shopping Center	Very much needed	21 (12.7%)	19 (19.2%)	3 (2.2%)	43 (10.8%)
	Somewhat needed	60 (36.1)	46 (46.5)	17 (12.6)	123 (30.5)
	Not much needed	38 (22.9)	15 (15.2)	28 (20.7)	81 (20.9)
	Not at all needed	43 (25.9)	16 (15.2)	85 (63.0)	144 (35.4)
	No opinion	4 (2.4)	3 (3.0)	2 (1.4)	9 (2.4)
	Total	166 (100%)	99 (100%)	135 (100%)	400 (100%)

selling space in most major markets, and an acute shortage of prime sites for development. Indeed, current business was so weak that Ralston Development would have to dismantle a substantial portion of the organization if a big center were not started within six months.

The only live prospect on the horizon was in Beaverdale, a prosperous suburban town of 40,000 residents that was part of a major metropolitan area. Five months earlier the Beaverdale Planning Commission had agreed to a staff feasibility study of a development proposal by Ralston Development. The effect of the proposal would be to expand a small local shopping center, with one existing department store, into a regional center with four department stores and numerous specialty shops, all connected by a covered mall. There would be enough selling space to attract shoppers from a radius of six to seven miles. A major advantage of the site was the proximity to the arterial freeway passing through the town. The attraction to the planning commission was the opportunity for substantial local employment, plus tax revenues of more than a million dollars a year.

Unfortunately for Joe Ralston, a local family holding undeveloped farmland near the freeway decided they had an equally good site for a regional shopping center. Their site was one mile from the site Ralston wanted to develop. Since the Santini family was highly visible in the local government, the planning commission was in no position to deny their request for equal consideration.

During a series of public meetings to discuss the competing proposals, a great deal of local opposition surfaced. Some opposition came from a loose coalition of environmental groups with previous success in thwarting large developments in the area. They were joined, somewhat uneasily, by a group of local residents anxious about the strain that the traffic from the shopping center would put on the congested local roads. Joe Ralston was sure these opposition groups were not representative of the community; however,

he had to concede that this was only intuition. In the meantime, the opposition was becoming more strident and much more active, with the evident encouragement of at least one and possibly two of the five planning commissioners. It was this situation that led him to decide that the best way to blunt the opposition was to conduct a survey of the residents in the portion of the town adjacent to the proposed developments.

While the principal research objective was to measure the support for a regional shopping center, Ralston also expected the results to show the superiority of his proposal over the Santini's. A further objective was to clarify the sources of opposition and support to help develop a campaign to mobilize support for his project.

Residential Survey

The consultants were well aware that the results of their study would be subject to hostile cross-examination by the opposition groups and the other developer. They also knew that Joe Ralston would have to use either the entire study or none of it.

During a series of focus-group interviews it became clear that many people were badly informed about the issues and consequently had very shaky opinions. Thus it was decided that respondents should be given complete descriptive information to ensure they had a proper basis for a choice. This meant a personal interview study of heads of households.[5] Respondents were to be given a map showing each proposed shopping center, and a lengthy written description would be read by the interviewer. Great care was taken in writing these descriptions to eliminate any bias that would favor one proposal over the other, or provide anything other than purely objective information. Descriptions were simply labeled R or S (corresponding to Ralston or Santini), to minimize the effect of the sponsor. The description for Proposal R is shown in Exhibit III-5. The order of presentation would be randomized to avoid bias. To ensure maximum response, three call-backs were to be used and a supervisor would attempt to convert refusals.

[5] The sample was drawn randomly from a list of utility customers in Beaverdale. Apartment dwellers paid their bills directly to the utility company.

PART IV

SPECIAL TOPICS IN DATA ANALYSIS

18

CORRELATION ANALYSIS AND REGRESSION ANALYSIS

Learning Objectives

▶ Understand the use of correlation as a measure of association.

▶ Distinguish between simple correlation and partial correlation.

▶ Discuss the objectives of regression analysis.

▶ Explain the procedure adopted to estimate the regression parameters.

▶ Interpret the meaning of the parameter estimates.

▶ Discuss the applications of regression analysis.

▶ Understand the concept and use of multiple regression.

Oftentimes in business research, the researcher is interested in determining whether there is any association (relationship) between two or more variables and, if so, the researcher would like to know the strength of the association and the nature of the relationship. In the previous chapter we discussed the chi-square goodness-of-fit test as a measure of association. We also discussed the limitations of the chi-square test as an association measure. In this chapter we will discuss the more commonly used measure of association—the **correlation coefficient. Correlation analysis** involves measuring the strength of the relationship between two variables. For example, the correlation coefficient provides a measure of the degree to which there is an association between two variables (X and Y).

Regression analysis is a statistical technique that is used to relate two or more variables. Here, a variable of interest, the **dependent** or **response** variable (Y) is related to one or more **independent** or **predictor** variables (X's). The objective in regression analysis is to build a regression model or a prediction equation relating the dependent variable to one or more independent variables. The model can then be used to *describe, predict,* and *control* the variable of interest on the basis of the independent variables. For example, when a new product or concept is being explored, one of the key variables of interest is usually the respondent's attitude or intentions toward it. Is it something that the respondent would consider buying and/or using? The goal may be to predict the ultimate usage of the product or concept under a variety of conditions. Another goal might be to understand what causes high intentions to purchase so that when the product does emerge, the marketing program can be adjusted to improve the success probability.

In this chapter we will discuss in detail the most simple form of regression analysis—the **bivariate** analysis. In the bivariate analysis, we will study how the variable of interest is related to *one* independent variable. Regression analysis that involves more than one independent variable is called **multiple regression** analysis.

CORRELATION ANALYSIS

The **Pearson correlation** coefficient measures the degree to which there is a linear association between two intervally scaled variables. A positive correlation will reflect a tendency for a high value in one variable to be associated with a high value in the second. A negative correlation reflects an association between a high value in one variable and a low value in the second variable. If the data base included an entire population, such as all adults in California, the measure would be termed the **population correlation** (ρ). If, however, it is based on a sample, it is termed as **sample correlation** (r).

If two variables are plotted on a two-dimensional graph, termed a **scatter diagram,** the sample correlation reflects the tendency for the points to cluster systematically about a straight line rising or falling from left to right. The sample correlation r always lies between -1 and $+1$. An r of $+1$ indicates a perfect positive linear association between the two variables, whereas if r is -1 there is perfect negative linear association. A zero correlation coefficient reflects the absence of any linear association.

Figure 18-1 illustrates five scatter diagrams. In Figure 18-1a, there is a rather strong tendency for a small Y to be associated with a large X. The sample correlation is -0.80. In Figure 18-1b, the pattern slopes from the lower left to the upper right, and thus the sample correlation would be $+0.80$. Figure 18-1c is an example of a sample correlation of $+1$. It is a straight line running from the lower left to the upper right. Figure 18-1d is an example in which there is no relationship between X and Y. Figure 18-1e shows a plot in which there is a clear relationship between the two variables, but it is not a linear or straight-line relationship. Thus, the sample correlation is zero.

Simple Correlation Coefficient

The concept of simple or bivariate correlation can be best understood by following the methodology for calculating it. First, the points are plotted in a scatter diagram. In the sample shown in Figure 18-2, the Y axis indicates the sales in thousands of dollars per day of stores in a retail chain, and the X axis indicates the distance in travel time to the nearest competing store. Six stores are located on the scatter diagram. A reasonable measure of association between the two variables would be the covariance between the two variables.

$$Cov(x,y) = \Sigma(X_i - \overline{X})*(Y_i - \overline{Y})$$

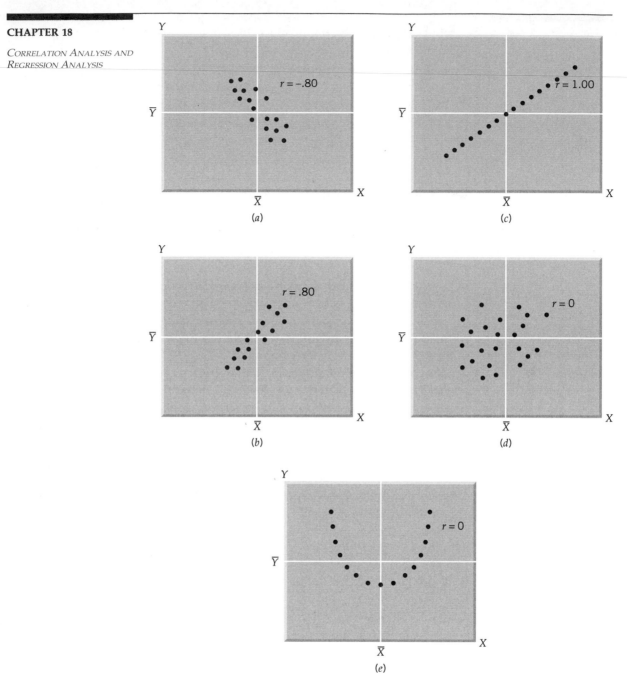

FIGURE 18-1
Scatter plots

Points in quadrants I and III would suggest a positive association, so large values of X would be associated with large values of Y. For store E, for example, the $(X_i - \overline{X}) * (Y_i - \overline{Y})$ term equals five times six, or 30. Table 18-1 provides a summary of this calculation.

If the data point had been higher (farther away from Y) or farther to the right (farther from X), then the value of the $(X_i - \overline{X}) * (Y_i - \overline{Y})$ term for store

FIGURE 18-2
Store sales vs. distance

TABLE 18-1
Determining the Sample Correlation Coefficient

	Daily Sales (thousands) Y_i	$Y_i - \overline{Y}$	Distance to Nearest Competing Store (min) X_i	$X_i - \overline{X}$	$(X_i - \overline{X})(Y_i - \overline{Y})$
Store A	3	−6	7	−4	24
Store B	8	−1	13	2	−2
Store C	17	8	13	2	16
Store D	4	−5	11	0	0
Store E	15	6	16	5	30
Store F	7	−2	6	−5	10
Total	54	0	66	0	$78 = \sum_i (X_i - \overline{X})(Y_i - \overline{Y})$
Average	$\overline{Y} = 9$		$\overline{X} = 11$		$15.6 = \dfrac{1}{n-1}\sum_i (X_i - \overline{X})(Y_i - \overline{Y})$

$$r_{YX} = \frac{1}{n-1}\frac{\sum (X_i - \overline{X})(Y_i - \overline{Y})}{s_X s_Y} = \frac{78}{5(3.85)(5.76)} = .70$$

$$s_X = 3.85 = \sqrt{\frac{1}{n-1}\sum_i (X_i - \overline{X})^2}$$

$$s_Y = 5.76 = \sqrt{\frac{1}{n-1}\sum_i (Y_i - \overline{Y})^2}$$

E would have been greater. On the other hand, a point near one of the dotted axes would contribute little to the association measure. Store D is located on the X line and, as shown in Table 18-1, contributes zero to the association measure. Similarly, points in quadrants II and IV suggest a negative association. Thus, store B, which is in quadrant II, has a negative contribution to the association measure. Table 18-1 shows this contribution to be −2.

The second step of the method for calculating the sample correlation is to divide the association expression by the sample size:

$$\frac{1}{(n-1)}*\Sigma(X_i - \overline{X})*(Y_i - \overline{Y})$$

To ensure that the measure does not increase simply by increasing the sample size (one of the limitations associated with the use of chi-square as an association measure), it is divided by the sample size. The association between retail store sales volume and distance to competitive stores should not get larger simply because the association measure is calculated using data from 20 stores instead of 10. Thus, we divide by the sample size (strictly speaking, by [n − 1]). Table 18-1 shows that this association measure would then be 15.6. This expression is termed as the sample **covariance.** Thus, the covariance between X and Y (denoted as COV_{XY}), measures the extent to which X and Y are related.

But the size of the covariance measure could be changed simply by changing the units of one of the variables. For example, if the sales were measured in dollars instead of thousands of dollars, then the association measure would be 15.6 million instead of 15.6. Such a dependence on the units of measure makes the measure difficult to interpret. The solution is to divide the measure by the sample standard deviations for X and Y.[1] The result is the sample correlation coefficient, which will not be affected by a change in the measurement units of one or both of the variables:

$$r_{XY} = \frac{1}{(n-1)}*\Sigma \frac{(X_i - \overline{X})}{s_X}*\frac{(Y_i - \overline{Y})}{s_Y}$$

$$r_{XY} = \frac{COV_{XY}}{s_X*s_Y}$$

This expression for the sample correlation coefficient (r) is termed the **Pearson product-moment correlation coefficient.** If the correlation coefficient is calculated for the entire population, it is denoted by ρ the population correlation coefficient. Like the case of the sample mean being an estimator of the population mean, the sample correlation coefficient "r" is an estimate of the population correlation coefficient "ρ."

The product-moment correlation coefficient has several important properties. First, as the methodology has demonstrated, it is independent of sample size and units of measurement. Second, it lies between −1 and +1. Thus, the interpretation is intuitively reasonable. Further, when regression analysis is discussed later in this chapter, a rather useful interpretation of the square of the sample correlation (r^2) will be presented that will provide additional insights into its interpretation.

Here, it should be stressed that, even though the correlation coefficient (r) provides a measure of association between two variables, *it does not imply any causal relationship* between the variables. A correlation analysis or, for that matter, even a regression analysis can measure only the nature and degree of association (or covariation) between variables; they cannot imply causation. Statements of causality must spring from underlying knowledge and theories about the phenomena under investigation and not from mathematical measures of association.[2] Further, the sample correlation coefficient can be seriously affected by outliers or extreme observations.[3]

The correlation coefficient provides a measure of the relationship between two questions or variables. The underlying assumption is that the *variables are intervally scaled,* such as age or income. At issue is to what extent a variable must satisfy that criterion. Does a seven-point agree-disagree scale qualify? The answer depends in part on the researcher's judgment about the scale. Is the difference between -2 and -1 the same as the difference between $+2$ and $+3$? If so, it qualifies. If not, a correlation analysis may still be useful, but the results should be tempered with the knowledge that one or both of the scales may not be intervally scaled.

Testing the Significance of the Correlation Coefficient

As discussed earlier, the calculation of the correlation coefficient r assumes that the variables whose relationship is being tested, are metric. If this assumption is not met either partially or completely, it affects the value of r. A simple test of hypothesis can be performed to check the significance of the relationship between two variables, measured by r. This involves testing

The null hypothesis $\quad\quad H_0: \rho = 0$ against
The alternative hypothesis $\quad H_a: \rho \neq 0$

Consider the example presented in Table 18-1. Here, the relationship between the sales per day of stores in a retail chain and the distance in travel time to the nearest competing store is determined using the sample correlation coefficient r, and is calculated to be 0.70. To test the significance of this relationship, the test statistic "t" can be computed using

$$t = r\sqrt{(n-2)/(1-r^2)}$$

In our example, $n = 6$ and $r = 0.70$. Hence,

$$t = 0.70\sqrt{(6-2)/(1-0.70^2)} = 1.96$$

If the test is done at $\alpha = 0.05$ with $n - 2 = 4$ degrees of freedom, then the critical value of t can be obtained from the tables to be 2.78. Since, $1.96 < 2.78$, we fail to reject the null hypothesis.

What does this mean? The statistical test of significance reveals that the value of the sample correlation r (found to be 0.70) is not significantly different from zero. In other words, the strength of the relationship between store sales and the distance from competing stores at best can be attributed to a chance occurrence. If the same value of r (0.70) had been obtained from a larger sample (say $n = 50$), then one could possibly conclude that there is a systematic association between the variables.

As an exercise, retest the hypothesis that $\rho = 0$, assuming that the value of $r = 0.70$ was obtained from a sample size of 50. Do you still fail to reject the null hypothesis? Why not?

Partial Correlation Coefficient

The Pearson correlation coefficient provides a measure of linear association between two variables. But when there are more than two variables involved in the relationship, the partial correlation analysis is used. The **partial correlation coefficient** provides a measure of association between two variables after controlling for the effects of one or more additional variables. For example, the relationship between the advertising expenditures and sales of a brand is influenced by several other variables. For sake of simplicity, let us assume the relationship to be affected by a third variable, the use of coupons. If the brand manager is interested in measuring the relationship between the dollar amount spent on advertisements (X) and the associated sales of the brand (Y), he or she has to control for the effect of coupons (Z). The partial correlation coefficient can thus be expressed as

$$r_{XY.Z} = \frac{r_{XY} - r_{XZ} * r_{YZ}}{\sqrt{(1 - r_{XZ}^2)} * \sqrt{1 - r_{YZ}^2}}$$

Although the correlation analysis provides a measure of the strength of the association between two variables, it tells us little or nothing about the nature of the relationship. Hence, the *regression analysis is used to understand the nature of the relationship between two or more variables.*

REGRESSION ANALYSIS[4]

As mentioned earlier, **regression analysis** is a statistical technique that is used to relate two or more variables. Here, a variable of interest, the **dependent** or **response variable** (Y) is related to one or more **independent** or **predictor** variables $(X's)$. The objective in regression analysis is to build a regression model or a prediction equation relating the dependent variable to one or more independent variables. The model can then be used to *describe, predict,* and *control* the variable of interest on the basis of the independent variables.

For example, consider the HMO study. In this study, the intention to enroll was one of the variables of interest. One motivation was prediction: to predict the enrollment if the plan were to be implemented. Thus, the intention question was analyzed to help predict the acceptance of the concept among the sample of respondents. However, it would be desirable to determine how the intentions to enroll were related to the distance to the HMO. If such a relationship were known, it might be possible to predict intentions for neighborhood areas just by knowing the distance to the HMO. Similarly, if the relationship between enrollment intentions and the health plan now used were known, some knowledge would be available about the possible intentions of others just by knowing their health plan. Furthermore, if the relationship between the coverage of the HMO (what services are included) and people's intentions were known, the prediction could be adjusted, depending upon the coverage actually used when the plan was implemented.

Prediction is not the only reason that a knowledge of the relationship between intentions and other variables is useful in the HMO study. Another motivation is to gain an understanding of the relationship so that the marketing program can be adjusted. If the relationship between intentions and the distance to the HMO is known, then a decision as to where to focus the marketing program geographically can be made more intelligently. It would make little sense to expend marketing effort on groups with little potential. Further, the relationship of intentions to the health plan of participants might provide information as to what competitive health plans are most vulnerable, and could help guide the development of the marketing program. The relationship between intentions and an HMO characteristic, such as coverage, could influence the exact type of plan introduced. A "product feature" such as coverage should be specified, so that the costs of the feature can be balanced with its impact on enrollment.

Regression analysis provides a tool that can quantify such relationships. Further, unlike cross-tabs and other association measures, which deal only with two variables, regression analysis can integrate the relationship of intentions with two, three, or more variables simultaneously. Regression analysis not only quantifies individual relationships but it also provides statistical control. Thus, it can quantify the relationship between intentions and distance while statistically controlling for the health plan and coverage variables.

Simple Linear Regression Model

The construction of a simple linear regression model usually starts with the specification of the dependent variable and the independent variable. Suppose that our organization, Midwest Stereo, has 200 retail stores that sell hi-fi and related equipment. Our goal is to determine the impact of advertising on store traffic; that is, the number of people who come into the store as a result of the advertising. More specifically, we are concerned with the number of people entering the store on a Saturday as a result of advertising placed the day before. The following regression model might then be hypothesized:

$$Y_i = \beta_0 + \beta_1 X_i + \varepsilon_i$$

where

Y = the number of people entering the store on Saturday (dependent variable)

X = the amount of money the store spent on advertising on Friday (independent variable)

β_0 = a model parameter (it represents the mean value of the dependent variable [Y] when the value of the independent variable X is zero). It is also called the Y-intercept.

β_1 = a model parameter, it represents the slope that measures the change in the value of the independent variable associated with a one-unit increase in the value of the independent variable.

ε_i = is an error term that describes the effects on Y_i of all factors other than the value of X_i

Several aspects of the model are worth emphasizing. First, the hypothesized relationship is linear; it represents a straight line, as shown in Figure 18-3. Such an assumption is not as restrictive as it might first appear. Even if the actual relationship is curved, as illustrated by the dotted arc in Figure 18-3, the relationship still may be close to linear in the range of advertising expenditures of interest. Thus, a linear relationship still may be very adequate.[5]

The error term is central to the model. In reality, store traffic is affected by variables other than advertising expenditures; it also is affected by store size and location, the weather, the nature of what is advertised, whether the advertising is in newspapers or on radio, and other factors. Thus, even if advertising expenditures are known, and our hypothesized linear relationship between advertising expenditures and store traffic is correct, it will be impossi-

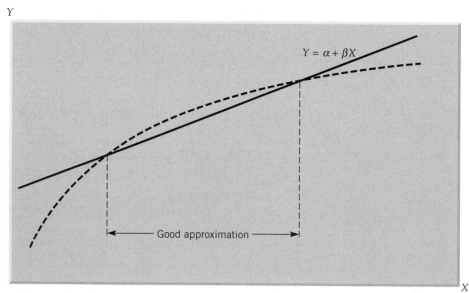

FIGURE 18-3
The linear approximation

ble to predict store traffic exactly. There still will be a margin of error. The error term explicitly reflects the error. Several assumptions surrounding the error term are made when estimating the parameters of the model and during significance testing. These are called the **assumptions of the regression model.**

Assumptions of the Regression Model. There are five major assumptions associated with the simple linear regression model.[6] These are

▶ The error term is normally distributed (i.e., for each value of X, the distribution of Y is normal).

▶ The mean or average value of the error term is zero ($E\{\varepsilon_i\} = 0$).

▶ The variance of the error term is a constant and is independent of the values of X.

▶ The error terms are independent of each other (the observations are drawn independently).

▶ The values of the independent variable X are fixed (for example, by an experimenter).

▶ Figure 18-4 provides an illustration of the model.

Estimating the Model Parameters. The parameters, β_0 and β_1, that characterize the relationship between X and Y are of prime interest. One of the goals of the regression analysis is to determine what they are. Although we do not know the true values of the parameters β_0 and β_1, we can calculate point estimate b_0 and b_1 of β_0 and β_1. The procedure is used to obtain a random sample of stores and to use the information from it to estimate β_0 and β_1. For example, assume that a random sample of 20 stores was selected. For each store in the sample, the number of people entering the store on a given Saturday was determined.

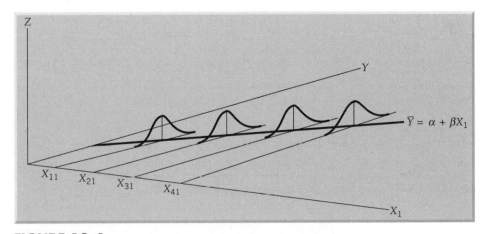

FIGURE 18-4
Simple linear regression model-A graphical illustration

Further, for each store the amount spent on advertising for the previous day was recorded. Table 18-2 presents the data for the 20 stores in our sample. The results are plotted in Figure 18-5.

The next step is to obtain a line that has the best "fit" to these points. Of course, a line could be drawn freehand; in practice, however, a computer program is used. The computer program generates a line that has the property that the squared vertical deviations from the line are minimized. Such a line is termed a **least-squares** line and is denoted by the following expression:

$$\hat{Y}_i = b_0 + b_1 X_i$$

The values of the least squares estimates b_0 and b_1 are calculated using the formulas

$$b_1 = \frac{n\Sigma x_i y_i - (\Sigma x_i)(\Sigma y_i)}{n\Sigma x_i^2 - (\Sigma x_i)^2}$$

TABLE 18-2
Advertising vs. Store Traffic Data

No. of Stores	Store Traffic Y_i	Advertising Dollar X_i	$X_i * Y_i$	X_i^2
1	90	40	3,600	1,600
2	125	75	9,375	5,625
3	320	100	32,000	10,000
4	200	110	22,000	12,100
5	600	190	114,000	36,100
6	450	200	90,000	40,000
7	400	300	120,000	90,000
8	700	310	217,000	96,100
9	800	380	304,000	144,400
10	810	410	332,100	168,100
11	1,000	480	480,000	230,400
12	1,170	500	585,000	250,000
13	1,200	520	624,000	270,400
14	1,500	550	825,000	302,500
15	1,000	560	560,000	313,600
16	900	580	522,000	336,400
17	700	690	483,000	476,100
18	1,000	700	700,000	490,000
19	1,300	710	923,000	504,100
20	1,350	800	1,080,000	640,000
Mean	780.75	410.25		
Sum	15,615	8,205	8,026,075	4,417,525

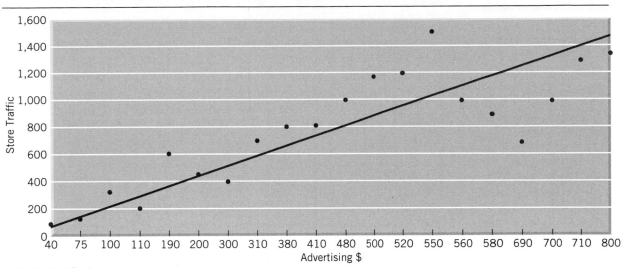

FIGURE 18-5
Advertising vs. store traffic

and

$$b_0 = \bar{y} - b_1\bar{x}$$

where

$$\bar{y} = \frac{\Sigma y_i}{n}; \bar{x} = \frac{\Sigma x_i}{n}$$

In this case, from Table 18-2, we can calculate b_0 and b_1 to be 148.64 and 1.54, respectively. In the case of the simple linear regression model involving one dependent and one independent variable, the parameter estimates and other model values easily can be hand-calculated. But, as the number of independent variables increases, the model becomes large, and hand computation is no longer feasible. In such situations, statistical packages such as SAS and SPSS normally are used. Subsequent sections and chapters, dealing with multiple regression analysis and other advanced multivariate techniques, provide the relevant SAS outputs along with the interpretations.

The value b_0 (148.64) is an estimate of the parameter β_0 and the value b_1 (1.54) is an estimate of the parameter β_1. These estimates are termed **regression coefficients** and are based on the random sample. The term $\hat{Y}$ (read as "Y hat") indicates the points on the line, and is an estimate of store traffic based on the regression model. For example, when X is 600, then $\hat{Y} = 148.64 + 1.54*600 = 1073$ (approx). Thus, if advertising expenditures of 600 were planned, our estimated store traffic would be 1073. In contrast, Y is the actual sales level. For example, for one store the advertising expenditure (X) was 500, the store traffic (Y) was 1170, and the store traffic estimate ($\hat{Y}$) was calculated to be 919. The difference between the actual and predicted values is called the **residual** and is an estimate of the error in the population.

If another random sample of 20 stores were to be obtained, undoubtedly it would contain different stores. As a result, the plot of X and Y would differ from Figure 18-5 and the regression coefficients, b_0 and b_1, would be different. Every random sample would have associated with it a different b_0 and b_1. In general, if any particular values of b_0 and b_1 are good point estimates of β_0 and β_1, they will, for $i = 1, 2 \ldots n$, make $\hat{Y}_i$ fairly close to Y_i. Therefore, the ith residual

$$e_i = y_i - \hat{y}_i$$
$$= y_i - (b_0 + b_1 x_i) \text{ will be fairly small}$$

The regression coefficients can be estimated using a number statistical techniques. Each of the techniques is based on some criterion to get the best measure of the population coefficients from the sample. One of the most commonly used techniques to estimate these coefficients is based on the **least squares criterion.** According to this criterion, the regression coefficients are calculated so as to minimize the residual sum of squares. In a mathematical form, this can be represented as

Minimize

$$SSE = \Sigma \, e_i^2 = (\Sigma \, (y_i - \hat{y}_i)^2$$
$$= \Sigma \, [y_i - (b_0 + b_1 x_i)]^2$$

Thus, the point estimates b_0 and b_1, *minimize the residual or error sum of squares (SSE).* Hence, these estimates are called the **least square estimates.**

Standard Error of Estimate. An examination of Figure 18-5 reveals that, although the least squares regression line provides a reasonable fit of the data points, there are some deviations in the sample data about the line. An estimate of the population variation about the regression line provides a reasonable measure of goodness-of-fit of the model (called the **mean square error MSE**), and can be calculated using the formula

$$s_{Y/X}^2 = \frac{SSE}{n - 2} = \frac{\Sigma e_i^2}{n - 2} = \frac{\Sigma (Y_i - \hat{Y}_i)^2}{n - 2}$$

The square root of the mean square error given by $s_{Y/X}$ (or more commonly denoted simply as "s") is called the **standard error of estimate.** In our example, the standard error can be calculated to be 218.40.

The standard error of estimate (s) is interpreted to mean that, for any given value of the independent variable X_i, the dependent variable tends to be distributed about the predicted value $\hat{Y}_i$, with a standard deviation equal to the standard error of the estimate. Hence, the smaller the standard error of estimate, the better the fit. Further, the standard error of estimate is the same for any given value of the independent variable. In other words, as the value of the independent variable X_i changes, the predicted value of $\hat{Y}_i$ will also change, but the standard deviation of the distribution of Y_i about $\hat{Y}_i$ remains a constant.

Interpretation of the Parameter Estimates. The parameter estimates have a very precise meaning. The parameter β_1 indicates that if the variable X is changed by one unit, the variable Y will change by β_1 units. Thus, if \$1 is added to the advertising budget, regardless of the level at which the budget is set, an extra β_1 customers will be expected to visit the store. Similarly, the parameter β_0 reflects the number of customers expected, on average, if no advertising is run the previous day. When understanding the phenomenon of interest is the motivation behind the data analysis, the prime interest is in b_1, the estimate of the β_1 parameter. The size of b_1 will be a reflection of the influence of advertising on store traffic.

Earlier we mentioned that the parameter estimates b_0 and b_1 vary from sample to sample. A measure of this variation of the parameter estimates is given by their standard errors. Thus, just as the sample mean, $\overline{X}$, has a standard error, which is estimated by s_x, b_0, and b_1 also each has a standard error associated with it. If the constant variance and independence assumptions of the simple linear regression model hold good, the standard error of b_1 can be shown to be

$$s_{b_1} = \frac{s}{\Sigma(x_i - \overline{x})^2} = \frac{1}{n-2} * \frac{\Sigma(Y_i - \hat{Y}_i)^2}{\Sigma(x_i - \overline{x})^2}$$

Similarly, the standard error of b_0 can be shown to be

$$s_{b_0} = s\sqrt{\frac{1}{n} + \frac{\overline{x}^2}{\Sigma(x_i - \overline{x})^2}}$$

In this example, the standard error of b_0 and b_1 can be calculated to be 100.10 and 0.21, respectively.

Testing the Significance of the Independent Variables. If β_1 were zero, there would be no effect of advertising on store traffic, and hence the model specified does not serve any purpose. Before using the model, it is useful to consider the hypothesis that β_1 is zero. If the evidence that β_1 is zero (namely, a non-zero estimate b_1) is impressive, we may want to discard the model.

As indicated previously, the estimate b_1 has a variation associated with it (measured by s_{b_1}) because it is based on a sample of stores. Thus, it could happen that b_1 is non-zero even if the parameter β_1 is zero. In fact, it would be highly likely that, even if there were no relationship between advertising (X) and store traffic (Y), any given random sample would produce a non-zero value for b_1. One way to evaluate the magnitude of b_1, taking into account its variation, is to use a statistical hypothesis test. The null hypothesis is that there is no linear relationship between the dependent and the independent variables. The hypothesis test can be formally represented as

Null hypothesis $H_0: \beta_1 = 0$
Alternate hypothesis $H_a: \beta_1 \neq 0$

The test statistic is given by

$$t = \frac{b_1 - \beta_1}{s_{b_1}} = \frac{1.54 - 0}{0.21} = 7.33$$

The calculated test statistic has a t-distribution. Hence, if we fix α as 0.05, the table value of t corresponding to $v = n - 2 = 18$ degrees of freedom is 2.10. Applying the rejection rule for a two-tailed test of hypothesis, we reject the null hypothesis that there is no linear relationship between the dependent and independent variables (since $t_{calc} > t_{table}$). Therefore, one can conclude that advertising expenditure affects store traffic.

In this example, the test of hypothesis resulted in the rejection of the null hypothesis. If it had resulted otherwise—that is, if the hypothesis test had failed to reject the null—it does not immediately indicate that the independent variable is not significant. It is perfectly possible that the dependent and independent variables are in fact related, *albeit* in a nonlinear manner. Also, before any hasty decision is made regarding the significance of the independent variable, the researcher needs to ascertain that a Type II error is not being committed.

Testing $H_0: \beta_1 = 0$ vs $H_1: \beta_1 \neq 0$ Using Prob-Values. The rejection rule is then: *Reject $H_0: \beta_1 = 0$ if $\alpha > p$ value.* In our case, the p-value (computed by SAS) was found to be 0.0001, resulting in the rejection of the null hypothesis. Hence, smaller the p-value, the stronger is the evidence to reject H_0.

Predicting the Dependent. The regression model can also be used as a predictive tool. Given an advertising expenditure, the model will predict how much store traffic will be generated. For example, if an advertising expenditure level of \$200 is proposed, a model-based estimated store traffic would be

$$\hat{Y} = b_0 + b_1 X_{01} = 148.64 + (1.54*200) = 457$$

Two cautionary comments: *First,* prediction using extreme values of the independent variable (such as $X = 2000$ in our example) can be risky. Recall Figure 18-3, which illustrated that the linearity assumption may be appropriate for only a limited range of the independent variables. Further, the random sample provided no information about extreme values of advertising. *Second,* if the market environment changes, such as if a competitive chain opens a series of stores, the model parameters probably will be affected. The data from the random sample were obtained under a set of environmental conditions; if they change, the model may well be affected.

How Good Is the Prediction? A natural question is, How well does the model predict? Assume that we have n observed values of the dependent variable, but we do not have the n observed values of the independent variable x with which to predict Y_i. In such a case the only reasonable prediction of Y_i would be

$$\overline{Y} = \frac{\Sigma Y_i}{n}$$

The error of prediction would then be $Y_i - \overline{Y}$.

While adopting the simple linear regression model, we predict Y_i using the formula $\hat{Y}_i = b_0 + b_i x_i$. The error of prediction here is $Y_i - \hat{Y}_i$.

Therefore, by using the independent variable, the error of prediction has decreased by an amount equal to

$$(Y_i - \overline{Y}) - (Y_i - \hat{Y}_i) = (\hat{Y}_i - \overline{Y})$$

It can be shown that, in general

$$\Sigma(Y_i - \overline{Y})^2 \quad \Sigma(Y_i - \hat{Y}_i)^2 = \Sigma(\hat{Y}_i - \overline{Y})^2$$

Or, by rearranging it can be shown that the

$$\Sigma(Y_i - \overline{Y})^2 = \Sigma(\hat{Y}_i - \overline{Y})^2 + \Sigma(Y_i - \hat{Y}_i)^2$$

Total Variation = Explained Variation + Unexplained Variation

where

Total Variation (SST)	is the sum of squared prediction error that would be obtained if we do not use X to predict Y.
Unexplained Variation (SSE)	is the sum of squared prediction error that is obtained when we use X to predict Y.
Explained Variation (SSM)	is the reduction in the sum of squared prediction errors that has been accomplished by using X in predicting Y. That is, the explained variation measures the amount of the total variation that can be explained by the simple linear regression model.

The measure of the regression model's ability to predict is termed the **coefficient of determination** (r^2) and is the ratio of the explained variation to the total variation,

$$r^2 = (SST - SSE)/(SST)$$
$$= (SSM)/(SST)$$

For our example, r^2 is equal to 0.74. Thus, 74 percent of the total variation of Y is explained or accounted for by X. The variation in Y was reduced by 74 percent by using X and applying the regression model.

The r^2 term is the square of the correlation between X and Y. Thus, it lies between zero and one. It is zero if there is no linear relationship between X and Y. It will be one if a plot of X and Y points generates a perfect straight line. Another way to interpret r, the sample correlation, is to interpret r^2 instead. A reduction or increase in r^2 can be interpreted as the percentage of reduction or increase in the explained variation.

So far, we have discussed the concepts and issues related to the simple linear regression model. As the number of independent variables increases, the regression analysis used is termed **multiple regression.**

Multiple Regression

Recall from the earlier discussion that the error term included the effects on the dependent variable of variables other than the independent variable. It may be desirable to include explicitly some of these variables in the model. As predictions, their inclusion will improve the model's ability to predict and will decrease the unexplained variation; in terms of understanding, they will introduce the impact of other variables and therefore elaborate and clarify the relationships. When more than one independent variable is included in a single linear regression model, we get a multiple regression model.

The general form of the multiple regression model can be expressed as

$$Y = \alpha + \beta_1 X_1 + \beta_2 X_2 + \ldots + \beta_k X_k + \varepsilon$$

where $\beta_1, \beta_2, \ldots, \beta_k$ are regression coefficients associated with the independent variables $X_1, X_2, \ldots, X_k$ and ε is the error or residual. The assumptions discussed in relation to simple linear regression apply equally to the case of multiple regression, except that instead of the one X used in the former, more than one X is used in the latter. As was the case in simple linear regression, a solution is sought for the constants (α and the β's) such that the sum of the squared errors of prediction ($\Sigma \varepsilon^2$) is minimized, or that the prediction is optimized. It is worth noting that the equations cannot be solved if (1) the sample size, n, is smaller than or equal to the number of independent variables, k; or (2) one independent variable is correlated perfectly with another.

The prediction equation in multiple regression analysis is

$$\hat{Y} = a + b_1 X_1 + b_2 X_2 + \ldots + b_k X_k$$

where $\hat{Y}$ is the predicted Y score, and $b_1, \ldots, b_k$ are the partial regression coefficients.

To understand the meaning of a partial regression coefficient, let us consider a case in which there are two independent variables, so that

$$Y = a + b_1 X_1 + b_2 X_2 + \text{error}$$

First, note that the relative magnitude of the partial regression coefficient of an independent variable is, in general, different from that of its bivariate regression coefficient. In other words, the partial regression coefficient, b_1, will be different from the regression coefficient, b_1, obtained by regressing Y on only X_1. This happens because X_1 and X_2 usually are correlated. In bivariate regression, X_2 was not considered, and any variation in Y which was shared by X_1 and X_2 was attributed to X_1. However, in the case of multiple independent variables, this is no longer true.

The interpretation of the partial regression coefficient, b_1, is that it represents the expected change in Y when X_1 is changed by one unit keeping X_2 constant or controlling for its effects. Similarly, b_2 represents the expected change in Y for a unit change in X_2, when X_1 is held constant. Therefore, b_1 and b_2 are called partial regression coefficients. It can also be seen that the combined effects of X_1 and X_2 on Y are additive. In other words, if X_1 and X_2 are each changed by one unit, the expected change in Y would be $(b_1 + b_2)$. Similar interpretation holds good for the case of k variables.

The regression coefficients would be unique to the random sample that happened to be selected. If another random sample were taken, the regression coefficients would be slightly different. This sampling variation in the regression coefficients is measured by the standard error (discussed in the previous chapter) associated with each of them. The procedure installed in most software packages calculates this standard error and provides it as one of the outputs.

Consider the following example where a researcher did a survey of the CEOs of some small businesses to explore the firm's interest in exporting to foreign markets. The description of the variables and the associated scale values are presented in Table 18-3. Two hundred small businesses received the questionnaire, and 98 were returned. Eight instruments could not be used because

TABLE 18-3
Description of Variables

Variable Description		Corresponding Name In the Computer Output	Scale Values
Willingness to export	(Y_1)	Will	1 (definitely not interested) to 5 (definitely interested)
Level of interest in seeking government assistance	(Y_2)	Govt	1 (definitely not interested) to 5 (definitely interested)
Employee size	(X_1)	Size	Greater than zero
Firm revenue	(X_2)	Rev	In millions of dollars
Years of operation in the domestic market	(X_3)	Years	Actual number of years
Number of products currently produced by the firm	(X_4)	Prod	Actual number
Training of employees	(X_5)	Train	0 (no formal program) or 1 (existence of a formal program)
Management experience in international operation	(X_6)	Exp	0 (no experience) or 1 (presence of experience)

of random responding and incomplete information. Out of the 90 usable questionnaires (45 percent response rate), data for 60 firms were used for model estimation and the remaining 30 observations were held for model validation (discussed later in this chapter). The information obtained from the survey instrument is given in Table 18-4.

The estimated regression equation is

$$\hat{Will} = 1.927 + 0.026 \text{ Size (Model 1)}$$
$$\text{where } \hat{will} = \text{predicted value for will}$$

Table 18-5 shows the results of this simple linear regression model (model 1).

The regression coefficient for size is 0.026 and is significant at the 10 percent level ($\alpha = .10$). The amount of variance in "will" explained by size is about 5.8 percent ($R^2 = 0.058$). R^2 cannot decrease as more independent variables are added to the regression equation. Yet, diminishing returns set in, so that after the first few variables, the additional independent variables do not make much of a contribution. For this reason, R^2 is adjusted for the number of independent variables and the sample size. The adjusted R^2 (adjusted for the degrees of freedom) is 0.041 in this example and is computed from the following formula:

$$R^2(\text{adjusted}) = 1 - (1 - R^2)\frac{n - 1}{n - k - 1}$$

where

$\quad n$ = number of observations
$\quad k$ = number of parameters

Since the variation explained is low, the researcher might consider adding a few more independent variables to explain additional variation in the dependent variable. It might be that the researcher considers adding variables X_2, X_3, and X_4 to the original regression equation. The resulting model (model 2) is
$Y = b_0 + b_1X_1 + b_2X_2 + b_3X_3 + b_4X_4 + \text{error}$

Parameter Interpretation in Multiple Regression

When the parameters of model 2 are estimated using OLS, the result is

$$\text{Will} = -2.153 + 0.032 \text{ size} + 0.344 \text{ Rev} + 0.483 \text{ years} + 0.042 \text{ Prod}$$

Table 18-6 shows the results of model 2.

A major assumption of multiple regression is that the model includes all the important and relevant variables. If an important variable is omitted, the model's predictive power is reduced. Further, if the omitted variable is correlated with an included variable, the estimated coefficient of the included variable will reflect both the included variable and the omitted variable.[7] In our example, the coefficient of size in the simple linear regression model (model 1) was about 0.03, and in the multiple regression model (model 2) it still remained around 0.03. This indicates that the additional variables (Rev, Years, and Prod) did not have large correlations with size and that the size coefficient remains unaffected to a large extent. From the results of model 2, one can interpret that the score on a firm's willingness to export would go up by 0.03 units for every one unit increase in the firm's size, keeping other variables (X_2, X_3, and X_4) at a constant/fixed value. Similar interpretations hold true for other variables.

Tests of Significance and Their Interpretations

There are several tests of significance that one may apply to the results of multiple regression analysis. Three of them are presented here: (1) test of R^2, (2) tests of regression coefficients, and (3) tests of increments in the proportion of variance accounted for by a given variable or a set of variables.

Test of R^2. Significance testing involves testing the significance of the overall regression equation as well as specific partial regression coefficients. The null hypothesis for the overall test is that the coefficient of multiple determination in the population, R^2_{pop}, is zero.

$$H_0: R^2_{pop} = 0$$

This is equivalent to the following null hypothesis:

$$H_0: \beta_1 = \beta_2 = \beta_3 = \ldots = \beta_k = 0$$

The overall test can be conducted by using an F statistic:

$$F = \frac{R^2/k}{(1 - R^2)(N - k - 1)}$$

with k and $N - k - 1$ df, where k = number of independent variables, and N = sample size. For the data of Table 18-6, $R^2 = 0.329$, $N = 60$.

$$F = \frac{.329/4}{(1 - .329)/(60 - 4 - 1)} = \frac{.0823}{.012} = 6.75$$

with 4 and 55 df, $p < .01$. The results clearly indicate that H_0 is rejected, meaning the independent variables do have a systematic association with the dependent variable in the model.

If the independent variables are statistically independent (uncorrelated), then R^2 will be the sum of bivariate r^2 of each independent variable with the dependent variable.

Tests of Regression Coefficients. If the overall null hypothesis is rejected, one or more population partial regression coefficients have a value different from 0. To determine which specific coefficients (β_i's) are nonzero, additional tests

TABLE 18-4
Export Data Set

Company	Willingness to Export (Y₁)	Level of Interest in Seeking Government Assistance (Y₂)	Employee Size (X₁)	Firm Revenue (million) (X₂)	Years of Operation in the Domestic Market (X₃)	Number of Products (X₄)	Training of Employees (X₅)	Management Experience in International Operations (X₆)
1	5	4	54	4.0	6.5	7	1	1
2	3	4	45	2.0	6.0	6	1	1
3	2	5	44	2.0	5.8	11	1	1
4	4	3	46	1.0	7.0	3	1	0
5	5	4	46	3.0	6.5	8	1	1
6	1	2	37	0.9	5.0	2	0	1
7	2	1	42	0.9	5.0	2	0	1
8	3	3	29	3.6	6.5	3	0	0
9	3	2	46	0.9	6.0	5	0	1
10	2	3	28	0.9	6.0	2	0	1
11	4	1	39	3.6	7.0	3	0	1
12	3	2	31	4.0	7.0	3	1	0
13	4	5	65	1.0	7.0	9	1	1
14	1	4	50	1.0	7.0	9	1	1
15	4	1	30	2.0	7.5	3	1	0
16	5	4	58	1.0	6.0	5	1	1
17	3	4	54	2.0	6.5	4	1	1
18	4	5	58	1.0	7.0	9	1	1
19	2	1	37	1.0	7.0	9	1	1
20	5	5	35	2.0	9.5	5	1	0
21	4	3	49	2.0	8.5	4	1	0
22	3	2	37	2.0	7.0	2	0	1
23	3	4	34	0.9	6.0	5	0	1
24	2	5	66	1.0	5.5	10	1	1
25	5	4	50	0.3	6.5	6	1	1

26	4	3	43	1.0	7.0	3	1	0
27	4	3	54	1.0	7.0	4	1	1
28	3	4	49	1.0	6.5	7	0	1
29	3	2	43	1.8	6.0	2	0	1
30	2	4	52	1.8	5.0	7	0	1
31	4	5	29	0.9	4.5	11	0	1
32	2	3	37	0.9	5.5	2	0	0
33	3	1	27	0.9	7.0	3	0	0
34	3	2	32	0.9	6.5	3	0	1
35	2	2	34	2.7	6.5	2	0	0
36	3	4	48	1.8	5.0	4	0	1
37	3	5	53	0.9	4.5	5	0	0
38	4	3	41	0.9	5.5	2	0	1
39	5	4	47	2.7	5.5	4	0	0
40	1	2	31	1.8	6.0	4	0	0
41	3	2	34	0.9	6.5	3	0	0
42	1	1	28	0.9	7.0	2	0	1
43	2	3	39	0.9	5.5	2	0	0
44	1	4	45	0.9	5.5	4	0	0
45	2	2	29	1.8	7.0	2	0	1
46	2	3	37	1.8	6.0	3	0	1
47	2	5	49	0.9	4.5	9	0	0
48	2	1	33	0.9	6.5	2	0	1
49	3	1	27	1.8	7.0	3	0	1
50	2	4	49	1.0	5.5	6	0	0
51	4	3	46	1.0	6.5	4	0	1
52	4	5	54	1.0	6.0	7	1	1
53	2	2	31	0.9	6.0	3	1	0
54	3	2	31	3.0	6.0	5	1	1
55	3	4	50	2.0	6.5	7	0	1
56	2	5	69	1.0	5.5	9	1	0
57	5	1	34	1.0	7.0	6	1	1
58	4	5	62	2.0	5.5	7	1	1
59	3	4	49	1.0	7.0	5	1	0
60	4	3	43	2.0	7.5	4	1	1

TABLE 18-5
Results of Model 1

Model: MODEL1
Dependent Variable: WILL

Analysis of Variance

Source	df	Sum of Squares		Mean Square	F Value	Prob > F
Model	1	4.601		4.601	3.595	0.0629
Error	58	74.248		1.280		
C Total	59	78.850				
	Root MSE		1.131	R-square	0.058	
	Dep Mean		3.050	Adj R-sq	0.041	
	C.V.		37.096			

Parameter Estimates

Variable	df	Parameter Estimate	Standard Error	T for H0: Paramter = 0	Prob > |T|	Standardized Estimate
INTERCEPT	1	1.927	0.609	3.161	0.002	0.000
SIZE	1	0.026	0.013	1.896	0.062	0.241

are necessary. Testing for the significance of the β_i's can be done in a manner similar to that in the bivariate case, by using t-tests. The significance of the partial regression coefficient for size may be tested by the following equation:

$$t = \frac{b}{S_b}$$

$$= 0.032/0.014$$

$$= 2.215$$

which has a t distribution with $n - k - 1$ degrees of freedom. If the significance level (α) is 0.05, then this t-value is significant. All the regression coefficients are significant at the 5 percent level, with the exception of Prod.

Tests of Increments in the Proportion of Variance Accounted for by Additional Variables. One of the typical questions that a manager asks is whether adding three more variables helped to explain more variation in the dependent variable. This can be learned by assessing the difference in R^2 between the larger (more variables) model and the smaller (less variable) model. In this example, the difference in R^2 amounts to 0.271 (0.329 − 0.058), and suppose the question is, *Is this a significant difference at the 1 percent level?* One can use an F-statistic to evaluate the statistical significance of this difference.

$$F = \frac{R^2_l - R^2_s}{1 - R^2_l} * \frac{d_l}{d_s - d_l}$$

TABLE 18-6
Results of Model 2

Model: MODEL2
Dependent Variable: WILL

Analysis of Variance

Source	df	Sum of Squares		Mean Square	F Value	Prob > F
Model	4	25.976		6.494	6.755	0.0002
Error	55	52.873		0.961		
C Total	59	78.850				
		Root MSE	0.980	R-square	0.329	
		Dep Mean	3.050	Adj R-sq	0.280	
		C.V.	32.146			

Parameter Estimates

Variable	df	Parameter Estimate	Standard Error	T for H0: Parameter = 0	Prob > |T|	Standardized Estimate
INTERCEPT	1	−2.153	1.131	−1.903	0.062	0.000
SIZE	1	0.032	0.014	2.215	0.030	0.298
REV	1	0.344	0.140	2.442	0.017	0.279
YEARS	1	0.483	0.146	3.294	0.001	0.385
PROD	1	0.042	0.060	0.690	0.492	0.092

Where R^2_l and R^2_s are the total variance explained by the larger and smaller models and d_l and d_s are the degrees of freedom in the larger and smaller models, respectively,

$$F = \frac{(0.329 - 0.058)}{(1 - 0.329)} * \frac{55}{(58 - 55)}$$
$$= 7.4$$

The table value for F at 1 percent level of significance for 3 and 55 degrees of freedom is about 2.19. The computed F-value of 7.4 exceeds the table F value of 2.19 (corresponding to $\alpha = 0.01$), and therefore the difference in R^2 is statistically significant at the 1 percent level. In other words, the larger model significantly explains more variation in the dependent variable than the smaller model.

Evaluating the Importance of Independent Variables. When regression analysis is used to gain understanding of the relationships between variables, a natural question is: *Which of the independent variables has the greatest influence on the dependent variable?* One approach is to consider the *t*-values for the various coefficients. The *t*-value, already introduced in the single-variable regression case, is used to test the hypothesis that a regression coefficient (i.e., β_1) is equal to zero and a nonzero estimate (i.e., b_1) was simply a sampling phenomenon.[8] The one with the largest t-value can be interpreted to be the one that is the least likely to have a zero β parameter.

A second approach is to examine the size of the regression coefficients; however, when each independent variable is in a different unit of measurement (store size, advertising expenditures, and so on), it is difficult to compare their coefficients. One solution is to convert regression coefficients to "beta coefficients." Beta coefficients are simply the regression coefficients multiplied by the ratio of the standard deviations of the corresponding independent variable to the dependent variable.

$$\text{Standardized } \beta_i = b_i \left(\frac{\text{standard deviation of } X_i}{\text{standard deviation of } Y} \right)$$

The beta coefficients can be compared to each other: The larger the beta coefficient, the stronger the impact of that variable on the dependent variable. The beta coefficients are the partial regression coefficients obtained when all the variables (Y, X_1, X_2, . . . X_k) have been standardized to a mean of 0 and a variance of 1 before estimating the regression equation. In Table 18-6, an analysis of the beta coefficients indicates that years (0.385) and firm size (0.298) have the most explanatory power, the same conclusion that the analysis of t-values showed. Comparing the unstandardized b directly does not achieve this result because of the different units and degrees of variability of the X variables. The regression equation itself should be reported for future use in terms of the unstandardized coefficients, so that prediction can be made directly from the raw X values.

The manager is quite excited about the ability to explain more variation in model 2 with the addition of some variables. In the interest of explaining some more variation, the manager adds the two remaining variables (X_5 and X_6) to the equation and then estimates the model (model 3). Table 18-7 shows the results of the OLS estimation of the model with all the six predictor variables.

An important thing to note in the latest results (model 3) is that the coefficient values of some predictor variables in model 2 have changed in model 3, and so have their level of significance. This change of value can occur due to **multicollinearity,** which represents the correlations among the predictor variables. The problem of multicollinearity cannot be viewed as dichotomous (no or yes), but should be viewed as the degree of multicollinearity (in a continuous form). Since the two new variables Train and Exp are highly correlated with Size and Years (in the range of 0.4 to 0.5, obtained through computing correlation coefficients), the variation to be explained in the dependent variable probably is shared by all the correlated variables, resulting in changed coefficients, inflated standard errors, and lack of statistical significance for some of the variables in the model.

One simple way to check for multicollinearity is to examine the correlations among the X variables. If, for example, X_1 and X_2 are highly correlated (say greater than 0.95), then it may be simpler to use only one of them, inasmuch as one variable conveys essentially all of the information the other contains.

TABLE 18-7
Results of Model 3

Model: MODEL3
Dependent Variable: WILL

Analysis of Variance

Source	df	Sum of Squares		Mean Square	F Value	Prob > F
Model	6	27.652		4.608	4.771	0.0006
Error	53	51.197		0.966		
C Total	59	78.850				

	Root MSE		0.982	R-square	0.350	
	Dep Mean		3.050	Adj R-sq	0.277	
	C.V.		32.224			

Parameter Estimates

Variable	df	Parameter Estimate	Standard Error	T for H0: Parameter = 0	Prob > |T|	Standardized Estimate
INTERCEPT	1	−1.824	1.578	−1.156	0.252	0.000
SIZE	1	0.019	0.018	1.062	0.293	0.181
REV	1	0.344	0.155	2.220	0.030	0.257
YEARS	1	0.474	0.193	2.450	0.017	0.377
PROD	1	0.027	0.067	0.400	0.690	0.059
TRAIN	1	0.216	0.417	0.518	0.606	0.094
EXP	1	0.409	0.328	1.248	0.217	0.166

In the current example, the coefficient for Size changed from 0.032 to 0.019 and, further, the significance level changed from 0.03 to 0.29 when variables X_5 and X_6 were added. If one comes to the conclusion that size is not an important predictor, one is wrong. Therefore, it is always necessary to check for multicollinearity in multiple regression analysis. The R^2 for this full model is 0.35, which is larger than the model with four predictors ($R^2 = 0.329$); however, the adjusted R^2 for the full model (0.277) is less than that for the four-predictor model (0.28). This implies that the addition of the two remaining variables did not add much to explaining the variation in "willingness to export."

One can also use **stepwise regression** to select, from a large number of predictor variables, a small subset of variables that account for most of the variation in the dependent or criterion variable. Here, the predictor variables enter or are removed from the regression equation one at a time. There are several approaches to stepwise regression:

Forward addition. To start with, there are no predictor variables in the regression equation. Predictor variables are entered one at a time, only if they meet certain criteria specified in terms of F ratio. The order in which the variables are included in the model depends on the contribution to the explained variation.

Backward elimination. At the beginning, all the predictor variables are included in the regression equation. Predictors are then removed one at a time based on the *F* ratio for removal.

Stepwise method. The forward addition is combined with the removal of predictors that no longer meet the specified criterion at each step.

Interactions

Another issue in model fitting is to determine whether the *X* variables interact. If the effects of two variables X_1 and X_2 are *not* interactive, then they appear as $b_1x_1 + b_2x_2$ in the regression equation. In this case the effects of the *two* variables are said to be *additive*. On the contrary, if the effect of X_2 on *Y* depends on the level of X_1, then interaction of X_1 and X_2 is said to be present. This phenomenon can be observed in many situations. For example, the influence of shelf displays on product sales could depend on the price-reduction level. A commonly used practice is to add the product X_1X_2 to the set of *X* variables to represent the interaction between X_1 and X_2. The model is

$$y = b_0 + b_1x_1 + b_2x_2 + b_3x_1x_2 + \text{error}$$

Analyzing Residuals

While high R^2 and significant partial regression coefficients are comforting, the efficacy of the regression model should be evaluated further by an examination of the residuals.

A **residual** is the difference between the observed value of Y_i and the value predicted ($\hat{Y}_i$) by the regression equation. Residuals are used in the calculation of several statistics associated with regression. In addition, scattergrams of the residuals, in which the residuals are plotted against the predicted values, $\hat{Y}_i$, time, or predictor variables, provide useful insights in examining the appropriateness of the underlying assumptions and the regression model fitted. Figure 18-6 provides illustrations of four plots (a through d) of residual analysis.

Figure 18-6*a* shows that the residuals are distributed randomly when plotted against the predicted value of *Y*, indicating no major violation of the assumption of constant variance. However, in Figure 18-6*b*, the residuals show an increasing pattern, with increasing values of $\hat{Y}$ indicating a nonconstant error variance. This problem is referred to as **heteroskedasticity.** A weighted least-squares procedure can be used to correct for this problem when estimating the parameters of the regression model. Figure 18-6*c* shows a nonlinear pattern of residuals, with $\hat{Y}_i$ indicating that possibly some nonlinear terms (basically nonlinear in variables such a X_1^2) should be included in the model. Finally, in Figure 18-6*d*, the plot of residuals with time shows a trend indicating the violation of independence of error/residual terms. This problem is referred to as **autocorrelation** and can be corrected for by using procedures such as the Cochran-Orcutt procedure.

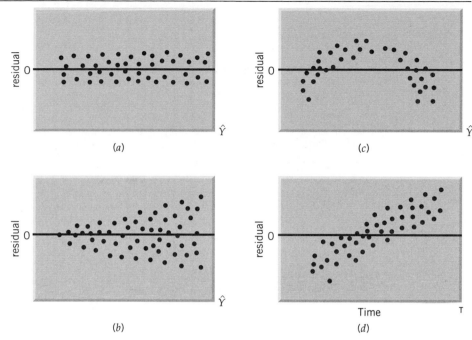

FIGURE 18-6
Residual plots

Predictive Validity

All multivariate procedures tend to capitalize on chance variations in the data. This could result in a model that is unduly sensitive to the specific data used to estimate the model. **Predictive validity** examines whether any model that is estimated with one set of data continues to hold on comparable data that are not used in the estimation. The predictive validity can be assessed in many ways. The three most commonly used methods are

1. The data are split into the **estimation sample** and the **validation sample.** The estimation sample contains more than half of the total sample, and the coefficients from both the samples are compared.
2. The coefficients from the estimated model are applied to the data in the validation sample to predict the values of the dependent variable Y_i in the validation sample, and then the model fit is assessed.
3. The sample is split into halves. One-half serves as the estimation sample, and the other is used as a validation sample in conducting cross-validation. The roles of the estimation and validation halves are then reversed, and the cross-validation is repeated.

Regression with Dummy Variables[9]

Nominal or categorical variables may be used as predictors if they are coded as dummy variables. The concept of **dummy variables** was introduced in Chapter 15. In that chapter, we explained how a categorical variable with four categories can be coded in terms of three dummy variables, D_1, D_2, and D_3, as shown.

Dummy Variable Coding

Consumer Types	Original Variable Code	D_1	D_2	D_3
Brand loyalty	1	1	0	0
Variety seeker	2	0	1	0
Impulse buyer	3	0	0	1
Rational buyer	4	0	0	0

Assume that the researcher is interested in running a regression analysis of the effect of consumer types on coupon redemption. The dummy variables D_1, D_2, and D_3 can be used as predictors. A *regression with dummy variables* would then be

$$Y_i = a + b_1 D_1 + b_2 D_2 + b_3 D_3 + \text{error}$$

Here the "rational buyer" has been chosen as the base level and has not been directly included in the regression equation. However, for the rational buyer group, D_1, D_2, and D_3 assume a value of 0, and the regression equation becomes

$$\hat{Y}_i = a$$

For brand-loyal consumers, $D_1 = 1$, and $D_2 = D_3 = 0$, and the regression equation becomes

$$\hat{Y}_i = a + b_1$$

Thus, the coefficient b_1 is the difference in predicted Y_i for brand-loyal, as compared to rational buyers. The coefficients b_2 and b_3 have similar interpretations. The concept of dummy variable regression analysis is widespread in the use of another multivariate technique, conjoint analysis (see Chapter 21).

Summary

In this chapter we discussed two of the more commonly used data analysis techniques in business research, **correlation analysis** and **regression analysis.**

Correlation analysis involves measuring the strength of the relationship between two or more variables. **Regression analysis** is used (a) to predict the dependent variable, given knowledge of independent variable, and (b) to gain an understanding of the relationship between the dependent variable and independent variables.

Applications. Regression analysis is used (1) to predict the **dependent variable,** given knowledge of independent variable values, and (2) to gain an understanding of the relationship between the **dependent variable** and **independent variables.**

Inputs. The model inputs required are the variable values for the dependent variable and the independent variables.

Outputs. The regression model will output **regression coefficients**—and their associated beta coefficient and *t*-values—that can be used to evaluate the strength of the relationship between the respective **independent variable** and the **dependent variable.** The model automatically controls statistically for the other independent variables. Thus, *a regression coefficient represents the effect of one independent variable when the other independent variables are held constant.* Another output is the R^2 value, which provides a measure of the predictive ability of the model.

Statistical Tests. The hypothesis that the regression parameter is zero and the parameter estimate is nonzero only because of sampling is based on the t-value.

Assumptions. The most important assumption is that the selected independent variables do, in fact, explain or predict the dependent variable, and that there are no important variables omitted. In creating and evaluating regression models the following questions are appropriate: *Do these independent variables influence the dependent variable? Do any lack logical justification for being in the model? Are any variables omitted that logically should be in the model?* A second assumption is that the relationship between the independent variables and the dependent variable is linear and additive. A third assumption is that there is a "random" error term that absorbs the effects of measurement error and the influences of variables not included in the regression equation.

Limitations. *First,* a knowledge of a **regression coefficient** and its *t*-value can suggest the extent of association or influence that an independent variable has on the dependent variable. However, if an omitted variable is correlated with the independent variable, the regression coefficient will reflect the impact of the omitted variables on the dependent variables. A *second* limitation is that the model is based on collected data that represent certain environmental conditions. If those conditions change, the model may no longer reflect the current situations and can lead to erroneous judgments. *Third,* the ability of the model to predict, as reflected by R^2, can become significantly reduced if the prediction is based on values of the independent variables that are extreme in comparison to the independent variable values used to estimate the model parameters. *Fourth,* the model is limited by the methodology associated with the data collection, including the sample size and measures used.

Questions and Problems

1. A random sample of eight introductory marketing texts yielded the figures shown in the table for annual sales (in thousands) and price (in dollars):

SALES	12.2	18.6	29.2	15.7	25.4	35.2	14.7	11.1
PRICE	29.2	30.5	29.7	31.3	30.8	29.9	27.8	27.0

    a. Determine the sample correlation between sales and price.

    b. Test at the 5 percent level that the population correlation coefficient is zero.

2. A college administers a student evaluation questionnaire for all its courses. For a random sample of 12 courses, the accompanying table shows both the instructor's average student ratings (on a scale from 1 to 5), and the average grades that the students expected (on a scale from A = 4 to E = 0).

INSTRUCTOR RATING	2.8	3.7	4.4	3.6	4.7	3.5
EXPECTED GRADE	2.6	2.9	3.3	3.2	3.1	2.8
INSTRUCTOR RATING	4.1	3.2	4.9	4.2	3.8	3.3
EXPECTED GRADE	2.7	2.4	3.5	3.0	3.4	2.5

    a. Find the sample correlation between the instructor ratings and expected grades.

    b. At the 10 percent significance level, test the hypothesis that the population correlation coefficient is zero against the alternative that it is positive.

3. Some regression models are used to predict, some to gain understanding, and some to do both. Consider a product manager for Betty Crocker cake mix: Give an example of each of the three types of models in the context of this product manager.

4. If an estimated regression model $\hat{Y} = a + bX$ yielded an r^2 of .64, we could say (choose one):

    a. 64 percent of the variation in the dependent variable was explained by the independent variable.

    b. The sample correlation between Y and X was 0.80.

    c. 64 percent of the data points lie on the regression line.

    d. a and b only.

    e. None of the above.

5. A company sets different prices for a pool table in eight different regions of the country. The accompanying table shows the numbers of units sold and the corresponding prices (in hundred of dollars).

SALES	420	380	350	400	440	380	450	420
PRICE	5.5	6.0	6.5	6.0	5.0	6.5	4.5	5.0

    a. Plot these data, and estimate the linear regression of sales on price.

    b. What effect would you expect a $150 increase in price to have on sales?

6. An attempt was made to evaluate the forward rate as a predictor of the spot rate in the Spanish treasury bill market. For a sample of 79 quarterly observations, the estimated linear regression,

$$\hat{y} = .00027 + .7916x$$

was obtained, where

$\hat{y}$ = Actual change in the spot rate

x = Change in the spot rate predicted by the forward rate

The coefficient of determination was .1, and the estimated standard deviation of the estimator of the slope of the population regression line was .27.

a. Interpret the slope of the estimated regression line.

b. Interpret the coefficient of determination.

c. Test the null hypothesis that the slope of the population regression line is 0 against the alternative that the true slope is positive, and interpret your result.

d. Test the null hypothesis that the slope of the population regression line is 1, and interpret your result.

7. An analyst for an oil company has developed a formal linear regression model to predict the sales of 50 of their filling stations. The estimated model is

$$\hat{Y} = b_0 + b_1 X_1$$

where

$\hat{Y}$ = average monthly sales in gallons

X = square foot area of station property

$X_1 = X - \overline{X}$ (difference from the mean)

Some empirical results were

Variable	Mean	Range of Data	Reg. Coefficient	t-value	r^2
Y		5,000 – 80,000 gal	$b_0 = 10,000$		
X	10,000	3,000 – 20,000 sq ft	$b_1 = 3.1$	2	.3

a. What does r^2 mean?

b. Interpret the parameter estimates b_0 and b_1.

c. Is the X_1 variable significant? At what level?

d. A new station is proposed with 30,000 sq ft. What would you predict sales to be? What assumptions underlie the estimate?

8. Consider the problem of predicting sales for each store in a chain of 220 bookstores. The model will have two functions. First, it will be used to generate norms that will be used to evaluate store managers. Second, it will be used to evaluate new site locations. What independent variables would you include in the model? How would you measure them?

9. The following table represents two other regression analyses completed in the HMO study. The dependent value of the first is the respondent's overall evaluation of the proposed HMO. The independent variables were the response to the question: "How satisfactory does this plan appear to you with respect to the following factors?" The scale was 1 to 5. The second analysis was the same, except the focus was on the respondent's present

plan instead of the HMO. Provide an interpretation of the results. What does a beta coefficient of 0.18 for the first variable mean? Interpret the table footnote. What do the two regressions show? What are the management implications?

Independent Variables	Proposed HMO Beta Coefficient	Respondent's Present Plan Beta Coefficient
Ability to choose doctor	.18[a]	.02
Coverage provided	.21[a]	.45[a]
Distance to doctor or hospital	.12[a]	.01
Participation	.13[a]	.08[a]
Efficiency in operations	−.03	.15[a]
Quality of care	.28[a]	.17[a]
Personal attention	.04	.09[a]
r^2	.38	.47
Dependent variable	Overall evaluation of proposed HMO	Overall evaluation of respondent's present plan

[a] Significant at the .01 level.

10. Refer to Question No. 7. If two additional variables are now added to the model in that question, then

$$\hat{Y} = b_0 + b_1 X_1 + b_2 X_2 + b_3 X_3$$

where

$X_2 =$ average daily traffic flow—cars
$X_3 =$ number of competing filling stations

The empirical results now are

Variable	Variable Mean	Variable Range	Regression Coefficient	t-value
Y	10,000			
X	10,000	3,000–20,000	$b_1 =$ 4.0	1.3
X_2	6,000	2,500–12,500	$b_2 =$ 4.0	1.0
X_3	12	0–25	$b_3 = -1000$	1.0
$r^2 = .45$			$b_0 = 10,000$	

a. Which independent variable seems now to be the most significant predictor?
b. Are X_1, X_2, and X_3 significant at the 0.05 level?
c. How might you explain why b_1 is now larger?
d. Interpret b_2.
e. Provide a prediction of sales given the following inputs:

$$X_1 = 5000$$
$$X_2 = 2000$$
$$X_3 = 0$$

How might you qualify that prediction? What model assumptions may be violated?

    f. A skeptic in upper management claims that your model is lousy and cites as evidence a station in Crosby, North Dakota, where

$$X_1 = 5000$$
$$X_2 = 2000$$
$$X_3 = 0$$

Yet, sales are 50,000, which is far more than predicted by the model. How would you answer this attack?

11. The following regression model was estimated to explain the annual sales from a direct marketing campaign:

$$S_t = 55 + 1.5P_t + 6.0M_t + 0.25C_i; \quad R^2 = 0.92$$
$$\quad\quad\quad (2.1) \quad (0.5) \quad (0.55)$$

where

S_t = \$ sales in year t
P_t = \$ promotional expenditure in year t
M_t = \$ product mailing expenditures in year t
C_t = Number of pamphlets distributed in year t

The estimated standard errors are given (in parentheses) corresponding to the coefficient estimates. The marketing director suggests that we should increase our mailing expenditures next year by sending more shipments first class, rather than via parcel post, since the mailing expenditure coefficient is "significant" in the regression. What would you advise?

End Notes

1. Recollect that the sample standard deviation is obtained using the formula:

$$s_x = \sqrt{\frac{\Sigma(X_i - \overline{X})^2}{(n - 1)}}$$

2. See Gilbert A. Churchill, Jr. *Marketing Research: Methodological Foundations*, 5th edition (Orlando, Florida, The Dryden Press), 1991, 824–825.

3. A measure of correlation that is not susceptible to serious influence by extreme values and on which valid tests can be based for very general popula-

tion distributions is obtained through the use of ranks. The ranks of x_i and y_i are used to compute Spearman rank correlation (r_s) given by

$$r_s = 1 - \left[\frac{6\Sigma d^2}{n(n^2 - 1)} \right]$$

where
$\quad\quad d$ = difference in ranks, and
$\quad\quad n$ = sample size

4. For a more detailed and comprehensive discussion on regression, see Bruce L. Bowerman and

Richard T. O'Connell. *Linear Statistical Models: An Applied Approach* (Boston, Mass., PWS-KENT Publishing Company) 1990; or David G. Kleinbaum, Lawrence L. Kupper, and Keith E. Muller. *Applied Regression Analysis and Other Multivariable Methods* (PWS-KENT Publishing Company), 1988; or any other advanced applied statistical textbook.

5. Further, a simple transformation of the independent variable can change some types of nonlinear relationships into linear ones. For example, instead of advertising, we might replace the advertising term with the logarithm of advertising. The result would be a model such as

$$Y_i = \beta_0 + \beta_1 \log X_i + \varepsilon_i$$

6. Violation of these assumptions can cause serious problems in applying and interpreting the regression model. For a more detailed discussion of the regression assumptions and remedies for violations of model assumptions, see Kmenta. *Elements of Econometrics*, 2nd edition (New York: MacMillan Publishing Company), 1986.

7. Recall the assumption that the error term is not correlated with the independent variables. If the error term includes an omitted variable that is correlated with an independent variable, this assumption will not hold.

8. Three qualifications. First, like any hypothesis test, the t-test is sensitive to the sample size. A small but nonzero regression parameter (i.e., β_1) can generate a low "p-level" if the sample size is large enough (and therefore s_b is small enough). Second, if the independent variables are intercorrelated (multicollinearity exists) the model will have a difficult time ascertaining which independent variable is influencing the dependent variable, and small t-values will emerge (the s_b terms will get large). Thus, small t-values an be caused by intercorrelated independent variables. Third, in addition to testing each independent variable using the t-test, it is possible to test (using an F-test) the hypothesis that all regression parameters are simultaneously zero. If such a hypothesis is not "passed," the entire model might be dismissed.

9. Adapted from Naresh K. Malhotra. *Marketing Research* (Englewood Cliffs, New Jersey: Prentice Hall), 1993; and Kumar V., A. Gorh, and G. Tellii. "A Decomposition of Repeat Buying," *Marketing Letters*, 1992, 3(4), 407–417.

CASE 18-1
The Seafood Grotto[1]

A study involving 158 families, selected randomly from a large New England city, was designed to help The Seafood Grotto, operators of several fine seafood restaurants, to determine who their customers were. Four segmentation variables were explored: age, income, social class, and life cycle. Social class was determined using Warner's Index of Status Characteristics, which uses the variables of occupation, income source, house type, and dwelling area. Life cycle was based on four categories: under 40 without children, under 40 with children, 40 and over with children in the household, and 40 and over without children in the household.

Each segmentation variable was correlated with frequency-of-use descriptions of various entertainment activities, ranging from about once a year to more than once a week, and with a variable that simply noted whether the selected entertainment activities were used during the past year. Using Table 1, answer the following questions:

Questions for Discussion

1. Can you say which segmentation variable is the most relevant for expensive restaurants?
2. Looking at the data across activities, which variables are the most relevant?
3. Explain the statistical test that is reported.

---

[1] Prepared by Robert D. Hisrich, Michael P. Peters, and David A. Aaker as a basis for class discussion.

TABLE 1

Correlation Coefficients for the Use/Nonuse and Frequency of Use of an Entertainment Activity

Entertainment Activity	Use/Nonuse				Frequency of Use			
	Income	Social Class	Age	Life Cycle	Income	Social Class	Age	Life Cycle
Bowl	−.08	−.15[b]	.28[a]	.38[a]	.12	−.04	.35[b]	.25[b]
Movies	.25[b]	.01	.38[a]	.46[a]	−.14	.35[a]	−.44[b]	−.49[a]
Ski	.18[b]	−.02	.27[a]	.36[a]	−.05	−.25[b]	−.08	−.07
Golf	.43[a]	.06	−.08	.04	.06	.32[b]	.15	.15
In-state travel	−.20[a]	−.02	.26[a]	.25[a]	.09	.06	.14	.05
Out-of-state travel	−.24[a]	.10	−.07	.06	.13	−.05	−.03	−.07
Foreign travel	.14	.09	−.01	.01	—[c]	—[c]	—[c]	—[c]
Dine at expensive restaurant	.27[a]	.02	.08	.17[b]	.12	.23[a]	.13	.17[b]
Dine at moderately priced restaurant	−.22[a]	−.03	.17[b]	.20[a]	.19[b]	−.12	.17[b]	.08
Dine at inexpensive restaurant	−.14	−.16[b]	.25[b]	.31[a]	.10	−.25[a]	−.07	−.07
Nightclubs	.12	.08	.32[a]	.41[a]	.28[a]	.11	−.42[a]	−.34[a]
Cocktail parties	−.23[a]	.03	.03	.16[b]	.15	−.02	.05	.01
Professional athletic events	−.32[a]	.01	.21	.33[a]	−.13	.07	−.09	−.12
College/high school athletic events	−.25[a]	−.06	.11	.17[b]	.35[a]	.23[b]	−.12	−.22[b]

[a] Significant at .01 level or better.
[b] Significant at .05 level or better.
[c] Foreign travel was excluded from this part of the analysis because it rarely occurs more than once a year.

CASE 18-2
Ajax Advertising Agency

As a model builder in the marketing services group of a large advertising agency, you are pondering your latest assignment. The task is to develop a model that will predict the success of new, frequently purchased consumer products. Many clients rely heavily on new products and need to be able to predict the likelihood of success before undertaking expensive test markets. They also need guidance in developing products and marketing programs that will be successful in the test market and, ultimately, in national distribution.

Preliminary discussions with a set of client representatives and other agency people already have provided some tentative conclusions:

1. It has been decided that to support the model developing and testing process, a panel of 1200 households would be established in a city often used as a test market. Thus, as new products were introduced into this city, the panel could be used to monitor their performance. Over a period of three years it was expected that 50 or 60 products could be observed.
2. It was suggested that product success depends on obtaining consumer knowledge of the product,

enticing people to try the product, and then achieving respectable levels of repurchase. Thus, it was concluded that a useful model would be one that was capable of predicting and explaining the following three variables: (a) product knowledge, (b) trial, and (c) repeat purchase.

Operationally, these variables would be measured by taking a consumer survey covering 250 homemakers randomly selected from the 1200-member panel. These homemakers would be contacted by telephone. The variables would be defined as follows:

1. *Product knowledge:* Percentage who were able to recall advertising claims accurately at the end of 13 weeks.
2. *Trial:* Percentage who made one or more purchases of the product during the first 13 weeks.
3. *Repeat purchases:* Percentage who had purchased and used the product who repurchased it or planned to do so.

The immediate task was to develop three sets of explanatory or independent variables that would explain and predict the three dependent variables. In addition, it would be necessary to specify the nature of the causal relationship—whether it would be, for example, additive or multiplicative and/or linear or nonlinear.

One variable seemed obvious. Product knowledge should depend on the level of advertising. Advertising could be measured in several ways. It would be possible, by monitoring local and national media, to estimate the average number of media impressions (advertisement exposures) per household. It was not clear, however, if advertising's impact on product knowledge was linear.

Several other tasks must be faced eventually. For instance, the model will need to be tested and validated. The database to be collected could be used for this purpose. The variables to be included in the database will need to be specified soon. Also, thought will have to be given to how and when managers should use the model.

Assignment 1

Develop a model of product knowledge. Specify variables, indicating precisely how they should be measured in any test application of the model. Indicate how such a model could be tested. Prepare a one-page paper summarizing your model.

Assignment 2

Develop a model of trial purchase and a model of repeat purchase. Indicate how you would use such a set of models if you were coming out with a new type of packaged cake mix.

CASE 18-3
Election Research, Inc.[2]

Election Research, a marketing research firm specializing in political campaigns, did an analysis on the 1972 California state legislature elections. Data were obtained for 72 districts and included the total number of registered voters by district, their party affiliation, the number of votes received by each candidate, the campaign expenditures of each candidate, and the identity of the incumbent, if one existed.

Of the 72 districts used, 27 had Republican winners and 45 had Democratic winners. There were 55 incumbent winners and 17 nonincumbent winners. The winners received an average of 66.6 percent of the votes cast and incurred 63.2 percent of the advertising expenses. The winner's advertising expenditure averaged $18,031 per district ($22,805 without an incumbent and $10,710 with an incumbent).

The following are the results of three regression runs (the numbers in parentheses are the t-values):

All districts:
$WSV = .240 + .174WSTE$ (4.82) $+ .414WSRV +$
$.0751$ (7.01) (4.60)$r^2 = .535$, $N = 72$

Incumbent districts:
$WSV = .329 + .157WSTE$ (3.67) $+ .409WSRV$
(6.07) $r^2 = .440$, $N = 55$

Nonincumbent districts:
$WSV = .212 + .234WSTE$ (3.39) $WSV +$
$.399WSRV$ (3.21) $r^2 = .615$, $N = 17$

where
WSV	=	the winner's share of total votes cast
$WSTE$	=	the winner's share of total advertising expenditures
$WSRV$	=	the proportion of registered voters that are registered to the winner's political party
I	=	the winner's incumbency dummy variable. A dummy variable is a 0-1 variable. In this case $I = 1$ for an incumbent district and $I = 0$ for a nonincumbent district.

Questions for Discussion

1. Interpret the regression coefficients. For all districts, what exactly does the coefficient .174 mean? Interpret the coefficients .141 and .075 as well. Why is the coefficient for the WSTE variable different in the three equations?
2. Explain exactly what the t-value means. Determine the p-value associated with each. Interpret r^2. Why is r^2 different for each equation?
3. Why does the incumbency dummy variable appear only in the first equation?
4. Could this model be used productively to predict? What insights could a candidate get from the model?

---

[2] Prepared by Scott Vitell and David A. Aaker of the University of California at Berkeley as the basis for class discussion.

19 DISCRIMINANT AND CANONICAL ANALYSIS

Learning Objectives

▶ Understand the concept of discriminant analysis and canonical analysis.

▶ How to use these techniques for business applications.

▶ How to interpret the results of these techniques.

▶ Identify the potential limitations (through violations of the assumptions) of these techniques.

▶ Illustrate an application of all these techniques with a computer system.

DISCRIMINANT ANALYSIS

Discriminant analysis techniques are used to classify individuals into one of two or more alternative groups (or populations) on the basis of a set of measurements. The populations are known to be distinct, and each individual belongs to one of them. These techniques also can be used to identify which variables contribute to making the classification. Thus, prediction and description, as in regression analysis, are the two major uses of discriminant analysis.

As an example, consider a mortgage company loan officer who wishes to decide whether to approve an applicant's mortgage loan. This decision is made by determining whether the applicant's characteristics are more like those of persons in the past who repaid loans successfully than those of persons who defaulted. Information on these two groups, available from past records, would include factors such as age, income, marital status, outstanding debt, and ownership of certain durable goods. Similarly, a researcher interested in business failures may be able to group firms according to whether they eventually failed or did not fail, on the basis of independent variables such as location, financial ratios, or management changes. The challenge is to find the discriminating variables to use in a predictive equation that will produce better-than-chance assignment of the individuals to the two groups.

Objectives. Discriminant analysis has four major objectives:[1]

▶ Determining linear combinations of the predictor variables to separate the groups by maximizing between-group variation relative to within-group variation (objects in different groups are maximally separated).

▶ Developing procedures for assigning new objects, firms, or individuals, whose profiles but not group identity are known, to one of the two groups.

▶ Testing whether significant differences exist between the two groups, based on the group centroids.

▶ Determining which variables count most in explaining intergroup differences.

Basic Concept. Suppose that an individual may belong to one of two populations. We begin by considering how individuals can be classified into one of these populations on the basis of a measurement of one characteristic, say X. Suppose that we have a representative sample from each population, enabling us to estimate the distribution of X and their means. Typically these distributions can be represented as in Figure 19-1.

From the figure, it is intuitively obvious that a low value of X would lead us to classify an individual into population II, and a high value would lead us to classify an individual into population I. To define what is meant by *low* or *high*, we must select a dividing point. If we denote this dividing point by C, then we would classify an individual into population I if $X > C$. For any given value of C, we would be incurring a certain percentage of error. If the individual came from population I but the measured X were less than C, we would incorrectly classify the individual into population II, and vice versa. These two types of errors are illustrated in Figure 19-1. If we can assume that the two populations have the same variance, then the usual value of C is

$$C = \frac{\overline{X}_I + \overline{X}_{II}}{2}$$

where, $\overline{X}_I$ and $\overline{X}_{II}$ are the mean values for the two groups, respectively. This value ensures that the two probabilities of error are equal. In actual applications,

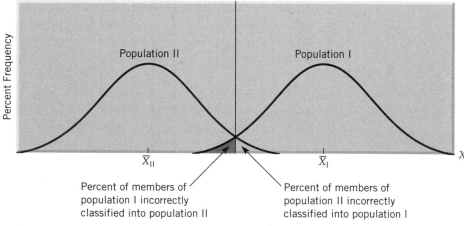

FIGURE 19-1
Distribution of two populations

a researcher is faced with more than one predictor variable and, therefore, needs to develop a linear combination of the predictor variables.

Methodology. **Discriminant analysis** involves deriving the linear combination of the two (or more) independent variables that will discriminate best between the *a priori* defined groups. This is achieved by the statistical criteria of maximizing the between-group variance relative to the within-group variance. The linear combination (known as the discriminant function/axis) for a discriminant analysis is derived from an equation that takes the following form:

$$Z = b_1X_1 + b_2X_2 + b_3X_3 + \ldots + b_nX_n$$

where

Z = Discriminant score
b = Discriminant weights
X = Predictor (independent) variables

Discriminant analysis (and ANOVA) are the appropriate statistical techniques for testing the hypotheses that the group means of two or more groups are equal. In discriminant analysis one multiplies each independent variable by its corresponding weight and adds these products together (see the preceding equation). The result is a single composite discriminant score for each individual in the analysis. By averaging the discriminant scores for all of the individuals within a particular group, we arrive at the group mean. This group mean is referred to as a **centroid.** The number of centroids corresponds to the number of groups. The centroids indicate the most typical location of an individual from a particular group, and a comparison of the group centroids shows how far apart the groups are along the discriminant function being tested.

The test for the statistical significance of the discriminant function is a generalized measure of the distance between the group centroids. It is computed by comparing the distribution of the discriminant scores for two or more groups. If the overlap in the distribution is small, the discriminant function separates the groups well; if the overlap is large, the function is a poor discriminator between the groups.

Figure 19-2 is a scatter diagram and projection that shows what happens when a two-group discriminant function is computed. Let's assume that we have two groups, A and B, and two measurements, X_1 and X_2, on each member of the two groups. We can plot in a scatter diagram the association of variable X_1 with variable X_2 for each member of the two groups. Group membership is identified by the use of large dots and small dots. In Figure 19-2 the small dots represent the variable measurements for the members of group B, and the large dots represent the variable measurements for group A. The ellipses drawn around the large and small dots would enclose some prespecified proportion of the points, usually 95 percent or more in each group. If we draw a straight line through the two points where the ellipses intersect and then project the line to a new Z axis, we can say that the overlap between the univariate distributions A' and B' (represented by the shaded area) is smaller than would

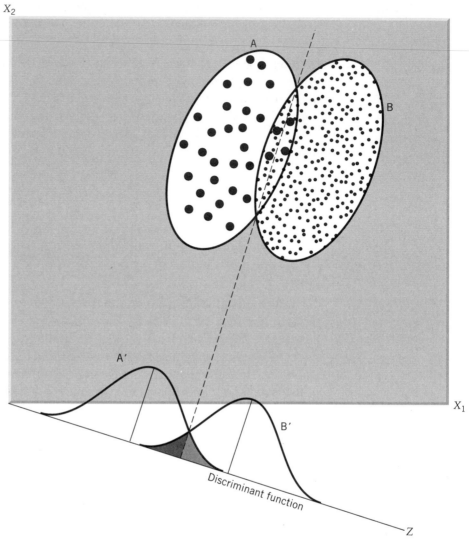

FIGURE 19-2
A graphical illustration

be obtained by any other line drawn through the ellipses formed by the scatter plots.[2]

The important thing to note about Figure 19-2 is that the Z axis expresses the two-variable profiles of groups A and B as single numbers (discriminant scores). By finding a linear combination of the original variables X_1 and X_2, we can project the result as a discriminant function. For example, if the dots and circles are projected onto the new Z axis as discriminant Z scores, the result condenses the information about group differences (shown in the X_1X_2 plot) into a set of points (Z scores) on a single axis. The mean value for the discriminant Z scores for a particular category or group is known as the **centroid.** A two-group discriminant analysis has two centroids, one for each of the groups. When the analysis involves two groups, the percentage of cases correctly classified (hit ratio) is determined by computing a single "cut-off" score. Those entities whose

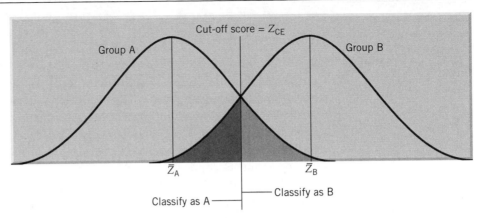

FIGURE 19-3
Equal groups sizes

Z scores are below this score are assigned to one group, while those whose scores are above it are classifed in the other group.

Group Assignment. The effects of equal and unequal sample sizes on the classification rule can be better understood by examining Figures 19-3 and 19-4. The critical cut-off point for equal sample sizes in each group is shown in Figure 19-3. The effect of one group being larger than the other is shown in Figure 19-4. Figure 19-4 illustrates both the weighted and unweighted critical cut-off points. The **Cut-off score** is the criterion (score) against which each individual's discriminant score is judged to determine into which group the individual should be classified. It is apparent from Figure 19-4 that if group A is much smaller than group B, then the optimal cut-off score will be closer to the centroid of group A than it is to the centroid of group B. Note also that if the difference in sample sizes is ignored, then use of the unweighted cut-off point results in perfect classification in one group (group B), but substantially misclassifies members of the other group (group A).

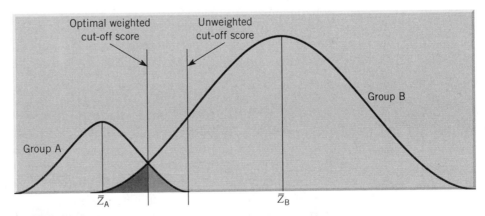

FIGURE 19-4
Unequal group sizes

For equal group sizes:

$$Z_{cut\text{-}off} = \frac{\overline{Z}_A + \overline{Z}_B}{2}$$

For unequal group sizes:

$$Z_{cut\text{-}off} = \frac{n_B\overline{Z}_A + n_A\overline{Z}_B}{n_A + n_B}$$

Comparing Regression and Discriminant Analysis. First, recall that in regression analysis the assumption is that the dependent variable Y is normally distributed and the independent variables are fixed. In discriminant analysis the situation is reversed: the independent variables are assumed to be normally distributed, and the dependent (i.e., grouping) variable is fixed, with values of zero or one. Second, the objective of regression analysis is to predict the mean population value of the dependent variable on the basis of the known and fixed values of the independent variables. In contrast, the objective in discriminant analysis is to find a linear combination of the independent variables that maximizes the discrimination between the two groups and minimizes the probability of misclassifying individuals or objects into their respective groups. In **regression analysis,** certain assumptions are made in order to generate parameter estimates that have desirable statistical properties. **Discriminant analysis** invokes a strategy for finding a means of accurately classifying individuals or objects into groups. Thus, these two techniques, though computationally similar, are conceptually different.

Application. In the export data set (Tables 18-3 and 18-4 in Chapter 18), one can create a nonmetric or categorical dependent variable by rescaling the "willingness to export" (Y_1) variable. A new variable "export interest" (EI) can be formed from the original (Y_1) variable. In other words, the "EI" variable will assume a value of 2 if one includes all the companies who responded with a value of four or five on the "willingness to export" scale. The "EI" variable will assume a value of 1 if one includes all the companies that responded with a value less than or equal to three on the "willingness to export" scale. Now that the two groups with export interest = high (2) and export interest = low (1) have been formed, one can perform the discriminant analysis. The independent variables for the discriminant analysis are the workforce size (X_2), firm's revenues (X_4), years of operation in the domestic market (X_5), and number of products currently produced by the firm (X_6). With two $(m = 2)$ levels for the dependent variable and four $(p = 4)$ independent variables, the number of discriminant functions that can be generated is given by the minimum of the number of levels in the dependent variable minus one and the number of predictor variables (denoted by Min $[m\text{-}1,p]$), which is one in this example.

Estimation. The **direct method** involves estimating the discriminant function so that all the predictors are included simultaneously. In this case, each indpendent variable is included, regardless of its discriminating power. This method is appropriate when the researcher has *a priori* reasons for the discrimination to be based on all the predictors. The parameters of the discriminant function are estimated subject to maximizing the between-group variation relative to the within-group variation. In other words, the discriminant weights are described such that the discriminant function provides maximum separation of groups (see Figure 19-2). Because there are two groups, only one discriminant function is estimated. Table 19-1 shows the results of the discriminant analysis for the export data. The canonical correlation (just like multiple R in regression analysis) associated with this function is 0.483. The square of this correlation, $(0.483)^2 = 0.233$, indicates that 23.3 percent of the variance in the dependent variable (export interest) is explained or accounted for by this model. The next step is determination of significance.

DETERMINATION OF SIGNIFICANCE

The null hypothesis, namely, that in the population the means of all discriminant functions in all groups $(H_o: \mu_A = \mu_B)$ are equal, can be tested statistically. In testing for significance in the export example (see Table 19-1), it may be noted that the Wilks' λ (defined as the ratio of within-group variance to the total variance) associated with the function is 0.766, which corresponds to a F-value of 4.1927 with 4 numerator degrees of freedom and 55 denominator degrees of freedom. This is significant beyond the 0.05 level. Wilks' λ assumes a value between 0 and 1. Larger values of λ indicate that group means do not appear to be different, and vice versa. If the null hypothesis is rejected, indicating significant discrimination, one can proceed to interpret the results.

INTERPRETATION[3]

The interpretation of the discriminant weights, or coefficients, is similar to that in multiple regression analysis. The value of the coefficient for a particular predictor depends on the other predictors included in the discriminant function. The signs of the coefficients are arbitrary, but they indicate which variable values would result in large and small function values, and associate them with particular groups. Generally, predictors with relatively large standardized coefficients contribute more to the discriminating power of the function than do the predictors with smaller coefficients.

The relative importance of the predictors also can be obtained by examining the structure correlations, also called **canonical loadings** or **discriminant loadings.** These simple correlations between each predictor and the discriminant function represent the variance that the predictor shares with the function. We use these correlations for substantive interpretations (e.g., to name the underlying constructs that the discriminant function represents). Like the standardized coefficients, these correlations must be interpreted with caution. Unless the sample size is large relative to the number of predictors, both the standardized coefficients and the loadings are very unstable. In other words, the results in one sample will not likely hold good in another sample from the same population. It is advised that the ratio of the number of observations to the predictors be at least 20:1.

Based on examining the standardized discriminant function coefficient for the predictor variables, one can conclude that workforce size (.83) and years of operation in the domestic market (.82) are the two most important discrimi-

TABLE 19-1
Results of Two-Group Discriminate Analysis for Export Data

Canonical Discriminant Analysis

60 Observations	59 df Total
4 Variables	58 df Within Classes
2 Classes	1 df Between Classes

Class Level Information

Export Interest	Frequency	Weight	Proportion
High	22	22.000	0.366
Low	38	38.000	0.633

Multivariate Statistics and Exact F Statistics

$S = 1$	$M = 1$	$N = 26.5$

Statistic	Value	F	Num df	Den df	$Pr > F$
Wilks' Lambda λ	0.766	4.192	4	55	0.004

Test of H_O: The canonical correlations in the current row and all that follow are zero.

	Likelihood Ratio	F	Num df	Den df	$Pr > F$
1	0.76632980	4.192	4	55	0.004

Pooled Within Discriminant Loadings
DIS1

SIZE	0.585
REV	0.249
YEARS	0.541
PROD	0.358
Canonical Correlation = 0.483	

nating variables of the level of export interest. This indicates that the larger the workforce size and more the years of operation in the domestic market, the more likely it is for the firm to have a greater interest in exporting. The unstandardized (or raw) discriminant function coefficients are given also. These

TABLE 19-1 *(continued)*

Total-Sample Standardized Discriminant Coefficients
DIS1

SIZE	0.825
REV	0.196
YEARS	0.824
PROD	0.156

Raw Canonical Coefficients

SIZE	0.077
REV	0.300
YEARS	0.895
PROD	0.061

Class Means on Discriminant Variables
Export Interest   CAN1

High	0.713
Low	−0.413

Classification Summary using Linear Discriminant Function
Number of Observations and Percent Classified into Export
Interest (EI):

From EI	High	Low	Total
High	16	6	22
	72.73	27.27	100.00
Low	9	29	38
	23.68	76.32	100.00
Total	25	35	60
Percent	41.67	58.33	100.00
	Hit Ratio: (16 + 29)/60 = 75%		

can be applied to the raw values of the variables in the data set for classification purposes.

The group means or centroids based on the discriminant function for each group are 0.713 for the high-export interest group and −0.413 for the low-export interest group. Given that the two groups have unequal sizes, the cut-off score on the discriminant function for classifying companies into one of the two groups is computed to be

$$\frac{38(.713) + 22(-0.413)}{60} = .0.3.$$

In terms of assigning firms to one of the two groups, if a firm has a Z-score greater than 0.3, then that firm belongs to the high-export interest group. If the firm's score is below 0.3, then it belongs to the low-export interest group.

Classification and Validation.[4] Validation of the discriminant function is necessary to avoid any sample or data-specific conclusions, in which case the results are not generalizable. The results should hold good for other samples from the same population.

The **holdout method** splits the total sample in two. One subsample is used to construct the classification rule, and the other is used for validation. **Classification matrix** is a matrix containing numbers that reveal the predictive ability of the discriminant function. The numbers on the diagonal of the matrix represent correct classifications, and the off-diagonal numbers are incorrect classifications (see Table 19-1). The **hit ratio,** or the percentage of cases correctly classified, can then be determined by summing the diagonal elements and dividing by the total number of cases. For validation, the discriminant weights, estimated by using the estimation sample, are multiplied by the values of the predictor variables in the holdout sample to generate discriminant scores for the cases in the holdout sample. The cases are then assigned to groups, based on their discriminant scores and an appropriate decision rule. For example, in two-group discriminant analysis, a case will be assigned to the group whose centroid is the closest. A variation of this method is to split the sample into K randomly chosen pairs of sets of equal size.

The **U-method,** or **cross-validation,** makes use of all of the available data without serious bias in estimating error rates. Frequently, it is inaccurately referred to as a jackknife procedure. Originally proposed by Lachenbruch (1967),[5] it holds out one observation at a time, estimates the discriminant function based on $n_1 + n_2 - 1$ observations, and classifies the held-out observation. This process is repeated until all observations are classified. If we denote by m_1 and m_2 the numbers of sample observations misclassified in G_1 and G_2, respectively, then the estimated classification error rates are given by $P_1 = m_1/n_1$ and $P_2 = m_2/n_2$.

Most discriminant analysis programs estimate a classification matrix based on the estimation sample. Because they capitalize on chance variation in the data, such results are invariably better than the classification obtained on the holdout sample. The hit ratio, or the percentage of cases correctly classified, is $(16 + 29)/60 = 0.75$, or 75% for the estimation sample. One might suspect that this hit ratio is artificially inflated, as the data used for estimation were also used for validation. Conducting classification analysis on an independent holdout set of data (with 60 additional observations) results in the classification matrix with a hit ratio of $(16 + 29)/60 = .75$, or 75%. If the chance classification is based on the size of the largest group, then it is called maximum chance criterion. Given two groups of unequal sizes, if everyone is assigned to the larger group (to maximize the percentage correcly classified), the maximum chance criteria is $38/60 = 63.3\%$. The proportional chance criteria (where the members are assigned to groups based on the original proportions) is given by $(22/60)^2 + (38/60)^2 = 53.5\%$. The hit ratio in our example exceeds both criteria, and thus it is probably worthwhile pursuing the discriminant analysis.

MULTIPLE DISCRIMINANT ANALYSIS

In **multiple discriminant analysis,** the goal is much the same, in that we wish to find an axis with the property of maximizing the ratio of between-group to within-group variability of projections onto this axis. A complicating feature in the case of three or more groups is that a single axis may not satisfactorily distinguish the groups, and much discrimination potential still remains. In general, with m groups and p predictor variables, there are, $\min[p, m - 1]$ (i.e., the minimum of the number of predictors and the number of groups minus one) possible discriminant axes (i.e., linear combinations). In most applications, since the number of predictor variables far exceeds the number of groups under study, at most, $m - 1$ discriminant axes will be considered. However, not all of these axes may show statistically significant variation among the groups, and fewer than $m - 1$ discriminant functions actually may be needed. Thus, in such cases, a good deal of parsimony will have been achieved.

Application. In the export data set, the original dependent variable can be split into three levels of export interest (EI). The EI variable will assume a value of 3 (high) if "willingness to export" exceeds the value of 3; EI = 2 (medium) if the value = 3; and EI = 1 (low), if "willingness to export" is below 3. Thus, a three-group discriminant analysis can be performed. Since there are three groups and four predictor variables, two discriminant functions will be generated. Table 19-2 shows the results of the multiple discriminant analysis.

Discussion of Results

If several functions are tested simultaneously (as in the case of multiple discriminant analysis), the Wilks' λ statistic is the product of the univariate λ for each function. In this export example, the Wilks' λ is 0.637 and is significant at the 0.05 level. Among two discriminant functions, the first function is significant at the 0.05 level of significance. Note that the second function is not significant at the prespecified level ($\alpha = .05$). However, the process of interpretation remains the same for both the functions.

As in the two-group discriminant analysis, the discriminant loadings (pooled within) can be interpreted. For example, in the pooled-within discriminant loadings, "years" has the highest correlation (0.649) and "prod" has the lowest correlation (0.171) with the first discriminant function. However, the second function exhibits higher correlation with "size" and "rev." Since only the first function is significant, we interpret only the results of the first discrimi-

TABLE 19-2
Results of Multiple Discriminant Analysis of Export Data

Canonical Discriminant Analysis

60 Observations	59 df Total
4 Variables	57 df Within Classes
3 Classes	2 df Between Classes

Class Level Information

Export Interest	Frequency	Weight	Proportion
High	22	22.000	0.366
Low	21	21.000	0.350
Mid	17	17.000	0.283

Multivariate Statistics and F Approximations

$S = 2$	$M = 0.5$	$N = 26$

Statistic	Value	F	Num df	Den df	$Pr > F$
Wilks' Lambda λ	0.636	3.418	8	108	0.001

Test of H_O: The canonical correlations in the current row and all that follow are zero.

	Likelihood Ratio	Approx F	Num df	Den df	$Pr > F$
1	0.636	3.414	8	108	0.001
2	0.903	1.965	3	55	0.129

Pooled Within Discriminant Loadings

	DIS1	DIS2
SIZE	0.352	0.741
REV	0.510	−0.698
YEARS	0.649	−0.208
PROD	0.171	0.585

TABLE 19-2 *(continued)*

Total-Sample Standardized Discriminant Coefficients

	DIS1	DIS2
SIZE	0.676	0.547
REV	0.511	−0.677
YEARS	0.851	0.140
PROD	0.032	0.323

Raw Discriminant Coefficients

	DIS1	DIS2
SIZE	0.063	0.051
REV	0.300	−0.400
YFARS	0.925	0.152
PROD	0.012	0.127

Class Means on Canonical Variables

Export Interest	DIS1	DIS2
High	0.688	0.233
Low	−0.795	0.164
Mid	0.091	−0.505

CLASSIFICATION FUNCTION
Export Interest

	High	Low	Mid
CONSTANT	−58.540	−44.319	−50.858
SIZE	0.749	0.651	0.673
REV	0.002	0.001	0.002
YEARS	11.637	10.254	10.972
PROD	0.222	0.194	0.120

nant function. The standardized and the raw discriminant coefficients can be interpreted similarly to the two-group discriminant analysis.

In two-group discriminant analysis, the members are classified to a particular group based on their discriminant score being above or below the cut-off score. The group assignment in multiple discriminant analysis becomes complicated when there are multiple discriminant functions and multiple groups. In such cases, a classification function is used to assign each object or individual to one of the three groups. This classification function is based

TABLE 19-2 *(continued)*

Classification Summary Using Linear Discriminant Function
Number of Observations and Percent Classified into Export Interest:

From Export Interest	High	Low	Mid	Total
High	15	4	3	22
	68.18	18.18	13.64	100.00
Low	4	14	3	21
	19.05	66.67	14.29	100.00
Mid	4	5	8	17
	23.53	29.41	47.06	100.00

on the concept of Mahalnobis distance (euclidean distance adjusted with the variance-covariance matrix—a matrix containing variances in the diagonal and covariances in the off-diagonal). A score is obtained on each of three classification functions for an object, and the object is assigned to the group that yields the maximum score.

The classification matrix yields a hit ratio of $(15 + 14 + 8)/60 = 61.7\%$ on the estimation sample and 60% on the hold-out sample. The maximum chance criteria for the three groups (of sizes 22, 21, and 17) is $(22/60) = 36.6\%$, and the proportional chance criteria is $(22/60)^2 + (21/60)^2 + (17/60)^2 = 33.7\%$. The hit ratio for the three-group discriminant analysis in our example far exceeds the maximum-chance and the proportional-chance criteria by providing a significant improvement of at least 68.5% $(61.7 - 36.6)/(36.6)$.

Summary of Discriminant Analysis

Application. Discriminant analysis is used primarily to identify variables that contribute to differences in the a priori defined groups with the use of discriminant functions. The analysis is also used for classifying objects into one or more groups that are already defined.

Inputs. The model requires variable values for the independent variables and the dependent variable (nonmetric).

Outputs. The discriminant analysis will provide the characteristics of the discriminant function such as the variables that contribute to each discriminant function (through discriminant loadings). The significance of the function is also given. The raw and the standard discriminant weights are given to assist in the classification of objects. Finally, the usefulness of the discriminant analysis for classification is evaluated through the hit ratio.

Statistical Tests. The significance of the discriminant function (through Wilks' λ) and the variables are evaluated through an F-statistic.

CANONICAL
CORRELATION ANALYSIS

Assumptions Underlying the Discriminant Function

1. The p independent variables must have a multivariate normal distribution.
2. The $p \times p$ variance-covariance matrix of the independent variables in each of the two groups must be the same.

Limitations. Some of the limitations are similar to that of regression analysis such as intervariable correlations in the model, correlation of variables with the omitted variables, and change of environment condition. The assumption of the discriminant analysis has to be tested and it is often possible that the assumption of equal variance-covariance matrix of the independent variable in each group is not met. In such cases, we have to resort to alternate techniques such as logit analysis (beyond the scope of this book).

CANONICAL CORRELATION ANALYSIS

When the researcher has two criterion variables (dependent variables) and multiple predictor variables (independent variables), **canonical correlation analysis** is an appropriate statistical technique. Multiple regression analysis investigates the linear relationship between a single dependent or criterion variable and multiple independent variables. Canonical correlation is an extension of multiple regression. It focuses on the relationship between two sets of interval-scale variables. For example, the relationship between the performance of a brand (measured as sales, market share, growth in sales, profit, etc.) and marketing-mix variables (price, promotion, distribution, advertising, and so forth) can be evaluated through canonical analysis.

Application. In the export data example (see Tables 18-3 and 18-4 in Chapter 18), suppose we wish to evaluate the association between a set of export-interest variables (the criterion set) and some firm characteristics (the predictor set). We want to know how several firm characteristics influence export-interest behavior such as willingness to export (Y_1) and level of interest in seeking government assistance (Y_2). The relationship between the Y-set and the X-set of variables is assessed by computing the canonical correlation. *Canonical correlation can be defined as the correlation between the linear combination (also called "linear composite") of the dependent variables and the linear combination of the independent variables.*

Calculation of the canonical correlation maximizes the correlation between two linear combinations. For example, the linear combination for firm characteristics might be

$$W = a_1X_1 + a_2X_2 . . . + a_qX_q$$

The linear combination for the export interest variables might be

$$V = b_1Y_1 + b_2Y_2 . . . + b_pY_p$$

and the correlation between W and V is defined as canonical correlation. As in regression analysis, a set of canonical coefficients or weights is identified for the predictor set of variables. Further, a set of canonical coefficients or weights is identified for the criterion set. To interpret the canonical analysis,[6] the researcher examines the relative magnitude and the signs of the several weights defining each equation, and sees if a meaningful interpretation is possible.

Here are a few facts about canonical analysis. First, the number of canonical functions that can be obtained is given by the min (p,q) where p and q are the number of variables in the criterion and the predictor set. Each canonical factor is interpreted based on the level of significance of the factors, the magnitude of the canonical correlation, and the amount of variance in one set of variables explained by the other set of variables. Also, canonical loadings, which represent the correlations between the original variables and the canonical factors, can be used to interpret the function.

Discussion of Results. Table 19-3 shows the results of the canonical analysis of the export data example. The number of canonical functions generated in this example is two ($p = 2$, $q = 4$).

Based on the raw canonical coefficients for both the criterion variables,

$$V_1 = 0.744 \text{ level} - 0.066 \text{ will} \quad \text{(first function)}$$
$$V_2 = 0.042 \text{ level} + 0.872 \text{ will} \quad \text{(second function)}$$

Similarly, based on the raw canonical coefficients for the predictor variables,

$$W_1 = 0.053 \text{ size} + 0.061 \text{ rev} - 0.426 \text{ years} + 0.149 \text{ prod}$$
$$W_2 = 0.042 \text{ size} + 0.559 \text{ rev} + 0.791 \text{ years} + 0.044 \text{ prod}$$

The canonical correlations for the first (between V_1 and W_1) and second factors (between V_2 and W_2) are 0.85 and 0.57, respectively, and both the functions are significant at $\alpha = 0.01$ level. The amount of variance shared by the linear composites (V_1 and W_1) of the first function (V_2 and W_2) and the second function are given by squared canonical correlation: 0.72 and 0.32 respectively. Canonical correlations are analogous to simple correlation coefficients. The difference is that a canonical correlation measures the association between the canonical variates, and not the original variables.

Although standardized canonical coefficients can be used to determine the relative importance of the variables, it is better to use canonical loadings (for similar reasons to those in the discriminant analysis). Based on the canonical loadings for the criterion set, the first function, V_1, is represented by level (0.99) and the second function, V_2, by will (0.99). Similar interpretations can be made for the predictor variable set. Based on the canonical cross-loadings, the criterion variable "level" produces the highest correlation (0.85) with the first linear composite (w_1) of the predictor variables and the criterion variable "will" by a larger correlation (0.57) with the second linear composite of the predictor variables. In simple terms, the variation in the criterion variable "level" is

TABLE 19-3
Results of Canonical Correlation Analysis

Canonical Correlation Analysis

	Canonical Correlation	Adjusted Canonical Correlation	Approx Standard Error	Squared Canonical Correlation
1	0.8503	0.8400	0.0360	0.7230
2	0.5712	0.5590	0.0877	0.3263

Test of H_0: The canonical correlations in the current row and all that follow are zero

	Likelihood Ratio	Approx F	Num df	Den df	Pr > F
1	0.18659015	17.7528	8	108	0.0001
2	0.67367729	8.8805	3	55	0.0001

Multivariate Statistics and F Approximations

$S = 2$	$M = 0.5$	$N = 26$

Statistic	Value	F	Num df	Den df	Pr > F
Wilks λ	0.186	17.752	8	108	0.0001

Raw Canonical Coefficients for the Criterion Variables

	V_1	V_2
LEVEL	0.7443	−0.0662
WILL	−0.0440	0.8723

Raw Canonical Coefficients for the Predictor Variables

	W_1	W_2
SIZE	0.0533	0.0420
REV	0.061	0.559
YEARS	−0.4268	0.7915
PROD	0.1496	0.0441

TABLE 19-3 *(continued)*

Standardized Canonical Coefficients for the Criterion Variables

	V_1	V_2
LEVEL	1.0058	−0.0896
WILL	−0.0510	1.0085

Standardized Canonical Coefficients for the Predictor Variables

	W_1	W_2
SIZE	0.5686	0.4485
REV	0.0531	0.4841
YEARS	−0.3930	0.7289
PROD	0.3801	0.1121

Canonical Loadings

Correlations Between the Criterion Variables and Their Linear Composite

	V_1	V_2
LEVEL	0.9987	0.0505
WILL	0.0887	0.9961

Correlations Between the Predictor Variables and Their Linear Composite

	W_1	W_2
SIZE	0.8583	0.3108
REV	−0.1131	0.6215
YEARS	−0.5716	0.7359
PROD	0.7716	0.2091

Canonical Cross-Loadings

Correlations Between the Criterion Variables and the Linear Composite of the Predictor Variables

	W_1	W_2
LEVEL	0.8492	0.0288
WILL	0.0754	0.5690

Correlations Between the Predictor Variables and the Linear Composite of the Criterion Variables

	V_1	V_2
SIZE	0.7298	0.1775
REV	−0.0962	0.3550
YEARS	−0.4861	0.4204
PROD	0.6561	0.1195

explained to a large extent by the first linear composite of the predictor variables, and the variation in "will" is explained to a large extent by the second linear composite of the predictor variables. Overall, the results indicate that both functions are necessary to explain variations in the two dependent/criterion variables.

Summary of Canonical Correlation Analysis

Application. *Canonical analysis is a technique to assess relationships between multiple dependent and multiple independent variables.*

Inputs. The inputs are the variable values for both the dependent and the independent variables (usually metric or dummy variables).

Outputs. The relationship between the dependent variables set and the independent variables set is assessed by **canonical correlation.** Canonical functions help to assess the relationship between the linear composites of the dependent variables with the linear composites of the independent variables. **Canonical loadings,** which represent the correlation between the variables and its linear composite, help to interpret the canonical function. Similarly, **canonical cross-loadings** can also be used for evaluating the contribution of variables in one linear composite in explaining the variation in the other linear composite.

Assumptions. This technique places very few (if any) assumptions on the scaling of the variables.

Limitations. Most of this technique's limitations come from the interpretation of the analysis.[7] First, canonical weights are derived to maximize the correlation between the linear composites, and not the variance extracted. Second, canonical correlation reflects shared variance between the linear composites, and not the variance extracted. As a result, canonical correlation could be high, yet the variance extracted could be low. Finally, the canonical weights are subject to a great degree of instability as are other techniques'.

Questions and Problems

1. A researcher wishes to perform a three-group multiple discriminant analysis and is interested in using information from the three variables that he or she collected during the study. How many discriminant functions are possible? Do you need all of them?
2. Are discriminant loadings better than discriminant weights for interpretation purposes?
3. If you have only one sample of 30 observations and use all of them to estimate the coefficients of the discriminant function, how would you validate the results?
4. If you violate the assumptions of the linear discriminant analysis, what other alternatives would you have in terms of statistical analysis?

5. Your consulting firm is approached by a leading consumer products manufacturer, General Mills, who just introduced a new brand of cookie in a test-market city. General Mills would like your company to use a discriminant analysis to see if it is possible to predict the people who will try a new brand, compared to those who will not try the new brand. You know that the market share of the new brand is only 10 percent, and observe that you can predict 90 percent of the population correctly by simply assuming each person did not try the new brand. This assumes that the market share of the new brand should be zero. From past experience, you know that it is difficult to predict 90 percent correctly with a discriminant analysis model, so you are reluctant to suggest such an investigation. Can anything possibly come out of the discriminant analysis research that might justify the cost of the investigation? Why?

6. A research study was concerned with assessing the difference between personalities of innovators and noninnovators in the purchase of a new home appliance.

   In that study, 50 innovators were compared with 40 noninnovators on five demographic variables (see the table that follows). The discriminant coefficients indicate that income is the best discriminator (among the six demographic measures studied) and that work experience is the worst.

Differences Between Innovators and Noninnovators

Variables	Innovator Mean	Noninnovator Mean	Discriminant Coefficient
Income	4.44	3.82	3.59
Age	3.93	3.20	3.08
Education	3.68	3.25	2.04
Family Size	3.13	2.78	2.44
Work Experience	2.00	1.73	0.95

The group centroids for both the innovators and the noninnovators are 3.0 and 1.8.

a. Develop the cut-off score for classification purposes.

b. You may notice that the size of the discriminant coefficients produces a ranking different from that which would be generated by looking at the differences in the means on the variables. Why?

7. How is canonical analysis different from regression analysis?

8. Is redundancy analysis necessary? How does it add value above the canonical correlation?

9. Consider the following example concerning the relationship between breakfast evaluations and the usage of breakfast products. Results for the first two canonical variate pairs are reported. Interpret the findings.

Variables	Variate 1		Variate 2	
	Canonical Loadings	Canonical Weights	Canonical Loadings	Canonical Weights
Predictor set				
Extensive	0.53	0.21	0.35	0.17
Sober	−0.43	−0.04	0.00	0.13
Imaginative	0.50	0.10	0.24	0.01
Varied	0.69	0.30	0.15	−0.17
With family	0.14	−0.07	0.53	0.09
With care	0.24	−0.09	0.58	0.22
Fast	−0.26	−0.29	−0.43	−0.45
Neat	0.08	−0.02	0.66	0.41
Good looking	0.26	−0.18	0.57	−0.19
Explained variance	15.7%		19.6%	
Criterion set				
Bread	0.48	0.23	0.12	−0.32
Meats	0.72	0.65	0.06	−0.33
Cheese	0.45	0.08	0.21	0.05
Eggs	0.39	0.15	0.30	0.03
Tablecloth	0.13	0.15	0.72	0.69
Dishes	0.05	−0.10	0.46	0.33
Explained variance	18.7%		14.7%	
Canonical correlation	0.95		0.80	
Redundancy $R^2_{(i) y/x}$	0.17		0.09	

Source: Kuylen and Verhallen (1981).

End Notes

1. P. E. Green, D. Tull, and G. Albaum. *Research for Marketing Decisions* (Englewood Cliffs, New Jersey: Prentice Hall), 1988.

2. This section is drawn from Joseph Hair, et al. *Multivariate Data Analysis with Readings* (New York: MacMillan, 1992.

3. C. J. Huberty. "Issues in the Use and Interpretation of Discriminant Analysis," *Psychological Bulletin,* 95, 1984, 156–171; W. D. Perreault, D. N. Behrman, and G. M. Armstrong. "Alternative Approaches for Interpretation of Multiple Discriminant Analysis in Marketing Research," *Journal of Business Research,* 7, 1979, 151–173.

4. M. Crask, and W. Perreault. "Validation of Discriminant Analysis in Marketing Research," *Journal of Marketing Research,* 14, February 1977, 60–68.

5. P. A. Lachenbruch. "An Almost Unbiased Method of Obtaining Confidence Intervals for the Probability of Misclassification in Discriminant Analysis," *Biometrics,* 23, 1967, 639–645.

6. Mark I. Alpert, and Robert A. Peterson. "On the Interpretation of Canonical Analysis," *Journal of Marketing Research,* 9, May 1972, 187; Mark I. Alpert, and Warren S. Martin. "Testing the Significance of Canonical Correlations," *Proceedings, American Marketing Association,* 37, 1975, 117–119; M. S. Bartlett. "The Statistical Significance of Canonical Correlations," *Biometrika,* 32, 1941, 29.

7. Z. Lambert and R. Durand. "Some Precautions in Using Canonical Analysis," *Journal of Marketing Research,* 12, November 1975, 468–75.

CASE 19-1
Southwest Utility[1]

In view of the national energy situation, it was felt that a need existed for an in-depth baseline study of consumer attitudes and perceptions of energy-crisis-related issues. As a result a study was conducted in February of 1974 (at the peak of the oil embargo) on a variety of energy-related issues.

A mail questionnaire was sent to 2500 residents of three medium-sized cities. A total of 922 respondents returned the questionnaire. A sample of 574 of the respondents was selected for the initial analysis. One key question asked if the respondent would be willing to give up degrees of heat in the home in order to

achieve less air pollution, assuming that such a trade-off were possible. One analysis was to determine how those willing to give up some heat in their homes differed from those that were not willing. Accordingly, the two groups are profiled in Table 1 on the basis of 10 variables.

The table shows the mean values for each group, the F-ratio, which reflects the statistical significance of the difference between the means, and the standardized discriminant coefficients.

Interpret the table elements. What is the appropriate interpretation of each term? Which variables are the most helpful in identifying the characteristics of the group? What are the appropriate hypothesis tests to be used in the analysis?

TABLE 1
Discriminant Analysis for Two Home Heat Preference Groups

Variable[a]	F-Ratio	Group 1 Prefer Less Heat $n = 171$ Mean (Standard Deviation)	Group 2 Prefer Same Heat $n = 378$ Mean (Standard Deviation)	Standardized Discriminant Coefficients
Family member 15–19 years	5.87	0.39 (0.69)	0.25 (0.58)	.35
Paid family members	3.81	2.16 (1.31)	1.93 (1.28)	.28
Education	14.34	4.05 (1.30)	3.55 (1.48)	.31
Income	5.67	3.64 (1.59)	3.28 (1.66)	−.08
Television	4.42	2.64 (1.04)	2.43 (1.09)	.14
Magazines	7.08	2.05 (1.16)	1.76 (1.20)	−.03
Civic clubs	7.68	1.44 (1.22)	1.14 (1.16)	.28
Spouse	4.80	1.27 (1.14)	1.04 (1.14)	.18
Amount each family should pay	16.94	3.55 (2.87)	2.57 (2.42)	−.05
Amount family is willing to spend	18.29	3.98 (3.13)	2.89 (2.61)	.12
Mean discriminant score (significant at .001 level)		0.44	−.20	

[a] Nonsignificant (at the 0.05 level) variables include the following demographics: sex, marital status, family size, age distribution of persons 0–14 and over 20 living at home, mobility, race, age (of respondent), and length of time as area resident. Only variables with an F-ratio included at the 0.05 level of significance are displayed.

[1] Prepared by David J. Barnaby, Richard C. Reizenstein, and David A. Aaker as a basis for class discussion.

20 FACTOR AND CLUSTER ANALYSIS

Learning Objectives

▶ Understand the concept and the need for factor and cluster analysis.

▶ Discuss the different methods of factor and cluster analysis.

▶ How to retain the correct number of factors and clusters.

▶ How to interpret the factor and cluster solutions.

▶ What to do with the output of both factor and cluster analysis.

Factor analysis and cluster analysis are techniques that serve to (1) combine questions or variables to create new factors and (2) combine objects to create new groups, respectively. Often these are termed the **analysis of interdependence** techniques, because they analyze the interdependence of questions, variables, or objects. The goal is to generate understanding of the underlying structure of questions, variables, or objects, and to combine them into new variables or groups. These two techniques can be illustrated by the following simple example.

Suppose we are interested in determining how prospective students select universities. The first step might be to determine how prospective students perceive and evaluate institutions. To generate relevant questions, students might be asked to talk informally about schools. More particularly, the students could be asked why they prefer one school or why they regard two as similar. The result could be 100 or more items, such as *large, good faculty, expensive, good climate, dormitories, facilities, athletic program, social aspects, impersonal,* and so on. A second step might be to ask a group of prospective students to evaluate how important each of these attributes is to them. At this point the analysis can get bogged down simply because there are too many attributes or variables. Furthermore, many of the attributes are redundant, really measuring the same construct. To determine which are redundant and what they are measuring, the analyst can turn to factor analysis. One result will be a set of new variables (or factors) created by combining sets of school attributes.

In another phase of the study, groups of students might be identified by what they are looking for in a college. We might hypothesize that one group is concerned about individual attention; another, low cost; another, proximity to home; and still another, quality education. If such groups exist and can be identified, it might be possible to isolate several, describe them, and develop a communication program—tailored to their interests—that could be directed toward them. **Cluster analysis** can be used to identify such groupings. It is used to identify people, objects, or variables that form natural groupings or clusters. A new variable is defined by cluster membership.

HMO enrollment intentions, for example, were based on a single question. However, it often will be theoretically and practically desirable to combine several questions, thereby creating a new variable that is based on more than one question. The fact that some constructs require more than one question to represent them generated a need to combine questions or variables. Social class, for example, often is represented best by a set of questions including income, education, and occupation. The need to combine questions also is partially due to the fact that sets of questions measuring such complex areas as life-style or image often are redundant. If questions on life-style or if image-question sets were not combined, the analysis would be most unwieldy and confused. A variable that is based on a combination of questions, of course, can be tabulated, just as the original questions or variables can (and are).

FACTOR ANALYSIS

Purpose

Researchers can use **factor analysis** for two primary functions in data analysis. One is to identify underlying constructs in the data. Thus, the variables "impersonal" and "large" in our school study actually may be indicators of the same theoretical construct.

A second role of factor analysis is simply to reduce the number of variables to a more manageable set. In reducing the number of variables, factor analysis procedures attempt to retain as much of the information as possible and to make the remaining variables meaningful and easy to work with.

Methodology

The two most commonly employed factor analytic procedures in marketing applications are **principal component** and **common factor** analysis. When the objective is to summarize information in a larger set of variables into fewer factors (our second purpose), principal component analysis is used. On the other hand, if the researcher is attempting to uncover underlying dimensions surrounding the original variables (first purpose), common factor analysis is used. So the researcher's objective dictates which procedure will be used. Conceptually, principal component analysis is based on the total information in each variable, whereas common factor analysis is concerned only with the variance shared among all the variables.

In general, factor analysis can be summarized as a method of transforming the original variables into new, noncorrelated variables, called the factors. Each factor is a linear combination of the original variables. One measure of the amount of information conveyed by each factor is its variance. For this reason the factors are arranged in the order of decreasing variance. Thus, the most informative factor is the first, and the least informative is the last. In other words, the objective of the principal components is to generate a first factor that will have the maximum explained variance. Then, with the first factor and its associated loadings fixed, the principal components will locate a second factor that maximizes the variance it explains. The procedure continues until there are as many factors generated as variables or until the analyst concludes that the number of useful factors has been exhausted. How to determine the number of factors to include will be considered shortly.

A Geometric Perspective

It often is helpful to consider a geometric interpretation of factor analysis. **Principal components** analysis, normally the first step in a factor analysis, will be described from a geometric perspective in the context of an example. Suppose that a group of prospective students rated, on a -5 to $+5$ scale, the importance of "good faculty" and "program reputation" in their decision as to which school to attend. Thus, a -5 rating would mean that the individual does not really care if the school has a good faculty (or rather, she or he might be more concerned about the athletic program). The respondents are plotted with respect to their ratings on the X_1 (good faculty) scale and on the X_2 (program reputation) scale. At this point, two questions arise. First, are there really two dimensions operating, or are both variables really measuring the same thing? If people value a good faculty, it seems likely that they also would value program reputation. Thus, these two dimensions might be measuring the underlying construct of overall quality. Second, there is the practical question of whether the number of variables could be reduced from two to one without sacrificing information.

Principal components analysis provides an approach to these questions. It will generate a new dimension, shown as F_1 in Figure 20-1, which retains as nearly as possible the interpoint distance information, or variance, that was contained in the original two dimensions. The new axis is termed F_1, or the first factor. It also is termed the **first principal component** or the **first principal factor.** Each person has a "score" or projection on the new dimension, just as he or she had on the original X_1 and X_2 dimensions. For example, in Figure 20-1, person 7 has a coordinate on factor 1 that is shown to be $F_{7,1}$. This projection is termed the **factor score** for person 7 on factor 1.

An important statistic is the percentage of the original variance that is included in the first factor. The original variance is the variance on the X_1 axis plus the variance on the X_2 axis. In this case, the variance of the factor scores on factor 1 might be 90 percent of the total original variance. This statistic indicates how well the factor serves to represent the original data.

In Figure 20-1, the points do not all lie exactly on the line represented by the first factor. There is variation about the first factor. To capture this variation, a second factor, F_2, is added perpendicularly to F_1. The two factors together will represent the data completely. They will account for all the variation along the two axes, X_1 and X_2. Just as there were factor scores for the first factor, there also will be factor scores or projections on the second. The projection for factor 2 for person 7 is shown in Figure 20-1.

In Figure 20-1, since there are only two dimensions, the second factor is positioned automatically. However, if a third dimension such as "school size"

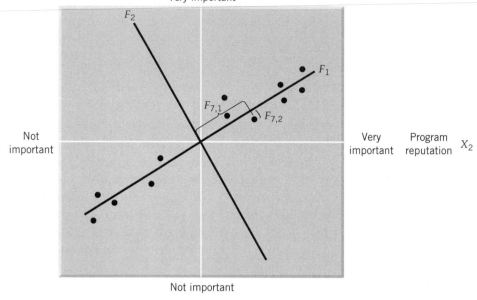

FIGURE 20-1
A factor analysis solution

were added to the original analysis (it would be shown coming out of the page), the position of the second factor would have to be determined. It could be a dimension tilted at any angle to the figure and still be perpendicular to the first factor. With three original variables, the second factor is selected so that the variance of the factor scores on the second factor is maximized.

The analysis can continue to select factors until the process is stopped (using one of the rules of thumb) or until the number of factors equals the number of original variables. Each factor will have a statistic associated with it—the percentage of the variance explained by that factor. After factors have been generated by principal components, they can be rotated using one of the many rotation schemes, such as **varimax rotation.**

Assume for the moment that data reduction is the objective. In that case, principal component analysis is used for data reduction.

Principal-Component Analysis

A (hypothetical) study was conducted by a bank to determine if special marketing programs should be developed for several key segments. One of the study's research questions concerned attitudes toward banking. The respondents were asked their opinion on a zero-to-nine, agree–disagree scale, on the following questions:

1. Small banks charge less than large banks.
2. Large banks are more likely to make mistakes than small banks.
3. Tellers do not need to be extremely courteous and friendly; it's enough for them simply to be civil.

4. I want to be personally known at my bank and to be treated with special courtesy.
5. If a financial institution treated me in an impersonal or uncaring way, I would never patronize that organization again.

For illustrative purposes, assume that a pilot study was conducted using 15 respondents. An actual pilot study probably would have a sample size of 100 to 400 respondents. Table 20-1 shows the pilot study data and the correlations among the variables. The correlation matrix shown in Table 20-1 has unities in the diagonal, implying that the researcher is interested in the total variance as opposed to the shared variance. A factor analysis program usually will start by calculating the variable-by-variable correlation matrix. In fact, it is quite possible to input directly the correlation matrix instead of the raw data. In any case, the factor analysis program will provide the correlation matrix as one of its outputs. It is a good idea to examine these correlations to see what information and hypotheses can be obtained. Which correlations are the largest? What does this imply?

Since the objective of factor analysis is to represent each of these variables as a linear combination of a smaller set of factors, we can express this as

$$x_1 = l_{11}F_1 + l_{12}F_2 + e_1$$
$$x_2 = l_{21}F_1 + l_{22}F_2 + e_2$$
$$\vdots$$
$$\vdots$$
$$x_5 = l_{51}F_1 + l_{52}F_2 + e_5$$

where x_1 through x_5 represent the standardized scores, F_1 and F_2 are the two standardized factor scores, $l_{11}, l_{12}, \ldots, l_{52}$ are the factor loadings, and e_1 to e_5 are the error variances.

What Is a Factor? To interpret the balance of Table 20-1, it is first necessary to understand the concept of a factor. The input variables very likely will contain redundancy. Several may be measuring in part the same underlying construct. This underlying construct is what is termed a factor. A **factor** is thus simply a variable or construct that is not directly observable but needs to be inferred from the input variables. It also might be viewed as a grouping of those input variables that measure or are indicators of the factor. In the factor model, just as in the regression model, there is a small set of independent variables, here termed **factors,** which are hypothesized to explain or cause the dependent variable. The regression coefficients, here termed **factor loadings,** link the factors to the variables and are used to help interpret the factors. In this context, the factor loadings are the correlations between the factors and the variables. The error term in both the factor and regression models absorbs measurement error and variation in the dependent variable that are not caused or explained by the factors. The **source** of the unexplained variation in the

TABLE 20-1
Principal Component Analysis

	Input = Variable Values					Output = Factor Scores	
OBS	**X1**	**X2**	**X3**	**X4**	**X5**	**FACTOR1**	**FACTOR2**
1	9	6	9	2	2	−0.91581	1.03767
2	4	6	2	6	7	0.93263	−0.00767
3	0	0	5	0	0	−1.05059	−1.94294
4	2	2	0	9	9	1.64856	−1.03405
5	6	9	8	3	3	−0.44159	1.04045
6	3	8	5	4	7	0.44671	0.30815
7	4	5	6	3	6	−0.00002	−0.03933
8	8	6	8	2	2	−0.80081	0.80036
9	4	4	0	8	8	1.44238	−0.39930
10	2	8	4	5	7	0.69027	0.09916
11	1	2	6	0	0	−1.10436	−1.35569
12	6	9	7	3	5	−0.11766	1.03863
13	6	7	1	7	8	1.27690	0.50694
14	2	1	7	1	1	−1.01006	−1.23345
15	9	7	9	2	1	−0.99654	1.18107

CORRELATION ANALYSIS

	X1	**X2**	**X3**	**X4**	**X5**
X1	1.00000	0.60980	0.46870	−0.01795	−0.09642
X2		1.00000	0.23048	0.18969	0.31863
X3			1.00000	−0.83183	−0.77394
X4				1.00000	0.92732
X5					1.00000

PRINCIPLE COMPONENT ANALYSIS
Prior Communality Estimates: ONE
Eigenvalues of the Correlation Matrix: Total = 5 Average = 1

	1	2	3	4	5
Eigenvalue	2.754602	1.774869	0.377091	0.064964	0.028474
Difference[a]	0.979733	1.397778	0.312127	0.036491	
Proportion[b]	0.5509	0.3550	0.0754	0.0130	0.0057
Cumulative[c]	0.5509	0.9059	0.9813	0.9943	1.0000

2 factors will be retained by the MINEIGEN criterion

	Factor Pattern			Rotated Factor Pattern Rotation method: Varimax		
	FACTOR1	**FACTOR2**	**Communalities**	**FACTOR1**	**FACTOR2**	**Communalities**
X1	−0.29	0.85	0.81	−0.17	0.89	0.81
X2	0.05	0.92	0.83	0.17	0.90	0.83
X3	−0.94	0.28	0.94	−0.89	0.41	0.94
X4	0.95	0.23	0.94	0.97	0.09	0.94
X5	0.94	0.27	0.96	0.97	0.13	0.96

TABLE 20-1 *(continued)*

Variance explained by each factor		Variance explained by each factor	
FACTOR1	**FACTOR2**	**FACTOR1**	**FACTOR2**
2.754602	1.774869	2.735	1.794

Standardized Scoring Coefficients		
	FACTOR1	**FACTOR2**
X1	−0.03915	0.49096
X2	0.08936	0.51083
X3	−0.31526	0.20227
X4	0.35929	0.07915
X5	0.35906	0.10182

[a] Difference represents the difference in eigenvalues between that factor and the subsequent factor.
[b] Proportion denotes the amount of variance explained by the factor relative to the total variance.
[c] Cumulative indicates the total proportion of variance explained by all the factors. For example, the first two factors explain a total of 90.59 percent of all the variations in the original variables.

dependent variable is an important concept in both factor analysis (percentage of variance explained and communality) and regression analysis (R^2).

Factor Scores. Although a factor is not observable like the other five variables, it still is a variable. One output of most factor analysis programs is the values for each factor for all respondents. These values are termed **factor scores** and are shown in Table 20-1 for the two factors that were found to underlie the five input variables. Thus, each respondent has a factor score on each factor, in addition to the respondent's rating on the original five variables. In subsequent analysis it may be convenient and appropriate to work with the factor scores instead of the original variables. The factor scores might be preferred because they have simply fewer factors than variables and (if the analyst is lucky) the factors are conceptually meaningful.

The factor is a derived variable in the sense that the factor score is calculated from a knowledge of the variables associated with it. Factors themselves can be represented as linear combinations of the original variables. For example,

$$F_j = b_{j1}x_{s1} + b_{j2}x_{s2} + \ldots + b_{jk}x_{sk}$$

where

F_j = factor scores for the jth factor
b_j = factor score coefficients on the jth factor
x_{sk} = k^{th} variable (standardized)

Table 20-1 provides the factor score coefficients for the bank example. For instance, the first subject's factor 1 score would be computed as

$$-0.91 = -0.039x_{s1} + 0.089x_{s2} - 0.315x_{s3} + 0.359x_{s4} + 0.359x_{s5}$$

These computed factor scores can be used as predictor variables in regression, discriminant, or other statistical analysis.

Factor Loadings. How is the factor interpreted if it is unobservable? Interpretation is based upon **factor loadings,** which are the correlations between the factors and the original variables.[1] The factor loadings for our bank study are shown at the bottom of Table 20-1. For example, the correlation between variable 1 and factor 1 is -0.29. The factor loadings thus provide an indication of which original variables are correlated with each factor, and the extent of the correlation. This information then is used to identify and label the unobservable factors subjectively.

Clearly, variables 3, 4, and 5 combine to define the first factor, which might be labeled a "personal" factor. This is so because the variables 3, 4, and 5 stress the "personal" aspects of the transaction in the banks. A larger value for variable 3 might indicate that the customers agree that the tellers need not be courteous. However, variable 3 has a high negative loading on factor 1, which indicates that customers do care for courteous service. Both variables 4 and 5 load positive on the first factor stressing the personal nature of the business.

The second factor is correlated most highly with variables 1 and 2. It might be termed a "small-bank" factor because both variables 1 and 2 have a positive loading on the second factor, and a high value on these variables indicate that the statements hold true for small banks.

Communality. Each of the five original input variables has associated with it a variance that reflects the differences among the 15 respondents. The amount of the variable 1 variance that is explained or accounted for by the factors is the communality of variable 1, and is shown in Table 20-1 to be 81 percent. **Communality** is the percentage of a variable's variance that contributes to the correlation with other variables or is "common" to other variables. In Table 20-1, variables 3, 4, and 5 have higher communalities; therefore, their variation is represented fairly completely by the two factors, whereas variable 1 has a lower communality. Just over 80 percent of the variance of variable 1 is due to the two factors.

Variance Explained. The percentage of variance explained is a summary measure indicating how much of the total original variance of all the five variables the factor represents.[2] Thus, the first factor explains 55 percent of the total variance of the five variables and the second factor accounts for 36 percent more variance. The percentage-of-variance-explained statistic can be useful in evaluating and interpreting a factor, as will be illustrated shortly.

Why Perform Factor Analysis on Data? One reason to perform **factor analysis** on data is to obtain insights from the groupings of variables that emerge. In particular, it often is possible to identify underlying constructs that might have practical and theoretical significance. Another reason is to reduce the number of questions or scales to a manageable number. This variable reduction can be accomplished in either of the two following ways:

1. Select one, two, or more of the input variables to represent each factor. They would be selected on the basis of their factor loadings and a judgment as to their usefulness and validity. In the example in Table 20-1, question 2 might be selected to represent the second factor. If the factor analysis is based on a pilot study, the larger study to follow then will have fewer questions to include. A set of 100 questions in a pilot study might be reduced to a group of 20 to 30 in the larger study.

2. Replace the original input variables with the factor scores. In the example represented by Table 20-1, the result would be two interpretable factors replacing five variables. In a larger problem, 50 input variables might be replaced by eight or nine factors. Subsequent data analysis would become easier, less expensive, and have fewer interpretation difficulties.

Factor Rotation. Factor analysis can generate several solutions (loadings and factor scores) for any data set. Each solution is termed a particular **factor rotation** and is generated by a **factor rotation scheme.** Each time the factors are rotated, the pattern of loadings changes, as does the interpretation of the factors. Geometrically, rotation means simply that the dimensions are rotated. There are many such rotation programs, such as **varimax rotation** (for orthogonal rotation) and **promax** (for oblique rotation). In the **varimax** rotation, each factor tends to load high (-1 or $+1$) on a smaller number of variables and low, or very low (close to zero), on other variables, to make interpretation of the resulting factors easier. In other words, the variance explained by each unrotated factor is simply rearranged by the rotation. The total variance explained by the rotated factors still remains the same.

Here, the first rotated factor will no longer necessarily account for the maximum variance. The amount of variance each factor accounts for has to be recalculated. In the **oblique rotation,** the factors are rotated for better interpretation, such that the orthogonality is not preserved anymore. Examples of both orthogonal and oblique rotation are provided in Figure 20-2.

In Figure 20-2, before the rotation, variables 1 and 2 have a high positive loading on both factors. Variables 3, 4, and 5 load positive on factor 1 and negative on factor 2. After the orthogonal rotation, variables 1 and 2 load high only on factor 1, and the remaining variables load high only on factor 2, thus facilitating easier interpretation of the factors. If the original factors are subjected to an oblique rotation, the results obtained will be similar to those of the orthogonal rotation (in this example); however, the two rotated factors will be correlated. In oblique rotation, you sacrifice orthogonality of factors for better interpretation.

In the bank example, the unrotated factor loadings themselves provide somewhat clearer interpretation. When the orthogonal varimax rotation was employed, the overall interpretation of the two factors did not change much; however, individual loadings did change to some extent. Table 20-1 shows both the unrotated and the rotated factor loadings for the bank example.

How Many Factors? Since factor analysis is designed to reduce many variables to a smaller number of underlying factors or constructs, a central question is,

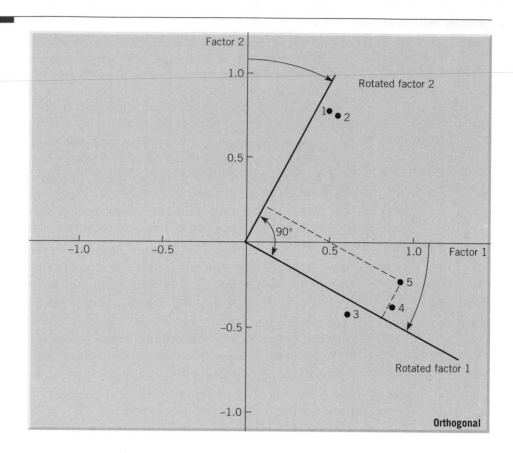

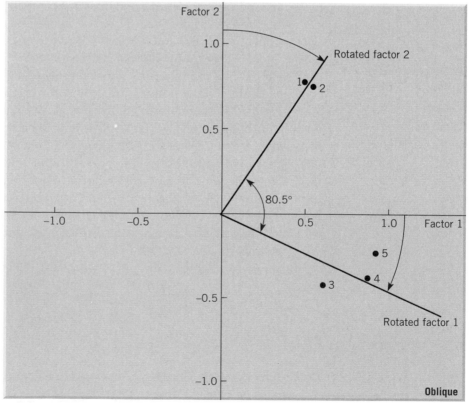

FIGURE 20-2
Factor rotations

How many factors are involved in the model? It is always possible to keep generating factors until there are as many factors as original variables, but such a practice would defeat one of the primary purposes of the technique.

Theoretically, the answer to the question is clear. There is a certain number of constructs that the input variables are measuring. These constructs are identified before the analysis from our theory and knowledge of the situation; then the data are factor analyzed until these constructs emerge as factors. Unfortunately, our theory is rarely that well defined. We therefore add some rules of thumb to the theoretical answer.

The rule of thumb we most heavily rely on in factor analysis studies is that all included factors (prior to rotation) must explain at least as much variance as an "average variable." In Table 20-1 the average variable would explain one-fifth, or 20 percent, of the variance. Actually, the second factor explained 36 percent, and the third factor, which was not shown, explained only 7 percent of the variance. The logic is that if a factor is meaningful and capable of representing one or more of the variables, it should absorb at least as much variance as an average original input variable.

Just because a lot of variance is explained, of course, does not mean that a factor is valid or meaningful or useful. If an irrelevant scale or question were repeated many times, each with a small modification, a factor underlying that question would explain much of the variance, but would not be a very interesting construct because the questions on which it was based were not very interesting.

A related rule of thumb is to look for a large drop in the variance explained between two factors (in the principal components solution). For example, if the variance explained by five factors (before rotation) were 40 percent, 30 percent, 20 percent, 6 percent, and 4 percent, there is a drop in variance explained in the fourth factor. This drop might signal the introduction of meaningless, relatively unimportant factors. A brief description of other criteria are provided next.

Eigenvalue Criteria. An **eigenvalue** represents the amount of variance in the original variables that is associated with a factor. Here, only factors with eigenvalues greater than 1.0 are retained; the other factors are not included in the model. In other words, the sum of the square of the factor loadings of each variable on a factor represents the eigenvalue, or the total variance explained by that factor. Hence, only factors with eigenvalues greater than 1.0 are included. A factor with an eigenvalue less than 1.0 is no better than a single variable, since, due to standardization, each variable has a variance of 1.0. Therefore, a factor should explain at least the amount of variance in one variable; otherwise it is better to have the original variable.

Scree Plot Criteria. A **scree plot** is a plot of the eigenvalues against the number of factors, in order of extraction (see Figure 20-3). The shape of the plot is used to determine the number of factors. Typically, the plot has a distinct break between the steep slope of factors with large eigenvalues and a gradual trailing off associated with the rest of the factors. This gradual trailing off is referred to as the "scree." Experimental evidence indicates that the point at which the scree begins denotes the true number of factors. Based on Figure 20-3, one would choose three factors. However, the third factor has a very low eigenvalue, which makes it not practically useful. Therefore, we would retain two factors.

Percentage of Variance Criteria. In this approach the number of factors extracted is determined so that the cumulative percentage of variance extracted by the factors reaches a satisfactory level. The level of variance that is satisfactory depends on the problem.

Significance Test Criteria. It is possible to determine the statistical significance of the separate eigenvalues and retain only those factors that are statistically significant. A drawback is that with large samples (sizes greater than 200) many factors are likely to be statistically significant, although, from a practical viewpoint, many of these account for only a small proportion of the total variance.

Perhaps the most appropriate rule is to stop factoring when the factors stop making sense. Eventually, the smaller factors will represent random varimax rotation and should be expected to be uninterpretable. Clearly, the determination of the number of factors, like the interpretation of individual factors, is very subjective.

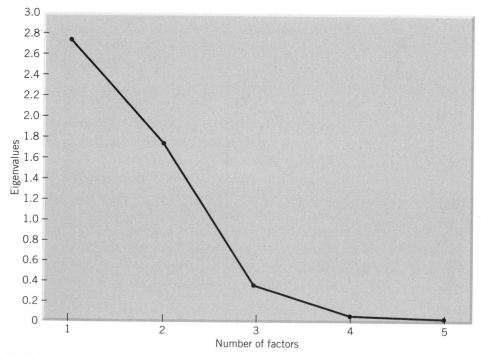

FIGURE 20-3
Scree plot

Common-Factor Analysis

As stated earlier, if the purpose is to recover underlying factors in the original variables, then common factor analysis is used. The factor extraction procedure is similar to that of principal component analysis except for the input correlation matrix. Communalities, or shared variance, are inserted in the diagonal instead of unities in the original variable correlation matrix. Communalities are defined as the amount of variance a variable shares with all the other variables. Since common factor analysis focused on shared variance (to recover the underlying construct), communalities are used in the diagonal of the correlation matrix rather than inserting "1's." Therefore, the total amount of variance that can be explained by all the factors in **common-factor analysis** would be the sum of the diagonal elements in the correlation matrix. Table 20-2 shows the results of common-factor analysis.

The total amount of variance (eigenvalue) to be explained in the principal component analysis was 5, and it is 4.28 for the common-factor analysis. Overall, the results of common-factor analysis do not seem to vary from those of principal-component analysis. However, this need not always be true, because the output of common-factor analysis depends on the amount of shared variance. If the shared variance is high among the variables, then the two procedures will yield similar solutions. Otherwise, differences can be observed between principal-component and common-factor analysis.

Summary of Factor Analysis

Application. Factor analysis is used to identify underlying dimensions or constructs in the data and to reduce the number of variables by eliminating redundancy.

Inputs. The input to factor analysis is usually a set of variable values for each individual or object in the sample. It is possible instead to input the matrix of correlations between the variables.[3] Actually, any type of square matrix whose components provide a measure of similarity between variables could be factor analyzed. The similarity measure does not have to be a correlation, although most often it is.

Outputs. The most important outputs are the factor loadings, the factor scores, and the variance-explained percentages. The factor loadings—that is, the correlations between the factors and the variables—are used to interpret the factors. Sometimes an analyst will pick one or two variables that load heavily on a factor to represent that factor in subsequent data collection or analysis. It also often is appropriate and useful to calculate the factor score and use that as a variable in the subsequent data analysis. The **percentage-of-variance explained** and other criteria help to determine the number of factors to include and how well they represent the original variables.

Key Assumption. The most important assumption is that there are factors underlying the variables and that the variables completely and adequately

TABLE 20-2
Common Factor Analysis

	Input = Variable Values					Output = Factor Scores	
OBS	X1	X2	X3	X4	X5	FACTOR1	FACTOR2
1	9	6	9	2	2	−0.84037	1.09086
2	4	6	2	6	7	0.88018	−0.19022
3	0	0	5	0	0	−1.09151	−2.00037
4	2	2	0	9	9	1.74028	−0.61231
5	6	9	8	3	3	−0.43271	1.04976
6	3	8	5	4	7	0.40098	0.32186
7	4	5	6	3	6	0.02497	0.15184
8	8	6	8	2	2	−0.77007	0.72030
9	4	4	0	8	8	1.43499	−0.46909
10	2	8	4	5	7	0.64349	0.13451
11	1	2	6	0	0	−1.14897	−1.44074
12	6	9	7	3	5	−0.14974	0.93232
13	6	7	1	7	8	1.19589	0.10743
14	2	1	7	1	1	−0.93920	−0.90774
15	9	7	9	2	1	−0.94820	1.11161

CORRELATION ANALYSIS

	X1	X2	X3	X4	X5
X1	0.75495	0.60980	0.46870	−0.01795	−0.09642
X2		0.72752	0.23048	0.18969	0.31863
X3			0.91853	−0.83183	−0.77394
X4				0.95004	0.92732
X5					0.92883

PRINCIPLE FACTOR ANALYSIS
Prior Communality Estimates: SMC

X1	X2	X3	X4	X5
0.754955	0.727517	0.918529	0.950038	0.928834

Eigenvalues of the Reduced Correlation Matrix:
Total = 4.27987218   Average = 0.85597444

	1	2	3	4	5
Eigenvalue	2.682061	1.538428	0.165240	−0.039876	−0.065981
Difference[a]	1.143633	1.373187	0.205116	0.026105	
Proportion[b]	0.6267	0.3595	0.0386	−0.0093	−0.0154
Cumulative[c]	0.6267	0.9861	1.0247	1.0154	1.0000

Two factors will be retained by the NFACTOR criterion.

TABLE 20-2 (*continued*)

	Factor Pattern			Rotated Factor Pattern Rotation method: Varimax		
	FACTOR1	**FACTOR2**	**Communalities**	**FACTOR1**	**FACTOR2**	**Communalities**
X1	−0.26	0.79	0.69	−0.16	0.82	0.69
X2	0.05	0.84	0.78	0.16	0.82	0.78
X3	−0.92	0.30	0.94	−0.87	0.42	0.94
X4	0.95	0.20	0.94	0.97	0.09	0.94
X5	0.93	0.25	0.93	0.96	0.13	0.93

Variance explained by each factor		Variance explained by each factor	
FACTOR1	**FACTOR2**	**FACTOR1**	**FACTOR2**
2.68	1.54	2.66	1.56

Standardized Scoring Coefficients		
	FACTOR1	**FACTOR2**
X1	−0.04508	0.30071
X2	0.01872	0.27600
X3	−0.16960	0.82512
X4	0.48129	0.51197
X5	0.36845	0.23793

[a] Difference represents the difference in eigenvalues between that factor and the subsequent factor.

[b] Proportion denotes the amount of variance explained by the factor relative to the total variance.

[c] Cumulative indicates the total proportion of variance explained by all the factors. For example, the first two factors explain a total of 98.61 percent of all the variations in the original variables.

represent these factors. In practical terms, this assumption means that the list of variables should be complete; that is, each factor among them is measured at least once and, hopefully, several times from several different perspectives. If for some reason the variables list is deficient from the beginning, it will take a large dose of luck to emerge with anything very useful.

Limitations of Factor Analysis. The greatest limitation of factor analysis is that it is a highly subjective process. The determination of the number of factors, their interpretation, and the rotation to select (if one set of factors displeases the analyst, rotation may be continued indefinitely) all involve subjective judgment.

A related limitation is that no statistical tests are regularly employed in factor anlysis.[4] As a result, it is often difficult to know if the results are merely accidental or really reflect something meaningful. Consequently, a standard procedure of factor analysis should be to divide the sample randomly into two or more groups and independently run a factor analysis of each group. If the same factors emerge in each analysis, then one may be more confident that the results do not represent a statistical accident.

CLUSTER ANALYSIS

All scientific fields have the need to cluster or group similar objects. Botanists group plants, historians group events, and chemists group elements and phenomena. It should be no surprise that when marketing managers attempt to become more scientific they should need procedures for grouping objects. Actually, the practical applications in marketing for **cluster analysis** are far too numerous to describe; however, it is possible to suggest by example the scope of this basic technique. **Cluster analysis** is a technique for grouping individuals or objects into unknown groups. It differs from discriminant analysis because the number and characteristics of the groups derived from the data in cluster analysis usually are not known prior to the analysis.

One goal of marketing managers is to identify similar consumer segments so that marketing programs can be developed and tailored to each segment. Thus, it is useful to cluster customers. We might cluster them on the basis of the product benefits they seek. Thus, students could be grouped on the basis of the benefits they seek from a college. We might group customers by their life-styles. The result could be one group that likes outdoor activities, another that enjoys entertainment, and a third that likes cooking and gardening. Each segment may have distinct product needs and may respond differently to advertising approaches.

We might want to cluster brands or products to determine which brands are regarded as similar and therefore competitive. Brands or products also might be grouped with respect to usage. If two brands or products are found to be bought by the same group of people, a tie-in promotion might be possible. If a test-market experiment is planned, it might be useful to identify similar cities so that different marketing programs could be compared by trying them out in different cities. To identify similar cities, we might cluster them on the basis of variables that could contaminate the test, such as size or ethnic composition. In marketing-media decisions, it often is helpful to know which media appeal to similar audiences and which appeal to different audiences.

In general, while employing any cluster analytic procedure, the user should be cautious about the following:[5]

▶ Most cluster-analysis methods are relatively simple procedures that usually are not supported by an extensive body of statistical reasoning.

▶ Cluster-analysis methods have evolved from many disciplines, and the inbred biases of these disciplines can differ dramatically.

▶ Different clustering methods can and do generate different solutions to the same data set.

▶ The strategy of cluster analysis is structure-seeking, although its operation is structure-imposing.

As with other techniques, the first step in performing cluster analysis is defining the problem. After defining the problem, a researcher should decide on the appropriate similarity measure. Next, decisions on how to group the objects are made. Later, the number of clusters must be decided. When groups, or clusters, are formed, the researcher should then attempt to interpret, describe, and validate them for managerial relevance.

Problem Definition

Let us consider the bank example once again. Assume we are interested in grouping individuals based on their similarity of responses to questions x_1 through x_5:

Measures of Similarity

In order to group objects together, some kind of similarity or dissimilarity measure is needed. Similar objects are grouped together and those farther apart are put in separate clusters. The commonly used measures for cluster analysis are (1) distance measures, and (2) correlation coefficients, and (3) association coefficients.

The most popular distance measure is the euclidean distance. The formula for squared euclidean distance is

$$d^2_{ij} = \sum_{m=1}^{P} (X_{im} - X_{jm})^2$$

where X_{im} and X_{jm} represent the standardized (to mean zero and unit standard deviation) values of the mth attribute for objects i and j and d_{ij}, the euclidean distance.

Inasmuch as the variables in a data matrix often are measured in different units, the formula above usually is applied *after* each variable has been standardized to zero mean and unit standard deviation. Standardization can remove the influence of the unit of measurement; however, it can also reduce the differences between groups on variables that may best discriminate clusters. Observations with extreme values (outliers) should be removed. A major drawback of the distance measures is that variables with both large size-differences and standard deviations can essentially swamp the effects of other variables with smaller absolute sizes and standard deviations.

Correlation coefficients (see Chapter 18) can also be computed between the five variables and input into cluster analysis. A major problem with the use of correlation coefficients is their sensitivity to the pattern of ups and downs across the variables at the expense of the magnitude of differences between the variables.

Association coefficients are used to establish similarity between objects when binary (1–0) variables are used. Suppose we want to create association coefficients between two brands (A and B) based on the presence or absence of eight attributes for each brand.

	A1	A2	A3	A4	A5	A6	A7	A8
Brand A	1	1	0	1	1	0	1	1
Brand B	1	0	0	0	1	1	1	0

One measure of a simple matching/association coefficient, s, is given by

$$s = \frac{(a + d)}{(a + b + c + d)}$$

where

a = number of attributes possessed by Brands A and B
b = number of attributes possessed by Brand A but not by Brand B
c = number of attributes possessed by Brand B but not by Brand A, and
d = number of attributes not possessed by both the brands

In this illustration,

$$s = \frac{(3 + 1)}{(3 + 3 + 1 + 1)} = \frac{4}{8} = 0.5$$

This measure has received little attention in our literature so far because of its exclusion in many software packages.

Clustering Approach

There are two approaches to clustering, a hierarchical approach and a nonhierarchical approach. **Hierarchical clustering** can start with all objects in one cluster and divide and subdivide them until all objects are in their own single-object cluster. This is called the "top-down," or decision, approach. The "bottom-up," or agglomerative, approach, in contrast, can start with each object in its own (single-object) cluster and systematically combine clusters until all objects are in one cluster. When an object is associated with another in a cluster, it remains clustered with that object.

A **nonhierarchical clustering** program will differ only in that it will permit objects to leave one cluster and join another as clusters are being formed, if the clustering criterion will be improved by doing so. In this approach, a cluster center initially is selected, and all objects within a prespecified threshold distance are included in that cluster. If a three-cluster solution is desired, three cluster centers are specified. These cluster centers can be random numbers or the cluster centers obtained from the hierarchical approach.

Each approach has advantages. Hierarchical clustering emerges as relatively easy to read and interpret. The output has the logical structure that theoretically always should exist. Its disadvantage is that it is relatively unstable and unreliable. The first combination or separation of objects, which may be based on a small difference in the criterion, will constrain the rest of the analysis. In doing hierarchical clustering, it is sound practice to split the sample into at least two groups and do two independent clustering runs to see if similar clusters emerge in both runs. If they are entirely different, there is an obvious cause for caution.

The advantage of nonhierarchical clustering is that it tends to be more reliable; that is, split-sample runs will tend to look more similar than those of hierarchical clustering. If the program makes a close decision early in the analysis that subsequently proves wrong with respect to the clustering criterion, it can be remedied by moving objects from cluster to cluster. The major disadvantage is that the series of clusters is usually a mess and very difficult to interpret. The fact that it does look messy is sometimes good in that the analysis does not convey a false sense of order when none exists. But the fact remains, it can be very difficult to work with. Further, we have to choose the number of clusters a priori, which could be a difficult task.

Actually, both approaches can be used in sequence. First, a hierarchical approach can be used to identify the number of clusters and any outliers, and to obtain cluster centers. The outliers (if any) are removed and a nonhierarchical approach is used with the input on the number of clusters and the cluster centers obtained from the hierarchical approach. The merits of both approaches are combined, and hence the results should be better.

Hierarchical Clustering. There are several methods to group objects into clusters under both the hierarchical and the nonhierarchical approach. In the **hierarchical** approach, the commonly used methods are single linkage, complete linkage, average linkage, Ward's method and the centroid method. Figure 20-4 illustrates the different methods of hierarchical clustering.

Single Linkage. The **single linkage** procedure is based on the shortest distance. It finds the two individuals (objects) separated by the shortest distance and places them in the first cluster. Then the next shortest distance is found, and either a third individual joins the first two to form a cluster or a new two-individual cluster is formed. The process continues until all individuals are in one cluster. This procedure is also referred to as the **nearest-neighbor** approach.

Complete Linkage. The **complete linkage** procedure is similar to single linkage except that the clustering criterion is based on the longest distance. For this reason, it is sometimes referred to as the **furthest-neighbor** approach. The distance between two clusters is the longest distance from a point in the first cluster to a point in the second cluster.

Average Linkage. The **average linkage** method starts out the same as single linkage and complete linkage, but the clustering criterion is the average distance from individuals in one cluster to individuals in another. Such techniques do not use extreme values, as do single linkage or complete linkage, and partitioning is based on all members of the clusters rather than on a single pair of extreme members.

Ward's Method. **Ward's method** is based on the loss of information resulting from grouping objects into clusters, as measured by the total sum of squared deviations of every object from the mean of the cluster to which the object is assigned. As more clusters are formed, the total sum of squared deviations (known as the error sum of squares) increases. At each stage in the clustering procedure, the error sums of squares is minimized over all partitions (the

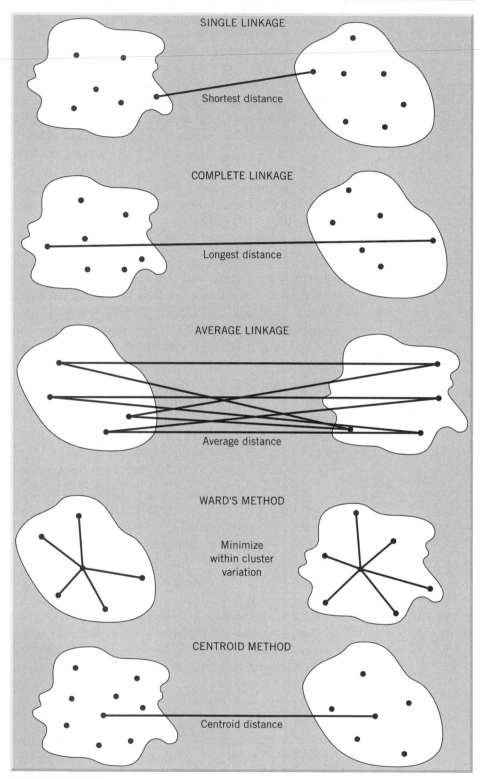

FIGURE 20-4
Hierarchical clustering methods

complete set of disjoint or separate clusters) obtainable by combining two clusters from the previous stage. This procedure tends to combine clusters with a small number of observations. It is also biased toward producing clusters with approximately the same number of observations.

Centroid Method. In the centroid method the distance between the group centroids (the centroid is the point whose coordinates are the means of all the observations in the cluster). If a cluster has one observation , then the centroid is the observation itself. The process continues by combining groups according to the distance between their centroids, the groups with the shortest distance being combined first.

An Example. Table 20-3 shows the results of using Ward's hierarchical clustering method on the bank data. Fifteen individuals are clustered hierarchically and the results show what objects are grouped together at each step. The error sums of squares (clustering criteria) associated at each step is also given. An elegant hierarchical arrangement of clusters known as the dendrogram is shown in Figure 20-5.

Interpretation of Table 20-3. The objective of the analysis in Table 3 is to identify clusters among the 15 objects. To start with there are 15 clusters. As shown in the table, objects 1 and 8 are combined first to produce a cluster, since those two objects are the closest to each other among other pairs of objects. However, objects 6 and 10 are also close (in fact the same distance as objects

TABLE 20-3
Hierarchical Cluster Analysis

Number of Clusters	Clusters Joined		Frequency of New Cluster	Error Sums of Squares	Tie
14	OB1	OB8	2	0.002	T
13	OB6	OB10	2	0.002	
12	CL14	OB15	3	0.003	
11	OB5	OB12	2	0.004	T
10	OB11	OB14	2	0.004	
9	OB2	OB13	2	0.006	
8	OB3	CL10	3	0.008	
7	OB4	OB9	2	0.008	
6	CL13	OB7	3	0.018	
5	CL9	CL7	4	0.038	
4	CL12	CL11	5	0.042	
3	CL5	CL6	7	0.105	
2	CL4	CL8	8	0.297	
1	CL2	CL3	15	0.463	

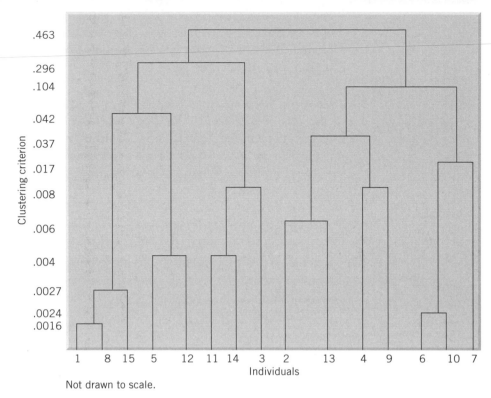

Not drawn to scale.

FIGURE 20-5
A dendrogram for hierarchical clustering of bank data

1 and 8) and they form another cluster. Now only 13 clusters are left, with no significant loss of information. As the process of forming clusters evolves, the error sums of squares (ESS) increases. A substantial increase in ESS is observed when we try to go from a four-cluster solution to a three-cluster solution, and a big increase in ESS when a two-cluster solution is obtained.* Therefore, an analyst would probably decide to stop with either a four-cluster or a three-cluster solution. As discussed earlier, the bias of Ward's method to produce equal-size clusters can be seen clearly in the two-cluster solution (with sizes of 8 and 7, respectively).

Nonhierarchical Clustering. In **nonhierarchical** methods (also known as **iterative partitioning**), the three most commonly used approaches are the sequential threshold, parallel threshold, and optimizing procedures.

Sequential Threshold. In this case a cluster center is selected and all objects within a prespecified threshold value are grouped. Then a new cluster center is selected and the process is repeated for the unclustered objects, and so on. Once objects enter a cluster, they are removed from further processing.

---

* See also Figure 20-6.

Parallel Threshold. This method is similar to the preceding one except that several cluster centers are selected simultaneously, and objects within the threshold level are assigned to the nearest center; the threshold levels can then be adjusted to admit fewer or more objects to the cluster.

Optimizing. This method modifies the previous two procedures in that objects can later be reassigned to clusters by optimizing some overall criterion measure, such as the average within-cluster distance for a given number of clusters.

An Example. The results of the nonhierarchical clustering for the bank data are shown in Table 20-4. The number of clusters are specified to be three, and the initial cluster seeds for the three clusters in the original variable space are selected. Through iterative partitioning, the objects are reassigned to different clusters until no individual moves from one cluster to the other. The cluster listing indicates which individual belongs to what cluster.

Interpretation of Table 20-4. As shown in Table 20-4, a three-cluster solution is sought. The initial cluster centers, or seeds, are given for the three clusters on the five variables. These initial cluster centers may be random numbers or may be obtained from the hierarchical approach for a three-cluster solution. The distance of an object from each of the three cluster centers is compared and the object is assigned to the closest cluster. Each object is thus assigned to one of the three clusters. After all the objects have been assigned, the cluster seeds are recomputed. Then the assignment process begins all over again. In this example, there are four iterations used to converge on a solution.

The cluster listing identifies the cluster members and their distances from the cluster seeds. Descriptive information such as cluster means and standard deviations is provided.

Number of Clusters

A central question in cluster analysis is how to determine the appropriate number of clusters. There are several possible approaches. First, the analyst can specify in advance the number of clusters. Perhaps, for theoretical and logical reasons, the number of clusters is known. Or the analyst may have practical reasons for specifying the number of clusters, based on the planned use of the clusters. Second, the analyst can specify the level of clustering with respect to the clustering criterion. If the clustering criterion is easily interpretable, such as the average within-cluster similarity, it might be reasonable to establish a certain level that would dictate the number of clusters.

A third approach is to determine the number of clusters from the pattern of clusters the program generates. The distances between clusters at successive steps may serve as a useful guideline, and the analyst may choose to stop when the distance exceeds a specified value or when the successive distances between steps make a sudden jump. These distances are sometimes referred to as **error variability** measures. Figure 20-6 shows the plot of error sums of squares with the number of clusters, using the Ward's method. Based on the large jump from four to three clusters, one would probably choose four clusters. However,

TABLE 20-4
Nonhierarchical Cluster Analysis

Nonhierarchical Procedure

Replace = FULL   Radius = 0   Maxclusters = 3   Maxiter = 6   Converge = 0.02

Cluster	X1	X2	X3	X4	X5
1	6.00	9.00	7.00	3.00	5.00
2	2.00	2.00	0.00	9.00	9.00
3	0.00	0.00	5.00	0.00	0.00

Minimum Distance Between Seeds = 12.4499
Change in Cluster Seeds

Iteration	1	2	3
1	1.960	3.921	1.795
2	0.867	1.138	0
3	0.925	0.909	0
4	0	0	0

Cluster Listing

Obs	Cluster	Distance from Seed
1	1	2.82
2	2	0.99
3	3	1.79
4	2	5.38
5	1	2.30
6	2	4.54
7	1	4.96
8	1	1.91
9	2	3.16
10	2	3.69
11	3	1.10
12	1	3.05
13	2	2.99
14	3	1.69
15	1	3.21

Cluster Summary

Cluster	Frequency	RMS Std Deviation	Maximum Distance from Seed to Observation	Nearest Cluster	Centroid Distance
1	6	1.5642	4.9638	2	9.1591
2	6	1.8239	5.3826	1	9.1591
3	3	0.8563	1.7951	1	9.3853

TABLE 20-4 (*continued*)

Cluster Means					
Cluster	X1	X2	X3	X4	X5
1	7.00	7.00	7.83	2.50	3.16
2	3.50	5.83	2.00	6.50	7.66
3	1.00	1.00	6.00	0.33	0.33

Cluster Standard Deviations					
Cluster	X1	X2	X3	X4	X5
1	2.00	1.67	1.16	0.55	1.94
2	1.51	2.40	2.09	1.87	0.81
3	1.00	1.00	1.00	0.57	0.57

Distance Between Cluster Means			
Cluster	1	2	3
1	.	9.1591	9.3853
2	9.1591	.	11.7225
3	9.3853	11.7225	.

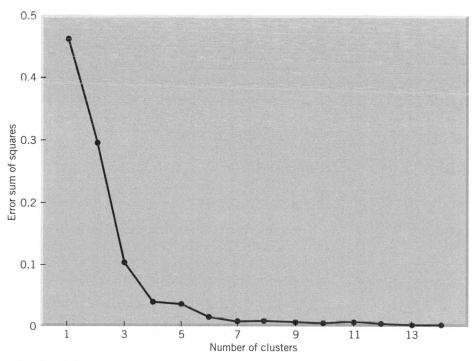

FIGURE 20-6
Plot of error sums of squares

based on the relative increase in error sums of squares, a three-cluster solution also appears possible.

Fourth, the ratio of total within-group variance to between-group variance can be plotted against the number of clusters. The point at which an elbow or a sharp bend occurs indicates an appropriate number of clusters. Increasing the number of clusters beyond this point probably is not useful, and decreasing the number can result in combining apples and oranges.

Whatever approach is used, usually it is useful to look at the total cluster pattern, such as those illustrated in Figures 20-5 and 20-6. It can provide a feel for the quality of the clustering and for the number of clusters that emerge at various levels of the clustering criterion. Usually more than one clustering level is relevant, and in the bank example it is clearly evident that three or four clusters are possible. Although cluster analysis can be used for identifying segments, a density estimation procedure may be a worthwhile alternative.[6]

Evaluating and Profiling the Clusters

Once clusters are developed, the analyst still faces the task of describing them. One frequently used measure is the **centroid**—the average value of the objects in the cluster on each of the variables making up each object's profile. If the data are interval scaled and clustering is performed in the original variables space, this measure appears quite natural as a summary description. Table 20-4 provides the cluster means and standard deviation on the original five variables for a three-cluster solution. The mean scores should help to describe/ profile the clusters.

If the data were standardized or if the cluster analysis was performed using factor analysis components (component factors), the analyst would have to go back to the raw scores for the original variables and compute average profiles using these data.

Often, it is helpful to profile the clusters in terms of variables that were not used for clustering.[7] These may include demographic, psychographic, product usage, media usage, and other variables. For example, the clusters may have been based on benefits sought. Further profiling may be done in terms of demographic and psychographic variables, to target marketing efforts for each cluster. The variables that significantly differentiate between clusters can be identified via discriminant analysis and one-way analysis of variance.

Statistical Inference

Despite attempts to construct various tests of the statistical reliability of clusters, no fully defensible procedures currently are available. The lack of appropriate tests stems from the difficulty of specifying realistic null hypotheses.

Despite the formidable problems associated with statistical inference in cluster analysis, analysts might try a few ad hoc procedures to provide rough checks on the clustering results. For example, they might apply two or more different clustering routines to the same data and compare results across algorithms. Or they may wish to split the data randomly into halves, perform separate clustering, and then examine the average profile values of each cluster across subsamples. Alternatively, analysts may delete various columns (variables) in the original profile data, compute dissimilarity measures across the remaining columns, and compare these results with the clusters found by using the full set of columns (variables).

Perform cluster analysis on the same data using different distance measures; then compare the results across measures to determine the stability of the solutions. We recommend the use of different methods of clustering and comparison of the results. Split the data randomly into halves; perform clustering separately on each half; compare cluster centroids across the two subsamples.

We also recommend another approach to validation. Use simulation procedures that employ random number generators to create a data set with the properties matching the overall properties of the original data but containing no clusters. Use the same clustering methods on both the real and the artificial data, and compare the resulting solutions.

Finally, when you use cluster analysis in a research study, the study should provide

▶ An unambiguous description of the clustering method.

▶ The similarity measure used in the study.

▶ The computer program used.

▶ The procedure used to determine the number of clusters.

▶ Adequate evidence of the validity of cluster analysis solution.

Summary of Cluster Analysis

Application. Cluster analysis is used to group variables, objects, or people. For example, people can be grouped into segments.

Input. The input is any valid measure of similarity between objects, such as correlations. It also is possible to input the number of clusters or the level of clustering.

Output. The output is a grouping of objects into clusters. Groupings are provided, such as those shown in Figure 20-5. Associated with each set of clusters will be the value of the clustering criterion. Some programs also output diagnostic information associated with each object. For example, they may provide the distance from each object to the center of its cluster and to the center of the next closest cluster. This information can help determine in more depth the cluster cohesion and the level of association between an object and a cluster.

Key Assumptions. The most important assumption is that the basic measure of similarity on which the clustering is based is a valid measure of the similarity between the objects. A second major assumption is that there is theoretical justification for structuring the objects into clusters. As with other multivariate techniques, there should be theory and logic guiding and underlying cluster analysis.

Limitations. Usually, it is difficult to evaluate the quality of the clustering. There are no standard statistical tests to ensure that the output is not purely random. The value of the criterion measure, the reasonableness of the output, the appearance of a natural hierarchy (when a nonhierarchical method is used), and the split-sample reliability tests all provide useful information. However, it is still difficult to know exactly which clusters are very similar and which objects are difficult to assign. Usually, it is difficult to select a clustering criterion and program on any basis other than availability.

Questions and Problems

1. How is a factor loading interpreted?
2. What is communality? What is the implication of low communality for a few of the variables?
3. How does principal components analysis differ from varimax rotation?
4. Why are factors rotated?
5. Identify a situation where you would expect the first factor to have high loadings on all variables and to account for almost all the variance.
6. Suppose five variables were factor analyzed and the percentage of variance explained was 80 percent, 12 percent, 5 percent, 2 percent, and 1 percent. How many factors would you include? What if the first three factors were interpretable and relevant?
7. Suppose you are conducting a large, 2000-respondent study for a bank. Among other elements the study includes:
    a. A 28-item image rating for three commercial banks, two savings and loans banks, and an "ideal" financial institution.
    b. A 75-item life-style question set.
    c. A 30-item set of questions to determine whether the respondents are opinion leaders, sources of product information, and so on.
    d. A 40-item set of questions on the importance of bank services.
    e. A set of questions on usage of 35 bank services.
    Specifically, how would factor analysis be employed in this study?
8. What labels would you attach to the varimax rotated factors in Table 20-1? Do you believe the varimax rotations are more valid than the principal components factors? More interesting?
9. Interpret and address factor loadings, factor scores, and factor score coefficients in Table 20-2.
10. Suppose similarity ratings for beer were cluster analyzed and three distinct clusters were found. How might those clusters differ? On what dimensions? On what characteristics?
11. When might hierarchical clustering be preferred over nonhierarchical clustering?
12. Respondents in a study were asked to indicate their activities (such as playing tennis, attending plays, attending dinner parties, etc.) on a 7-point

scale (from 1 = never to 7 = frequently). A correlation between respondents was obtained. Cluster analyze these respondents.

	1	2	3	4	5	6	7	8	9	10	11	12
1.	—	.32	−.10	−.10	−.30	.01	.50	−.12	−.40	.22	−.07	.32
2.		—	.02	.02	−.45	.12	.82	.05	−.10	.32	−.15	.15
3.			—	−.60	.16	.35	.50	.87	.01	−.15	.44	.20
4.				—	.34	.71	.35	.42	−.10	.19	.49	.26
5.					—	.40	−.01	−.12	.51	.49	−.11	.35
6.						—	.08	.26	.11	.09	−.46	−.01
7.							—	−.17	.20	.03	.07	.16
8.								—	.09	.33	.32	.32
9.									—	.16	.01	−.12
10.										—	.03	.11
11.											—	.40
12.												—

End Notes

1. Actually, the factor loadings will be correlations only when (1) the input variables are standardized [each variable has its mean subtracted and is divided by its standard deviation $(X - \overline{X})/\sigma_r$], and (2) the factors are perpendicular or independent (an explanatory comment appears in endnote 4), two conditions that normally are present. As previously noted, most factor analysis programs begin by calculating a correlation matrix, a process that standardizes the variables. If either condition is not present, the factor loadings, although not correlations, still can be interpreted as indicators of the association between the variables and the factors. Further, a matrix of variable-factor correlations, termed a factor structure matrix, is provided as an output of the factor analysis program. When the variables are standardized, the factor coefficients become "beta coefficients" in the regression context. Unlike regression analysis, where the independent variables usually are correlated, the factors are independent. That is why a factor loading is here a correlation, whereas a beta coefficient in the regression context is not a correlation.

2. The percentage of variance explained is proportional to the sum of squared loadings associated with that factor. Thus, a factor's percent of explained variance depends in part on the number of variables on which the factor has high loadings. A variable's communality actually is equal to the sum of the squared factor loadings on that variable.

3. Factor analysis could be conducted on a correlation matrix between people or objects instead of a between-variable correlation matrix. The resulting factors would then represent groups of people instead of groups of variables. This approach is called Q-factor analysis. The more common focus on relationships between variables is termed R-factor analysis.

4. David W. Stewart. "The Application and Misapplication of Factor Analysis in Marketing Research," Journal of Marketing Research, 18, February 1981, 51–62.

5. Mark S. Aldenderfer and Roger K. Blashfield. Cluster Analysis (Sage Publications), 1984.

6. V. Kumar and R. Rust. "Market Segmentation by Visual Inspection," Journal of Advertising Research, 29(4), August/September 1989, 23–29.

7. Girish Punj and David W. Stewart. "Cluster Analysis in Marketing Research: Review and Suggestions for Application," Journal of Marketing Research, 20, May 1983, 134–148.

Table 1 shows the output of a factor analysis conducted on the ratings of 82 respondents who were asked to evaluate a particular discount store using 29 semantic-differential, seven-point scales. The same respondents were asked to evaluate a supermarket. A second factor analysis was conducted on the supermarket data, and the results are shown in Table 2.

Questions for Discussion

1. Label the factors. Compare these factors with those found in the discount store analysis of Table 1. Why should they be different? *Hint:* It isn't because a discount store is different from a supermarket.

2. Analyze the communalities. Which are low? What are the implications? Contrast with Table 1.

TABLE 1
Factor Loadings for a Discount Store (Varimax Rotation)

Scale	I	II	Factor III	IV	V	Communality
1. Good service	.79	−.15	.06	.12	.07	.67
2. Helpful salespersons	.75	−.03	.04	.13	.31	.68
3. Friendly personnel	.74	−.07	.17	.09	−.14	.61
4. Clean	.59	−.31	.34	.15	−.25	.65
5. Pleasant store to shop in	.58	−.15	.48	.26	.10	.67
6. Easy to return purchases	.56	−.23	.13	−.03	−.03	.39
7. Too many clerks	.53	−.00	.02	.23	.37	.47
8. Attracts upper-class customers	.46	−.06	.25	−.00	.17	.31
9. Convenient location	.36	−.30	−.02	−.19	.03	.26
10. High quality products	.34	−.27	.31	.12	.25	.36
11. Good buys on products	.02	−.88	.09	.10	.03	.79
12. Low prices	−.03	−.74	.14	.00	.13	.59
13. Good specials	.35	−.67	−.05	.10	.14	.60
14. Good sales on products	.30	−.67	.01	−.08	.16	.57
15. Reasonable value for price	.17	−.52	.11	−.02	−.03	.36
16. Good store	.41	−.47	.47	.12	.11	.63
17. Low pressure salespersons	−.20	−.30	−.28	−.03	−.05	.18
18. Bright store	−.02	−.10	.75	.26	−.05	.61
19. Attractive store	.19	.03	.67	.34	.24	.66
20. Good displays	.33	−.15	.61	.15	−.20	.57
21. Unlimited selections of products	.09	.00	.29	−.03	.00	.09
22. Spacious shopping	.00	.20	.00	.70	.10	.54
23. Easy to find items you want	.36	−.16	.10	.57	.01	.49
24. Well-organized layout	−.02	−.05	.25	.54	−.17	.39
25. Well-spaced merchandise	.20	.15	.27	.52	.16	.43
26. Neat	.38	−.12	.45	.49	−.34	.72

[1] Based on the study by John Dickson and Gerald Albaum. "A Method for Development of Tailormade Semantic Differentials for Specific Marketing Content Areas," *Journal of Marketing Research*, 8 (February 1977), 87–91.

TABLE 1 (*continued*)

Scale	I	II	Factor III	IV	V	Communality
27. Big store	−.20	.15	.06	.07	−.65	.49
28. Ads frequently seen by you	.03	−.20	.07	.09	.42	.23
29. Fast checkout	.30	−.16	.00	.25	−.33	.28
Percentage of variance explained	16	12	9	8	5	
Cumulative variance explained	16	28	37	45	50	
Possible Factor Interpretations:						
Factor I Good service—friendly			Factor IV Spaciousness			
Factor II Price level			Factor V Size			
Factor III Attractiveness						

TABLE 2
Factor Loadings for a Supermarket (Varimax Rotation)

Scale	I	II	Factors III	IV	V	Communality
1. Well-spaced merchandise	.73	.10	−.11	.02	.12	.57
2. Bright store	.63	−.08	.45	−.11	.06	.62
3. Ads frequently seen by you	−.04	.08	−.02	−.12	.58	.36
4. High-quality products	.50	.32	.24	.01	−.03	.41
5. Well-organized layout	.70	.08	.05	−.00	.12	.51
6. Low prices	−.09	.64	−.02	.19	.18	.49
7. Good sales on products	.27	.73	−.00	−.10	−.01	.62
8. Pleasant store to shop in	.63	.36	.09	.12	.01	.55
9. Good store	.73	.37	.26	.19	−.06	.78
10. Convenient location	.18	.01	.59	−.10	.36	.52
11. Low pressure salespersons	−.15	.05	.40	−.06	−.11	.20
12. Big store	.08	−.02	.42	−.00	.14	.20
13. Good buys on products	.35	.73	.04	.18	−.10	.70
14. Attractive store	.68	.28	.38	.10	−.10	.70
15. Helpful salespersons	.43	.16	.34	.34	.45	.64
16. Good service	.60	.19	.21	.35	.01	.56
17. Too many clerks	−.06	.03	−.01	.62	−.08	.40
18. Friendly personnel	.48	.11	.17	.47	.36	.62
19. Easy to return purchases	.39	.10	.01	−.10	.43	.36
20. Unlimited selection of products	.10	.09	.48	.17	−.18	.31
21. Reasonable prices for value	.24	.71	.04	.01	.13	.58
22. Neat	.87	−.00	.11	.07	.04	.78
23. Spacious shopping	.72	.02	−.26	−.01	.18	.62
24. Attract upper-class customers	.38	−.37	−.17	−.06	.06	.32

TABLE 2 *(continued)*

Scale	I	II	Factors III	IV	V	Communality
25. Clean	.83	.11	.16	.12	.03	.74
26. Fast checkout	.22	.12	−.07	.68	−.13	.55
27. Good displays	.73	.19	.07	.14	.13	.61
28. Easy to find items you want	.57	.23	−.08	.03	−.01	.39
29. Good specials	.37	.62	.08	.06	.32	.63
Percentage of variance explained	26	11	6	5	5	
Cumulative variance explained	26	37	43	48	53	

CASE 20-2
Behavioral Research[2]

A considerable amount of the nation's resources are spent handling and replacing discarded products. Thus, it would be useful to modify consumer's behavior, encouraging product maintenance and repair and discouraging style-oriented replacement decisions.

Before addressing the task of modifying current consumer behavior regarding product disposal decisions, it seemed appropriate to researchers at Behavioral Research to conduct a study determining current behavioral patterns. They therefore proposed and received government funding for a study with an ultimate objective to use segmentation procedures to identify and describe the type of person who has "throwaway" tendencies and to contrast this consumer type with others who have different tendencies.

Description of the Research

In-home interviews were conducted with 311 residents of the city of Santa Monica, California. To be an eligible respondent, some member of their household had to have disposed of one of a selected list of 12 small electric appliances during the past year. The product list included appliances characterized by rapid technological innovation (e.g., toaster ovens), those for which style innovation is rapid (e.g., electric toothbrushes), and those considered "stable" (e.g., vacuum cleaners).

Respondents were asked how they disposed of the product. The following are the choices offered and the number of respondents in each category.

	Number of Respondents
Discarded the product	65
Stored the product	128
Sold, donated, or traded in the product	62
Gave the product to a friend	56
Total	311

Thus, a total of 65 of the 311 respondents discarded the product, whereas 246 of the respondents selected one of the alternate choices.

The research objective was to identify variables that would distinguish between individuals who chose different means of disposing of small electric appliances. Two sets of variables were included in the study. The first was a standard set of demographic variables including age, marital status, education, occupation, and family income. The second was a set of lifestyle or psychographic variables which were developed exclusively for this study. A total of 65 (5-point agree–disagree) statements were drawn from a review of the literature of consumers' opinions on matters such as product durability, the repair industry and the like and from statements made by participants in three focus groups conducted during the exploratory phase of the project. The lifestyle statements were thus all related to disposition behavior as opposed to being general lifestyle statements.

[2] Written by Marian Burke, W. David Conn, Richard J. Lutz, and David A. Aaker as a basis for class discussion.

TABLE 3
Factor Loadings of the Life-style Statements

	Factor 1
Products break down too soon these days.	.719
Products are built so cheaply today that they are meant to be thrown out rather than repaired.	.595
Today greater attention is devoted by manufacturers to performance standards and durability.	−.593
Products aren't built like they used to be.	.592
I am often disappointed with the durability of products I buy.	.541
Too many products are built in such a way that they can't be easily repaired.	.529
Today's products are vast improvements over products of the past.	−.461
TOTAL VARIANCE EXPLAINED	11.6%

	Factor 2
I like to have "the latest thing" in appliances.	.602
I like modern, stylish things.	.580
I sometimes replace a perfectly usable product with one that is more stylish.	.486
I sometimes replace a product even though it is still useful.	.473
Style changes in products are unimportant.	−.467
I am convenience oriented.	.400
TOTAL VARIANCE EXPLAINED.	9.5%

	Factor 3
I don't pay much attention to the use and care booklets that come with products.	.608
I read product labels and instruction booklets carefully.	−.596
I don't take care of products the way I should.	.459
I look for products with good warranties.	−.452
In general, I make wise purchase decisions.	−.409
TOTAL VARIANCE EXPLAINED	5.4%

	Factor 4
If a product costing less than $40 breaks down I'm likely to discard it without much hesitation.	.694
If a product costing less than $60 breaks down I'm likely to discard it without much hesitation.	.596
If a product costing less than $20 breaks down I'm likely to discard it without much hesitation.	.594
Once something on a product breaks, you might as well throw it away.	.491
I feel a responsibility to have a product repaired rather than replaced whenever feasible.	−.390
I often buy less expensive products so that I can throw them away without feeling guilty.	.370
It is often cheaper to buy a new product than to have an old one repaired.	.350
TOTAL VARIANCE EXPLAINED	4.8%

	Factor 5
It takes too long to have a product repaired.	.705
It is really hard to get a product repaired these days.	.613
Getting an item repaired is usually very inconvenient.	.514
The repair industry is a "rip-off."	.502
It is too expensive to get many smaller products repaired.	.430
You can't trust most repair shops.	.414
TOTAL VARIANCE EXPLAINED	3.6%

TABLE 3 *(continued)*

	Factor 6
I am a "pack rat."	.523
I often keep old appliances around the house rather than get rid of them.	.462
I often give away old products to relatives or friends.	.420
I like to fix things.	.400
I tend to keep old products until I move—then I throw or give them away.	.364
I always buy "new" rather than "used."	.350
TOTAL VARIANCE EXPLAINED	3.3%

	Factor 7
Consumers are more price conscious today than ten years ago.	.508
Labels on products should be more informative.	.459
Advertisements should be more informative.	.394
The repair industry should be regulated.	.349
TOTAL VARIANCE EXPLAINED	3.0%

A factor analysis was conducted on the 65 lifestyle variables. The results are shown in Table 3.

Questions for Discussion

1. Label and describe the factors.
2. Assume that a national probability sample was going to be obtained in a follow-up study. Identify two of three variables to represent each factor.
3. How many of these factors should be considered for subsequent analysis?
4. What analysis would you now recommend?
5. What set of variables do you feel will be more useful in identifying those who discard products: the demographic or the lifestyle variables?
6. Which of the factors will be the best predictors of disposal behavior? Which demographic variables? Be specific in your hypotheses.

21 MULTIDIMENSIONAL SCALING AND CONJOINT ANALYSIS

Learning Objectives

▶ Understand the concept and need for multidimensional scaling and conjoint analysis.

▶ Discuss the different types of input to create perceptual maps and partworth utilities.

▶ Explain the different types of procedures to create perceptual maps and compute the partworth utilities.

▶ Describe how to interpret the solution of MDS and conjoint analysis.

MULTIDIMENSIONAL SCALING

Multidimensional scaling (MDS) addresses the general problem of positioning objects in a perceptual space. Much of marketing management is concerned with the question of positioning. With whom do we compete? How are we compared to our competitors? On what dimensions? What positioning strategy should be followed? These and other questions are addressed by MDS.

Multidimensional scaling basically involves two problems. First, the dimensions on which customers perceive or evaluate objects (organizations, products, or brands), must be identified. For example, students must evaluate prospective colleges in terms of their quality, cost, distance from home, and size. It would be convenient to work with only two dimensions, since the objects could then be portrayed graphically. However, this is not always possible, because additional dimensions sometimes are needed to represent customers' perceptions and evaluations. Second, objects need to be positioned with respect to these dimensions. The output of MDS is the location of the objects on the dimensions, and is termed a **perceptual map.**

There are several approaches to multidimensional scaling. They differ in the assumptions they employ, the perspective they take, and the input data they use. Figure 21-1 categorizes the major approaches in terms of the input data and the methods used to produce perceptual maps. One set of approaches involves object attributes. If the objects were colleges, the attributes might be faculty, prestige, facilities, cost, and so on. MDS then combines these attributes into dimensions such as quality. Another set of approaches bypasses attributes and considers similarity or preference relationships between objects directly.

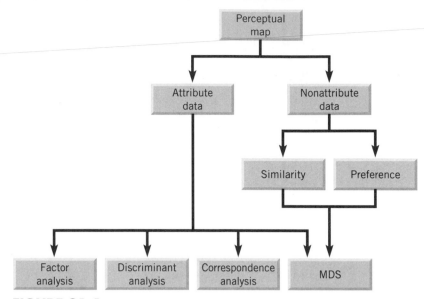

FIGURE 21-1
Approaches to create perceptual maps

Thus, two schools could be rated as to how similar they are or how much one is preferred over the other, without regard to any underlying attribute. This chapter will first describe the attribute-based approaches. An application of MDS based on the nonattribute-data will follow. Finally, it will discuss the ideal-object concept.

ATTRIBUTE-BASED APPROACHES

An important assumption of attribute-based approaches is that we can identify attributes on which individuals' perceptions of objects are based. Let us start with a simple example. Suppose that the goal is to develop a perceptual map of the nonalcoholic beverage market.[1] Suppose further that exploratory research has identified 14 beverages that seem relevant and nine attributes that are used by people to describe and evaluate these beverages. A group of respondents is asked to rate each of the beverages on the nine attributes, on a 7-point scale. An average rating of the respondent group on each of the nine attributes, termed profile analysis in Chapter 10, would be of interest. However, it would be much more useful if the nine attributes could be combined into two or three dimensions, or factors. Two approaches—**factor analysis** and **discriminant analysis**—usually are used to reduce the attributes to a small number of dimensions.

Factor Analysis

Since each respondent rates 14 beverages on nine attributes, he or she ultimately will have 14 factor scores on each of the emerging factors, one for each beverage. The position of each beverage in the perceptual space, then, will be the average factor score for that beverage. The perceptual map shown in Figure 21-2 illustrates this. Three factors, accounting for 77 percent of the variance, serve to summarize the nine attributes. Each beverage is then positioned on the attributes. Since three factors or dimensions are involved, two maps are required to portray the results. The first involves the first two factors, while the second includes the first and third. For convenience, the original attitudes also are shown on the maps as lines or vectors. The vectors are obtained based on the amount of correlation the original attitudes possess with the factor scores (represented as factors). The direction of the vectors indicates the factor with which each attribute is associated, and the length of the vector indicates the strength of association. Thus, on the left map the "filling" attribute has little association with any factor, whereas on the right map the "filling" attribute is strongly associated with the "refreshing" factor.

Discriminant Analysis

Whereas the goal of factor analysis is to generate dimensions that maximize interpretability and explain variance, the goal of discriminant analysis is to generate dimensions (termed **discriminant function** factors) that will discriminate or separate the objects as much as possible. As in factor analysis, each dimension is based on a combination of the underlying attributes. However, in **discriminant analysis,** the extent to which an attribute will tend to be an

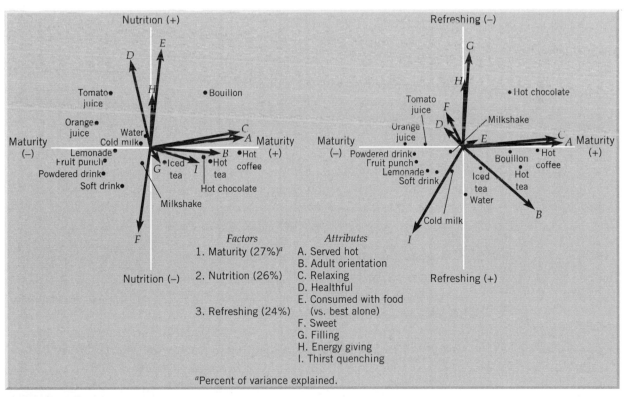

FIGURE 21-2
Perceptual maps of a beverage market

important contributor toward a dimension depends on the extent to which there is a perceived difference among the objects having that attribute.

Comparing Factor and Discriminant Analysis

Each of the approaches has advantages and disadvantages. **Discriminant analysis** identifies clusters of attributes on which objects differ. If all objects are perceived to be similar with respect to an attribute (such as an airline's safety), that attribute should not affect preference (such as the choice of an airline). Following that logic, the discriminant analysis objective of selecting attributes that discriminate between objects seems sensible. A second useful characteristic of discriminant analysis is that it provides a test of statistical significance. The null hypothesis is that two objects actually are perceived identically. The test will determine the probability that the between-object distance is due simply to a statistical accident. A third quality of discriminant analysis is that it will identify a perceptual dimension even if it is represented by a single attribute.

In contrast, **factor analysis** groups attributes that are similar. If there are not several attributes representing a dimension, it will tend not to emerge in the factor analysis solution. Factor analysis is based on both perceived differences between objects and differences between people's perceptions of objects. Thus, it tends to provide a richer solution, use more of the attributes, and result in more dimensions. All perceptual dimensions are included, whether they discriminate between objects or not. Hauser and Koppelman conducted a study of shopping centers in which they compared several approaches to multidimensional scaling.[2] They found that factor analysis dimensions provided more interpretive value than did those of discriminant analysis.

Introducing Importance Weights

Both factor analysis and discriminant analysis ignore the relative importance of particular attributes to customers. Myers and Tauber suggest that the attribute data be multiplied by importance weights and then be subjected to a factor analysis.[3] As a result, the attributes considered more important will have a greater tendency to be included in a factor analysis solution. Myers and Tauber presented a factor analysis perceptual map for snack food that included the dimensions of "convenience" and "nutrition." When that study was repeated, this time with importance weights introduced, a "child likes" dimension replaced the "convenience" dimension.

Correspondence Analysis

In both factor analysis and discriminant analysis, the variables are assumed to be intervally scaled, continuous variables. A 7-point Likert scale (agree–disagree) would usually be used. However, often it is convenient to collect binary or zero–one data. Respondents might be asked to identify from an attribute list which ones describe a brand. The result will be a row of zeros and ones for each respondent. Or the respondent could be asked to pick three (or k) attributes that are associated with a brand, or two (or k) use occasions that are most suitable for a brand. The result is again a row of zeros and ones for each respondent and each brand.

When the data consist of rows of zeros and ones reflecting the association of an attribute or other variable with a brand or other object, the appropriate MDS technique is termed **correspondence analysis.**[4] Correspondence analysis generates as an output a perceptual map in which the elements of attributes and brands are both positioned.

Binary judgments are used in several contexts. First, if the number of attributes and objects is large, the task of scaling each object on each attribute may be excessive and unrealistic. Simply checking which attributes (or use occasions) apply to a given object may be a more appropriate task. Second, it may be useful to ask respondents to list all the attributes they can think of for a certain brand or to list all the objects or brands that would apply to a certain use occasion. For example, what snacks would you consider for a party given to watch the Super Bowl? In that case, binary data would result, and correspondence analysis would be the appropriate technique.

Basic Concepts of MDS

MDS uses proximities among different objects as input. A proximity is a value that denotes how similar or different two objects are, or are perceived to be, or any measure of this type. MDS then uses these proximities data to produce a geometric configuration of points (objects), in a two-dimensional (preferably) space as output. Attribute-based data such as objects X attributes (profile matrix) and nonattribute-based data, including similarity and preference data, can be used to obtain proximities data. The euclidean distances (derived) between objects in the two-dimensional space are then computed and compared with the proximities data.

A key concept of MDS is that the derived distances (output) between the objects should correspond to the proximities (input). If we make the rank order of derived distances between objects/brands correspond to the rank order of the proximities data, the process is known as *nonmetric MDS.* On the contrary, if the derived distances are either multiple or linear functions of the proximities, then it is known as *metric MDS.* Nonmetric MDS assumes that the proximities data are ordinal but metric MDS assumes that they are metric. However, in both cases the output (derived distances) is metric.

Evaluating The MDS Solution

The fit between the derived distances and the proximities in each dimension is evaluated through a measure called *stress.* In MDS, the objects can be projected onto two, three, four or even higher dimensions. Since visual inspection is possible only with two, or possibly three, dimensions, we always prefer lower dimensions. Usually, the stress value increases when we decrease the number of dimensions. The appropriate number of dimensions required to locate the objects in space can be obtained by plotting the stress values against the number of dimensions. As with factor analysis (scree plot) and cluster analysis (error sums of squares plot), one chooses the appropriate number of dimensions, depending on where the sudden jump in stress starts to occur. Sometimes we directly seek a two-dimensional representation, since managers always prefer that because it is easier to interpret.

Determining the Number of Dimensions. Figure 21-3 plots the stress values against the number of dimensions. As you can see, higher dimensions are associated with lower stress values and vice versa. The plot indicates that probably two dimensions are acceptable, since there is a large increase in the stress values from two dimensions to one.

Labeling the Dimensions. To label the dimensions, one can correlate the object's attribute ratings with the dimension to determine which dimensions correlate highly with what attributes and, accordingly, name the dimensions. Multiple regression is used with dimensional coordinates as the criterion variables and the attribute ratings as the predictor variables. Table 21-1 is an example of naming the dimensions for a perceptual map of shopping locations.

The regression weights indicate that the first dimension be labeled "variety" because attributes such as variety of merchandise, "specials," store availability, and so forth, are associated with it. Similar interpretation for the second dimension yields the label "Quality vs. Price."

Interpreting the Dimensions. The perceptual map in Table 21-1 gives the location of the various shopping areas in Chicago. As you can see, the Chicago Loop location is the only one that offers a good value (quality/price) and variety. To the contrary, Korvette City offers low value and less variety. This location has a major opportunity to reposition, and can decide to move toward the origin by increasing both value and variety. It is evident that different shopping locations are perceived to be different from one another.

Once the dimensions are appropriately labeled, the locations of the objects/brands are evaluated and an appropriate strategy is implemented to

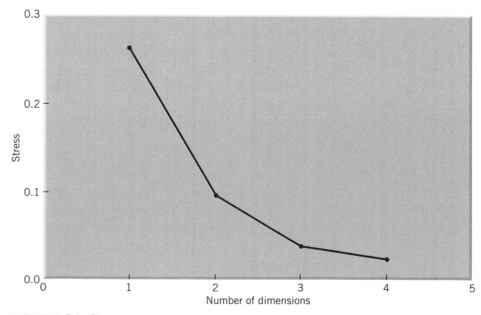

FIGURE 21-3
Plot of stress versus dimensionality

TABLE 21-1
Perceptual Map of Shopping Locations
(Hauser and Koppelman 1979)

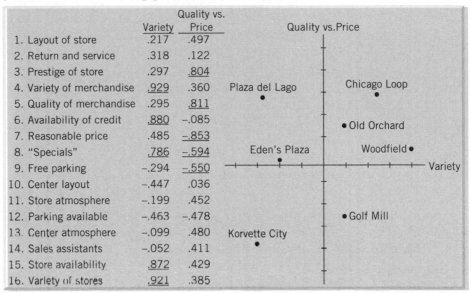

	Variety	Quality vs. Price
1. Layout of store	.217	.497
2. Return and service	.318	.122
3. Prestige of store	.297	.804
4. Variety of merchandise	.929	.360
5. Quality of merchandise	.295	.811
6. Availability of credit	.880	–.085
7. Reasonable price	.485	–.853
8. "Specials"	.786	–.594
9. Free parking	–.294	–.550
10. Center layout	–.447	.036
11. Store atmosphere	–.199	.452
12. Parking available	–.463	–.478
13. Center atmosphere	–.099	.480
14. Sales assistants	–.052	.411
15. Store availability	.872	.429
16. Variety of stores	.921	.385

either reposition (if necessary) or maintain that location in the eyes of the consumers.

MDS can also be used on attribute data to produce perceptual maps. When MDS is used on the attribute data, it is known as the **attribute-based MDS.** However, the attribute/profile data that usually are represented as an objects x attributes matrix (for example, see Table 20-1), are transformed to an object x object correlation/distance matrix (as in cluster analysis). For practical purposes, the transformed data appear similar to the similarity/dissimilarity data that could be collected directly from the respondents.

Attribute-based MDS has the advantage that attributes can have diagnostic and operational value and the dimensions can be interpreted in terms of their correlations with the attributes. Further, the Hauser and Koppelman study concluded that attribute data were easier for respondents to use and that dimensions based on attribute data predicted preference better than did dimensions based upon nonattribute data.[5]

However, attribute data also have several conceptual disadvantages. First, if the list of attributes is not accurate and complete, the study will suffer accordingly. Generating an attribute list can be difficult, especially when possible differences among people's perceptions are considered. Second, it may be that people simply do not perceive or evaluate objects in terms of underlying attributes. An object may be perceived or evaluated as a whole that is not decomposable in terms of attributes. Finally, attribute-based models may require more dimensions to represent them than would be needed by more flexible models, in part because of the linearity assumptions of factor analysis and discriminant analysis. These disadvantages lead us to use nonattribute data, namely, similarity and preference data.

Application of MDS with Nonattribute Data

Similarity Data. Similarity measures simply reflect the perceived similarity of two objects in the eyes of the respondents. For example, each respondent may be asked to rate the degree of similarity in each pair of objects. The respondent generally is not told what criteria to use to determine similarity; thus, the respondent does not have an attribute list that implicitly suggests criteria to be included or excluded. In the following example, the respondent judged Stanford to be quite similar to Harvard.

	Pair number 1	
	Stanford	Harvard

Extremely Similar						Extremely dissimilar
--	--	--	--	--	--	--
1	2	3	4	5	6	7

The number of pairs to be judged for degree of similarity can be as many as $n(n-1)/2$, where n is the total number of objects. With 10 brands, there could be 45 pairs of brands to judge (although fewer could be used).

Although at least seven or eight objects should be judged, the approach is easier to illustrate if only four objects are considered. First, the results of the pairwise similarity judgments are summarized in a matrix, as shown in Figure 21-4. The numbers in the matrix represent the average similarity judgments for a sample of 50 respondents. Instead of similarity ratings, the respondents could be asked simply to rank the pairs from most to least similar. An average rank-order position then would replace the average similarity rating matrix. It should be noted, however, that rank ordering can be difficult if 10 or more objects are involved.

A perceptual map could be obtained from the average similarity ratings; however, it is also possible to use only the ordinal or "nonmetric" portion of the data. Thus, the knowledge that objects *A* and *C* in Figure 21-4 have an average similarity of 1.7 is replaced by the fact that objects *A* and *C* are the most similar pair. Figure 21-4 shows the conversion to rank-order information.

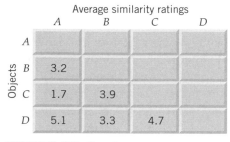
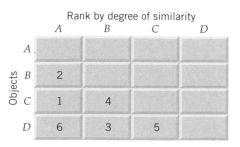

FIGURE 21-4
Similarity judgments

Ordinal or nonmetric information often is preferred, for several reasons. First, it actually contains about the same amount of information in that the output usually is not affected by replacing intervally scaled or "metric" data with ordinal or nonmetric data. Second, the nonmetric data often are thought to be more reliable.

Next, a computer program is employed to convert the rankings of similarity into distances in a map with a small number of dimensions, so that similar objects are close together and vice versa. The computer will be programmed to locate the four objects in a space of two, three, or more dimensions, so that the shortest distance is between pair (A, C), the next shortest between pair (A, B), and the longest pair between (A, D). One possible solution that satisfied these constraints in two dimensions is the following:

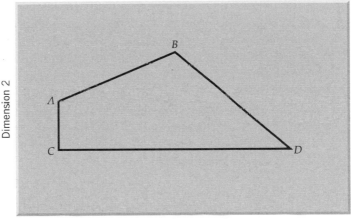

Dimension 1

The reader might be able to relocate the points differently and still satisfy the constraints so that the rankings of the distances in the map correspond to the rankings of the pairwise similarity judgments. This is because there are only a few points to move in the space and only six constraints to satisfy. With 10 objects and 45 constraints, the task of locating the points in a two-dimensional space is vastly more difficult, and requires a computer. Once a solution is found (the points are located in the space), it is unlikely that there will be a significantly different solution that still satisfies the constraints of the similarities matrix. Thus, we can argue that the intervally scaled nature of the distances between points really was hidden in the rank-order input data all the time.

The power of the technique lies in its ability to find the smallest number of dimensions for which there is a reasonably good fit between the input similarity rankings and the rankings of distance between objects in the resulting space. Usually, this means starting with two dimensions and, if this is not satisfactory, continuing to add dimensions until an acceptable fit is achieved. The determination of "acceptable" is a matter of judgment, although most analysts will trade off some degree of fit to stay with a two- or three-dimensional map, because of the enormous advantages of visual interpretations. There are situations where more dimensions are necessary. This happened in a study of nine different types of sauces (mustard, catsup, relish, steak sauce, dressing, and so on). Most respondents perceived too many differences to be captured with two or three dimensions, in terms of either the types of foods with which the sauces would be used or the physical characteristics of each sauce.[6]

A sample of 64 undergraduates provided similarity judgments for all 45 pairs of ten drinks including Coke, Diet Coke, 7-Up, Calistoga Natural Orange, and Slice. They were asked to rate the similarity of each pair such as Slice–Diet Coke, on a nine-point scale. The two-dimensional solution is shown in Figure 21-5. Note that Slice is considered closer to Diet 7-Up than to 7-Up, and Schweppes and Calistoga are separated even though they are very similar.

Interpreting the resulting dimension takes place "outside" the technique. Additional information must be introduced to decide why objects are located in their relative positions. Sometimes, the location of the objects themselves can suggest dimensional interpretations. For example, in Figure 21-2 the location of the objects suggests dimension interpretations even without the attribute information. Thus, the fruit punch versus hot coffee object locations on the horizontal axis suggest a maturity dimension. In Figure 21-5, the objects on the horizontal axis indicate a cola–noncola dimension. The vertical axis seems to represent a diet–nondiet dimension, because in both the cola group and the noncola group, the nondiet drinks tend to be higher than the diet drinks.

The concept of an ideal object in the space is an important one in MDS, because it allows the analyst to relate object positioning to customer likes and dislikes. It also provides a means for segmenting customers according to their preferences for product attributes.

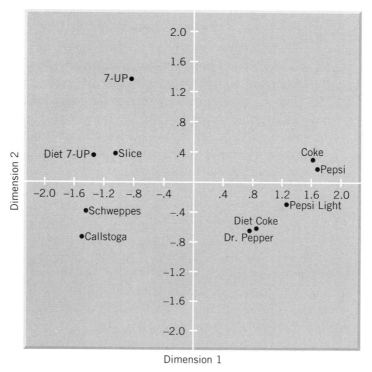

FIGURE 21-5
Perceptual map using similarity data

Preference Data. An **ideal object** is one that the customer would prefer over all others, including objects that can be conceptualized in the space but do not actually exist. It is a combination of all the customers' preferred-attribute levels. Although the assumption that people have similar perceptions may be reasonable, their preferences are nearly always heterogeneous—their ideal objects will differ. One reason to locate ideal objects is to identify segments of customers who have similar ideal objects.

There are two types of ideal objects. The first lies within the perceptual map. For example, if a new cookie were rated on attribute scales such as

```
Very sweet ...................Not at all sweet
Large, substantial ..........Small, dainty
```

a respondent might well prefer a middle position on the scale.

The second type is illustrated by a different example. Suppose attributes of a proposed new car included

```
Inexpensive to buy...............Expensive to buy
Inexpensive to operate.........Expensive to operate
Good handling...................Bad handling
```

then respondents would very likely prefer an end point on the scale. For instance, the car should be as inexpensive as possible to buy and operate. In that case, the ideal object would be represented by an ideal vector or direction rather than an ideal point in the space. The direction would depend on the relative desirability of the various attributes.

There are two approaches to obtaining ideal-object locations. The first is simply to ask respondents to consider an ideal object as one of the objects to be rated or compared. The problem with this approach is that conceptualizing an ideal object may not be natural for a respondent, and the result may therefore be ambiguous and unreliable.

A second approach is indirect. For each individual, a rank-order preference among the objects is sought. Then, given a perceptual map, a program will locate the individual's ideal objects such that the distances to the objects have the same rank order (or as close to it as possible) as the rank-order preference. The preferred object should be closest to the ideal. The second most preferred object should be farther from the ideal than the preferred, but closer than the third most preferred, and so on. Often, it is not possible to determine a location that will satisfy this requirement perfectly and still obtain a small number of dimensions with which an analyst would like to work. In that case, compromises are made and the computer program does as well as possible by maximizing some measure of "goodness-of-fit."

Issues in MDS

Perceptual maps are good vehicles through which to summarize the position of brands and people in attribute space and, more generally, to portray the relationship among any variables or constructs. It is particularly useful to portray the positioning of existing or new brands and the relationship of those positions to the relevant segments. There is a set of problems and issues in working with MDS[7]:

1. When more than two or three dimensions are needed, the usefulness is reduced.
2. Perceptual mapping has not been shown to be reliable across different methods. Users rarely take the trouble to apply multiple approaches to a context to ensure that a map is not method specific.
3. Perceptual maps are static snapshots at a point of time. It is difficult from the model to know how they might be affected by the market events.
4. The interpretation of dimensions can be difficult. Even when a dimension is clear, it can involve several attributes, and thus the implications for action can be ambiguous.
5. Maps usually are based on groups that are aggregated with respect to their familiarity with products, their usage level, and their attitude. The analysis can, of course, be done with subgroups created by grouping people according to their preferences or perceptions, but with a procedure that is ad hoc, at best.
6. There has been little study of whether a change in the perception of a brand, as reflected by a perceptual map, will affect choice.

Summary of MDS

Application. MDS is used to identify dimensions by which objects are perceived or evaluated, to position the objects with respect to those dimensions, and to make positioning decisions for new and old products.

Inputs. Attribute-based data involve respondents rating the objects with respect to specified attributes. **Similarity-based** data involve a rank order of between-object similarity that can be based on several methods of obtaining similarity information from respondents. **Preference** data also can provide the basis for similarity measures and generate perceptual maps from quite a different perspective.

Ideal points or directions are based either on having respondents conceptualize their object, or by generating rank-order preference data and using the data in a second stage of analysis to identify ideal points or directions.

Outputs. The output will provide the location of each object on a limited number of dimensions. The number of dimensions is selected on the basis of a goodness-of-fit measure (such as the percentage of variance explained in factor analysis) and on the basis of the interpretability of the dimensions. In attitude-based MDS, attribute vectors may be included to help interpret the dimensions. Ideal points or directions may be an output in some programs.

Key Assumptions. The overriding assumption is that the underlying data represent valid measures. Thus, we assume that respondents can compare objects with respect to similarity or preference or attributes. The meaning of the input data is rather straightforward; however, the ability and motivation of respondents to provide it often is questionable. A related assumption is that the respondents use an appropriate context. Some could base a rank-order preference of beer on the assumption that it was to be served to guests. Others might assume the beer was to be consumed privately.

With the attribute-based data, it is assumed that the attribute list is relevant and complete. If individuals are grouped, it is assumed that their perceptions are similar. The **ideal object** introduces additional conceptual problems. Another basic assumption is that the interpoint distances generated by a perceptual map have conceptual meaning that is relevant to choice decisions.

Limitations. A limitation of the attribute-based methods is that the attributes have to be generated. The analyst has the burden of making sure that the attributes represent the respondents' perceptions and evaluations. With similarity and preference data, this task is eliminated. However, the analyst then must interpret dimensions without the aid of such attributes, although attribute data could be generated independently and attribute-dimension correlations still obtained.

CONJOINT ANALYSIS

Before examining the technique of **conjoint analysis,** we first will take a look at three examples of the kind of management problems for which conjoint analysis is extremely well suited:

1. Modifying a credit card.
2. Identifying land-use attitudes.
3. Revamping an industrial product line.

Modifying a Credit Card.[8] A firm wanted to improve the benefits of its credit card to retailers, to get more of them to honor the card. Changes could be made to any of the following attributes:

▶ Discount rate (percentage of billings deducted by the credit card company for providing the service); the alternatives were 2.5 percent versus 6 percent.

▶ Speed of payment after receipt of week's vouchers (1 day versus 10 days).

▶ Whether card authorization was by computer terminal or toll-free billing number.

▶ Extent of the support payment for local advertising by the retailers (either 1.0 percent or 0.75 percent of billings).

▶ Provision of a rebate of 15 percent of charges on all billings in excess of the retailer's quota (which would be set at 25 percent more than the previous year's sales).

Because there are two levels for each of the five factors, 32 possible combinations of credit cards could be offered. The best combination would be both attractive to the retailers and profitable to the company.

Identifying Residential Land-Use Attitudes. Most suburban land development follows a "spread" or "urban sprawl" pattern, with large home lots and uniformly low population densities. Is this what home buyers want, or do they accept this alternative because it is the only one land developers offer? Specifically, would buyers be willing to sacrifice some elements of private space to gain a better view from their yard? More importantly, would they accept cluster developments—groups of small lots—surrounded by large areas of open land that may be scenically valuable or ecologically vulnerable? The answer to these questions depends on the importance potential home buyers attach to attributes such as the view from the back or front yard, versus measures of lot size such as back-yard size, distance between houses, and distance to the front sidewalk.[9]

Revamping an Industrial Product Line. The Brazilian subsidiary of the Clark Equipment Company was considering replacing their largest-selling forklift truck with two new models. One new model was to have slightly less performance than the current model but would sell at a 5 percent lower price. The other new model would offer an automatic transmission for the first time, plus better performance and reliability, but at a 5 percent higher price. For this move to be profitable, the company would have to gain and hold an additional 3 percent market share.[10]

Overview of Conjoint Analysis

Conjoint analysis is an extremely powerful and useful analysis tool. Its acceptance and level of use have been remarkably high since its appearance around 1970. One study concluded that over 400 conjoint studies for commercial applications were undertaken annually in the early 1980s.[11]

As the previous examples indicate, a major purpose of conjoint analysis is to help select features to offer on a new or revised product or service; to help set prices; to predict the resulting level of sales or usage; or to try out a new-product concept. **Conjoint analysis** provides a quantitative measure of the relative importance of one attribute as opposed to another. Chapter 10 introduced other methods to determine attribute importance weights. The most direct was simply to ask people which attribute is important. The problem is that respondents usually indicate that all attributes are important. In selecting a car, they want good gas mileage, sporty appearance, lots of room, a low price, and so forth. In conjoint analysis the respondent is asked to make trade-off judgments. Is one feature desired enough to sacrifice another? If one attribute had to be sacrificed, which one would it be? Thus, the respondent provides extremely sensitive and useful information.

Some characteristics of situations where conjoint analysis has been used productively are

1. Where the alternative products or services have a number of attributes, each with two or more levels (e.g., automatic versus manual transmission).
2. Where most of the feasible combinations of attribute levels do not presently exist.
3. Where the range of possible attribute levels can be expanded beyond those presently available.
4. Where the general direction of attribute preference probably is known. (Travelers want less noise, faster travel, more comfort, and so on.)

The usual problem is that preferences for various attributes may be in conflict (a large station wagon cannot get into small parking spaces), or there may not be enough resources to satisfy all the preferences (a small price tag is not compatible with certain luxury features). The question usually is to find a compromise set of attribute levels.

The input data are obtained by giving respondents descriptions of concepts that represent the possible combinations of levels of attributes. For example, one of the credit card concepts for retailers to evaluate would be

1. Discount rate of 6 percent.
2. Payment within 10 days.
3. Credit authorization by telephone.
4. 0.75 percent of billings to support payments for local retailer advertising.
5. No rebates.

Respondent retailers then evaluate each concept in terms of overall liking, intentions to buy, or rank order of preference compared to other concepts. Paired comparison judgments also can be obtained to provide the degree of preference of one profile over the other. However, ratings data are used in more than 50 percent of the commercial applications of conjoint analysis.

The computer program then assigns values or "utilities" for each level (also known as *partworth utilities*) of each attribute. When these utilities are summed for each of the concepts being considered, the rank order of these total value scores should match the respondents' rank ordering of preference as closely as possible. This process can be illustrated with the utilities from the credit card study shown in the table below as well as in Figure 21-6. The combination with the highest total utility should be the one that originally was most preferred, and the combination with the lowest total utility should have been least preferred:

Attribute	Combination Level	Utility	Combination Level	Utility
Discount rate	2.5%	0.9	6%	−0.9
Speed of payment	1 day	0.2	10 days	−0.3
Credit authorization	Computer	0.3	Telephone	−0.3
Marketing support	1.0%	0.05	0.75%	−0.05
Rebate	15.0%	0.1	None	−0.1
Total utility for combination		1.55		−1.65

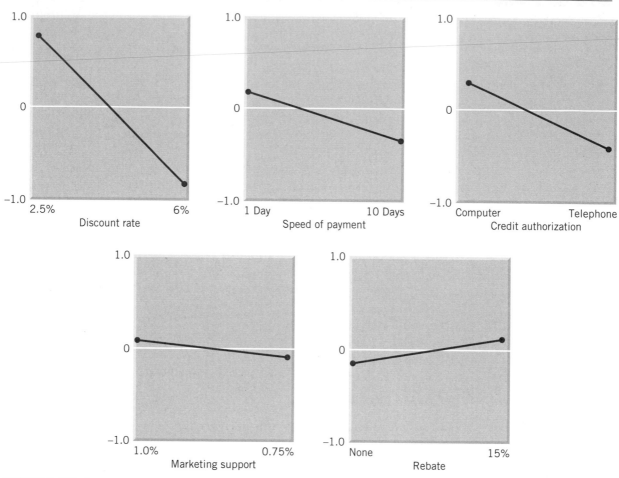

FIGURE 21-6

Utilities for credit card attributes (each separate interval scale measured in terms of a common unit)

Source: Paul E. Green. "A New Approach to Market Segmentation," *Business Horizons*, February 1977.

Interpreting Attribute Importance

The greater the difference between the highest and the lowest valued levels of an attribute, the more important the attribute. Conversely, if all the possible levels have the same utility, the attribute is not important, for it has no influence on the overall attitude. In the credit card study, the size of the discount was clearly the most important attribute. While this is not a surprising finding, it should be kept in mind that the magnitude of the difference in utilities for the two discount levels is strongly influenced by the choice of extreme levels. Had the chosen discount levels been 2.5 percent and 4 percent, the difference in utilities would have been much less. For this reason, it is often desirable to use three or even four levels of a complex attribute. For example, in Figure 21-6, the relative importance of the discount rate is obtained as 56.25 percent ((1.8) / (1.8 + 0.5 + 0.6 + 0.1 + 0.2)) where 1.8 is the difference in partworth utilities between the discount-rate levels. Similarly, the other numbers in the denominator represent the difference in utilities between the levels of the remaining attributes.

Usually, the measures of attribute importance obtained from a trade-off study are only a means to an end. The real pay-off comes from using the results to identify optimal combinations of attribute levels for new products, services, or policies. To see how this is done, we first need to look more closely at the way the trade-off data are collected from respondents, analyzed, and interpreted.

Collecting Trade-off Data

Respondents can reveal their trade-off judgments by either considering two attributes at a time, or by making an overall judgment of a full profile of attributes.

Full-Profile Approach. In a **full-profile** approach, respondents are given cards that describe complete product or service configurations. For example, two possible full-profile descriptions of package tour holidays are shown in Figure 21-7. Not all possible combinations of attribute levels have to be presented in order to estimate the utilities. For example, in Figure 21-7, even with six attributes, each described at three levels, there are 18 profiles to compare.[12] Respondents can be asked either to rank-order the profiles in order of preference, or assign each of the 18 cards to a category of a rating scale measuring overall preference or intentions to buy. The advantage of the rating scale is that it can be administered by mail, whereas a ranking task usually entails a personal interview.

Trade-off Approach (Considering Two Attributes Simultaneously). Respondents in a trade-off approach are asked to rank each combination of levels of two attributes, from most preferred to least preferred. The matrix shown in

Card 1	Card 2
Water temperature Just warm enough to swim	**Water temperature** Comfortably warm
Hotel location Five-minute walk to beach	**Hotel location** Facing beach
Size of nearest town Fishing village	**Size of nearest town** Major country town
Flight schedule Weekend	**Flight schedule** Weekday
Local entertainment Bars	**Local entertainment** Bars, nightclubs, theaters
Price $250	**Price** $300

FIGURE 21-7
Product descriptions
Source: This illustration is adapted from Dick Westwood, Tony Lunn, and David Bezaley. "The Trade-Off Model and Its Extensions," paper presented at the Annual Conference of the British Market Research Society, March 1974.

Figure 21-8 illustrates this approach, with the numbers in the cells representing one respondent's rankings. In this matrix, there are nine possible alternatives to be ranked. The best and the worst alternatives are obvious. The interesting evidence is that the respondent doing the ranking in this example is willing to walk five minutes to find comfortably warm water. However, there are six attributes in all, so potentially there could be

$$n(n - 1)/2 = 6(5)/2 = 15$$

such matrices for each respondent to fill in. Fortunately, it is not necessary to present all pairs in order to extract statistically the utilities without confusing the contributions of the various attributes.

Comparing Data Collection Approaches[13]

The arguments in favor of the full-profile approach are that (1) the description of the concepts is more realistic since all aspects are considered at the same time; (2) the concept evaluation task can employ either a ranking or rating scale; and (3) the respondent has to make fewer judgments than if the two-attribute trade-off approach were used. Unfortunately, as the number of attributes increases, the task of judging the individual profiles becomes very complex and demanding. With more than five or six attributes, there is a strong possibility of information overload, which usually leads respondents to ignore variations in the less-important factors. To get the flavor of this problem, look at Figure 21-8 and see how difficult it is to choose one package holiday over another.

The pairwise trade-off approach is not a panacea either. Because more judgments are required, the task can be tedious and time consuming. Consequently, respondents may lose their place in the matrix or develop a standardized response pattern just to get the job done. Since only two attributes are being considered, there is a potential loss of realism. This problem is most troublesome when there is substantial environmental correlation among attributes for technological or other reasons. For example, the 0 to 55 mph acceleration time, gas mileage, horsepower rating, and top speed of an automobile are not independent attributes. When only two of these four attributes are being considered, respondents may be unclear as to what should be assumed about the others. This problem also is encountered with price, because it may be used

		Facing beach	5 minutes walk to beach	More than 5 minutes walk to beach
	Comfortably warm	1	2	5
Water temperature	Just warm enough to swim	3	4	6
	Too cold to swim	7	8	9

FIGURE 21-8
Trade-off approach

as an indicator of quality. Of course, if environmental correlations are high it may be possible to create a composite factor. This means losing information about the component attributes.

Studies comparing the two methods typically show that the estimated utilities are roughly similar and that, for large numbers of factors which are not environmentally correlated, the trade-off approach yields somewhat higher predictive validity. In part because it is difficult to find factors that are not correlated, the full-profile approach is increasingly preferred. Almost 60 percent of recent studies used the full-profile approach, and another 10 percent used a combination of full-profile and two factors at a time. Only 6 percent of the studies used the trade-off approach.[14]

Analyzing and Interpreting the Data

The analysis of conjoint or trade-off studies, like all other marketing research, is guided by the research purpose. As an illustration, a manufacturer of automobile batteries with a lifetime guarantee wanted to know how much emphasis to place on the fact that the batteries never need water. A conjoint study was conducted in which respondents were asked to evaluate full-concept profiles made up of combinations of three attributes and three levels:

Attribute	**Levels**
Price	$30, $45, $60
Length of guarantee	Lifetime, 60 months, 48 months
Maintenance required	No water needed, add water once a year, add water as needed

The preference ranking of these stimulus profiles was input to the analysis. The first problem in the data analysis is to estimate a set of utilities (sometimes called *partworths*) for the nine attribute levels, such that

1. The sum of the attribute level utilities for each specific profile equals the total utility for the profile.
2. The *derived* ranking of the stimulus profiles, based on the sum of estimated attribute level utilities, corresponds as closely as possible to the respondent's *original* ranking.

Although the details of the techniques used to achieve this are beyond the scope of this discussion, the elements are straightforward. The partworth utilities can be obtained with an iterative procedure that starts with an arbitrary set of utilities and systematically modifies them until the total utility of each profile correlates maximally to the original ranks. The procedure continues until no change in the utility of an attribute level will improve the correlation. As a practical matter, most analysts use regression analysis (Chapter 19) to obtain the attribute weight utilities, because it provides very similar results and is much easier and cheaper to use than an iterative procedure.[15]

Once the utilities are estimated, they are displayed, and the relative importance of each attribute is determined. In the case of automobile batteries, the following graph displays the results.

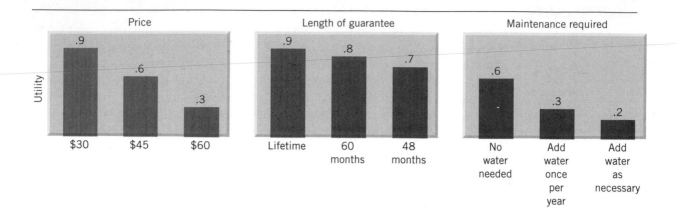

According to these utility values, both price and length of guarantee are more important than the maintenance attribute. However, the relative difference in the total utility from a change in the level of maintenance (0.6 − 0.2 = 0.4) is greater than for a change in the length of guarantee (0.9 − 0.7 = 0.2). Clearly, the fact that the battery doesn't need water should be emphasized as an advertising appeal, especially if potential buyers are not aware of this benefit.

Validity Issues

The conjoint model assumes that preference can be modeled by adding the utilities associated with attribute levels, and that these utilities can be estimated from either full-profile or trade-off data. There are several indications that the model has a substantial level of validity.

A bottom-line validity test is the remarkable acceptance of conjoint analysis in industry. The technique, introduced only in 1971, was estimated to have had over 5000 applications during the first 17 years. It now is used routinely by many market research firms and their clients.

The conjoint model has been found to predict the market share of transportation modes between two cities and the type of fare in North Atlantic air travel.[16] At the individual level, a conjoint model involving eight factors (including salary, location, need to travel, and so on) predicted subsequent job choice by M.B.A. students, with an impressive 63 percent hit rate. Another study used a conjoint model successfully to predict the acceptance of 13 new products introduced into supermarkets.

The reliability of conjoint analysis has been the subject of several studies. In general, reliability has been found to be high. One study exploring both the full profile and the trade-off approach, using five product classes, found that the output was not sensitive to which five of six attributes were included or whether three or five levels were used on the price attribute.[17] Another study concluded that reliability fell when the number of attributes was increased.[18] As in other multivariate techniques, the reliability of the profile evaluations or the partworth utilities can be assessed by the test-retest procedure. The internal validity can be evaluated through the holdout sample and the external validity can be assessed through observing respondents' behavior in the actual marketplace.

Application Issues

Four areas of application appear especially promising. First, the insights that are gained into how consumers make choices within an existing market,[19] coupled with information on the perceptions of the competitive alternatives, are valuable for guiding communications programs. Second, the analysis can suggest new product or service configurations with significant consumer appeal compared to alternatives. Finally, the utility measurements can be used to develop strategic marketing simulations.[20] These are used to evaluate the volume and profit implications of changes in marketing strategies. The following is a typical application, taken from Green and Wind:[21]

> As a case in point, a large-scale study of consumer evaluations of airline services was conducted in which consumer utilities were developed for some 25 different service factors such as on-ground services, inflight services, decor of cabins and seats, scheduling, routing, and price. Moreover, each utility function was developed on a route (city-pair and purpose-of-trip basis).
>
> As might be expected, the utility function for each of the various types of airline service differed according to the length and purpose of the flight. However, in addition to obtaining consumers' evaluations of service profiles, the researchers also obtained information concerning their perceptions of each airline (that is, for the ones they were familiar with) on each of the service factors for which the consumers were given a choice.
>
> These two major pieces of information provided the principal basis for developing a simulation of airline services over all major traffic routes. The purpose of the simulation was to estimate the effect on market share that a change in the service configuration of the sponsor's services would have, route by route, if competitors did not follow suit. Later, the sponsor used the simulator to examine the effect of assumed retaliatory actions by its competitors.

Although most applications have been in the private sector, conjoint and trade-off analyses also are well suited to conducting cost–benefit analyses of public policy decisions. A recent application (see Figure 21-9) to the problem of recruiting for the armed forces reserves shows what can be done.[22]

There are constraints on applications, however. The most useful applications have been in complex, expensive, or risky product or service categories such as remote computer terminals, transportation modes, and major appliances; or with problems such as retail-branch site selection. Even in these categories, the requirement that each attribute be divided into discrete levels is a potential limitation. The difficulty is with such attributes as durability or styling, which are difficult to divide sensibly into levels because there are no objective standards to define "very safe" or "smart styling." The value of trade-off analysis is limited further when used with products or services having only one or two important attributes or where little explicit attention is paid to trade-offs because the costs or risks are low.

Summary of Conjoint Analysis

Applications. Conjoint analysis is used to predict the buying or usage of a new product that still may be in concept form. It also is used to determine the relative importance of various attributes to respondents, based on their making

The Reserves have been facing declining strength because of an inability to attract and retain people. The question was, What actions should be taken to modify the "product" or the "communications" to increase enlistments among civilians as well as the likelihood of reenlistment?

The overall objective of the study was to examine in detail motivational factors in enlistment and retention. More specific objectives were to (1) measure young men's propensity to serve or reenlist, (2) determine current perceptions of the Reserves, (3) determine the relative importance of the 12 key job attributes that may provide the basis for influencing young men to join and remain in the Reserves, and (4) indicate what configurations of job characteristics, benefits, and incentives will enhance accessions and reenlistment intentions among various target groups.

These objectives were tailor-made for a trade-off analysis. Separate samples of 17- to 26-year-old males without prior service and current reservists were studied. A computer-based interactive interview was used, with subjects responding on a keyboard to questions presented on a cathode-ray tube. The trade-off questions were in the form of preferences for pairs of attributes. A typical question appeared as follows:

"Which would you prefer . . . "

A 4-year enlistment term and a $1000 bonus	OR	A 6-year enlistment term and a $3000 bonus?

Other attributes investigated included starting pay, educational assistance, hair regulations, retirement benefits, and hours of meeting each month.

The output of the study included the measurement of the relative importance of various attributes, and estimates of actual recruitment levels that would occur given any change in the attributes of the military "job."

FIGURE 21-9
Trade-off analysis

trade-off judgments. One motivation is prediction. What sales or usage level will a new concept achieve? A second is understanding relationships. How does changing one of the attribute levels affect preference?

Inputs. The **dependent variable** is the preference judgment a respondent makes about a new concept. The **independent variables** are the attribute levels that need to be specified. Respondents make judgments about the concept either by considering two attributes at a time (trade-off approach) or by making an overall judgment of a full profile of attributes (full-profile approach).

Outputs. A value of relative utility is assigned to each level of an attribute. Each respondent will have her or his own set of utilities, although an average respondent can be created by averaging the input judgments. The percentage of respondents who would most prefer one concept from among a defined set of concepts can be determined.

Assumptions. The basic assumption is that people evaluate concepts by adding up their evaluations of the concept's individual attribute levels. It is assumed that the individual attributes are not excessively redundant and that there are no interactions between attributes.

Limitations. In the **trade-off approach,** the problem is that the task is too unrealistic. It's difficult to make trade-off judgments about two attributes while holding all the others constant. In the **full-profile approach,** the task can get very demanding, even for a motivated and conscientious respondent. There is a very real limit on the number of attributes that can be used, especially in the full-profile approach.

Questions and Problems

1. Suppose an MDS study was to be made among high-school seniors for use by the University of Indiana. The goal was to see how Indiana was positioned with respect to the 10 to 20 colleges with which it competes and to determine how students evaluate colleges.
   a. How would you determine which colleges should be the object of the MDS study?
   b. Generate a list of attributes that you feel should be included in the study. What methods did you use to generate the list?
   c. Detail ten different ways to generate between-object similarities. Which one would you use in the study?
   d. Do you think the perceptual map would be different if preference data were used? Can you illustrate any hypothesized difference with an example?
2. How might a perceptual map like the one in Figure 21-2 be used to suggest a new-product concept? Be specific. How might the concept be developed? How might it be tested?
3. The claim is made that MDS is of little help in new-product planning, because most of the dimensions are "psychological" dimensions and not really actionable. Predicting psychological reactions to physical changes is very difficult. Furthermore, it is questioned, how much guidance do we gain from hearing that we need a "sportier" car or a more "full-bodied" beer. Comment.
4. How would you go about introducing ideal objects into Figure 21-2?
5. It is argued that people are not consciously aware of which dimensions they are employing to make similarity or even preference judgments. Further, respondents may base judgments on attributes to which they are unwilling to admit. The use of nonattribute data in MDS is, thus, rather like motivation research in that it allows the researcher to make judgments about information unavailable by direct methods. Comment.
6. Suppose, given Figure 21-5, an advertising objective was to reposition Pepsi as being more fun, light, active—closer to 7-Up. How could MDS be used to test proposed copy and evaluate the results of a campaign? Can you think of any possible problems with this kind of use of MDS?
7. An exciting use of correspondence analysis is using scanner data to generate maps. Scanner data provides information on which brands a family did and did not buy. Such a set of binary data can be used to generate a map positioning the brands in a space. Brands that are close will tend to be purchased by the same families, whereas brands that are far apart tend not to be purchased by the same family. Comment.
8. A relevant issue is whether respondents can provide directly similarity judgments that are meaningful. In particular,

a. Do consumers commonly make overall similarity judgments? If not, will their judgment be meaningful?

b. Does the perceptual map represent the internal cognitive structure, or does the nature of the task and memory limitation inhibit all the relevant dimensions from being recovered?

c. Do respondents share the same concept of what is meant by "similarity?"

9. Attempt to label the dimensions of Figure 21-2 using only the object location information.

10. Describe why cluster analysis might be appropriate both before and after an MDS study.

11. In either the full-profile or the trade-off approach, the respondent can rank-order the alternative choices or can arrange them on some scale, such as extremely desirable, very desirable, desirable, neutral, and undesirable. What are the advantages and disadvantages to using a rank-order approach?

12. Explain how conjoint analysis is used to determine attribute importance. Is the resulting attribute importance sensitive to the selection of levels for an attribute? Illustrate by using Figure 21-6.

13. Compare the full-profile approach to the trade-off approach. What are the advantages of each? Which would you use in the example of automobile batteries? If price were one of the attributes, would you be more likely to use the full-profile approach?

14. Do purchasers of major appliances, such as refrigerators and room air conditioners, treat price as an attribute in an additive model of preference that underlies conjoint analysis? That is, do they arrive at an overall judgment by summing the evaluative rating of each attribute (including price)? How would you test whether this model applied to this situation?

15. Do the following:

a. Reflect on the last airplane flight you took. What attributes did you consider in your choice of airline?

b. To learn more about the trade-offs you made in your choice of airline, conduct a trade-off analysis on yourself. Start with the attributes and then establish two or three feasible levels for each attribute. Prepare trade-off matrices of 10 or more possible pairs of attributes, and fill in the cells according to a criterion that seems appropriate. What have you learned?

16. Interview the manager of a local "quick copy" shop or an individual who recently bought or specified a copying machine, to learn which attributes were used to choose it. Can the buyer describe on which features trade-offs were made? Are there logical levels to the attributes that were used?

End Notes

1. This example is based on research reported in Thomas P. Hustad, Charles S. Mayer, and Thomas W. Whippie. "Consideration of Context Differ-ences in Product Evaluation and Market Segmentation."

2. John R. Hauser and Frank S. Koppelman. "Alter-

native Perceptual Mapping Techniques: Relative Accuracy and Usefulness," *Journal of Marketing Research, 16*, November 1979, 495–506. Hauser and Koppelman conclude that factor analysis is superior to discriminant analysis; however, many other experienced researchers prefer discriminant analysis for the reasons noted herein.

3. James H. Myers and Edward Tauber. *Market Structure Analysis* (Chicago: American Marketing Association), 1977, 48–55. The authors call this technique a *weighted covariance analysis.*

4. Donna L. Hoffman and George R. Franke. "Correspondence Analysis: Graphical Representation of Categorical Data in Marketing Research," *Journal of Marketing Research*, August 1986, 213–227. Michael J. Greenacre. "The Carroll-Green-Schaffer Scaling in Correspondence Analysis: A Theoretical and Empirical Appraisal," *Journal of Marketing Research*, 26, August 1989, pp. 358–365.

5. Hauser & Koppelman, op. cit.

6. James H. Myers and Edward Tauber, *Market Structure Analysis*, Chicago: American Marketing Association), 1977, 38.

7. V. Kumar and Robert P. Leone, "Nonlinear Mapping: An Alternative to Multidimensional Scaling for Product Positioning," *Journal of the Academy of Marketing Science*, 19(3), 1991, 165–176.

8. Paul E. Green. "A New Approach to Market Segmentation," *Business Horizons*, February 1977, 61–73.

9. Robert L. Knight and Mark D. Menchik, "Conjoint Preference Estimation for Residential Land Use Policy Evaluation," Institute for Environmental Studies, University of Wisconsin, July 1974.

10. *Clark Material Handling Group—Overseas: Brazilian Product Strategy*(A), HBS Case Services, 1981.

11. Dick R. Wittink and Philippe Cattin, "Commercial use of Conjoint Analysis: An Update," *Journal of Marketing*, 53(3), 1989, 91–96.

12. In fact, there are $(3 \times 3 \times 3 \times 3 \times 3 \times 3 =)$ 729 possible combinations. Fortunately, it is possible to use an experimental design, known as an *orthogonal array*, in which a small set of combinations is selected such that the independent contributions of all six factors are balanced, to reduce this to 18 combinations. See Paul E. Green. "On the Design of Choice Experiments involving Multifactor Alternatives," *Journal of Consumer Research*, 1, September 1974, 61–68.

13. This section draws on Paul E. Green and V. Srinivasan. "Conjoint Analysis in Consumer Research: Issues and Outlook," *Journal of Consumer Research*, 5, September 1978, 103–123; Paul E. Green and V. Srinivasan. "Conjoint Analysis in Marketing: New Developments with Implications for Research and Practice," *Journal of Marketing*, 54(4), 1990, 3–19.

14. Wittink and Cattin, op. cit.

15. In the regression approach, the rank ordering is the dependent variable and the independent variables are 0–1 variables for each level on an attribute, less one. Thus, for the price attribute there would be a 0–1 variable for $45 (coded as "1" only if the profile had a $45 price) and a 0–1 variable for $60 (coded as a "1," only if the profile had a $60 price). The profile with a $30 price would be the reference level and therefore would not have its own 0–1 variable. If the $45 variable is coded "0" and the $60 variable is coded "0," then the level must be $30.

16. The predictive studies are reviewed in David B. Montgomery. "Conjoint Calibration of the Customer/Competitor Interface in Industrial Markets," in Backhaus and D. Wilson (eds), *New Developments in Industrial Marketing* (Springer-Verlag), 1985.

17. David Reibstein, John E. G. Bateson, and William Boulding. "Conjoint Analysis Reliability: Empirical Findings," *Marketing Science*, Summer 1988, 271–286.

18. Naresh K. Malhotra. "Structural Reliability and Stability of Nonmetric Conjoint Analysis," *Journal of Marketing Research*, 19, May 1982, 199–207.

19. Paul E. Green and Abba M. Krieger. "Segmenting Markets with Conjoint Analysis," *Journal of Marketing*, 55(4), 1991, 20–31. Rajeev Kohli and Vijay Mahajan. "A Reservation-Price Model for Optimal Pricing of Multiattribute Products in Conjoint Analysis," *Journal of Marketing Research*, 28(3), 1991, 347–354.

20. Paul E. Green, J. Douglas Carrol, and Stephen M. Goldberg. "A General Approach to Product Design Optimization via Conjoint Analysis," *Journal of Marketing*, 45, Summer 1981, 17–37.

21. Paul E. Green and Yoram Wind. "New Way to Measure Consumers' Judgements," *Harvard Business Review*, July–August 1975, 107–117.

22. Public Sector Research Group of Market Facts, Inc., "Conjoint Analysis of Values of Reserve Component Attributes," a report prepared for theDepartment of Defense (Washington, DC: U.S. Government Printing Office), November 1977.

CASE 21-1
Nester's Foods

Nester's Foods is evaluating a group of concepts for new diet products. To evaluate the positioning of these new products, an MDS study was conducted. The respondents, women who were on a diet, were asked to group 38 food products, including 10 of the new diet concepts. The output of the MDS, based on these similarity ratings, is shown in Figure 1. "L.C." stands for low calorie, and "M/S" stands for meal substitute.

Questions for Discussion

1. Label the dimensions.
2. Group the products into clusters visually and describe the different clusters. What are the positioning implications?
3. What other information would you collect, and how would you use it in the analysis?

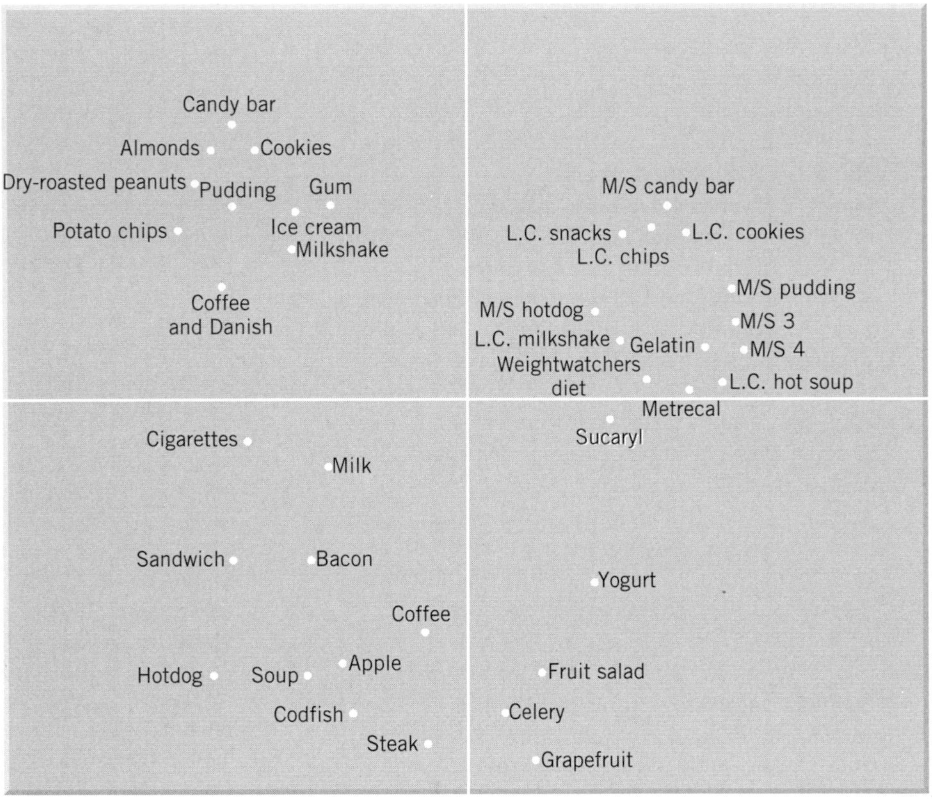

FIGURE 1

Two-dimensional perceptual configuration of 38 food products

Source: Adapted from Yoram Wind and Patrick J. Robinson. "Product Positioning: An Application of Multidimensional Scaling," in Russell L. Haley, ed. *Attitude Research in Transition* (Chicago: American Marketing Association), 1972.

CASE 21-2
Pepsi-Cola

Ed Sturdley, the marketing research manager for Pepsi, had commissioned a perceptual mapping study of Pepsi in the college market. He had been concerned with the fact that perceptual maps tended to be sensitive to the approach used. Therefore, he had insisted that the data contain information so that perceptual maps could be conducted using similarity, preference, or attribute data.

The study involved the following questionnaire, distributed to a representative sample of 64 undergraduates from U.S. colleges. Ten objects were included:

1. Pepsi
2. Diet 7-Up
3. Calistoga Natural Orange
4. 7-Up
5. Slice 10% Fruit Juice
6. Schweppes Sparkling Water
7. Dr. Pepper
8. Diet Coke
9. Coke
10. Pepsi Light

The analysis of the similarity data is shown in Figure 21-5. A perceptual map based on the preference data is shown in Figure 2. The two-dimensional fit was extremely good for both. If anything, the preference-based map had a slightly higher fit.

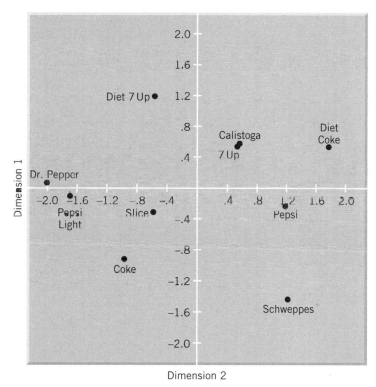

FIGURE 2
Perceptual map using preference data

Questions for Discussion

1. Critique the questionnaire. Was it complete? Would you have asked the questions the same way?
2. Compare the preference map with the similarities map. What differences do you see? What are their implications? Which is the "correct" map?
3. Conduct any other analysis that you believe would be useful. Interpret the results. Among the analyses that could be run would be analyses to compare perceptual maps obtained from

   ▶ Attribute, similarity, and preference data.

   ▶ Factor analysis vs. discriminant analysis of the attribute data.

▶ Subsets of the data such as males, those preferring a cola, those preferring a diet drink, or the heavy drinkers.

▶ Subsets of the objects such as the subset excluding all diet drinks or the subset excluding the nondiet colas.

▶ Converting the attribute data to binary by indicating whether the attribute rating was three or above and using correspondence analysis.

▶ Conducting a cluster analysis of the drinks using the attribute data and again using the similarity data.

▶ Conducting a cluster analysis of the respondents.

The questionnaire consisted of six sets of questions:

I. Please rate the following pairs of drinks as to how similar they are. Circle the appropriate number.

	Very Similar						Very Different		Coded Column
Pepsi–Diet 7-Up	1	2	3	4	5	6	7	8 9	1
Pepsi–Calistoga Natural Orange	1	2	3	4	5	6	7	8 9	2
Pepsi–7-Up	1	2	3	4	5	6	7	8 9	3
Pepsi–Slice 10%	1	2	3	4	5	6	7	8 9	4
					.				.
					.				.
					.				.
Dr. Pepper–Diet Coke	1	2	3	4	5	6	7	8 9	40
Dr. Pepper–Coke	1	2	3	4	5	6	7	8 9	41
Dr. Pepper–Pepsi Light	1	2	3	4	5	6	7	8 9	42
Diet Coke–Coke	1	2	3	4	5	6	7	8 9	43
Diet Coke–Pepsi Light	1	2	3	4	5	6	7	8 9	44
Coke–Pepsi Light	1	2	3	4	5	6	7	8 9	45

II. Indicate your attitude toward the following drinks.

	Dislike Strongly		Dislike			Like		My Favorite		Coded Column
Pepsi	1	2	3	4	5	6	7	8	9	46
Diet 7-Up	1	2	3	4	5	6	7	8	9	47
Calistoga Natural Orange	1	2	3	4	5	6	7	8	9	48
7-Up	1	2	3	4	5	6	7	8	9	49
Slice 10% Fruit Juice	1	2	3	4	5	6	7	8	9	50
Schweppes Sparkling Water	1	2	3	4	5	6	7	8	9	51
Dr. Pepper	1	2	3	4	5	6	7	8	9	52
Diet Coke	1	2	3	4	5	6	7	8	9	53
Coke	1	2	3	4	5	6	7	8	9	54
Pepsi Light	1	2	3	4	5	6	7	8	9	55

III. From the above list, circle the drink you bought last. (56) (ten brands coded 0 to 9 in order of question 2)

IV. Indicate your agreement or disagreement with the following statements.

	Agree Strongly							Disagree Strongly		Coded Column
Pepsi is:										
Refreshing	1	2	3	4	5	6	7	8	9	57
Sweet Tasting	1	2	3	4	5	6	7	8	9	58
Fruity	1	2	3	4	5	6	7	8	9	59
Full-Bodied	1	2	3	4	5	6	7	8	9	60
For the Young and Active	1	2	3	4	5	6	7	8	9	61
Fattening	1	2	3	4	5	6	7	8	9	62
Diet 7-Up is:										
Refreshing	1	2	3	4	5	6	7	8	9	63
Sweet Tasting	1	2	3	4	5	6	7	8	9	64
Fruity	1	2	3	4	5	6	7	8	9	65
Full-Bodied	1	2	3	4	5	6	7	8	9	66
For the Young and Active	1	2	3	4	5	6	7	8	9	67
Fattening	1	2	3	4	5	6	7	8	9	68
Pepsi Light is:										
Refreshing	1	2	3	4	5	6	7	8	9	111
Sweet Tasting	1	2	3	4	5	6	7	8	9	112
Fruity	1	2	3	4	5	6	7	8	9	113
Full-Bodied	1	2	3	4	5	6	7	8	9	114
For the Young and Active	1	2	3	4	5	6	7	8	9	115
Fattening	1	2	3	4	5	6	7	8	9	116

V. What is the number of times during the last week that you consumed one of these beverages _____ (117–118)

VI. I am male _____ I am a female _____ (119)
    (coded a 1 if male and 2 if female)

Identification Number (120–121)

CASE 21-3
The Electric Truck Case[1]

John Hirsch of Central Utility was attempting to develop conclusions from a conjoint analysis study of electrically powered trucks. The study objectives were (1) to determine the number of commercial applications that were compatible with the limitations of electric vehicles, and (2) to assess the perceived importance of those technical requirements as compared to other vehicle characteristics, such as initial costs and pollution levels.

In the first phase of the study, a sample of truck owners was interviewed and the nature of their applications was determined. They found that 11 percent of commercial truck applications could get along with the electric vehicle limitations of a 4-mile range, a maximum of 40 stops, a load limit of 1500 pounds payload, and "seldom" freeway travel. The most sensitive dimension was freeway travel. If that limitation were removed, the electric vehicle could be used for 19 percent of applications. In the second phase of the study, people responsible for purchases of commercial trucks were invited to an "electric vehicle seminar at which an operating electric truck was available for inspection and test driving." During the seminar they discussed the advantages and disadvantages of electric vehicles and participated in a conjoint analysis study.

[1] Prepared by George Hargreaves, John D. Claxton, Frederick H. Siller, and David A. Aaker as a basis for class discussion.

TABLE 1
Relative Utilities of Conventional Versus Electric Vehicles

Attribute	Conventional Vehicle	Utility	Electric Vehicle	Utility
Speed and range	Unlimited	+1.426	40 mph and 40 miles	−1.426
Operating costs	Standard: 10 cents/mile	−0.928	Reduced: 5 cents/mile	+0.928
Initial price	Standard: $5000	+0.901	Premium: $8000	−0.901
Pollution levels	Standard: Gasoline engine	−0.544	Zero	+0.544
Propulsion system	Conventional: Gasoline engine	−0.019	New propulsion system	+0.019
	Net utility	+0.836	Net utility	−0.836

As Table 1 indicates, the conjoint study involved five attributes, each of which had two levels associated with it. For example, the initial price was either $5000 or $8000. The respondents were those attending the electric vehicle seminars. Each respondent was asked to rank 16 alternative truck designs, based on the attributes shown in Table 1. The rankings of the respondents were averaged and provided the inputs to a conjoint analysis program. The output utilities also are shown in Table 1.

Questions for Discussion

Evaluate the study. Do you feel the attributes and the attribute levels were well selected? Interpret Table 1.

1. What information does it contain?
2. What are the underlying assumptions?
3. What additional analysis might be useful to do?

CASE 21-4
Fargo Instruments

Ed Heedam was an account executive for the marketing research firm, Boyle Research, and was designing a study for Fargo Instruments, makers of private-label calculators for major retailers. One of Fargo's retail chain customers wanted to review its line of calculators. The need was to determine what types of features to offer in the next generation of models. Among the features that could be included in a model were rechargeability, financial functions, statistical functions, warranty, and algebraic parentheses to assist calculation. The study needed to estimate how much the target customer group, college students, would pay for the various features. The tentative plan was to use a telephone interview.

One option was clearly conjoint measurement. If conjoint was used, there would need to be a decision as to whether a two-by-two trade-off or the full-profile approach should be used. However, Ed wondered if there might be alternatives to conjoint that may work in this case, alternatives that may be more amenable to telephone interviewing and provide the same information. In particular, he was considering two alternatives, a constant sum approach and a dollar metric approach.

In the constant sum approach the respondent would allocate ten points over the five attributes proportional to the attribute's importance to him or her. In the dollar metric, the respondent would be asked to indicate what attribute level would be least preferred (unless the answer was obvious) and how much he or she would pay to receive another attribute level. Both would force the respondent to chose between attributes and would thus address the "I like all the features" problem of simply asking directly for the importance of each attribute.

Questions for Discussion
1. What are the similarities and differences between the constant sum and dollar metric approaches

658

to conjoint? Which are best suited to telephone interviewing? Which would you select in this case? Under what circumstances would conjoint tend to be preferred? What about the dollar metric? What about the constant sum?

2. Would you select the full profile or the trade-off approach?
3. What other changes would you consider making in the design?

22 PRESENTING THE RESULTS

Learning Objectives

▶ Discuss the fundamentals of research presentation.

▶ Provide details on preparing the research report.

▶ Discuss issues related to successful oral presentation.

▶ Explain the importance of continued relationship with the client.

It is difficult to exaggerate the importance of the role that communication skills play in effective management. Along with the related skill of working with and motivating people, the ability to communicate effectively is undoubtedly the most important attribute a manager can have. There is also little doubt that managers are dissatisfied with the present level of communication skills. Business schools are criticized routinely and justifiably for focusing on techniques and neglecting communication skills. Further, managers frequently make harsh judgments about themselves and their colleagues with respect to communication skills. A senior advertising executive concluded that "advertising people are bright, presentable, usually articulate—but most of them are duds when it comes to making presentations."[1] A special *Business Week* report said, "So appalling is the quality of written reports in some companies that senior executives are sending their managers through writing courses, to try to put some point back into the reports that cross their desks and eliminate the extraneous material that increasingly obscures the point."[2]

Effective communication between research users and research professionals is extremely important to the research process. The formal presentation usually will play a key role in the communication effort. Generally presentations are made twice during the research process: First, there is the research proposal presentation, discussed in Chapter 4, when the client must decide to accept, change, or reject it. Second, there is the presentation of the research results, when decisions associated with the research purpose are addressed and the advisability of conducting further research often is considered. This chapter will focus on the presentation of research results, but much of the material will apply to the original research proposal presentation as well.

GUIDELINES FOR SUCCESSFUL PRESENTATIONS

The purpose of this chapter is to help readers avoid making presentations that are ineffective because they are dull, confusing, or irrelevant. Have you been exposed lately to any that hit the jackpot—that are all three? Presentations can be written, oral, or both. Later in the chapter, we will offer some tips on making both written and oral presentations. First, however, here are some guidelines that apply to both types of presentations. In general, a presenter should

1. Communicate to a specific audience.
2. Structure the presentation.
3. Create audience interest.
4. Be specific and visual.
5. Address validity and reliability issues.

Each of the guidelines will be discussed in turn.

Communicate to a Specific Audience

The first step is to know the audience, its background, and its objectives. Most effective presentations seem like conversations, or memos to a particular person, as opposed to an amorphous group. The key to obtaining that feeling is to identify the audience members as precisely as possible.

Audience identification will affect presentation decisions such as selecting the material to be included and the level of presentation. Excessive detail or material presented at too low a level can be boring or seem patronizing. However, the audience can become irritated or lost when material perceived as relevant is excluded or the material is presented at too high a level. In an oral presentation, the presenter can ask audience members whether they already know some of the material.

Frequently, there will be two or more different audiences to which a presentation must be addressed. There are several ways to deal with such a problem. In a written presentation, an executive summary at the outset can provide an overview of the conclusions for the benefit of those in the audience who are not interested in details. The presentation should respect the audience's time constraints. An appendix also can be used to reach some people selectively without distracting the others. Sometimes the introduction to a chapter or a section can convey the nature of the contents, which certain audiences may bypass. In an oral presentation, the existence of multiple audiences should be recognized with a statement such as, "I need to provide some information on instrumentation next. You engineers in the audience can help by making sure that I don't miss anything." Such an acknowledgement probably will please the engineers so that they will be helpful rather than bored and restless.

Structure the Presentation

Each piece of the presentation should fit into the whole, just as individual pieces fit into a jigsaw puzzle. The audience should not be muttering, "What on earth is this person talking about?" or "How does this material fit in?" or

"I'm lost." The solution is to provide a well-defined structure. As Figure 22-1 illustrates, the structure should include an introduction, a body, and a summary. Further, each of the major sections should be structured similarly. The precept is to tell the audience what you are going to say, say it, and then tell them what you said. Sometimes you want to withhold the conclusion, to create interest. In that case the audience could be told, "The objective here will be to come to a recommendation as to whether this new product should go into test market and, if so, with what type of pricing strategy." Further, use nontechnical definitions as much as possible to present the report in simple language. For example, critical path could simply be stated as "the list of activities that must be completed on time."

Introduction. The introduction should play several roles. First, it should provide audience interest, a task that will be discussed in detail in the next section. A second function is to identify the presentation's central idea or objective. Third, it should provide a road map to the rest of the presentation so that the audience can picture its organization and flow. Sometimes the only way to develop such a road map is to say something like, "This presentation has four parts. The research purpose and objectives will be discussed first. The second section will describe the research design. . . ." However, with a little effort and luck it is sometimes possible to develop and use a flowchart that will convey the structure in a more interesting way. For example, in this book such a structural role was played by Figures 1-1, 3-1, and 4-2. (The reader should attempt to identify other figures so used.) When such a device is used, the audience should be clear when each section will be addressed. The label for the section should use identical wording throughout, and the start of the section

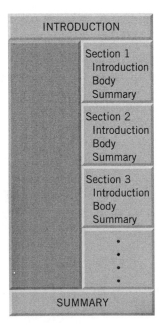

FIGURE 22-1
The presentation structure

should be made clear: "Having finished the second section, we now move to the third."

Body. Usually, it is best to divide the **body** of the presentation (or the major section) into between two and five parts. The audience will be able to absorb only so much information. If that information can be aggregated into chunks, it will be easier to assimilate. Sometimes the points to be made are not combined easily or naturally. In that case, it is sometimes necessary to use a longer list: "There are 12 problems in this new product concept." However, the presentation should never drift through the body with no structure at all.

One way to structure a presentation is by the research questions: "This research was conducted to address four research questions. Each of these will be considered in turn." Another method that is often useful when presenting the research proposal is to base it on the research process, as was illustrated in Chapter 4.

The most useful presentations will include a statement of implications and recommendations relevant to the research purpose. However, when the researcher lacks information about the total situation because the research study addresses only a limited aspect of it, the ability to generate recommendations may be limited.

Summary. The purpose of the **presentation summary** is to identify and underline the important points of the presentation and to provide some repetition of their content. The summary should support the presentation communication objectives by helping the audience to retain the key parts of the content. The audience usually will perk up when they realize the end is near and an overview of the presentation is coming, so the summary section should be signaled clearly. A section summary has the additional task of providing a transition to the next section. The audience should feel that there is a natural flow from one section to the next.

Create Audience Interest

The audience should be motivated to read or listen to the presentation's major parts and to the individual elements of each section. Those in the audience should know why the presentation is relevant to them and why each section was included. A section that cannot hold interest probably should be excluded or relegated to appendix status.

The research purpose and objectives are good vehicles to provide motivation. The research purpose should specify decisions to be made and should relate to the research questions. A presentation that focuses on those research questions and their associated hypotheses will naturally be tied to relevant decisions and hold audience interest. In contrast, a presentation that attempts to report on *all* the questions that were included in the survey and in the cross-tabulations often will be long, uninteresting, and of little value.

The researcher should point out those aspects of the results that are important and interesting. Suppose a chart is used that contains 10 descriptors of customers in 13 different markets. The presenter should circle three or so of those 130 numbers and be prepared to say, "Look at this number. We had hypothesized it to be higher than the others and it actually is lower. Let's look at the possible reasons and implications." The presenter should not feel compelled to wade through every detail of the questionnaire and the analysis.

As the analysis proceeds and the presentation is being prepared, the researcher should be on the lookout for results that are exceptionally persuasive, relevant, interesting, and unusual. Sometimes the deviant respondent with the strange answers can provide the most insight if his or her responses are pursued and not discarded. For example, in Figure 15-4, more respondents answered the age question than the income question. Of the 48 respondents who did not answer the income question, almost all of them were "moderately interested" in the new health plan. Why? Are there any implications? Sometimes a few or even one deviant respondent can provide useful ideas and insights.

The best way to provide interest is to make the content so relevant that the audience will be interested: however, one may not always have been absorbing the content. Especially in those cases, it is very useful to make the presentation a lively and interesting experience. One way is to interject humor. The best humor is that tied to the subject matter or to the presentation, as opposed to memorized jokes that really do not fit. It is good to reward the audience periodically, however, and humor often works. Another tactic is to change the pace of the presentation. Break up the text with graphs, pictures, or even cartoons. In an oral presentation, try a variety of visual aids and some audience-involvement techniques. For example, the audience may be asked a question periodically and given a chance to talk and become involved.

Be Specific and Visual

Avoid talking or writing in the abstract. If different members of the audience have different or vague understandings of important concepts, there is a potential problem. Terms that are ambiguous or not well known should be defined and illustrated or else omitted. Thus, in a segmentation study, an "active saver" might be unambiguously defined as one who added at least $500 to savings in each of the last two years.

The most interesting presentations usually use specific stories, anecdotes, studies, or incidents to make points. They will be much more interesting and graphic than a generalization, however accurate and scientific. Instead of "studies have shown that . . . ," it is more effective to say, "in the Topeka test market the 69-cent price had far less trial than the 89-cent price for product X when the bright blue package was used." In other words, give concrete examples. A utility company conducted a focus-group study to learn homeowners' motivations to conserve energy and their attitudes toward adding insulation. The marketing research director, in presenting the results to top management, played a 20-minute edited videotape recording of the focus groups, in which the key segments were illustrated graphically. The impact on the audience was greater than otherwise would have been possible. They actually heard specific customers, representative of the emerged segments, forcefully put forth their views.

The adage, "A picture is worth a thousand words," applies to both written and oral presentations. A mass of data often can be communicated clearly with

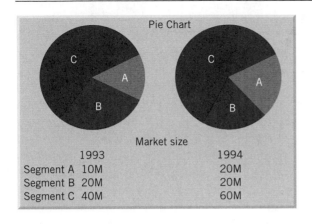

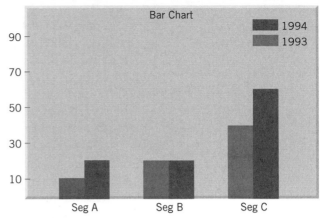

FIGURE 22-2
Graphically portrayed data

graphs. A wide variety is available, such as bar graphs, line graphs, and pie charts (see Figure 22-2). Color can be employed to add interest, to highlight findings, and to help deal with complexity. Also, use short "crisp" titles as opposed to longer titles (see Table 22-1).

Address Issues of Validity and Reliability

The presentation should help the audience avoid misinterpreting the results. Throughout Part II of this book, countless potential research design issues are raised that can affect the validity and interpretation of the results. The wording of the questions, the order in which they are asked, and the sampling design are among the design dimensions that can lead to biased results and misinter-

TABLE 22-1
Title of Tables/Figures

	Hypothetical, Longer, More Explanatory Titles Typical of Many Presentations	Short "Crisp" Titles
Example 1	Median incomes for families, by type of community, for 1940 through 1980	Family incomes by area (1940–1980)
Example 2	Projected incomes for families, by type of community, for 1990 through 2020	Income predictions: the next thirty years
Example 3	Critical path analysis, tasks, and slack time for 12-month work program	Next year's work program
Example 4	Effectiveness—cost ratios for alternative development projects for fiscal year 1989-90	Project recommendations for next year
Example 5	Unemployment rates and frequencies for major industries and communities for six-county area	Regional unemployment statistics

Source: Adapted from Witzling and Greenstreet, Presenting Statistics (New York: John Wiley & Sons). p. 224. 1992.

pretations. The presentation should not include an exhaustive description of all the design considerations. Nobody is interested in a textbook discussion of the advantages of telephone over mail surveys or how you located homes in an area sampling design. However, when the wording of a question or some other design issue can affect an interpretation and ultimately a research conclusion, that issue should be raised and its possible effect upon the interpretation discussed. For example, in a product-concept test, the method of exposing respondents to the concept may be crucial. Some discussion of why the method used was selected and its effect on the interpretation may be very useful. Try to identify those design issues that will affect interpretation and raise them in the context of the interpretation.

The presentation should include some indication of the reliability of the results. At a minimum, it always should be clear what sample size was involved. The key results should be supported by more precise information in the form of interval estimates or a hypothesis test. The hypothesis test basically indicates, given the sample size, what probability exists that the results were merely an accident of sampling. If the probability (or significance level) of the latter is not low, then the results probably would not be repeated. Do not imply more precision than is warranted. If 15 out of 52 respondents answered positively, do not give the precentage as 28.846. Rather, use 29 percent, or "nearly 30 percent." Consider the following exchange:

Speaker:	27.273 percent favored version B of the product.
Audience Member:	What was the sample size?
Speaker:	Around 11.
Audience Member:	Really? As large as that!

WRITTEN PRESENTATION

The general guidelines discussed so far are applicable to both written and oral presentations. However, it is important to generate a research report that will be interesting to read. Most researchers are not trained in effective report writing. In their enthusiasm for research, they often overlook the need for a good writing style. In writing a report, long sentences should be reconsidered and the critical main points should stand out. Here are some hints[3] for effective report writing.

▶ Use main heading and subheadings to communicate the content of the material discussed.

Main Heading: Probability Sampling
   Subheading: Statistical Issues in Probability Sampling—Systematic Sampling

▶ Use present tense as much as possible to communicate information.
   "Most of the consumers prefer Brand A to Brand B"

▶ Whether the presentation is written or oral, use active voice construction to make it lively and interesting. Passive voice is wordy and dull.

Active voice: Most consumers prefer Brand A.
Passive voice: Brand A is preferred by most of the consumers.

▶ Use computer-generated tables and graphs for effective presentation. Figures 22-3 and 22-4 are examples of graphical illustration, and Table 22-2 shows the results for a sample of questions in a table form.

▶ Use informative headings:
"Brand Quality is the Key Factor in Product Selection," as opposed to "Outcomes of Product Selection Analysis."

▶ Use verbations to communicate respondents' comments. Many times the way a customer expresses himself/herself means a lot to the brand manager.

▶ Use double-sided presentation if possible. For example, tables or graphs could be presented on the left side of an open report and their descriptions on the right side.

The Organization of the Report

A report can be organized in many ways, since no one format is suitable for all purposes. The nature of the topic, the type of study, and the nature of the audience will dictate the report's format. A general format for presenting a research report is given in Table 22-3.

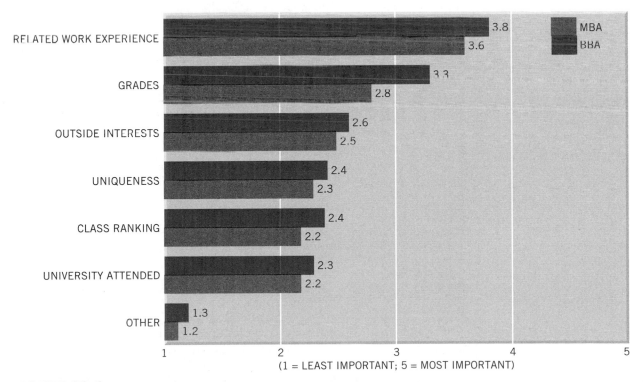

FIGURE 22-3
Ranking of resume screening factors

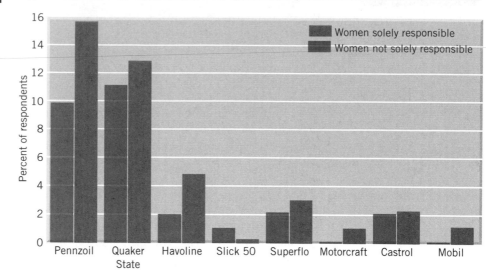

FIGURE 22-4
Unaided recall of brand name

Cover Page:	The cover page should provide information on the title of the study, the date prepared, for whom it is prepared, and the researcher(s)' names and organization.	
Executive Summary:	This must be brief, crisp, and informative, since most of the time executives pay attention only to this section. Present the research objectives and goals, findings, conclusions, and recommendations.	
Table of Contents:	This includes complete details of all the major sections and subsections and gives the associated page numbers. Table 22-4 is an example of a table of contents for a research report.	
Information:	This section should describe the nature of the problem, clearly state the research objectives and research questions, and give an overview of the report's organization.	
Methodology:	Describe the methodology used to conduct the study. All technical details should be presented in the appendix.	
Findings:	The results of the study usually occupy the bulk of the report. Describe the findings in detail along with the necessary tables and graphs. This is the place to give the managerial implications of the study results.	
Limitations:	Usually, assumptions are made while conducting a research study. This section should describe the limitations of the assumptions and any problems that may have arisen during the data collection, sampling, or survey process.	
Conclusions and Recommendations:	Here, you should clearly state the conclusions of the study and give possible recommendations. These recommendations would involve either suggesting a strategy or presenting ideas for implementing strategies, and so forth.	
Appendixes:	These contain all technical details of the study such as copies of questionnaires, coding instructions, data, sampling, plan, and so on.	

Finally, you should include a cover letter with the report. This cover letter provides details on the enclosed material—the research report, who is responsible for the project, and which people are receiving copies of the report. It should also communicate that the researcher will be happy to answer any questions that may arise from the report.

TABLE 22-2
Descriptive Information on the Responses

	Question	Statistic	Mean	Median	Min	Max	Standard Deviation
	Need for external marketing research great?[1]		2.68	2.50	1	5	1.04
	Importance of need for external marketing research[2]		2.50	2.50	1	5	1.18
M							
A	Duration too long?[1]		2.90	3.00	2	5	1.01
R	Duration too short?[1]		2.45	3.00	1	4	0.85
K	Importance of duration[2]		2.09	2.00	1	4	1.06
E							
T	Frequency good?[1]		2.72	3.00	1	4	10.7
I	Importance of Frequency[2]		2.13	2.00	1	4	0.99
N							
G	Price Good?[1]		2.90	3.00	1	5	1.15
	Importance of Price[2]		2.68	3.00	1	5	1.17
R							
E	Results Confidential?[1]		4.04	5.00	2	5	1.55
S	Importance of Confidentiality[2]		3.90	4.00	1	5	1.41
E							
A	Benefits to UH Great?[1]		4.00	4.00	2	5	0.81
R	Importance of UH Benefits[2]		2.45	2.00	1	5	1.14
C							
H	Sponsor time too long?[1]		2.27	2.00	1	4	0.82
	Sponsor time too short?[1]		2.90	3.00	2	4	0.68
	Importance of Sponsor time[2]		2.27	2.00	1	4	0.88
	Value of Project?[1]		3.18	3.00	1	5	1.05
	Importance of Value[2]		3.50	3.00	1	5	1.10

[1] 1 = Strongly Disagree, 2 = Disagree, 3 = Neither Agree nor Disagree, 5 = Agree, 6 = Strongly Agree
[2] 1 = Of No Importance, 2 = Moderately Important, 3 = Important, 4 = Very Important, 5 = Extremely Important

TABLE 22-3
General Format for a Research Report

   I. Cover Page
  II. Executive Summary
 III. Table of Contents
 IV. Introduction
  V. Methodology
 VI. Findings
VII. Limitations
VIII. Conclusions and Recommendations
 IX. Appendixes

TABLE 22-4
Table of Contents of a Research Report

I. Introduction 1

II. Description of Research 3

III. Research Design 4
  Overview of the Marketing Issue 4
  Methodology 4
    Mode of Data Collection 4
    Sampling Procedure 5
    Data Analysis 6
    Description of Cross-Tabulation 7

IV. Analysis of Results 8
  How Maintenance is Managed 8
  Selection of Shampoo 9
    Frequency Distribution 9
    Cross-Tabulations 10
  Advertising and Maintenance 11
  Demographics 11
    Age 12
    Marital Status 13
    Education 14
    Income 15

V. Limitations of the Study 16

VI. Conclusions and Recommendations 17
  Conclusions 17
  Strategic Recommendations 18

VII. Appendixes
  Appendix A. Interview Questions
  Appendix B. Questionnaire
  Appendix C. Coding Instructions
  Appendix D. Frequency Distribution Tables
  Appendix E. Variable Relationships Studied

ORAL PRESENTATION

The ability to communicate orally is extremely important to effective management in general and to the marketing research functions in particular. What can be done to ensure that the oral presentation is as effective as possible? The following five suggestions will be discussed in this section:

1. Don't read.
2. Use visual aids.
3. Make sure the start is positive.
4. Avoid distracting the audience.
5. Involve the audience.

Don't Read

Not everyone will agree with this first suggestion; however, these authors firmly believe that the risks and disadvantages of reading outweigh the advantages. The biggest problem with reading is that it usually is boring for the reader and for the audience. Very few can make a script sound interesting, and those few usually do even better without a script. Further, it is necessary to develop the ability to communicate orally in front of a group without a script, to prepare for those occasions when there is no time to prepare a script or when the presenter must adapt to new developments in the middle of a presentation. If you rely too heavily on a script and use it in what may be limited opportunities to give presentations, you will not develop this important capability.

The advantages of reading from a written report are that the time of the presentation and the choice of words are not left to chance, and you are protected from an attack of stage fright. The alternative is good preparation, a set of notes, and rehearsal. The notes should provide (1) an outline so that the proper flow is maintained, and (2) a list of items that should be included. You may want to consult the notes occasionally to make sure you have not omitted anything. More detailed notes can be consulted more frequently. To avoid distraction, keep the notes on a lectern or on cards or a clipboard, positioned so that you can manage them easily with one hand. Especially when the length of the presentation needs to be carefully controlled, rehearsal is essential. Often, five or more rehearsals can be worthwhile. It is even better if feedback is available in the form of a practice audience or a videotape. You can combat stage fright with deep breathing, pauses, and experience. There is no substitute for experience.

Use Visual Aids

Visual aids perform several functions. First, they give impact to the information and focus attention on important points. Second, ideas that are extremely difficult to express in words often can be communicated easily with visual aids. Finally, they help to give the presentation variety. Visual aids include transparencies, charts, handouts, slides, videotapes, films, samples, demonstrations, and role playing. Transparencies, charts, slides, and handouts are probably the most widely used.

Transparencies are easy to make and can be carried in a folder. They have the advantage of controlling the audience's attention. The transparency can be exposed one line at a time by covering the rest with a piece of paper. The audience thus focuses on what is being uncovered at the moment and does not wander ahead of the presentation. You can write on the transparency to make a point during the presentation. The key to successful use of transparencies is using readable, large type, and minimizing the number of words or numbers used. Experienced and skilled users of transparencies often use only five or fewer lines per transparency, with each line containing only a few words or numbers. One rule of thumb is that a single transparency should contain no more then 30 words or items of data.

Similar guidelines apply to charts and slides, which share most of the characteristics of transparencies. Charts are more versatile than transparencies but are less convenient to make and carry. Slides are better for large audiences, since they can be seen more easily, but they require time to prepare and are not easily modified. Thus, they are not suitable for a presentation that is still being developed and refined.

The use of handouts provides the audience with something to take notes on and to take with them. As a result, the audience burden of taking notes is greatly reduced. Sometimes when transparencies are used, the audience's note-taking task is so difficult that it becomes distracting. Handouts free listeners to attend to and participate more fully in the presentation. Their disadvantages are that they must be prepared beforehand and the audience is tempted to look ahead. Further, there is always the distraction of making sure everyone is on the right page, although numbering the pages helps.

Make Sure the Start Is Positive

The start should be positive in tone, confident, and involving. Sometimes a period of silence can be used effectively to get attention. It is useful to stimulate and involve the audience immediately, perhaps by a provocative question or statement. Absolutely, never apologize at the outset, even in jest. If you tell the audience you are nervous, unprepared, or unknowledgeable, even in the context of a humorous line, it will tend to believe you.

Avoid Distracting the Audience

The presenter needs to be aware that the audience is easily distracted. The following do's and don'ts address some common causes of distraction:

1. Take everything out of your pockets and make sure there is nothing on the lectern other than your notes. Remove pens, pointers, keys, clips— everything. It often happens, without your even being aware of it, that you will pick up objects and manipulate them until the audience is severely distracted, if not driven bananas.
2. Try to avoid the extremes of either obvious pacing or hiding behind a lectern. It can be as distracting to see a speaker clutch a lectern for support as to see someone pace back and forth. The speaker's movements should be purposeful and natural, such as stepping aside to point to a chart, standing or sitting beside the lectern, or moving closer to the audience for a short portion of the presentation.
3. Maintain good eye contact. This allows audience feedback, stimulates trust and confidence in what you are saying, and involves the audience. A speaker who avoids eye contact by looking up or down or somewhere else risks distracting the audience.
4. Be concerned with the sound of your voice. Listen to a tape of your presentation if possible. A presentation can be distracting if it is too soft, loud, fast, slow, or monotoned. Be sure to use pauses to break up the presentation and to allow the audience time to digest the material.

Involve the Audience

An involved audience will be more interested. An effective technique is to intersperse questions throughout. If time does not permit a discussion, a pause at least gives the audience members a chance to reflect. Sometimes it is useful to ask each person to write down his or her opinion on a piece of paper; for example, personal judgment on a key value in the data analysis. Another technique is to refer to the ideas of people in the audience, saying, for example, "As John mentioned last week . . ."

The question-and-answer part of the presentation is particularly important. This often concludes the talk, but it can be permitted to occur during the presentation. Pause and make sure that the question is understood; then, if possible, give a short positive or negative response and as compact an explanation as possible. If you do not know, say so, adding (if appropriate) that you will get the answer by the next day. A good technique is to write the question down so you do not forget it. Equally as important, those in the audience see that you are taking them seriously. Anticipate questions beforehand, and rehearse the answers. Sometimes it is even effective to leave things out of the presentation if they could be covered more effectively during the question-and-answer period.

Relationship with the Client. It is important to work with the client or at least be available to clarify or interpret the research results when the findings are implemented. The continued relationship not only helps researchers to evaluate the project's usefulness, but gives them a sense of confidence about the quality of their work. Since most of the marketing research projects are obtained through word-of-mouth referrals, not through advertising, it is important to satisfy the client. It may be useful for the researcher to sit with the client and get feedback on various aspects of the research project.

Summary

Communication skills are important to the marketing research process; this includes the presentation of both the research proposal and the research results. An effective presentation involves several elements. The audience should be clearly identified so that the presentation will be on target. It should include an introduction with an overview of the presentation structure, a body, and a summary. Motivation can be provided by relating the presentation to the research objectives and purpose, by focusing on the most interesting findings, and by having an interesting presentation style. The use of specific examples and visual material can help you communicate more effectively and interestingly. You should discuss those elements of methodology that affect interpretation.

Several guidelines can help improve both written and oral presentations. Reading a report tends to be boring and should be avoided. Visual aids such as transparencies and handouts can add punch and improve communication. Make sure the start is positive. Try to involve the audience, and avoid distracting mannerisms.

Questions and Problems

1. By what criteria would you evaluate a written presentation? Develop an evaluation form. Would it differ depending on whether the research proposal or the research results were being presented?
2. By what criteria would you evaluate an oral presentation? Develop an evaluation form.
3. Observe three specific oral presentations outside of class. Consider the following:
   a. Were there any distracting mannerisms?
   b. What did the presenters do with their hands?
   c. How was the audience involved, if at all?
   d. Evaluate the visual aids used. Would you recommend the use of other visual aids?
   e. Did you ever become confused or bored? Was there anything the presenter could have done differently to counteract that tendency?

End Notes

1. Ron Hoff. "What's Your Presentation Quotient?" *Advertising Age*, January 16, 1978, 93.
2. "Teaching the Boss to Write," *Business Week*, October 25, 1976, 56.
3. Adapted from H. L. Gordon. "Eight Ways to Dress a Research Report," *Advertising Age*, October 20, 1980, S-37.

CASES FOR PART IV
Special Topics in Data Analysis

CASE IV-1
Smith's Clothing (B)

In the Smith's Clothing (A) case a research project was developed in which the following types of information were gathered:

1. Image data using 20 attributes for four different stores, including Smith's.
2. Patronage data: where respondents shopped and where they last bought.

3. A bank of 30 life-style questions relating to shopping and women's clothing.
4. A 10-question scale that measures opinion leadership in women's fashions and the tendency to discuss women's fashions.
5. A set of importance weights on the 20 attributes used in the image question-bank.
6. Demographic variables.

Develop an analysis strategy using the various multivariate techniques that have been covered. The sample size is 1000.

CASE IV-2
Newfood[1]

Mr. Conrad Ulcer, newly appointed New Products marketing director for Concorn Kitchens, was considering the possibility of marketing a new highly nutritional food product with widely varied uses. This product could be used as a snack, a camping food, or as a diet food. The product was to be generically labeled Newfood.

Because of this wide range of possible uses, the company had great difficulty in defining the market. The product was viewed as having no direct competitors. Early product and concept tests were very encouraging. These tests led Mr. Ulcer to believe that the product could easily sell 2 million cases (24 packages in a case) under the proposed marketing program involving a 24-cents package price and an advertising program involving $3 million in expenditures per year.

The projected P & L for the first year national was

Sales	2.00 million cases
Revenue	$8.06 million (assumes 70 percent of the retail price is revenue to the manufacturer)
Manufacturing costs	$3.00 million ($1 million fixed manufacturing costs plus $1 per case variable)
Advertising	$3.00 million
Net margin	$2.06 million

There were no capital expenditures required to go national, since manufacturing was to be done on a contract pack basis. These costs were included in the projected P & L. Concorn has an agreement with the contract packer requiring that once a decision to go national is made, Concorn is obligated to pay fixed production costs ($1 million per year) for three years even if the product is withdrawn from the market at a later time.

Even though there are no capital requirements, it was the company's policy not to introduce new products with profit expectations of less than $.5 million per year (a 3-year planning horizon was usually considered).

Because there was considerable uncertainty among Concorn management as to either probable first-year or subsequent-year sales, or the best introductory campaign, it was decided that a six-month market test would be conducted. The objectives of the test were to

▶ Better estimate first-year sales.

▶ Study certain marketing variables to determine an optimal—or at least better—introductory plan.

▶ Estimate the long-run potential of the product.

These objectives were accomplished through the controlled introduction of the product into four markets. Conditions were experimentally varied within the gro-

---

[1] Reproduced with permission from Prof. Gerald Eskin, and the Board of Trustees, Leland Stanford Junior University, Stanford, CA.

cery stores in each of the four markets. Sales were measured with a store audit of a panel of stores. Preliminary results had been obtained. Now it was up to Mr. Ulcer to decide what they meant for the introductory strategy of Newfood.

Design of Experimental Study

The three variables included in the experimental design were price, advertising expenditures, and location of the product within the store. Three prices were tested (24 cents, 29 cents, 34 cents); two levels of advertising (a simulation of a $3 million introduction plan and a $6 million plan); and two locations (placing the product in the bread section versus the instant breakfast section). Prices and location were varied across stores within cities while advertising was varied across cities. The advertising was all in the form of spot TV. The levels were selected so that they would stimulate on a local basis the impact that could be achieved from national introduction programs at the $3 million and $6 million expenditure levels. Due to differential costs between markets and differential costs between spot and network (to be used in national introduction), an attempt was made to equate (and measure) advertising inputs of gross advertising impressions generated, normalized for market size. Unfortunately, it was not possible to achieve exactly the desired levels. This was due to the problem of nonavailabilities of spots in some markets and discrepancies between estimate of TV audiences made at the time the test was being planned and the actual audiences reached at the time the commercials were actually run.

The advertising plan and actual gross rating points (GRPs) achieved, by city, are as follows:

City	Advertising Plan—Simulation of First Year National Program	Desired GRPs per Week	Actual GRPs Achieved
3	$3.0 million	100	105
4	$3.0 million	100	110
1	$6.0 million	200	165
2	$6.0 million	200	190

Complete information is not available on the distribution of spots over the six-month period, but it is known that about as many spots were run in the first two months as in the next four months combined.

The test design is summarized below. Treatment was held constant over the entire six-month period. Each cell contained three stores. Each store was audited monthly.

		P = 24 cents		P = 29 cents		P = 34 cents	
City	ADV Level	L1	L2	L1	L2	L1	L2
3	Low						
4	Low						
1	High						
2	High						

P = Price
L = Location
3 stores per cell

The design generated the following sample sizes:

	Per Month	Total for Six Months
Per Price	24	144
Per Location	36	216
Per Adv Level	36	216
Per City	18	108
Total	72	432

The data were analyzed on a bimonthly basis. The response measure used in the analysis was average unit sales per month per experimental cell.

Control Measures

In the selection of cities and stores for the tests, attempts were made to match cells and cities on such variables as store size, number of checkout counters, and characteristics of the trading area. Because it was not certain that adequate matches had been achieved, it was decided to obtain measurements on some of these variables for possible use in adjusting for differences in cell characteristics. It was also felt that it might be possible to learn something about the relationships between these variables and sales, and that this information would be of assistance in planning the product introduction into other markets.

The data are listed in Exhibit IV-1. Exhibit IV-2 presents a matrix of simple correlation coefficients. Thus the correlation between the first two months sales ($S1$) and price was $-.70$.

Questions for Discussion

1. The correlation between price and sales is large and negative for all three time periods. What does this say about how price works?

EXHIBIT IV-1

Average Unit Sales Per Month								
First 2 Months S1	Second 2 Months S2	Last 2 Months S3	Price P	Adv (1 if High, 0 Otherwise) A	Location (1 if Instant Breakfast, 0 Otherwise) L	Income (000) I	Store $ Vol (000) V	City #
225	190	205	24	0	0	7.3	34	3
323	210	241	24	0	0	8.3	41	4
424	275	256	24	1	0	6.9	32	1
268	200	201	24	1	0	6.5	28	2
224	190	209	24	0	1	7.3	34	3
331	178	267	24	0	1	8.3	41	4
254	157	185	24	1	1	6.9	23	1
492	351	365	24	1	1	6.5	37	2
167	163	145	29	0	0	6.5	33	3
226	148	170	29	0	0	8.4	39	4
210	134	128	29	1	0	6.5	30	1
289	212	200	29	1	0	6.2	27	2
204	200	175	29	0	1	6.5	37	3
288	171	247	29	0	1	8.4	43	4
245	120	117	29	1	1	6.5	30	1
161	116	111	29	1	1	6.2	19	2
161	141	111	34	0	1	7.2	32	3
246	126	184	34	0	0	8.1	42	4
128	83	83	34	1	0	6.6	29	1
154	122	102	34	1	0	6.1	24	2
163	116	116	34	0	1	7.2	32	3
151	112	119	34	0	1	8.1	36	4
180	100	75	34	1	1	6.6	29	1
150	122	101	34	1	1	6.1	24	2
Mean 236	164	171	29	.5	.5	7.0	32	

EXHIBIT IV-2

		(S1)	(S2)	(S3)	(P)	(A)	(L)	(I)	(V)
Matrix of Simple Correlation Coefficients									
(S1)	1	1							
(S2)	2	.88	1						
(S3)	3	.92	.90	1					
(P)	4	−.70	−.73	−.77	1				
(A)	5	.12	.03	−.16	0	1			
(L)	6	.01	−.04	.04	0	0	1		
(I)	7	.18	.00	.34	−.13	−.75	0	1	
(V)	8	.39	.30	.54	−.18	−.74	−.04	.81	1

2. Explain the correlations between advertising and sales. What is happening to the advertising effect over time?

3. Note that the intercorrelations between advertising location and price are all zero. Why?

4. Run regressions for each of the three sales variables (S1, S2, S3) using P, A, and L as independent variables. What do these regressions imply about the effect of price? Of advertising? Of location?

5. Rerun the regressions adding the variables I and V. Do your judgments about the effects of price, advertising, and location change? Why?

6. If possible, obtain an output of residuals (differences between the model predicted Y and the actual Y). Check the residuals to identify observations that do not seem to fit the model. Why don't they fit? For example, the residual for the second observation of the S1 variable would be the difference between 323 (the observed value) and the prediction made by the model, i.e., the intercept

   plus P (24) times the price regression coefficient

   plus A (0) times the advertising regression coefficient

   plus L (0) times the location regression coefficient

   plus I (8.3) times the income regression coefficient

   plus V (41) times the store regression coefficient

7. What additional regression runs, if any, should be made to complete the analysis of this data?

PART V

APPLICATIONS

23

TRADITIONAL APPLICATIONS OF MARKETING RESEARCH: PRODUCT AND PRICE

Learning Objectives

▶ Introduce the major applications of marketing research.

▶ Discuss the information requirements for new product research.

▶ Provide discussion on the various techniques used for concept generation, product evaluation and development, and pretest and test marketing.

▶ Briefly discuss the forecasting techniques usually used for assessing product demand potential in various organizations.

▶ Introduce the applications of marketing research in pricing of the product.

Now that we have considered the various steps in the marketing research process in detail, it is time to think about what to do with it. In Part V we again talk briefly about the various applications of marketing research, which can be applied to every stage of the marketing process. Traditionally, marketing decisions have been divided into 4Ps—product, price, promotion, and place (henceforth, distribution) decisions. In the first two chapters of Part V, we discuss the information needs for the 4P decisions and the various techniques available in the industry to obtain that information. The last chapter in this part deals with the marketing research applications for contemporary issues like total quality management, brand equity, and customer satisfaction.

This chapter deals with product and price decisions. The main product decisions that need to be considered are the physical design of the product and its demand potential. Many companies spend millions of dollars in R&D in order to come up with a new product that will satisfy consumer needs. The various information requirements and techniques used for this purpose are covered in the following section called New Product Research. The other major decision regarding new products is how to forecast sales potential. Various methods of forecasting are discussed briefly. Once the product is available, its price must be determined. We also discuss two methods of pricing and their informational requirements.

NEW PRODUCT RESEARCH

New products development is critical to the life of most organizations as they adapt to their changing environment. Since, by definition, new products contain unfamiliar aspects for the organization, there will be uncertainty associated with them. Thus, it is not surprising that a large proportion of marketing research is for the purpose of reducing the uncertainty associated with new products.

New-product research can be divided into four stages, as shown in Figure 23-1. The first stage is generating new product concepts; the second is evaluating and developing those concepts; the third is evaluating and developing the actual products; and, finally, comes testing the product in a marketing program.

Concept Generation

There are two types of concept generation research. The first might be termed **need identification research.** The emphasis in need research is on identifying unfilled needs in the market. The second is termed **concept identification.** Here, an effort is made to determine concepts that might fill an identified need.

Need Identification. There are various ways by which marketing research can identify needs. Some are qualitative and others, like segmentation studies, can be quantitative. The following are some examples:

▶ **Perceptual maps,** in which products are positioned along the dimensions by which users perceive and evaluate, can suggest gaps into which new products might fit. MDS typically is used to generate these perceptual maps.

▶ Social and environmental **trends** can be analyzed. For instance, a trend away from low-calorie foods was the reason that Pizza Hut introduced the Big Foot Pizza and McDonald's reintroduced the Quarterpounder.

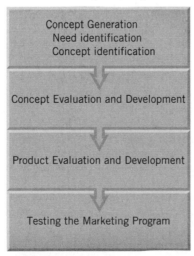

FIGURE 23-1
Phases in new product research

▶ An approach termed **benefit structure analysis** has product users identify the benefits desired and the extent to which the product delivers those benefits, for specific use applications. The result is an identification of benefits sought that current products do not deliver.[1]

▶ Product users might be asked to keep a diary of a relevant portion of their activities. Analyzing such diaries can provide an understanding of unsolved problems associated with a particular task.

▶ In focus-group interviews, product users might discuss problems associated with product-use situations. Thus, office managers might, for example, discuss problems they have experienced with the postal service.

▶ **Lead user analysis** is another approach that many companies now use more often. Using this approach, instead of just asking the users what they have done, their solutions are collected more formally. First, lead users are identified. **Lead users** are those who early on face needs that later will be general in a marketplace; they are positioned to benefit significantly by solving problems associated with these needs. Once a lead user is identified, the concepts that company or person generates are tested.

The advertising agency BBDO, which relies heavily on "problem detection" to generate new-product concepts and ideas for advertising campaigns, has developed a procedure for rating problems.[2] The agency asks each respondent who is a potential prospect to rank each problem as to whether it

▶ Is important.
▶ Occurs frequently.
▶ Has a solution.

A "problem score" is obtained by combining these ratings, and the score is used to screen ideas. Using this technique, BBDO found that buyers of a dog food felt that it

▶ Smelled bad.
▶ Cost too much.
▶ Did not come in different sizes for different dogs.

Subsequently, the company developed products that were responsive to the criticisms.

Concept Identification. There are various ways to identify concepts. Some are neither user-based nor follow from an identification of unfilled needs. For example, a technological breakthrough can suggest concepts, as when the freeze-dry process suggested freeze-dried fruit in cereal; or competitors may introduce a new product that represents either a threat to or an opportunity for an organization. One role of marketing research is to monitor the environment systematically to learn of technological or competitive developments that may suggest new concepts.

During the new-product development process usually there is a point where a concept is formed but there is no tangible usable product that can be tested. The concept should be defined well enough so that it is communicable. There may be simply a verbal description, or there may be a rough idea for a name, a package, or an advertising approach. The role of marketing research at this stage is to determine if the concept warrants further development and to provide guidance on how it might be improved and refined. Conjoint analysis typically is used to obtain an ideal combination of the concept's various features. Thus, research questions might include

► Are there any major flaws in the concept?

► What consumer segments might be attracted to it?

► Is there enough interest to warrant developing it further?

► How might it be altered or developed further?

There are approaches to concept testing that do not involve obtaining reactions from relevant people. One is to attempt to identify a set of similar products and to learn what the market response to them has been. Thus, a new crossword puzzle aid might be partly evaluated by determining the sales of similar products such as crossword puzzle dictionaries or of such complementary products as crossword puzzle magazines.

Most concept testing, however, involves exposing people to the concept and getting their reactions. In exposing people to the concept, the market researcher needs to address a series of questions:

► How are the concepts exposed?

► To whom are the concepts exposed?

► To what are they compared?

► What questions are asked?

There always will be a trade-off between the timing of the concept test and the development of the marketing program. The whole point of concept testing is to determine if it is worthwhile to develop a marketing program. So it is not realistic to hold off concept testing until a marketing program exists. Still, there is always the danger that a missing element in the final marketing program could distort the test.

Normally, the concept is exposed through personal contact, either in the respondent's home, office, or plant, or in some central location like a shopping center. Normally, respondents should include those who would be among the target segments. Since the goal of concept testing is to determine if a viable market exists, the researcher should be careful to avoid omitting a potential segment from the study.

Usually, the concept test will explore several versions of a concept or several product concepts responsive to a user need. For example, in the mid-1960s, in response to an identified need for a household garbage disposal system, Whirlpool engineers tested four concepts: a disposable garbage can, a garbage compactor that would hold two weeks' worth of garbage, a built-in kitchen compactor, and a portable kitchen compactor.[3] The concept test showed the last two alternatives to be definitely superior.

For the evaluative aspects of concept testing, it is necessary to include some overall indication of attitudes, interest, and likelihood of purchase. The purchase likelihood, for example, could be scaled as

Definitely Buy	Probably Buy	Might or Might Not Buy	Probably Not Buy	Definitely Not Buy

Researchers must interpret the results cautiously, particularly when they are encouraging, since the exposure, even if presented in a relatively neutral way, will sensitize the respondent to the product. The result actually is an exaggerated tendency to indicate that the respondent will buy the product.

Concept testing is particularly important for durable goods and many industrial products, because they rarely employ use testing or test markets. The Ford Taurus, Mitsubishi large-screen TV sets, or the Sony Camcorder were never in test markets, for example. The problem is that it really is not practical to develop or produce such equipment on a pilot basis. A major commitment is required and it would not be realistic economically to withdraw the product after market-testing it.

Product Evaluation and Development

Product evaluation and development, or product testing, is very similar to concept testing, in terms of both the objectives and the techniques. The aim is still to predict market response to determine whether or not the product should be carried forward.

Use Testing. The simplest form of **use testing** gives users the product, and, after a reasonable amount of time, asks their reactions to it, including their intentions to buy it. Researchers can contact the respondents in shopping centers, by personal visit to their homes or offices, or, initially, by telephone. Burlington Industries, producer of fabrics, calls randomly selected telephone numbers to locate adult women who make many of their own clothes and who would be willing to evaluate a new dress fabric.[4] The fabric then is sent by mail, and a second telephone interview two months later solicits their description of their experience with it. Now market researchers can use the latest in computer technology and can do **virtual product testing,** which is explained in Exhibit 23-1.

There are several problems associated with use tests. First, because of unclear instructions, a misunderstanding, or lack of cooperation, respondents may not use the product correctly and may therefore report a negative opinion. Or they may not use it at all and simply fabricate an opinion. Second, the fact

EXHIBIT 23-1

Virtual Testing

MarketWare Corp. believes it has captured real marketing research on consumer behavior in its new software, Visionary Shopper. The suburban Atlanta-based firm, already a leader in pegboard-display product space management software with its Pegman product, now is trying to take its technology into the rest of the store with its new virtual reality-based software. The system, which runs on PCs, allows consumers to stroll through store aisles on a computer screen, allowing examination of packages as though the shelf was really in front of them. MarketWare believes a multitude of marketing variables can be measured in impact through the process, which for most brands and categories runs about 30 minutes per consumer.

Most significantly, though, according to MarketWare's Stephen Needel, who directs the firm's simulation efforts, "it feels like fun" for the consumer. "We can extend the time we have them in there" doing the testing because of the appeal of the three-dimensional presentation and real-shelf look. Consumers can actually remove products easily from a shelf, examine labels, study prices and other product options, and react to shelf-layout changes or promotional and pricing considerations—all without setting foot in a store. And for consumers sensitized to batteries of direct marketing and marketing research mail and phone calls, the system is a pleasant break, because "it's not survey work," said Needel. "It's virtual reality."

Consumers are recruited through store and mall intercepts and given about five minutes' training on the software. Then MarketWare personnel leave them alone to do their shopping so that they'll rely on themselves rather than a proctor to walk through the virtual store aisles. The anonymity also helps boost real consumer responses to the variables being tested. Literally, the software gives consumers a grocery-store look, allowing for zoom-ins on shelves and packages, and real handling of packages to study labels, right down to rotating the package, seemingly by hand. Prompts allow the consumers to place the package in their grocery carts for purchase and/or replace it on the shelf. If designated for purchase, it appears in the cart with other purchased items, while the hole it created in being removed from the shelf appears on the computer screen image of that shelf.

In combination with the firm's market-leading Pegman software, shelf rearrangement and different marketing variable examinations are rapidly and easily done. "We can test as many variables at the same time as you want," said Needel. Needel also believes the system will get beyond some consumer responses that otherwise might not be accurately attained. For instance, the amount of beer a consumer might remove from a shelf in such a virtual reality test might be more in line with reality than what the consumer might say in survey research to avoid presenting an image of drinking too much.

Source: Howard Schlossberg. "Shoppers Virtually Stroll Through Store Aisles to Examine Packages," *Marketing News,* June 7, 1993, p. 2.

---

that they were given a free sample and are participating in a test may distort their impressions. Third, even when repurchase opportunities are made available, such decisions may be quite different than when they are made in a more realistic store situation with special displays presenting the new brand and those of its competitors. Fourth, there is the issue of whether the users will accept the product over a long time period. This problem is especially acute when repurchase data cannot be or are not obtained. Finally, they may inflate their intentions-to-buy question. Consumers may say that they will buy the product but may end up not doing so.[5]

A particular type of use test is the **blind-use test,** which is most appropriate just after the product emerges from the research-and-development laboratory. Even though a product may be proved superior in the laboratory, the consumer may not perceive it to be superior. For example, one consumer product company developed a window cleaner that was a definite improvement over existing products. The new product, however, was clear in color, whereas the existing products had a bluish tint. A blind-use test, however, showed that consumers preferred the existing products. One hypothesis was that the blue color of the existing products was the reason consumers preferred them over the new, clear product. To test this hypothesis, a blind-use test pitted the new product against blue-colored water. Over 30 percent of the respondents preferred the water. Thus, the color of the new window cleaner was identified as the problem in the blind-use tests and was addressed in subsequent product development. The blind taste tests used for New Coke, described in Exhibit 23-2, is a classic example of how these tests can lead to false results.

Predicting Trial Purchase. Several models have been developed to predict trial levels of new, frequently purchased consumer products.[6] The model termed ESP (estimating sales potential) is typical.[7] Data from 45 new-product introductions were obtained and used to estimate the model. Trial levels (the percentage of a sample of consumers who had purchased the product at least once within 12 months after launch) were predicted on the basis of three variables:

▶ Product class penetration (PCP)—the percentage of households purchasing at least one item in the product class within one year[8]

▶ Promotional expenditures—total consumer-directed promotional expenditures on the product

▶ Distribution of the product—percentage of stores stocking the product (weighted by the store's total sales volume)

EXHIBIT 23-2

The Introduction of New Coke

During the early 1980s, Pepsi gained share at the expense of Coca-Cola in part because Pepsi had a sweeter, smoother taste. Pepsi ads show that in "Pepsi Challenge" blind taste tests, people actually did prefer Pepsi over Coke. As a result, Coca-Cola ran tests of a new cola formula which involved 190,000 consumers in 35 cities, costing over $4 million dollars. They found that with brands not identified, the new Coke flavor was preferred to the original Coke by 55 percent to 45 percent. When the same consumers were told what they were tasting, their preference for the new flavor was 61 percent. The new flavor was preferred to Pepsi by as much as 56 percent to 44 percent.

Encouraged by this market research, Coca-Cola on May 9, 1985, replaced the Coca-Cola drink with "New Coke." It was a disaster. Coke users rebelled and demanded that the original Coke be returned. By July, a poll found that 60 percent of those who tried New Coke thought that the now unavailable original Coke tasted better. On July 10, 1985, Coca-Cola reintroduced the original product as "Classic Coke" and just a few months later Classic Coke was outperforming New Coke by as much as nine to one in some markets. In 1986 New Coke fell to a 2.3 percent share.

How did the research go so wrong? In retrospect, it seems clear that consumer reaction to the withdrawal of Coca-Cola should have been examined. New Coke was tested but not as a replacement to the original Coke. In the market introduction of New Coke, the original Coke was no longer available and thus consumers no longer had the freedom to choose. The fact that a choice was imposed was clearly resented and affected the acceptance and, in fact, the perceived taste of the product.

The Coke experience illustrates that it is very tenuous to use an attitude measure for an object in one context to predict the opinions in another context.

Source: Debra Jones Ringold. "Consumer Response to Product Withdrawal: The Reformulation of Coca-Cola." *Psychology and Marketing*, Fall 1988, 189–210.

Knowledge of these three variables enabled ESP to predict trial levels of the 45 new products extremely accurately. (The regression model explained 95 percent of the variance of the three variables.) Once the model is estimated, it can be applied to other new products. The manager simply estimates the percentage of households using the product class, the total promotional expenditures planned for the new product, and the expected distribution level. The model will then estimate the trial level that will be obtained.

Trial also can be estimated directly using controlled shopping experience. A respondent is exposed to the new product promotion and allowed to shop in a simulated store or in an actual store in which the product is placed. The respondents then will have an opportunity to make a "trial" or first purchase of the product.

Pretest Marketing. Table 23-1 is an overview of a laboratory test design (a form of pretest marketing) called ASSESSOR.[9] Two approaches are used to predict the new brand's market share. The first is based on the preference judgments. The preference data are used to predict the proportion of purchases

TABLE 23-1

The ASSESSOR Laboratory Test Market Research Design and Measurement[a]

Design	Procedure	Measurement
O_1	Respondent screening and recruitment (personal interview).	Criteria for target group identification (e.g., product class usage).
O_2	Premeasurement for established brands (self-administered questionnaire).	Composition of "relevant set" of established brands, attribute weights and ratings, and preferences.
X_1	Exposure to advertising for established brands and new brand.	
(O_3)	Measurement of reactions to the advertising materials (self-administered questionnaire).	Optional, (e.g., likability and believability ratings of advertising materials).
X_2	Simulated shopping trip and exposure to display of new and established brands.	
O_4	Purchase opportunity (choice recorded by research personnel).	Brand(s) purchased.
X_3	Home use/consumption of new brand.	
O_5	Postusage measurement (telephone interview).	New brand usage rate, satisfaction ratings, and repeat purchase propensity. Attribute ratings and preferences for "relevant set" of established brands plus the new brand.

Source: Adapted from Alvin J. Silk and Glen L. Urban. "Pre-Test-Market Evaluation of New Packaged Goods: A Model and Measurement Methodology." *Journal of Marketing Research, 15* (May 1978). 178.

[a] O = measurement; X = advertising or product exposure.

of the new brand that respondents will make given that the new brand is in their response set. These estimates for the respondents in the study are coupled with an estimate of the proportion of all people who will have the new brand in their response set, to provide an estimate of market share. A useful byproduct of this approach is an analysis of the concomitant market share losses of the other brands. If the firm has other brands in the market, such information can be critical.

The second approach involves estimating trial and repeat purchase levels based on the respondent's purchase decisions and intentions-to-buy judgments. A trial estimate is based on the percentage of respondents who purchase the product in the laboratory, plus an estimate of the product's distribution, advertising (which will create product awareness), and the number of free samples to be given away. The repeat-purchase rate is based on the proportion of respondents who make a mail-order repurchase of the new brand and the buying-intentions judgments of those who elected *not* to make a mail-order repurchase. The product of the trial estimate and the repeat purchase estimate become a second estimate of market share. ASSESSOR has been modified and other models have also been proposed for pre-test marketing.[10]

The method has a host of limiting assumptions and limitations. Perhaps the most critical assumption is that the preference data and purchase and repurchase decisions are valid predictors of what actually would happen in the marketplace. The artificiality of the product exposure and such surrogates for purchase decisions in the marketplace is a problem common to all laboratory approaches. Another problem is related to the convenience-sampling approach and the fact that there will be attrition from the original sample (in one study, 16 percent of the respondents did not use the brand and another 16 percent could not be reached for the telephone interview).[11]

Laboratory tests have a number of advantages also. First, compared with test markets, they are fast, relatively cheap, confidential, and flexible. A basic ASSESSOR test can be conducted in three months with a cost that starts around $75,000 (most tests will compare alternative tactics and cost more), much less than test markets. The time and lack of confidentiality of test markets can be damaging. Further, for a relatively modest incremental cost, a laboratory test market can evaluate alternative executions of elements in the marketing program such as packaging, price, advertising, product features, and location within the store. Second, the accuracy experience is impressive.

Test Marketing. Test marketing allows the researcher to test the impact of the total marketing program, with all its interdependencies, in a market context as opposed to the artificial context associated with the concept and product tests that have been discussed.

There are two primary functions of **test marketing.** The first is to gain information and experience with the marketing program before making a total commitment to it. The second is to predict the program's outcome when it is applied to the total market.

There are really two types of test markets: the sell-in test market and the controlled-distribution scanner market. **Sell-in test markets** are cities in which the product is sold just as it would be in a national launch. In particular, the product has to gain distribution space. **Controlled-distribution scanner markets** are cities for which distribution is prearranged and the purchases of a panel of customers are monitored using scanner data.

Designing the Sell-In Market Test[12]

Selecting the Test Cities

1. **Representativeness.** Ideally, the city should be fairly representative of the country in terms of characteristics that will affect the test outcome, such as product usage, attitudes, and demographics.
2. **Data availability.** It often is helpful to use store audit information to evaluate the test. If so, it would be important to use cities containing retailers who will cooperate with store audits.
3. **Media isolation and costs.** It is desirable to avoid media spill-over. Using media that "spill out" into nearby cities is wasteful and increases costs. Conversely, "spill-in" media from nearby cities can contaminate a test. Media cost is another consideration.
4. **Product flow.** It may be desirable to use cities that don't have much "product spillage" outside the area.

Table 23-2 lists the cities that are the most representative metropolitan areas in the country. Another issue is the number of test cities to use. A single test city can lead to unreliable results because of the variation across cities of both brand sales and consumer response to marketing programs.[13]

"I can't remember the brand name, but it has a commercial with a lot of people running in all directions."
Copyright © Ned Hilton/Consumer Reports.

TABLE 23-2
Test Market Cities

Rank	Metropolitan Area	1990 Population	Cumulative Index	Housing Value Index	Age Index	Race Index
1	Detroit, MI	4,382,000	22.8	11.8	1.5	9.5
2	St. Louis, MO–IL	2,444,000	22.8	15.1	1.6	6.2
3	Charlotte–Gastonia–Rock Hill, NC–SC	1,162,000	24.1	13.5	2.7	7.9
4	Fort Worth–Arlington, TX	1,332,000	25.0	17.0	5.9	2.2
5	Kansas City, MO–KS	1,566,000	25.4	17.9	2.7	4.8
6	Indianapolis, IN	1,250,000	25.5	16.7	2.4	6.3
7	Philadelphia, PA–NJ	4,857,000	26.7	18.0	1.7	7.1
8	Wilmington, NC	120,000	27.2	15.1	4.1	8.0
9	Cincinnati, OH–KY–IN	1,453,000	27.2	19.1	1.6	6.6
10	Nashville, TN	985,000	27.6	18.5	2.9	6.2
11	Dayton–Springfield, OH	951,000	27.6	19.5	1.9	6.2
12	Jacksonville, FL	907,000	27.6	17.2	2.5	7.9
13	Toledo, OH	614,000	27.8	20.0	2.4	5.5
14	Greensboro–Winston–Salem–High Point, NC	942,000	27.8	17.6	2.9	7.3
15	Columbus, OH	1,377,000	28.4	19.0	3.8	5.7
16	Charlottesville, VA	131,000	28.5	16.9	6.3	5.2
17	Panama City, FL	127,000	28.6	20.1	2.6	6.0
18	Pensacola, FL	344,000	28.7	21.8	2.2	4.7
19	Milwaukee, WI	1,432,000	28.8	23.4	1.4	4.1
20	Cleveland, OH	1,831,000	28.9	18.2	3.4	7.4

Judith Waldrop, "All American Markets," *American Demographics*, January 1992, 27.

Implementing and Controlling the Test. A second consideration is to control the test by ensuring that the marketing program is implemented in the test area so as to reflect the national program. The test itself may tend to encourage those involved to enhance the effectiveness of the marketing program. Salespeople may be more aggressive. Retailers may be more cooperative. There is also the reaction of competitors. At one extreme they can destroy the test by deliberately flooding the test areas with free samples or in-store promotions. More likely, however, they will experiment with retaliatory actions and monitor the results themselves.

Timing. A third consideration is timing. If possible, a test market normally should be in existence for one year. An extended time period is needed for several reasons. First, there are often important seasonal factors that can be observed only if the test is continued for the whole year. Second, initial interest is often a poor predictor of a program's staying power. There is usually a fatigue factor that sometimes can take a long time to materialize.

Measurement. A crucial element of the test market is the measure used to evaluate it. A basic measure is sales based on shipments or warehouse withdrawals. Store audit data provide actual sales figures and are not sensitive to inventory fluctuations. They also provide variables such as distribution, shelf facings, and in-store promotional activity. These already have been discussed in detail in Chapter 6. Knowledge of such variables can be important in evaluating the marketing program and in interpreting the sales data.

Measures such as brand awareness, attitude, trial purchase, and repeat purchase are obtained directly from the consumer, either from surveys or consumer panels. Such variables as brand awareness and attitude also serve as criteria for evaluating the marketing program and can help interpret sales data. The most useful information obtained from consumers, however, is whether they bought the product at least once, whether they were satisfied with it, and have either repurchased it or plan to.

Costs of a Test Market. In making cost–benefit judgments about test markets, all costs need to be considered. Many costs are relatively easy to quantify; these might be the development and implementation of the marketing program, preparation of test products, administration of the test, and collection of data associated with the test.

The costs and risks that may delay the launch of a new product are more difficult to quantify. If a new-product launch is delayed by six months or a year, an opportunity to gain a substantial market position might be lost.

Controlled Distribution Scanner Markets (CDSM). These are termed **controlled distribution** because there are generally agreements with retailers to allow new products under test to have access to shelf space. An example of a CDSM is IRI's BehaviorScan, which was discussed earlier in Chapter 6.

CDSMs have four major advantages over test markets. First, they are less expensive. Although it is difficult to generalize, they probably cost from one-sixth to one-third the cost of a full test market. Second, there is the potential to do more experimenting with marketing variables in a CDSM. The advertising seen by panel members is controllable. Further, the in-store activities such as promotions and pricing are under more control than they would be in a sell-in test market. Third, the scanner-based data probably are more accurate, timely, and complete than the data available in a sell-in test market. Fourth, there is the potential to provide accurate early estimates of the test market results using the consumer panel information.

The most obvious disadvantage of a CDSM is that it provides no test of the product's ability to gain shelf space, special displays, in-store promotions, and so on. Since gaining distribution can be a crucial issue for some products, leaving it unaddressed can be troublesome. Another major CDSM disadvantage is the limited choice of test cities.

Projecting Trial, Repeat, and Usage Rates Using Panel Data. To estimate the ultimate trial level, the percentage of product class buyers who will try the new brand at least once is monitored over time. Each person who tries the new product is then monitored again, and the time between the first (trial) purchase and second purchase is noted. The market share estimate is thus the product of the percentage of people who tried and the percentage of people who repeat-purchased the product. Market share and sales projections made using this modeling logic can be very accurate, as the experience of Parfitt and Collins illustrates.[14] Exhibit 23-3 gives an example of test marketing.

FORECASTING

The previous section dealt with how to design the right product. An estimate of the initial repeat purchase rate, market share, and sales also can be obtained from test marketing programs. But the decision to introduce the product will

EXHIBIT 23-3

Nivea's Path to the Bath

Picking the best test-market methodology for a new product is a process that's almost always shaped by both the realities of the marketplace and a company's position in that market. Few marketers know that better than Irena Valles, a group product manager for Beiersdorf, USA, the Norwalk, Conn., manufacturer of Nivea moisturizing products. Always competing against such skin-care powers as Chesebrough-Pond's and Jergens', she uses live test markets to try strategies for products she describes as "nichey."

Carving out a wider niche is what Beiersdorf sought with its new line of bath and shower additives, Nivea Bath Silk, when it went into live test market in Chicago and Seattle at the end of 1988. "Both cities were very good Nivea markets," says Valles, "and we could count on the cooperation of the accounts [chain drugstores] in both. Also, we could isolate magazines for print advertising in these two markets." Although the bath additive category was flat when Nivea entered test market, Valles thought Bath Silk could build sales by appealing to loyal Nivea users, and she was proven right. Beiersdorf supported the product in test market with full-scale advertising promotion and couponing. "This was almost a mini-launch," recalls Valles. "We also cross-ruffed Nivea bath pacquettes with our lotions and gave samples with coupons to generate trial and cross-purchase with Nivea consumers. We put a questionnaire in the bath products and found that 80 percent of the users were previous Nivea users and were happy to see a new product from us."

One of the objectives of the test was to find out whether Bath Silk had the potential to achieve the same market position (No. 3) and share (8%) that Nivea already held in the cream and lotion category. "We're a player, but not really a major one," says Valles, "and our capital investment was fairly low because we were adapting a product that was already very prominent and ready for us to take over from Europe." (The Beiersdorf parent, headquartered in Hamburg, West Germany, is a European market leader in shower, bath, and soap products). Initially, Bath Silk was advertised separately from the rest of the Nivea line, but that strategy was jettisoned. "We changed our strategy for the national launch," says Valles. "Instead of advertising Bath Silk to the bath user and putting it in the bath category in stores, we decided to capitalize on the Nivea trademark and put the bath line where we're strongest, in the skin-care section. We found that by putting all our products together in the same place in the store, we tracked far better."

Although the changes in advertising and store positioning made it difficult to project test results, Valles remains a firm believer in live testing. "To us, the live test market is the most real world," she says. "It really gives us a very true indication of what we can expect when we go national. "No one's going to argue with success. Since the Bath Silk line went national August 1989, all the signs are good. What's more, the entire $150 million bath additive category is picking up.

Source: Leslie Brennan. "Meeting the Test," *Sales and Marketing Management*, March 1990, p. 58.

depend on the forecast of the demand for the product and the profits it will bring. Hence, forecasting methods are an integral part of product research. They also are the basis for almost all planning and control. This section will focus on forecasting methods for existing products or services.

Qualitative Methods

Jury of Executive Opinion. This approach involves combining the judgments of a group of managers about the forecast. The group normally would include a variety of concerned and informed managers representing such functional areas as marketing, sales, operations, manufacturing, purchasing, accounting, and finance. They each would bring to the forecast a different background, perspective, and set of biases. Often, their judgments would be supported by background information that might include past data, economic and industry developments, competitive actions, and relevant news from customers or distributors.

This technique has several advantages. First, it tends to be fast and efficient. Second, it tends to be timely in that the forecast is generated on the basis of the most current situation. Third, the knowledge on which the forecast is based is extremely rich. It includes, at least potentially, all the collective knowledge and experience of the involved managers. Fourth, it has no formal requirements in terms of historical data.

The disadvantages are due to the subjectivity involved.

Sales Force Estimates. The **sales force estimate** involves obtaining the judgments from the sales force. Usually, each salesperson will provide a forecast for each product or product type, by customer. Uncertainty can be introduced in several ways. One way is to allow the salespeople to provide a sales estimate range in addition to the single number representing the expected sales level. Another is to have them estimate the probability of each potential sale. The sales forecast then will be the sum of all the potential sales, each weighted by its probability of occurring.

Forecasts generated from the sales force are based on the salesperson's knowledge of the customer or client, which often is extremely complete, sensitive, and current. Like the jury of executive opinion approach, it allows the introduction of subjective judgments that draw on rich experience. Salespeople often lack relevant information about a company's plans and overall industry trends. In addition, there is a greater tendency for biases to occur. Individual salespeople can be naturally optimistic or pessimistic, and such biases often are more serious when the forecast is linked to their performance measures.

Surveys of Customer Intentions. The third judgment method is a survey of customer intentions. Customers are asked to make their own forecast about their usage and buying intentions. Customer intentions will be based on subjective judgments about future requirements. The right person in the customer organization must be contacted, and questions must be addressed with care. As the last chapter indicates, various biases can emerge. Obviously, the advantage of the approach is that the user-customer has the best information on which to base a forecast. It works best when the customers, or at least the major customers, are few in number. Surveys can become expensive and time consuming, of course, and thus are inappropriate for some forecasting tasks. They also are difficult when a sensitive purchase decision is involved and those surveyed may be reluctant to provide information.

Delphi Approach. In the jury of executive opinion, a group of people gather and reach a consensus on a forecast. Such an effort is subject to group effects. In particular, judgments might be swayed by the persuasions of some group members who have strong personalities, special interests, or special authority. A method to retain the wisdom of a group while reducing the effect of group pressure is the Delphi approach. In the **Delphi approach,** group members are asked to make individual judgments about a forecast. These judgments then are compiled and returned to the group members, so that they can compare their own previous judgments with those of the others. They then are given an opportunity to revise their judgments, especially if they differ from the others'. They also usually can state why they believe that their judgment is accurate, even if it differs from that of the other group members. After three or four iterations, group members usually reach their conclusions.

Quantitative Methods

Time-Series Extrapolation. A reasonable approach to forecasting is simply to extrapolate historical data forward. This approach, termed **time-series forecasting,** can be very effective, especially for short-term forecasting. A time-series is simply data that are collected over time, such as weekly sales data for a three-year period.

Trend Projection. An advantage of time-series forecasting is that it is easy to understand conceptually. Historical data simply are plotted and extrapolated forward. The process can be done completely visually, or it can be done by using a regression program. In either case, a plot of historical data usually provides a useful feel for the data that a computer output sometimes lacks.

The simplest trend is the straight line. The equation is simply,

$$y = a + bt$$

where t is time.

In a linear or straight-line model, the growth is assumed to be a constant amount. The appropriate model is the exponential model. Another useful curve, that is often used in time series forecasting, is an S-shaped curve.

Weighting the Data. How much historical data should be used? At first glance, it would seem that all available data should be used. However, data that are too old will represent conditions that have changed and therefore actually could tend to detract from the forecast. There are three intermediate positions that deserve mention: moving average, exponential smoothing, and past turning points. In the **moving average** method the average of the last n data points is used to weight the data. In **exponential smoothing,** instead of weighting the last n data points equally, we use exponentially decreasing sets of weights, so that the more-recent data are weighted more heavily than less-recent data. If a **past turning point** (a point in time where there was substantial change in the growth rate caused by an environmental change) can be identified, a forecast might be based on data acquired since that point in time.

Seasonal and Cyclical Indexes. It is important to distinguish between a trend and a seasonal or cyclical fluctuation. A growth pattern simply may represent a cyclical upturn or even a seasonal fluctuation. Further, in short-term forecasting, the time period involved will be weeks, months, or quarters, and it becomes necessary to forecast the seasonal and cyclical effects as well as the trend. The solution is to develop indexes that will represent the seasonal and cyclical effect. The **seasonal index** represents the effect of seasonal fluctuations. It can be created in a variety of ways.[15] A commonly used index, developed by the Bureau of the Census, is based on the ratio of a given month's sales to the average monthly sales, over a 12-month period. Trends can be estimated and forecasts made using seasonally adjusted data. Then the seasonal index can be used to convert the forecast to actual numbers. **Cyclical indexes** can be developed in the same manner as seasonal indexes; however, most cycles, like business cycles, do not behave as regularly as seasonal factors, and it can be very difficult to determine even the length of the cycle.[16]

Causal Models

Time-series approaches are limited by their simplistic assumption that the future will be the same as the past, and they use only historical data on the variable to be forecast. **Causal models** introduce into the analysis, factors that are hypothesized to cause or influence, either directly or indirectly, the object of the forecast.

Leading Indicators. Perhaps the simplest form of causal analysis is the attempt to identify **leading indicators** of the object to be forecasted. These indicators then could be monitored. An example of a leading indicator is as follows: The sales of color televisions are a leading indicator of the demand for components of color television sets. The sales of a product class are always a leading indicator of the sales of a supplier.

Regression Models. A more formal causal model would be in the regression context. The dependent variable would be the object of the forecast. The independent variables would be the causal factors that are thought to cause or influence the forecast. The task, then, is to identify the causal factors and to obtain data representing them. An example of the regression model is as follows.

The sales of the Simmons Company, makers of Beautyrest Mattresses, were hypothesized to have a linear trend and, in addition, to be caused by marriages during the year, housing starts, and annual disposable personal income.[17] The resulting model was

$$S = 49.85 - 0.07M + 0.04H + 1.22D - 19.54T \quad r^2 = .92$$
$$ (1.2) \quad (3.1) \quad (2.0) \quad (8.4) \quad (7.3)$$

where

S = annual sales
M = annual number of marriages
H = annual housing starts
D = disposable income
T = time in years (the first year is 1, the second 2, etc.)

The numbers in parentheses, which are the t-values, indicate that the trend is highly significant, as is the disposable-income variable.

PRICING RESEARCH

Research may be used to evaluate alternative price approaches for new products before launch or for any proposed changes in products already on the market. As in the case of test marketing, the question of "reality" applies, and it has been found that the sales response to products at different prices in actual stores produced far more discriminating results than the sales response in an artificial store.

There are two general approaches to pricing research. The first is the well-established Gabor and Grainger method.[18] Here, different prices for a product are presented to respondents (often by using test-priced packs) who then are asked if they would buy. A "buy-response" curve of different prices, with the corresponding number of affirmative purchase intentions, is produced.

A second approach, in which respondents are shown different sets of brands in the same product category, at different prices, and are asked which they would buy. This multibrand-choice method allows respondents to take into account competitors' brands, as they normally would outside such a test. As such, this represents a form of simulation of the point of sale.

Decisions concerning the price range for a new product have to be made early in the development stage. A product concept cannot be tested fully, for example, without indicating its price, so when the product is ready to be introduced, a decision must be made about its specific price. Decisions concerning changing prices—Should we change the price and, if so, in what direction and by how much?—will then need to be made over the life of the product.

Two general pricing strategies can be followed. The first is a profit-oriented strategy, in which the objective is to generate as much profit as possible in the present period. In this strategy, the product is priced at a premium as long as the market is prepared to buy it at that price. The other is a share-oriented strategy, whose objective is to capture an increasingly larger market share. This is accomplished, insofar as pricing is concerned, by entering the market at a low price and continuing to reduce it as the increasing volume results in lowered production costs. Some potential profits in the early stages of the product life cycle are forgone in the expectation that higher volumes in later periods will generate sufficiently greater profits, so that over the life of the product the highest overall profits will result.

There is a substantial difference in the information required for pricing under the two strategies. It follows that pricing research for the two different approaches differs substantially in terms of the information sought.

Research for Profit-Oriented Pricing

The manager using a profit-oriented pricing strategy is attempting to price the product at the point at which profits will be the greatest until market-condition changes or supply costs dictate a price change. The optimal price using this strategy is the one that results in the greatest positive difference between total revenues and total costs. This means that the researcher's major tasks are to forecast the costs and the revenues over the relevant range of alternative prices. The forecasting methods discussed in the previous section can be used for this purpose.

Research for Share-Oriented Pricing

A requisite for successfully using share-oriented pricing is that average unit production costs continue to go down as cumulative output increases. For some products, this reduction takes the form of an experience curve.

The pricing pattern that is followed for the purpose of increasing market share is to

1. Enter the market at a price that is substantially low. It can be even below cost.
2. Hold the entering price constant until unit costs have fallen to the point that a desired percentage mark-up on cost is being obtained.
3. Reduce price as costs fall to maintain mark-up at the same desired percentage of costs.

The pricing pattern is illustrated in Figure 23-2.

Share-oriented pricing decisions require information that either is not required or is different in nature from the information required for more traditional pricing. The types of information required for this pricing method are

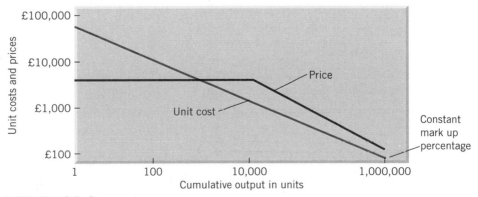

FIGURE 23-2
Share-oriented pricing

1. The nature of the experience curve.
2. Break-even points.
3. Cost of units sold to additional market segments.
4. Competitor costs.
5. Forecast of the "decline" stage of the product life cycle.

The research techniques that have already been described in this text can generate the information required for this type of pricing.

A simple typology of the various pricing strategies that are followed in practice and the informational requirements for these strategies are given in Table 23-3.[19]

Summary

The first stage in new-product research is **concept generation,** which involves research, first to identify needs, and second to identify concepts that will be responsive to those needs. The second stage is **concept evaluation and development**—getting relevant people's reactions to concepts. The purposes usually are to help make a judgment as to whether to proceed and to suggest some directions in the subsequent development phase. The third stage is **product evaluation and development,** where a more realistic product exposure is possible because the product and much of the marketing program have been developed. In particular, the product will be available for use tests, where potential customers try it and provide reactions. The laboratory test market, where respondents are exposed to the product and then given the opportunity to make a trial purchase in a simulated supermarket, are used for product trials. The fourth stage is the test market, where the product and the marketing program actually are implemented in the field. In a sell-in test market, the product is sold just as it would be in a national launch. In a **controlled distribution scanner market (CDSM) test,** distribution is prearranged and purchases are monitored using scanner data.

There is a set of qualitative approaches to forecasting that includes the **jury of executive opinion,** the **sales force estimates,** the **survey of customer intentions,** and the **Delphi approach.** These approaches are fast, inexpensive, flexible, and can integrate large quantities of information, but they suffer from the biases, uncertainties, and inconsistencies inherent in the subjective judgments used. **Time-series** forecasting, the projection of historical data, is well suited to short-term forecasts of data containing a clear trend or seasonal or cyclical patterns. It is not capable of forecasting turning points, where the environment changes. **Causal models** refer to the introduction of factors that directly or indirectly cause or influence the forecast. It can simply be the identification of leading indicators or the use of a formal regression model.

There are two approaches to pricing research. One is to present respondents with the product at different prices and ask them to buy. The second is to show respondents different sets of brands in the same product category, at different prices, and ask them which they would buy. The information to be obtained by pricing research depends on whether a profit-oriented or a share-oriented pricing strategy will be adopted.

TABLE 23-3
Informational Requirements for Pricing Strategies

Strategy	Description	Informational Requirements	Sources of Information
Random Discounting	If some consumers have heterogeneous search costs, firms discount their prices in a random manner to take advantage of those consumers. These consumers buy at the undiscounted price instead of searching for the lowest price, whereas consumers with low search costs will buy at the low price.	Knowledge of consumer segments in the market Characteristics of consumers (their search costs, etc.) Product and cost information Information on legal constraints	Demographic consumer data Analysis of scanner data Internal records Legal data
Second Market Discounting	If distinct markets exist and if the consumers in one market incur transaction costs to buy in another, the firm can discount its price in the other markets to below its average cost. In the international context this is called dumping.	Knowledge about the different markets and their characteristics Product and cost information Information on the legal aspects of the other markets Information on the transaction cost incurred by the consumer when he/she buys from the different market	Internal records Legal data Secondary data sources that give the demographic profile of the markets
Periodic Discounting	When some consumers in the market have differential reservation prices, firms can start at high prices and periodically discount them in order to draw consumers with lower reservation prices.	Information about the consumers' reservation prices Product and cost information	Internal records Survey research to determine the consumers' reservation price Legal data
Price Signaling	When consumers in the market are willing to pay more for a product despite lack of knowledge regarding its quality, then price signaling can be used. Essentially the strategy is to produce an inferior product and sell it at the same price as the better-quality product another firm produces, in the belief that consumers will assume that the product is of high quality and buy it because of its high price.	Information about your competitor's prices and costs Information about the legal constraints of price signaling Product and cost information	Internal records Secondary data on competitor prices Legal data Inferential information on competitor costs

TABLE 23-3 *(continued)*

Strategy	Description	Informational Requirements	Sources of Information
Penetration Pricing	Penetration pricing is used in situations similar to that in periodic discounting, except in this case competitors are also free to enter at the same price. Hence, the threat of competitive entry and price-sensitive consumers force the firm to price its products at a low price.	Product and cost information Information about competitor prices and costs	Secondary data and inferential information on competitor prices and costs Internal records
Geographic Pricing	Geographic pricing strategies are used by firms that sell in markets that are separated geographically. The difference in pricing is due to transportation costs rather than reservation prices or transaction costs.	Information on the characteristics of the different markets Product and cost information Information on the transportation costs and about any legal aspects that may hinder this particular type of pricing strategy	Internal records Secondary data and inferential information on competitor prices and costs
Premium Pricing	This strategy and price signaling are very similar. The difference stems from the fact that in price signaling the firm produces only the inferior product and prices it high, whereas here the firm produces both the inferior and the better product and sells them at the same price to exploit the joint economies of scale.	Product and cost information Information on the competitor's price and cost Information on the characteristics of the consumers (like the maximum price they are willing to pay for this product)	Secondary sources of legal data Internal records Secondary sources of information on markets and transportation costs
Price Bundling	Bundling strategy is adopted when the products are nonsubstitutable, perishable, and there is an asymmetric demand structure for them. An example of this strategy is selling a car with the maximum number of options. The perishability in the case of durables is with regard to the purchase occasion.	Information on the demand characteristics for the various components of the bundle Product and cost information Information on the consumer preferences for the various combinations of the bundle	Internal records Survey data on consumer characteristics and preferences Secondary sources of information on competitor costs and prices
Complementary Pricing	Complementary pricing is the strategy used by firms to price complementary products. They usually price the main product at low price while the price of the complement is high. The classic example is Japanese pricing of their cars and the spare parts.	Product and cost information	Internal records

1. Develop a research design to provide a demand estimate for the following new products:
    a. A plastic disposable toothbrush that comes in a cylinder 5/8 in. in diameter and 3 in. in length. Its unique, patented quality is that the toothpaste already has been applied.
    b. A lemon condiment. Lemon enhances the flavor of many foods, including corn-on-the-cob, fish, and melons. The lemon condiment would be in a crystallized form that would capture the essence of lemon and be served in a "lemon shaker" that would complement the salt and pepper shakers.
    c. A clear plastic umbrella attachment for bicycles, which folds away behind the handlebars when not in use.
    d. A vibrator secretarial chair which contains a gentle vibrator device designed to provide relaxation and blood circulation for people who must sit for long periods of time.
    e. A battery-powered, two-passenger automobile with a top speed of 40 mph and a range of 120 miles.
2. In benefit structure analysis, 500 or so respondents are asked to react to a large number (75–100) of specific product benefits and to many product characteristics. The reactions are in terms of both the desire for and perceived deficiencies in current brands with respect to each benefit and characteristic. The focus is on a specific use occasion. For example, if a household cleaner were involved, the respondent would focus on a single cleaning occasion. The brand used also would be asked. How would you generate the list of benefits and product characteristics? Develop a sampling plan. What data analysis would you conduct?
3. In evaluating a new product idea, what criteria should be used? What role should marketing research play in evaluating the idea against each of the criteria?
4. How would you find a name for a new brand of soda that is a new "natural drink" made out of carbonated apple juice with some ginger and lemon added?
5. Identify five new products. Consider a concept test for each. Which could be exposed via a mail questionnaire? Via a phone interview? Via cable television? Which, if any, of these products would you take directly to market, bypassing a test market? Why?
6. How can the bias of a purchase-intention question in a concept test be measured?
7. What are the key assumptions of the ASSESSOR laboratory test market? What changes could you make to improve its validity?
8. Compare and contrast the controlled distribution scanner markets with selling test markets. What are the advantages and disadvantages of each? When would you want to use a selling test market?
9. Beecham sued the research firm Yankelovich Clancy Shulman (YCS) when its laboratory test market prediction for the new product, Delicare, proved

to be wrong. Beecham argued that one of the model inputs, the percentage of households using fine-fabric detergents, was assumed by YCS to be 75 percent when it was actually 30 percent. In general, should a research firm be held liable for an inaccurate prediction based on a market research study if the model used:

a. Had an incorrectly entered key number?

b. Had a structure that was found to be faulty (for example—a new product model failed to take into account that distribution might not be widespread)?

c. Used a sample that was not representative of the market to be served by the new product?

10. Assume you are the director of a large private hospital, which is one of four hospitals serving a medium-sized Midwestern community. What types of forecasting information do you think the director will need? Answer this question for:

a. A university art museum.

b. A small retail sporting goods store.

c. A university.

d. Delta Airlines.

e. A maker of small computers sold primarily to educators of grades 1 through 8.

11. Design a short-term (four months) sales forecasting system for an electronics company that makes instruments to test such electronic components as transistors and integrated circuits. The instruments are sold to a variety of industries through a 20-person sales force. Although there are thousands of customers, only about 300 provide about 85 percent of annual sales. The instrument normally has to be approved by people in manufacturing, purchasing, and quality control before it is purchased. Evaluate the various qualitative approaches in this context. Consider also the problem of forecasting sales potential five years out. The need is to make some basic decisions as to in what product markets the company wants to operate.

12. What causal variables would you want to explore if you were forecasting:

a. Furniture sales by region?

b. Student applications at Northwestern University over a 24-year period?

c. Attendance at the Chicago White Sox games by day, for purposes of planning the staff and food requirements?

d. Sales of a pizza sandwich at the Round Table pizza chain?

13. When is periodic discounting preferred to random discounting? Is one better than the other?

14. A major airline announced that it was reducing its fares by 30 percent for off-peak travel. (Off-peak travel is defined as travel time between 8:00 P.M. and 8:00 A.M. on weekdays, and all weekend.) Do you consider this as price signaling or second-market discounting?

15. The top management of your company has come up with a concept they think is exciting and has tremendous potential. It wants to find out the

demand for this product. It plans to skim the market if the demand is high for the product. You have been given the responsibility to design a prototype and determine the demand. Further you have also been asked to find out whether skimming would be the best pricing strategy to adopt? What information will you require to answer these questions and how will you obtain it?

End Notes

1. James H. Meyers. "Benefit Structure Analysis: A New Tool for Product Planning," *Journal of Marketing,* 40, October 1976, 23–32.
2. E. E. Norris. "Your Surefire Clue to Ad Success: Seek Out the Consumer's Problem," *Advertising Age,* March 17, 1975, 43–44.
3. E. Patrick McGuire. *Evaluating New-Product Proposals* (New York: The Conference Board, 1973, 47.
4. McGuire, op. cit., 58.
5. James W. Taylor, John J. Houlahan, and Alan C. Gabriel. "The Purchase Intention Question in New Product Development: A Field Test," *Journal of Marketing,* 40 January 1975, 90–92.
6. Henry J. Claycamp and Lucien E. Liddy. "Prediction of New Product Performance: An Analytical Approach," *Journal of Marketing Research,* 6, November 1969, 414–420; Gert Assmus. "NEWPROD: The Design and Implementation of a New product Model," *Journal of Marketing,* 39, January 1975, 16–23.
7. Gerald J. Eskin and John Malec. "A Model for Estimating Sales Potential Prior to the Test Market," *1976 Educators Proceeding* (Chicago: American Marketing Association), 1976, 230–233.
8. In situations where no definition of the product class exists, a product appeal measure obtained from a concept test is used to estimate the size of the relevant product class for that particular product.
9. As discussed in Chapter 12, the symbols O_1, O_2, etc., refer to a measure or observation and X_1, X_2, etc., refer to experimental treatments.
10. Glen L. Urban, J. R. Hauser, and J. H. Roberts. "Prelaunch Forecasting of New Automobiles: Models and Implementation," *Management Science,* 36(4), April 1990, 401–21; Glen L. Urban, J. S. Hulland, and B. D. Weinberg. "Premarket Forecasting of New Consumer Durables: Modeling Categorization, Elimination, and Consideration Phenomena," *Journal of Marketing,* 57, April 1993.
11. Ibid., 12.
12. This section draws in part on the excellent overview of market testing by Alvin A. K. Achenbaum entitled, "Market Testing: Using the Marketplace as a Laboratory," in Robert Ferbar, ed., *Handbook of Marketing Research* (New York: McGraw-Hill), 1974, 4–31 and 4–54.
13. Valentine Appel. "Why a Single Pair of Markets Is Still Not Enough," ARF Advertising Heavy Spending Tests Workshop, April 1985.
14. J. H. Parfitt and B. J. K. Collins. "Use of Consumer Panels for Brand Share Prediction," *Journal of Marketing Research,* 5, May 1968, 131–145.
15. One approach is simply to use an additive term reflecting the amount, on the average, that a given month differs from the average monthly level. It could be estimated by introducing a dummy variable for a season in a regression. The coefficient would reflect the average difference between demand in that month and demand in other months. If, however, there is a growth trend, it might be more appropriate to say that October averages 15 percent more than the average month than to say it is 34,000 units more than average. In that case, an index based on a ratio should be used.
16. For a discussion of market cycles that applies cycles of lengths of 40 months, 9 years, 18 years, and 54 years, see Henry O. Pruden, "The Kondratieff Wave," *Journal of Marketing,* 42, April 1978, 63–70.
17. George G. C. Parker and Ediberto L. Segura. "How to Get a Better Forecast," *Harvard Business Review,* March–April 1971, 99–109. The firm is identified in Robert A. Levy. "A Clearer Crystal Ball," *Dun's Review,* 98, July 1971, 50.
18. Gabor A. and Grainger C. Price as an indicator of quality. *Economics,* 33, 1966, 43–70.
19. This table was adapted from Gerard J. Tellis. "Beyond the Many Faces of Price: An integration of Pricing Strategies," *Journal of Marketing,* 50 (4), 1986, 146–160.

Brown Microwave was one of the leaders in the area of microwave ovens for the home, with about 15 percent of the market in 1977. Although microwave cooking had been around for many years, its use in homes was in a major growth stage.

Brown was considering two new cabinet designs for its 1979 line of countertop microwave cookers. Both represented a sharp departure from the modern chrome designs that had been available from Brown and its competitors. One was an "early American" design and the other was made out of heavy dark wood and was more of a Mediterranean design. The concept was to add charm, warmth, and style to a product that had a "chrome-computer" image. The new design would add about 15 to 20 percent to the price of the unit.

The new designs would have to provide a net increase of Brown's sales of 15 to 20 percent to be considered worthwhile. There would be a substantial investment required to produce them, and their introduction would require a large percentage of the marketing budget and sales effort.

Before committing the company to one or both of these designs, a product test was proposed. The concept was to modify a large van so that half of it would simulate three kitchen segments. The segments would differ in the type of paneling and cabinets used. One was dark, Mediterranean in appearance, another was light-oak "early American," and the third had a contemporary look. In this setting five counter-top microwave ovens were displayed: two were competitive models, one was the existing Brown design, and the remaining two were the proposed Brown designs. Each had very comparable features and specifications. The major difference was the cabinet.

The plan was to bring the van into five cities throughout the eastern United States, and in each city to recruit 100 women. The women would be recruited from shopping areas near or connected to office buildings. The hope was to obtain a reasonable number (like 25 percent of the sample) of working women who would be on a lunch break or would be shopping after work. The women would be asked to help evaluate some new kitchen appliances. A gift was promised for participants. The cities would be selected from cities frequently used as test markets.

Each woman would be shown each of the five models. The common performance capabilities would be explained, but it would be emphasized that the major difference was appearance and price. The price of each would be noted on an attached sign. After the women saw the five models, they would be asked to indicate their first, second, and third choices, assuming they were buying such an appliance now. The following information also would be obtained regarding the respondents' status prior to exposure to the new models:

1. Did the respondents own a microwave oven?
2. If so, what type and make?
3. If not, were they familar with microwaves and did they plan to purchase one during the next year?

   After exposure to the new models:

1. What were their intentions of buying a microwave oven during the next year?
2. What were their age, education, income, and family size?
3. Size of home or apartment? Rent or own?
4. Occupation?
5. What type of outlet would they go to if they were considering buying a microwave oven?

Assignment

Evaluate the research design. Would you make any changes? Plan a data analysis strategy.

CASE 23-2
National Chemical Corporation (B)

The Tiger-Tread spray product designed to free cars stuck in ice or snow had been delayed due to problems with packaging. In the summer of 1980, the problems were solved and the product was ready to go. There were, however, a host of basic decisions that needed to be made, and Charley Omsrud was considering the value of delaying a national introduction of the product and running a test market.

One issue involved the amount of production capacity to plan both for the 5-oz can (good for two or three use occasions) and the 10-oz can (good for four to six use occasions). Although the 200 people from the Toledo lab that tried product samples did not seem to have problems using it, there was always the lingering concern that unanticipated product problems could materialize in a broader test.

An issue that had recently emerged was whether the market should be restricted to fleets of cars. A colleague of Charley Omsrud, the marketing manager, had observed that for every fleet car there were well over ten other potential customers. If a consumer effort were mounted, the nature of the marketing program needed to be decided. In the test market used in 1970, extensive advertising and distribution was obtained. Charley felt that a middle course might make sense. His idea was to distribute the product through service stations and support it with point-of-purchase display stands and brochures. After all, the consumer did rely on the service station to provide antifreeze and other winterization services.

Charley was evaluating a proposal from a local marketing research firm to conduct a test market through the coming winter in a snowbelt city of around two million people. The plan was to reach fleet owners with the existing sales force and to reach individual car owners through service stations supported by point-of-purchase advertising. The cost would be $50,000 for running the test and evaluating the results. Among the outputs would be:

1. The percentage of households that
   ▶ Were aware of the product
   ▶ Purchased the product
   ▶ Made a repeat purchase.
2. The number and size of fleets that
   ▶ Were aware of the product
   ▶ Were aware but did not order the product
   ▶ Ordered the product
   ▶ Ordered the product and made repeat purchases.
3. The type and incidence of any product problem.

Questions for Discussion
1. What will be learned from the test?
2. What would you add or change about the test?
3. What else would you like to know before making a decision about the test?

CASE 23-3
U.S. Department of Energy (B)

The U.S. Department of Energy wanted to determine public attitudes toward six different windmill designs, including the familiar old Dutch windmill design and more futuristic designs such as the Darrieus (egg-beater) design. One proposal was to show 300 adult respondents slides of the six designs. Each design was to be shown in three different scenes, a flat-land setting, a setting of hills, and a shore setting. The respondents were to be recruited from six locations, one of which was near a large working windmill.

Questions for Discussion
1. Evaluate the research design. How would you select the cities and recruit the respondents?
2. How would you have them evaluate the six designs (actually the 18 different slides).
3. Would you use an evaluative scale or a paired or triad comparison?

24 TRADITIONAL APPLICATIONS OF MARKETING RESEARCH: DISTRIBUTION AND PROMOTION

Learning Objectives

▶ Introduce the various distribution decisions that require marketing research inputs.

▶ Discuss the information requirements and the techniques used for making place decisions.

▶ Introduce the various measures used to evaluate advertisements.

▶ Describe the techniques used in the actual industry to obtain the measures used to evaluate advertisements.

▶ Briefly mention the methods used to obtain information for other media decisions.

The previous chapter discussed the information requirements for the product and pricing decisions and the various methods used to obtain them. In this chapter the focus on the traditional marketing applications is extended to place and promotion decisions. The distribution decisions that are discussed here are (1) the number and location of warehouses and retail outlets, and (2) the number and location of salespersons (territory allocation decisions). The section on promotional research briefly discusses sales promotion research. Then, various methods of copy testing and the research required for other media decisions are described.

DISTRIBUTION RESEARCH

Traditionally, the distribution decisions in marketing strategy involve the number and location of salespersons, retail outlets, warehouses, and the size of discount to be offered. The discount to be offered to the members in the channel of distribution usually is determined by what is being offered by existing or similar products, and also whether the firm wants to follow a "push" or a "pull" strategy. But it is in the number and location decisions that marketing research plays an important role. In this section we discuss these issues.

Warehouse and Retail Location Research

Warehouse and retail location decisions are important, because they have substantial effects on both the costs and the time required to deliver products to customers. The essential questions to be answered before a location decision is made are, "What costs and delivery times would result if we chose one location over another?"

Some form of simulation is required to answer these questions. It can be a relatively simple, paper-and-pencil simulation for the location of a single warehouse in a limited geographic area, or it can be a complex, computerized simulation of a warehousing system for a regional or national market.

Center-of-Gravity Simulation. The center-of-gravity method of simulation frequently is used for locating a single warehouse or retail site. It is a method for finding the approximate location that will minimize the distance to customers, weighted by the quantities purchased.

The location giving the minimum weighted average distance from the customers is the point where the warehouse/retail site may be located.

A single center-of-gravity calculation provides an approximate location of the least-cost and least-delivery-time location for a single warehouse or a retail store. The greater the symmetry of customer locations and weights, the more nearly the initial calculation approximates the optimal location. The location indicated by the first calculation can be checked to determine if it is optimal (or near optimal) by using a "confirming" procedure. If it is not, successive calculations can be made as necessary to "home in" on the optimal location.[1]

To illustrate the method, assume that (1) five retail stores are located as shown in Figure 24-1; (2) stores 1 and 5 each buy, on the average, one

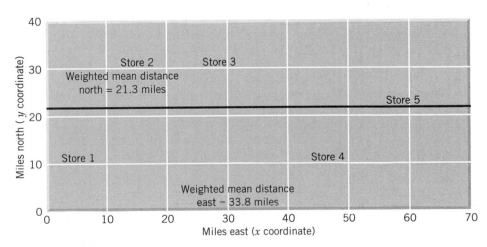

FIGURE 24-1
Center-of-gravity warehouse location to serve five retail stores

ton of merchandise per year, and stores 2, 3, and 4 each buy an average of two tons per year; and (3) straight-line distances (measured on the grid lines) are the appropriate ones for estimating transportation costs and delivery times.

The procedure for determining the location that will give the minimum weighted average distance from the warehouse to the customers is as follows:

Q1 Compute the weighted mean distance north* (y coordinate) from the zero point for the stores:

$$\text{Distance} \times \text{weight} = \text{weighted distance}$$

Store 1	10 miles $\times$ 1 ton	= 10 ton-miles
Store 2	30 miles $\times$ 2 tons	= 60 ton-miles
Store 3	30 miles $\times$ 2 tons	= 60 ton-miles
Store 4	10 miles $\times$ 2 tons	= 20 ton-miles
Store 5	20 miles $\times$ 1 ton	= 20 ton-miles

*Weighted mean distance north = 170/8 = 21.3 miles.

Q2 Compute the weighted mean distance east* (x coordinate) from the zero point for the stores:

$$\text{Distance} \times \text{weight} = \text{weighted distance}$$

Store 1	10 miles $\times$ 1 ton	= 10 ton-miles
Store 2	20 miles $\times$ 2 tons	= 40 ton-miles
Store 3	30 miles $\times$ 2 tons	= 60 ton-miles
Store 4	50 miles $\times$ 2 tons	= 100 ton-miles
Store 5	60 miles $\times$ 1 ton	= 60 ton-miles

*Weighted mean distance east = 270/8 = 33.8 miles.

Q3 The location giving the minimum weighted average distance from the customers is the point for which the two weighted means are the coordinates. For the example, the location indicated is 33.8 miles east (x) and 21.3 miles north (y) of the zero point. The zero point can be chosen arbitrarily, but all of the initial calculations have to be made based on the selected zero point.

The confirmation procedure is as follows:

1. Calculate confirming coordinates x, y using the formulae

$$x = \frac{\sum_{j=1}^{n} \frac{x_j W_j}{V_j}}{\sum_{j=1}^{n} \frac{W_j}{V_j}} \quad y = \frac{\sum_{j=1}^{n} \frac{y_j W_j}{V_j}}{\sum_{j=1}^{n} \frac{W_j}{V_j}}$$

where x_j and y_j are the coordinates of the jth customer, W_j the weight for that customer, and V_j the distance of the customer from the point defined by the coordinates. V_j is computed from the center-of-gravity calculation and is calculated using the following equation:

$$V_j = [(x_j - x_g)^2 + (y_j - y_g)^2]^{\frac{1}{2}}$$

where x_g and y_g are the coordinates of the location of the store.

2.   If the center-of-gravity coordinates and the confirmation model coordinates are the same (or nearly the same), no further calculations need be made. If they are not reasonably similar, replace the center-of-gravity coordinates with the initial confirmation model coordinates, and calculate a second set of confirmation coordinates.

3.   Repeat step (2) as necessary until the new confirmation coordinates match those being confirmed.

Computerized Simulation Models. Although the center-of-gravity method is an adequate method in most situations for locating a single warehouse, it is not designed to cope with the complexities involved in determining how many warehouses should be used and where they should be located in an overall regional or national distribution system. A computer is required to work on multiple warehouse location problems because of the large amounts of data that have to be processed for each of the many possible configurations of numbers and locations of warehouses.

The central concept involved in simulations for this purpose is very simple. Data that describe the customer characteristics (location of plants, potential warehouse and retail sites) and distribution costs (costs per mile by volume shipped, fixed and variable costs of operating each warehouse, the effect of shipping delays on customer demand) are developed and read into the computer. The computer is then programmed to simulate various combinations of numbers and locations of warehouses, and to indicate which one(s) gives the lowest total operating cost. Some very effective results have been achieved by using computer simulations to design distribution systems.

The role of marketing research in such simulations typically is used to validate the simulation model and to develop the data needed to operate it. As in the case of validating sales force decision models, the first step in the validation procedure should be to compare historical data with the model's predictions for some previous year. Warehouse locations, warehousing costs, transportation rates, and demand data for the year can be entered, and the model's predicted costs can be compared with the actual costs. A second step is to run sensitivity analyses by making changes in the historical data (adding/subtracting a warehouse or a retail store, moving the location of a warehouse/retail outlet, increasing the fixed cost of operating), such that the model outcomes are at least qualitatively predictable.

Catchment Area Analysis. Suppose you manage a store in a regional shopping center. You are considering a direct mail advertising campaign. How would you decide where to send the advertisements? This is just one of the several uses for trading-area data. They include creating mailing lists, evaluating a store's or shopping center's market positioning, measuring competitive customer bases, determining the potential of new locations, and evaluating regional retail chains and acquisition plans.[2]

Formal models have been developed that can be used to predict the trading area of a given shopping center or retail outlet based on relative size, travel time, and image.[3] A variety of other techniques can also be used to establish trading areas. An analysis of the addresses of credit card customers can provide a useful estimate of the trading area. This method assumes that credit customers and noncredit customers live in the same general areas. Check clearance data can be used to supplement this information.

The best, but also the most expensive, way of establishing trading area boundaries is to conduct surveys to determine them. Shopping center intercept surveys are commonly conducted for this purpose. When information on market potential and market penetration is desired, the shopping center intercept survey needs to be supplemented by a survey of nonshoppers at the shopping center or store. The nonshopper surveys are often conducted by telephone, with screening to eliminate shoppers. To avoid selection bias when merging the two samples, appropriate weightings based on shopping frequencies must be used.[4]

Outlet Location Research. Individual companies and, more commonly, chains, financial institutions with multiple outlets, and franchise operations, must decide on the physical location of their outlet(s). The cost and inflexible nature of the decision makes it one of critical importance.

Three general methods are in use for selecting specific store sites. The first is the **analogous location method.** This method involves plotting the area surrounding the potential site in terms of residential neighborhoods, income levels, and competitive stores. Regression models have been used for location studies for a variety of retail outlets including banks, grocery stores, liquor stores, chain stores, and hotels.[5] Data for building the model and for evaluating new potential locations are obtained through secondary data analysis and surveys.

Multiple regression models can be used to generate a relationship between store turnover and a range of store, population, and competitor characteristics. The advantage of multiple regression analysis is that the relationship between turnover, as the dependent variable, and a range of independent variables, can be assessed more systematically. Multiple regression analysis allows more complex relationships to be investigated. Numerous variables, and even different forms of model, can be adopted and tested very quickly.

The multiple regression equation will take the following form:

$$Y = a + b_1 x_1 + b_2 x_2 \ldots + b_m x_m + b_{m+1} x_{m+1} \ldots + b_n x_n$$

$$\underbrace{}_{\substack{\text{store} \\ \text{characteristics}}} \qquad \underbrace{\phantom{+ b_m x_m + b_{m+1} x_{m+1}}}_{\substack{\text{catchment area} \\ \text{characteristics}}}$$

where Y is store sales, and the x's are the independent variables, those concerned with the characteristics of each store (typically store size, car parking facilities, and so on) and those concerned with the characteristics of the catchment area (population and competition). This approach can then be used in forecasting sales for a proposed store.

The third type of model, the so-called **location-allocation** model, encompasses a number of associated techniques that are used to allocate demand to each potential site/store design combination.[6]

Location-allocation models are concerned with the location of facilities and the allocation of consumers, population, or trips to those facilities. Other models are based on allocations of consumers on a probability basis, reflecting the distance-decay effect away from centers and the preferences of shoppers.

The **gravity** model has existed for a long time and it has proved its worth in helping to explain certain types of human spatial behavior. Gravity theory holds that more people will travel from a particular origin to a given destination than will travel to a more distant destination of the same type and size. In more formal terms, it posits that preference to shopping in a store is directly proportional to the store size and inversely proportional to the square of the distance of that store.

Number and Location of Sales Representatives

How many sales representatives should there be in a given market area? There are three general research methods for answering this question. The first, the sales effort approach, is applicable when the product line is first introduced and there is no operating history to provide sales data. The second involves the statistical analysis of sales data and can be used after the sales program is under way. The third involves a field experiment and is also applicable only after the sales program has begun.

Sales Effort Approach. A logical, straightforward approach to estimating the number of sales representatives required for a given market area is to:

1. Estimate the number of sales calls required to sell to, and to service, prospective customers in an area for a year. This will be the sum of the number of visits required per year 'V_i', to each prospect/customer 'P', in the territory, or

$$\sum_{i=1}^{n} V_i P, \text{ where } n \text{ is the number of prospects/customers}$$

2. Estimate the average number of sales calls per representative that can be made in that territory in a year, c.
3. Divide the estimate in statement (1) by the estimate in statement (2) to obtain the number of sales representatives required, R. That is,

$$R = \sum_{i=1}^{n} V_i P / c$$

Statistical Analysis of Sales Data. Once a sales history is available from each territory, an analysis can be made to determine if the appropriate number of sales representatives is being used in each territory. An analysis of actual sales versus market potential for each sales representative may yield a relationship of the kind shown in Figure 24-2.

If so, further analysis will very likely indicate those areas in which the average market potential is less than X_1 per sales representative but which have too many representatives, and those with average market potential of more than X_2 but which have too few sales representatives.

Field Experiments. Experimenting with the number of calls made is another method of determining the number and location of sales representatives. This may be done in two ways: (1) making more frequent calls on some prospects/customers and less frequent calls on others in order to see the effect on overall sales (in this method the number of sales representatives remains unchanged) and (2) increase the number of representatives in some territories and decrease them in others to determine the sales effect.

Again, the design of the experiment(s), and the advantages and limitations of conducting them for determining the appropriate number of sales representatives for each territory are very similar to those for conducting other experiments.

Computerized Models of Sales Force Size and Allocation by Market and by Product Line. There are a number of computerized models, spreadsheet and others, for determining sales force size and for allocating the sales force by market and by product line. Examples are CALLPLAN, which is an interactive salesperson's call planning system, and DETAILER, a decision calculus model for the question of sales force allocation. When management is considering using a formal model to assist in making sales-force-related decisions, marketing research often becomes involved in one or more of three ways:

1. Determining what models are available and recommending which, if any, should be adopted.

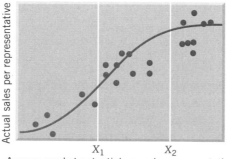

X_1 X_2

Average market potential per sales representative

FIGURE 24-2

Actual sales versus market potential per sales representative

2. Developing the data needed to operate the model selected (market potential) by product and by market, desirable call frequencies by class of customer, and so on.
3. Operating the model.

The model selected should be valid and require data that can be obtained at a reasonable cost. A workable approach to testing the validity of a model is to run analyses with it under different conditions and to see how it performs. A first step is to run the model with actual sales force data from the past two or three years and to see if it reasonably accurately replicates the actual sales (and, depending upon the model, by sales territory and product as well). After making any necessary calibrating adjustments, the model's "predictions" and the actual results ought to be reasonably close. Following that, one should set up and run a range of cases that might actually occur. Examining the model's output for each of them and determining whether they seem reasonable will further check on the model's probable validity.

PROMOTIONAL RESEARCH

This section focuses on the decisions that are commonly made when designing a promotional strategy. The decisions for the promotional part of a marketing strategy can be divided into groups: (1) advertising and (2) sales promotion. Sales promotion affects the company in the short term, whereas advertising decisions have long-term effects. Companies spend more time and resources on advertising research than on sales promotion research because of the greater risk and uncertainty in advertising research. We first discuss the use of marketing research in advertising decisions, and then briefly talk about the use of marketing research in sales promotion.

Advertising Research

Most of the promotional research companies do concentrate on advertising because advertising decisions are more costly and risky than sales promotion decisions. Advertising research typically involves generating information for making decisions in the awareness, recognition, preference, and purchasing stages. Most often, advertising research decisions are about advertising copy. Marketing research helps to determine how effective the advertisement will be. Another area this section discusses relates to media decisions.

Criteria. What separates an effective advertisement from a dud? The criteria will depend, of course, on the brand involved and its advertising objective. However, there are four basic categories of responses used in advertising research in general and copy testing in particular: (1) advertisement recognition, (2) recall of the commercial and its contents, (3) the measure of commercial persuasion, and (4) the impact on purchase behavior.

Recognition. One level of testing recognition is whether respondents can recognize the advertisement as one they have seen before. An example of recognition testing is the Bruzzone Research Company (BRC) tests of television commercials.[7] Questionnaires are mailed to 1000 households. The sample is drawn from the Donnelley list of all households that have either a registered automobile or a listed telephone. Interest in the subject matter and a one dollar payment usually generates a response of 500. The recognition question is at the top of the questionnaire; at the bottom is the brand-association question, a critical dimension of most campaigns.

Starch has been measuring printed-advertisement recognition since 1923. In the Starch survey, respondents are asked to read a magazine and, for each advertisement, are asked if they saw it in the issue. The noted score, usually the measure of recognition, is the percentage who answer affirmatively.

Recall. The **day-after-recall (DAR)** measure of a television commercial, first used in the early 1940s by George Gallup, then by Young & Rubicam, is closely associated with Burke Marketing Research.[8] The procedure is to telephone 150 to 300 program viewers the day after a television commercial appears. They are asked if they can recall any commercials the previous day for a particular brand. They are then asked if they can recall anything about the commercial: what was said, what was shown, and what the main idea was. DAR is the percent of those in the commercial audience who were watching the show, before and after the commercial was shown, who remembered something specific about it such as the sales message, the story line, the plot, or some visual or audio element.

The DAR is an "on-air" test in that the commercial exposure occurs in a natural, realistic, in-home setting. It is well established and has developed extensive norms over the years.

Gallup and Robinson, Mapes and Ross provide a similar measure for print media. They place a magazine with 150 of its regular readers and ask that it be read in a normal manner. The next day the readers are asked to describe ads for any brands of interest.

DAR scores have many limitations. First, their reliability is suspect. Extremely low test-retest correlations (below .30) have been found when commercials from the same product class are studied. Second, DAR scores are unduly affected by whether viewers like the particular program and the nature of the program. Third, of eight relevant studies, seven found practically no association between recall and the measure of persuasion it generated.

Persuasion. The **forced exposure, brand preference change** test measures the change in brand preference after watching the advertisement. Since the respondents view the advertisement in a theater, the test is called the *forced exposure, brand preference change test.* Theater testing, pioneered by Horace Schwerin and Paul Lazarsfeld in the 1950s, is now done by McCollum/Spielman, ASI, and ARS.[9]

The McCollum/Spielman test uses a 450-person sample, spread over four geographically dispersed locations.[10] Forced exposure tests recruit the respondents by telephone and ask them to come to a central location to preview television programming. Seated in groups of 25 in front of television monitors, they respond to a set of demographic and brand/product-usage questions that appear on the screen. The respondents view a half-hour variety program featuring four professional performers. At midpoint in the program seven commercials, including four test commercials, are shown in a pattern like the one diagrammed here:

Performer A	Performer B	T 1	C	T 2	C	T 3	C	T 4	Performer C	Performer D

C = constant commercials   T = test commercials

After the audience expresses its reactions to the program, an unaided brand-name-recall question is asked that forms the basis of the **clutter/awareness** score (the percentage who recalled that the brand was advertised). The clutter/awareness score (C/A) for 30-second commercials averages 56 percent for established brands and 40 percent for new brands.[11] The four test commercials are then exposed a second time, surrounded by program material, in the following pattern:

Program Intro.	T 1	Program	T 2	Program	T 3	Program	T 4	Program

T = test commercials

An attitude shift (AS) measure is obtained. For frequently purchased package goods, such as toiletries, the preexposure designation of the brand purchased most often is compared with the postexposure brand selection in a market-basket-award situation. The respondents are asked to select brands they would like included if they were winners of a $25 basket of products. In product fields with multiple-brand usage, such as soft drinks, a constant sum measure (i.e., a total of 10 points is allocated to brands, which are apportioned according to audience preference) is employed before and after exposure. For durables and services, the pre- and postpreference is measured.

Finally, diagnostic questions are asked. Some of the areas that are frequently explored include

▶ Comprehension of message/slogan.

▶ Communication of secondary copy ideas.

▶ Evaluation of demonstrations, spokesman, message.

▶ Perception of brand uniqueness/brand differentiation.

▶ Irritating/confusing elements.

▶ Viewer involvement.

The ASI and ARS also have similar tests to obtain a measure of persuasion.

Customized Measures of Communication/Attitude. Standardized-copy test measures are useful because they come with norms sometimes based on thousands of past tests. Thus, the interpretation of a test becomes more meaningful. Some objectives, particularly communication objectives, necessarily are unique to a brand, and may require questions tailored to that brand. Customized measures of communication/attitude have to be developed for such applications.

On-Air Tests—Brand Preference Change. In the Mapes and Ross on-air test, commercials are aired on a radio station in a preselected prime-time position in each of three major markets. Prior to the test, a sample of 200 viewers (150 if it is an all-male target audience) are contacted by phone and asked to participate in a survey and a cash award drawing that requires viewing the test program. During the telephone interview, respondents provide unaided brand-name awareness and are questioned about their brand preferences for a number of different product categories. The day following the commercial exposure, the respondents again answer brand-preference as well as DAR questions. The key Mapes and Ross measure is pre-and postbrand preference change. There are other measures of brand preference change also, like the one done by ASI Apex System, which differs slightly from the Mapes and Ross test.[12] Exhibit 24-1 is a sample proposal for a Mapes and Ross on-air test.

Purchase Behavior

Coupon Stimulated Purchasing. In the Tele-Research approach, 600 shoppers are intercepted in a shopping center location, usually in Los Angeles, and randomly assigned to test or control groups. The test group is exposed to five television or radio commercials or six print ads. About 250 subjects in the test group complete a questionnaire on the commercial. Both groups are given a customer code number and a packet of coupons, including one for the test brand, which can be redeemed in a nearby cooperating drugstore or supermarket, depending on the product. Selling effectiveness score is the ratio of purchases by viewer shoppers divided by the purchases by control shoppers. Purchases are tracked by scanner data. While the exposure context is highly artificial, the purchase choice is relatively realistic in that real money is spent in a real store.

Split-Cable Tests. Information Resources, Inc.'s (IRI) BehaviorScan is one of several **split-cable testing** operations (Burke and Nielsen being two others). BehaviorScan was described in part in Chapter 6. Behavior Scan monitors the purchases of the panel members as well as in-store information such as special prices, features, and displays.

An additional capability of split-cable testing makes it extremely important in advertising research. The panelists have a device connected to their TV sets that not only allows the channel selection to be monitored, but also allows the advertiser to substitute one advertisement for another in what are called "cut-ins." Thus, a host of tests can be conducted such as the impact of specific commercials, sets of commercials, advertising budget levels, the time of day

EXHIBIT 24-1

Mapes and Ross 24-Hour Recall Marketing Research Project Proposal

Project:	Mapes and Ross on-air test
Brand:	Diet Coke
Background and Objectives:	The agency has changed the slogan used in the commercials to a new one. The objectives of this test will be a) To measure the new slogan's effectiveness in generating attention (related recall). b) To measure the new slogan's communication effectiveness.
Research Design:	The traditional Mapes and Ross on-air test method will be used. The sample will consist of 400 male and female respondents, aged 18 and older, in the program audience. The sample specifications will follow recent Mapes and Ross on-air tests. The data will be broken out by the age group 18–34, 35–49, and 50–65-year olds, as they fall naturally in the program audience. The commercial will be shown in Houston, Kansas City, and Chicago on UHF television channels, using movie programs. There will be one exposure. In each of the three metropolitan areas, interviewers will telephone a sample of men, age 18 and over, and invite them to view the test program that night. The follow-up telephone interviews the next day will probe whether the prerecruited respondents watched the program. Then the respondents will be asked what commercials they recall and what they recalled about the Diet Coke commercial, followed by a measure of liking of the slogan.
Information to Be Obtained:	1. Total commercial recall 2. Slogan recall 3. A measure of liking for the slogan
Action Standard:	The new slogan will be compared to the original slogan and the Mapes and Ross norms on the following measures:

Old slogan

Total commercial recall	18%
Percent recalling the slogan	35
Measure of liking for the new slogan on a 5-point scale	3.8

If the new slogan scores below the above scores for the original slogan, we will not move forward with the test slogan. Additionally, if new slogan scores lower than old slogan on the measure of liking in the 18–34 age group, we will not move forward with the new commercial.

Timing and Cost:	The time schedule for this research will be

1 1/2	weeks	to set up test/insert commercial into UHF movie programs
1	day	field work
1	week	top-line
2	weeks	computer tabulations
2	weeks	final report
7 1/2	weeks	total

The cost for this research will be $11,250 ± 10

---

or the program in which the ad appears, the commercial length, or the interaction with promotion programs.

Tracking Studies

When a campaign is running, its impact often is monitored via a tracking study. Periodic sampling of the target audience provides a time trend of measures of interest. The purpose is to evaluate and reassess the advertising campaign, and perhaps also to understand why it is or is not working. Among the measures that often are traced are advertisement awareness, awareness of elements of the advertisement, brand awareness, beliefs about brand attributes, brand image, occasions of use, and brand preference. Of particular interest is knowing how the campaign is affecting the brand, as opposed to how the advertisement is communicating the message. The Eric Marder firm provides an approach to obtaining tracking data without doing customized studies.[13] On a continuous basis, they maintain a panel of women from whom they obtain the various measures just described. Table 24-1 gives a comprehensive view of the measures of advertisement effectiveness and the various tests the industry uses to obtain them.

Diagnostic Testing

A whole category of advertising research methods is designed primarily not to test the impact of a total ad but rather to help creative people understand how the parts of the ad contribute to its impact. Which are weak and how do they interact? Most of these approaches can be applied to mock-ups of proposed ads as well as finished ads.

Copy Test Validity

Copy test validity refers to the ability to predict advertising response. Figure 24-3 is an overview of some of the important ways in which copy tests can differ. Each dimension involves validity issues and trade-offs with cost. Hence,

TABLE 24-1
Measures and Tests of Ad Effectiveness

Measure of Advertising Effectiveness	Test Used in the Industry
Recognition	1) BRC tests of television commercials 2) Communicus recognition measures of radio and television advertisements 3) Starch Scores
Recall	1) DAR measure by Young and Rubicam 2) Gallup & Robinson and Mapes and Ross provide similar measure for the print media
Persuasion	1) Forced Exposure Brand Preference Change Tests done by McCollum/Spielman, ASI and ARS 2) On-Air Tests of brand preference change done by Mapes and Ross and ASI Apex system 3) Customized Measures
Purchase Behavior	1) Coupon-stimulated purchasing done by Tele-Research 2) Split-cable testing by IRI (BehaviorScan)
Tracking Studies	1) Customized studies 2) Eric Marder's TEC audit

Advertisement Used
    Mock-up
    Finished advertisement

Frequency of Exposure
    Single-exposure test
    Multiple-exposure test

How It's Shown
    Isolated
    In a clutter
    In a program or magazine

Where the Exposure Occurs
    In a shopping center facility
    At home on TV
    At home through the mail
    In a theater

How Respondents are Obtained
    Prerecruited forced exposure
    Not prerecruited/natural exposure

Geographic Scope
    One city
    Several cities
    Nationwide

Alternative Measures of Persuasion
    Pre/post measures of attitudes or behavior
    (that is, pre/post attitude or behavior shifts)
    Multiple measures
    (that is, recall/involvement/buying commmitment)
    After-only questions to measure persuasion
    (that is, constant sum brand preference)
    Test market sales measures
    (that is, using scanner panels)

Bases of Comparison and Evaluation
    Comparing test results to norms
    Using a control group

FIGURE 24-3
Alternative methods of copy testing

each of these issues has to be considered carefully before a copy test can be designed.

Qualitative Research. Focus-group research is widely used at the front end of the development of an advertising campaign. In such groups, people will discuss their opinions about the product and the brand, their use experiences, and their reaction to potential advertisement concepts and actual advertisements.[14]

Audience Impressions of the Ad. Many copy test approaches append a set of open-ended questions designed to tap the audience's impressions of what the ad was about, what ideas were presented, interest in the ideas, and so on. One goal is to detect potential misperceptions. Another is to uncover unintended associations that may have been created. If too many negative comments are elicited, there may be cause for concern.

Adjective Checklist. The BRC mail questionnaire includes an adjective checklist that allows the advertiser to determine how warm, amusing, irritating, or informative the respondent thinks that the ad is. Several of their phrases tap an empathy dimension. "I can see myself doing that," "I can relate to that," and so on. Some believe that unless advertisements can achieve a degree of empathy they will not peform well.

Eye Movement. Eye movement devices, such as those used by Perception Research and Burke, record the point on a print ad or package where the eye focuses, 60 times each second. An analysis can determine what the reader saw, what he or she "returned to" for reexamination, what point was "fixed on."

Physiological Measurement. Of particular interest in advertisements that are intended to precipitate emotional responses is the use of measures that reflect physiological arousal that the respondent normally can't control. Among the measures used are galvanic skin response (GSR), skin resistance, heart beat, facial expressions, muscle movement, and voice pitch analysis. The difficulty is in the interpretation, because a variety of reactions can stimulate arousal.[15]

Budget Decision

Arriving at analytical, research-based judgments as to the optimal advertising budget is surprisingly difficult. However, there are research inputs that can be helpful. Tracking studies that show advertising is either surpassing or failing to reach communication objectives can suggest that the budget should be either reduced or increased. Forced-exposure testing of multiple exposures can suggest the optimal number of exposures per month for an audience member. Such a number can help guide advertising budget expenditures. More direct approaches include regression analysis of internal sales and advertising data, field experimentation, and split-cable experimentation.

Media Research

In evaluating a particular media alternative such as *Time Magazine* or "Dynasty," it is necessary to know how many advertising exposures it will deliver and what will be the characteristics of the audience. A first cut of the vehicle's value is the cost per thousand (circulation), the advertisement insertion cost divided by the size of the audience.

Measuring Print-Vehicle Audiences. Print-vehicle circulation data are easily obtained, but neglect pass-along readers both inside and outside the home. Thus, to measure a vehicle's audience, it is necessary to apply approaches such as recent-reading, reading-habit, and through-the-book methods, to a randomly selected sample.

In the **recent-reading method,** respondents are asked whether they looked at a copy of a weekly publication within the past week, or during the last month if it is a monthly publication.[16]

The **reading-habit method,** which askes respondents how many issues out of the last four they personally read or looked at, is also sensitive to memory difficulties. In particular, it is difficult to discriminate between reading the same issue several times and reading several issues. The **through-the-book** readership attempts to reduce the problem resulting from faulty memory. Respondents' readership is ascertained only after they are shown a specific issue of a magazine, and asked whether they read several articles, and if they were interesting. The approach, which requires an expensive personal interview, is sensitive to the age of the issue.

Measuring Broadcast-Vehicle Audiences. Television audience size is estimated by an audimeter and a diary. The audimeter is attached to a television set and monitors the set's activity 24 hours a day, recording any change or activity that lasts over 30 seconds. Nielsen has recently introduced the "people-meter," which is discussed in Chapter 6.

Nielsen, in its national ratings estimates, supplements the audimeter with a matched sample **diary panel.** A diary household notes the viewing activity, including who is doing the watching. A clocklike meter keeps track of how long the set is on so that Nielsen can make sure that the diary is complete. Using the diary information, Nielsen can break down the audience estimates by age, sex, and geographic area. Mediamark and Simmons are two other major audience-measuring services.[17]

Sales Promotion Research

There are three major types of sales promotion: consumer promotions, retailer promotions, and trade promotions.

Figure 24-4 depicts the major agents involved in sales promotion. In general, the consumer, or end user, is the ultimate target of all sales-promotion activities. In consumer promotion, manufacturers offer promotions directly to consumers, whereas retail promotions involve promotions by retailers to consumers. Trade promotions involve manufacturers offering promotions to retailers or other

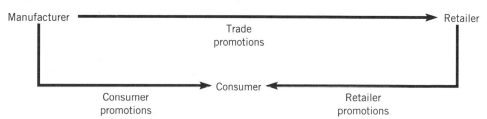

FIGURE 24-4

A schematic framework of the major types of sales promotion

trade entities. Trade entities can also promote to each other. For example, a distributor can offer a steep temporary price cut to retailers in order to sell its excess inventories. We call these **trade promotions** since the recipient of the promotion is a marketing intermediary.

Sometimes several manufacturers or several retailers combine in one promotion. These are called **cooperative promotions** or **promotion partnerships.** Partnership promotions often "tie in" a sample or other promotion for one product with the purchase of another. For example, a snack food company that offers coupons for a soda brand on its package is engaging in a tie-in consumer promotion.

Strategically, trade promotions and the resultant retailer promotions are elements of the "push" component of a manufacturer's marketing effort, whereas consumer promotions are part of the "pull" effort. It is important that the push and pull elements of sales promotion strategy work hand-in-hand with the push and pull elements of the rest of a firm's marketing strategy. For example, trade promotions often must be coordinated with sales activity, whereas consumer promotions often are coordinated with advertising.

Table 24-2 provides a list of specific retailer, trade, and consumer promotions. This list is by no means exhaustive.

The most commonly researched sales promotions are coupons, trade allowances, and retailer promotions. Even among retailer promotions, only recently have researchers begun to distinguish among price cuts, displays, and features, and even now, those are often subsumed under one "promotion" or "deal-offer" variable.

Unfortunately, much of the research on sales promotion has concentrated on only a few types or has considered promotion more generically. For example,

TABLE 24-2
Specific Sales Promotional Tools

Retailer Promotions	Trade Promotions	Consumer Promotions
Price cuts	Case allowances	Couponing
Displays	Advertising allowances	Sampling
Feature advertising	Display allowances	Price packs
Free goods	Trade coupons	Value packs
Retailer coupons	"Spiffs"	Refunds
Contests/premiums	Financing incentives	Continuity programs
	Contests	Financing incentives
		Bonus packs
		Special events
		Sweepstakes
		Contests
		Premiums
		Tie-ins

couponing by far is the most researched form of consumer promotion. In one sense, this is appropriate, since coupons are clearly the most important consumer promotion for packaged goods marketers.[18] However, contests and sweepstakes, continuity offers, price packs, and premiums are clearly underresearched. Rebates, which are the durable goods analog of couponing, have received very little attention. The use of premiums and financing incentives in a durable goods context is also vastly underresearched.

With scanner data so easily and widely available, most of the informational requirements for decisions on sales promotions can be readily extracted from them. Both Nielsen and IRI have installed scanner-based information-collection systems (both store and panel) in the major markets of the country. In five years' time they plan to cover all the markets in the country, so researchers will have a wealth of information to rely on. They also have a number of ready-to-use expert systems, some of which were discussed in Chapter 6, which provide information such as sales and market share in that store in the week there was a promotion so managers can easily find out whether the promotion was effective.

Summary

The distribution decisions that typically require a lot of information from outside the firm are those that deal with the number and location of warehouses, retail outlets, and salespersons. Marketing research aids managers in making these decisions by providing the necessary information. The **center-of-gravity method, computerized simulation, catchment-area analysis,** and **outlet location research** are some of the more commonly used analytical tools managers use in this area of decision making. Marketing research also helps in conducting field experiments, statistical analysis of sales data, and setting up of computerized models for determining sales force size and allocation of sales amounts.

Criteria used in copy testing can be usefully grouped into four types: recognition, recall, persuasion, and behavior. BRC uses mail questionnaires to measure television commercial recognition and brand name association. Communicus (for television) and Starch (for print ads) use personal interviews. Day-after-recall is widely used but controversial because of its inability to predict persuasion or behavior, especially for emotional appeals. Persuasion has been measured in forced exposure or on-air contexts, by change in brand preference, change in prize list brand preference, comparison of its effect on brand preference with a nonexposed control group, measures of advertisement involvement and brand commitment, and measures tailored to particular advertising objectives. Behavior measures include coupon-stimulated buying after a forced exposure to an ad, and scanner-based monitoring of panelists in a split-cable testing operation.

Copy test validity concerns usually focus on the naturalness of the exposure, the reactive effect of being in an experiment (especially when the exposure setting is not natural and when an attitude measure is required), the representativeness of the sample, and the appropriateness and validity of the response measure. A tracking study provides measures of advertising impact over time by taking periodic (monthly, quarterly, or yearly) surveys of audience response. **Diagnostic testing,** to evaluate the advertisement content at all stages of the process, includes qualitative research, audience and impressions, adjective checklists, eye movement, physiological measures, and monitoring audience response during the commercial. **Media research** includes measuring vehicle audiences by asking people about their reading habits, and using audimeters connected to television sets.

There are different ways by which a product/service can be promoted. **Couponing** is the most common way of sales promotion, and most of the marketing research has concentrated on coupon promotion. Scanner data can provide most of the informational requirements for sales promotion decisions.

Questions and Problems

1. Why measure recognition, anyway? Why would it ever be of value to have an audience member recognize an ad when he or she could not recall it without being prompted and could not recall its content? Why not just measure recall?

2. Compare the BRC recognition method with the Communicus method. What are the relative strengths and weaknesses?

3. Is DAR widely used? Why? Would you use it if you were the product manager for Lowenbrau? For American Express? Under what circumstances would you use it?

4. Review the validity problems inherent in the McCollum/Spielman theater testing approach. Compare these to
   a. Mapes and Ross method
   b. Apex method
   c. Tele-Research approach
   d. Sherman BUY test
   e. BehaviorScan approach

5. Why conduct tracking studies? Why not just observe sales?

6. How will adjective checklists help a creative group? What about eye-movement data?

7. DuPont conducted a field experiment for an improved version of Teflon several years after they first introduced Teflon. Four cities received 10 daytime commercial minutes per week during the fall months, five cities received 5 minutes per week, and four cities (the control group) received no advertising. Cities were randomly assigned to each of the three test conditions. The sales measure was a purchase of Teflon cookware as reported by telephone interviews with 1000 housewives in each of the test cities. The total purchases turned out to be about 30 percent higher in the

heavy advertising cities than in those cities with no or low advertising, but there was no real difference between the low and no advertising groups. Critique this test. What validity problems do you see? What changes would you make? Would you conduct the same test if the product change had been out for three years?

8. Mediamark estimated the total adult readers of *Family Circle* magazine as 32.1 million, while Simmons estimated it as 18.3 million. Why the difference? Which is right?

9. In a survey of homemakers, the readership of *Harper's* was exaggerated and the readership of *Modern Romance* seemed much less than circulation figures indicated. Why would respondents incorrectly report their readership in this manner? Can you think of ways to avoid this bias?

10. What are the weaknesses of the audimeter? Of the diary? If cost was not a problem, do you believe a camera in the room would be a reasonable solution? Identify and evaluate other alternatives.

11. You are the sales manager for a firm that sells photocopying machines, laser printers, and fax machines. Design a system for finding the number and location of the salespersons in your company. Describe clearly the input, the method(s) of calculation, and the output of your system.

12. What is the significance of "trade area"? How does one decide the trading area for a retail store?

13. Conduct research on the computerized models that are available for locating warehouses and salespersons? Give a detailed report on their capabilities, advantages, and disadvantages.

End Notes

1. S. Van Auken. "The Centroid Locational Model: A Study in Situational Dependency, *The Logistics and Transportation Review*, 2, 1974, 149–63.

2. J. A. Paris and L. D. Crabtree. "Survey License Plates to Define Retail Trade Area," *Marketing News*, 19, 1985, 12.

3. D. L. Huff and R. R. Batsell. "Delimiting the Areal Extent of a Market Area," *Journal of Marketing Research*, 14, 1977, 581–5.

4. E. Blair. "Sampling Issues in Trade Area Maps Drawn from Shoppers Surveys,"*Journal of Marketing*, 14, 1983, 98–106.

5. C. S. Craig, A. Ghosh, and S. McLafferty. "Models of the Retail Location Process: A Review," *Journal of Retailing*, 60, 1984, 22.

6. M. F. Goodchild. "ILACS: A Location-Allocation Model for Retail Site Selection," *Journal of Retailing*, 60, 84–100.

7. Donald E. Bruzzone. "The Case for Testing Commercials by Mail," presented at the 25th Annual Conference of the Advertising Research Foundation, New York, October 23, 1979.

8. Benjamin Lipstein. "An Historical Perspective of Copy Research," *Journal of Advertising Research*, 24 December 1984, 11–15.

9. Lipstein. op. cit.

10. *AC T Advertising Control for Television*, Undated publication of McCollum/Spielman Research.

11. *Ibid.*

12. Descriptive material from Mapes & Ross.

13. The TEC audit, New York: TEC Measures, Inc.

14. Benjamin Lipstein and James P. Neelankavil. "Television Advertising Copy Research: A Critical Review of the State of the Art," *Journal of Advertising Research*, 24, April/May 1984, 19–25.

15. David A. Aaker, Douglas M. Stayman, and Michael R. Hagerty. "Warmth in Advertising: Measurement, Impact and Sequence Effects," *Journal of Consumer Research*, March 1986.

16. William S. Blair. "Observed vs. Reported Behavior in Magazine Reading: An Investigation of the Editorial Interest Method," *Proceedings of the 12th Annual Conference of the Advertising Research Foundation*, New York City, 1967.

17. "ARB and NSI Defend Their TV Diaries," *Media Decisions*, October 1973, 72–74.
18. Robert C. Blattberg, and Scott A. Neslin. *Sales Promotion: Concepts, Methods and Strategies* (Englewood Cliffs, New Jersey: Prentice Hall), 1990.

CASE 24-1
Levi Strauss & Co.

Sue Swenson, a member of the research group at Foote, Cone & Belding/Honig, a San Francisco advertising agency, was reviewing four copy testing techniques, all of which cost about $10,000 per commercial (plus media costs where required):

1. Burke DAR (spots are purchased in three markets for the test ads)
2. Mapes and Ross
3. McCollum/Spielman
4. Tele-Research

A meeting was scheduled with the Levi Strauss account group for the next day to decide on which copy tests to employ on two new Levi's campaigns. The following week a similar meeting was scheduled involving a campaign for a new bar of soap for another client. In each case the task was to determine which testing approach would be used to help make the final selection of which commercials to use in the campaigns. Swenson knew that she would be expected to contribute to the discussion by pointing out the strengths and limitations of each test and to make her own recommendations.

Levi Strauss & Co. had grown from a firm serving the needs of miners in the Gold Rush era of the mid-1800s to a large, sophisticated clothing company. In 1979 it had sales of over $2 billion, drawn from an international and domestic operation. The domestic company, Levi Strauss USA, included six divisions: Jeanswear, Sportswear, Womenswear, Youthwear, Activewear, and Accessories. In 1979, Levi Strauss was among the 100 largest advertisers, with expenditures of $38.5 million, primarily on television.

Concerning the Levi's campaigns, Swenson recognized that two very different campaigns were involved. The first was a corporate-image campaign. The overall objective was to build and maintain Levi's brand image. The approach was to build around the concepts of "quality" and "heritage," the most meaningful, believable, and universal aspects of the Levi's corporate personality. Unlike competitors who claimed quality as a product feature, Levi's 128-year-heritage advertisements had an important additional dimension. More specifically, the advertising involved the following strategy:

1. Heritage-quality: communicate to male and female consumers, ages 12 to 49, that Levi's makes a wide variety of apparel products, all of which share in the company's 128-year commitment to quality.
2. Variety-quality: communicate to male and female consumers, ages 12 to 49, that Levi's makes a wide variety of quality apparel products for the entire family.

Figure 1 shows one of the commercials from the pool that was to be tested for the corporate campaign.

The second campaign was for Levi's action suits. In 1979, the Sportswear division responsible for action suits spent approximately $6 million on network television commercials and co-op newspaper ads to introduce Actionwear slacks, which topped the sales of both leading brands of men's slacks, Haggar and Farah, in that year. The primary segment was middle-aged males, who often suffer from middle-aged spread. Actionwear slacks, a blend of polyester and other fabrics with a stretchable waistline, were presented as a solution to the problem. The advertising objectives for the new campaign were guided by the following:

Focus: Levi's action garments are comfortable dress clothes.

Benefits: Primary—comfortable; secondary—attractive, good-looking, well made, long-wearing.

Reasons why:

1. Levi's Action slacks are comfortable because they have a hidden stretch waistband and expandable shell fabric.
2. Levi's Action suit jacket is comfortable because it has hidden stretch panels that let you move freely without binding.
3. The Levi's name implies quality, well-made clothes.

Brand character: Levi's Action clothing is sensible, good-value menswear manufactured by Levi Strauss & Co., a company dedicated to quality.

LEVI'S® "ROUNDUP"

(Music) Yessir, this drive started over a hundred years ago, back in California.

Just a few head of Levi's Blue Jeans, and a lot of hard miles.

Across country that would've killed ordinary pants.

But Levi's? They thrived on it! If anything, the herd got stronger —and bigger.

First there was kid's Levi's. Ornery little critters...seems like nothing stops 'em.

Then there was gal's pants, and tops, and skirts. Purtiest things you ever set eyes on.

And just to prove they could make it in the big city, the herd bred a new strain called Levi's Sportswear.

Jackets, shirts, slacks a bit fancy for this job, I reckon, but I do admire the way they're made.

Fact is, pride is why we put our name on everything in this herd.

Tells folks, "This here's ours!" If you like what you got, then c'mon back!

We'll be here. You see, fashions may change...

...but quality never goes out of style!

FIGURE 1
A corporate commercial
Levi Strauss & Co. Two Embarcadero Center, San Francisco, CA 94106

Figure 2 shows a commercial from the pool for the Levi Action campaign.

Swenson also knew that previous Levi's commercials had proved exceptionally memorable and effective, owing to their distinctive creative approach. In part, their appeal lies in their ability to challenge the viewer's imagination. The advertising assumes that viewers are thoughtful and appreciate advertising that respects their judgments.

In preparing for the next day's meeting with the Levi account group, she decided to review carefully the four copy testing services. The immediate problem

TV. 30 Sec.
Title: "Action Suit/Bus"

ANNCR: If a man's suit jacket fits
       like a straight jacket . . .
WIFE: Hold on, Joe!
JOE: I can't raise my arms.

ANNCR: If his pants fit their worst
       around his waist,
WIFE: Sit down.
JOE: I can't—these pants are too
     tight.

ANNCR: Then he needs Levi's•
       Action Suit . . . perhaps
       the most comfortable suit
       a man can wear.

ANNCR: The waistband strrrr-
       retches to give more room
       when you need it.

JOE: Comfortable.
ANNCR: The jacket lets you
       move your arms without
       binding.

JOE: I can sit.
OLD LADY: Hmmmmmmph!

JOE: I can stand, too.

ANNCR: Levi's Action Suit from
       Levi's Sportswear.

FIGURE 2
An action suit commercial
Levi Strauss & Co. Two Embarcadero Center, San Francisco, CA 94106

was to decide which of the services to recommend for testing commercials from the two Levi's campaigns. She knew that similar issues would be raised in discussions with another of the agency's clients the following week concerning a national campaign for a bar-soap line extension. Positioning for the bar-soap essentially involved a dual cleanliness-fragrance theme. A demonstration commercial focused on these two copy points.

Questions for Discussion

1. What copy testing service or services should Sue Swenson recommend for testing the two Levi Strauss commercials?

2. What service or services should she recommend for testing the bar-soap commercial?

25 APPLICATIONS OF MARKETING RESEARCH IN THE NINETIES

Learning Objectives

▶ Introduce the agenda for marketing research in the nineties.

▶ Discuss the concept of **competitive advantage** and the various ways of measuring it.

▶ Discuss **brand equity** and the various techniques used to measure it.

▶ Discuss **customer satisfaction** and the different methods of operationalizing it.

▶ Describe the concept and methodologies used to measure the different dimensions of **total quality management.**

▶ Briefly discuss the other emerging strategies like **relationship marketing,** and **integrated marketing communications** and mention how marketing research satisfies their information requirements.

Companies operate in a constant state of flux. With the environment characterized by increasing dynamism and uncertainty, firms have to innovate continuously to remain competitive. To survive in the nineties, firms must not only provide goods/services to the consumer efficiently but should also possess sustainable competitive advantage. Hence, there has been a shift of focus in marketing, from delivering goods/services to consumers (satisfying their needs) to achieving a competitive advantage. Companies are embracing new tools, techniques, and strategies in order to remain competitive. This has resulted in a new agenda for marketing research in the nineties.

Some of the strategies that companies have begun to adopt are **total quality management** (TQM), **relationship marketing,** and **integrated marketing communications** (IMC). To decide on and implement these strategies managers require dramatically different information than they need for making marketing mix decisions. Hence, marketing research has to rise to the challenge and provide managers with the requisite information. Moreover, tremendous advances in the field of statistics and computational capabilities have led market researchers to adopt more and more sophisticated techniques.

This chapter discusses various new methods of operationalizing well-established constructs like competitive advantage, brand equity, and customer satisfaction, and a few of the emerging strategies in the field of marketing such as TQM, relationship marketing, and so forth. Then it enumerates the informational requirements to implement these strategies. This chapter also briefly touches upon various techniques and methods that marketing research companies use to satisfy these informational requirements.

COMPETITIVE ADVANTAGE

The notion that achieving superior performance requires a business to gain and hold an advantage over competitors is central to contemporary strategic thinking. Businesses seeking advantage are exhorted to develop distinctive competencies at the lowest delivered cost, or to achieve differentiation through superior value. The promised payoff is market-share dominance and above-average profitability. Michael Porter's pioneering text on competitive strategy changed the way many companies think about their competition.[1] Porter identified five forces that shape competition: current competitors, the threat of new entrants, the threat of new substitutes, the bargaining power of customers, and the bargaining power of suppliers.

Assessing Competitive Advantage[2]

Assessing competitive advantage can be done in a number of ways. They can be broadly classified as market-based assessment and process-based assessment. **Market-based assessment** is direct comparison with a few target competitors, whereas **process-based assessment** is a comparison of the methods employed by the competitors in achieving their distinctive advantage. The different methods of assessing competitive advantage are given in Table 25-1.

Market-Based Assessment

Market Share. This is measured as a percentage of total industry sales over a specified time period. In terms of Porter's typology, market share is one of the measures used to assess current competition. About 70 percent of the companies in the 1990 Conference Board study tracked their competitors' market share, because market share identifies who the major players are, and

TABLE 25-1
Methods of Assessing Competitive Advantage

Market-based	Process-based
Market share	Marketing skills audit
Recall share	Comparison of relative costs
Advertising share	Comparison of winning versus losing competitors
R&D share	Identifying high-leverage phenomena

changes in market share identify who has become more or less competitive in the marketplace (that is, who gained share from whom).

But clearly there are problems in assessing competitive advantages using market share. A company's market share can change dramatically depending on whether the market is defined as global, a particular export market, the U.S. market, a region of the United States, a city, or a segment of users, or is based on product usage. The scope of the market normally is specified by a realistic assessment of company resources and by company growth objectives. Operationally, the market often is specified by the way market researchers are able to collect sales and market share information.

The change in market share over time is a vital indicator of competitive dynamics, particularly during the growth stage of a product or market. It indicates whether a firm is ahead, abreast of, or behind the market's total growth rate. Part of the reason that Japanese companies are concerned about gaining market share is that they often compete in high-growth markets, and they understand that this is the crucial time to develop brand loyalty. For example, the Japanese production of calculators grew 200 times during the 1970s. A firm had to expand its sales by this multiple just to keep its market share; Casio raced ahead of its rivals and increased its market share from 10 percent to 35 percent.[3]

Recall Share. This is the percentage of customers who name the brand when they are asked to name the first brand that comes to mind when they consider buying a particular type of product. This indicates the consumer's top-of-mind brand awareness and preferences. This gives a measure of advantage to that brand over others in the market.

Advertising Share. This is the percentage of media space or time a brand has of the total media share for that industry, often measured simply as dollars spent on advertising. This is likely to lead to a change in recall share. The advertising share is another measure of current competition that a firm faces.

R&D Share. This is a company's research and development expenditure as a percentage of the total industry R&D expenditure. This is a long-term predictor of new product developments, improvements in quality, cost reductions, and, hence, market share. It is a very important measure of future competitiveness in many high-technology markets. All of the above share measures can be obtained from either survey data or secondary data.

Process-Based Assessment

Marketing Skills Audit. Skills are "the most distinctive encapsulation of the organization's way of doing business." One vehicle for assessing skills is the **marketing audit.** It is a comprehensive, systematic, independent, and periodic examination of a business unit's marketing environment, objectives, strategies, and activities. The audit should be based on customer orientation or focus on customer satisfaction as the overriding theme to guide the audit. The audit is nothing but a marketing research project whose objective is to critically evaluate the way the firm performs in its environment.

Comparison of Relative Costs. Another measure of advantage is a comparison of the firm's costs versus those of competitors. The company gains a cost advantage when its cumulative costs are lower than its competitors'. Competitors' costs can be estimated from public data or interviews with suppliers and distributors. Secondary data can be used to obtain such data. Techniques such as "reverse engineering" are also used to obtain competitor's costs.

Comparison of Winning Versus Losing Competitors. Key success factors can be inferred by analyzing differences in performance among competitors. For this approach to yield useful insights, three difficult questions must be answered. First, which competitors should be included in the comparison set? Second, what criteria should be used to distinguish the winners from the losers (e.g., profitability, growth, market share, creation of markets)? Third, what are the reasons for the differences in performance? This procedure is a good place to start to determine a competitive advantage. Secondary sources or qualitative research methods can provide this information.

Identifying High-Leverage Phenomena. Ideally, these are causal relationships that describe how controllable variables such as plant scale, production-run length, and sales force density affect outcomes such as manufacturing and sales costs per unit. The analysis task is formidable because a myriad of potential relationships must be examined, but only a few will be found to have significant leverage. The researcher determines the current position of each leading competitor for each significant relationship and estimates how these competitors will change their positions. Marketing research can play a very useful role in gathering this information.

BRAND EQUITY

Brand equity is defined as a set of assets and liabilities linked to a brand that add to or subtract from the value of a product or service to a company and/or its customers.[4] The assets or liabilities that underlie brand equity must be linked to the name and/or symbol of the brand. The assets and liabilities on which brand equity is based will differ from context to context. However, they can be usefully grouped into five categories:

1. Brand loyalty.
2. Name awareness.
3. Perceived quality.
4. Brand associations in addition to perceived quality.
5. Other proprietary brand assets: patents, trademarks, channel relationships, etc.

The concept of brand equity is summarized in Figure 25-1, which shows the five categories of assets that are the basis of brand equity. The figure also shows that brand equity creates value for both the customer and the firm.

Research Questions under Brand Equity

An appraisal of the brand based upon the five dimensions involves addressing and obtaining answers to the questions that follow. Marketing research can help to provide answers to these questions:

> *Brand Loyalty.* What are the brand-loyalty levels, by segment? Are customers satisfied? What do "exit interviews" suggest? Why are customers leaving? What is causing dissatisfaction? What do customers say are their problems with buying or using the brand? What are the market-share and sales trends?

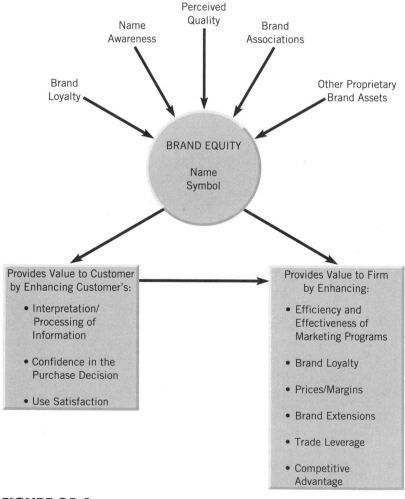

FIGURE 25-1
Brand equity

Awareness. How valuable an asset is brand awareness in this market? What is the company's brand awareness level as compared to that of competitors? What are the trends? Is the brand being considered? Is brand awareness the problem? What could be done to improve brand awareness?

Perceived Quality. What drives perceived quality? What is important to the customer? What signals quality? Is perceived quality valued—or is the market moving towards a commodity business? Are prices and margins eroding? If so, can the movement be slowed or reversed? How do competitors stack up with respect to perceived quality? Are there any changes? In blind-use tests, what is our brand name worth? Has it changed over time?

Brand Associations. What mental image, if any, does the brand stimulate? Is that image a competitive advantage? Does it have a slogan or symbol that is a differentiating asset? How are the brand and its competitors' positioned? Evaluate each position with respect to its value / relevance to customers and how protected / vulnerable it is to competitors.

Other Brand Assets. Are sustainable competitive advantages attached to the brand name that are not reflected in the other four equity dimensions? Is there a patent or trademark that is important? Are there channel relationships that provide barriers to competitors?

Typically, marketing research is used to obtain answers to these questions.

Measuring Brand Equity

It is important to develop approaches that place a value on a brand, for several reasons. First, since brands are bought and sold, a value must be assessed by both buyers and sellers. Which approach makes the most sense? Second, investments to enhance brand equity need to be justified, as there always are competing uses for funds. A bottom-line justification is that the investment will enhance the value of the brand. Thus, some "feel" for how a brand should be valued may help managers address such decisions. Third, the valuation question provides additional insight into the brand-equity concept.

What is the value of a brand name? Consider Compaq, Boeing, Betty Crocker, Ford, Weight Watchers, Bud, and Wells Fargo. What would happen to those firms if they lost their brand name but retained the other assets associated with the business? How much would they have to spend to avoid damage to their business if the name were lost? Could any expenditure avoid a loss of business, perhaps permanently?

At least four general approaches have been proposed to assess the value of brand equity. One is based on the excess price that the name can command in the marketplace. The second looks at how much it would cost to replace the brand with a new one. The third is based on the stock price. The fourth focuses on a brand's earning power.[5] Many other methods have also been proposed to measure brand equity. We shall now consider these in the listed order.

Excess-Price Approach. Brand equity assets such as name awareness, perceived quality, associations, and loyalty all have the potential to provide a brand with a price premium. The resulting extra revenue can be used (for example) to enhance profits, or to reinvest in building more equity.

Observation. One way to measure the excess price a brand can support is simply to observe the price levels in the market. What are the differences, and how are they associated with different brands? For example, what are the price levels of comparable automobiles? How much are the different brands depreciating each year? How responsive is the brand to a firm's own price changes, or to competitors' price changes. These observations inform the manager about the brand's equity. With the emergence of scanner technology, observing price levels of different products has become relatively easy. In fact, both IRI and Nielsen sell syndicated products giving the prices of various products over a period of time.

Customer Research. Price premiums can also be measured through customer research. Customers can be asked what they would pay for various features and characteristics of a product (one characteristic would be the brand name).[6] Termed a dollarmetric scale, this survey provides a direct measure of the brand name's value. Using a variant of the dollarmetric measure, American Motors tested a car (then called the Renault Premier) by showing an "unbadged" (unnamed) model of it to customers and asking them what they would pay for it.[7] The same question was then asked with the car identified by various names. The price was around $10,000 with no name, and about $3,000 more with the Renault Premier name on it.

Obtaining buyer-perference or purchase-likelihood measures for different price levels furnish additional insight. Such studies can gauge buyer resistance to competitors' price decreases, and determine consumer response to one's own company's decrease in price. A high-equity brand will lose little share to a competitor's lower price, and (up to a point) can gain share when its own relative price is decreased.

Trade-off Analysis. *Trade-off (conjoint) analysis* is still another approach. Here, respondents are asked to make trade-off judgments about brand attributes. For example, suppose that a computer's attributes included on-site service (supplied vs not supplied), price ($2,200 vs $1,700), and name (Compaq vs Circle). A respondent would prefer on-site service, low price, and an established brand name. To determine the relative value of each, the respondent would be asked to choose between:

Circle at $1,700 vs Compaq at $2,200
Service at $1,700 vs no service at $2,200
Compaq with no service vs Circle with service

The output of trade-off analysis would be a dollar value associated with each attribute alternative. The dollar value of the brand name would thus be created in the context of making judgments relative to other relevant attributes of the product class. Given that a price premium can be obtained, the value of the brand name in a given year would be that price differential multiplied by the unit sales volume. Discounting these cash flows over a reasonable time would be one approach to valuing the brand.

Impact on Customer Evaluation. Considering the price premium for a brand may not be the best way to quantify brand equity, especially for product classes like cigarettes and air travel, where prices are fairly similar. An alternative is to consider the impact of the brand name upon the customer evaluation of the brand, as measured by preference, attitude, or intent to purchase. What does the brand name do to the evaluation?

The value of the brand would then be the marginal value of the extra sales (or market share) that the brand name supports. Suppose, for example, it was believed that sales would be 25 percent less if the brand name were discarded, or sales would decline 25 percent over a five-year period if the advertising support for the name were eliminated. The profits on the lost marginal sales would represent the value of the brand.

The size of any price premium and the preference rating of a brand can both be measured and tracked over time using survey research. However, this approach is static, in that it looks at the brand's current position—a view that does not necessarily take into account the future impact of changes (such as improvements in quality).

Replacement-Cost Approach. Another prespective is the cost of establishing a comparable product that can bring in the same amount of business. If it were felt that it would cost $200 million to develop and introduce a product and that the chance for success was 25 percent, on average four products costing a total of $800 million would need to be developed to ensure one winner. A firm should thus be willing to pay $800 million for an established brand with prospects comparable to those being developed. Hence, the equity of the brand can be valued at $800 million.

Stock-Price Approach. Another approach, suggested by financial theory, is to use stock price as a basis to evaluate the value of a firm's brand equities.[8] The argument is that the stock market will adjust the price of a firm to reflect the future prospects of its brands.

The approach starts with the market value of the firm, which is a function of the stock price and the number of shares, from which the replacement costs of the tangible assets (such as plant and equipment, inventories and cash) are subtracted. The balance, intangible assets, is apportioned into three components: the value of brand equity, the value of nonbrand factors (such as R&D and patents), and the value of industry factors (such as regulation and concentration). Brand equity is assumed to be a function of the age of a brand and its order of entry into the market (an older brand has more equity), the cumulative advertising (advertising creates equity), and the current share of industry advertising (current advertising share is related to positioning advantages).

The problem with this approach is that if a firm has more than one brand, it is difficult to evaluate the value of each brand to the firm. The internal records of the company are sufficient to evaluate brand equity by this method.

Future-Earnings Approach. The best measure of brand equity would be the discounted present value of future earnings attributable to brand-equity assets.[9] The problem is how to provide such an estmate.

Discounting the Future Profit Stream. One approach is to simply discount the profit stream that is projected for the brand. Such a plan should take into account brand strengths and their impact on the competitive environment. One firm that uses the brand's plan to provide a value for brand equity adjusts the manufacturing costs to reflect the industry average rather than the actual costs. The logic is that any above- (or below-) average efficiency should be credited to manufacturing and not to brand equity. **Scenario analysis** is done to ascertain the most likely scenario that will occur. Based on this scenario, the profit stream is projected for the brand. Marketing research helps in building credible scenarios and deciding which is the most likely.

Applying an Earnings Multiplier. Another approach that researchers can use, even when a brand profit plan is unavailable or unsuitable, is to estimate current earnings and apply an earnings multiplier. The earnings estimate could be current earnings, with any extraordinary charges backed out. If the current earnings are not representative because they reflect a downward or upward cycle, then some average of the past few years might be more appropriate. If the earnings are negative or low due to correctable problems, an estimate based on industry norms of profit as a percent of sales might be useful.

The earnings multiplier provides a way to estimate and place a value on future earnings. To obtain a suitable earnings multiplier range, the historical price earnings (P/E) multipliers of firms in the involved industry and in similar industries should be examined. For example, a multiplier range for a brand might be 7 to 12 or 16 to 25, depending on the industry.

The use of an industry-based P/E ratio provides a judgment that stock-market investors have placed upon the industry prospects—its growth potential, the future competitive intensity from existing and potential competitors, and the threat of substitute products. The question remains, which P/E multiplier within the identified range should be used for the brand?

To determine the actual multiplier value within that range, an estimate of the competitive advantage of the brand is needed. Will the brand earnings strengthen over time and generally be above the industry average, or will they weaken and be below average? The estimate should be based on a weighted average of a brand appraisal on each of the five dimensions of brand equity.

In evaluating brand equity, one also needs to deal with the problem of evaluating other firm assets. First, some part of the discounted present value of a business is due to such tangible assets as working capital, inventory, buildings, and equipment. What portion should be so attributed? One argument is that such assets are book assets that are being depreciated, and their depreciation charge times an earnings multiplier will reflect their asset value. Another method would be to focus on cash flow instead of earnings and estimate such assets by using book value or market value. This estimate would then be subtracted from the estimate of discounted future earnings.

Evaluation of Brand Extensions. It is difficult to estimate the earnings streams from **brand extensions** (the use of the brand name to enter new product classes—for example, Kellogg's bread products, or Hershey's ice cream). Usually, the value of potential brand extensions will have to be estimated separately.

The extension value will depend on the attractiveness of market area of any proposed extension, its growth and competitive intensity, and the strength of the extension. The extension strength will be a function of the relevance of the brand association and perceived quality, the extent to which they could translate into a sustainable competitive advantage, and the extent to which the brand will fit the extension.

The methodology followed by *Financial World* to measure the brand equity of Coca-Cola during its annual evaluation of global brands is given in Exhibit 25-1.

CUSTOMER SATISFACTION

In recent years American business has become increasingly committed to the idea of **customer satisfaction** and **product-service quality.** The measurement of customer satisfaction and its link to product-service attributes is the vehicle for developing a market-driven quality approach.[10] In this section, we will discuss customer satisfaction research.

Customer satisfaction research has been around for a long time. However, it has become a fixture at most large corporations only in recent years. The growth in the popularity of customer satisfaction research is, of course, a corollary to the quality movement in American business. The idea that the customer defines quality should not be new to marketers. However, its recognition in the Baldridge criteria has given this idea a credibility that was previously lacking.

Satisfaction research, like advertising tracking research, should be conducted at planned intervals so as to track satisfaction over time. Thus, satisfaction research can be put in the context of an interrupted, time series, quasi-experimental design. Over time, management will do various things to improve customer satisfaction, take measurements following these changes, and evaluate the results to see if the changes that were implemented had a positive effect on customer satisfaction.

This approach requires a sequential research design that uses the results from each research phase to build and enhance the value of subsequent efforts. During this process, it is imperative to study customers who were lost, to

EXHIBIT 25-1

Estimation of Brand Equity of Coke

Financial World (*FW*) determined, for example, that the Coca-Cola brand family had 1992 world-wide sales of $9 billion. According to the best estimates of consultants and beverage experts, Coke enjoys an operating margin of around 30%, so operating profits for the Coke brand were $2.8 billion.

Coke's elaborate bottling and distribution system generated another $27 billion in revenues, and operating profits of $3 billion. But *FW* did not take these numbers into consideration in valuing the Coca-Cola name, because to some extent that would be an overvaluation. We include only the value added by Coke directly, not the value added by the bottlers or distributors. "It is important to recognize that not all of the profitability attributed to a brand should be used in the calculation of brand value to avoid overvaluation and double counting," says Noel Penrose, executive vice president of the Interbrand Group.

Even if Coca-Cola's bottling and distribution network does contribute to brand image, it will be reflected in higher sales and margins of the product itself. The value of the distribution system, though significant, is not the value of the brand. Were we to include the bottling and disbribution system, we would have added another $40 billion to our value of Coca-Cola.

Which brings us to the next step: Once product-related profits have been determined, we deduct from a brand's operating profit an amount equal to what would be earned on a basic, unbranded, or generic version of the product. To do this we estimate the amount of capital it takes to generate a brand's sales. On average, analysts believe that it requires 60 cents worth of capital, which is generally a little higher than net property, plant and equipment plus net working capital, to produce each dollar of sales. Using that yardstick, the capital used in production in Coke's case comes to $5.5 billion. Second, we assume that a 5% net return on employed capital after inflation can be expected from a similar nonbranded product. So we deduct 5% of Coke's capital employed ($273 million) from the $2.7 billion in operating profits to obtain the profit attributable to the brand name alone.

For Coke, that leaves an adjusted operating profit figure of $2.4 billion. We then make a provision for taxes, and the remainder is deemed to be net brand-related profits. Finally, we assign a multiple based on brand strength as having seven components: leadership, or the brand's ability to influence its market; stability, the ability of the brand to survive; market, the brand's trade environment; internationality, the ability of the brand to cross geographic and cultural borders; trend, the ongoing direction; support, effectiveness of the brand's communications; and protection, the brand owner's legal title. Obviously, the stronger the brand, the higher the multiple applied to earnings. This year, we used multiples ranging from 9 to 20. Coke was assigned the highest multiple, which results in a brand value of $33.4 billion.

Source: Alexandra Ourusoff. "How the Brand Values were Assigned," *Brand Week,* August 1993, 27.

determine why they left. This issue must be addressed early on in the system design.

A useful step is to provide management with a framework for understanding, analyzing, and evaluating the status of customer satisfaction in the firm. A sequential design provides some level of comfort, because it allows for the luxury of making critical decisions after you have sufficient data to reduce the risk of error inherent in establishing a customer satisfaction system.

Customer Satisfaction Measurement Process

A "no frills" customer satisfaction program involves the following:[11]

Define Goals and How Information Will Be Used. A common failure of customer satisfaction research is lack of clear, comprehensive, and measurable goals. Given the strategic nature of the quality improvement process, key parts of a company must be involved in setting objectives for customer satisfaction measurement and management. This helps to clarify the needs of various users of the information, creates a sense of ownership of the process, and identifies how various levels of a company may have to cooperate to plan action.

Equally important is determining how the information will be used once it is developed. Careful analysis of strategic and tactical organizational applications will ensure that issues of design, sample, analysis, reporting, and deployment are structured to provide customer-focused information that can be acted on most effectively.

Discover What Is Important to Customers and Employees. This discovery phase of data collection is intended to identify, in customers' and employees' own language, the attributes that comprise their perceptions and expectations for quality and satisfaction. This information is gathered through various qualitative techniques, notably, depth interviews with senior managers and focus groups or on-site interviews with customers and customer-contact personnel.

The research will generate a comprehensive list of everything that customers and employees consider important. It is now necessary to use similar associative techniques, to group related or redundant attributes and agree on candidates for subsequent measurement as key drivers of satisfaction.

Measure Critical Needs. Measuring the relative importance of the attributes identified in qualitative discovery and a company's competitive performance on those attributes is accomplished through critical-needs assessment. This phase uses in-depth telephone, mail, or personal interviews with a representative sample of customers, lost customers, and competitors' customers to gather quantitative information. Using trade-off techniques, instead of traditional importance scaling, provides improved discrimination on the relative importance of attributes.

This phase should provide a broad array of actionable information. It should include the relative importance of key drivers of satisfaction; competitive performance on these critical attributes; site-specific performance, depending on sample size; cross-market segments with specific service needs; value-adding performance relative to expectations; and specific gaps between importance and performance.

Act on the Information. Action planning organizes activity to improve customer satisfaction by operationally defining and functionally deploying customer requirements. This makes it possible to establish cross-functional quality improvement teams. Using techniques such as quality function deployment, flow charts, check sheets, Pareto charts, and cause-and-effect diagrams, teams can improve processes, based on external customer needs, internal chains of customers, work-flow analysis, and work-process analysis.

Measure Performance over Time. Periodic measurement of how a company and its competitors perform on the key drivers of satisfaction reveals the rate at which customer satisfaction is improving or declining. Using the same sample criteria and interviewing techniques applied in critical needs assessment, measurement should involve a brief interview on current performance and include an opportunity for open-ended comments. The frequency of measurement should be determined by market dynamics and should allow sufficient time for change to become measurable.

Consideration also should be given to periodic qualitative monitoring to provide information on changes in environment. Using the model described in the preceding paragraph, to improve and measure customer satisfaction requirements can greatly enhance existing total quality management and other quality improvement programs. It also can stand alone as a first step in focusing an organization on improved customer satisfaction as the key to improved market share and financial performance.

In either case, success ultimately is determined by the organization's top-down commitment to meet and exceed the customers' requirements in the marketplace. For example, knowing that customers want "quick service" is helpful: knowing that "quick service" means having their problems solved in less than five minutes is actionable. Exhibit 25-2 talks about the various measures that are used to determine customer satisfaction in Europe.

Issues in Questionnaire Design and Scaling in Satisfaction Research. Each customer-satisfaction study utilizes questions that are, to some degree, unique. However, as in the other types of studies discussed in this chapter, certain general types of information are collected in most customer satisfaction studies:

▶ *Screening questions.* The question begins with screening questions to make sure that the person contacted falls into the target group. If the goal is to

EXHIBIT 25-2

Customer Satisfaction Measurement in Europe

Most European markets have undergone an important shift in what drives satisfaction. Service factors (so-called "soft factors") have surpassed quality and price in importance. In Germany's consumer electronics market, for example, soft factors determine customer satisfaction with dealer performance 55% of the time. According to Role Crooner, marketing director of McDonald's, Germany, "Measuring customer satisfaction is an important issue. If you don't measure customer satisfaction, you can't identify customer trends in the long term and won't be able to react in a timely fashion."

Customer satisfaction can be measured in a variety of ways: Volkswagen, Europe's automobile market leader, uses questionnaires to survey about 660,000 customers in Germany every two years. Panasonic attaches reply cards to each product sold. Dell Computer in its European operations includes a questionnaire diskette when it delivers computers, and IKEA furniture gives its customers point-of-purchase questionnaires, which can be dropped off in specially designated boxes. Additional incentives increase the amount of customer feedback: Bang & Olufsen, the Danish consumer electronics manufacturer, extends its guarantee for another year for customers who respond to its questionnaire. Dell Computer thanks its respondents with 10 free diskettes.

It is also important to formulate and implement two categories of satisfaction targets: performance and value-shaping. Performance targets define the desired level of overall satisfaction; for example, at Swissair no more than 3% negative ratings for overall performance should occur in each quarter. Value targets describe the desired standards of customer values; IKEA stipulates 10 minutes as the maximum waiting time in the checkout line.

Source: Wolfgang Muller. "European Firms Set Management Principles for Customer satisfaction," *Marketing News*, February 4, 1991, 6.

interview current customers, and current customers are defined to include those individuals who have patronized Wendy's in the last 30 days, the questionnaire will begin with a series of questions designed to determine whether the particular individual meets these requirements.

▶ *Overall ratings.* Some experts argue that it is important to get an overall satisfaction rating from respondents very early in the interview. This might be done by asking, "Please indicate your overall satisfaction with Wendy's on a scale of 1 to 10, where 1 is poor and 10 is excellent." This rating can be the dependent variable in the regression analysis.

▶ *Performance ratings.* The researchers are interested in measuring customer perceptions of Wendy's performance on a number of specific aspects of the product or service. The specific aspects are the key satisfaction factors discussed previously. The researcher will use a numerical rating scale to gauge the satisfaction with each element.

▶ *Intent to use or purchase product or service in the future.* Satisfaction surveys usually include some measurement of customer likelihood to do business with the firm in the future. This provides a basis for determining whether to purchase or use the product or service. The researcher would hypothesize that the higher the satisfaction level, the higher is the likelihood to do business with the organization in the future.

▶ *Category or brand usage information.* This information will be used for classification purposes in cross-tabulation analysis. For example, does the respondent also patronize McDonald's, Burger King, Arby's, or Little Caesar's?

▶ *Demographic and life-style information.* This information is used for classification purposes. The researcher often is interested in determining whether any particular demographic or life-style group is more or less satisfied than Wendy's average customer.

A few of the scales used in satisfaction research are given below.

▶ *Asking customers whether they agree or disagree that Wyatt's Cafeteria satisfactorily serves them.* For example
Overall, I am extremely satisfied with the service I receive from Wyatt's Cafeteria.

strongly agree	somewhat agree	neither agree nor disagree	somewhat disagree	strongly disagree
____	____	____	____	____

▶ *Having the customer rate the performance of a company from excellent to poor.* For example
Overall, how would you rate the service you receive from Wyatt's Cafeteria? Would you say

excellent	very good	good	fair	poor
____	____	____	____	____

▶ *Asking customers how satisfied they are with the food quality.* For example
Are you

very satisfied	somewhat satisfied	neither satisfied nor dissatisfied	somewhat dissatisfied	very dissatisfied
_____	_____	_____	_____	_____

▶ *Having customers interpret their satisfaction based on a 5- or 10-point scale.* For example
Using a 10-point scale, where 10 means extremely satisfied, how satisfied are you with Wyatt's Cafeteria overall?

All of these scales attempt to pinpoint a quantitative interpretation of the customer's feelings and attitudes in response to their experiences with a company's products and/or services.

Scale selection for customer satisfaction research usually follows considerations similar to those found in product and attitude testing. More specifically, selection is guided by the properties inherent in each of four different levels of measurement: nominal, ordinal, interval, and ratio.

For most behavioral marketing research, interval scales typically are the best measurements. From the standpoint of the marketing researcher, commonly used descriptive statistics (arithmetical mean, standard deviation) and tests of significance (*t*-tests, ANOVA) assume the customer satisfaction data are at least interval-scaled.

There are advantages and limitations of scales with respect to at least four other aspects: (1) respondent interpretation and understanding, (2) appropriateness and ease of administration, (3) statistical analysis and description, and (4) ease and meaningful interpretation of results.[12]

TOTAL QUALITY MANAGEMENT

Recent years have witnessed a renewed emphasis on delivering superior quality products and services to the customers.[13] With foreign competition steadily eating away the profitability and the market shares of American companies, more and more of them are adopting total quality management (TQM) to become more competitive.[14] TQM is nothing but a process of managing complex changes in the organization with the aim of quality improvement. In Figure 25-2 the process of managing complex change and the effects when one of the links in the chain is missing is depicted.

The total quality management concept essentially is a business philosophy that was used by the Japanese to gain competitive advantage. It is now being discovered and used by the American organizations. Total quality management can be defined as a systematic effort at continuous quality improvement of all processes, products, services, and human resources throughout the organization, undertaken with an objective of improving customer satisfaction. The

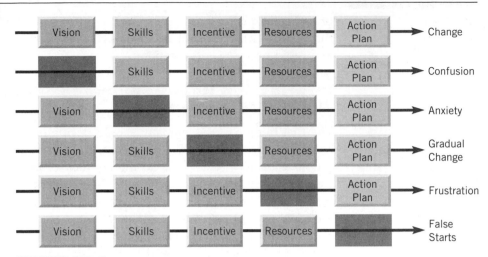

FIGURE 25-2
Managing complex change
Source: American Productivity Council.

characteristics of an organization that has successfully implemented TQM are as follows:

▶ A TQM company strives for a continuous improvement in quality. To achieve this continuous improvement process (CIP), everyone in the organization must be trained and educated continuously.

▶ Teams and teamwork are another cornerstone of the total quality management organization. Cross-functional teams must be formed, and they must work together. The teams must be inherently motivated and should be empowered to set their own objective.

▶ Quantifiable measures of progress must be established, and rewards should be based on these measures. One of the most commonly used tools to set quantifiable measures is **benchmarking.** Competitive benchmarking is nothing more than comparing the company's processes, practices, and products against the world's best, including those in other industries.

▶ The TQM companies use a number of formal tools, techniques, and processes to ensure the quality of their products/services and processes. Almost all of them use some form of **statistical quality control** and **statistical process control.** TQM companies aim at zero defects. The most commonly used tools in a TQM company are **flowcharting, cause and effect diagrams, Pareto charts, control charts,** and **scatter diagrams.** Techniques such as **Taguchi methods, quality function deployment (QFD), Poka-Yoke and Robust designs** are commonly employed. **Just-In-Time** process, the **plan-do-check-act** cycle and **activity-based costing** are also frequently used in TQM companies.

The federal government has recognized the need for a quality imperative and has recently introduced the Malcolm Baldridge Award for Quality. Adoption of total quality management is one of the prerequisites for competing for the award. The number of companies competing for this award has increased at a rapid pace since its inception.

Information Requirements for Total Quality Management

The first thing a TQM company should decide on are the guiding principles behind its data choices. Why these data, and not those data? As usual, the best rationale usually refers back to the bedrock of customer satisfaction. There should be a clear link between the kinds of data collected and maintained and the quality values of the company.[15] If short-term financial measurements drive the company, measures like market value to book value and price-to-earnings multiples will dominate management reports and meetings. If, on the other hand, quality lies at the center of business strategy and planning, a larger share of the measurement and reporting will focus on quality issues. When companies are truly committed to quality values, many data issues resolve themselves.[16]

Many companies struggle with how to develop measures in order to plan, control, and implement their total quality management program. Most of the Baldridge award winners have explicit methodologies and measures for their TQM programs. Honeywell created a guide to total quality management for its managers.[17] The manual identifies the following "Principles of Measurement":

1. Measurement must be specific. You need to know exactly what you want to measure.
2. Measure the outputs of highest value to the customer. This entails converting customer information into measures, which means you must first know exactly what your customers expect.
3. Measures can be applied to all performance dimensions, external as well as internal. It is not enough to achieve an internal goal if you fail to meet customers' expectations or your competitors' performance.
4. Understand the game before you decide how you will keep score. Tracking the wrong measure will not improve your quality.
5. Measure process as well as results. If you just measure results, you will always be fixing mistakes instead of preventing them.
6. You can't hit tomorrow by shooting at yesterday. You can't even hit tomorrow by shooting at today. The science of anticipating future customer and process requirements is called "leading the duck."
7. There is no single perfect measure. First identify the indicators for your objective, then measure all those indicators.

Federal Express uses specific measurements to track events that negatively affect a customer as they happen, using their service quality indicator (SQI). Twelve types of events are weighted by degree of importance to the customer. FedEx's goal is an SQI score of zero. SQI results are broadcast weekly over the company's private television network. Identifying actual failure creates an intense focus on the relatively few service breakdowns. Exhibit 25-3 gives the details about Federal Express Service Quality Indicator.

EXHIBIT 25-3

Service Quality Indicators:
How FedEx Measures Its Performance

Customers are the best judges of the quality of services. That's why, in developing a composite quality indicator, Federal Express looked for factors reflecting its customers' view of performance. It identified twelve components as key elements in successfully delivering what customers want. Some failures have much more impact than others. Losing or damaging a package, for example, is much more serious than simply delivering one a few minutes late. Therefore, the company assigns weighting factors according to the customer's perception of their importance.

The service quality indicator (SQI) is the weighted sum of the average daily failure points for the 12 components, and it is reported weekly and summarized monthly. Some 60 million weighted opportunities for error exist each day, yet SQI scores have steadily dropped until they now run about 0.4 of 1%. The company now calculates a similar SQI figure for the international delivery service. The purpose of the service quality indicator is to help Federal Express identify and eliminate causes of failures but *not* to place blame. If courier mislabeling of packages was found to be a cause for wrong-day-late failures, for example, the SQI team would work on creating effective methods for preventing miscoding at the source rather than on developing an elaborate and expensive expediting system. Finding out what dissatisfies customers is a first step, but then a cooperative effort within the context of all the goals of the organization is needed to find optimum solutions to any problems—so that employees do the *right* things right.

Following are the SQI components:

Failure	Weight	Description
Right day late	1	Delivery after the commitment time but the right day.
Wrong day late	5	Delivered the wrong day.
Traces unanswered by COSMOS	1	Number of proof of performance requests by customers where exception information, proper scans, or proof of delivery (POD) data are not in COSMOS.
Complaints reopened by customers	5	Includes customer complaints on traces, invoice adjustments, missed pickups, etc., reopened.
Missing proof of performance	1	Billing documents that don't match a POD in COSMOS or from the field POD queue on a timely basis, including prepaid and metered packages as well as those that are invoiced.
Invoice adjustment requested	1	Packages on which customers request an invoice adjustment, including those not granted because a request indicates the customer perceives a problem.
Missed pick-ups	10	Complaints from customers recorded as missed pick-ups.
Damaged packages	10	Includes packages with either visible or concealed damage and weather and water damage. Also includes contents spoiled or damaged due to a missed pickup or late delivery.
Lost packages	10	Includes both packages missing and those with contents missing due to pilferage.
Overgoods	5	Packages received in Lost & Found (no label or identifying data inside package).
Abandoned calls	5	Any call to FedEx that is not answered, which is any call in which caller hangs up without speaking to an agent after 20 seconds from receipt of call.
International	1	Includes components from the performance measurement of international operations.

Source: Robert Haavind. *The Road to the Baldridge Award,* (Stoneham: Butterworth-Heinemann), 1992, p. 76.

The kind of data a company should collect also depends on the nature of its business. Accounting firms, for example, do not need extensive data on worker safety; their workers are not usually in physical danger. Chemical or mining companies, on the other hand, cannot afford to ignore that kind of data. Data and information relating to customers, employees, and suppliers should be collected. External, independent contractors, such as market-research companies, law firms, and insurance providers, all qualify as suppliers. The company must control and monitor the quality of its goods and services. Data on support functions like accounting and internal legal services are also important and should be collected.

The presentation of data is also important in a TQM company. The data should be grouped into categories, such as customer-related data, data on internal operations, supplier data, and so on, giving brief, thumbnail descriptions explaining the use and relevance of each database. The data can also be labeled according to whether they are generated by the company itself or by outside vendors.

Analysis of Data in a TQM Company. Analysis is the second phase of the data-and-information-gathering and problem-solving/quality-improvement process. The aim of analysis is to comb through the raw data you have collected and to turn it into useful information for such functions as planning, performance review, design of products and services, and quality-improvement projections. The key questions in this item are

▶ Who performs the analysis?

▶ What analytical techniques are used?

▶ Which data are analyzed and at what level of detail?

▶ How are data aggregated and how are relations between data groups cross-referenced?

▶ How does the company improve its analytical capabilities? (This last question relates to continuous improvement.)

In responding to this item, applicants should concentrate on how analysis, as it is performed for each major function, affects evaluation and decision making, especially at the corporate level.

Choosing the Right Analytical Method. TQM companies typically employ a handful of sophisticated analytical techniques, including formal statistical analyses, as well as informal tools such as "lessons learned." The analysis should be performed systematically, and problems should be analyzed efficiently and effectively. The idea here is to identify a problem in one operating area, and then to see if that problem is occurring elsewhere. The company must determine what, if any, connection there is between the two problems; if there is a connection, chances are there is a basic system flaw. A large, widespread system problem would trigger additional, more comprehensive analyses. Analyzing data in ways like this, which allow identification of system issues from among seemingly different sets of operating-group data, is the hallmark of organizations that have learned to effectively analyze information.

Managing and Maintaining the Data. Once the analyses are performed and the databases are assembled, the TQM companies have well-developed methods for managing and maintaining them. In particular, these companies have specific methods and techniques that they use to ensure the quality of data and their rapid assimilation throughout the company.

Data Quality. Data quality is measured in terms of validity, reliability, consistency, timeliness, and standardization. Periodic audits of the *processes* used to collect, analyze, and report data are a good way to ensure that the data are fundamentally sound. Some companies use cross-functional teams whose express responsibility is data-and-information management and measurement control. Outside, independent reviewers can be used to perform audits to corroborate internal findings. Because information and analysis is such a critical function, though, such audits should be aggressively monitored by senior management.

Comparisons and Benchmarks. Competitive and benchmark data are so absolutely critical to quality improvement that companies adopting total quality management devote special attention to them. Vigorous benchmarking is a key indicator of external focus and in integral element in the strategic management of quality.[18]

Broadly speaking, **benchmarking** is the practice of searching outside one's company for new ideas for improvement of processes, products, and services. Benchmarking involves "either adopting the practices or adapting the best features, and implementing them to obtain the best of the best." Benchmarking also means establishing numerical operating targets for particular functions, based on the best possible industry or out-of-industry practices. This concept is very new for most companies and stands in contrast to their current practices, which project the future from the company's own past trends, without any reference to what competitors and other leading companies are doing. In addition, benchmarking validates and adds credibility to the goal-setting process by its concentration on best practices. The key questions in this item are

▶ What elements do you compare, and how do you select information for comparison?

▶ What is the full scope of comparison data?

▶ How do you get reliable information from the companies or the industry you've selected?

▶ How do you use benchmark information to encourage new ideas and innovation?

▶ How do you improve the benchmarking capabilities you already have?

The Xerox benchmarking model has been held up as the global standard against which other companies ought to benchmark *their* benchmarking. This version requires ten steps:[19]

1. *Identify what is to be benchmarked.* A team selects a product, a service, a process, or a practice; even a level of customer satisfaction. The goal is to determine whether the area of interest is managed the best way possible.

2. *Identify comparative companies.* Benchmarking partners can be other operating units within Xerox, Xerox competitors, or noncompetitors who are judged the leaders in the area to be benchmarked.

3. *Determine data-collection method, and collect data.* In true "apples-to-apples" fashion, teams determine what measurements will be used in the benchmarking process. Then a trip is often made to the selected company, and face-to-face exchanges are conducted with principals of both firms. Often, a tour of the benchmarked area is included.

4. *Determine current performance levels.* Once the team has gathered the necessary data and compared them with current performance levels, the results are analyzed. Generally, they reveal a negative or positive performance gap.

5. *Project future performance levels.* The benchmarking team forecasts the expected improvement by the company under study, and sets the new Xerox goals based on this forecast of the benchmark. This step ensures that the Xerox goals will still equal or perhaps exceed the performance of the studied organization after whatever time it takes to implement the team's findings.

6. *Communicate benchmark findings and gain acceptance.* The team presents its methodology, findings, and proposed strategies to senior management. This information is also communicated to employees who will be asked to help implement the new strategies.

7. *Establish functional goals.* After concurrence, the team then presents final recommendations on ways in which the organization must change, based on benchmark findings, to reach the new goals.

8. *Develop action plans.* The team develops specific action plans for each objective, and develops strategies for obtaining full organizational support.

9. *Implement specific actions, and monitor progress.* The plans are put into place. Data on the new level of performance are collected. Adjustments to the process are made if the goals are not being met, and problem-solving teams may be formed to investigate.

10. *Recalibrate benchmarks.* Over time, the benchmarks are reevaluated and updated to ensure that they are based on the latest performance data from the benchmarked company.

Quality Function Deployment. The power of measurements is clearly visible in applications of quality function deployment, or QFD, a Japanese import used to make product designs better reflect customer requirements. In QFD, a multifunctional team measures and analyzes in great detail both customer attitudes and product attributes. Marketing research plays a crucial role at this stage of the process. Then the team creates a visual matrix in order to find ways to modify product attributes (engineering characteristics) so as to improve the product on the customer-based measures of product performance. Along the way, the team must develop a series of measures of several different types. Here is how it works.[20]

Step 1. Attributes that the customer looks for in the product (CAs) are defined. These are descriptions of what the customer wants, often in the customers' own words and phrases. There may be dozens of them, and it may be expedient to group them into groups of related attributes. CAs are also given relative importance weightings, often through trade-off (conjoint) analysis and other forms of survey research. (Usually weightings are in relative percents such that they total 100 percent.)[21]

Step 2. Customer evaluations of competing products are obtained for each of the customer attributes determined in Step 1. (Usually, survey research is needed.) Competitive position is often measured on a relative scale where $1 = $ worst and $5 = $ best. This comparative data help product engineers and managers understand how to best achieve competitive advantage through their work on the attributes.

Step 3. Engineering characteristics (ECs) that may affect the attributes are listed. Usually the design team does this after reviewing attributes in detail (in order to help them develop descriptors that are meaningful from the customer's perspective). Some engineering characteristics affect more than one of the attributes. Some of the proposed ECs will not appear to affect any attributes, which means either that they may be unnecessary, or that there may be a flaw in the customer research. ECs are described quantitatively: weight, length, number, and so forth. This exercise presents a good opportunity for rethinking both the design and the existing quality measures for it.

Step 4. The extent of the impact of each EC on each CA is determined or estimated. This is often done on a four-point scale in the body of the matrix, such as

1. Strong positive impact.
2. Medium positive impact.
3. Medium negative impact.
4. Strong negative impact.

Step 5. All this information is summarized in a chart, often called the house of quality. (The reason is obvious when you look at the diagram.) The chart shows customer attributes on the vertical, and engineering characteristics on the horizontal dimension. The resulting grid is filled in with the relationship scores from Step 4.

Step 6. The impact of changes in any engineering characteristic on other ECs is evaluated. (A scale such as the one in Step 4 can be applied to this step.) Interactions among ECs in which changes in one EC have an impact on another are represented in a "roof" diagram above the matrix. A simplified "house of quality" is shown in Figure 25-3.

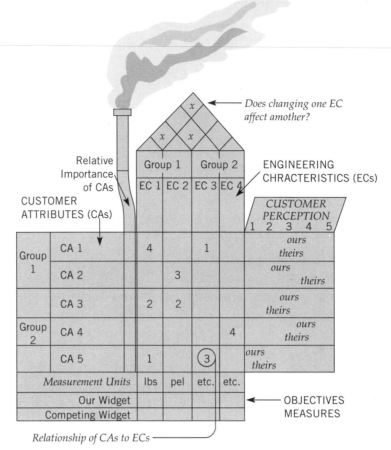

FIGURE 25-3
House of quality

Step 7. As the team develops the measures and fills in the matrix, it naturally begins to focus on customer attributes in which the product appears weak and also begins to develop ideas concerning how to improve various engineering characteristics. Now that the matrix is complete, the team turns its attention completely to the task of redesign, using the house of quality diagram as a guide. Because the diagram integrates a great many measures having to do with customer perception, competitive position, and engineering characteristics, the team is far better able to keep all these considerations in mind during redesign than it could without this tool.

A brief example helps make the benefits of QFD more tangible. Here is one from two professors who described the method in an academic journal when it was first introduced to the United States:

> *Consider the location of an emergency brake lever in an American sporty car. Placing it on the left between the seat and the door solved an engineering problem. But is also guaranteed that women in skirts could not get in and out gracefully. In contrast, Toyota improved its rust prevention record from one of the worst to one of the best by coordinating design and production decisions to focus on the customer concern. Using the house of*

quality, designers broke down "body durability" into 53 items covering everything from climate to modes of operation. They obtained customer evaluations and ran experiments on nearly every detail of production, from pump operation to temperature control and coating composition. Decisions on sheet metal details, coating materials, and baking temperatures were all focused on those aspects of rust prevention most important to customers.[22]

Marketing Research

Marketing research is an invaluable part of QFD. The customer attributes are obtained through conjoint analysis or through other forms of survey research. The customer evaluations on competing products are also obtained through survey research. Hence, a thorough knowledge of marketing research is required.

RELATIONSHIP MARKETING

Relationship marketing combines elements of general advertising, sales promotion, public relations, and direct marketing to create more effective and more efficient ways of reaching consumers.[23] It centers on developing a continuous relationship with consumers across a family of related products and services.

The relationship marketing process incorporates three key elements:

1. Identifying and building a database of current and potential consumers, which records and cross-references a wide range of demographic, life-style, and purchase information.
2. Delivering differential messages to these people through established and new media channels based on the consumer's characteristics and preferences.
3. Tracking each relationship to monitor the cost of acquiring the consumer and the lifetime value of his or her purchases.

Exhibit 25-4 talks about how Huggies and a few other companies used relationship marketing as successful competitive strategy.

Three Keys to Relationship Marketing

There are strategic opportunities for companies on the leading edge of relationship marketing techniques.[24] Successfully addressing the trend will depend on a three-pronged effort discussed below.

Identify and Build Marketing Databases of Present and Potential Purchasers. In the age of relationship marketing, the **customer database** will be as important a strategic asset for manufacturers as the brand itself. Advertisers will need the capability to use mass media and more targeted media channels as ways of prospecting for customers. Once potential customers have been identified, advertisers must capture their names and information on their lifestyles in a database for future communications.

It's important to keep in mind that not all consumers are appropriate targets for relationship marketing, and not all targets are customers. Consequently,

EXHIBIT 25-4

Relationship Marketing in Practice

The diaper manufacturer previously described is a good example. Huggies has spent over $10 million to set up a system that provides it with the names of over 75 percent of the expectant mothers in the United States. The names are obtained from doctors, hospitals, and childbirth trainers. During their pregnancies, the mothers-to-be receive personalized magazines and letters with ideas on baby care, thus building a bond between the mothers and Huggies.

When the baby arrives, a coded coupon is delivered which Huggies can track to know which mothers have tried the product. Later, as new technologies fall into place, Huggies will be able to know which mothers continue to purchase Huggies. In this case, Huggies' parent, Kimberly Clark, is not only building diaper sales but also establishing relationships with mothers which can be leveraged across other products. The cost of linking the consumer to the brand can be justified since the per-baby consumption of single-use diapers averages more than $600 annually.

Other innovative programs include: Kraft's "Cheese and Macaroni Club," which sends children a packet of goodies; MTV's custom magazine, which viewers get when they respond to MTV's 800 number; and Isuzu's personalized inserts in *Time*, which list nearest dealerships and are redeemable for a premium.

Source: Michael J. Wolf. "Relationship Marketing: Positioning for the Future," *Journal of Business Strategy*, July/August 1990, 16–21.

---

the initial database must be carefully refined and segmented. Designed and developed properly, the marketing database will allow companies to expand their internal capabilities to include relationship marketing. Marketers leading the way include Procter & Gamble, which is using "800" telephone numbers in its ads for Cheer Free detergent to target people with sensitive skin; Porsche, which has created a database of 300,000 affluent prospective purchasers of its cars; and Citicorp, which is setting up a database of customer information collected from retail outlets for its own use and for sale to third-party marketers. **Marketing research** will play a crucial role in developing these databases. Most of these databases can be built using secondary data.

Deliver Differentiated Messages to Targeted Households. Advertisers must develop the ability to communicate with a defined audience of the existing and potential users of their products. The media choices they make must therefore offer the ability to not only broadcast the message to the entire circulation or audience, but also to target precisely defined demographic slices. For advertisers, more precise targeting means greater impact.

Mass circulation magazines are responding to advertisers' needs with selective binding and personalized ink-jet printing. Applying these two technologies, an automobile manufacturer, for example, can send an ad for a high-end car to one household and an ad for a midrange car to another household. In addition, the automobile manufacturer can add a personalized message to the ad with ink-jet printing and even list the names of the nearest dealers.

Recently, MCI diverted money from its TV budget to pay for a subscriber-personalized ad in *Time*. Clearly, publishers can exploit mass reach with niche ads that provide more targeted messages.

Broadcast media are also relinquishing their positions as passive media. Telemarketing innovations will allow broadcast media to become increasingly interactive. At the same time, addressability will become an important factor in both cable and broadcast.

Track the Relationship to Make Media Expenditures More Effective and More Measurable. Common wisdom has it that half of all advertising dollars are wasted; the difficulty is knowing which half. The media innovations just described will allow advertisers to pinpoint what works and what doesn't. Consequently, relationship marketing's most important effect will be a shift in the way decisions are made about where to advertise. Traditionally, decisions have been based on various *ex ante* measures of exposure, such as cost-per-thousand, audience, or circulation. In the future, however, decisions will be made on *ex post* factors such as evidence of penetration of the required target audience or even evidence of sales results.

In this new environment, the basis of measurement changes and emphasis will shift from cost-per-thousand to the value of reaching a target market. Advertisers must evaluate the cost of gaining and maintaining a customer relationship over several years. Once again, **marketing research** will play a significant role in this phase of the relationship marketing strategy. Tracking usually will be done by survey research.

INTEGRATED MARKETING COMMUNICATIONS

Integrated marketing communications (IMC) is the process of developing and implementing various forms of persuasive communications programs with customers and prospects over time.[25] The goal of IMC is to influence or directly affect the behavior of the selected communications audience. IMC considers all contacts which a customer or prospect has with the product or service as potential delivery channels for future messages.[26] Further, IMC makes use of all forms of communication that are relevant to the customer and prospects, and to which they might be receptive. In sum, the IMC process starts with the customer or prospect and then works back to determine and define the forms and methods through which persuasive communications programs should be developed.

IMC, from the consumers' view, means that the marketing organization tries to understand their wants and needs. The concept makes sense if the need is clearer communication, or if the goal is to make it easier for consumers to understand the offers or products or services that are available. If the idea of integration is to help consumers sort through all the information overload that now exists, then there is value in the concept. If integration helps consumers work through all the various media alternatives to find the information they are seeking, then IMC is a worthwhile concept.[27]

The real impetus behind integrated marketing is in realizing that your company's products and services don't exist to increase profits and maximize shareholder value; they exist to benefit customers better than the competition.

That's the way to advance profitability and expand shareholder value. It's a long-term view to be sure, and it's one held by many Japanese companies.

The change that integrated marketing invariably calls for requires that organizations first test the waters by focusing on a particular business or product area, and following one of two approaches.[28] The first step, common to both, however, is an infrastructure creating cross-functional teams of people who can recognize and represent the needs of the customers at every point of contact with the organization. This group can include finance, sales, marketing channels, communications, and so forth. The next step is choosing the approach.

Path A takes existing products and services, communications, and infrastructure and focuses on a particular business area. The cross-functional team redefines the marketing communications and operational aspects of that area. The team develops specific and measurable goals with regard to communications, relevancy, and productivity, and it creates specific plans to measure the achievement of those goals.

This path is not to be confused with broad-based TQM, because the scope of this cross-functional team's effort is narrow and focused. The intent is to evaluate the marketing program within a specific business area and, assuming positive rewards, broaden its scope.

Path B establishes a separate laboratory created expressly for a new product or service that has no preexisting processes. The cross-functional team for this lab is empowered to develop specific and measurable customer-based goals, and all the necessary plans, programs, and processes to achieve and measure these goals.

Both paths minimize your risk by creating pilot programs for testing these new approaches. Whichever path you choose, it is essential to establish research components. Preresearch regarding customer needs must go beyond features and benefits to determining the ways products and services are best delivered, priced, serviced, and supported. Postresearch needs to provide accurate measurement of how well the organization did in improving customer perceptions and behavior, and which areas of contact require improvement.

On both paths, the teams need the authority to make decisions and changes in the business area. They also must include people with expertise in direct marketing, which is essential to determining the value of the investment to the marketer. Both paths need a financial commitment, as well as a long-term view of capturing realistic results.

Summary

With the nineties characterized by burgeoning globalization and heightened competition among firms, the future seems to be more uncertain and unpredictable than ever before. The consumer of the nineties has also undergone a dramatic transformation. Armed with more information and ever-increasing choices, the consumer of the nineties has become more and more demanding. With cheaper store brands invading the supermarkets and with recession a persistent phenomenon, loyalty has become a scarce commodity in the current marketplace. Marketing managers are trying many new strategies to cope with this uncertain environment and the fickle consumer. A market researcher has to have thorough knowledge of these emerging strategies and concepts in order to survive. But the uncertainty in the environment has a rather fortunate consequence for the market researcher. Managers are turning increasingly to research to understand the complex global environment and the nature of the capricious consumer. Hence, marketing research has to rise up to this challenge and provide the managers of the nineties the right kind of information to make their decisions.

This chapter has introduced the emerging concepts and strategies in marketing. Even though the concept of competitive advantage has been there for a long time it is only in the last decade that it has been receiving a lot of attention. More and more companies are trying to gauge their competitive advantage and trying to hold on to it. There are many ways of measuring competitive advantage, a few of which have been mentioned in this chapter. The term **brand equity** has no clear definition nor a single methodology to measure it. A synthesis of the various definitions and measures of brand equity are given in the chapter. **Customer satisfaction** is another construct that has received a lot of attention. The basic methodology to measure customer satisfaction is discussed. The three most popular strategies that are emerging in this decade are **TQM, relationship marketing,** and **integrated marketing communications.** There is a brief description of these strategies, of the various data requirements necessary for managers trying to implement these strategies, and of the methodologies to be adopted to obtain these data.

Questions and Problems

1. You are a startup entrepreneur who employs about 100 people. You supply mainly grade items (such as nuts, bolts, etc.) to a big NASA contractor. The contractor has threatened to cancel its future orders until you adopt TQM in your company. He or she wants you to establish specific, tangible measures to achieve TQM in your company. Specify some of the measures you will have to show to your contractor to convince it that you have adopted TQM, and also describe the informational requirements for those measures.
2. What type of data need to be collected to build long-term relationships with your consumer if you are
   a. A consumer product company.
   b. An industrial product firm.
   c. A service-oriented organization.
3. Do you think the customer-satisfaction-measurement methodology described in the text is a valid one? Why or why not? How will you check on the reliability and validity of your customer satisfaction measurement?
4. The concept of brand equity is nebulous. Do you agree with the statement? Give reasons for your answers.
5. Why is measuring competitive advantage so important? Discuss the advantages and limitations of the various measures of competitive advantage given in the text.

6. You're the advertising agency for a retail store. You had talked about the concept of integrated marketing communications to the top management of the retail store. Management doesn't want to implement IMC in its store because it feels that the costs of integrating outweigh the benefits. Conduct a cost–benefit analysis to convince the retail store management that IMC is a worthwhile strategy to adopt.

End Notes

1. Michael E. Porter. *Competitive Strategy* (New York: The Free Press), 1980.

2. George S. Day and Robin Wensley. "Assessing Advantage: A Framework for Diagnosing Competitive Superiority," *Journal of Marketing,* 52, April 1988, 1–20.

3. Subrata N. Chakravarty, "Economic Darwinism," *Forbes,* October 6, 1986, 52–56; and J. W. Brittain and D. R. Wholey. "Competition Coexistence in Organizational Communities: Population Dynamics in Electronics Components Manufacturing," in *Ecological Models of Organizations,* Glenn R. Carrol, ed. (Cambridge, Massachusetts: Ballinger), 1988.

4. David A. Aaker. *Managing Brand Equity* (New York: The Free Press), 1991.

5. Wagner A. Kamakura and Gary J. Russell. "Measuring Brand Value with Scanner Data," *International Journal of Research in Marketing,* 10, March 1993, 9–22; Joffre Swait, Tulin Erdem, Jordan Louviere, and Chris Dubelaar. "The Equalization Price: A Measure of Consumer-Perceived Brand Equity," *Internation Journal of Research in Marketing,* 10, March 1993, 23–45; Kevin Lane Keller. "Conceptualizing, Measuring, and Managing Customer-Based Brand Equity," *Journal of Marketing,* 57, January 1993, 1–22.

6. Lewis C. Winters. "Brand Equity Measures: Some Recent Advances," *Marketing Research: A Magazine of Management & Applications,* 4, December 1991, 70–73.

7. Allan L. Baldinger, "Marketing, Finance Must Work Together to Measure Brand Equity," *Marketing News,* 25, September 2, 1991, 36.

8. Carol J. Simon and Mary W. Sullivan. "The Measurement and Determinants of Brand Equity: A Financial Approach," *Marketing Science,* 12, Winter 1993, 28–52.

9. B. G. Yovovich. "What Is Your Brand Really Worth?" *Adweek's Marketing Week,* August 8, 1988, 18–24.

10. William Boulding, Ajay Kalra, Richard Staelin, and Valarie A. Zeithaml. "A Dynamic Process Model of Service Quality: From Expectations to Behavioral Intentions," *Journal of Marketing Research,* 30, February 1993, 7–27.

11. James M. Salter. "The Systematic Approach to Measuring Satisfaction," *Marketing News,* 25, February 4, 1991, 9.

12. Robert A. Peterson and William R. Wilson. "Measuring Customer Satisfaction: Fact and Artifact," *Journal of the Academy of Marketing Science,* 20, Winter 1992, 61–71.

13. Mary Jo Bitner. "Evaluating Service Encounters: The Effects of Physical Surroundings and Employee Responses," *Journal of Marketing,* 54, April 1990, 69–82; A. Parasuraman, Valarie A. Zeithaml, and Leonard L. Berry. "A Conceptual Model of Service Quality and Its Implications for Future Research," *Journal of Marketing,* 49, Fall 1985, 41–50; John R. Hauser and Don Clausing. "The House of Quality," *Harvard Business Review,* May–June 1988, 64.

14. *Special Report,* "Quality—Small and Midsize Companies Seize the Challenge—Not a Moment Too Soon," *Business Week,* November 30, 66–74.

15. Albert C. Hyde. "Rescuing Quality Measurement from TQM," *Bureaucrat,* 19, Winter 1990–1991, 16–20.

16. C. E. Bogan and C. W. L. Hart. *The Baldrige* (New York: McGraw-Hill), 1992.

17. *The Honeywell Quality Improvement Owner's Manual.*

18. Stephen George. *The Baldrige Quality System* (New York: John Wiley & Sons), 1992; Robert Camp. *Benchmarking: The Search for Industry Best Practices that Lead to Superior Performance* (Milwaukee: Quality Press), 1989.

19. From *Competitive Benchmarking: What It Is And What It Can Do For You* (Xerox Corporate Quality Office), 1987, 17.

20. Alexander Hiam. *Closing The Quality Gap* (Englewood Cliffs, New Jersey: Prentice Hall), 1992.

21. Abbie Griffin and John Hausser. "The Voice of the Customer," *Marketing Science,* 12, Winter 1993, 1–27.

22. Op. cit.

23. John J. Harrison. "Transforming Data Into Relationships," *National Underwriter,* 97, August 2, 1993, 7, 12; D. Edelman, D. Schultz, and M. Winkleman. "Up Close and Personal," *Journal of Business Strategy,* 14, July / August 1993, 22–31.

24. Regis Mckenna. "Relationship Marketing," *Executive Excellence*, 9, April 1992, 7–8; Jonathan R. Copulsky and Michael J. Wolf. "Relationship Marketing: Positioning for the Future," *The Journal of Business Strategy*, July/August 1990, 16–21.

25. Tom Duncan. "Integrated Marketing? It's Synergy," *Advertising Age*, 64, March 8, 1993, 22; Don E. Schultz. "Integrated Marketing Communications: Maybe Definition is in the Point of View," *Marketing News*, 27, January 18, 1993, 17.

26. Thomas R. Duncan and Stephen E. Everett. "Client Perceptions of Integrated Marketing Communications," *Journal of Advertising Research*, 33, May/June 1993, 30–39; Don E. Schultz. "Why Ad Agencies are Having So Much Trouble with IMC," *Marketing News*, 27, April 26, 1993, 12.

27. Don E. Schultz. "Integration Helps You Plan Communication From Outside-In," *Marketing News*, 27, March 15, 1993, 12.

28. Kerri L. Acheson. "Integrated Marketing Must Bring 2 Perspectives Together," *Marketing News*, 27, August 16, 1993, 4, 7; Don E. Schultz, "How to Overcome the Barriers to Integration," *Marketing News*, 27, July 19, 1993, 16; Don E. Schultz. "Just What are We Integrating? And Who Should Benefit?," *Marketing News*, 27, May 24, 1993, 10.

Tables

A-1   Standard Normal Probabilities
A-2 χ^2 Critical Points
A-3 F Critical Points
A-4 t Critical Points

TABLE A-1
Standard Normal, Cumulative Probability in Right-Hand Tail for Positive Values of z; Areas Are Formed by Symmetry

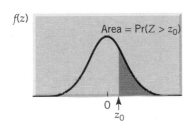

| | | | | **Second Decimal Place of Z_0** | | | | | | |
Z_0	.00	.01	.02	.03	.04	.05	.06	.07	.08	.09
0.0	.5000	.4960	.4920	.4880	.4840	.4801	.4761	.4721	.4681	.4641
0.1	.4602	.4562	.4522	.4483	.4443	.4404	.4364	.4325	.4286	.4247
0.2	.4207	.4168	.4129	.4090	.4052	.4013	.3974	.3936	.3897	.3859
0.3	.3821	.3783	.3745	.3707	.3669	.3632	.3594	.3557	.3520	.3483
0.4	.3446	.3409	.3372	.3336	.3300	.3264	.3228	.3192	.3156	.3121
0.5	.3085	.3050	.3015	.2981	.2946	.2912	.2877	.2843	.2810	.2776
0.6	.2743	.2709	.2676	.2643	.2611	.2578	.2546	.2514	.2483	.2451
0.7	.2420	.2389	.2358	.2327	.2296	.2266	.2236	.2206	.2177	.2148
0.8	.2119	.2090	.2061	.2033	.2055	.1977	.1949	.1922	.1894	.1867
0.9	.1841	.1814	.1788	.1762	.1736	.1711	.1685	.1660	.1635	.1611
1.0	.1587	.1562	.1539	.1515	.1492	.1469	.1446	.1423	.1401	.1379
1.1	.1357	.1335	.1314	.1292	.1271	.1251	.1230	.1210	.1190	.1170
1.2	.1151	.1131	.1112	.1093	.1075	.1056	.1038	.1020	.1003	.0985
1.3	.0968	.0951	.0934	.0918	.0901	.0885	.0869	.0853	.0838	.0823
1.4	.0808	.0793	.0778	.0764	.0749	.0735	.0722	.0708	.0694	.0681
1.5	.0668	.0655	.0643	.0630	.0618	.0606	.0594	.0582	.0571	.0559
1.6	.0548	.0537	.0526	.0516	.0505	.0495	.0485	.0475	.0465	.0455
1.7	.0446	.0436	.0427	.0418	.0409	.0401	.0392	.0384	.0375	.0367
1.8	.0359	.0352	.0344	.0336	.0329	.0322	.0314	.0307	.0301	.0294
1.9	.0287	.0281	.0274	.0268	.0262	.0256	.0250	.0244	.0239	.0233
2.0	.0228	.0222	.0217	.0212	.0207	.0202	.0197	.0192	.0188	.0183
2.1	.0179	.0174	.0170	.0166	.0162	.0158	.0154	.0150	.0146	.0143
2.2	.0139	.0136	.0132	.0129	.0125	.0122	.0119	.0116	.0113	.0110
2.3	.0107	.0104	.0102	.0099	.0096	.0094	.0091	.0089	.0087	.0084
2.4	.0082	.0080	.0078	.0075	.0073	.0071	.0069	.0068	.0066	.0064

$f(z)$

Area $= \Pr(Z > z_0)$

0   z_0

Z_0	.00	.01	.02	.03	.04	.05	.06	.07	.08	.09
					Second Decimal Place of Z_0					
2.5	.0062	.0060	.0059	.0057	.0055	.0054	.0052	.0051	.0049	.0048
2.6	.0047	.0045	.0044	.0043	.0041	.0040	.0039	.0038	.0037	.0036
2.7	.0035	.0034	.0033	.0032	.0031	.0030	.0029	.0028	.0027	.0026
2.8	.0026	.0025	.0023	.0023	.0023	.0022	.0021	.0021	.0020	.0019
2.9	.0019	.0018	.0017	.0017	.0016	.0016	.0015	.0015	.0014	.0014
3.0	.00135									
3.5	.000 233									
4.0	.000 031 7									
4.5	.000 003 40									
5.0	.000 000 287									

TABLE A-2
χ^2 **Critical Points**

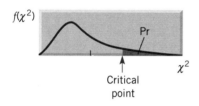

df \ Pr	.250	.100	.050	.025	.010	.005	.001
1	1.32	2.71	3.84	5.02	6.63	7.88	10.8
2	2.77	4.61	5.99	7.38	9.21	10.6	13.8
3	4.11	6.25	7.81	9.35	11.3	12.8	16.3
4	5.39	7.78	9.49	11.1	13.3	14.9	18.5
5	6.63	9.24	11.1	12.8	15.1	16.7	20.5
6	7.84	10.6	12.6	14.4	16.8	18.5	22.5
7	9.04	12.0	14.1	16.0	18.5	20.3	24.3
8	10.2	13.4	15.5	17.5	20.1	22.0	26.1
9	11.4	14.7	16.9	19.0	21.7	23.6	27.9
10	12.5	16.0	18.8	20.5	23.2	25.2	29.6
11	13.7	17.3	19.7	21.9	24.7	26.8	31.3
12	14.8	18.5	21.0	23.3	26.2	28.3	32.9
13	16.0	19.8	22.4	24.7	27.7	29.8	34.5
14	17.1	21.1	23.7	26.1	29.1	31.3	36.1
15	18.2	22.3	25.0	27.5	30.6	32.8	37.7
16	19.4	23.5	26.3	28.8	32.0	34.3	39.3
17	20.5	24.8	27.6	30.2	33.4	35.7	40.8
18	21.6	26.0	28.9	31.5	34.8	37.2	42.3
19	22.7	27.2	30.1	32.9	36.2	38.6	43.8

TABLE A-2 *(continued)*

df \ Pr	.250	.100	.050	.025	.010	.005	.001
20	23.8	28.4	31.4	34.2	37.6	40.0	45.3
21	24.9	29.6	32.7	35.5	38.9	41.4	46.8
22	26.0	30.8	33.9	36.8	40.3	42.8	48.3
23	27.1	32.0	35.2	38.1	41.6	44.2	49.7
24	28.2	33.2	36.4	39.4	42.0	45.6	51.2
25	29.3	34.4	37.7	40.6	44.3	46.9	52.6
26	30.4	35.6	38.9	41.9	45.6	48.3	54.1
27	31.5	36.7	40.1	43.2	47.0	49.6	55.5
28	32.6	37.9	41.3	44.5	48.3	51.0	56.9
29	33.7	39.1	42.6	45.7	49.6	52.3	58.3
30	34.8	40.3	43.8	47.0	50.9	53.7	59.7
40	45.6	51.8	55.8	59.3	63.7	66.8	73.4
50	56.3	63.2	67.5	71.4	76.2	79.5	86.7
60	67.0	74.4	79.1	83.3	88.4	92.0	99.6
70	77.6	85.5	90.5	95.0	100	104	112
80	88.1	96.6	102	107	112	116	125
90	98.6	108	113	118	124	128	137
100	109	118	124	130	136	140	149

TABLE A-3
F Critical Points

	Pr	Degrees of Freedom for Numerator										
		1	2	3	4	5	6	8	10	20	40	∞
1	.25	5.83	7.50	8.20	8.58	8.82	8.98	9.19	9.32	9.58	9.71	9.85
	.10	39.9	49.5	53.6	55.8	57.2	58.2	59.4	60.2	61.7	62.5	63.3
	.05	161	200	216	225	230	234	239	242	248	251	254
2	.25	2.57	3.00	3.15	3.23	3.28	3.31	3.35	3.38	3.43	3.45	3.48
	.10	8.53	9.00	9.16	9.24	9.29	9.33	9.37	9.39	9.44	9.47	9.49
	.05	18.5	19.0	19.2	19.2	19.3	19.3	19.4	19.4	19.4	19.5	19.5
	.01	98.5	99.0	99.2	99.2	99.3	99.3	99.4	99.4	99.4	99.5	99.5
	.001	998	999	999	999	999	999	999	999	999	999	999
3	.25	2.02	2.28	2.36	2.39	2.41	2.42	2.44	2.44	2.46	2.47	2.47
	.10	5.54	5.46	5.39	5.34	5.31	5.28	5.25	5.23	5.18	5.16	5.13
	.05	10.1	9.55	9.28	9.12	9.10	8.94	8.85	8.79	8.66	8.59	8.53
	.01	34.1	30.8	29.5	28.7	28.2	27.9	27.5	27.2	26.7	26.4	26.1
	.001	167	149	141	137	135	133	131	129	126	125	124
4	.25	1.81	2.00	2.05	2.06	2.07	2.08	2.08	2.08	2.08	2.08	2.08
	.10	4.54	4.32	4.19	4.11	4.05	4.01	3.95	3.92	3.84	3.80	3.76
	.05	7.71	6.94	6.59	6.39	6.26	6.16	6.04	5.96	5.80	5.72	5.63
	.01	21.2	18.0	16.7	16.0	15.5	15.2	14.8	14.5	14.0	13.7	13.5
	.001	74.1	61.3	56.2	53.4	51.7	50.5	49.0	48.1	46.1	45.1	44.1
5	.25	1.69	1.85	1.88	1.89	1.89	1.89	1.89	1.89	1.88	1.88	1.87
	.10	4.06	3.78	3.62	3.52	3.45	3.40	3.34	3.30	3.21	3.16	3.10
	.05	6.61	5.79	5.41	5.19	5.05	4.95	4.82	4.74	4.56	4.46	4.36
	.01	16.3	13.3	12.1	11.4	11.0	10.7	10.3	10.1	9.55	9.29	9.02
	.001	47.2	37.1	33.2	31.1	29.8	28.8	27.6	26.9	25.4	24.6	23.8

Degrees of Freedom for Denominator

Degrees of Freedom for Denominator

df	α											
6	.25	1.62	1.76	1.78	1.79	1.79	1.78	1.77	1.77	1.76	1.75	1.74
	.10	3.78	3.46	3.29	3.18	3.11	3.05	2.98	2.94	2.84	2.78	2.72
	.05	5.99	5.14	4.76	4.53	4.39	4.28	4.15	4.06	3.87	3.77	3.67
	.01	13.7	10.9	9.78	9.15	8.75	8.47	8.10	7.87	7.40	7.14	6.88
	.001	35.5	27.0	23.7	21.9	20.8	20.0	19.0	18.4	17.1	16.4	15.8
7	.25	1.57	1.70	1.72	1.72	1.71	1.71	1.70	1.69	1.67	1.66	1.65
	.10	3.59	3.26	3.07	2.96	2.88	2.83	2.75	2.70	2.59	2.54	2.47
	.05	5.59	4.74	4.35	4.12	3.97	3.87	3.73	3.64	3.44	3.34	3.23
	.01	12.2	9.55	8.45	7.85	7.46	7.19	6.84	6.62	6.16	5.91	5.65
	.001	29.3	21.7	18.8	17.2	16.2	15.5	14.6	14.1	12.9	12.3	11.7
8	.25	1.54	1.66	1.67	1.66	1.66	1.65	1.64	1.63	1.61	1.59	1.58
	.10	3.46	3.11	2.92	2.81	2.73	2.67	2.59	2.54	2.42	2.36	2.29
	.05	5.32	4.46	4.07	3.84	3.69	3.58	3.44	3.35	3.15	3.04	2.93
	.01	11.3	8.65	7.59	7.01	6.63	6.37	6.03	5.81	5.36	5.12	4.86
	.001	25.4	18.5	15.8	14.4	13.5	12.9	12.0	11.5	10.5	9.92	9.33
9	.25	1.51	1.62	1.63	1.63	1.62	1.61	1.60	1.59	1.56	1.55	1.53
	.10	3.36	3.01	2.81	2.69	2.61	2.55	2.47	2.42	2.30	2.23	2.16
	.05	5.12	4.26	3.86	3.63	3.48	3.37	3.23	3.14	2.94	2.83	2.71
	.01	10.6	8.02	6.99	6.42	6.06	5.80	5.47	5.26	4.81	4.57	4.31
	.001	22.9	16.4	13.9	12.6	11.7	11.1	10.4	9.89	8.90	8.37	7.81
10	.25	1.49	1.60	1.60	1.59	1.59	1.58	1.56	1.55	1.52	1.51	1.48
	.10	3.28	2.92	2.73	2.61	2.52	2.46	2.38	2.32	2.20	2.13	2.06
	.05	4.96	4.10	3.71	3.48	3.33	3.22	3.07	2.98	2.77	2.66	2.54
	.01	10.0	7.56	6.55	5.99	5.64	5.39	5.06	4.85	4.41	4.17	3.91
	.001	21.0	14.9	12.6	11.3	10.5	9.92	9.20	8.75	7.80	7.30	6.76
12	.25	1.56	1.56	1.56	1.55	1.54	1.53	1.51	1.50	1.47	1.45	1.42
	.10	3.18	2.81	2.61	2.48	2.39	2.33	2.24	2.19	2.06	1.99	1.90
	.05	4.75	3.89	3.49	3.26	3.11	3.00	2.85	2.75	2.54	2.43	2.30
	.01	9.33	6.93	5.95	5.41	5.06	4.82	4.50	4.30	3.86	3.62	3.36
	.001	18.6	13.0	10.8	9.63	8.89	8.38	7.71	7.29	6.40	5.93	5.42
14	.25	1.44	1.53	1.53	1.52	1.51	1.50	1.48	1.46	1.43	1.41	1.38
	.10	3.10	2.73	2.52	2.39	2.31	2.24	2.15	2.10	1.96	1.89	1.80
	.05	4.60	3.74	3.34	3.11	2.96	2.85	2.70	2.60	2.39	2.27	2.13
	.01	8.86	6.51	5.56	5.04	4.69	4.45	4.14	3.94	3.51	3.27	3.00
	.001	17.1	11.8	9.73	8.62	7.92	7.43	6.80	6.40	5.56	5.10	4.60
16	.25	1.42	1.51	1.51	1.50	1.48	1.43	1.46	1.45	1.40	1.37	1.34
	.10	3.05	2.67	2.46	2.33	2.24	2.13	2.09	2.03	1.89	1.81	1.72
	.05	4.49	3.63	3.24	3.01	2.85	2.74	2.59	2.49	2.28	2.15	2.01
	.01	8.53	6.23	5.29	4.77	4.44	4.20	3.89	3.69	3.26	3.02	2.75
	.001	16.1	11.0	9.00	7.92	7.27	6.81	6.19	5.81	4.99	4.54	4.06

df (denom)	α											
6	.25	1.62	1.76	1.78	1.79	1.79	1.78	1.77	1.77	1.76	1.75	1.74
	.10	3.78	3.46	3.29	3.18	3.11	3.05	2.98	2.94	2.84	2.78	2.72
	.05	5.99	5.14	4.76	4.53	4.39	4.28	4.15	4.06	3.87	3.77	3.67
	.01	13.7	10.9	9.78	9.15	8.75	8.47	8.10	7.87	7.40	7.14	6.88
	.001	35.5	27.0	23.7	21.9	20.8	20.0	19.0	18.4	17.1	16.4	15.8
7	.25	1.57	1.70	1.72	1.72	1.71	1.71	1.70	1.69	1.67	1.66	1.65
	.10	3.59	3.26	3.07	2.96	2.88	2.83	2.75	2.70	2.59	2.54	2.47
	.05	5.59	4.74	4.35	4.12	3.97	3.87	3.73	3.64	3.44	3.34	3.23
	.01	12.2	9.55	8.45	7.85	7.46	7.19	6.84	6.62	6.16	5.91	5.65
	.001	29.3	21.7	18.8	17.2	16.2	15.5	14.6	14.1	12.9	12.3	11.7
8	.25	1.54	1.66	1.67	1.66	1.66	1.65	1.64	1.63	1.61	1.59	1.58
	.10	3.46	3.11	2.92	2.81	2.73	2.67	2.59	2.54	2.42	2.36	2.29
	.05	5.32	4.46	4.07	3.84	3.69	3.58	3.44	3.35	3.15	3.04	2.93
	.01	11.3	8.65	7.59	7.01	6.63	6.37	6.03	5.81	5.36	5.12	4.86
	.001	25.4	18.5	15.8	14.4	13.5	12.9	12.0	11.5	10.5	9.92	9.33
9	.25	1.51	1.62	1.63	1.63	1.62	1.61	1.60	1.59	1.56	1.55	1.53
	.10	3.36	3.01	2.81	2.69	2.61	2.55	2.47	2.42	2.30	2.23	2.16
	.05	5.12	4.26	3.86	3.63	3.48	3.37	3.23	3.14	2.94	2.83	2.71
	.01	10.6	8.02	6.99	6.42	6.06	5.80	5.47	5.26	4.81	4.57	4.31
	.001	22.9	16.4	13.9	12.6	11.7	11.1	10.4	9.89	8.90	8.37	7.81
10	.25	1.49	1.60	1.60	1.59	1.59	1.58	1.56	1.55	1.52	1.51	1.48
	.10	3.28	2.92	2.73	2.61	2.52	2.46	2.38	2.32	2.20	2.13	2.06
	.05	4.96	4.10	3.71	3.48	3.33	3.22	3.07	2.98	2.77	2.66	2.54
	.01	10.0	7.56	6.55	5.99	5.64	5.39	5.06	4.85	4.41	4.17	3.91
	.001	21.0	14.9	12.6	11.3	10.5	9.92	9.20	8.75	7.80	7.30	6.76
12	.25	1.56	1.56	1.53	1.55	1.54	1.53	1.51	1.50	1.47	1.45	1.42
	.10	3.18	2.81	2.61	2.48	2.39	2.33	2.24	2.19	2.06	1.99	1.90
	.05	4.75	3.89	3.49	3.26	3.11	3.00	2.85	2.75	2.54	2.43	2.30
	.01	9.33	6.93	5.95	5.41	5.06	4.82	4.50	4.30	3.86	3.62	3.36
	.001	18.6	13.0	10.8	9.63	8.89	8.38	7.71	7.29	6.40	5.93	5.42
14	.25	1.44	1.53	1.53	1.52	1.51	1.50	1.48	1.46	1.43	1.41	1.38
	.10	3.10	2.73	2.52	2.39	2.31	2.24	2.15	2.10	1.96	1.89	1.80
	.05	4.60	3.74	3.34	3.11	2.96	2.85	2.70	2.60	2.39	2.27	2.13
	.01	8.86	5.51	5.56	5.04	4.69	4.46	4.14	3.94	3.51	3.27	3.00
	.001	17.1	11.8	9.73	8.62	7.92	7.43	6.80	6.40	5.56	5.10	4.60
16	.25	1.42	1.51	1.51	1.50	1.48	1.48	1.46	1.45	1.40	1.37	1.34
	.10	3.05	2.67	2.46	2.33	2.24	2.18	2.09	2.03	1.89	1.81	1.72
	.05	4.49	3.63	3.24	3.01	2.85	2.74	2.59	2.49	2.28	2.15	2.01
	.01	8.53	6.23	5.29	4.77	4.44	4.20	3.89	3.69	3.26	3.02	2.75
	.001	16.1	11.0	9.00	7.94	7.27	6.81	6.19	5.81	4.99	4.54	4.06

Degrees of Freedom for Denominator

Cut-off points for the Student's *t* Distribution

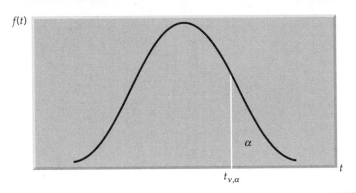

df(v)	.100	.050	α .025	.010	.005
1	3.078	6.314	12.706	31.821	63.657
2	1.886	2.920	4.303	6.965	9.925
3	1.638	2.353	3.182	4.541	5.841
4	1.533	2.132	2.776	3.747	4.604
5	1.476	2.015	2.571	3.365	4.032
6	1.440	1.943	2.447	3.143	3.707
7	1.415	1.895	2.365	2.998	3.499
8	1.397	1.860	2.306	2.896	3.355
9	1.383	1.833	2.262	2.821	3.250
10	1.372	1.812	2.228	2.764	3.169
11	1.363	1.796	2.201	2.718	3.106
12	1.356	1.782	2.179	2.681	3.055
13	1.350	1.771	2.160	2.650	3.012
14	1.345	1.761	2.145	2.624	2.977
15	1.341	1.753	2.131	2.602	2.947
16	1.337	1.746	2.120	2.583	2.921
17	1.333	1.740	2.110	2.567	2.898
18	1.330	1.734	2.101	2.552	2.878
19	1.328	1.729	2.093	2.539	2.861
20	1.325	1.725	2.086	2.528	2.845
21	1.323	1.721	2.080	2.518	2.831
22	1.321	1.717	2.074	2.508	2.819
23	1.319	1.714	2.069	2.500	2.807
24	1.318	1.711	2.064	2.492	2.797
25	1.316	1.708	2.060	2.485	2.787
26	1.315	1.706	2.056	2.479	2.779
27	1.314	1.703	2.052	2.473	2.771
28	1.313	1.701	2.048	2.467	2.763
29	1.311	1.699	2.045	2.462	2.756
30	1.310	1.697	2.042	2.457	2.750
40	1.303	1.684	2.021	2.423	2.704
60	1.296	1.671	2.000	2.390	2.660
∞	1.282	1.645	1.960	2.326	2.576

For selected probabilities, α, the table shows the values $t_{v,\alpha}$ such that $P(t_v > t_{v,\alpha} = \alpha$, where t_v is a Student's *t* random variable with *v* degrees of freedom. For example, the probability is .10 that a Student's *t* random variable with 10 degrees of freedom exceeds 1.372.

Accuracy a criterion used to judge whether a market research study is logical and presents correct information.

Additive Causal Relationship a causal relationship in which the causal effects of two variables on a third variable are added.

Administering Error error that occurs during the administration of a survey instrument to the respondent.

Affective/Liking Component that part of attitude representing the person's overall feelings of liking or disliking for the object, person, or event.

Aided Recall a questioning approach that attempts to stimulate a respondent's memory with clues about an object of interest.

American Marketing Association the premier association of marketing practitioners and academicians in the United States, which publishes journals and organizes conferences for the dissemination of marketing knowledge.

Analysis of Dependence any multivariate analysis where one or more variables are predicted or explained by other variables.

Analysis of Interdependence any multivariate analysis where the interrelationships within a set of variables are examined and no variable is seen to be a dependent variable.

Analysis of Value an estimate of the benefits gained by undertaking a market research study.

Analysis of Variance (ANOVA) a method of testing a hypothesis regarding the difference between several means.

Artificiality the conditions that differ from the real world in experimental treatment so that projections become difficult and risky.

ASSESSOR a computer model for predicting market share of a new packaged good brand using laboratory test market data.

Associative Scaling a scale in which the respondent is asked to associate alternatives with each question.

Attitudes mental states used by individuals to structure the way they perceive their environment and to guide the way in which they respond. A psychological construct comprised of cognitive, affective, and intention components.

Attribute a characteristic or property of an object or person.

Attribute Judgment the judgment an individual makes about the numerous characteristics or attributes that are possessed by an object.

Automatic Interaction Detection (AID) a technique for finding interactions in a sample by using nominally scaled independent variables to find subgroups that differ with respect to a dependent variable.

Averaging a memory error whereby something is reported as more like the usual, the expected, or the norm.

Bar Graph a graph of bars whose length indicates relative amounts of the variable.

Before Measure Effect the alerting of respondents to the fact that they are being studied, due to the presentation of a before measure, causing unnatural responses.

Behavior the past and present overt responses of subjects.

Behavior Recording Device a mechanical observation method, such as a traffic counter, that continuously monitors behavior, usually unobtrusively.

Benefit Segmentation a type of market segmentation based on the benefits that people seek from products.

Bipolar Scale a scale bounded at each end by polar adjectives that are antonyms.

Blind Use Test a use test where consumers are asked to evaluate product alternatives without being aware of brand names.

Blocking a procedure by which a nonmanipulated variable is introduced into the experiment to ensure that the groups are equalized on that variable.

Bottom-Up Measurement a method of determining market potential that has as its starting point the identification of product use situations or applications.

Brand Equity the concept wherein the brand is considered an asset insofar as it can be sold or bought for a price. A powerful brand is said to have high brand equity.

CALLPLAN an interactive model designed to aid a salesperson in his or her call planning process. Its objective is to determine call-frequency norms for each client and prospect.

Canonical Correlation Analysis an analysis method used in the case of two dependent variables and multiple independent variables. It focuses on the relationship between two sets of interval-scale variables.

Case Study a comprehensive description and analysis of a single situation.

Causal Relationship a precondition influencing a variable of interest, or, more strictly, a change in one variable that produces a change in another variable.

Causal Research research having very specific hypotheses that is usually designed to provide the ultimate level of understanding—a knowledge that one construct under certain conditions causes another construct to occur or to change.

Census Tract a group of city blocks having a total population of more than 4000 and generally used to approximate neighborhoods.

Centroid the average value of the objects contained in the cluster on each of the variables making up each object's profile.

Chi-Square Statistic a measure of association between two nominally scaled variables.

City Block the smallest identifiable unit in the U.S. Census, being bounded by four streets or some other physical boundary.

Classification Variables used to classify respondents, such as demographic and socioeconomic measures.

Closed-Response (or Structured) Question a question accompanied by the presentation of responses to be considered by the respondent.

Cluster Analysis a set of techniques for grouping objects or persons in terms of similarity.

Cluster Sampling a sampling method where a random sample of subgroups is selected and all members of the subgroups become part of the sample.

Clutter/Awareness the percentage who recalled a brand was advertised when exposed in a "clutter" of seven ads in a McCollum/Speilman test.

Coding the categorization and numbering of responses.

Cognitive/Knowledge Component that part of attitude representing a person's information about an object, person, or event.

Communality the proportion of a variable's variance explained by all of the factors in a factor analysis solution.

Comparative Scale a type of scale with some form of explicit or implicit comparison built into the scale.

Compensatory Model any multi-attribute model in which one attribute compensates for another in the overall preference for an object.

Complementary Pricing the pricing strategy used by firms to price complementary products. They usually price the main product at a low price while the complement is charged at a higher price.

Completion Test a projective technique in which the respondent is asked to complete a series of sentences.

Compositional Approach an attitude measurement approach in which the overall preference judgment for each object is obtained by summing the evaluative rating of each attribute times the importance of that attribute.

Computer-Retrievable Databases secondary records accessible by a computer system.

Concept Test a test of a product concept where the concept is evaluated by a sample of the target segment.

Concurrent Validity criterion validity that is established by correlating the measurement score with the criterion variable, both measured at the same time.

Conjoint Analysis a method of obtaining the relative worth or value of each level of several attributes from rank-ordered preferences of attribute combinations.

Consideration/Evoked Set all the alternatives that potential buyers would consider in their next purchase of the product or service.

Constant Sum Scale a scale in which the respondent must allocate a fixed number of points among several objects to reflect the relative preference for each object.

Construct a concept, usually psychological such as attitudes and values, that is not directly observable.

Construct Equivalence deals with how the researcher and the subjects of the research see, understand, and code a particular phenomenon.

Construct Validity the ability of a measurement instrument to measure a concept or "construct"; generally, construct validity is demonstrated by showing both convergent and discriminant validity.

Content Analysis a technique used to study written material by breaking it into meaningful units, using carefully applied rules.

Controlled Distribution Scanner Markets (CDSM) distribution for new product test is prearranged and results are monitored with scanner data.

Contingency Coefficient a chi-square statistic corrected for sample size.

Continuous Purchase Panel a fixed sample of respondents who are measured on several occasions over a period of time.

Contrived Observation an observation method in which people are placed in a contrived situation so that their responses will reveal some aspects of their underlying beliefs, attitudes, and motives; examples are tests of variation in shelf-space, product flavors, and display locations.

Control Group the group of subjects not exposed to the experimental treatment.

Convenience Sampling a sampling method in which convenient sampling units are contacted, such as church activity groups or student classes.

Convergent Validity the ability of a measurement instrument to correlate or "converge" with other supposed measures of the same variable or construct; the opposite of discriminant validity.

Copy Test Validity the ability to predict advertising response.

Correlation a number between +1 and −1 that reflects the degree to which two variables have a linear relationship.

Correspondence Analysis a technique for producing perceptual maps using binary data.

Criterion/Empirical Validity the validity of a measurement instrument as determined by empirical evidence that correlates the measurement instrument with other "criterion" variables.

Cross-Tabulation/Contingency Table Analysis the determination of a frequency distribution for subgroups.

Cyclical Indexes a representation of the effects of business cycle fluctuations in making a forecast.

Data unassimilated facts about the market.

Data Analysis Error errors that arise due to the faulty procedures employed in coding, editing, analyzing, and interpreting data.

Database an organized store of data, usually within a computer.

DAR (Day-After-Recall) the percentage of the audience who can recall something specific about the commercial the next day.

Decision Support System (DSS) a collection of rules, procedures, and models for retrieving data from a database, transforming it into usable information, and disseminating it to users so that they can make decisions.

Decompositional Approach attitude measurement approach in which the utilities of each attribute are obtained from the overall preference judgment for each object.

Delphi Approach a group judgment method where each member makes an individual judgment and then each member is given an opportunity to revise his or her judgment after seeing the others' initial judgments, until, after several iterations, the group members reach their conclusion.

Demographic Shifts changes in physical and socioeconomic characteristics of a population such as age, ethnicity, income, and so on.

Descriptive Research research that usually is designed to provide a summary of some aspects of the environment when the hypotheses are tentative and speculative in nature.

DETAILER a decision calculus model for determining the salesforce allocation by market and by product line.

Diary Panel the basic data-gathering instrument for local TV and radio ratings.

Direct Observation an observation method in which the researcher directly observes the person or behavior in question.

Discriminant Analysis a statistical technique for developing a set of independent variables to classify people or objects into one or more groups.

Discriminant Function the linear combination of variables developed by discriminant analysis for the purpose of classifying people or objects into one or more groups.

Discriminant Validity the ability of a measurement instrument to not correlate with supposed measures of other variables or constructs; the opposite of convergent validity.

Drop-Off Approach the hand delivery of a questionnaire to sampling points.

Dummy Variable a variable taking on the values of either 0 or 1, which is used to denote characteristics that are not quantifiable.

Efficiency a criterion used to judge whether a market research study produces the maximum amount and quality of information for the minimum expenditure of time and money.

Expected Value the value obtained by multiplying each consequence by the probability of that consequence occurring and summing the products.

Experimental Control the control of extraneous variables through experimental procedures such as randomization or block designs.

Experimental Error error that arises due to the improper design of the experiment.

Experimental Group the group of subjects exposed to the experimental treatment.

Experimental Treatments alternative manipulations of the independent variable being investigated.

Experiments studies that require the intervention by the observer beyond that required for measurement.

Exploratory Research research that usually is designed to generate ideas when the hypotheses are vague or ill-defined.

Exponential Smoothing in time-series extrapolations, the weighting of historical data so that the more recent data are weighted more heavily than are less recent data, by exponentially decreasing sets of weights.

External Source a marketing data source found outside of the organization.

External Validity the applicability of experimental results to situations external to the actual experimental context.

Extraneous Variable variables other than the manipulated variable that affect the response of the test units and hence the results of the experiment. Also known as the confounding variables.

F Statistic the statistic used in the analysis of variance to test for differences in groups.

Face/Consensus Validity the validity of a measurement instrument as determined entirely by subjective argument or judgment.

Factor an underlying construct defined by a linear combination of variables.

Factor Analysis a set of techniques for the study of interrelationships among variables, usually for the purposes of data reduction and the discovery of underlying constructs or latent dimensions.

Factor Loading the correlation (or sometimes the regression weight) of a variable with a factor.

Factor Rotation the generation of several factor analysis solutions (factor loadings and scores) from the same data set.

Factor Scores a respondent's score or value on a factor.

Factorial Design an experimental design in which two or more experimental variables are considered simultaneously by applying each combination of the experimental treatment levels to randomly selected groups.

Field Experiments experiments in which the experimental treatment is introduced in a completely natural setting.

Focus Group a group discussion focused on a series of topics introduced by a discussion leader; the group members are encouraged to express their own views on each topic and to elaborate or react to the views of each other.

Forced Exposure respondents are exposed to an ad in a facility as opposed to an ''on-air'' test in the home.

Foreign Market Opportunity Analysis acquisition of information that would help the management to narrow the possibilities for international marketing activities. The aim of such an exercise is to gather information to aid in managerial decision making.

Frequency Distribution a report of the number of responses that a question has received.

Full-Profile Approach a method of collecting data for trade-off analysis in which respondents are given cards that describe complete product or service configurations.

Genotypic Sources of Refusal these pertain to why survey respondents refuse to participate on account of their inherent characteristics such as age, sex, occupation, and so on.

Goodman and Kruskall's Tau a measure of association for nominally scaled variables based on a proportional reduction in error.

Hierarchical Clustering a method of cluster analysis that starts with each object in its own (single-object) cluster and systematically combines clusters until all objects are in one cluster.

History Effect any influence on subjects, external to an experiment, that may affect the results of the experiment.

Hold-Out Sample a sample used to test a model developed from another sample.

Home Audit a method of collecting continuous purchase panel data in which the panel members agree to permit an auditor to check their household stocks of certain product categories at regular intervals.

Humanistic Inquiry a method in which the researcher is immersed in the group or system under study.

Hypothesis a possible answer to the research question.

Ideal Object the object the respondent would prefer over all others, including objects that can be conceptualized but do not actually exist; it is a combination of all the respondent's preferred attribute levels.

Independence in statistics, the property that the knowledge of one variable or event offers no information as to the identity of another variable or event.

Individual Depth Interview a qualitative research method designed to explore the hidden (deep) feelings, values, and motives of the respondent through a face-to-face interview with the researcher.

Industrial Market a market for goods and services composed of industrial firms, other businesses, government agencies, and organizations in general, rather than individual consumers.

Information data that have been transformed into answers for specific questions of the decision makers.

Information System a system containing marketing data and marketing intelligence.

Instrumentation Effect the effect of changes in the measuring instrument on the experimental results.

Integrated Marketing Communications a concept of marketing communications planning that recognizes the added value of a comprehensive plan that evaluates the strategic roles of a variety of communication disciplines and combines these disciplines to provide clarity, consistency, and maximum communication impact through the seamless integration of discrete messages.

Intention/Action Component the part of an attitude that represents the person's expectations of future behavior toward the object, person, or event.

Interactive Effect the case where the effect of one variable on another variable depends on the level of a third variable.

Interference Error error that occurs due to the failure of the interviewer to adhere to the exact procedure while collecting the data.

Internal Records a marketing data source found within the organization.

Internal Validity the ability of an experiment to show relationships unambiguously.

Interval Estimation the estimation of the interval in which an unknown population characteristic is judged to lie, for a given level of confidence.

Interval Scale a scale with the property that units have the same width throughout the scale (i.e., thermometer).

Intervening Variable any variable positioned between two other variables in a causal path.

Interviewer Error a source of error in personal interviews due to the impression the respondent has of the interviewer and the way the interviewer asks questions, follows up partial answers, and records the responses.

Itemized Category Scale a scale in which the respondent chooses among one of several response options or categories.

Judgmental Sampling a nonprobability sampling method in which an "expert" uses judgment to identify representative samples.

Jury of Executive Opinion an efficient and timely qualitative research approach that combines the judgments of a group of managers about forecasts, most commonly used in consumer products and service companies.

Laboratory Experiment an experiment in which the experimental treatment is introduced in an artificial or laboratory setting.

Laboratory Test Market a procedure whereby shoppers are exposed to an ad for a new product and then taken on a simulated shopping trip in a laboratory facility.

Latin Square Design an experimental design that reduces the number of groups involved when interactions between the treatment levels and the control variables can be considered relatively unimportant.

Leading Indicators a variable that tends to predict the future direction of an object to be forecast.

Likert Scale a scale developed by the Likert method in which the subject must indicate his or her degree of agreement or disagreement with a variety of statements related to the attitude object and which then are summed over all statements to provide a total score.

Lockbox Approach the delivery by mail of a small, locked metal box containing a questionnaire and other interviewing exhibits.

Magnitude Scaling a technique for measuring opinions using a ratio scale instead of an interval scale.

Mail Diary Method a method of collecting continuous purchase panel data in which panel members record the details of each purchase in certain categories and return a completed mail diary at regular intervals.

Mail Panel a representative national sample of people who have agreed to participate in a limited number of mail surveys each year.

Mail Survey the mailing of questionnaires and their return by mail by the designated respondents.

Market Potential the sales for the product or service that would result if the market were fully developed.

Market Segmentation the development and pursuit of marketing programs directed at subgroups or segments of the population that the organization could possibly serve.

Marketing Planning and Information System a system of strategic and tactical plans and marketing data and intelligence that provides overall direction and coordination to the organization.

Marketing Program Development the stage of the market planning process which deals with segmentation decisions, product decisions, distribution decisions, advertising and promotion decisions, personal selling decisions, and pricing decisions.

Marketing Research the specification, gathering, analyzing, and interpretation of information that links the organization with its market environment.

Manipulation the creation of different levels of the independent variable is known as manipulating the variable.

Matching a procedure for the assignment of subjects to groups that ensures each group of respondents is matched on the basis of the pertinent characteristics.

Maturation during a research study, changes within respondents that are a consequence of time.

Mean the number obtained by summing all elements in a set and dividing by the number of elements.

Measurement the assignment of numbers by rules to objects in order to reflect quantities of properties.

Measurement Equivalence this deals with the methods and procedures used by the researcher to collect and categorize essential data and information.

Measurement Error error that occurs due to the variation between the information sought by the researcher and the information generated by a particular procedure employed by the researcher.

Monopolar Scale a scale bounded at each end by polar adjectives or phrases, one of which is the negation of the other.

Mortality Effect the effect on the experimental results of respondents dropping out of an experiment.

Moving Average using the moving average of the last n data points (e.g., the monthly averages for a year) to forecast.

Multiattribute Model any model linking attribute judgments with overall liking or affect.

Multidimensional Scaling a set of techniques for developing perceptual maps.

Multistage Designs a sampling procedure that consists of several sampling methods used sequentially.

Multivariate Analysis the simultaneous study of two or more measures on a sample of objects.

Need a want, an urge, a wish, or any motivational force directing behavior toward a goal.

Need Research/Identification a type of concept-generation research with the emphasis placed on the identification of unfulfilled needs that exist in the market.

New-Product Research Process a sequential four-stage process consisting of concept generation, concept evaluation and development, product evaluation and development, and product testing.

Nielsen Retail Index a retail store audit–conducted by A. C. Nielsen for four major groups of stores: grocery products, drugs, mass merchandisers, and alcoholic beverages.

Nominal Scale a measurement that assigns only an identification or label to an object or set of objects.

Nondirective Interview a type of individual depth interview in which the respondent is given maximum freedom to respond, within the bounds of topics of interest to the interviewer.

Nonparametric Procedures analysis techniques that are applicable only if the data are nonmetric (nominal or ordinal).

Nonprobability Sampling any sampling method where the probability of any population element's inclusion is unknown, such as judgmental or convenience sampling.

Nonresponse Bias an error due to the in ability to elicit information from some respondents in a sample, often due to refusals.

Nonresponse Error error that occurs due to nonparticipation of some eligible respondents in the study. This could be due to the unwillingness of the respondents to participate in the study or the inability of the interviewer to contact the respondents.

Observation a data collection method where the relevant behaviors are recorded; examples are direct observation, contrived observation, physical trace measures, and behavior recording devices.

Omission a memory error where a respondent leaves out an event or some aspect of it.

Omnibus Survey a regularly scheduled personal interview survey comprised of questions from several separate firms.

On-Line Telephone Interview an interview where the interviewer (1) reads the questions from an on-line cathode-ray-tube (CRT) terminal that is linked directly to a computer and (2) records the answers on a keyboard for entry to the computer.

Open-Response/Unstructured Question a question with either no classification of responses or precoded classification of responses.

Optimizing (*in Cluster Analysis*) a nonhierarchical method of clustering wherein the objects can later be reassigned to clusters on the basis of optimizing some overall criterion measure.

Order Bias the bias of question responses due to the order of question presentation.

Ordinal Scale a measurement that assigns only a rank order (i.e., "less than or greater than") to a set of objects.

On-Air Test a test ad is shown on a channel viewed at home.

Paired Comparison a scale in which the objects to be ranked are presented two at a time so that the respondent has to choose between them according to some criterion.

Parallel Threshold a nonhierarchical clustering method wherein several cluster centers are selected simultaneously and objects within threshold level are assigned to the nearest center. Threshold levels can be adjusted to admit fewer or more objects to cluster.

Parameter a number constant in each model considered, but varying in different models.

Parametric Procedures analysis techniques that are applicable only if the data are metric (interval or ratio).

Partial Correlation Coefficient examining the association between a dependent and independent variable after satisfactorily factoring out the effect of other independent variables.

Part-Worth Utilities utilities associated with particular product or brand attributes that are added together to obtain an overall utility for a product or brand alternative in conjoint analysis.

Past Turning Point a point in time where a substantial change in growth rate can be identified by an environmental change; a forecast can be based on data since that point.

Perceptual Map/Reduced Space a spatial representation of the perceived relationships among objects in a set, where the objects could be brands, products, or services.

Periodic Discounting the strategy adopted by the firm wherein the firms can start at a high price and periodically discount their prices in order to draw consumers with lower reservation prices. This is useful when markets have consumers with differential reservation prices.

Personal Interview a face-to-face interview between the respondent and the interviewer.

Phenotypic Sources of Refusal these pertain to why survey respondents refuse to participate on account of the characteristics of the data collection procedure such as which questions are asked, how they are asked, length of the interview, and so on.

Phi-Squared a chi-square statistic corrected for sample size.

Physical Trace Measures an observation method, such as a home audit, in which the natural "residue" or physical trace of the behavior is recorded.

Picture Interpretation a projective technique based on the Thematic Apperception Test (TAT), in which the respondent is asked to tell a story on the presentation of a series of pictures.

Population Specification Error error that occurs when an inappropriate population is chosen for the study.

Potential Rating Index Zip Markets (PRIZM) the classification and grouping of residents of zip code areas based on demographic and lifestyle data derived from the census.

Predictive Validity criterion validity that is established by correlating the measurement score with a future criterion variable.

Pretest the presentation of a questionnaire in a pilot study to a representative sample of the respondent population in order to discover any problems with the questionnaire prior to full-scale use.

Price Bundling the pricing strategy adopted to products that are nonsubstitutable, are perishable, and have an asymmetric demand structure. An example is pricing a car that includes many options.

Price Signaling the pricing strategy adopted when the consumers in the market are willing to pay more for a product despite lack of knowledge regarding a product's quality. The firm produces an inferior product and sells it at the same price as the better quality product produced by another firm, in the hope that customers will associate high quality with high price.

Primary Data data collected to address a specific research objective (as opposed to secondary data).

Principal Components/Principal Factor Analysis a type of factor analysis that seeks to explain the greatest amount of variance in a data set, thus providing data reduction.

Probability Sampling any sampling method where the probability of any population element's inclusion is known and is greater than zero.

Problem or Opportunity Definition a process of understanding the causes and predicting the consequences of problems or a process of exploring the size and nature of opportunities; the second phase of marketing program development.

Profile Analysis the comparison of evaluations of the alternatives in a consideration set, on the important and determinant attributes.

Projective Techniques a set of presentation methods of ambiguous, unstructured objects, activities, or persons for which a respondent is asked to give interpretation and find meaning; the more ambiguous the stimulus, the more the respondent has to project him or herself into the task, thereby revealing hidden feelings, values, and needs; examples are word association, role playing, completion tests, and picture interpretation.

Purchase Interception Technique a consumer survey technique for collecting data through personal interviews by instore observation of purchase behavior and then interception of consumers in the shopping environment to determine the reasons behind that behavior.

Qualitative Research research designed primarily for exploratory purposes, such as getting oriented to the range and complexity of consumer activity, clarifying the problem, and identifying likely methodological problems; examples are individual and group interviews, projective techniques, and case studies.

Quick Clustering one method of cluster analysis.

Quota Sampling a judgmental sampling method that is constrained to include a minimum from each specified subgroup in the population.

Random Error measurement error due to changing aspects of the respondent or measurement situation.

Randomization a procedure in which the assignment of subjects and treatments to groups is based on chance. Randomization ensures control over the extraneous variables and increases the reliability of the experiment.

Randomized Block Design an experimental design in which the test units first are grouped into homogeneous groups along some prespecified criterion and then are assigned randomly to different treatments within each block.

Rank-Order Scale a scale in which the respondent is required to order a set of objects with regard to a common criterion.

Ratio Scale a measurement that has a true or meaningful zero point, allowing for the specification of absolute magnitudes of objects.

Reading-Habit Method measuring print media exposure by asking how many issues of the last four you have read.

Recent-Reading Method measuring print media exposure by asking whether someone looked at a copy in the past week for a weekly or in the past month for a monthly.

Recording Error error that occurs due to the improper recording of the respondents answers.

Refusal Rate a measure of any data collection method's ability to induce contacted respondents to participate in the study.

Refusals a source of nonsampling error caused by a respondent's refusing to participate in the study.

Regression Analysis a statistical technique that develops an equation that relates a dependent variable to one or more independent (predictor, explanatory) variables.

Relationship Marketing establishing, developing and maintaining long-term, trusting relational exchanges with valued customers, distributors, suppliers and dealers by promising and delivering high-quality services and products to the parties over time.

Relative Market Potential the market potential of one segment relative to other segments.

Relevance a criterion used to judge whether a market research study acts to support strategic and tactical planning activities.

Reliability the random error component of a measurement instrument.

Research Approach one of the following six sources of data—the information system, secondary and standardized data sources, qualitative research, surveys, observations, and experiments.

Research Boundary a delineation of the scope of the research study in terms of items such as population characteristics, locations, and product markets.

Research Objectives a precise statement of what information is needed, consisting of the research question, the hypotheses, and the scope or boundaries of the research.

Research Process the series of stages or steps underlying the design and implementation of a marketing research project, including the establishment of the research purpose and objectives, information value estimation, research design, and implementation.

Research Proposal a plan for conducting and controlling a research project.

Research Purpose the shared understanding between the manager and the researcher regarding the decision alternatives, the problems and opportunities to be studied, and who the users of the results shall be.

Research Question the statement(s) of what specific information is required for progress toward the achievement of the research purpose.

Research Tactics the development of the specific details of the research, including the research approach, sampling plan, and choice of research supplier.

Response Bias the tendency of respondents to distort their answers systematically for a variety of reasons, such as social desirability and prestige seeking.

Response Error error that occurs due to the respondents providing inaccurate information (intentionally or unintentionally). This might be due to the inability of the respondent to comprehend the question or misunderstanding the question due to fatigue or boredom.

Response Style the systematic tendency of respondents to select particular categories of responses regardless of the content of the questions.

Retail Store Audits audit data collected by research firms whose employees visit a sample of stores at fixed intervals for the purpose of counting stock and recording deliveries to estimate retail sales.

Role-Playing a projective technique in which the respondent assumes the role or behavior of another person so that the respondent may reveal attitudes by projecting him or herself fully into the role.

Sample a subset of elements from a population.

Sampling Equivalence deals with the question of identifying and operationalizing two comparable populations and selecting samples representative of other populations and comparable across countries.

Sampling Frame a listing of population members that is used to create a random sample.

Sampling Frame Error error that occurs when the sample is drawn from an inaccurate sampling frame.

Sampling Unit any type of element that makes up a sample, such as people, stores, and products.

Scale Transformation manipulation of scale values to ensure comparability with other scales.

Scanner Data the scanner is a device that reads the universal product code off a package as it is processed at a retailer's checkout stand. Scanner data include data on all transactions including size, price, and flavor. It also normally includes in-store information like special displays.

Scatter Diagram a two-dimensional plot of two variables.

Scree Plot used in factor analysis, a plot of the eigenvalues against the number of factors in order of their extraction. The shape of the plot is used to determine the number of factors.

Screening Sample a representative sample of the population being studied that is used to develop or pretest measurement instruments.

Seasonal Index a representation of the seasonal forecast.

Secondary Data data collected for some purpose other than the present research purpose.

Second Market Discounting the pricing strategy adapted wherein the firm discounts its prices in the other markets below its average cost.

Selection Bias differences among subjects, prior to an experiment, that affect the experimental results.

Selection Error error that occurs in a nonprobability sampling method when a sample obtained is not representative of the population.

Sell-In Test Market the new product being tested must be sold to the retailer. Shelf space is not prearranged.

Semantic Differential Scale a scale in which the respondent is asked to rate each attitude object in turn on a five- or seven-point rating scale bounded at each end by polar adjectives or phrases.

Semistructured/Focused Individual Interview a type of individual depth interview in which the interviewer attempts to cover a specific list of topics or subareas.

Sensitivity the ability of a measurement instrument to discriminate among meaningful differences in the variable being measured.

Sequential Sampling a sampling method in which an initial modest sample is taken and analyzed, following which, based on the results, a decision is made regarding the necessity of further sampling and analysis; this continues until enough data are collected.

Sequential Threshold a nonhierarchical clustering method wherein a cluster center is selected and all objects within a prespecified threshold value are grouped. Then a new cluster center is selected and the process repeated. Once objects enter a cluster they are removed from further processing.

Significance Level the probability of obtaining the evidence if the null hypothesis were true.

Similarity/Judgment the judgment an individual makes about whether two objects are similar or different without specifying specific attributes.

Simple Random Sampling a sampling method in which each population member has an equal chance of being selected.

Single-Source Data data on product purchases and causal factors such as media exposure, promotion influence, and consumer characteristics that come from the same households as a result of advances in scanner and information technology.

Situation Analysis the stage of the market planning process that deals with understanding the environment and the market, identifying opportunities and threats, and assessing the firm's competitive position.

Snowball Design a judgmental sampling method in which each respondent is asked to identify one or more other sample members.

Social Indicators statistical series that describe trends in social rather than economic variables.

Spilt-Ballot Technique the inclusion of more than one version of a question in a questionnaire.

Spilt-Cable Testing exposing two or more groups of a cable system to different ads and monitoring their purchases.

Spurious Association an inappropriate causal interpretation of association due to an unmeasured variable influencing both variables.

Standard Deviation the square root of the variance.

Standard Error of Estimate in regression analysis, the standard deviation of the sampling distribution of the regression model parameter estimates.

Standard Industrial Classification (SIC) System a uniform numbering system developed by the U.S. Government for classifying industrial establishments according to their economic activities.

Standard Metropolitan Statistical Area (SMSA) census tracts that are combined in counties containing a central city with a population of at least 50,000.

Standardized Marketing Data Sources external sources of marketing data collected by outside organizations for several information users who have common information needs.

Stapel Scale a 10-category, unipolar rating scale with categories numbered from -5 to $+5$. It modifies the semantic differential by having the respondent rate how close and in what direction a descriptor adjective fits a given concept.

Statistic any of several characteristics of a sample.

Statistical Control the control of extraneous variables through statistical methods.

Strategic Plans plans that focus on strategic decisions of resource allocation with long-run performance implications, usually having time horizons of more than one year.

Stratified Sampling a sampling method that uses natural subgroups or strata that are more homogeneous than the total population.

Surrogate Information Error error that occurs due to the difference between the information that is required for a marketing research study and the information being sought by the researcher.

Survey Method a method of data collection, such as a telephone or personal interview, a mail survey, or any combination thereof.

Syndicated Services services from firms like A. C. Nielsen, Information Resources Inc., and SAMI/Burke who make available standardized and recurrent marketing research reports to subscribers, usually manufacturers of frequently purchased consumer packaged goods.

Systematic Error the measurement error due to constant aspects of the person or measurement situation.

Test Marketing the introduction of the new product in selected test cities that represent the typical market, so that the results of the performance in these markets can be projected on a national basis.

Third Person Techniques a technique of ascertaining the respondents' views by asking them to answer for a third person.

Through-the-Book measurement of exposure to print media by asking respondents if they recognized articles in an issue.

Thurstone/Equal-Appearing Interval Scale a scale developed by first having a group of judges categorize a set of items and then selecting those items that were similarly categorized; the scale is administered by having respondents choose those statements to which they agree.

Times-Series Forecasting data collected over time, such as weekly sales data for three years, especially effective for short-term forecasting.

Top-Down/Chain-Ratio Approach a method of determining market potential that has as its starting point the identification of the total and available markets.

Total Quality Management the concept of creation of value to the consumer through enhanced product and service quality, thereby enhancing customer satisfaction.

Tracking Studies monitoring the performance of advertising by regular surveys of the audience.

Trade-Off Approach a method of collecting data for trade-off analysis in which the respondent is asked to rank each combination of levels of two attributes from most preferred to least preferred.

Unaided Recall a questioning approach in which the respondent is asked to remember an object of interest without the assistance of clues from the researcher.

Uniform Product Code (UPC) a standard code assigned to each manufacturer's brand and pack size so that its purchases can be tracked through a store scanner system.

U.S. Bureau of the Census the Federal agency that conducts the U.S. Census once every 10 years and compiles demographic statistics on the population. It also conducts one-shot surveys for other federal agencies.

Use Test a type of product evaluation where the product is given to consumers; after a reasonable period of time, the consumers are asked for their reactions to it.

Utility in trade-off analysis, the worth or value of each level of each attribute relative to the other levels.

Validity the ability of a measurement instrument to measure what it is supposed to measure.

Values and Lifestyles Survey (VALS) a survey conducted by the Stanford Research Institute which classified the U.S. population into nine lifestyle segments based on individual values and lifestyles of survey respondents.

Variable Respecification a procedure by which existing data are modified to create new variables or a large number of variables are collapsed into fewer variables.

Variance a measure of dispersion based on the degree to which elements of a sample or population differ from the average element.

Varimax Rotation a rotation method that searches for simple structure, a pattern of factor loadings where some loadings are close to one, and some loadings are close to zero.

Warehouse Withdrawal Services syndicated services offered by firms like SAMI/Burke in which periodic audits are done at the warehouse or wholesale level and reports are produced on product shipments made to retail stores served by those warehouses.

Weighting a procedure by which each response in the database is assigned a number according to some prespecified rule.

Word Association a projective technique in which the respondent is asked to give the first word that comes to mind on the presentation of another word.

INDEX

A Classifiction of Residential
  Neighborhoods (ACORN),
  133–134
Administering errors, 81, 82–83
Alternate hypothesis testing, 470
American Shoppers Panel, 145
Analysis of interdependence, *see*
  Cluster analysis; Factor analysis
Analysis of variance (ANOVA), 458,
  460, 491–492, 495, 503, 504–513
  between-treatment vs. within-
    treatment variance, 506–510
  one-factor (one-way), 505–506
  table, 508–513
  within-treatment variance, 506
Anchor strength, in rating scales, 264
ANOVA, *see* anaysis of variance
Arbitron, 156, 158, 192
Attitudes:
  accuracy of measurements of,
    277–280
  behavior and, 253–254
  choosing a scale to measure, 274,
    276–277
  components of, 254–255
  definition of, 254
  interpreting scales that measure, 274,
    275
  measurement of, 255
  surveys and, 200, 253–281
  types of rating scales to measure,
    258–270

Bayesian decision theory, 64–66
Behavior recording devices, 192
Benefit structure analysis, 682
Binary variables, 447
Bivariate analysis/correlation, *see*
  Correlation analysis; Regression
  analysis
Blind comparison testing, 9–10
Blind-use test, 685–686
Brand awareness scale, 265
Budgeting, for research projects, 83–85

Call reports, 225
Canonical:
  analysis, 460–461
  correlation, 460–461
  loadings, 579

Case studies, 73
Causality, determination of in research,
  322–326
Census(es), 126–129
  industrial and services data, 128–129
  vs. sampling, 358–359
  types of, 127
Centroids:
  definition of, 575, 576
  in cluster analysis, 620
Chi-square:
  distribution, 477–479
  goodness-of-fit test, 460, 484–485
  statistic, 479–480
  test of independence, 459, 477–484
  tests, 458, 459, 475–485
Classical experimental designs, 328–
  336
Cluster analysis, 461, 595, 596, 610–622
  centroids in, 620
  hierarchical clustering, described,
    612–613
  nonhierarchical clustering, described,
    612–613, 616–617
Cochran Q test, 459
Coding of data, 444–447
Common factor analysis, 596
Communality, in factor analysis, 602
Comparative rating scales, 260–261
Completion tests, 185–186
Computer-assisted telephone
  interviewing (CATI), 233, 235
Conference Board Survey of Consumer
  Confidence, 231
Confidence interval, in hypothesis
  testing, 491
Conjoint analysis, 461, 641–651
Consolidated metropolitan statistical
  areas (CMSAs), 128
Constant-sum rating scale, 262–263
Construct equivalence, in international
  marketing research, 90
Consumer purchase panels, 141,
  144–148
Contingency table analysis, 453–454
Continuous purchase panel, 147
Continuous-rating scales, 274
Controlled distribution scanner markets
  (CDSM), 691

Correlation analysis, 536–542
  bivariate analysis/correlation,
    537–542
  correlation coefficient, 536–542
    partial, 542
    testing significance of, 541–542
  Pearson correlation coefficient, 537,
    540
  scatter diagrams in, 537–539
  simple correlation, 537–542
Council of American Survey Research
  Organizations, 229
Critical values, 471–475
Cross-tabulation, 453–454
Customer databases, 119
Customer feedback, 119

Data analysis:
  coding, 444–447
  cross-tabulations in, 453–454
  descriptive statistics and, 450–453
  error, 82
  factors determining statistical
    technique, 454–457
  factors in, 599–601
  frequency distribution and, 449–450
  fundamentals of, 442–462
  means and percentages in 450–454
  multivariate analysis, 448
  preparation of data for, 443–448
  statistical techniques for, 458–462
    ANOVA, 458, 460
    canonical correlation analysis,
      587–591, 460–461
    cluster analysis, 461
    conjoint analysis, 461, 641–651
    discriminant analysis, 460, 573–587
    factor analysis, 461, 595–609
    multidimensional scaling, 461
    multiple linear regression, 460
    simultaneous equation regression
      analysis, 461–462
  statistically adjusting data, 447–448
  strategy for, 448–454
  tabulation of, 449–454
Data collection methods, 77–78
  ethical issues in, 211–213
  factors affecting choice of, 207–211
  impact of culture on, 78
  observational methods, 189–193

qualitative research, 173–189
surveys, 199–213, 218–241
Data sources:
   primary, 77, 114. *See also* Data
      collection methods
   secondary, 77, 114–137, 141–158
      applications of, 131–134
      appraising, 129–131
      benefits of, 115
      census data, 126–129
      external sources of, 119–126
      for international marketing
         research, 134–137
      internal sources of, 117–119
      limitations of, 116–117
      standardized, 141–158
      uses of, 115–116
Data, standardized, 114
Degrees of freedom, 471, 474
Demand estimation, using secondary
   data, 131–132
Design errors, 81
Dichotomous variables, 447
Discriminant analysis, 460, 573–587
   determining significance of of
      discrimination, 579
   interpretation of coefficients in,
      579–586
   in multidimensional scaling, 630,
      631–632
   multiple, 583
   vs. regression analysis, 578
Discriminant loadings, 579
Door-to-door interviews, 219
Dummy variables, 447–448, 563–564

Eigenvalue criteria, definition of, 605
Electronic mail (e-mail) surveys,
   237–238
Equal-appearing intervals scaling
   method, 267–268
Estimating sales potential (ESP),
   686–687
Ethics, 14–17, 211
Executive interviewing, 219
Experimental error, 82
Experimentation, 321–352
   vs. descriptive research, 322–324
   determination of causality and,
      322–326
   guidelines for conducting
      experimental research, 347–349
   issues in, 326–328
   laboratory vs. field experiments,
      343–345
   limitations concerning, 349–352
   types of experimental designs,
      328–343
   validity, 345–347

F-ratio (*F*-statistic), 509
Factor analysis, 461, 595–609
   common factor analysis, 607

communality in, 602
eigenvalue criteria, definition of, 605
factor loadings in, 602
factor rotation schemes in, 603
factor scores in, 601–602
in multidimensional scaling, 630–631,
   632
percentage of variance criteria, 606
scree plot criteria, definition of,
   605–606
significance test criteria, 606–607
Factor rotation schemes, described, 603
Factors, in data analysis, 599–601
Fax surveys, 237
Field experiments, 343–345
Focus groups, 7, 177–183
   analyzing/interpreting results,
      182–183
   key factors for success of, 179
   moderating, 181–182
   planning agenda for, 179–180
   recruiting participants for, 180–181
   telephone technique, 183
   trends in, 183
   two-way, 183
   types of, 178–179
   via television network, 183
Frequency distribution, 449–450
Funny faces scale, 264, 281

Genotypic source of refusal, 202
Geocoding, 133
Goodman and Kruskal's tau, 481,
   482–484
Green marketing, 7

Hidden-issue questioning, 177
Hierarchical clustering, described,
   612–613
Histogram, 449–450
HMO (health maintenance
   organization) study, 55–59
   choice of survey methods for, 238
   rating scale example from, 259–260
   regression analysis of data from,
      542–543
   research approach for, 78–79
   research objectives for, 292, 293
Humanistic inquiry, 191
Hypothesis development, 51
Hypothesis testing:
   basic concepts of, 470–475
   commonly used tests in marketing
      research, 494–501
   confidence interval and, 491
   of differences between means,
      495–499
   of differences between proportions,
      500–501
   introduction to, 467–469
   probability-values approach to, 491,
      501–502

of proportions, 499–500
sample size effect in, 502–503
of single mean, 492–495
steps in, 469

Inaccuracy in response, on surveys,
   202–204
Independence, statistical, 475–484
Information system(s), 23–25
   application to marketing research, 25
   databases and, 23–24
   decision support system (DSS) and,
      23–25
Inoculation treatments, 510–511
Instrumental variables, 447
Interference error, 83
International marketing research:
   construct equivalence in, 90
   data sources for, 134–137
   measurement equivalence in, 90
   personal interviews in, 238–239
   questionnaires in, 311–314
   research design for, 86–91
   sampling equivalence in, 90–91
   sampling frame selection, 382–383
   sampling procedure in 383–384
   scales/scaling in, 280–281
   Self-Reference Criterion in, 60
   surveys in, 238–241
   telephone interviews in, 239–240
Interval estimation, and sample size,
   399–401
Interval scale, 256–257
Interviewers, surveys and, 205–206
Interviews:
   in-depth, 176–177
   in international research, 178,
      238–239
   personal, 218–222
   telephone, 222–227, 239–240
   unstructured, 73
Itemized-category rating scales,
   259–260
Iterative partitioning, described,
   616–617

Kelly's triad, 177
Kolmogorov-Smirnov tests, 458

Laboratory experiments, 343–345. *See
   also* Experimentation
Laddering technique, 177
Lead user analysis, 682
Likert scale, 266–267, 297, 298
Literature reviews, 73

Mail panels, 230–231
Mail surveys, 227–232, 240–241
Mall intercept surveys, 219–220
Mall sampling (shopping center
   sampling), 380–382
Market planning process, stages of,
   4–11

implementation, 4, 11
marketing program development, 4, 8–10
situation analysis, 4, 5–7
strategy development, 4, 7–8
Marketing decision support systems (MDSS), 25–30
Marketing research:
  application of Bayesian decision theory in, 64–66
  applications for, 680–697, 706–723, 730–756
    advertising research, 713–716
    benefit structure analysis, 682
    brand equity, 733–739
    competitive advantage, 731–733
    concept generation, 681–684
    customer satisfaction, 739–744
    distribution, 706–713
    forecasting, 692–696
    integrated marketing communications, 755–756
    lead user analysis, 682
    media research, 721
    new product research, 681–692
    number and location of sales representatives, 711–713
    pricing, 696–698
    product evaluation and development, 684–692
    promotional research, 713–724
    purchase behavior, 716–718
    relationship marketing, 753–755
    sales promotion research, 721–723
    total quality management, 744–755
    tracking studies, 718–719
    warehouse and retail location research, 707–711
  budgeting projects, 83–85
  career opportunities in, 37–38, 40–41
  categories of:
    evaluative, 22
    programmatic, 22,
    selective, 22
  definition of, 2, 4
  ethics in, 14–17
  factors that influence decisions in, 11–13
  information systems and, 23–25
  international, 17–18, 37, 59–60. See also International marketing research
  overview of process, 42–43
  preliminary stages of, 43–59
  role in managerial decision making, 4–11
  scheduling projects, 83–85
  suppliers of, 30–37
    corporate/in-house departments, 32–33
    external, 33–36
  use of, 13–14

McNemar test, 459
Measurement equivalence, in international marketing research, 90
Measurement error, 82
Measurement, definition of, 255
Memory distortions, 203
Metropolitan statistical areas (MSAs), 128
Micromarketing, 3–4
Multi-item scales, 266–274
  guidelines for developing, 272–274
Multidimensional scaling, 461, 629–651
  application with nonattribute data, 636–639
  attribute-based approaches, 630–636
  basic concepts of, 633
  discriminant analysis in, 630, 631–632
  factor analysis in, 630–631, 632
  stress measure in, 633–635
Multimedia services, as standardized data sources, 156
Multiple regression analysis, see Regression analysis
Multivariate analysis, 448, 458–459

National Family Opinion (NFO), 145, 230–231
National Purchase Diary (NPD) Panel, 145, 158
Nielsen Food Index (NFI), 150
Nielsen Retail Index, 143–144
Nielsen Television Index (NTI), 36, 155, 158
Nominal scale, 255, 256
Nonhierarchical clustering, described, 612–613, 616–617
Nonresponse errors, 81, 83, 201–202
Nonsampling error, 359–360
Null hypothesis testing, introduction to, 470

Observational methods:
  behavior recording devices, 192
  benefits of, 189
  content anlaysis, 190–191
  contrived observation, 190
  direct observation, 190
  humanistic inquiry, 191
  limitations of, 192–193
  physical trace measures, 191
  types of, 190–192
Omnibus surveys, 220–221
One-tail test, 474–475
Order bias, in questionnaires, 305–308
Ordinal scale, 256, 257

Perceptual map, in multidimensional scaling, 629
Phenotypic source of refusal, 202
Physical trace measures, 191

Pictorial rating scales, 263–264, 280–281
Picture interpretation, 186
Pictured Aspirations Technique (PAT), 188
Population specification error, 82
Power of the hypothesis test, 474
Presentations, research, 660–673
  guidelines for, 661–666
  oral, 670–673
  written, 666–669
Principal component analysis, 596, 600–609
Probability distribution, 471
Profile analysis, 269–270
Projective research techniques, 183–189
  case studies, 187
  completion tests, 185–186
  picture interpretation, 186
  role rehearsal procedure, 187
  third-person techniques, 186
  word association, 184–185
Purchase intercept technique (PIT), 220

Q-sort scaling, 262
Qualitative research:
  focus group discussions, 177–183
  in-depth interviews, 176–177
  limitations of methods, 189
  need for, 173–174
  projective techniques, 183–189
  uses for, 174–175
Qualitative variables, 447
Questioning error, 83
Questionnaires, 290–314
  for international marketing research, 311–314
  pretesting of, 307–311
  sequence and layout of questions in, 305–311
  steps for developing, 290–311
  types of questions used in, 292–300
  wording of questions in, 300–305

Random-digit dialing, 223
Rank sum tests, 458
Rank-order scales, 261–262
Ratio scale, 255–256
Recall awareness, 254
Recording error, 83
Regression analysis, 536, 542–563
  vs. discriminant analysis, 578
  dummy variables in, 563–564
  HMO study example of, 542–543
  multiple regression, 552–555
    parameter interpretation in, 554–555
    residuals in, 562–563
  simple linear regression model, 543–552
  simultaneous equation, 462
  unobservable variables in, 462
  validity of, 563

Relationship marketing strategies, 119
Relevancy, of attitude measurements, 279
Reliability, of attitude measurements, 278–279
Research approach, 71, 73–79
    causal, 75–77
    descriptive, 73–74, 76–77
    exploratory, 73, 76–77
    for HMO study, 78–79
    research tactics in, 71
Research design, 71–83
    errors in, 81–83
        nonsampling errors, 81–83
        sampling errors, 81
    for international marketing research, 86–91
Research objective, 49–54
Research presentations, see
        Presentations, research
Research proposal, 85–86
Research purpose, 43–49
Research question, 49, 50
Research tactics, 79–81
Response biases, 203–204
Response errors, 81, 83
Role playing, 186–187
Role rehearsal procedure, 187
Runs tests, 458

Sample size:
    ad hoc methods of determining, 392–394
    budget constraints and, 393–394
    determining population standard deviation in, 402
    effect on hypothesis testing, 502–503
    factors determining, 394
    interval estimation and, 399
    multistage sampling design and, 408
    population characteristics/parameters, 394–395
    proportions in, 402–404
    reliability and, 397–399
    sample characteristics/statistics, 395–397
    sequential sampling and, 408
    statistical techniques of determining, 394–408
    statistical theory and, 392–408
Sampling equivalence, in international marketing research, 90–91
Sampling plan, 80
Sampling:
    vs. census taking, 358–359
    cluster, 371–372
    convenience, 376–377
    disproportional stratified, 371
    error, 359–360
    frame, 82, 363–366
    fundamentals of, 358–384

in international marketing research, 382–384
    judmental, 375–376
    multistage design, 373–375, 408
    nonprobability, 375–378
    nonresponse problems in, 378–380
    probability, 367–373
    procedure, selection of, 366–367
    process, 360–367
    proportional stratified, 370–371
    quota, 377–378
    sequential, 408
    shopping center, 380–382
    simple random, 367–368
    snowball, 376
    stratified, 369–370, 406–407
    systematic, 372–373
    target population, determining, 361–363
Scale transformation, 448
Scales/scaling:
    accuracy of attitude measurements, 277–280
    choosing a scale to measure attitude, 274, 276–277
    in cross-national research, 280–281
    definition of, 255
    interpreting, 274, 275
    properties of, 255–258
    types of:
        associative, 266, 270
        brand awareness, 265
        comparative, 260–261
        constant-sum, 262–263
        continuous-rating, 274
        funny faces, 264, 281
        interval, 256–257
        itemized-category, 259–260
        Likert, 266–267, 297, 298
        multiple-item, 266–274
        nominal, 255, 256
        ordinal, 256, 257
        paired comparison, 266
        pictorial, 263–264
        Q-sort, 262
        rank-order, 261–262
        ratio, 255–256
        semantic-differential, 266, 268–269, 297
        single-item, 258–266
        single-pole, 264
        Stapel, 264, 270
        summated, 267
        thermometer, 264, 281
        Thurstone, 266
        used in HMO study, 259–260
        verbal purchase intent, 265
Scatter diagrams, 537–539
Scheduling, of research projects, 83–85
Scree plot criteria, definition of, 605–606

Secondary data sources, see Data sources, secondary
Segmentation marketing, data sources for, 133–134
Selection errors, 81–82
Self-administered questionnaires/interviews, 220
Self-Reference Criterion (SRC), 60
Semantic-differential scales, 266, 268–269, 297
    in cross-national research, 280
Sensitivity, of attitude measurements, 279
SIC (Standard Industrial Classification) System, 33, 128–129
Sign test, 458, 459
Significance level, 471–474
Single-item rating scales, 258–266
Single-pole scales, 264
Single-source systems of data sources, 142, 148, 151–154
Standard Industrial Classification (SIC), 33, 128–129
Standard metropolitan statistical area (SMSA), 128
Standardization, 448
Standardized sources of marketing data, 141–158
Stapel scales, 264, 270
Starch Readership Survey/Scores, 36, 156, 158
Statistical experimental designs, 336–343
Store audits, 141,
Store-specific marketing, 3–4
Summated scale, 267
Surrogate information error, 82
Surveys, 199–213, 218–241
    advantages of, 199
    consumer, 7
    inaccuracy in response, 202–204
    information obtained from, 200
    interviewer errors in, 205–206
    in international marketing research, 238–241
    mall intercept, 219–220
    methods of conducting, 206–207
        choice of in HMO study, 238
        combinations of, 232–233
        computer hardware and software technology, 235–237
        computer interactive interviewing, 235
        computer-assisted telephone interviewing, 233, 235
        electronic mail (e-mail) surveys, 237–238
        fax surveys, 237
        mail surveys, 227–232, 240–241
        personal interviewing, 218–222, 238–239

Code of Ethics of Marketing Research Association

The Code of Professional Ethics and Practices

1. To maintain high standards of competence and integrity in marketing and survey research.
2. To maintain the highest level of business and professional conduct and to comply with Federal, State and local laws, regulations and ordinances applicable to my business practice and those of my company.
3. To exercise all reasonable care and to observe the best standards of objectivity and accuracy in the development, collection, processing and reporting of marketing and survey research information.
4. To protect the anonymity of respondents and hold all information concerning an individual respondent privileged, such that this information is used only within the context of the particular study.
5. To thoroughly instruct and supervise all persons for whose work I am responsible in accordance with study specifications and general research techniques.
6. To observe the rights of ownership of all materials received from and/or developed for clients, and to keep in confidence all research techniques, data and other information considered confidential by their owners.
7. To make available to clients such details on the research methods and techniques of an assignment as may be reasonably required for proper interpretation of the data, providing this reporting does not violate the confidence of respondents or clients.
8. To promote the trust of the public for marketing and survey research activities and to avoid any procedure which misrepresents the activities of a respondent, the rewards of cooperation or the uses of data.
9. To refrain from referring to membership in this organization as proof of competence, since the organization does not so certify any person or organization.
10. To encourage the observance of principles of this code among all people engaged in marketing and survey research.

Source: Reprinted by permission of the Marketing Research Association, Inc., Chicago, IL.

telephone interviews, 222–227,
239–240
nonresponse errors due to refusals,
201–202
overview, 199–200
questionnaires for, 290–314
response biases in, 203–204
sources of errors in, 200–206
Symbolic analysis, 177
Systematic random-digit dialing,
223–224

T-tests, 458
Target marketing, data sources for,
133–134

Target population, determining,
361–363
Thematic Apperception Test (TAT), 186
Thermometer scale, 264, 281
Third-person techniques, 186
Thurstone scale, 267–268
Two-pole scales, 264
Two-tail test, 474–475
Type I/Type II errors, 471–474

Univariate analysis, 458–459

Validity, in experimental research,
345–347

Validity, of attitude measurements,
277–278
Variable respecification, 447–448
Verbal purchase intent scale, 265
Virtual product testing, 684–685

Walker Industry Image Study, 207
Weighting (of data), 447
Wilcoxon test, 459
Word association, 184–185

Z-tests, 458